WILLIAM SHAWCROSS became a writer after leaving University College, Oxford in 1968. He was in Czechoslovakia during the Soviet occupation; this inspired his first book, a biography of Alexander Dubček, the Czechoslovak leader, which was published in 1970. Since then he has written and travelled widely. In 1995 he wrote the BBC Television series *Monarchy*. In 2002 his BBC Television series and book, *Queen and Country* celebrated the Queen's Golden Jubilee and examined the changing face of Britain during her reign. He lives in England.

WILLIAM SHAWCROSS

QUEEN ELIZABETH

THE QUEEN MOTHER

The Official Biography

PAN BOOKS

First published 2009 by Macmillan

First published in paperback 2010 by Pan Books
an imprint of Pan Macmillan, a division of Macmillan Publishers Limited
Pan Macmillan, 20 New Wharf Road, London N1 9RR
Basingstoke and Oxford
Associated companies throughout the world
www.panmacmillan.com

ISBN 978-0-330-43430-0

1 3 5 7 9 8 6 4 2

A CIP catalogue record for this book is available from
the British Library.

Typeset by SetSystems Ltd, Saffron Walden, Essex
Printed in the UK by CPI Mackays, Chatham ME5 8TD

Visit **www.panmacmillan.com** to read more about all our books
and to buy them. You will also find features, author interviews and
news of any author events, and you can sign up for e-newsletters
so that you're always first to hear about our new releases.

She had all the royal makings of a Queen.

Shakespeare, *King Henry VIII*, IV, i, 87

CONTENTS

Contents

Contents

List of Illustrations

PREFACE

HER MAJESTY THE QUEEN did me the signal honour, in July 2003, of inviting me to write the official biography of Queen Elizabeth The Queen Mother. I was given unrestricted access both to Queen Elizabeth's papers and to members of her family, Household and staff. I am deeply grateful to The Queen for the help I have received, and I thank The Duke of Edinburgh, The Prince of Wales, The Duke of York, The Earl of Wessex, The Princess Royal, The Duke of Gloucester, The Duke of Kent, Princess Alexandra, The Duchess of Cornwall, Viscount Linley, Lady Sarah Chatto and The Earl of Snowdon for their invaluable assistance. I thank The Queen for permission to quote from material in the Royal Archives, as well as from letters in other collections subject to her copyright, and, above all, I thank Her Majesty for giving me absolute freedom to write as I wished.

The Royal Archives at Windsor Castle, where Queen Elizabeth's private and official papers are housed, are at the top of a long steep staircase in the Round Tower. I have rarely worked in a more delightful place. During my numerous visits there I was treated with the greatest patience by the Registrar, Pam Clark, and her staff, including Jill Kelsey, Allison Derrett and Angie Barker, and by the former Curator of the Royal Photograph Collection, Frances Dimond. The present Curator, Sophie Gordon, and the Assistant Curator, Lisa Heighway, with Paul Stonell and Alessandro Nasini have done sterling work providing illustrations from Queen Elizabeth's photograph collection.

Among the papers to which I was given access in the Royal Archives were the transcripts of conversations which Queen Elizabeth had in 1994 and 1995 with Eric Anderson, who had just retired as head master of Eton College. These, together with Queen Elizabeth's letters to her family and friends,* were vitally important in providing her own commentary on her life.

---

* In this book the misspellings of Queen Elizabeth's childhood letters have been left as

At Glamis Castle, ancestral home of the Bowes Lyon family, by kindness of the eighteenth Earl of Strathmore and Kinghorne I was able to read more of Queen Elizabeth's letters among her parents' papers, as well as other family correspondence which shed light on her early life. I was greatly assisted in my research there by the Archivist, Jane Anderson, who also provided valuable help with picture research. My thanks are due to Lord Strathmore for permission to quote from papers at Glamis and to reproduce photographs from his family albums. Many members of his family were very kind to me; they include his mother Mary, Dowager Countess of Strathmore, who answered my innumerable questions about the family, and his sister Lady Elizabeth Leeming, to whom I am deeply indebted. On my behalf she carried out superb research in the archives at Glamis and elsewhere, interviewed members of her family, and compiled a series of richly informative notes on the family and its homes. Her expertise as both a researcher and an editor was invaluable throughout.

At St Paul's Walden Bury, the Queen Mother's other childhood home, Sir Simon and Lady Bowes Lyon kindly allowed me access to yet more family letters and papers. Among other members of the Bowes Lyon family, I am grateful to Queen Elizabeth's nieces Lady Mary Clayton, Lady Mary Colman and the Hon. Mrs Rhodes (née Margaret Elphinstone), whose help I have greatly appreciated, and also to Queen Elizabeth's nephew the Hon. Albemarle Bowes Lyon, to her cousin John Bowes Lyon, and to Rosie Stancer, her great-niece, and her husband William.

I thank Her Majesty Queen Fabiola of the Belgians for permission to quote a letter she wrote to Queen Elizabeth, Her Majesty The Queen of Denmark for permission to quote from a letter from the late Queen Ingrid, Her Majesty The Queen of the Netherlands for permission to quote from a letter from the late Princess Juliana, and His Majesty The King of Norway for permission to quote from a letter from the late Queen Maud.

I am indebted to all those who have allowed me to read, and to quote from, their family papers; some of them I have to thank also for permission to quote from letters in which they own the copyright among Queen Elizabeth's papers at Windsor. They include: the Earl of Airlie,

---

written, but her occasional mistakes as an adult have been corrected (as have those of a few other writers) on the grounds that they are an unnecessary distraction from the sense of the letters. She herself was well aware that spelling was not her strong point. 'It all smacks to me of BUREAUCRACY!!!' she once wrote in a note inveighing against that particular bugbear. 'How fortunate that I have just learnt to spell this valuable word!' (RA QEQM/PRIV/MISCOFF)

Anne, Countess Attlee, John Dalrymple Hamilton, Viscount Davidson, Eric and Sir Geoffrey de Bellaigue, Lady Katharine Farrell, George Fergusson, Sir Edmund Grove, the Earl of Halifax, Kate Hall, Richard Hall, Mrs David Hankinson and the Hon. Mrs David Erskine, Lord Hardinge of Penshurst and the Hon. Lady Murray, Mrs Sylvia Hudson, Carol Hughes, Lady May, David Micklethwait, Viscount Norwich, Wilfred Notley, Rev. Jonathan Peel, Lady Penn, the Earl of Rosslyn, the Marquess of Salisbury (whose archivist, Robin Harcourt-Smith, I wish also to thank for his help), Susannah Sitwell, Earl Spencer (whose archivist, Bruce Bailey, I thank likewise), Margaret Vyner and her daughter Violet, Robert Woods and the Earl of Woolton.

I wish also to express my thanks to those who have given me permission to quote from their letters, or letters from their forebears, among Queen Elizabeth's papers or in other collections I have consulted. They include Lord Annaly, Sir Toby Anstruther, Bt, Bryan Basset, Winston Churchill, Mrs Alan Clark, the Duke of Devonshire, the Rev. Canon Dendle French, Lord Gage, Lord Gladwyn, Sir Carron Greig and Geordie Greig, James Joicey-Cecil, Candida Lycett Green, Sir Ian Rankin, Sir Adam Ridley, Lady Elizabeth Shakerley, the Earl of Stockton, Sir Tom Stoppard, Viscount Stuart of Findhorn and Baroness Thatcher.

My thanks are due for assistance with my research and, where appropriate, permission to publish material from the collections in their care, to Allen Packwood and Andrew Riley at the Churchill Archives Centre, Churchill College, Cambridge (Churchill Papers, Lascelles Papers, Lloyd Papers, Norwich Papers), Helen Langley and her staff at the Bodleian Library, Oxford (Attlee Papers, Beck Papers, Isaiah Berlin Papers, Monckton Papers, Bonham Carter Papers, Violet Milner Papers, Woolton Papers), Dr Frances Harris and William Frame at the British Library (Airlie Papers), the staff of The National Archives (Foreign Office Papers), the staff of the National Library of Scotland (Ballantrae Papers), Christine Penney and her staff at Birmingham University Archives (Chamberlain Papers), Michael Meredith at Eton College Library (Diana Cooper Papers), the staff of the Borthwick Institute, University of York (Hickleton Papers), Dr Richard Palmer and his staff at Lambeth Palace Library (Lang Papers, Alan Don Papers), the staff of the Centre for Kentish Studies, Maidstone (Hardinge of Penshurst Papers), the staff of Library and Archives Canada, Ottawa, in particular Denis Boulé, Bill Russell, Paulette Dozois and Jennifer Mueller, and the staff of the Archives Nationales du Québec, especially Louis Fournier, Pierre Rainville, Jacques Morin and Rénald Lessard. I gratefully acknowledge the permission of Balliol College, Oxford to publish an extract from the Monckton Papers, and that of the Isaiah Berlin Literary Trust to quote from a letter from Sir Isaiah Berlin.

Many people in the Royal Household, past and present, have helped me in different ways. They include Sir Robin (now Lord) Janvrin, the Queen's Private Secretary when I was invited to write this book, and his successor, Christopher Geidt. I have benefited greatly from their encouragement. I am also indebted to the Royal Librarian, the Hon. Lady Roberts, for her constant support, her invaluable knowledge and her eye for detail; she and her colleagues, Bridget Wright, Emma Stuart and Paul Carter, helped with enquiries about Queen Elizabeth's extensive book collection. Sir Hugh Roberts, Director of the Royal Collection, provided much useful information and kind guidance throughout. Shruti Patel, Karen Lawson, Daniel Partridge and Eva Zielinska Millar of the Royal Collection Photographic Services assisted with illustrations. In the office of The Duke of Edinburgh, Brigadier Sir Miles Hunt Davis, the Duke's Private Secretary, and Dame Anne Griffiths were most helpful. At Clarence House I was greatly helped by Sir Stephen Lamport, Private Secretary to the Prince of Wales, and his successor Sir Michael Peat, as well as by David Hutson, Virginia Carington and Paddy Harverson.

I thank Penny Russell Smith, Press Secretary to the Queen when I began this book, for her help. In the later stages, her successor, Samantha Cohen, was impeccably wise and kind; I am very grateful to her. In her office several others, in particular Ailsa Anderson, were of great assistance. I am also grateful to others at Buckingham Palace, including Helen Cross, Doug King and Mrs Margaret Mattocks and her fine team on the Buckingham Palace switchboard.

Other members or former members of the Royal Household to whom I owe my thanks include the late Sir Richard Bayliss, Dr Ian Campbell, Lord Fellowes, the late Sir Edward Ford, Sister Gillian Frampton, Dr Jonathan Holliday, the late Lieutenant Colonel Sir John Johnston, the late Sir Oliver and Lady Millar, Peter Ord, Canon John Ovenden, Sir Richard Thompson and Mr Roger Vickers.

Among the members of The Queen Mother's Household to whom I am greatly indebted are Sir Alastair Aird, her last Private Secretary, and Lady Aird, who were unfailingly helpful; I was also given much assistance by the Hon. Nicholas Assheton, Dame Frances Campbell-Preston, the late Lady Margaret Colville, Fiona Fletcher, Mrs Michael Gordon-Lennox, the late Sir John and Lady Griffin, Elizabeth, Lady Grimthorpe, Martin and Catriona Leslie, Jamie Lowther-Pinkerton, Jeremy Mainwaring Burton, Lucy Murphy and Major Raymond Seymour. Sir Michael and Lady Angela Oswald gave me enormous assistance, especially in regard to Queen

Elizabeth's passion for steeplechasing. Ashe Windham, former equerry and friend of Queen Elizabeth, was my delightful guide to the Castle of Mey and much more. Lady Penn, former lady in waiting to Queen Elizabeth, has given me consistent and excellent advice.

Many former members of Queen Elizabeth's staff helped me with obvious delight in the subject; they include Leslie Chappell, Sadie Ewen, Nancy McCarthy, Danny and Sandy McCarthy, Jacqui Meakin, Michael Sealey, the late Clifford Skeet, the late William Tallon, June Webster, Ron Wellbelove and the late Charlie Wright.

A multitude of other people, some of them friends of Queen Elizabeth, assisted me. They included the Countess of Airlie, Christiane Besse, Lord and Lady Brabourne, John Bridcut, Donald Cameron, George Carey, Lord and the late Lady Carrington, Sir Edward Cazalet and Mrs Peter Cazalet, Rev. Professor Dr Owen Chadwick, Lady Charteris, Rosemary Coleman, Sir Timothy Colman, Dr Anita Davies, Deborah, Duchess of Devonshire, Annabel Eliot, Alwyne Farqharson, Julian Fellowes, Andrew Festing, Lord and Lady Nicholas Gordon-Lennox, the Earl and Countess of Gowrie, the Duke and Duchess of Grafton, Dame Drue Heinz, Heather Henderson, Nigel Jaques, Lady Sarah Keswick, Sarah Key, Patricia, Countess Mountbatten of Burma, Mrs Timmy Munro, James Murray, Lady Rupert Nevill, Patty Palmer Tomkinson, Brigadier Andrew Parker Bowles, Major Johnny Perkins, Johnny Robertson, Leo Rothschild, Clare and Oliver Russell, Lord and Lady Sainsbury, the late Bruce Shand, Christine Shearer, Anne Sloman, Lizzie Spender, Betty Berkeley Stafford, Margaret, Dowager Viscountess Thurso, the Duchess of Westminster, Galen and Hilary Weston, Lynne Wilson and the late Lord Wyatt and Lady Wyatt.

I benefited from valuable insights into Queen Elizabeth's private visits to France and Italy provided by the Marquise de Ravenel, daughter of Prince Jean-Louis de Faucigny-Lucinge, the orchestrator of many of the tours, Bertrand du Vignaud de Villefort, the Prince's successor as tour organizer, Laure, Princesse de Beauvau-Craon, Queen Elizabeth's hostess in Lorraine, and Madame Servagnat, survivor of Ravensbrück, whom she met during her visit to Epernay in 1983. I thank them all for their kind help. In Australia, Sir James Scholtens reminisced with great charm about Queen Elizabeth's tours there in which he was involved.

In Canada, where my research was conducted by Sheila de Bellaigue, I thank: at Rideau Hall, Ottawa, Rosemary Doyle-Morier for valuable contacts and information, and Patricia McRae for arranging access to Governor Generals' papers; also in Ottawa, Martin and Louise Tetreault and Roger and Huguette Potvin; in Montreal, Robin Quinlan, for kind hospitality and introductions to Mrs Tom Price, Colonel Bruce Bolton,

Colonel Victor Chartier, Tom Bourne and Elspeth Straker, all of whom provided useful information about Queen Elizabeth's links with The Black Watch (Royal Highland Regiment) of Canada, and Mrs Alan Gordon, in whose house Queen Elizabeth stayed in 1987; in Toronto, Walter Borosa, former Chief of Protocol for Ontario, who was involved with many of her visits, Colonel Hugh Stewart, former Colonel of The Toronto Scottish (The Queen Mother's Own) Regiment, and David Willmot, who supplied tales of Queen Elizabeth's visits to the Woodbine races; also Harris Boyd, Federal Co-ordinator of Queen Elizabeth's later tours, and Jean-Paul Roy, his deputy, both of whom provided further enlightenment about her visits and her occasionally wilful, but highly popular, deviations from the official programme; and Beverly McLaughlin, Chief Justice of Canada, who drew my attention to Queen Elizabeth's speech on laying the foundation stone of the Supreme Court building in Ottawa in 1939.

Others to whom I owe warm thanks for advice, information or help in many different ways are Dr Joanna Marschner of Historic Royal Palaces and Joanna Hashagen of the Bowes Museum, for information on Queen Elizabeth's clothes; Lucia van der Post, for an assessment of Queen Elizabeth's style of dress; Wendy Moore, for information on Mary Eleanor Bowes; Donald Gillies, for information on Archie Clark Kerr; Clare Elmquist, for information on Lydie Lachaise; Dr Christina de Bellaigue, for information on private education for girls; Gladys Noble, for information on Lord Roberts Memorial Workshops; Ian Shapiro, for kindly showing me a letter from King George VI in his collection; Bob Steward, for research on Catherine Maclean; Charles Sumner, for information regarding his aunt, Beryl Poignand.

All writers owe debts to other writers. As well as those already mentioned, many eminent historians assisted me with great kindness; they include my old friend Kenneth Rose, author of, *inter alia*, an authoritative biography of King George V, and Philip Ziegler, a particular source of wisdom on the role of the official biographer. I am grateful also for the most generous advice of Sir Martin Gilbert, official biographer of Winston Churchill, and I thank D. R. Thorpe, official biographer of Lord Home. Sir Eric Anderson and his wife Poppy gave me wonderful support. Vernon Bogdanor, Professor of Government at Oxford University and author, among other distinguished works, of *The British Constitution*, was a peerless guide to me throughout the writing of this book.

Much has already been written about Queen Elizabeth. The first biography of the then Duchess of York was written by Lady Cynthia Asquith with the Duchess's assistance, and was published in 1927. In the 1960s Dorothy Laird was given official assistance to prepare what was called the 'first authorised biographical study of Her Majesty'. Queen Elizabeth was such a compelling subject that these books were followed by many more, including *The Queen Mother* (1981), by Elizabeth Longford, a great historian whom I was fortunate to know from my childhood, *My Darling Buffy* (1997) in which Grania Forbes explored Elizabeth Bowes Lyon's youth and, especially, *Queen Elizabeth*, by Hugo Vickers (2005). In her *George VI* (1989) Sarah Bradford naturally wrote at length about Queen Elizabeth too. All of these books contain valuable original material which I have used and credited and I am grateful to the authors for their help.

I had an exceptional group of people helping me with my research – Patricia Lennox-Boyd, Douglas Murray and Rachel Smith delved in various archives and libraries and on the internet; Julia Melvin and Gill Middleburgh chronicled particular areas of Queen Elizabeth's life from the records in the Royal Archives and elsewhere, and helped in many other ways; Lucy Murphy, after serving for thirty-four years in Queen Elizabeth's office, brought her invaluable knowledge to my aid. The person who helped me most throughout these six years was Sheila de Bellaigue, former Registrar of the Royal Archives. I am deeply indebted to her for her diligent research, her wit, her meticulous attention to detail and her scholarly advice. I could never have written this book without her.

My literary agents – Carol Heaton in London and Lynn Nesbit in New York – have both been, as usual, immensely supportive; and my publishers, Macmillan in London and Knopf in New York, have been most forbearing and helpful. In particular Georgina Morley, and her colleagues at Macmillan, guided me and the book to publication with skill and fortitude. In New York, Sonny Mehta displayed his usual élan, kindness and judgement. In London I was given excellent advice by Charles Elliott and towards the end I was wonderfully assisted by Peter James, the doyen of copyeditors. I count myself very fortunate to have persuaded the legendary Douglas Matthews to compile the index.

My family has had to live with my work on this book for a long time and I thank especially my wife Olga for her understanding, and Conrad, Ellie, Alex and Charlie for their tolerance. My sister Joanna and my brother Hume have also helped me kindly. And I thank my late parents, Hartley and Joan, for years of encouragement. One of my earliest memories, from February 1952, is of my mother weeping in our garden; when I asked her why, she replied, 'The King has died.'

*

The nature of official biography inevitably changes over time. In his inaugural lecture as Queen Elizabeth The Queen Mother Professor of British History at the University of London, David Cannadine remarked that until the end of the 1950s, royal biographers 'were specifically instructed to write nothing that was embarrassing to the institution of monarchy, or critical of the particular individual who was being thus commemorated and memorialised'. By Harold Nicolson's account, such strictures were indeed placed upon him when he began work on King George V's biography. John Wheeler-Bennett, official biographer of Queen Elizabeth's husband, King George VI, thought that royal biography was almost a sacred enterprise which, like matrimony, ought 'not to be entered into inadvisedly, or lightly; but reverently, discreetly, advisedly, soberly and in the fear of God'.

No such instructions were issued and no such fears were instilled in me; on the contrary, I was encouraged to write what I wished. When I showed members of Queen Elizabeth's family, Household and staff sections of the manuscript, they offered many helpful suggestions to ensure accuracy and completeness, but the decision on what to publish remained mine alone. I have been guided by the advice of Hamlet – 'Be not too tame neither, but let your own discretion be your tutor.'

Any biography, even one as long as this, is selective; the writer has to choose which aspects of the subject to concentrate upon. I have quoted at length from Queen Elizabeth's private letters because few of them have been seen before and because I found them remarkable – from childhood to old age she wrote with a rare clarity and verve. Her letters illuminate sides of her character which were not always clear to people beyond her immediate family. Not all her letters, written or received, survive; sadly I was able to find few between her and her mother, Lady Strathmore. As happens in any family, other letters have been lost or thrown away over the years. Nevertheless, I have sought wherever possible to use the primary sources uniquely available to me when narrating the trajectory of Queen Elizabeth's life.

The English philosopher Roger Scruton has, in a happy phrase, described the British monarchy as 'the light above politics'. It is the light that Queen Elizabeth cast over the life of the nation that I have tried to describe.

WILLIAM SHAWCROSS
July 2009

PROLOGUE

WEDNESDAY 19 JULY 2000 was the day chosen for the pageant celebrating the hundredth birthday of Queen Elizabeth The Queen Mother. In London, the day did not begin well. There were bomb scares, the controlled explosion of a suspicious bag, and many trains were cancelled. Senior police officers considered whether the whole event should be abandoned. It was not.

The celebration, on Horse Guards Parade in Whitehall, had been designed as a joyful tribute to Queen Elizabeth and the hundreds of organizations with which she was connected. In warm afternoon sunshine, as the National Anthem was performed by massed military bands, the Royal Philharmonic Orchestra and a choir of a thousand singers, Queen Elizabeth, dressed in pink, arrived with her grandson the Prince of Wales in a landau escorted by the Household Cavalry.

After she had inspected the troops, she and the Prince sat on a flower-bedecked dais (though she stood much of the time) to watch the parade together. It began with a march-past of the regiments of which she was colonel-in-chief, followed by the King's Troop of the Royal Horse Artillery and the Mounted Bands of the Household Cavalry. One hundred homing doves were released as a young boy sang 'Oh for the Wings of a Dove'.

Then came a cavalcade of the century, a light-hearted look at the hundred years she had lived through; more of a circus than a parade, it included 450 children and adults, with a variety of stars. Among the scenes and players who passed in front of her were soldiers of the First World War, ballroom dancers from the 1920s, a Second World War fire engine and ambulance, Pearly Kings and Queens from the East End of London, and people in 1940s dress celebrating victory in 1945. Then came a series of post-war cars – Enid Blyton's Noddy in his yellow car, the first Mini Minor, James Bond's Aston Martin, an E-type Jaguar. More recent – and perhaps more surprising – twentieth-century memories were recalled by Hell's Angels on their bikes, punk-rock youths in black and the television characters, the Wombles.

After this eclectic depiction of the previous ten decades, representatives of 170 of the more than 300 civil organizations, charities and other groups with which Queen Elizabeth was associated marched past her. This part of the parade began with Queen Elizabeth's page leading two of her corgis, the breed of dog which had for so long shared her life. There were more animals: camels (ridden by members of the Worshipful Company of Grocers, whose emblem is a camel), horses, an Aberdeen Angus bull, North Country Cheviot sheep, chickens, racehorses. The groups waving gaily as they passed included the Girls' Brigade, Queen Elizabeth's Overseas Nursing Services Association, the Cookery and Food Association (a hundred chefs all in their whites), the Mothers' Union, the Poultry Club of Great Britain, the Royal National Lifeboat Institution, the National Trust, the Royal College of Midwives, St John Ambulance Brigade, the Royal School of Needlework, the Colditz Association, the Battle of Britain Fighter Association, the Bomber Command Association and, bringing up the rear, twenty-two holders of the Victoria and George Crosses, Britain's highest awards for heroism, followed by the venerable Chelsea Pensioners marching stiffly but proudly in their bright red uniforms. Everyone in the stands stood up as these brave men and women passed.

RAF planes from the Second World War – a Spitfire, a Hurricane, a Lancaster bomber, a Bristol Blenheim – flew overhead, followed by the Red Arrows trailing red, white and blue vapour trails. And all the while the bands and the orchestra played on and the choirs sang. Hubert Parry's glorious anthem 'I Was Glad', which had been sung at King George VI and Queen Elizabeth's Coronation in 1937, was followed by First World War music-hall favourites such as 'Pack Up Your Troubles in Your Old Kit Bag', 'Keep the Home Fires Burning' and (nicely vulgar) 'My Old Man Said Follow the Van'. Three hundred children from the Chicken Shed Company danced. Altogether some 2,000 military personnel and more than 5,000 civilians celebrated on Horse Guards Parade.

The whole event lasted an hour and a half, and at the end the Queen Mother made a short speech of thanks saying it had been a wonderful afternoon and 'a great joy to me'. The crowd cheered, the National Anthem was sung again, and Queen Elizabeth got into her car to make a lap of honour past thousands of happy, cheering people before driving off to St James's Palace, where she climbed the stairs to the State Rooms and spent the next hour and a half at a reception, sitting down only to talk to the singer Dame Vera Lynn.

Two weeks later, on the morning of her actual hundredth birthday, 4 August, a large crowd gathered outside her London home, Clarence House. The gates were opened and Queen Elizabeth came out to take the salute when the King's Troop, the Royal Horse Artillery, marched past. In front of the crowd the royal postman, Tony Nicholls, delivered her the traditional message sent by the Queen to all her subjects who reach their hundredth birthday. The Queen Mother started to open it and then passed it to her equerry. 'Come on, use your sword,' she said. Captain William de Rouet unsheathed his ceremonial blade and slit the envelope open. The message was written in the Queen's own hand and read, 'On your 100th birthday all the family join with me in sending you our loving best wishes for this special day. Lilibet'.[1]

Then, with the Prince of Wales, Queen Elizabeth climbed into a landau decked with flowers in her racing colours of blue and gold, and was driven to Buckingham Palace past the large crowds lining the Mall. The Prince was deeply moved by the rapturous reception for his beloved grandmother. It was, he thought, 'the British at their best – and you always manage to bring the best out in people!'[2] At the Palace, Queen Elizabeth appeared alone on the balcony. She waved to the crowds as she had first waved after her marriage in 1923 and, most famously, on Victory in Europe (VE) Day in May 1945. As the Band of the Coldstream Guards played Happy Birthday and the crowd roared its approval, she was joined by twenty-seven of her children, grand-children, great-grandchildren, nephews, nieces and many of their spouses.

In her long life the world had undergone technological change with unprecedented speed, and political transformations of exceptional violence. It had moved from the age of travel by horse to that of travel through space. The First World War and the Russian Revolution had toppled the emperors of Austria, Germany and Russia. Many other European kings and queens had subsequently departed their thrones. The United Kingdom had suffered the trauma of the Great War and then faced almost continuous challenge from economic and political turmoil, from war and the threat of war – through a world slump, the abdication of King Edward VIII, the Second World War, the Cold War. Queen Elizabeth had come to terms with massive changes – loss of empire, the growth of a modern multi-racial Commonwealth of newly independent states in Asia and Africa, and a social revolution in Britain itself which had begun with the first majority Labour government elected in 1945.

The British monarchy was not isolated from the political and social changes. Indeed the abdication in 1936 was a self-inflicted wound from which it might not have recovered. It had adapted itself, and it had survived; more than that, it had retained the consent of the people essential to constitutional monarchy. This adaptation was largely due to the efforts of successive sovereigns and their advisers. But a key question, explored in this book, is the extent to which the consent necessary for its survival was generated by the woman who was for almost eighty years at its heart – as Duchess of York, Queen and Queen Mother.

In any biography of a public person there is a danger of over-emphasizing the role of the individual in shaping events. This is particularly true when the individual has, like Queen Elizabeth, great prestige but no real power. Nevertheless, it remains legitimate to ask how Queen Elizabeth responded to the great personal and public crises of her life and what wider effect this had.

How did she do it? What combination of qualities had enabled this young Scottish aristocrat to come into the Royal Family and play such a central role in the life of the nation for almost eighty years? What part did she play in her unique family, as a young married woman, as a mother, as grandmother and great-grandmother? And on the national stage, how did she earn and, more remarkably, how did she retain her popularity through all of the turbulent twentieth century? What were the drawbacks to her very particular style? What did she really contribute to the monarchy and to the nation in times of crisis and social revolution? Would the British monarchy have evolved in a very different way without her influence? And would that have helped or hindered the institution and the country? All these questions can perhaps be examined in the context of a few words from Walter Bagehot, the mid-nineteenth-century writer who is often seen as the greatest interpreter of modern monarchy: 'The nation is divided into parties, but the crown is of no party. Its apparent separation from business is that which removes it both from enmities and from desecration, which preserves its mystery, which enables it to combine the affection of conflicting parties – to be a visible symbol of unity.'

CHAPTER ONE

AN EDWARDIAN CHILDHOOD

1900–1914

'The sun always seems to be shining'

ELIZABETH ANGELA Marguerite Bowes Lyon, the ninth child and the fourth daughter of Lord and Lady Glamis, was born at the end of the Victorian era, on 4 August 1900. Her family was of distinguished and colourful lineage in both England and Scotland.

Lord Glamis was the son and heir of the thirteenth Earl of Strathmore and Kinghorne. The Strathmores trace their ancestry back to the fourteenth century. John Lyon of Forteviot, the Chamberlain of Scotland from 1377 to 1382, married the daughter of King Robert II in 1376 and was knighted the following year. He was granted the thaneage of Glamis, a Crown possession in the Vale of Strathmore in eastern Scotland, some twelve miles north of Dundee, and this remained thereafter the principal seat of the family, although the transformation of a hunting lodge on the land into a castle did not begin until the early fifteenth century. Sir John Lyon's grandson Patrick was created the first Lord of Glamis.

In 1537 Janet, Lady Glamis, a Douglas by birth, wife of the sixth Lord Glamis, was burned at the stake in Edinburgh on charges trumped up by James V of Scotland. Then, having disposed of Lady Glamis and imprisoned her two sons, the King seized the lands and Castle of Glamis. He occupied the Castle and held court there, on and off, between 1537 and 1542.

Their estates for the most part restored after James V's death, the family continued to play a prominent role in Scottish royal history. The ninth Lord Glamis was created earl of Kinghorne by James VI of Scotland (James I of England) in 1606 and in 1677 Patrick, third Earl of Kinghorne, took the additional title of Strathmore. He became known as Earl of Strathmore and Kinghorne, the titles held by his successors ever since. Earl Patrick's *Book of Record*, a diary written between 1684

and 1689, is a treasured item in the family archives at the Castle. In it
he wrote that he was four years old when his father died and 'the debt
which my father left behind him was, by inventories whereof some
are yet extant, no less than four hundred thousand pounds.'[1] That this
young man not only paid off such enormous sums but was also able
to carry out extensive building works and improvements to the Castle
says much for his qualities of character.

In 1767 John, the ninth Earl of Strathmore, married Mary Eleanor
Bowes. She came from a well-established north of England family
which owned the estates of Gibside and Streatlam Castle in County
Durham.* As she was the only child and heiress of her parents, the
family name was perpetuated through her marriage: the ninth Earl and
his Countess by Act of Parliament took the surname of Bowes, to be
used 'next, before, and in addition to, their titles of honour'.[2] Under
the eleventh Earl it became Lyon Bowes, and finally, with the accession
of the thirteenth Earl in 1865, Bowes Lyon.[†]

The Bowes family had acquired both power and wealth since Sir
Adam Bowes, a fourteenth-century lawyer, was granted land at Streatlam, near Barnard Castle. And in 1691 Sir William Bowes married
Elizabeth Blakiston, heiress of Gibside, thereby adding a large estate
rich in coal to the Bowes possessions.

Mary Eleanor's father, George Bowes, third son of Sir William,
was both a considerable landowner and one of the first to make a
fortune from coal. He was said by his daughter in her *Confessions*[‡] to
have been 'a great rake in his youth', but he was astute too, and 'a
great sportsman with a real appreciation of beauty in art, architecture
and nature'.[3] The landscaped gardens at Gibside, created between 1729
and 1760, are testament to his energy and vision.

---

* One account of the origin of the Bowes family traces it to William, cousin of Alan the
Black, Earl of Richmond, who came over with William the Conqueror, and who put his
cousin in command of 500 archers in the tower of Bowes to protect the region from attacks
by the men of Westmorland and Cumberland. (Charles E. Hardy, *John Bowes and the Bowes
Museum*, Friends of the Bowes Museum, 1989, p. 6)

† Official documents from the time of Queen Elizabeth's marriage use the hyphenated
version of her surname, Bowes-Lyon. But when she was young, she and her family tended to
call themselves plain 'Lyon', and when they used both names, it was without a hyphen. The
senior branch of the Strathmore family continues to omit the hyphen.

‡ Mary Eleanor wrote her *Confessions* in 1778 on the orders of her second husband, who used
them against her in their divorce case and later published them, probably to raise money when
he was imprisoned for his maltreatment of her.

Mary Eleanor was born in 1749 to George and his second wife, Mary Gilbert, whose father Edward owned St Paul's Walden Bury in Hertfordshire. She inherited her father's charm, and he imbued her with his own enthusiasm for all kinds of knowledge.[4] Her marriage to John Lyon, celebrated on her eighteenth birthday in 1767, produced five children, but it was unhappy. The ninth Earl of Strathmore was known as 'the beautiful Lord Strathmore'; he was not uncultivated,* but his wife's biographer, Jesse Foot, characterized him as a bluff, hearty man and 'a good bottle companion', who was 'not exactly calculated to make even a good learned woman a pleasing husband'.[5] He believed that Mary Eleanor's intellect needed to be restrained. She had a serious interest in botany, and in 1769 she published a poetical drama called *The Siege of Jerusalem*. Her husband thought such pursuits frivolous.[6]

The Earl developed tuberculosis and he died at sea in March 1776 while on a voyage to Lisbon where he had hoped to recover his health. On board ship he wrote a kind last letter to his wife suggesting that she should protect her fortune by placing it in trust. He included another word of advice which perhaps illustrates the differences between the couple. 'I will say nothing of your extreme rage for literary fame. I think your own understanding, when matured, will convince you of the futility of the pursuit.'[7]

After his death, Mary Eleanor was left 'one of the richest widows in Britain'.[8] However, her personal life was tumultuous and in autumn 1776 she fell in love with Andrew Robinson Stoney, who became known as Stoney Bowes. One of the chroniclers of the Bowes Lyon family was frank in his description of Stoney Bowes: 'This man was surely the lowest cad in history ... He was the type of seedy, gentlemanly bounder, calling himself "Captain", which has flourished in every era of society ... [He] was cunning, ruthless, sadistic with rat-

---

* In a history of the Lyon family which Queen Elizabeth's mother, Lady Strathmore, began writing late in life, he is described as well educated and knowledgeable about architecture and paintings. The history was far advanced but not finished when she died in 1938. There is correspondence with John Murray Publishers and it was clearly a serious project. She received advice from the Rev. John Stirton, minister of Crathie and chaplain to the King, whose *Glamis Castle: Its Origin and History* was published in 1938. Lady Strathmore's enthusiasm jumps from the page. A note found in the box containing the text reads 'ANOTHER DISCOVERY! I can now tell you what Queen Mary <u>ate</u> when at Glamis in 1562!! and who accompanied her.' (Glamis Archives)

like cleverness and a specious Irish charm. He was a fortune hunter of the worst type.'[9] He had driven his first wife to death; but he charmed and seduced Mary Eleanor and they married in January 1777.

Shortly afterwards Stoney Bowes discovered to his fury that his bride had taken her first husband's advice and secured her fortune in trust. Four months after their marriage he managed to force Mary to sign a document revoking her prenuptial deed and he dissipated her wealth as swiftly as he could. When Mary Eleanor's mother died in 1781 she left her daughter St Paul's Walden Bury, which Stoney Bowes began to use as a safe house from his creditors in the north. Eventually Mary Eleanor managed to escape from him and file for divorce on grounds of his adultery and cruelty. In May 1786 this was granted, with Bowes being ordered to pay Mary £300 a year in alimony. However, he appealed, and began 'a ferocious war of propaganda'.[10]

He then had her abducted by force and taken north to Streatlam Castle, where he incarcerated her and tried to compel her at gunpoint both to sign documents suspending the divorce and to cohabit with him again, which would have invalidated her case.[11] She refused and he then dragged her around the north of England in appalling winter conditions while her solicitor searched for her in vain and had warrants issued for Stoney Bowes's arrest. Eventually, after wild chases which excited wide public interest, she was rescued. Bowes and his accomplices were sentenced to three years in prison and fined £300. He continued a campaign of lawsuits and public vilification of his ex-wife until she died in 1800. Stoney Bowes himself died in 1810.[12]

Mary Eleanor's son John had become the tenth Earl of Strathmore on his father's death in 1776. Unlucky in love, he threw himself into the restoration and improvement of the estates at Streatlam and Gibside, and then fell for Mary Millner, the daughter of George and Ann Millner of Stainton, a village close to Streatlam Castle. She bore his son, John Bowes, on 19 June 1811, and he married her in July 1820, the day before he died.

The earldom of Strathmore and Kinghorne devolved on Mary Eleanor's second surviving son, Thomas, who won the titles and estates after a lawsuit against his nephew John. He became the eleventh earl. But John Bowes inherited Gibside and Streatlam and, an accomplished man, he founded a great business empire. John Bowes and Partners operated twelve collieries and his income from coal alone was said to be immense. As MP for South Durham for fifteen years, he was a supporter of electoral reform, the anti-slavery movement and religious toleration. He bred four Derby winners at his Streatlam stud. In 1847 he went to live in Paris, where he met his first wife Joséphine Benoîte Coffin-Chevallier. Together they collected works of art and then built the Bowes Museum in the town of Barnard Castle, an imposing edifice in elaborate French Renaissance style, which is filled with fine paintings, tapestries, furniture and porcelain and thrives today, a striking monument to its founders.[13]*

By contrast, the eleventh Earl, although fortunate in his lawsuit against John Bowes, lacked financial acumen and died in the debtors' sanctuary at Holyroodhouse in 1846. His son Thomas, Lord Glamis, had already died at Honfleur in 1834; he too was in debt and his wife, Lady Glamis, née Charlotte Grinstead, was left with very little money to bring up four young children.† Her son Thomas became the twelfth earl on the death of his grandfather. He too lived beyond his means and died, a ruined man, in 1865. However, he achieved the distinction of riding twice in the Grand National. Later, his great-niece Queen Elizabeth adopted his racing colours of buff and blue stripes, blue sleeves and a black cap.

Thomas was succeeded by his brother Claude, the thirteenth Earl, who finally brought the spendthrift era to an end. Life at Glamis under Earl Claude reflected all that was best in Victorian society, and his diaries‡ show that it was neither stiff nor dull.[14] In his book, *The Days before Yesterday*, published in 1920, Lord Frederick Hamilton looks back fondly on his stays with the thirteenth Earl of Strathmore and his family: 'I like best, though, to think of the Glamis of my young days . . . when the whole place was vibrant with joyous young life, and the stately, grey-bearded owner of the historic castle, and of many broad

---

* Queen Elizabeth took great interest in her Bowes ancestry. She collected John Bowes memorabilia whenever she could, buying back many pictures and pieces of silver which had been sold at Christie's at the time of the sale of Streatlam Castle in 1922. She was patron of the Friends of the Bowes Museum from 1962 until her death.

† The legend of the 'Monster of Glamis' which originated in the nineteenth century may have arisen from the birth and death of the first child of Lord and Lady Glamis in 1821. The story ran that a deformed creature was kept alive, hidden in the Castle, until some time between 1865 and 1876. There appears to be no credible evidence for this story.

‡ The thirteenth Earl kept meticulous diaries from 1861 until shortly before his death in February 1904.

acres in Strathmore besides, found his greatest pleasure in seeing how happy his children and his guests could be under his roof.'[15]

No more charming family could be imagined, according to Lord Frederick. Lord Strathmore's seven sons and three daughters were all 'born musicians', and they were always singing: 'on the way to a cricket-match; on the road home from shooting; in the middle of dinner, even, this irrepressible family could not help bursting into harmony.' They sang madrigals and part-songs after dinner, and at services in the family's private chapel. They were equally good at acting and had a permanent stage at Glamis where they performed highlights from the latest Gilbert and Sullivan operas. All the sons were excellent shots and good at games; one brother was lawn tennis champion of Scotland, and another won the doubles championship of England.[16]

The thirteenth Earl's life was a continual struggle to repair the damage done to the family by the reckless extravagance of his grandfather, father and brother. In 1853 he married Frances Dora Smith who shared his deep Christian faith. The first of their eleven children, Elizabeth Bowes Lyon's father Claude George, was born in 1855. He held the courtesy title of Lord Glamis, before succeeding as the fourteenth earl in 1904. Educated at Eton, he served in the Life Guards from 1876 to 1881, the year he married Cecilia Cavendish-Bentinck.

Cecilia too came from a well-connected and devout family. She was the great-granddaughter of the third Duke of Portland, who was twice prime minister in George III's reign. Had she been a boy, she would have succeeded her uncle, the fifth Duke. Cecilia's father, Charles Cavendish-Bentinck, was a clergyman who died in 1865 aged only forty-seven, when Cecilia was just three. Her mother Caroline* married again in 1870, becoming Mrs Harry Scott of Ancrum; she was widowed again in 1889. In later years she spent a good deal of her time in Italy, first at the Villa Capponi in Florence,† and then in San Remo and Bordighera, on the Italian Riviera west of Genoa.

---

* Née Caroline Burnaby (1833–1918), daughter of Edwyn Burnaby of Baggrave Hall, Leicestershire.

† The Villa Capponi was bought by Mrs Scott's mother-in-law, Lady Elizabeth Scott, in 1882, and was sold by Mrs Scott in about 1908. Mrs Scott seems to have rented houses in San Remo before moving in late 1907 to Bordighera, where she rented the Villa Bella Vista, and later

Cecilia and Claude met in the 1870s. Some of the letters written during their courtship survive; they often corresponded more than once a day between Whitehall, where Claude was stationed with the Life Guards, and Forbes House, Ham, just west of London, where Cecilia lived with her mother. 'Darling Claudie,' Cecilia wrote from Ham not long before their marriage, 'I wish you weren't on guard – & could come out for a ride with me – do you remember our last ride? in the pelting rain? . . . I think I will write to you again by the 3 o.c. post – I'm longing for a letter from you dear Claudie – it is the next thing to seeing you.' 'My darling Cecilia,' he responded the same afternoon, 'I have just received your sweet letter . . . You ask me if I remember our last ride together? Of course I do, how awfully wet we got, but the ride before that I remember much better. I shall never forget that little corner, after passing the park-keeper's hut (where I once left my cover-coat) . . . Hoping to get yr letter all right tomorrow morning and longing to see your sweet face again, I am, my darling Cecilia, Ever your most loving Claudie.'[17]

Their wedding took place at Petersham Church on 16 July 1881. Cecilia was given away by her cousin, the sixth Duke of Portland. After 'cake and lunch', as Lord Strathmore described it in his diary, Claude and Cecilia caught the 5.05 train to Hitchin en route to St Paul's Walden Bury, the Hertfordshire house left to the groom by his paternal grandmother, Charlotte.[18] Claude resigned his commission and they started their lives together as Lord and Lady Glamis.

Their first child, Violet Hyacinth, was born in April 1882 at St Paul's Walden Bury, and the second, Mary Frances (May), born in August 1883, was followed by a line of sons – Patrick (September 1884), John (Jock) (April 1886), Alexander (Alec) (April 1887), Fergus (April 1889). Next came another girl, Rose, born in May 1890, and then Michael (October 1893).

The family's financial situation continued to improve as the new generation grew. John Bowes died in 1885 and, as he was childless, his houses returned to the main branch of the family. But in 1893 the family was struck by tragedy when Violet, Claude and Cecilia's eldest

bought Poggio Ponente which she left to one of Cecilia's sisters on her death. The Strathmores also owned a house in Bordighera, Villa Etalinda, which the thirteenth Earl bought in 1896. It was later sold to Queen Margharita of Savoy who built the enormous Palazzo Regina Margharita in the twenty-acre garden. She gave the palace and the villa to the War Association for the use of the war-wounded, their widows and orphans.

child, contracted diphtheria. She died of heart failure on 17 October, just two weeks after the birth of her brother Michael. She was only eleven, and was always said in the family to have been a beautiful child – there is a portrait of her at Glamis which would seem to bear this out. Lady Glamis bore her daughter's loss with as much courage as she could muster.

After Michael's birth in 1893 there was an interlude in the nursery at St Paul's Walden Bury until Elizabeth was born seven years later in August 1900. Her mother was thirty-eight. There is a small mystery surrounding the actual place of her birth.

The birth certificate filed at the register office in Hitchin by her father, Lord Glamis, states that she was born at St Paul's Walden Bury. The 1901 census return for the house, which Lord Glamis as head of the household was responsible for completing, also states that Elizabeth (by then eight months old) was born there.[19] Her first biography, published in 1927, for which she gave the author Lady Cynthia Asquith some assistance, says the same. There is a plaque in the parish church of All Saints at St Paul's Walden, unveiled by Queen Elizabeth herself in 1937, which commemorates her birth in the parish and baptism at the church.

She therefore caused some surprise when, close to her eightieth birthday, she said that she had been born in London.* In fact various records in her archives show that this was nothing new. The passport issued to her in 1921, despite the evidence of her birth certificate, showed her place of birth as London.[20] In the early 1950s the press office at Buckingham Palace repeatedly confirmed that the Queen had been born in London.[21] In 1978 the President of the British Astrological and Psychic Society wrote to Queen Elizabeth in a quandary because he had just read that she had been born in Hertfordshire, whereas the astrological chart he had lately presented to her was calculated on Edinburgh as her place of birth. Which was correct? She wrote at the top of his letter: 'I was born in London & christened in Hertfordshire.'[22] Unfortunately no comment by her seems to have survived as to why St Paul's Walden was officially recorded as her birthplace, or why she willingly unveiled a plaque containing wrong information.

---

* The Clarence House press officer was asked to clarify the question in August 1980, when the Queen Mother was in Scotland; her lady in waiting, Dame Frances Campbell-Preston, put it to her directly. Her unhesitating response, 'London,' was passed back by telephone.

The birth of a ninth child is unlikely to attract as much attention as the first, and Elizabeth Bowes Lyon's birth was no exception. Her grandfather's diary does not even mention it, although he does record her father's delayed arrival at Glamis on 22 August, causing him to miss the start of the grouse season by ten days.[23] Nor has any correspondence about it come to light among the Strathmore papers. If the birth took place in London it was perhaps at the flat in Belgrave Mansions, Grosvenor Gardens, which Elizabeth's paternal grandparents rented, and where Lord and Lady Glamis lived when they were in London.* Or it could have been at Mrs Scott's home, Forbes House, where the couple's third daughter, Rose, was born in 1890.

In her account of Queen Elizabeth's early years, *My Darling Buffy* (1997), the writer Grania Forbes investigated the problem with diligence. She speculated that Elizabeth could have been born in a London hospital and then driven straight to Hertfordshire, or even that she was born en route between London and St Paul's Walden. Either is no doubt possible, but the hospital hypothesis is unconvincing, because women of Lady Glamis's station normally had their babies at home and also because it is likely that some record of a hospital birth would subsequently have emerged. Another possibility advanced by Forbes was that Elizabeth's father, an absent-minded man, actually made a mistake when he registered his daughter's birth, more than six weeks after the event.[24]

In his 2005 biography Hugo Vickers points out that Dorothy Laird – who received authorization and help from the Queen Mother for her 1966 biography – does not mention a place of birth.[25] Vickers suggests that she might have wished to draw a veil over the whole subject.[26] Perhaps she preferred not to discuss the matter both because she was uncertain of the truth and because she thought it of purely private interest. At least in her youth, details of births would have been considered too delicate an issue to be discussed even within the family.

The belief persists in some quarters, nevertheless, that her birth did indeed take place in Hertfordshire. Canon Dendle French, chaplain of Glamis Castle and formerly vicar at St Paul's Walden, has done what he can to resolve the mystery.

Canon French traced Miss Margaret Valentine, daughter of the

---

* Belgrave Mansions is shown as their address on the invitation list for the Buckingham Palace garden party on 11 July 1900. (RA LC/CER/GP)

Rev. Henry Tristan Valentine, the vicar of St Paul's Walden who baptized the baby Elizabeth in September 1900. Miss Valentine was 'a very sprightly 91 year old, very lucid, and said she remembered very clearly August 4th 1900. "I was practising the piano at the Vicarage, and a maid came over from the Bury to say that Lady Glamis had given birth to a baby girl." I asked her if this had been at the Bury and she said that it was. She did not seem to have any doubt about this at all.' Moreover, among the letters Canon French received was one from a man who said that his father-in-law, Dr Bernard Thomas, a GP in Welwyn, always insisted that he was present at the birth. He was the family doctor, but it seems unlikely that a Hertfordshire doctor would be called to attend a birth in London.

Canon French also discovered that there had been a certain amount of gossip in the village, including the rumour that Lady Glamis had actually been en route from London when the contractions began and that the birth took place in or near Welwyn. One story passed down, but acknowledged as only hearsay, was that the baby started to arrive en route from London and that Lady Glamis was taken to Dr Thomas's home, Bridge House, Welwyn, where the infant was delivered. At the same time, one of Canon French's elderly parishioners told him that her aunt had been in charge of the laundry at the Bury and her work made her certain that the birth had taken place there. 'So there you are!' concluded the Canon. 'Conflicting stories – and perhaps we shall never know – but I have to say that London is the least likely place, given the evidence, and I still think it was in (or near) the Bury!'[27]

*

WHEREVER HER birth took place, the new century into which Elizabeth Bowes Lyon was born seemed to many to be a dawn of optimism. Europeans could look back on at least 200 years of growth and most of them would have assumed that it was progress. European industrialization in the nineteenth century had brought the greatest expansion of wealth the world had ever seen. There was no reason to expect this to end.

As John Roberts pointed out in his magisterial *History of the World*, the flow of commodities had increased exponentially: oil, gas and electricity had joined coal, wood, wind and water as sources of energy. Railways, electric trams, steamships, motor cars, even bicycles, brought remarkable changes to communications – indeed it was the greatest revolution in transport since animals had been tied to carts thousands of years before. Industrialization at the end of the nineteenth century was more than enough to keep pace with population growth. Those Europeans who considered such matters had reason to believe that their history since the Middle Ages showed a continual advance towards goals which were so evidently worth while that few of them were ever questioned. Since European civilization had spread across the globe, the entire world seemed set fair on a progressive course.

There were of course pessimists; some of them felt that civilization was drifting away from its moorings in religion and absolute morality, 'carried along by the tides of materialism and barbarity probably to complete disaster'.[28] Distribution of the newly created wealth was uneven and most Europeans were still poor. More and more of them lived in cities and towns, for the most part in wretched conditions which seemed to many to breed the inevitable conditions for revolution. Socialists stoked the rhetoric which sustained the notion of revolution – in Britain socialism was a moral creed rather than a materialistic one. It meant not Marxism but trade unionism and parliamentary methods. Yet in 1896 the Second International, an organization of socialist parties, had confirmed the supremacy of Marxism and the dogma of the class struggle.

This was frightening for the middle classes throughout the continent, but Marxist rhetoric tended to ignore the reality that, although the majority was still poor, the capitalist system had improved the lives of huge numbers of people in recent decades. It had also, in many places, advanced democracy. The suffrage was spreading inexorably, at least among males, and the discussion of women's rights had grown ever fiercer in the late nineteenth century. Henrik Ibsen had intended his play A Doll's House to be a plea for the individual, but it was taken as a call for the liberation of women. The development of advanced capitalist economies created massive opportunities for employment for women as typists, telephonists, shop assistants and factory workers. The accretion of such jobs changed domestic economics and family life for ever.

Another force was the ever faster march of technological progress. Together with piped water, clean sources of energy for both light and heat began to spread in the new century. These developments, and others such as electricity, preserved food, cookers, washing machines with mangles, helped to start the transformation of domestic life, at least for the middle classes. Later, the gradual spread of knowledge about contraception began to enable women to think that they could try to control the demands of procreation in ways which had been unimaginable to their mothers and to all their ancestors before them.

As we look back over the horrors of the twentieth century it is easy to say that the pessimists won the argument. In fact neither optimists nor pessimists were wholly right.[29] Hindsight can be a disadvantage – sometimes today it is difficult to see how the optimists could have been so certain. But they included men and women of great intelligence and wisdom.

It is also true that, although the end of the nineteenth century really did have an ominously decadent *fin de siècle* feeling for some people, they were a minority, even among artists and intellectuals. Revolutionaries like to see history as a state in which, after long periods of nothing happening, cataclysm occurs. An alternative view is that progress (or any change) tends to be slow and is often almost unnoticed. Thus electric light is invented and is indeed revolutionary, but its adoption is gradual, spread over many decades. The changes, intellectual and technological, which were so much to affect the life of Elizabeth Bowes Lyon and all others born on the cusp of the century at first did little to disturb the traditional rhythms of her world.

*

ON 22 JANUARY 1901, almost six months after Elizabeth's birth, Queen Victoria died at Osborne, her home in the Isle of Wight. It was a momentous event. Her funeral took place amid unprecedented pomp and ceremony and was attended by representatives of over forty nations. There are nineteen stout volumes in the Royal Archives containing the outpourings of the British press alone on the passing of the Queen Empress, who had reigned for nearly sixty-four years.

She was succeeded by her son, King Edward VII. Although it is tempting to see a new reign and a new century as marking a distinct change, these were but artificial breaks in a continuous process. The new monarch differed in style but not much in substance from the old; the monarchy itself remained firmly grounded in a society in which aristocratic families like the Strathmores could still be confident of the privileges, but also conscious of the responsibilities, which their place in the social order brought them.

King Edward VII's reign was to be short, less than ten years. He was seen much more in public than his revered mother and he mixed more freely with his subjects. Enthusiastic for lavish spending and for pageantry, he resumed the tradition, only occasionally followed by Queen Victoria in her widowhood, of attending the state opening of Parliament in person.

King Edward visited the watering places of Europe frequently, sometimes to the detriment of communications with his ministers. He was a genial extrovert who enjoyed meeting people and made them feel at ease. By his friendships he did a great deal to help secure the social acceptance of Jews. He sought, also, to achieve good relations with other countries, and his visit to France in 1904 created the atmosphere which helped to bring about the Entente Cordiale with Britain's hitherto hereditary enemy. In his personal life, he enjoyed the company of attractive and amusing women and acquired the reputation of a philanderer. But he treated his wife Queen Alexandra with affection and respect, and loved his children, three daughters, Princesses Louise, Victoria and Maud, and two sons, Prince Albert Victor ('Eddy') who died in 1892, and Prince George (later King George V) on whom he lavished affection after his elder brother's death.

The Edwardian years have been described as the Indian summer of the country-house way of life.[30] Despite the agricultural depression which set in after 1875 and which to a great extent broke the old reliance of the landed classes on land as a source of income, the mystique of ownership of a country property lived on. White table-cloths were still spread and the silver teapot still set out for tea on spacious lawns. Much had changed, however, and the families who weathered the changes best were those with resources beyond their broad acres – property in London, for example, or coalmining interests. Thanks to the arrival of the railways and then the motor car, travel to and between country properties was faster than ever before. Industrialization brought wealth and the newly rich wanted the highest status symbol of all – a stake in the land, but for purposes of recreation and display rather than income. Field sports, especially shooting, were the great pastime of the aristocracy of the age. According to the official history of Purdey's, the gun makers, the Edwardian years were some of the busiest and most profitable the firm has ever known. 'Individual cartridge orders of 10,000 per season are commonplace in the books of the time, and the cartridge-loading shop was busy far into the night. The orders for guns never slackened and profits boomed.'[31]

In the homes of great families, change was slow. Many country houses were still run on Victorian lines, so that family, guests, servants and children each had their separate areas. *Country Life* in 1911 commented approvingly of Crathorne Hall in Yorkshire: 'The whole of the nursery quarters are isolated, as they should be, and served by a separate corridor.'³² That was not the case at St Paul's Walden Bury, a handsome Queen Anne house of rose-red brick, its walls covered with magnolia and honeysuckle, set in the green Hertfordshire countryside. The house was comfortable and slightly shabby; it had none of the imposing, slightly eerie romance of Glamis. It was large but not grand; the nursery wing was easily accessible from the rest of the house.³³

Elizabeth's childhood was not formal or restrictive – indeed it was idyllic, all the more so after the birth in May 1902 of her brother David, the last of Cecilia and Claude's children. He and Elizabeth became so close and there was such a gap between them and their elder siblings that their mother called them her 'two Benjamins'. Within the family Elizabeth was known as Buffy.

After their mother, the most important presence in the children's lives was their nanny. Clara Cooper Knight, known as Alah, was the daughter of a tenant farmer on the Strathmores' Hertfordshire estate, and was taken on by Lady Strathmore when Elizabeth was only a month old. She later described Elizabeth as 'an exceptionally happy, easy baby: crawling early, running at thirteen months and speaking very young'.³⁴ Kind but firm, devoted and utterly dependable, Alah remained in charge of the nursery until Elizabeth was eleven and stayed with the family thereafter. She went to work for Elizabeth's elder sister May, and then took charge of Princess Elizabeth when she was born in 1926.

Elizabeth Bowes Lyon spent most of her childhood at St Paul's Walden Bury. Her brother David told Lady Cynthia Asquith that he and Elizabeth regarded Glamis as 'a holiday place, Streatlam as a visit, and St Paul's as "Home" '.³⁵ Cynthia Asquith commented: 'Its atmosphere of a happy English home recalls to one's memory so many of the familiar delights of childhood – charades, schoolroom-tea, home made toffee, Christmas Eve, hide-and-seek. Nowhere in this well-worn house, one feels, can there ever have been very strict rules as to the shutting of doors, the wiping of boots or the putting away of toys . . . least of all any edict that children must be seen, not heard.'³⁶

The garden outside was both lovely and mysterious, with barns and other outhouses making irresistible places to play. Elizabeth loved being in the stable around the smell of horses and leather, bits of which the groom gave her to polish. 'Absolute bliss,' she recalled.[37] Beyond the garden lay woodland, intersected by long grassy avenues lined with beech hedges and connected by lateral rides. Statues stood at the end of vistas and a maze of walks criss-crossed the wood; there were ponds, a rock garden and a huge knobbled oak tree. Once within this wood it was hard not to believe that one was in a vast forest.[38]

The adult Elizabeth gave Cynthia Asquith a whimsical description of this magical childhood world. 'At the bottom of the garden, where the sun always seems to be shining, is THE WOOD – the haunt of fairies, with its anemones and ponds, and moss-grown statues, and the BIG OAK ... where the two ring-doves, Caroline-Curly-Love and Rhoda-Wrigley-Worm, contentedly coo in their wicker-work "Ideal Home".'[39]

The two children had a favourite hiding place which they called the Flea House. It was in the attic of the decrepit brewhouse – a 'blissful retreat', David said, in which they hid from grown-ups and escaped from their morning lessons. 'In it we kept a regular store of forbidden delicacies acquired by devious devices. This store consisted of apples, oranges, sugar, sweets, slabs of Chocolat Menier, matches and packets of Woodbines.'[40] Years later Queen Elizabeth recalled the fascination of the farm buildings for the two children: 'I loved wandering round the old Barns and Flea House, & remembering some of the old characters who seemed to live there. Will Wren's parlour and Charles May's shed were always full of fascinating & exciting objects when we were children, and the Brew House, with its dangerous deep well, and chaff cutting machine, were very special and rather frightening!'[41]

'We did all the usual country-life things together,' David told his sister's biographer. 'We were never separated if we could avoid it.'[42] Their interests were not identical: she loved horses, he did not; she loved parties, he did not. When visitors came she would explain, 'David is rather shy.'[43] Mrs Thompson, the housekeeper, wrote after Elizabeth had married and become duchess of York:

> They were the dearest little couple I have ever seen and the Duchess always took the lead. She would come tripping down the stairs and it would be 'Mrs Thompson, have you any of those

nice creams left for us?' and she would herself open the cupboard and help herself to what she liked best . . . I can see her now coming outside the window of the housekeeper's room with her tiny pony Bobs, and making him beg for sugar, and often she would come up by herself and pop her head up suddenly and make us all jump, at which she would have a good laugh. She had a very happy childhood, and always good health to enjoy it.[44]

If St Paul's Walden Bury was a delightful family home, Glamis Castle was a thrilling place to spend holidays. It is one of the most splendid buildings in Scotland. The oldest part of the Castle, the south-east wing, dates from the fifteenth century but it was not until the early seventeenth century, when the first and second earls of King-horne set about remodelling the Castle, that it acquired its impressive height, its turreted profile and some of its finest rooms. The soaring central staircase, with eighty-six wide stone steps winding round to the top of its tower, was built at this time. Its hollow newel may once have been intended to heat the house with warm air rising from a fire at its base; but since 1686 it has held the mighty weights of the Castle clock, the steady ticking of which, muffled by the thickness of the stone, has been described by one family member as 'the heartbeat of the castle'.[45]

The first Earl installed the imposing chimneypiece and overmantel in the great hall, now the Drawing Room; the second Earl was responsible for the handsome arched ceiling, dated 1621. After a period of neglect, towards the end of the seventeenth century the Castle acquired its present spectacular approach and façade thanks to the inspiration of Patrick, first Earl of Strathmore and Kinghorne, who moved the entrance to the stair tower and the avenue leading up to it. He also installed the chapel next to the Great Hall, richly decorated with paintings by Jacob de Wet, which survives, after a mid-nineteenth-century restoration. Earl Patrick's much admired gardens and policies (parkland) were destroyed in the eighteenth century. However, the more open setting of the Castle today allows for dramatic effect, the turrets appearing to rise up as one makes one's way down the long, straight drive. (In 2008, the Prince of Wales opened the Queen Mother Memorial Gates at the end of the drive, thus allowing a view of the Castle from Glamis village for the first time.)

Through the ages the Castle has resounded with superstition, legend and tales of ghosts and even monsters, and has received the visits of kings and queens of Scotland. James VI of Scotland visited often to see his friend the ninth Lord Glamis, who then accompanied his sovereign south on his accession to the throne of England (as James I) in 1603 and became one of his Privy Counsellors in 1606. It is possible that Shakespeare heard tales of the many historical connections between Glamis and the Scottish Crown at the English Court. Whatever inspired the playwright's imagination, the Castle continues to have a stirring association with the grim tragedy of *Macbeth*.[46] Before the installation of gas lighting in 1865, climbing the stairs to bed with a flickering candle could have unsettled the thoughts of even the most unimaginative soul. After spending a night at Glamis, Sir Walter Scott wrote, 'I must own that when I heard door after door shut, after my conductor had retired, I began to consider myself as too far from the living, and somewhat too near the dead.' Scott drew on the Castle and the circumstances of the family in two of his novels, *Waverley* and *The Antiquary*.[47] By the end of the Victorian period the Castle had become somewhat more domestic. In the last decade of the century the thirteenth Earl, Elizabeth's grandfather, embarked on building work to accommodate his growing number of grandchildren.[48] Plans for the new nursery wing show large south-facing rooms on the second floor. Electricity came to the Castle only in 1929.

One of Elizabeth's earliest memories was of her grandparents' golden wedding celebration at Glamis in 1903, when she sat on her grandfather's knee and watched the fireworks.[49] His diary records that the Strathmores invited 571 children from five schools in the neighbourhood to tea, sports and a conjuring show, followed by fireworks arranged by the house steward, Charles Collingwood. 'All went perfectly. They said there were 2000 people to see the fireworks. We saw them from my window with some of the children.'[50]

On 16 February 1904 Elizabeth's grandfather died and, at the age of forty-nine, her father became fourteenth earl of Strathmore and Kinghorne.* The diary of her elder sister May records that she and her mother sent their clothes off to be dyed black.[51] Years later Elizabeth recalled that in her childhood they always seemed to be in mourning for someone.[52]

---

* As daughters of an earl, Elizabeth and her sisters acquired the courtesy title of 'Lady'. Thus she was now Lady Elizabeth Bowes Lyon.

Home remained at St Paul's Walden Bury but now that her father had inherited Glamis as well – not to mention Streatlam and Gibside – her family's visits north became more prolonged. The winter, spring and summer until July were generally spent in Hertfordshire and London, where from late 1906 the Strathmores rented 20 St James's Square, a magnificent house designed by Robert Adam for Sir Watkin Williams-Wynn in the 1770s. In August they moved to Glamis, staying there until October or sometimes November before returning south. The autumn was also the period for visits to Streatlam. Decamping to Glamis was a major operation. It was not just the family but the household which moved to Scotland. As well as clothes they took silver, china and everything else that they might need for several weeks' holiday and entertainment north of the border. Everyone boarded the overnight train which took them to the little station at Glamis.

By the standards of the day, and of their acquaintances, the Strathmores did not run a grand household. The 1901 census return for St Paul's Walden Bury lists a housekeeper, a cook, a lady's maid, a dairy maid, a nursery maid, two housemaids, a kitchenmaid, two footmen, a page, a coachman and a groom (who doubled as a chauffeur when motor cars were acquired in about 1908). For many decades, the most cherished was Arthur Barson who served the family through several generations as footman, valet and butler. 'Nothing would go on without him – he keeps everything going,' the young Elizabeth informed a newcomer to the household.[53] She later told a relative that the family all liked Barson so much that they insisted he be included in the portrait of the family showing them gathered in the drawing room at Glamis, with Elizabeth and David in the foreground building houses of cards on the floor. It was painted in 1909 by a young Italian painter, Alessandro Catani-Chiti, and still hangs at St Paul's Walden Bury.[54]

Later Elizabeth recalled that Glamis, like St Paul's, was filled with local people working for the family. Outside there were gardeners, grooms and agricultural workers. Inside there were housemaids, kitchenmaids and laundry maids. 'It was really like a little village,' she remembered, and she thought it was a happy one. 'They were all our friends.'[55] For many years the family cook was Etta Maclean, known as Mrs Eeta. She had been trained by Lady Strathmore and travelled with the family. Her two sisters also worked for the Strathmores; one,

Catherine (Catta), later became Elizabeth's lady's maid and stayed with her for many years after her marriage.[56]*

*

THE FATHER of this great family was thin, rangy and unconventional. He had a thick moustache which greyed quite early in his life. He was not extrovert; indeed he was said to be 'a quiet, courteous, religious man, conscientious to a degree'.[57] He had a strong sense of duty which he imparted to his children; he was a dedicated landowner who was said to be generous to his tenants; he was a sportsman, a good if not first-class cricketer, and an excellent shot. But above all he loved forestry and was known for the eccentric delight he took in chopping up trees.

A family anecdote tells something of his character. One day when working with his trees, he was looking sufficiently unkempt and unrecognizable for a wandering tramp to stop and talk to him. They got on so well that the tramp stayed to help him with a bonfire. The Earl then told the tramp that he had heard that, if one went to the back door of the big house, one would be given some money, and advised him to try this the next day. Lord Strathmore then gave the butler a sovereign to pass on. Next day the tramp reappeared and told the Earl with jubilation that he had received a half-sovereign. History does not relate what happened to the butler, who was surely not the beloved Barson.[58]

If Claude was eccentric and loved by his family and retainers, Cecilia was simply much loved – by all her children, her servants and her friends. She dominated her family and household, running both with affection and care. One of her daughters recalled: 'Mother was a very wonderful woman, very talented, very go-ahead, and so upright. She had a terrific sympathy; the young used to pour their troubles out to her and ask her for advice, often when they would not go to their own parents.'[59] Her granddaughter Lady Mary Clayton spoke of her as 'the wisest person one could meet', and described her 'delicious' laugh.[60] Devoid of snobbery, Cecilia had a great capacity for friendship. She had a zest for living and was constantly developing new enthusiasms, but

---

* Catherine Maclean (c. 1890–1966), dresser to the Duchess of York and Queen Elizabeth 1923–52. Owing to ill health she did not work after 1941 and finally retired in 1952. In the 1950s and 1960s the three Maclean sisters ran the Dores Inn on Loch Ness, where Queen Elizabeth sometimes visited them.

she was casual to the point of apparent carelessness. When a visitor could no longer bear to watch water pouring down the wall of a room at St Paul's Walden Bury and pointed it out to her, she merely remarked, 'Oh dear, we must move that sofa.'[61]

She gave wonderful parties. Raymond Asquith, the eldest son of the future Prime Minister, described a ball at Glamis in September 1905: 'The place is an enormous 10th century dungeon. It was full of torches and wild men in kilts and pretty women pattering on the stone stairs with satin slippers . . . I was glad to find I had enough illusibility left to fancy myself in a distant century.'[62]

A lively and imaginative storyteller, Cecilia entertained her children with tales of life at Glamis in centuries gone by. Gradually, she inculcated in them a sense of history and romance, a love of tradition and a sense of duty. She was strict but not harsh; her children were brought up according to firm principles, but they recalled that these were never enforced unkindly. 'Work is the rent you pay for life' was one of her maxims; another was 'Life is for living and working at. If anything or anyone bores you, then the fault is in yourself.'[63] She was artistic and creative, and her embroidery, especially crewel-work, was outstanding in its design and execution. She also had a good ear for music and was an accomplished pianist. Another of her loves was gardening, and at Glamis between 1907 and 1910 she designed and created what is now called the Italian Garden. A major project, it involved felling about four acres of trees and levelling and draining the ground, all carried out by men from the estate.[64]

Christianity was fundamental to both Cecilia and Claude; they instilled a strong sense of religion in their children. The family said prayers daily at St Paul's Walden Bury and in the Glamis chapel. Lady Strathmore considered that women's hair should be covered for worship and provided white lace caps for guests. On Sundays she played the harmonium to accompany the hymns. She taught each of her children to kneel and pray beside their beds every night. Elizabeth continued to do this until the end of her life. The Strathmore children were brought up – like so many other British children from different backgrounds – with a love of nation as well as a love of God. Loyalty to King and Country were imbibed early on, along with decent behaviour. Their generation, like their parents', was proud of the spread of Christianity, law and technical progress throughout the British Empire.

It was a happy household and, according to contemporary accounts, Elizabeth was a vivacious child who, from an early age, loved the company of adults as well as children. Her grandmother found her 'quite a companion', even at the age of three, and enjoyed 'her coaxy little ways'.[65] Her mother once found the three-year-old pouring tea (which she had ordered herself) and talking to neighbours who had arrived early. On another occasion, according to Cynthia Asquith, she approached a distinguished visitor with the words 'Shall us sit and talk?' As Lady Cynthia commented, 'The sentence was a command rather than an invitation,' and the man was gently detached from the rest of the party and led away for a long conversation.[66]

Being ninth of ten children had its benefits: adults took a more indulgent view of one's behaviour. Elizabeth was mischievous as well as precocious, although her first biographer found no reports of 'sensational naughtiness' beyond the occasion when, aged about six, she used a pair of scissors to cut up her sheets. When she confided this to a visitor, she was asked, 'What will Mother say when you tell her?' 'Oh! Elizabeth,' she replied – and she was correct.[67]

Lord David Cecil, who was introduced to Elizabeth in London when they were both children, later wrote: 'I turned and looked and was aware of a small, charming rosy face around which twined and strayed rings and tendrils of silken hair, and a pair of dewy grey eyes . . . From that moment my small damp hand clutched at hers and I never left her side . . . Forgotten were all the pretenders to my heart. Here was the true heroine. She had come. I had seen and she had conquered.'[68] Another admirer, Lord Gorell,* whom she used as a child to call 'old boy', remembered later that she had said to him, when aged eight, that she was sure she had 'bothered' him when she was only six. On the contrary, he recalled: 'there are children, of course, who bother grown ups; but Lady Elizabeth was never one of them . . . She had, even then, that blend of kindliness and dignity that is the peculiar characteristic of her family. She was small for her age, responsive as a harp, wistful and appealing one moment, bright-eyed and eager the next, with a flashing smile of appreciative delight.'[69]

One of the many photographs of Elizabeth and David as children shows them at Glamis with their dancing master, Mr Neill of Forfar. It is almost like a painting by Rembrandt; the bearded old man, standing

---

* Ronald Gorell Barnes, third Baron Gorell (1884–1963), Liberal peer and author.

with his fiddle, watches as Elizabeth poses in a long Jacobean dress
said to be of rose pink and silver, while David wears the multi-coloured
jerkin, tights, cap and bells of a court jester. Mr Neill took his job as
teacher seriously; though he used to skip around the room after his
pupils as he played, he maintained a solemn mien so that David and
Elizabeth knew that they must learn their steps. Only when the dance
was complete and any audience present clapped them could they
relax.[70] On one occasion they danced for the minister of Glamis, Dr
John Stirton, who was later appointed chaplain to King George V at
Balmoral. He recalled that when Cecilia Strathmore sat at the piano
and played a few bars of a 'quaint old minuet', suddenly 'as if by a
magician's touch, two little figures seemed to rise from the floor and
dance, with admirable precision and grace, the stately measure so
characteristic of the eighteenth century.' When the dancers bowed and
curtsied, 'little choruses of praise were heard on every side, and Lady
Elizabeth, on being asked the name of the character she had adopted,
said with great *empressement*: "I call myself the Princess Elizabeth."'[71]

Among Elizabeth's abiding childhood memories were her trips to
Italy with her mother, to stay with her grandmother Mrs Scott in her
various villas in Florence, San Remo and Bordighera. These visits are
not well documented, but the first was probably to San Remo in
February 1907, when she was six years old. On 14 February, Claude
wrote to his mother at the Strathmores' villa in Bordighera: 'Cecilia
and my darling Elizabeth are starting from Charing X tomorrow
morning and you will see her soon I hope.'[72] Eight days later Elizabeth
wrote to her father, with some assistance, for the spelling is faultless:
'This is a most lovely place and there is an orange tree in the garden
and lots of flowers I pick them before breakfast.'[73]

There were several more trips over the next few years and they
made a deep impression on the young girl. Later she spoke to her first
biographer of 'the thrill of night travel and restaurant-car meals, and at
the end of the journey the glamour of being "abroad", the gabble and
gesticulations of foreigners, and all the colour and beauty of this Italian
home'. Mrs Scott's Villa Capponi in Florence had a wonderful garden,
'with magnificent cypresses standing out against the blue distant
mountains behind Fiesole' and views over the city of Florence; the
house itself was filled with beautiful furniture, pictures and flowers.[74]
On another trip, this time to Bordighera, Elizabeth reported back to
her father that she had been playing on the rocks on the sea shore.

'There is a dear little donky here called Marguarita and we put it in a little carriage and I drive it is so quiet have got nothing more to say exept it is a lovly garden my best love to yourself good by from your very loving Elizabeth.'[75]

In November 1908 Elizabeth's eldest brother Patrick, Lord Glamis, married Lady Dorothy Osborne, daughter of the Duke of Leeds. 'Me and Dorothy's little brother are going to be bridesmaids,' she wrote.[76] It was to prove a problematic marriage for the family: none of them found Dorothy Glamis easy.[77] In early 1910, the birth of John, the eldest son of Patrick and Dorothy, made Elizabeth an aunt for the first time, at the age of nine. She proudly recorded the event in the first of her surviving diaries, which she began on the first day of 1910.

The diary is a red morocco leather book about the size of a large postcard, perhaps given to her as a Christmas present in 1909. Her handwriting is strong and even, in black ink. On the flyleaf she wrote: 'Written by Elizabeth Lyon, begun Jan 1 1910, at St Paul's Walden.'

> Jan 1 1910. I had my first nevew great excitement. Same day went to Lady Litten's Fancy dress party and had great fun. Jan 2 Sunday – did nothing went to church. Jan 3 lessons in the morning – in the afternoon I went to a party at King's Walden there was a Xmas tree. Jan 4 had lessons in the morning. At 7 in the evening May, Rosie, David and I went to Lady Verhner in fancy dress it was great fun, there were proggrams too and supper at half past nine. We went away at ten. It was from 7 to 12.[78]

The diary was kept well for January 1910 but, in the way of diaries, tailed off thereafter. It recounted her lessons, a 'not very nice' fancy-dress party, enjoying *Aladdin* in London, lessons, rain, more lessons, tobogganing and church, and on the 21st she went for a long walk and 'met people going to vote. David and I wore the right color. Vote for Hillier.'[79] Alfred Hillier was the Conservative candidate for Hitchin, and his victory gave Elizabeth some happy news to send to her French governess: 'Le conservatives a allee dedans ici n'est e pas ces gentil.'[80]

It was a time of political change. In 1906 the Conservatives had been swept away at Westminster by a landslide Liberal victory, and twenty-nine of the new Members represented the Labour Party. The January 1910 election was called after the unprecedented rejection by the House of Lords of a Finance Bill – Lloyd George's controversial 'People's Budget' of 1909. He had proposed to raise income tax and other taxes. Land taxes, in particular, aroused the fury of the Conservative majority in the Lords.

The election resulted in a hung Parliament. The Liberals lost their large majority and were returned with a majority of just two. They now had to rely on the support of Labour and Irish MPs. King Edward VII was not pleased. He complained to his son that 'our great Empire' was now being ruled by Irish nationalists, 'aided and abetted by Messrs Asquith, L. George and W. Churchill'.[81] And indeed the new government was compelled to bring in an Irish Home Rule bill in return for Irish nationalist support for Lloyd George's budget. But the Conservative majority in the House of Lords rejected the proposals of the Liberal government to reduce the powers of the Lords and this brought about a constitutional crisis which eventually did lead to a reduction in those powers.

The crisis was unresolved when, on 6 May 1910, Edward VII died. His son, King George V, wrote in his diary, 'At 11.45 [p.m.], beloved Papa passed peacefully away & I have lost my best friend and the best of fathers.'[82] Lady Strathmore noted that all the shops were 'crammed' when she went out to buy mourning clothes. On 20 May, a beautiful day, she and her two elder daughters watched the funeral procession from Apsley House at Hyde Park Corner.[83] Nine European monarchs came to bury the King, including his nephew Kaiser William II of Germany; none could foresee that four years later their nations would all be engulfed in war.

*

IN JULY 1910 Elizabeth's eldest sister May married Sidney Herbert, sixteenth Baron Elphinstone, at St Margaret's, Westminster. He had an exciting personality: formerly a big-game hunter and an explorer, in 1900 he had travelled to the Ta Hingan Shan mountains on the Sino-Russian border. Elizabeth loved being a bridesmaid at the wedding.[84] She was by now well into her lifetime habit of writing chatty letters and wrote several to May as soon as her sister had departed on her honeymoon.

> Darling May-di-kin,
>   This letter will reach you just after the one I wrote last night, perhaps you will think it funny me writing so soon, but I have

got such a lot more to ask and tell you that I am writing before I forget it. (Please tell me if I am to call Sidney Darling or Dear). . . . wasen't it funny when they showered Sidney and you with rice, how far did you go with the shoes fastened on the motor, the boys told Charles May to stand in front of them so you would not see.[85]

May replied to her promptly from her honeymoon, for three days later Elizabeth wrote again, apologizing that 'I cant help writing so often because I have got such a lot to tell you, so please don't answer all my letters unless you like.'[86]

For her birthday on 4 August, she told May, her father had given her ten shillings 'because I was ten', her mother gave her a ring, her grandmother a tennis racket and some cut coral. Her brother Michael teased her by refusing to go and buy her a present, then handed her a penny which he increased to four shillings – 'so I am very rich'. May and Sidney sent her a present too. 'I absolutely don't know how to thank you and Sidney for the lovely beautiful [underlined often] clock it will be so usefull, I thank you and Sidney a thousand times.'[87]

When Cecilia Strathmore had to go to London or to Streatlam without her, Elizabeth wrote a stream of affectionate letters to her 'Darling Sweetie Lovie Mother', telling her that they had been to look for wild hyacinth bulbs in the wood, or that one of the dogs was lame, or that she was doing her lessons – 'essays, music, Geografy and sums'.[88] After Christmas 1910 she wrote, 'I am [underlined seven times] so longing to see you lovie. Rosie said that perhaps you are going to let us go to Jack and the Beanstalk. Do write or telephone and tell us if we are going to any parties.'[89]

The telephone was part of the exhilarating technological revolution of the time. It was still a marvel but, like the motor car, was becoming more and more widely used. In 1900 there were 36,000 horses pulling trams in Britain. Over the next fourteen years, the internal combustion engine caused their number to fall to fewer than a thousand.[90] Even more astonishing were adventures in the air. The ten-year-old Elizabeth wrote an essay entitled 'A recent invention, Aeroplanes': 'An aeroplane, to look at, is like a big, great bird. They are very clever inventions. An aeroplane is usualy shaped like a cigar, and has a propeller at one end, and on each side the great white wings, which makes it look so like a bird. An aeroplane can fly very high and it makes a great noise. They are not quite safe, yet, and many, many axidents have happened.'[91]

Next year more domestic interests dominated a letter in which she recounted a typical day at St Paul's Walden:

Dear Miss Ela Collins,

I hope you are feeling quite well. We are at St Paul's Walden, and it is a lovely day. This morning David and I got up at 6 o'clock. We first went and let out – Peter, Agiratem, Bumble bee, Lion-mouse, Beauty and Delicate, our six silver blue Persian kitten cats. After that we went to see the ponies, then we fed the chickens, there are over three hundred. Then we went to get Judy, Juno, her four puppies, and Major. Then we went to look for eggs for our breakfast, then went for a ride. After that lessons till lunchtime. Then lessons till half past four, then we took our tea into the wood and when we came home I begun to write this letter. Goodbye Miss Ela & with

Love from

Elizabeth A M B Lyon[92]

Much later she recalled that her early years were spent in 'a quiet world' of horses. In St James's Square 'the footman would whistle once for a hansom and four times for a Growler',* and Hyde Park on Saturdays was filled with ponies and carriages. At St Paul's Walden the family had dog carts to take them through the lanes to and from the railway station. And at Glamis she remembered all her life a frightening incident when, the coachman by her side, she was driving a pair of horses and they started to run away with her. 'We were hanging on, making straight for the gates which were shut and I said to our coachman, "What are we going to do?" and he took his bowler hat off and he said, "Trust in the Lord," with which we hung on and, do you know, as we got nearer the gates, they opened. We flew through them at great speed. Trust in the Lord.'[93]

The quiet horse-world began to end when her father acquired the first family car – 'Huge. It made such a noise you really couldn't hear what the other person was saying.' It could go uphill only backwards.

---

* The Growler was a spacious Victorian four-wheeled cab; it was eventually replaced by the lighter, faster two-wheeled hansom cab.

'I remember my father sitting on the back seat tapping on the window with his stick saying to the chauffeur "Take a run at it."' Those early cars were both hazardous and exciting, she said – and grooms did not always make good drivers.[94]

Life took on a more boisterous note when Elizabeth and David were joined by their elder siblings and parties of friends for weekends at St Paul's Walden Bury and for the summer holidays in Scotland. Lord Gorell recalled that nothing was as friendly as the pre-war summer house parties at Glamis, when, 'under the gracious guidance' of Cecilia Strathmore, 'the old castle re-echoed with fun and laughter'. The boys played cricket constantly. The games were fun – 'serious-non-serious' rather than in deadly earnest. One match at Arbroath depended on the ability of Fergus, 'a great wag as well as a dear and gallant fellow, but no cricketer, to achieve the unusual and make a run, and amidst cheers for once he managed a fluke shot'.[95]

Shooting was at the heart of life at Glamis. There were two high points in the year – August–September for grouse and September–October for partridges. Horses and carts took the guns (the shooting party) up to the moor; the keepers would walk. The party would spend most of the day on drives such as Ingliston Bogs, West Dunoon, Tarbrax, Hayston Hill, The Warren. Every male member of the family had his own gamebook; these were meticulously kept and reveal that an average of five guns, sometimes only two and rarely more than seven, went out at a time. Often it was just members of the family who shot, along with the factor and occasionally friends and neighbours. The gamebook of Elizabeth's brother Fergus shows a good grouse day on 15 August 1913. The guns that day were all family – Pat, Jock, Mike, Fergus and their father. They shot 133 grouse, two woodcock, six hares, twelve rabbits and one 'various'. On another occasion, when Fergus shot at Glen of Ogilvie by himself, he recorded: 'ripping day. Most enjoyable I ever had.'[96]

The evenings were also lively. The Castle was lit by hundreds of candles; there were immense fires; there was dinner in the great dining room, which the twelfth Earl had renovated in 'Jacobean' style and which boasted an enormous carved sideboard, family portraits and wooden armorial shields illustrating family alliances. After dinner the family and their guests adjourned to the drawing room, where logs burned constantly in the fireplace to banish the chills as summer died into autumn. The focus of the room was often the piano at which

Lady Strathmore or one of her daughters would play in the evenings while the rest of the party gathered around to sing traditional Scottish ballads or popular songs of the day such as 'Would You Like Me for a Father, Mary Ann?', 'The Little Nipper' by Albert Chevalier or 'The Vamp' from *Bran Pie*.[97] If one of the children had a birthday, the older siblings made comic toasts which aroused general laughter. Gorell commented that there was:

> no stiffness, no aloofness anywhere, no formality except the beautiful old custom of having the two pipers marching around the table at the close of dinner, followed by a momentary silence as the sound of their bagpipes died away gradually in the distance of the castle. It was all so friendly and so kind ... No wonder little Elizabeth came up to me once as my visit was nearing its end and demanded 'But why don't you *beg* to stay?'[98]

A friend and admirer of Elizabeth's sister Rose, a young naval officer named Frederick Dalrymple Hamilton,* came for the first time in the summer of 1911; his diaries over the next three years contain vivid glimpses of life in the Strathmore family, and of the young Elizabeth. 'Very pleased to see Lady Rose again,' he wrote on arriving at Glamis. 'Made the acquaintance of her younger sister Elizabeth for 1st time who is a little angel!! After tea Rosie took me up to the gardens & we fed on gooseberries. Played a new gambling game after dinner.' The next days were filled with cricket matches, shooting, tennis, raids on the fruit garden and picnics. After one 'enormous lunch' on the moor, 'the more energetic ones set out to climb a hill about 3 miles off. Mike & Elizabeth & I thought this quite beyond our strength & so we coiled ourselves down & went to sleep on the top of the first hill!' In the evening they 'sang ribald songs in the Billiard room and later on danced in the drawing room'. The next day they all dressed up for dinner, and Rose pinned her friend into a velvet costume with a sword and wig. 'Rose as Joan of Arc was topping also Elizabeth in an early Georgian kind of rig ... After dinner we danced

---

* Frederick Dalrymple Hamilton (1890–1974), entered Royal Navy 1905. Captain of the Royal Naval College, Dartmouth 1936–9; Captain, HMS *Rodney* 1939–41. During the Second World War he held various commands, and was naval secretary to the First Lord of the Admiralty 1942–4. Flag Officer Commanding Scotland and Northern Ireland 1946–8, and Admiral, British Joint Services Mission, Washington 1948–50. KCB 1945. He married, 1918, Gwendolen Peek.

reels in the middle of which my trousers fell off & I had to make a quick exit!!!'[99]

Sitting next to Mike in the Castle chapel at the first of two services he attended on Sunday, Freddy 'had much ado not to laugh' but was deterred by the presence of Lord Strathmore behind them; in the afternoon he went with the two sisters for 'a trout tickling expedition & had great fun though the number of trout tickled was exactly nil!' In the garden later, he recorded, 'E. nearly killed herself eating green apples!' He hated leaving next day – 'I don't think I've ever had such a good time,' he wrote. He said goodbye sadly at the station to a large party including Elizabeth and that evening he sent her a box of chocolates.[100] His later visits both to Glamis and to St Paul's Walden were equally filled with fun and carefree games – in Freddy's pre-war diaries there is a sense of eternal play.

But there was grief in the Strathmore family also. Alec, Elizabeth's third brother, had been badly injured at Eton when a cricket ball hit his head. This seems to have caused a tumour. In July 1911 his brother Jock, who was a year older, wrote to their mother from Boston, Massachusetts, where he was working in a bank, 'I am so sorry to hear you don't think Alec is so strong. I wonder why it is? What do the doctors say about the condition of his head? Poor Alec, what an awful long time it has been for him.'[101] Alec's gamebook records that towards the end of his life he often had to stop shooting early because of headaches. In October 1911 Jock wrote to a friend, 'I am very much afraid that he is not getting any better.'[102] Jock took a boat home, but he was too late to see his brother. Alec died in his sleep in the early hours of 19 October 1911, aged twenty-four. Cecilia was devastated. Her mother wrote to her from Bordighera: 'I am so thankful to feel that you have Jock with you but so grieved for him not getting home in time to see his Companion Brother. With his deep feeling heart it must be hard to bear.'[103]

*

IN EARLY 1912 Elizabeth took up her diary again with a brief entry for the weekend of 17–18 February. She was at St Paul's Walden Bury with Rose, her father and David; her mother was at Glamis. On Saturday she and Rose went riding from 11 to 3. '<u>Great</u> fun. <u>Lovely</u> day.'[104] On Sunday they all went to the parish church of All Saints, which lay at the end of a grassy ride cutting through the woods below the house.

At the beginning of March Freddy Dalrymple Hamilton found both Elizabeth and David 'down with measles or up rather' when he lunched with the family at St James's Square; he was there again the next day to take Mike and Rose to a show at the Coliseum, and noted in his diary that suffragettes, whose campaign to win the vote for women was at its height, were 'busy smashing windows all day'.[105] In April he spent a weekend at St Paul's Walden, where he joined a young house party: there was tennis and other games, and after church on Sunday 'we were beautifully idle all the rest of the day lying in various attitudes of repose on the lawn.' The next morning 'Mike, Lady Rosie, Elizabeth & David & I went down to the Grotto & had certain adventures with an old Boat which Mike & I succeeded in sinking.' On the drive back to London that night, he saw billboards announcing 'the awful news about the Titanic'.[106] The great liner, supposedly unsinkable, had sunk on her maiden voyage after hitting an iceberg; more than 1,500 people died.

Elizabeth's spasmodic diary omits these events, but records that she had a fitting for her bridesmaid's dress for Violet Anson's wedding* – 'White satin, chiffon & lace'. The family gathered at St James's Square to say goodbye to Jock, who was returning to America for six months. The following week she had another fitting and returned to Hertfordshire in the middle of a violent thunderstorm. 'Celler 3 feet deep'. The next day she felt quite unwell and took some 'Gregory Powder' (a universal panacea in those days). She feared she might have 'influenzer', and was not at first allowed to see Mrs Scott and Aunt Vava,† who had just arrived. But the doctor told her she just had a chill, so she was able to come downstairs to see the visitors. 'Grannie gave me a little cup,' she recorded. With that she finally lost interest in her diary, which ends decisively: 'Good night.'[107]

May 1912 found the two Benjamins still at St Paul's Walden, without their parents and busy with their lessons. David was given a bicycle for his tenth birthday; Elizabeth wrote to her mother, 'I cant help envying him. It is <u>so</u> hot today that its uncomfortable, one person

---

* Lady Violet Anson (1886–1974), third daughter of third Earl of Lichfield. She and her brother Rupert, friends of the young Bowes Lyons, had been among the August 1911 house party at Glamis. She married Lancelot Mare Gregson in July 1912.

† Violet Cavendish-Bentinck (1864–1932), Cecilia's unmarried younger sister.

in London has already died of the heat . . . I simply must fly to lessons, but I will write you a longer letter tomorrow.' The letter ended with many kisses.[108] Two days later she wrote:

> There are no lessons today so I can write you a nice long letter. It was _very_ hot yesterday, and I started out riding in the afternoon, but I had to come back because it was _so_ hot, and there was _no_ ginger beer. (I am sure you will say 'I am glad.') . . . David's getting on very well with his bicycle, I _do_ so wish I had one, do you think it would stop me growing if I had one, if I only rode little distances. I must stop now Love, as I have got to write to Father before Church, goodbye Precious Darling, from your very _very_ _very_ _very_ loving Elizabeth.[109]

★

ALL ELIZABETH'S brothers went to Eton, but, although boarding schools for girls were becoming more fashionable, they were not yet the norm for aristocratic families. Lady Strathmore herself taught Elizabeth and David to write and introduced them to drawing as well as music and dance. But she did not deem her own teaching to be enough. The two children had a series of governesses and teachers at home, and also attended day school when in London. At St Paul's Walden, where the children spent most of their time, their governess was Miss Mary Wilkie, who remained with them for nine years.* At Glamis they were taught for a time by Miss Laurel Gray, who later recalled saying to Elizabeth at their first meeting, 'I expect that you can spell quite long words,' to which the little girl instantly replied, 'Oh yes, I can spell capercailzie & ptarmigan.'[110] Miss Gray also recounted that Lady Strathmore had asked her to keep an account book of the children's progress. 'When they were good, a good mark and a penny. And of course a bad mark, that was shocking. Elizabeth wasn't too good but she always had a good mark, she was naturally a good scholar. A bad mark made no difference to David. I was as strict as I could be, he was terrible.'[111]

In London, when they were eight or nine, Elizabeth and David attended a school in Marylebone run by a Fröbel-trained teacher, Miss

---

* Mary Wilkie worked as a governess and taught in private schools for twenty-three years, and at a boys' grammar school for a further eighteen. She died in 1955, aged eighty-one. (RA QEQMH/GEN/1955/May; RA QEQMH/PS/W)

Constance Goff.* According to the reminiscences of a fellow pupil, Joan Ackland, Elizabeth and David wore tussore smocks, had very good manners and were inseparable. Years later during the Second World War, Joan, by now Mrs Edgar Woollcombe, met Queen Elizabeth; the Queen recalled the French and German plays they had performed at school, the boxing for the boys and fencing for the girls. She also remembered being called a show-off when she had begun an essay on the sea with the Greek words for 'The Sea, the Sea!'[112]†

Lady Strathmore also engaged both French and German governesses. Mademoiselle Lang was known by the children as Madé (for Mademoiselle, a nickname they also used for later French governesses); she was with the family from about 1901 to 1910, and appears to have been peripatetic, unlike Miss Wilkie and Miss Gray, moving with her pupils between Hertfordshire, London and Glamis.‡ A few surviving letters to Madé Lang show that the nine-year-old Elizabeth had not yet made great progress with her French.

Apart from formal lessons, Elizabeth and David were sent to dancing classes in London with Madame D'Egville. Elizabeth showed early talent for dancing: her elder sister May taught her the Cake Walk at the age of four, and commented that she did it 'very well for such a tiny girl'.[113] In her twenties she was noted among her contemporaries as an exceptionally good dancer, and for the rest of her life she took to the floor at every opportunity.

She had music lessons at Madame Mathilde Verne's Pianoforte School. Madame Verne's first impression of her was of 'a very pretty, vivacious little girl'. She was said to have a good ear for music but on one occasion Madame Verne watched her defying her teacher's attempts to make her persist with a particularly difficult exercise. 'I

---

*   No contemporary reference to Elizabeth and David's attendance at this school has been found in the Glamis Archives; but in 1964 Miss Goff sent Princess Margaret a letter written by her mother as a child. (RA QEQMH/GEN/1964/G) Friedrich Fröbel (1782–1852) had pioneered the kindergarten system, developing children's abilities through play and activity.

†   Elizabeth is quoting the cry uttered by Greek mercenaries when, after a 1,000-mile flight from the Babylonian interior in 401 BC, they at last saw the Black Sea and knew they were back among Greek cities (according to Xenophon's *Anabasis*).

‡   Mademoiselle Lang left St Paul's Walden in early 1910 and went to work for Lady Leven and Melville; later she returned to France and married, becoming Madame Guérin. She kept in touch with Queen Elizabeth, and her daughter Georgina, later Madame Reinhold, came to England each year for a few weeks in 1936–9 to teach French to Princesses Elizabeth and Margaret. Madame Guérin died in 1965.

looked at the child. Though reverent in face, there was a warning gleam in her eyes as she said to the teacher, "Thank you very much. That was wonderful," and promptly slid off the music-stool, holding out her tiny hand in polite farewell.' But she was coaxed back to end the lesson.[114]

*

IN SEPTEMBER 1912, when he was ten, David was sent to St Peter's Court preparatory school in Broadstairs, where two of King George V's younger sons, Prince Henry and Prince George, were also pupils. Cynthia Asquith quoted a tear-stained letter written by Elizabeth just after this sad event. 'David went to school for the first time on Friday. I miss him horribly.'[115]

She herself had already had to face the horrors of a new school and new teachers. As she recalled many years later: 'In London I went to what was called classes. One terrifying person [was] called Miss Wolff.'[116] What this lady's classes consisted of is not clear, but they were held in South Audley Street, and an earlier pupil was Lady Delia Spencer,* whose younger sister Lavinia, Elizabeth's contemporary and great friend, probably also went to Miss Wolff's.

Early in 1912 Lady Strathmore enrolled Elizabeth in the Misses Birtwhistles' school in Sloane Street, which she attended for a time while the family was in London. She and her nanny would walk – it was quite a long way – from their home in St James's Square. Elizabeth was told to avert her eyes as they passed the gentlemen's clubs in Pall Mall.[117] She said later that she did not think she learned anything at the Birtwhistles'. 'A little bit of poetry I certainly remember. So I'm afraid I'm uneducated on the whole.'[118] In fact she seems to have prospered at the school. A few weekly reports for 1912 and 1913 survive in the Glamis Archives, and show her doing well in most of the thirteen subjects she studied. English was a strong suit: she had good marks in grammar, spelling, composition, literature and recitation. Then there was French, French history, geography, history, scripture, arithmetic, geometry and natural history; she did best in

---

* Lady Delia Spencer (1889–1981), daughter of sixth Earl Spencer. She married Sidney Peel in 1914. After his death in 1938, she was appointed woman of the bedchamber to Queen Elizabeth. Miss Wolff's classes are mentioned in Priscilla Napier, *A Memoir of The Lady Delia Peel*, J. & J. Peel, 1984, p. 23.

scripture – her mother's training, no doubt – and history. Her lowest mark was 7 out of 20 for arithmetic, although she redeemed herself with 17½ the following week, and her place in class varied from sixth out of six to second out of seven. She received the maximum mark for conduct every week.[119]

Day school in London could never be a satisfactory solution, however, for a child whose family spent so much time away from the capital. Elizabeth did not return to the Birtwhistles after the Easter holidays in 1913. The highlight of that holiday was what proved to be her last trip to Italy as a girl; it is also the best documented, as she briefly resumed her diary to record it. She and David travelled with their mother, first to stay with Mrs Scott at Bordighera and then on to Florence. They stayed at the Hotel Minerva, next to Santa Maria Novella, visited the principal galleries and churches and motored up to Fiesole. They went to see the painter Ricciardo Meacci,* and Aunt Vava bought Elizabeth, David and their mother paintings by him. There was more shopping: Elizabeth purchased some 'very pretty old cups and saucers'.[120] She loved her visit. But she would be eighty-five before she saw Florence again.

Back in Hertfordshire she resumed her lessons with a new governess. Lady Strathmore seemed to have found the ideal educator in a young German woman, the twenty-one-year-old Käthe Kübler, daughter of a Prussian official living in Erlangen in Bavaria. Fräulein Kübler later published her memoirs, in which she recalled her first day at St Paul's Walden Bury – it was a glorious spring afternoon and she arrived to find the family having tea in the garden room, which looked out over the park. She was received with warmth and kindness, and Elizabeth, whom she described as charming to look at, 'with a small, dainty figure, a narrow, finely shaped, rather pale little face, dark hair and lovely violet-blue eyes', took her to see the horses and her dog Juno, who had five puppies. 'As soon as she noticed that I loved animals I knew that I had won her over,' the governess remarked.[121]

A fortnight later Lady Strathmore asked Käthe if she would be

---

* Ricciardo Meacci (1856–after 1928), a Florentine painter popular among the expatriate British community in the area. Aunt Vava later commissioned from him an elaborate painting in the style of a Renaissance altarpiece, symbolizing the marriage of the Duke and Duchess of York, as a wedding present; Meacci also painted a headboard incorporating the arms of the Strathmores and of the British Royal Family and the date of the marriage, for another wedding present.

willing to stay on as Elizabeth's full-time governess, responsible for
her entire education, including piano lessons, drawing, needlework
and gymnastics. 'I was very willing to do so, and so we both set to
work with zest. Hitherto Lady Elizabeth had had only French governesses, and she had been to school only for a very short time. A
regular education, as we understand it in Germany, was something
quite unknown to her. With true German thoroughness I drew up a
timetable for her lessons and a plan of study, both of which were
approved by Lady Strathmore.'[122] The day began with a pre-breakfast
piano lesson; after breakfast with the family, formal lessons began
at 9.30 and continued in the afternoon until 4 p.m. They included
history, geography, mathematics, science, French and German. Fräulein Kübler taught her pupil in English, but outside the schoolroom
spoke only German with her. She found Elizabeth intelligent and
mature beyond her years and eager to learn; she soon spoke German
fluently.

Käthe Kübler was a companion as well as a teacher. A photograph
in her memoirs shows her arm in arm with Elizabeth, walking in the
park at St Paul's Walden, a solid figure in a sensible hat and long-
skirted suit with collar and tie, a head taller than her pupil, who
wears a shady brimmed hat adorned with a feather and a patterned
scarf. After lessons, they would go for walks, play tennis or golf, or
eat strawberries and gooseberries in the kitchen garden, where 'Lady
Elizabeth was adept at crawling under the netting and filling herself
with strawberries while lying on her stomach.'[123] Their greatest
delight was to go out in a pony cart taking a basket of sandwiches
and cakes, and picnic in the woods, building a fire in a clearing to
make tea.

Fräulein Kübler was struck by Elizabeth's passionate love for her
mother. 'How often I heard her high, clear voice calling through the
house: "Mother darling, where are you?" Every morning when she
woke, she went to her mother's bedroom, where they would read a
chapter of the Bible together.'[124] Käthe too came to love Lady
Strathmore, 'almost more than my pupil', for her graceful kindness.

Lessons continued in St James's Square when the family migrated
to London for the season. Ballet and dancing classes interrupted the
regime, with walks in Hyde Park and trips to the cinema by way of
further diversion. Once they went to Earl's Court, where Elizabeth
took a switchback ride, screaming with delight when it roared through

a tunnel. Käthe Kübler's memoirs also offer a glimpse of the lively social life the family led: Elizabeth's beautiful and musical elder sister Rose enjoyed a constant round of balls, parties and concerts, and the Strathmores gave evening parties which Elizabeth and her governess watched from the stairs above the main reception rooms. But they were allowed to attend luncheons at which statesmen and other notables might be present: Fräulein Kübler recalled proudly having sat next to Lord Rosebery, Lord Curzon and Lord Lansdowne.

Every weekend they returned to the relaxed informality of St Paul's Walden. 'On Sunday morning we all went to the little village church together,' Käthe recounted, 'and at 4 p.m. there was often a cricket match; Lord Strathmore and his four eldest sons would play with the village lads, and the butler and the valet played too. Lady Rose, Lady Elizabeth and I sat in the field and watched with the villagers.' She could never understand the game despite Elizabeth's patient explanations; but 'there was always much merriment when we had tea at five o'clock. My pupil's brothers competed with each other telling funny stories, and I often wept with laughter over Lord Strathmore's comic jokes.'[125]

With the approach of the 1913 summer holidays Käthe went back home for a month and Elizabeth looked forward to David's return from school. She wrote to him from St Paul's Walden using phrases which suggest that her lifelong devotion to the novels of P. G. Wodehouse may already have begun:

We have come down here for good now, at least till you come home. Fräulein goes to Germany on Tuesday 22nd next. Well and 'ow are yer, Hay? Boo, you haint no good, you haint woggling yer tooth. Oi ham. Dur. What's the good o' not woggeling. Hay? Ant no good at all. Arthur Duff has givn me a NEW PONY. Its 16 years old, but awfully good still.

Only 11 more days now.

HOORAY.

WHAT HO!

PIP. PIP.

It's a very short time. Everybody's well. Do write me a letter soon.

Please do Ducky.

Goodbye your very very very very very very loving Elizabeth[126]

Freddy Dalrymple Hamilton, still smitten with Rose, spent a hot July weekend at St Paul's Walden, playing tennis and cricket with Elizabeth's brothers and going on a 'garden robbing expedition' with Rose and Elizabeth, 'who did most of the eating. I fell backwards into a gooseberry bush which was rather a painful business. A gorgeous day in every way.'[127] Freddy was not the only one to celebrate Elizabeth's appetites – earlier that year someone had filled in her neglected diary to tease her for her gluttony. The hand could be that of Mike or Jock:

January 1st
Overeat myself.

Thursday Jan 2nd
Headache in the morning. very good tea. Christmas cake, Devonshire Cream, honey, jam, buns & tea. eat too much.

Friday Jan 3rd
Not quite the thing today Breakfast very good. Sausages, kedgeree, Brown Bread, Scones & honey. Excellent lunch – beefsteak – 3 helps – ham and roley poley. I eat a good deal . . .

Tuesday Jan 7th
Barrel of apples arrived today – had one for breakfast. 10 am eat an apple. 11 am had an apple for 11 oclock lunch. 12. had an apple. Roast pigeons and chocolate pudding & apples for lunch! 3 pm eat an apple. 3.15 pm David and I fought and have got bruise on my leg because he said I was greedy. eat two apples for supper.[128]

In August 1913 Käthe Kübler went to Glamis for the first time. She was impressed by its splendour, and Elizabeth did not spare her any of its ghost stories and legends. The German governess wrote a full account of life there:

During the shooting season, in September and October, there were often more than twenty guests in the castle; the gentlemen brought their valets and the ladies their maids. At the head of the whole household was the butler, assisted by the housekeeper, who ruled over the female servants and was also in charge of the linen room. Huge piles of snow-white tablecloths, sheets, towels and napkins were stacked there, and were also used, for guests were constantly coming and going. Glamis Castle had its own laundry, in which half a dozen laundry maids worked. The kitchen was ruled by a French chef, who received his orders from Lady Strathmore every morning. He in turn was in command of a number of kitchen maids and scullery maids. Liveried servants waited at table; several motor cars, carriages and riding horses were at the disposal of the guests ... Lord Strathmore did not belong to the celebrated large landowners known for their wealth; nevertheless it seemed to me that life was lived in the greatest style on his estates.

... Lord Strathmore sometimes took Lady Elizabeth and me with him when he went shooting. The pheasants are put up by the beaters, and the guns must be good shots if they want to hit the birds, which fly high above the trees. Then there was fly-fishing for trout in the Glamis burn, the stream that flows through the park.[129]

In November life was quieter; there were no more house guests, and often there were only five – Lord and Lady Strathmore, their two younger daughters and the governess – around the great table in the dining room. They returned to St Paul's Walden in time for Christmas 1913, and Elizabeth sent another letter to David at school: 'My darling David, Thank you so much for your delightful pc. I'm afraid Ive been a dreadfull long time writing but Ive been <u>horribly</u> busy, trying to knit Xmas presents and doing lessons. Only 18 days to the holidays. 2 weeks and 4 days. Its nice to think about. Mother got two enormous stockings ... I do look forward to us two opening them.' She was not sure what to give Fergus, who was serving with the Black Watch in India, for Christmas. 'Its so awfully difficult to give a man something which he really likes, except guns and motors. Good thought. I might send him a motor. Shall we give it between us? Only a few hundreds!'[130]

Christmas in Hertfordshire was followed by a visit to Glamis in early 1914. Elizabeth and David went tobogganing. After David went back to school, Käthe Kübler began drilling her pupil for the Oxford Local Preliminary Examination. 'We worked at such a pace that Lady Elizabeth grew pale and thin. Her mother made us stop, and said with a smile: "Health is more important than examinations,"' the governess recalled.[131] Lady Strathmore was also receiving complaints from Elizabeth: 'I <u>do</u> hate my lessons sometimes, and [get] sicker every day of this beastly exam. I know less and less!'[132] But Fräulein Kübler's efforts were rewarded: Elizabeth passed the examination and was awarded a certificate, still preserved in the Glamis Archives.

To Käthe's delight, Lady Strathmore asked her to stay on four more years until Elizabeth's eighteenth birthday – to teach her languages, music and history of art and even take her abroad, to Germany, Austria and Italy. The only problem was David. He had taken a violent dislike to Fräulein Kübler, and picked quarrels with her at every opportunity. A distraught Elizabeth reported to her mother from Glamis in June 1914:

> My darling Mother,
>
> Most terrible goings-on here.
>
> At this present moment Fräulein is crying and sobbing in her room, and David is doing lessons with Mr Hewett. They had a dreadful quarrel just before tea, two at lunch, and I really don't know what to do. For the last week I have'nt had one single moment of peace, even in my room, and its too awful. I cant tell you how I look forward to Thursday, oh it will be nice. I really cant help just one tear now and then . . . Everybody is very well, I don't know about Fräulein, but I do pity her poor thing, and I'm afraid she'll go away for good, with a bad feeling against this family, though I believe she quite likes me.[133]

One bone of contention – literally – between David and Fräulein Kübler passed into the annals of Glamis history: when David shot his first hare, the governess ate the whole animal herself, leaving him only the head.[134] Elizabeth was alarmed. 'I don't know what is going to happen at lunch today,' she lamented in another letter to her mother, 'as David swears he's not going to let Fräulein have any rabbit pie. He killed the rabbits.'[135]

Fortunately there were lighter moments: Elizabeth went fishing with David and was pleased with her own progress. 'I am really casting quite well, no splashes!'[136] Jock came to stay, which cheered her, and she sent one of her mock-Cockney missives to Mike.

> Thank you most awfully for your delightful episal. I was glad to get it, and it made me laugh some, you bet. I suppose you'r moving around pretty slick just now, dinner, balls ect. I hope you are having plenty of champenge, clarit, 'oc, mosel, and baeer, Baaeer, Baaeer, wonderful baaer, fill yourself right up to here (neck). That was by Shakespeare. Oi ad an horful noice toime

yesterday playing 'opscotch with Fairweather,* or can taal you he got a talent for 'opscotch. We are coming down on Thursday next, it will be nice seeing you all again. It's not very peaceful here![137]

Käthe Kübler did go away for good, but not because of David. As the governess expressed it in her memoirs, 'Then came the day when the world was jolted awake by the shots at Sarajevo. When I came into the breakfast room in the morning I saw distraught faces. Lord Strathmore gave me the "Morning Post". "Here, read this. It means war." I would not and could not believe it.'[138] It was the end of June 1914. Fräulein Kübler was no doubt being wise long after the event; it would have been remarkable if Lord Strathmore had understood so early that the assassination in Sarajevo would lead to more than local fighting in the Balkans. When Käthe left for Germany on 12 July to attend her parents' silver wedding and take her month's holiday, Lady Strathmore embraced her and made her promise to come back. By the time the month was over, it was too late for her to return and she volunteered for the German Red Cross in Erlangen.†

The Great War broke out late on Elizabeth Bowes Lyon's fourteenth birthday, 4 August 1914. Her mother had taken her and other members of the family to the London Coliseum to see a vaudeville programme with Charles Hawtrey, G. P. Huntly and the Russian ballerina Fedorova. That same evening King George V held a Privy Council meeting at Buckingham Palace, attended by one minister and two officials. The Council proclaimed a state of war with Germany from 11 o'clock that evening. The King recorded in his diary that the declaration of war was 'a terrible catastrophe but it is not our fault'.[139]

In the Coliseum the audience was filled with people exhilarated by the prospect of war. 'I think they honestly thought it was going to be about a month and it would be finished,' Elizabeth commented much

---

* William Fairweather, head keeper at Glamis.

† By the end of August Käthe was caring for a constant stream of wounded soldiers. Remarkably, she continued to correspond with Elizabeth after the outbreak of war, via the British Consulate in the Hague. Two of Käthe's wartime letters survive at Glamis; one was written from Cambrai in northern France in September 1915, responding to a letter from Elizabeth, who had written telling her that three of her brothers had been wounded, and the second from Erlangen in 1917, asking for a reference from Lady Strathmore. She was to write to her former pupil again in more sinister circumstances in 1933 after the Nazis had come to power, and to visit her in 1937, the year in which her memoirs were published.

later. As she went to bed in St James's Square, vast, exultant crowds were pushing down the Mall to Buckingham Palace. Ever after she remembered, 'The streets were full of people shouting, roaring, yelling their heads off – little thinking what was going to happen.'[140]

CHAPTER TWO

TENDING THE WOUNDED

1914–1918

'It's so dreadful saying goodbye'

THE WAR CAME to dominate everyone's lives. Home was a Front for the first time ever; patriotism and commitment were expected from people of every age and every background. The values on which the British establishment prided itself – courage, self-sacrifice, duty, honour – were deemed to be easily and properly transferable from the playing fields to the battlefields. The young Eric Blair (later George Orwell) published a poem entitled 'Awake! Young Men of England' in the *Henley and South Oxfordshire Standard* that summed up the feelings of the time:

> Oh! give me the strength of the lion,
> The wisdom of Reynard the Fox,
> And then I'll hurl troops at the Germans,
> And give them the hardest of knocks.
>
> Awake! oh you young men of England,
> For if, when your Country's in need,
> You do not enlist by the thousand,
> You truly are cowards indeed.[1]

Chauvinism was not peculiar to Britain. One of the new forces in the first two decades of Elizabeth's life was the growth in the power of nationalism throughout Europe. Since the Crimean War separatist battles against Ottoman rule had created Serbia, Greece and Romania. By the end of the nineteenth century the new countries of Montenegro and Bulgaria had emerged, and the Balkans remained a place of violent change. There had been wars in 1912 and 1913 as the new states fought over the spoils of the decaying Ottoman Empire. Britain's nationalist problem was lesser, but still real – in Ireland. Indeed, in the view of some historians, the danger of civil war in Ireland was avoided only by the outbreak of war on a larger scale.

At the turn of the century European states might have congratulated themselves that they had avoided war between the major powers since 1870, when Germany had defeated France and seized Alsace and Lorraine. But Germany and Italy were both newly united powers, and their leaders encouraged nationalist enthusiasms. Meanwhile the two great European empires of Russia and Austria-Hungary faced massive internal problems of their own. Austria-Hungary seemed stretched almost beyond endurance and here too the demands of industrialization were creating new tensions. In Russia, economic progress coincided with a political revolution after the introduction in 1905 of a parliament, the Duma, albeit with very limited powers. Russia remained dependent on her foreign suppliers, in particular her closest ally, France. The French, after the loss of Alsace-Lorraine, knew that they must have allies against any further threat from the German army.

Since 1870 the balance of power had preserved peace in Europe but through the early years of the twentieth century the likelihood of war increased. Austria-Hungary was prepared to resort to local wars to eliminate threats to her position from nationalism in the Balkans, while Germany was willing to risk war – even a European war – to extend her own imperial reach. Europe began to divide into two camps, and Germany used commercial and colonial issues to exacerbate tensions with France. The German General Staff made plans to fight a two-front war – first to inflict a quick defeat on France and then to deal with her slower-moving ally, Russia.

In Britain, patriotism was allied to a sense of pride both in the achievements of empire and in the supremacy of the British navy. The continued expansion of German ambitions convinced the British that they would have to involve themselves more directly in the continental balance of power unless they wished to see Germany dominate all of Europe. When Germany began to develop her navy, this could only be seen as a threat to British domination of the seas. By 1911 the race for naval superiority had led to a marked increase in tensions between the two powers. Britain's Liberal government reluctantly allied the country to France.

In the event the catalyst came not in the North Sea but in the southern Slav lands. On 28 June 1914 Archduke Franz Ferdinand, heir

to the Austrian throne, and his wife were assassinated by a Bosnian
Serb at Sarajevo, in Bosnia Herzegovina, which was under Austrian
rule. The Austrians, with German support, blamed Serbia and declared
war on her; a week later the mesh of alliances across Europe had
begun to drag the rest of the continent into war.

Few people immediately understood the implications of the Archduke's assassination. It was three weeks before *The Times* considered
its consequences on its main page.[2] Until then, summer sunshine,
holidays, pageantry were greater preoccupations. But power was also
on display. On 17 and 18 July King George V made an 'informal' visit
to the Royal Navy and reviewed the fleet at Spithead. He saw before
him forty miles of ships – 260 vessels in all, including twenty-four of
the new Dreadnought battleships – which resembled, in Winston
Churchill's words, 'scores of gigantic castles of steel, wending their
way across the sea like giants bowed in anxious thought'.[3]

Even while the King was inspecting his kingdom's apparently
impregnable defences, the war machinery of Europe was engaging
gear. Austria's declaration of war on Serbia aroused Serbia's ally Russia;
Austria in turn called upon Germany. Russia appealed for French
support and Germany was thus given the rationale for the first phase
of her battle plan – a quick assault upon France through Belgium to
destroy the threat from the west before she dealt with the massive
Slav menace from the east. The principal uncertainty was whether the
British would actually fulfil their recent assurances to come to the
assistance of their new friend and traditional enemy across the
Channel.

London hesitated. It seemed to some that if Britain refused to be
drawn in, a war would have disastrous consequences but it just might
remain limited. On the other hand, if Britain entered, the chances of a
widespread conflagration were much greater. Moreover the British
government had serious domestic concerns. That spring, Britain had
been closer to civil war than at any time in the previous hundred years
– because of the demand for Home Rule in Catholic Ireland and the
absolute refusal of the Protestant north to be governed by the Catholic
south. The crisis had split the British army and had divided the parties
in Parliament more bitterly than any issue in living memory.

On 28 July the British fleet moved to face Germany in the North
Sea. The next day the Foreign Secretary, Sir Edward Grey, rejected a
German request for a guarantee of British neutrality, Russia ordered

partial mobilization, Belgrade was shelled. On 1 August France, Germany and Belgium mobilized; Germany declared war on Russia, demanded unlimited passage through Belgium and sent her troops into Russia and Luxembourg. Next day her troops were in France as well. And on 3 August France and Germany declared war on one another.

Huge patriotic crowds appeared outside Buckingham Palace. That evening King George V and Queen Mary had to show themselves on the balcony three times, to tremendous cheering. In his diary the King recorded that public opinion agreed that the German fleet should not be allowed into the English Channel to attack France, nor German troops permitted to march through Belgium. 'Everyone is for war & our helping our friends,' he wrote.[4]

The German war plan demanded the overthrow of France within forty days. Berlin launched thirty-four infantry and five cavalry divisions westwards. The Belgians resisted bravely and managed to check the overwhelming German advance, but only for a time. Within a fortnight the fighting had displayed the terrible destructive force of modern industrial weapons, massed machine guns and gigantic artillery pieces.

In London Field Marshal Lord Kitchener of Khartoum was appointed secretary of state for war on 5 August; he alarmed some of his colleagues in the War Cabinet when, contrary to the conventional wisdom, he warned that the war could be a long one. He insisted on keeping two divisions in Britain, against the threat of invasion.[5] On 7 August Kitchener called for 100,000 volunteers. The response was instant. *The Times* reported, 'The crowd of applicants was so large and so persistent that mounted police were necessary to hold them in check, and the gates were only opened to admit six at a time.' Some 2,500 men a day were volunteering and in London a hundred men were sworn in every hour.[6] When reports came back of Austrian atrocities in Serbia and of German atrocities in Belgium and France, opinion hardened.

The enthusiasm and eagerness to get to the Front were widely shared. One young aristocrat was 'afraid of missing anything before the war was over'. Lord Tennyson, grandson of the poet, dressed and packed in feverish haste to get there on time.[7] Many of those who were stationed around the Empire with their regiments felt they were missing the most important moment in their country's – and their own – life. Families with landed estates sent their sons off to war and did everything they could to help their staff and their tenants do the same. Many landowners kept jobs open for men who volunteered, and allowed families to live rent free until their menfolk returned.

*

FOR ELIZABETH's four surviving elder brothers – Patrick, Jock, Fergus and Michael – there was simply no alternative. Patrick was already in the Scots Guards, Jock and Fergus were in the Black Watch and Michael, who had just completed his first year reading agriculture at Magdalen College, Oxford, volunteered for the Royal Scots at once. He wrote to his mother, 'It's rather funny thinking of me as a soldier, I don't quite feel one yet and I'm afraid I'll never look the soldier Fergie looks.'[8]

Wars – even those expected to be short – add a sense of urgency. Marriages took place quickly all over the country. On 9 September Fergus wrote to his mother that he and his fiancée Lady Christian Dawson-Damer* had decided to get married the following week.[9] Almost immediately afterwards there was a second family wedding – Jock married Fenella Hepburn-Stuart-Forbes-Trefusis.† Both bridegrooms then went off to join their regiments.

Elizabeth later recalled the thrill of those first days of anticipation and upheaval. Schoolroom routine collapsed and she remembered 'the bustle of hurried visits to chemists for outfits of every sort of medicine and to gunsmiths to buy all the things that people thought they wanted for a war and then found they didn't'.[10] A week after her birthday and the declaration of war, she travelled up to Scotland as the family did every year in early August, to prepare for the Glorious Twelfth and the opening of the grouse season. This year was different. Gone were the convivial gatherings of the house party, the candle-lit dinners, the songs around the piano, the hearty breakfasts, the assembly for shooting every day, the fierce but friendly cricket matches.

---

* Lady Christian Dawson-Damer (1890–1959), daughter of fifth Earl of Portarlington. A daughter, Rosemary (1915–89; m. 1945 Edward Joicey-Cecil), was born of this marriage. Lady Christian married again in 1919 (Captain William Martin, d. 1947).

† The Hon. Fenella Hepburn-Stuart-Forbes-Trefusis (1889–1966), known in the Strathmore family as Neva, younger daughter of twenty-first Baron Clinton. She and Jock had five daughters.

Like many great country homes, Glamis was at once converted for hospital use, receiving wounded or sick soldiers sent to convalesce after treatment at Dundee Infirmary. The great table was taken out of the dining room and beds were moved in. A nurse, Helen Anderson, was appointed to supervise medical care. Casualties were dispatched from Southampton to Dundee by train – a thirteen-hour journey – often wrapped only in blankets, their uniform cut away around their wounds.[11] Many of the men had never seen such a place as Glamis, and they gazed at the great castle and grounds in astonishment. They were shown around and each given a white bed along the panelled walls of the dining room, as well as a nightshirt and a set of warm clothes.[12]

The billiard room became a collecting depot for winter clothing for soldiers and the billiard table was stacked with thick shirts and socks, mufflers, belts and sheepskins to be made into coats and painted with a waterproofing varnish. Official supplies, not least of greatcoats, lagged behind demand, and the Strathmores aimed to provide every man in the thousand-strong local Black Watch battalion with a sheepskin. Socks were packed with presents of cigarettes, tobacco, pipes or peppermints in the toe.[13] As Elizabeth recalled, 'during these first few months we were so busy knitting, knitting, knitting and making shirts for the local battalion – the 5th Black Watch. My chief occupation was crumpling up tissue paper until it was so soft that it no longer crackled, to put into the lining of sleeping bags.'[14]

Lord Strathmore too was involved in war preparations: as lord lieutenant of Forfarshire he chaired the local territorial defence associations, and was also charged with instructing farmers and landowners in the county what to do with their crops and livestock in case of invasion. This required caution, so as not to alarm people; there was already an atmosphere approaching paranoia, as reported by his daughter's governess: 'Mysterious lights have been seen all along this coast at night & cannot be traced. Forfar is supposed to be a hotbed of spies. Lady S is very funny. She heard that 2 Dundee butchers (I think it was) were willing to supply sheepskins for the famous coats at a reduced rate – one of them named Miller she said she would not employ as she suspected him of being a spy & wishing to ingratiate himself – & also that his name was in reality Müller!'[15]

*

WHILE ELIZABETH Bowes Lyon's relations were each doing what they could for the war effort, one of the most significant events for her personally at this time was the arrival in the family of a new governess. Beryl Poignand was to be a friend, almost a co-conspirator, throughout Elizabeth's teenage years and an important confidante thereafter.* Elizabeth's letters to Beryl give not only a glimpse of the world in which she grew up, but also a unique insight into her character. She was a fine letter writer all her life and her personality – lively, kind, mischievous – sparkles across the folded pages in their small blue envelopes. Beryl's own letters home provide further valuable information and a vivid picture of the family in wartime.

Miss Poignand's appointment seems to have come about through a French 'holiday governess', Madeleine Girardot de Villers, whom Lady Strathmore had engaged to take over – temporarily, as they all thought – from Käthe Kübler in July 1914. Elizabeth evidently got on well with Mademoiselle Girardot. A sheaf of *dictées* in the Glamis Archives dating from August and September 1914 shows a diminishing number of mistakes, with increasingly pleased comments by the governess. To one of these Elizabeth added cheekily, 'elle est la meilleure pupille que j'ai eue'.¹⁶

Madeleine Girardot had been a trainee teacher at the Maison d'Education de la Légion d'Honneur, the school founded by Napoleon for the daughters of members of the order, at Saint-Denis on the outskirts of Paris. There she had made friends with Beryl Poignand, a young Englishwoman who also taught at the school. Beryl, who was born in India in 1887, was the daughter of an Indian Army officer; the Poignand family claimed descent from a physician at the Court of Louis XVI who had fled to England. She had had a good education and, having returned from France in the summer of 1914, was now

---

* Dorothy Irene Beryl Poignand (1887–1965), daughter of Colonel George Poignand and his wife Catherine Maud. Governess to Lady Elizabeth Bowes Lyon 1914–17. Under the pseudonym Anne Ring, she wrote two books about Princess Elizabeth and Princess Margaret in the 1930s and several magazine articles about the Royal Family in the 1940s. During the Second World War she was temporarily employed by the Royal Household in the Central Chancery of the Orders of Knighthood, and stayed on until 1949. In 1947 she helped organize the exhibition of Princess Elizabeth's wedding presents and compiled the catalogue. Until her death in 1965 she remained in touch with Queen Elizabeth The Queen Mother, whose letters to Beryl were subsequently returned by her cousin, Mrs Leone Poignand Hall. These letters, together with Beryl's letters to her mother, to which access has been generously given by Mrs Hall's son Mr Richard Hall, have not been available to previous biographers.

living with her recently widowed mother in Farnham in Surrey. It was
probably at Madeleine Girardot's suggestion that she wrote to Lady
Strathmore offering her services as governess.

Lady Strathmore, struggling to balance the demands of two convalescent hospitals (she had set up another at St Paul's Walden), four
sons at the Front or about to set off, and a husband and two daughters
for whom she had to maintain a home, was relieved. She replied to
Beryl Poignand that she sounded very much like what she was looking
for, 'a lady who can teach and speak French and also able to teach
English', and asked if she would be prepared to come for a few
months.[17] The offer was accepted; Lady Strathmore wrote again
promising to order the necessary books from the Army & Navy Stores
and added: 'I do hope you will be happy here. Elizabeth is really a
delightful companion – very old for her age – and very sensible. So
that you will not have a <u>child</u> with you always.'[18]

Miss Poignand arrived at Glamis station from London one evening
in late November 1914, and was shown to a spacious tower bedroom,
with a fire burning brightly and supper awaiting her in the comfortably
furnished schoolroom. 'No electric light here – chiefly lamps everywhere & gas in the corridors,' she reported to her mother. 'It is an old
place, you would love it, all nooks & corners & stairs up & down &
long passages – many floors of stone of course.'[19] Bathing arrangements
were a matter of wonder after the more modest comforts of a villa in
Farnham.

> The maid brings in tea – lights my candles & goes off with my
> sponge & towels to a Bathroom some little way away – of which
> I think I have the sole use – to get to it I pass through a large
> bedroom & along a corridor & down a few stairs. Arrived there I
> find a huge hot bath set – the Bath is enormously deep – a large
> blanket spread on the ground & beside the Bath a carpeted step
> ladder by which one mounts in order to descend into the Bath.
> There is also a spray & douche apparatus.[20]

With her pupil there was an instant rapport. 'I like Elizabeth very
much & I think we shall be great friends,' Beryl wrote. Their daily
routine was quickly established: chapel – wearing the prescribed lace
cap – and piano practice for Elizabeth, breakfast at 8.45, two hours of
lessons followed by three-quarters of an hour out of doors and a
further hour's lesson before lunch. Then they were free to go out

again until the last lesson from 4 to 5. There was family tea around a large table at 5, Elizabeth's last meal – except for the occasional apple – until her bedtime at 8 p.m., after which Beryl was served her supper in the schoolroom. This was a mere four hours of lessons a day, and three on Saturday: it was probably at least an hour a day shorter than Fräulein Kübler's timetable. Even so, it was a challenge for the new governess. Despite her immediate affection for Elizabeth, she worried that 'it is not too easy teaching her. I have to make things as interesting as possible or she would easily get bored I think. She is intelligent – it is a wonder to me that she knows all she does – her education has been rather quaint.'[21] Moreover, Lady Strathmore's enthusiasm for a more rigorous academic education for her daughter was lukewarm. 'I don't know if very advanced mathematics are required for Elizabeth's exam,' she said to Beryl; 'but I do not wish her to take anything very advanced. I am not a believer in very high mathematics for girls.' Beryl was amused and relieved, since maths was not her own strong point. She reassured her employer that 'ordinary Arithmetic' was all that was required.[22]

Elizabeth enjoyed the new regime: three years later, looking back on 'those happy days', she described a typical day. The timetable has evolved a little, starting at 8 a.m. with a history lesson which is interrupted by the breakfast gong. Afterwards she and Beryl do some arithmetic, also interrupted, this time by Nurse Anderson, who comes rustling and panting up the stairs for a chat. This is followed by a trip down to the Oak Room for hot chocolate, biscuits and jokes, 'the first & last manufactured by the Lady Rose Lyon', and a walk through the pinetum. At lunch they 'eat an 'orrid amount', and go for another walk afterwards. Then 'back to the schoolroom for a bit. Eat enormous quantities of Vida bread, at tea, & a few "plaisanteries" with Mike.' After tea, she added innocently, 'I sleep before the fire while Medusa [her nickname for Beryl] reads about Queens of England.' Then they would visit the soldiers' ward for a lively game of whist before supper, and eventually 'wander bedwards, tired, but let us hope happy!!!'[23]

Beryl Poignand noted her pupil's liveliness and quick interest in the world about her. When the newspapers arrived in the morning, Elizabeth 'simply pounced' on the *Daily Mail*, provided for her personally. Her loving relationship with her parents was plain to see: they were devoted to her, and she was very attentive to both of them. The governess's letters home paint an appealing portrait of Lord Strathmore as a gentle, humorous man who was immensely fond of his children and grandchildren, 'especially of E. who is very sweet with him, always looking round to see if he wants anything – & lighting his cigarettes etc'. He was occasionally querulous, a characteristic which Beryl observed that his family ignored; but like many fathers of the less domineering sort, he was used to that. 'No one ever communicates with me unless they want to be paid something,' he was once heard to say. There was nothing stiff or pompous about him or his wife. 'He always arrives late for meals, & consequently is miles behind everyone else – if the footmen have left the room he sometimes asks Lady S. to throw him some pudding & if the sweet is a "dry" one she throws it across the table & he catches it in his hands or on his plate or sometimes doesn't catch it at all.'[24]

Lady Strathmore emerges from Beryl's letters as the hub of the family, energetic and admirably generous in her provision for the convalescent soldiers. She and her daughters dressed very simply, Lady Strathmore mostly in black 'with lace ruffles', while Rose wore a white silk blouse and a tweed walking skirt with a golf jacket. Elizabeth's usual garb was a navy-blue dress with a white yoke and cuffs, often with a jacket like her sister's. There was no need, Beryl assured her mother, for smart clothes at Glamis.[25]

Letters arrived sporadically from the two Bowes Lyon sons at the Front. One beautiful November morning when the sun sparkled on a thick frost at Glamis, Beryl recorded that Lady Strathmore had heard from Patrick and Jock in northern France, where the 5th Battalion The Black Watch had just come under fire. They had taken German trenches but had not advanced. A fortnight later Jock wrote again: they usually spent three days and nights in the trenches, or longer if the firing was lively, before being relieved, which meant walking nine miles back out of enemy artillery range before they could have any rest. He had not seen a mattress since leaving Dundee, he said. Sleep was impossible at the Front: as an officer he had to remain alert, for they were barely 200 yards from the German lines. Another letter spoke of the intense cold, of the slimy mud in the trenches, and of Jock's bitter disappointment to find that some of the cooked pheasants his mother had sent him had been badly packed and had rotted before arrival. The Glamis cook at once set to work preparing more.[26]

Fergus, by now a captain, was still at Aldershot, where he had been sent at the beginning of the war to train new recruits in the 8th

Battalion The Black Watch; it was not until the spring of 1915 that he went with the battalion to France. Michael's reserve battalion of the Royal Scots had at first been sent to Weymouth; in November they were suddenly moved to Sunderland and ordered to dig trenches. At Glamis the family could only suppose there was an invasion scare. In December he was sent to France, not to the Front but to Rouen, whence he dispatched cheerful letters home. It was a beautiful city full of fine churches, he wrote; but he had no intention of entering any of them, having had far too much sightseeing forced on him by his mother and sister Rosie in the past. He had been given the task of censoring soldiers' letters home, and quoted some of them: 'P.S. please excuse writing but I am rather drunk'; 'What is Tom a'doin' – 'as 'e 'listed or is 'e a coward – or is 'e after Nell – 'cos if so tell 'im I'll break 'is d— neck when I come back.'[27]

Elizabeth was still in touch with Fräulein Kübler. Her former governess sent her a long letter from Belgium, where she was nursing German soldiers. She was convinced that her country's cause was a righteous one and that the Kaiser had done all he could to stop the war.[28] Elizabeth seems not to have been impressed; her new governess recorded that she wanted to give up her German lessons and learn Russian instead, a wish frustrated by Beryl's ignorance of that language.[29]*

It was now clear that the war would not be over by Christmas. Young British women also wanted to play their part, and Elizabeth's sister Rose decided to train as a nurse. She enrolled at the London Hospital, which was offering three-month courses, and left Glamis in early January 1915 to join several of her friends training in the capital.

At the end of its first year, the convalescent hospital at Glamis was commended for its good work, especially with men suffering from shattered nerves. It was run with the minimum of regulations – 'this hospital treated its inmates neither as prisoners nor as children, but as privileged guests.'[30] Several were Highlanders, young and shy; one who had barely spoken a word had a visit from his sister: 'the nurse said he was so pleased & his eyes filled with tears when he knew she

---

* Elizabeth did, however, have some lessons in Italian in 1917, as appears from a letter to her in the Glamis Archives, from Laura Baldi, her teacher, who regrets that the lessons have come to an end and hopes her pupil will not forget what she has learned. (Glamis Archives, Letters from friends)

was coming,' Beryl wrote to her mother.[31] Those members of the family who were there 'contended with one another to make the wounded soldiers feel at home'. One of their patients told a visitor, 'my three weeks at Glamis have been the happiest I ever struck. I love Lady Strathmore so very much on account of her being so very like my dear mother, as was; and as for Lady Elizabeth, why, she and my fiancay are as like as two peas!'[32]

Lord Strathmore found it harder to make contact with the soldiers: 'he is terribly shy,' Beryl Poignand commented; but after a few days he was talking animatedly to those with whom he had a cavalry background in common. 'Today he very politely (Elizabeth says) introduced himself to the 5th Dragoon ... Elizabeth is very funny about him & takes him off sometimes – quite nicely of course – she is devoted to her parents.'[33]

In this environment most of the soldiers quickly relaxed; they explored the Castle and its grounds, they were taken for outings in the motors, attended the chapel, played billiards and gathered around the piano singing heartily. Until she departed, Rose played such favourites as 'We Don't Want to Lose You' or 'The Sunshine of Your Smile'.[34] One evening Rose dressed David up in her own clothes, with a hat and a thick veil, and introduced him to the soldiers as her cousin. He played the gracious lady so successfully that the deception was complete. When the soldiers discovered their mistake there was much mirth, and serious danger that future lady visitors would be greeted with guffaws of 'I know *you*!' After Rose left for London a gramophone was acquired for the men, but it was considered a poor substitute for her piano playing.[35]

Elizabeth was too young to train as a nurse; her task was generally to make the soldiers feel at home. She did rounds of the ward, talked to them all, made friends with many and went to the village shop to arrange large quantities of vital purchases – Woodbines, Gold Flake and Navy Cut tobacco.[36] She was intrigued by the soldiers and tried to draw them out: one, a Canadian named Baker who had been as far afield as Nepal, Egypt and South Africa, she discovered had been educated at Malvern; Beryl suspected him of being a wandering black sheep. They gave nicknames to their favourites: one sprightly Cockney named Bill became 'Twinkly Eyes'.[37]

The irony was that the better the care the soldiers received at Glamis, the sooner they were sent back to the Front. There were noisy farewells in the Castle crypt, with crackers and group photographs; next morning the soldiers signed the Visitors' Book* and were driven to Dundee. The motors that took them brought back ten more invalids, who came with harrowing tales and dreadful wounds from the Front; one was an eighteen-year-old shot in the stomach at Ypres, another had been shot through the lungs, and a third had a damaged spine and was likely to remain disabled for life. There was a 'London Scottie' (the London Scottish Regiment), of whom Nurse Anderson reported in awestruck tones that he had beautiful shaving things and pyjamas with a silk stripe.[38] He was the author of some suitably polished lines in Elizabeth's autograph book:

> Farewell! lovely Glamis, for soon I go
> From thy dear old walls to which I owe
> Deep gratitude for the days here spent
> Since welcomed here – a convalescent.[39]

This year, 1914, was the first time for twenty years that the Strathmores had spent December at Glamis. Beryl reported to her mother that Lady Strathmore had come into the schoolroom and said, 'At last I have got out of Father that we are staying here for Xmas.' At this, Elizabeth 'jumped up in delight & kissed her Mother exuberantly, as for some reason or other she wanted much to spend Xmas here'.[40]

It was a depleted family party: of Elizabeth's siblings only Rose and David were there. Rose wrote to her friend Delia Peel that she hoped that 'this horrible time' would be over soon. 'Pat, Jock & Mike are all out now, & I suppose Fergus will be going out soon.'[41] Despite all the anxieties, family and staff at Glamis did their best to bring good cheer to the soldiers, setting up an immense tree in the crypt and distributing presents. 'The fun was fast and furious,' according to Elizabeth. Everyone ate too much, and she and David danced wildly with the soldiers in the ward. All in all, she said, it was 'a dandy Xmas, you bet your bottom dollar'.[42]

Freddy Dalrymple Hamilton, on leave from his ship, came for the New Year and recorded that there were twenty wounded soldiers at Glamis. 'We played various doubtful card games etc. with them in the evening which was very amusing and after a bit, quite heating! It was a most cheerful evening. Heard several new & wonderful trench

---

* The Visitors' Books with the soldiers' signatures are in the Glamis Archives.

stories & I can't say I envy the soldiers much!' He could not help recalling his previous visit, playing cricket with the Bowes Lyon brothers, who were now away on active service. 'I never dreamt then the conditions under which I should be there next! We none of us sat up for the New Year.'[43] Next day he left by train with Rose.

Behind the face of gaiety and good cheer that she wore for her guests, Lady Strathmore was always worrying about her sons. On 3 January 1915 she wrote to her married daughter May with news of acquaintances and friends who had been killed or wounded. She had heard that 'one of our spys' who had been sent to Germany claimed that the Germans would run out of ammunition by May '& that all the educated people in Berlin knew they could not possibly win – & were talking of what terms we were likely to accept. That is good news – but thousands more will be killed & maimed before then. We have several new wounded here – one or two old ones have been x-rayed – & will have to have operations – which I am very sorry for.'[44] Later she was visited by a brother officer of Mike, who told her of a day of carnage on the Kaiser's birthday, 27 January: 'hundreds & hundreds of dead Germans everywhere – & not 10 yards of ground unshelled'.[45]

A terrible new form of warfare had developed. On the battlefields, machine-gun fire mowed men down like grass; only truly massive bombardment by artillery, which became heavier and heavier in the course of the war, could help suppress this murderous fire. Once the enemies had mobilized their industrial resources to produce such weapons, they turned the battle zones into wastelands, annihilated by iron, through which men edged fitfully, agonizingly forward and back.

The Germans' sweep westwards in August 1914 had not awarded them the instant victory that their war plan required, but they had captured almost all of Belgium and much of northern France. In the east the Germans and Austrians had stopped Russian offensives. Brutal and unexpected stalemate everywhere was the norm as 1915 began.

In mid-January 1915 Lady Strathmore took her two youngest children back to London, where Jock was home on leave and staying at St James's Square with his wife Fenella. He was confident that the war would be over in the summer; others were more pessimistic. Rose was busy, studying for her first nursing examination. 'Rosie told us some 1st hand experiences of the London Hospital,' Freddy recorded after lunching with them all at St James's Square in mid-January. 'It didn't sound very nice & I hope she won't kill herself over it!' Barely a month later she had passed her exam and was on a surgical ward.[46]

With David back at school, Elizabeth now had one of her greatest friends for company: Lady Lavinia Spencer,* who lived near by at Spencer House on the edge of Green Park. Lavinia was equally high-spirited, and she and Elizabeth shared a passion for the theatre and the cinema. They exchanged teasing girlish letters about their respective idols. 'She is most awfully nice, very pretty & too charming,' Lavinia wrote to her brother about Elizabeth.[47] Their respective governesses also got on well, and the quartet visited the Wallace Collection and went to concerts at the Albert Hall and to a performance of *The Mikado*. There were to be frequent visits to the theatre in the next few years.

Life resumed something of its pre-war pattern. Elizabeth spent the weekdays in London, with lessons in the morning and outings for tea with friends in the afternoon, matinées at the theatre, and occasional visits to the cinema in Regent Street or a bus-ride away at Marble Arch – she and Beryl were impressed by newsreels of the sinking of the *Blücher* and of an air raid on the east coast, but thrilling adventures featuring their favourite actors were the main attraction. Occasionally Elizabeth might be invited out in the evening by family friends like the Countess of Crawford, who asked her to dinner followed by a performance of the musical *Florodora*,† as company for her fourteen-year-old son David. Once she narrowly missed a royal encounter: Lavinia Spencer invited her to a tea party for Princess Mary, King George V's seventeen-year-old only daughter, which had to be cancelled at the last minute because the Spencers' chauffeur had the measles and the whole house was quarantined.[48]

As before, weekends were spent at St Paul's Walden if possible,

---

* Lavinia Emily (1899–1955), second daughter of sixth Earl Spencer; married, 1919, Hon. Luke White, later fourth Baron Annaly. Lady in waiting to the Duchess of York on East African tour 1924–5; extra lady in waiting thereafter. She was a great-aunt of Lady Diana Spencer.

† *Florodora* was one of the most successful musicals of the early twentieth century, both on Broadway and in London. Its famous song, 'Tell Me Pretty Maiden', was hugely popular and another attraction of the show was its sextet of beautiful singers, called 'the English Girls' in the score, but soon popularly dubbed 'the Florodora girls'. These six roles were filled by identically sized women, all five foot four inches; they became popular fantasy figures and the turnover on stage was high as young male admirers persuaded many to leave the show to marry them.

and Beryl's first visit there in February 1915 produced a descriptive letter home. The house seemed small and homely compared to Glamis, quaint, but 'so beautifully furnished & bright & clean looking . . . Eliz: simply loves the place – she has all her precious belongings – books, childish toys & clothes & dresses here. Books! I have never seen so many books anywhere. Shelves in every room – hundreds of them.' Her pupil took her on a long ramble in the grounds, to the lake inhabited by sleepy old carp, where once monks fished for their Friday dinner and now an ancient punt and a waterlogged boat lolled; the walled garden of fruit trees and bushes full of promise for summer raids; the apple-house where they pocketed apples to eat on the way home; the dairy, fowl houses and stables, where Elizabeth's pony Bobs lived along with Rose's hunter, still too tall for her diminutive younger sister, who longed to ride her. They picked snowdrops in the woods; crocuses, daffodils and jonquils were beginning to appear everywhere. Beryl was shown the long grassy alleys leading away between the tall trees and copses, and was introduced to 'Arkles' – the Hercules statue at the end of one – and 'the Bounding Butler', the discus-thrower figure on the lawn.

Lady Strathmore had returned to Glamis, where Lord Strathmore was ill with flu and needing company, so Elizabeth and her governess were alone at St Paul's Walden. On Sunday they walked to church, where they sat at the front and felt eyes boring holes into their backs: behind them sat some of the wounded soldiers who were convalescing in the nursery wing of the house, cared for by Red Cross nurses; there were eight men there at this time, and Elizabeth and Beryl spent that evening talking to them. They spoke of friends and companions they had seen wounded or killed; 'they none of them when once they have been out there want to go again,' Beryl recorded. 'Poor things they say the sufferings & privations especially in the early part of the war were too awful.' The nurses reported that the nerves of one man were quite shattered; he constantly called out in his sleep, and woke up in terror. Elizabeth was pleased to find that another of them had been in the Highland Light Infantry unit to which Mike was attached, and knew him.[49]

Back in London after the weekend they found that Jock had returned to Flanders. News came from Mike, who was well but finding life 'dull'. Remarkably, Lady Strathmore considered going to visit him, but decided against this because the sea crossing – at the mercy of

German submarines – was too dangerous; furthermore, her husband, eldest son and youngest daughter were all unwell, so she was 'rather required'.[50]

Lord Strathmore's influenza and the feverish chill from which Elizabeth had been suffering were not serious; more so was Patrick's condition. He had been sent home in late February 1915 with a wounded foot. His battalion, the 5th Black Watch, had suffered terrible losses: of the thousand men who had gone out, only 350 were still standing. There was a dearth of recruits; the regiment was counting on Patrick, a major, to raise a third reserve battalion, as 'he only could do it,' Lady Strathmore reported to May Elphinstone. As she said, he would have to make his appeal on crutches, 'which might not inspire, but all the men adore him'.[51]

Patrick was a strikingly handsome, popular and charming man ('He looked really as if he'd stepped down from Olympia,' his eldest niece later said of him).[52] But he was now suffering badly from shell shock, and although at first he was reported to be in high spirits, 'hopping all over the house with his wounded foot in the air',[53] his nervous condition deteriorated, and with it his physical health: he could not eat, and spent three weeks recuperating in a nursing home. A spell at Glamis with his brother Jock, to whom he was close, helped; but he did not fully recover and was invalided out of active service.

Towards the end of March 1915 Mike had been able to snatch a few days' home leave before returning to France. It may have been on this occasion that Elizabeth accompanied her mother to Victoria station to see him off. Many years later she recalled, 'There was a very young little officer going off, and his mother – I can see her now – was weeping. And I remember my brother leaning out of the train and saying, "Don't worry I'll look after him." And do you know, he was killed the next day. It was so awful when one thinks about it.'[54] Two months later a telegram arrived announcing that Mike was in hospital in Rouen suffering from shell shock. He proved to have a head wound as well, and was sent by river steamer to Le Havre and shipped home. Lady Strathmore's concerns about this son were different: 'now Lady S. is worrying about how in the world she will manage to keep him at all quiet – he is so headstrong & will want to be going to theatres etc all the time,' Beryl Poignand recorded.[55]

Jock too had been wounded. In early May the first finger of his left hand was shattered by a bullet. He sailed to Southampton among 850 casualties on a ship intended to carry half the number. His damaged finger had to be amputated. Lady Strathmore was relieved that his injury was not worse, while his youngest sister, to her delight, found herself quoted in the *Daily Mail*, to whose reporter she had spoken when he rang up St James's Square asking for information about her brother's wound.[56]

For all Lady Strathmore's preoccupations with her soldier sons and her hospitals, she did not neglect the upbringing of the two Benjamins and stuck to her principles on the profitable use of holiday time. Elizabeth and David had French conversation lessons with yet another Madé, Lydie Lachaise,* while Beryl went home for a fortnight, and David had drawing lessons, which his sister was annoyed to have to take in his place when he fell ill.[57]

In July 1915 Elizabeth was overjoyed to be taken to the Haymarket Theatre to see a new romantic comedy, H. A. Vachell's *Quinneys*,† starring her particular idol Henry Ainley,‡ whom she had been thrilled to glimpse from the window of a taxi a few days earlier.[58] Her letters at this time overflow with swooning references to this actor; and she was mercilessly teased about him by her family – particularly her brothers – who told her he was fat and old. They sent her 'vulgar and insulting telegrams' on her birthday, 'about darling Henry's stomach, was it real or a cushion, he was just having his 25th anniversary on the stage & such insults'.[59]

To her delight, later that summer she was able to send Beryl 'perfectly wonderful, marvellous, absolutely indescribable news'. Her friend Lavinia had a first cousin 'who KNOWS Darling HENRY VERY

---

* Lydie Lachaise (1888/9–1982) was French governess to the children of Sir James Reid, Bt, Queen Victoria's physician for many years. Sir James's wife was Lavinia Spencer's Aunt Susan (née Baring; her sister Margaret had married the Hon. Robert Spencer, Lavinia's father. Margaret had died in 1904 soon after the birth of her third daughter, also Margaret, and the motherless Spencer children grew up close to their Reid cousins). Mlle Lachaise was holiday governess to Lady Elizabeth and her brother again in August 1915. She stayed in England and married Raphael Aboav in 1920.

† Horace Annesley Vachell (1861–1955), novelist and playwright. *Quinneys*, his most successful play, was adapted from his novel of the same name. It was made into a film in 1927.

‡ Henry Ainley (1879–1945) was a major classical actor who appeared in hundreds of productions over a forty-five-year career. He starred in many films, the last of which was *As You Like It* (1936) in which he played the exiled Duke while the young Laurence Olivier played Orlando. Ainley was known for his superb elocution and much loved for his rendering of great soliloquies.

WELL!!!! He is 35 (Hahahoo, Rosie and Mike will be squashed!) and she is going to write and find out the colour of his eyes, & everything, also get his signature. Isnt it absolutely unbelievable . . . Darling Henry. I am so pleased. I feel that it was quite worth sticking up for him all this time. Oh my sacred Aunt in pink tights, perhaps we shall even meet him, help I shall die in a minute. Yours, Elizabeth.'[60] She afterwards acquired a signed photograph of Ainley in his role as Joe Quinney, and continued to follow him in all his stage and film roles. 'I bet all the housemaids think that he's my young man!' she wrote to Beryl after hanging the latest picture of her hero over her mantelpiece at Glamis.[61] She and Lavinia, who had a crush on another actor, Basil Hallam,* signed themselves 'Henriette' and 'Basilette' in the facetious letters they exchanged about their adoration of these idols.

The two also shared a penchant for handsome sailors, and corresponded irreverently as King George V (Lavinia, who signed one letter in a passable imitation of the King's writing, 'Your Lord and Sovereign George R') and Queen Mary (Elizabeth, rebuked by her friend in the same letter for flirting with sailors: 'For shame! Tut! Remember your queenly dignity, & don't make eyes at men in The service, Mary – although, of course, I own it's a temptation').[62]

Another admirer of sailors came into Lady Elizabeth's life at around this time: she was Katie Hamilton,† daughter of the Duke of Abercorn, who was to become a lifelong friend. Lavinia wrote that they were both dying to hear about the captivating specimens of nautical manhood Elizabeth had met while staying with her sister May in Edinburgh.[63] Katie was determined to marry a sailor, and indeed fell for one – Lavinia's brother Cecil, a sub-lieutenant in the navy. 'Wouldn't it be splendid if you & Lavinia & I all married sailors,' she wrote to Elizabeth; 'there would be a lifelong feud between us if by any chance one of the 3 got promoted first!'[64]

Handsome men in uniform did not have to be sailors to attract Elizabeth's attention. In London she and Beryl had taken to watching

---

* Basil Hallam (1889–1916), actor and singer. His most famous role was as Gilbert the Filbert in the revue *The Passing Show* at the Palace Theatre in London in 1914–15. He joined up in 1915 but was killed in a parachute jump on the Western Front in 1916.

† Lady Katharine Hamilton (1900–85), daughter of third Duke of Abercorn. She married, in 1930, Lieutenant Colonel (later Sir) Reginald Seymour, equerry to King George V, and became a lady in waiting to Queen Mary for some time before transferring to Queen Elizabeth's Household in 1937.

the Red Cross chauffeurs outside their headquarters in St James's Square. Elizabeth dubbed one of these drivers 'The Beautiful One', and he appears frequently in her letters of these years. 'I received the most seraphic, glorious, delightful, beautiful, wonderful smile from the Beautiful One yesterday,' she wrote to Beryl in July 1915. 'He was perfectly charmed to see me, (whato).'[65]

On Elizabeth's fifteenth birthday, also the first anniversary of the outbreak of war, they went to the Hippodrome. The cast threw hundreds of soft balls into the auditorium which the audience could then fling at each other. Elizabeth, with her usual enthusiasm, embraced this challenge vigorously.[66]

Friday 6 August was 'a fairly decent' last day in London before she left for Scotland, after seven months in the south. She went shopping and bought a hat and a pink dressing gown and 'lots of chocs'. Perhaps best of all, she had 'a wonderful last smile from the Beautiful One, we waved to each other for the <u>first and last</u> time, a fitting goodbye'.[67] That night she and David travelled 'alonio' on the night sleeper to Glamis. She found that 'two <u>most</u> beautiful sailors' were travelling in the same coach. 'We had long conversations in the corridor in the morning.'[68]

At Glamis she slipped happily back into her role of friend to the soldier patients. Her unaffected curiosity about them and enjoyment of their company are evident from her letters throughout the war. There seems to be no doubt that the experience of welcoming and cheering men from all walks of life and many parts of the world had a major impact upon her – indeed, one can surmise that everything she learned from this stood her in extremely good stead in the life that lay before her. The soldiers were charming, she reported to Beryl, who was away for the summer holidays; and this time there was a sailor among them, to her delight. 'My dear Miss Poignand, you <u>are</u> missing something! One is a fisherman and a Naval Reserve, he has been shipwrecked five times. Blue eyes, black hair, <u>so</u> nice. Reminds me of Henry.'[69]

Another of the new patients was Corporal Ernest Pearce of the Durham Light Infantry, whose right shoulder had been shattered at Ypres in May 1915. Soon after he arrived, he saw a girl in a print dress swinging a sun bonnet in her hand. It was Elizabeth. He thought she had beautiful eyes and found her delightful; whenever he met her in the weeks ahead, he said later, 'she was always the same. "How is your shoulder?" "Do you sleep well?" "Does it pain you?" "Why are you not smoking your pipe?" "Have you no tobacco?" "You must tell me if you haven't and I'll get some for you" . . . For her fifteen years she was very womanly, kind-hearted and sympathetic.'[70]

Corporal Pearce said that everyone in the Castle 'worshipped' Elizabeth. For her part, she described Pearce as 'A most delightful Corporal, nice boy indeed'. His name appears frequently in her letters thereafter, often as her partner in the boisterous games of whist they played in the evenings. He returned to service in 1916 and survived the war; Elizabeth kept in touch with him throughout, helped him in the post-war years and later gave him a job as a gardener which he kept for the rest of his life.*

There was joy at Glamis in late August 1915 – Fergus came back from France for five days' leave. It was almost a year since he and Christian had married and their daughter Rosemary had been born on 18 July. But after this holiday he had to return to the Front. Lydie Lachaise, the French governess, never forgot the sadness in Lady Strathmore's face when he left.[71]

At the beginning of September Lady Strathmore and David travelled south – David to begin his life at Eton – while Elizabeth went to visit May at Carberry Tower, the Elphinstone family home near Edinburgh. From there she sent her mother a request: 'Darling Mother, don't forget, a little white fox neck thing, a really chic hat, the "dernier cri" in shirts & a warm winter coat, the newest mode!!!!!!'[72] She replied to a letter from Beryl, who was still in London, with a mixture of low badinage and high politics: 'Yes, of course my dear Ass, you may call at St James's Square for your luggage. Please give my best love to the dear B.O. and old goggle eyes . . .'. Quoting from a letter from Sidney Elphinstone, she continued:

> London is full of dreadful rumours . . . But much the worst is that Kitchener is going to resign, Winston will take his place and Lloyd George will be Prime Minister. But Sidney, who wrote about it, says that he doesn't think that this long suffering country would stand that, for they have such faith in K of K. I hear the Russians

---

* Ernest Pearce (1893–1969), served in 1/7th Durham Light Infantry, wounded at Ypres in May 1915; promoted lance sergeant December 1916. He worked in a shipyard in Sunderland after the war. His niece Mary Ann Whitfield Pearce also worked for Queen Elizabeth at Royal Lodge from 1946 to 1981, latterly as head cook.

are getting a much better supply of ammunition now, perhaps they will pick up a bit . . .

How terribly you would have envied me. I spent the whole afternoon on the shores of the Forth. So near the ships that I could see people. And a conversation with a most beautiful sailor, with blue eyes and black lashes and so good looking. That was yesterday. He pointed out all the ships to me . . . They looked too fine for words. I simply revelled in 'em. And simply hundreds of beautiful brown Lieutenants, Subs, Snotties [midshipmen], Admirals and sailors. Oh my! They were all most amorous! . . . Beatty's fleet I suppose.[73]

Back at Glamis a few days later she found a 'fairly cheerful' letter from David at Eton, and new soldiers – 'one is a ventriloquist; another has a huge cut across his head and is rather "queer", no wonder'.[74]

Then came the news that every family dreaded throughout the war. Only a month after his return from Glamis to the battlefields, Fergus had been killed at the Battle of Loos.

*

FERGUS WAS a delightful, cheerful and energetic young man, a country-man through and through. He took great pleasure in being on his own, and particularly loved Glamis. He was said to have made friends with two poachers and to have imbibed a great deal of their lore.[75]

In December 1910 Fergus had become a second lieutenant in the 2nd Battalion The Black Watch, and in 1911 he was sent to serve in the Punjab. He and his mother corresponded frequently and one teasing letter from him to the ten-year-old Elizabeth survives in the Glamis Archives. He wonders whether she has been to Gunter's tea shop lately, and describes his ideal dinner: '1. Buttered eggs 2. Fillets of salmon 3. Roast pigeon (fried potatoes, peas, collieflower) 4. Lamb cutlets 5. Macedoine of fruits 6. Lemon water ice 7. Fruit (peaches, grapes etc) 8. Coffee 9. Probably very very sick.'[76]

Fergus would have been content to remain in his regiment, but by his early twenties he knew that he had to earn more money. In February 1914 he decided, reluctantly, to go into the City.[77] But on the outbreak of war he immediately rejoined the Black Watch. Sent to the Front in early 1915, he wrote home about the gas being used by the

Germans. 'They are fiends,' he said. 'These are trying times and I'm sure we'll all be overjoyed when the war is over.'[78]

In the spring of 1915 the Germans and Austrians mounted a huge and successful assault on Russian positions to the east. In order to relieve the pressure on their Russian allies, the French decided to attack German lines in Champagne and Artois. The British government was a reluctant partner in this venture – London agreed only for fear that the Russians might make a separate peace. Through the summer the Germans strengthened their positions. Fergus wrote home in June describing the German trenches his troops were facing as 'quite impregnable – rows & rows of them . . . & all lined with concrete & with murderous machine guns'.[79] It would have been wise to delay an attack. But the British were not even allowed to choose their own terrain; General Joffre insisted that they fight side by side with the French through the ruined villages of Loos and Lens, not in the more open countryside that Kitchener preferred.[80]

After his brief visit home in August, Fergus rejoined his battalion as final preparations were under way. Despite the season, it was pouring with rain and the trenches were filled with mud. Around 800,000 British and French soldiers were poised to attack on 25 September. General Haig, in command of I Corps of the British Expeditionary Force, wrote in his diary, 'The greatest battle in the world's history begins today.' General Joffre told the French, 'Votre élan sera irrésistible.'[81]

Not so. The French advanced in Champagne but then were stopped by the Germans. The British, using poison gas for the first time, pushed forward strongly at first, but reinforcements were called up too slowly. One soldier who was there said, 'Jerry did himself well at Loos and on us innocents. We went into it, knowing no more than our own dead what was coming. And Jerry fair lifted us out of it with machine guns.' The losses were appalling.[82] Private Carson Stewart of the 7th (Service) Battalion The Queen's Own Cameron Highlanders recalled: 'When they took the Roll Call after Loos, those not answering, their chums would answer, "Over the Hill." '[83]

In the early morning of 27 September Fergus was ordered to drive out a party of Germans who had infiltrated a trench by the Hohenzollern Redoubt, a German stronghold which the Black Watch had captured the day before. He and his men, exhausted from the previous two days and nights of fighting, had only just been relieved at 4 a.m. and were preparing themselves some breakfast when the orders came. As Fergus led his party forward a German bomb exploded at his feet, blowing off his right leg and wounding him in the chest; at the same time he was hit by bullets in the chest and shoulder. He died at about 11.30 a.m.

The news did not reach Glamis until four days later, on 1 October. Lieutenant G. B. Gilroy of the 8th Battalion The Black Watch wrote to Lady Strathmore telling her what had happened and assuring her that her son could not have suffered any pain but must have died instantly.[84] Perhaps mercifully, it was several weeks before Lady Strathmore learned that Fergus's death had been neither instant nor painless. His soldier servant, Lance Corporal Andrew Ross, and Sergeant Robert Lindsay, who had been with him when he died, came to Glamis to see her. Both men, and his fellow officers, spoke of Fergus with affection and admiration.[85] Sergeant Lindsay gave her the name of the stretcher bearer who had carried Fergus away for burial; she later wrote to him to ask for details, saying that she planned 'to go out & try & find his grave when the war is over'.[86]

The entire community of Glamis was thrown into deep sorrow. Corporal Pearce recalled later that the soldiers all agreed not to go up to the billiard room, to stay off the lawns and not to play the gramophone. They wrote a letter of sympathy to the Countess. She thanked them and said she hoped that, as her guests, they would carry on using the Castle just as before.[87] On 3 October 1915 Fergus was remembered in the parish church at Glamis with the words: 'How hard to realise that all that personal quickening, that lovableness and charm, that brightness and vivacity, that thoughtfulness have passed and gone.'[88]

Few records of Elizabeth's reaction to Fergus's death have survived. She wrote Lavinia Spencer a letter described by her friend as 'brave' in her sympathetic reply, which is in the Glamis Archives. Beryl Poignand recorded that 'poor little Elizabeth' had managed to remain 'gay and bright' when she accompanied the Glamis convalescents to the local picture palace in Forfar soon after the sad news arrived.[89] Her writing paper for most of 1916 was black-edged in mourning for Fergus.

A few weeks after the battle Winston Churchill, then a battalion commander on the Western Front, heard a lecture on Loos and wrote to his wife, Clementine, that it was a tale 'of hopeless failure, of sublime heroism utterly wasted and of splendid Scottish soldiers thrown away in vain . . . Alas, alas.'[90]

Among the many thousands killed at Loos was John, the only son of Rudyard Kipling; his body was never found. The poet wrote of the death of all the young men:

That flesh we had nursed from the first in all cleanness as given . . .
To be blanched or gay painted by fumes – to be cindered by fires –
To be senselessly tossed and retossed in stale mutilation
From crater to crater. For this we shall take expiation.
  But who shall return us our children?[91]

*

LIFE ON THE Home Front continued. Elizabeth had resumed her lessons with Beryl; she claimed in a letter to Beryl's mother that she was not doing very well. 'I am hopelessly rotton at Arithmetic, Literature, Drawing, History and Geography,' she wrote. Beryl, she added, was 'really in despair about my exam, you see I'm so frightfully stupid & don't know anything except what I've learnt with her about – Julius Caesar, Napoleon, French History, & a lot of little things about the Gods & Goddesses, Hades etc.'[92]

At the end of October she and her mother travelled down to London to see David, on his first long leave (half-term) from Eton. It was not the best of journeys – the train was three hours late and filled with troops – 'my word how drunk the sailors were!' They arrived in thick fog in London, and Elizabeth discussed a new threat – the Zeppelin airships – 'don't be surprised if the Zepps come, for they love fogs,' she wrote to Beryl.[93] It was a warning with resonance; the Zeppelins inspired real terror and recently five of them had dropped 189 bombs on London and the Home Counties, killing seventy-one people.[94]* Elizabeth's attitude remained insouciant. She and David went to see *The Scarlet Pimpernel* at the Strand Theatre. 'When the

---

* Before the war the enormous, lighter-than-air machines had caused amazement as they flew over Europe. When war came, millions of people feared them as no other weapon. One of the Zeppelin's historians wrote that it was 'the H-bomb of its day, an awesome sword of Damocles to be held over the cowering heads of Germany's enemies'. (Quoted in Martin Gilbert, *First World War*, p. 42)

Zepps were last here, they dropped a bomb into the pit at the Strand and killed 6 people so of course we went there.'[95]

A crisis for Glamis arose just before Christmas 1915 when the medical authorities in Dundee considered closing the hospital at the Castle. Elizabeth and her mother were horrified and went to Dundee to argue their case. 'I waited outside, trembling, the fate of the hospital was in the balance, but, hooray, its all right,' Elizabeth wrote. Lady Strathmore had been effective and Dr Fraser at the Infirmary told them that Glamis had done 'wonderful good work, especially with "nervy" men' and he would continue to send patients there.

When they got back to the Castle, Nurse Anderson was 'simply dancing with impatience at the top of the stairs'. The rejoicing was compounded by Jock, who had telephoned to say he was coming home that night. So he did, with a whole group of friends. 'You can (or rather cannot) imagine the row they made in the motor, "Auld Lang Syne" etc. I have just seen Jock (it is about 11.15) he is so happy.'[96]

The Strathmores again spent Christmas at Glamis, and Elizabeth prepared a tree for the soldiers. They each got presents from the family – an electric torch, a shirt, chocolates and crackers. 'I believe the noise last night at "lights out" was something appalling, trumpets & squeaky things going like mad,' she wrote to Beryl. 'Of course we drank "To Hell with the b— Kaiser" last night.'[97]

The year ended forlornly. Massive loss of life had gained little ground for either side. Neither had broken through the other's lines of trenches. The British Expeditionary Force in France had now grown to over a million men. Many of these were poorly trained divisions upon which General Haig knew he could not really depend. More and more of the young volunteers in Kitchener's New Armies presented themselves to army medics with what the official medical history of the war described as 'definite hysterical manifestations (mutism and tremors)'.[98] The Germans held stronger positions at the end of the year than they had at its start. Resignation, if not cynicism, had replaced enthusiasm and euphoria. On New Year's Eve Elizabeth wrote again to Beryl: 'Today is the last day of 1915. Isn't it dreadful? If this war doesn't come to an end next year, it never will, I don't think so.'[99]

★

IN THE FIRST few weeks of 1916 Elizabeth had to cram for the Junior Examination of the Oxford Local Examinations Board. She and Beryl still had some fun. They went to the theatre in Dundee together and Elizabeth teased Beryl's mother that Beryl had behaved 'in a disgraceful manner', singing so loudly that the manager asked her to stop, 'whereupon she sang most aggressively to him (the poor man had a red nose) "Put a bit of powder on it", which is a vulgar song. To crown all that, she drank three cocktails on reaching home, and had to be carried up to bed by Barson, who seemed to enjoy the job!!!'[100]

The examination took place in east London. At eight o'clock on the morning of 17 March Elizabeth took the bus and tram from St James's Square to the Hackney Examination Centre, which she described to her mother as 'about the last house on that side of London, green fields beyond'. First she had to do a 'memory drawing paper' which ended at 10.45, so she travelled home again for lunch and then back to Hackney in the afternoon for the 'model drawing' paper. After four hours of travel 'I'm what you might call "slightly fatigued",' she wrote to her mother.[101] The next week she had a paper on Walter Scott which she found 'difficult'. All in all she was afraid that she had failed her exams. 'The geography and Arithmetic were quite hopeless, much too complicated for me!'[102] At some stage she appears to have been fed tapioca pudding in Hackney, which added to her misery.

A trip to the theatre to see Henry Ainley restored her spirits. 'I've seen old Henry in "Who is He" and simply loved it. He's so good looking, (do tell Mike & Rosie, and make him as young and beautiful as you can) with BLUE eyes and BLACK hair, and quite THIN, not too thin, but just right. I am so triumphant, you'd love him, he's so funny,' she told Lady Strathmore.[103]

In the midst of her examinations she had actually received a letter from Ainley, who had heard she was coming to the play. 'I shall myself look forward with keen pleasure to Friday evening,' he wrote, adding: 'at the end of the first act I shall raise my eyes to that part of the house where you & your friend will be seated, & may I hope to meet a smile of appreciation & pleasure.' Better still, he had sent her a photograph of himself and said he had heard that she was 'at present engaged on a most difficult advanced examination' and was sure she would come through 'with flying colours'.[104]

Alas she did not. A few weeks later she received an impersonal form from the Examination Board. 'You do not appear to be entitled to a Certificate,' it announced. Furthermore, no questions 'respecting the cause or extent of your failure' could be answered.[105] She was disappointed, if defiant. 'All that I say is, DAMN THE EXAM!! I always was good at poetry wasn't I?!!' she wrote to Beryl. 'I'm not going to tell anyone about it anyhow, till they ask me!! Good heavens! What was the use of toiling down to that – er – place Hackney? None, I tell you none. It makes me boil with rage to think of that vile stuff, tapioca, eaten for – nothing? Oh hell . . . Yes, I am very disappointed, but I daresay I shall get over it, if I go and see Henry.'[106]

Less enthralling than the theatre was the prospect of a tea party at Spencer House on 2 April 1916. 'Lavinia wants me to go to tea, to meet Princess Mary and Prince Albert next Sunday,' she wrote to her mother, adding, 'They don't frighten me quite as much as Queens.'[107] Afterwards, however, she declared the tea party 'was rather frightening – in fact, very'. She had had a table all to herself and 'nearly burst' trying to think of something to say to her neighbours, Mr Robinson and Mr Dill. She added: 'Prince Albert was next door, he's rather nice.'[108] Beryl Poignand reported to her mother that the Prince and his sister had enjoyed themselves so much that 'long after their carriage was announced they kept on staying & staying – they played games after tea – "Up Jenkins" & "Clumps", a guessing game'.[109]

Prince Albert, the second son of King George V, was a twenty-year-old naval sub-lieutenant; he was at this time on sick leave from his ship. He and Elizabeth were later said to have met for the first time at a children's tea party many years earlier;* but their Spencer House meeting was the first of which either of them left a record. No comment by the Prince has survived, however, and Elizabeth made little of the encounter. The remainder of her letter to her mother was taken up with enthusing about Henry Ainley – his wonderful voice and his dreadful shyness.[110]

In the second half of April 1916, she had a holiday in Glamis with her father. A new batch of convalescent soldiers was about to arrive;

---

* In January 1923 Lord Strathmore was reported in the press as saying that it had been at a party given by Lady Leicester when the two were children (*Evening News*, 16 January 1923); King George VI's official biographer John Wheeler-Bennett stated that it had happened at Montagu House (where their hostess would have been the Duchess of Buccleuch) in 1905.

she spent a lot of time writing letters and listening to records of Henry Ainley singing patriotic songs. At the end of the month she took the train back to London, leaving her father and Barson, she said, 'sorrowfully drinking cocktails'.[111]

Back in St James's Square, she was much taken up with the rush towards her sister Rose's wedding. Rose was the beauty of the family. A kind and intelligent girl, she was closest of all to her brother Michael, and she had nursed Alec when he was dying. She had many admirers – her daughter Mary Clayton recalls her grandmother saying that, after Rosie's twentieth proposal, she gave up counting.[112]

To the chagrin of Freddy Dalrymple Hamilton – always 'the unlucky third' in affairs of the heart, he felt – Rose's choice fell on a fellow naval officer, William Spencer Leveson-Gower (who later became the fourth Earl Granville).[113] He was known as Wisp, partly because of his Christian names and partly because as a child he had straw-coloured hair.

The preparations for the wedding – held barely a month after the engagement was announced – gave rise to much family hilarity at Rose's expense. 'We thought of getting the chorus from the Gaiety for bridesmaids, and the two waiters also from the same theatre, because they are so amusing for the reception affair afterwards!' wrote her younger sister. 'Also a band of the Royal Scots, and some sailors to pull the carriage to the church and back, and all sorts of such suggestions have been made!!! It would be rather amusing if it could be done!!'[114] Elizabeth thought the trousseau needlessly extravagant. 'I should never be able to use 2 dozen of everything, lingerie I mean, good heavens, I'm thankful to say no.'[115] She went to buy her shoes at Pinet, one of the best shops in Bond Street – 'the first and last time for poverty stricken me I expect, as they were demned expensive' – over thirty shillings.[116]

Wisp and Rose were married on 24 May 1916. 'The "best man" is very nice – Commander Tom Goldie RN,' Elizabeth reported to Beryl. But evidently not that nice. 'Jock says the best man has got to kiss the bridesmaid but he's jolly well not going to kiss me!!'[117]

Not long after the wedding Elizabeth discovered that society magazines were describing Dorothy Cavendish,* Lavinia and herself

---

* Lady Dorothy Cavendish (1900–66), daughter of ninth Duke of Devonshire, married in 1920 Harold Macmillan MP.

as 'coming Beauties'. 'Did you ever hear such absolute <u>rot</u> in your life? DC is positively ugly, Lavinia is very pretty, but not even a Beauty, and as for me!' News of the war preoccupied her more. Worried about friends in the navy, she commented, 'It seems a "damn silly" thing to go and do, only part, and a small part, of our fleet to go & take on the whole Hun fleet, but its very brave.'[118] She was referring to the Battle of Jutland on 31 May, in which 259 warships were deployed to fight each other – Winston Churchill called it 'the culminating manifestation of naval force in the history of the world'. Prince Albert saw active service in the battle, aboard HMS *Collingwood*.

It had been German strategy since before the turn of the century to deploy a fleet so large that the British (or any other enemy) would be fatally weakened by any decisive engagement.[119] At the end of May, the German High Seas Fleet succeeded in luring the British Grand Fleet out into the North Sea. Sixteen U-boats attacked British ships as they left their ports, though none of the torpedoes succeeded in striking its target. But the next afternoon, within half an hour of each other, *Indefatigable* and *Queen Mary* were both sent to the bottom of the sea, with the loss of over 2,200 men. Two hours later as visibility, made more murky by the smoke from 250 funnels and by cordite, began to fail, Admiral Hood's flagship, *Invincible*, was blown up and more than a thousand men were drowned. In the dark of that night the German fleet escaped and fled back to its havens.

Despite the immense losses of ships and men, the British navy had not been defeated; but when Admiral Beatty took over the command of the Grand Fleet he concluded that British strategy should be not to engage the German navy but to keep it bottled up in its harbours. The war had to be won in the mud of Flanders.

*

ON 1 JULY 1916 the greatest British catastrophe of the war began. The British and French attempted a mass infantry attack on German lines along the north bank of the River Somme. Almost a quarter of a million shells were fired at German positions in an hour that morning; the noise of this massive barrage was so intense it could be heard on Hampstead Heath. Then the heavily laden men of eleven British divisions hauled themselves out of their trenches to advance against German positions on the north bank of the Somme.

They sang:

> We beat them on the Marne,
> We beat them on the Aisne,
> We gave them hell at Neuve Chapelle,
> And here we are again![120]

The weather in northern France was glorious. As Harold Macmillan, then a captain in the Grenadier Guards, wrote to his mother, it was 'not the weather for killing people'.[121]* The horror unfolding on the Somme was not quickly understood in Britain. At first even the General Staff did not grasp the scale of the tragedy. Indeed, one war correspondent wrote that 1 July was 'on balance, a good day for England and France'.[122]

By nightfall that day, the army had suffered over 57,000 casualties of whom 20,000 were dead. One eyewitness, Brigadier General F. P. Crozier, recorded: 'I glance to the right through a gap in the trees. I see the 10th Rifles plodding on and then my eyes are riveted by a sight I shall never see again. It is the 32nd Division at its best. I see rows upon rows of British soldiers lying dead, dying or wounded in No Mans Land. Here and there I see an officer urging on his followers. Occasionally I see the hands thrown up and then a body flops to the ground.' Altogether the Battle of the Somme lasted 141 days. The horrors were almost indescribable.

While the battle was in its early stages, Elizabeth and her mother went to visit 'dear old Pegg' (Trooper J. Langfield Pegg of the New Zealand Mounted Rifles, who had been a convalescent at Glamis in December 1915) in the New Zealand hospital at Walton on Thames. He showed them around; there were more than 350 men there, some of them just arrived from the Front, looking very pale, tired and dirty. Returning to Glamis in early August, they found a new batch of soldiers. As Elizabeth reported to Beryl, 'They've most of them been in this new thing [the Somme] & a Scotch one said that only 52 men were left of his batt: by the time they'de reached the German trenches. It must have been awful.'[123]

*

ON SATURDAY 16 September 1916 Elizabeth's father and David went shooting with Gavin Ralston, the Glamis factor, and some neighbours.

---

* Harold Macmillan (1894–1986) was prime minister 1957–63.

Elizabeth and her mother remained at the Castle tending to the soldiers. In the afternoon nine of the soldiers and the Sister went to the pictures in Forfar. Fortunately some of the soldiers stayed behind. One of them, Sergeant Cowie, whom Elizabeth described as 'remarkably good looking. Very quiet and Scotch and huge', suddenly smelt smoke and realized that the Castle was on fire. He raised the alarm.[124] Elizabeth at once took charge, telephoning for the fire brigades from both Forfar and more distant Dundee. She wrote to Beryl later that she, four soldiers and all the maids 'rushed up and handed buckets like old Billy-o. The more water, the more smoke, we absolutly could not find the fire.'[125]

The whole village ran up to help, but still the fire spread and 'the little flames were sort of creeping through the roofs ... It was too awful.' The Forfar fire brigade arrived full tilt but were 'absolutly no use', having only a hand pump which was quite unable to get water ninety feet up the tower. Fortunately the Dundee brigade were prompt and reached the Castle only twenty-six minutes after being called out. With their powerful engines they were able to spray water all across the roofs of the tower.

Gradually the fire was brought under control, but then a new crisis developed. The cold-water storage tank in the roof suddenly burst with the heat and its contents cascaded down, along with the water from the firemen's hoses. Elizabeth at once saw the danger to the contents of the Castle and organized David – now back from shooting – and some of the maids to brush the water down the stairs, away from the rooms. 'From 6.30 till about 10 o'c I stood just outside the drawing room door, sweeping down the water.'[126] At the same time, she directed about thirty people into a line to remove all the pictures, valuable objects and furniture at risk and store them in dry rooms. When night fell she searched for candles so that they could continue as best they could.

'I can't tell you all the little incidents, but it was too dreadful, we thought the whole place would be burnt,' Elizabeth wrote. It was indeed a close call. Next day the wind strengthened, and Captain Weir, the chief of the Dundee fire brigade, told Elizabeth that nothing would have saved the Castle had the wind been as strong the previous day. In the end only the rooms at the very top of the Castle were destroyed by fire, but the water damage was serious throughout. 'It was pouring into the drawing room all night, and the Chapel is a wreck. All the pictures with <u>huge</u> smudges, it's beastly.'[127]

Elizabeth's crucial role was clear to all. She had been vital in organizing both the fire brigades and the rescue of the Castle's artefacts. When Lord Strathmore thanked one of the tenants for his help, he replied, 'It was her little Ladyship told us how to do it and kept us to it.'[128] The *Dundee Courier* reported that she 'was a veritable heroine in the salvage work she performed even within the fire zone'.[129] According to Cynthia Asquith Elizabeth was toasted with 'Highland Honours' in every house and cottage for miles around. From the trenches of northern France, her brother Michael wrote, after hearing the news, 'My darling old Buffy . . . The fire must have been awful! And I hear you worked like the devil himself.'[130]

Her mother told Beryl, 'Eliz[th] was wonderful – she worked without ceasing & long before I had time to think of anything <u>inside</u> the Castle, she had gathered up all the treasures & put them in safety – & then she <u>directed</u> & saved all the furniture possible. She really is a wonderful girl, poor darling she was quite worn out after & ached all over for days.'[131]

For the next few weeks, as the clearing, cleaning and repairs proceeded, Elizabeth spent a good deal of time with the soldiers. She told Beryl that one day she took three of them, Blencoe ('the wag'), Randle ('a dear ugly nice Scotch boy, rather shy') and 'Sergeant Shell Shock, as I call him, because I don't know his name', for a drive in the pony carriage. On another occasion she gave Blencoe a lift to the village and back when she saw him limping down the avenue. He told her that whenever in future he saw her name in the paper he would say, 'Ah, I had a drive with <u>that</u> young lady.'[132]

She was playing frequent card games with the 'boys' – in particular Hearts, 'a new game, in which nobody wants the Queen of Spades as she counts 13. So of course, their one aim and object was to give her to me!!'[133] There was 'wild laughter' when she got the Queen of Spades time after time – and she discovered that they had been passing it under the table to give to her. 'They are such babies!'[134] She and her mother both loved 'Sergeant Shell Shock' in particular. She also thought that another soldier, Nix, was 'angelic. I love him. You would too. 'e's very small and merry with a golden heart as you might say.'[135] She wrote a poem about Sergeant Little because Sister teased him after he put a postal order in the fire by accident:

'His mental state' said Sister
   'Gives me quite a fright
He talks such dreadful nonsense
   Morning, noon and night.

'He was'nt sane when first he came
   It's getting worse and worse,
And if he stays much longer,
   I think that I shall curse!

'He received a postal order
   (Don't call me a Liar)
For he looked at it one moment
   Then PUT IT IN THE FIRE!!

'Is'nt it sad, in so young a lad,
   Such lunacy to see,
For he drank his cup and saucer
   And forgot about the tea!!

'Though Sergeant Little's brain is weak
   His arm is very strong,
He strafes the Bosche like anything
   Here's Luck to him life long![136]*

The soldiers apparently loved this poem. 'They really thought I
had brains!' Encouraged, she wrote another one for Private Harding,
one of those who had 'delighted' in slipping her the Queen of Spades.

   I sometimes go into the Ward
      And play a game or two;
   And if I get the Queen of Spades
      T'is only due to you –
         Private Harding!

---

*   She wrote this poem in Sergeant Little's autograph book; he responded with one in hers:

         There is a young lady so charming and witty
         (I'm really not forced to tell you she's pretty)
         But she is

         She wrote some nice verses about where the sense ended
         Of a Patient whom she thought would be rather offended
         But he isn't

(Sergeant J. Little, 8th East Yorkshire Regiment, poem in Lady Elizabeth Bowes Lyon's
autograph book, October 1916. RA QEQM/PRIV/PERS)

> Are you not ashamed and sorry
> That cheating should go on?
> Something's wrong about the dealing
> I put the blame upon –
> Private Harding![137]

Mr Dunn, the local photographer who had recorded the fire, came to the Castle to photograph Elizabeth and the soldiers. They all dressed up and pretended they were the Glamis Band, complete with gramophone, dinner horn, penny rattle, drum, penny whistles. 'The noise is infernal! . . . They are quite mad. Harding was the Queen of Spades!! That was a great joke! Nix was "His Lordship's Jockey" and frightfully pleased with himself.'[138] Next day she had to present the prizes at the whist drive, which she was dreading. In the event it was not too bad, she thought. Harding won first prize, six handkerchiefs – and then they all danced; her partner whisked her round and round until she became quite giddy. Then reels, recitations and the evening ended with a whisky toddy at 12.30 a.m.

After breakfast the following day ten of the soldiers left and Elizabeth waved them goodbye. 'They were all dreadfully unhappy and too darling . . . I do wonder if they caught their train! Because every two steps, they stopped, threw their kit bags into the air, and waved frantically, and of course all the kit bags fell down, so that took about 3 minutes to pick them all up. They all enjoyed themselves frightfully last night.'[139]

She remained in touch with many of them – Nix, 'the angelic little one', wrote to her from Hull. Pegg wrote to tell her that he had won the Distinguished Conduct Medal and was going back to New Zealand. Ernest Pearce wrote to say that he had been made a lance sergeant. Some of those who were left at Glamis celebrated Hallowe'en. 'They all dressed up and got married. It was very profane and most amusing.'[140]

More serious matters were on her mind because she was about to be confirmed. The Bishop was coming to stay for the weekend,* she wrote to Beryl, and added, ' 'elp!' She was being prepared for confirmation by Mr Tuke, the rector of St John's Episcopal Church in Forfar. She sent Beryl a sketch of her confirmation dress – white crêpe de

---

* Rt Rev. Charles Edward Plumb, Bishop of St Andrews, Dunkeld and Dunblane.

Chine trimmed with white fur, and with buttons down one side. She thought it would be 'quite useful for dancing classes and things afterwards'.[141]

The confirmation took place on Sunday 5 November 1916. Instead of a private ceremony in the chapel at home – 'that's the one thing I will not have. I'm quite determined. I know exactly what it would be. Rows of gaping soldiers and domestics,' she declared firmly – she elected to be confirmed at St John's in Forfar.[142] She and the other girls wore white veils above their white dresses. Margaret Cadenhead, who was also being confirmed, said, 'she had her hair tied back with a bow. Lovely hair and lovely eyes, beautiful blue eyes.'[143] Afterwards Elizabeth and her mother returned to the south.

In February 1917 she had to take to her bed for about ten days suffering from a bronchial complaint. She followed the war news and rumours. 'The news is really quite cheerful isn't it? Germany howling for peace (silently so far), and we are catching their mouldy subs. This is hush news, two of their biggest and newest surrendered (tho its probably untrue) minus their officers. They'd shot them all. Pip pip. Hurrah to heaven.'[144]

She remained in the south – at St Paul's Walden and St James's Square, where her mother had undertaken another patriotic duty: entertaining overseas officers. This sometimes took the form of *thés dansants*, which Elizabeth attended. Many of the guests were Australian officers. 'Thursday is our Australian day. At least every day is that now, we are simply inundated with them!' she wrote to Beryl. 'Do come and join the gory throng that goes fox trotting along. You wear a hat & your best dress I believe at these sort of things! The men are very nice and quite RESPECTABLE, so your Mother wont mind letting flighty flirtatious Beryl come & dance.'[145] Beryl accepted the invitation, and they both clearly enjoyed themselves. 'Wasn't it too too funny? I was never so much amused in my life!! One man was too horrible for words, he was disgusting, & yet even he amused me. The sailor was very nice. Did you dance with him? . . . And did you dance with Captain Phillips in plain clothes? He is so nice, he's often been here for lunch and dances simply divinely.'[146]

The next week, that same Captain Phillips came to tea with her at St James's Square, 'tete a tete!! Rather funny. He's such a nice person, & we talked solidly in the dark from 5 till 7.15!! He's an excellent talker, & told me stories. Its nice talking to an intelligent person occasionally . . . Captain P asked me if I was interested in letters from the front?'[147] This was followed by several rows of question marks.

Back at Glamis for a snow-covered Easter 1917, she found there were only seven soldiers at the Castle. With George Robey rattling away on the gramophone, she played cards with them and, as always, she won their hearts. One of them wrote presciently in her autograph book,

> May the owner of this book be
> Hung, Drawn, and Quartered.
> 'Yes'.
> Hung in Diamonds, Drawn in a Coach and Four and
> Quartered in the Best House in the Land.[148]

Behind the fun, the war. By now Germany and Britain were each determined to starve the other out by means of naval blockades. The French had suffered more than 3,350,000 casualties and the British over a million. The Germans had lost nearly two and a half million and were still fighting their enemies on both Eastern and Western Fronts. Food riots in Germany were increasing, infant mortality was growing fast. The German General Staff decided to resort to unrestricted submarine warfare – ships of neutral nations, including the United States, were now targeted. The US Congress responded by voting for war. A million American men were under training, but the Germans gambled that they could destroy Britain and France before the US army could be deployed in Europe.[149]

Attitudes became more intransigent. In April 1917 Albert Einstein wrote from Berlin to a friend in Holland of the way in which nationalism had altered the young scientists and academics he knew. 'I am convinced that we are dealing with a kind of epidemic of the mind. I cannot otherwise comprehend how men who are thoroughly decent in their personal conduct can adopt such utterly antithetical views on general affairs. It can be compared with developments at the time of the martyrs, the Crusades and the witch burnings.'[150]

Soon after Easter, George Dawson-Damer, brother of Fergus's widow Christian, was killed. Elizabeth was shocked. 'He was <u>very</u> nice, gay, good looking & very amusing. Its dreadful.'[151] Bad news came even closer. On Thursday 3 May Lord Strathmore received a telegram at Glamis from the War Office to say that his son Michael was missing in northern France. He immediately telegraphed to Rose in London:

'BAD NEWS. MICHAEL MISSING APRIL 28. WAR OFFICE WILL WIRE FURTHER NEWS. TELL MOTHER THEY SAY NOT MEAN NECESSARILY KILLED OR WOUNDED.'[152]

Michael was adored in the family, and for Elizabeth he had always been an admired and amusing elder brother.[153] From Glamis she immediately wrote to Beryl, 'I don't know what to say, you know how we love Mike, and it would be so terrible if he's killed. It's horrid & selfish of me to write you a miserable letter, but I'm so unhappy, & added to that I cant help worrying about Mother in London. I thank the Lord that Rosie is there. It's dreadful, and somehow I never thought Mike could get killed. If he's all right, he must be, I'll tell you. Your loving Elizabeth.'[154] One can only imagine how Lady Strathmore must have suffered from this latest blow. But she knew how Elizabeth must also be feeling and wrote to her that very afternoon: 'Isn't this terrible news of darling Mikie – however Sidney has just been to the W. Office – with great difficulty was allowed to see the casualty lists – & in the R. Scots 16th Bat 2 officers were wounded, & nine missing, so that is all we can hear for the present – he may be a prisoner with the other 8, or they may all be killed. Goodbye sweet darling. I wish you were here.'[155]

Michael's commanding officer, Colonel Stephenson, wrote to Lord Strathmore with more details: on 28 April Michael had been leading his company in an attack at the village of Roeulx, near Arras, when they were heavily counter-attacked. Some of the brigade's troops were captured, but Stephenson did not know to which battalion they belonged.[156] On 8 May he wrote again saying that there were reports from German prisoners that a considerable number of British troops had been surrounded and captured at Roeulx village. But there was still no news of who they were, and this would not be known until the lists arrived from Germany.[157]

Elizabeth found the waiting almost unbearable. 'Somehow I never thought anything could happen to Mike,' she wrote to Beryl; 'everybody is so fond of him, but one forgets that doesn't count in a War.' Her mother was in a terrible state, she reported. Patrick was also at St James's Square waiting for a medical board, and he too was in a bad way. She apologized for writing 'such a depressed letter, and how I hope the next one will be mad & full of the usual rubbish. He [Mike] said in his last letter you know, "If I'm pipped, I think little John had better have my guns," and so he knew they were going to have a bad time I suppose.'[158] (John was Patrick's son.) Feeling utterly wretched, Elizabeth took the train down to London on 7 May to be with her mother. By 12 May she was in bed with a temperature and a swollen face and neck, either one of her bad colds or perhaps, she thought, even measles.[159]

According to family legend, David was the only one who remained optimistic. He was thought to have some powers of second sight; he maintained, apparently, that he knew Mike was not dead because he had 'seen' him, in a house surrounded with fir trees, with his head bandaged.[160] His sister's anxious letters at this time make no mention of this, but if the story is true, David was proved right. On the morning of 22 May, the telephone rang at St James's Square. It was Cox's bank saying that they had just received a cheque drawn by Mike since he went missing. He was a prisoner of war. Elizabeth wrote at once to Beryl:

Ma Chère Medusa,
     I'm quite and absolutely stark, staring, raving mad. Do you know why? Canst thou even guess? I don't believe you can!
               AM I MAD WITH MISERY OR WITH JOY?
                         WITH
                           !
                       !! JOY !!
                           !

Mike is quite safe! Oh dear, I <u>nearly</u>, nearly burst this morning, we had a telephone message from Cox's to say they'de received a cheque from Mike this morning, so we <u>rushed</u> round, and it was in his own handwriting, & they think he's at Carlsruhe. Isnt it <u>too</u>, <u>too</u> heavenly. I cant believe it, yes I can but you know what I mean, & how awful the last 3 weeks have been. Yours madly, Elizabeth[161]

A stream of friends and relations called at the house to give their congratulations on Mike's survival. Barson, the devoted butler, naturally 'had a good old bust-up in honour of Mike! Mosh (hic) aushpishush auccashun (hic). What o,' Elizabeth wrote to Beryl as she lay in front of the fire drying her hair. She suggested they go to the theatre together to celebrate.[162]

Soon there came a postcard from Mike himself. Dated 4 May, it had taken over a month to be delivered. He wrote:

A postcard to let you know my address which is under my name. [It was the officers' prisoner-of-war camp at Karlsruhe.] You can send me various things chiefly food, but I want an Auto-strop razor & lots of blades most of all. Did you get a letter from me? Got here last night after a long journey. I've arrived here with absolutely nothing except what I stand up in, but am getting a cheque cashed today. Nothing much to tell you of here I'm afraid but I hope I shall be able to write a letter shortly. Just going to have a bath, I'm perfectly filthy & a long beard. Love to all. Ideal Milk, butter & bread & tea would be good, also shirts, vests, drawers, socks, flannel trousers (grey). Mike[163]

Eventually Elizabeth received a long letter in Mike's familiar bantering style, addressed to 'My darling Buffy' and written from a prisoner-of-war camp at Ströhen, Hanover. Two or three lines of it – apparently about the camp food – were heavily inked out by the censor. Mike hoped his sister was having a good time dancing with Captain Phillips and could remember all the steps of the foxtrot. Not surprisingly, food and drink were his main interest. He asked for a weekly supply of flour, dripping and baking powder to make scones, and also macaroni, Cadbury's peppermint creams, plain chocolate and some cheap tobacco to roll his own cigarettes. He thought longingly of home: 'PW must be heavenly now & I suppose the strawberries are ripe now. How I should love to be crawling flat on my stomach under a net! We don't git no champagne, clarit, mosal or beeeer here wust look. I expect someone will censor that, at least I don't suppose they will realise that it is Hertfordshire, and concerns wet things.'[164]

Mike received his first letters, from May and Elizabeth, at the end of June. 'Great joy!' To his consternation, however, the letters did not mention sending food.[165] By August the message had got through: he wrote to say that he had received sixty-nine parcels.[166] In September he was moved to comparative luxury at Neu Brandenburg, where he reported that he was able to bathe daily in a lake, and had a soft bed and a balcony;[167] later he was transferred to Schweidnitz in Silesia. His letters to his mother show that Elizabeth continued to write to him with lively accounts of her social life, but her letters have not survived.[168]

On her return to Glamis in glorious weather in the middle of June 1917, Elizabeth found new patients – 'sixteen strange shy enormous men' lying on the lawn, she reported to Beryl. They politely saluted her and she talked to some of them at once, but she was more self-conscious than she had been when younger. 'We are so mutually afraid of each other!' The Clerk of the Forfar School Board had written to ask her to present medals and prizes at the school. She was terrified but her mother made it clear that it was her duty to agree. 'I had to accept, and I know I shall die. It's too dreadful, and the worst of it is, I KNOW Sister & the boys will want to come, oh it's terrible. I dream, or rather have nightmares about it!'[169] Beryl was evidently not much impressed with her nervousness and Elizabeth complained that she was 'horribly unsympathetic . . . It's too awful! Swine!'[170] Afterwards she protested that she had been 'petrified'. There were many speeches; 'I, of course, made a long one, touching on many points including The Food Question, Education, Star Worship etc etc. It was greatly appreciated I assure you.'[171]

When she got to know the new soldiers, she liked them – as she usually did. Just one of them was 'very good looking'. She was curious about people and was becoming more discriminating; she was meeting not only convalescent soldiers, but officers from the Dominions needing hospitality while on leave from the Front. As well as giving parties for Australian officers at St James's Square, the Strathmores opened Glamis to them – and their Canadian and New Zealand counterparts. 'One very "interesting" one yesterday,' Elizabeth wrote. 'That's the only way I can describe him. Tall, blue eyes, very keen kind of face, clever & a terrific accent.'[172] She was somewhat embarrassed by a New Zealander, Lieutenant J. B. Parker. 'He is rather an old fashioned young man, & he paid me wonderful & weird compliments at all times.' She asked him how he thought of so many polite things to say, and he replied that 'he did'nt think of them, they came from his heart! I laughed. I could'nt help it! Poor young man – he'll recover all right.'[173]

She was beginning to distinguish between men. 'Its funny how dull some men are, whilst others are so interesting. On one hand a little pipsqueak, with pink cheeks & a toothbrush moustache, whose only conversation is about theatres, the War & himself. And on the other hand a man who could'nt look a pipsqueak if he tried, who has lived by himself & observed nature – there are such a lot of pipsqueaks!!! I shall be seventeen soon. Damn. I don't want to get any older.'[174]

The rain that July was terrible; the crops at Glamis were flattened.

Soon after her birthday Elizabeth took to her bed for two weeks with what seemed like severe influenza. It was her fourth bout of feverish illness that year and Dr Morris, the Glamis doctor, was concerned lest she had caught from the soldiers some kind of trench fever, which could affect the heart. He ordered her to bed 'as my heart didn't beat enough or something'.[175] By the beginning of September she was still unsteady on her feet and 'dash it all' she was not even allowed to walk, let alone play tennis 'as me 'eart is still weak'.[176] At the end of the month she was still being dosed with raw eggs and brandy, and felt limp and tired.[177]

By 4 October, however, she had regained her spirits enough to enjoy a concert thrown by the soldiers at Glamis for the benefit of their colleagues at Forfar Hospital, who descended on the Castle for tea. It was a hilarious occasion.[178] There was now something of a routine at Glamis. Elizabeth and her mother played and sang with the soldiers almost every evening. They would get through dozens of songs a night. One which they liked to hear her sing was 'Wonderful Girl, Wonderful Boy, Wonderful Time'.[179]

Always the war continued to strike the heart – Patrick Ogilvy, third son of the Strathmores' close neighbour, Mabell, Countess of Airlie, was killed on 9 October; his eldest brother, Lord Airlie, was home from the war 'with very bad nerves'; and they heard that Zeppelins had dropped bombs all around St Paul's Walden, breaking windows.[180] Hopes for peace seemed to have disappeared; when General Sir Horace Smith-Dorrien, who had commanded the Second Army on the Western Front in 1915, came to lunch at Glamis in September, Elizabeth was depressed to hear that 'he didn't think that there was any likelihood of the War ending for some time'.[181]

She was ever more aware of the human costs of the war. The motors that took the rested soldiers back to Dundee still brought an inexhaustible stream of more wounded men to fill their places. One day she went to Dundee Infirmary herself to visit one of her favourite patients at this time, Private C. Morris. His chest had been crushed on the battlefield, and he had been sent back from Glamis for more treatment. He was in no doubt of what he owed Elizabeth and her mother. 'I must say that I was never treated better in any part of the British Empire than I was treated at Glamis Castle,' he wrote to her, 'and I don't quite know how to thank the Strathmore family for all the kindness they have shown towards me.'[182] He finally recovered and

Elizabeth was delighted when her parents offered him a job as a gardener at St Paul's Walden.[183]

She found nothing so difficult as saying goodbye to men returning to the Front. At the end of November she had 'a nerve racking and terrible experience – bidding goodbye to FOURTEEN men!' Among them was a sergeant to whom she had taken 'a violent affection' at the last minute – he was dreadfully ugly but so nice that she 'begged Sister to push him downstairs or give him a blister or something' so that he could remain at Glamis. 'It's so dreadful saying goodbye, because one knows that one will never see them again, and I hate doing it.'

She always went to make her farewells after dinner, because the men would be driven away in the early morning and also because 'Sister likes to show me off in evening dress, because they never have seen evening dresses which embarrasses me too dreadfully. They invariably look at my shoes, except the ones that gaze rapturously into my eyes sighing deeply all the while . . .' She was aware how much she had changed since she was a child at the start of the war: 'oh! the difference from Dec. 1914! I was just remembering this evening, that night when Mr Brookes, Harold Ward, Teddy Daird (in pyjamas) & I had a bun fight in the crypt, and David chased Nurse A round the Ward with cocoa & water to pour, & how it all got spilt on the floor, & her black fury!! It was fun – weren't they darlings?'[184]

Meanwhile groups of Australian and New Zealand officers came and went, to mixed reactions from their young hostess. There was a Mr Stubbins, who insisted on trying to teach her all about motors '& I don't understand & go to sleep'. To avoid him and other boring men, 'Mother & I have to pretend that we are going away on Saturday! . . . It's always worse when there is no male member of the family, I don't count Father because he so rarely appears.' Elizabeth was exasperated by Stubbins – 'the first time I've ever scolded a man, & very successful it was. He was most penitent & I forgave him!! Just like a dog, the more you beat him (for a reason) the more he likes you – alas!'[185] Few people elicited such negative reactions.

At around this time Elizabeth had what appears to have been her first proposal of marriage; it was from the New Zealander, Lieutenant Parker. He asked her if her birthday were between 1 and 10 August, claiming that he had read an astrological book from which he had calculated that 'the' person for him would be born between those dates.[186] To Beryl she wrote Mr Parker had sent her 'a – no, I don't think I'll tell you. I can't.'[187]

She thought they would 'be migrating south soon to the land of bombs & war alarms & "excursions" '.[188] In the event they had to stay at Glamis while a new ward of twelve more beds was created and an additional nurse recruited.[189] But on 12 December, after tearful farewells, Elizabeth and her mother boarded the night train to London. When they arrived they heard that her sister Rose and Wisp Leveson-Gower had had a daughter. 'Isn't it exciting!' Elizabeth wrote. 'They'll have to call her Wisperina or Wisperia or something!'[190]

At around the same time Jock and Neva also had a daughter, Anne, and Elizabeth hoped that she would help take the place of Patricia, their firstborn who had died aged only eleven months in June 1917. Jock had been invalided out of the army, joined the Foreign Office and been sent to Washington. To Elizabeth's delight, Neva had written to say that her maid in Washington had met an English soldier who had been at Glamis: 'He apparently raved about it, & its heavenliness, & about me, & said he'd never forget me (!!), and who do you think it was? Dear Sergeant Broadhead!! Isn't that a curious coincidence? In all that <u>huge</u> continent, that the maid should have met a man who knew our family! He is training American recruits. <u>Such</u> a darling he was.'[191]

Christmas 1917 was spent quietly at St Paul's Walden. Two weeks later, on 8 January 1918, Elizabeth went to her first ball.* She chose a dress, had her hair done and rushed around looking for shoes. 'I'm going to my first real dance on Wednesday & feel rather terrified!' she wrote to Beryl. 'I'm sure I shall know nobody!' She was astonished to be lectured by her mother and David who told her 'that I ought to be more flirtatious. I nearly died of surprise. You know I daresay I've got rather quiet from having all those Australians and NZ (!!!) at Glamis, as one simply <u>must</u> sit on them!'[192]

She 'trembled all afternoon' before the dance, as she reported to

---

* The dance was for Margaret Sutton, the niece of the Hon. Edward Wood (1881–1959), later third Viscount Halifax, whom Elizabeth came to know very well as foreign secretary, and his wife Lady Dorothy, née Onslow, who became her lady in waiting. The young Elizabeth dined with the Woods before the dance.

Beryl; but there is no doubting the excitement and pleasure it gave her. 'I danced every single dance,* & Mother came to fetch me, & we departed at about 1.30. They had part of Ciro's black Band ... I enjoyed it <u>very</u> much. One could only dance with such few people tho' because the dances were <u>so</u> long, but I loved it, and enjoyed it fearfully. Do you know I think my dress really looked quite pretty.'[193] From his prisoner-of-war camp in Germany Mike wrote to Lady Strathmore saying he was longing to hear about the ball. Elizabeth had sent him her photograph with her hair up, and he commented, 'what a pretty little thing Buffy has become'.[194]

On 7 February 1918 the Strathmores had a dance at St James's Square. It began as a 'tiny' party to pay back people who had invited Elizabeth out. But it grew as 'millions of people' asked themselves and by the day itself 'nearly <u>everybody</u> is coming. I really had no idea that the Strathmore family was so popular, it's awful,' she claimed to Beryl. A young naval lieutenant on whom she had taken pity at an earlier dance had rung her up '& we had a I-don't-know-how-to-describe-it talk.' She felt sorry for him. 'You know I've got a soft spot in my 'eart for a bhoy in blue, so 'ave you, and he was so pathetic!' She had written a four-page letter to Lieutenant Parker, 'but I simply <u>can't</u> get the last bit in! I wish I could talk to him, it's so difficult writing ... These young men <u>do</u> worry me so, I <u>wish</u> they wouldn't. Do come round, & give me some more of your sage (?) advice!'[195] Ten years later she was to meet Parker again in New Zealand.

Men were fascinated by her. At dinner a few weeks later she met a young man from the American Embassy named Morgan.† She thought he was 'the cutest thing out. He fair gives me the goat – gee – he's <u>some</u> kid – cut it out Rube – sling us no more of the canned goods, I'm fair up against this stunt, etc.'[196] At Lady Hastings's dance in March she danced with Lord Settrington and many others. Charles Settrington was the eldest son of the eighth Duke of Richmond, and

---

* Among Elizabeth's dancing partners were the Hon. Michael Biddulph (1898–1972), later third Baron Biddulph, whose sister Adèle was a friend of Elizabeth; Archie Balfour (1896–1966), son of Captain Charles Balfour and Lady Nina Balfour, a friend of Lady Strathmore; the Hon. Bruce Ogilvy (1895–1976), son of the eighth Earl of Airlie and Mabell, Countess of Airlie, Queen Mary's lady in waiting; and Captain Henry Courtney Brocklehurst (1888–1942), who was married to Lady Airlie's daughter Helen and whom Elizabeth was to meet in very different circumstances in 1925.

† Probably Stokeley Williams Morgan, Second Secretary at the American Embassy.

the brother of Doris Gordon-Lennox, with whom Elizabeth began a long and close friendship at this time.[197]

It was during this period that she met the Prince of Wales, widely spoken of as the most glamorous man in London. She danced with him twice at the Cokes' dance,* where she also danced with Lord Cranborne,† who was to become another lifelong friend. At the Harcourts' a few nights later she sat between the Prince of Wales and Count Michael Torby.‡ She found it both terrifying and enjoyable. 'As usual I danced the first dance with P.W., I don't know why, but I usually do!' In fact she danced three times with the Prince that night and several times with Victor Cochrane Baillie,§ a round young man with a large moustache whom she described as a faithful friend, 'very nice, but extremely ugly, poor thing'.[198] Cochrane Baillie was smitten with her and wrote to ask her if she would 'deign' to write to him sometimes.[199]

The gaiety of her social life could not shut out the painful realities of the war, as her letters to Beryl Poignand in the spring of 1918 show. 'It was the last dance for some time, so tho' I enjoyed it very much, I felt slightly depressed at moments. Such a lot of these boys are going out quite soon – in fact nearly everybody I know. I suppose they expect fearful casualties. They are so young, a great many only nineteen.'[200] She worried about Ernest Pearce, now in the field near Arras. She heard that Lord Settrington was missing. (He had been taken prisoner.) 'I wonder if Peace will ever come. I feel as if I never want to go to a dance again, one only makes friends and then they are killed.'[201] A few days later she wrote, 'Doesn't it make you curse & swear inside you when one thinks that if we'd had a decent Government the War might be over?'[202]

---

* Thomas William, Viscount Coke, later fourth Earl of Leicester (1880–1949), and his wife Marion.

† Robert ('Bobbety') Arthur James Gascoyne-Cecil, Viscount Cranborne (1893–1972). In 1947 he succeeded his father as fifth Marquess of Salisbury, and in the 1950s he served in the Churchill, Eden and Macmillan governments.

‡ Count Michael Torby (1898–1959), son of Grand Duke Michael Michailovich of Russia, and descendant of Tsar Nicholas I. Brother of Lady Zia Wernher and of Nadejda, Marchioness of Milford Haven.

§ Hon. Victor Cochrane Baillie (1896–1951), son of second Baron Lamington; succeeded 1940 as third baron; married 1922 Riette Neilson. He served in the Scots Guards 1914–17, and was mentioned in dispatches and awarded the MC.

George Thirkell,* an Australian officer who had stayed at Glamis, wrote to her from 'In the Field, France': 'Just a note to let you know that I am still all OK though we have had a fairly strenuous time the last 6 weeks.' He had just escaped a German gas barrage and he now enclosed some 'souvenirs' for her, namely pieces of fabric from three 'Bosche' planes.† The red piece came from the wing of Baron von Richthofen's plane, which had been shot down 'almost on top of my dug-out'. The Baron had brought down eighty Allied planes, Thirkell wrote. 'He was chasing a British plane when he was brought down by an Australian Lewis Gunner on the ground.'[203]

At the end of May Elizabeth went to Harwich to visit her brother-in-law Wisp on his destroyer, HMS *Scott*. She described the trip to the ship on board a launch, climbing the 'wavy ladder' up the side, saluting the sailors at the top; 'then one falls heavily down the hatch (is it?) into the waiting arms of a Sub or (preferably) a Lieut!'

The commanding officer, Admiral Tyrwhitt, came to dinner: everyone was frightened of him – everyone except Elizabeth, and he invited her to lunch on his flagship. She went and was shown around by a very nice flag lieutenant – 'it was unfortunate that when the time came to go, I was found eating chocolates in his cabin!! . . . I <u>do</u> like sailors, they are such darlings. Soldiers, or the most <u>beautiful</u> officers, never awaken such thrills as a darling Lieut – don't you agree? Pip pip.'[204]‡

In June 1918 she had 'a very riotous' lunch with Freddy Dalrymple Hamilton, who always made her laugh. At a dinner dance with Lord and Lady Powis she danced with both 'a funny little American with nice eyes, from the Embassy' and Lord Erskine, who walked her home. Each was furious when she danced with the other. 'I have suddenly taken to blushing again, I do hope it will go soon, it's such a bore.'[205]

The eager young American was called Sam Dickson, Third Secretary at the US Embassy; he began to telephone her and invited her to dinner. She had to explain to him 'that young ladies did <u>NOT</u> dine

---

* He later married Angela Mackail, the writer Angela Thirkell.

† The pieces of fabric are in the Royal Archives, still in the envelope in which they were sent, inscribed in King George VI's hand with the statement that it contained a piece of von Richthofen's plane.

‡ HMS *Scott* was torpedoed a few months later with the loss of twenty-six men. Wisp Leveson-Gower survived.

alone with young men at well known restaurants!!!' So her mother chaperoned them to dinner at the Berkeley and they then invited him back to the house where he and Elizabeth ate strawberries and talked till 11 p.m. He seemed lonely and told her all about his family life in the States. 'It sounds exactly what we imagine cowboys to be!'[206]

On 22 June her maternal grandmother, Mrs Scott, died at her home in Dawlish. Cecilia Strathmore went straight to Devon to organize the funeral, leaving Elizabeth to run the household in London. 'Oh dear! I do miss her so dreadfully,' Elizabeth wrote to Beryl. 'I never knew before how much I depended on her – and more things seem to crop up for me to decide than I've ever known. It's always the way.'[207]

When she returned to Glamis in early August 1918 she found sixteen new soldiers; she did her best to get to know them all. She was also kept busy with duties in the local community: a bazaar at Glamis in aid of prisoners of war, at which they raised £300 despite a violent storm which blew down the marquee and ruined the lavender bags and trimmed hats which Elizabeth had made for her stall; a Baby Show at Arbroath; a charity sale at Forfar which, to her terror, she had to open with a speech. Meanwhile she made friends with an amusing Canadian, Lieutenant J. S. Reynolds, who had 'grasped me by the arrrm, & hurrrled me into safety!' in the storm at Glamis.[208]

By now the might of America was at last turning the war. The Allies had managed, at enormous cost, to halt the last great German offensive. In August 1918 many of the positions lost during the Battle of the Somme two years before were regained. The Allies attacked the length of the Western Front in a final mood of exhilaration. But the casualties mounted.

Elizabeth was worried for Lieutenant Reynolds, but in September he wrote to tell her that he and his unit were now advancing through northern France. They had collected 'tons of souvenirs from the Huns' and 'if I get out of this mess alive will send you an Iron Cross if you think it will be OK.'[209] She copied a part of this letter to Beryl saying, 'Rather a nice letter don't you think? I think he thought he might get killed don't you?'[210] A little later, he did indeed send her an Iron Cross, and she was delighted.[211]

At Holy Communion on Sunday 29 September four soldiers came to worship with Sister. Elizabeth was touched to see them all kneeling in their hospital blues before the altar. 'It really was a beautiful sight, tho' it gave me a lump in my throat. I keep on thinking of it. Poor dear boys.'

That month Austria began to sue for peace and German forces started to withdraw from the Western Front. As the warriors wound wearily towards peace, a new killer, influenza, began to rage. Twenty thousand American soldiers died of the disease in two months. Anarchy spread through Germany. On 9 November 1918 the Kaiser fled Berlin and, having finally agreed to abdicate, drove into exile in Holland. By now three of the dynastic empires of Europe had fallen, the Habsburgs, the Hohenzollerns and the Romanovs. Tsar Nicholas II and his family, King George V's cousins, had been brutally murdered in July 1918 by the Bolsheviks, who had seized power in Russia following the October Revolution in 1917.

At the eleventh hour of the eleventh day of the eleventh month of 1918, the Armistice effectively ended the war. Elizabeth was at Glamis and ever after she remembered the patients from the Castle, all dressed in their hospital blues, marching happily together up the long avenue to the pub. 'They went straight to the village to celebrate and I think they drank too much. Seats got broken up to make a bonfire and all that sort of thing. I can see them now, all going to enjoy this wonderful moment.'[212]

In London thousands of people rushed into the street and danced around bonfires all over town, even at the foot of Nelson's Column. King George V and Queen Mary appeared on the balcony of Buckingham Palace before the exultant crowds. In the next week they drove five times through London in an open carriage and everywhere they were cheered by ecstatic people. In a speech to the assembled Lords and Commons in the Palace of Westminster, the King said, 'May goodwill and concord at home strengthen our influence for concord abroad. May the morning star of peace, which is now rising over a war-worn world, be here and everywhere the herald of a better day, in which the storms of strife shall have died down and the rays of an enduring peace be shed upon all nations.'

Three-quarters of a million people from the United Kingdom had been killed. Another 200,000 from the Empire also died. France lost many more, both actually and proportionately. No one knows just how many people died around the world. Some say about ten million; others more. Russia alone is thought to have lost between 1,700,000 and 3,000,000 dead and another five million wounded. Typhus killed another million in the Balkans. Millions more were wounded, families were carved into pieces. Europeans were shocked by what they had done to themselves. Perhaps it is not quite true to say that an entire generation was lost, but it was scarred for ever.

Winston Churchill described well the nature of the war that had just ended.

> No truce or parley mitigated the strife between the armies. The wounded died between the lines: the dead mouldered into the soil. Merchant ships and neutral ships and hospital ships were sunk on the seas and all on board left to their fate, or killed as they swam. Every effort was made to starve whole nations into submission without regard to age or sex. Cities and monuments were smashed by artillery. Bombs from the air were cast down indiscriminately. Poison gas in many forms stifled or seared the soldiers. Liquid fire was projected upon their bodies. Men fell from the air in flames, or were smothered, often slowly, in the dark recesses of the sea. The fighting strength of armies was limited only by the manhood of their countries. Europe and large parts of Asia and Africa became one vast battle field on which after years of struggle not armies but nations broke and ran.[213]

The economic heart of the continent had been ravaged too. Millions were starving. Economic output in 1919 was a quarter below what it had been in 1914. And at the centre of the destruction lay shattered the country which had been the power of Europe before the war, Germany herself. 'We are at the dead season of our fortunes,' wrote John Maynard Keynes, a young economist. 'Never in the lifetime of men now living has the universal element in the soul of man burnt so dimly.'[214]

A letter that Elizabeth wrote to Beryl at the end of the month reflected the uncertain mood in the country after the initial euphoria of victory. Two Australian officers who had convalesced at Glamis had been to see her. They had had a nice and silly time, '& we yelled songs round the piano after tea'. Perhaps because of the long-drawn-out suspense of the war, she was now feeling depressed. 'Can't think why. No reason on earth. Everything is wonderful. So long waiting for Mike perhaps.'[215]

Mike finally came home. In the first week of 1919, Elizabeth and her mother were at St Paul's Walden when they received a telephone call to say that he was on a train. They rushed up to London. At the station they had to wait as five trains unloaded wounded, sick and disoriented soldiers whose appearance shocked Elizabeth. Finally Mike's train came in and they were able at last to embrace him. He seemed fairly well and cheerful, but he brought with him a friend called Lathom who looked very ill and was completely dazed. 'He merely sat & looked at the fire,' she told Beryl. 'Poor boys, they must have had a <u>beastly</u> time, they hate talking about it.'[216]

*

IN EARLY APRIL 1919 Elizabeth gave a play party. She and her sister-in-law, Jock's wife Neva, Emma Thynne, Mike, Captain Keenan and Charlie Settrington dined at the Ritz and then went to see George Robey perform in *Joybells* – she thought he was 'too priceless'.[217] Then she did something rather daring. Decades later she recalled 'creeping out of the house in St James's Square, round the corner into Duke Street and going off to lunch with a very nice young gentleman in one of those horrible little low cars'. They 'whizzed off' down the Portsmouth Road to a pub.[218]

The young gentleman was Charlie Settrington. It appears that they motored to Walton for lunch and then took a long walk on Box Hill. They had tea 'at an extraordinary place, where the waiter winked, & said he <u>also</u> came from London!' Writing to Beryl about it, Elizabeth maintained firmly that Charles was a dear, but just a friend. 'One's family always thinks that a man must be violently in love with one, which is <u>so</u> annoying if one is friends.'[219]

Although there was now a spate of engagements and weddings among her circle of friends, she seems to have had no desire to follow suit, and was sorry when Lavinia married Luke White in April.* 'It's rather a sad thing a wedding, don't you think?' she wrote to Beryl before setting off for Althorp with Katie Hamilton for the ceremony. 'Poor old Lavinia! Her last two days of spinsterhood.' 'I do hate weddings!' she commented afterwards.[220]

Later in the month she and David took her Canadian friend Lieutenant Reynolds to see a revue, *Buzz-Buzz*.† She was amused by

---

* Luke Henry White (1885–1970) succeeded as fourth Baron Annaly in 1922.

† *Buzz-Buzz*, with music and lyrics by Herman Darewski, was on at the Vaudeville Theatre, starring Margaret Bannerman, Nelson Keys and Gertrude Lawrence, and included such

the officer's wildness and his fondness for alcohol; he was perhaps an early example of the appeal that raffish but entertaining characters had for her throughout her life. Towards the end of May the Lieutenant left England; he came to say goodbye one morning, bearing roses; she was still in bed. 'I was so sad at not seeing him . . . he is so nice and wild!!!'[221]

On 28 June 1919 the Versailles Peace Treaty was signed. The King appeared again and again before ecstatic crowds on the balcony of Buckingham Palace. 'Please God,' he wrote in his diary, 'please God the dear old Country will now settle down and work in unity.'[222] It later became conventional to decry the peace that was reached at Versailles. In truth it deserves a certain respect. The task facing its authors was almost impossible – it was to reconcile ideals and expectations with recalcitrant realities. This was the first great European peace treaty which had to be drawn up with the views of democratic electorates in mind. France needed to believe herself protected from a third dose of German aggression, the British and the Americans had to deal with the overriding problem of central European security. Poland was resurrected. Serbia was enlarged into Yugoslavia, and Czechoslovakia was created out of the ruins of Austria-Hungary.* All these countries survived for most of the rest of the century and Poland thrives still today.

The peace agreement had to be a world settlement – of the twenty-seven countries which signed the principal treaty, seventeen were outside Europe. The harshest parts of the treaty were the economic reparations which were imposed on Germany. The main intent was to recompense France and Belgium for the devastation they had suffered and to give both as much guarantee as possible that Germany could never rise to threaten them again.

When the treaty was signed at Versailles, smaller wars were still being fought. British troops were fighting alongside Generals Koltchak and Denikin and the White Russian forces still holding out against the new Soviet Union. They were there partly to secure British investments in Russia and partly to identify the British army with an anti-

---

numbers as 'There Are So Many Girls', 'If I Went into Parliament', 'Winnie the Window Cleaner' and 'Everything is Buzz-Buzz Now'.

* Versailles was followed by five separate treaties with the nations on the losing side, the last of which, the Treaty of Sèvres, was signed by Turkey and the Allies on 20 August 1920.

revolutionary cause. Their presence gave Elizabeth one of her greatest heartbreaks of those years.

August 1919 found her, as always, at Glamis. It was a parched summer – they had had no rain for three months. Plans to make a new tennis court had had to be postponed because the ground was so hard. There were still Canadian and Australian officers around for tea and she and her mother went to a sale of Friesian cattle, where her mother bought two bulls. Elizabeth had taken driving lessons and was now driving the family Wolseley all over the Glamis estate – which she found 'great fun'.[223]

But then came awful news – Charlie Settrington, fighting in the White Russian cause, had been badly wounded.[224] He died on 24 August. Elizabeth was inconsolable. 'He is my only real friend, & one feels one can never have another like him. He was a real friend, I wasn't shy of him, and he was so delightful. It's a dreadful thing, and his family simply adored him . . . I think I must have been fonder of him than I realised, because now there seems a kind of blank – if you understand what I mean?' He had been the only male friend she had to whom she could talk naturally. 'I liked him specially because he never tried to flirt, or make love or anything like that – which always spoils friendships. Even that day spent down at Box Hill.'[225]

Elizabeth had entered the war in 1914 as a carefree girl; she emerged from it as a young woman mature for her years. She was joyous, vivacious, and delightful company. But as a result of the war she had moved among, and learned about, a wider circle of people than she would otherwise ever have met. She had also acquired, through her experience of the suffering of family, friends and soldiers from all over the world, an understanding of pain, and of the difficulties of others, which served her and her country well in the years to come.

CHAPTER THREE

PRINCE ALBERT

1918–1923

'It takes so long to ponder these things'

'LUCKILY ONE DOESN'T "come out" much in War time,' Elizabeth had written at the end of 1916, referring to the 'awful thought' that Lavinia Spencer, a year older than her, was about to be launched into society as a debutante.[1] For although the war had by no means put a stop to dances, dinners and parties – and Elizabeth had found them far from awful when her turn came in early 1918 – the formalities of the 'season', in particular the glittering royal occasions, had been suspended since 1914. Presentation at Court, the sine qua non of social recognition, which for debutantes meant parading in evening dress with ostrich-feather headdresses and long trains before the King and Queen at Buckingham Palace, had ceased. There were no levées (at which men were presented), no Court balls, no garden parties and no Royal Ascot. Similarly, country-house entertaining on the grand pre-war scale had come to a halt; shooting was much reduced, with parkland ploughed up, coverts felled for timber, and keepers, beaters, loaders and the sportsmen themselves away in the forces.

With the end of hostilities, however, social life at Court and in the great houses of the land gradually resumed its old pattern. Presentation ceremonies were resumed,* with one startling innovation: the King abolished the ban on presenting actors and actresses, provided of course that they were ladies and gentlemen of irreproachable character.[2] It

---

* In 1919 there were three special garden parties at Buckingham Palace to which 15,500 were invited, including thousands of debutantes who had missed their presentation at Court. The traditional Courts began again in 1920, although at first 'shorn in some small measure of [their] former full magnificence by the decision not to permit the wearing of feathers and full Court train', as *The Times* recorded of the first peacetime Court on 10 June 1920. Feathers and trains reappeared in a modified form in 1922 and continued to be worn until 1939, with a brief interruption in 1936 when King Edward VIII decided not to hold Courts.

was a small signal of the increasing social mobility which the war had accelerated.*

Royal Ascot reappeared on the social calendar in glorious weather in June 1919. Queen Mary was pleased by the good turnout after five years of war, and the King recorded that everyone wore 'a high hat' as in the old days.[3] Elizabeth was there for the first time and enjoyed it very much. That summer she was constantly busy 'in a dissipated way', as she put it, with dinners and dances.[4] In September 1919 Glamis was once more filled with young people dancing and dining by candlelight, laughing and singing around the fireplaces. Elizabeth's grief at Charles Settrington's death overshadowed the gaiety for her, but her friends pronounced the party a great success.[5] Christmas at St Paul's Walden, going out shooting with Mike and David, and playing with Jock and Fenella's children, revived her spirits. 'I can hardly write sense, as the grammy is blazing forth "Indianola", the best dancing tune in the world!' she told Beryl; and then there was the Hertford Ball to look forward to and dread a little.[6]

For that ball, in early January 1920, she was invited to join a house party with the Salisbury family at Hatfield, quite close to St Paul's Walden. She found them delightful, particularly Lord David Cecil, whose heart she had captured when they were both children and who remained a lifelong friend. 'He is _very_ clever, & _most_ entertaining. Quite vague like they all are.'

She had been afraid that she would know no one, but the party included two of her dancing partners from her first ball in 1918, Count Willy de Grünne, a Belgian diplomat who danced 'too divinely', and Bruce Ogilvy, son of the Strathmores' neighbour in Scotland, Lady Airlie. Several other friends, including Helen Cecil, a Salisbury cousin,[†] and Lord Dalkeith, the eldest son of the Duke of Buccleuch, were also there. They played tennis in the real tennis court and violent games of hockey, and one night of dancing ended with 'a terrific game of follow-

---

* It may also have reflected the King's predilections: like his future daughter-in-law he was an avid theatregoer. But he had given up this pastime for the duration of the war, as well as racing, most other social activities and the consumption of alcohol, as part of the exercise in setting an example of restraint which the government had urged upon him.

† Helen Cecil (1901–79), daughter of Lord Edward Herbert Gascoyne Cecil, married in 1921 Major the Hon. Alexander Hardinge (1894–1960), later second Baron Hardinge of Penshurst, equerry and Assistant Private Secretary to King George V and later Private Secretary to King Edward VIII and King George VI.

my-leader right round the house, which is immense, under the dining room table & even across the roof!!' The Hertford Ball was 'heavenly' and she had worn her new white frock. 'Several people admired it, which pleased me immensely!!' Walter Dalkeith drove her back to St Paul's – it was a hair-raising drive as he had hardly ever driven before. They swerved into ditches and crashed into the Strathmores' gate. 'I wonder that I am alive.'[7]

In March more decorum was required when Elizabeth went to Buckingham Palace for the first time, with a group of Scottish ladies led by her elder sister May. They had embroidered new covers for a set of chairs in the Palace of Holyroodhouse, and were presenting Queen Mary with their handiwork. Elizabeth stood in for Rosie. 'Only ¼ of her chair is finished, so I shall be chucked out for certain!'[8] she told Beryl. Fortunately the Queen noticed neither the missing work nor the substitute delegate and was delighted with the offering.[9]

Coincidences are not necessarily the work of fate; nevertheless it is tempting to describe as fateful the week in July 1920 when Elizabeth was at last formally presented at Court. For in that same week she also dined with the King and Queen and, by sheer chance, had her first significant meeting with Prince Albert. That it happened at a propitious moment in his life was yet another operation of chance.

Social life in Edinburgh reached its peak every year in early July when King, Queen and Court took up residence at Holyroodhouse. As today, there were garden parties, receptions, presentations and investitures at the Palace and a variety of external royal visits and functions. In 1920 the King and Queen arrived on Saturday 3 July and on the following Monday they gave a dinner for forty. Their guests were Edinburgh dignitaries with a sprinkling of Scottish peers, including the Elphinstones and Lord and Lady Strathmore, who were accompanied by Elizabeth. Apart from the twenty-three-year-old Princess Mary, she was the youngest by far and the only woman unmarried. She had perhaps been invited as company for the Princess, although the two did not know each other well. Elizabeth enjoyed herself, seated between the Lord Justice General and the Admiral Commanding at Rosyth, both of whom she pronounced 'very nice'.[10]

Next day, 6 July, the King and Queen held an afternoon reception in the Throne Room at which Elizabeth was presented, along with 150 other young ladies and hundreds of other 'presentees', both male and female: the King and Queen shook hands with 1,100 people in the space of an hour and a half. There was one more royal occasion – a large garden party on the following day – after which Elizabeth and her mother took the night train back to the south.

Thursday 8 July, the day on which she arrived back in London, was the most momentous of the week. That night Elizabeth went to the Royal Air Force ball at the Ritz. 'It was really most amusing, & there were some <u>priceless</u> people there,' she reported to Beryl. 'All the heroes of the Air too.' Prince Albert had also come to the ball. With him was his new equerry, James Stuart, youngest son of the Earl of Moray.* Stuart and his elder brother Lord Doune belonged to Elizabeth's circle of friends and neighbours in Scotland. Many years later, in his memoirs, he wrote that Prince Albert had asked him that evening 'who was the girl with whom I had just been dancing. I told him that her name was Lady Elizabeth Bowes Lyon and he asked me if I would introduce him, which I did.'[11]

The Prince invited the young woman on to the floor. Elizabeth continued in her letter to Beryl: 'I danced with Prince Albert who I hadn't known before, he is quite a nice youth.'[12]† She seems to have forgotten their tea-party meeting in 1916 and this new encounter apparently made little impression on her. For the Prince it was different – he is reported to have said subsequently that 'he had fallen in love that evening, although he did not realize it until later.'[13] He became determined to win Elizabeth's favour and eventually her hand. That was not to be easy. She was widely admired and was much in demand, and she enjoyed the carefree, open, happy lifestyle in which her parents had brought her up. It was almost the opposite

---

* James Stuart (1897–1971), third son of seventeenth Earl of Moray, captain 3rd Battalion Royal Scots and brigade major 15th Brigade (dispatches), First World War. Equerry to the Duke of York 1920–1. MP for Moray and Nairn 1923–59, Joint Parliamentary Secretary to the Treasury 1941–5, Conservative Chief Whip 1941–8, Secretary of State for Scotland 1951–7. Created Viscount Stuart of Findhorn 1959.

† This letter clinches the vexed question of when their meeting took place. James Stuart's memoirs put it at the right place – the RAF ball – but in the wrong year, 1921. King George VI's official biographer, John Wheeler-Bennett, and Hugo Vickers in his biography of Queen Elizabeth place it at a dance given by Lord Farquhar on 2 June 1920. Prince Albert went with Queen Mary, Princess Mary and Prince Henry to the dinner Lord Farquhar gave before the dance, but James Stuart did not go with him. Stuart and Elizabeth may have been among the 150 guests at the dance afterwards, but it was evidently at the RAF ball that she first danced with the Prince.

of the Court routine with which Prince Albert had been surrounded since childhood.

*

PRINCE ALBERT was a sensitive young man, whose upbringing had been fraught rather than idyllic. He was born in 1895, in the early hours of the morning of 14 December, the anniversary of the death of his great-grandfather, Prince Albert, and therefore a day which Queen Victoria held sacred. His parents, the Duke and Duchess of York, were concerned lest the old Queen should be upset.[14] They need not have been.

Queen Victoria's journal for the day begins: 'This terrible anniversary returned for the 34th time.' But she went on to record that she received 'telegrams from Georgie and Sir J Williams, saying that dear May had been safely delivered of a son at 3 this morning, Georgie's first feeling was regret that this dear child should be born on such a sad day. I have a feeling it may be a blessing for the dear little Boy, and may be looked upon as a gift from God!'[15] The baby's grandfather the Prince of Wales (later King Edward VII) suggested that he be called Albert, his parents agreed readily, and the Queen was touched. She wrote, 'I am all impatience to see the new one, born on such a sad day, but rather the more dear to me, especially as he will be called by that dear name which is the byeword for all that is great and good.'[16] He was christened Albert Frederick Arthur George.

Albert's childhood was not easy. His elder brother Edward (known in the family by the last of his seven Christian names, David), whom he adored, had enormous, easy charm, which he deployed at will. Albert, by contrast, was born with knock knees and was left handed, a condition considered in need of correction in those days. He was obliged as a child to write with his right hand and for several years he wore splints on his legs which day and night caused him great pain.

His parents were devoted to their children but each found it hard to establish intimate relationships with them. King George V's official biographer, Harold Nicolson, asked delicately but properly how it was that 'a man who was by temperament so intensely domestic, who was so considerate to his dependents and the members of his household, who was so unalarming to small children and humble people, should have inspired his sons with feelings of awe, amounting at times to nervous trepidation?'[17] From both his parents Prince Albert learned at an early age that he must always be obedient. His infancy was made all the more difficult by the fact that he had for many years a cruel nurse who appears to have fed him so badly that he was afflicted for the rest of his life by digestive problems.[18] He also suffered from both a crippling stammer and a fearsome temper which he always found hard to control.

Like his father and elder brother before him, Prince Albert was destined for the navy and was enrolled in the Royal Naval College at Osborne in January 1909. He was small and at first found the rough-and-tumble of school life hard. His stammer made lessons difficult for him. In his final examinations at Dartmouth, the senior naval college to which he went after Osborne, he was shown no favouritism and was placed sixty-first of sixty-seven students. At the same time, however, he enjoyed both colleges for the friendships he was able to form with boys of his own age. People liked him, despite his volatility. He was well mannered, kind and generous and impressed everyone with his determination and character. He rose a little from the bottom of his class and in due course progressed to join the Royal Navy.

When his grandfather King Edward VII died in May 1910 the fourteen-year-old Prince Albert walked behind the gun carriage bearing the King's coffin past mourning crowds to Westminster Abbey. One biographer has speculated that 'he must have been aware, perhaps for the first time now that he was old enough to realise it, of the importance of the public face of kingship and the deep emotions which centred on the person of the King'.[19] His father, now King George V, proved to be a conciliatory monarch, bluff and straightforward, no intellectual but with a wisdom conferred upon him by simplicity and honour. During his reign of almost twenty-six years five emperors and eight kings would disappear, and many other dynasties with them. But the British monarchy emerged stronger than ever.[20]

The King and Queen and their six children now had to move from their London home, Marlborough House, into Buckingham Palace – a soulless office with residential rooms attached, which has inspired little affection among members of the Royal Family since it was transformed in the nineteenth century from an unassuming house into a grandiose official residence. They were able to enjoy both Windsor Castle and Balmoral, where Queen Mary attempted to lighten the decor without interfering with her husband's affection for his childhood memories.

At Sandringham little changed, because King Edward VII had bequeathed the house to his widow Queen Alexandra for her lifetime. The new King and his family continued to live near by at York Cottage, a small house which he and Queen Mary had been given on their marriage.

Now that their father was king, the Princes' status was enhanced. Prince Edward (David) became heir apparent and was created prince of Wales in 1911. Prince Albert, only eighteen months younger, had always felt unequal to his more obviously gifted brother and now he seemed more overshadowed than ever.[21] One of their tutors wrote of him, 'One could wish that he had more of Prince Edward's keenness and application.'[22] Comparisons between the two were all the more likely because their next sibling was a girl – the tomboyish Princess Mary, who became a passionate horsewoman – and five years separated Prince Albert from his next brother. Prince Henry, a cheerful boy destined for a military career, and Prince George, the most debonair and self-assured of the brothers, were the first monarch's sons to be sent away to preparatory school. The youngest in the family, Prince John, born in 1905, suffered increasingly from epilepsy and died in 1919.

Fortunately for Prince Albert, he was better at sports than his glamorous elder brother. His prowess in shooting was especially important because this drew him closer to his father, one of the best shots in the land. He had made his first entry – three rabbits – in his first gamebook at Christmas 1907, just after his twelfth birthday. From then on shooting and recording his bag meticulously became a lifelong passion.

His dedication to sport reflected other qualities in which he outdid his brother: determination and conscientiousness. His confirmation in the Church of England at Easter 1912 was an important event for him. Two years later he wrote to the Bishop of Ripon, who had conducted the service, 'I have always remembered that day as one on which I took a great step in life. I took the Holy Sacrament on Easter Day alone with my father and mother, my eldest brother and my sister. It was so very nice having a small service quite alone like that, only the family.'[23] A deep and simple commitment to the Christian faith gave him comfort and strength throughout his life.

In January 1913 he set sail from Devonport in the cruiser HMS *Cumberland*. His six-month training voyage was not easy – he suffered from seasickness and then from too much publicity. When the ship berthed in Tenerife and the Caribbean he was mobbed by excited crowds. In Jamaica he was prevailed upon to open an extension to a yacht club but his stammer made the ordeal almost insufferable and neither here nor in Canada later in the cruise did he enjoy the enthusiastic attentions which young women attempted to bestow upon him. He also came to understand for the first time how unwelcome the attentions of the press could be.

In September 1913 the Prince was appointed midshipman on the 19,250-ton battleship *Collingwood*. For security reasons he was known as Johnson. He received no preferential treatment; like all other midshipmen, known as snotties, he slept in a hammock outside the gunroom and took his turn at all the same tasks.

When the Archduke Franz Ferdinand was assassinated in Sarajevo on 28 June 1914, Prince Albert was on board his ship off Portland. On 29 July, the day after Austria declared war on Serbia, squadron after squadron of the British Grand Fleet was dispatched north to Scapa Flow, Orkney, to guard the northern entrance to the North Sea. When Britain declared war on 4 August, Prince Albert was on station in the dark sea off Scotland. He was the only one of the royal children to be in the line of fire and his father wrote in his diary, 'Please God that it will soon be over & that he will protect dear Bertie's life.'[24] To the Prince himself, the King wrote, 'May God bless and protect you my dear boy is the earnest prayer of your very devoted Papa. You can be sure that you are constantly in my thoughts.'[25]

To the Prince's dismay, his chronic ill health prevented him from giving full wartime service. He had an appendectomy in September 1914, and over the next three years severe gastric problems forced him to spend long periods in sick bays or convalescing at home.

'I am longing and have been longing for centuries to get back to my ship,' he wrote, and at last in May 1916 his wish was granted.[26] He was thus aboard *Collingwood* when she was ordered into action against the Germans at the Battle of Jutland on 31 May 1916. He later wrote a lengthy factual account of what had happened, concluding with his own impressions:

At the commencement I was sitting on the top of A turret and had a very good view of the proceedings. I was up there during a lull, when a German ship started firing at us, and one salvo 'straddled' us. We at once returned the fire. I was distinctly startled and jumped down the hole in the top of the turret like a shot rabbit!! I didn't try the experience again. The ship was in a fine state on the main deck. Inches of water sluicing about to prevent fires getting a hold on the deck. Most of the cabins were also flooded.

The hands behaved splendidly and all of them in the best of spirits as their heart's desire had at last been granted, which was to be in action with the Germans.[27]

He was disappointed that his ship had not played a more important part in the battle that day. But perhaps he was fortunate, because the losses were terrible.

By July 1916 the Prince's stomach pains were worse than ever and he was diagnosed as suffering from a duodenal ulcer. After months of convalescence he joined the battleship *Malaya*. Shortly afterwards Louis Greig, the naval doctor who had looked after him at Osborne and had been ship's surgeon in the *Cumberland*, was appointed to the *Malaya* too. Prince Albert was delighted. Already a friend, Greig came to play an important role in his life, not just as doctor but as mentor. His wise medical advice won him the trust of the King as well, and this led to his appointment as equerry to the Prince. Fifteen years older, and a first-class rugby player, he did not usurp the role of the King as father but he became the man in whom the diffident young Prince found it most easy to confide. From 1917 onwards Greig was constantly by the Prince's side, advising him on matters spiritual, temporal and romantic, and the Prince acknowledged how much he owed to Greig in helping him onward towards maturity.

The Prince's health did not improve in the course of 1917 and Greig supported his desire for an operation to relieve his gastric problems, over the usual objections of cautious royal doctors. The operation, in November, was successful; it was evident that the Prince could have been saved two years of pain and anguish. In February 1918, fully recovered, he transferred to the Royal Naval Air Service, which was soon to join with the Royal Flying Corps to become the Royal Air Force. He reported for duty at the new flight training school at Cranwell in Lincolnshire and became the first member of the Royal

Family to take to the air, a dangerous venture in those early days of flight. (After the war was over, he continued his training and passed the required flying tests, although he was not allowed to fly solo.)

By the autumn of 1918, with the German army collapsing in retreat, the Prince was keen to see action once more and was delighted to be posted to Major General Trenchard's Air Force staff in northern France. Soon after, on 11 November, the Armistice was declared and the King wrote to his son, 'The great day has come and we have won the war. It has been a long time coming but I was sure if we stuck to it, we should win & it is a great victory over one of the most perfect military machines ever created.'[28]

The end of the war brought the monarchy anxiety as well as relief. Revolution had swept across Europe, and in early 1919 demobilization led to serious disorders which frightened many people into thinking that revolution could curse Britain as well. The government had planned badly, ordering those called up last to be demobilized first. This caused understandable anger among the longer-serving men; there were riots in Glasgow and Belfast and Luton Town Hall was burned down by a mob. Winston Churchill was transferred to the War Office and completely rewrote the demobilization plan, introducing a new scheme which allowed the longest serving and the wounded to be released first. This quelled any prospective mutinies but industrial relations deteriorated during 1919 as more and more aggrieved soldiers returned to their workplaces and discovered that the 'homes fit for heroes' promised by the government would be a long time in coming.

The radical New Statesman complained: 'Meanwhile, round about, shoots are going on, hounds are killing or drawing blank. Estimates are being prepared for the refitting of yachts. The merits of rival designs for new motor cars are being discussed, and dodges for enticing young women into domestic service ... And the necessity of a bathroom for each guest room in the afterwar house is frankly admitted. It is almost astonishing: it is wildly funny, having regard to the fact that millions of people are starving in Europe.'[29] Unemployment soared and strikes proliferated. There was talk of the Red Flag flying over Buckingham Palace. Anger at the sacrifices demanded of everyone during the war was widely felt, and the dread of class war if not of Bolshevism spread among the establishment and the middle classes.

In the so-called khaki election that Lloyd George called at the end of 1918, which was the first time that women were allowed to vote, his Coalition government comprising Conservatives and one wing of the Liberal Party was returned with a large majority. Asquith and his (Independent) Liberals were swept away, and Labour became the largest party in opposition. Nevertheless discontent grew.

The King had long been conscious of the danger. He was remarkably well informed about public opinion and was given intelligent advice by friends of the monarchy.* He took it. As the historian Frank Prochaska later observed, 'the Crown did not lack initiative or resolve. Galvanized by the drift of politics and social malaise, it could do something positive to protect itself.'[30] The King deliberately sought to strengthen the ties of affection and respect between Crown and people. In the latter part of the war he and the Queen had redoubled their visits to the armed forces, munitions factories, hospitals and other institutions up and down the land; and Colonel Clive Wigram, the King's Assistant Private Secretary, had successfully campaigned for better press coverage of their work.[†] In 1917 the King had founded the Order of the British Empire, which opened up the honours system to the mass of the people, both in Britain and throughout the Empire, a hugely popular measure. The same year he had dropped the Royal Family's German titles and adopted the name of Windsor for the dynasty. Now, in the post-war climate of social unrest, the King was urged to cultivate contacts with the Labour movement and to take an active interest in the problems of the working classes. The people must be persuaded, his Private Secretary Lord Stamfordham argued, to regard the Crown as 'a living power for good'.[31]

To advance such aims, both at home and in the Empire, the King's advisers encouraged him also to increase the public appearances of his elder sons and his daughter. At Lloyd George's suggestion, the Prince of Wales was sent on a series of lengthy imperial tours, beginning with Canada, to convey the King's thanks to the countries which had come to Britain's aid in the war. As for Prince Albert, he was given an

---

* His papers in the Royal Archives include a file entitled 'Unrest in the Country' containing letters between his Private Secretary, Lord Stamfordham, and various correspondents offering information and advice from 1917 onwards. See Frank Prochaska's *The Republic of Britain*, pp. 159–80, for details of these and related papers, which show both the concerns of the King's advisers and their views on how the monarchy should adapt itself to meet them.

[†] This led to the appointment in 1918 of the first full-time press secretary at Buckingham Palace.

unprecedented task – to establish closer royal links with the world of industry.

In the words of his biographer, this was 'a veritable *terra incognita* to the Royal Family',[32] but by a lucky chance the Rev. Robert Hyde, who had founded the Boys' Welfare Association in July 1918, decided to seek royal patronage just as Prince Albert returned from France in early 1919. The organization, which was soon broadened into the Industrial Welfare Society, aimed to improve basic conditions for workers, and thus, it was hoped, improve industrial relations.

The King approved the idea of Prince Albert becoming president of the Association. Prince Albert willingly accepted, 'provided there's no damn red carpet about it'.[33] He began work at once, visiting factories and other industrial sites across the land; he soon won the praise of the popular press for his unostentatious style and sense of purpose. He showed a keen interest in the places he visited and helped raise enough money to put the society on a sound footing. Over the years he came to acquire a unique first-hand knowledge of the workings of different industries throughout the kingdom; there is no doubt that his work helped reinforce the bonds between monarch and people.[34]

In October 1919 Prince Albert was sent for a year to Trinity College, Cambridge, with his younger brother Prince Henry, and under the watchful eye of the benign Louis Greig. There he studied history, economics and civics, and in particular the development of the British constitution.[35] He was not confined to Cambridge, but was frequently called to London and elsewhere, whether on behalf of the Industrial Welfare Society or for other royal representational duties.

But all was not work. Both the Prince of Wales and Prince Albert were keen to have their share of the gaieties of post-war social life. The King, however, worried incessantly about his sons and the new world in which they lived. Although active and conscientious in fulfilling their public duties, in private the King and Queen preferred dignified seclusion, eating alone with each other, protected by the walls of their palaces from the post-war kaleidoscope of socialism, jazz and fast young women. (The King especially feared the last for their ability to corrupt his sons.)[36] And so, it must be said, the overriding quality of the Royal Family's homes was tedium. Prince Albert told his mother's lady in waiting Lady Airlie that even Ascot week at Windsor was boring. 'No new blood is ever introduced, and as the members of the party grow older every year there's no spring in it, and no originality in the talk – nothing but a dreary acquiescence in the order of the day. No one has the exciting feeling that if they shine they will be asked again next summer – they know they will be automatically, as long as they are alive. Traditionalism is all very well, but too much of it leads to dry rot.'[37]

Yet the King and Queen could not afford to discourage youth and 'new blood', especially in the form of well-born young ladies for their sons to meet. In 1917, as a logical next step to casting off their German titles, they had decided that their children should be allowed to choose British spouses,* rather than looking to royal families abroad (many of which were German or with German origins) for spouses of equal rank. Not long afterwards Queen Mary had begun to make enquiries about suitable girls, and even to invite them to Ascot parties.† She was not a natural matchmaking mama, however; these efforts cannot have come easily to so reserved a person.

At this stage in his life Prince Albert was particularly close to his brother the Prince of Wales. Indeed they shared romantic secrets. At first both had seemed attracted by girls of good family of whom their parents might have approved – the Prince of Wales by Portia (Lady Sybil) Cadogan, daughter of Earl Cadogan, and Lady Rosemary Leveson-Gower, daughter of the Duke of Sutherland, and Prince Albert by Lady Maureen Vane-Tempest-Stewart, Lord Londonderry's daughter, one of the girls Queen Mary had invited to Ascot.

In 1918, however, the Prince of Wales fell deeply in love with a married woman, Freda Dudley Ward. She was pretty, amusing and intelligent, married to a man sixteen years her senior from whom she had drifted apart. As if in emulation of his brother, in 1919 Prince Albert became infatuated with a close friend of Freda, another unhappily married woman, whom he had met at a ball at the end of 1918.[38]

---

* In the King's diary entry recording the Council meeting at which he made his declaration about the House of Windsor, he went on to say: 'I also informed the Council that May and I had decided some time ago that our children would be allowed to marry into British families. It was quite an historical occasion.' (RA GV/PRIV/GVD/1917: 17 July, quoted in Kenneth Rose, *King George V*, p. 309)

† In 1920 Queen Mary invited two girls to Windsor with their parents for the Ascot house party; in 1921 she selected eight other girls, including Lady Elizabeth Bowes Lyon, to invite to lunch at Ascot, two each day, when Prince Albert and Prince Henry were there. (RA MRH/MISC/227, 228; list by Queen Mary, [1921], British Library, Add MSS 82748)

She was Lady Loughborough, née Sheila Chisholm,* a beautiful Australian whose marriage to Lord Loughborough, eldest son of the Earl of Rosslyn, had suffered because of his alcoholism and gambling. According to Lady Loughborough's memoirs, she and Freda often danced with the two Princes at balls, 'which annoyed some of the dowagers. However, we didn't care. We knew no party was complete without us – and them!'[39†]

News of Prince Albert's friendship with Sheila Loughborough eventually came to his parents' ears, and it added greatly to the worry their eldest son's liaison was already giving them. The King had intended to make Prince Albert a duke in June 1920, when his year at Cambridge was over, and at the same time to give him his own establishment and financial independence. But Prince Albert's relationship with a married woman, and the risk of a scandal if she divorced, threatened to undo much of the good work, to which the Prince himself had contributed so much, in consolidating the monarchy and winning over disaffected public opinion.

In April 1920 the King confronted his second son. 'He is going to make me Duke of York on his birthday provided that he hears nothing more about Sheila & me!!!!' wrote the Prince to his elder brother, now away on his second tour, to New Zealand and Australia.[40] He felt trapped, for at twenty-four he longed for his independence. Although he privately railed against his father and declared to his brother that Sheila was 'the one & only person in this world who means anything to me', it is evident that his feelings were not as deep as his brother's for Freda. He explained the situation to Sheila, who was understanding and promised to remain friends, and in May he accepted his father's terms.[41]

The King created him duke of York on 3 June, and wrote him a letter that, like many of his letters to his children, expressed

---

* Margaret Sheila Mackellar Chisholm, daughter of Harry Chisholm of Sydney, NSW; married in 1915 Francis Edward Scudamore St Clair-Erskine, Lord Loughborough, eldest son of fifth Earl of Rosslyn; divorced 1926; she married secondly, 1928, Sir John Milbanke, eleventh baronet (d. 1947), and thirdly, 1954, Prince Dimitri of Russia. She died in 1969.

† In her memoirs she also recalled one evening when she had been dancing with Prince Albert, and noticed 'a young girl standing alone by the doorway with no partner and felt sorry for her. I asked somebody who she was and they told me she was a debutante called Elizabeth Bowes Lyon.' (Princess Dimitri, 'Waltzing Matilda' (unpublished memoirs of Lady Loughborough), 1948, p. 40, private collection)

the affection which his gruffness so often concealed from them in person:

> Dearest Bertie,
>   I was delighted to get your letter this morning, & to know that you appreciate that I have given you that fine old title of Duke of York which I bore for more than 9 years & is the oldest Dukedom in this country. I know that you behaved very well, in a difficult situation for a young man & that you have done what I asked you to do. I feel that this splendid old title will be safe in your hands & that you will never do anything which could in any way tarnish it. I hope that you will always look upon me as yr. best friend & always tell me everything & you will find me ever ready to help you & give you good advice.
>   Looking forward to seeing you to-morrow.
>   Ever my dear boy,
>   Yr. very devoted Papa[42]

The Prince had written to his father the day before, saying that he was proud to be duke of York and hoped that he would live up to the title. He added, 'I can tell you that I fulfilled your conditions to the letter, and that nothing more will come of it.'[43] However, Prince Albert was not entirely happy. He had not been looking forward to June and July, he wrote to his brother; he would be spied upon at dances by people longing to carry gossip back to his parents. He was not going to give them any chances; but 'Oh! if only one could live one's own life occasionally.' He added incredulously, 'You wouldn't think it possible but Mama actually talked about marriage to me the other day!!!!!!!'[44]

With the dukedom came an independent household for the Prince. Louis Greig became his comptroller; James Stuart, who had been with his army unit in Brussels in November 1918 when Prince Albert had been on an official visit there, and had helped entertain him, was appointed his equerry.

★

MEANWHILE, FOR Elizabeth the end of the war had brought more suitors. Among the proposals of marriage she received were yet more from Commonwealth soldiers who had stayed at Glamis. She sometimes found it hard to compose letters of rejection and asked Beryl for help with one which had to be sent 'thousands of miles'.[45] She had become friendly with a Captain Glass in 1918; in March 1920, however, to her consternation he asked her to marry him. 'Awful thing happened on Thursday!' she told Beryl. 'C . . . n G . . . s proposed to me!! Oh Gosh, I couldn't help it, wasn't it <u>awful</u>?'[46] He continued to write to her, but she was unmoved. 'My dearest old egg,' she remarked to Beryl, 'it never had the <u>slightest</u> tinge of Ro-mance about it at all, at any time, I hated it all!'[47] She had to grow accustomed to deflecting suitors. 'People were rather inclined to propose to you in those days,' she recalled many years later. 'You know, it was rather the sort of thing, I suppose. And you said "No thank you", or whatever it was.' As for the rejected suitor, she said, he would often reply, 'Oh, I thought you wouldn't,' so she felt 'it was all very nice and light-hearted.'[48]

Among the young men who constantly sought her attention several stood out. One was Prince Paul of Serbia.* The Prince, born in St Petersburg in 1893, had had a rather miserable childhood, abandoned by his parents. His Oxford career, reading Greats at Christ Church, was happy but interrupted by the war. He became a popular member of young London society, and a close friend of Elizabeth's brother Michael. He praised Elizabeth's prettiness 'with her shining, lively eyes and beautiful smile'.[49] Many thought he was keen to marry her.

Prince Paul and Michael Bowes Lyon shared a flat in London with Lord Gage,† whose family had long lived in a beautiful house, Firle Place, on the South Downs near Lewes in Sussex. A slightly dour man whose nickname was Grubby, George Gage had great hopes for his friendship with Elizabeth. Their mutual friend the diarist Chips Channon‡ later noted, 'Poor Gage is desperately fond of her – in vain, for he is far too heavy, too Tudor and squirearchal for so rare and patrician a creature as Elizabeth.'[50]

There was also Bruce Ogilvy, son of Lord and Lady Airlie and

---

* Prince Paul (1893–1976) was the son of Prince Arsène Karageorgević (brother of King Peter I of Serbia) and his Russian wife Aurora Demidoff. After his parents separated he was taken in by King Peter, who brought him up with his own sons.

† Sir Henry Rainald ('George') Gage (1895–1982), sixth Viscount Gage, lord in waiting to King George V, King Edward VIII and King George VI; Parliamentary Private Secretary to Secretary of State for India 1924–9. Married 1931 Hon. Alexandra Grenfell.

‡ Henry 'Chips' Channon (1897–1958), knighted 1957, Conservative politician and diarist.

Elizabeth's neighbour at Glamis. He was an amusing companion, 'very "norty"', as she described him; but she dismissed him, along with Captain Glass, as 'silly nice fools', in comparison with real friends like Charles Settrington.[51] A more dependable, older friend was Arthur Penn,* a charming, witty and kindly man who had been her brother Jock's contemporary at Eton; Elizabeth had met him during the war and had found him entrancing. Penn had fought heroically, winning both the Military Cross and the Croix de Guerre.

The suitor who came closest to winning her hand, however, was James Stuart. Born in Edinburgh in 1897, Stuart was still at Eton when war began; he immediately joined the Royal Scots, despite being under age. He trained with Michael Bowes Lyon and they became lifelong friends. Stuart fought with great courage during the war and was awarded the Military Cross and bar. His heroism added lustre to his enormous personal charm. There were those who said that the war had induced a depression in him, as in many other young men. But he was very attractive to women.

James Stuart had been one of the guests at that first post-war house party at Glamis in September 1919, when Elizabeth had been grieving over the death of Charles Settrington. He was engaged to Evelyn Louise Finlayson but broke off the engagement in the second half of 1920, and around that time became romantically involved with one of Elizabeth's friends, Mollie Lascelles.† It is not clear when Elizabeth was first drawn to him, or he to her, but her letters to Beryl Poignand contain only passing references to him until the end of 1920.

The London season of 1920 was filled with events and dances galore. For Elizabeth, it was sadly interrupted when she and her family had to move out of their home in St James's Square‡ in mid-June, into

---

* Arthur Horace Penn (1886–1960), son of William and Constance Penn of Taverham Hall, Norfolk. Served in Grenadier Guards in 1914–18 war (MC, mentioned in dispatches). Afterwards practised as a barrister, then worked in the City. Appointed groom in waiting to King George VI 1937. Rejoined his regiment in Second World War and served as regimental adjutant, combining this with working as acting private secretary to Queen Elizabeth. Remained in her service as private secretary, and then treasurer, until his death.

† Vreda Esther Mary ('Mollie') (1900–93), daughter of Major William Frank Lascelles. In April 1921 she married the Earl of Dalkeith, eldest son of seventh Duke of Buccleuch, who succeeded as eighth duke in 1935.

‡ The Strathmores were unable to renew the lease on the house. Elizabeth was heartbroken at leaving 'this darling house', so full of happy memories. They rented 20 Eaton Square and

a rented house in Eaton Square, a neighbourhood she disliked.[52] (Later
the family moved permanently to Bruton Street in Mayfair.) Soon after
the move to Eaton Square, she went to Ascot and Henley, and then to
the RAF ball at which, it seems, Prince Albert lost his heart to her.

Nine days later, on 17 July, the Prince went to Bisham, on the
Thames near Henley, to spend the weekend in a house party given by
Lady Nina Balfour.* It was probably there that he had his next meeting
with Elizabeth. Her friend Helen Cecil later wrote, 'Apparently when
they were all at Lady Nina's he held Elizabeth's hand under Nina's
very nose in the famous electric launch. Elizabeth says it was quite
worth it just to see Nina's face.'[53] For Elizabeth it was perhaps no
more than an amusing game; for Prince Albert it probably meant
more. However, three days afterwards he was still writing wistfully to
the Prince of Wales about Sheila Loughborough, and reproaching his
brother for advising him, as Queen Mary had, to marry and settle
down. 'I haven't thought about that yet,' he protested. But he seemed
to view the prospect of Sheila's coming departure for Australia with
equanimity.[54]

*

AS USUAL, the Strathmores took the night train to Glamis in early
August 1920, and soon guests began to arrive for a succession of house
parties. In early September Elizabeth and her brothers Michael and
David, the only unmarried members of the family, welcomed a
particularly large group of their friends for the annual Forfar County
Ball on the 8th. Her dance card for the ball is preserved in the Glamis
Archives. She danced with many admirers, Prince Paul, Lord Gage,
James Stuart and Victor Cochrane-Baillie. The ball was only half of the
fun. A house party at Glamis was always exhilarating, an informal,
ever moving tableau with a panoply of entertainments – tennis, cricket,
shooting, walking and, in the evenings, dressing up, charades, dancing,
cards and singing around the piano.

In all this gaiety Elizabeth was the carefree and enchanting centre.
One of her admirers, Lord Gorell, recalled to another biographer,

---

then 6 Upper Brook Street until moving into their new permanent home at 17 Bruton Street,
Mayfair, in late 1921 or early 1922.

* Lady Helena ('Nina') Balfour (1865–1948), daughter of fifth Earl of Antrim, married 1888
Captain Charles Barrington Balfour. She was a great friend of Cecilia Strathmore.

Elizabeth Longford, 'I was madly in love with her. Everything at Glamis was beautiful, perfect. Being there was like living in a Van Dyck picture. Time, and the gossiping, junketing world, stood still . . . But the magic gripped us all. I fell *madly* in love. They all did.'[55]

At the end of the week Elizabeth reported to Beryl that she was completely exhausted by it all. 'We dressed up & ragged about, & now that the hard tennis court is finished, we played all day.' But at one point the fun and games had got a little out of hand. 'The most awful thing happened. Victor proposed to me the night we all dressed up! He looked too awful with great black smudges all over his face! I did hate it! Don't tell anybody. Still a few people here, must fly and dress for dinner.' As a PS, Elizabeth wrote across the top of the page: 'Prince Albert is coming to stay here on Saturday. Ghastly!'[56]

The Prince had invited himself, from Balmoral, where he and Princess Mary were staying with their parents in gloomy isolation, with none but elderly guests and familiar royal cousins for company. It is unlikely that he had yet confided in the King and Queen about his interest in Elizabeth; but the idea of going to Glamis may have occurred to him because Princess Mary had been invited by Mabell, Countess of Airlie, to stay with her at Airlie Castle, only a few miles away.*

Elizabeth was nervous and asked as many friends and members of her family as possible for assistance. Helen Cecil wrote to her mother from Glamis, 'Elizabeth is here & a perfect angel as usual . . . They have the Duke of York coming here & Elizabeth specially asked me to stay & help with him.'[57] Helen was by this time engaged to Captain Alexander Hardinge, who had recently been appointed assistant private secretary to the King. He was at Balmoral, and exchanged frequent letters with his fiancée. Quite unaware of Prince Albert's feelings, Hardinge was 'green with envy' that he was off to Glamis. 'Oh the lucky brute – and it means so little to him – and all the world to me, and I cannot go.' Worse still, James Stuart would be accompanying

---

* The Prince may also have received encouragement from someone else who knew Glamis and Elizabeth very well. The minister at Crathie, the church attended by the Royal Family at Balmoral, was now the Rev. Dr John Stirton, who had previously been minister at Glamis. 'I am really responsible for the Duke having first gone there,' he recorded in his diary two years later, as Prince Albert set out for Glamis again. (Rev. John Stirton, Diary, 26 September 1922, RA AEC/GG/026)

the Prince. 'You won't let James cut me out, will you, Helen!'
Hardinge wrote. 'He is so attractive that there would be every
justification for it.'[58]

Other friends there to help Elizabeth included Katie Hamilton,
Diamond Hardinge,* Doris Gordon-Lennox and James Stuart's elder
brother Lord Doune. Helen's letters give a lively picture of the
atmosphere at Glamis before the Prince arrived. 'Elizabeth is playing
"Oh Hell" on the piano on purpose for me & Diamond is singing it
which is most distracting! . . . It is very nice being here & Elizabeth is
the greatest darling.'[59] The morning of the Prince's arrival she wrote,
'There is a fearful fuss over tonight & the week-end in general. We
are to have reels & all sorts of strange wild things tonight which will
be awful.'[60]

The guests were a little on edge when the Prince arrived to stay
and Princess Mary came with Lady Airlie for dinner. 'Everybody made
awful floaters that night, it became simply comic in the end,' Helen
wrote; but after dinner they danced reels boisterously, with the
dowagers giving the lead: 'Lady Airlie & Mrs James† having sliding
races up and down the extremely slippery floor was quite a good sight
too!' Afterwards Doris and Katie courted disaster by doing 'a marvellous imitation' of the royal visitors 'when P.A. came round the screen
& nobody could warn them that they were rushing on their fate!'[61]

At breakfast the next morning only Helen arrived on time; she did
her part in helping entertain the Prince 'mostly by singing hymn
choruses in a high falsetto which made him laugh'.[62] There was tennis,
and in the afternoon a service in the family chapel for which Princess
Mary came over again from Airlie. Here Elizabeth takes up the tale in
a letter to Beryl: 'Afterwards I showed her & the Duke [of York] the
castle, & terrified them with ghost stories! We also played ridiculous
games of hide & seek, they really are babies! She didn't leave till 6.30,
& then we all played General Post, & Flags etc till dinner time – I had
played tennis all the morning, so you can imagine how tired I was!!

---

* Alec Hardinge's sister, another of Elizabeth's friends. Born in 1900, she married Major
Robert Abercromby in June 1923. She suffered from ill health and died in 1927 following a
serious illness.

† Venetia James, née Cavendish-Bentinck (1863–1948), a cousin of Lady Strathmore, and
Elizabeth's godmother. She married, in 1885, John Arthur James of Coton House, Rugby, who
died in 1917.

. . . Poor P. Mary really did enjoy herself – she is most awfully nice.'[63]
At one point during the games Helen had hoped to slip away and
write to Alec Hardinge, but 'Elizabeth's signals of distress' at being left
alone with her royal visitors were so obvious that she felt she had to
stay.[64]

After dinner they sang noisily all evening '& it was all quite fun',
Elizabeth recorded.[65] According to Helen the repertoire included 'the
most appalling songs' and Prince Albert joined in 'with more gusto
than any of them'. At midnight Elizabeth and her girl friends slipped
upstairs and made apple-pie beds for her brother David and for James
Stuart, to whom they had just said a mocking goodnight, dropping
him 'a deep curtsey, in a row like the chorus'. Helen teased her fiancé
by writing to him that Stuart was indeed 'quite delightful . . . I wonder
he isn't spoilt with all the women making such fools of themselves
over his good looks.'[66]

On the last day of Prince Albert's stay the whole party went out
for a walk after breakfast. 'Elizabeth & Prince A. were allowed to go
on miles ahead which agitated the former rather but we thought
ourselves awfully tactful!' Helen reported. The rest of the party chased
each other about, the girls hiding and the men pelting them with mud
to avenge the apple-pie beds.[67] Later Helen wrote to Elizabeth, 'Do
tell me any particularly odious things that the Duke of Y. said about
me when you betook yourselves to the garden. It would be such a
waste if after my efforts to please him by leaving him in peace with
you I didn't hear his remarks!! I'm sure he's grateful about that anyway
tho' I'm not so certain about you! I trust you will forgive me, sweet
love, because you are such an angel.'[68]

The Prince would have agreed with that. He was enchanted by it
all. The contrast between the formality of his own family life and the
relaxed joy of Glamis whirling around Elizabeth was intoxicating. The
happy relationships between the Strathmores and their children and
the affectionate teasing between Elizabeth and her brothers and sisters
were pure delight. The weekend seems to have convinced him that
Elizabeth Bowes Lyon was the woman for him.

After her guests had left, Elizabeth wrote to Beryl that she was in
bed with a cold and 'utterly exhausted after 3 weeks of entertaining
people!' Prince Albert's visit had 'kept us pretty busy! He was very nice,
tho', & very much improved in every way.'[69] The Prince wrote to
thank Lady Strathmore for his stay at Glamis: 'I did enjoy my time

there so much, & I only wish I could have stayed there longer, I hope you will forgive me for the very abrupt way in which I proposed myself.'⁷⁰ This was echoed by James Stuart, who wrote, 'Prince Albert really did enjoy it, I know and in no other house in the United Kingdom could it have been done so well, or anywhere near it. It was perfect. Princess Mary also has talked of nothing else but her visit. I need hardly add how much I enjoyed myself also: one could not do otherwise at Glamis.'⁷¹ Elizabeth's friends too wrote her letters overflowing with thanks and praise. 'The moment I set foot in your house I feel a different person,' wrote Doris; Helen told Elizabeth she was 'just the most perfect person that ever was'; she and Diamond were driving the Hardinge family to distraction 'both talking at once & all about Elizabeth & Glamis!'⁷² Women as much as men adored Elizabeth.

She was by now, it seems from Helen's comments, uncomfortably aware of the Prince's interest in her, but she did not yet mention it to Beryl. Meanwhile her autumn continued much as before, with friends to stay at Glamis, and house parties elsewhere. And she was seeing more of James Stuart. He came back to Glamis on 2 October for a week to shoot, and a few days later she drove with him to Ballathie House on the River Tay near Perth, where Doris Gordon-Lennox was staying in a house party with her sister Amy's parents-in-law, Sir Stuart and Lady Coats. Doris wrote to her afterwards that the whole family adored seeing her, and she tried to put her mind at rest about her arrival alone with James Stuart – a rather risqué thing for a young woman to do. 'Of course we didn't think anything of you & James coming! No one thought it a bit funny. I think everyone here now realises how fashionable it is to tour round Perthshire & Forfarshire with "Les frères Stuart" & I assure you it was quite alright. I do so understand it – it is such a joy to have real friends like that.' She ended by saying, 'I wish I could thank you for your saintliness to me – perhaps one day I'll have an opportunity – until then I can only attempt to tell you how I've adored the last two months – thanks chiefly to you.'⁷³

In November, back in London, Elizabeth sent a cryptic note to Beryl which indicates that Prince Albert came to call on her when she had been expecting to see Beryl. She asked why Beryl had not come, adding: 'As a matter of fact our Bert stayed till 7, talking 100 to 20, or even 200 to a dozen. I am just off to a smart dance, & I know I shan't know a soul, & will be miserable. I must see you some time – when on earth can it be? I <u>do</u> wish he hadn't come this evening, but I simply couldn't stop him, & I am longing to see you.'[74]

She and Beryl did get together, and had a long talk, catching up on all that had happened. Writing to her friend afterwards, she had an urgent request:

Don't say one word about what I told you <u>please</u>, as that sort of thing is <u>too</u> awful if it gets about, & would make things very uncomfortable – so <u>do</u> keep it strictly to yourself – it is very important. You are the only person I have told about it except Katie, so you will be discreet I know. I thank thee. Not even your Mother. Au revoir – are you jazzing this week?[75]

One can but conclude that the Prince had begun to pay court to her in earnest, and that it worried her. At about this time she and the Prince began to correspond: her first surviving letter to him was written on 13 December 1920, in answer to one from him (which does not survive). She had been invited to a dinner which was to be given for him on 15 December, the day after his twenty-fifth birthday, by a well-known society hostess. She wrote:

Dear Prince Albert,
    Thank you so much for your letter. I am looking forward very much to Mrs Ronnie Greville's party – though the very thought of it <u>terrifies</u> me! I haven't been to a proper dinner party for months and months, and have quite forgotten how to behave! I expect it will be great fun though. Have you been very gay? Dancing every night I expect. Only a short note, as Wednesday is so soon.
    I am, Sir, Yours sincerely
        Elizabeth Lyon[76]

In the event she enjoyed Mrs Greville's party,* as she told him in her next letter, written from St Paul's Walden. Prince Albert sent her

---

* The Hon. Mrs Ronald Greville, née Margaret McEwan (1863–1942), the presumed only child of the Scottish brewer and philanthropist William McEwan MP, whose fortune and fine collection of pictures she inherited when he died in 1913. In 1891 she married the Hon. Ronald Henry Fulke Greville: he died in 1908. Her husband was a friend of King Edward VII, which led to a continuing friendship with the Royal Family. She entertained generously and in grand style at her London house in Charles Street, Mayfair, and at her Surrey mansion, Polesden Lacey. A forceful character, notorious for her acerbic wit, she had many critics, but she could also be kind and generous, and she was shrewd, witty, interested in people and an excellent

a little box for Christmas, for which she thanked him 'a thousand times'. Her mother was unwell and she did not expect to go to another dance for months – 'I lead such a deadly existence here, that there is simply nothing to tell you – oh except that I have just fallen into a pond!'[77]

On the last day of 1920 she wrote to Beryl saying she had been very worried about her mother. Although Lady Strathmore's health was now improving the doctor said it would take a long time for her to recover her strength. Ironically Elizabeth seems once again to have been waiting in vain for a visit from Beryl when James Stuart had called to see her. 'It was rather funny, that evening that you might have been coming round, James Stuart came in.' She added: 'he is an angel, and I should like you to see him, as you hardly know any of my friends now.'[78]

The dances resumed in January 1921. One was given by Lord Winterton at Shillinglee Park in Surrey, for which Elizabeth stayed with the Leconfields at Petworth.* In a letter to Prince Albert the next day she wrote, 'I am quite mad this morning, as we danced till 3 last night, and I didn't go to sleep till 5, so you must forgive me if this letter is rather odd!!' There was an enormous party of people staying at Petworth, 'some nice and some nasty! At the moment I feel, that if anybody even spoke to me, I should bite them, so I hope nobody will!' As a postscript along the side of the page she wrote, 'This is an awful letter – I really believe I am going mad.'[79]

The next day she was at the other side of Sussex, staying with George Gage at Firle, for the Southdown Ball at which she danced until five in the morning. She returned, exhausted, to St Paul's Walden. Sitting in the billiard room, listening to the gramophone playing 'all the most delicious tunes – I feel most sentimental!' she wrote to Beryl. 'Swanee always makes me feel worst. Such memories!! Tut tut Elizabeth, compose yourself.' She loved Firle but it was 'such a funny visit. Because apparently all the servants & people there, think he [Lord Gage] is going to marry either Doris or me, and they were

---

hostess whose cuisine and cellars were renowned. During the First World War, like the Strathmores, she set up a convalescent hospital at her house, and for this and for other war work she was in 1922 made DBE – Dame Commander of the British Empire.

* Charles Henry Wyndham, third Baron Leconfield (1872–1952), and his wife Beatrice, whose home, Petworth House, is renowned for its Grinling Gibbons carvings and its fine collection of paintings.

intensely excited! I don't think it's either of us personally, he is merely
a great friend of us both, but it was so funny.'[80]

That month the Prince came to St Paul's Walden for the first time.
Replying to his letter proposing a visit, Elizabeth invited him to lunch
on 17 January:

> the only thing is, would you mind having it alone? Not alone by
> yourself I don't mean – (it sounds so funny that, as if you would
> have it in one room, and me in another!!) But you see my mother
> has been very ill, and she & I are really only having a sort of
> picnic down here by ourselves, and I am so afraid you would be
> bored to <u>tears</u>. It would be delightful though if you are <u>sure</u> you
> wouldn't mind not having a large luncheon party? Please do say
> if you think you might! This is <u>quite</u> a small house, and <u>no</u> ghosts
> like at Glamis!

She gave him directions, telling him to 'keep to the right all the way,
till you come to a tumbledown old white gate on the left. Then you
go up a bumpy road full of holes, and eventually reach an even more
tumbledown old house, and a tumbledown little person waiting on the
doorstep – which will be <u>ME</u>!!! . . . I am Sir, Yours sincerely, Elizabeth
Lyon.'[81]

No account of the lunch survives, but they met again on 8
February when Elizabeth was a bridesmaid to Helen Cecil at her
marriage to Alec Hardinge. 'I bet you I look too disgusting at it,'
Elizabeth wrote to Beryl, as her dress was to be blue, a colour she
then disliked.[82] Diamond Hardinge, Doris Gordon-Lennox and Mollie
Lascelles were also bridesmaids, and Arthur Penn was best man. The
King and Queen, Princess Mary and Prince Albert were guests.

Each time he saw Elizabeth the Prince evidently fell more in love.
Early in 1921 he told his parents that he was planning to propose to
her. Queen Mary consulted Mabell Airlie about her son's choice and
was reassured;[83] thereafter, as both friend of the Strathmores and lady
in waiting to the Queen, Lady Airlie became a valued mediator
between the two families.* On 16 February the Prince went to tea
with Lady Airlie; Lady Strathmore was there too.

---

* Her edited memoirs, *Thatched with Gold*, much quoted by other biographers, tell the story
but are not wholly reliable and are imprecise about the sequence of events in the courtship.

The Prince asked himself to lunch again on Sunday 27 February. There were no servants, Elizabeth warned him, except the 'all-important' cook. 'So if you come to luncheon there would be nobody to wait on us! So if you have something more amusing to do, please don't worry to come. Otherwise if you don't mind having no servants & things, do come! This is extremely ill expressed I'm afraid, but I thought I'd just let you know about Sunday.'[84]

It was scarcely a pressing invitation; it may even have been a hint that he should not come. If so, the Prince ignored it. That afternoon he evidently proposed to Elizabeth and she refused him. It was upsetting and the next day she wrote:

> Dear Prince Bertie, I must write one line to say how <u>dreadfully</u> sorry I am about yesterday. It makes me miserable to think of it – you have been so <u>very</u> nice about it all – please do forgive me. Also <u>please</u> don't worry about it –, I do understand so well what you feel, and sympathise so much, & I hate to think that I am the cause of it. I honestly can't explain to you how terribly sorry I am –, it worries me <u>so</u> much to think you may be unhappy – I do hope you won't be. <u>Anyway</u> we can be good friends can't we? Please do look on me as one. I shall <u>never</u> say anything about our talks I promise you – and nobody need ever know. I thought I must just write this short letter to try and tell you <u>how</u> sorry I am. Yours very sincerely, Elizabeth[85]

It was the first time she had signed with her Christian name only.

He immediately tried to put her mind at rest; his letter does not survive, but she wrote again: 'Dear Prince Bertie, Thank you so much for your letter, which much relieved my mind. I feel just the same as you do about it, and am <u>so</u> glad . . . Yes, I feel I know you so much better this last few weeks – I think it is so much easier to get to know people in the country – even if it's only for an hour or two – don't you? One is more natural I expect.' The rest of the letter is certainly 'natural' – she asked him about his hunting, congratulated him on his recent speeches, which she had read in the paper, and told him she was going to Glamis for Easter. This time she signed herself Elizabeth Lyon.[86]

Both sets of parents, and their go-between Mabell Airlie, were sad that the relationship seemed to have foundered. Lady Strathmore wrote to Lady Airlie:

My dearest Mabel

I have written to the young man as you advised – & told him how truly grieved we are that this little romance has come to an end. I also suggested the alternative reason he might give to his Father, in case he had not already spoken about it. I will tell you, if he replies to this letter.

You have been so angelically kind to E. & me, all through this little episode in her life, that I shall always be grateful to you dear Mabel.

I do hope that the Queen is not very much annoyed with E. & me, altho' it wd be quite natural that she shd be, but I shd be so unhappy to cause her (the Queen) any worry in her strenuous life. I hope 'he' will find a very nice wife, who will make him happy – as between you & me, I feel he will be 'made or marred' by his wife.

No one except you knows what a keen disappointment it has all been to me, but I daresay it is all for the best, & my worldliness will be well squashed!![87]*

Queen Mary appears not to have been annoyed, for a few days later she invited Lady Strathmore to see her at Buckingham Palace.[88] No record of the conversation has survived.

The Prince may have been downcast but he was determined to maintain his pursuit of Elizabeth and they continued to correspond. On Good Friday she wrote to him from Glamis to say she was happy that 'depressing' Lent was nearly over. She hoped to come to London soon but 'It is so impossible to make plans with my mother ill like this – sometimes I get rather depressed, but I suppose that is silly of me!'

Elizabeth was busy getting up a sale for the troop of Girl Guides she had started at Glamis in 1920. 'You ought to see me in my uniform of Lord High Admiral of the Guides,' she told the Prince. 'I am an awe-inspiring figure & look most commanding. Have you been doing anything amusing lately? Please forgive such a deadly letter, I think my brain is going, through not having seen anyone for such ages.'[89] She signed herself 'Elizabeth'.

*

---

* This letter is quoted, inaccurately, in *Thatched with Gold*, p. 167.

PRINCE ALBERT, too, was busy – with his work for the Industrial Welfare Society. Such work was needed. Throughout 1920 industrial unrest had been growing. In the first three months of 1921 unemployment almost doubled to 1,300,000, the export price of coal collapsed, and the government announced its intention to denationalize the mining industry. At the beginning of April the miners declared a strike and the railwaymen and transport workers threatened to join them. The King immediately returned from Windsor to London. 'There is no doubt that we are passing through as grave a crisis as this country has ever had,' he wrote. 'All the troops have been called out, Kensington Gardens are full of them . . . The Government have made all their preparations for distributing food &c and the public are entirely with the Govt, so perhaps these delightful people who want a revolution, will come to their senses before it is too late.'[90] Prince Albert too had been at Windsor: cancelling out all else in his engagement diary are the words 'Return to London on account of Coal Strike.'[91]

The general sense of nervousness that the prevailing social system would not survive affected the Bowes Lyon family. In the second week of April Lord Strathmore, taking his butler Arthur Barson with him, hurried from St Paul's Walden to Glamis to raise volunteers to break the transport strike. Elizabeth wrote to Beryl, 'Bad times my dear M[edusa], but I love the calm way the British people take it all! Nothing but talks of Revolution and Ruin, & yet everybody moons along in the same old way, except that the "Boys" join anything they can. Mike has joined something, and goes to Hertford tomorrow. Very bored, but I suppose he's right.'[92]

The government made elaborate plans for feeding London and other cities but at the last minute, on 'Black Friday', 15 April, the railways and transport unions called off their strike. The King was relieved when, shortly afterwards, he attended a football match watched by 73,000 people: 'at the end they sang the National Anthem and cheered tremendously. There were no Bolsheviks there! At least I never saw any. The country is all right: just a few extremists are doing all the harm.'[93]

It was in these troubled circumstances that Prince Albert took up a suggestion by Alexander Grant, an industrialist. Grant argued that increasing contacts between young people of different backgrounds would benefit society as a whole. The Prince, who had been impressed by a football game between young Welsh steelworkers and pupils from Westminster School, hit upon the idea of a camp. Two hundred boys from public schools and 200 from firms which had joined the Industrial Welfare Society would be brought together with the aim of breaking down social divisions through a week of shared games and entertainment.

The first camp, paid for by Grant, took place in August 1921 on Romney Marsh in Kent. It was unprecedented: although camps had been held by organizations such as the Boys' Brigade and the Scouts, this was the first to mix groups which had never met. There were of course teething troubles and problems of communication, but the camp went well.* 'Your Boys Camp was a great success wasn't it?' Elizabeth asked the Prince. 'I hope so anyway, as it is such an excellent idea, and a wonderful thing for the boys.' The camps became an annual summer event for the next eighteen years. Prince Albert always spent one full day, the Duke's Day, at the camp, joining in meals and games, and in the singing of what became the camp song, 'Under the Spreading Chestnut Tree'. Although inevitably limited and too easily dismissed as naive by a more cynical generation, these camps were a genuine attempt to mitigate the harsh realities of industrial life between the wars.

The Prince of Wales, too, was playing his part, in a welcome year off from his Empire tours. He visited industrial areas and was enthusiastically received even by convinced republicans in Glasgow and Lancashire.[94] In May 1921 he went on a ten-day tour of Devon and Cornwall, during which he stayed for two days with Lord and Lady Clinton† at Bicton in Devon. The Clintons were the parents of Elizabeth's sister-in-law Fenella, and they had invited her to join their house party for the Prince's visit. Elizabeth was struck by his industry. 'The Prince was away all day working hard, & only got back at tea time – he does have a hellish life – that's the only word for it.' For her it was a pleasant interlude: the party played tennis, 'lazed about, &

---

* The first Duke of York's Camp started on 30 July 1921, when the Duke welcomed the 400 participants at the Royal Mews at Buckingham Palace, after which they were taken to the camp site at New Romney. The Duke visited them there on 3 August. Despite an unsympathetic press beforehand, the camp was indeed a great success.

† Lord Clinton (1863–1957) was a member of the Council of the Duchy of Cornwall, Keeper of the Privy Seal to the Prince of Wales, and Lord Warden of the Stannaries at this time, and the Prince's visit (16–25 May) was in his role as duke of Cornwall.

occasionally did a few official Prince of Wales things and had great fun'.[95]

There was more amusement to come. Diamond Hardinge's father, Lord Hardinge of Penshurst, had been appointed ambassador to France in 1920. He was a widower and the twenty-year-old Diamond, a lively, humorous girl given to daring practical jokes,[96] was his only daughter. She invited Elizabeth to go to Paris with her at the end of May 1921. Prince Paul had also written to Elizabeth from Belgrade to say that he was visiting the French capital too and hoped they would meet: he was 'simply longing' to see her again, '& also we might have some of our fast parties in the gay French Metropolis.'[97]

She loved this, her first visit to Paris. She and Diamond escaped from the Embassy and dined with Prince Paul and Lord and Lady Dalkeith – Walter Dalkeith had married Mollie Lascelles in April. 'It was such fun,' she wrote to Prince Albert, 'and delicious seeing Mollie again – also it felt very odd being chaperoned by her!'[98] Afterwards they danced at Ciro's club. Then, as she told Beryl, but not the Prince, they went on to 'a low place, full of the most astounding people! . . . We threw balls at each other, and danced, and at 1.30 Maurice and Leonora Hughes danced divinely.* At 2 we staggered out – me exchanging a rapid fire of little pink balls with a sinister gentleman in a black beard! It <u>was</u> such fun, & so indescribably Parisien as to atmosphere!' Another night they dined at the Café de Madrid:

> One ate and danced out of doors, under trees lit up with little pink lights. I do wish you could see them dancing the shimmy here!! It's too disgusting! And at the place we finished up at last night, honestly none of the women wore any clothes under their frocks! Too odd it is! The food is so good here – alpine strawberries, huge asparagus & horse shoe rolls are the things I like!

There was serious sightseeing too: the two girls went to the Louvre, and Lord Hardinge drove them to Malmaison and Chartres.[99]

---

* Maurice Mouvet (1888–1927), professional dancer in cabarets and nightclubs, and his partner Leonora Hughes. They danced with great success in London and Paris in the early 1920s; Maurice was particularly famous for his skill in the tango, the Brazilian maxixe and the Apache.

Elizabeth wrote to the Prince that she had decided to stay on for at least a week, 'as London is so dull now, and this is amusing. Are you going to Ascot? I know you <u>love</u> it!!'[100] On 9 June she wrote again. She had been to a ball the night before 'and I am in the last stages of exhaustion! They dance the Tango a great deal out here – rather an amusing dance I think. I danced it with a Russian called Constantine Somebody the other evening – I never found out his other name! It was so funny, one is suddenly hurled into the air, and then bounced on the floor till one is gaga, ou la la! Very painful.'[101]

Back in England she continued to correspond with the Prince, to meet him at dances and to play tennis with him. They were not well matched on the court – he had won the RAF Doubles Competition in 1920, playing with Louis Greig, whereas she was 'getting worse & worse!' as she told him.[102] There was more tennis, without the Prince, at a lively house party at Welbeck Abbey, home of Elizabeth's relations the Duke and Duchess of Portland.* 'We played tennis violently all day, & danced violently all night, so I'm now even more of a wreck than I was!' she reported to the Prince in a letter thanking him for a book he had sent for her birthday.[103] She was expecting him at Glamis at the end of September 1921, just as the year before. She was happy to be friends with him, she said in her letters. This must have encouraged his ambitions.[104]

Queen Mary came to see for herself. On 5 September she arrived at Airlie Castle to stay with Lady Airlie, and Lord Strathmore and Elizabeth were invited for tea; Lady Strathmore was unwell and could not come. Four days later the Queen lunched at Glamis. 'Went over the Castle which is most interesting,' she recorded, with characteristic brevity.[105] According to Mabell Airlie, 'Lady Elizabeth filled her mother's place as hostess so charmingly that the Queen was more than ever convinced that this was "the one girl who could make Bertie happy".' But Queen Mary was determined not to interfere. 'I shall say nothing to either of them. Mothers should never meddle in their children's love affairs.'[106]

On 24 September Prince Albert duly arrived at Glamis. While he was there his mother wrote, sending 'many messages to the Strathmores and E' and hoping he was enjoying himself.[107] He replied, 'It is

---

* The sixth Duke of Portland (1857–1943) was a first cousin of Cecilia Strathmore, the son of her father's younger brother.

delightful here and Elizabeth is very kind to me. The more I see her the more I like her.'[108] With her mother still in bed, Elizabeth continued to play hostess. Her father, Michael and David were there; so were Rose and Wisp, together with Mida Scott,* Katie Hamilton, Doris Gordon-Lennox and James Stuart. After three days of partridge driving, which the Prince enjoyed, although he felt he had not shot as well as he could, he joined his brother David on the London train at Glamis. James Stuart, alone of the party, stayed on at Glamis for three more days.

Back at Buckingham Palace the Prince wrote to his father that his week at Glamis had been 'delightful' and 'they were all so kind to me'.[109] To Elizabeth he wrote:

> My dear Elizabeth, Thank you ever so very much for all your kindness to me last week at Glamis. I did so love my time there, & hated having to leave you all on Friday night to come South ... It is very sad to think that we shall not meet now for some time, but do please write to me & let me know when you are coming back to London ... Thanking you again ever so much for asking me up to Glamis, & being <u>so</u> kind to me in every way.[110]

On 2 October Lady Strathmore had an operation; a tumour had been feared but fortunately the surgeon found and removed only a large gallstone.[111] Nonetheless, she suffered shock and the doctors feared for her life, Elizabeth told Beryl. 'I can't tell you how awful it is – this is the 6th day of suspense, but I believe she will recover somehow.'[112] She began to do so.

To the Prince Elizabeth wrote, 'I'm afraid this is a very depressed letter, but you know, it is such a relief to write about it, & does one so much good, that I hope you don't mind. I'm afraid I must have made a lugubrious hostess last week, but I enjoyed having everybody here, and I only hope that it wasn't too depressing for you ... Shall I write a little later on, & let you know how my mother is? You are very sympathetic about it all – worry <u>is</u> awful, isn't it? ... Thank you again for your letter, it is <u>such</u> a help to have the sympathy of one's

---

* Lady Margaret Ida Montagu-Douglas-Scott, daughter of seventh Duke of Buccleuch and elder sister of Lady Alice, the future Duchess of Gloucester. She married Captain Geoffrey Hawkins in 1926.

friends on these occasions.'[113] She had found that she could rely on him in times of stress; she welcomed that at difficult moments, an important element of their developing relationship.

The Prince wrote back at once and on 11 October Elizabeth was able to tell him that her mother was better. 'The relief is so intense that I don't know what to do! . . . It was nice of you to take so much interest.' Under her signature, she wrote: 'Don't lead too fast a life in London, & above all don't have anything to do with "FASTY": she's dangerous.'[114] (Fasty was a nickname for Doris Gordon-Lennox.) To this the Prince replied that he was 'so happy that all anxiety and worry for you are over' and assured her that London life was dull 'with no fast little parties as you call them . . . I heard from "Fasty" yesterday who sent me her photos which she took at Glamis, & they are so good. She is not in London now, but I will keep your warning about her in mind!!!!'[115]

At the end of October, however, Lady Strathmore had a relapse and developed pleurisy. Once again, the burden of looking after both her mother and the household fell upon Elizabeth. She shouldered it. Lady Strathmore wrote to a friend after she had recovered, 'I can't tell you how wonderful my little Elizabeth has been all this time, looking after everybody & everything, in fact I have hardly been missed at all.'[116]

Inevitably it was a strain upon Elizabeth. 'My brain is a blank,' she wrote in one letter to the Prince.[117] On the advice of her mother's doctor she decided to take a break, and went to London. Prince Albert visited her after consulting a French therapist who claimed to be able to cure stammering by the use of will power and imagination.[118] She wrote to him afterwards, 'I was so interested to hear about the Frenchman – is your will power becoming intense? Next time I see you, you will probably have your will under such marvellous control, that having said to yourself "I don't know Elizabeth" – I shall receive a stony stare.'[119]

There was someone else she saw in London. 'I got off quite alright the other evening,' she wrote to Beryl after her return to Glamis, 'as James Stuart turned up and insisted on taking me to Euston, where he placed me in the train & stalked off! Rather funny.'[120] Elizabeth's comment suggests that all was not well between them. Stuart had just left Prince Albert's service; by his own account the job was neither well paid nor congenial enough for him to want to remain.[121]

Queen Mary had taken a kindly interest in Elizabeth and her family; Lord Strathmore sent her telegrams recounting his wife's progress and Elizabeth wrote to her. The Queen replied that she 'felt so deeply for you all during your time of anxiety, & shared your feelings to the full, for I have become much attached to your dearest Mother, especially since my delightful afternoon at Glamis'.[122] Now, in late November, although Lady Strathmore was improving, she was still too weak to leave her bed, and the Queen sent her a present of a basket for her letters.[123]

Elizabeth returned to her duties at Glamis, with little prospect of travelling south again before January when, she told the Prince, she would have to buy some clothes. 'What colours do you like? Most men like blue or black for ladies' dresses, both of which I look like nothing on earth in!'[124] In mid-December she was cross with herself because she had missed his birthday; she wrote to apologize and to wish him 'a very happy and successful 26th year'. It was impossible to buy presents in Glamis, she said, 'otherwise I should have bought a large and magnificent offering. The only thing one can buy are bull's eyes – very sticky and they won't travel!'[125]

Christmas at Glamis that year was muted. Lady Strathmore was still unwell and Elizabeth also spent much of the time in bed with flu. The Prince was, as usual, with his parents at York Cottage at Sandringham, and she wrote to him in pencil to thank him for 'the most darling little clock', a present perhaps inspired by her habitual tardiness. 'It really is too pretty for words, and besides being pretty is useful too. I am enchanted with it. Also that is an excellent photograph of you – I wish I had got something to send you too.'[126]

There was just one guest at Glamis over the New Year holiday – James Stuart.[127] He was saying goodbye. Early in 1922 he left for the United States, where he had been offered a job in the oil business through Sir Sidney Greville, a long-serving courtier whose sister was one of Queen Mary's ladies in waiting. Much later Stuart claimed that he and Elizabeth had been in love, and that Queen Mary had intervened to remove him as a rival to her son.[128] If Queen Mary was indeed involved in his departure, no evidence has been found in the Royal Archives. However, many years later King George VI told Princess Margaret that her mother had almost married James Stuart, but that he had gone abroad.[129] Later still, Queen Elizabeth herself acknowledged that her 'very serious' suitor had gone away to America.[130]

★

MEANWHILE PRINCESS MARY had become engaged to Viscount Lascelles;* Prince Albert had written to tell Elizabeth that they had 'fixed it up themselves, and are frightfully happy'.[131] The Princess invited Elizabeth to be one of her bridesmaids at the wedding in February 1922. She added, 'Bertie tells me you are coming south shortly and he is so looking forward to seeing you.'[132]

Elizabeth and the Prince saw each other on the weekend of 13–15 January at her godmother Mrs James's house, Coton, near Rugby, where they had both been invited to stay for the Atherstone Hunt Ball. Prince Albert drove her and Katie Hamilton to the ball. The party at Coton was 'quite good fun', he told his mother afterwards, without elaborating.[133] Queen Mary replied at once from York Cottage, 'I was longing to hear how Elizabeth had behaved & whether she is beginning to thaw or not! Your letter does not enlighten me on this point so I must have patience till we next meet.' She reminded her son that Lady Airlie was ready to assist in any way.[134]

In fact, as the Prince revealed to the Queen, he was 'rather depressed' about the weekend at Coton. The weather had been bad and everyone was cooped up in the house. He did not think Elizabeth was very well, as she had 'lost her good spirits after the first evening'. He had danced with her both nights 'and I think things were going better, but I would like to have a talk with you some time on your return on this subject. I am sure Lady Airlie could help a lot now.'[135] In a letter to the Prince of Wales, away on tour in India, he said he was making only very slow progress towards the engagement he hoped for.[136]

In early February Elizabeth's paternal grandmother† died, and the Prince sent his commiserations, hoping that this bereavement would not prevent her being a bridesmaid to his sister. She replied that, while Glamis would be filled with relations and the burial in the family cemetery would be sad, her death had been long expected.[137]

---

* Henry George Charles Lascelles (1882–1947), Viscount Lascelles, succeeded his father as seventh Earl of Harewood in 1929.

† Frances Dora, widow of the thirteenth Earl of Strathmore (1832–1922).

On 28 February there were large, enthusiastic crowds outside Westminster Abbey* for Princess Mary's wedding. Elizabeth thought her bridesmaid's dress – white satin and silver lace – was very pretty.[138] At the rehearsal she found it quite difficult to walk slowly and steadily in the high heels she had to wear. 'I am so afraid I shall appear intoxicated, which would be awful,' she wrote to the Prince.[139] In the event she managed her heels perfectly well, and afterwards she and the other bridesmaids lunched with members of the Royal Household and wedding guests at Buckingham Palace.† Years later her biographer Elizabeth Longford pointed out that this occasion gave her 'her first glimpse of what it was to participate in a royal public event. With her flair for happiness, she could not but find it enjoyable.'[140]

But this brief experience did not at once persuade her to change her mind about marrying into the Royal Family. On 7 March 1922 Prince Albert provoked another crisis in their relationship: he proposed to her again. She was apparently taken by surprise and once more she said no. She wrote to him next day from Bruton Street:

> Dear Prince Bertie,
>   I am so terribly sorry about what happened yesterday, & feel it is all my fault, as I ought to have known. Will you please forgive me? You are one of my best & most faithful friends, & have always been so nice to me – that makes it doubly worse. I am too miserable about it, and blame myself more than I can say. If you ever feel you want a talk about things in general – I hope you will come and see me, as I understand you know. I do wish this hadn't happened. Yours Elizabeth[141]

The same afternoon he replied that her letter had somewhat depressed him:

> I have been thinking over what happened yesterday all today & I feel that you must think so badly of me. For my sake please do

---

* The first royal wedding in the Abbey for 650 years was that of Princess Patricia of Connaught, King George V's cousin, to the Hon. Alexander Ramsay in 1919; it started a new and popular trend, and Princess Mary's wedding attracted even more attention because she was the King's only daughter and also the first of his children to follow their parents' decision in favour of marriage into British families.

† It is not true, as has been stated, that she sat next to the Duke of York at the wedding breakfast. This was held in a different room and was restricted to the Royal Family, royal guests and the bridegroom's family.

not make yourself miserable or worried about it, as I should never forgive myself. I was entirely in the wrong to bring up the question in the way I did without giving you any warning as to my intentions. Ever since last year I have always been hoping to get to know you better & to let you know my thoughts, but I see that I failed to enlighten you. How were you to guess what they were when we never really had any good talks like we did yesterday? I see it all now and blame myself entirely for what happened.

He took comfort in the fact that she said they could talk more about it. He seems to have felt that her refusal might not be final.

I thank you with all my heart for having said it. I am so so sorry for making you miserable, & it is far more to the point when I ask you to forgive me. Will you? Do please think over what I have told you in this letter & I think you will see how it is all my fault. When shall I have a hope of seeing you again as I feel we cannot leave things in this uncertain state. It is so bad & unsettling for us both, & whatever you decide will I know be best for both.[142]

A few days later she thanked him 'for your very nice letter – it relieved my mind tremendously in a way, and I do hope you are not worrying about it all any more'. She was off to Scotland, 'so we shall not meet for several weeks I expect. Please do try & forget about this, as I hate to think that you worry over it – things are hard for you anyway, and I can't bear to think that they are any harder through me . . . Au revoir – till I don't know when.'[143]

His immediate fear was that he was the reason for her sudden departure to Glamis. 'I do hope I was not the cause as that would be too sad for me.' He felt she did not want him to discuss matters any more, 'but I feel I must tell you that I have always cared for you & had the hope that you would one day care for me. Things were difficult for both of us weren't they from the start, & I understand from your letter that you want me to forget it. I have no other alternative I am afraid so I will try.' He thought that her mother had a right to be told what had happened. 'But I know you will keep it a secret from everyone else in this world as I shall.' He was unable to disguise his pain. 'This letter as you may imagine is one which I have found very difficult to write & I only hope that you will always look upon me as more than an ordinary friend. If you will do this I shall feel much happier after what has happened. Ever, Yours very sincerely, Albert.'[144]

As usual, Elizabeth replied as kindly as she could, telling the Prince that he wrote 'the nicest letters of anyone I know'. She agreed that it had been difficult for both of them,

> but especially for you, and thank you so much for being so nice about it. I do hope we can go on being friends, as it would be too sad if a happening like this should come between our friendship, and I don't see why it should, do you?
>
> I shall always be glad to see you if you ever feel like dropping in to tea, & having a talk. As I do understand you know, and when people are as good friends as you & I are – there is always a lot to talk about. I wish I could put into words what I feel about it all, & I think it is wonderful of you to have gone on caring – oh why didn't I guess. How silly I've been, and, as you say in your letter, of course I shall look on you as more than an ordinary friend.

She said that she had already told her mother of what had happened 'but nobody else in the world and never shall'.[145]

Her letter cheered him: 'You wrote too nicely to me, & I do feel now that you are not angry with me for what happened. So long as we can still be great friends that is all I was worrying about, & you say you hope we shall always be that & so do I. Your mother very kindly wrote to me about it all after what you had told her. I do hope she was not very upset.' With that, he changed the subject and talked of his beloved hunting, and of how sad it was that the season was nearly over.[146] He did not write again for three weeks.

★

IN THE AFTERMATH of the Prince's unexpected proposal, Elizabeth exchanged letters with James Stuart in New York. He was lonely and unhappy there – and he was jealous. He was particularly troubled by one remark in her letter to him. 'You say in it that you are returning to Glamis and that "The most extraordinary things have happened to me the last 3 weeks, so perhaps it's just as well that I should be."' He had spent most of the day worrying about what this meant; then, that evening, he had received a letter which told him 'that you and

Glenconner are seldom apart, so I suppose that it's that: or is it Michael? Not that it's any of my business but you know what a fool I am – I hope he's very nice. Well, well – It's a curious world. I am just about to destroy your letter as that paragraph upsets me too much, if I should read it again. Jealousy is a very bad trait, and I have always tried to get rid of it.' Here he broke off. 'Interval of ten minutes,' he wrote. 'I have just been controlling myself with a cigarette and feel better. After all, I want to do what I am doing and I am a dashed bit luckier than most people . . . In fact, "it's fair enough by me" as they say here – or I'm going to think so anyway . . . I am afraid this is rather a waily letter – but I hope not very unpleasant. Yours James.'[147] There is no reference to Prince Albert in the letter. Nor are its sentiments those of a man sent away against his will. But he makes no effort to conceal his feelings for Elizabeth.

The identity of 'Michael' is not clear; possibly it was Michael Biddulph, brother of Elizabeth's friend Adèle; but her letters at this time do not mention him. Christopher Glenconner,* however, was indeed a new recruit to the ranks of Elizabeth's suitors. A year older than Elizabeth and described as 'the most straightforward and sensible member of a wildly eccentric family',[148] he lived at Glen in Peebleshire and Wilsford in Wiltshire. There his mother Lady Glenconner, formerly Pamela Wyndham, one of the poetic and literary circle known as the Souls, created an aura of romance and mysticism which Elizabeth later recalled with pleasure. Lord Glenconner's friendship with Elizabeth probably began in early 1922. That they were 'seldom apart' was certainly an exaggeration, for she was at Glamis from early March until late May. But they exchanged letters. 'I have been having a wonderful soulful correspondence with Lord Glenconner!' Elizabeth reported to Beryl from Glamis in May. 'He does write most excellent letters, & <u>most</u> high brow – so funny.'[149] And perhaps filled with more longing than he revealed. But the letters do not survive.

*

THE PRINCE KEPT his second proposal secret from his parents to begin with. But in early May 1922 Queen Mary wrote to tell Lady Strathmore that she and the King were 'much disappointed that the little

---

* Christopher Tennant, second Baron Glenconner (1899–1983), married first, 1925, Pamela Winifred Paget; secondly, 1935, Elizabeth Harcourt Powell.

"romance" has come to an end as we should so much have liked the connection with your family. My son feels very sad about it but he is quite good and sensible and they are to remain friends. I hope you and E. will not reproach yourselves in any way, no one can help their feelings & it was far better to be honest. I am so sorry to hear that you are still so far from well ... With my love to you and E. and many regrets.'[150]

Both Elizabeth and her mother, still at Glamis, were ill again. Lady Strathmore had another operation on 7 May, when the surgeon discovered that an abscess had been causing her chronic raised temperature and poor health. After it was drained she made a good recovery. Meanwhile Elizabeth took to her bed with tonsillitis and a high temperature. She looked like 'a ghost, so white & thin', her mother wrote to May Elphinstone on 16 May;[151] and there was no prospect of her returning to London yet. A letter from Prince Albert in mid-April, saying he hoped she would come back south soon, remained unanswered for a month.

When she did reply, telling him that she was better and hoped to be 'hopping around in London Town very shortly', she kept to light-hearted talk of dinners and dances, slipping in almost casually the briefest of references to what had happened between them: 'Do you know the Queen wrote Mother a most charming letter, which was very nice of her indeed. I thought it was so kind of her.'[152] As far as she was concerned, there seems to have been no more question of a romance. Writing to her sister May she said, 'Yes, I did put an end to that affair you mentioned, last Feb: but did not tell anyone except Mother.'[153]

James Stuart wrote from the oilfields of Texas; she told Beryl, 'he says it's exactly like books there. Everybody packs a gun, & the Sheriff has got nine nicks in his for the 9 men he's killed. It must be very uncomfortable!'[154] At the end of May she received an injured letter from another admirer, George Gage, who seems to have understood that the intensity of his feelings for her was not reciprocated. 'My dear Elizabeth, You are awful & don't care how much you hurt the feelings of your friends if they don't amuse you for half a minute. You did hurt mine the other night & I don't pretend that I didn't mind.' But he went on to issue a humorous invitation to Firle in June, promising that 'the chaperonage system will be perfect & everything will be conducted (as it always is here) on the best Victorian lines.'[155]

In late May Elizabeth returned to London en route to Paris to stay with Diamond Hardinge again. This time she was reluctant to go, for there were friends to see and balls to attend in London after her long absence in Scotland. But Diamond had been ill, and Elizabeth did not want to disappoint her. Of this trip no account by Elizabeth herself survives; but her visit coincided with Christopher Glenconner's arrival in Paris. They had lunch together, and spent the afternoon at Versailles, where it rained heavily, as he recollected. He told her nine years later that he remembered every moment vividly, and that he had been deeply in love with her.[156]

Back in London, June and July were filled with a delightful whirl of dances, dinners, theatres, nightclubs and country weekends for Elizabeth and her friends – including Prince Albert. For the Prince there were also foundation stones to be laid, war memorials to be unveiled and meetings of charitable organizations to attend. There were two royal weddings – the marriage of King Alexander of Yugoslavia to Princess Marie of Romania, for which the Prince travelled to Belgrade in early June to represent his father; and that of his cousin Lord Louis Mountbatten to Edwina Ashley in mid-July. Then, on 25 July, he sailed to Dunkirk in a destroyer to lay the foundation stone of a memorial to the Dover Patrol.*

On the return journey a curious incident occurred. John Campbell Davidson,† a member of the Parliamentary delegation which had attended the ceremony in Dunkirk, was introduced by Louis Greig to the Prince and was left with him in the wardroom of the ship. Davidson later wrote an account of the meeting.

> I had not been in the Duke's presence more than a few minutes before I realised that he was not only worried, but genuinely unhappy. He seemed to have reached a crisis in his life, and

---

* The Dover Patrol, created in summer 1914, became a vital wartime command. It could call upon a motley array of sometimes obsolete cruisers, monitors, destroyers, armed trawlers, paddle minesweepers, armed yachts, motor launches and coastal motor boats, submarines, seaplanes, aeroplanes and airships. The Patrol's many tasks in the southern North Sea and the Dover Straits included escorting merchantmen and hospital and troop ships; laying sea-mines and sweeping up German mines; bombarding German military positions on the Belgian coast; and sinking U-boats.

† John Colin Campbell Davidson (1889–1970), at this time MP for Hemel Hempstead and Parliamentary Private Secretary to the Prime Minister. Created 1937 Viscount Davidson. Married 1919 Hon. Frances Joan Dickinson.

wanted someone to whom he could unburden himself without reserve. He dwelt upon the difficulties which surrounded a King's son in contrast with men like myself, who had always had greater freedom at school and University to make their own friends, and a wider circle to choose from. We discussed friendship, and the relative value of brains and character, and all the sort of things that young men do talk about in the abstract, when in reality they are very much concerned in the concrete.

He told me that sometimes the discipline and formality of the Court proved irksome, and I sensed that he was working up to something important. I felt moved with a great desire to help him if I could. He was so simple and frank and forthcoming.

Then, out it came. He declared that he was desperately in love, but that he was in despair for it seemed quite certain that he had lost the only woman he would ever marry. I told him that however black the situation looked, he must not give up hope; that my wife had refused me consistently before she finally said 'yes', and that like him, if she had persisted in her refusal, I would never have married anyone else.[157]

Davidson's personal experience probably explains why Greig had introduced him to the Prince and, perhaps, why the Prince confided in him. The conversation does seem to have helped embolden the Prince – he pursued his suit quietly and doggedly through the rest of 1922. He later described his tactic as 'playing the waiting game'.[158]

As it happened, the day after his conversation with Davidson, Elizabeth wrote to invite the Prince to Glamis. 'How sick I am of London!' she said. 'It is a very depressing sort of end-of-everything feeling, isn't it?' He should let her know when he was coming, 'so that I can collect a few charmers & Society Beauties for the same week'.[159]

For herself she had unwittingly collected another admirer in London: Archibald Clark Kerr,* a diplomat eighteen years older than herself whom she met at a party given by Lady Islington that summer while he was on leave from his post as senior adviser to Lord Allenby in Egypt. He later wrote that he found her 'wonderful, beautiful, and

---

* Archibald Clark Kerr (1882–1951), diplomat; served under Lord Allenby in Cairo 1922–5; British Minister to the Central Americas 1925, Chile 1928, Sweden 1931. Knighted 1935; Ambassador in Iraq 1935, Peking 1938, Moscow 1942, Washington 1946. Created Baron Inverchapel 1946. Married 1929 Maria Theresa Diaz Salas, daughter of a Chilean millionaire.

so gentle', and his letters to his mother and to friends show that he hoped to marry her.[160]

Elizabeth invited Clark Kerr to Glamis, but he felt that he had been 'dull and inarticulate' there. Nonetheless, 'If anything can be perfect it must be the Lyon family. I had come to think that the type was extinct. Thank God it isn't.'[161] He wrote her long entertaining letters and she remained on cordial terms with him. Her friendliness shows that apart from the spirited young admirers of her own age, she was also drawn to older, cultivated and witty men. Arthur Penn was one such; another was Jasper Ridley, a barrister by training who became a banker, and who was a discriminating collector of contemporary art. He was to become an adviser on her own art collection.* A third was Francis Godolphin D'Arcy Osborne,† a cousin of the Duke of Leeds and thus also of Dorothy, the wife of Elizabeth's eldest brother Patrick. Elizabeth seems to have met him first in 1919 or 1920, and they became lifelong friends, exchanging both jovial and serious letters. He remained one of the few people outside her family to whom she could express her feelings. In late October 1922 she wrote to him, 'You seem to have spent rather a pleasant autumn – I spent the time entirely at Glamis, entertaining a series of guests, some were nice and some were NOT.'[162]‡

The guests at Glamis had already included Lord Glenconner, George Gage, Prince Paul and Francis Doune, together with a succession of Elizabeth's girl friends. Before Prince Albert arrived, Elizabeth wrote to warn him that the partridge shooting would be poor because of the wet weather, but she was looking forward to seeing him. 'It is such ages since we met. I do hope you won't be terribly bored here. I noticed some old chickens flying quite high down at the farm the other day, we might have a chicken drive to vary the

---

* Jasper Ridley (1887–1951), second son of Sir Matthew Ridley (later Viscount Ridley), married 1911 Countess Nathalie Benckendorff. A member of the Contemporary Art Society, he later became chairman of the Trustees of the National Gallery and the British Museum, and also chairman of Coutts Bank.

† Francis Godolphin D'Arcy Osborne (1884–1964), great-great-grandson of fifth Duke of Leeds; Envoy Extraordinary and Minister Plenipotentiary, Washington DC, 1931–5; Ambassador to the Holy See 1936–47; succeeded his distant cousin, Lady Dorothy's brother John, eleventh Duke, as twelfth duke of Leeds 1963.

‡ One guest who had amused her was the American actor James K. Hackett, who had come to absorb the atmosphere of Glamis in the hope of improving his performances as Macbeth. She had never seen a man drink so much, she said.

monotony. Wouldn't that be fun?'[163] The 'charmers' and 'Society Beauties' she had assembled for him were 'Fasty' Doris, Bettine Malcolm,* and Rachel and Mary Cavendish.† Prince Paul returned for the week, and Chips Channon and Arthur Penn completed the party. Elizabeth's brothers Michael and David were there. And there was an extra guest: Lady Airlie.

The shooting was not good but Prince Albert reported to his mother, 'Lady Strathmore is so much better and is much stronger than she was, and does everything again now. We were not a large party but a happy one. The Lyon family were all so kind to me.'[164] He made no reference to Elizabeth. But his feelings for her were hard to disguise. Chips Channon later recalled, 'One rainy afternoon we were sitting about and I pretended that I could read cards, and I told Elizabeth Lyon's fortune and predicted a great and glamorous royal future. She laughed, for it was obvious that the Duke of York was much in love with her. As Queen she has several times reminded me of it. I remember the pipers playing in the candlelit dining-room, and the whole castle heavy with atmosphere, sinister, lugubrious, in spite of the gay young party.'[165]

John Stirton, the minister at Crathie, commented in his diary that the Prince had wanted to marry Elizabeth, 'but it is said (I do not believe this) she refuses to accept him as a husband. An understanding therefore has been made that he must not speak again on the subject. I am very sorry for him as Lady Elizabeth is the only girl the Duke has wished to marry. I do think he ought not to have gone to Glamis just now.'[166]

But the Duke knew what he was doing. On his return to London he carried out a small commission for Elizabeth: buying her some new gramophone records. These, she wrote, 'arrived in record time. (Oh, a joke, accident I promise).' She posted him 'two crackly sovereigns' by way of payment, which he sent back. She was particularly enjoying 'Stumbling', 'Limehouse Blues' and 'I'm Simply Mad about Harry', she said. He also sent her a photograph of himself and she told him she had put it up in her room.[167]

---

*   Bettine Malcolm (1899–1973), married in December 1922 Captain Henry Somerset, kinsman of tenth Duke of Beaufort; their son David succeeded as eleventh duke.

†   Lady Rachel Cavendish (1902–77), daughter of ninth Duke of Devonshire. Mary Cavendish (1903–94), first cousin of Rachel, married Lord Balniel in 1925, and became Countess of Crawford in 1940 when he succeeded his father as twenty-eighth earl of Crawford.

Prince Albert's unhappiness in love had at least one good effect: it brought him and his mother closer, and she wrote him an affectionate letter of praise in early October. He protested that he did not deserve all the nice things she said. 'But you have made me very happy telling me what you have, and I greatly appreciate it.'[168]

The Prince continued with a busy programme of public engagements throughout the autumn of 1922, and although he and Elizabeth wrote to each other, it was some time before they met again. In early November she went to stay for the first time at Holwick Lodge in County Durham, a Strathmore property which was usually let for the shooting. She wrote to tell the Prince that 'the family are amusing themselves by shooting at huge packs of grouse that fly over the butts at lightning speed! It is rather fun, and such lovely country . . . From the window where I am writing, I can see about 30 miles right down a wide valley – it is all nice & wild & lovely in the daytime. But nothing to do in the evenings, so I play the records you gave me.' She added that she was longing to hear about what he had been doing. 'So do come around one day.'[169]

'I do so want to see you as I have so much to tell you about what I have been doing & I am sure you have been doing a lot too,'[170] he wrote, in a letter which crossed with hers. He came to lunch at Bruton Street on 11 November, and Lord Strathmore invited him to shoot at St Paul's Walden for the weekend of 24 November. The Prince and Elizabeth had an enchanting time together. He wrote to her afterwards, 'Wonderful day, wonderful shoot & wonderful time. Of all the days' shooting I have ever had I can't remember any I have enjoyed more than last Saturday . . . It was so nice of you to spend all the afternoon with me that day. I am sure it spurred me on to greater efforts.'[171]

Elizabeth herself, however, was troubled that their friendship had given rise to gossip. She wrote to him of her concern, and he replied asking if he could come and see her to discuss it. 'I do not think really that people will start talking about us again as they must know by now what friends we are. But of course it is just as you wish & we can talk it over tomorrow.'[172] The weeks before Christmas were filled with invitations, and Elizabeth's anxieties centred on a house party to which she and the Prince had both been invited for the Pytchley Hunt Ball in January. She asked him, 'Do you think it will start all these horrible people talking again?'[173]

Gossip or no, the two dined in a party at Claridge's on 12 December before going to Lady Anne Cameron's dance, and the next evening they were together again at a dinner and dance given by Mrs Greville. Afterwards the Prince wrote to thank Elizabeth for being 'very kind to me ... in giving me so many dances & all the rest of it. I have never enjoyed an evening more, & I rather think, at least I hope, that you did too. I only wished that we had sat next to each other at dinner. That was a slight mistake on our hostess's part!! What do you think?'[174] They met again on 21 December when the Prince took Elizabeth, her sister-in-law Fenella and her brother David to dinner and the theatre. Then they parted for Christmas, she to St Paul's Walden and he to York Cottage at Sandringham.

By now Queen Mary was becoming concerned by the rumours about a relationship she thought had ended. The confidence which had lately existed between mother and son seems to have disappeared, for she now used Lady Airlie as her intermediary even with him. The burden of the messages transmitted by Lady Airlie was that Elizabeth should not attend the Pytchley Ball. She told Lady Strathmore that she had been asked to 'hint' that Elizabeth should stay away 'as it is perhaps wiser for the sake of the young man as your letter written early in this year made it clear that nothing further could come of the friendship, to the parents' very deep regret'.[175]

On Christmas Day Elizabeth wrote an unhappy letter to the Prince in which she said she understood his family's point of view and would not attend the ball. She did not want to behave badly towards him – 'you know that, don't you? I think it is so nice of you to be such a wonderful friend to me, and I don't want you to regret it ever ... It is all very sad, and must be so annoying to you. We've had such fun these last few weeks. I do hope you don't think I've behaved badly – I'm just beginning to wonder.' She was sorry to bore him with 'such a rambling and ill-expressed letter, but I felt I must tell you what I was going to do. Please tell me, have I done right? Yours in perplexity, Elizabeth.' Across the top of the last page she wrote, 'Perhaps you had better tear this up.'[176]

They were able to meet and discuss such irritating problems at another ball, at Holkham Hall near Sandringham, on 28 December. At 3.30 a.m., as soon as he got home to York Cottage, the Prince sat down to write to her. 'It is the limit the way other people mix themselves in things which do not concern them.' He urged her to go and see Lady Airlie, who had just written them a letter which does not survive but which appears to have encouraged them to resolve the situation.[177] He advised Elizabeth to be frank with Lady Airlie 'and tell her exactly what great friends we are; & I will do the same.'[178] He was angry and ready to confront his parents. Elizabeth however was cautious and anxious to avoid a fracas. She advised the Prince to do nothing until she had seen Lady Airlie.[179]

Elizabeth had not written to Beryl, who was away in Germany, for some time. But now, thanking her friend for a Christmas present, she confided, 'I don't seem to be able to like anybody enough to marry them! Isn't it odd? I love my friends but somehow can't do more, I daresay I shall end my days a spinster, & probably be much happier! However, one can't tell, can one?'[180]

The Prince returned to London on 2 January 1923. The next day he took Elizabeth to dinner at Claridge's and then to the theatre, with his equerry Captain Giles Sebright and Lady Anne Cameron. After the show they returned to Claridge's to dance. It must have been a happy evening because the Prince seems to have been emboldened, perhaps on the dance floor, to ask Elizabeth once again to marry him. The following day Elizabeth went to talk to Lady Airlie and then wrote to the Prince at length about his proposal:

It is so angelic of you to allow me plenty of time to think it over – I really do need it, as it takes so long to ponder these things, & this is so very important for us both. If in the end I come to the conclusion that it will be alright, well & good, but Prince Bertie, if I feel that I can't (& I will not marry you unless I am quite certain, for your own sake) then I shall go away & try not to see you again. I feel there are only those two alternatives – either it will all come right, which I hope it will, or the other. I do hope you understand my feelings – I am more than grateful to you for not hurrying me, and I am determined not to spoil your life by just drifting on like this. You are so thoughtful for me always – oh I do want to do what is right for you. I have thought of nothing else all today – last night seems like a dream. Was it? It seems so now.

Perhaps you had better not say anything just yet to <u>anybody</u> – what do you think? Do as you think best.[181]

At this complicated, emotional moment of her life, she took up her diary again.* She wrote, 'I went to see Lady Airlie – talked a long time & explained everything. She was so nice. I ma tsom dexelprep.'[182] Elizabeth used mirror writing several times in her diaries at this time for her most private thoughts.

She also recorded that George Gage had been to lunch with her, and had 'bullied' her into going down to Firle next day for the Lewes Hunt Ball. On Friday 5 January she woke feeling tired, and wrote in her diary, 'Ma gnikniht oot hcum. I hsiw I wenk.' Troubled, she set off for Firle. Someone brought evening papers from London and she noted in her diary that they reported 'that I was engaged to the Prince of Wales – not mentioning my name, but quite obvious enough. <u>Too</u> stupid & unfounded.'[183] The report in the *Daily Star* declared, 'Scottish Bride for Prince of Wales; Heir to the throne to wed Peer's daughter; an Official Announcement imminent . . . One of the closest friends of Princess Mary'. The paper's description of the 'young Scottish lady of noble birth . . . daughter of a well-known Scottish peer, who is owner of castles both north and south of the Tweed' could fit no one else.[184]

Chips Channon, a member of the house party, thought that she seemed perturbed. 'The evening papers have announced her engagement to the Prince of Wales. So we all bowed and bobbed and teased her, calling her "Ma'am": I am not sure that she enjoyed it. It couldn't be true, but how delighted everyone would be! She certainly has something on her mind . . . She is more gentle, loving and exquisite than any woman alive, but this evening I thought her unhappy and distraite. I longed to tell her that I would die for her, though I am not in love with her.'[185] Even so, according to her own account she enjoyed the evening. 'Great fun. Danced with some very nice old friends – John Bevan, Tom Bevan, Ian Melville, Mr Wethered, besides our party. Danced till nearly 4! Home 4.30. Ate biscuits & sherry. Bed 5.'[186]

A few hours later she arose, returned to London and drove down to St Paul's Walden with her parents. After a quiet weekend, breakfast on Monday brought 'a sheaf of cuttings about my rumoured engage-

---

* Apart from her childhood diaries, her first surviving diary is that of 1923.

ment to the Prince of Wales. Too silly.'[187] She wrote to Prince Albert to thank him for his latest letter; she repeated that the evening at Claridge's seemed like a dream to her. 'I think the great thing is to be with the person, or it all seems too unreal – do you feel that at all?' She asked if he had seen the stories about her and the Prince of Wales. 'It's too extraordinary, why can't they leave one alone? And in this case, it was so utterly absurd. I'm so sleepy, I must go to bed – thank you again so [underlined four times] much for your letter. God Bless you, Yours Elizabeth.'[188]

She went to another ball, this time at Longleat, for her friend Lady Mary Thynne,* daughter of the Marquess of Bath. Back in London on 11 January, Doris Gordon-Lennox came to lunch and they had a long talk. The Prince then arrived for tea and they talked until 7.30, which led to another cryptic entry in her diary. 'I ma yrev deirrow oot.'[189]

By now the King and Queen had been made aware that their son was still pursuing Elizabeth and she was resisting him. They were not pleased. The Queen wrote to Lady Airlie on 9 January thanking her for her help 'in this tiresome matter. The King & I quite understand from yr & Com: Greig's letters what is going on. I confess now we hope nothing will come of it as we both feel ruffled at E's behaviour!'[190] Her own family was concerned too; she acknowledged later that one of her brothers said to her, 'Look here. You know you must either say yes or no. It's not fair.' 'I think he was right,' she said. 'It's a good thing having brothers.'[191]

The Prince felt that this was the moment to tell his parents what was really happening. On Friday 12 January he wrote to his mother at Sandringham, saying he hoped she and his father would not think badly of him for having left them with the impression that it was all over between him and Elizabeth. In the last two months 'a distinct change' had come over her and he had seen a good deal of her 'in a quiet way', and she had been charming to him 'in every way'. He said that on his return from Sandringham at the New Year he had told Elizabeth how he felt and she had asked for time to think over what he had said. If her mother gave him permission, he was intending to go to St Paul's Walden at once; Elizabeth had promised him 'a definite

---

* Lady Mary Thynne (1903–74) married in 1921 third Baron Nunburnholme (divorced 1947). She was lady in waiting to Queen Elizabeth 1937–47; in 1947 she married Sir Ulick Alexander, Keeper of the Privy Purse to King George VI.

answer one way or the other' on Saturday. 'This is all very difficult to write to you darling Mama, but I know that you and Papa will give me your blessing if this all comes right & I shall be very happy.' He knew it had all taken a very long time but he was certain that he had been right 'to play the waiting game' because 'I know she would have said no, had I pressed her for an answer before now.'

He was still waiting for Lady Strathmore's response. 'I am sending this by messenger if I know I am going down to her family & will send you a telegram at once; if her answer is as I hope it will be, in 3 words "All right. Bertie." Not another soul will know what has happened until I hear from you & I will let you know where I am.' As he was finishing this letter, he heard that he was indeed invited to St Paul's Walden. 'So I do hope you will wish me luck. I am very very excited about it all. Best love to you darling Mama, I remain Ever Your very devoted boy Bertie.'[192]

While the Prince had been waiting and writing at Buckingham Palace, Elizabeth awoke in Bruton Street feeling 'very tired. Up by 11. Doris came round & talked till 12.30 . . . I sat before the fire in a stupor till 1.30. Dashed off to be photographed for Vogue.' Back at the house she telephoned the Prince on her father's behalf – 'he was out, so left a message to bring guns . . . Home ¼ to 6. Prince Bertie called for me at 6 & we motored down to St Paul's Walden.'[193]

There has till now been some uncertainty about just when Elizabeth finally accepted the Prince. Records in the Royal Archives and at Glamis tell a coherent story of the weekend. According to her diary, on the morning of Saturday 13 January she had 'breakie' at 10.30 and then went for a walk with the Prince. After lunch they both went to saw wood with her father. 'Prince Bertie sawed hard. Talked after tea for hours – dediced ot tiaw a elttil – epoh I ma ton gnivaheb yldab.'[194] So, on Saturday night, the Prince once again went to bed uncertain.

On Sunday morning after breakfast she sat and talked with the Prince until 12.30 '& then went for a walk in the enchanted wood. Long walk after lunch & long talks after tea & dinner.' She did not record it in her diary, but late that evening she did finally accept his proposal of marriage. Lady Stathmore's account, written to her daughter May, put it like this: 'He came down to St. P.W. suddenly on Friday, & proposed continuously until Sunday night, when she said Yes at 11.30!! My head is completely bewildered, as all those days E was hesitating & miserable, but now she is absolutely happy – & he is radiant.'[195]

On Monday morning the happy Prince drove Elizabeth up to London and dropped her at Bruton Street. Later he took her to lunch with Princess Mary and Lord Lascelles at Chesterfield House. The Prince of Wales came to congratulate them and then escorted her home while Prince Albert set off with Louis Greig to Sandringham to tell his parents. He appears not to have sent the agreed telegram. The King recorded in his diary, 'Bertie with Greig arrived after tea and informed us that he was engaged to Elizabeth Bowes Lyon, to which we gladly gave our consent. I trust they will be very happy.' The Queen was less reserved. 'We are delighted and he looks beaming. We sent off telegrams, wrote letters & were very busy.'[196]

The same was true of Elizabeth. At home in Bruton Street with her mother, she wrote 'lots' of letters, including one to her friend Arthur Penn. 'I must tell you, I am going to marry Prince Bertie – I do hope you like him – I feel terrified now I've done it – in fact no one is more surprised than me. Arthur, you have been my best friend for years please please don't cast me off as one now, will you?'[197] She went out to tell Lady Nina Balfour and Lady Airlie. Back home she wrote more letters. Then the news was released from Sandringham. 'The telephone rang the whole evening – hundreds of reporters clamouring! Last day of peace I suppose! Bed 11.'[198]

CHAPTER FOUR

A ROYAL WEDDING

1923

'You are perfectly safe in the hands of a Scots lassie'

ON TUESDAY 16 January 1923 the papers were filled with news of the engagement.* Elizabeth read them in bed in Bruton Street. 'Great headlines & lots of rot!' she wrote in her diary. 'Telegrams poured in all day, letters & reporters tumbling over each other.'[1]

The King and Queen both wrote at once to their future daughter-in-law. The King told her that he was delighted she was to become a member of his family. Bertie, he wrote, was 'radiant with happiness & I most gladly give my consent to your marriage with him. I know you will do all you can to help him in his many duties . . . God bless you my dear Elizabeth.'[2] The Queen wrote, 'The King and I are delighted to welcome you as our future daughter in law and we send you our warmest congratulations. The news has come as a great surprise and we feel very much excited!' She invited Elizabeth and her parents to Sandringham the following weekend and promised a warm welcome. 'I hope you will look on me as a "second mother" and that we shall become great friends. May God bless you both, my beloved children, is the heartfelt prayer of your loving future mother in law, Mary R.'[3] To Lady Strathmore, the Queen wrote how delighted she and the

---

* The *Dundee Advertiser* even claimed prior knowledge: 'Today's announcement of the betrothal of the Duke of York and Lady Elizabeth Bowes Lyon, youngest daughter of the Earl of Strathmore, will be received with great gratification throughout the Kingdom and with very special emotions of pleasure in Forfarshire. But, in Forfarshire, at any rate, the news will contain little of the element of surprise. Rumour, which does not always lie, has prepared the public to hear that a very charming romance was maturing which would link the Royal House with the ancient and historic family of romantic Glamis. It is just the kind of wedding which the British public would like – a wedding of free choice yet in every way charmingly right. The Duke, if nobody else, has reason to thank his stars that the war has been fought. Otherwise a dread convention of pre-war Royalty might have sent him to meet his fate in Germany instead of Strathmore.' (16 January 1923)

King were that Bertie's 'great wish' had come true '& that he is really engaged to dearest Elizabeth'.[4]

Lady Strathmore replied thanking the Queen 'many times' for her most kind letter. She was sure that Prince Bertie would make Elizabeth happy and was 'quite certain that she will make him the best & most loving of wives, & a very loyal & affectionate child to Your Majesty'.[5]

The Prince was overjoyed by everything. He thanked his mother for being so charming about his engagement. 'I am very very happy & I can only hope that Elizabeth feels the same as I do ... She was delighted with your letters, though feels rather shy about how to answer them.'[6] In the event she did well, writing to the King, 'I am so grateful to Your Majesty for welcoming me so kindly as a future member of your family and I only hope that I shall be able to help Bertie in all his many duties, and in many other ways also.'[7] To the Queen she wrote, 'my greatest wish is to be a real daughter to Your Majesty. I shall look forward intensely to my visit to Sandringham on Saturday, and I do hope you will think I shall make Bertie a good wife, we are both so happy, and it is all wonderful.'[8]

On Tuesday the Prince returned from Sandringham for lunch at Bruton Street, and afterwards they faced a crowd of photographers and well-wishers when they drove off to the Palace together for the first time. There they chose the engagement ring from a selection brought by the jeweller Bert of Vigo Street: it was a large sapphire flanked by diamonds in a platinum setting.

Back at Bruton Street, Elizabeth made a mistake. She talked to two Scottish reporters.* And she also saw another journalist, 'the most fearful bounder of the gentleman class', as Lady Strathmore described him, 'whom Father had been much too kind to'.[9] This was Charles Graves, brother of the writer Robert Graves and reporter for the London *Evening News*. He had at first driven down to St Paul's Walden, where, stealing a march on the newsmen waiting outside the house, he simply rang the doorbell and produced his personal visiting card. The affable Lord Strathmore apologized for his daughter's absence and gave him a letter of introduction to her. Armed with this and seated in a large Daimler provided by his newspaper, Graves was able to bypass crowds, rival reporters and police in Bruton Street, and to gain

* One of these may have been from the *Glasgow Herald*, which published a well-informed article next day.

admittance to the house. His interview, describing Elizabeth seated at a table stacked with telegrams, 'a charming picture of English girlhood, in a simple dark-blue morning dress edged with fur', her 'brilliant eyes . . . alight with happiness as she talked of the goodwill that had been shown her by high and low',[10] appeared on the front page of the *Evening News* and was picked up by the daily newspapers next day. Graves claimed in his memoirs that pressure was brought to bear on Elizabeth 'by royal circles' to deny the interview, which she refused to do.[11] This may not be strictly true – Queen Mary, for example, simply commented, 'How tiresome the newspaper people have been interviewing poor E., such a shame,'[12] and Elizabeth herself, to judge from her diary, was both thrilled and appalled by the press interest. But whether as a result of a royal warning or her own decision there were no more interviews.*

Wednesday was another day of newspaper stories and the constant delivery of sacks of letters, scores of telegrams. Several of her girl friends – Betty Cator, Doris Gordon-Lennox and Diamond Hardinge – came to see her. Christopher Glenconner dropped in too. Elizabeth and Doris slipped out for a walk in what must have been for once welcome fog: 'Talked hard – she is so pleased.' The Prince went hunting during the day but came to dinner and they talked till midnight. Thursday was the same, with hundreds more letters and telegrams, and she posed for photographers for an hour. 'When we went out at 4, there was a large crowd – most embarrassing.' That evening the Prince had to go to an Industrial Welfare Society dinner, but he came around to Bruton Street afterwards to see her. 'Talked nonsense till 12!'[13]

The Prince of Wales sent Elizabeth a warm letter of congratulation. 'I'm so glad & I do so hope you will both be very very happy.'[14] Arthur Penn wrote with emotion to her and she replied at once that his letter was 'far the nicest I've had yet . . . It was all so surprising and I am very pleased with being engaged!'[15] Penn wrote also to Lady Strathmore and she thanked him, praising his understanding of Eliza-

---

* A journalist on the *Daily Sketch* wrote on 19 January 1923: 'The interviews granted to the Press, for which, let me add, both Press and public are duly grateful, by Lady Elizabeth Bowes Lyon are surely without precedent. Never before has the bride-to-be of a prince of the blood-royal established such a link between the teeming millions and the private affairs of the exalted few. But I shouldn't be at all surprised to find a complete cessation of these interviews in the very near future.'

beth's character. 'She is such a perfect being in every way that I am naturally very anxious about her future, because outside, or rather inside that bright character is a terribly acute <u>sensitiveness</u>, which makes life much more difficult for her. However Prince Bertie simply adores her, and I think grasps her true worth – although I think he will have to grow a little older to fully appreciate her character.'[16]

In reply to D'Arcy Osborne's congratulations, Elizabeth wrote, 'You must come round and "'ave one" soon, you have no idea how tiring it is being engaged! I am quite gaga already!!'[17] On Friday 19 January they were again swamped with letters which she endeavoured to go through with the help of a secretary, Norah Chard, enlisted by Louis Greig. After lunch she and the Duke drove to Richmond Park to look at the garden of White Lodge, the house the King and Queen were planning to let them have. Once again, they talked long into the evening.[18]

*

ON SATURDAY MORNING she had to prepare herself for her first formal meeting with her future parents-in-law. She came downstairs at 11 o'clock, and then she and the Duke set off in his car to Liverpool Street station. Her parents followed in the Daimler. 'We got to Liverpool St in about 10 minutes. Vast crowd there, & hundreds of photographers.'[19] Together with the Duke and her parents, she journeyed in a special carriage attached to the 11.50 train to Wolferton, the station which served Sandringham. A cold lunch was served en route.

King George VI's biographer, John Wheeler-Bennett, commented decades later that her first meeting with the King and Queen as her future parents-in-law was 'an ordeal not to be underestimated but Lady Elizabeth came through with flying colours'.[20] The King and Queen were awaiting them at York Cottage. Both immediately thought Elizabeth pretty and charming; the King wrote in his diary, 'Bertie is a very lucky fellow,' and the Queen noted that she was 'engaging & natural', adding next day, 'I am much taken with Elizabeth.'[21] They took her and her parents straight to Sandringham House for tea with Queen Alexandra. Many years later Elizabeth recalled that the Queen 'looked beautiful in her old age, and tho' practically stone deaf, managed with those Danish gestures to convey quite a lot!'[22] Also there to examine her were four more royal ladies: Queen Alexandra's youngest daughter Queen Maud of Norway, her sister the Empress Marie Feodorovna of Russia, mother of Tsar Nicholas II, and Queen Alexandra's eldest daughter Princess Louise, Duchess of Fife, with her daughter Princess Maud. After tea she was taken upstairs to meet Princess Victoria, Queen Alexandra's second daughter, who was ill.

Elizabeth enchanted them all and Queen Mary thought it was 'a very happy cheerful party'.[23] When they returned to York Cottage Elizabeth and the Duke spent much of the rest of the weekend reading through more piles of letters, and writing replies to their friends, relations and well-wishers. To Lady Leicester, a neighbour at Holkham, the Prince wrote, 'I am very very happy to know that my dream of some years has come true, & that the most wonderful person in the world is going to be my wife.'[24]

Elizabeth told her sister May that she was 'almost gaga with writing'. She said that she had just been through 'the most ghastly ordeal of going to tea with Queen A and all the old ladies. They were all too angelic to me, but it is a strain! The King & Queen are both so charming to me, but it's most terrifying! . . . I really feel so happy, it's so surprising, I never thought I'd say yes.'[25] To Beryl Poignand she wrote, 'I've had a ghastly time this week with reporters & photographers curse them, but hope they will very soon get tired of us.' Meeting all the relations had not been easy. 'They have all been so very kind & charming, but I'm feeling utterly exhausted.' She had already received letters from two of the former patients at Glamis, Ernest Pearce and Norman Jepson* – 'such delicious letters. I was so pleased.' After exclaiming, 'I am so happy, & most surprised, as I never thought I'd marry him!!!' she added, 'I am so tired already – I think I shall probably die long before I get married. How delighted the papers would be – after the ROMANCE the TRAGEDY! What ho. Best love, I've got at least 500 letters to write.'[26]

Mike, her wittiest brother, wondered what the weekend at Sandringham was like. 'I do hope Father is behaving nicely & not pouring his cocoa backwards and forwards in four cups & two tumblers under the Queen's nose at breakfast . . . Well, what ho Cheerie ho, What ho what! Your loving Mike.' In a postscript, he asked, 'Have you written to James? I think you ought to. Poor James! He will be angry, won't

---

* Lance Corporal Norman Jepson had written a sixteen-verse 'Ode to Glamis' in Elizabeth's autograph book, singing her praises as 'a maiden, charming and rare'.

he?'[27] James Stuart had indeed heard the news; he sent a telegram of congratulations from New York.[28] George Gage's disappointment was acute, but he admitted, 'You ought to be a princess – you are one naturally.' He asked for her photograph.[29] From Cairo came a letter from Archie Clark Kerr, who said that he was speechless with envy but sent her every possible kind wish.* The Prince, he thought, 'is the luckiest person in the world to have for his own your happiness, your goodness, your beauty, your serenity, your everything that makes you what you are.'[30]

*

BY SUNDAY NIGHT the atmosphere at York Cottage was more relaxed. The Hardinges – Elizabeth's friend Helen and her husband Alec, the King's Assistant Private Secretary – came to dinner, and afterwards, watching the King and Prince Albert playing billiards, Elizabeth and Helen 'sat on hot water pipes & talked'.[31]

On Monday 22 January, the Prince and Elizabeth, with the Strathmores, left Norfolk by train from Wolferton, in the same private carriage. At Liverpool Street, there was another large, friendly crowd to greet them. He returned to Buckingham Palace, she to Bruton Street. At the Palace, the Prince immediately wrote to his mother thanking her for being so charming to Elizabeth.[32] The Queen replied, 'You ask what Papa & I think of Elizabeth, well we are simply enchanted with her & think her too dear & attractive for words & you have made a wonderful choice.'[33] In the King's eyes she possessed the added advantage of being 'so unlike some of the modern girls', and she would be 'a great addition to our family circle'.[34] To Lady Strathmore, Queen Mary wrote that the weekend had given her and the King 'the greatest happiness and it was such a joy to see the radiant faces of "our children". We are simply enchanted with your darling little Elizabeth and one and all here rave about her.'[35]

That afternoon the Prince and his fiancée took tea with Princess Mary. Back home, Elizabeth found that her decision was proving

---

* Many years later, in a letter to David Bowes Lyon, Clark Kerr asked him 'to tell me how the devil you knew that I loved your sister so much. It is quite true. I did . . . I didn't tell anyone and I am sure that she didn't, for she was quite determined that I should not tell her either! I know that it took me seven years to get over it, if ever I really did.' (10 February 1944, Bowes Lyon Papers, SPW)

contagious. 'Doris came in – she is engaged to Clare Vyner.* I am so glad.'[36] That was only the start of it. A few days later Diamond Hardinge announced that she was engaged – to Bobby Abercromby.†

Next day, 23 January, the betrothed couple went with Lord Farquhar to inspect White Lodge. Farquhar,‡ a friend of the King and until recently Lord Steward, had leased the house from the Crown since 1909, and now relinquished it for them. It had been Queen Mary's family home before her marriage, and she liked the idea of her son and his wife taking it over.[37] Situated in the middle of Richmond Park, White Lodge was built by King George II between 1727 and 1729 'as a place of refreshment after the fatigues of the chace'. Queen Caroline, his wife, decided to live in it; later their daughter Princess Amelia was made Ranger of the Park and she took over the house and extended it.[38] 'We went all over the house. Charming place,' Elizabeth commented in her diary.[39] 'I was simply enchanted by it all,' she wrote to the Queen. 'There is nowhere I should like to live in more, and I have fallen in love with it.'[40] She did not remain enamoured for very long.

The rest of the week was spent dealing with the continuing deluge of letters, seeing Diamond Hardinge, Arthur Penn, Freddy Dalrymple Hamilton and other friends, choosing new notepaper for herself, visiting her dressmaker, Madame Handley Seymour, for new clothes, dining at Claridge's with the Duke and friends, and going with May and David to see a revue, *The Co-Optimists*§ – to find that a verse about her and the Duke had been added to one of the songs in the show. She also paid a visit to her doctor, Dr Irwin Moore, to have her throat treated. 'It makes one feel awfully tired.'[41] The treatment for tonsillitis, from which she suffered frequently, could be harsh in those days: she described it as having her throat 'burnt'. She had eight more

---

* Lieutenant Commander Clare George Vyner (1894–1989) of Fountains Abbey and Studley Royal.

† Major Robert Alexander Abercromby MC (1895–1972), later ninth Baronet.

‡ Horace, first Earl Farquhar (1844–1923), Master of the Household to Edward VII 1901–7; Lord Steward to George V 1915–22; friend of both Kings. He had a house in Grosvenor Square as well as White Lodge, and Castle Rising, near Sandringham, which King George V, who had leased the house and its shooting, sub-let to him.

§ The revue, originally devised by Davey Burnaby, ran for 500 performances from June 1921 at the Royalty Theatre in London. It included songs by Irving Berlin, and among the cast was Stanley Holloway.

weekly sessions until the doctor pronounced her throat better in early April.

On 25 January the Prince took the night train to Glasgow for two days of official visits. Released by their engagement from the conventions of formality, he and Elizabeth wrote to each other with a new tenderness. 'My dear Darling, I am just writing you a very little letter,' she began. 'I shall be thinking about you when you get this, & hoping that everything will go off wonderfully well. I am quite sure it will. Also, I might add that I do [underlined several times] love you Bertie, & feel certain that I shall more & more. I shall miss you terribly. You are such an Angel to me. Goodbye till Sunday – may it come quickly. From your always & forever loving E.'[42]

This letter crossed with one written by the Duke in pencil on the train.

My own little darling one,

How I hated leaving you this evening after our delightful little tete a tete dinner . . . This is my first letter to you since you made me such a very happy person that Sunday at St Paul's Walden & you don't know what a wonderful difference it has made to me darling, in all ways. I think I must have always loved you darling but could never make you realise it without telling you actually that I did & thank God I told you at the right moment.

As soon as he reached Scotland, he wrote again in ink, 'My darling, I have just arrived safely & am told a letter will reach you by the morning. I wrote you a line in the train in pencil which goes as well, though I know you don't like pencil letters . . . I feel it terribly to be parted from you for so long darling.'[43]

By the weekend, when she drove with her mother and her sister May to St Paul's Walden, the excitement had taken its toll. 'Felt very tired & rather depressed through feeling so tired,' she wrote in her diary.[44] She spent Sunday morning in bed; the Duke arrived at lunchtime, in a new car. That evening they danced a little and talked a lot.

They returned to York Cottage on Monday 29 January to spend the week with the King and Queen. The days that followed were calm and predictable, as the King liked them to be, his future daughter-in-law absorbed into the routine without further ado. The men went shooting in the morning; the ladies joined them for lunch. The King wrote to his son Prince George of Elizabeth: 'The more I see of her the more I like her.'[45]

There were two more visits to the old ladies at Sandringham House – 'Everybody as old as the hills!'[46] wrote Elizabeth – a trip to Newmarket to see the King's horses, lunch and a walk round the gardens at Holkham. The evenings were not lively. In other company she would certainly have preferred to dance to the gramophone, play games or sing, but she had evidently been advised to bring some kind of 'work' with her. 'Knitted my blue thing after [dinner] until nearly 11,' she noted in her diary on the first evening; and knit she did, for two more evenings. Her lack of skill at knitting socks later became a joke she shared with the King. Throughout the week, she and the Duke continued to reply to letters and to thank people for the gifts they had received.

The Duke wrote an affectionate letter to his future mother-in-law to tell her how very happy he was that Elizabeth was to be his wife.

> I feel it must have come through all your great kindness to me during the last 3 years, when you were angelic enough to let me come to Glamis, St Paul's Walden & Bruton Street after all the difficulties which seemed invariably to come up year after year. Elizabeth has always been angelic to me ever since I first knew her in 1920, & even after the various vicissitudes she was always the same wonderful friend to me. And now it has all changed into something much more wonderful, and I only hope that I am worthy of her great love. I can assure you that I will do my utmost to make her happy all our lives.[47]

Lady Strathmore responded equally warmly. 'All I ask & pray for, is that she sh^ld be happy, & this I feel she will be with your love surrounding her. Dear Bertie you have been so kind to me too, that I know, that tho' I must in a sense lose E. I am gaining a son who will always be very dear to me.'[48]

To Mabell Airlie the Duke wrote joyously, 'How can I thank you enough for your most charming letter to me about the wonderful happenings in my life which have come to pass, & my one dream which has at last been realized. It all seems so marvellous to me & for me to know that my darling Elizabeth will one day be my wife. We are both very very happy & I am sure we shall always be.' Her earlier letter after Christmas, he said, had been 'an inspiration' to them. 'It only wanted very little to make us both make up our minds, and I am sure it was your words that did it . . . we can only bless you for what you did.'[49]

Elizabeth wrote again to Beryl Poignand, saying that she had had a 'delicious and restful week' in Norfolk. 'It is a bit of a strain staying with one's future in-laws, whoever they are. Mine have been all too angelic to me, I must say.'[50]

*

ON 6 FEBRUARY James Stuart, who had just returned from New York, came to call. He was very depressed, Elizabeth thought, to find all his friends 'engaged & scattered'. She recorded in her diary, 'He is just the same – Very slow!'[51] This private comment reveals, perhaps, that she had no regrets about him.

Later that week she had a difficult day, driving with the Queen, the Duke and Louis Greig to White Lodge to go over the house again. Queen Mary loved the house as she knew it and considered that it was 'in excellent order'.[52] It was not easy for a young bride to suggest changes.[53] After touring the upper floors for two hours they had a picnic lunch; then they descended to the basement, whereupon Sir John Baird, the First Commissioner of Works, arrived with the architects and they had to go all around the house again. It was exhausting.[54]

But over the next few days a brief escape into the company of her own family and friends brought relief. With 'les frères Stuart', James and Francis, and her brother Mike, she drove to Oxford to see David, stopping in Henley for a cherry brandy. After lunch and a walk at Magdalen, she drove for some of the way home; they stopped at Maidenhead and took tea at Skindles Hotel on the Thames – 'lovely day'. That evening, however, she wrote in her diary, 'Leef rehtar desserped.' It was, perhaps, the painful recognition that she would soon have to put such carefree days behind her.[55] That weekend was easier, because she and her fiancé could be with her parents at St Paul's Walden. They relaxed. After he left her to return to London alone on Sunday 11 February, the Prince wrote to say, 'I loved the weekend with you & hated leaving you this evening, just a month tonight isn't it darling when you told me you loved me. What a day that was for me!!! & for you too.'[56]

Her time was filled now. She sat for the portraitist John Singer

Sargent so that he could sketch her in charcoal, for Prince Paul's wedding present to them;* she was also sitting to L. F. Roslyn† for a bust. She visited White Lodge (or 'Whiters' as she called it) again, with 'about twelve architects, plumbers etc'. She was taken to meet members of the wider Royal Family. On 17 February she and her mother went to 'Buck House' (another nickname she had begun to use) where, in a gesture symbolic of the importance of precedent in the world Elizabeth was about to enter, Queen Mary gave her 'some wonderful lace, in the same room that Queen Victoria gave her presents in'. She went to Thomas Goode's, one of London's best glass and porcelain shops, with the Duke to choose glass, and to Zyrot, a fashionable milliner, to choose hats: 'Such fun! Also country suits!' She saw her doctor for further attention to her throat. Then there were constant visitors to be entertained – and all the time there was the problem of more photographers, more crowds. Thus on 23 February she recorded in her diary that 'a horrible photographer' had been lying in wait for her when she went for a sitting to Mabel Hankey, the miniaturist.‡ 'So a crowd collected. Such a nuisance.'⁵⁷

Everyone wanted to meet her, or to reaffirm acquaintanceship. But although she continued to see her friends, she was already expected to take part in some of the formal life of the Royal Family. On 21 February Elizabeth's name appeared for the first time in the Court Circular as a member of the royal party at a public event, when the King and Queen took her and the Duke to the Shire Horse Society's annual show at the Royal Agricultural Hall in Islington. On Monday 5 March, at Buckingham Palace, she had her first experience of a royal ritual, standing with the Duke beside the King and Queen while

---

* John Singer Sargent (1856–1925) drew her in a single two-hour sitting on 17 February; she commented in her diary: 'simply marvellous'. He did another charcoal portrait of her on 2 March. One of the two portraits, a profile, belonged to Lady Strathmore before passing into Queen Elizabeth's collection. Sargent also drew Prince Albert's portrait, commissioned by the American Ambassador, George Harvey, as his wedding present to the couple. (Susan Owens, *Watercolours and Drawings from the Collection of Queen Elizabeth The Queen Mother*, pp. 66–9)

† Louis Frederick Roslyn (1878–1940). The bust is now at Clarence House (RCIN 100975), and is illustrated in John Cornforth, *Queen Elizabeth The Queen Mother at Clarence House*, p. 118.

‡ This was for the Countess of Strathmore's present to her future son-in-law, a miniature framed in diamonds (RCIN 422497). Mabel Hankey also painted a charming watercolour portrait of Lady Strathmore in 1923, which was given to Elizabeth as a wedding present (RCIN 453428). She had painted Elizabeth as a child in 1907 (RCIN 453421). (Owens, *Watercolours and Drawings from the Collection of Queen Elizabeth The Queen Mother*, pp. 64, 62)

'privileged bodies' read addresses of congratulation on their engagement. This was the custom by which certain institutions, for example
Oxford and Cambridge Universities, the Corporations of London and
Edinburgh, the Church of England and the Free Churches, traditionally
present loyal addresses to the sovereign in person. 'Some very funny,'
she remarked.[58]

A week later she and Lady Strathmore took the night train to
Scotland. 'I love Glamis,' she wrote to the Duke. 'When I arrived this
morning the sun was just rising over the Sidlaw hills, and made the
snow on the Grampians look pink & heavenly. It was wonderful to
be able to see about twenty miles instead of down one London street!
It would be more delicious if you were here too – I hate to think of
you in horrible London all by yourself.'[59] This letter caught the night
mail and was with him the next morning at Buckingham Palace. He
replied at once to say how much it had cheered him up. He hoped
she was getting a rest – there would not be much chance before the
wedding. 'Why couldn't we be married first and do all this work
afterwards?'[60]

The difficulties they faced in arranging their future home to their
own satisfaction preoccupied them both. The Duke was irked by
Queen Mary's insistence on keeping control of changes at White
Lodge. He praised his fiancée's constant cheerfulness and said his own
patience had been 'tried very high on one or two occasions don't you
think? All I want is that you should have what you want & that you
should get the benefit & pleasure of going round & finding them for
yourself & not having things thrust at you by other people.'[61] Elizabeth
tried to soothe and reassure him – as she would throughout their
marriage. 'Don't worry about White Lodge and furniture. I am quite
certain we shall make it enchanting – you and I; so please don't fuss
yourself, little darling. You are such an angel to me always, and I hate
to think of you worrying about anything. "Keep calm and don't be
bullied – rest if you can" is my advice!!'[62]

Several busy days followed, looking for furniture, discussing the
wedding cake, to be baked by McVitie and Price in Edinburgh, even
attending a rugger match with the Duke. Everywhere, she made a
good impression. The Duke's papers include a letter from Jock Smith
of the Scottish Football Union to Louis Greig in which he remarks that
'HRH is d—d lucky in his choice & the couple have made a most
astonishing impression on our hard-headed, hard-hearted people.'[63]

A crowd saw them off on the night train to London. Next day the Duke took her to both lunch and tea with his family. Everything was very formal – Elizabeth's diary and, to a lesser extent, her letters suggest that she already well understood the constraints under which the Royal Family lived. Inevitably there were times when she found the new pomp and new circumstances of her life difficult and daunting. By 21 March she was feeling tired and depressed by the way in which her life was being circumscribed. The Duke came to dinner and she had a 'long talk to him about interference etc'.[64] In the morning she 'dashed off' to see Lady Airlie, lunched at the Palace and chose her bridesmaids' dresses; she had decided on the design for her wedding dress at Madame Handley Seymour's a few days earlier. Next day a series of rather formal presentations – 'very pompous,'[65] she declared in her diary – to the betrothed couple began at Buckingham Palace: silver dishes from the City of London, more from the Army Ordnance Corps. But there were moments alone with the Duke or members of her family that were fun, high spirited and to be treasured. One weekend at St Paul's Walden Bury, 'Mike, Bertie and I made a bonfire & baked potatoes. Marvellous day, sat & watched it.'[66]

More sittings, more fittings, more presents. On 28 March she and the Duke 'ordered the wedding ring, bought a gramophone and a dressing table'. That evening Chips Channon came for cocktails and then she and the Duke and some of her siblings had a 'very merry' evening dancing at the Savoy.[67] More humdrum matters brought them back to earth. They debated how much should be spent on their new linen. Mrs Greville had apparently offered to buy it, or at least to contribute towards it. They had been advised that it would cost £1,500, but Elizabeth thought this excessive. 'Whoever is buying it for us must remember that we are not millionaires (what ho!) and don't you think £1,000 ought to do it?'[68]

Meanwhile, the letters kept flooding in, among them another mournful missive from Archie Clark Kerr in Cairo,[69] and more cheerful ones from many of the soldiers who had known her at Glamis. Gordon George wrote that as a New Zealander he rejoiced 'that your charm and goodness and delightfulness are to shine where the whole Empire will get the good of you'. It was four years since he had been recuperating at Glamis 'but I have always gratefully remembered how kind to me you were when I was often perplexed and disturbed: and how you won us all, as an angel that moved among us, to love you with an enthusiastic, distant, revering love'. He sent her as a present Spenser's *Wedding Songs*.[70]

Easter was early that year and at the end of March they had to separate – the Duke to Windsor and she home to St Paul's Walden. He wrote to her from the Castle: 'How I hated leaving you today after lunch with the thought of not seeing you my darling till next Wednesday morning . . . Only 4 more weeks darling, & then we can take a rest away from everybody & everything. I wonder how you are looking forward to that time. I know I am very much indeed & I do hope you are too, I know it is all going to be so marvellous darling for us, don't you think?'[71] A letter came from her: 'Bertie my darling, I haven't got anything special to say, but am just writing this note, in case nobody else writes to you!!'[72] On Easter Saturday she wrote again and said she had read in the paper that he had walked from the Castle to Frogmore.* 'Having never seen Frogmore, I imagine it as a large white Tomb full of frogs! I can't think why, but that is the impression it gives me – isn't it silly?' She informed him that he had 'a most changeable face. It is too odd. Sometimes you look a completely different person, always nice though, but I must not flatter you because then your head will swell, & you will have to buy new hats.' She wished he had a small aeroplane so that he could fly over to see her for an hour or two.[73]

Instead the Duke spent the Easter weekend at Windsor, riding, playing squash with the Prince of Wales and golf with all three of his brothers, but always feeling constrained by the precise timetables laid down by his father. By Sunday he was keen to break away. He would rather they spent the next weekend at her home, 'where there are no fusses or worries', he told his fiancée, 'as here there is no rest & the day is so marked out into minutes for this thing & the other, which is always such a bore, & we never get any real peace'. At Windsor everything was orders – 'Life is not as easy as it should be but the change is coming & you my little darling I hope are going to help me with this change. You must take them in hand & teach them how they should do these things.'[74] He knew how much the Royal Family would benefit from her gaiety and spontaneity.

---

* Frogmore House, set in the private Home Park at Windsor Castle, is famous for its beautiful landscaped garden and eighteenth-century lake. Queen Victoria loved Frogmore and built a mausoleum for herself and her husband, Prince Albert, in the grounds.

On 4 April, at Buckingham Palace, she had to make her first speech in her new role. 'The Pattenmakers presented me with a chest full of rubber footwear, & I read a speech back,' she recorded in her diary.[75] She worried about it for days and rehearsed it endlessly, telling the Duke that if she failed, he would have to step in. She did not fail, but it was perhaps a relief, after receiving this bounty of gumboots and galoshes, that she was able to escape to Pinet in Bond Street and buy shoes. That afternoon she and the Duke, along with Louis Greig, motored to Windsor, stopping for tea with Mrs Greig on the way. After dinner at the Castle, the Royal Family and Household crossed the river to Eton to listen to a gala performance of Mendelssohn's *Elijah*.[76]

For the next two days Elizabeth had her first taste of the ordered life of the Royal Family at Windsor Castle. In fact her diary conveys a surprising informality, and none of the rigidity of which the Duke complained. She chatted with the Prince of Wales while the Duke went out riding; the King showed her his room and played gramophone records for her; the Queen gave her a tour of the Castle; Sir John Fortescue, the Librarian, took her and the Duke to see the treasures of the Royal Library. Queen Alexandra came to lunch and gave her a pearl and amethyst chain. And at dinner Elizabeth had an amusing neighbour: Dick Molyneux,* a member of the King's Household with a distinguished military past and a lively sense of humour who was to become a particular friend to her at Court.

On Saturday, to the regret of the King and Queen, they left for London (where they opened more presents) and then drove on to the haven of St Paul's Walden. There indeed they relaxed – after tea she and the Duke made a bonfire and then 'sat & drank a cocktail & ragged about'; after dinner they played the 'grammy'.[77]

The weeks and then the days before the wedding became more and more crowded. Elizabeth tried to find time for herself at home in Bruton Street in the afternoons. On Tuesday 10 April she dressed in

---

* The Hon. Richard Molyneux (1873–1954), son of fourth Earl of Sefton, decorated for his services in the Tirah Campaign on the North-West Frontier of India in 1897–8, fought under Kitchener in the Sudan in 1898, badly wounded at the Battle of Omdurman. Served in the South African War 1899–1901 and in the First World War. Groom in waiting to King George V c. 1919–36. Extra equerry to Queen Mary 1936–53. He also acted as an unofficial artistic adviser on picture hangs and the arrangement of rooms, to Queen Mary and later to Queen Elizabeth.

one of her new Handley Seymour outfits: a loose-fitting brown coat edged with fur and an elaborately trimmed cloche hat, and went with the Duke to Goodwood for Doris's wedding to Clare Vyner at Chichester Cathedral. Next day, at Buckingham Palace, she and the Duke received deputations bringing them loyal addresses and wedding presents, and she was created a Lady of Grace of the Order of St John of Jerusalem. That afternoon she went with her mother to Catchpole and Williams to have strung the two rows of pearls her father had given her. 'Then to Handley S. to try on my wedding dress. Rather nice I hope.'[78]

Next day, after choosing chintzes for White Lodge with her mother and being photographed by Hoppé for the *Graphic* magazine,[79] she wrote an affectionate letter to D'Arcy Osborne thanking him for the two 'divinely bound' books of poetry he had sent her; infinitely more pleasurable, she said, than 'eight ropes of pearls from a new oil Lord . . . I wish you would come in one evening if you can, & drink a cocktail & exchange a few ideas on MAGIC and POLITICS and SPIRITUALISM and RELIGION, and GEORGE ROBEY and AMERICANS and all the terribly interesting things in this world.'[80]

After her marriage, when Osborne asked her how he should address her, she replied in a manner which typified her spirit: 'I really don't know! It might be <u>anything</u> – you might try "All Hail Duchess", that is an Alice in Wonderland sort of Duchess, or just "Greetings" or "What Ho, Duchess" or "Say, Dutch" – in fact you can please yourself, as it will certainly please me.'[81] In fact there had been much public speculation about what she would be called after her marriage. The Press Association reported that 'The future style and title of the bride is a matter for the King's decision. Recent times supply no precedent . . . but the Press Association believes that Lady Elizabeth will share her husband's rank and precedence, but until the King's wishes are known, no official information is available.'[82]

As to what the King's decision should be, there was lively discussion between Lord Stamfordham, his Private Secretary, and the Home Office. Stamfordham asked if she would become *ipso facto* HRH the Duchess of York. And how should she sign her name? He presumed she would not be a princess. So she could not sign simply 'Elizabeth' as Princess Mary signed herself 'Mary'. Presumably she should use 'Elizabeth of York'. The Home Secretary disagreed with the Private Secretary and said that Lady Elizabeth would indeed acquire the status of princess on marriage, though she would style herself Duchess of York; she should certainly sign herself 'Elizabeth'. Lord Stamfordham acquiesced.[83] After the marriage an official announcement was issued that 'in accordance with the settled general rule that a wife takes the status of her husband Lady Elizabeth Bowes-Lyon on her marriage has become Her Royal Highness the Duchess of York with the status of a Princess.'

Stamfordham's initial attitude amounted almost to treating the marriage as morganatic, which seems curious in a country where such an alliance was an alien concept.* But he, like everyone else, was feeling his way in a situation with few helpful precedents. As has already been mentioned, the King and Queen had decided as early as 1917 that their children should be allowed to marry into British families. Princess Mary's marriage to Lord Lascelles had helped accustom the public to this idea, although it was nothing new as far as princesses were concerned: Queen Victoria's fourth daughter and King Edward VII's eldest daughter had both married compatriots and commoners.[†] But princes were different: no sovereign's son had married – at least not publicly and with official sanction – into a non-royal family since an earlier Duke of York, the future King James II, had married Lady Anne Hyde in 1660.[‡] Now the effect of King George V's decision was to be demonstrated for the first time by one of his sons.

The novelty and the quandaries were not only on the bridegroom's side. The Strathmores too were entering uncharted territory: there were no guidelines for marrying a daughter into the Royal Family, and

---

* A morganatic marriage is one between a man of exalted rank and a woman of lower rank in which the wife does not acquire the status of her husband. Such marriages occasionally happened in European royal families but there was no provision for them in Britain.

[†] Princess Louise (1848–1939), fourth daughter of Queen Victoria, married the Marquess of Lorne, later ninth Duke of Argyll, in 1871; Princess Louise of Wales (1867–1931), eldest daughter of King Edward VII, married the Earl (later first Duke) of Fife in 1889. Queen Victoria's granddaughter Princess Patricia of Connaught had also married a commoner, the Hon. Alexander Ramsay, in 1919, and had taken the name Lady Patricia Ramsay.

[‡] They were married secretly at Breda in 1659 but publicly in England the following year, after the Restoration. Two of King George III's brothers secretly married commoners of whom the King did not approve (this led to the Royal Marriages Act of 1772, under which the sovereign's approval of marriages of members of the Royal Family, whether or not to commoners, has to be secured). His son (the Duke of Sussex) and grandson (the second Duke of Cambridge) subsequently also married commoners.

1. Lord Strathmore.

2. Lady Strathmore.

3. Elizabeth Bowes Lyon
in 1902.

4. The Strathmores at Glamis in 1907. Back row, left to right: Alec, Fergus, Jock, Patrick, May and Rose. Front row, left to right: Michael, Elizabeth, Lord Strathmore, Lady Strathmore with David on her lap.

5. Elizabeth aged two, with her sister Rose at St Paul's Walden Bury.

6. Elizabeth and David in the Italian Garden at Glamis.

7. Elizabeth, being held aloft by her elder brother Patrick, with her sister Rose on the far right.

8. Elizabeth with her father on the cricket pitch at Glamis.

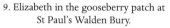

9. Elizabeth in the gooseberry patch at St Paul's Walden Bury.

10. Beryl Poignand in 1915.

11 & 12. Elizabeth with convalescent soldiers at Glamis
(*above*) in January 1915 and (*below*) in 1916.

13. A house party for the Forfar Ball, 9 September 1920. Left to right: Katie Hamilton, Grisell Cochrane-Baillie, Lady Strathmore, Hilda Blackburn, Diamond Hardinge, Elizabeth, Lord Gage, Francis Doune (seated, front), James Stuart, Prince Paul of Yugoslavia.

14. Elizabeth with Arthur Penn (left) and Freddy Dalrymple Hamilton at a house party at Molecomb, January 1921.

15. Elizabeth, centre, with (clockwise) her sister Rose Leveson Gower and friends Katie Hamilton, Doris Gordon-Lennox and Mida Scott in 1921.

16. With the Duke of York in a photograph from Elizabeth's own album, captioned by her, September 1920.

17 &18. The Duke of York and Elizabeth at Glamis (*below left*) in 1921 and (*below*) at a shoot.

A luncheon party at Glamis Castle, Forfarshire, the Earl of Strathmore's seat, where the Duke of York has been staying. Standing, from left to right: the Hon. Michael Bowes-Lyon, the Hon. David Bowes-Lyon, the Duke of York, the Earl of Strathmore, Captain the Hon. W. Leveson-Gower and the Hon. James Stuart. Seated: Lady Doris Gordon-Lennox, Lady Margaret Scott, Lady Elizabeth Bowes-Lyon, Lady Katharine Hamilton and Lady Rose Leveson-Gower

19. A cutting from the society pages showing the Duke of York as a guest at Glamis.

20. Elizabeth at her first royal engagement, as a bridesmaid at Princess Mary's wedding, 28 February 1922.

PHOTO,
VANDYK, LTD.
LADY D. GORDON-LENNOX. LADY E. BOWES-LYON.
LADY MARY CAMBRIDGE. PRINCESS MAUD.

THE ROYAL WEDDING.
VISCOUNT   PRINCESS
LASCELLES.   MARY.   MAJOR SIR VICTOR MACKENZIE   LADY D. BRIDGEMAN.
LADY RACHEL CAVENDISH.

532.W.
BEAGLES POSTCARDS
LADY MAY CAMBRIDGE.
LADY MARY THYNNE.

21. The Duke of York and Elizabeth soon after their engagement.

they were soon to discover that the traditional roles of the respective parents in arranging a wedding would be reversed. At first Lord and Lady Strathmore evidently expected to play the part of the bride's parents in entertaining the wedding guests. They assured Gunters, the bakers, that they would receive the order for the cake and refreshments if these were to be provided by Lord Strathmore.[84] They told the Queen that they would rent a large house in London 'in order to entertain and do the usual things inseparable from a wedding'. But, as the Lord Chamberlain recorded, 'this idea was of course put aside, as The King and Queen decided that a Royal Wedding should follow its usual course.'[85] This meant that the responsibility – and expense – of entertaining fell on the King and, perhaps to the relief of the bride's parents, the Lord Chamberlain's Office took control of all the arrangements, merely consulting Lady Strathmore on the guest lists and the seating plan in Westminster Abbey.

The numbers involved were so great that it was decided to hold parties at Buckingham Palace on the three days before the wedding for those who could not be fitted into the Abbey: an evening party on Monday 23 April, an afternoon party for servants the next day, and another afternoon party on the eve of the wedding. Lady Strathmore was in constant touch with the Palace about her guest list, at the last minute asking despairingly for more Lyon cousins to be invited. 'Presents are pouring in, & I am at a loss what to do!'[86] She was also concerned that the Strathmore servants and local farmers should not be overlooked, and asked for eighty tickets to the afternoon party. 'People are coming all the way from Scotland to attend it, not to mention Yorkshire & Durham! ... P.S. How many people may I ask to stand in the Fore Court to see the Bride & Bridegroom depart?'[87]

For Elizabeth, the fortnight before the wedding was an exhausting round of formal receptions at Buckingham Palace, last-minute shopping with friends, dodging photographers, and evenings filled with dining and dancing. She loved Paul Whiteman's band, which played at a dance given by the Mountbattens and again at Audrey Coats's dance on 18 April.* Among her many dance partners were Dickie

---

* Audrey Coats, née James (1902–68), sister of Edward James of West Dean, well known for his patronage of surrealist art. One of Elizabeth's good friends, Audrey had married Dudley Coats in 1922.

Mountbatten, Prince Paul, Prince George and Fruity Metcalfe, amiable equerry and friend to the Prince of Wales. James Stuart called in one evening for cocktails and chatter.[88]

For the Duke, work continued. He was determined to ensure that industrial welfare and the wellbeing of the young remained at the core of his public interests. On 18 April he made what appears to have been the first visit by a member of the Royal Family to a trades union: the Amalgamated Engineering Union, at its offices in Peckham Road in south-east London. He had met the President, James Brownlie, and other members of the union at the annual Duke of York's Camp the previous year. According to *The Times*, Brownlie told him that the union had 320,000 members and 1,800 branches. 'The Duke might suppose that in coming to the headquarters of a great trade union he was visiting some sort of Bolshevik organisation more concerned to promote strife than peace. But nothing could be further from the fact.' After they had toured the building, Brownlie proposed a toast to the Duke's marriage. 'Take my assurance that you are perfectly safe in the hands of a Scots lassie,' he said.[89] A week later, at a reception at the Palace, the Duke introduced Brownlie to his bride with the words, 'Here is the Scottish lassie, Mr Brownlie.'[90]

Elizabeth's last weekend as an unmarried woman was that of 21–22 April. She went to the Palace again on Saturday for lunch with the King and Queen, who gave her their principal presents: a tiara and a complete suite of diamonds and turquoises from the King, a diamond and sapphire necklace from the Queen. From her father she received a diamond tiara and a rope necklace of pearls and diamonds, while her mother gave her a diamond and pearl necklace and bracelet. The bridegroom's own present to her was a diamond and pearl necklace with a matching pendant. As the soldier at Glamis had hoped, Elizabeth was now hung with jewels. Her gift to her fiancé was a platinum and pearl watch-chain.[91]

After lunch Queen Mary and Princess Mary motored over to Bruton Street to see the trousseau* and presents there; other gifts

---

* The dresses made by Madame Handley Seymour for the trousseau were shown to the press on 20 April. *The Times* listed twelve, and remarked on their simplicity; more striking for those remembering their wearer in her later years are the colours: black, navy, beige, very little blue or green and no yellow, although mauve, pink, silver and white appear. Full details of her wedding dress and going-away outfit – which was of a grey/beige tint – were also given to the press in advance. (*The Times* and *Morning Post*, 23 April 1923)

were displayed at Buckingham Palace. The Livery Company of Needle-
makers had presented a thousand gold-eyed needles; South African
ostrich farmers had sent an ostrich-feather mantlet, tied with ribbons;
there was a gift of silver inkwells, stamp-boxes and candlesticks from
the members of the Cabinet, a set of tea-trays, a hammock and a
waste-paper basket made by blind ex-soldiers at St Dunstan's, and
dressing-cases from the Glamis tenantry, and much more.[92] A present
which gave the Duke of York particular pleasure was one of the battle
ensigns worn by HMS *Collingwood* at Jutland.*

That evening Elizabeth went home to St Paul's Walden and spent
Sunday morning resting in bed. After lunch she went for short walks
in between writing letters and noted in her diary, 'Feel very odd &
sad at leaving home.'[93] On Monday 23 April, back in London, she
went to the Abbey with the Duke and all the bridesmaids for the
wedding rehearsal. She was tired when she got home at 7 p.m., but
after dinner, wearing her 'new pink', she set off for Buckingham
Palace with her parents to attend the first of the pre-wedding receptions given by the King and Queen. There were about 800 guests –
members of the two families, their friends, members of the diplomatic
corps and donors of wedding presents, which were on display in large
glass cases. H. H. Asquith, the former Prime Minister, described the
evening to a friend: 'I went in my knee-breeches and medals after
dinner to Buckingham Palace, where the rooms, big as they are, were
very nearly crowded ... The bride, everyone says, is full of charm
and stood in a row with the King and Queen. We all shook hands
with her as we passed ... The whole of what is called the "world"
was there in its best frocks.'[94]

In the course of the evening Asquith inadvertently stood on the
train of a lady's dress, anchoring her to the floor for two minutes, a
mishap observed by another guest, Freddy Dalrymple Hamilton. He
recorded in his diary that Elizabeth was 'splendid & looked lovely &
seemed to take everything very calmly as I never had any doubt she
would ... I didn't manage to talk to Elizabeth but we had to content

---

* Later HMS *Collingwood* became the name of the Royal Navy's training establishment at
Fareham, Hampshire, and in June 1968 Queen Elizabeth presented the ensign to the new HMS
Collingwood at a ceremony attended by 3,000 sailors. She said, 'Today I hand you this flag for
safe keeping; guard it well, for this White Ensign is a symbol of the loyalty and courage of
those who served in the Collingwood during that great battle.' It was an emotional moment
for her. (RA QEQMH/PS/ENGT/1968/11 June)

ourselves with making ugly faces at each other across the room!'[95] The King gave Elizabeth his personal Order;* the Queen commented in her diary on how pretty she looked in pink.[96] Her own diary entry ended, 'Shook hands with hundreds & talked till 11.15. Home 11.30. All the family went. Bed 1.'[97]

On Tuesday Elizabeth worked for a time on letters with Miss Chard and then she and the Duke attended the afternoon party at the Palace for Royal Household and Strathmore staff – about a thousand in all – and took tea with the King and Queen. That evening came the unexpected announcement that James Stuart was betrothed to Lady Rachel Cavendish. Everyone seemed very happy. Elizabeth and the Duke dined at Claridge's with the newly engaged couple and ten of their mutual friends and then went on to the Hippodrome and later to the Berkeley Hotel, fashionable then and later, dancing all the while. 'I was in good form! Went home, & talked to Bertie. Then talked to Mike for ages. Bed 3.30.'[98]

Next morning, the eve of her wedding, she awoke at 10 o'clock 'feeling very ill!' Beryl Poignand and Betty Cator both came to give her last-minute cheer. 'I talked on the telephone and did a million things before lunch.' The Duke came to settle a few final details and afterwards they drove together through the usual crowds to the Palace. In the Duke's room, Mrs Lindsay Carnegie presented the gift of the people of Forfarshire.[99]

Soon after their engagement, the County Clerk of Forfarshire had written to Lord Strathmore to seek his advice on a suitable present. Lord Strathmore had consulted his daughter, who had made it clear that she did not want the people of Forfar to go to any unnecessary expense. He had therefore replied 'that she would infinitely prefer that no money was spent on a wedding gift for her when unemployment and distress are so prevalent, and when almost everyone is feeling the pinch of the bad times. I entirely agree with those sentiments, which Lady Elizabeth holds strongly, although she does not wish to tie the hands of those at the meeting unduly, and, above all, does not wish to appear ungrateful.'[100] After this letter was read at a public meeting, the

---

* Sovereigns since King George IV have followed the practice of presenting Family Orders, consisting of a portrait of the sovereign set in diamonds and suspended from a ribbon, to female members of the Royal Family.

Council decided to present her with an illuminated book, full of illustrations of her home county.*

At the third Palace party she had to shake hands with hundreds more people. It was very tiring, but at 6 p.m. she and her mother went home for a quiet family evening at Bruton Street, her last as a single woman. 'Felt terribly moved when I said good-night to the darling boys & mother. I adore them. Bed 11.'[101]

*

ON THE MORNING of the wedding, crowds gathered early in Bruton Street and all along the route to the Abbey. Spring was only beginning to touch the trees of London. It was a cold, damp, blustery day, but, in the words of Queen Mary, 'the sun came out between showers.'[102] The King had commanded that flags be flown on government buildings on the day of the wedding. But there were no decorations in the Mall, for in the current economic climate he was mindful that extravagance might not be popular. There was nothing to discourage firms or private individuals from putting up bunting should they wish. School-children were given the day off school and the King requested that His Majesty's ships be dressed overall and fire a salute at noon.[103]

As the bride prepared, her family left for Westminster Abbey as and when the meticulous schedule required. Just after 11 a.m., Queen Alexandra left Marlborough House. One minute later the King and Queen drove out of Buckingham Palace, accompanied by the sovereign's escort of the Household Cavalry. At 11.13 the bridegroom, attended by the Prince of Wales, followed them. One minute before that, Elizabeth had set off from Bruton Street with her father. There is a famous photograph of her as she left the family home, glancing somewhat tentatively at the camera, about to step into the carriage and away from her family. She and her father drove in a state landau escorted by four mounted Metropolitan policemen. According to one of her biographers, she seemed to be both surprised and touched by the warmth of her welcome along the streets. But her father was

---

* *The Illuminated Address from the County of Angus* contained watercolours by the renowned painter David Waterson from Brechin in Angus and a poem specially composed by J. M. Barrie. It remained among her possessions; after her death in 2002, it was sent back from Clarence House to Glamis.

reported to be in low spirits at the prospect of giving away his daughter.[104]

This was the first marriage of a king's son in the Abbey and only the third royal marriage to take place there since Richard II had married Anne of Bohemia in 1382. It had since become the custom for royal marriages to be celebrated privately, until Princess Patricia of Connaught's marriage in Westminster Abbey in 1919, followed by that of Princess Mary in 1922.

Among the guests were three prime ministers, present and past – Bonar Law, Lloyd George and Asquith – the first two, according to the *Yorkshire Post*, not flattered by the gold lace and breeches they wore as Privy Counsellors. Asquith was 'smiling and serene in his Trinity House uniform', his wife swathed in an almond-green marocain wrap. Lord Curzon, 'appearing very pleased with himself, slouched in wearing an overcoat, and with his hands in his pockets', the *Post*'s reporter noted. Present also were Winston Churchill, looking 'chubby and sleek', Austen Chamberlain and his wife, she in a silver cloak and a gold turban decked with tall osprey feathers, while Mrs Neville Chamberlain wore an elegant gown by Worth. All parties in the House of Commons were 'well represented', as *The Times* pointed out – Labour leaders included Ramsay MacDonald, J. R. Clynes and Arthur Henderson.[105] Another notable Labour MP, Will Thorne of the Gas Workers and General Union, had asked for and obtained seats for his wife and daughter.[106]

Asquith, writing next day about the ceremony, remarked that the crowds in the streets were enormous and must have been drenched to the skin by the persistent showers throughout the day. 'As a pageant it was extremely well done. I sat in the stalls with a curious little knot of neighbours: Ramsay MacDonald and Clynes (who were in black frock-coats), Buckmaster,* Simon† and Winston Churchill! The ennui of the long waits was relieved for me by being next to Winston, who was in his best form and really amusing.'[107] Duff Cooper, with his wife

---

* Stanley Owen, Baron Buckmaster of Cheddington, later first Viscount Buckmaster (1861–1934), Lord Chancellor 1915–16.

† Sir John Simon, later first Viscount Simon (1873–1954). Home Secretary 1915–16. Successively Foreign Secretary, Home Secretary and Chancellor of the Exchequer 1931–40, and Lord Chancellor 1940–5.

Diana, was pleased to have good seats.* 'The Mosleys† were next to us and the Dudley Wards immediately behind. I enjoyed it.'[108] Perhaps the best view of the ceremony was that enjoyed by fifty-two boys seated high up in the Triforium. They had been invited at the Duke's special request to represent young industrial workers.[109]

There were considerably fewer guests than had been invited to Princess Mary's wedding: in his anxiety to keep costs low the King had ruled out the construction of the special stands which were used to increase seating in the Abbey in 1922, thus reducing the places available from 2,680 to 1,780.[110] Nevertheless, as the *Morning Post* reported, there was 'a large and brilliant congregation which included many of the leading personages of the nation and Empire',[111] with an estimated million spectators lining the processional route. As well as the huge press coverage, the ceremony and its aftermath, up to the appearance of the couple on the balcony at Buckingham Palace, were filmed – the first time this had been done, and the films were ready to be shown the same evening.‡

The service began with the ecclesiastical procession into the Abbey. It was led by the Archbishop of Canterbury, the Most Rev. Randall Davidson, who had held the post for a quarter of a century; the Archbishop of York, the Most Rev. Cosmo Lang; then the Primus of

---

* Duff Cooper, later first Viscount Norwich (1890–1954), Conservative politician, diplomat and author. In 1935 he was appointed secretary of state for war, and in 1937 first lord of the Admiralty. He publicly opposed Neville Chamberlain's policy of appeasement and resigned over the Munich Agreement in 1938. In 1940 he became minister of information in Churchill's War Cabinet; in 1944 he was appointed British ambassador to France, a post which he held with great success until 1947. He had married in 1919 Lady Diana Manners (1892–1986), one of the most beautiful women of her time, a vivid personality who was in her element as ambassadress in Paris.

† Sir Oswald Mosley, sixth Baronet (1896–1980), and his wife Lady Cynthia, daughter of the statesman Lord Curzon. Mosley was distantly related to the Strathmores through Frances Dora Smith, wife of the thirteenth Earl, who was the great-granddaughter of Sir John Mosley, first Baronet. Although chiefly known as the founder of the British Union of Fascists, in 1923 he was an independent Conservative MP. He joined both the Labour Party and the Independent Labour Party in 1924; he developed his fascist sympathies in the 1930s. In 1936, after the death of Lady Cynthia, he married Diana Guinness, née Mitford.

‡ One of the film companies, Gaumont Graphic, used the wedding as a test for a new developing and printing plant, and boasted that by 9 o'clock that night they had produced 25 million feet of film. (Nigel Arch and Joanna Marschner, *Royal Wedding Dresses*, exhibition catalogue, Historic Royal Palaces, 2003, p. 21)

the Episcopal Church of Scotland, Elizabeth's Church, the Most Rev. Walter Robberds.

The King was wearing the uniform of an Admiral of the Fleet; Queen Mary was striking in a dress and turban of aquamarine blue and silver. With the King and Queen were Queen Alexandra and her sister the Dowager Empress Marie Feodorovna, Prince George and Princess Mary, together with some fourteen other members of the Royal Family. On the other side of the nave was the bride's family. According to the press accounts of the time, Lady Strathmore was wearing 'a handsome gown of black marocain' under a black cloak with a collar of blue roses. Her eldest daughter, May Elphinstone, was dressed in a spectacular embroidered outfit of dove-grey satin with jade and gold roses, a large plumed hat and a sable wrap. Dorothy Glamis, both beautiful and elegant, wore what was described as 'one of the most successful costumes in the Abbey' of soft silver.[112]

The Duke of York was the first member of the Royal Family to be married in the dress uniform of the Royal Air Force. He wore the Garter Riband and Star and the Star of the Order of the Thistle, which the King had bestowed upon him in honour of his Scottish bride. His row of medals included those he had earned by service in the war. He was supported by the Prince of Wales, wearing the uniform of the Grenadier Guards, and by Prince Henry, in the uniform of the 10th Hussars. Freddy Dalrymple Hamilton, seated with his wife Gwendolen close to the aisle, watched the Duke as he walked by. 'We managed to catch his eye as he passed or thought we did as he ½ grinned at us.'[113]

Awaiting the bride were her eight bridesmaids – Queen Mary's nieces, Lady Mary and Lady May Cambridge, and four of Elizabeth's old friends, Lady Katharine Hamilton, Lady Mary Thynne, Betty Cator and Diamond Hardinge, and then her two nieces, Elizabeth Elphinstone and Cecilia Bowes Lyon. All wore ivory-coloured dresses of crêpe de Chine with bands of Nottingham lace, covered with white chiffon. Around their waists they had leaf-green tulle sashes held in place by a white rose and a silver thistle. In their hair they wore bandeaux of white roses and myrtle leaves. Each bridesmaid also wore her gift from the bridegroom – a carved crystal brooch in the form of the white rose of York with a diamond centre carrying the initials E and A. The older bridesmaids wore silver shoes, the two young ones, who were carrying the train, white shoes. They all carried bouquets of white roses and white heather.

The bride arrived punctually, just as the sun came out from behind the clouds. She was wearing a dress of cream chiffon moiré with appliquéd bars of silver lamé, embroidered with gold thread and beads of paste and pearl. It had a deep square neckline and short sleeves, a straight-cut bodice and a slightly gathered skirt with a short train set into the waist seam at the back. Over the dress she wore a long train of silk net with a lace edging, and a *point de Flandres* lace veil, both of which Queen Mary had lent her. The veil was drawn down low over her forehead; a simple wreath of myrtle leaves, white roses and white heather held it in place. Her shoes were of ivory silk moiré embroidered with silver roses, and she carried a bouquet of roses and lily-of-the-valley.

When Elizabeth and her father entered the Abbey, one of the clergy preceding her fainted. As they waited for the procession to reform, she suddenly left her father's side and went to lay her bouquet of white roses on the Tomb of the Unknown Warrior, placed at the west end of the nave in honour of the countless British dead of the Great War whose bodies had never been found and who had had no proper burial.* This gesture was unexpected. People speculated afterwards that at the door of the Abbey she might have thought suddenly of her brother Fergus, killed in 1915 at the Battle of Loos.

On the arm of her father, Elizabeth then moved towards her future. Freddy Dalrymple Hamilton reflected the emotion of many of her friends and family in the account he wrote in his diary.

The organ which had been crashing loudly for some time suddenly broke into 'Lead us Heavenly Father lead us' very softly which gave a most wonderful effect I thought & there was Elizabeth with her father & looking extraordinarily nice & I couldn't help feeling most extraordinarily proud of her as if she'd been my own sister. She did it amazingly well & even appeared to be enjoying it as she smiled up at Lord S when he bent down & asked her something.[114]

---

* The tomb contains the body of an unidentified British soldier from a European battlefield which was buried in Westminster Abbey on 11 November 1920, the second anniversary of the end of the war.

According to *The Times*, 'The Duke of York faced with shining eyes and a look of happiness the girl who, hand in hand with her father, was advancing in her lovely old fashioned dress, gleaming with silver and veiled in old lace . . . they seemed to think of no one but each other.'

The bride and groom had asked Cosmo Lang to give the address. He pleased everyone with his words. 'Will you take and keep this gift of wedded life as a sacred trust?' he asked. 'With all our hearts we wish that it may be happy. You can and will resolve that it will be noble. You will not think so much of enjoyment as of achievement. You will have a great ambition to make this one life now given to you something rich and true and beautiful.' He commended the Duke for his work in industrial welfare and then, turning to the new Duchess, he said, 'And you, dear bride, in your Scottish home, have grown up from childhood among country folk and friendship with them has been your native air. So have you both been fitted for your place in the people's life. The nations and classes which make up our Commonwealth too often live their lives apart. It is . . . a great thing that there should be in our midst one family which, regarded by all as in a true sense their own, makes the whole Empire kin and helps to give it the spirit of family life.'[115]

While the families signed the registers in the chapel of Edward the Confessor, the choir sang an anthem composed by Sydney Nicholson for Princess Mary's wedding, 'Beloved, Let Us Love One Another'. After the signing, the principal guests took their places again in the Sanctuary. Then as Mendelssohn's Wedding March began, the Duke and Duchess of York returned to the heart of the Abbey. They smiled at Lady Strathmore, who had tears in her eyes. She was feeling both moved and saddened by it all; she thought that her daughter looked 'lovely . . . so dignified and restful, just her own sweet little self as usual'.[116] The couple then bowed and curtsied respectively to the King and the Queen before walking back through the full length of the nave, and then emerging from the Abbey into a sunnier day. Elizabeth Bowes Lyon had arrived at the Abbey as a commoner; she left as the fourth lady in the land.

She and the Duke stepped into their scarlet and gold coach and drove by a long route back towards the Palace, through Marlborough Gate, St James's Street, Piccadilly, around Hyde Park Corner and finally down Constitution Hill. All the way they were cheered. When she arrived at Buckingham Palace, her bridesmaids and her friends, who had returned directly from the Abbey, all curtsied to her. As her sympathetic biographer Dorothy Laird put it, 'she had stepped across the barrier into the closed circle of the Royal Family for ever.'[117]

At the Palace, the wedding breakfast for over sixty people, mostly from the two families, was prepared by the royal chef, Gabriel Tschumi, and included *Consommé à la Windsor, Suprêmes de Saumon Reine Mary, Côtelettes d'Agneau Prince Albert, Chapons à la Strathmore* and *Fraises Duchesse Elizabeth*.[118] There was just one toast, proposed by the King. 'I ask you to drink to the health, long lives and happiness of the bride and bridegroom.'

The wedding cake was cut in the Blue Drawing Room. It was nine feet high and weighed 800 pounds. It was the one that they had helped design on their visit to the McVitie and Price biscuit factory in March, and was a gift of the Chairman, Alexander Grant. Its three tiers were decorated with the coats of arms of the Strathmores and the Duke of York, and surmounted by an ornamental confection symbolizing love and peace. At the couple's request, Grant arranged that slices of identical cake were distributed at the Duke's expense to thousands of poor children at wedding tea parties arranged for them in London and other cities.[119]

While the Duchess and her family, old and new, lunched at the Palace, other friends and guests at the Abbey were meeting and lunching all over London. Duff and Diana Cooper had 'skipped out' by the North Door of the Abbey and got an excellent view of the couple driving away. In the crowd they met Jasper Ridley, and drove him home. 'In an outburst of confidence he told us that he had long been in love with Elizabeth Lyon and that he was miserable about her marriage. He had never believed she would do it and it had been a very sudden volte face on her part as she had refused the Duke of York several times.'[120]

At the Palace, the Duchess changed into her going-away dress, a soft shade of dove-grey crêpe romain, over which she wore a travelling coat wrap. Her brown hat was small, with an upturned brim and a feather on the side. She chose it, apparently, so that the crowds would not find their view of her impeded.[121] As they left for their honeymoon in an open landau, their friends and relations threw rose petals over them. The Duke's brothers and the bridesmaids ran into the arch of the forecourt after the landau, throwing more petals, and were pushed against the wall of the arch as the escort of cavalry moved briskly after the carriage – 'for an alarming moment they were caught between the stone wall and the quarters of the great black horses.'[122]

Cheering crowds accompanied the couple to Waterloo where a special train awaited them. Their carriage was, according to *The Times*, 'upholstered in old gold brocade and decorated with white roses, white heather, white carnations and lilies of the valley'. The train drew out at 4.35 p.m. and after a gentle ride through south London into the Surrey countryside arrived at Bookham at 5.10 p.m. There the newly-weds received bouquets and listened to an address of welcome before they were taken by car to Polesden Lacey, the home of Mrs Ronnie Greville, who had been delighted to offer it to them. One of the first things that the new Duchess did there was to send a telegram to her mother saying, 'Arrived safely deliciously peaceful here hope you are not all too tired love Elizabeth'.[123]

Her diary records her wedding day thus:

Thur 26 Apr. Woke at 8.30. Up by 10. Put on my wedding dress, aided by Suzanne & Catherine. It looked lovely. All the family went off early, also mother. Miss Chard came & talked to me. At 11.12 the carriage came, & father & I started off for the Abbey. Lots of people in B St., & crowds in the streets. Did not feel very nervous. Bertie smiled at me when I got up to him – & it all went off well. We had a long drive home to B.P. Crowds very kind. We were photographed, & also went out on the balcony. Then luncheon. Sat between Bertie & the King. After lunch talked & cut cake etc. Went to change about 3.20. Mother & Anne* came – then May & Rosie, Mike & David & father. Awful saying goodbye. B & I drove off at 4.15 & had a special to Bookham. Very tired & happy. Bed 12.[124]

---

* Elizabeth's five-year-old niece, daughter of Jock and Fenella.

CHAPTER FIVE

DUCHESS OF YORK

1923–1924

'Bertie do listen to me'

ON THE FIRST day of her married life the Duchess of York awoke at 11, had breakfast in bed and looked at all the papers. She still felt exhausted and did not get up until lunchtime. She dressed herself comfortably in an old blue tweed suit – to the dismay of her maid. 'Poor Catherine is miserable,' she wrote to her mother, 'because I won't wear anything new – I hate new things!'¹ That afternoon the Duke and Duchess sat together in the sun, strolled around Mrs Greville's garden and sat down to write to their parents and friends.

The Duchess told her mother she was worried that she had been exhausted by the events of the last three months. 'I could not say anything to you about how utterly miserable I was at leaving you and Mike & David & father. I could not <u>ever</u> have said it to you – but you know I love you more than anybody in the world mother, and you do know it, don't you? Bertie adores you too, & he is being too marvellous to me, & so thoughtful. He really is a darling – I <u>hope</u> you all like him.'² Lady Strathmore replied at once, thanking her for her '<u>darling</u>' letter – 'I just love it & shall always keep it.' She continued in a way which exposed the depth of her feelings. 'I won't say what it means to me to give you up to Bertie – but I think you know that you are by <u>far</u> the most precious of all my children, & always will be. I do <u>love</u> Bertie – & think very highly of his <u>character</u>, but above everything I love his really worshipping <u>you</u>, & I go on telling myself that when I get low about you. However I do wish he was not a Royalty – but his own dear plain self, (I don't mean plain in <u>looks</u>.)' She ended by saying that she liked the Prince of Wales immensely, 'but he is not a <u>patch</u> on Bertie!'³

The Duke wrote also to 'Darling Lady Strathmore' thanking her and Lord Strathmore for letting him marry Elizabeth. 'You know how

I love her & will always take care of her, & I do hope you will not look upon me as a thief in having taken her from you. I know only too well what Elizabeth is to you, & to me she is everything.'[4] Lady Strathmore's reply was reassuring, saying she felt 'very much at peace about you & my darling Eliz[th] who I know is so very happy with you'.[5]

Letters were dispatched to the Duke's parents too. The Duke told the King what happiness it had brought him to be allowed to marry Elizabeth, and thanked him for all his kindness since their engagement. He hoped that his parents had been satisfied with the wedding arrangements 'as I was so anxious that everybody would be pleased & of course especially you & Mama. I am afraid you must both have been very tired after it all.'[6] To his mother, the Duke wrote, 'I do hope you will not miss me very much, though I believe you will as I have stayed with you so much longer really than the brothers. I am very very happy now with my little darling so perhaps our parting yesterday was made easier for me but still I did feel a pang at leaving my home.'[7]

Queen Mary replied that she and his father would indeed miss him, as 'you have always been such a good son,' and 'we always turned to you in difficulties, knowing how reliable you always are.' But their sadness was softened by the knowledge that Elizabeth 'will make you such a perfect little wife', and they were already devoted to her.[8] Similarly the King wrote to 'Dearest Bertie' to congratulate him once more on having 'such a charming and delightful wife as Elizabeth'. 'I am sure you will both be very happy together . . . I miss you very much & regret your having left us, but now you will have your own home which I hope will be as happy as the one you have left.' He went on to make a pointed contrast between Prince Albert and his eldest son, the Prince of Wales. 'You have always been so sensible & easy to work with & you have always been ready to listen to any advice & to agree with my opinions about people & things, that I feel we have always got on very well together (very different to dear David).' He was quite certain that 'Elizabeth will be a splendid partner in your work & share with you & help you in all you have to do.'[9]

Many years later, King George VI's biographer John Wheeler-Bennett commented, 'No prophecy could have been more completely fulfilled, no expression of confidence more entirely justified. The

Duchess was not only to be the partner of his happiness but his inspiration of encouragement in the face of adversity, his enduring source of strength in joy and sadness.'[10]

*

THEY WERE comfortable at Polesden Lacey.* A large mansion near Dorking in Surrey, it was built in 1821 to designs by Thomas Cubitt, and the exterior retained some of its Regency flavour. After the Grevilles bought it in 1906, however, the interior was redesigned to Mrs Greville's taste by Mewes and Davis, the architects of the Ritz hotels in London and Paris. One of her additions was a grandiose saloon fitted with elaborate carved and gilded panelling dating from the early eighteenth century, and richly furnished with large mirrors and Persian carpets. The atmosphere she created was one of opulence and comfort. There were extensive gardens, tennis courts and a golf course, and the house was well supplied with all kinds of produce from the estate, on which there were cattle and sheep, vegetable gardens, orchards and hothouses. Mrs Greville was generous with staff, food and everything else her guests needed.

They walked around the golf course, the Duke with a club, they went to church in the rain on Sunday, they listened to gramophone records, they 'Talked very hard'.[11] And they enjoyed the unaccustomed privacy and solitude. They allowed one photographer to come and take pictures of them in order to deter all the others. On Thursday 3 May 1923, a hot day, reality intruded with a slightly unwelcome visit to London. They drove up to Bruton Street, where the Duchess 'talked hard' to her brothers David and Mike and to her mother. After lunch she and the Duke went to the Palace where she 'argued in vain' with

---

*   At this time Mrs Greville in fact intended to leave the house to the Duke of York. As a childless widow, she wrote to King George V in 1914 to say that, in recognition of King Edward VII's kindness to her after her husband's death in 1908, she wanted to leave Polesden Lacey to one of the King's sons. The King accepted, because she had no near relations, and Queen Mary went to visit Mrs Greville at Polesden Lacey. (RA GV/PRIV/AA48/8–10) It was evidently decided between them that Prince Albert should be chosen (the Prince of Wales, as heir to the throne, enjoyed the income of the Duchy of Cornwall and had no need of such munificence), and thereafter Mrs Greville took a special interest in him, writing to Queen Mary about him and inviting him to parties in London and Surrey. His accession to the throne before Mrs Greville's death meant that he had no need of Polesden Lacey, and Mrs Greville left it to the National Trust.

Commander Greig. The cause of this particular disagreement is not known, but she was apparently becoming impatient with her husband's principal aide.[12]

In the afternoon, to their relief, they were able to drive back to Polesden Lacey and went for a warm evening stroll in Mrs Greville's garden, before writing more letters. On Monday 7 May they left the house and motored up to London, lunching with the Strathmores at Bruton Street. That evening the Duchess had a cocktail with Mike and then changed into her blue travelling suit. The Prince of Wales arrived and 'We had a very gay dinner – & sang at the piano afterwards.' Then they drove to Euston to take the 11 o'clock sleeper to Scotland.[13] The train pulled into Glamis station at 10 a.m. and the platform was thronged with well-wishers. The Duchess's troop of Girl Guides, as well as the Boy Scouts and the local schoolchildren, were among those who had come to welcome them. 'Very nice of them,' she remarked.[14]

Her parents had prepared a suite of rooms in the oldest part of the Castle for them, and these they used from now on. On the first floor, the sitting room had latticed windows on either side of the blue and white Dutch-tiled fireplace. There were eighteenth-century tapestries on the walls and Chippendale chairs for which Lady Strathmore had worked tapestry seats. In the main bedroom, the fringe around the top of the four-poster bed was embroidered with the names and birth dates of all Lady Strathmore's children (and the dates on which Violet and Alec had died); the bed was covered with a quilt she had made. The dressing room had been converted into a bathroom for them, with another dressing room next door.

It was 'delicious' to be back at Glamis, as the Duchess wrote to Beryl; but the weather was dreadful – icy cold, with hail, sleet and snow showers.[15] Nevertheless they went out for walks, shot rabbits, visited friends in the neighbourhood or read, relaxed and wrote more letters. By the middle of the next week the Duchess had developed a 'rather troublesome' cough. Despite this, on Thursday 17 May they drove over to Cortachy Castle to lunch with the Airlie family and that evening, after playing bezique before dinner, they took the sleeper to London. The Duchess was touched by the crowd who gathered at the station to cheer them off.[16]

Next morning her cough was worse; they went straight to Bruton Street for breakfast, and the doctor came and gave her cough mixture. In the evening they drove down to Frogmore House in the Home

Park at Windsor, which the King had lent them, as White Lodge was not yet ready. The cough was by now 'very uncomfortable'. They spent the weekend resting at Frogmore, but were not constantly prudent. On Tuesday the Prince of Wales came to dine and then suggested they went dancing at the Embassy Club, 'so we dashed up to London in his car, & joined Paul's party there'. Among Prince Paul's guests were the Prince of Wales's friend Freda Dudley Ward, Sheila Loughborough,* Alice Astor, Prince Serge Obolensky† and Lord Cranborne. 'Danced hard till 2.30. David sent us back in his car. Very tired & enjoyed it awfully. Coughed a good deal.'[17]

The following morning, she recorded, 'Woke up very tired. We are not used to dancing!' On Friday 25 May she was diagnosed with whooping cough. 'Most annoying, but glad to know what it is.'[18] It was in the papers the following day. 'I hope Her Royal Highness likes Bananas,' wrote the dowager Lady Bradford solicitously to Queen Mary, 'for they are so good in whooping cough.'[19] The Duke told his mother that they could not come to her birthday party next day. 'You can imagine how very disappointed we both are about it, as it is so unromantic to catch whooping cough on your honeymoon!'[20]

Meanwhile Queen Mary was still busying herself with the refurbishment of White Lodge. She acted from the best of motives – her own first married home had been furnished in advance by Maples on the orders of her future husband, in the mistaken belief that he was doing her a kindness.‡ No doubt she wanted to ensure not only that her old home retained its character but also that it would be suitably

---

* Lady Loughborough had just returned from Australia, as she recorded in her memoirs. Her friend 'Ali' Mackintosh gave a party at the Embassy Club that night – no doubt the occasion to which the Duchess's diary refers. Lady Loughborough wrote: 'The Prince of Wales was with us and Freda, of course, also the Duke and Duchess of York. (Prince Bertie, now the Duke of York, had married the little debutante we had seen in the doorway of Eresby House three years before, Elizabeth Bowes Lyon).' (Princess Dimitri, 'Waltzing Matilda', p. 48)

† Prince Serge Obolensky (1890–1978), a Russian émigré, with whom, according to her memoirs, Sheila Loughborough had been in love at the time of the Duke of York's infatuation with her. Obolensky was formerly married to Princess Yurievsky, daughter of Tsar Alexander II. In 1924 he married Alice Astor (1902–56), daughter of John Jacob Astor IV; he was the first of her four husbands. She was a patron of the arts, especially the ballet.

‡ This was York Cottage at Sandringham. The Duke had chosen all the carpets, wallpapers and furniture with the help of his father, his sister and a man from Maples, a sadly frustrating experience for his wife, who loved arranging rooms. (James Pope-Hennessy, Queen Mary, pp. 275–8)

elegant. It cannot have been easy, however, for the Duchess to feel at home in a house so dominated by her mother-in-law's taste.

The young couple finally moved into White Lodge on 6 June. Together they arranged their possessions, old and new, fitting in as well as they could with the furniture that Queen Mary had chosen. The Duchess's diary records a two-hour visit of inspection by her mother-in-law a month later. 'We went all over the house till 5.15. Felt quite exhausted about the legs!'[21] She later confided to her mother that her bedroom was 'HIDEOUS', and asked if she could have two of her pictures from Glamis, one of them a Madonna, to hang on the walls.[22] It was a small but very natural rebellion.

It quickly became clear that White Lodge was not ideal for a young couple in the public eye whose lives were centred in London. The house was big and expensive to run. Richmond Park was no longer the sylvan fastness that George II had enjoyed 200 years before, but a weekend attraction for thousands of people. Many of them wanted nothing so much as a glimpse of the new Duchess and her husband. So when they were at home, privacy was a problem. When they left it, distance was the difficulty.

The road to London was nothing like as crowded as it was to become, but it was busy nonetheless. After an afternoon or early-evening engagement, the Duke and Duchess often had to drive to Richmond to change into evening wear and then drive back to town. In the winter, fog often descended upon the Park and it was sometimes hard to find the house at all. Although they had rooms at Buckingham Palace which Queen Mary urged them to use whenever they wanted – 'I have done my best to make them as nice as possible for Elizabeth,' she wrote[23] – they quickly began to wish they could move to London. But that was not easy, partly because of the need to avoid offending the King, let alone the Queen, and partly because delicate negotiations with the Crown Estate Commissioners and the Ministry of Works were involved. Royal expenditure may not then have been scrutinized as carefully as in later years, but it was an issue.

Three years were to pass before a suitable house in London could be found for them and the hurdles to moving were overcome. In the meantime the Duchess made the best of it. She invited D'Arcy Osborne, busy at the Foreign Office, to visit her – 'So some time you must throw the Eastern question firmly aside, turn your most magic stone three times from East to West, & start for Richmond.'[24] (She and Osborne had a long-running whimsical dialogue about how magic stones could ward off trouble. As one historian wrote of Osborne, 'he would have liked to believe in witches and the god Pan . . . with only a half-sceptical smile he wore a charm against cosmic rays.')[25]

Despite its drawbacks, White Lodge gave the Duke and Duchess a degree of independence and freedom: they were able to entertain family and friends informally, to play tennis and to go out riding (which the Duchess enjoyed, remarking in her diary that she had not ridden for years).[26] Nor did the distance prevent them from driving frequently to London to dine and dance with friends.

All this helped counterbalance the new restraints in the Duchess's life. Entry into the Royal Family, with its rituals and its orderliness, really was a sort of golden incarceration. The young Duchess could no longer go shopping alone; she could not travel on trains alone, or on buses at all. She was no longer able to see her friends as spontaneously as she loved to do, and when she met them at Court or at official functions there was a certain distance imposed by the formality required of the Royal Family. Helen Hardinge commented in her memoirs that older members of Queen Mary's entourage disapproved of the Duchess seeing 'too much' of her old friends, for fear that they would be too familiar towards her. As a result, Helen herself made a point of being 'very formal and decorous – so that it took the Duchess of York some time after her marriage to come to terms with all our conventional efforts to treat her correctly'.[27] Although later the Duchess was able to appoint friends to her entourage, her first lady in waiting was a stranger, a generation older and no doubt chosen by Queen Mary as someone whose experience would be helpful. She was Lady Katharine Meade,* formerly lady in waiting to the Duchess of Albany. She received the lukewarm description 'quite nice' on her first appearance in the Duchess of York's diary in June 1923; Helen Hardinge described her as a 'well-meaning old cup of tea',[28] but she never became close to the Duchess and resigned in 1926.

All in all, the Duchess was isolated and restricted in a way she had never been before. Her own family life had been so relaxed that the rules of the Palace, the Court and the King himself cannot have been

---

* Lady Katharine Meade (1871–1954), daughter of fourth Earl of Clanwilliam. The Duchess of Albany, to whom she had been lady in waiting, was the widow of Queen Victoria's youngest son Prince Leopold, Duke of Albany.

easy to assimilate. The King's life, as the Duke of Windsor later wrote, was a 'masterpiece in the art of well-ordered, unostentatious, elegant living'. The King and male members of the Household wore frock coats every day. Ladies of the Household dressed in formal clothes and wore, or at least carried, gloves at all times. In the evenings, dinners were sumptuous and formal. The King wore white tie and tails and the Queen wore full evening dress with tiara, even when they were dining alone. At Windsor, men wore the Windsor Coat, a dark-blue evening dress coat with scarlet collar and cuffs, gilt buttons and knee breeches. In Ascot Week, before dinner, guests gathered in the Green Drawing Room. Ladies would mingle on one side of the room, men on the other.

Members of the family would wait in the Grand Corridor until the King and Queen arrived. In the State Dining Room the dinner table was laden with the Grand Service of silver gilt, originally made for George IV. When the Queen led the ladies out at the end of the meal, they each dropped the King a deep curtsy. In the drawing room, the Queen had her own settee to which one or two women were brought to talk to her, while the others talked rather formally in small groups. The King and the men then came out of the dining room, paused for a moment with the ladies and went on into another room where they smoked cigars and talked.[29]

The Duchess, whose family dinner parties were far less formal and considerably more fun, did what she felt she could to enliven Court life. She found that she was able to put nervous guests at ease in ways which the King and Queen could never have done. When possible, she would sit down at the piano after dinner, play and sing and encourage other guests to join her.[30]

The King and Queen were perhaps surprised by how much they enjoyed this breath of informality. They quickly became fond of their new daughter-in-law and were openly affectionate towards her. They asked her to call them Papa and Mama, their own children's names for them; fortunately she had always called her own parents Mother and Father. The King made concessions to the Duchess that other members of the family would have thought quite impossible. Of them, he demanded perfection in every detail, and precision was essential to perfection. Sir Frederick Ponsonby, Keeper of the Privy Purse, wrote subsequently that there was no greater crime than being late. 'When I say late, the ordinary meaning of the word hardly conveyed the wonderful punctuality of the King and Queen. One was late if the clock sounded when one was on the stairs, even in a small house like York Cottage.'[31]

Punctuality was not known to be a passion of the Duchess. Remarkably, that did not seem to matter. It was soon part of Court lore that on one occasion early in her marriage she and the Duke arrived two minutes late for lunch and she apologized. To the delighted amazement of others at table, the King replied, 'You are not late, my dear, I think we must have sat down two minutes too early.' On another occasion when someone mentioned to the King her tendency to tardiness, he replied, 'Ah, but if she weren't late, she would be perfect, and how horrible that would be.'[32]

Adding to the King and Queen's affection for her was the fact that Prince Albert was clearly so happy. He had rarely appeared to be a very confident young man; his stammer compounded his general nervousness and his nervousness exaggerated his stammer. He was hard to get to know, but those who did know him valued him highly. It is a cliché but nonetheless true that he blossomed on marriage. He revelled in having achieved both freedom (at least some) and love (of an abiding sort). He found life in a new home with the Duchess to be an enchanting adventure, which not even the problems of White Lodge could diminish. Whenever he was upset – whether by a chance remark or request from his parents, or a failure on the tennis court or in the butts, or a problem with making a speech – she gently calmed and reassured him. 'I shall never forget the Duchess's wonderful gentleness with him in the car afterwards,' said one of her ladies in waiting after he was trounced at tennis at Wimbledon.[33]

At the end of June she had to prepare for a stressful moment – entertaining her parents-in-law to a meal at White Lodge for the first time. The Duchess may well have been concerned – the Duke wrote to his mother in advance, 'I had better warn you that our cook is not very good, but she can do the plain dishes well, & I know you like that sort.' The lunch went well, and Queen Mary thought that they had made the house 'very nice'.[34]

*

PUBLIC LIFE began to demand the Duchess's attention. The politics of the time was dominated by the problems of the economy and, in particular, by the decline of Britain's principal export industries – coal, steel and shipbuilding. The brief post-war boom had ended by 1921, and unemployment remained above one million until the Second World War. Hopes that the sacrifices of 1914–18 would bring about a better world were shrinking, and by 1922 the idealism of the immediate post-war years had almost entirely disappeared. For, instead of prosperity, peace had brought deflation, higher unemployment, lower wages and lower profits.

Economic gloom was accompanied by cultural questioning, a reaction against what were thought to be the stuffy and traditional values of the Victorian era. Writers began to question these values. In *Eminent Victorians*, published in 1918, Lytton Strachey had satirized celebrated Victorians such as Dr Arnold, General Gordon and Florence Nightingale, treating them as plaster saints. Where Strachey led, lesser talents followed. By the end of the 1920s, many people were coming to believe that Britain had blundered through the Great War under the leadership of incompetent politicians and bloodthirsty generals. The new atmosphere of cynicism and questioning posed difficulties for the Royal Family, who were forced to redefine their role in a society greatly changed from that which they had known before 1914.

In politics new men were coming to power. The Lloyd George era ended with the fall of his Coalition government in October 1922. The Coalition had been widely condemned for its policy of repression in Ireland, for its aggressive attitude towards organized labour, and for corruption in the sale of honours. In the general election which followed in November 1922, two-party politics was restored, but with the Labour Party replacing the Liberals as the main party of the left. The Conservatives, however, under their new leader Bonar Law, won the election, although Law was forced to resign on grounds of ill health in 1923, and died shortly afterwards. The new Conservative leader, who, with Labour's Ramsay MacDonald, was to dominate the inter-war years, was Stanley Baldwin. Both of these men believed in moderation. MacDonald sought to wean the Labour Party away from doctrines of class war and direct action. Baldwin, a former West Midlands ironmaster, tried to persuade the Conservatives and the leaders of industry to adopt a more conciliatory attitude towards organized labour. In a speech to the House of Commons in 1923, shortly after becoming prime minister, he declared: 'Four words of one syllable each are words which contain salvation for this country and for the whole world. They are "Faith", "Hope", "Love" and

"Work". No Government in this country today which has not faith in the people, hope in the future, love for its fellow-men, and which will not work and work and work, will ever bring this country through into better days and better times.'[35]

Baldwin's conciliatory sentiments naturally endeared him to George V and the Royal Family. In modern times, the constitutional monarchy has become a unifying institution, and so successive monarchs have been temperamentally inclined to conciliation and moderation. Between the wars, George V, Edward VIII and George VI all saw themselves as having a role to play in helping to mitigate class feeling.

The Duchess's first public engagement as a member of the Royal Family came on 30 June 1923 when she and the Duke attended the Royal Air Force Pageant at Hendon. Aeroplanes, still an awe-inspiring novelty, provided an increasingly popular spectacle. Attempts to fly the Atlantic had excited huge publicity since 1919 when two RAF pilots, Captain John Alcock and Lieutenant Arthur Brown, had managed to cross from Newfoundland to Ireland, some eight years before Charles Lindbergh made his epic solo flight. An airmail service between London and Paris had been opened in 1919 and in 1923 a regular passenger service was just gaining popularity; aircraft became a little more comfortable – made of metal rather than wood and wire – and safer, as radio communications were developed. In the summer of 1923, some 80,000 people came to the Hendon show to see the de Havillands which had been formed into a special new squadron to defend London and had a top speed of 150 mph.[36]

In early July the Duke and Duchess visited Edinburgh, where they drove through the city with the King and Queen, cheered by large crowds. For the next five days they stayed at the Palace of Holyroodhouse – which the Duchess loved, as she wrote to D'Arcy Osborne. She was pleased to find herself back among her Scottish countrymen. 'They are so romantic, & sentimental, & generous & proud that they have to hide it all under a mask of reserve and hardness, & they seem to take people in very successfully!!'[37] She and the Duke accompanied the King and Queen on engagements in and around Edinburgh, they toured the Border country together by motor, and on 13 July they went to Dunfermline. Although the press photographs of these visits show the Duchess in an obviously secondary role, a girlish figure in pretty summery clothes, often just in the background, a sharp-eyed reporter at Dunfermline noticed her particular talent with crowds, which was to endear her to the public in the future. At the Carnegie Orthopaedic Clinic, she 'suddenly recognised among the ex-Service men one whom she had met in a war hospital' – presumably Glamis. 'She at once went across to the patient, shook hands with him, and chatted with him for some minutes.'[38]

Later that month, on 19 July, she undertook what appears to have been the first solo engagement of her public life. She spent the morning with her husband visiting a thousand children from the slums of London who were on a holiday in Epping Forest organized by the Fresh Air Fund. That afternoon she set off without the Duke to visit the children's hospital in Cheyne Walk.[39] A few weeks before, she had tactfully declined an invitation to open the new open-air ward on the roof of the hospital because Queen Alexandra was its president. But she had indicated that she would 'be very glad indeed to pay a visit to the Hospital' once the new ward was opened. The Cheyne Hospital was set up for handicapped and incurable children, and in the years ahead she became closely associated with her patronages of similar homes and hospitals.[40]

Over 24–25 July the Yorks spent two days in Liverpool where, among other duties, they laid the foundation stone of a new wing for the Infirmary. While they were there victims of a serious street accident were brought into the casualty department; most were children. The Duke and Duchess offered to contribute to a relief fund and continued to request reports on the injured after they had returned to London. While there, the Duchess also judged a children's essay competition. In his letter of thanks, the Lord Mayor of Liverpool wrote, 'On all hands one hears beautiful tributes to the kindness of the Duke and the wonderful charm of the Duchess.'[41]

Her particular gift for engaging with individuals was evident privately as well as publicly. Sergeant Ernest Pearce, whom she had befriended when he was a convalescent at Glamis in 1915 and with whom she had kept in touch ever since, had fallen on hard times. With barely enough money to feed and clothe his family as a result of a strike, her letter and gift of £10 came as a 'godsend'. 'The children are all rigged out in boots & clothes and I do not care who sees them now – they all look neat & smart and we have just enjoyed the best Sunday dinner we have had for many a bright week,' he told her, going on to vent his anger at the strike leaders, 'a d—d rotten lot . . . – all out for themselves – yet the men has not the blinking courage to shift them . . . it makes me mad to think these are the men who stop an honest working man from a full week's work.' Sergeant Pearce also expressed the hope that she had recovered from her whooping cough, as the papers said she was not looking very well. 'I'm afraid Richmond Park is not a Glamis Castle – pardon me saying so.'[42]

*

AFTER THEIR Liverpool trip there was a break from public duties. They spent five days at Molecomb, Lady Doris Vyner's childhood home in Sussex. 'So delicious seeing Doris again – the first time since we married,' wrote the Duchess. They attended the races at Goodwood, played the piano and the banjo or danced in the evenings, and held a married couples' tennis tournament, which the Yorks won 'easily!'[43]

Wherever she went the Duchess's appearance was, understandably, a focus of attention. She clearly enjoyed clothes and the press loved reporting on her outfits. She quickly evolved a way of dressing which not only suited her but became instantly recognizable. When she first stepped into the public eye, while slim young flappers dressed in somewhat mannish clothes and sported cropped hair, she was photographed with her hair prettily curled, wearing cloche hats, shoulder-hugging fur collars and long skirts. At Goodwood the *Daily Telegraph* described her attire each day. One outfit was 'a café au lait-coloured crepe marocain dress, with a long straight bodice and draped skirt' and 'a brown lace hat over gold tissue . . . having a bunch of brown grapes shaded to gold at one side'.[44] Her preferred colours seem to have been darker than they later became, and she often chose brown or grey, fashionable colours at the time.*

The Duchess's twenty-third birthday on 4 August had an even greater significance than usual. Not only was Prince Paul of Serbia's engagement to Princess Olga of Greece announced that morning – 'so glad', she noted – but James Stuart and his fiancée Rachel Cavendish had chosen the day for their wedding. The Yorks did not attend it; in the afternoon the Duchess sat for a portrait by Savely Sorine,† while

---

* The fashion correspondents whose descriptions of the outfits worn by ladies attending the Yorks' wedding appeared in the London press commented on the preponderance of these muted colours among the smartest ensembles.

† Savely Sorine, Russian portrait painter (1887–1953). Sorine was a student of Repin at the Academy of Beaux Arts in Petrograd, where he won the Prix de Rome. He went into exile

the Duke played polo at Worcester Park. Her diary for the day was melancholy. Of James and Rachel she wrote, 'hope it will be alright'. She found sitting for her portrait boring and she felt depressed. She did not state the reason, but perhaps memories of past, more carefree birthdays and other times confronted her, particularly after the light-hearted interlude with old friends at Molecomb.[45] A sense of sadness does seem to infuse the portrait. Sorine showed her in a white dress on a brownish-red sofa, partly covered by green drapery. A straw hat hangs from her right arm, her engagement ring is prominent on her left hand. Her face is almost square, her eyebrows exaggerated, her eyes have little sparkle.

As usual, she left for Scotland soon after her birthday. But this year, for the first time, Glamis had to share her with Balmoral. She and the Duke went to her home first and the Prince of Wales came to stay. He wrote an unusually cheerful letter to his father shortly afterwards, saying how much he had enjoyed his visit: 'they are a very happy family there – I'm so fond of Elizabeth; she is too sweet for words & she was the life and soul of the party – I'm so glad she's going to be at Balmoral.'[46]

Once at Balmoral, the Duke spent as much time as possible out grouse shooting or stalking. The Duchess had fewer opportunities to escape the house. She wrote to her mother saying, with poetic licence, that most people at Balmoral were over ninety. She and the Duke were looking forward to returning to Glamis. 'It will be heavenly. There is no "family" feeling at all in this family. They are all very nice to me, & horrid to each other!'[47]

Her brothers-in-law in particular valued her presence. Prince George wrote to her after she had left saying how much they all missed her. 'You managed to keep the King in a good temper which was the main thing & which very few people can do least of all his sons.'[48] The King and Queen were also sad to see her go. The King wrote to his son, 'We miss you very much. The better I know & the more I see of your dear little wife the more charming I think she is & everyone fell in love with her here.' The Queen's letter repeated the

after the Russian Revolution and exhibited his work widely, including at the Salon d'Automne in Paris in 1922–3, and at the International Exposition of Pittsburgh in 1923–4. In 1948 he painted a portrait of Princess Elizabeth, intended as a companion piece to that of Queen Elizabeth: both are painted in watercolour on paper. The two portraits (RCIN 453400, 453399) today hang in Clarence House.

sentiments: 'the more I see of her the more I love her, we are indeed lucky to have got such a charming daughter in law & you such a delightful wife.'[49]

*

DURING THE first year of her marriage the Duchess attended three royal weddings and one christening, each increasing her acquaintance with her husband's extended family. The most daunting, perhaps, was the first, a double celebration in Belgrade. The son and heir of Alexander, King of the Serbs, Croats and Slovenes (the new Yugoslavia), was to be christened, and a day later King Alexander's cousin and Elizabeth Bowes Lyon's admirer Prince Paul was to marry Princess Olga of Greece.* The Duke and Duchess of York had agreed to be godparents to the child but had not originally intended to attend either service.

The Foreign Office initially put no pressure on them to do so, but then, at short notice, Lord Curzon persuaded the King that the presence of the Duke and Duchess would be an important way of showing British solidarity with the newly established Triune Kingdom. On 23 September the King telegraphed the Duke, who had just begun a short holiday with his wife at Holwick Lodge. The Duke was incensed not only by the sudden change of plan, but also because he felt that the request did not give his wife enough time to prepare for the trip. He wrote intemperately to Louis Greig, 'Curzon should be drowned for giving me such short notice. I have written to him for his reasons & also asked him to see me before leaving.' Referring to his new married status, he added, 'He must know things are different now.'[50]

The Duke and Duchess had to make swift preparations. On 27 September the Duchess left Holwick for a brief visit to London to find suitable clothes for the festivities in Belgrade. On the train from Darlington (the nearest station to Holwick) she scribbled a note to her husband in blue pencil on the inside of the dust jacket of a P. G. Wodehouse novel, *Psmith in the City*. 'My darling Darlington . . . I wish you were here, but I'm glad for you to be out on the "mower" instead

---

* The other two royal weddings in 1923 were those of Lady Louise Mountbatten to the Crown Prince of Sweden on 4 November and of Princess Maud, daughter of Louise, Princess Royal, to Lord Carnegie on 12 November.

of in this stuffy beastly train.' She had had difficulty stopping herself laughing at the extreme politeness of the waiter who served lunch on the train. 'There was the usual crowd of slightly hysterical females at Darlington, who murmured "Isn't she sweet," gazing fondly at Catherine [Maclean, her maid].'[51] Later that day, after she had arrived in London, she wrote again, self-mockingly, to 'Darling Angel', saying, 'I've really got nothing to say except that all London was decorated in honour of my arrival, and they are having fireworks everywhere tonight, in token of their delight in my return. Isn't it touching? . . . Your extremely loving E.'[52] In preparation for the trip, the Duchess had a new passport photograph taken, ordered new clothes from Mrs Handley Seymour and bought 'some very pretty hats' in Curzon Street.[53] A pair of candlesticks was bought from Garrard as a wedding present for Prince Paul.[54]

From Holwick the Duke wrote saying how lonely he felt without her. He had had an unsatisfactory, wet, cold day's shooting. 'Lunch was not a success. There was not enough whiskey to keep us warm & your father's brandy bottle was filled with Italian Vermouth by mistake!! Poor Barson got it in the neck!! However all is now well & peace is restored.' He was looking forward to seeing her back at Glamis on the Sunday. 'Hope you will have a good day for your clothes, hair, teeth and nose. Darling don't overtire yourself please trying on or choosing clothes as it is so bad for you.' It was nearly cocktail time as he wrote 'and there is no you to make them. Mike no doubt will blow our heads off with his concoction.'[55]

In early October they returned to London and to their public duties. The Imperial Conference – at which the British government recognized the rights of Dominions within the Empire to negotiate and ratify treaties with foreign powers – had opened on 1 October. On 11 October the King gave a dinner at Buckingham Palace for the Dominion and Indian delegates at which the Yorks were present. The Duchess, wearing a tiara and white satin embroidered with pearls, was seated between the King and Stanley Bruce, the Australian Prime Minister. She also talked to the other premiers, notably General Smuts, the Prime Minister of South Africa, whom she described as 'A super man & a great one'[56] – this was to remain her view all her life – and to Mackenzie King, the Canadian Prime Minster. All three were to act as her hosts in the years to come.

Next day they had a rather hair-raising drive (the accelerator jammed and the car ran away with them for a mile) to Northampton-shire. Shaken but not harmed, they looked over and decided to rent the Old House in Guilsborough. It was tiny (by royal standards) but the Duchess thought it was furnished with 'wonderful taste';[57] it would be a charming place in which to be alone together for winter weekends and would enable the Duke to indulge his passion for hunting with the Pytchley and Waddon Chase, both near by.[58]

The following week was filled with more fittings of clothes, dinner at Claridge's, a trip to the theatre to see a musical, *Stop Flirting*, starring Fred and Adele Astaire, and a dance at the Savoy. The Duchess loved musicals: 'I think there is nothing to beat them, & the worse, the better,' she wrote to D'Arcy Osborne, adding that she thought the Astaires 'delicious'.[59] She was soon to find herself in a real-life musical comedy.

D'Arcy Osborne sent her some books to read on the train to Serbia. He appears, somewhat surprisingly for a confirmed bachelor, to have asked her opinion of the merits of marriage to a young American woman named Isabel. So she gave it:

> Is a bell necessary on a bicycle. That's one point against her poor girl. Now let me see –
>
> | Against. | For. |
> | --- | --- |
> | 1. Her name. | Sense of Humour. |
> | 2. American. | |
> | 3. Eight millions. | |
> | 4. Indifferent features. | |
> | 5. No parents. | |
>
> Yes, I think you ought to marry her. The sense of humour balances everything.

She ended, 'I must stop now, and turn over the clocks, wind up the piano, & generally prepare for Adventure in the Balkans.'[60]

*

THEY AROSE early on the morning of Thursday 18 October to start their three-day journey. They were accompanied by Lieutenant Colonel Sir Ronald Waterhouse,* Lady Katharine Meade, the Duchess's lady in

---

* Waterhouse had been private secretary and equerry to the Duke of York in 1921, but had

waiting, two valets and two ladies' maids, one of them Catherine Maclean. A newspaper photographer, Arthur Ferguson, from Personality Press Ltd, travelled with the group.

The Simplon Express took them from Paris to Milan, where they visited the Cathedral before rejoining the train for Venice and then Zagreb. There, on Saturday morning, their carriage was hitched to a special but ancient train to take them on the long, hot journey over the plains to Belgrade.[61] They were attended by footmen in pale-blue liveries with spats and vast silver buttons. At Belgrade station that evening they were met by King Alexander and his sister, Princess Helen, as his wife Queen Marie, known as Mignon, was unwell.

After the formal greetings, the band played 'God Save the King' several times and very fast; then they were swept off to the Royal Palace 'in tiny blue victorias with white horses'. There the Duchess met for the first time the redoubtable 'Cousin Missy', Queen Marie of Romania, Mignon's mother and King George V's first cousin. She was an effusive and irrepressible lady, granddaughter of Queen Victoria and ever eager to promote family ties with Britain. The Duchess had to change swiftly for a large family dinner, which included most of the Romanian Royal Family, Queen Elizabeth of Greece and Princess Olga's family. She was seated between the King of Romania and her old friend Prince Paul. After dinner she was taken to see Mignon and her baby, Prince Peter, whose christening was next day. By the time she went to bed at 10.30, she was, she wrote, 'Tired!'[62]

The Palace was crowded, the midday temperature was over 70 degrees in the shade, and there was no hot water, but she enjoyed it all. 'Everything is very funny here, just like a musical comedy!' Perhaps it was all the more enjoyable because it was the opposite of Palace life in London – everything was delayed.[63]

On Sunday morning the Duchess was given 'a sort of embroidered frock' to wear for the christening. She was godmother (*koomitsa*) and the Duke was godfather (*koom*). The Duke's role was, as she wrote, 'very complicated'.[64] He had to carry the baby on a cushion into the church; the baby's grandmother Queen Marie of Romania and his aunt Princess John unswathed him and then the Duke handed him to the

---

become principal private secretary to the Prime Minister a year later. He was seconded to act as equerry to the Duke for this trip.

Patriarch for total immersion, as the Serbian Orthodox rites required. Unfortunately the Patriarch lost his grip on the infant, who fell into the font. The Duke reacted fast, grabbed the baby and returned him to the shaking hands of the Patriarch.[65] The Duke, preceded by a deacon, then had to carry the loudly protesting child three times around the altar. He was 'simply terrified', according to his wife.[66]

After the service, at which the Duchess thought the singing was lovely, the royal party appeared on the balcony of the Palace. The crowd below cheered 'Zhivio Petar!' (Long live Peter).* That afternoon the Duke and Duchess drove around steaming-hot Belgrade with Prince Paul and Princess Olga and took tea on the Romanian royal yacht in the Danube. Most of the Romanian Royal Family were living on board – because there was no room at the Palace.[67]

Next day, 22 October, the Duchess wore an embroidered velvet gown for their friends' wedding. 'Olga looked lovely, I thought, & it went off very well, and Paul is so happy. He was enchanted at having us there, & otherwise he had no real friends.' After a late lunch she 'skipped away', changed, and went to visit a children's hospital run by a Scottish doctor, Dr Katherine Mcphail.† That evening they met the British colony at the Legation: 'Very small and all Scotch!' Meeting expatriate Scots was to become a constant of her visits abroad.

Afterwards they dined – still in their day clothes, she noted – before driving to the station with King Alexander.[68] They had an amusing formal departure ceremony – amusing because they were not really departing. The train was due to leave early in the morning but they had decided to spend the night in their own *wagon lit* in a siding. 'So we went through all the usual pomp, & a guard of honour, looking exactly like the male chorus of a revue, & a band, & rows of ladies with bouquets, & kisses all round, & then we steamed triumphantly out of the station, for about 20 yards, where we stopped all night! It was so funny, because it was all a sham, & they all knew it too!! You

---

* Crown Prince Peter came to the throne only eleven years later when his father, King Alexander I, was assassinated while in Marseilles. The young King Peter II was forced into exile after the German invasion in 1941. He took refuge in Britain and later joined the RAF. He was deposed *in absentia* in 1945 and died in the United States in 1970.

† This was the Anglo-Serbian Children's Hospital. 'It is the only one in all Serbia, and does marvellous work,' the Duchess recorded. (RA QEQM/PRIV/DIARY/3)

have no idea how odd they are, & so nice!'[69] They liked her too: the Duke reported to his father that 'they were all enchanted with Elizabeth'.[70]

They arrived back in England on 25 October, having spent five of the previous seven nights on trains.* It had been an exhausting but fascinating experience for the Duchess, and one that she had taken entirely in her stride.

*

CHRISTMAS 1923 was politically a difficult period. Stanley Baldwin was facing increasing problems at home and abroad. He wished to introduce Protection to defend British producers against cheap imports and on 12 November he asked the King for a dissolution of Parliament so as to seek a mandate from the nation. The King, who worried about the turmoil across Europe and believed that Baldwin would lose his gamble, attempted to dissuade him, but in vain.

Baldwin's proposal to impose import taxes raised an outcry against the prospect of expensive food, and the election was fierce. The Liberals, split between Lloyd George and Asquith, reunited under the banner of Free Trade. Lloyd George, in typically spirited fashion, called the Tories 'tinned crabs' and 'tinned salmon', the sorts of foods on which people were warned they would have to subsist, if tariffs were introduced. The *Daily News* published electioneering songs which proved popular enough actually to be sung at political meetings. One, a parody of the popular American song 'Yes, We Have No Bananas', went:

> No, we won't have Protection,
> We won't have Protection today.
> 'Twould rush up the prices
> And squeeze us like vices
> And we'd have to pay, pay, pay . . .[71]

The years of slump had given ex-servicemen, now on the electoral register, ample time to think. As Robert Graves pointed out, they might dislike 'Socialist clap trap' but they felt they had been let down by both the major, older parties. ' "Them Socialists can't make no bigger box-up nor the old lot didn't" was the mood on many mean streets.'[72]

When the results came in on 6 December, Baldwin and the

Conservative Party had lost eighty-eight seats; they now had only 258 Members of Parliament. The relatively new, completely untried Labour Party increased its representation from 144 seats to 191 and the number of Liberal MPs rose to 158. It was an unprecedented crisis. For the first time ever in British politics there was a three-way split; no one party could govern alone, but each of them could try to form a coalition with one of the others. In effect the Liberals held the balance of power between left and right. The King's role became critical.

Baldwin wished to resign at once, but the King considered that this would not be proper – he reminded the Prime Minister that the Conservatives were still the single largest party and so it was Baldwin's duty to confront the new House of Commons and thus determine whether or not he could actually form a government. The King insisted that the sovereign 'ought not to accept the verdict of the Polls, except as expressed by the representatives of the Electorate across the floor of the House of Commons'.[73]

Baldwin agreed but he stressed that he was not prepared to form another coalition with the Liberals in order to keep Labour out. This caused further dismay among Conservatives, in and out of Parliament. Labour politicians were thought of by many traditionalists as 'Wild Men' who would destroy the established order, just as their comrades had in Russia. All sorts of schemes were proposed by which the monarch might use his prerogative to keep Labour out. These suggestions aroused Labour anger and one Labour leader, George Lansbury MP, warned at a meeting in Shoreditch, 'Some centuries ago, a King stood against the common people and he lost his head.'[74] In similar vein, the 'Marseillaise' and 'The Red Flag' were sung at a meeting at the Albert Hall over which the Labour leader, Ramsay MacDonald, presided. All this was alarming, but the King remained calm, saying that he must rely upon his own judgement.[75] He knew that, if and when Baldwin was defeated in Parliament, he would have to send for Ramsay MacDonald as the leader of the next-largest party. He also made it clear that he would not hamper MacDonald by imposing conditions of any sort upon him.

The run-up to Christmas was thus a period of political uncertainty, if not fear, but that did not get in the way of traditional festivities. The Yorks were busy. On 11 December they attended a concert given by the Royal Amateur Orchestral Society at the Queen's Hall in central

London, and the same evening went to a charity ball. They attended the Christmas Party of the 'Not Forgotten' Association and on 18 December the Duchess had a solo engagement to present the prizes at the Francis Holland School in Clarence Gate on the edge of Regent's Park. Christmas itself was to be spent at Sandringham. The contrast between the stiff formality of the royal occasion and the happy hilarity of all her Christmases past was something to which the Duchess did not look forward.[76]

She and the Duke took the train to Norfolk with other members of the Royal Family on 22 December and, after arrival at York Cottage, called that afternoon at the big house to see 'Granny, Aunt Toria & the Norways* etc. Everybody looking even older!'[77] On Christmas Eve they watched the distribution of Christmas food to the tenants of the estate and then returned for tea at Sandringham House, where all the presents were laid out on a long table. The King and Queen gave their daughter-in-law a pretty bracelet and a number of smaller presents. On Christmas Day itself they all walked to church and then had lunch at York Cottage. Afterwards the Duke and Duchess went for a long walk. Dinner that night, for which she dressed in red velvet, was at the big house. She sat between General Sir Dighton Probyn, Queen Alexandra's ancient, eccentric, bewhiskered Comptroller, and Olav, the Crown Prince of Norway. It seems to have been a more relaxed evening than she had feared, for she recorded in her diary, 'crackers and much laughter'.[78]

*

NINETEEN-TWENTY-FOUR opened with another attempt by the Duke to get them rehoused. It was not easy. First of all there were not many suitable houses easily available in London and, secondly, there was the problem of the public money already spent at White Lodge; they could not simply walk away. The Duchess's diary recorded, 'Greig telephoned after tea to say that edeh [sic] dah a klat tuoba etihw egdol, & taht ti dah deliaf. Cifirret tnemtnioppasid.'[79]

At the same time, she got into a rare scrape with the King. On Tuesday 8 January they had returned to London from Northampton. She went to the dentist who 'froze my face', then she drove on to

---

* Queen Alexandra, her daughter Princess Victoria, King Haakon VII of Norway, his wife Queen Maud (Queen Alexandra's youngest daughter) and their son Crown Prince Olav.

White Lodge. There was a busy evening ahead. They drove back into London and picked up the Prince of Wales at St James's Palace; they dined with him, and Prince George, at Claridge's and then went to the theatre. After a brief stop at St James's Palace they went on to the Midnight Follies, a nightclub and cabaret in the Metropole Hotel. There they danced. They did not get home till 3 a.m.[80]

Dancing and jazz had become widespread passions since the end of the war. There were many new dance crazes – the Twinkle, the Jog Trot, the Vampire, the Shimmy and later the Charleston. Journalists wrote, with typical prurience, of shocking 'Nights in the Jazz Jungle'. A *Daily Mail* article described 'Jazzmania' thus: 'Women dressed as men, men as women; youths in bathing drawers and kimonos. Matrons moving about lumpily and breathing hard. Everybody terribly serious; not a single laugh, or the palest ghost of a smile. Frantic noises and occasional cries of ecstasy came from half a dozen negro players. Dim lights, drowsy odours and futurist paintings on the walls and ceiling.'[81] With dancing came more drinking. The Licensing Act of 1921 allowed alcohol to be served with food (often just sandwiches) after 11 p.m. But physicians expressed great concern that the younger generation were drinking more. Cocktails were denounced as 'the most reprehensible form of alcoholic abuse'.

The Metropole was the first hotel to offer dancers a large cabaret as well, and this attracted a certain notoriety. When the King heard of the Duke and Duchess's visit to the Follies, he was not pleased, and told Louis Greig so. Greig passed on the reprimand and the Duchess noted in her diary, 'Apparently na lufwa wor tuoba eht thgindim seillof.' She wrote at once to her father-in-law. 'I am <u>so</u> sorry about this, as I hate to think of you being annoyed with us, or worried in any way,' she said; they had gone only to have supper there after the theatre, 'and it really is a most respectable place. I promise you we would not go anywhere that we <u>ought not</u> to.' She hoped he did not mind her writing, because she knew how busy he was. However, she could not resist adding a rather risky reference to fast behaviour: 'I only hope I shall not be under the influence of a drug!! As whilst you are opening Parliament, I shall be opening my jaw to the dentist, and he told me he was going to inject some "dope" into my face.'[82]

If his daughter-in-law's charm had its usual mollifying effect, no written response has survived; perhaps the King wrote none because he was indeed busy with matters of government. On 15 January 1924 he conducted the state opening of the new Parliament; afterwards, the Yorks had lunch with him at the Palace. The King advised the Duke to attend the House of Commons when he could – 'there will be some very interesting debates which will become historical.'[83] On 21 January Baldwin confronted the Commons. The Conservatives were defeated after the Liberals decided to side with Labour.

The next day Baldwin came to the Palace to tender his resignation. The King sent for Ramsay MacDonald. In his diary he noted, 'I had an hour's talk with him, he impressed me very much, he wishes to do [the] right thing.' He added: 'Today 23 years ago dear Grandmama died, I wonder what she would have thought of a Labour Govt.'[84] In the event, MacDonald appointed a Cabinet with wise regard to the sensibilities of those who feared revolution. He and the King quickly established great confidence in each other. The King made a point of meeting each of his new ministers personally; he recorded in his diary that he had a very interesting conversation with the most left-wing minister of all, John Wheatley, now Minister of Health. He was impressed, writing to Queen Alexandra: 'I must say they all seem to be very intelligent & they take things very seriously. They have different ideas to ours, as they are all socialists but they ought to be given a chance & ought to be treated fairly.'[85]

The new men thought well of their king. One of them, J. R. Clynes, Lord Privy Seal, a former mill-hand, wrote in his *Memoirs*, 'I had expected to find him unbending; instead he was kindness and sympathy itself. Before he gave us leave to go, he made an appeal to us that I have never forgotten: "The immediate future of my people, and their whole happiness, is in your hands, gentlemen. They depend upon your prudence and sagacity." '[86]

On the day of Baldwin's defeat, the Yorks had awoken at their rented house at Guilsborough; the Duke went hunting while the Duchess ventured on the train from Northampton – there was a train drivers' strike that day and it was not clear she would get through. But a few trains were running and the station master at Northampton put on a saloon for her. She reached White Lodge at about 6.30, just after her husband had arrived by car. He left to dine with the Prince of Wales and then went to the House of Commons to witness the moment at which the Labour Party took power for the first time.[87]

The rest of that winter the Duke and Duchess spent many

weekends at Guilsborough. She liked him to hunt but she was aware of the dangers and got nervous – and sometimes cross – if he returned late from the field. Apart from hunting, their lives were busy – with official engagements, and an enormous amount of driving to and from White Lodge – not to mention late nights in plenty. Thus on Tuesday 26 February the Duchess went out to lunch at the Berkeley with her friend Dorothé Plunket 'and I admired her baby'. (Patrick Plunket, who was born in September 1923, was to become an intimate friend of the family; his parents died in a plane crash in 1938.) This was followed by a long night out with the Prince of Wales, ending with another visit to the Metropole, despite the King's opinion of the place. They got to bed at 3 a.m. and next day, although both felt tired and unwell, they drove to London, had tea with Lady Airlie at Bruton Street and then drove back to 'Whiters' to change for a great ball at the Londonderrys'.[88]

On 28 February, accompanied by Louis Greig, she opened the Ideal Home Exhibition at Olympia. This outing was almost the last duty that Louis Greig undertook as the Duke of York's Comptroller. He and the Duke had agreed that he should retire, to be replaced by Captain Basil Brooke. It was a major break – Greig had served the Duke with sympathy, loyalty and inspiration since 1916, as his principal and essential bulwark and friend. His departure was perhaps inevitable once the Duke had a wife who was not only anxious but also well able to offer him even greater support and encouragement.

In October 1923 the Prince had written to reassure his parents that the decision was mutual and necessary. 'I feel that now I am married it is better to have a change as things have not been working too smoothly and we both feel the time has come.'[89] The King and Queen were nonetheless alarmed and told him so. The Prince replied to his father saying how sorry he was to have worried them and he now wished he had told them of his plan to relinquish Greig before he had done it. 'I wish I had known what I do now about how much you liked him & all the different things he did for you.'[90]

Inevitably rumours circulated that the Duchess was responsible for Greig's departure. She was dismayed by such talk and, in a letter to him the following month, she took care to express both her own and the Duke's gratitude to him, adding that the Duke was troubled by these unfounded accusations. Greig replied:

I was tremendously bucked up with your letter, because, although the question of ingratitude never entered my mind, I began honestly to think that I ought to have gone years ago & that Prince Bertie had been keeping me on against his will & that I ought to have seen this earlier than I did.

Your charming letter has made a tremendous difference to this feeling & Prince Bertie has also been very kind, so that all is absolutely clear again, & I can assure both you & Prince Bertie that I am at your service as long as I am needed.[91]

In a fond letter of 29 February 1924, the day after he left, the Prince himself assured Greig of his gratitude and affection. 'A parting between two friends is always a painful ordeal, but a parting between us, I hope, is an impossibility, even an official one . . . I hope and trust we shall always be the best of friends and that we shall see something of each other in the days to come.'[92] At the insistence of the King and Queen, Greig remained a member of the Household, even while he embarked on a new career in the City.[93]

That spring, the Duchess was again afflicted by bouts of flu and tonsillitis. On 7 March, after attending a party for Members of Parliament at Buckingham Palace, she 'went straight back to White Lodge, & felt like death'.[94] She had to spend ten days in bed. She wrote in pencil to D'Arcy Osborne, asking if he would come and see her. 'I am bubbling with talk at the moment.' She wanted to hear all about the new Labour regime at the Foreign Office. She was not, she wrote, enthusiastic about Labour, but she was very fond of her Scottish nurse from Dundee who was 'deliciously enthusiastic' about everything. 'How I love the little things of life.'[95]

On 23 April the Duke and Duchess went with the King to the opening of the British Empire Exhibition at Wembley. The King was patron of the exhibition, the Prince of Wales president, and Queen Mary patron of the Women's Section. The Duchess, unlike her husband, also had an important role – she was president of the Women's Section. The exhibition was a major event in which sovereign and Empire were once again fused in the public imagination. In retrospect it is easy to say that by 1924 the days of empire were fading fast, but at the time it did not seem so. The Empire Collect, read at the opening ceremony by the Bishop of London, beseeched the Almighty to 'raise up generations of public men who will have the

faith and daring of the Kingdom of God in them, and who will enlist
for life in a holy warfare for the freedom and rights of all Thy children'.
The exhibition was designed to celebrate the extraordinary achievements of Britain in the world and to draw the peoples of the Empire
together.[96]

The Royal Family drove by car most of the way from Windsor to
Wembley, and then, despite the cold, they transferred to horse-drawn
carriages, in which they paraded around the packed and enthusiastic
stadium. The Prince of Wales then formally invited his father to open
the huge imperial collection gathered in his honour and in celebration
of the Empire. The Duchess recorded it thus: 'David asked the King
to open it and he was broadcasted.'[97] In fact it was a much more
momentous occasion than her words suggest – this was the first time
that the infant British Broadcasting Company had ever broadcast the
words of the King live, the first time that millions of his subjects –
perhaps ten million – had ever heard the King's voice.[98]

Wireless was still a new phenomenon. In 1919 the Marconi
Company had begun transmissions from Chelmsford and the following
year Dame Nellie Melba was paid the fabulous sum of £1,000 by the
Daily Mail to sing into the microphone. 'Listening in' became more
and more popular and in 1922, when the Post Office agreed to allow
the formation of a company just to transmit, the British Broadcasting
Company was created. (It was elevated to the dignity of a Corporation
four years later.) It was to be organized by wireless manufacturers, and
from the start it was run with close supervision by the state. The
medium boomed. Stations were set up all around the country. Enthusiasts created 'crystal' sets from odds and ends to pick up whatever
transmissions they could. Tall poles were erected in gardens for aerials
and young boys all over the country were seen hunched over sets,
earphones clamped to their heads, fingers twisting dials.

Inevitably there were technical problems with the King's broadcast.
The BBC had set up large Marconi polarized moving-coil microphones
on either side of the royal dais, and the sound was run through a
nearby BBC booth down Post Office lines to Savoy Hill. The first
few minutes of the broadcast were lost, but by the time the King rose
the system had been repaired. At the end of his speech he said, 'We
believe that this Exhibition will bring the peoples of the Empire to
a better knowledge of how to meet their reciprocal wants and aspirations . . . And we hope further that the success of the Exhibition will

bring lasting benefits not to the Empire only, but to mankind in general.'[99]

The Times reported the moment with enthusiasm. 'There were no chatterings nor scufflings among the children now. There was not a whisper, scarce even a stifled cough (and we are still in April and this is England) in all the great assembly. So great was the silence that a creaking door and an echo ... were the only sounds that crossed in the smallest degree His Majesty's clear, rich tones.'[100] The broadcast was relayed around the world, marking the beginning of a revolution in communications which would transform society and, within Britain, have far-reaching repercussions on the role and image of the monarchy.

The Royal Family toured the exhibition, where visitors could watch a re-enactment of the Zulu wars and journey from pavilion to glamorous pavilion on the 'Neverstop Train', viewing the verities of Australia, the exoticism of Malaya, the glorious pagodas of Burma and, above all, the fabulous treasures of the Jewel in the Crown, India.* Among the most popular exhibits – and certainly the longest lasting – was the intricate miniature mansion designed by Lutyens and known as Queen Mary's Doll's House, which is still viewed, at Windsor Castle, by hundreds of thousands of people every year. For the Duchess, there was probably more panoply than refreshment at Wembley that day. It was impressive, but cold, and by the time she arrived back in Windsor she had a chill and went to bed feeling 'rotton'.[101]† She was advised to have a series of inoculations against tonsillitis; the injections were unpleasant and not obviously helpful.[102]

There were not, in those days, many female members of the Royal Family able to undertake public duties. If the Duchess wished to play a significant role in the public life of the monarchy, there was much she could do. Before her marriage she had already undertaken more public activities than many of her age; she had been a commissioner

---

* Bertie Wooster, one of the Duchess's literary heroes, went to the exhibition with his friend Biffy (in the 1924 short story 'The Rummy Affair of Old Biffy'), and it is perhaps fair to say that his mind was on other things than the glory of empire: 'By the time we had tottered out of the Gold Coast and were working towards the Palace of Machinery, everything pointed to shortly executing a quiet sneak in the direction of the rather jolly Planter's Bar in the West Indian section ... A planter, apparently, does not consider he has had a drink unless it contains at least seven ingredients, and I'm not saying, mind you, that he isn't right.'

† The spelling she invariably used, from childhood onwards.

in the local Girl Guides and she had often helped her mother in church and village functions. But she knew very little about life in the cities or about the industrial world.

During her long life she was to become patron of a large array of charities and organizations. But she began this part of her career in an almost haphazard manner. The first charities she took over were those which Princess Christian, Queen Victoria's third daughter, who had been much interested in nursing and other charities, had patronized until her death in June 1923. These included the North Islington Welfare Centre and Wards, the Young Women's Christian Association, the Mothercraft Training Society and the National Society for the Prevention of Cruelty to Children. Another was the Royal Hospital and Home for Incurables at Putney. She took a keen interest in the work of the hospital over the decades that followed; at one stage she asked whether its name might not be changed, but the patients themselves wished it to continue as it was.[103]*

As her gift for raising funds for charities was already clear, she was ideally suited to play a leading role in what later became known as the 'welfare monarchy'.† In early November 1923 she and the Duke visited Manchester to help one of its hospitals raise money to clear a £70,000 debt; on 23 November she opened the bazaar at the Working Men's College in St Pancras.

On 29 November the Duke and Duchess visited the Queen's Hospital for Children in Bethnal Green and that night they were the patrons of a ball at Claridge's in aid of the hospital. The next day they visited the Royal Free Hospital in the Gray's Inn Road on behalf of the Scottish Women's Hospitals' Association, of which the Duchess had recently become president. That same evening they attended the St Andrew's Eve Ball (again at Claridge's) in aid of the Royal Free Hospital's Women's and Babies' Annexe. Writing to invite the Duchess to the ball, the Association's secretary had been blunt about the 'royal effect' which helped charities so much: 'The sale of tickets would be mere child's play, if Her Royal Highness would graciously consent to this.'[104]

---

* The Royal Hospital's name was changed to the Royal Hospital and Home, Putney, in 1988, and to the Royal Hospital for Neuro-Disability in 1995.

† The term was coined by Frank Prochaska in his influential study, *Royal Bounty: The Making of a Welfare Monarchy* (1995).

She already possessed an enduring and deeply felt interest in the armed forces. This grew naturally from her childhood, from her brothers' service, the death of Fergus and her experiences in caring for sick and wounded servicemen at Glamis. The war-wounded became a particular focus for her. At the time of her marriage there were still almost 19,000 wounded soldiers in hospital. In July 1924 she and her husband attended a garden party for a thousand disabled soldiers, sailors, airmen and their nurses in the grounds of Hampton Court. She talked with many people. A letter of thanks afterwards said, 'Her Royal Highness was absolutely wonderful, you cannot imagine it without seeing it, the way the unfortunate, disabled men crowded round her gave one a lump in the throat, no wonder she is so popular.'[105]

At the same time she became accustomed to the rituals of royal public life: laying foundation stones, opening new buildings, attending anniversaries – events by which the institutions involved set great store.

*

SATURDAY 26 APRIL was the Duke and Duchess's first wedding anniversary, and the Duchess gave her husband a pair of cufflinks from Cartier. That afternoon they stood in for the King at the Cup Final at Wembley. Newcastle was playing Aston Villa before an enormous, enthusiastic crowd; the Duchess sat next to Ramsay MacDonald, who was very talkative, she recorded; and there was 'terrific excitement' when Newcastle won with two goals in the last five minutes.[106]

Summer gaiety was breaking out and they spent many evenings at dinners and balls in great London houses, or at one of the many thriving clubs and grand hotels. They frequently went out dining and dancing with the Prince of Wales, to whom they were both very close, and his friends.

By the beginning of June they had managed, to their relief, to move to Chesterfield House in Mayfair, loaned to them for the summer by Princess Mary and her husband Viscount Lascelles. On 3 June they gave a party for about seventy people and danced until the early hours. Among those who came were Fred Astaire and his sister Adele, and sixty-five years later Queen Elizabeth could still recall the 'thrill' of dancing with Fred.[107]

There were several royal visits to occupy them as well. On 12 May they formally welcomed the King and Queen of Romania at Victoria station at the start of their state visit, and attended the banquet in their honour that night. On 26 May it was King Victor Emmanuel III and Queen Elena of Italy who came; the Yorks went to the Guildhall lunch in their honour the following day and took their children, Princess Mafalda and Crown Prince Umberto ('Beppo'), to a polo match at Ranelagh.[108] In July they were on duty again for the visit of the heir to the throne of Ethiopia, Ras Taffari (later Emperor Haile Selassie).

More testing was their trip to the most difficult part of the United Kingdom, Northern Ireland, which was still riven with tensions between the Protestant Unionist majority and the Catholic nationalists. This was their most significant official visit to date, the first time any member of the Royal Family had been to Northern Ireland since the King had opened the new Ulster Parliament in June 1921.[109] The formal invitation came in March 1924 from the Duke of Abercorn, the Governor of Northern Ireland, 'on behalf of the people of Northern Ireland'.[110]

They spent a week in the province, from 19 to 26 July, and were welcomed everywhere with great enthusiasm by Ulstermen fiercely loyal to the United Kingdom. The Duchess's diary gives the flavour of a remarkable week. To avoid civic ceremonies before reaching Northern Ireland, they sailed from the small port of Stranraer rather than Liverpool, on the morning of Saturday 19 July. Even at Stranraer, official presentations and crowds were inescapable. 'At 9.30 the Provost appeared with an Address of welcome & a huge crowd. At 10 we went on board HMS Wryneck & sailed for Bangor. Marvellous day. We sat on the bridge & drank champagne & had great fun.' They landed some three hours later, to a 'great reception – thousands of people'.[111]

They then drove to the Governor's official residence, Clandeboye,* near Bangor, where the fun continued. The Duke of Abercorn's wife was ill, so his daughter, the Duchess's old friend Katie Hamilton, acted as hostess. She had invited their mutual friend Helen Hardinge to help. Having her friends there made the stay much more enjoyable for the Duchess, and Helen wrote a lively account of it all in her diary. The Duchess asked her to sing 'The Bells of Hell', they played poker until the early hours and constantly gossiped together. At one point she

---

* Clandeboye was the family home of the Marquess of Dufferin but was used as an official residence by the Duke of Abercorn, whose own home, Barons Court in County Tyrone, was too far from Belfast.

recorded that the Duke, absorbed in looking at some jungle prints, did not come when his wife called him. 'The corners of her mouth went down after the third attempt & putting both hands on his shoulders she said angelically: "Bertie do listen to me." He kissed her and came at once. The wisdom of the serpent!'[112]

On Monday 21 July, they set off for Belfast. Messrs Armstrong Siddeley had lent them two Landaulette convertibles in which they could be better seen. They were given honorary degrees at Queen's University and then the Duke unveiled the University's war memorial. After a luncheon 'with speeches and much noise', they moved on to the Ulster Hall, where the Duke received addresses and made a speech which his wife judged to have gone very well. That evening they attended a dinner and a reception at Stormont Castle.[113] After the reception there was a supper, but according to Helen Hardinge's diary the Duchess complained that it went on too long, preventing her from shaking hands with enough of the guests. 'When I do a thing I like to do it well and feel people are satisfied.'[114]

The following day was filled with engagements. The Duke laid the foundation stone of the new City Art Gallery, and they visited the York Street Spinning Mills. At a lunchtime banquet in City Hall the Lord Mayor, seated next to the Duchess, seems to have set light to himself with his cigar. According to her diary, he 'burst into flames! Very nice speeches & great excitement.'[115] The Duke received the Freedom of the City, the Duchess a present of silver from the women of Belfast. Finally, in a last-minute addition to the schedule, they fitted in a crowded reception for about 2,000 people, before leaving on a special train. That night was spent with the Abercorns at their home, Barons Court; the Duchess was tired and went to bed at 10.30. A day of recuperation in the company of Katie and Helen followed; in her characteristic phrase, she 'talked hard' with Katie.[116]

The Duchess was surprised by how warm the welcome was even in Londonderry, the heart of republicanism, where they went on 24 July. 'Up by 9.30 in my grey cloak and hat. Rainy morning . . . Arrived Derry at 11. Considering that more than half are Nationalists, we had a marvellous welcome. Drove to Town Hall, & got the Freedom.' They toured the City and County Infirmary, attended yet another civic luncheon and reception, and left by train for Belfast, stopping at Coleraine, Ballymoney and Ballymena, where the Duke laid the foundation stone of the new town hall. Arriving in Belfast in the evening, they were met by 'more huge crowds, who shrieked & yelled', before continuing on to Mount Stewart, the home of Lord and Lady Londonderry, where they were to spend the next two nights. It had been 'a very long day!' as the Duchess recorded; and the next day was spent quietly at Mount Stewart. On their last evening their hosts gave a dinner at which the Duchess sat between Lord Londonderry and the Primate of Ireland (the Most Rev. Charles D'Arcy, Archbishop of Armagh), and then 'danced hard, until 2!', with their host, her husband and others.[117]

On Saturday, a lovely day, the Duchess went for a walk along the seashore with Dorothé Plunket. After lunch she changed into a grey crêpe de Chine dress with a pink hat, and she and the Duke then made their way by car and train through cheering crowds, stopping to be presented with bouquets, and ending eventually at Belfast Harbour. At 6.15 they set sail in HMS *Wryneck* once more. 'The visit was a great success I think. We sat on the bridge & talked & drank champagne. Very nice people.'[118]

The visit was indeed deemed a success. The Duke wrote afterwards to his father to say that their reception had been astounding. 'Elizabeth has been marvellous as usual & the people simply love her already. I am very lucky indeed to have her to help me as she knows exactly what to do & say to all the people we meet.'[119]

*

ON 11 AUGUST their happy time at Chesterfield House came to an end. Reluctantly they had to move back to White Lodge. First, though, there was the pleasure of late summer in Scotland. They went north, stopping at Studley Royal near Ripon to stay with the Vyners and then on up to Edinburgh, where they saw the Duchess's sister May Elphinstone and her children, of whom the Duchess was very fond.* Then it was further north to Glamis and Balmoral for the rest of August and September. It is clear from correspondence and diaries that they both found Glamis the more congenial and more restful home.

The King's regime at Balmoral had not relaxed. No cocktails were

---

* Throughout their lives, the Elphinstone children called her Peter and she signed all her letters to them with that name. This tradition appears to have begun when, in her childhood, Elizabeth Elphinstone found the name Aunt Elizabeth difficult and called her Peter instead. And Peter it remained ever after.

allowed, no card games either. The guest lists rarely changed and included a succession of ministers invited more for business than for pleasure, and two old friends of the King, Canon Dalton and Sister Agnes. Dalton, a formidable autocrat, had been George V's tutor and was a canon of Windsor.* Now in his eighties, he was tall and stooped and some thought he looked as if he had been quarried from the same stone as the Castle. He was arrogant with his peers in the Chapter and his humour, though boisterous, was not always well considered. According to George V's biographer, Kenneth Rose, he took to reading the lessons in a dramatic manner – 'he endowed the Almighty with a thundering bass and Isaiah with a piping falsetto.'[120]

Miss Agnes Keyser, known as Sister Agnes, was the founder and Matron of King Edward VII's Hospital for Officers, which in those days was in Grosvenor Crescent off Hyde Park Corner. She had been a friend of King Edward and it was said that she had enabled him to meet his companion Mrs Keppel in her house. She liked to have patients from the Household Cavalry and the Brigade of Guards and she is reported to have been rather malicious. Harold Nicolson observed that she 'enjoyed repeating to the King, not always with useful results, the talk of the town'.[121] This talk often included the latest gossip about the adventures of the King's sons, in particular the Prince of Wales. She was one of the few people privileged to have her own key to Buckingham Palace garden and so she had ample opportunity to repeat to the King whatever stories she had acquired about the Princes and 'bad women', a source of continual anxiety to the monarch. At Balmoral she cut a remarkable figure striding across the moors dressed in mauve and wearing an orange wig.[122] But she and Canon Dalton were perhaps not ideal companions for young people who had driven many miles for dinner. When on one occasion the King asked the Labour minister J. H. Thomas, a former railwayman whose company he enjoyed, why his sons did not spend more time at Balmoral, Thomas was frank: 'It's a dull 'ouse, Sir, a bloody dull 'ouse.'[123]

In September 1924 the Duchess wrote to her mother from Balmoral, saying that she had been meaning to write every day 'but

---

* Rev. John Neale Dalton (1839–1931), Canon of St George's Chapel, Windsor 1884–1931, was the father of Hugh Dalton (1887–1962), Chancellor of the Exchequer in Attlee's government 1945–7.

somehow it is so boring that I felt there was nothing to tell you!!
However the King & Queen are in very good form, and we are both
very popular!' There were consolations. 'There are one or two quite
nice old men here, who only appear at meals.' And there was about to
be a ghillies' ball – 'the Queen is simply thrilled', the Duchess
commented – for Queen Mary loved dancing.[124] The 'old men' were
Lords Rawlinson and Revelstoke. Rawlinson was Commander-in-Chief
of the Army in India and a much decorated First World War
commander. John Baring, second Baron Revelstoke, was Receiver
General of the Duchy of Cornwall and a director of the family bank.
For all the boredom of Balmoral, both there and elsewhere it was part
of her apprenticeship as the King's daughter-in-law to meet men (and
some women) of consequence, and such encounters no doubt helped
form her abiding interest in the nation's welfare, the Empire and the
role of the monarchy.

They returned to the more convivial circumstances of Glamis in
the second half of September. When the Duke drove back up to
Balmoral at the end of the month for more stalking, they exchanged
affectionate letters across the hills. In one he told the Duchess how
much he missed her and was thinking of her. 'Don't get frightened at
night sleeping all alone darling in that enormous bed,' he wrote.[125] She
replied at once: 'I miss you dreadfully and am longing for Monday,
when I hope you will arrive here sunburnt, manly & bronzed, bearing
in your arms a haunch of venaison rôti as a love offering to your
spouse . . . Goodbye darling, it seems all wrong that we shouldn't be
together, doesn't it – from your very, very loving Elizabeth.' She added
a PS asking if 'Mama', the Queen, might have any trifle for a bazaar in
Dundee in aid of a charity she would cherish all her life. This was the
Lord Roberts Workshops, which offered training and employment to
disabled servicemen and became for many decades part of the fabric of
British society.* They were raising funds to help some 300 disabled

---

* The charity, Lord Roberts Memorial Workshops, was inspired by Field Marshal Lord
Roberts of Kandahar, known as Bobs, one of the most distinguished and popular military
commanders of the Victorian era. He was dedicated to the cause of disabled ex-servicemen
and, after his death in 1914 while visiting troops at the Front, workshops bearing his name
were expanded around Britain in his memory. After both world wars they rescued thousands
of severely wounded soldiers from destitution and taught them skills; for decades soldiers
earned a living producing furniture, brushes, toys, baskets and other household goods.
The Duchess of York sustained her support and affection for this charity all her life. In

men, she wrote. 'It's not so much a matter of money to keep them alive, it's a matter of money to keep their self respect alive by giving them work & saving them from the street corners. I am very keen about it.'[126] He responded with equal affection, saying that it was too cold to enjoy stalking and that he was bored at Balmoral. He was longing for Monday – and would be back at Glamis in time for lunch.[127]

On Thursday 9 October they went to the bazaar together, and were met by officials at the Dundee City Boundary. They drove in an open car to the Caird Hall, where the Duchess opened the bazaar with a short speech. Then she and the Duke fought their way through the crowd who had come to see them and spent some time selling goods at the Forfarshire stall. Afterwards, the Duke wrote to his mother that the items she had sent fetched £20 and altogether they made a good deal of money 'as everybody wanted to buy things from Elizabeth'.[128] The sale easily sped past its goal of £10,000, raising twice as much.

The Dundee bazaar coincided with another political crisis which had the King hurrying down by night train from Balmoral to London. Ramsay MacDonald had called a vote of confidence on his handling (or mishandling) of a charge of sedition first brought and then dropped against the acting editor of a communist paper which had incited troops to disobey orders to move against strikers. MacDonald lost the vote and went to the Palace on 9 October to ask the King to dissolve Parliament. King George V was reluctant, fearing the harmful impact of a third election within two years. But there was no alternative.

The resultant election in November 1924 was dominated by dubious allegations about the Labour government's closeness to the Bolshevik government in Russia. MacDonald lost and the Conservatives were returned to power under Baldwin. The King showed no pleasure in Labour's defeat and warned Baldwin against humiliating the socialists; he was concerned above all about the danger of class war. The Conservatives, he thought, should at once get to grips with the problems of housing, unemployment and the cost of food and education. The Duchess greeted the change of government with more enthusiasm. In her diary she exclaimed, 'The election news wonderful,

---

1938, as queen, she gave the Royal Warrant of Appointment to all eleven Lord Roberts Workshops. She made over sixty visits to the Dundee workshop, the last in 1994, following its merger with Blindcraft to create Dovetail Enterprises.

already great Conservative majority. Everybody relieved – hopes for a year or two of comparative peace.'[129] To her mother she wrote, 'wasn't the election <u>marvellous</u> especially in Scotland. One feels so much safer.'[130]

In the next few weeks the Duchess made her final preparations for what would be a defining experience. She and the Duke were to visit East Africa. King George VI's official biographer, John Wheeler-Bennett, wrote of the origins of the tour only that the Duke had long wanted to 'see something of the British Empire at first hand' and that, an exhausting year and a half after their marriage, he and his wife badly needed a holiday. The Duchess's biographer Dorothy Laird speculated that the Duke also hoped to help his wife avoid the winter bouts of tonsillitis with which she had been repeatedly afflicted. There is probably truth in both explanations. It was a joy for them to get away together and the four-and-a-half-month journey was unforgettable – both for the thrill of discovering Africa and for the freedom which they could never enjoy at home.

CHAPTER SIX

ON SAFARI

1924–1925

'Best bit of one's life'

ON 27 JUNE 1924 the Duchess had sat next to Winston Churchill at dinner and had an 'interesting conversation' with him.[1] They talked about Africa – Churchill had his own personal experience as a guide. He had made an East African journey himself in 1907, as under secretary of state at the Colonial Office in the Campbell-Bannerman government. He described the trip in his book *My African Journey* and one can imagine that at dinner he excited her interest with his vivid memories.

Recalling her own African tour seventy years on, Queen Elizabeth explained, 'Winston was extraordinary. I remember sitting next to him at dinner just after we were married and he said, "Now look here, you're a young couple. You ought to go and have a look at the world. I should go to East Africa," he said. "It's got a great future, that country." So we did . . . And I have always been grateful to him, you know, because I don't think we would have thought of going.'[2]

Her memory of his intervention was quite correct. Churchill followed up their conversation. On 10 July, he wrote to her to say he had approached Edward Marsh,* private secretary to J. H. Thomas, the Colonial Secretary, about 'Your Royal Highness's wishes & plans about a tour in East Africa and Uganda'. Marsh had reported back that Thomas was 'vy favourably impressed with the idea'. But he added that Thomas wanted to see how the couple's forthcoming trip to Ulster went before committing himself to a full-scale colonial tour.[3]

---

* Edward Marsh had been Churchill's private secretary at the Colonial Office in 1905 and had accompanied him on his African journey; he stayed with Churchill in subsequent ministerial appointments, including his period as colonial secretary in 1921–2, and remained a lifelong friend.

Like everyone else, he was unprepared for the extraordinary success of the Irish visit, due in good measure to the personality of the Duchess herself.

Quite apart from securing the permission of the government, there was also the small matter of the King, whose acquiescence could never be taken for granted. The Duke seems – not for the first time – to have approached his irascible father through his more sympathetic mother. On 14 July the Duchess's diary has a rare entry in her husband's hand: 'Good day.' The reason is soon clear. While the Duchess was replying to Churchill's letter, the Duke went to see the Queen 'about our winter trip', and that very evening they received the King's consent. 'Marvellous,' the Duchess wrote.[4]

Over the next few months she had the pleasure of looking for clothes, and the discomfort of being inoculated against many diseases. The King and Queen offered to give the Duke as a Christmas present something that he needed for the trip; their son asked if they would pay for the tin cases he had had to get – these, he said, would cost 'certainly not more than £20'.[5]

The prospect was thrilling. For the Duchess, the first year of marriage had meant learning to live under the watchful eye of both the public and the Royal Family; apart from their winter weekends in Northamptonshire she and her husband had had little time alone together. And for a passionate sportsman like the Duke the idea of a big-game safari had immense appeal. This was the heyday of such adventures. Firms like Safariland Ltd of Nairobi and London were practised in supplying tents and equipment. White hunters were there to guide and protect inexperienced and nervous travellers, and numerous African trackers, gun-bearers, porters, cooks and 'boys' were provided to ensure that life was as comfortable in the bush as could be managed. In Kenya the building of the Uganda Railway (1895–1903) from Mombasa to its terminus on Lake Victoria had opened up the untouched interior of a country which teemed with wildebeest, buffalo, zebra, eland, giraffe, oryx, gazelle, waterbuck, lions, cheetahs, leopards and hyenas. Plentiful opportunities for duck shooting and fishing existed. In Uganda there was the extra attraction of elephant and white rhino, while the Sudan held out the prospect of sailing down the Nile aboard a comfortable paddle-steamer, with exciting expeditions ashore after more elephant, antelope of all kinds and even crocodiles.

Many young women of the Duchess's background might have

been daunted by the prospect of four months in the wilderness. She had never been out of Europe before; travelling in Africa even with the service they would enjoy still held elements of risk and unpredictability; and although most of the trip was to be holiday, she and the Duke would still at all times be representing the British Crown. She did have misgivings, writing to D'Arcy Osborne, 'I am feeling slightly mingled in my feelings about going to Africa, as I hate discomfort, and am so afraid that I shall not like the heat, or that mosquitoes will bite my eyelids & the tip of my nose, or that I shall not be able to have baths often enough, or that I shall hate the people. On the other hand I think it is good for one to go away and see a little LIFE, and then think how pleased I shall be to get home again.'[6] She need not have been concerned. This was to be one of the formative experiences of her life.[7] She took from it a great affection for Africa and a sense of astonishment at the achievements of the British Empire.

The Empire had been called upon to make substantial sacrifices for Britain during the First World War – almost 150,000 white troops from Australia, New Zealand, Canada and South Africa had lost their lives. So had an estimated 54,000 Indians. Of African losses there are no reliable figures, but some 40,000 black Africans served as labourers and porters with the British armies in France – their casualty rates are likely to have been high.[8]

The war inevitably weakened loyalties and raised doubts about the basis of empire. Nonetheless, at Versailles, American ideas of self-determination were largely superseded by a new division of colonial territories and the British Empire actually grew. Since the British navy had switched from coal to oil, influence over the oil-producing countries and the Suez Canal was more important than ever. The Germans had made the Middle East a theatre of war and their defeat meant that Iraq, Transjordan and Palestine now became British 'mandates' while Syria and Lebanon were handed to France. In Egypt an end to the British protectorate was demanded – and dismissed. Instead the British installed a monarchy there, as they did in Iraq and Transjordan.

Britain took over the German colonies of Togoland, Cameroon and German East Africa (Tanganyika). Altogether almost two million more square miles were now coloured red on the map and thirteen million more people found themselves to be subjects of the King. But the strains of holding the Empire together were growing inexorably.

The costs that Britain had incurred in defeating Germany (estimated at some £10 billion) were only slowly counted, but from the early 1920s onwards their effect was real. The imperial economy was hard to sustain; after the wartime boom, demand for British products diminished sharply. The Dominions were developing their own industries and Britain's share of world markets had begun a fall which was never really to be reversed. At the same time America and Japan were dramatically increasing their output and exports – and their power. British industrialists found themselves barely able to meet such new realities and responded only by demanding longer working hours or lower wages. As we have seen, industrial relations became increasingly bitter as strikes and lock-outs spread and became frequent and intense.[9] All of this made it harder and harder actually to pay for the Empire.[10] By the mid-1920s there were more criticisms and doubts but, at least on the surface, Britain's sway was still extraordinary and exhilarating.

The most difficult of the countries the Duke and Duchess were to visit was the Sudan. Britain had first occupied the Sudan and Egypt in 1882 but a revolt against British rule, led by the so-called Mahdi (Guided One), culminated in the fall of Khartoum and the murder of General Gordon in 1885. The Mahdi created a strict Islamist state but the British re-established their control over the Sudan following General Kitchener's victory in 1898 at the Battle of Omdurman. In 1899 Anglo-Egyptian rule was established, but in effect the Sudan was administered as a British colony.

The Sudan Civil Service, created by the British Colonial Office, became one of the finest in the world, but British rule also stoked nationalist resentment in both Egypt and the Sudan. In 1924 a group of Sudanese military officers led an uprising against the British, and Sir Lee Stack, the Governor General of the Sudan, was assassinated in Cairo on 19 November. This revolt was put down by the British army, but tension remained high when the tour of the Duke and Duchess was being planned. In Whitehall there was considerable discussion about whether the country was too dangerous for them to visit. The Chief Secretary of the Sudan government, H. A. MacMichael, asked that the Sudan should not be mentioned in the public announcement of the tour, as he feared that the Egyptian press would 'start howling, & will attribute some low motive to the trip'; they would assume that it was connected with the current political negotiations between Britain and Egypt.[11] During the tour the Duke's Private Secretary kept in touch with the Colonial and Foreign Offices in case it became necessary to rearrange the route to avoid the Sudan. By the end of the year the official view was that the journey could go ahead as planned, but that a final decision would be taken in early February.

*

THE DUKE AND Duchess set off on Monday 1 December 1924, having taken leave of their families, who were concerned about the voyage. The King warned them never to be without a doctor and not to run unnecessary risks 'either from the climate or wild beasts'.[12] Queen Mary wrote that she 'hated saying "good bye" to you two beloved children', but she hoped they would have a delightful and enjoyable tour. 'God bless you both, my precious children.'[13] Lady Strathmore found saying farewells even harder, and so the Duchess had written to her from White Lodge, 'My darling Sweet, Alright, I won't come round, as I also hate saying goodbye. I expect the time will pass very quickly and you won't worry about me will you darling, as I will take great care of myself in every way, I promise you . . . Au revoir Angel, from your very very loving Elizabeth.'[14]

To avoid the high winter seas of the Bay of Biscay, they had decided to board their ship, the SS *Mulbera*, at Marseilles. This had the added advantage of allowing them to travel by train via Paris; the Duchess told her mother that she was looking forward to buying an evening dress there.[15] They stayed in Lord Derby's apartment on the Avenue d'Iéna and enjoyed themselves, despite the fact that they were followed everywhere by two French detectives – actually, the Duchess found them amusing. Apart from shopping, there was tea at the Ritz and dinner at the British Embassy; they also visited the Casino de Paris, 'where for the first time in my life I saw ladies with very little on, & somehow it was not in the least indecent'. They danced in rather risqué nightclubs, including Les Néants, where 'we drank off a coffin, surrounded by skeletons & exchanging very vulgar badinage with a man carrying a huge Bone. Then to a Russian place where I enjoyed myself so much being very fast, & throwing balls at rather a nice American, & then to a tiny place with several Negroes with delicious voices who sang & sang.' They strolled in the gardens at Versailles, 'so lovely & forlorn & empty'.[16] All in all, she noted, 'We had great fun in Paris and feel very well.'[17]

On the evening of 4 December they were driven to the railway station at Pierrefitte, north of Paris, where the P&O Express made a special stop to pick them up. After the overnight journey they arrived in Marseilles at noon. Their party consisted of their Comptroller Captain Basil Brooke, the Duke's equerry Lieutenant Commander Colin Buist, Lavinia Annaly, the Duchess's childhood friend, who was acting as her lady in waiting, the Duke's valet Victor Osborn and the Duchess's maid Catherine Maclean. When they embarked on the *Mulbera* they discovered that they had been wise to come by train; the ship's voyage across the Bay of Biscay had been very disagreeable.[18] But the Mediterranean was calm and, after six restful days on the 'Old Mulberry' as the Duchess called her, they steamed through the Suez Canal. She and the Duke arose at dawn to see 'the marvellous early light' across the desert. They were happily surprised to pass HMS *Wryneck*, the destroyer which had carried them to Belfast in July. 'They turned out & cheered us. It was quite a homesick feeling!'[19]

They sailed south and arrived at the British port of Aden on 16 December.* There they were met by the British Resident, General Scott, who took them on a tour of the town. Surrounded by people, 'we saw Cain's tomb, & the place where the Queen of Sheba embarked, & the Water Tanks made by King Solomon', the Duchess recounted to her mother; later they met a magnificently attired sultan over tea at General Scott's residence.[20] Further south shipboard rituals became more exotic. There was a fancy-dress ball, judged by the Duchess, who was dressed in a red Spanish shawl with a floppy hat and a rose. Lavinia Annaly, decked out as a cowgirl, played the violin in a band, which she had organized for the occasion. The Duchess was relieved to be able to avoid a ducking in the Crossing the Line Ceremony – her husband was not spared – but she was nonetheless awarded a certificate of allegiance to King Neptune and the Order of the Old Sea Dog.[21]

Two days later, on 22 December, they landed in Africa. 'It was a lovely sight in the early morning with the sun astern, seeing native huts and tropical vegetation. Our first view of Kenya,' recorded the Duke as the *Mulbera* approached Mombasa.[22] This was the first royal

---

* Aden, a strategic port on the south-west corner of Yemen, dominated the entrance to the Red Sea. It had always been an important landfall for seamen and merchants, lying roughly equidistant between the Suez Canal, Bombay and Zanzibar, which were all important British possessions in the nineteenth century. It was controlled by Britain from 1839 to 1967.

visit to East Africa since 1910* and crowded on the quayside with the Governor, Sir Robert Coryndon, and other officials were large numbers of people from the British colony, as well as Kenyans, Somalis, Indians and Arabs, all of whom helped to cheer them ashore.

There was no escaping formalities, ceremony, receptions, or the endless gaze of the public. But this was all much more exciting than civic receptions at home. As part of the formal welcome, they received many addresses from the non-African communities – the Duchess wrote mischievously to her father-in-law that 'at Mombasa all the Portuguese communities presented very loyal Addresses, which I am sure must give you vast pleasure!!'[23] That evening 5,000 tribal dancers from all over East Africa and from the Congo region performed in a spectacular *ngoma* to welcome them. There were stilt walkers and leapers from among the Kikuyu people of Kenya and Kipindi-Pindu clowns from the Yao tribe of Nyasaland.

Later that night they left by train for Nairobi. The next day they sat on special seats fixed to the front of the engine and saw 'zebra, hartebeeste, ostrich, baboons & wildebeeste quite near the line', the Duke wrote to his father.[24] In Nairobi they were taken over by the British colony for two days – they opened the City Park, danced at the fashionable colonial watering hole, the Muthaiga Club, attended Christmas Day services in both an English and an African church, and met British residents at a party at Government House.

On Boxing Day they were able to escape and they drove north to establish their first camp on the Siolo plain beyond Meru. There they were joined by their shooting party. One of these was Major G. H. 'Andy' Anderson, an experienced hunter who had reconnoitred the trip for them. Also with them were Captain C. A. Palmer-Kerrison, the Governor's ADC, and Dr J. L. Gilks, Kenya's Principal Medical Officer and the expedition's medical man. At Siolo they were also joined by Pat Ayre, a local settler and sawmill owner, who was to be their second white hunter, and Captain Keith Caldwell of the Kenya Game Department, who was to remain with them throughout their Kenyan and Ugandan safaris.

---

* Prince Arthur, Duke of Connaught, his wife and their daughter Princess Patricia made a safari trip to Kenya (then known as the East Africa Protectorate) in 1910. (It became 'The Kenya Colony and Protectorate' by Order in Council in July 1920, the Protectorate consisting of the mainland dominions of the Sultan of Zanzibar.)

The Duchess was already enthralled. 'We arrived at the camp two days ago,' she wrote to her mother, 'and it is simply wonderful. The country is quite unlike anything I expected, and it is <u>beautiful</u>. We took two days motoring here, and the camp is in the middle of a huge plain exactly like an English Park, and on every side there are mountains . . . The flowers coming here were too <u>wonderful</u>. I saw great masses of Morning Glory & thought of you, also arum lilies, orchids, carpets of bright blue forget me nots, and wonderfully coloured daisies – big ones like marguerites.' They slept in small round huts called *bandas* and they could hear lions 'who growl all night, but they don't appear much'. She had an African servant whom she liked very much* and she loved the climate. 'The sun is hot in the morning, but it's quite cool all the time. I am wearing flannel trousers & a jumper and sun hat.'²⁵ She was unaccustomed to trousers; to the Prince of Wales she wrote, 'I don't look <u>too</u> bad in my trousers and shirt. It makes me look very <u>small</u> which annoys me, but as thank God there are no tall women here, I don't really mind.'²⁶

Perhaps the relative comfort of the Siolo camp was intended to break them in gently before they began their real safari under canvas and on the march. They spent three weeks there, during which the Duke went on a five-day safari without the Duchess – and she learned to forget her fondness for late mornings and late nights. To her own surprise, she was soon rising at 7 a.m. and going to bed soon after sundown at 7 p.m., and she even enjoyed getting up before dawn to join her husband on excursions. On 29 December she wrote to her mother, 'we got up at 4 and went out to try & get a lion. It was <u>too</u> thrilling. They had left a rhino and zebra out, & as it was getting light we crept up behind bushes & found two lions growling over the zebra. Before we saw them we heard the most blood curdling growls and grumbles, and all felt petrified with fear! We all shot together but it was still too dark to see properly, and they were off like a streak of lightning . . . I saw about 12 giraffes too the other day – quite close.'²⁷

The Duke often went out for a day's hunting with Pat Ayre, looking for lion or eland, while the Duchess and Lady Annaly set off with Keith Caldwell on foot or in the large open Rolls-Royce which

---

* He was Seyai, a Yao from Nyasaland, who worked for Major Anderson and his wife. Anderson recorded that the Duchess liked him so much that she kept him on for the entire trip. (G. H. Anderson, ms account of the Yorks' trip, 1943, RA Lascelles Papers, Box A)

Caldwell drove throughout the expedition. 'The birds are simply marvellous,' the Duchess told her brother David. 'Thousands of partridges – a little bigger than ours, and flocks of guinea fowl, & quail & pigeons & anything you like. It is exactly like a warm summer evening at Glamis here – nice & cool & Scotch.'[28] The Duke returned from his short hunt in time for the second anniversary of their engagement on 14 January. They celebrated with champagne. Five days later they began a more strenuous part of the safari, setting off on foot, moving camp almost every day. The days became hotter, the terrain more difficult – 'walked on over 2 miles of lava rock the size of footballs. Simply awful walking,' the Duchess noted.[29]

Africa began to affect her more and more. 'I rise at 4.30 (I can hear you say "My God"),' she wrote to D'Arcy Osborne,

> & go walking around with my spouse and the white hunter [Pat Ayre], who is a charming man with an imagination, an accent & a sense of humour. He is exactly like what I imagine the Scarlet Pimpernel to be, very slow & sleepy & long, and if he wasn't so brown he would be rather good looking. He is English South African & talks American. Everyone talks American here, and so do I. We usually hunt till ten or eleven, and then join the camp which has moved after us like magic, & drink & sleep till about 3.30, when we sally forth once again.

They walked at least twelve miles a day and she had been lucky enough to see quite a number of lions. 'The game is amazing, & it is such fun to watch them. Rhino are very funny; very fussy, like old gentlemen, & very busy all the time, quite ridiculous in fact. Giraffes I adore – they are utterly prehistoric, and very gentle. Also they move like a slow motion movie. I never knew that I could like this sort of life so much – out all day long, and one never even knows the day of the week. I feel it must be good for one. England seems so small & full & petty and unhappy in contrast to Africa.'[30]

They spent one night in a mosquito-ridden camp by a swamp and next morning she and the Duke set off with Ayre '& walked steadily across a plain for 2 hours. Came to trees & a swamp where we hoped to see buffalo, but no. Sat down under some trees, & suddenly decided to send for our tents & stay. Had seen rhino spoor etc, & hope for lions. Saw thousands of zebra – I shot two dead with two shots for lion kills. Hated doing it.'[31] They stayed in this little unexpected camp for two days. But they could not sleep for the calls of the lions and hyenas and the barking of their dogs. Early next morning they crept up to the dead zebra and 'we saw two [lions] running away – one big black-maned beauty ... We are having great fun – B & I & Pat Ayre & Inglebrecht.'[32]*

When they rejoined the main safari they found that their African trackers had located rhinoceros, and it was here that the Duchess showed her shooting skills. She told her father-in-law, who she knew disapproved of women with guns, 'When we went on our shooting trip, I took to shooting with a rifle, which I do hope you won't dislike me for. But really there was nothing else to do, and I enjoyed it so much, and became very bloodthirsty. First of all I shot birds as big as capercailzie for the pot, and then I shot buck, and by great flukes managed to kill and not wound, and then I shot a rhinoceros which nearly broke my heart. I am sure you would have laughed at me, and I was quite glad you weren't there!'[33] The party then retraced its steps back to Siolo camp; at Archer's Post, where they had left the cars, they found Martin Johnson, an American photographer, and his wife Osa, whose car was stuck in the mud of the Uaso Nyero river. They helped pull it out, and the Johnsons, who were on an expedition to film big game, took this opportunity of filming their rescuers too, to their amusement.[34]

On 4 February, feeling 'very sad', they drove over 200 miles back to Nairobi, where they stayed at Government House with Sir Robert Coryndon. There were compensations for the loss of their carefree life on safari. 'Had my hair washed & waved at 9. Feel clean again!' the Duchess noted in her diary next day. But she added, 'I adore safari!'[35]

If the trip was a revelation for the Duchess, she could see that its liberating effect on her husband was even more stunning. His health and morale had both improved. She wrote to her mother that he looked 'a different person'.[36] In similar vein she told the Prince of Wales, 'It's a good life here, and you have no idea what it has done for Bertie. He is a different being, quite calm and losing all his nerviness.' And she knew it was not just the climate and the exercise. 'Darling David, I know now your feelings of relief and freedom when you get away from England on your own – away from all the petty little annoyances and restrictions that drive one crazy. It's marvellous,

---

*   J. H. Engelbrecht was another hunter who had joined the party.

isn't it?'[37] She was struck by how much braver she was here than at home, where she thought she was 'a loathsome little coward'. Her African servant looked after her far better than a maid, she wrote. 'Wouldn't Mama be shocked?' She was not looking forward to their return – she loved coming home, 'but I hate being always under the eye of a narrow minded autocrat'. This was also an expression of sympathy for the Prince of Wales, for she knew well his resentment of his father's heavy hand and of the 'stunts' he was obliged to attend. 'Dear David,' she went on, 'I hope your affairs are going well, and that neither your heart or your staff are giving you cause to worry. Those two seem to give you most trouble in life, and also of course you are very very naughty, but delicious.'[38]

The Prince replied with equal affection, recognizing her contribution to his brother's happiness. He added a word of advice that was redundant to her of all people – but it was revealing: 'What a lot of things are Hell. But not for you I hope – now & never. You deserve so much happiness & I believe & pray you have it . . . You are divine to me & such a wonderful friend . . . Take care of yourself darling & don't get too brave & don't let the family worry you this Summer. It's not worth it & they are harmless really if you stand up to them a bit & do things to please them once in a while. I find that helps a lot & it's not much trouble really & then they don't mind bigger things so much.'[39]

The Duke reported proudly to his father on their expedition, which he described as:

> a proper safari. By this I mean we have moved every day shooting on the way & sleeping in tents in camp under trees . . . Elizabeth has surprised all of us especially me in what she has done both walking & in shooting. She has been wonderful & is not at all tired & has thoroughly enjoyed it & what is most important has not overdone it in any way. She has done very little shooting but with great success has killed an Oryx, a Giant Gazelle & a Rhino. I bought her a light .275 Rigby for this & she has also shot lots of birds of all sizes with a small double barrelled .300 bore rifle. The birds were on the ground & not flying as stated!! She is a very good rifle shot but of course has not shot with a gun. I know you don't approve of ladies shooting at home but out here things are so different & one's whole life is changed from all points of view.[40]

To his mother he added that the climate had done 'worlds of good' to his wife's health and that she had had no recurrence of tonsillitis.[41]

Back in Nairobi the world of officialdom called once more – there were addresses to be received, and the Duke made a visit to the War Graves Commission cemetery; then there was another glimpse of social life in the colony at dinner at the Muthaiga Club, with dancing till 3 a.m. But soon they were packing to take happily to the road again. The Duke noted in his diary that they had brought too much luggage with them, 'but we shall know in future'. He would have been sad to think that they would never return. They said goodbyes to their Scarlet Pimpernel, Pat Ayre, and to Major Anderson and embarked on the train to Nakuru on 7 February, on the way to Uganda to begin the next part of their tour.

En route they stopped for two days with Lord Francis Scott* and his wife at Deloraine, the Scotts' house near Njoro, where they saw a little of the life of the settlers in what were then called the White Highlands. The Duchess was impressed by the settlers.[42] On 10 February they rejoined the train for Eldoret where they were to make their next stop and carry out more public engagements. But as the train climbed through lovely country to the Uasin Gishu plateau, the news reached them that their kind host in Nairobi, Sir Robert Coryndon, had suddenly died after an attack of pancreatitis. His death was a shock; the Duke immediately cancelled all their remaining engagements in Kenya and drove back to Nairobi for the funeral, while the Duchess returned to Deloraine.

Early on 12 February she was driven back to the station at Njoro to rejoin her husband; they rattled along the narrow-gauge railway for the rest of that day, up to Kisumu on Lake Victoria. This was the terminus of the Uganda Railway which, despite its name, had not yet reached Uganda. They embarked on the steamer *Clement Hill* and sailed through the night across the lake. After stopping at Jinja to see the source of the White Nile at the Ripon Falls, they reached the dock at Entebbe on St Valentine's Day. About a hundred canoes, filled with

---

* Lord Francis Scott was the uncle of the future Duchess of Gloucester, Lady Alice Montagu-Douglas-Scott, who lived at Deloraine for a time before her marriage to Prince Henry, third son of King George V, in 1935. Kenya and Deloraine would have been an added bond between the sisters-in-law, whose families knew each other in Scotland. Lady Alice's elder sister Margaret Ida ('Mida') was a friend of Lady Elizabeth Bowes Lyon and a frequent guest at Glamis.

Africans 'paddling like mad and shouting and singing',[43] sped out from the shore to welcome them. They were greeted by the acting Governor, Edward Jarvis;* the former Governor, Sir Geoffrey Archer, who had made all the arrangements for their trip, had recently been appointed governor general of the Sudan following the assassination of Sir Lee Stack.

They found that Keith Caldwell's reliable open-topped Rolls-Royce was there to meet them and to carry them around, first to Government House to meet the Kabaka of Buganda† and other African chiefs. The next day, Sunday, they drove to Kampala to attend a service at the Anglican Cathedral at Namirembe – 'simply packed', noted the Duchess – and afterwards they visited Roman Catholic missions. That evening their doctor advised them to take quinine against malaria – this had not been necessary in the high altitudes of Kenya. The drug was unkind to the Duke – he succumbed to quinine poisoning and had to cancel all his engagements next day as he lay abed, sick and perspiring, with swollen eyes.[44]

One day later he was well enough for them to resume their public engagements; they received addresses from the non-African communities in Kampala and then proceeded to the Bugandan parliament, the Lukiko, where they were welcomed by the Kabaka, whom the Duke invested as an honorary KCMG.‡ They then watched a spectacular *omwoleko*, a parade of warriors accompanied by thunderous drumming.

Describing her first impressions of Uganda to her mother, the Duchess remarked that it was 'more tropical' and 'softer' than Kenya, and less developed in some ways – she was surprised to find that there was no running water or electric light at Government House – but 'the cotton in this country is doing wonderfully well, and it is all native. They are fine big men, and apparently are successful because they are left under the Chiefs and not interfered with. Kenya, of course, is a white man's country, and this is all black.'[45] Broadly speaking, she was right – that was, in a nutshell, the difference between

---

* Edward Blackwell Jarvis (1873–1950), Chief Secretary, Uganda, and acting Governor on various occasions.

† HH Daudi Chwa (1896–1939), King of Buganda 1897–1939.

‡ KCMG – Knight Commander of the Order of St Michael and St George. This Order was founded by King George III in 1818 and is awarded to British subjects who have rendered extraordinary and important services abroad or in the Commonwealth.

Kenya as a British colony and Uganda as a protectorate. Uganda had no white settlers – tea and coffee planters were not allowed to own land, but only to lease it – and the country was governed under a system which maintained tribal hierarchies and encouraged the chiefs to practise their traditional forms of government at the local level, while the network of British provincial and district commissioners provided centralized control.

On 18 February they drove some 200 miles west to Fort Portal, where they met the Mukama (King) of Toro and his subordinate chiefs and exchanged gifts. The formalities over, they could begin their next safari. At Fort Portal a new team and a new adventure awaited them. There were two hunters, Captain Roy Salmon and Dr Duke, a safari manager, Brodrick Ashton Warner, and a new doctor, W. H. Keane. Salmon was an exuberant character who was known as Samaki, meaning 'fish'; he had been recommended by the former Governor as 'simply a magnificent hunter, fearing nothing & without a nerve in his body'.[46] Both the Duke and the Duchess took to him at once, and often chose to go shooting with him alone.

'The Duke & Duchess have started the trip I am doing with them,' Salmon wrote home from their first camp, in the Semliki Valley. They had walked down the steep escarpment into the valley, a drop of over 2,000 feet in about six miles, to reach their *banda* camp of bamboo and elephant-grass huts in the early evening. Salmon liked his royal charges at once; they were not at all stiff, and immediately called him by his nickname. 'She is awfully pleasant to look at & topping manners. He speaks very slowly but has practically no stammer as a rule though occasionally he does.' He added – perhaps there were after all limits to his fearlessness – that the Governor had told him that their safety was his personal responsibility, 'which is rather terrifying'.[47]

The party dined in traditional safari style, the Duchess seated between the two hunters. 'She looked perfectly adorable in silk pyjamas & dressing gown with long mosquito boots,' wrote Samaki. 'The Duke wore a sort of Jaeger pyjama suit & Lady Annaly a wonderful pair of painted silk pyjamas. Great chatter all the time & a very good dinner.' He was happy, noting with approval that the royal couple had left it entirely to him to decide at what time they would leave for the next camp in the morning. 'So we get off at 5 a.m.'[48]

Their departure must have been a remarkable spectacle in the dawn light: the safari procession 'seemed unending, as we have 600

porters', the Duke of York recorded.[49] The Duchess rode a monowheel
– a kind of rickshaw consisting of a seat and canopy fixed to a bicycle
wheel – for part of the sixteen-mile trek. But she abandoned it to go
after a buffalo, to the alarm of her companions Dr Duke and Keith
Caldwell, who had spotted another two buffaloes near by. She dispatched hers successfully. From Naindikwa, where they next camped,
she went out with the Duke and Samaki and caught her first sight of
elephants, feeding among palms about 200 yards away. 'So off we
went & crept right up to within about 20 or 30 yards, and watched
them. It was very amusing – they poured sand over their backs, and
then picked bunches of grass (about five foot high) and wiped it off
and flapped their huge ears,' she later reported to her mother.[50]

Next day the trio left the main camp and set out on a separate
expedition, accompanied (no doubt mindful of the King's strictures
against travelling without a doctor) by Dr Keane and Ashton Warner.
'It's much nicer being a small safari,' the Duchess noted in her diary.[51]
But now there was an unofficial addition to their reduced party in the
shape of a hunter named Bezindenhout, whom the Duchess immediately nicknamed the Hoot. He was a well-meaning Dutchman who
tried, not always successfully, to locate game for them. 'We went on
& walked for miles in the boiling sun without seeing anything but
millions of Uganda kob,' the Duchess recorded on a day when the
Hoot had promised to find a leopard. 'We walked & walked & walked,
& got back to camp about 6.30 – very tired.'[52] She was gratified,
nevertheless, by the compliments her stamina – and her shooting –
earned her. 'You can't imagine what a reputation I have acquired as to
walking and shooting! I walk nearly twenty miles a day sometimes, &
feel most frightfully well, and the hunters are all amazed. It's too
funny,' she wrote to her mother. 'I love this life.'[53]

Captain Salmon's letters show that she was not quite as hardy as
she wished her mother to believe. 'They were both wonderful walkers
which amazed [the Duke] as at home she is renowned for never
walking a yard. She really was a funny little girl in her khaki shirt &
slacks & red silk neckerchief. Not being used to walking her feet
naturally blistered & she did seem a pathetic little person when in the
middle of the day we rested for a couple of hours & we took her
boots & socks off to cool her feet.'[54]

On 25 February they reached Lake Albert, the goal of their walking
safari. They boarded the SS *Samuel Baker*, a flat-bottomed paddle-

steamer, which the Duchess described as a 'very hot little boat'[55] and which was to be their stuffy and uncomfortable base for the next week. First there was another unplanned excitement: with Samaki and Dr Keane, they were rowed across the lake in search of elephant. 'We landed on a tiny bit of sand,' the Duke recorded, '& at once struck off into very thick bush. In a small clearing we saw at least 30 crocodiles, great big ones basking in the sun. They all waddled off back into the reeds on the lake at our approach. We did not see any elephant as they had gone further inland as the waterholes had started to fill up. The thick bush was my idea of Africa & it felt very creepy & sinister.'[56]

The next day they arrived at the port of Butiaba on the eastern shore of the lake, to be welcomed by the Mukama of Bunyoro, who hoped that they would have a successful safari. 'A large and very famous elephant called "Kakogi" lives in Bugungu, and we hope that Kakogi's tusks will go back with you to England to remind you of your visit to Lake Albert and the Bunyoro country.'[57]

The Mukama's good wishes bore fruit the very next day, though history does not relate whether it was in fact Kakogi whose tusks became Prince Albert's trophy. The party had planned to settle in a *banda* camp built for them at Ndandimiri by the local tribal chief; but, hearing that there were no elephants within forty miles, they returned instead to the *Samuel Baker*, steaming across to the White Nile and down to Katengiri where they camped. The next morning Salmon set off with the Duke and a small safari, leaving the Duchess and the rest of the party behind, for, as the hunter wrote, 'I was not sure of the country we would be shooting in. The Duke & I went off with one tent & bath between us & we shot a very big elephant the first evening out so we sent back for her to come out to breakfast with us.'[58]

The Duchess was thrilled. 'I started at 6 with Mr Warner to join Bertie & Samaki. On the way, we heard a lion roaring quite close. Then we heard 3 shots, & we imagined Bertie had shot it. The shots frightened an elephant, & it came bearing down on us at full speed, so we slipped behind an ant hill & it flew past. We got to their camp in the middle of borassus palms at 7.30, & they weren't in yet. We had breakfast, & then they arrived. Had raked the lion, but it got away. We started off at 8.30, looked at his elephant – HUGE!'[59]

Salmon's comments on that morning give a glimpse both of the young couple together and of the real risks of safari life.

It really was pleasing to see them meeting again & left no doubt
as to whether it was a love match. Before breakfast he & I went
off to try for a lion & she coming along with Ashton-Warner
heard us shooting & the lion grunting & was no end pleased to
have her husband handed back safe & sound. He utterly adores
her & could hardly bear it when I took her into thick country
after heavy game. He used to say when we were alone that
though he did not want any special care taken of himself he did
want me to make her as safe as possible without spoiling her
sport . . . Sometimes he said 'You know you ought to be jolly
flattered as I would not let her do this with another living man,'
& I certainly did especially when she said 'But I would not do it
with anyone else.'[60]

The Duchess expressed her delight at these excursions into the bush
with Samaki in a letter to her sister: 'One day I spent walking amongst
elephants – It was simply wonderful, and made one feel such a worm
looking at those <u>enormous</u> creatures. One could watch for <u>hours</u> –
they are so amusing, and frightfully dangerous, but the man we were
with is a great elephant hunter, and we walked about amongst the
herds quite easily.'[61]

A few days later it was the Duke who ran into danger while out
alone with Samaki in pursuit of an elephant. 'I really did run too big a
risk that time & was thoroughly scared at one time & tried to leave
him behind,' Samaki admitted. 'But he kept on my back & when I had
emptied my rifle calmly began firing & killed the bull.'[62] In his diary
the Duke reported, 'Had he [the elephant] come down the donga
towards us we should not have had much prospect of stopping him; as
I don't think we could have climbed up the sides as the banks were
covered with thick reeds like bamboos.'[63] That evening Samaki somewhat nervously admitted the incident to the Duchess. She replied, 'I
shall write & tell you what I really think of you but take this in the
meantime' – whereupon she picked up a menu card and wrote, 'Dear
Samaki, I think you charming & very brave. E.'[64]

By this time the Duke had accumulated a sizeable number of
trophies, which was at the time the chief aim of an African safari. But
he was reluctant to shoot one rare species and admitted in his diary,
'The White Rhino is only found in this part and is looked upon as a
great trophy. It is not at all difficult to shoot, but only three or four
are allowed to be shot a year as they are becoming scarce. I did not

want to shoot one on hearing this, but they wanted me to get one.'
He did so.[65]

That same afternoon Roy Salmon took them on an escapade which
earned him a rebuke from the acting Governor. He borrowed a car
and drove them to Arua, a hill station forty miles from the Nile to the
west, arriving unannounced at the house of a 'jolly young couple' he
knew. The wife rushed to tell her husband that Samaki had brought
the Duke and Duchess of York for tea. ' "Don't you believe it old girl,"
he retorted; "it's one of his leg pulls." To which the Duke said,
laughing like a boy, "I am the D. of Y. you know, really I am & this
lady is my wife." '[66]

That night they were unable to leave as planned for Nimule on
the Sudan border, where the Uganda trip was to end; the rudder on
their 'horrid little boat', the *Samuel Baker*, broke. Furthermore the
Duchess fell ill with a stomach upset, which her husband blamed on
the ship's bad food. She had scarcely recovered two days later when
they finally left Uganda on 5 March, feeling 'all very sad & quite
sentimental' at saying goodbye to their companions of the last
fortnight.[67]

Salmon, who was undoubtedly bewitched by the Duchess and
flattered to have become a favourite, recorded that at their last dinner
he sat between her and the Duke, which caused jealousy among other
members of the party. He recorded several conversations about the
Prince of Wales, of whom both the Duke and Duchess spoke with
great affection. 'She says David is a perfect dear & a great pal of hers
& the strongest man in the way of endurance in England ... He is
apparently greatly beloved by them both & they are both scared of the
King I imagine.'[68] A final glimpse of the Duchess by Salmon is worth
quoting in full:

> Her complexion is the most perfect I ever saw. One day she was
> powdering it on the march & he [the Duke] said 'come along,
> don't bother about that now' & I remarked that I had never seen
> anything more worth bothering about & then he said 'As a matter
> of fact you are quite right & do you know she has never washed
> her face in her life? I did not believe it before I was married but I
> know it's so. She puts some grease stuff on at night & it rubs off
> on the pillow by morning & that is all she ever does. I think it a
> very grubby way of living.'

She most indignantly denied the latter part of the description, said she used lots of water but no soap as the cream* took its place & certainly the result was glorious to look upon. She has perfectly wonderful eyes & uses them at times in a thoroughly mischievous way. She used to say 'Watch so & so while I catch his eye' & proceed to startle some man with a glance & then laugh like a child.[69]

The playful girl of the Beryl letters was not far away; the mischief and charm were enduring traits of her character.

The last lap of the tour began with a ninety-mile car drive over bumpy roads – these were testing for the Duchess, who was still feeling quite unwell – skirting the unnavigable section of the Nile and rejoining it at Rejaf. They had been met at Nimule by the team which was to accompany them through the Sudan: Captain Courtney Brocklehurst, Game Warden of the Sudan, Major R. H. Walsh his assistant, and the Provincial Medical Officer, Dr Biggar. The Duchess already knew Captain Brocklehurst, who was married to Mabell Airlie's daughter. He was a remarkable man, a professional soldier of great bravery who had found a new vocation as a game warden, acquiring a deep knowledge of the wild animals in his charge and publishing a book about them, *Game Animals of the Sudan;*[†] he was also in charge of the Khartoum Zoo. A conservationist as well as a hunter, he deplored indiscriminate killing of animals for the sake of it, and regarded photographing them in their natural habitat as much more worth while than gathering trophies.[70]

This stage of the tour was still potentially difficult because of the anti-British rebellions in the Sudan. But on 29 January Basil Brooke had been informed that the Foreign Office saw no reason for avoiding the Sudan, and that 'in the absence of any further telegram present

---

* This was Cold Cream of Roses, a special formula made for the Duchess by Malcolm Macfarlane, a pharmacist in Forfar, who had sent her a jar of it as a wedding present. In her letter of thanks she said she would use it all her life. She did, receiving fresh supplies from the pharmacy until 1990, when Mr W. Main, the pharmacist who had taken over the business from Malcolm Macfarlane's widow, retired.

† Published by Gurney & Jackson, Edinburgh, 1931. Brocklehurst served with the 10th Hussars in the First World War; he rejoined his regiment in the Second World War and was drowned in Burma in 1942 trying to save his porters' lives when they got into difficulties while crossing a river in spate.

plan can hold good.'[71] No further telegram was received and so the journey went ahead. Nonetheless, they did run a certain risk.

At Rejaf, to the Duchess's relief, they joined the *Nasir*, a river steamer, which was larger and better appointed than the *Samuel Baker*. 'This is a very comfortable boat,' she informed her sister Rose; 'and it is rather nice to have a real bath & wc, after having neither for about six weeks – tho' personally I love a tent, and will you believe it – I get up with the greatest ease at 5!'[72] In fact they had joined not so much a boat as a flotilla: they were accompanied by three barges, one housing the Sudan game wardens and their staff, gun-bearers and porters, another for their five touring Ford cars and four lorries, the last carrying ten donkeys and wood for fuel.[73]

For the next two days the Duchess stayed on board to recuperate with Lavinia Annaly, while the men went hunting. The Duke wrote her a worried letter, but she was able to join him next day at his camp.[74] For his part, he continued to revel in the safari life, writing enthusiastically to his elder brother: 'Never once during this trip have I felt I wanted to be home again. All this is so new & original in what one sees & the life one leads.'[75] The Duchess was no less exhilarated, and not a little proud of herself. 'I have become mad about shooting, and simply adore it. I have been walking twenty miles a day, starting at 5.30 am & getting in at 6 pm, and tiring out tough hunters in the most extraordinary way!! I cannot understand it unless it is the lust of the chase. I went out every day with Bertie, & loved it all . . . One day I went out the whole day after elephants, and it was the most thrilling & wonderful thing that I've ever done.'[76]

The party rejoined the *Nasir* at Juba on 10 March and steamed to Mongalla, where they visited a miniature zoo. The Sudan was much hotter than either Kenya or Uganda: the Duchess complained that she was 'dripping' for the first time. 'One is called at 6 always here, and gets up almost at once, & breakfast about 7.30. It really is too hot later, and the sun rises punctually at 6 & goes down at 6 in the evening, when it is nice & cool and lovely stars.'[77] Expeditions ashore meant floundering through tall papyrus or over sharp-edged swamp grass which cut the knees, gave way under one's weight and was infested with biting red ants.[78] Although the Duchess did not always go out with the hunters, her husband noted approvingly that on one expedition with Captain Brocklehurst she crawled some distance through this unpleasant terrain to shoot a gazelle.[79] She herself had no complaint, commenting 'we have had a very peaceful time going down the Nile on this very comfortable boat, and shooting a little here and there ... The birds are very wonderful here – marvellous colours, & lovely crested cranes & storks & every sort of duck & geese.'[80]

From 16 to 19 March they went further afield, leaving the comforts of the *Nasir* and driving westwards in 'boiling' heat into the province of Bahr-el-Ghazal, the Duke at the wheel of one of the Ford tourers with his wife beside him.[81] After two unsuccessful days in pursuit of the giant eland they returned to the Nile, where the Duchess turned ship's barber and cut Basil Brooke's hair. She stayed up late talking to him and Major Walsh.[82] As in both Kenya and Uganda, the atmosphere was relaxed and congenial, and the new team found as much favour with the Duchess as had Pat Ayre and Roy Salmon. She also enjoyed the cooling drinks of shandy to which Major Walsh seems to have introduced her. 'My goodness you deserve a good [leave],' she wrote to him later, 'after battling with Brock & five utter strangers for 6 weeks on the dear old Nile. It _was_ fun, I'd give anything to be coming out again this year, to chase elusive animals & drink shandy & talk.'[83]

Their next major landfall was at Tonga, from which they motored to Talodi* to see the Nuba Gathering on 25 March. This remarkable assembly of 10,000 tribesmen armed with ancient rifles marched past the royal couple for an hour, and then took part in wrestling, spear-throwing and dancing displays. An amused English observer of the scene thought that it was the guests of honour who seemed outlandish here. Noting that the Duke was wearing a light-grey lounge suit and a double terai hat, he went on: 'The writer knows nothing about ladies' fashions and cannot attempt to describe ladies' dresses, he only knows that HRH the Duchess of York looked charming in something blue and a glance into the royal enclosure where all the ladies were

---

* After the assassination of Sir Lee Stack on 19 November, Lord Allenby delivered an ultimatum to Zaghlul Pasha, the Egyptian Premier, demanding, among other things, the immediate withdrawal from the Sudan of all Egyptian officers and the purely Egyptian units of the Egyptian army. At Talodi, where there was only one British officer, the Egyptian officers refused to obey orders to leave and were arrested. They broke out and caused 'mutinous disorder' in the battalion on 25 November, but after Sudanese troops had arrived three days later, they were evacuated without further trouble. (Sir Harold MacMichael, *The Anglo-Egyptian Sudan*, Faber & Faber, 1934, pp. 154–8)

assembled reminded him of ASCOT – Ascot frocks at Talodi – what are we coming to?'[84] It must certainly have felt odd to the Duchess; as her husband remarked later, she had got so used to trousers that she had almost forgotten how to wear a dress.[85]

That night there was a gale and torrential rain, 'which was not nice as we were all sleeping outside', commented the Duke. They moved into tents, and then on to a verandah when the Duchess's tent collapsed at 4 a.m., but by morning both were thoroughly drenched. Next day, rather sadly, they parted company with their gun-bearers and personal boys at Tonga, for their camping safaris were over. Instead, the *Nasir* steamed up the Bahr-el-Ghazal river and the party made day excursions inland in pursuit of exotically named game: tiang, white-eared kob and red-fronted gazelle.

Continuing their voyage down the Nile, on 31 March they arrived at Kodok, where they went ashore to be met by the Governor of the Upper Nile Province and to watch 'a very good native dance . . . done by Shilluks. They have a little leopard skin round their waists & huge bracelets & painted faces, & sing very well – rather like a violoncello, & the dances are most amusing. They act all the time, & have lion-hunts & sham battles.'[86] In the few remaining days of shooting, the Duchess endured an attack by a swarm of bees during breakfast, walked for two hours in gruelling heat, and dispatched a sizeable bull roan antelope, a nine-foot crocodile and a gazelle.[87] And then it was time for their life of informality and privacy to come to an end, symbolized by the Duchess's regretful entry in her diary for 6 April: 'Got up in my blue crepe de chine, & said good-bye to my dear & hideous trousers.'[88]

On 6 April they finally disembarked from the *Nasir* at Kosti, some 180 miles south of Khartoum, and boarded a train for Makwar where they were taken to see the new Sennar dam across the Blue Nile, which, as part of the great Gezira irrigation scheme, was expected to contribute to the prosperity of the Sudan by allowing the cultivation of cotton and other crops over a hugely expanded area. The Duke jotted down the statistics of the dam in his diary; his wife's entry was equally characteristic: 'Joined the train, & puffed off to Makwar, having bidden Capt. Flett [captain of the *Nasir*] a fond farewell. Very hot. Got to Makwar at 4, & went to see the Great Dam. Lots of engineers, & DCs [district commissioners] & Governors. Very interesting, but too long. Went back to the Chief Engineer's house, & sat & drank lemonade. I was very tired & cross. Had a cocktail with Major Walsh. Bed 10.'[89]

The idyllic days in the wild were over – they had to yield their private lives to their public personae. At Khartoum next day they were met by the Governor General, Sir Geoffrey Archer. Also there to receive them was the Duchess's old friend (and disappointed suitor) Archibald Clark Kerr. Now *en poste* in Cairo as acting counsellor, he had persuaded Lord Allenby to send him to greet the Duke and Duchess on his behalf, since the unsettled political situation in Egypt did not allow them to visit Cairo on their way home. He had written her a long, disillusioned letter about Egyptian affairs on 10 March, at the same time enjoining her 'not to tell me Big Game stories. I do hope that you have adequately survived your appalling expedition. It was a splendidly courageous thing to do and I know that you did not rejoice over the inevitable killing of jolly animals.'[90]

After their weeks of safari, Khartoum did not impress. Although she found the Governor General 'very nice, and everything is done so well here,' the Duchess wrote dispiritedly to Queen Mary: 'I have never seen a more horrible town, and what makes it worse, there is nothing to see!'[91] No doubt for political reasons, they were advised against visiting the battlefield at Omdurman, the site of the British victory over the Khalifa in 1898. The ship in which they were to sail home from Port Sudan was delayed, but with their friends Captain Brocklehurst and Major Walsh they visited the zoo which the former had founded, and enjoyed an evening reception in the cool of the garden of the Governor General's Palace, meeting 'all the big Sheikhs and notables'; 'very fine old men', the Duchess remarked.[92]

On 9 April they left Khartoum by train, still accompanied by Brocklehurst and Walsh. The station was heavily guarded, since shots had been fired at the dining car of the train the previous evening when they should have been on board. Neither seemed perturbed; nor – perhaps deliberately – does either seem to have reported this incident in writing home. After a night and a day passing through desert and rocky hills ('No shots at the train yet!' observed the Duchess), they reached Port Sudan and boarded the SS *Maloja*, having said reluctant goodbyes to their two travelling companions. 'We are all very sad it is all over – it has been <u>marvellous</u>,' she lamented in her diary, adding next day, when woken at the by now accustomed early hour, 'It is very sad having nothing to get up for now!'[93]

The voyage home, to judge from the Duchess's letters, was the least enjoyable part of the trip; there was a sense of the real world and all its obligations closing back in on them; she and the Duke missed the thrill of safari, and she felt cold, 'all shrunken & small & blue'; she had no appetite for the ship's fancy-dress ball this time. The only compensation was that the English cricket team was on board the *Maloja*. She enjoyed talking to them – 'The cricketers are very nice, and all excellent accents – not at all refined thank God.'[94] They had a 'real old Whitwell XI feel about them, 'Obbs, & 'Earns and 'Endren, & Woolley, & Sutcliffe & Douglas & Gilligan. It really makes one feel very pre-war to hear about l.b.w.'s etc. once again,' she told her sister.[95] (Whitwell is a Hertfordshire village close to St Paul's Walden.)

They again shortened the journey by taking the train across France, but this time there were no delightful frivolities in Paris. On 19 April 1925 they crossed from Boulogne to Dover. As if to prove her husband's point in removing her from the chilly English climate, the Duchess almost immediately fell ill with tonsillitis; but, as she wrote to her friend D'Arcy Osborne, 'I am bubbling inside with Africa.'[96] The affection continued all her life. The safari trip, she said many years later, had been 'Wonderful. Best bit of one's life.'[97]

CHAPTER SEVEN

BIRTH OF A PRINCESS

1925–1927

'Elizabeth of York sounds so nice'

'IT'S AWFUL COMING back to the social and unnatural atmosphere again!' the Duchess confided to her diary soon after their return from Africa.[1] London seemed drab after their months in the wild, the restrictions of life in the Royal Family and at Court more stifling than ever. In Britain the shadow of the war still hung over everything and everyone, and for many that shadow never fully passed. One distinguished lawyer, a boy during the war, remembered ever after those schoolfriends who had perished; he thought they showed 'a certain uncomplainingness, an acceptance, without dramatics and without self pity, of their sad and untimely fortune. Those young men, who were only promoted boys, took their lot with a dignity that we now forget.'[2] War memorials were erected in villages and market towns across the land, and plaques listed the names of all those who had been sacrificed. Yet few of the new homes which Lloyd George had promised the heroes returning from war had been built.

Other homes were being constructed at speed. London was expanding outwards – 'dormitory suburbs' were being created by the extension of the Underground and Metropolitan railways. The first such extension was on the Northern Line, as it became known, to Golders Green and then Hendon in autumn 1923. The President of the Board of Trade, Sir Philip Lloyd-Graeme, switched on the current on the new line with a golden key and his ten-year-old son, wearing a bowler hat, drove the first train through to Hendon. Then came the turn of south London, with the Morden line extension.[3]

New necessities were purchased easily from the multiple stores which spread into the modern housing estates – W. H. Smith the newsagent, Sainsbury the grocer, Dewhurst the butcher, the Victoria Wine Company, MacFisheries, the tailor Montagu Burton, Woolworths, British Home Stores, Marks and Spencer – all had more and more outlets as middle-class housing spread. Architects struggled on tight budgets to make the same red-brick houses, built a dozen times in one street, different from each other. One would have a round stair window, another an unexpected gable, a third an unusual porch or a wooden garage. They could cost about £1,000 each and they rejoiced in names like Rosslyn, The Elms, Mon Abri.[4]

Hire purchase or 'never-never' schemes were becoming more and more popular, allowing people to acquire furniture, vacuum cleaners, gas ovens, wirelesses, even motor cars, as never before. The car greatly increased the emigration to suburbia. By 1924 the Baby Car, the Austin Seven, was on the market. It sold for £165 and was described as the Mighty Miniature but more widely as the Bed Pan. It was soon followed by the Morris Minor. The growth of the motoring population, together with the popularity of extended bus services, led to practical but ugly ribbon developments along main roads. Stanley Baldwin with reason declared, 'It is no exaggeration to say that in fifty years at the rate so-called improvements are being made, the destruction of all the beauty and charm with which our ancestors enhanced their towns and villages will be complete.'[5]

At the same time as this erosion of the countryside was beginning, urban unemployment remained high and the problems of the working class were imperfectly addressed. This was true in all of Europe, not just in Britain. The crumbling of old economic patterns of exchange since 1914 made poverty and unemployment more intractable and created fertile soil for revolutionaries to till.

After the triumph of the Bolsheviks in Russia, it was inevitable that every European country would spawn its own revolutionary communist party. Leadership was provided by the Comintern, created by Moscow in 1919 to ensure that national communist parties followed the policies of the Soviet Union. The communists may have been more alarming than effective, and in Britain they never acquired large membership. But alarming they were nonetheless, particularly after they came to power in Hungary and then, for brief periods, in Germany. In almost every European country socialists were divided into two camps – those who were loyal to Moscow and called themselves communist and those who wished to remain loyal to their own nations and remained socialists. The two factions were bitter rivals for working-class support.

In 1925 the production of food and raw materials in Europe for the first time reached the levels of 1914 and manufacturing industry revived. There were grounds for confidence – it was still possible to hope for and even believe in the future of liberal democracies. But the rather efficient pre-1914 economic system had been fatally damaged and the new prosperity rested on shallow foundations. The crisis of employment for the growing working class was a constant concern. The spectre of violent revolution and totalitarianism was ever present in Europe – and it was to dominate the era.

*

IT WAS A COLD spring and the Duchess's nostalgia for Africa's warmth was intensified by the return, all too soon, of her tonsillitis.[6] An additional sadness for both the Yorks was that, the day after they returned, the Prince of Wales left for a long journey to West and South Africa and South America. The Duke wrote to his brother saying, 'Between ourselves we were not very glad to get back from our travels . . . We miss you terribly, of course, & there is an awful blank in London of something missing, & that blank is you.'[7] They missed calling on him at lunchtime at St James's Palace for a cocktail, they missed evenings out at slightly risqué clubs with him, and they missed being able to share complaints about life with him.

For the Duke there was one compensation for his brother's absence: he replaced the Prince of Wales as president of the British Empire Exhibition. After the great success of the exhibition in 1924 it had been decided that there should be a new one in 1925, to be opened in May. Now that the Duke had experienced the Empire at first hand, he brought a personal enthusiasm, even a zest, to the task.[8]

As president, the Duke had to make a speech at the opening ceremony on 9 May, inviting his father to open the exhibition. He was nervous at the prospect, above all because his speech would be broadcast by the new British Broadcasting Company. He practised it many times. The closer to the day of the opening the more nervous he became. Not only did he have to speak in front of the stadium, the nation and much of the world – he also had to perform in front of the sternest judge of all, his father. He wrote to the King, 'I hope you will understand that I am bound to be more nervous than I usually am.'[9]

He had several sleepless nights before the ordeal and on the day itself, Saturday 9 May, he set out for Wembley 'very downhearted', according to his wife's diary. When the moment finally came, his legs were trembling, but his voice was quite steady and although he had difficulty articulating some words, he persevered.[10] The Duchess had remained at White Lodge where she listened to the speech on the wireless. 'It was marvellously clear & no hesitation. I was <u>so</u> relieved,' she wrote.[11] Afterwards the Duke said he thought that the speech was 'easily the best I have ever done'. Perhaps even more important, 'Papa seemed pleased which was kind of him.'[12] The King wrote to Prince George, 'Bertie got through his speech all right, but there were some rather long pauses.'[13] The Duke's speech defect remained a real tribulation and source of anxiety for him and his family for some time to come.

For the Whitsun weekend at the end of May the Duke and Duchess had a welcome short trip to Glamis, where they shot rabbits and took their dog Glen for walks with the Duchess's father and brothers. It was much easier for them to relax there, but the Queen took to writing slightly querulous letters reproaching them if they spent weekends away.[14] They returned to London in time for Trooping the Colour – the Duchess rode in the same carriage as the Queen and Princess Mary and then watched the ceremony from a room over the Horse Guards Arch. The next day they went together to Dudley in support of the Duke's interest in the Industrial Welfare Society and their now recognized sympathy for social and relief work. Their official files on the trip illustrate the local impact of royal visits, of which this was but one of many.

They visited T. W. Lench Ltd, manufacturers of nuts and bolts; Harry Lench, regarded as a pioneer in welfare work and one of the most progressive employers in the Black Country, wrote afterwards of their visit that it would 'never be forgotten by my workpeople or by me'.[15] Another firm, Stevens and Williams Ltd, which had been suffering badly from foreign competition, received a similar boost from the royal visit to its Brierley Hill art glass works. The couple also went to the Guest Hospital, where the Duchess received cheques on behalf of the hospital – this was common practice in institutions supported by voluntary donations: the cheques or 'purses' tended to be more generous if a distinguished guest were on hand to accept them. On this occasion, apparently, the hospital's debt was completely wiped out.[16]

On 15 July the Duchess had to undertake a major engagement of her own at the British Empire Exhibition – she opened the First International Conference of Women in Science, Industry and Commerce, of which she had agreed to be president. The conference was chaired by Lady Astor;* also on the platform with the Duchess were three formidable older women: Ellen Wilkinson, the suffragette leader, trade unionist and Labour MP; Viscountess Rhondda, 'the Welsh Boadicea', another suffragette; and the distinguished physiologist Professor Winifred Cullis. Margaret Bondfield, a prominent trade unionist and Labour politician, spoke at the lunch afterwards.

The Duchess was in daunting company; she felt 'very frightened', but nevertheless delivered her short prepared speech with sufficient verve to attract effusive, if patronizing, praise from one of the men present. F. S. Dutton of the Industrial Court wrote afterwards: 'Her Royal Highness's speech was a real treat! It was very bravely and charmingly done & all the women folk were lyrical about it. We men will soon have to look to our laurels!'[17] She pointed out that this was the first conference of its kind for women, and also the first she had opened; referring to 'the ever-increasing scope of women's work' and 'the importance of women's activities in so many spheres', she hoped it would lead to many similar gatherings. Lady Astor, thanking her for coming, complimented the Duchess on her 'very practical interest in industrial welfare'. For Caroline Haslett, who as secretary of the Women's Engineering Society had organized the conference, the important thing was that the Duchess had allied herself publicly with women's causes.[18]

Emerging as a public figure, the Duchess was an increasing asset to the Royal Family. The press noticed, and commented. According to one article, 'She has, in fact, the genius of friendship, and this is perhaps why she has the happy faculty, as Viscountess Astor MP said on one notable occasion, of "never being bored".'[19] The Duke realized more and more how invaluable his wife's assistance was. He wrote to the Prince of Wales, 'She is marvellous the way she talks to old mayors & the like at shows, & she never looks tired even after the longest of days. She is a darling & I don't know what I should do without her.'[20]

On 17 July they gave a reception at St James's Palace for visitors

---

* Nancy Astor, Viscountess Astor (1879–1964). Born Nancy Langhorne in Virginia, USA, she married Waldorf Astor, second Viscount Astor, in 1906. A prominent and controversial politician and society hostess, in 1919 she became the first woman to take a seat in Parliament.

from the Empire and the press. According to her diary, 'I put on white & a tiara. At 9.30 B & I went to St James's Palace, & we gave an Evening Party to Overseas Visitors. About 600. Went quite well. Home 12 – Very tired & quite hoarse!'[21] Duties were mixed with pleasures, however – their friend Major Walsh, home on leave from the Sudan where they had hunted with him, came to town. They were always eager to see him; later that summer they invited him to lunch to see their African trophies, which had been mounted. 'Having been entertained to a tête à tête breakfast with you, my dear white hunter on that wicked old Nile, I feel it would be proper & decent of you to partake of our hospitality, just by way of a change,' the Duchess wrote to him. On his next leave there was another invitation: 'Dear Walshie, Welcome home again to dear old England, the home of BEER ... All white hunters should visit their charges on instant arrival in London, so I fear that you haven't done too well. However, there is always a drink waiting here for you, or even two.'[22]

On 10 August they started on their annual summer holiday in Scotland, split between the gaiety of Glamis and the dull routine and restrictions of Balmoral. For some of the time the Duchess left her husband with his parents while she visited her sister in Edinburgh. Although she played her part in the Royal Family with enthusiasm, she was still detached enough to see it clearly. In one letter written from her sister's house she urged her husband to stick up for himself 'and remember that you are an elderly married man' not to be patronized. 'I miss you frightfully.'[23] He replied at once that he had loved getting her letter. 'I am longing for Monday when you come here. I miss you terribly darling in this awful room. It wants some of your letters lying about & a few papers on the floor!! to make it at all homely.'[24]

*

THE AUTUMN OF 1925 brought moments of both joy and sadness. The Prince of Wales returned from his long tour to Africa and South America. 'Your trip has been the most marvellous success from all accounts,' the Duke of York had written to him. 'I hope the people here will realise it when you return.'[25] In fact, the Prince received a spectacular welcome home. The Royal Family and government ministers gathered at Victoria station to greet him. 'Great embracings,' Queen Mary recorded in her diary later.[26] Despite the rain, crowds cheered the King and his sons as they drove back to Buckingham Palace (the Queen and Duchess returned by a shorter, drier route), and cheered again when the family appeared on the balcony, before dining together that evening. It was a clear indication of the popularity of the Prince of Wales.

A few weeks later, however, family and nation were in mourning. On 20 November Queen Alexandra died at Sandringham aged eighty, after a heart attack. It was sixty-two years since she had been welcomed from Denmark as 'the Sea-King's daughter from over the sea'.[27] A woman of beauty, gaiety and generosity, after the death of her husband she had continued to carry out royal duties and support her charitable causes, but she had grown very frail in the last five years. She lost her hearing completely and much of her vision, and became confused. She was tended with great affection by her unmarried daughter Princess Victoria, and her son the King visited her constantly.

He was greatly saddened by her death. 'Darling Motherdear', he wrote in his diary on 22 November, 'was taken this morning to our little church where she had worshipped for 62 years.'[28] The next day the Queen's funeral took place at Westminster Abbey and she was buried beside her husband in St George's Chapel, Windsor. The Duchess wrote to her 'dearest Papa' to tell him how much she was thinking of him. 'Words, I know, are useless in a tragic time, but I hope you will allow me to send you my deepest & truest sympathy from the very bottom of my heart.'[29]

For the Duchess and her husband there was joyous news that autumn. They had both had one overriding preoccupation for some time. In a letter to the Prince of Wales in August, the Duke, speaking of his happiness with his wife, had added, 'I still long for one thing which you can guess, & so does she.'[30] It was around this time, in fact, that the Duchess became pregnant. She soon felt the symptoms of it. 'I am feeling much better now, tho' the sight of wine simply turns me up! Isn't it extraordinary?' she wrote to her husband in September. 'It will be a tragedy if I never recover my drinking powers.'[31] She need not have worried.

They waited until the middle of October before they told their parents. The Duke wrote to Lady Strathmore, hoping that she was as delighted as he was at the news.[32] He added that it would be much easier to turn down engagements for his wife now and she clearly could not motor up and down to White Lodge – a house in central

London was all the more urgently needed. The Duchess's pregnancy was also a reason not to make constant weekend trips to Sandringham. The Queen agreed, writing to her son, 'It is most necessary that E. should take the greatest care of her precious self. It is a great joy to Papa & me to feel that we may look forward to a direct descendant in the male line of our family & the country will be delighted when they are allowed to know.'[33]

The Duke and Duchess discovered that Curzon House, in Curzon Street, was available for rent, and decided to move there and shut up White Lodge for the winter.[34] They both wrote to Queen Mary explaining the idea; the Duchess said, 'It is rather an attractive old house, and we can all squeeze in, which will make things much more convenient. I am sure you will think this a good idea, as after October it gets very foggy and lonely in the Park here.' As for her health, she was feeling well, except for headaches, and she thought they would soon pass. 'Bertie & I are so pleased and excited about it all, & talk endlessly on the subject, which is perhaps a little previous!'[35] Given the Duchess's condition, the Queen could hardly object to the move back into London – she just hoped that it would not be too expensive.[36]

The Duchess kept many, though not all, public engagements during the first months of her pregnancy. In the second half of October she did not travel with the Duke to Sunderland, nor did she go with him to the University of Leeds, whose appeal he had headed as patron. The reason given in both cases was her 'very heavy list of engagements during the next few weeks'.[37] But she did go to Hackney – the site of her unsuccessful examination and the disagreeable tapioca pudding back in 1916. She had a long day there, opening both Hackney's Maternity and Child Welfare Centre and a nurses' home of the Hackney District Nursing Association, as well as visiting the head-quarters of the British Legion.

In the middle of November she went to Cheltenham to visit the County of Gloucester Nursing Association's bazaar, at the invitation of the Dowager Duchess of Beaufort. Once she had agreed to this, other local worthies applied for parcels of her time. The Cheltenham branch of the British Legion asked her to visit them. The programme stated, 'After the vote of thanks the Dowager Duchess will ask Her Royal Highness if she will be so good as to come through the Bazaar to a concert in a side room, for a short time.' The Dowager Duchess added a further request: could two of her granddaughters make a presentation?[38] In the way of royal programmes, more was constantly required, and generally given. The only invitations which the Duchess was always glad to refuse were formal dinners.[39]

After the funeral of Queen Alexandra the Duke was expected to stay on at York Cottage with his parents; the Duchess, feeling unwell, remained in London. He went shooting during the day but found the evenings without his wife very dull. He loved talking to her on the telephone. Because it was so easy for telephone operators to listen in, they could not say much to each other, 'but we hear each other's voices, which is the nearest we can get to each other. Darling I do feel so sorry for you feeling wretched as you do at this time, but I do hope as time goes on you will not find things such an effort.'[40]

She was able to join him for the traditional Royal Family Christmas in Norfolk, still at York Cottage.* On Christmas Eve he wrote her a letter recalling that it was three years since he had been waiting for her to say yes. His heart, he said, still went 'pit-a-pat' for her in the same way as it did then. This letter was one which he had to post across the abyss of only a few feet. 'Why I have written these letters to you when you're in the room, I don't know. But I just have. All my love darling.'[41] They tried to cheer up the traditional Christmas events by bringing with them from London their own entertainment. 'We brought down a cinema, & a radio, & a gramophone, which are all hard at work at different ends of the house, which is much the same here as being in the same room!' the Duchess reported to her sister May. Christmas went off quite well, she said.[42]

In the New Year the Duke resumed his hunting in Leicestershire; his wife apparently felt some pangs of loneliness, telling D'Arcy Osborne that she was 'a hunting widow now, & singularly free from visitors'.[43] The roads were treacherous and so she did not go to St Paul's Walden as much as she might have liked.[44] She seems to have made her husband aware of her irritation for he wrote an apologetic letter to his 'own little Elizabeth darling', declaring, 'my conscience has pricked me and your letter tonight made me feel that I had been very unkind to you.'[45]

---

* The King and Queen did not move into Sandringham House until 1926. Both were sad to leave York Cottage, despite its cramped rooms, uninspiring furnishings and cooking smells, for they had lived there for thirty-three years. But they soon came to appreciate the advantages of the main house.

Early in 1926 the Duchess made sure that the maternity nurse who had looked after her sisters and their babies would be able to come to her in April. Annie Beevers,* known as Nannie B, 'tall and dark and very Yorkshire', as Queen Elizabeth later described her, was a widow who had trained in midwifery after the death of her husband. Writing to Nannie B to confirm the arrangement, the Duchess asked her to recommend a tonic 'as I get rather tired (& irritable I fear!)'.[46]

As their lease of Curzon House was coming to an end, the Duke and Duchess had planned to rent another house, in Grosvenor Square, where their child would be born and where they would spend the summer. But when difficulties arose over the new house in March, they abandoned the idea and decided to go instead to the Duchess's parents' house, 17 Bruton Street.[47]

The baby was due at the end of April. Towards the middle of the month the Duchess's doctors decided that the birth should be induced. The King's physician, Sir Bertrand Dawson, lunched with the King and Queen at Windsor Castle on 17 April and explained the situation. They both wrote at once to the Duke to say that they were sorry for the extra anxiety this would cause. Queen Mary was full of affectionate concern for the future parents but also, characteristically, for the future of the dynasty. She wished she could be with them, 'but I am afraid to go to Bruton Street on account of the Press, as the last thing one wants is for any inkling of this to appear in the papers, so I hope you will both understand & will not think me a heartless wretch as indeed my heart & thoughts are with you at this time, which is of such great importance to our family.' Alive to the ever present danger of eavesdroppers, she said that if the Duke wanted to telephone her 'you need not mention E's name as we shall understand.'[48] Both the King and Queen suggested that, as Lady Strathmore had a temperature and could not be with her daughter for the birth, they should send for May Elphinstone. 'Someone who has had a baby & knows is such a comfort to one at such moments,' Queen Mary wrote.[49]

A little girl was born early in the morning of 21 April. It was a

---

* Anne Beevers (1862–1946), née Greaves, born in Clayworth, Nottinghamshire, daughter of a carpenter from Yorkshire. Her husband died following a rugby accident, leaving her with a small son. After training as a midwife at the London Hospital, she became a much loved private maternity or monthly nurse employed by many society families, and the Duchess remained in touch with her until her death in 1946.

difficult labour and the doctors decided to perform a Caesarean section.
The Duke was 'very worried & anxious',[50] and paced the house, as
well as looking after the Home Secretary, Sir William Joynson-Hicks,
who had been summoned in accordance with the convention that this
minister must always be present at the birth of a child in the direct
royal succession to see that no substitution took place.* The first
medical bulletin, signed by Henry Simson† and Walter Jagger,‡ stated
that 'The Duchess of York has had some rest since the arrival of her
daughter. Her Royal Highness and the infant Princess are making very
satisfactory progress. Previous to the Confinement a consultation took
place, at which Sir George Blacker§ was present, and a certain line of
treatment was successfully adopted.'

Queen Mary recorded in her diary that at Windsor Castle she and
the King were woken at 4 a.m. to be given the news that 'darling
Elizabeth had got a daughter at 2.40. Such a relief & joy.'[51] The new
child was the King's first granddaughter and third in line to the throne,
after the Prince of Wales and the Duke of York.

That afternoon the King and Queen motored up from Windsor to
Bruton Street. A small crowd cheered them outside the house. 'Saw
the baby who is a little darling with a lovely complexion & pretty fair
hair,' the Queen noted in her diary.[52] To her son she wrote, 'I am so
thankful all is going well with our darling Elizabeth & that adorable
little daughter of yours, she is too sweet & pretty & I feel very proud
of my first grand daughter!'[53] Next day the Duke wrote to thank his
mother. 'You don't know what a tremendous joy it is to Elizabeth &
me to have our little girl. We always wanted a child to make our
happiness complete, & now that it has at last happened, it seems so
wonderful & strange ... I do hope that you & Papa are as delighted,
as we are, to have a grand daughter, or would you have sooner had

---

* This practice had been established following the rumours, probably untrue, that a baby had
been substituted for the rightful heir to King James II and his second wife, Queen Mary of
Modena. The custom was suspended during the Second World War, and King George VI,
who thought it 'archaic', later abolished it.

† Sir Henry Simson (1872–1932), obstetric surgeon at the West London Hospital. He had
attended Princess Mary at the births of her two sons.

‡ Dr Walter Jagger (1871–1929), physician. He also attended the Duchess of York during
bouts of influenza after the birth of Princess Elizabeth.

§ Sir George Blacker (1865–1948), obstetric physician at University College Hospital.

another grandson?* I know Elizabeth wanted a daughter. May I say I hope you won't spoil her when she gets a bit older.'⁵⁴

Among the hundreds of letters and telegrams they received was one from Beryl Poignand. The Duke wrote to thank her and to tell her how overjoyed they were with their baby. 'You have known Elizabeth for so long & I can tell you how very proud I am of her for the way she has gone through this last week.'⁵⁵ Lady Strathmore also sent a letter to Beryl saying, 'The baby is a lovely, healthy little creature . . . Eliz is getting on but is still very tired & weak – but the Drs are pleased with her progress, so all is well. She often talks of you & the old days & is exactly the same as ever.'⁵⁶

The most urgent task was the choosing of the new Princess's names. On 27 April the Duke wrote to his father to say that their choice was Elizabeth Alexandra Mary – the names of the baby's mother, her great-grandmother and her grandmother. 'We are so anxious for her first name to be Elizabeth as it is such a nice name & there has been no one of that name in your family for a long time. Elizabeth of York sounds so nice too.'⁵⁷ The King approved the choices at once.⁵⁸

*

THE BIRTH OF the Princess provided a welcome diversion in troubled times. Indeed a few days later Britain appeared to some (particularly in sections of the press) to be on the cusp of revolution. Both the King and the Duke had been preoccupied with the danger of a general strike, threatened by the Trades Union Congress in support of the coalminers.

Coal had for over a century been the basis of Britain's industrial power and, to a significant extent, of her imperial expansion. Mining was the biggest industry in Britain, the only one employing over a million people. It had been temporarily nationalized during the war – now it had become a symbol of class struggle.⁵⁹ In summer 1925 the owners gave notice that they intended to lower wages and enforce longer hours. The Miners' Union was led by a charismatic former

---

* The first grandchild of King George and Queen Mary was George, the elder son of Princess Mary and Lord Lascelles, who had been born on 7 February 1923. A second son, Gerald, was born on 21 August 1924.

Baptist lay preacher, A. J. Cook, who saw himself as 'a humble follower of Lenin'. He decided to take the government and the owners' ultimatums as a challenge to join a class war. His ambition was at the very least to refuse all concessions.[60] The King was worried, writing in his diary in July 1925 that a strike 'will play the devil with the country. I never seem to get any peace in this world. Felt very low & depressed.'[61]

At the last minute the government surrendered, deciding to continue the subsidies pending the report of a Royal Commission. The report in March 1926 recommended complete reorganization of the industry, the end of the subsidies and a smaller reduction in wages than the owners had wanted. This last Cook refused to accept. The miners' slogan 'Not a minute on the day, not a penny off the pay' was supported by many other unions. They felt that at last organized labour should show its strength. The TUC announced a general strike for 3 May; it was to include all workers except those in the public health services.

Such dread swept the country that it might have seemed that the Day of Judgement was nigh. Many government ministers, and many members of the upper and middle classes, their concerns whipped up by the *Daily Mail* and other papers, feared that this was the start of the British Bolshevik revolution. Duff Cooper recorded in his diary, perhaps with irony, that his wife Diana had asked him on 5 May how soon they could with honour leave the country. 'I said not until the massacres began.'[62]

Facing the threat of a national strike, the government formed an Organization for the Maintenance of Supplies and enlisted volunteers from the middle and upper classes as drivers to move food between cities. On 3 May itself Hyde Park was closed to the public and used as a milk depot. Troops were moved into Whitehall and used to convoy food. There was no public transport but people walked or hitch-hiked to work. Power plants were taken over by the government but illuminated signs were prohibited. Fog made life more confusing. Amateur train and bus drivers managed to get some buses and trains running, but such 'scabs' risked having the windows of their vehicles broken. Members of the gentlemen's clubs in St James's turned up for lunch in policemen's uniforms.[63]

Newspapers were published only with difficulty in Britain. Winston Churchill, the Chancellor of the Exchequer, expressed government demands for the 'unconditional surrender' of the unions with his usual forthrightness; he published a government broadsheet, the *British Gazette*, which declared that the General Strike was a threat to the constitution and warned that the army might have to assist the government more robustly. The King made it clear that he thought this imprudent.[64] In the event troops were needed only in the London docks, where violence was never far distant.[65]

The *Daily Mail*, the government's principal cheerleader, printed editions in Paris and flew them over to London. It brandished headlines such as 'The Pistol at the Nation's Head' and under the headline 'For King and Country' (the paper's slogan) on 3 May it printed an editorial which declared, 'A general strike is not an industrial dispute. It is a revolutionary movement intended to inflict suffering upon the great mass of innocent persons in the community ... This being so, it cannot be tolerated by any civilised government, and must be dealt with by every resource at the disposal of the community.'

The strike caused the King great anxiety; he came to London on the morning it began and stayed there throughout. He had consistently shown his sympathy for the poor of his kingdom as well as his affinity with the rich. Just before the strike began he told Lord Durham, a mine owner, that he was sorry for the miners. When Durham complained that they were 'a damned lot of revolutionaries', the King retorted, 'Try living on their wages before you judge them.'[66]

The Duke of York, with his specific interest in industrial matters, was also worried and attended five of the debates in the House of Commons during the strike; on 11 May he went to see the food transport organization in Hyde Park. The King urged the government to protect those who were trying to maintain essential services but was opposed to anything that might make the strikers desperate.[67] He discouraged the government from introducing legislation or even orders in council that might be seen as confiscating money from strikers and thus provoke more fury. However, while the King was sympathetic to the plight of the poor, he was absolutely opposed to intimidation or any other breach of the law by strikers.[68] At one stage during the General Strike he urged new legislation to prevent intimidation of those who were trying to break the strike. The Prime Minister thought this unwise.[69] On the other hand, he subtly and successfully discouraged the government from legislating to control trades union funds. As his Private Secretary Lord Stamfordham recorded, on 9 May he told the Home Secretary and the Attorney General that the situation so far was 'better and more peaceful than might have been expected. The spirit of the miners was not unfriendly, as shown by such instances as Saturday afternoon's Football Match at Plymouth between the police and the strikers: but any attempt to get hold of or control the Trades Union Funds might cause exasperation and provoke reprisals.'[70]

There was not much support for the miners among the well-to-do, who found that they were able to get by surprisingly well. They rallied to voluntary organizations, as they had during the war, and paid attention to the BBC, which now had around two million regular listeners and which urged them to 'do their bit'.[71] After the strike had continued for eight days it became clear that the strikers would succeed neither in intimidating the public nor in coercing the government. A rift grew between the TUC and the Miners' Union over terms for settlement and the TUC called off the General Strike on 12 May. The *Daily Mail* was triumphant: 'Surrender of the Revolutionaries' and 'A Triumph for the People' were among its favoured headlines. The King wrote in his diary, 'our old country can well be proud of itself, as during the last nine days there has been a strike in which four million people have been affected, not a shot has been fired and no one killed. It shows what a wonderful people we are.'[72]

Not everyone returned at once to work. The dockers, printers and transport workers remained out for another five days and some of the abandoned miners held out for another six months. By then they were utterly impoverished, winter was closing in and they were compelled to drift back to work. The coal strike finally came to an end only in November 1926.

The trades unions realized that they had been beaten and did not voice any strong objection when, in 1927, much more draconian legislation made general strikes illegal.[73] Instead they began to co-operate with industrialists and took part in a new National Industrial Council formed in 1927. But many workers remained suspicious and gradually the feeling grew that the miners had not been fairly treated. Coal remained the largest single employer in the country until the Second World War and nationalization of the mines was one of the first acts embarked upon by the Labour government elected in 1945. Harold Nicolson, King George V's official biographer, put it well when he wrote that the strike 'was felt to be a common tragedy and not a purely class tragedy; there was little heresy hunting and no victimisation. Every section of the community felt sorry for the other sections, as well as for themselves.'[74]

But at the same time the strike seemed to reduce militancy. The Communist Party had doubled its membership during 1926 – it lost large numbers of recruits afterwards. And many middle-class 'blacklegs' suddenly realized for the first time how difficult manual labour could be, and began to harbour a new respect for workers. The historian A. J. P. Taylor was surely exaggerating when he declared that 'The general strike, apparently the clearest display of the class war in British history, marked the moment when class war ceased to shape the pattern of British industrial relations.'[75] But perhaps he was right in the sense that 1926 showed that Britain might be able to deal reasonably with the issues of industrial discontent and thus avoid the totalitarian responses which began to scar Europe.

*

IN THE IMMEDIATE aftermath of the strike, the Royal Family could afford some happiness. It centred upon Princess Elizabeth who straight away became the focus of attention in her extended family. The newspapers had reported the birth with enthusiasm and reflected the affection in which the Duchess was already held, after three years of marriage. Not only that – they tried to assume the mantle of fairy godparents around the crib, each bearing good wishes and glorious predictions. The *Morning Post* remarked, 'For the Royal Family the day was one of congratulation and satisfaction, a feeling which the public cordially shared, because in three short years the Duchess has become universally and outstandingly popular.' The *Daily Telegraph* declared, 'The Duchess has taken a full share in our national life, working for all sorts of philanthropical institutions, and with her husband she has visited many centres of industry.' The *Daily Graphic* showed remarkable foresight when it wrote that the family's happiness was shared by the nation and added, 'The possibility that in the little stranger to Bruton Street there may be a future Queen of Great Britain (perhaps, even a second and resplendent Queen Elizabeth) is sufficiently intriguing; but let us not burden the bright hour of its arrival with speculation of its Royal destiny.'

On 26 May (Queen Mary's birthday) a photograph of the Duchess with her baby was published in the *Sketch*, and the *Daily Mirror* reported 'a charming incident' outside Buckingham Palace. 'About noon two nurses came out into the courtyard, and one of them was carrying the Duchess of York's baby.* The infant Princess was shown to the crowd which lined the railings, and people were obviously delighted to enjoy this homely privilege. Later the Duke and Duchess of York drove up to the Palace and were very cordially greeted by the sightseers.'[76]

The baby was christened on 29 May in the private chapel at Buckingham Palace, with water from the River Jordan. She was dressed in the same cream satin and Honiton lace robe which her father had worn at his christening; it had been made for Queen Victoria's eldest child in 1841 and royal babies had been christened in it ever since. The service was conducted by Cosmo Lang, Archbishop of York, and the godparents were the King and Queen, Princess Mary, the Duke of Connaught, May Elphinstone and Lord and Lady Strathmore. The choir of the Chapel Royal, St James's Palace, sang and the Princess cried forcefully during the service. Afterwards there was a christening tea at Bruton Street at which the Duchess of York cut a cake bearing a single silver candle. The next day her photograph appeared in the papers, smiling broadly.

In early August the family went up to Glamis as usual, with the baby now in the care of Alah Knight, the Duchess's own nanny. The Scottish air agreed with the little Princess – she put on weight and she slept soundly in her pram in the open air, in the Italian garden designed by her grandmother, the rhythmic sounds of tennis from the court near by. Queen Mary was anxious that Princess Elizabeth should visit Balmoral too, but this the Duchess parried, writing to her mother-in-law, 'I am longing for you to see her. She has grown so round and pink [and] merry. The country air suits her marvellously well I am glad to say. I would have so loved to bring her up, but I am sure you will agree that so many changes is not a good thing.'[77] When the Yorks made their own trip to Balmoral at the end of September, they left the baby with the Duchess's mother at Glamis.

---

* The nurse carrying the Princess was Nannie B. She stayed with the family for about two months; in July the Duchess wrote to her to say she was glad she had been so happy, and hoping that 'the next time' would be the same. She sent a gold wristwatch as a memento of 'us three here who are so fond of our dear Nannie B'. (Duchess of York to Nannie B, 7 and 9 July 1926, private collection)

The Prince of Wales asked the Duchess if he could come and stay with them at Glamis. She was delighted and told her mother, 'he would love to come unless he's in the way. Do tell me when I come up. He is so frightfully modest, & is terrified of pushing in where he's not wanted.'[78] He did come, and afterwards wrote euphoric letters of thanks to both Lady Strathmore and her daughter.[79] To the Duchess he wrote, 'Darling Elizabeth, It _was_ fun at Glamis & very sweet of your family to have me stop there & I was sad to leave you all last night . . . I miss you both & you've been so sweet to me these last days – Yes – you really have & I mean that absolutely.' He gave her the good news that he had received 'a parcel of new records from N.Y. & there are some peaches of tunes – fine for Charleson – Carleston'.[80]

But Glamis was no longer just for holidays – the Duchess had official functions to perform in Scotland. She opened the Dundee Horticultural Society's Flower Show and, accompanied by the Duke, she enjoyed launching the new Montrose lifeboat.[81] In the second week of October, the end of their Scottish sojourn, they went to stay with the Elphinstones at Carberry Tower for a round of engagements in Edinburgh on 9 October, which marked the Duchess's full return to public life. Their schedule helps to show the role which the Royal Family played in attracting funds for civic institutions which at that time depended on philanthropy and public subscription.

First the Duke opened the new radiology department at the Royal Infirmary. The Infirmary was maintained entirely by voluntary contributions, and the staff of physicians and surgeons – the leading members of the medical profession in Edinburgh – gave their services voluntarily. Afterwards the Duke was presented with the Freedom of the City, and the Duchess inspected the Edinburgh Company of the Girls' Guildry, of which she was patron, before a civic luncheon. (This was her first patronage; she had accepted it during her engagement.) In the afternoon, the Duchess unveiled a plaque commemorating the new installation of the Edinburgh Corporation's gas works. Later they visited the club rooms of the Cameron Highlanders' Association (the Duke was colonel-in-chief of the 4th Battalion), and finally they went to visit the Royal Soldiers' Home at Colinton. This last visit was arranged only because of the persistence of a Miss Mina Davidson who had known Lady Strathmore as a girl. Like the administrators of the Royal Infirmary, she knew how important the patronage of members of the Royal Family was to ensure the flow of voluntary support.[82]

*

THE DUCHESS'S delight in her infant daughter was overwhelming, but she had one cause for serious concern. The Prime Minister of Australia, Stanley Bruce, had asked that one of the King's sons come out in early 1927 to open the new Federal Parliament buildings in Canberra.

Australia had become a federation on 1 January 1900. Under the Commonwealth of Australia (Constitution) Act, the colonies of New South Wales, Victoria, Queensland, South Australia, Western Australia and Tasmania became states federated together under one Dominion government. It was the last great imperial measure of the Victorian era. In May 1901 the first session of the Commonwealth Parliament was opened by the Duke of Cornwall and York, the future King George V.[83] At that time the Commonwealth government had been housed in Melbourne, the capital of Victoria, but in 1911 the government obtained an area of some 900 square miles from the government of New South Wales on which to create a new capital, Canberra. These plans were delayed by the First World War, but the construction of the town finally began in 1923 and the government intended to have the new Parliament buildings ready to be opened in 1927.

The Prince of Wales had made a very successful tour of Australia in 1920; he had been welcomed with rapture and became known as 'the travelling salesman of Empire'. Robert Graves wrote of him, 'He became a symbol of industrious go-ahead youth, fully acquainted with all the world's problems; having, it is true, no plan by which to solve them, but at least a determination to tackle them and to struggle through.'[84]

The Prince would have been welcomed back to Australia. But the Duke of York was keen to go, and had told Leo Amery, the Dominions Secretary, that he had 'much enjoyed his unofficial visit to Kenya and would welcome an opportunity of obtaining further experience of the Empire'.[85] Amery put the Duke's name forward, but the King was initially sceptical. Lord Stamfordham replied to Amery that 'the Duke of York is the only one of the Princes who could undertake this duty; and for many reasons His Majesty cannot, at this distance of time, hold out much hope of such an arrangement being carried out.'[86] In early April 1926 the Governor General, Lord Stonehaven, wrote to Stamfordham urging the importance of the royal visit, and asking him to help persuade the King: 'The Crown is becoming more and more the only real link which unites the Empire.'[87] In July, finally, it was announced that the Duke and the Duchess of York were to go.

Since there was, in those days, no question of children, let alone infants, accompanying their royal parents on such a tour, this would mean that they would be parted from their daughter for at least six months. The Duchess was dismayed by this prospect. There was another anxiety. Both the King and Bruce were anxious that the Duke might not be able to sustain all the pressures of such a tour. In particular there was apprehension – which the Duke himself shared – that his stammer would make it impossible for him to deliver all the speeches that a formal tour would require.[88] Bruce was said to be appalled by the inhibitions that the Duke's speech defect would necessarily impose upon him.[89] For the Duke himself the crisis was far worse. Despite the support and reassurance of the Duchess, he had begun to despair about his stammer and his failure to conquer it. According to his official biographer, he had even begun to fear that the problem might be a mental rather than a physical one. But help was at hand.

The Duke's first broadcast speech at Wembley had been heard by an Australian therapist named Lionel Logue. He had originally trained as an engineer, but he later discovered he had a power of healing and had taken up speech therapy in order to help Australian soldiers traumatized in the First World War. In 1924 he had come to Britain and taken rooms in Harley Street in which to practise. He was recommended to the Prince's Private Secretary, Patrick Hodgson. The Duke himself was not keen to try yet another therapist; he had had his hopes raised too many times, always to be dashed. It was the Duchess who persuaded him to have 'just one more try'.[90]

Lionel Logue recorded this impression of the Duke's first appointment with him on 19 October 1926. 'He entered my consulting room at three o'clock in the afternoon, a slim, quiet man, with tired eyes and all the outward symptoms of the man upon whom habitual speech defect had begun to set the sign. When he left at five o'clock you could see that there was hope once more in his heart.'[91] Logue evidently did have an extraordinary gift. He saw his first task as being to persuade stammerers that there was nothing 'wrong' or fundamentally different about them, that they were normal people with a common affliction which could usually be cured.

The first stage of his treatment was to teach patients to breathe correctly. He showed the Duke how to regulate his lungs and breathing so as to enable himself the better to relax. He had to do exercises at home, lying on the floor and reciting devilishly difficult tonguetwisters. The Duchess encouraged him in the whole process. She often went with him to Logue's Harley Street rooms or to his flat in South Kensington for his sessions. But in the end he could only cure himself and Logue said later that the Prince was 'the pluckiest and most determined patient I ever had'.[92]

It is hard to exaggerate the almost instant, indeed superb effect Logue had upon the Duke's self-confidence. As the tour of Australasia loomed closer, his fear of it diminished rather than grew. This was remarkable and deeply heartening for him, and for his wife. Shortly before he left, he wrote to Logue, 'I must send you a line to tell you how grateful I am to you for all that you have done in helping me with my speech defect. I really do think you have given me a real good start in the way of getting over it & I am sure if I carry on your exercises and instructions that I shall not go back. I am full of confidence for this trip now.'[93]

Before they left there was still much to do. They had finally found a house in place of White Lodge. Number 145 Piccadilly was perfect, a stone-built house, close to Hyde Park Corner and facing south with a view over Green Park towards Buckingham Palace. They were able to lease the house, and in return White Lodge was leased out by the Crown.

The new house needed a great deal of attention. Queen Mary was, naturally, keen to be deeply involved in all the works. She insisted on inspecting the house early on, declaring, 'I should like to see it before the improvements are commenced as it is always interesting to see a house before & after it has been done up.' She also warned her son not to mention to the King loans of furniture to them belonging to the Crown, 'because the dear soul does not understand about these things'.[94] She thought they should keep all the furniture they wanted from White Lodge and she promised them a cheque for £750 to do up a room at her expense. She found them some chandeliers at Osborne and the King lent them another from Balmoral.[95] Other furniture, including a walnut bureau and an octagonal card table, came from Lady Strathmore. The Duchess was grateful for all help – like everyone moving house she found the expense much greater than she had anticipated. None of the curtains from White Lodge were big enough for the windows at 145 Piccadilly – she had to get fourteen new pairs, all four or five yards long – and she found that decent material cost more than £1 a yard. 'However if it is good wearing stuff, we shall be able to move it and use it for years and years,' she told her mother.[96]

For the Duchess, moving home was a diversion from the thought of parting from her baby for the tour. Princess Elizabeth was the object of her parents' adoration. 'I am longing for you to see her,' the Duchess wrote to Nannie B. 'She is growing so big and is as sharp as a needle, & so well. She sleeps beautifully, and has always got a smile ready.' She asked Mrs Beevers to visit them at Bruton Street, where they were busy preparing for 'this horrible trip'.[97] Perhaps nothing before had brought home to her so clearly the conflict between duty and family, work and pleasure. She told Major Walsh, 'by next June I shall be old & worn & grey after our Australasian tour. You must prepare for a cynical & hardened old woman of the world by the time I've finished with the Aussies.' She thought she would have to come to Africa, to recover. 'I'll bring my gramophone and my '275, & we'll vary the Charleston with a little letting off at crocs & other four-legged animals.'[98]

They stayed at Sandringham House for Christmas that year for the first time, returning to London soon afterwards to make final preparations for their departure to Australia and New Zealand at the end of the first week in January. As the date approached everything became more hectic. 'I don't dare think of the 6th it is so awful,' the Duchess confessed.[99] She felt in a complete whirl and all the arrangements she had to make reduced her brain, she said, to 'chaos'.[100]

They spent New Year's Eve, as they preferred, with her family at St Paul's Walden. On the first day of 1927 the men went shooting and she had 'a lovely long lie in!' reading a thriller by Edgar Wallace. 'Mother and I had lunch and talked hard' – her way of recording in her diary that she and her mother, on whom she still relied a great deal, had a serious conversation. On Sunday they went as usual to the Church of All Saints. The vicar, Mr Whitehouse, 'boomed' at them and after lunch they drove back to London where she found

Catherine Maclean, her maid, exhausted from the packing. That night she had a typhoid inoculation and, unusually for her, she had a bad reaction – she hardly slept and felt ill next morning.[101]

As the departure date grew closer, the Duchess became 'more and more miserable'.[102] 'The baby was too delicious having her bottle & playing & being naughty,' she wrote in her diary.[103] One of her friends supposed that the child would spend the time with Lady Strathmore in the country, but there were other claims upon her, as the Duchess explained. 'I expect I shall have to divide her! You see the Queen wants to have her for at least three out of the six months.'[104]

On Tuesday 4 January, the Duchess tried on clothes and had 'dozens of questions to answer & decide at home'. James Stuart came to lunch and then she and her sister Rosie went to Heal's to buy nursery things. That evening the Prince of Wales threw a farewell party for them. Many of their friends came to say goodbye, including Fred Astaire and his sister Adele. The Plantation Orchestra played 'marvellously'. It was a moment for abandonment: 'I did a Charleston with David [the Prince of Wales] for nearly 20 minutes!! Home at 3.30! Bed 4. Oh Lord.'[105] Wednesday was another day of goodbyes; George Gage came to see her; so did Adele Astaire, who brought her a gramophone record and a book. She 'felt ill all today'.[106] The paediatrician to whom she was entrusting the Princess, Dr George F. Still, came to talk to her about his charge and promised to send her regular reports. They dined with her parents and the King and Queen at Buckingham Palace.

On the morning they had to leave, she awoke and rose early. 'Feel very miserable at leaving the baby. Went up & played with her & she was so sweet. Luckily she doesn't realize anything.'[107] When they were finally ready to depart, Alah Knight brought the baby downstairs for the final goodbye. The Duchess was very emotional. Watching Princess Elizabeth play with the buttons on her father's uniform 'quite broke me up'.[108] The Duke was miserable too and felt that his daughter 'will be so grown up when we return'.[109] The Duchess knew she had to drag herself away and so she 'drank some champagne & tried not to weep'.[110]

At Victoria station Queen Mary saw that her daughter-in-law was being as brave as possible, and so she said nothing about the little Princess – as she put it in a letter, 'I purposely did not allude to yr leave taking of yr angelic baby knowing only too well you would be bound to break down.'[111] After long farewells on the platform, the special train drew them away on the start of their journey towards the furthest reaches of the Empire.

At Portsmouth Harbour the Duke and Duchess had a rousing send-off from large, enthusiastic crowds. One of the officials with them wrote next day, 'If you wanted evidence that the country was not going Bolshevik, you could not have had better proof than was afforded yesterday.'[112]

CHAPTER EIGHT

AN AUSTRALASIAN ASSIGNMENT

1927

'I could never have done the tour without her help'

FOR THE NEXT six months their home was a great ship, HMS *Renown*. Lead ship of a class of two fast 26,500-ton battlecruisers, she was launched in Glasgow in 1916. Designed by the Admiralty to have great speed, she served with the Grand Fleet in the North Sea during the remaining two years of the Great War. In 1919–20 she carried the Prince of Wales on a voyage to Australasia and America. Since then she had been extensively refitted to increase her protection against gunfire and torpedoes – and to carry the Duke and Duchess and their entourage around the world.

The tour was seen to be of great importance – not only to the government of Australia, which had inspired it, but also to the King. After they had put to sea the Duke wrote to his father, 'This is the first time you have sent me on a mission concerning the Empire, & I can assure you that I will do my very best to make it the success we all hope for.'[1]

The British Empire was one of the most astonishing international organizations the world has ever seen. As we have noted, during the war a third of the troops that the mother country, Britain, had raised came from the Empire, and when the peace settlement of Versailles handed German colonies to the victors, the British Empire in the 1920s reached its greatest extent ever – it covered a quarter of the world. But the price of victory had been immense and the costs of administering the expanded Empire grew ever less easy for Britain to support. Throughout the 1920s, the imperial defence budget was continually cut. The rationale was that after the Great War Britain would not be involved in another major war for at least ten years and that no expeditionary force was required for that purpose. The armed forces were therefore principally to provide garrisons for India, Egypt and all other territories under British control. Manpower became scarcer and controlling the increasingly restless colonies between the wars became more and more difficult. The arrogance of power gave way to hesitation as the self-confidence vital to any imperialist venture gradually diminished. But in 1927 the Empire seemed still to be a permanent part of the world order. The Duke and Duchess had no reason to doubt its lasting strength before they set out from Portsmouth and almost everything that happened to them from then on confirmed that view.

Despite the importance which both the Australian and British governments attached to the trip, they were constrained to operate it within a very tight budget. In October the Dominions Office had pressed the Treasury as to whether a government grant-in-aid would be voted to help the Yorks' expenditure in undertaking the tour. The Prince of Wales, who was unmarried, had been given £25,000 for his tour of Canada, Australia and New Zealand in 1919–20. (When the King and Queen, as Duke and Duchess of York, had been to Australia twenty-five years before, they were allowed £20,000.)

In the difficult economic circumstances following the General Strike, the government felt unable to provide as much. Basil Brooke wrote to the Treasury in November 1926: 'His Royal Highness wishes me to emphasise the fact that the assistance for which he is asking is solely to meet expenses connected with the official and extraordinary nature of the tour. The Duke is fully prepared to pay out of his own purse any charges which he and the Duchess would normally be called upon to bear in their daily routine.'[2] In the end the government offered £3,500 up front with another £3,500 promised in March 1927. Of this £175 was apportioned, as a clothes allowance, to each of the five male members of the staff, £125 to each of the Duchess's two ladies in waiting and £325 for the Duke and Duchess between them. They had to spend a great deal more out of their own resources to cover the expenses of the trip. Even so, several Labour Members of Parliament objected to the £7,000 grant – the trip was referred to in Parliament as 'a joy ride'. It was in fact arduous.

One of the Duke and Duchess's duties was to represent the trading interests not just of Britain herself, but of the whole British Empire. The Duke agreed to carry on board the All British Campaign's 'Emblem of Empire Industries'. The British Industries Fair in Birmingham sent him a telegram of loyalty and support, referring to 'the valuable service HRH is always willing to render to the development [of] British Trade'.[3]

They were not only to travel in *Renown*, but also to use her as their base for much of the tour of Australia. The officer in charge of fitting the ship out, Admiral Parker, had been a little nervous about just what to do. In August 1926 he had written to Basil Brooke wondering whether the Duchess's request that all the cabins be painted entirely blue was wise. 'I do think she will be tired of all Blue.'[4] But the Duchess was fairly determined and even rejected the first blues that the Admiralty suggested, as she did the suggestion of stripes.[5]

Parker accepted the required blue, ordered more cushions and sent the ship's barber to Trumper's in Curzon Street, to learn how the Duke liked his hair cut. He worried that the ladies would be bored if they had nothing but their knitting to do on the long voyages, and arranged for the ship's library to be supplemented – the Times Book Club agreed to loan the ship 120 books for a charge of twelve guineas.[6] The chosen selection very much reflected popular taste of the time: it included Edgar Wallace, P. G. Wodehouse and John Buchan – all favourites of the Duchess – John Galsworthy, Agatha Christie, Radclyffe Hall (whose notorious lesbian novel *The Well of Loneliness* she later described to a friend as 'terrible'),[7] John Masefield, Arthur Conan Doyle and 'Sapper', the ultimate adventure-story writer.

Parkers of Piccadilly lent a selection of framed prints for the cabins in the hope that they would 'help in some way to take away the bareness of the bulkheads and steel walls and make the suite a little more homelike for the cruise'.[8] Pathé Frères Cinema Ltd sent films for viewing on board – they included three comedies starring Harold Lloyd and Bebe Daniels (*Modes and Madness, Heap Big Chief, Hustling Harold*), and two 'song films with music' (*Swanee River, Coming thro' the Rye*).[9] Alfred Hays' Gramophone Agency lent them an electric gramophone, while 78 rpm records were provided by the Gramophone Company and chosen according to Basil Brooke's assessment of the Duke and Duchess's tastes – they included a selection of Kreisler, the Brahms Hungarian Dances, some of the older Harry Lauder songs, Gilbert and Sullivan and some Chopin.[10] An Ampico Reproducing Piano was lent by Sir Herbert Marshall and Sons for shipboard dances. These clever machines reproduced foxtrots performed by some of the most celebrated pianists of the time. Like the gramophone, the piano endured much damage from rough seas on the voyage and needed serious repairs afterwards.[11]

The scale of the floating cellar was impressive, even for a six-month voyage for the Duke's party of ten. There were more than sixty cases of vintage champagne from various suppliers, fifty-eight cases of the Duke's favourite whisky, Buchanan's, twelve cases of brandy from Justerini and Brooks, twelve cases of Gordon's gin, French and Italian Vermouth, forty cases of port and eighteen cases of sherry, as well as over thirty cases of claret.[12] The Duke and Duchess liked cocktails before lunch and dinner and often drank champagne throughout the meal. (In 1931, when they made an official visit to Paris, this had to be explained to their bemused hosts.) Bulgarian cigarettes were provided by the navy. The Duke enjoyed smoking.

The Duke and Duchess could not have realized the extent to which the tour was to plunge them into the limelight across the Empire as never before. It would do a great deal to develop their sense of their own public personalities. This was one of the first royal tours to be organized along modern lines with the interests of the media taken (at least partly) into account. There was an official photographer, W. J. Fair, and two movie cameramen were assigned to the tour. An official film was produced by the Commonwealth government of Australia and distributed by the European Motion Picture Company. A similar film was produced in New Zealand. Hundreds of thousands of people all over the world could thus share in the royal progress. Nor was the written word neglected. There was a writer in residence aboard *Renown* – an Australian journalist, Taylor Darbyshire, who produced a book of the voyage.

The King had appointed the Earl of Cavan* as chief of staff for the tour. Cavan had commanded the Guards Brigade and then the Guards Division during the war and had served as Chief of the Imperial General Staff from 1922 to 1926. His wife Joan was asked to be one of the Duchess's two ladies in waiting. Lord Cavan had rather a formal manner, and neither Duke nor Duchess was immediately drawn to him, but he represented them well, often in unseen ways.

Cavan's task was to see that everything ran as smoothly as possible and that all the protocols and formalities demanded by the King, an exacting if distant supervisor of the tour, were met. The King was

---

* Field Marshal Frederick Rudolph Lambart, tenth Earl of Cavan (1865–1946).

especially insistent that the Duke and Duchess should wear the correct dress for every different occasion. He sent frequent instructions, advice and complaints by coded telegram. (Fortunately, letters to and from London took weeks, sometimes more than a month, to arrive, which tended to diminish the urgency of some strictures.)

The Duchess's other lady in waiting, Victoria Gilmour,* was quite another matter. Known as Tortor, she proved to be a delightful companion and became a close and lifelong friend of the Duchess. Patrick Hodgson, the Duke's Private Secretary, described her in a letter to Queen Mary, 'Mrs Gilmour is also much liked and keeps us all amused. She is perhaps a little vague at times and has the most wonderful way of losing her own possessions which invariably are found in the one place "where she knows she never put them!" But these trifles are more than compensated for by her keenness and her companionship to the Duchess.'[13] Two equerries, Colin Buist and a newcomer, Major Terence Nugent,† were also in the party, and the Duke was allotted a political secretary for the tour, Harry Batterbee,‡ as the official representative of the British government. The party's health was in the hands of Surgeon Commander H. E. Y. White, a physician who was to show his worth.

On the voyage out they went the Atlantic route, via Las Palmas, Jamaica and then through the Panama Canal to the Pacific. The weather was at first quite disagreeable – there was a storm off Ushant and after the first night aboard the Duchess wrote in her diary, 'Hardly slept at all last night, and kept on jumping up to put things away. Even the big gramophone fell over.'[14] The Duchess proved to be a hardier sailor than some of the others. She wrote to D'Arcy Osborne that the ship was 'very beautiful in a clean large way' and the food

---

* The Hon. Mrs Little Gilmour (1901–91), née Cadogan, fifth daughter of Viscount Chelsea, and granddaughter of fifth Earl Cadogan; she married in 1922 John ('Jock') Little Gilmour, later second baronet; the marriage was dissolved in 1929. They were the parents of Sir Ian Gilmour MP, who became a minister in the Conservative governments of Edward Heath and Margaret Thatcher.

† Terence Edmund Gascoigne Nugent (1895–1973), Comptroller, Lord Chamberlain's Department 1936–60, extra equerry to King George VI and Queen Elizabeth II, created Baron Nugent of West Harling 1960; permanent lord in waiting to the Queen 1960–73.

‡ Harry Batterbee (1880–1976) was an assistant secretary in the Dominions Office. Created Knight Commander of the Royal Victorian Order in 1927, he served as UK high commissioner in New Zealand from 1939 to 1945.

was quite good. She begged him to write to her. 'I already feel cut off.'[15]

As the weather improved both Duke and Duchess made themselves popular with all ranks on board. The Duke made casual visits to the wardroom to talk to the senior officers, which pleased them. They dined with the junior officers in the gunroom and played charades and nursery games and danced the tango and Charleston with some of the midshipmen. The Duchess had time to rest and read and talk – and above all to miss her daughter. 'Felt depressed – I miss the baby all the time, & am always wondering what she is doing,' she noted in her diary.[16] This was a constant, if private, agony for her through the entire voyage. There were diversions – clay-pigeon shooting from the deck, the ship's rifle range and squash court. Every Sunday there was a church service on board, at which the Duchess enjoyed the hearty singing of the crew.

On Monday 10 January they anchored off the Canary Islands in warm weather, but there was a heavy swell. Spanish officials in Las Palmas were supposed to come aboard but declined, saying that the sea was too rough. The Duke and Duchess were more adventurous. Indeed, the Duchess impressed all on board with her disdain for the waves. Lord Cavan wrote to the King that with 'gazelle-like agility' she managed to get aboard the barge to be taken ashore. It was hard to recognize the National Anthem as played by a local band. The British Consul and his wife were somewhat eccentric – he was very deaf and appeared very old while she, according to Lord Cavan, had 'steadfastly refused to change her fashion of clothing – so I am told – since the age of small waists, large sleeves & a bustle!'[17]

The next day *Renown* set sail for Jamaica. The first and relatively easy stage of the trip had gone well. But the criticism from the King had already begun. A telegram arrived from Clive Wigram, the King's Assistant Private Secretary, warning Cavan that the King objected to some of the press coverage of the tour. Cavan responded robustly, saying that the telegram had caused 'some little disturbance'. No offensive articles could have come from the journalists aboard because he personally vetted all messages they sent. Whatever caused upset in London 'must therefore have come from some source for which I am not & obviously cannot be responsible'.[18]

The King evidently complained also about descriptions of the Duchess's clothing because Cavan insisted, 'As regards "descriptions of

clothing" Her Royal Highness's departure frock from London &
landing frock at Las Palmas are all that have been passed by me – & I
may observe that if the authorized Pressmen are not to send this
information, the uncensored Press of every place of landing most
certainly will. However our three men will not mention the dresses
worn except at official functions & this the public absolutely demand.'[19]

Lord Cavan understood that strictures from the King could be very
demoralizing for the young, nervous Duke and Duchess, for he wrote
to Wigram:

> Very Private . . .
> This is not for HM eyes! I think you & I must realize that T.R.H.
> are both sensitive, frightfully anxious to do well & therefore they
> feel it more acutely than old warriors like myself, if the very first
> telegram from Home is couched in a critical vein. If H.M. by any
> chance ever does say an approving word, it wd work wonders, if
> a very short encouraging telegram cd be sent especially before the
> difficult & arduous work in Australia.
>
> All is really going very well but T.R.H. get plunged into
> depths of woe if their efforts are misconstrued.
>
> At Las Palmas none but British subjects wd have even
> attempted a landing. The Spanish Governors Civil & Military &
> Mayor made no effort to come on board! & so we most carefully
> said 'By mutual arrangement the international courtesies were
> exchanged ashore' – tho' it is obvious that our people went
> through all the dangers & difficulties.
>
> A word of recognition of this really plucky effort is the sort of
> 'encouragement' that I refer to.[20]

Cavan's plea evidently paid off – some weeks later. On 21 February,
after they had arrived at Auckland, he wrote to Wigram: 'I cannot
thank you enough for His Majesty's splendidly timed message of
encouragement just before arrival at Auckland.' His letter crossed with
one to him from Wigram saying that he hoped Their Majesties'
message to the Duke and Duchess on arrival acted as 'a good pick-me-
up'.[21]

On 20 January, when the Duke and Duchess landed at Kingston,
the streets were lined with cheering people. The next three days
provided the Duchess with her first glimpse of what a fully fledged
tour could involve. At an evening reception, Lord Cavan told the

Palace, more than a thousand guests 'of all hues' passed before Their Royal Highnesses. Although the Governor of Jamaica and Lord Cavan considered that it was unnecessary for them to venture beyond Kingston, the Duke and Duchess decided otherwise. On the second day of their three-day tour they visited the cathedral at Spanish Town and then went to a garden party in the centre of the island. People were delighted; this was the first time, they were told, that any member of the Royal Family had visited the interior. Cavan reported to the King that 'The Duchess is looking so fresh and well.'[22] Back at the King's House in Kingston the Duke's enthusiasm for tennis was useful; he played a doubles match in which he partnered a Jamaican 'of colour', one of the best players in the island, thus acknowledging equality among sportsmen and giving great satisfaction locally.[23]

This first short visit confirmed what was in little doubt: that the appeal of the Duchess's personality worked as well abroad as at home, and that it would contribute greatly to the success of the tour. Lord Cavan sent the King an editorial from the *Daily Gleaner* of Kingston, describing how she 'smiled her way into the hearts of the people . . . her kindly glances, the sweetness of her manner, her whole attitude of gracious charm have won for her a love which must last as long as those who have seen her shall live.'[24] The power of her smile became a leitmotif of the entire voyage. Praise of this kind was to be lavished on her throughout the many decades to come.

From Jamaica they began to sail into the heat. Cabin temperatures rose to an almost unbearable 86 degrees and they took to sleeping on deck. Their destination was one of the modern wonders of the world, the Panama Canal, carved through the isthmus only just as the First World War began, linking Atlantic and Pacific oceans for the first time. Many of the labourers on the Canal were British subjects from the West Indies who welcomed the couple warmly.[25]

The Duchess was intrigued by the extraordinary workings of the Canal. She watched as the ships were dragged into the locks by the 'mules' – little electric tractors on rails – and then rose or fell as vast amounts of water were pumped in or out of the locks. From Panama she wrote to the Prince of Wales. Her letters to him were affectionate, frank and humorous, not unlike those she wrote to her brothers. She teased him for being a 'naughty little wicked little Empire builder. You are also an Empire destroyer too, as in my daily radio news I read that the Prince of Wales helped to finish off the old Empire – promenade & all.'[26]* She told him of an archly flirtatious encounter with the President of Panama: 'I have got off with the President here which was rather hot making. We had some interesting conversations with him . . . The language of the eye I had to fall back on, and gee he fell too.'[27] The Duke's account to his father of the same episode was more restrained: 'the President of Panama came on board. He was not very exciting & spoke very little English.'[28]

As they steamed through the Canal the Panamanian press was enchanted by the Duchess. Indeed the King complained again – this time directly to his son – that the newspapers were publishing 'all sorts of stuff which we thought twaddle . . . such as what clothes Elizabeth wore'.[29] This type of reportage, however, gives a vivid picture of the impression they made. One description stands out: 'On the upper after deck stood a slight, slender English boy, dressed in the white uniform of a captain of the English Navy . . . Beside him was a sweet, pretty, charming young woman gowned in a fetching morning gown of pale lavender and carrying a white silk parasol. The man raised his hand to his helmet in a salute, and the little woman waved her handkerchief in goodbye. These two personages were the Duke and Duchess of York.'[30]

Great crowds waited for them as they went through the locks at Pedro Miguel. The local newspaper reported that 'a young Britisher, resident on the isthmus, waved his hat and shouted to Her Royal Highness, "How's the baby?"' At which 'the Duchess leaned over the railing and replied "Baby's fine."'[31] In fact she was increasingly miserable about Princess Elizabeth; they both found the terse telegrams from Alah – 'ALL RIGHT KNIGHT' – inadequate. Dr Still had dispatched his first report but, of course, it was still afloat on the ocean, with weeks to go before it was delivered.† From Panama the

---

*   On 22 January 1927 the Prince of Wales attended the last performance (*Lady Be Good*) at the Empire Theatre, Leicester Square, before it was demolished and replaced by a cinema. The promenade was a broad corridor running behind the private boxes at the back of the Grand Circle.

†   Dr Still reported on 15 January on the Princess's weight gain; her increased alertness (listening to his watch, holding out her arms to be picked up, beginning of teething); he said that Queen Mary had been very disappointed that he had advised against the baby yet going to Sandringham. 'I hope Your Royal Highness will not be bored with all these details, but I expect you may not hear all you would like to hear in the cable.' (RA QEQM/PRIV/PAL)

Duchess telegraphed home, 'No message arrived. Please send news at once.'[32]

As they crossed the Pacific both the Duke and the Duchess seemed to dread the exhaustion that lay ahead. The Duke wrote to his brother complaining about the length and monotony of the voyage, and confessed that he had been feeling very depressed.[33] They felt cut off from home; all the news they had was from the regular wireless bulletin 'which only mentions China and football results', the Duchess told the Queen in early February. She fretted at the thought that her child might become unwell. 'I do hope you like having the Baby, and that she continues to be well and happy, and no colds . . . I miss her quite terribly, and the five weeks we have been away seem like five months.'[34]

The Queen wrote to tell them that she had heard that Princess Elizabeth had 'cut her first tooth which is good', news which could only emphasize all that they were missing. Queen Mary also complained that Dr Still had prevented Princess Elizabeth from visiting them at Sandringham because she had eye trouble and was teething: 'this was a great disappointment to us but of course we agreed. As a matter of fact the weather here has been & is so much better than anywhere else that I think the fine air wld have done the child good.'[35] As soon as the King and Queen returned from Sandringham to London, the little Princess arrived to stay at Buckingham Palace. Queen Mary wrote: 'she is looking too sweet & seems happy in her new surroundings, she was delighted with the parrot Charlotte this morning at breakfast & watched the bird eating pips with an air of absorption. How nice "Alla" is & baby is turned out too beautifully.'[36]

The King wrote kindly about the Princess as well, but he was unable to resist making criticisms of his son's appearance or sense of protocol when he saw fit. He had studied the press photographs of them in Las Palmas and wrote to the Duke, 'I send you a picture of you inspecting Gd. of Honour (I don't think much of their dressing) with yr. Equerry walking on yr. right next to the Gd. & you ignoring the Officer entirely. Yr. Equerry should be outside & behind, it certainly doesn't look well.' When the Duke eventually received this complaint at the other side of the world, he replied good-naturedly that he had noticed the same thing '& I can explain it easily. I had just finished inspecting the guard of honour and was walking back to join

Elizabeth. Buist was taking a message from me. It was an unfortunate moment for the photograph to be taken.'[37]

They spent a fortnight at sea, steaming south and west and when they reached the equator they both went through the traditional Crossing the Line Ceremony, with all due deference to King Neptune's domain. The Duchess was presented with the Order of the Golden Mermaid by a member of the ship's crew dressed as Queen Amphitrite.

They were much in demand on that empty ocean – even the French population of Tahiti were hoping that *Renown* would call upon them. Instead they spent two days on the island of Nuka Hiva, in the French Marquises, Gauguin's earthly paradise. It was a simple place; only about four ships a year called there. They found it a delight to leave the ship to walk, to fish and to bathe. One evening the islanders danced for them. The Duchess's reaction was perceptive, if romantic; she wrote to Queen Mary that 'it was really most remarkable, and very interesting. They are brown and the men quite nice-looking, but very diseased and are rapidly dying out. Instead of being strong healthy cannibals with strange religions and no clothes, they are now weakly half hearted Roman Catholics with European clothes. It seems all wrong, but that is what happens.'[38]

The Duke and Duchess were by now fully able to enjoy the banter of shipboard life; she took pleasure in the dancing on the quarterdeck – finding the midshipmen especially light on their feet. Patrick Hodgson, who had originally had some misgivings about whether the Duchess had understood the importance of the tour, was by now completely won over, writing to Queen Mary, 'I now feel I was mistaken and that she is alive to all that is involved.'[39] Lord Cavan felt the same.[40] They came to Fiji, which was then governed through the Dominion of New Zealand, on 17 February. They landed at Suva, where they presented walking sticks to the tribal chiefs, but the traditional dances of welcome could not take place because of an outbreak of measles. The heat was too intense for midday appointments but they made a late-afternoon drive upcountry to Rewa, visited the War Memorial Hospital and made a trip around the harbour in one of *Renown*'s launches.

The civic welcome was followed by a dinner and ball at the Governor's House. The *Fiji Times* recorded the impression the Duchess made: she looked 'radiant. She wore a lovely gown of ivory georgette heavily beaded, with a green rose on one side. She had a white tulle scarf, and carried a beautiful shaded pink feather fan. Her silver shoes had the heels studded with brilliants. She wore a charming diamond tiara and a valuable pearl necklace adorned her neck.' The report of the ball was enlivened by an episode that conveyed both her sense of fun and her presence of mind, and contributed to a new image of the Royal Family. 'When all the guests had shaken hands, a lone dog, which had managed to get into the ballroom, quietly trotted up to Her Royal Highness and held up its paw. The Duchess smilingly shook hands and patted doggy on the head. Apparently perfectly satisfied, the dog followed precedent and quietly passed out of the hall.'[41]

*

As THEY HEADED south from Fiji, the temperatures began to drop to a delightful 78 degrees, which everyone enjoyed. They were able to gather their strength for the most important stages of the tour. Making their landfall in New Zealand had originally upset the Australian government, which had proposed the tour. The problem was that if the tour had begun in Australia instead, then the subsequent trip to New Zealand would have compelled the Duke and Duchess to endure the worst of New Zealand and Pacific winter weather. The Duke had been determined that his wife should not be subjected to any avoidable strain. In trying to persuade his government to accept this, the Australian High Commissioner in London, Richard Casey, went so far as to suggest that the Duchess's medical advisers were anxious not to do anything which might prevent her from having another child, something ardently desired by the British public.[42] In the end, the Australian government had accepted the decision with good grace.

Two days before they arrived in New Zealand, after a voyage lasting almost seven weeks, they received a cable from the King and Queen reminding them of the seriousness of their task: 'You are about to land in New Zealand and start on the first stage of your mission; and we shall more than ever follow your doings with affectionate interest. There is a strenuous time before you but we know that you both will do everything to secure the success which has already attended your efforts.'[43] At dawn on 22 February *Renown* passed through the straits into the bay of Waitemata, the port of Auckland. Later that morning, as rain fell heavily, they stepped ashore to be greeted by the Governor General, Sir Charles Fergusson, and their official visit began.

The Duchess liked New Zealand and its people at once.[44] And she made an impact on her hosts which one could call extraordinary – were it not for the fact that it was becoming normal wherever she went. Lord Cavan reported to the King that she looked radiant as they landed and were taken to the packed town hall for the official welcome. There the Duke replied to the address. 'It was really very well delivered,' Cavan said, 'and after the first two or three sentences it was fluently and forcefully spoken.'[45] The Duke was also pleased. He told his mother that he had had to make three speeches on the first day they arrived: 'I had perfect confidence in myself & I did not hesitate at all. Logue's teaching is still working well, but of course if I get tired, it still worries me.'[46]

It had been intended that the New Zealand leg of the tour would be less demanding than that which awaited them in Australia. However, the long days of public exposure in New Zealand were exhausting for both of them. Their welcome was ecstatic – and endless. Engagements were piled upon each other; as the Duke wrote to his mother, 'these tours are always arranged by the Ministers whose one & only idea is more votes, and they see to it that we go to all the small towns in their constituencies.'[47] New Zealand had only a small police force of about a thousand men and there was no way they could keep control as the enthusiastic crowds stormed their visitors. In many places, their car (often roofless despite the rain) could scarcely move for the throngs that pressed around them. At one civic welcome the Duchess chose to carry, instead of the official bouquet, a posy of wild flowers tossed at her by a child at the roadside, bearing the message 'God bless the wee baby Princess'.

The *New Zealand Herald* noticed that the Duchess 'smiled her way into the hearts of the people'. This smile was even said to have touched a man who was well known as an active communist agitator in Auckland. On the second day of the visit he met Joseph Coates, the Prime Minister, and said to him, 'I've done with this —— Communism.' Coates asked why such a sudden conversion had taken place and the man replied, 'Why, they're human! Yesterday I was in the crowd with the wife and one of the children waved his hand, and I'm blessed if the Duchess didn't wave back and smile right into my face, not two yards away. I'll never say a word against them again. I've done with it for good and all.' Coates relayed this story to Sir Charles Fergusson who, in turn, sent it on to the King. The tale was retold by John

Wheeler-Bennett, King George VI's biographer, who used the incident to illustrate his argument that 'the vivid charm of the Duchess of York was a very real factor in the success of the tour. A more responsive personality than the Duke, she was able to complement his greater shyness by a radiance which carried all before it. "She shines and warms like sunlight," a young Scotsman wrote of her at this time.'[48]

The Duke too rose to the challenge of the trip, if in a less demonstrative manner. His clearly sincere interest in the country and in the views of its people won him affection. His love of riding, fishing and shooting endeared him to a population which was dedicated to the sporting ethic. Both he and his wife were moved by the evidence of fidelity to the Crown that their visit produced. The Duchess wrote to Queen Mary, 'The marvellous loyalty of the people of N.Z. is quite amazing, and any mention of "the King and Queen", "the Mother Country", "The Empire" or "Home" or any other expression brings out such very genuine and whole hearted cheers that it gives one quite a lump in the throat.'[49]

Perhaps because of their forced parting from their daughter, both of them expressed a particular interest in children and their welfare. The Duke coined a phrase which he used often – 'Take care of the children and the country will take care of itself.'[50] They liked what they saw of the antipodean approach to children. The Duchess was able to analyse it for the Queen.

> The children are so well looked after here – so different to England, in that they come first in everything. They are taught to be loyal to the Crown before anything, and then they are taught to be well & healthy & clean. Everywhere that we have been, we have been intensely struck by the appearance of the children. Apparently the teachers are very good, and they have to take most stupendous oaths of loyalty to the Crown before they are allowed to teach. Considering that it is the Crown that keeps the Empire together, I think it is a pity they are not more particular about teachers at home.[51]

New Zealand was the home of Sir Truby King, the doyen of mothercraft and babycare in the first half of the twentieth century.*

---

* Truby King (1858–1938) was one of New Zealand's foremost physicians and a prominent medical reformer. He received worldwide recognition for his pioneering work in the feeding

The Duchess of York already had a strong interest in his work and she had now the opportunity of directly supporting it. On 7 March, in Wellington, she opened the Karitane Home for babies and the training of nurses. She also visited Truby King at home and wrote to Queen Mary about his 'most amazing work in lowering the death rate for babies. I hope that it will really spread in England, tho' of course his ideas will have to be adapted to suit conditions in England.'[52] With her new-formed enthusiasm, she described to her sister May how strong and healthy and good-looking the New Zealand children appeared. 'Not like your puny, pale, small delicate & hideous children,' she jokingly added, the badinage masking her desperate homesickness.[53]

But there was a consolation. Farming in New Zealand and the promise of new life and prosperity in Australia had drawn several generations of Scotsmen to settle there. Everywhere the Duchess went she was approached by kindly, welcoming people, many no less homesick than she, whose families had been tenants of her father's, or who were the sort of people she would, as a girl, have encountered in Dundee or Montrose. She knew instinctively how to deal with her countrymen and women from north of the border. Out of the woodwork appeared people more intimately connected with the past. 'I saw Mr Parker here!! I danced with him. He proposed to me during the war, but I don't believe I ever answered him,' the Duchess recounted to her sister.[54]

The New Zealand and Australian press both served a strongly matriarchal society. Women longed for details of the fashions brought from London by the Duchess, and whether the King liked it or not as he read the reports, her soft and feminine style was reported at length. 'The Duchess of York . . . was in periwinkle blue flowered georgette, draped at one side, worn under a beautiful wrap shot in blue and gold, with a heavy collar of squirrel fur lined with blue velvet in the same tone and a small hat turned up from the face in periwinkle blue.' And again, 'The Duchess of York was lovely in palest pink ninon encrusted with diamante and with a draping of tulle from the shoulder caught with a diamond and emerald pendant, with ropes of pearls.'[55] The Duke was beginning to feel that it was his wife they wanted to see, not him; she tried to assure him that it was not so. 'All the sentimental

---

and management of infants, but also made important contributions to knowledge in fields of psychological medicine, health education and plant acclimatization.

twaddle they write about me is obviously absurd – they always like a bit of romance, & the baby too helps the women to get silly – horribly silly.'[56]

The demands of the tour were so intense that it was hard to ensure that they had any free time. On their first Sunday morning, deferring worship until the evening at a Maori church, they motored to the Green and Blue Lake. The Duchess found the hot springs and geysers at Rotorua somewhat alarming – she told Queen Mary, 'I expect we saw much the same things that you did in 1901. I must say I hated walking round the geysers, although I was so interested, thinking that every moment we would all disappear through a thin crust into the unknown!'[57]

More welcome was a weekend fishing trip. In the Bay of Islands, the Duke caught a 150-pound shark and the Duchess had 'considerable success with a snapper'.[58] On another happy fishing break they were the guests of the New Zealand government at the Kowhai fishing camp at Tokaanu, which they loved. 'The most marvellous camp I have ever seen,' the Duke wrote in his tour diary. 'All tents beautifully furnished & fitted up with electric light & a water supply even in the lavatories.' Nothing was caught to equal the Duke's shark, but the Duchess had a small triumph. 'I found Elizabeth playing an 8 lb trout which she landed, & was highly delighted. Her first trout in her life,' the Duke recorded.[59] It was the first of many in a long life of happy fishing. Looking less than regal, but clutching her rod, she smiles with pleasure out of the photographs.

In his rather dry report back to the King, Lord Cavan praised the Duke for his new confidence and said that the Duchess 'has been quite splendid; she never appears to be tired'.[60] Alas, he was wrong. Taylor Darbyshire's account of the trip, *The Royal Tour of the Duke and Duchess of York*, describes how, at this point, the exhaustion of the long days of public exposure finally defeated her. 'The pace set, necessarily, was rather fast, and the combined exertion of sitting erect all day smiling – as only the Duchess can smile – at all the spectators at the roadside, or meeting the local dignitaries at the half-dozen towns which were passed through, proved too much.'[61] It was thought that dust from the roads might have settled on her throat, and she was too exhausted to resist it having a toxic effect. At root, the programme was far too crowded and she was completely exhausted.

By the evening of 9 March she had a temperature of 102 degrees and her tonsils were inflamed. There was alarm among the party; Surgeon Commander White, the medical officer in *Renown*, advised her that it was impossible for her to continue in this condition. She bowed to his advice. Her illness was a serious blow for the Duke. His staff knew that he could be 'nervy' and snap when he was tired[62] – and this happened more often when his wife was not around to soothe him. Sure that she was the major attraction for the eager crowds, his first thought was to cancel the remainder of the tour, to the South Island of New Zealand.[63] South Island was expected to be harder – the mining communities were thought unlikely to be so welcoming. 'It is a political tragedy that the Duchess could not go to Westport to soften the hard miners,' wrote Lord Cavan.[64] The prospect of tackling them alone was daunting for the Duke. But he decided that duty demanded that he do it, and so he did.

'Next day's journey began under saddened circumstances. The Duchess had so identified herself with the life and spirits of the party that everybody felt that some savour had gone out of the tour,' wrote Darbyshire.[65] But the Duke's spirit in shouldering the rest of the tour alone was much admired, and he earned unexpected ovations from the miners of South Island. In country districts people 'thronged about him with a gladness and a sympathetic loyalty that was the warmer for their appreciation of his coming to them at the cost of a certain self-sacrifice'.[66] Harry Batterbee commented to Lord Stamfordham that the Duke's journey was politically important '& did a great deal of good in encouraging the conservative as opposed to the bolshevist element'.[67] The crowds at last convinced him that it was for him they cheered, not just his wife.

The Duchess, meanwhile, rested in the less than luxurious Commercial Hotel in Nelson. After three days' total rest she was well enough to sail in *Renown* back to Wellington where she convalesced at Government House under the care of Commander White. She finally met Lady Alice Fergusson, the wife of the Governor General, who had been ill and unable to receive the Duke and Duchess on their arrival in New Zealand. The two invalids recuperated in deckchairs in the sunshine.

During this enforced separation she and her husband exchanged letters which testify to their feelings for each other. She told him that everyone had been very kind to her in Nelson – 'the baker sent me bread, the bookseller books, the ladies cakes & flowers, the fruiterer pears and grapes'. It was wonderful but not quite enough – 'all I wanted really was a nice comforting kiss from you.' She knew how much easier it was for them to work as a pair: 'when you tackle the Mayor, I can tackle the Mayoress!' But she thought the way he carried on was marvellous and she tried to reassure him that she was not the only focus of attention. 'Darling when you are feeling very depressed and tired, remember what wonderful work you are doing. They all loved you in N Island, and quite rightly.' She feared that she had shown the weakness of her sex. 'I never dreamt that I would be such a failure, but no doubt women are not made for the life we were leading, or men either if it comes to that . . . Well darling, I do pray that you will get through this nightmare of a programme, and I shall only look forward to the moment when I shall see you again. I send you all my love and hundreds of kisses & several hugs.'[68]

The Duke replied from Christchurch. 'My own little darling E, I have just received your darling letter which has spurred me on to greater efforts. Millions and millions of thanks for it you darling; it is just what I wanted & nothing could have given me greater help and encouragement.' He agreed that the work was too much for one person alone and he missed her terribly every day. But it was only a week to go before they met again; meanwhile she should not worry about him, but should just 'have a real rest and get the throat strong again'.[69]

From Wellington the Duchess also wrote to her sister May. 'The programme here was simply ghastly, & I stuck it for 16 days, & then suddenly cracked. It's really not a suitable life for women & we are having fearful trouble to keep the Australian programme down. They cannot believe that we are made of flesh and blood . . . so if you see me coming home old & haggard & ugly, don't be surprised!'[70]

Back in London, the King was both sympathetic and concerned. The real goal – Australia – was still ahead and for this the Duchess must recover her strength.[71] He hoped, he wrote to the Duke, 'that she will arrive in Australia quite fresh & well. If you find she is getting tired, she must do less, otherwise she will get ill again. You have certainly been through a strenuous time.' The couple were finally reunited on board *Renown* off Bluff, a desolate place on the southern tip of South Island. The weather was so bad that day that the official embarkation plans had to be scrapped and the Duke was taken out to the ship in the harbour tug, the only vessel which could stand the high seas caused by a north-westerly gale against the tide. In squalls of wind and rain, his wife watched as he tried to board. She reported to Lady Alice Fergusson, 'I was glad to be on board when I saw my husband being thrown (literally) from the bridge of the tug on to our quarter-deck at Bluff. It looked most unpleasant, but he did not seem to mind much.'[72]

As they set sail for Sydney, there seemed little doubt that the tour of New Zealand had been an outstanding success, in spite of the Duchess's illness. Sir Charles Fergusson wrote to the King, 'from New Zealand's point of view it could not possibly have given greater pleasure.'[73]

*

SATURDAY 26 MARCH 1927 was a perfect autumn morning in Sydney. *Renown* glided past The Heads and into one of the greatest natural harbours in the world. The bays were filled with boats which had come out to greet the battlecruiser, but they had all been requested to refrain from hooting or whistling while she was under way. The silence made her arrival all the more impressive. She dropped anchor in front of Admiralty House exactly to the minute scheduled, whereupon a cacophony of welcome broke out.

The Duke and Duchess then had their first taste of the intense political rivalries which have always characterized Australia and which complicated their visit. They had been invited by the Federal government to visit all of the states in the Commonwealth of Australia. But since they were landing in Sydney, the government of New South Wales demanded the right to welcome them. This was objected to by other state governments and by the Commonwealth government. No one would budge and the impasse was solved only by building a pontoon into the harbour and declaring it to be Federal territory. On this stick of wood the Federal ministers performed the first greetings and, a few yards behind them on the shore, the ministers of the government of New South Wales waited to favour the Duke and Duchess with a repeat of the process.

Politics aside, the welcome was remarkable. Lord Stonehaven, the Governor General, felt that the pride and happiness of the Australian people in receiving such a royal visit was a tribute to the strength of the British Empire.[74] Some of the visiting party were a little more surprised by the rather raucous and familiar nature of Australian society. Everything seemed much rougher than in New Zealand, including the press. There was great good humour, but less organization and less reverence. At every turn the Australians loudly cheered not only their royal guests, but also their little daughter, whom everyone referred to as Princess Betty. The Duke may have been surprised that he was repeatedly greeted by shouts of 'Albie!'[75]

It quickly became clear that in Australia there was little concept of fatigue. One of the greatest problems for the couple's staff was to ensure that their programme was not completely overloaded. Everyone was worried lest the Duchess fall ill again. That first weekend was already crowded. They attended a ball at the town hall, divine service in St Andrew's Cathedral, and a garden party. They also undertook a tour of the Prince of Wales Repatriation Hospital for sick and disabled war veterans. The visit was more harrowing than might have been expected; by mistake they were led into a room where a woman was weeping beside her dying husband.[76]

The weather did not favour the garden party – the royal visitors and their hosts took tea under cover – watched by about 2,000 people standing in the rain with, apparently, scarcely 200 umbrellas between them.[77] Later, while the Duke of York received an honorary degree from Sydney University, the Duchess attended a large reception given in her honour by the National Women's Council, whose members, according to a scandalized Lord Cavan, were the only people who behaved badly: 'When the Duchess got there – they not only presented an address but called her "the Representative of the Queen"!! Luckily we just managed to stop the address going to the Press – but if it does leak out please explain to His Majesty that Batterbee and the Governor were both assured that there wd be no such thing.'[78] The children of New South Wales presented her with a gold and silver tea-set for 'Princess Betty'.

The King was delighted with the enthusiastic reception reported in the British press. He wrote to his son: 'I hope Elizabeth will not do too much & rest as soon as she feels she is getting tired ... Your daughter is very flourishing & is more delightful every day & more pleased with herself.'[79] Queen Mary was more forthcoming, writing to the Duke, 'Baby is as sweet as ever, she is so lively always trying to jump & to stand up, & makes funny little noises & screams & shouts for fun, really too delightful, happy & carefree.' A week later the King and Queen went to Windsor Castle 'bringing with us in our car your adorable child who was awfully good, giving shrieks of delight at each dog she saw'.[80]

By now Dr Still had sent the Duchess several more reports on the Princess's progress. In early February she was trying to stand on her nurse's lap. A month later she was sitting up, was above average weight and had discovered how to roll over and over and how to wave goodbye and say 'Ta-Ta'. By the end of March she was growing fast, cutting more teeth and could now say 'By-ee'. She enjoyed listening to the band outside the Palace.[81]

So as not to detract in any way from the principal purpose of the royal couple's presence in Australia – the opening of the new Federal Parliament – their engagements were carefully selected to serve a few chosen patronages. Much of their programme reflected Australian reverence for the Anzacs (Australia and New Zealand Army Corps – the soldiers who had fought in the Great War). They progressed northwards from Sydney towards Queensland and Brisbane, inspecting returned sailors, soldiers, nurses, Boy Scouts and Girl Guides. The schedule was punishing. They stopped at a bewildering array of places whose names were either curiously familiar or else phonetic aborigine: Newcastle, Wallangarra, Stanthorpe, Warwick, Clifton, Toowoomba, Gatton, Laidley, Ipswich. Near Blackheath the Duchess laid the foundation stone of the Anzac Memorial Hospital at Govett's Leap.

She had many communications from soldiers who had convalesced at Glamis and officers who had been entertained at St James's Square during the war, and she made certain that as many as possible could get through the barriers of officialdom to speak to her.[82] Expatriate Scots competed with old soldiers for her attention. A Mrs Leach, whose husband farmed at Borung in Victoria, wrote about her grandfather who had served his apprenticeship as a painter-decorator at Glamis. Mr and Mrs Leach had called their farm Glamis. Miss Vivian Eastland wrote from St Kilda, 'It was very difficult seeing you on Thursday to realise that you were the little girl of 4 years I last saw in Glamis Castle nursery when I was maid to Lady Mary and Lady Rose, who I hope are both well; your nurse Clara [Alah] was very kind to me & I often amused you while she did your pretty hair, because it used to get in such tangles.'[83]

The Duke and Duchess finally reached Brisbane on the afternoon of 6 April. They had been told to expect the capital of Queensland to be unsympathetic. In fact their reception could not have been more enthusiastic. Their progress through the streets was constantly delayed by the unexpectedly huge crowds and by people desperate to present the Duchess with bouquets and presents. Batterbee wrote in amazement to a colleague in the Colonial Office, 'Anything like the enthusiasm of the welcome at Brisbane, which is supposed to be the home town of Bolshevism, I have never seen. The Labour Ministers there simply tumbled over themselves to get near the Duke and Duchess.'[84] The Duchess genuinely liked Forgan Smith, the acting Premier of Queensland – they got on very well when she discovered he came from Longforgan. He later sent her some samples of Queensland timbers in which she had expressed an interest. 'The people were so nice and friendly, even tho' they are called the Bolshie State . . . The children are so healthy to look at, but very spoilt, and completely without discipline,' she informed the Queen. 'Please forgive me for setting out my opinions in this manner. They are probably completely wrong, but just what I think personally, and only after a glance really!'[85]

By now they were aware that they had reached the middle of their tour and were looking forward to completing the second half. In Queensland they were able to rest a few days on a cattle station named Tamrookum; the weather was lovely – warm with cool breezes. The Duke enjoyed mustering cattle and the Duchess liked the grass, the trees and the hills – she thought it was the prettiest place they had been to. She told her mother, 'The people are so nice and friendly, & the distances are so vast that it keeps them simple . . . all the Scotch people are very glad to see me!! They are so nice & sentimental about each other.' All the governments were Labor, while that of New South Wales 'is composed of very Red people'. But she got on well with them all; she thought the trip was a success. 'One forgets that the people are terribly loyal, & never see anybody, so it is very hard work.'[86]

But it was worth while; as the Duke told his father, 'The people here have got a most wonderful spirit of loyalty to you & the Empire.'[87] Patrick Hodgson wrote to Queen Mary, 'Her Royal Highness has captivated everyone with her charm of manner.'[88] Public perceptions of her seemed to verge on adoration. Schoolgirls travelled hundreds of miles from outback sheep stations to see her. A blind girl wrote in Braille: 'Mother has described you to me, and I know just how sweet and dainty you are'; she received a reply saying that the

Duchess was 'greatly touched' by her 'kind message of welcome'. Another girl wrote, 'I was so happy when Mummie told me she had seen you at the Royal Garden Party. She said you looked like a beautiful fairy Princess in your beautiful dress and diamonds. We are quite lonely now you are gone.'[89] It may be hard to credit in a more blasé and cynical age, but the upward turning of her face and her constant smile fired the imaginations of many women and girls. An old widow saw her smile, and her 'loneliness and weakness were forgotten'. A schoolgirl enlarged on the theme of 'how pleased the poor wounded soldiers must have been to have you hovering near their bedside.'[90]

From Brisbane they returned to Sydney and embarked again in *Renown* for Tasmania. They found the weather there chilly after the heat of Queensland. Their welcome in Hobart, the capital, was affectionate but quieter than in either Brisbane or Sydney. They visited Launceston as well, if only to slake the bitter rivalry between the two towns. 'We are leading a strenuous life & opportunities for rest get fewer as time goes on,' the Duke wrote to his father.[91] The Duchess was beginning to feel the strain again; fortunately they were able to rest at the sheep station of the Cameron family at Mona Vale.

From Tasmania *Renown* set course for Melbourne and, though the sea was rather rough, the Duchess had time to compose a letter to Queen Mary. 'I am afraid I have not written for a long time, but we have been so terribly busy, that letters are extremely difficult to write.' She hated to admit physical weakness, but she did not conceal how hard she had found it all. 'I think this sort of tour is far too strenuous for a woman, and I do get terribly tired.' Suggesting discreetly that it was much harder than when Queen Mary had been in Australia as Duchess of York in 1901, she added, 'Of course wireless, cars and the Press complicate things enormously, and one is expected to do the impossible, with never a moment's rest.' But she was conscious of the good the tour was doing her husband. After commenting on the unfortunate Australian political rivalries and jealousies, she said, 'Bertie has been wonderful, and is far less shy & more sure of himself. I expect this Tour will mean a great deal to him. Do you remember you told me at Sandringham what a help such experience would be to him?'[92]

As they approached Melbourne, the cruisers escorting *Renown* fired a twenty-one-gun salute to mark the first birthday of Princess Elizabeth. Missing her dreadfully, the Duke and Duchess sent their daughter a birthday telegram. At Windsor, Queen Mary wrote in her diary on 21 April, 'Beautiful day. Darling baby's first birthday. We gave her lots of presents after breakfast.' The King recorded that they gave her a jewelled safety-pin brooch, frocks and toys. 'She gazed on everything & beamed & I think rather liked it all.'[93]

Next day the Duke and Duchess received a telegram: 'I send you my best love on my first birthday and thank you for telegram. Wish you were here with me. I have lots of lovely presents. Hope to see you very soon. Little Elizabeth.'[94] Subsequently more reports, including 'a birthday review', arrived from Dr Still. In one he informed the Duke and Duchess that the Princess now weighed twenty-three pounds and 'You will be delighted with her, she is so sweet, and it is not merely sweet looks but a sweet nature that makes her such a darling.' Nonetheless, 'when Her Royal Highness decides that things are not just as she requires, she is becoming very emphatic in saying so, in fact proceeded to battery and assault upon Nurse once when not allowed to come to me today: you will have to come home and do the Stern Mother!' Her vocabulary was growing – she had pointed to the electric light 'and said distinctly: "Yight" '.[95]

Meanwhile, Melbourne was preparing itself. The *Argus* reported that day, 'Everything possible has been done to make the programme worthy of the occasion. The city is bright with colour that will give it a carnival aspect by day, while by night the streets will be ablaze with illumination. All that remains now is for the army of the people, an army that will probably number 500,000, to do their part.'

The royal couple stepped ashore to be welcomed by a large number of schoolchildren singing the National Anthem and waving. The Duchess seemed delighted and repeatedly waved at them, which pleased them. According to the *Argus*, she was wearing 'a small blue hat with a large cluster of blue velvet forget-me-nots which drooped over the brim at one side, and these exactly matched her blue eyes'. The paper described her as petite and slender, with rose-petal skin and grace and charm. 'Then there is the smile of which so much has been heard, and the strange thing is that everyone who has seen it feels it is for him or her alone. It seems to create an intimacy which, while purely imaginary, is nonetheless delightful.'

They drove in a horse-drawn carriage down the fine processional route of St Kilda's Avenue into the city, Sydney's historic rival. Just as they entered the grounds of Federal Government House, a terrible thing happened. The wingtips of two of the planes in their Royal Australian Air Force escort touched and the planes crashed, killing the crews in front of their eyes. The Duchess, already under strain, was very upset and, although she continued with the programme for the next two days, Commander White decided she should spend the weekend resting at Government House. The Duke sent a message of heartfelt sympathy.[96]

Three days later, on 25 April, came Anzac Day, perhaps the most emotional in the Australian and New Zealand calendar, evoking memories of sacrifice in Flanders, Palestine and above all Gallipoli. Thousands upon thousands of people from all over Victoria poured into Melbourne to see the salute taken by the son of the monarch in whose name those sacrifices had been made. After laying a wreath on the Cenotaph in front of Parliament House, the Duke joined the Governor General and the Governor on the saluting base. *Renown's* Marine Band led the parade, followed by Australia's most distinguished officer, General Sir John Monash, and his staff. Then 25,000 men from all over Australia and New Zealand marched past, almost all in plain clothes but wearing all their medals, including twenty-nine recipients of the Victoria Cross. According to Lord Cavan, they marched 'with a glorious swing – pride in themselves, and first rate dressing'.[97]

After the march-past the Duchess and her ladies in waiting set off for Government House but were prevented from leaving by 'one of Australia's really extraordinary outbursts', as Lord Cavan described it. The crowds surged forward, with the police powerless to stop them. Dozens of people climbed on to the car. 'However, with the curious instinct that just prevents an Australian undisciplined crowd from going too far, the situation was saved by a lot of Diggers* forming a voluntary ring round the Duchess' car, and so allowing it to progress at a yard a minute to Government House.'[98]

Commander White continued to keep a close eye on his charge, determined to restrict her programme whenever necessary to ensure she got through the remaining three weeks which were to culminate in the all-important ceremony in Canberra. From Melbourne they proceeded to Ballarat and Adelaide, where 12,000 people attended a public reception and 12,000 children then danced for them. En route

---

* Australian military slang for Australian soldiers. The term originated in the Great War.

to Canberra they rested privately with Mr and Mrs Macfarlane of Tailem Bend, where the Duke took part in the unusual sport of a kangaroo hunt and the Duchess joined the picnic party. And then it was on to Canberra.

The new capital of the Commonwealth could not have been more different from the vibrant cities of Sydney and Melbourne – it was little more than a village set in fields filled with grazing cattle and sheep. When the Prince of Wales had visited it in 1920, he had called Canberra 'a city of hope and foundation stones'. Now many of those foundations had grown buildings upon them but Canberra was still tiny and pastoral.[99] The ceremony was imperial. On the warm, sunny morning of 9 May the Duke and Duchess travelled in a procession of carriages, with postilions dressed in scarlet and outriders in perukes and cockaded hats, to the new Parliament House. The Duke had slept badly and was nervous, because he understood only too well that this was a momentous occasion for Commonwealth, for Crown – and for himself.[100]

He inspected the guard of honour and was then presented with a golden key by the Australian Prime Minister, Stanley Bruce, and invited to unlock the door of the new building. At his own insistence, he then spoke on the steps to the crowds outside; many thought it the most moving speech he made on the whole tour. On this day, he said, 'one feels the stirrings of a new birth, of quickened national activity, of a fuller consciousness of your destiny as one of the great self-governing units of the British Empire.' This was the beginning of a new epoch, a moment to dream 'of better things'.[101]

Dame Nellie Melba sang 'God Save the King' and the procession entered Parliament House. After formally unveiling the statue of King George V in the King's Hall the Duke sat in the chair of the President of the Senate with the Duchess near by. Conditions were not ideal: the Senate Chamber was small and the lights of the film cameramen increased the temperature to 80 degrees within minutes. (The film of the event was distributed by Pathé News – the first time members of the Royal Family were seen around the Empire taking part in such a ceremony.) But the Duke spoke well, saying that the British Empire had advanced to a new concept of autonomy – 'to the idea of a system of British nations, each freely ordering its own individual life, but bound together in unity by allegiance to one Crown and co-operating with one another in all that concerns the common weal'.[102] After a fanfare of trumpets and a twenty-one-gun salute, the clock struck twelve and the Parliament of the Commonwealth was open. The only sadness in an otherwise flawless event was the death of another pilot, Flying Officer F. E. Ewen, whose plane crashed in front of Parliament House during a review of troops that afternoon. The Duke and Duchess were shocked and sent a wreath; Ewen's mother later wrote to thank them.

Their journey was almost done. From Canberra they returned to Melbourne to rejoin *Renown*. They chose to make the last part of the journey in open cars and stopped at the town halls of South Melbourne to say goodbye. After sailing from Melbourne on 12 May, they had a rough crossing of the Great Australian Bight. The Duchess related to the King, 'I got washed out of bed at 3 am by a huge sea which crashed suddenly over the ship, & I had to spend an hour drying my hair at the radiator! I could not help laughing, but it was very annoying too.'[103]

They had one more Australian destination, Fremantle, the principal port in Western Australia, where they had to gird themselves one more time for the familiar programme of addresses, bouquets, speeches, openings and inspections. Their effect on the crowds and the press there was the same as in the rest of the continent. The Albany *Dispatch* recorded, in unusually purple prose, that the Duchess persuaded her husband, anxious to keep to the timetable, to make an impromptu stop at the Anzac Memorial Hospital at Albany.

> The Duke was obdurate ... Then happened the little incident which is being repeated in the backblock homesteads to the mothers and the children there ... it is with a tremble of the voice and a glistening of the eye that the little Royal Lady, having the true heart of a woman and the gracious grandeur of a queen, begs her lord to accede to the request, and he consents to do so ... in the days that are yet to be, the most memorable spot along that road will be the Anzac Memorial Hospital, which his wife's plea induced a prince to visit.

After they had finally embarked in *Renown* for home, one man in the crowd in Perth wrote to the Duchess to say that he had heard the remark of a twelve-year-old schoolboy who had seen her pass: ' "She looked at me and I got a smile too" ... I could judge by the tone of his voice you had won his little heart.' He ended, 'Hoping that if one day the people of the British Empire are fortunate enough to have you as our Queen, you will not lose the power of your winning smile nor your happy service of kindly thought and deed.'[104]

*

It was an appropriate tribute to the Duchess and to her husband. They had each discovered qualities and powers within themselves of which they had scarcely known. Sir Tom Bridges, Governor of South Australia, wrote to the King, 'His Royal Highness has touched people profoundly by his youth, his simplicity and his natural bearing, while the Duchess has had a tremendous ovation and leaves us with the responsibility of having a continent in love with her.'[105] Other reactions were similarly enthusiastic. Lady Strathmore told the Queen that she had received many letters from ex-soldiers who were veterans of Glamis showing the impact her son-in-law and daughter were having.[106] Harry Batterbee wrote to Lord Stamfordham, 'We are all feeling rather tired after our strenuous time, but I do not think that there can be any doubt whatever that the Australian Tour has been a great success and done a great deal of good. A nail has been driven into the coffin of Bolshevism, which will securely hold it down, I trust, for some time to come.'[107]

On board ship, the Duke had time to start a long letter to his father. It was with some pride, as well as relief, that he could tell the King that his Canberra speeches had gone off without a hitch. He paid credit again to Lionel Logue and added:

I have so much more confidence in myself now, which I am sure comes from being able to speak properly at last.

It is a great relief to me that the object of our mission is now over, & more especially when I played my part successfully, at least I think & hope so . . . Elizabeth has done wonders & though I know she is tired she never had a return of her tonsillitis & went about with me every day. I could never have done the tour without her help; that I know, & I am so thankful she came too.[108]

Both his parents wrote to the Duke in terms which must have pleased him. Queen Mary said, 'We have had such delightful letters from various people about the Tour, telling us of your & E's popularity & of the trouble you both gave yourselves to make the Tour the success it has been. You must both of you feel rewarded for all the trouble you have taken & for the fatigue you have undergone. Of course the whole thing has been too strenuous & people have been too "exigeant" & wanted you to do too much, it is always difficult to make people realise that their "show" is not the only one!'[109]

They had hardly had time to start to relax in the heat of the Indian Ocean when, three days out from Fremantle, on Queen Mary's birthday, a serious fire broke out in *Renown*'s engine room. It was caused by an overflow of fuel oil between tanks; the engine room soon became an inferno and four of the boiler-room staff were gassed and burned as they tried in vain to douse the blaze. There was a grave risk that the ship's principal oil tanks could explode, in which case *Renown* would almost certainly have been totally destroyed. Plans to abandon ship were readied, but as a result of the storms through which she had passed on her journey many of her lifeboats were out of action. The firefighters continued to struggle and after about eight hours they finally managed to extinguish the flames. It was a near-disaster, but the Duke was laconic when he told the King about it: 'Oil is a dangerous substance for a fire & it might have been serious.'[110] Harry Batterbee was perhaps nearer the mark in observing, 'It was really great luck that we didn't go up sky high. What a sensation it would have caused if we had just disappeared.'[111] Years later Queen Elizabeth recalled that 'the nearest ship was a thousand miles away. Totally empty sea. So we had to prepare to leave. The deck got quite hot and I couldn't think of anything to take in the boat except a bottle of Malvern water and my [book of] prayers. I couldn't leave them behind.'[112]

They broke the journey home in Mauritius, where the Duke enjoyed a rather exotic *chasse* or gigantic deer drive with more than sixty beaters, and the next day they attended the races, which enabled a lot of islanders to see them. *Le Mauricien* declared that the people of the island had been simply swept off their feet by the royal visit. Two cases of dolls'-house furniture were sent from the island as a gift for Princess Elizabeth. They had one more stop before the Suez Canal, at Great Hanish Island in the Red Sea, a strategic oiling station for the British navy. The Duke hunted and shot an Arabian gazelle, but Lord Cavan enjoyed it less, writing to Stamfordham: 'if ever you have a public man to get rid of – send him to Great Hanish Island where we stopped for 24 hours to oil. I have never seen or smelt anything more awful! & temperature is never under 95° & no shade!'[113]

Now that they were finally nearing home, the Duchess wrote to the King to say how much they were looking forward to seeing him and the Queen again.

> It seems such a long time since we left you in January, & I cannot believe that we are really getting home at last – older, & I hope wiser!
>
> I hope you will not think me looking old & ugly, but a week in the Red Sea in June does not help the complexion to look its best! It has been very hot, & my cabin (sleeping) has been 105, which is most uncomfortable . . .
>
> I am looking forward more than I can say to the Baby & a good rest. I have missed her all day & every day, but am so grateful to you & Mama for having been so kind to her. It will be wonderful to see her again.
>
> With much love dearest Papa,
> Ever your affect. daughter in law,
>   Elizabeth[114]

After they had passed through the Suez Canal into the Mediterranean the weather grew much more agreeable, but their work was not yet finished. They stopped for a fairly formal three-day visit in Malta, to find that Lord Louis Mountbatten was also there in his yacht *Shrimp*. After a brief stop at Gibraltar they finally approached Portsmouth on 27 June 1927. The King was, as throughout their trip, meticulous in his instructions on the dress required. On their arrival, he told the Duke, he should wear 'Frock coat & epaulettes with star' and he added, 'We will not embrace at the station before so many people. When you kiss Mama take yr. hat off.'[115]

Queen Mary had been busy at 145 Piccadilly, where the Duke and Duchess and their daughter were now to live. Together with Lady Strathmore she had been furnishing the Princess's nursery and had provided the baby with a cupboard for her toys. The Princess and Alah moved into the house just before her parents returned and Queen Mary suggested to Lady Strathmore that they both go to the house 'with some flowers to arrange the rooms & just put a few finishing touches to make the rooms look homely'.[116]

The Duke and Duchess had travelled 30,000 miles by sea and several thousand miles by land around the world. At Portsmouth they were greeted by the Duke's three brothers and together they boarded a special train to Victoria station where, on a platform bedecked with flowers, they met their families again. Cecilia Strathmore had requested ten platform tickets. Tortor Gilmour's two children and their nanny were there to greet their mother. Despite the King's strictures, the families all embraced warmly.

The Yorks drove in an open carriage through cheering crowds down Whitehall and up the Mall to the Palace, to be greeted again by their parents more privately and – most importantly – to be reunited with their daughter. The whole family, including Princess Elizabeth, then appeared on the Palace balcony. The crowds were ecstatic and the newspapers were generous in their praise of the 'envoys'. They commented on the Duchess's sense of duty in leaving her baby behind for so long; almost all of them remarked upon her obvious joy on her return. The *Daily Mirror* described 'Britain's affectionate welcome home for the Duke and ever smiling Duchess' while *The Times* recorded, 'Twice the Duchess, her face radiant with smiles, brought the Princess forward.'

The voyage had been of immense significance to them both. The exuberant loyalty of so many millions of people to Britain and to the Crown was impressive, as well as moving. It gave each of them a real feeling for the strength of the Empire – perhaps it seemed to them more resilient than it really could be. Above all the voyage gave the Duke new confidence in his ability to confront the world with his wife at his side. And it gave the Duchess the knowledge that, wherever she went, she was able to use her personality to win immense affection for herself and, more importantly, for her husband and her country. The experience and the lessons were not forgotten.

CHAPTER NINE

THE LONG WEEKEND

1927–1936

'The world is in such a bad way'

IN THE LATE 1920s the world was nearing the middle of what later came to be called 'the long weekend' between the two great wars.* Fear may not always have been present, but it was always in the background. The future seemed constantly under threat as traditional systems of government and long-standing social arrangements attempted to adapt to the vast changes imposed by the industrialization of the last century, the destruction of the war and the extension of the franchise.

At first the most obvious external danger came from the growth of the new empire of Soviet communism. Ever since the triumph of Bolshevism in Russia and the murder of the Tsar and his family, all European states had seemed at risk, if not living on borrowed time. Not for nothing did King George V and many around him worry constantly about the impact of communist ideology and subversion by communist agitators, particularly as millions of men were demobbed after the Great War and unemployment grew.

Perhaps almost as alarming, notions of republicanism if not out-right revolution were attractive and fashionable among the intellectual elite of Britain. To many in the 'smart set', monarchy symbolized the failures of the past, and Bolshevism was the promise of the future. At the end of the 1920s, Joseph Stalin began the forced industrialization of Russia by herding the peasants into collectives. This meant in effect a new civil war, in which this time the party fought the peasantry and killed or transported millions of them.[1] Russia's 'success' became an example to Western idealists and intellectuals who were ignorant of,

---

* *The Long Weekend* was the title of a 1940 book by Robert Graves and Alan Hodge drawn upon here.

or chose to ignore, the appalling sacrifices by which industrialization was achieved.

To combat the siren song of revolution, the King and his advisers had, as we have seen, sought from the start of the long weekend to strengthen the engagement of the monarchy with working people. New relationships with trades union leaders and Labour politicians were forged. At the same time members of the Royal Family continued reaching out to people through the welfare monarchy, their network of philanthropic patronages.

On her return from her long voyage, the Duchess felt a conflict of emotions. There was, above all, the longed-for reunion with her daughter, Princess Elizabeth, which was not easy after such a long separation at the Princess's age. With perception, the King wrote to the Duke soon after their return: 'I trust yr sweet little baby begins to know her parents now & likes them.'[2] She did, and the Duchess rejoiced in that. As she wrote to Nannie B, her daughter was 'too delicious, and was nice to me at once, which was a great relief!'[3]

On the other hand, she now lost the intimate intensity which she and her husband had shared throughout their voyage. The tour had been gruelling, but it was their own tour; their days were often exhausting, but they and they alone were the principals, they were far from parental supervision, and everything they did was new, exciting and shared. Back in London they had to play their supporting roles in formal Court rituals in which they were only pieces of an elaborate jigsaw, presided over by the King, who could be kind but was often critical and irritable.

But the crucial point was that the Yorks' success had impressed the King and Queen. This alone gave the Duke a new confidence in his own abilities and as a result his stammer had improved. He told his voice coach, Lionel Logue, 'I have been talking a lot with the King, & I have had no trouble at all. Also I can make him listen, & I don't have to repeat everything over again.'[4] His father was very happy. 'Delighted to have Bertie with me,' he wrote to Queen Mary from Balmoral; 'he came yesterday evening, have had several talks with him & find him most sensible, very different to D[avid]'.[5]

The King was still not prepared for the Prince of Wales to have access to confidential information.[6] The Prince was a charismatic and popular figure, but he seemed to the King, and to many of his own staff, to be increasingly careless of the duties of his office. There were those who considered that adulation and a café-society lifestyle had warped him. Throughout the late 1920s and early 1930s these fears grew. By contrast, the stock of the Duke of York was rising and he had acquired a new sense of purpose. He was eager to acquire more understanding of Commonwealth affairs. The day after he and the Duchess returned, the Duke called on the Prime Minister and the Colonial Secretary, Leo Amery, and he gave Amery a longer report on the tour over lunch at 145 Piccadilly a few days later.[7]

For her part, the Duchess had by now won herself a rather remarkable role within the family – everyone seemed to confide in her, especially her brothers-in-law. Her letters from the Prince of Wales were full of affection, gossip and sometimes mischievous comments on his parents and his duties. On a voyage to Canada with his younger brother Prince George in August 1927, the Prince of Wales wrote a birthday letter to his sister-in-law promising that 'we will drink a toast to you. (We aren't as tight as we seem altho it is cocktail time!)' They were bored with the 'bromidic' first-class passengers – 'We long to probe into the 2nd class where we have already had opportunity to mark down some choice pieces from the Middle West. Pity we can't travel 2nd class – Yes a pity!'[8] Prince George, too, regarded her as an ally and, knowing how well she got on with the King, occasionally asked her to intervene with his father on his behalf.[9]

Meanwhile her own success on the tour meant that public demands on the Duchess were growing too – often indeed, she, rather than the Duke, was the focus of attention. That summer was marked by the first of many biographies to be written of the future Queen Elizabeth. The author was Lady Cynthia Asquith, whose most celebrated book was her wartime diary.* The Duchess agreed to assist her on condition she was allowed to see the manuscript before publication. Asquith asked for help from many of the Duchess's relations and friends, including Beryl Poignand and Sergeant Ernest Pearce, the former patient at Glamis who had remained in touch with her. Asquith told Pearce that the Duchess had described him as 'a very old friend' and asked him 'if you could tell me any little incidents or impressions of her in the old hospital days at Glamis'.[10] Pearce was flustered and flattered and wrote to the Duchess saying that Asquith's request for an

---

* Lady Cynthia Mary Evelyn Asquith (1887–1960), diarist, novelist and biographer. Daughter of eleventh Earl of Wemyss. She married Herbert Asquith (son of the Prime Minister) in 1910.

interview put him 'in a juice of a fix'.[11] After receiving the Duchess's approval he gave the author a vivid account of his time at Glamis and of his acquaintance with the young Elizabeth Bowes Lyon. The biography, later updated, was useful for such first-hand recollections.

The Duke and Duchess had a pleasant summer relaxing in Scotland with the eighteen-month-old Princess Elizabeth, who was now walking, which her mother at first found nerve-racking.[12] In the third week of September she and the Duke left their daughter at Balmoral to undertake two days of public engagements in Glasgow. On this occasion she was very much the centre of attention, and he was her support. In pouring rain, she visited Ralston Hospital for paralysed ex-servicemen and the Elder Park Child Welfare Centre at Govan. She was made a guild sister of the Trades Guildry of Glasgow and she opened the Health and Housing Exhibition in the Kelvin Hall; the Girls' Guildry provided a guard of honour. She was also given the freedom of the city and in the presentation speech she was praised for her interest in movements for social and educational advancement. Afterwards she sent a personal donation towards the fund being raised to establish a Scottish academy of music in Glasgow.[13]

The Duchess told the Queen that she had enjoyed the whole visit, despite the rain and the usual rush, and went on: 'I visited a child welfare centre in Govan on Tuesday, & had a marvellous reception from every shade of socialist, crimson, red & pink! . . . I miss the baby horribly, but am so glad that you are enjoying her (how swelled headed I am about her).'[14] The King sent congratulations on the success of the visit, adding, 'Your sweet baby is very flourishing & more delightful than ever & walks about everywhere.'[15]

Eventually, the sojourn in the Highlands came to an end and they returned south with the slightly heavier hearts that weigh on everyone at the end of a summer holiday as winter and work loom. At least they were no longer isolated in Richmond and had a home in central London which they enjoyed – and which, the King reminded them, Queen Mary had taken a lot of trouble to prepare for them.[16]

In early November they went to Woolwich and visited the Arsenal before the Duke opened the Woolwich Memorial Hospital. At the Imperial Institute a few days later they went to a sale of work for the benefit of war-disabled servicemen – a recurring theme of their philanthropic work. The Duchess bought some of the men's handiwork, produced under the auspices of a charitable enterprise named

Painted Fabrics,* and subsequently gave permission for her name to be used on the firm's writing paper. As with many charities, one favour led to requests for others, and she continued to support this cause in later years.

On 16 November the Duke and Duchess went together to Exeter to open a new orthopaedic hospital. A few weeks later, the opening of a new wing at Walthamstow General Hospital in east London became something of an event. Their route took in much of the East End and Stratford and Leyton, some of the poorest boroughs in London. They were given a warm reception throughout and their presence helped raise £3,190 for the hospital's funds. The strongly socialist local council went so far as to present the Duchess with £100 to be spent on the hospital, a sum which impressed the local MP, Sir Hamar Greenwood. 'Their Royal Highnesses, and they alone, have commanded the respect and won the allegiance of certain extremists who have hitherto worked against some of England's cherished ideals,' he wrote to the Duke's Private Secretary. 'Believe me, this is literally a Royal achievement; and those of us who know the difficulties and dangers are profoundly grateful to Their Royal Highnesses.'[17] Both the language and the threat might appear exaggerated today, but in 1927, one year after the General Strike, perceptions were different.

On 13 December the Duke and Duchess attended a performance of *A Message from Mars* given by the Lena Ashwell Players in Notting Hill Gate, in support of a movement to take drama to the urban poor. 'We actually made a profit for a change, such is the magic wrought by their interest,' declared the organizers afterwards.[18] Two days later the Duchess was in Aldershot visiting the King's Own Yorkshire Light Infantry, the first of the regiments of which she became colonel-in-chief. She had been appointed on 12 August 1927 and maintained a lifelong association with the regiment.[19]

That Christmas, as usual, the family travelled by train to Sandringham. Princess Elizabeth was now attracting increasing press attention; this could be irritating but it enhanced the Yorks' popularity as an ideal

---

* Painted Fabrics grew out of painting classes run by students from the Sheffield School of Art for severely injured servicemen during the First World War. Its founder, Annie Carter, set up a business employing the men to produce fabrics for a well-off clientele, and its workshops were taken over to make aircraft parts during the Second World War. Fabric production continued afterwards, but business declined and the firm was wound up in 1958.

young family. On this occasion she was reported to have worn pink velvet and fur on the journey and white silk for a Christmas party for the Sandringham estate workers. The *Westminster Gazette* described the Princess at the party as 'chattering and laughing and bombarding the guests with crackers handed to her by her mother'. This story seems to have been accurate. 'Baby was too sweet & threw crackers & joined in the fun,' wrote Queen Mary in her diary.[20]

After Christmas, the Princess's parents acceded to the King and Queen's constant requests for more time with their grandchild – she stayed on with her grandparents at Sandringham, where she loved playing with Snip, the King's dog.[21] After she returned home in late January 1928, the King wrote to the Duke, 'I miss your sweet baby more than I can say, breakfast & tea are quite different without her ... I think the air here agreed with her & she has come on a lot.'[22] The Queen was equally devoted and told her son, 'I don't think you & Elizabeth realize what a great joy your child is to us & how we love having her with us now & again in the house, she is so sweet & natural & so amusing.'[23]

The year was filled with both official and private events, but that autumn there was pleasure as well as work. The Yorks had taken Naseby Hall in Northamptonshire so that the Duke could enjoy the hunting season. The Duchess loved being there, although she thought the countryside ugly and bleak. She liked the wind and the rain tearing at the house. 'Hi! A slate has fallen. And another! Hooray, a large piece of lead now. The whole roof is coming off,' she wrote to D'Arcy Osborne.[24]

The end of 1928 brought a real crisis for the family, and the country. On 11 November the Duke and Duchess accompanied the King and Queen at the Armistice Day ceremony at the Cenotaph. The King caught a chill and by 21 November he had become unwell. He had to dictate that day's entry in his diary to the Queen. 'I was taken ill this evening. Feverish cold they called it, and retired to bed.'[25] There were no more diary entries, except a few written by the Queen, for the next five months. Penicillin had not yet been developed and the King very nearly died.[26] His physician Lord Dawson understood at once that his patient was seriously ill. Tests showed that he had a streptococcal infection of the chest, and he developed septicaemia over the next few days. He began to suffer serious bronchial pain and became delirious. The Palace did not reveal this grim news to the public but by early December the medical bulletin did acknowledge 'a decline in the strength of the heart'.

The King's children were summoned. The Duke of York had only to come from Naseby; the Duchess was in London. She came at once 'and was a great comfort to us', her sister-in-law Princess Mary wrote.[27] The Prince of Wales had to make a longer journey. He was on safari in Kenya with Denys Finch Hatton, the celebrated white hunter. On 27 November he received a coded telegram from the Prime Minister informing him that the King was seriously ill. Baldwin thought that the British people would be profoundly shocked if the Prince did not come home.[28]

The Prince did not react well, according to the subsequent account of his Private Secretary, Alan Lascelles. His immediate response was apparently to dismiss the telegram. 'I don't believe a word of it,' he declared. 'It's just some election dodge of old Baldwin's.'[29] Lascelles wrote that at this he lost his temper. 'Sir, the King of England is dying, and if that means nothing to you, it means a great deal to us.' At which the Prince apparently looked at him, said nothing, left the room and spent the rest of the evening getting to bed the wife of a local British official. He told a friend it was the best thing to do after a shock. Once he was convinced of the gravity of his father's condition – and the fact that he might soon become king himself – the Prince made his way home as swiftly as possible by land and by sea. He was borne on a British cruiser through the Suez Canal to Brindisi where the Italian government had laid on a special train to speed him across the continent.[30]

London was rife with rumours – such as that the King had died but that news of this was being delayed until the return of the Prince of Wales. Other gossip had it that the Duke of York planned to usurp the throne in his elder brother's absence. Amused, the Duke wrote to tell his brother that there was a story going about that the reason for his rushing home was that 'in the event of anything happening to Papa I am going to bag the Throne in your absence!!! Just like the Middle Ages.'[31]

By the time the Prince of Wales finally arrived home on the evening of 11 December, the King's condition was critical. The Duke met his brother at Victoria station and, on the short drive to the Palace, warned him how shocked he would be by his father's changed appearance. Dawson, he said, felt he would have to perform an operation very soon.[32] The Duke also told the Prince how calm and strong their mother had been. But he was concerned for her. 'She keeps too much locked up inside of her. I fear a breakdown if anything awful happens. She has been wonderful.'[33]

Next day the end seemed near – the King's gifted nurse, Sister Black, wrote, 'The doctors had done everything that could be done. Human skill ended there.'[34] But Dawson, watching his unconscious patient, decided that he really must make one more attempt to locate the source of the fatal poison – an abscess just behind the diaphragm.[35] With great dexterity, he managed to find the site, plunged in a needle and drew off over a pint of pus. That night the King had a rib removed and the draining of the abscess was completed.[36]

Over the next few days constant medical bulletins were issued and churches all over England were kept open day and night so that people could come to offer prayers for their monarch. Gradually it seemed that such prayers were being heard. The King's decline had been arrested. But he was by now so frail that it was some weeks before his doctors could be confident that he would actually recover.[37] The Royal Family remained in London over Christmas; on 6 January 1929 Queen Mary recorded in her diary that for the first time in nearly six weeks the King had been able to hold a conversation with her, which cheered her greatly. There was relief and gratitude throughout the country.

At the beginning of February the King was able to travel with the Queen to the south-coast resort of Bognor to convalesce. They hoped to have their granddaughter to stay with them, but both the Duchess and the Princess were ill with chest infections at the time.[38] The Princess's trip to the seaside was finally arranged for the middle of March. 'She is looking forward wildly to digging in the sand, and talks knowingly of pails & spades!' the Duchess wrote, adding a warning: 'She is very sensible really & understanding, but like a piece of quicksilver nowadays!'[39] The Queen recorded in her diary how delighted the King was to have his granddaughter close to him again. The gardener made a sandpit for her and the King watched her playing while the Queen sometimes joined her making sand pies; the Princess's sunny personality was said to have helped her grandfather's recovery.

While the Princess stayed beside the English Channel, her parents crossed it en route to Oslo for the wedding of Crown Prince Olav of Norway to Princess Märtha of Sweden; the Duke, who was the Crown

Prince's first cousin, was to be best man.* They had hoped that the
Royal Navy might make a ship available to them, but the King was
concerned that the expense of this might lead to questions in Parliament and so the Duke and Duchess travelled by train and ferry via
Berlin.[40]

They arrived in the German capital on the morning of 15 March.
After breakfasting at the British Embassy they looked around the
Schloss where Kaiser Wilhelm II had lived, which the Duchess found
'most interesting & rather sad'. The Kaiser's own rooms were bereft
of his furniture (he had taken it into exile in Holland), but she coveted
Hoppner's portrait of Frederick, Duke of York, which she spotted in
his dressing room. They went to Potsdam and saw Frederick the
Great's rococo palace of Sans Souci; the Duchess was very much
taken with the collection of Watteau paintings there. 'Then, just to
see a little of modern Germany, we had tea at a tea & dance place
in Berlin. It was most amusing.'[41] She told Queen Mary she had
enjoyed her day in Berlin, but writing to her friend D'Arcy Osborne
she allowed herself to be a little more mischievous, saying, 'I will
reserve my opinions (if you care to hear them) of our late enemies
until I meet you again.'[42]

The night train and ferry of 15/16 March carried them to Malmö.
The Duchess instantly preferred Sweden to Germany, marvelling at
the exquisitely clean and magnificently appointed hotel to which they
were taken. They were invited to tea in a beautiful pink-brick castle
where everyone behaved with great courtesy and friendliness. 'We
arrived with dozens of other guests all bearing flowers & clicking their
heels. A birthday party! & such a deliciously old fashioned atmosphere
of compliments and clicks, & tea handed in boiling hot rooms by
Rectors of neighbouring Universities. I enjoyed it so much, and they
all talked such good English.' She was impressed with Swedish efficiency – 'So well educated and every cottage with electric light and
telephone'. But their journey was beginning to seem endless – 'our
train, which started in such a businesslike way from Calais, every
second being of importance, has now deteriorated into a kind of

---

* Crown Prince Olav was the only son of King Haakon VII of Norway and his wife Queen
Maud, King George V's sister. He was also related to the Duke through his father, who was
Queen Alexandra's nephew.

Oriental timeless affair, & I feel that we may be days before we reach our destination.'[43]

They did reach Oslo in good time for the wedding on 21 March. At the pre-wedding ball at the Royal Palace on 19 March, the *Daily Telegraph*'s reporter recorded that the Duchess 'looked lovely in a silver beaded frock and a diadem of diamonds'; the 'gay party of 600 – Kings, Princes, Dukes, Counts, dignitaries, and their wives' danced until 2 a.m.; the Duchess, it was noted, danced mostly with her husband. Oslo was brilliantly illuminated for the occasion, with 'flaming ice pillars' and dance floors laid down in the streets, where the crowds whirled the night away. For the wedding, the Duke of York, in naval full-dress uniform, accompanied the bridegroom to the Church of Our Saviour, while the Duchess, wearing a white fur coat and the 'new pinky gold dress' she had had made for the wedding,[44] was escorted by Prince George of Greece. 'We loved having dear Bertie and darling Elizabeth,' Queen Maud wrote to Queen Mary. 'Everyone of course lost their hearts to Elizabeth, she was so sweet to all.'[45]

When they returned to London, Queen Mary brought Princess Elizabeth back to them. They spent the next few weeks between London and Naseby, where the Duchess had now made friends with local farmers and the parson, 'a tall heavenly man with an immense white collar who catches moths!'[46] In London they gave a number of dinner parties at 145 Piccadilly and considered giving a ball at St James's Palace but abandoned the idea after a warning from the Queen: 'Papa hates the thought of those new dances being danced in his Palaces, old fashioned no doubt but difficult to combat!'[47]

Immediately after their return it was announced that the King had decided to nominate the Duke to the post of lord high commissioner to the General Assembly of the Church of Scotland. The holder, appointed annually, was the King's representative at the Assembly. It was an important compliment to the Duke and the first time that a member of the Royal Family had held this ancient office. Moreover, 1929 marked the Reunion of the Church of Scotland and the Free Church after more than eighty years of schism.[48]

The Duke and Duchess took up residence in the Palace of Holyroodhouse on 20 May, and the next day they were driven, with great pageantry, through large and enthusiastic crowds to St Giles's Cathedral and then to the Tolbooth Church where the Assembly met. There the Duke delivered the King's commendation on the reunion of the churches, and he and the Duchess were greeted with tremendous applause. Alongside the official ceremonies there was a great deal of socializing. They were both seen to enjoy themselves; the Duchess was described in one newspaper as 'a winsome Scotswoman, before whose smile the whole capital fell enchanted'.[49] She was moved by the Assembly itself, writing to Queen Mary: 'They, the Assembly, are, I think, really pleased at us being here, and their feeling for you & Papa makes tears come to one's eyes. They are so delightfully sincere in Scotland!'[50] Basil Brooke, the Duke's Comptroller, wrote: 'The Duke and Duchess had the most terrific reception. They could hardly get through Princes Street on their way to the Station on Wednesday night and the Edinburgh crowd let themselves go properly and cheered like a Londoner.'[51] The *Scotsman* even went so far as to declare that 'it may well be that the frail ghost of Mary Queen of Scots revisiting the Castle felt the stirrings of jealousy.'[52]

The Duchess missed her daughter 'dreadfully' and many people in Edinburgh were disappointed she was not with them. 'Not that they would have seen her, but they would have liked to feel that she was here,' she wrote to Queen Mary. 'In the solemn old Assembly, the Moderator mentioned in his welcoming address "our dear Princess Elizabeth", which is, I believe, almost unique. It almost frightens me that the people should love her so much. I suppose that it is a good thing, and I hope that she will be worthy of it, poor little darling!'[53] The Princess, known to herself and her family as Lilibet, was now at Windsor Castle, happily playing with her cousins, Princess Mary's children. From there she wrote her mother a letter (which perhaps had a hand guiding her own): 'Darling Mummy, Do come here and see the soldiers and the band I am very well and very busy. Love from Lilibet XXOO.'[54]

On 30 May the first general election with full female franchise took place and, appropriately, its result was almost revolutionary. Labour became the largest party in the Commons for the first time, though it lacked an overall majority. Stanley Baldwin resigned on 4 June. The King was back at Windsor but he was ill again – another abscess had formed at the site of his earlier operation, and it had burst on 31 May. The Labour Party leader, Ramsay MacDonald, recorded that the King received him in a yellow Chinese dressing gown.[55] Three days later the members of the new government came by train to Windsor to be sworn in by the King, who managed this time to struggle into a frock coat. The new Minister of Labour, Margaret Bondfield, was the first ever female member of the Cabinet. She recalled, 'When my turn came, he broke the customary silence to say "I am pleased to be the one to whom has come the opportunity to receive the first woman Privy Councillor." His smile as he spoke was cordial and sincere.'[56]

On 7 July the King participated in a service of thanksgiving for his recovery, although all was not yet well. 'Fancy a Thanksgiving Service,' he said, 'with an open wound in your back.'[57] A week later he had a second operation: another rib was removed and the abscess was successfully drained. The King and Queen were not able to make their cherished summer trip to Balmoral that year. Only by the end of September was the wound finally healed.

This long period of recovery alternating with relapse inevitably threw more burdens – and also more limelight – on to the King's children. Most of all, it was the Duke and Duchess of York who came into prominence this year. Were there presentiments of their future role in the minds of some around them? The rumour that the Duke was out to usurp the throne from his brother has already been mentioned; and in the Royal Household misgivings were growing about the prospect of the Prince of Wales's succession. Those who worked with him and knew him best acknowledged his charm and his popular appeal, but privately they despaired of his lack of seriousness.

Many years later Queen Elizabeth revealed that at this time the King himself had doubts that his eldest son would ever succeed him, and told her and her husband so. She recalled that while they were staying with the King during his convalescence he said to the Duke of York, 'You'll see, your brother will never become King.' She remarked that her father-in-law was 'extraordinary. He had such wisdom. He was a practical sort of man. He must have seen something we didn't, because I remember we thought "how ridiculous", because then everybody thought he was going to be a wonderful King. I remember that very very well. I remember we both looked at each other and thought "nonsense".'[58]

There is nothing to show that they gave any further thought to what was to them, evidently, a very remote possibility. They simply continued to play their supporting role to the King and the Prince of Wales. The 1929 summer season was both fun and hard work. They gave several dinner parties at 145 Piccadilly. Their guests were a mixture of their friends and people prominent in public life or literature; they included the Prime Minister Ramsay MacDonald, Sir Samuel and Lady Hoare,* Stanley Baldwin and his wife, the German and French Ambassadors, the writers John Buchan, Rudyard Kipling and J. M. Barrie (Barrie was born in Kirriemuir, five miles from Glamis). Both together and separately, they carried out busy programmes of functions and visits; they were now operating their public life in an increasingly professional manner.

The Duchess was becoming ever more active in her charitable work. In July she opened a new block of flats for the Kensington Housing Trust and attended a garden party for the National Council for Maternity and Child Welfare; with the Duke she supported a gala in aid of the Save the Children Fund and visited the free hospital for animals run by Our Dumb Friends' League of which she was already the patroness. Sometimes friends enlisted her support: one such was Lord Gorell, who had played cricket with her brothers at Glamis house parties in the early years of the century. He was chairman of King's College Hospital, which she visited in July to present badges to the children who had subscribed to a cot to be called the Princess Elizabeth Cot. But she firmly declined to allow Princess Elizabeth to be patroness of the Jolly Juveniles.

Such public engagements (like other members of the family she now called them 'stunts' in private) continued throughout the summer. But all too often she felt that the press undid her work. She wrote to D'Arcy Osborne, 'I think that half the good of a long slaving day in Birmingham or Manchester is undone by a few paragraphs in the Daily Sketch or Mirror describing my very frequent new dresses and my alterations to this house. Already this year I have done up my sitting room five times, and the number of dresses trimmed with diamonds would keep ten families going for ten years. It is very annoying isn't it? However, we must take the rough with the smooth & keep the old flag flying. Hooray. With kindly & Christian thoughts to ALL, I remain yours sincerely if a trifle sourly Elizabeth.'[59]

They spent a few days at Glamis before going on to Deeside. The Duke had asked his parents if they could rent a house on the Balmoral estate. Eventually the Queen suggested Birkhall. This charming small

---

* Sir Samuel Hoare, second Baronet (1880–1959), Conservative politician, and his wife Lady Maud, née Lygon, daughter of sixth Earl Beauchamp. Hoare was created Viscount Templewood in 1944.

house a few miles from Balmoral Castle had been acquired by Queen Victoria and Prince Albert in 1849 for the Prince of Wales (the future Edward VII), and it proved to be a godsend for the Duke and, even more so, for the Duchess of York. Thanking the King just a few days after they moved there, she wrote, 'I am sure that we are going to love being here, in fact I already feel that I have lived here most of my life.'[60] In the event, that was exactly what she did. Her delight in the place fills a letter she wrote about it to D'Arcy Osborne:

> I must tell you that Scotland just around this house is looking too lovely & beautiful for words of mine to describe. The birches are golden & silver, the river is an angry black & blue, every other tree is scarlet & yellow, & I feel very satisfied every time that I look out of my window. It really is delicious to be able to see so much beauty, & I find it most helpful and calming. This little house is enchanting. It is very small, & lined with caricatures of the 90s,* with extremely comfortable & ugly beds of the late Victorian era, & is badly lit with neo-Edwardian oil lamps, with an ever present smell.[61]

The river was the Muick, which ran through the garden past the house to join the River Dee; she found the rushing sound of the waters very soothing at night.[62] The windows looked on to the wild hillsides of Glen Muick. It was a small house by the standards of most of the places they lived in – certainly compared to Balmoral. There were few bedrooms, so they were unable to have many people to stay, but the Duchess saw this as an advantage. 'It is a very nice feeling to know that one can't have a lot of guests, & it is so much more peaceful.'[63]

Milk, butter and eggs came from a farm near by. The Duchess rose most mornings at 8 o'clock and came home at sundown, weary and, in her phrase, 'terribly contented'. The air was like wine. 'I felt so well at the end of the Autumn that I kept on saying to myself, "My goodness, how well I feel." '[64] She found time to read and that autumn finished *A High Wind in Jamaica* by Richard Hughes, Graham Greene's

---

* These were prints of famous people by the Victorian satirical cartoonists Spy (Leslie Ward) and Ape (Carlo Pellegrini) collected by Sir Dighton Probyn VC (1833–1924), who had lived in the house. He had won the Victoria Cross in the Indian Mutiny of 1857 and was the founder of Probyn's Horse. He was Keeper of the Privy Purse to King Edward VII and Comptroller to Queen Alexandra in her widowhood.

The Man Within, which irritated her,* and a new book by Osbert Sitwell, *The Man Who Lost Himself*, which he had sent her.[65] She had met Sitwell through the well-connected Mrs Ronnie Greville; she enjoyed his wit, his books and his company – over the years he became a good friend.

A few guests did come – Clare and Doris Vyner, the Duke's brother Prince Henry, and King George of Greece.† The pleasure of it all was complete when Lilibet joined them from Glamis; she was 'in seventh heaven' there, the Duchess told Queen Mary.[66]

Before they ended their Scottish holiday they were faced with a major public duty: the first Assembly of the newly united Church of Scotland on 2 October. The Duke had to stand in for his father, who was to have come but was not yet well enough. Once more he and the Duchess stayed in state at Holyroodhouse, and they invited the elderly and frail Lord Davidson of Lambeth, the former Archbishop of Canterbury, who was to speak at the ceremony, to stay with them. Despite gales, torrents of rain and the depressing surroundings of the only hall large enough for the 10,000 people present – 'really a garage', wrote the Duke – it went well. The King wrote a brief line of congratulation to his son on the two speeches he had been obliged to make.[67]

The Duchess also had solo engagements. On 1 October she laid the foundation stone of the Edinburgh Hospital for Crippled Children. On 5 October it was the turn of the Scottish National Monument to David Livingstone at Blantyre. To a plea that Princess Elizabeth might attend the reply came: 'it will be quite impossible for Princess Elizabeth to accompany Her Royal Highness on that occasion, as she is never allowed to take part in public ceremonies.'[68]

---

* *A High Wind in Jamaica* by Richard Hughes was published to great acclaim in 1929; it did away with Victorian sentimental visions of childhood. Set against a tropical landscape and the ever present sea, it told the story of a family of English children who, on the voyage home from Jamaica, fell into the hands of pirates. *The Man Within* was Graham Greene's first novel, published in 1929. The title was taken from a line by Sir Thomas Browne (1605–82), 'There's another man within me that's angry with me.'

† King George II of Greece (1890–1947), Queen Alexandra's great-nephew, succeeded his father Constantine I as King of the Hellenes in 1922, was deposed 1924 and lived in exile at Claridge's Hotel in London until restored to his throne by plebiscite in 1935. During the Second World War he again lived in exile in England from 1940 before returning to Greece in 1946, not long before his death.

Back in England, the autumn work began, with visits for both Duke and Duchess to different areas of London and to Birmingham. For 29 October a day of functions in Eastbourne was planned. They firmly pushed away any suggestions that were too elaborate: no Scottish pipers at luncheon in the Grand Hotel, no giant box of chocolates to be presented for Princess Elizabeth, street decorations provided only they did not put the people of Eastbourne to expense and certainly no mounted escort, because recently in Edinburgh a horse had been alarmed by the enthusiasm of the crowd, and a nasty accident had nearly occurred in front of the Duchess.[69]

The public acquisition of the beautiful Downs and the Beachy Head area near Eastbourne was marked by a ceremony at which the Duke and Duchess unveiled commemorative stones. The afternoon was given over to the Princess Alice Memorial Hospital and the Conference of the British Commercial Gas Association. The Duke put personal emphasis on this because of the interest that he and the Duchess took in industrial questions and the significant part played in industrial life by the Association.

*

AFTER CHRISTMAS 1929 the Yorks left Princess Elizabeth with her grandparents at Sandringham, from where she wrote, 'Darling Mummy, A hapy new year to you and Papa. Wet day. Grandpa cant shoot. I had lovely presents this morning. Will you come back to your darling E.'[70]

In January 1930, the Duke had to go to Rome for the wedding of Crown Prince Umberto of Italy and Princess Marie José of Belgium. The Italians were disappointed that the Duchess did not come, but she was at home suffering from another attack of bronchitis. More importantly, she had discovered that she was pregnant, and had written to her monthly nurse Nannie B to say she would be needed in August. But she hoped to keep it a secret for some time.[71] In the event it was just as well the Duchess stayed at home – the Duke did not enjoy the trip and was relieved his wife had not had to endure it.

Italy was the first country in Europe to abandon liberal democracy. The Italian fascist movement had been founded by a journalist and ex-soldier, Benito Mussolini, in 1919. His Fasci Italiani di Combattimento ('union for struggle') grew through the 1920s. Initially its members were gangs of thugs who terrorized socialists and working-class organizations; the elected authorities were unable to stop their violence. In 1922 the King of Italy felt compelled to ask Mussolini to form a government. The violence ceased. Mussolini gradually created a dictatorship, and gave himself the title Il Duce.

The Duke reported to the Duchess: 'Every station in Italy was covered with the Fascisti & Italian detectives galore, looking for any signs of anti fascist people.' He went on a shoot in which he was expected to kill fallow deer, which he refused to do; to please his chasseur he shot one buck. He saw the Sistine Chapel, which he thought was 'marvellous', but the wedding was the worst-organized ceremony he had ever attended. The delays were endless, there was no singing and the Cardinal seemed 'gaga'. There were 'literally millions' of 'Kings, Queens, ex Ks, ex Qs, ex enemies, ex allies, all mixed up together, to say nothing of ex neutrals'. The only people with whom he could have a decent conversation, he found, were their old friends Paul and Olga of Yugoslavia. Princess Olga – who had had to spend 'goodness knows what' on her clothes – was very envious of the Duchess for having been able to stay at home. 'Thank God there is only one more day now before I start back. I have started to count the hours darling before I see you again . . . All my love to you darling angel.'[72]

No sooner were the Duke and Duchess reunited than, on 7 February 1930, her brother Jock died of pneumonia at the age of forty-three. He was the fourth child that Lady Strathmore had lost and she was distraught; 'He was so loving, so interesting & interested in everything – & this world will be much poorer without him,' she wrote to Beryl Poignand. She worried about his wife Fenella and their four young daughters.[73] Two of them had inherited a mental condition through Fenella's family and needed special care.*

---

* Their first child, Patricia, born in 1916, had died at eleven months. The second, Anne (1917–80), married, first, Viscount Anson in 1938 and, second, Prince George of Denmark in 1950. Diana, the fourth (1923–86), married Peter Somervell in 1960. Their other two daughters, Nerissa (1919–86) and Katherine, born in 1926, inherited a mental condition from which three of their cousins, children of Fenella's sister, also suffered. Their grandfather Lord Clinton paid for the five children to be looked after at a home not far from St Paul's Walden Bury. They later moved to a hospital in Surrey. Their cousin Lady Mary Clayton, daughter of the Duchess of York's sister Rose, described them as 'lovely children . . . like easily frightened does'. She added, 'Though none of these children recognised their mothers they knew each other and used to walk together in the park which interested the doctors very much.' Their aunt Elizabeth sent Nerissa and Katherine presents each year.

The Duchess too was very distressed. 'It was a terrible thing to happen, and even now I can hardly believe that it's true,' she wrote to Nannie B.[74] To D'Arcy Osborne she observed that although Jock could be 'sarcastic & a little difficult to please, he was intensely affectionate, and a really good friend. If I needed good advice I always asked Jock, because though it might not be as palatable as one could wish, it was always right.' She concluded that none of her brothers should live in town – they all loved the countryside too much. 'It kills people in the end if they are parted from the land. It's too strong a thing to understand.'[75] Queen Mary was sympathetic. 'Your poor Mother, my heart aches for her, knowing her love for all her children, & what a devoted family you are, a rare occurrence in these days.'[76]

*

BY APRIL THE Duchess could no longer put off announcing that she would not be carrying out any more engagements that summer. Like most women of the time, pregnancy made her modest. 'My instinct is to hide away in a corner when in this condition, which I know is silly, but I suppose it is a feeling handed down from many generations back,' she told Queen Mary. 'I should really like to live quietly in the country for the last few months, and then reappear afterwards as if nothing had happened!'[77] The Queen agreed.[78]

The Duchess had spent the first three months of the year quietly at Naseby, telling Nannie B in early April that she felt very well indeed, 'touch wood. It is such a long time, nearly 4 years, since little Elizabeth arrived, that I have quite forgotten what it's like!'[79] She and the Duke decided that their second child should be born at Glamis and so, in mid-July, a few weeks before the baby was due, they repaired there. The weather was fine and at first the Duchess enjoyed sitting in the sun, awaiting her time. She seems to have suspected that the baby would be another girl, for she wrote to the Queen on 21 July, 'I will write again soon, and only hope that our new daughter (?) will not delay too long after August 8th.'[80]

By the end of July the weather had turned wet. The Duchess was, she said herself, getting 'slightly irritable' waiting, and longing for 'the whole business' to be over. By now Scotland's remoteness seemed a disadvantage; she thought that the next time she had a baby, she would try to have it in London, in winter, 'as it is much more agreeable for both of us I think, as when one is in the country one misses all the lovely flowers and cadeaux for the baby, & little excitements like that!!' The royal gynaecologist, Sir Henry Simson, was now in attendance, 'and the more he hovers the slower it all seems!'[81]

Simson was assisted by Frank Neon Reynolds, a thirty-five-year-old obstetrician and gynaecologist. He was conscious of the honour of attending upon the Duchess, but, as the waiting extended, he became nervous about all his own patients in London. Invited to lunch at Glamis on Sunday the 27th, he sat next to Lady Strathmore, 'a dear old thing with white hair who absolutely fitted into the picture, even to her Elizabethan collar standing up round the back of her neck'. He liked the Duchess and her 'lovely expression'; she showed him around the Castle. The Duke he found rather shy, 'and it makes one wonder if one is being backward and gauche, but it seems it is the same with everybody.'[82] The following Sunday Sir Henry and Dr Reynolds moved into the Castle so as to be there when labour began. Princess Elizabeth showed Reynolds the stables and her pony, and asked about his own daughter, Petronelle, who was three. The days were long but the evenings were cheerier – they all dined together, talked and played bridge.

The weather on the Duchess's thirtieth birthday was wretched. Queen Mary sent her a clock. Princess Elizabeth gave her a large pot of white heather. The Duchess was sure that the baby would not arrive for another week. But Dr Simson thought it might be earlier and, on his advice, the Home Secretary, John Robert Clynes, former President of the National Union of General and Municipal Workers, was sent for and arrived in Scotland promptly on 5 August. The Strathmores gratefully accepted Lady Airlie's offer to put him up at Airlie Castle, not far from Glamis.

The Duchess was beginning to feel oppressed, writing to Queen Mary that she was sure that everyone had come 'very previous'. She supposed that she would be given 'all sorts of horrid drinks, so as not to keep these foolish people waiting ... and here they all are waiting & hovering like vultures! I <u>shall</u> be glad when they are gone.'[83] The Duke felt the same. 'I shall be very thankful when this is all over, as I find I get very nervous & anxious about everything,' he wrote to his mother. 'I know it is unnecessary & silly but I can't help it.'[84] To add to the tension, the village was swarming with newspapermen all desperately speculating on what was happening, although they were being told absolutely nothing. Frank Reynolds described them as 'sort of waiting with their mouths open for something to drop into them!'[85] The Duke went shooting as much as he could to kill time, his nerves and a few snipe, duck and rabbits. He celebrated the opening of the grouse-shooting season on 12 August by bagging enough for the Castle's dinner that night.

Finally, after about six hours' labour on the night of 21 August, the Duchess was delivered of her second daughter. It was a far easier birth than that of Princess Elizabeth. Frank Reynolds wrote to his wife: 'A very nice baby and everything went smoothly without any trouble.'[86] Lady Strathmore was delighted to tell her son David that this time his sister felt 'wonderfully well; in fact, she can hardly believe she is herself, she feels so different to last time . . . Now she is perky & well & interested in everything.'[87]

The news was immediately telephoned to the King and Queen. The Queen's immediate reaction was to be sorry it was not a boy, but the King said he was glad it was a girl; one could play with girls longer than with boys, and the parents were young and had plenty of time to have a son.[88] Queen Mary was relieved by this response, and sent congratulations to her son.[89] She wondered how Lilibet had taken the arrival of her sister; she need not have worried – the Princess was said to be 'enchanted'.[90] David Bowes Lyon's father-in-law Colonel Spender-Clay, who was staying at Glamis, wrote, 'That wonderful child Elizabeth is very excited & thought first of all that it was a wonderful Dolly & then discovered it was alive. She then took each of the three Doctors by the hand & said "I want to introduce you to my baby sister." '[91]

The doctors in attendance issued an official bulletin stating that 'The Infant Princess is doing fine' – 'doing fine' was a Scottish colloquialism and was used to emphasize the fact that the Princess had been born north of the Tweed.[92] In London the bells of St Paul's pealed in salute and at the Tower of London forty-one guns were fired – twenty-one for the Royal Salute and another twenty on behalf of the Lord Mayor and Corporation. At Glamis itself, the arrival of 'the lassie's bairn' was greeted by an enormous bonfire of larch, spruce and oak branches on Hunter's Hill. It was lit by four small girls with the same torches as had been used to light the fire that had celebrated the wedding of the baby's mother seven years before.[93] According to Lady Strathmore, more than a thousand motor cars full of people came, and as many motorcycles, with people from Edinburgh, Glasgow and even further afield. 'It was most extraordinary.'[94]

The press managed to upset the family by reporting that 'twilight sleep'* was used for the birth. Patrick Hodgson, the Duke's Private Secretary, wrote to the editor of the *Sunday Express* 'to protest emphatically' that such stories were 'absolutely without foundation and have caused Their Royal Highnesses the greatest possible annoyance'. Simson also issued a statement declaring, 'I desire to emphasise the fact, which has been noted in all the Bulletins, namely, that everything was and continues to be absolutely normal.'[95]

Anxious to be closer to their new grandchild, the King and Queen travelled from Sandringham to Balmoral. Rather against his wishes, the Duke left his wife, daughter and new baby to visit them. His mother thought he looked 'pleased & relieved'.[96] He found the discussions at Balmoral a little frustrating and wrote at once to his wife:

> My own darling Angel Elizabeth,
>
> How I hated going away yesterday & leaving you my Angel, & that lovely precious new born baby of ours, to say nothing of our adorable Lilibet. You don't know how happy I am about it all, & how thankful that you my Angel are going on so well & strong. I don't mind at all that it's a girl. I would have liked a boy & you would too I know, but at last Lilibet has a playmate in the nursery. We still have plenty of time, we are still young, though I think in London in the Spring for the next one.

He said that he had been irritated by his father telling him that he should have dealt differently with the press, the doctors and everyone concerned. 'The dear man does not & never will understand the present day Press & I told him so. 30 years ago when we were born things were very different, but he cannot grasp that.'[97]

The reporters outside the Castle gates would have been delighted to learn that the naming of the King's new granddaughter was proving

---

* 'Twilight sleep' was a form of anaesthetic consisting of injections of morphine and scopolamine, used especially to relieve the pain of childbirth. It fell out of favour because it provided inadequate relief and could be dangerous for the baby.

contentious within the family. The Duke and Duchess wanted to call her Ann but, for reasons which were not clear, the King did not like that name. From the start he and the Queen wanted Margaret, 'after Margaret of Scotland, our ancestress'.[98] Without acknowledging that she knew that the King and Queen had this preference, the Duchess wrote to the Queen to thank her for two little pill boxes she had sent her as a present. She went on to report that her baby was 'nice & round & neat I am glad to say. I do hope you will be pleased with her.' Then she broached the name. 'I am very anxious to call her Ann Margaret, as I think that Ann of York sounds pretty, & Elizabeth & Ann go so well together. I wonder what you think? Lots of people have suggested Margaret, but it has no family links really on either side, & besides she will always be getting mixed up with Margaret the nurserymaid.'[99]

The King and Queen were not swayed even by this argument, and the Yorks reluctantly bowed to parental will and decided to call their daughter Margaret Rose instead of Margaret Ann. 'I hope that you will like it,' the Duchess wrote to the Queen.[100] The Duke took Princess Elizabeth to Balmoral and reported to his wife that his parents liked the names. He included a letter which he said Lilibet had dictated:

> Darling Mummie,
>   I miss you very much. I came over the Devil's Elbow [the dangerous pass at Glenshee] & we stopped twice on the way, & arrived here safely at half past four. Grannie & Grandpapa were please to see me & I fed Snip at tea with biscuits. Papa came to see me in my bath & put me to bed in my big little bed. It has no sides & I am very quiet in it.

The Duke added that she was 'very proud of her bed. She is terribly sweet & was in my room the whole evening.' In her own hand the child sent a page of pencilled kisses – half 'For Mummy' and the rest 'For our new baby'.[101]

The Duchess, sitting in a chair in the sunlight at Glamis, wrote back to her husband, 'It's such a lovely day, I do wish you were here duckie.' She told him that she had thought of a new exercise for him – when he returned to Glamis he could 'lug' her around the garden in a bath chair. 'I miss you horribly.'[102] The Duke sent her another letter from Lilibet:

My darling Mummy,

I am looking forward to coming on Saturday to see my Mummy & my baby. I have been missing my Mummy very much indeed. I drove in the carriage to the gate of Birkhall but we did not go in. It has been raining all day & I walked in the puddles this afternoon. Best love to Mummy & Baby Margaret Rose.

Your very loving daughter

LILIBET[103]

There was still the question of where the new baby should be christened. The Duchess was keen for the new Archbishop of Canterbury, her friend Cosmo Lang, who was coming to stay at Balmoral, to perform the ceremony in the family chapel at Glamis. She wanted her daughter to be received into the Church as soon as possible; she worried about taking her on the long journey back to London while still 'a pagan'.[104] Sadly, the official advice was that the established (Presbyterian) Church of Scotland might not view with enthusiasm the senior Anglican prelate performing the christening in Scotland.* The Duchess was upset and she also felt that too much fuss was being made of her second daughter. 'After all,' she explained to Queen Mary, 'the little angel is not of supreme importance at the moment, and I do hate the way that the papers make it of such moment. I always hope & pray that David will marry someone suitable – he ought to have some nice children.'[105]

She wrote to Cosmo Lang to say how disappointed she was that he could not conduct the service quietly at Glamis.[106] Perhaps realizing the Duchess's nervousness about the delay in administering the sacrament, he suggested that when he came to lunch at Glamis, 'if I see the little Princess ... may I be allowed to give her my Blessing – anticipating the Christening which will come later'.[107] The Archbishop did come to lunch at Glamis to bless the new Princess; they agreed

---

* Clive Wigram, the King's Assistant Private Secretary, recorded that when the idea was broached after dinner at Balmoral, he, the King's Private Secretary Lord Stamfordham and Dr Stirton, the Minister at Crathie Church, 'raised a cry of horror. Firstly the Church of Scotland is recognised in Scotland as the C of E is in England ... There might be something in the proposal of her baptism in the C of Scotland ... At the same time we said that there would be an awful outcry in England if the possible heir to the throne was baptized in the C of S. – Should this Princess ever succeed there would be a shout for her Coronation in St Giles.' (Sir Clive Wigram to Lady Wigram, 27 August 1930, copy, RA AEC/GG/6)

that the christening should be at the end of October in the private chapel at Buckingham Palace. The Duchess was still quite weak and she did not move much outside her room until the end of September.[108] When she finally came back south with Margaret Rose she told the Queen, 'It really does take a whole year to have a baby, and I cannot manage much standing yet.'[109]

Princess Margaret Rose's christening took place at 3.15 p.m. on Thursday 30 October. Her godparents were the King's sister Princess Victoria, the Prince of Wales, Princess Ingrid of Sweden,* Rose Leveson-Gower and David Bowes Lyon. The Duchess knew already that her second child had a very different character from her first. She told Archbishop Lang, 'Daughter No. 2 is really very nice, and I am glad to say that she has got large blue eyes and a will of iron, which is all the equipment that a lady needs! And as long as she can disguise her will, & use her eyes, then all will be well.'[110]

*

BY NOVEMBER THE Duchess felt strong enough to resume her public engagements: she attended the reopening of the newly restored St George's Chapel in Windsor Castle on 4 November, the annual sale of war-disabled men's work at the Imperial Institute a week later, and she was again at Queen Mary's side for the Armistice Day service at the Cenotaph. She also went on several shopping expeditions with the Queen – one of the ways in which she fostered good relations with her mother-in-law. They went to Fortnum and Mason, the General Trading Company and favourite antique shops. She and the Queen planned a birthday lunch for the Duke on 14 December, but the day before he was kicked in the leg while out hunting.

He had to have the wound stitched and he was given an antitetanus injection which itself gave him great pain for over a week. He was attended by Dr Varley of 21 Cadogan Place but, like many members of the Royal Family, the Duke believed in homeopathic medicine. The Duchess later came to be convinced by homeopathy but at this stage she seems to have been rather suspicious of it. She wrote to Dr Varley, saying she was ignorant of etiquette but she

---

* The future Queen of Denmark, she was the daughter of King George V's cousin Princess Margaret of Connaught, Crown Princess of Sweden. She married Crown Prince Frederick of Denmark in 1935.

wondered if he would mind if Dr Weir* came and saw the Duke as well. Her husband, she said, 'has great faith in his little homeopathic powders, & Dr Weir is a homeopathic doctor . . . If it is alright, my husband thought that he might look on whilst you are looking at the leg, and then he can swallow down his powders with joy.'[111] She thought that 'the idea even of these little doses will make him feel more cheerful.' Dr Varley raised no objection – he could hardly do otherwise – but neither conventional nor homeopathic treatment produced a quick cure. The Duke continued to suffer considerable pain.

On Christmas Eve they travelled up to Sandringham and that evening – as was their custom – the family celebrated with Christmas tree and presents. 'The children delighted with their toys. Baby Margaret very composed and sweet,' Queen Mary recorded in her diary. Christmas Day was spent as always – church in the morning, presents to the servants after lunch. After tea they went to the ballroom, where the children played.[112] Over the rest of the holiday the Queen, the Duchess and Princess Elizabeth amused themselves by having dancing lessons in the ballroom. The Duchess later wrote to the Queen that 'Lilibet and I miss our evening "hops" very much, & often wish that we were marching or polkaing in the ballroom with you!'[113] Instead they were in Northamptonshire, so that as soon as he was fit enough the Duke could once again indulge his passion for hunting.

*

NINETEEN-THIRTY-ONE opened with the death of the King's eldest sister, the Princess Royal.† 'A bad beginning for a New Year,' he wrote in his diary. 'I feel very depressed.' Only two weeks later, his oldest friend Sir Charles Cust, with whom he had been a naval cadet in 1877, also died. Cust, his equerry for almost forty years, was the only man who could ever contradict and even criticize the King to his face. In March, perhaps worst of all, Lord Stamfordham, the King's Private Secretary, died. The Private Secretary to the monarch fills a position

---

* Sir John Weir (1879–1971), homeopathic doctor who was physician to many members of the Royal Family.

† Louise, Princess Royal, Duchess of Fife (1867–1931). She married in 1889 Alexander Duff, sixth Earl of Fife, who was created duke of Fife by Queen Victoria. He died in 1912.

of immense importance and trust – none more so than Stamfordham. The King's official biographer, Harold Nicolson, later wrote, 'Protective, cautious, imaginative and stimulating had been the guidance which, for more than thirty years, King George had obtained from this wise man. George V was right when he said "He taught me how to be a King." '[114]

That was not the end of it. In April the King was shocked by the latest turmoil in Europe: revolution forced King Alfonso XIII of Spain and Queen Victoria Eugenia, George V's cousin Ena, to flee their country. Ferment and unrest were widespread; monarchies were again under threat. The world, and Europe in particular, was still trying to adjust to the way in which the Great War had destroyed the international economic system. Nations attempted to shore up their struggling economies with protectionism. The indefinite reparations imposed on Germany by the Treaty of Versailles, while understandable, seriously restricted the development of the most powerful economy in Europe. The USA was truly the only engine of growth – it produced almost 40 per cent of the world's coal and more than half its manufactures. When at the end of the 1920s the long American boom seemed to be ending and short-term money became less available, loans to Europe were called back and European businesses began to suffer. The stock market collapse of October 1929 spelled the beginning of the end of American business confidence and of overseas investment. There was a rally in 1930 but then the world fell into slump.

By the summer of 1931 banks began to close their doors across Europe, foreign deposits were withdrawn from London, the collapse of the German mark appeared imminent and a seven-power conference hurriedly called in London failed to reach a solution, largely because France refused to help the Germans. Many Germans became convinced that they had to have a more assertive policy of national self-sufficiency to preserve themselves from total ruin. Prices tumbled all over the world, the burden of national debts rose, world trade declined, markets shrank, foreign exchanges teetered, and financial crashes followed each other with terrifying speed.[115]

Throughout Europe, unemployment rose inexorably. In summer 1931 grim forecasts of a colossal deficit and the need for massive (though temporary) cuts in British government spending, including unemployment benefit, led to a further collapse of confidence. The run on the pound was more like a rout. Ramsay MacDonald's minority government had to obtain hasty loans from Paris and New York. It was clear that it was incapable on its own of dealing with the financial crisis which was engulfing Britain and the world. The government reached the point of collapse on 23 August. Panic spread and there were fears that the entire financial system might disintegrate. The King knew he had to act quickly 'to prevent the old ship running on the rocks'[116] and he encouraged MacDonald and the leaders of the Conservative and Liberal parties to come together to form a national government. They did so and the new administration pledged itself to economies of £78 million including a temporary 10 per cent cut in government wages and in the dole.[117]

The National Government was originally conceived merely as an emergency expedient, but by October 1931 ministers had decided that they needed longer and went to the country asking for a 'doctor's mandate'. On 27 October the government won one of the most sweeping victories in electoral history. The King was overjoyed. 'Please God I shall now have a little peace and less worries,' he wrote.[118] Queen Mary was perhaps more prescient; she thought the majority 'rather too large for internal peace'.[119]

The day after the election the Duke and Duchess went with the King and Queen, the Prince of Wales and Prince George to Drury Lane to see Noël Coward's play Cavalcade. Queen Mary recorded that the house was packed, and that the Royal Family had a wonderful reception; the audience sang the National Anthem at the end.[120]

Very much part of the cultural attempt to overcome the Depression, Cavalcade was a magnificent variety show which evoked the patriotic and progressive values of the Victorian era. It was a remarkable piece of stagecraft – a cast of 400 people were brought up on to the stage on six hydraulic lifts. On the opening night, Coward himself delighted the audience by declaring, 'In spite of the troublous times we are living in, it is still a pretty exciting thing to be English.' Theatregoers loved him for it and the Daily Mail ran the script of Cavalcade as a serial.[121] The Duchess thought it a marvellous pageant, and very moving.[122] Coward later became a firm favourite of hers over many decades.

That autumn the political and economic crisis dominated everything. The King decided to reduce the Civil List, the sum voted by Parliament to meet the official expenses of the Royal Household, by £50,000 a year. The Duke of York gave up hunting and sold his horses,

Lord Strathmore debated whether he should shut up Glamis. 'I really feel rather worried about everything Mama,' the Duchess wrote to the Queen. 'The world is in such a bad way, & we seem to be going from bad to worse here too.'[123] She realized that her engagements had to reflect the difficulties of the times. This applied to private as well as public events – she even worried that the press would find out about a small dance being given for the wedding of Lady May Cambridge, the Queen's niece, to Henry Abel Smith at which Princess Elizabeth was to be a bridesmaid for the first time. 'Not that there is the slightest harm in a small dance, it is only the vulgar way that papers put such items before the public.'[124] In fact the press coverage was kind. *The Times* described the Duchess at the wedding as a smiling and attractive figure in a golden-brown lace frock matched by a fine cloth coat finished with a luxurious roll collar of blue fox fur; the *Telegraph* reported that the most excitement was caused by the appearance of Princess Elizabeth in her bridesmaid's dress of blue velvet with a little Juliet cap.

Both Duke and Duchess found that the deeper the Depression bit the more charities and other organizations needed their support in raising funds, and it was an indication of their growing workload that they had to take on more administrative help. Their office moved from 145 Piccadilly to a rented flat near by. The Duke had appointed Commander Harold Campbell* assistant private secretary in 1929, partly to help with the Duchess's engagements. This relieved the pressure on the Duchess's sole lady in waiting, Lady Helen Graham, who had managed most of her employer's official correspondence since her appointment in 1926.† She was joined by a second lady, Lettice Bowlby,‡ in 1933.

One of the charitable causes strongly supported by both Duke and Duchess was the Housing Association Movement, which aimed to provide affordable housing; it grew strongly in the inter-war years. In December 1931 the Duchess attended a fundraising event for the

---

* Captain Sir Harold Campbell (1888–1969), Assistant Private Secretary and equerry to Duke of York 1929–33, Private Secretary 1933–6, Groom of the Robes and equerry to King George VI 1937–52, Groom of the Robes and equerry to Queen Elizabeth II 1952–4.

† Lady Helen Graham (1879–1945), daughter of fifth Duke of Montrose.

‡ The Hon. Mrs Geoffrey Bowlby (1885–1988), née Annesley, daughter of eleventh Viscount Valentia. Her husband Captain Geoffrey Bowlby was killed in the First World War.

London branches of the movement.* She and the Duke continued to choose their engagements carefully: the Duke, for instance, decided that he should not attend the dinner of the Merchant Taylors' Company 'in view of the state of the country'. As his Private Secretary explained, 'the actions of the Royal Family are very carefully watched by the public, and the Duke feels it might be misunderstood if he attended a City Company's Dinner at a time when unemployment and consequent distress were rife.'[125]

The power of the Duchess's presence was already clear. She acquired a reputation for responding warmly to the lives of ordinary men and women. At the end of 1931 the Mayor of Cardiff pleaded for the Duchess to come on her own for just one day to raise people's spirits.[126] (In the event she made a joint visit with her husband the following spring.) After she opened the Post Office Exhibition of Arts at Mount Pleasant in north London, the organizer reported that hundreds of people had expressed their gratitude to him 'and it seems that Her Royal Highness has captured the hearts of all, men and women alike'; she agreed to become patroness of the Post Office Arts Club.[127]

She took all the hardship inflicted on the country seriously, but she retained her sense of humour and tried to see whatever silver lining there might be. Writing to D'Arcy Osborne in Washington she said, 'This country seems to have settled down to being poor, & everybody is quite cheerful, but only because it is inevitable to change one's circumstances.' Everything was simpler now and 'it is quite fashionable to be sentimental, you may like music – weaker cocktails, less food, & a slight very slender streak of patriotism starting again'. She thought people were less brittle and more serious. 'I forgot to tell you that conversation is becoming the fashion. Isn't it fun – conversation & Beer & eggs instead of Embassy & champagne & twitter.'[128]

*

---

*   The Duchess was patron of the St Marylebone Housing Association; after she had laid the foundation stone of the Association's first block of flats in 1928 the Honorary Secretary commented on the effect on 'what is supposed to be a "Red" neighbourhood. Anything less "Red" than the demonstration on June 9th it would be hard to imagine – yet the Police had asked me if it would be wise to allow Her Royal Highness to visit one of the cottages.' (Letter to Lady Helen Graham, 17 July 1928, RA QEQMH/PS/PS/St Marylebone Housing Association)

AT THE HEIGHT of the economic crisis in 1931 the King offered the Yorks the use of Royal Lodge, a charming and unpretentious house in Windsor Great Park. It was a welcome offer because, now that the Duke had given up his horses, they no longer rented houses in hunt country. Royal Lodge changed their lives and became one of the places the Duchess loved and lived in most for decades to come. Indeed, she died there seventy-one years later.

Royal Lodge had been the country home of the Prince Regent, later King George IV. He chose not to live in Windsor Castle where his father, George III, was confined for his last years of sickness and delusion and where Queen Charlotte and her daughters also lived. The cottage, as it was called, became a favourite residence, and even after he became king in 1820 he continued to use it.

George IV enjoyed grandiose schemes and he asked the architects John Nash and Sir Jeffry Wyatville to expand and improve the house. When the King died in 1830 Wyatville was in the process of building a large banqueting saloon. This room and the small octagonal room adjoining it were the principal features to be retained when most of the house was demolished after the King's death. Thereafter the Lodge was little used until the late 1860s, when it became a grace-and-favour residence, lived in mostly by members of the Royal Household, until the arrival of the Yorks. Alterations and additions had been haphazardly made. The front door was reached only through a long conservatory. Wyatville's splendid saloon with its five bays of tall Gothic windows had been divided into three rather poky rooms and additional rooms built above it. The rest was cramped and poorly maintained.

Queen Mary, ever practical, was at first opposed to her son and daughter-in-law taking on the property. She urged the Duke to turn it down on the grounds that the house was very small, the garden was expensive to keep up, they would be expected to contribute to all the Windsor charities, and they would need a caretaker. In a word, she was concerned that they could not afford it. 'I tender my advice for what it is worth but I believe you will agree with me, both of you.'[129] They did not. They saw past the dilapidation and, like George IV – always a favourite of the Duchess, who called him 'Old Naughty' – they both loved the house at once.

The Duchess wrote to Queen Mary saying that they thought it was 'the most delightful place & the garden quite enchanting, also the little wood'. There were not quite enough bedrooms for the four of them, but they could manage if her husband took one of the small downstairs rooms as his dressing room. 'It would be wonderful for the children, and I am sure that they would be very happy there.'[130] She understood the financial constraints – they had already had to make economies – but she thought they could manage. Thriftily, she told the Queen that to save on carpets they would 'fill up with linoleum'.[131] (Much of that linoleum was still there when she died.) Queen Mary was not displeased that her initial advice had been ignored; once it was clear that they had set their hearts upon it, she entered into the project with enthusiasm.[132]

Inevitably, the more they considered it all, the more work needed to be done. The first thing was to take out the partitions in the big saloon and restore it to Wyatville's intended glory. The floor there turned out to be in bad condition and so they put down parquet. They changed the old kitchen into a dining room, and moved the kitchen towards the back of the house – the Duchess thought that would cut down on the smell of cooking around the house and would allow the staff to be more self-contained.[133]

Having then decided that they should demolish the enormous conservatory and build a new family wing, they found a firm of builders who would do the whole job – largely to the Duke's own designs – including all new bathroom and other fittings for a little over £5,000. As he observed in the history of the house which he later compiled, economic conditions in 1931 were 'not propitious for approaching the Treasury for a grant'.[134] Instead, the Duke proposed to his father that they should go ahead and pay for the work themselves. He hoped his father would approve the scheme.[135] The King did. Dust and debris reigned, but by the end of 1932 the rather gloomy, run-down house had been successfully transformed into a charming and comfortable home.

Their hopes for Royal Lodge, in the words of the Duke's biographer, were that it should be 'their real home', where they could relax, where 'the keynote was to be gaiety and love and laughter; above all a home where their children might grow up with the boon and the blessing of a family life replete with affection and understanding, such as the Duchess had enjoyed, and the Duke had never known'.[136] He might have added that it was to be another St Paul's Walden.

The garden was just as important to them as the house. It offered the Duchess her first chance to indulge the love of gardening she had absorbed from her mother, and it gave the Duke scope to develop his talent for landscaping. He liked being out in all weathers, and would sally forth 'clad in a blue overall and armed with a double edged javelin chopper, clippers and saw' and followed by 'a small army of household servants', supplemented during Ascot week by any available visitors, to help clear the grounds.[137] With the advice of Eric Savill, the Deputy Surveyor of Windsor Parks and Woods, he and the Duchess created what was later described as 'one of the most beautiful smaller gardens in the country'.[138] They replanted and extended the existing garden, bringing in a waterfall and a series of pools to enlarge the rock garden. A woodland area containing many fine old trees was also added, and in this they took special interest and pleasure. Within it they made glades of flowering shrubs and trees and grassy walks interspersed with statues, including one, *Charity*, copied from the original at St Paul's Walden. The Duke loved rhododendrons, about which he became knowledgeable, and planted many new varieties; the Duchess had a special affection for magnolias.

In addition to its echoes of her childhood home, the garden acquired another link with the Duchess's youth: her convalescent soldier friend Ernest Pearce, who in 1935 was unemployed. She offered him a job as gardener at Royal Lodge, where he remained until his death in 1969.* There was also a miniature garden for the little thatched and fully furnished house called Y Bwthyn Bach, which the people of Wales presented to Princess Elizabeth on her sixth birthday in 1932, and which still stands there today. The two Princesses were given the task of looking after its garden.

In 1936 the Duke and Duchess called in the architect and landscape designer Geoffrey Jellicoe, who designed new terraces to link the house more harmoniously with its setting.[139] The garden remained a great source of pleasure to the Duchess throughout her life.

*

---

* Rhododendrons were not Ernest Pearce's favourite plant, however, to judge by the letter he wrote asking for a boiler suit to wear while doing the 'long dirty sticky job' of picking the blooms. 'I have to get right inside some of them . . . and I get in a very dirty mess – much to the annoyance of Mrs P. when it comes to washing day.' (Letter from Ernest Pearce to the Privy Purse, 3 June 1956, RA QEQMH/HH/INDIV/PEARCE)

PREOCCUPIED AS they were by their new home, their public duties continued. In early March 1932 the Duke made an informal industrial tour of Lancashire and later in the month they both went to Cardiff. They were touched by the courage of the unemployed miners and their families and lent their support to fundraising efforts for the Blaina and District Hospital which was perilously short of money. Afterwards the Duchess received a letter from a voluntary social worker in Blaina, thanking her for 'all the immense joy you gave to that sad, disgruntled people. They felt they were forgotten by all the world, & then you came – & a new force of life thrilled thro' them.'[140]

Her involvement in the arts was developing and she was showing an interest in contemporary work. She gave her support, for instance, to the Camargo Society for the Production of Ballet,* and the matinée she attended on 29 February was devised and performed by some of the most exciting artists of the time: she met their Vice-President, Madame Tamara Karsavina, and Lydia Lopokova (wife of the economist John Maynard Keynes), Ninette de Valois and Frederick Ashton.[†] William Walton's *Façade* and Darius Milhaud's *La Création du monde* were performed. Constant Lambert and Alicia Markova were also present. The Duchess was developing her own style, and although her relationship with the King and Queen was never confrontational, her tastes were quite distinct, and in the case of the ballet and art could be considered relatively avant garde. She became an enthusiastic balletomane over the years ahead, and it was a passion that she passed on to Princess Margaret.

Other organizations she supported that spring and early summer included the Royal General Theatrical Fund, the Royal Cancer Hospital, the Child Haven children's home near Brentford, the National Council of Girls' Clubs in Liverpool, and the Forty-Five Churches Fund, through which she was involved in welfare work in east London – a particular interest to her. She paid a visit to Plymouth which had had to be cancelled the year before. In June she and the Duke visited

---

* The Camargo Society, named after Marie Camargo, a renowned eighteenth-century ballerina, was created by ballet lovers in 1930 with the intention of stimulating the idea of a national ballet. It gave a platform to Frederick Ashton, Ninette de Valois and other choreographers. The society staged the first British productions of *Giselle* and *Swan Lake*, Act II. In 1933 its repertoire was incorporated into the Vic-Wells (later the Royal) Ballet.

† Sir Frederick Ashton (1904–88), leading ballet dancer and choreographer. Director of the Royal Ballet 1963–70, he was a friend of Queen Elizabeth till the end of his life.

the Ex-Services Welfare Society in Leatherhead, which provided a home and workshops for those suffering severe mental breakdown as a result of the war. Ex-servicemen and their work always appealed to her and at the end of June she received purses in aid of the Duke of Richmond's Convalescent Home for Discharged Soldiers.

For her birthday that August the King and Queen gave her a shared present with the Duke – it was a Chinese screen for Royal Lodge.[141] She was delighted and thanked the King 'a thousand times for your great kindness'. The bad news, however, was that with her birthday 'I am beginning to feel pretty aged, & today I found TWO GREY HAIRS!! I suppose one must expect this at 32, or shall I pay a visit to my hairdresser, & come out a platinum blonde!'[142] The King had been, as usual, racing his yacht at Cowes and she hoped that sailing had given him 'a rest from the cares of these troubled times'. In a touching and significant statement of her feelings, she thanked him for all that he and the Queen had done for her. 'I was very young & ignorant of the world when I married & had no idea at all of what I would be plunged into – the pitfalls were many; but Bertie was so good, and you & Mama so kind & forgiving of my mistakes that I shall always feel very grateful to you for your understanding & affection. It means so much to me, & it has helped me tremendously. I do hope that you don't mind me saying this – it somehow just came as I wrote.'[143]

This summer they had once more asked the King to lend them Birkhall, rather than have them to stay at Balmoral. The Queen was not happy as she relied on the Yorks to be the most attentive of her children; she professed to be surprised.[144] In the end she and the King did allow them to base themselves at Birkhall – on one condition, that the little Princesses came to stay at Balmoral for a week as well.[145]

Once again Birkhall seduced them and they put off their return to London as long as they could. The Duchess loved the feeling of isolation in the wild, the beauty of the trees and the tumbling river outside her window. 'I am so happy here,' she wrote. 'In fact I am certain that I am a most simple creature and am most ill suited to my present calling. I inherit a hermit complex from my Lyon family side, & the older I get, the more exclusive I feel.'[146] (She probably meant 'reclusive'.)

During their summer in Scotland the Duke and Duchess had visited Glasgow. The horror of unemployment was very clear in all the villages they drove through and she told Queen Mary, 'It was very sad to see the sad & lean faces of the men. I am afraid there is a great deal of misery.' The Depression was indeed causing more and more misery and on 1 November hunger marchers reached London. Both the Duchess and Queen Mary were frustrated that they could not do more to help. The Duchess had her own solution: 'It is the men who need work so much – women do not need employment in the same way – they can be happy when idle, but a man ought to work. I would like to make all the women who have jobs that men could do, give them up. I know that this is impossible, but I wish that it was not.'[147]

Writing to D'Arcy Osborne, she said, 'I am feeling very thwarted at this moment. There is so much to be done in this country, things that I could easily do, but a combination of Press & Precedent make it impossible. And I am quite sure that it is not only useless, but almost dangerous to flout convention. Curse it!' Making the same point as she had to Queen Mary, but in stronger terms, she wrote:

> I cannot see how the older men can ever work again. It is a tragedy, & unless the land can absorb some work & unless some women will give up their jobs, I fear that a lot of men will be workless all their lives. Women can be idle quite happily – they can spend hours trying their hair in new ways, & making last year's black coat into this year's jumper, & all this on 3 cups of tea and some buns. But a man must be seriously busy, & eat meat. Therefore, I think it a crime for women to take jobs that men can do as well.

She added, 'I am writing very wildly I am afraid.'[148]

Her belief that women were automatically less fitted for most jobs than men was outdated, as D'Arcy Osborne pointed out to her in response, even as he sympathized with her 'frustration complex over unemployment & other national affairs'. He suggested ironically, 'perhaps one day you will be able to take things in hand and order the women of the country from the plough and the counting house to their proper place, the home'.[149] In the event, when her day did come she was to praise young women who put their hand to the plough during the Second World War and to give her whole-hearted support to organizations, both civilian and military, which provided work for women. She called herself 'anti-feminist' in 1934,[150] and would still have done so a lifetime later; but her position made her a valuable catch for working women's organizations needing publicity or funds, and she gave patronage and active help to many of these, avoiding only those of 'a political complexion'.[151]

On Christmas Day 1932, for the first time, the King broadcast a message to the Empire, speaking into a microphone installed at Sandringham. The message was relayed widely, including to the congregation in Canterbury Cathedral. Cosmo Lang wrote to the Duchess to say that the worshippers had been deeply moved. 'I suppose hardly any of them had ever heard his voice before.' Dr Lang also congratulated the Yorks on the way they carried out their duties.[152] The Duchess appreciated his 'nice and cheering letter' and told him how much she enjoyed her '(alas) rare' talks with him. She hoped to be able to see him soon. 'Life becomes more complicated daily. I am lucky in having a very happy family life, which, of course, gives one great strength, and I am indeed grateful, as without it, the hurry & rush would be too much to bear.'[153]

Early in the new year of 1933 she left the children with their grandparents at Sandringham. The Queen was, as always, delighted and reported that Princess Margaret 'is a great pickle & does all kinds of things to annoy Papa, tho' she seems to be very fond of him, she thinks it is funny & looks up at him with wicked eyes after she has done it, she is very attractive'.[154]

The Duke and Duchess continued to work on Royal Lodge; she had bought chairs for her bedroom, 'a rather battered but good clock', some china, and other furniture, pictures and chintzes. There were still pungent smells of new paint and fusty carpets which she hoped time and fresh air would banish. They had to put up a shed for garden furniture and build a meat larder. There was time also to relax; they went skating on the lake near by in the Great Park.[155] The next need was for a dog and in summer 1933 the family took delivery of Dookie, the first of a long line of Welsh corgis, supplied by Miss Thelma Evans, of Rozavel Kennels in Reigate.[156]* From now on generations of corgis grew up with the Duchess and her daughters.

The demands of their public life in the early 1930s, as well as those of home and family, were slowly changing their priorities. Days, and

---

* Dookie's kennel name was Rozavel Golden Eagle; when he was sent for training, servants in the house, knowing he was destined to live with the Duke of York, called him Dookie – he learned to respond to that name and so it remained with him.

sometimes evenings too, were filled with public engagements, and their social life shrank in consequence. Often they dined with a few friends and went to see a film or a play afterwards; sometimes they went to the cinema by themselves, but they did not go as often to dances and balls as in earlier years.

There was increasing pressure year by year to involve their children, or at least Princess Elizabeth, in public events. This was a pressure that the Duchess tried to resist, determined to give her children the kind of happy and unfettered life she herself had enjoyed. In 1933 she took on a young Scottish teacher, Marion Crawford, as governess to Princess Elizabeth. Since finishing her two-year teacher-training course at the Moray House Training College in Edinburgh in 1930 Miss Crawford had been governess to the daughter of the Duchess's sister Rose. It is evident from the letter she wrote to the Duchess setting out her qualifications that she had received a good theoretical and practical grounding, and her teacher's certificate, she said, described her as 'Very Promising'.[157] Dermot Morrah, who talked to Marion Crawford for his authorized book on Princess Elizabeth in 1949, described her as attractive and very human, kindly but with 'the high sense of intellectual discipline which is an honourable tradition of Scotland'.[158]

Miss Crawford was invited for a trial visit to the family at Easter, and began teaching Princess Elizabeth in the autumn of 1933; Princess Margaret joined the class in due course. A schoolroom was set up at 145 Piccadilly and lessons were from 9.15 to 12.30 with half an hour's break. The Princesses then lunched with their parents, if they were at home. In the early years at least, there were no more lessons after that; the children spent the afternoons out of doors whenever possible, and at 5.30 they went to their mother in her sitting room for an hour before supper and bedtime.

To judge from Marion Crawford's letters and timetables preserved in the Royal Archives, she was a serious-minded young woman who did her best to give her pupils the kind of solid education, self-discipline and wide-ranging instruction that would enable them to participate intelligently in conversation and make sense of the world around them, rather than to excel academically. That Crawfie, as they called her, remained with the Princesses for the next fifteen years is evidence that she got on well with them and that her efforts satisfied their parents.

The Duchess seems to have been content to leave timetable and curriculum to the governess and intervened very little, except in those respects which echoed her own education. Like her own mother, she wished to teach her daughters Bible stories herself, and they came to her bedroom each morning for this. Like her mother, who had curtailed her lessons and told her governess that health was more important than examinations, she insisted on the children getting plenty of fresh air. Later, when the Princesses were a little older, she copied Lady Strathmore's practice of employing a French 'holiday governess', Georgina Guérin, the daughter of her own governess 'Madé' Lang.* When the Linguaphone Institute wrote offering her their First Course in Latin, a French literary course and a set of French songs for Princess Elizabeth, she ordered only the songs.[159]

As time went by, Marion Crawford did not find the Duchess very supportive; she commented that sometimes 'things are not made easy for me.' Even when Princess Elizabeth was eleven her mother was reluctant to allow a full school day. 'I have been more or less commanded to keep the afternoons as free of "serious" work as possible,' the governess recorded.[160] To her credit Miss Crawford made the best of this, giving the girls lessons as they walked in the garden and devising educational games for them. Not always successfully: she tried giving them a geographical Happy Families to take downstairs after tea, when they went to see their parents, 'but I am afraid if I am not there to play too,' she reported, 'Racing Demon wins the day.'[161]

Worse still, Crawfie's timetables were all too often disrupted by 'distractions like dentists, tailors and hair-dressers who seem very unwilling to come any other time of day than the morning'. When morning swimming lessons were introduced she won her point by persuading the Duchess to allow afternoon lessons in the garden to make up for the lost time. But she complained that her pupils often went to bed too late, so that they missed their morning piano practice and there was much yawning in class.[162]

The governess found an ally in Queen Mary, who took a close interest in the children's education; her replies to the Queen's enquiries reveal the governess's frustrations with her employer.[163] Another

---

* Mlle Guérin came several times in 1935–9; her letters home give a glimpse of life at Birkhall and Balmoral, and reveal that she detested Crawfie. She was succeeded in 1939 by Madame Montaudon Smith, 'Monty', who taught the Princesses in term-time as well, and to whom they were devoted. They also had a German governess, Hanni Davey.

supporter was Owen Morshead, the Royal Librarian, who gave the Princesses regular historical tours of Windsor Castle when they were older. A 1941 letter from Queen Mary to Morshead shows her disapproval of her daughter-in-law's lackadaisical attitude to the Princesses' education. 'Between ourselves,' she wrote, 'I asked nice Miss Crawford about your talks to the Princesses which she is so keen about, she says it is so awkward to fix definite hours or days for these as her dear Majesty constantly wants the children at odd moments, a fatal proceeding when one has lessons to do, & one which the late King & I never indulged in where lessons were concerned!'[164] Morshead shared Queen Mary's view, writing to her later that Miss Crawford was 'apt to feel discouraged about her work from time to time'. He added: 'I will forbear from enlarging on this delicate point, in which I know Your Majesty's feelings are deeply engaged.' However he made clear that he was not impressed that the eighteen books recently ordered for Princess Elizabeth by her mother were all by P. G. Wodehouse.[165]

All this seems to show that the Duchess did not consider it necessary for her daughters to have any more rigorous or extensive an education than she had received herself. Instead, she wanted them to have plenty of fresh air, exercise, fun – and light reading. In academic terms the education she arranged for her children was similar to that given to daughters of aristocratic families at the time, many of whom were still taught at home. But it was, inevitably, an imperfect education, dispensed mostly by a governess whose experience and expertise were narrow. Moreover the Princesses lacked the companionship and stimulation of other children as classmates, although activities outside the schoolroom, such as Madame Vacani's dancing classes and the Girl Guides,* made up for this to some extent.

When it became clear that Princess Elizabeth needed a better training for her future role, her mother followed wise advice in arranging for Henry Marten, the Vice-Provost of Eton, to give her history lessons from 1939. For the first of these tutorials Princess Elizabeth was taken by carriage to Marten's study at Eton, where she sat and listened, surrounded by piles of books on the floor – an unfamiliar sight for her. Later the carriage was sent to bring Marten to

---

* A Girl Guide company was formed at Buckingham Palace, into which friends of the Princesses and daughters of Royal Household staff were enrolled.

the Castle. Marie-Antoinette de Bellaigue, an intelligent and cultivated woman who taught both Princesses European history as well as French from 1942 and remained a trusted friend to them for many years, also helped give them a wider outlook. She felt strongly, however, that their mother took too little interest in their academic education.[166]

What always mattered most for the Duchess was moral and spiritual education, and here her mother's influence ran deep. She brought up her own children in the Christian principles she had learned; her letters to her daughters remind them to be kind, to be thoughtful to others, and to keep their temper and their word.[167] She was also keenly aware of children's sensitivities, and believed encouragement and understanding vital to their development – something that she felt her husband's upbringing had lacked. Among her private papers is a note she wrote for him 'in case of anything happening to me':

1. Be very careful not to ridicule your children or laugh at them. When they say funny things it is usually quite innocent, and if they are silly or 'show off' they should be quietly stopped, & told why afterwards if people are there.
2. Always try & talk very quietly to children. Never shout or frighten them, as otherwise you lose their delightful trust in you.
3. Remember how your father, by shouting at you, & making you feel uncomfortable lost all your real affection. None of his sons are his friends, because he is not understanding & helpful to them.[168]

*

AT CHRISTMAS 1933 Archbishop Lang sent the Duchess another of his annual letters of praise for her public work. She replied hoping that the new year would be 'a happier one for many people in this land, and their happiness will certainly make us happier. One cannot help worrying over the misery & hardship suffered by so many good people, and their courage in facing hardship is the thing that I admire most in them. It is a great example to all of us luxurious minded creatures – not you, but us – I mean!'[169]

Her public commitments continued as usual. On 16 February 1934 she opened the X-ray department of the Marie Curie Hospital in

Hampstead and that evening she and the Duke attended the Jubilee Ball at the Dorchester Hotel of the London Angus Association. Aberdeen Angus cattle were to be a lifelong interest to her, and she felt very much among friends at this gathering.[170] The Toc H League of Women Helpers was an organization in which she took a special interest and she agreed to open their new headquarters, New June, in the City of London, to be dedicated by the founder of Toc H, the Rev. Tubby Clayton, on 21 February. Her friendship with him lasted for years.[171] She continued to work for 'her' hospital, St Mary's Paddington, and many other organizations claimed her time and attention over the next months.

That summer Lady Strathmore was ill again and the Duke suffered acute pain from a poisoned hand, which required surgery. He was out of action for weeks and the Duchess had to make a long-planned trip to Sheffield on her own. The fifth-largest city in the country, Sheffield had a substantial working-class population and had borne the Depression and unemployment bravely. She had a full programme and she was delighted with the warm welcome she received. She visited the Painted Fabrics workshops and the disabled ex-servicemen it employed.* On the way she stopped at the home of one of the workmen, a much decorated but badly injured old soldier, Sergeant 'Taffy' Llewellyn, who was too weak to go to the workshops for her visit. She talked to him, according to the administrator, 'with such perfect understanding, that his poor shattered body and entire system received just the tonic it needed to put up a fresh fight against the terrible depression from which he has been suffering for so many months, and for which the doctor could do nothing'.[172]

Her private account of her visit to the city, in a letter to Osbert Sitwell, was exuberant. She declared, 'It took me three baths and three

---

* In 1935 the enterprise's fundraising campaign in London, essential to give its disabled employees a summer holiday, had been a complete flop owing to the illness of its royal patron, the Princess Royal. They turned to the Duchess for help, asking her to come to a special sale at Claridge's. She hesitated, not wishing to encroach on her sister-in-law's territory. But as her lady in waiting wrote, 'the Duchess of York, having seen the men at work and met their families, is deeply interested and intensely anxious that they should not have to forgo their holidays this year.' She went; the sale raised enough to guarantee the men their holiday, and there was great jubilation, the administrator reported. (Captain Scott to Lettice Bowlby, 19 June 1935, and to Lady Helen Graham, 18 July 1935, RA QEQMH/PS/ENGT/1935/17 July)

days to become clean after my two days in Sheffield – never have I been so dirty. Smoke, steel filings, oil & coal dust all gathered to cast a dusky hue over my person, & five hours on end with the charming and very Labour Lord Mayor completed my rout.'[173]

Later that year she had an artistic diversion. Oswald Birley, one of the most successful painters of the time, was commissioned to paint a group of her friends known to each other (and to no others) as the Windsor Wets' Club. The club had been founded a few years earlier with the Duchess as patroness and it reflected her sense of mischief. The Wets were, in a phrase, a secret group of like-minded tipplers intent on raising their collective spirits. Their motto was *Aqua vitae non aqua pura*. 'The great thing was', she explained many years later, 'that being a SECRET SOCIETY we had to have a secret sign, & this was, to raise the glass to other members without being seen by the disapprovers!'[174] Most of its devotees were members of the Royal Household, and their clandestine association enlivened the tedium of many a Court function.*

The Duchess's chief co-conspirator was Dick Molyneux, the club's Honorary Treasurer, to whom she wrote a spoof letter in June 1931 accepting the post of patroness: 'It is with pride and pleasure that I accept this responsible position, and if the occasion arises, you may rest assured that your Patroness will be with you to the last glass.' They kept up a humorous correspondence about club business, including her suggestion of a club tie with champagne stripes on a claret ground.[175]

In May 1934 the lure of immortality encouraged the Wets to have their portrait painted. The Duchess was also enthusiastic; she had liked Birley's work – he had painted her portrait for one of her regiments, the King's Own Yorkshire Light Infantry. In August that year, when she was staying with the Elphinstones at Gannochy, she wrote to Molyneux – although he was in the same house party – to inform him that:

---

* The roll-call of members, eventually, was the Duke of York, the ninth Earl of Airlie, Sir Reginald Seymour, the ninth Duke of Devonshire, the tenth Duke of Beaufort, the ninth Duke of Rutland, the fifth Earl of Erne, the Hon. Sir Richard Molyneux, the fourth Earl of Eldon, the nineteenth Duke of Norfolk and the third Viscount Halifax (later first Earl); apart from the Duchess there were only two lady members, the Duchess of Beaufort and the Countess of Eldon.

I have decided to make Lady Eldon (spouse of our valued
Secretary) an honorary Lady Member of the Club. And no
interference from you please. It's quite time that I took the reins
again I can see.

   Well, aqua vitae non aqua pura still holds good, & I hope that
you will have a good week here & will live up to the motto of
the Club. Elizabeth (Patroness).[176]

Birley accepted the commission; his excellent and humorous portrait
still hangs at Windsor Castle.[177] It shows a number of the gentlemen
members of the Club sitting and standing around a table laden with
port and wine after dinner at Windsor. Since women were not
supposed to participate in such occasions, the Duchess of York and the
Duchess of Beaufort are present only as portraits on the wall, while
Lady Eldon peers from around a screen; the Duke of York's membership is also signalled by his portrait. 'It was a silly, but most enjoyable
underground movement,' Queen Elizabeth said later, '& we laughed a
lot.'[178]

*

AT THE END of July 1934 the Duchess went to Cowes with the King
and Queen. She looked forward to it. 'I like the feel of yacht racing –
it is very exciting, & very peaceful. No noise, except the creak of the
sails & the water rushing by – & a glow of health after a few days at
sea!!'[179] In the event the weather was poor and she only had one day
racing on *Britannia*;* they spent more time than they expected aboard
the royal yacht, the *Victoria and Albert*.† The Duchess made the best of
it, writing to Osbert Sitwell 'in a little house on the top deck. It has
leather seats, silver fittings and too many tassels to count. Extremely
Edwardian, & of course extremely comfortable. I am looking at a

---

* *Britannia* was King George V's racing yacht, built on the Clyde in 1893 for his father the
Prince of Wales (later King Edward VII). She was a 121.5-foot steel-framed, cutter-rigged yacht
and won many races in the 1890s. King George V inherited *Britannia* and his father's love of
racing, and the yacht continued to compete successfully at Cowes in the inter-war years. She
was scuttled after the King's death in 1936, in accordance with his wishes.

† *Victoria and Albert* was the third of three royal yachts of this name built for Queen Victoria,
launched in 1901. She was used for cruises around Britain and to the Mediterranean by King
Edward VII and King George V; she was replaced in 1953 by the new royal yacht *Britannia*,
named in honour of King George V's racing yacht.

battleship as I write, hundreds of seagulls are crying & <u>nobody</u> bothers me, so I am happy.'[180]

She left Cowes on her thirty-fourth birthday – and that day *Britannia* had a spectacular win, beating her rival *Astra* by twelve seconds.[181] The Duchess wrote to the King to say that she 'would have blown up with excitement!' if she had been there. 'It is very odd, but nothing in the whole year gives me such pleasure as my few days at Cowes, I feel quite different, & <u>so</u> happy ... there is something so exhilarating about the elements, the sea & the wind & the sun, and one feels far away from the horrors of modern civilization with its noise and eternal hurry.'[182]

She and the Duke and their daughters now travelled, as every August, to Scotland where they divided their time between Glamis and Birkhall. It was an idyllic interlude; the girls in particular loved it. They took Princess Margaret for the first time to the Braemar Gathering; this display of Highland Games was a regular engagement for the Royal Family but not one in which many members rejoiced. This year the King escaped it, on grounds of a slight chill. At the end of their holiday the family was as sad as ever to leave Birkhall. The Duchess told the King, 'Lilibet nearly wept when we left the other day.'[183]

However, they were soon caught up in the preparations for the major royal event of the year. In the autumn of 1934 the King's fourth son Prince George, Duke of Kent, became engaged to and married Princess Marina of Greece. The Duchess had discussed this possibility with the Prince himself and with Queen Mary while they were together in Cowes. She told the Queen that she hoped something would come of the idea but 'He <u>must</u> get to know her well, because with his character it would be madness to marry somebody who was not congenial to him.'[184] Before the Duke left to meet the Princess in Yugoslavia in August, he wrote to the Duchess to say that he doubted anything would happen. In the event, he was pleasantly surprised by the beautiful Greek Princess – by the end of the month he was engaged and the Duchess wrote to congratulate him. 'She is so sweet, & so pretty, and do tell her that nobody will welcome her more than her future sister in law ... Darling, Bertie & I, the old married couple, pray that you will both be as happy as we are.'[185]

In mid-September the bride-to-be and her parents, Prince and Princess Nicholas of Greece, accompanied by Prince George, came to Balmoral to meet their future in-laws. The Duchess may well have sympathized with Princess Marina, whose introduction to the Royal Family was, in its way, as daunting as her own had been. Ironically, Princess Marina would have been perfectly at ease with the bevy of royal cousins and aunts gathered at Sandringham to inspect Lady Elizabeth Bowes Lyon in 1923. Lady Elizabeth, on the other hand, would have seen nothing odd in the King and all the male members of his family turning out in kilts to greet her, nor in the Ghillies' Ball to which the Greek visitors were subjected two days later. But they at least 'seemed to enjoy' the ball, as the King noted cautiously in his diary.[186]

The Duchess then arranged for Beryl Poignand to come in to deal with Princess Marina's correspondence. 'Don't forget to make a nice curtsey to Marina, her mother & father, & anybody that should be curtseyed to!' she warned her old friend. 'Practise shaking hands & bending those proud knees of yours. A curtsey in the morning ought to get you through the day!' But of course, she added, 'this doesn't apply to you & me. It's only for other members of the Royal family ... Au revoir and sharpen up the old pencil. Your loving E.'[187]

Most of the important members of the remaining royal houses in Europe came to London for the wedding on 29 November 1934. At the first 'family' dinner, for seventy-five, the Duchess sat between Prince Charles of Sweden and Prince Nicholas of Greece, the father of the bride. Her old friend Prince Paul of Yugoslavia was also at her table. Another guest was Princess Marina's thirteen-year-old cousin Prince Philip of Greece, who was at school at Gordonstoun. The next night the King and Queen gave a party for 800 people at the Palace.

The wedding day was overcast but fortunately there was no fog as had been feared and the marriage was clearly popular. Princess Elizabeth was again an excited bridesmaid. The four-year-old Princess Margaret was keen to go to the wedding too; the King and Queen agreed on condition that the Duchess could 'really guarantee that Margaret will behave like an angel & that you will keep her near you'.[188] The Duchess complied. She wore what *The Times* called 'an unusual shade of japonica-pink velvet. The coat had a collar of blue fox fur and wide sleeves drawn into a band at the cuffs. Her close fitting hat had two tufts of shaded pink feathers at the side.'[189] She led Princess Margaret, who was wearing a cream satin coat and bonnet trimmed with narrow bands of beaver, by the hand into the Abbey. The Princess sat on a stool at her mother's feet and, according to her grandfather, Lord Strathmore, she was 'as good as gold' during the service.[190] The *Daily Telegraph* recorded that when her sister appeared, holding the train, only a few feet from her, Princess Margaret waved to attract her attention, whereupon Princess Elizabeth gave her a stern look and shook her head. 'Thenceforth all exuberance was quelled.'[191]

★

DURING 1935 THE Duke and Duchess of Kent began to play an active part in public life, which relieved the pressure upon the Prince of Wales and the Yorks. This was welcome to them all, because it was an especially busy year, the year of the King's Silver Jubilee. The Duchess of York's files show her turning down as many engagements as she accepted. She rejected most charitable film premieres because she believed that they did more for the film companies than for the charities. She was firm about where she wanted to go and what she would do, but flexible and generous in her approach to the people on the ground, and ready to change dates or times to suit them. Charity organizers were often pleasantly surprised by her willingness to shake more hands and spend more time than expected, because she knew the pleasure it gave.

The King and Queen asked them to attend more functions at Court than usual this year, but both she and the Duke much preferred their relatively independent public work with their own patronages and charities to the predictable and repetitive formalities of Court life. The Duchess scored a small but important victory in this respect by writing the King a cleverly worded letter asking him to allow her to accept the honorary colonelcy of the London Scottish Regiment. If he agreed, she said, 'I promise you that I should behave very quietly and not traipse about Hyde Park in a grey kilt!'[192] She pointed out that the Scots so easily felt left out and she would be sorry if she had to cancel her attendance at the regiment's annual prize-giving and concert in order to attend a Court. As usual her charm worked – the King gave way to her on both issues.

The Jubilee was a much greater success than anyone, in particular the King, had dared to hope. Indeed it was in every way a vindication of the King's low-key but steadfast approach to his task, his devotion to his duty, his acceptance of political change and his strategy of reaching out to his people.

On 6 May, the actual anniversary of the King's accession, the four

Yorks led the royal carriage procession to St Paul's for the thanksgiving service. The King wrote in his diary, 'A never to be forgotten day, when we celebrated our Silver Jubilee. It was a glorious summer's day 75° in the shade. The greatest number of people in the streets that I have ever seen in my life, the enthusiasm was indeed most touching.' After returning to Buckingham Palace he was gratified to be cheered by an enormous crowd. 'By only one post in morning I received 610 letters. At 8.0 I broadcast a message of thanks to the Empire. After dinner we went out on the balcony again & there must have been 100,000 people.'[193]

Every night that week, the King and Queen appeared on the Buckingham Palace balcony and every night it was the same. Every day he and the Queen were driven in an open coach through London. In all the poorest areas – Lambeth, Whitechapel, Battersea, Kennington, Limehouse – they were greeted by rapturous crowds. Hordes of children waving flags and shouting, their parents smiling, laughing and clapping, greeted the dignified elderly couple everywhere. Houses were exuberantly decorated with streamers, flags and bunting and the King remarked in his diary that all this decoration had been put up 'by the poor'. The King's official biographer, Harold Nicolson, noted later that students of mass behaviour were 'fascinated and perplexed' by this popular rejoicing. Among the reasons he gave were deep affection for the King, pride that Britain's monarchy, unlike so many others, had survived, reverence for the Crown as a symbol of patriotism, and more. 'Comfort in the realization that here was a strong benevolent patriarch personifying the highest standards of the race. Gratitude to a man who by his probity had earned the esteem of the whole world.'[194]

Dedicated left-wingers like the distinguished radical sociologist Beatrice Webb disliked what they saw. More flexible ones rejoiced. George Orwell suggested that it was possible to see in the expressions of loyalty 'the survival, or recrudescence, of an idea almost as old as history, the idea of the King and the common people being in some sort of alliance against the upper classes.'[195] The Jubilee gave a great fillip to thousands of charities which launched Jubilee appeals and enlisted different members of the Royal Family in their causes. The King's Fund sold £11,000 worth of seats at Jubilee processions. Canada raised £250,000 for a Silver Jubilee Cancer Fund within weeks of its being launched. All over the Empire Jubilee contributions came pouring in.[196] The King was surprised and moved by it all. After one happy drive through the East End, he said to his nurse Sister Black, 'I'd no idea they felt like that about me . . . I am beginning to think they must really like me for myself.'[197]

The Yorks played their part in the celebrations. On 9 May they went with the rest of the family to Westminster Hall where the King received loyal addresses. There were 2,000 people there – they sang the National Anthem robustly and cheered wildly. The next night the Duke and Duchess took the night train to Edinburgh to assist in Scotland's own Jubilee festivities.

The celebrations continued until early June. On the 8th (the day after Ramsay MacDonald resigned as prime minister on grounds of health, and Stanley Baldwin was sworn in) the King and Queen made the last of their triumphal drives around London. The emotion and enthusiasm engendered by such an event as the Jubilee produce many monuments. One of the most important from 1935 was King George's Jubilee Trust, a national appeal headed by the Prince of Wales to 'promote the welfare of the younger generation'. A total of £1 million was quickly raised and distributed between existing youth organizations and the Boy Scouts and Girl Guides.

Soon after the Jubilee Trust was launched, *Punch* published a cartoon of a man in uniform looking angry as he read in the *Daily Mail* the news of the 'King's Call to Youth' and saying, 'I thought I had the best youth movement in Europe, but I begin to think I am mistaken.' The uniformed man was Adolf Hitler.[198]

*

THROUGHOUT MOST of the 'long weekend', successive British governments of the early 1930s had encouraged the people to believe that another appalling war could be best avoided by the magic of collective security. The League of Nations, created with great optimism in 1919, was portrayed by most people as by far the best hope of avoiding the cataclysm of war. Mutual restraint and the spirit of co-operation under the aegis of international law were offered as the best deterrents to aggressors. Such hopes were completely understandable given the horrors of 1914–18 but, after the rise of the dictators, less and less realistic. In Britain governments and most people believed that, after Passchendaele and the Somme, no one would ever wish to go to war again. They failed to reckon with the fascist mentality, which derived an entirely different lesson from the Great War – that their countries had not been ruthless enough.

In September 1930 the German people, terrified by the economic crisis and the threat of runaway inflation, awarded Hitler's National Socialist Party 107 seats in the Reichstag. In January 1933 Hitler was invited to form a national government and the Reichstag fire a few weeks later gave him an excuse to arrest all communist deputies; that summer he asserted that Nazism was now the only legitimate force in Germany. His dictatorship was established. In March 1935, he defied the Treaty of Versailles by introducing conscription. As Harold Nicolson put it, 'to attentive ears there came, in the last months of George V's life, the distant grumble of the thunder of a second war.'[199] But not everyone wished to hear it and those, like Winston Churchill, who heard it most clearly were often denounced as selfish warmongers.

Soon after Hitler seized total power, Käthe Kübler, who had been the Duchess's governess at Glamis from 1913 until the outbreak of war in 1914, had written to her former pupil protesting that the British press was horribly biased against Herr Hitler and assuring her that the stories attacking him were completely untrue.[200] No reply from the Duchess has been found, but Fräulein Kübler may have come to regret her pro-Hitler views. Queen Elizabeth said later, 'She was the headmistress of a big school in Munich and then those horrible Nazis discovered she was a Jew and she was out in a day. She was sacked.'[201]*

More influential with the Duchess was undoubtedly her friend D'Arcy Osborne, still at the British Embassy in Washington. By early 1934 he was increasingly alarmed by the breakdown of democracy and the rise of authoritarianism in Europe. Nazism appalled him: 'what a nauseating and ridiculous affair it all is with its spurious Aryanism and its Germanic theology.' He evidently shared the Duchess's misgivings about Germany. 'Apparently the Germans are miserable unless they can be drilled and driven like a mob of halfwits. I would dearly like to wipe Germany and Japan off the map of the world with two neat

---

* After the abdication Käthe Kübler wrote to the Duchess, now Queen, saying she would like to come to see her, and asking permission to dedicate her memoirs to her. She did come, and took tea with the Queen on 13 October 1937. Her book, *Meine Schülerin, die Königin von England*, was published that year.

smudges of the thumb and I am sure we would all be a lot better off.'[202] In another letter he asked if she was as depressed about the world as he was. 'What are we going to do to stop the Germans from planning and making a new war in their own good time?'[203]

On this matter the Duchess and the King were not far apart. George V had always distrusted and disliked both Mussolini and the Nazis. He talked of 'those horrid fellows, Goering and Goebbels'. He detested the Nazis' Jew-baiting and the brutality with which the fascists achieved power. In April 1934 he warned the German Ambassador that his country's massive rearmament was threatening Europe with war and 'ridiculed' the Ambassador's explanation.[204] In September 1934 the British Ambassador to Berlin, Sir Eric Phipps, wrote to the King predicting that the regime would not change – 'The Nazis have their hands on every lever now; besides, and this also is important, large numbers of Germans regard Hitler with a species of mystic adoration: some pick up the earth upon which he treads to keep as a precious souvenir.'[205]*

The King understood. A few months later, in January 1935, his Private Secretary Sir Clive Wigram wrote to the Ambassador saying the King felt that 'we must not be blinded by the apparent sweet reasonableness of the Germans, but be wary and not taken unawares.'[206] But, like millions of his subjects, the King dreaded the prospect of another war. In May 1935 he told Lloyd George, 'I will not have another war. *I will not.* The last one was none of my doing and if there is another one and we are threatened with being brought into it, I will go to Trafalgar Square and wave a red flag myself sooner than allow this country to be brought in.'[207]

As the joy of the Jubilee celebrations faded, the King and his government were compelled to spend more and more time contemplating the threats from the dictators. In October 1935, deriding the notions of collective security and international law, Mussolini declared war on and invaded Abyssinia.† The King was more concerned about

---

* Phipps recounted also how Mrs Greville, the Yorks' friend and benefactor, had sought an appointment with Hitler while a guest of the German government in Nuremberg. A short meeting had been arranged with some difficulty. 'Mrs Greville was, it seems, delighted.'

† This attack by Italian forces on the Ethiopian Empire – also known as Abyssinia – began the Second Italo-Abyssinian War (October 1935–May 1936). Abyssinia never surrendered but it was annexed into the newly created colony of Italian East Africa. The crisis demonstrated the ineffectiveness of the League. Both Italy and Abyssinia were member nations and yet the

the future than ever; he repeatedly consulted the new Foreign Secretary, Sir Samuel Hoare, who later wrote, 'I believe that it was the
anxieties of Abyssinia, coming as they did on the top of the Silver
Jubilee celebrations, that killed the King.'[208]

★

ON 6 NOVEMBER Prince Henry, Duke of Gloucester, was to be married
to Lady Alice Montagu-Douglas-Scott, who became one of the most
dedicated and beloved members of the Royal Family. She was the
sister of the Duchess's girlhood friend Mida (Lady Margaret Ida
Montagu-Douglas-Scott). The two Princesses were to be bridesmaids.
The bride and maids were dressed by Norman Hartnell; and the
Duchess took her daughters to his shop for a fitting. 'I noticed then,
for the first time,' Hartnell wrote in his memoirs, 'the intentionally
measured and deliberate pace of Royal ladies. With lovely smile and
gracious movement the Duchess of York acknowledged on either side
the reverences of the women present and very slowly moved on and
out of sight.'[209] She liked Hartnell's ideas and he subsequently became
one of her most important dress designers. Alice Scott's father, the
Duke of Buccleuch, died shortly before the wedding; instead of
postponing the ceremony, the families decided that it should take place
privately in the chapel at Buckingham Palace. 'Now all the children
are married but David,' the King recorded laconically in his diary.[210]

On 29 November the Duke and Duchess of York left London on
the Golden Arrow for Paris. There they were to attend the annual
banquet of the Caledonian Society of France, which wanted to make a
special Silver Jubilee occasion of its annual dinner on St Andrew's
Day.[211] They had accepted on condition that there was no general
election taking place in Britain at that time and that the political
situation in France was quiet.[212]

In the event the expected election had taken place on 14 November
– the National Government, led by Stanley Baldwin, was returned. As
for the French political situation, the British Ambassador, Sir George
Clerk, advised that Prime Minister Laval might well fall before the end
of November, but that this would not necessitate cancelling the visit.
'The only doubt that would arise would be if the Italo-Abyssinian

League was unable to control Italy or to protect Abyssinia. Italy's invasion was accepted by
Britain and France because they sought to retain Italy as an ally in case of war with Germany.

situation leads to fresh unjustifiable attacks upon our policy in the French press, and Anglophobia shows its head again.' He would watch out for this.[213]

In Paris they stayed at the British Embassy, and had a full three-day programme. The Duchess had time to order some dresses from Lanvin. Afterwards the Ambassador reported to the King through Sir Clive Wigram on the success of the visit. Sir George was loud in his praise of the Duke. 'Such contacts with our Royal Family do an immense amount of good and I personally have every reason to be grateful, for they are a real help to me in my work . . . The Duchess was of course her charming self, and won every heart. To you, who know her, I need not, and indeed I cannot say more.'[214]

The visit encouraged the Duchess in her somewhat wry love for France. She gave her friend D'Arcy Osborne a vivid description of its high points. She was particularly struck when at one dinner an 'enormous' Frenchman:

> practically sank on to his knees beside me, & gurgled 'If only we had people like you both in France' etc etc whilst I pretended that it was quite O.K. to have a Huge Frenchman with a Légion d'Honneur in his buttonhole kneeling violently beside one. They don't mean a word they say, but they are so nice, & so nasty. I like their sense of humour – it's so delicious, & yet, how can one trust them? They are so unsentimental when it comes to politics, & horribly straight seeing. What do you think of them?[215]

They returned to London on 2 December, a sad night – the King's beloved sister Princess Victoria died at Coppins. The King was grief-stricken – they had supported each other through every year and talked to each other every day. For once he allowed his personal feelings to come before his duty and cancelled the state opening of Parliament due to take place later that day – he simply felt he could not endure this very public occasion while assailed with such sorrow.[216]

By the middle of December, the Duchess had come down with a serious attack of flu while at Royal Lodge. Her daughters were upset, and Princess Margaret wrote to her from London, 'Darling Mummy, I hope you are better today. You must be better for Xmas. When will the doctor let you come to LONDON? XXXXXX.'[217] Her doctors were in fact very concerned; the influenza developed into pneumonia and her temperature soared to 103 degrees. There was no question of her being able to go to London, let alone Sandringham, for Christmas. The two Princesses travelled to Norfolk with the King and Queen on 21 December and the rest of the family, including the Prince of Wales, the Kents and their new baby Edward and the Gloucesters, and other guests arrived on Christmas Eve.

The Duke and Duchess had to spend Christmas at Royal Lodge, separated from their children. While she stayed in bed, he worked in the garden, moving many of the rhododendron bushes. The children's nurse Alah Knight, Jean Bruce, a lady in waiting to Queen Mary, and others at Sandringham kept the Duchess informed about the children and the Duchess and her daughters wrote each other cheerful letters. According to Jean Bruce, Princess Margaret sat through a long sermon 'looking adorable and minute' between Queen Mary and Lord Athlone.[218] Alah took them to see the King in his room every morning at 9.15 and they saw him again at teatime. Both girls had fun playing in a snow storm, dressed in their new pink coats and velvet hats.[219]

The Duchess wrote to Princess Elizabeth saying she hoped she was having a lovely time and being very polite to everybody. 'Mind you answer very nicely when you are asked questions, even though they may be silly ones . . . Give Margaret some GREAT BIG KISSES from me, and a great many to your darling self. Good bye angel, from your very loving Mummy.'[220] Princess Margaret wrote, 'I hope you will be better tomorrow. And ask the doctor to let you come. It is all white mist out and you cannot see. We have millions of cards. We made a lovely Xmas tree – lots of things on it. I love your letter.'[221] The Duchess sent Princess Elizabeth news of their corgi, Dookie, and said that as soon as she was better she would come to Sandringham '& I shall give you and Margaret such an ENORMOUS HUG, that you will be quite squashed.'[222]

She wrote to Queen Mary to say how absurd it seemed to be spending Christmas in bed, '& poor Bertie ploughing through a turkey all by himself poor darling'.[223] To the King, she sent an affectionate end-of-year letter recalling the joy of his Jubilee celebrations; she must have been feeling better because she ended it with a joke, 'Have you heard what the Abyssinian soldier said about Mussolini? "He is my enema the Douche."'[224] In continued good humour she wrote to her fellow Windsor Wet Dick Molyneux:

I am much better, but the doctor told me this morning that I can't get up just yet. It is too sickening, but apparently I've had that old fashioned flu that has pneumonia with it, and it's very slow to get rid of. I expect that when I am well again I shall be VERY well. Oh Boy. Well, be good if you can, which I doubt, and I should stay away from Abyssinia if I were you just for a bit. I know it's very tempting, but make it one of your New Year resolutions & stick to it. I couldn't give you better advice – remember what happened last time. A very happy New Year to you from your suffering President Elizabeth.[225]

The King was not able to go shooting any more; he could manage only short walks to the stables and the stud – even then he constantly had to pause to take his breath. He made his Christmas broadcast with considerable difficulty. The Royal Librarian, Owen Morshead, who was at Sandringham, wrote to his wife, 'I didn't like his colour at all, and gather that his circulation is bad. In fact I believe the machine is worn out, and I seriously doubt if we shall ever come here again . . . Poor dear man; he was ever so friendly and kind, but clearly tired out.'[226] Only his grandchildren now seemed to rouse his interest. 'Saw my Kent grandson in the bath,' he recorded.[227] He gave Princess Margaret a silver box that had belonged to Princess Victoria. After thanking him nicely, Princess Margaret said, 'Grandpapa I've got such a good idea – if you filled the box with chocolates I could eat them in the morning when I wake up.'[228]

By Thursday 16 January the King's condition was worse; he wrote in his diary that he 'didn't feel very grand'.[229] The Queen was worried and sent at once for the Duke of York. The Duchess was still feeling wretched but she agreed he must go that afternoon. The Duke did not yet understand the full seriousness of his father's condition. Travelling up to Sandringham by train, he met Tommy Lascelles, who had just been appointed assistant private secretary to the King. Lascelles wrote to his wife that the Duke was 'very amiable . . . I thought him much changed for the better since I last saw him 8 years ago.'[230] Over the next few days Lascelles became much less cheerful about the behaviour and attitudes of the Prince of Wales; indeed, his misgivings about the Prince, which had led to his resignation from his staff in 1928, were reinforced.[231]

When the Duke arrived at Sandringham he found Queen Mary

presiding over tea while a large company, including his children, played a game of Happy Families. He realized now how ill his father was and how remarkably calmly and bravely his mother was facing the end. The Duchess was still not well enough to travel to Sandringham, and she wrote to the Queen, 'I must send you one little line to tell you that I am thinking & praying for you & Papa all the time. I cannot think of anything else, my life has been so bound up with yours the last twelve years, and I cannot bear to think of your anxiety.'[232]

On Saturday the guests left – the little Princesses were taken back to their mother at Royal Lodge. The first bulletin about the King's ill health was issued. Sandringham was at once besieged by reporters and photographers. 'Too heartless,' commented the Queen.[233] Emotion ran through the house with the Prince of Wales seeming particularly distraught, though he was less close to his father than the other siblings. On Monday 20 January the King held in his bedroom a last meeting of his Privy Counsellors to set up a Council of State to act on his behalf. With great difficulty he spoke his assent and signed what looked something like GR on the document. As the Counsellors left he smiled at them – many were in tears. That night another bulletin was read on the BBC: 'The King's life is moving peacefully to its close.'

Just before the end, according to Lord Wigram, the Prince of Wales 'became hysterical, cried loudly and kept on embracing the Queen'.[234] 'His emotion was frantic and unreasonable', according to Helen Hardinge.[235] At the moment her husband died, Queen Mary turned to her eldest son and kissed the hand of her new king, Edward VIII. In her diary she wrote of King George V: 'The sunset of his death tinged the whole world's sky.'[236]

She was not wrong. King George had been widely and greatly loved. The next day's newspapers appeared with heavy black borders; all broadcasting was cancelled, theatres and cinemas were closed. Millions of people across the land went to church to pray.

The following day, Wednesday 22 January, the Duchess was at last well enough to travel to Sandringham. The whole family was now there. On Thursday the 23rd the coffin was taken by train from Wolferton station to London; all the way, people stood bareheaded by the track and on the hills above it, watching the King on his last journey. From King's Cross, King Edward and his brothers followed their father's coffin on foot to Westminster Hall. The coffin was enfolded in the Royal Standard and on top of it was fixed the Imperial Crown. As the procession turned into the Palace of Westminster, the jewelled Maltese cross on the top of the crown was shaken loose and tumbled into the gutter. The officer in charge of the bearer party picked it up. 'A most terrible omen,' Harold Nicolson thought.[237]

As relations and other dignitaries arrived for the funeral, almost a million men and women passed silently by the coffin in the dim and misty Westminster Hall. At midnight on 27 January, the eve of the funeral, the King and his three brothers stood guard over the coffin for twenty minutes in dim candlelight – 'a very touching thought', their mother recorded.[238]

The next day the Queen described as 'a terrible day of sadness for us'. The coffin was drawn on its gun carriage to Paddington station 'through wonderful crowds of sorrowing people mourning their dear King'. It was then carried by train to Windsor, past thousands upon thousands of people lining the track, and then taken through more throngs of mourners into the Castle and St George's Chapel. After the funeral service, attended by many kings and heads of state from a Europe teetering again on the edge of horror, King George was laid to rest. Queen Mary wrote, 'We left him sadly, lying with his ancestors in the vault. We returned to London by train & got home by 3.30.'[239]

Over the next few weeks the Duke and Duchess and other members of the family were constantly with the Queen, whose dignity and strength throughout moved everyone. Like other members of the family, the Duchess received and replied to many letters of sympathy. Arthur Penn was sure she felt the loss, 'but if anything can cheer you, I think it may well be the knowledge that nothing can have added so much to the happiness of the King's later years [as] his first daughter in law'.[240]

Schoolchildren all over the world wrote to Queen Mary and other members of the family. Messages from African chiefs and Tibetan lamas were widely and, it should be said, gratefully read. The poets did their best. Edmund Blunden penned an elegy in *The Times*. The Poet Laureate, John Masefield, cabled his tribute to the King from Los Angeles, praising 'His courage and his kindness and his grace'. More evocative of the past and perhaps more prescient of the uncertain future was the young John Betjeman:

Spirits of well-shot woodcock, partridge, snipe
Flutter and bear him up the Norfolk sky:
In that red house in a red mahogany book-case
The stamp collection waits with mounts long dry.
The big blue eyes are shut that saw wrong clothing
And favourite fields and coverts from a horse;
Old men in country houses hear clocks ticking
Over thick carpets with a deadened force;
Old men who never cheated, never doubted,
Communicated monthly, sit and stare
At a red suburb ruled by Mrs Simpson,
Where a young man lands hatless from the air.[241]

CHAPTER TEN

ABDICATION

1936–1937

'We are not afraid'

NINETEEN-THIRTY-SIX was one of the unhappiest years of the Duchess's life. She began it in bed with pneumonia and ended it ill again, with the virulent influenza that attacked her so frequently. She began it as the daughter-in-law of King George V and she ended it, to her astonishment and dismay, as Queen Consort to King George VI. The abdication of King Edward VIII was the most serious constitutional crisis affecting the British monarchy since the seventeenth century. There were many, and they included the Duchess of York and her husband, who feared that the institution might not survive it.

King Edward VIII came to the throne on a wave of public enthusiasm. He was a hugely popular figure of whom much was expected, and he was widely seen as a talented, exuberant and sympathetic young man who could bridge the gap between generations. People thought that as an ex-serviceman he would be able to relate to the needs of former soldiers. His travels, much wider than those of any previous Prince of Wales, would give him a special understanding of the lands of the Empire and those beyond. He would be as steadfast as his father but more up to date, more flexible.

At first he enjoyed extra sympathy because it was clear to everyone that, as an unmarried and childless man, his difficult job would also be a very lonely one. During the interment of King George V in St George's Chapel, Lady Helen Graham, the Duchess of York's lady in waiting, looked at the new King and said to the member of the Royal Household beside her, 'I feel so sorry for him. *He* is not going home to a wife behind the tea pot and a warm fire, with his children making toast for him.'[1] A similar fear was expressed by Chips Channon, who wrote that his heart went out to King Edward 'as he will mind so terribly being King. His loneliness, his seclusion, his isolation will be almost more than his highly strung and unimaginative nature can bear.'[2]

*

As HEIR TO the throne, the Prince of Wales had had a long and not always easy apprenticeship. But he had perhaps suffered less than his younger brother Prince Albert from their father's hypercritical attitude, being more obviously attuned to the demands of public life and not having to endure the terror of a crippling stammer.

The Prince of Wales joined the Grenadier Guards just before the outbreak of war in 1914; he had a 'good war', insisting that he be allowed to serve on the Western Front, but was chagrined that he was not allowed to fight in the trenches. The war over, he embarked on what was perhaps the finest public period of his life – a series of overseas tours in which his youth, his looks and his charm captivated hearts and strengthened links across the Empire. He was particularly gifted at reaching out to veterans. Lloyd George called him 'our greatest ambassador' and even his father wrote a rare letter of unqualified praise.[3] However, the Prince made clear from early on that he found many of his official duties irksome. Lloyd George warned the Prince that if he was to be a constitutional monarch he must first be a constitutional Prince of Wales. The King was more severe and saw in his son's insouciance a lack of respect for manners and morals which he believed would damage if not destroy the monarchy.

The Prince had always had a much more 'modern' point of view. He enjoyed throughout the 1920s and early 1930s a more fashionable, and perhaps cynical, world, a society in which the colour of fingernails, the length of skirts and the height of heels were more important than middle-class virtues. In this he was quite unlike his younger brother Bertie. Nonetheless the two brothers were close and the Duchess of York loved the Prince's rather 'naughty' company; their letters to each other testify to the affection that developed between them from the moment of her engagement to the Duke. During the early 1930s, however, the Prince's lifestyle contrasted more and more sharply with that of the Yorks. While the Yorks lived in domestic bliss, the Prince of Wales was a man about town. He took up flying, he summered on the Riviera rather than on Deeside, he spent many long evenings entertaining his friends in chic London nightclubs.

His favourite home was Fort Belvedere, which he had been granted by the King in 1929, just down the road from Royal Lodge. The Fort was a folly, a little Georgian eye-catcher at the southern end of Windsor Great Park, close to Virginia Water. It was, according to Diana Cooper, 'a child's idea of a fort' with its castellated walls and tower.[4] In this sense it was the complete opposite of Windsor Castle, the greatest castle in the land. Under the Prince of Wales's stewardship, the Fort became something of a byword (not in the press, of course, but among those who knew) for fun. There the Prince and his guests could relax and enjoy themselves with little protocol.[5]

His parents dearly wanted him to marry and to have children. But the Prince was more interested in liaisons than in wedlock. During the 1920s and early 1930s, instead of searching for a bride who could eventually bring lustre to the throne, the Prince indulged in a series of affairs with married women, interspersed with many shorter relationships. The most durable of his romances were with Freda Dudley Ward, the MP's wife who became the principal object of his affection from 1918, and then with Thelma Furness, twin sister of Gloria Vanderbilt, a pretty and gay creature who, like the Prince, enjoyed simple if not superficial pleasures.[6] The Yorks liked Thelma Furness and the two couples often spent time together, particularly over weekends at Fort Belvedere or Royal Lodge.

One winter weekend in January 1933, the Yorks went skating near the Fort with the Prince and Thelma Furness. Both the Duchess and Thelma were new to this sport and Prince Albert found them kitchen chairs to push before them and help them stand up straight. Thelma wrote, 'The lovely face of the Duchess, her superb colouring heightened by the cold, her eyes wrinkled with the sense of fun that was never far below the surface, made a picture I shall never forget.'[7]

There was another member of that skating party, a new American friend of the Prince. She was Mrs Ernest Simpson.

*

BOOKSHELVES HAVE been filled with works about Wallis Warfield Simpson. And with some reason. She so fascinated the Prince of Wales that he laid down his crown for her and thus altered for ever the course of the British monarchy.

Born in 1896 into a good Baltimore family, her early life was penniless. Her father died when she was an infant and her mother for a time ran a boarding house. From childhood onwards she understood that security came with money. Her first husband, Winfield Spencer, was a handsome pilot but he turned out to be an alcoholic, and she divorced him in 1922 to lead a rackety life which took in China as well as New York. In 1928 she remarried. Her new husband was Ernest Simpson, a kindly Anglo-American, also good-looking, and they settled in London.

She was socially ambitious, and a friend of Thelma Furness, through whom she met the Prince of Wales. He was attracted by her glamour and her sharp wit. She was clever, she was brusque, she was self-possessed and, unlike any of the English women the Prince knew, she was completely unimpressed by royalty. She was probably the first person he had ever known who talked down to him. She said what she wanted, and what she wanted she generally got.

In early 1934 Thelma Furness made a three-month trip to the United States and, apparently, asked Wallis Simpson to keep an eye on the Prince in her absence. Lady Furness had chosen her chaperone badly. Within weeks of her departure the Prince had become enthralled by Wallis Simpson and frequently invited her and her husband to weekends at the Fort, while taking her dancing, during the intervening weeks, often without her husband. When Thelma Furness returned from America she found that her friend had usurped her position as favourite.[8] She and Freda Dudley Ward were cut off.

The Prince's own family soon had similar reasons for concern. Prince George, the closest of all the family to the Prince of Wales, lived with him at St James's Palace and spent many weekends at the Fort. He realized quickly that Mrs Simpson was intent on dominating his brother and isolating him from his family. He later said that after she came into the Prince of Wales's life, his family never saw him 'as in days gone by'.[9] Through 1934 and 1935 the Prince grew ever more bold in displaying his infatuation with Mrs Simpson. Although the British press still observed a total and astonishing silence on the affair out of deference to the monarchy, the American press rejoiced in the story and in London society the whispers grew louder. People in and around the Court talked of Mrs Simpson's total control over the Prince.[10] The King confronted his son, who denied any impropriety.[11]

Unlike most people, the King took him at his word. Nonetheless he was dismayed by his son's conduct. 'He has not a single friend who is a gentleman. He does not see any decent society. And he is 41.'[12] Some months before his death the King is reported to have said, 'I pray to God that my eldest son will never marry and have children, and that nothing will come between Bertie and Lilibet and the throne.'[13]

By 1935 it was clear to his family and close friends that the Prince was in thrall to Mrs Simpson. There was private speculation at the time – and much more later – that her hold was at least partly sexual. His biographer considered that this may well have been true but there was more to the relationship than just sex. 'Until the day he died his eyes would follow her around the room; if she went out he would grow anxious . . . It was her personality, not her appearance or her sexual techniques, which captivated him.'[14]

There were those who came to believe that, even before the death of his father, the Prince had already decided to renounce his right to the succession and abscond with Mrs Simpson. That was certainly the opinion of two of King George V's Private Secretaries, Alan Lascelles and Alec Hardinge.[15] Lascelles later stated that King Edward himself told him in the summer of 1936 that he had not wanted to become king.[16] His brother confirmed this: shortly after the abdication, the new King George VI remarked to Owen Morshead, perhaps relying more than he realized on hindsight, 'he never meant to take it on . . . You see Papa's death fell wrongly for his plans . . . It would have been easy, comparatively, to chuck it while yet he was P. of Wales; he would have had a rough crossing with Papa, but he would have faced up to that.'[17] In fact it would not have been simple for the Prince of Wales to 'chuck it': legislation would have been required, in Britain and the Dominions, to alter the line of succession. But it is true that, with his father's death, he was trapped – by the Court, by ceremony and by the whole machinery of government. Perhaps it was no wonder that, though less close than the Duke of York to their father, he reacted to the moment of his death with a far greater display of emotion.

His anguish was deepened two days later when the late King's will was read to the family. He discovered that his father had left him a life interest in Sandringham and Balmoral but, unlike his siblings, he was to receive no money. Clive Wigram and the King's solicitor, Sir Bernard Bircham, explained to him that King George V had expected that (like previous Princes of Wales) he would have built himself a nest egg out of his Duchy of Cornwall revenues, and that his siblings had had no such income. (It was indeed later discovered that he had accumulated a considerable fortune.) The Prince was furious – and with a face like thunder, according to Lascelles, strode out of the room to telephone the bad news to Mrs Simpson.[18]

Senior members of the Household soon began to despair at the priorities of the new King. Sir Godfrey Thomas, his Private Secretary for many years as Prince of Wales, was convinced that he was 'not fitted to be King and that his reign will end in disaster'.[19] Alec Hardinge, who had been Assistant Private Secretary to George V and whom the new King was soon to appoint his private secretary, found it even more difficult than he had expected to adjust. His wife Helen's diary entries reflect his problems:

> March 10th Alec late as usual owing to the new King's strange hours!
> March 27th Confusion in the King's affairs because he's so impractical.
> March 31st Alec very much depressed by His Majesty's irresponsibility.[20]

★

FOR THE DUCHESS of York the death of the King brought vast changes, both private and public. In a personal sense it created a void. She wrote revealingly of her relationship with her father-in-law to Lord Dawson:

> Unlike his own children I was never afraid of him, and in all the twelve years of having me as a daughter-in-law he never spoke one unkind or abrupt word to me, and was always ready to listen, and give advice on one's own silly little affairs. He was so kind, and so <u>dependable</u> . . . I am really very well now, and, I think, am now only suffering from the effects of a family break up – which always happens when the head of a family goes. Though outwardly one's life goes on the same, yet everything is different – especially spiritually, and mentally.[21]

She was now the wife of the heir presumptive. Since the new King was unmarried and since Queen Mary, in mourning, would inevitably withdraw from public life for some time, her responsibilities were bound to increase. But whereas the Yorks had been an essential part of King George V's Court, they were not nearly so close to that established by Edward VIII. The new King quickly seemed to withdraw from his family and into the bosom of his friends. That, if anything, made the relationship between Queen Mary and the Yorks closer than ever. The Queen had conducted herself during her husband's last illness and since his death with her usual reserve and dignity. It was clear to those around her that she missed the King immensely, even though she remained quite calm.

Still convalescing from her pneumonia, the Duchess was prescribed a period of sea air, and in early March she and her daughters went to stay at the Duke of Devonshire's house in Eastbourne, Compton Place. The Duke of York came to join her in between bouts of public engagements. She went up to London briefly to see the Gainsborough exhibition held by Sir Philip Sassoon at his Park Lane house. She was accompanied by Kenneth Clark, the director of the National Gallery and the Surveyor of the King's Pictures, who was becoming an important adviser to her and was helping her build up a collection of pictures herself.* He complimented her on her appreciation of art. 'So few people seem to enjoy pictures: they look at them stodgily, or critically – or acquisitively; seldom with real enthusiasm,' he wrote.[22]

After a month at Compton Place the family returned to London, and then went home to Royal Lodge for Easter, which was very different that year. The tradition of many years had been abandoned; the Court did not move to Windsor Castle as it had throughout the reign of King George V. The King spent Easter with friends at Fort Belvedere. Queen Mary, by contrast, moved into Royal Lodge with the Duke and Duchess for almost three weeks. The Duchess gave up her bedroom and bathroom for her mother-in-law, who was also given the Octagon Room as her own sitting room, so that she could be as independent as possible.

Queen Mary's presence meant that Royal Lodge became in effect the focus of the Royal Family at this time, with the King and other members of the family coming and going, to lunch, dine or stay. The Duchess, like everyone else in the family, was keenly aware that, with the death of King George V, Queen Mary's role had changed. 'I feel that the Family, as a family, will now revolve round you. Thank God

---

* Sir Kenneth Clark (1903–83), Director of the National Gallery 1934–45, Surveyor of the King's Pictures, 1934–44. Later Slade Professor of Fine Art, Oxford, Professor of the History of Art, Royal Academy, and chairman of the Arts Council of Great Britain. Author of many art-historical works, he was also an inspiring lecturer and broadcaster who reached a broad audience through his television series, notably *Civilisation* in 1969, the year in which he was created a life peer as Baron Clark of Saltwood.

22. Elizabeth leaving Bruton Street for the Abbey, 26 April 1923.

23. The bridal party immediately after the wedding. Left to right: Mary Cambridge, Katie Hamilton, Mary Thynne, Ronnie Stanniforth, Betty Cator, Cecilia Bowes Lyon, Michael Bowes Lyon.

24. The bride and groom's carriage progressing along Constitution Hill.

25. The wedding party on the balcony at Buckingham Palace. Left to right: Queen Alexandra, Queen Mary, the Duchess of York, the Duke of York, King George V.

26. Honeymooning at Polesden Lacey.

27. Arthur Penn's characteristic souvenir of the wedding.

Portrait of the Artist — who has been asked to depict a humorous incident in connection with a wedding — trying to remember one.

Arthur Penn
1923.

E at 6.0 a.m.   *A at 6.0 a.m.*

28–30. The Duke and Duchess on safari in East Africa, 1925,
captioned by the Duke.

Looking for Rhino on the Plain below

31. The Duchess holding a monkey.

32. The Duchess with the Duke wearing, according to his own caption, 'a tribal headdress given to me by the Mukama of Toro and made of beads and colobus monkey skin'.

33. Visiting the Makwar Dam near Khartoum on the way back from safari. Left to right: J. W. Gibson, the Duchess, G. L. Prouse and the Duke.

34. The Duke and Duchess driving through Belfast during their official visit in July 1924.

35. The Duchess fishing at Tokaanu while on tour in New Zealand.

36. With the Duke at the state opening of the Australian Parliament in Canberra, 9 May 1927.

37. Returning from the continent.   38. The Duke and Duchess at a hunt meet.

39. The first photograph of the Duchess and the newborn Princess Elizabeth, April 1926.

40. The Duchess with Princess Margaret and Princess Elizabeth, September 1930.

41. The Duchess with the King and the Duke of York at a summer fête at Balmoral.

we have all got you as a central point, because without that point it might easily disintegrate.'[23] On Good Friday the King joined them at the Royal Chapel, immediately next to Royal Lodge, and next day, which was cold with showers of sleet, the Duke and Duchess and the Princesses arranged the flowers in the chapel as Queen Mary watched. On Easter Sunday they all exchanged eggs and gifts at breakfast and then went to a shortened matins in the Private Chapel at Windsor Castle with the King.[24]*

On 25 May the entire family supported Queen Mary on one of her first semi-public engagements since the death of her husband: she had been invited by the Cunard White Star Company to see the *Queen Mary* the day before she departed on her maiden voyage from Southampton to New York. All the Queen's sons and daughters-in-law came; Princess Elizabeth was there too – her mother had asked if she could come as she was 'madly keen' to see the ship.[25] The King flew down from Fort Belvedere; the rest of the family took the train. They had lunch on board with Sir Thomas and Lady Royden and the company directors.

Queen Mary recorded that it was a lovely day. They were shown all over the ship, from first class to third, inspecting the swimming pool and the Turkish bath, the restaurant adorned with a circus painting by Dame Laura Knight, the lounges, library and children's rooms (where, according to the *Morning Post*, Princess Elizabeth played with the toys, slid down the slide, tried her hand at the toy piano and saw a Mickey Mouse cartoon), and the cabins, which Queen Mary pronounced very comfortable. On the King's departure his scarlet and blue biplane circled over the ship and dipped 'as if in salute to the world's greatest liner'.[26] Next day, 26 May, was Queen Mary's birthday and, as every year, the family gathered at Buckingham Palace for lunch. For the Queen it was a sad occasion.

The loss of King George V's dominating but reassuring presence, and the sense of unease brought by the new reign, sapped even the

---

* The small Private Chapel in the royal apartments at the Castle is used only by the Royal Family. The Royal Chapel in the grounds of Royal Lodge is also a private chapel, originally built for King George IV and enlarged by Queen Victoria for the use of the Royal Family and people who lived and worked in the Great Park. It has its own chaplain, and members of the Royal Family regularly attend Sunday services there when staying at Windsor, rather than in St George's Chapel in the Castle. St George's is the chapel of the Order of the Garter, and the annual Garter service is held there, as well as some royal weddings and funerals.

Duchess's positive spirit. She valued the efforts of her friends to support and cheer her. Dick Molyneux took her to see the paintings at Greenwich and in the Courtaulds' collection at Eltham Palace in south-east London. She loved it all, writing afterwards, 'I am deeply grateful to you, my dear old friend and fellow Wet, for arranging such a good outing, and honestly, it did me all the good in the world. I still feel a bit sad about everything, & last Wednesday was a really bright moment in a gloomy summer.'[27]

Other friends kept her up to date with more sombre events. Nineteen-thirty-six was another year in which the power of the dictators, Hitler and Mussolini, grew. Having watched the world, and in particular the League of Nations, fail to stop Italy invading Abyssinia, the Nazi government reoccupied the demilitarized zone of the Rhineland. Nothing happened and the continent continued its descent into the twilight of barbarism. D'Arcy Osborne, who had now arrived in Rome as British ambassador to the Holy See, began to send the Duchess letters filled with drumbeats of warning about the march of fascism. He was concerned that Britain was far too smug and complacent. 'Disarmed to the gums, we can't afford to go throwing our morals and ideals in the faces of gangster dictators.'[28]

*

THE DUCHESS's public life in the new reign was busier than ever; she was as much in demand, and her presence worked its familiar magic for charitable causes. She used her influence with the new King as she had with the old, appealing to Edward VIII on behalf of her charities. Not surprisingly, perhaps, she seemed more confident and more willing to express opinions and to intervene with friends in high places than she had been in the lifetime of King George V, in particular over the unemployment and poverty she saw on visits to industrial areas.

As patroness of the Toc H League of Women Helpers she went to several different events celebrating the group's coming of age in June. The text of her handwritten speech for their festival at the Crystal Palace survives; she used the themes of family and home to welcome visitors from the 'family' of Empire to the home country. In one intriguing passage she said, 'In these rather puzzling days [these words were underlined in red], it is both inspiring and comforting to feel, that all here tonight are united by the spirit of fellowship in the desire to keep burning the light of sacrifice & service, and to contribute by personal effort to the common good.'[29] It is not clear whether her 'puzzlement' referred to the worsening international situation or to events nearer home.

Later in June the Duchess was hostess at a tea party at 145 Piccadilly which she may well have approached with mixed feelings: the Duke was President of the Imperial War Graves Commission, and the Anglo-German-French Committee of the Commission was visiting England. At the beginning of June the Duke decided to invite the Committee to tea, together with the French and German Ambassadors. So the Duchess found herself entertaining the former Chief of the General Staff of the German army and several other German officials, as well as their French and British counterparts.[30]

At the end of July the Duke and Duchess visited Jarrow, the origin of one of the hunger marches. Much of Britain was by now recovering, but in Jarrow about 40 per cent of the people were still out of work. Feelings were running high in the area, and Walter Runciman, the President of the Board of Trade, was perturbed by the timing of this royal visit.[31] In fact, it proved a public success, although a disturbing experience for the Duchess, who was horrified by the poverty she saw. 'I always dread going up to Tyneside,' she wrote to Duff Cooper, now the Secretary of State for War, 'because I admire the people there with all my heart, & it darkens my thoughts for months afterwards, to know how desperate they are.' But at least despair had not given way to apathy. She went to Palmer's Shipyard, the only source of employment in the town, which she thought a scene of desolation. On the streets they drove 'through large crowds of emaciated, ragged, unhappy & undaunted people, who gave us a wonderful reception'. Their courage made her weep, she said; she found it terrible that so many good men should be wasted. She wished that more of these unemployed young men could join the army – to that end she asked Duff Cooper if the standards of fitness for recruits could not be reduced to allow more men to benefit from army training. He replied that his Ministry would act upon her suggestion.[32]

The Duke and Duchess then went to stay with the Duke of Northumberland at Alnwick Castle. From there they drove with their friends Clare and Doris Vyner to the Fountains Abbey Settlement at Swarland, where Clare Vyner had created an environment of small-holdings for unemployed people from Tyneside. Each family was given an acre and a half on which to build a bungalow and very quickly a new community had been created of former industrial workers, shipyard craftsmen and clerks. The Duke and Duchess were both impressed; she wrote to Queen Mary about the trip, and he congratulated Clare Vyner on his personal efforts to give people new lives.[33]

After a hard-working summer the Yorks embarked with their daughters on their annual visit to Scotland, to the intense pleasure of the Princesses. Two weeks at Glamis were to be followed by several at Birkhall. Meanwhile, in early August Queen Mary finally forced herself to return to Sandringham for the first time since her husband's death. While she was there, sadly sorting through his rooms, the King flew up for lunch but immediately afterwards returned to London, leaving his mother to her mournful tasks.[34]

*

THERE WERE VERY different preoccupations and pleasures at Fort Belvedere. Mrs Simpson dominated the King's life; most weekends she played the part of hostess at the Fort, with or without her husband. Helen Hardinge described in her diary an evening at Windsor Castle. The King had brought his party over from the Fort; they included Mr and Mrs Simpson, and an unknown American woman. They watched a film of the Grand National. 'The unknown American lady was the one already selected to be Mr Simpson's wife! Mrs Simpson was very friendly and agreeable, and admired my Victorian jewellery. It was from this evening that I felt sure the King and Mrs Simpson meant to marry.'[35]

Many of the staff hated what was going on: Osborne, the King's butler, was frightened he would lose his job because 'Mrs S had got her knife into him and he felt he was doomed.' He also said that he had picked up a label in Mrs Simpson's writing which read, 'To our marriage' – and that this had obviously been attached to some present from her to him.[36] The British press was still exercising remarkable self-control about Mrs Simpson's very existence, but London's great salons and the Houses of Parliament were buzzing with gossip about the King's adventures and his friend's requirements. The King was said to be less than diligent in reading the daily government papers sent to him in his boxes and, perhaps worse, to leave them lying around at the Fort for anyone to see. His sackings within the Household were also widely discussed. The Duchess of Devonshire, Queen Mary's Mistress of the Robes, told Lady Airlie that there was a rumour that everyone over sixty would have to go. 'I daresay', she continued, 'Mrs S. would have the good sense not to push really unsuitable men in. Can you think of a suitable office for Mr S.?? "Guardian of the Bedchamber" or "Master of the Mistress" might do.'[37]

On 28 May 1936 the names of Mr and Mrs Simpson appeared for the first time in the Court Circular as guests of the King at dinner the previous evening. The Prime Minister, Stanley Baldwin, was also present and was introduced to the Simpsons for the first time. According to her own later autobiography, the King had persuaded Mrs Simpson to come by telling her, 'It's got to be done. Sooner or later my Prime Minister must meet my future wife.'[38] In June the King was prevented by continued official mourning from attending Royal Ascot but he sent Mrs Simpson in a royal carriage. Shortly afterwards Ernest Simpson moved out of the marital home and the King rented Mrs Simpson a house in Regent's Park. To the horror of even the King's supporters, divorce proceedings were now imminent.[39]

Helen Hardinge described a dinner which the King gave in July 1936. The Yorks were there, as were the Churchills. Mrs Simpson acted as hostess.

> The King was in good form. He circulated among his guests, talking to each of them for a while, and his social technique was admirable ... Winston Churchill was one of the few people around the dinner table that night who found Mrs Simpson acceptable. Curiously enough, he considered that she just did not matter and had no great significance; he believed that, in the ultimate analysis of the Monarchy, she simply did not count one way or the other. Moral and social considerations apart, he considered her presence to be irrelevant to King Edward's performance as Sovereign. The King thought the exact opposite. He considered she was the only thing that mattered.[40]

Churchill's support was perhaps surprising. He was greatly concerned about the growth of fascist power in Europe, and the King was widely suspected of being too sympathetic to the new Germany. The evidence for this has been thoroughly examined and convincingly analysed by King Edward VIII's official biographer Philip Ziegler, and need not be revisited here.[41] Many years later the publication of official German documents proved that in 1936 the Nazi leaders were already planning to exploit the King's sympathy to achieve an Anglo-German entente and more. But the British Foreign Office gave little credence to reports of this nature at the time, and Churchill too may well have dismissed the rumours as exaggerated.

Mrs Simpson was another matter: senior Whitehall officials thought her to be 'in the pocket of the German Ambassador', as Lord Wigram recorded in February 1936.[42] Helen Hardinge noted in her diary that 'one of the factors in the situation was Mrs Simpson's partiality for Nazi Germans'.[43] Her alleged pro-German views certainly cannot have endeared Wallis Simpson to the Duchess of York. In any event, suspicions about Mrs Simpson, combined with the King's carelessness about official papers, were enough to give senior members of the Royal Household the impression that in both his public and his private conduct the King was not entirely sound.[44]

In early August the King set off on a controversial, indeed damaging voyage around the Mediterranean on a chartered yacht, the *Nahlin*, with Mrs Simpson and a few friends. All over the Mediterranean the couple were cheered and photographed and the American papers published every detail. Not all was heavenly on board the *Nahlin*. The Duff Coopers were among the guests and Diana Cooper recorded an unhappy scene when the King got down on all fours to release the hem of Mrs Simpson's dress from under a chair – to which Mrs Simpson responded by glaring at him and saying, 'Well, that's the *maust* extraordinary performance I've ever seen,' and began to attack him for other aspects of his behaviour. Diana Cooper now felt that 'Wallis is wearing very badly.' She also thought that Mrs Simpson was beginning to tire of the pleasure of the King's company.[45]

After the cruise, the King returned to London but Mrs Simpson stopped in Paris to shop. There she fell ill and had ample time, in her room at the Hôtel Meurice, to read all that the American newspapers had written about her and the King on their cruise. She appears to have been appalled by the enormity of what was happening and wrote to the King to tell him that it was all too much for her and she had decided to return to her husband. 'I am sure you and I would only create disaster together,' she wrote. 'I want you to be happy. I feel sure I can't make you so, and I honestly don't think you can me.' Whatever her real intentions, the King was horrified – he telephoned her immediately and threatened to cut his throat if she did not come to Balmoral.[46]

*

ON THE BALMORAL estate there was a good deal of concern about the King's plans. He had already attempted to introduce efficiencies at Sandringham, on which he had asked the Duke of York to advise, and he planned to do the same at Balmoral. The Duke had sought to soften the pain of the job losses which the King imposed in Norfolk, but in Scotland he had not been consulted. Both he and the Duchess were worried about the King's attitude.[47] Queen Mary shared such concerns. With restraint, she wrote to the Duke, 'What a pity David went abroad when there is so much for him to do here & at Balmoral.'[48]

Unfortunately, the new King showed that his interests were elsewhere. Much has been made, and with reason, of the Aberdeen Infirmary incident. Earlier in the summer the King had been invited to open the new Aberdeen Infirmary in September. He had declined, on the grounds that he would still be in official mourning for his father. He deputed the Duke of York to do it in his stead on 23 September.[49] A few days before the event the Duchess wrote to the Queen, 'I do wish that David could have done it, as they have all worked so hard for so long . . . But he won't, so there it is!' She told the Queen that she and the Duke had been paying visits in the neighbourhood and asked if there were any tenants or others whom the Queen would like them to see. She was not really looking forward to the King's arrival at Balmoral. 'I am secretly rather dreading next week, but I haven't heard if a certain person is coming or not – I do hope not, as everything is so talked of up here. I suppose it is natural, the place being empty for eleven months, that the time it is occupied every detail is discussed with gusto!'[50]

Then, on the day that the Duke and Duchess were opening the Infirmary, an astonishing incident occurred. The King, who had arrived at Balmoral four days earlier, suddenly appeared in Aberdeen. He drove himself the sixty miles, wearing driving goggles, to the railway station, in order to meet Mrs Simpson and her friends Mr and Mrs Herman Rogers off the London train. He put Mrs Simpson in the seat beside him and Mr and Mrs Rogers in the back. In other words, mourning allegedly stopped him from carrying out a duty in the city that day, but it was no barrier to his indulging his caprices. He could not have expected to pass unnoticed. The Aberdeen *Evening Express* published a photograph of him, with the words 'His Majesty in Aberdeen. Surprise visit in car to meet guests'. Next to it was a photograph of the Yorks opening the hospital. No clearer indication of the new King's priorities, and of the contrast with his brother and sister-in-law, could have been given to the people of Aberdeen. It was damaging to his reputation.[51]

Mrs Simpson's arrival at Balmoral was announced in the Court Circular; even Winston Churchill deprecated her going 'to such a highly official place upon which the eyes of Scotland were concentrated'.[52] At the Castle her influence over the King was evident. Understandably, he put her in the best spare bedroom but to the surprise of his Household he refused to occupy the King's room himself, preferring to be in the dressing room of her suite.[53]

The Balmoral staff were concerned that the King would act in as draconian a way against them as he had against the workers at Sandringham. Queen Mary hoped the Duke of York would advise him 'to do the right thing' but in the event the King made sweeping changes on Deeside with no reference to his brother.[54] The Duke was upset and wrote to his mother, 'David only told me what he had done after it was over, which I might say made me rather sad. He arranged it all with the official people up there. I never saw him alone for an instant.'[55]

The Duchess wrote to her mother-in-law to say that there was a great sadness and sense of loss on Deeside. 'You & Papa made such a family feeling by your great kindness & thought for everybody, but David does not seem to possess the faculty of making others feel wanted.'[56] The Duchess added that she felt more and more anxious; she knew where the problem lay, but there were so few people with whom she could discuss it all. 'I feel that the whole difficulty is a certain person. I do not feel that I can make advances to her & ask her to our house, as I imagine would be liked, & this fact is bound to make relations a little difficult.' She was quite certain that the Duke should not get involved. 'The whole situation is complicated & horrible, and I feel so unhappy about it sometimes, so you must forgive me darling Mama for letting myself go so indiscreetly. There is nobody that I can talk to, as ever since I married I have made a strict rule never to discuss anything of Family matters with my own relations – nor would they wish it, but it leaves so few people to let off steam to occasionally!' Thinking ahead, she asked, 'Has anything transpired about Xmas? Can we all spend it together – do suggest it to David as he loves & admires you & I am sure would arrange what you wished.'[57]

Queen Mary was grateful for this 'dear long letter' and replied at once, saying that the subject 'grieves me beyond words'. The King, she lamented, was 'so good in so many ways, & so ill-judged in others'. She knew that the Yorks had been very kind to the people on the Balmoral estate – she wished that the King had stayed there longer and had been 'less encumbered by guests', so that he could have dealt better with all estate matters. She had gathered that he did not want to spend Christmas or any part of the winter at Sandringham, so she had asked him to let her and the Duke and Duchess stay there for a few weeks; 'we 3 must arrange to run it together as we think best but this is for us to discuss & to see how best it can be arranged, for I must confess I should like to have a family party there as usual for Xmas, & to have the Xmas tree for our people, who will be so much disappointed if we are not able to give them some kind of happiness at that festive time of year, & I feel strongly that dear Papa would wish this – I am sure you will both agree.'[58]

But while the King's family struggled to convince themselves that life could go on in the old way, the stage was being set for the inevitable tragedy. After Balmoral Mrs Simpson took up residence in Felixstowe, because the next convenient Assizes in which the divorce could be heard happened to be near by in Ipswich. This proceeding caused some panic among those who knew of the King's friendship with Mrs Simpson; even Winston Churchill was alarmed at the prospect of her being free to marry again.[59]

On 20 October the Duke and Duchess arrived back in London on the night train from Scotland with their daughters. That same day the Prime Minister, Stanley Baldwin, after searching his conscience, finally confronted the King. He told him that thousands of letters had been received at Downing Street and elsewhere, many from British residents in the United States and most of them very critical of the King's relationship with Mrs Simpson. The Prime Minister showed some of these letters to the King and asked him if he could not be more discreet and if Mrs Simpson's divorce could not be postponed. The King refused, asserting that Baldwin had no right to interfere in the private matters of another person.[60]

Shortly after this Alec Hardinge, the King's Private Secretary, felt that he should inform the Duke of York of what was happening. Till now the Duke had convinced himself that, however strong his brother's feelings for Mrs Simpson, he would not sacrifice the throne for her. Now Hardinge informed him that the King's refusal to heed the Prime Minister suggested that he would indeed put Mrs Simpson before any other consideration. 'The possibility of abdication could no longer be ignored,' the Duke's biographer wrote, 'yet the Duke recoiled from it with consternation and incredulity. In his mind he sought to free himself from the nightmare web that was slowly enmeshing him, but in his heart he began to realise the inevitability of his destiny.'[61]

It was not easy. The Duke and the Prince of Wales had been friends as well as brothers all their lives, and since 1923 the Duchess had added to the gaiety of their relationship. Now the King had completely cut them off. If he really planned to marry Mrs Simpson after her divorce came through, it was clear to most of his family, though not yet to the King himself, that he could not remain on the throne. The Duke would become king, his wife queen, and Princess Elizabeth would be the heir to the throne. The prospect for all of them – although as yet the Princesses knew nothing of what was happening – was terrifying, and until his conversation with Alec Hardinge the Duke had not really believed it could happen.

Queen Mary was also suffering. In the country her public behaviour as dignified widow of the King won her admiration. Within the family, she relied more and more on her other children. So did they upon her: after visiting her at her new home at Marlborough House, the Duchess wrote, 'In these anxious & depressing days you are indeed "a rock of defence" darling Mama, & I feel sure that the whole country agrees.'[62] The Queen expressed her own anxiety to the Duke – 'how unsatisfactory it all is, so underhand and unpleasant. How will it end, you may imagine how worried I feel.'[63]

Mrs Simpson received her decree nisi on Tuesday 27 October. The people of Ipswich were astonished by the size of the international press corps which descended upon the town to cover the event, but they remained largely ignorant of the cause. Only the *News Chronicle* carried a story of any length about the divorce – without explaining its importance. The American newspapers had a field day talking of Mrs Simpson's forthcoming marriage to the King. They spun stories that

'Wally' had dined with Queen Mary and that she was going to be created a duchess before the wedding.[64]

At the Palace, there were formalities and illusions of normality to be maintained. Senior members of the Royal Household continued to plan the King's Coronation and engagements for him even though they had begun to fear that he might not be there to take part. The Duchess wrote a long letter to 'Darling David', in which she made no mention of the crisis which obsessed them all. Instead she thanked him for lending them Birkhall, without which she did not think she could cope with all the problems of modern life. 'I do thank you from my heart – you are always so sweet & thoughtful for us, and I wish that I could thank you as I would wish.' She added a plea that in summer 1937 he might review the St John Ambulance Brigade.

> It would do an incredible amount of good, because you know the men are practically all working men who give up holidays & ordinary leisure to do Ambulance service on great & little occasions – they hardly ever get a pat on the back, & yet are absolutely essential to us, and I cannot begin to tell you what a marvellous effect it would have if you could possibly spare a day next summer. Oh dear – I do hate to ask you this, but the St John gets things like Investitures for the grand people, and I do feel that the thousands of working men who give up their hard earned leisure to cope with accidents & public occasions would feel so set up if you could have a look at them. Please forgive me for asking you this, but you are so understanding about these things. Please don't give me away, as it really has nothing to do with me. I am being an interfering busybody ... If you possibly can – it would be wonderful if you could inspect them. Your loving sister in law Elizabeth.[65]

As the crisis built, the King continued to avoid his family. The Duke finally saw him on the morning of 6 November, and urged him to come to Sandringham for a day or two at Christmas, if only for their mother's sake. 'He is very difficult to see & when one does he wants to talk about other matters,' the Duke wrote to Queen Mary. 'It is all so worrying & I feel we all live a life of conjecture; never knowing what will happen tomorrow, & then the unexpected comes.'[66] The Queen agreed. 'As you say things are not very pleasant just now, everything appears to be in the air, & it is so difficult to get D. to think about what one wants to discuss with him, as he goes off the subject so quickly.'[67]

The King's own Private Secretary precipitated the denouement. On 13 November Alec Hardinge wrote to the King to warn him that the silence of the British press on the subject of his friendship with Mrs Simpson would last only for a matter of days and the effect of publicity was likely to be 'calamitous'. Moreover the government might resign and the King would then have to find another prime minister. If an election resulted, 'Your Majesty's personal affairs would be the chief issue.' Hardinge recommended that the only way of avoiding these dangers was for Mrs Simpson to go abroad *without further delay* – and I would *beg* Your Majesty to give this proposal your earnest consideration before the position has become irretrievable'.[68] It was wise advice but not tactful; the letter infuriated the King, who cut off all contact with Hardinge.

Nevertheless the King was moved to action. On the evening of 16 November he summoned Baldwin and told him that he intended to marry Mrs Simpson as soon as she was free. He would prefer to do this as king, but if he could not, then he would abdicate. Baldwin was appalled and told the King, 'Sir this is most grievous news, and it is impossible for me to make any comment on it today.'[69] That evening he passed on the news to his colleagues. Duff Cooper recalled that he said that 'he was not at all sure that the Yorks would not prove the best solution. The King had many good qualities but not those which best fitted him for his post, whereas the Duke of York would be just like his father.'[70]

The Prime Minister might be stunned, but the King apparently felt liberated. After his interview with Baldwin he went to dinner with his mother at Marlborough House, determined to tell her of his decision. Queen Mary's exact response is not known, but she commented later, 'I thought I was extremely outspoken and tried to express my displeasure, but I suppose he never listened to what I said.'[71]* She

---

* Subsequently Queen Mary was quoted by one of her ladies in waiting as saying that 'My son actually came to see me one day in November and said, "I'm going to marry Mrs Simpson on April 27 and be crowned on May 12." I said, "But my dear David you cannot do any such thing." Well, he said that was what he had decided to do.' (Note by Owen Morshead, 14 January 1937, RA AEC/GG/12/OS/1)

simply could not now and would not ever believe that Mrs Simpson was fit to be the wife of her son, let alone Queen. For her, duty came first, and only in duty came fulfilment. But she evidently did not make her feelings clear enough, and next day she wrote her son a letter which he took for encouragement: 'As your mother I must send you a letter of true sympathy on the difficult position in which you are placed. I have been thinking so much of you all day, hoping you are making a wise decision for your future.'[72] The King replied with affection, 'I feel so happy and relieved to have at last been able to tell you my wonderful secret; a dream which I have for so long been praying might one day come true. Now that Wallis will be free to marry me in April it only remains for me to decide the best action I take for our future happiness and for the good of all concerned.'[73]

The Queen was more explicit with her daughter-in-law, to whom she wrote on 17 November, the day after her dinner with the King: 'I am more worried than I can say at what is going on.' The tension, the sorrow and the loneliness were almost unbearable and she asked the Duke and Duchess to come and see her. 'There is no one I can talk to about it, except you two as Mary is away & one can't discuss that subject with friends. What a mess to have got into & for such an unworthy person too!!! Yr sad tho' loving Mama.'[74]

The same day the King had finally brought himself to tell his younger brother directly of what he planned. The Duke was shocked and incredulous and went straight home to tell his wife who immediately sat down to write to the Queen:

> My darling Mama
> Bertie has just told me of what has happened, and I feel quite overcome with horror & emotion. My first thought was of you, & your note, just arrived as I was starting to write to you, was very helpful. One feels so helpless against such obstinacy . . . God help us all to be calm & wise.
> Your devoted daughter in law Elizabeth[75]

The next morning, Wednesday 18 November, the Duke and Duchess went to see Queen Mary to discuss the crisis, which was still unknown to all but a very close circle. Indeed some of those in the know wished that the press were less 'responsible'. The Duchess of Devonshire, with whom the Yorks had spent the previous weekend at

Chatsworth,* wrote to Lady Airlie, 'What in the world is going to happen about Mrs S! one sees no good solution at all. I think it is getting time for the English Press to utter a few carefully chosen warnings.'[76]

At the end of the week, on 20 November, the Yorks went to stay for a shooting weekend with the Pembrokes at Wilton House, near Salisbury.† Their inability to discuss the matter with which they were totally preoccupied must have made the stay very difficult for them. The Duchess wrote to Queen Mary: 'Staying here, in a very normal English shooting party, it seems almost incredible that David contemplates such a step, & every day I pray to God that he will see reason, & not abandon his people. I am sure that it would be a great shock to everybody and a horrible position for us naturally. However, it is no good going over the same ground again, but I must repeat that I do not know what we should do without you darling Mama . . . It is a great strain having to talk & behave as if nothing was wrong during these difficult days – especially as I do not think anybody here dreams of what is worrying all of us.'[77]

His family found it almost impossible to reach the King. It was particularly distressing for the Duke of York, who wrote to his beloved brother on 23 November saying, 'I do so long for you to be happy with the one person you adore,' and adding, 'I feel sure that whatever you decide to do will be in the best interests of this Country and Empire.'[78] The Duchess wrote to the King on the same day with a plea on behalf of her unhappy, bewildered husband:

Darling David

Please read this. Please be kind to Bertie when you see him, because he loves you, and minds terribly all that happens to you. I wish that you could realize how loyal & true he is to you, and you have no idea how hard it has been for him lately. I know that he is fonder of you than anybody else, & as his wife, I must write & tell you this. I am terrified for him – so DO help him.

* According to a later chatelaine of Chatsworth, Deborah, Duchess of Devonshire, Queen Elizabeth never stayed at the house again, because of its association with this unhappy time in her life.

† Reginald Herbert, fifteenth Earl of Pembroke (1880–1960), and his wife Beatrice. Their daughter Patricia (1904–94) was a friend of the Duchess of York and later, as Lady Hambleden, became a long-serving lady in waiting to Queen Elizabeth.

And for God's sake don't tell him that I have written – we both
uphold you always. E.

Across the top of the page she wrote, 'We want you to be happy,
more than anything else, but it's awfully difficult for Bertie to say what
he thinks, you know how shy he is – so do help him.'[79] The Duchess's
concern both for her husband's inability to express himself and for his
future was understandable. In the event the King still declined to see
his brother.

The Duchess also wrote to Alec Hardinge's wife Helen, one of the
few people with whom she felt it safe to communicate: 'It's bad,
whichever way one looks at it, both from our point of view, and the
country's.' She felt, she said, 'very depressed and miserable'.[80] A few
days later, the Duke wrote to Sir Godfrey Thomas, the King's Assistant
Private Secretary, expressing the depth of his fears. 'If the worst
happens & I have to take over, you can be assured that I will do my
best to clear up the inevitable mess, if the whole fabric does not
crumble under the shock and strain of it all.'[81]

Meanwhile, the King went away on a tour of the mining villages
of South Wales. He displayed the best of himself, engaging sympathetically with the destitute, unemployed miners. He made the memorable
statement 'Something must be done' which, when reported, gave
many people hope that their monarch was advancing their cause,
while worrying some politicians that the King was trespassing beyond
his constitutional role. There was no doubt that he felt keenly the
plight of the unemployed, and there was equally no doubt that the
signs of his own popularity emboldened him to think that perhaps,
after all, he could stay.[82]

By the end of November a morganatic marriage – in which his
wife would not become queen but would hold some lesser title – had
become the King's ambition. The Prime Minister, however, considered
this a distasteful solution, which neither the public nor the Dominions
were likely to accept. The leaders of both Labour and Liberal parties
agreed with him.[83]

Early on the morning of 28 November Baldwin sent out telegrams
to the Dominions – Canada, South Africa, Australia, New Zealand,
the Irish Free State – to seek their views on the possibility of the
King's marriage. The answers varied in tone from Australian trench-
ancy to Irish coolness, but they allowed Baldwin to conclude that the

Dominions, collectively, would not accept the idea of a morganatic marriage, let alone the notion that Mrs Simpson might become queen.[84]

*

ON THE NIGHT of 29 November, the Duke and Duchess took the train to Edinburgh, so that the Duke could be installed as grand master mason of Scotland, succeeding the Prince of Wales, who had resigned the post upon becoming king. Upset and uncertain, the Duke wrote to his Private Secretary, 'I feel like the proverbial "sheep being led to the slaughter", which is not a comfortable feeling.'[85] They kept in touch by telephone.

While they were in Scotland the crisis finally became public. On 1 December the Bishop of Bradford, Dr Walter Blunt, addressed his Diocesan Conference with a criticism of the King – not for his association with Mrs Simpson but for his irregular attendance at church. He commended the King to God's Grace, which the King needed no less than others 'for the King is a man like ourselves.' And he added, 'We hope that he is aware of his need. Some of us wish that he gave more positive signs of his awareness.' Subsequently it was said that when he originally drafted his address the Bishop was not aware of the King's friendship with Mrs Simpson.[86]

The provincial papers immediately commented on the Bishop's remarks and the London press then finally followed suit. By Thursday 3 December all caution was gone, and when the Yorks stepped off the night train at Euston they were greeted with newspaper placards emblazoned 'The King's Marriage'. This was a terrible shock to them both. The Duke recorded later that the sight 'surprised and horrified' him.[87] 'We have just arrived back from Scotland, to be greeted with the bombshell of the daily papers – it is all so dreadful & wasteful,' the Duchess wrote to Dick Molyneux; 'we both are unhappy & terribly worried.'[88] That morning, 3 December, the Duke hastened to talk first to his mother and then to his brother, whom he found 'in a great state of excitement', saying he would ask the people what they wanted him to do and go abroad for a while.[89]

But first the King decided to send Mrs Simpson abroad, away from the public drama and private turmoil. She was receiving poison-pen letters and after a brick had been thrown through the window of her rented house in Regent's Park, she had taken refuge at Fort Belvedere.

She left that night, 3 December, for the villa of Mr and Mrs Herman Rogers in Cannes; she was accompanied by a friend, Lord Brownlow, and carrying some £100,000 worth of jewellery. She walked out of Fort Belvedere without saying goodbye to any of the staff. Weeping, the King said farewell to her and begged her to call him when she stopped for the night. According to her own later account, he said, 'You must wait for me no matter how long it takes. I shall never give you up.'[90] It took just eight more days for him to give up everything else.

After Mrs Simpson's departure the King went to Marlborough House and saw Queen Mary, the Duke of York and Princess Mary. He made what the Duke called the 'dreadful announcement' that he could not live alone as king and that he must marry Mrs Simpson.[91]

The hitherto silent press was now, to the astonishment of the overwhelming majority of the British people, filled with stories and photographs of the King and the hitherto completely unknown Mrs Simpson. Reading them in Cannes, Wallis Simpson was horrified by the often critical tone of the papers. So, for very different reasons, were members of the Royal Family. It was the first time that a monarch had been so roundly attacked since Queen Victoria had been criticized for shutting herself away after Prince Albert's death.

The effect of the news on many in Britain was illustrated by an entry in the diary of the Duchess's childhood friend, Freddy Dalrymple Hamilton (now Captain of the Royal Naval College at Dartmouth), on 3 December.

This morning we got the biggest shock of all the shocks we have had in the last 18 months when we read in the papers that the City was upset – Govt. stocks were falling & that there was some trouble about H.M. the King. In the 6 o'clock news we heard that The King was at variance with his Ministers on the subject of his private affairs ... Apparently he wishes to marry an American lady called Mrs Simpson, who it is said has already been twice divorced in America ... Heaven knows one wishes H.M. nothing but happiness but such a marriage would be so repugnant to the British people generally that it could never be approved by any Cabinet ... it seems incredible that H.M. with all his consideration & sympathy for others should really contemplate abandoning the ship in the middle of the storm especially as he is the most popular man in the British Empire.[92]

Public opinion was divided between those who held this view and those who felt that the King should be allowed to marry the woman he loved. At Buckingham Palace huge quantities of letters were received from the public at home and abroad, reflecting both sides. Susan Williams in her study *The People's King* examined the letters from the public preserved in the Royal Archives and concluded that the majority of ordinary people supported the King.[93] On the same evidence King George VI's biographer John Wheeler-Bennett came to the opposite conclusion, and Tommy Lascelles commented that 'the day-to-day realization of that [highly critical] opinion had, at the time, a deep influence on the thought of [the King's] brother, and still more of his mother, who read every word of the stuff . . . it was a constant feature of that nightmare month.'[94] Baldwin and Clement Attlee, the leader of the Labour Party, who both kept close to public opinion, were convinced that the King had little backing in the country. The King's supporters were a curious combination – Winston Churchill, Oswald Mosley, the fascist leader, and the press lords Beaverbrook and Rothermere. The aim of Beaverbrook and Churchill was, in Beaverbrook's words, to 'bugger Baldwin'.[95]

Over the weekend of 5–6 December much of the support the King enjoyed seemed to evaporate as the enormity of what he wished to do sank into the minds of the British people. Any notion of a 'King's Party' faded. The Duke wrote to his mother that he had spoken to David who seemed quite calm, though he could not be hurried in his decision. 'I feel so terribly sad for you darling Mama & I can well imagine through what anxiety you must have been going during this last 3 weeks. It has been awful for all of us, but much more so for you, when David has been trained for the great position he holds, & now wants to chuck away. I am feeling very overwrought as to what may befall me, but with your help I know I shall be able to carry on . . . I really cannot believe that David is going.'[96]

The Duchess was grateful to the many friends who wrote to offer their support. She replied to a letter from Osbert Sitwell, 'In these last few days, when every minute has seemed an hour, we have been sustained & helped by the sympathy of our friends . . . It is extraordinary how one's heart lightens at the kindness of friends.'[97]

★

ON 6 DECEMBER Baldwin went to see Queen Mary at Marlborough House. He was nervous because he always found her shyness rather difficult to overcome, but she greeted him with the words, 'Well, a pretty kettle of fish we're in now!' and this homely phrase revealed to him that he had no need to pick his words in describing the King's conduct.[98] She thought the idea of a morganatic marriage was the worst solution of all; she simply would not countenance it. Apart from anything else, she thought, it would create a court within the Court and would make her own position intolerable – she saw no reason why she should compete with Mrs Simpson.

Throughout the weekend, the King refused to see his brother, claiming that he had not yet made up his mind what to do; the Duke and Duchess waited anxiously just down the road at Royal Lodge. In fact the King was still trying to have his way. Mrs Simpson, now in an uncomfortable villa in the south of France, was constantly offering advice and threats down the crackling telephone lines of the time. These calls were often painful to the King, and to those who overheard him shouting down the line in the Fort. Sometimes he was reduced to tears. Walter Monckton, the distinguished lawyer whom Edward VIII had asked to liaise with the Prime Minister on his behalf, said that those who heard his end of the calls would never forget them.[99]

Mrs Simpson was, mostly, urging him to be strong, rely on his personal popularity, tough out the government and insist on his rights. On 6 December she issued a statement declaring herself ready 'to withdraw forthwith from a situation that has been rendered both unhappy and untenable'. But she was well aware that the King would not give her up, and she was equally determined that he should not give up the throne; the solution of a morganatic marriage – though after a decent interval during which the King would win popular support – was her ultimate aim, as Sarah Bradford pointed out in her biography of King George VI.[100]

On the evening of Monday 7 December the King finally agreed to see the Duke of York at Fort Belvedere. 'I was with him at 7.0 pm. The awful and ghastly suspense of waiting was over,' the Duke recorded. Pacing up and down the room, the King told his brother that he had decided to abdicate. The Duke went back to Royal Lodge for dinner before returning to the Fort. 'I felt having once got there I was not going to leave. As he is my eldest brother I had to be there to try & help him in his hour of need.'[101] Later that night the Duke returned to London with his wife.

At this point in the crisis the Duchess was struck by one of her frequent attacks of flu. She took to her bed at 145 Piccadilly and was thus absent for most of the dramatic events that followed. She was stunned by it all and, like her husband, could still scarcely believe what the King was doing, let alone the implications for her own family. The Duchess had a very definite view on the King's proposal that he should be able to remain on the throne while contracting a morganatic marriage to Mrs Simpson. She wrote to her sister May, 'Bertie & I are feeling very despairing, and the strain is terrific. Every day lasts a week, & the only hope we have is in the affection & support of our family & friends. I feel so sad, & yet there is only a very straightforward case – if Mrs Simpson is not fit to be Queen, she is not fit to be the King's morganatic wife.'[102] In a letter to Lady Londonderry she demurred from the suggestion that Queen Mary's views should discreetly be made known. 'I also think that it is <u>essential</u> for the Queen to remain outside any controversy – she <u>must</u> be above everything, and her calm & dignity will prove to the people the futility of the cheap Press.'[103]

Every day brought new uncertainties and wild rumours.[104] Negotiations between the King, his family, his advisers and the Prime Minister continued. On the evening of Tuesday 8 December there was a surprising interlude – a dinner at the Fort, which was attended by the Prime Minister, the Dukes of York and Kent, the King's advisers Walter Monckton and Edward Peacock, his solicitor, and Ulick Alexander, the Keeper of the Privy Purse. According to the Duke of York's own account, while all the guests 'were very sad (we knew the final & irrevocable decision he had made) my brother was the life & soul of the party ... I whispered to W.M. [Walter Monckton] "& this is the man we are going to lose." One couldn't, nobody could, believe it.'[105]

At the end of a harrowing day of discussions with the King and his advisers on 9 December, the Duke returned to London to his mother and wife. He went to see Queen Mary; Walter Monckton came, bringing the draft Instrument of Abdication to show them. As the Duke recorded, 'I broke down & sobbed like a child.'[106] His mother recalled this later, saying he was appalled. 'He was devoted to his brother and the whole Abdication crisis made him miserable. He sobbed on my shoulder for an hour – there, upon that sofa.'[107] Queen Mary was herself in shock. Her biographer pointed out that in her diary she rarely indulged in exclamation marks. On this occasion she clearly felt they were necessary. She still could not believe that her son, her firstborn, was determined to abdicate 'the Throne of this Empire because he wishes to marry Mrs Simpson!!!! The whole affair has lasted since Novr. 16th and has been very painful. It is a terrible blow to us all & particularly to poor Bertie.'[108]

The Duchess, still ill in bed, wrote to Queen Mary next day:

> I am so distressed that at this most vital and unhappy moment in the history of our country, I cannot leave the house to come & be with you. Old Weir insists that I remain in my room, at least for today and very unwillingly I have accepted his advice. My thoughts are continually with you, and we are sustained & encouraged more than I can say by your wonderful example of dignity and wisdom. Darling Mama, you are indeed a beacon of light to all the poor bewildered people who are now groping in the darkness of disillusionment, and with your leadership we must all combine to get the country back to what it was this time last year.

She ended the letter, 'I have great faith in Bertie – he sees very straight, & if this terrible responsibility comes to him he will face it bravely.'[109]

At about 10 a.m. on 10 December, in the presence of his brothers, the King signed the Instrument of Abdication, which declared his 'irrevocable determination to renounce the throne for Myself and for My descendants'. A few hours later the Prime Minister told the whole sorry story to the House of Commons and thus the world. In her diary that night Queen Mary recorded that this 'was received in silence & with real regret. The more one thinks of this affair the more regrettable it becomes.'[110]

That day negotiations became quite unpleasant on the subject of the financial settlement to be agreed with the King after his abdication. The most difficult questions involved Sandringham and Balmoral, in which, under the terms of King George V's will, his eldest son had a life interest. The properties now had to be passed to the Duke of York but the King wanted as generous a settlement for himself as he could obtain. He claimed that his total fortune was only £90,000 and that he could not survive without subsidy. He insisted that his brother should buy his life interest in Sandringham and Balmoral. The Duke agreed to pay him £25,000 a year if the government declined to do so. Later, however, it became clear that the King had lied to his brother about the true state of his finances in ways which seemed unforgivable. His wealth was later estimated to be closer to £1 million than to £100,000. 'It was a suicidal lie,' wrote King Edward VIII's biographer; and it drove further pain deep into the brothers' relationship over the years to come.[111]

Freddy Dalrymple Hamilton wrote in his diary the same day: 'The Duke of York is to be proclaimed King on Saturday & so Elizabeth will become Queen of England – a fate I never guessed for her in the old days of Glamis but which she will do as well as she does her present job.'[112]

The family rallied to the Duke and Duchess. Princess Mary* wrote at once to her sister-in-law:

> My darling Elizabeth,
>   I do want to tell you how very much you are in my thoughts at this most distressing time for us all but more especially for you and Bertie not knowing from day to day for over 3 weeks what your future life was to be. It is all a nightmare but I am truly thankful that at last the right solution has been found. I know that Bertie will carry on the great traditions of our monarchy and in this he will have you to help him. It is a great comfort at this time to realize what yours and Bertie's happiness can mean to this Country and the Empire . . . Now darling Elizabeth you must take care of yourself and get quite well. I am too sorry your being laid up just now.
>   Best love, darling Elizabeth, ever your most devoted Mary[113]

That night when the Duke returned to his home at 145 Piccadilly, as he later recorded, 'I found a large crowd outside my house cheering wildly. I was overwhelmed.'[114]

The next day, Friday 11 December, his brother's abdication was announced just before 2 p.m. The Duke was now King George VI – he had decided to take his father's name to strengthen the sense of

---

* She was now the Princess Royal, the title traditionally conferred on the eldest daughter of the sovereign, but held by only one princess at a time. So Princess Mary acquired it in 1931, on the death of the previous Princess Royal, Princess Louise, Duchess of Fife, the eldest daughter of King Edward VII.

continuity. For the new King it was 'that dreadful day'. He spent most of it occupied with arrangements for his Accession Council and Proclamation and with the difficult question of what his brother's title should now be. A decision was needed quickly because his brother insisted on making a farewell broadcast and Sir John Reith of the BBC was planning to introduce him on air that night as 'Mr Edward Windsor'. The King pointed out that that was quite wrong and instructed that his brother should be introduced as 'His Royal Highness Prince Edward'; he also declared his intention of giving the ex-King a new title. Indeed the first act of his reign was to make his brother duke of Windsor.[115]

That evening the final act of the tragedy took place at Royal Lodge. There the Royal Family dined together for the last time. Absent from the dinner, the new Queen wrote an affectionate letter of farewell to her brother-in-law.

Darling David

I am so miserable that I cannot come down to Royal Lodge owing to being ill in bed, as I wanted so much to see you before you go, and say 'God bless you' from my heart. We are all overcome with misery, and can only pray that you will find happiness in your new life.

I often think of the old days, & how you helped Bertie & I in the first years of our marriage. I shall always mention you in my prayers, & bless you, Elizabeth[116]

Afterwards Prince Edward was driven to Windsor Castle to make his farewell broadcast, which he had written himself, with some help from both Monckton and Churchill. He spoke well and moved many of his listeners to tears. Declaring his allegiance to the new monarch and his loyalty to Britain, he explained, 'I have found it impossible to carry the heavy burden of responsibility and to discharge my duties as King as I would wish to do without the help and support of the woman I love.' Determined to exonerate Mrs Simpson, he said, 'The other person most nearly concerned has tried up to the last to persuade me to take a different course.' He entrusted the nation to his brother 'with his long training in the public affairs of this country and with his fine qualities' and pointed out that 'he has one matchless blessing, enjoyed by so many of you and not bestowed on me – a happy home with his wife and children.' He ended with the words, 'And now we all have a new King. I wish him and you, his people, happiness and prosperity with all my heart. God save the King.'

The new Duke then returned to Royal Lodge to say goodbye to his family. Queen Mary had been relieved by the content of her son's speech. This was perhaps the lowest point of her life, but she concealed her feelings behind her mask of dignity and courage. 'And then', she wrote, 'came the dreadful good bye as he was leaving that evening for Austria. The whole thing was too pathetic for words.'[117] The new King embraced his predecessor and the Duke bowed to his new sovereign.[118]

The Duke was then driven away through the fog. In Portsmouth at 2 a.m. he boarded HMS *Fury* for the first leg of his journey into exile. To his astonishment, not one of his personal servants would agree to go with him.

As his brother was driving away, King George VI returned to London to his sick wife who, by her own later account, had lived the last week in a daze.[119] Queen Mary wrote to her to say how sorry she was her temperature still kept them apart. 'Thank God this awful crisis is at an end & people all welcome you both warmly, the P.M. has handled it so well and D. has acted with great dignity. You darling know how much I love you both & that you can always count on me to help you as much as I can.'[120]

The next morning, 12 December, at his Accession Council, the new King spoke with a low, clear voice but with hesitations which touched the hearts of many who heard him:

Your Royal Highnesses, My Lords and Gentlemen,

I meet you today in circumstances which are without parallel in the history of our Country. Now that the duties of Sovereignty have fallen upon Me I declare to you My adherence to the strict principles of constitutional government and My resolve to work before all else for the welfare of the British Commonwealth of Nations. With My wife and helpmeet by My side, I take up the heavy task which lies before Me.[121]

The following day, Sunday, prayers were offered for the new King and Queen throughout the country.

Reflecting on the abdication many years later in her series of conversations with Eric Anderson, Queen Elizabeth stressed the high hopes that everyone had held for King Edward VIII and the shock of his departure.

It was a terrible surprise to everybody when he decided that he had to leave. It was the whole Commonwealth who said no no, we don't want you to marry this lady. And it was just a terrible tragedy, it really was. We all loved the Prince of Wales and we all thought he was going to be a wonderful King. It was the most ghastly shock when he decided to go. It was a dreadful blow to his brother because, you see, they were great friends. It's a terrible, bitter blow when somebody you love behaves like that. Fortunately he was never crowned, and that was one of the good things he did. If he was going to make up his mind to go away, to do it before.

I wonder. I don't think he ever wanted to be King. I don't think he thought of it as something he ought to do. Very odd. People do change in a strange way. He had this extraordinary charm, and then it all disappeared. I don't know what happened. Nobody knows, really. He was frightfully popular. Everybody adored him. I think he may have thought he was so popular that people would want him back, whatever. I imagine that might have been in his mind. Oh, he was immensely popular all over the Commonwealth. He was extremely attractive. That makes it all the more strange, the whole thing. He must have been bemused with love, I suppose. You couldn't reason with him, nobody could. The whole Government tried, everybody tried. The only good thing is, I think he was quite happy with her.[122]

*

AFTER A YEAR of sadness and constant tensions, it was a time for rest, reflection and consolidation. Fortunately the Christmas and New Year holidays gave the new King and Queen, their family, their Household and, indeed, their country time to pause and take stock of the extraordinary events they had lived through.

Princess Elizabeth and Princess Margaret, aged only ten and six, also needed time to absorb what had happened. Their parents had protected them from the drama of the abdication, and they had been told nothing of it until it was over. Lady Cynthia Asquith, their mother's biographer, recorded that she saw the Princesses the day after their father's accession; Princess Margaret said, 'Isn't all this a bore? We've got to leave our nice house now,' while her elder sister was awestruck at the sight of an envelope addressed to 'Her Majesty The Queen'. 'That's *Mummie* now, isn't it?' she said. Princess Margaret later recalled that she asked her sister whether this all meant that she herself would one day be queen. 'She replied, "Yes, I suppose it does." '[123] After that, Princess Elizabeth did not mention it again. Meanwhile the two children had to come to terms with the imminent loss not only of their happy home at 145 Piccadilly but also of their relatively unconstrained family life. There was a new formality to get used to, now that the life of the Court revolved around their parents. Now both father and mother were always in the limelight – and so too were the children, although their mother continued to try to shield them from publicity. But her new role would also mean that she had less time to devote to her daughters. At least for now, her principal task undoubtedly had to be to support and encourage her husband.

She wrote at once to the Archbishop of Canterbury, to thank him for his sympathy and good advice. She said, 'I can hardly now believe that we have been called to this tremendous task, and, (I am writing to you quite intimately) the curious thing is that we are not afraid. I feel that God has enabled us to face the situation calmly.' They were, she said, 'so very unhappy over the loss of a dear brother – because one can only feel that exile from this country is death indeed . . . We pray most sincerely that we shall not fail our country, & I sign myself for the first time, & with great affection Elizabeth R.'[124] Cosmo Lang was touched by this letter, and his chaplain Alan Don urged him to keep it carefully for it showed the Queen's spirit – 'we are not afraid'.[125] The Archbishop told her he was eager to discuss the plans for the Coronation of not only the new King but also 'forgive me if I say Hurrah! – of the Queen'.[126] One decision had been already made. The Coronation was to be on 12 May 1937, the day planned for Edward VIII.

Dr Lang also made his own controversial intervention. In a post-abdication address to the nation, the Archbishop criticized the late King's conduct: 'Even more strange and sad is that he should have sought his happiness in a manner inconsistent with the Christian principles of marriage, and within a social circle whose standards and whose way of life are alien to all the best instincts and traditions of his people.'[127] These words aroused widespread distaste and hundreds of

critical, even abusive letters, were received at Lambeth Palace in the
next few days. A doggerel made the rounds:

> My Lord Archbishop what a scold you are!
> And when your man is down how bold you are!
> In Christian charity how scant you are!
> Oh! Old Lang Swine, how full of Cantuar!

Many of those who criticized him feared that his words would have
upset Queen Mary. On the contrary: Queen Mary told those around
her that she thought the Archbishop 'was quite right in saying what
he did'.[128] Queen Elizabeth agreed. To one friend she wrote of the
Archbishop's address, 'I think the nation vaguely _felt_ it, but _he_ put the
issue clearly and as no one else had the right to do. Nowadays we are
inclined to be too vague about the things that matter, and I think it
well that for once someone should speak out in plain and direct words,
what after all was the truth.'[129]

King George VI celebrated his forty-first birthday on 14 December
by bestowing upon his wife the Order of the Garter. She was delighted
and wrote at once to give the news to Queen Mary. Bertie, she said,
'had discovered that Papa gave it to you on his, Papa's, birthday June
3rd, and the coincidence was so charming that he has now followed
suit'.[130] His biographer pointed out there was more to it than that – it
was also 'a public declaration of gratitude and affection to one who
had shared with him so bravely the burdens of the past, and was to
bear with him so nobly the trials of the future'.[131]

Queen Mary, moved by the kind letters she had received, asked
her son's permission to issue a message of thanks to the British
people.[132] The King immediately gave his assent. 'It will be such a
great help to me,' he told her.[133] Cosmo Lang wrote the message for
her; this time, his words were without controversy, intended both to
give some credit to Queen Mary's eldest son and to beg for support of
her second. She declared that her heart had been filled with distress
when her dear son laid down his charge. 'I commend to you his
brother, summoned so unexpectedly and in circumstances so painful
to take his place ... With him I commend my dear daughter-in-law
who will be his Queen. May she receive the same unfailing affection
and trust which you have given to me for six and twenty years.'[134]

Queen Mary was indeed shattered – her daughter-in-law wrote to

Victor Cazalet* that the abdication 'very nearly killed poor Queen Mary, there is indeed such a thing as a broken heart and hers very nearly collapsed'.[135] Widowed and, as she saw it, abandoned by her firstborn, she wanted to gather the rest of her family around her to try and recreate as much as possible the atmosphere that she and King George V had created for both family and Household. On 22 December the family left for their traditional Christmas at Sandringham and, but for a short break, remained there until the end of January. Not surprisingly, after the stress of recent months Queen Mary spent most of Christmas week in her own set of rooms.

She was greatly relieved that the new King was able to act just in time to stop the sale, arranged by Edward VIII, of thousands of acres belonging to Anmer and Flitcham farms, part of the Sandringham estate. Unlike his brother, the King loved the place. To the relief of retainers and Household alike, he immediately reversed many of the other changes proposed by Edward VIII at both Sandringham and Balmoral.

Owen Morshead was invited to Royal Lodge the weekend after the accession, and then to Sandringham, and recorded that he found both King and Queen 'exceedingly kind and frank'. Understandably, there was only one topic of discussion: Edward VIII's almost casual manner of handing the reins to his brother. 'Here you are; I can't do it; you take it on.' The King and Queen dwelt upon his extraordinary personality – 'his amazing power of charming people, his flair for making any party go'. The Queen praised his 'unique talents' but was concerned that if he parted from Mrs Simpson 'it would be dangerous to have such a powerful personality, so magnetic, hanging about doing nothing.'[136]

There was no Christmas Broadcast this year, but the King released a New Year message dedicating himself to the peoples of the British Empire. 'I realize to the full the responsibilities of my noble heritage. I shoulder them with all the more confidence in the knowledge that the Queen and my mother Queen Mary are at my side ... To repeat the words used by my dear father at the time of his Silver Jubilee, my wife and I dedicate ourselves for all time to your service, and we pray that

---

* Lieutenant Colonel Victor Cazalet (1896–1943), MP for Chippenham 1924–43. He served as political liaison officer to General Sikorski, the Polish wartime leader, from 1940, and was killed in the same aeroplane crash as the General in 1943.

God may give us guidance and strength to follow the path that lies before us.'[137]

*

THE TWO QUEENS agreed on their principal shared duty – sustaining the King. In their letters they were solicitous of each other. The new Queen thanked her mother-in-law for 'your unfailing sympathy & understanding through those first bewildering days when we were still stunned by the shock of David's going . . . It was so wonderful having the old family atmosphere again. I feel sure that it is our great strength in these difficult days.'[138]

She was receiving support from the wider Royal Family as well. The King's great-aunt Princess Beatrice tried to reassure her: 'You are so sweet & good & have always adorned your position so well, that I am [sure] you need have no diffidence about becoming Queen.'[139] Queen Mary's niece Mary, Duchess of Beaufort, recalled how long ago they had danced about together – Elizabeth in a blue dress covered in red cherries. 'What ages ago it seems and what things have happened through the years that have gone. There is one thing that has never changed – and that is yourself. What a relief it is to find that!' The feelings of disquiet she had had during the previous ten months were gone now.[140] Princess Alice, Countess of Athlone, sent a long affection- ate letter full of sympathy for the loss of freedom and 'untrammelled family life' that lay ahead.[141]

Queen Mary wrote to thank Cecilia Strathmore for her sympathy over the ordeal she had suffered. But in the end, she thought, all was for the best and 'dear Bertie and Elizabeth will carry out things in the same way that King George V did . . . Elizabeth is such a darling and is such a help to Bertie.'[142] Lady Strathmore agreed. She had been horrified by the events of the last few months. 'I still can hardly believe that my darling little daughter is the Queen of this great Empire,' she wrote to Sir John Weir, who was treating the Queen's influenza, but she was sure that she and the new King 'will be great examples of all that is good & best in this world'.[143]

The Queen told Queen Mary that she felt very emotional at this time, and set enormous value on friendship – particularly from those whom she felt liked her and the King for their own sakes. One evening at dinner Owen Morshead told her that Eric Savill, the presiding genius of Windsor Great Park who had helped them create their garden at

Royal Lodge, was perfectly devoted to them both. At this she seemed on the verge of tears.[144] She and her husband were genuinely worried that people would not like them, and that King George VI would be seen as a poor substitute for King Edward. Friends and family advised them to take things quietly and allow the public to get to know them in their new role.

It was a role the King at first thought he could never properly play. Suddenly he had all the burdens of a constitutional monarch with, in Walter Bagehot's famous formulation, the right to be consulted by his ministers, the right to advise them and the right to warn them. These rights were in effect duties, and were only part of his myriad new obligations. His brother the Duke of Windsor later explained well the drudgery of much of the work. 'From long observation of my father's activities, I knew only too well what I was in for. The picture of him "doing his boxes", to use his own phrase, had long represented to me the relentless grind of the King's daily routine.'[145] Never had the new King more depended on his wife's reassurance and her ability to calm his 'gnashes'.

As well as calming and bolstering her husband and reassuring her daughters about the future, the Queen was kept busy replying to the flood of letters which now landed every day on her desk. Many, from both friends and strangers, expressed relief that the uncertainty was over and some reflected confidence that she and her husband would, much more than Edward VIII, embody the solid values of King George V and Queen Mary. Jasper Ridley was sure that the frightening task they were taking on 'must be lightened by the conviction you will have of goodwill around you. You see, we do want the Monarchy, and we must have it in hands like yours.'[146]

From the Embassy in Baghdad came a letter from her old suitor Archie Clark Kerr rejoicing in the fact that there was now a Scottish queen on the throne.[147] Osbert Sitwell wrote to her: 'I think the country is very fortunate in finding you both at such a time.'[148] She replied with characteristic brio: 'One can hardly believe that we could have survived such drama & tragedy, & yet, here we are, back at the old business – Buckling to, doing our best, keeping the old Flag flying hoorah, and of course it is the only thing that is worth doing now. I believe now, more than ever before, that this country is worth sacrificing a good deal for. In fact, if I was exiled, I should die, anyway in the spirit.'[149] She was aware that she and the King would probably be 'moderately unpopular' for some time, 'but as long as our friends stick to us, one can shoulder any amount of trouble. Certainly what is called the burden of Kingship is truly said. The whole thing is a burden – when you are youngish and an Aunt Sally for verbal skittles, especially; & yet, the more difficult it all is, the more worth while.'[150]

She thanked D'Arcy Osborne for his 'dear, understanding letter. I do wish that you had been here during these days of drama & tragedy and disappointment . . . – everything seems like a bad dream. But the curious thing is, that I am not afraid. Inadequate, but un-frightened.'[151]

*

AT THE BEGINNING of 1937 there was a malicious campaign of gossip against the King. He had decided, with great reluctance, to postpone an Accession Durbar in India that his brother had agreed for the winter of 1937–8. The announcement that the new King would not now undertake such an important trip and ceremony was taken by some to show that he was weak and frail. Concern on this score had been inadvertently augmented by Cosmo Lang. In his controversial post-abdication broadcast, he had not only criticized the Duke of Windsor's behaviour, he had also drawn attention to the new King's speech defect. He claimed, 'he has brought it into full control, and to those who hear it it need cause no sort of embarrassment, for it causes none to him who speaks.'[152] The Archbishop's remarks were unfortunate; they led the public to expect serious problems with the new King's diction and this in turn increased the King's nervousness. It was soon whispered that, although his appearance was tolerable, he was in fact quite unfit to be king. Supporters of the Duke of Windsor claimed that King George VI might not even be able to survive the Coronation, let alone all the subsequent duties of kingship.

The Duke of Windsor's own behaviour did not help. Queen Elizabeth was subsequently blamed, by some at least, for the fact that the relationship between the brothers, once so close, deteriorated further and further during 1937. But it is hard, in face of the evidence, to hold her responsible – her overriding concern was to sustain and encourage her husband, to give him the confidence to try and rebuild the monarchy in which they believed so strongly. The bad blood that arose between the brothers was sad but perhaps inevitable.

The Queen was convinced that her husband needed all possible help to resist the real but, she thought, improper demands of his brother. Almost alone in Austria, separated from Mrs Simpson until her decree absolute came through at the end of April, the Duke of Windsor spent a great deal of time on the telephone. He constantly called his brother, the King, and took easily to advising him on what he should do. George VI found these telephone calls difficult, as Walter Monckton recorded with sympathy. It was not just that he had always admired his brother. 'The Duke of Windsor was particularly quick in understanding and decision and good on the telephone whereas King George VI had not the same quickness and was troubled by the impediment in his speech.'[153]

Sometimes the Duke's unsought political advice ran counter to that which the new King was receiving from his government. More difficult were the personal matters. Even before the end of January 1937 the Duke was constantly telephoning about money, about returning to Fort Belvedere, about his attendance at the Coronation, about members of his family coming to his eventual wedding, and above all about Mrs Simpson's title when they married. Arguments over these issues were painful for all concerned throughout the early months of 1937 – and thereafter.

The King's brother-in-law Lord Harewood understood the threat that the Duke represented to the King, on a personal and a political level, and believed that it was absolutely essential to keep him out of the country for five, or even ten, years. He thought that the King should treat his brother's return as a matter for the Cabinet to decide.[154]

The King and Queen were aware that opinion at all levels of the country was still divided. Malicious rumours about both Kings continued to swirl around the smart houses of London as alliances changed and those who had been friendly with the former King or, worse, with Mrs Simpson found that they were now out of fashion. In fact, given the way in which the country and society had been riven by Edward VIII's priorities and his abdication, the new King and Queen were quite indulgent of those who had taken the side of the former King. Lord Brownlow, who had accompanied Mrs Simpson to the south of France in December, lost his position as lord in waiting, but no other major figures suffered for their involvement with King Edward and his set. Indeed, the new King embraced his brother's most trusted confidant, Walter Monckton. It was a tribute both to Monckton's extraordinary integrity and to the King's judgement that the King conferred on him the first knighthood of the new reign. He remained ever after a diligent and extraordinary servant of his country and his King and the only channel of communication who was also trusted by the exiled Duke of Windsor.

Others enjoyed mocking the former King's friends. Soon after the abdication Osbert Sitwell wrote a poem, 'Rat Week', in which he denounced all those who had sought the favour of Edward VIII and Mrs Simpson and then jumped ship.

> Where are the friends of yesterday
>   That fawned on Him,
>   That flattered Her;
> Where are the friends of yesterday,
> Submitting to His every whim,
> Offering praise of her as myrrh
>   To him?
> What do they say, that jolly crew,
> So new, and brave, and free and easy,
> What do they say, that jolly crew,
> Who must make even Judas queasy?

Sitwell was concerned that, despite their long friendship, the new Queen might not like his poem and he did not send it to her himself, telling her later that he thought it would be 'an impertinence'.[155] He had no reason to worry. She loved it, writing to him, 'I must tell you first of all, that we all thought your satire absolutely brilliant. It really is perfect – it hits hard (and never too hard for me) and is wickedly amusing.'

In this unusually acerbic letter, which perhaps betrayed the strain she was under at the time, she told him what a relief it was to have his amusing and friendly letter 'amongst the vast amount of begging letters, complaints, appeals, warnings, lunatic ramblings etc which go to make up one's daily postbag. Not forgetting bad poetry, bad drawings & paintings, bad music & other bad things sent by the mad & bad who seem to people the world. So you can imagine how one falls greedily on the few friendly letters that come, and yours was very welcome!'[156]

*

AFTER THE RELAXING sojourn at Sandringham, the family had the unwelcome prospect of beginning life at Buckingham Palace. None of them wished to leave the happy home at 145 Piccadilly for the rather grim 'office' of the Palace. Queen Elizabeth later described this as the worst house move of her life.[157]

The date chosen was 15 February. The King drove up from Royal Lodge and the Queen went first to an engagement at the British Industries Fair at White City in west London. *The Times* reported, 'The whole move was accomplished without ceremony, and no change in the exterior appearance of the Palace will be visible to the casual passer-by. The Royal Standard flew while Their Majesties were still living in Piccadilly, and no increase in the number of sentries at the gates is made. It is understood that the King and Queen will use the rooms on the first floor formerly occupied by King George and Queen Mary.' The rooms were not yet ready for them, and they lived temporarily on the ground floor. It was not very comfortable, but at least the young Princesses enjoyed playing in the broad corridors. With her mother-in-law's diligent advice – this time welcome – the Queen set about acquiring some new furnishings. At the suggestion of Queen Mary, Mrs Charles Rothschild gave her several sets of silk curtains from her family's house in Piccadilly. 'Hooray!' wrote the Queen, 'what splendid news about the curtains, and how wonderful a success your letter had! It really is a triumph, and most kind of Mrs Rothschild to offer us that lovely silk. One can get nothing to touch it nowadays.' Major Williams, the official responsible for the furnishings at Buckingham Palace, 'turned quite pale with excitement when I told him!' Queen Mary also tracked down a chandelier and wall lights for her.[158]

The Queen had started making appointments to her own Household. She was able to surround herself with people she knew well, liked and trusted. As duchess of York she had had just two ladies in waiting, Helen Graham and Lettice Bowlby (with her great friends Lavinia Annaly and Tortor Gilmour as temporary additions); now she had a hierarchy of nine ladies. Her most senior lady, the Mistress of the Robes, by tradition had to be a duchess, and she chose Doris Vyner's aunt, Helen, Duchess of Northumberland. Below the Mistress of the Robes came three Ladies of the Bedchamber: Countess Spencer (Cynthia, sister of the Queen's girlhood friend Katie Hamilton and future grandmother of Lady Diana Spencer), Viscountess Halifax (Dorothy, wife of the Lord Privy Seal and future Foreign Secretary),

Viscountess Hambleden and Lady Nunburnholme (both friends of her debutante years, and the latter a bridesmaid at her wedding). Then there were four Women of the Bedchamber: Helen Graham and Lettice Bowlby stayed on in this role, and Queen Elizabeth also appointed Katie Seymour (née Hamilton) and Marion Hyde,* with Lady Victoria Wemyss, a cousin on her mother's side, as Extra Woman of the Bedchamber. The Earl of Airlie – Joe, friend and neighbour at Glamis since the Queen's childhood – became her Lord Chamberlain, while Basil Brooke, the Duke of York's Comptroller since 1924, became her Treasurer. A little later she took on a private secretary of her own, Captain Richard Streatfeild.

Their first official engagement as monarchs was a visit to the East End of London on 13 February. Originally this visit was to have been made by King Edward VIII on 12 December – in the event the day after the abdication. The invitation had come from the mayors of five boroughs and it was then extended to King George VI, with the request that the Queen came too 'as she is so very popular in our district'.[159] Lord Cromer, Lord Chamberlain and head of the King's Household, thought it was important to accept, for 'there is a growing impression in the minds of the ignorant that the last King was "pushed out" largely because of the interest he took in the poor, which did not find favour in the eyes of the rich, nor of the Government people who are supposed to have disapproved of the interest taken in the Distressed Areas in Wales, and elsewhere . . . These ideas are, of course, fantastic but at the same time they appear to be rooted and to be spreading in the minds of the ignorant.' He recommended therefore that the King and Queen should visit the East End as soon as might be possible.[160] They agreed and the visit was a great success; the streets were filled with flags, bunting and cheering crowds.

In March the first official parties of the new reign were given – a tea party at Buckingham Palace for the Diplomatic Corps on 11 March was followed by an afternoon reception five days later, at which Countess Spencer took a select number of the 500 guests to talk to the Queen. The Queen, she wrote, 'did it beautifully, & appeared to <u>wish</u> to talk to each guest – a great gift'. Queen Mary was also there,

---

* Lady Hyde (1900–70), née the Hon. Marion Glyn, married in 1932 George, Lord Hyde, eldest son of sixth Earl of Clarendon. He was killed in a shooting accident in 1935. Their son Laurence became the seventh Earl.

'looking wonderful in dead black lace & <u>miles</u> of pearls – also the two little Princesses – most pleasing to the eye in the sombre atmosphere of the Palace'.[161]

Next day there was a formal dinner at the Palace. Afterwards, Harold Nicolson recorded, the Queen talked to her guests. 'She wears upon her face a faint smile indicative of how much she would have liked her dinner-party were it not for the fact that she was Queen of England. Nothing could exceed the charm or dignity which she displays, and I cannot help feeling what a mess poor Mrs Simpson would have made of such an occasion . . . The Queen teases me very charmingly about my pink face and my pink views.'[162]* At the end of that week the Queen had a more amusing engagement at what was to become her favourite sport – she went to the Grand National at Aintree.

Easter 1937 was like the old days: they spent it once again at Windsor Castle. They and the Princesses were warmly cheered by large crowds as they drove from Royal Lodge through the Great Park. Their party included Clement Attlee and his wife Violet. Attlee wrote to his brother Tom, 'The K and Q were very pleasant and easy to get on with.'[163] Osbert Sitwell was delighted to be among their guests, although he worried beforehand to his sister-in-law, Georgia, 'It will be lovely seeing it, and in grand state – Windsor liveries, gold plate, bands etc. – but I'm rather terrified.'[164]

Also invited were the Duff Coopers, who had been on the *Nahlin* cruise. Lady Diana Cooper decided it was best to be frank about her friendship with Edward VIII and told the King at dinner, 'I'm afraid I'm a Rat, Sir' – a remark that the King enjoyed passing on to Osbert Sitwell. When Lady Diana retired to bed, her husband stayed behind for 'an hour's so-called drinking tea with the Queen. She put her feet up on a sofa and talked of Kingship and "the intolerable honour" but not of the [abdication] crisis.' Lady Diana noted, 'Duff so happy, me rather piqued.' She thought that Windsor compared well with Fort Belvedere. 'That was an operetta, this is an institution.'[165]

---

* Sir Harold Nicolson KCVO CMG (1886–1968), diplomat, author, diarist and politician, married to the writer Vita Sackville-West. He entered Parliament as a member of the National Labour Party in 1935 and quickly became a strong voice in alerting the country to the dangers of fascism. His diaries are among the most important first-hand accounts of British political and social life in the mid-twentieth century. He wrote the official biography of King George V, published in 1952.

The figurehead of the institution was very happy. Queen Mary wrote to her son and daughter-in-law after Easter to say, 'what a joy it has been to me to feel that the beloved old Home is in such good hands & that you two dear beloved people will carry on the tradition which dear Papa & I tried to do, in memory of our ancestors & of the wonderful history of Windsor.'[166]

*

THROUGHOUT ALL THIS time the King and Queen were having to prepare for the greatest event in their lives – the Coronation. When they came unexpectedly to the throne, it was not just the date of the ceremony that had been fixed. Much of the basic planning had already been done, but five months was not long to complete the preparations, particularly now that a queen was to be crowned, as well as a king.

First, and perhaps most important of all, the Queen's crown had to be created. The crown jewellers, Garrard, were summoned to Sandringham in January to start to suggest designs. They produced sketches and those that the Queen and the King thought possible were mocked up in painted metal models. They found it difficult to decide whether to have one of eight arches or four. Eventually they chose a model with four arches.

The majority of the stones for the new crown came from the dismantled Regal Circlet made for Queen Victoria in 1853 and remounted for her in 1858. The band of the Circlet, which the new crown virtually replicated, but in platinum, had been set with sixteen large diamonds between sixteen crosses and surmounted by four fleurs-de-lis alternating with Maltese crosses. One of these was designed to hold the huge Koh-i-nûr diamond, which could be detached and worn as a brooch.* The Koh-i-nûr had subsequently been incorporated into Queen Alexandra's crown of 1902 and Queen Mary's of 1911. Now it became part of the new Queen's crown.

Queen Mary entered into the planning, as her biographer put it, 'with her characteristic vigour'.[167] She was determined to break with tradition and attend the ceremony – the first time that the widow of a king would be present in Westminster Abbey to see his successor

---

* The Koh-i-nûr (Mountain of Light) was the most famous of the jewels in the Lahore Treasury, ceded to Britain following the annexation of the Punjab in 1849. The diamond was presented to Queen Victoria in 1850 and recut under Prince Albert's direction in 1852.

crowned. She could not bear not to be present when her beloved second son went through the ritual which his brother had renounced. She accompanied the Queen to Garrard to examine the crown jewels, she went to the Abbey to see the preparations, in particular the creation of the Royal Box, she advised on the colour of the ribbon for the King's Order (the family order given to royal ladies by the sovereign – she thought it should be pink), she worried about how the Princesses should travel to the service.[168]

The Queen realized, according to Elizabeth Longford, that her old dressmaker, Madame Handley Seymour, would be heartbroken if she were not allowed to make the Coronation robes, and so she gave her the commission. The robe was traditional, resembling that which Queen Mary had worn in 1911, which in turn reflected that of Queen Alexandra in 1902. It had a combined cape and train; the white ermine shoulder cape was fastened on the shoulders with white satin bows, and with gold cord and tassels. The train was of purple velvet, forty-four inches wide and eighteen feet long. Symbols of the British Empire – the rose, thistle, shamrock, leek, maple, acacia, fern and lotus – were embroidered on the velvet with gold thread. The dress itself was fashionably bias-cut white satin with square décolleté and slashed sleeves flounced with old lace. It was embroidered by members of the Royal School of Needlework with diamanté emblems of the British Isles and Empire. Three rows of gold galloon lace ran around the edge of the train. The Queen's shoes, made by Jack Jacobus of Shaftesbury Avenue, were white satin high heels, decorated with English oak leaves and Scottish thistles.[169]

The two Princesses were measured for their own robes of purple velvet lined and edged with ermine, with ermine capes tied, like their mother's, with gold cords and tassels on the shoulder. For the maids of honour, Norman Hartnell created stiff white satin dresses with embroidered garlands in pearls, diamanté and crystal incorporating a Victorian wheat-ear motif suggested by the Queen herself.

As the Coronation approached, the King became increasingly nervous about how he would deal with the strain of it, and in particular whether his stammer would cripple his public responses in the Abbey and the live broadcast he would have to make from Buckingham Palace in the evening after the service. Cosmo Lang had the temerity to suggest a new voice coach, but Lord Dawson rejected this idea at once, saying that the King had full confidence in Lionel Logue. In fact, the King was also helped by a BBC sound engineer called Robert Wood, who spent many hours teaching him how best to use the microphone.[170]

At the end of April the King, Queen and Princess Elizabeth travelled by barge down the river to Greenwich to open the National Maritime Museum. This was the first royal progress along the Thames since 1919. The Queen unlocked the door of the newly restored Queen's House with a gold key. They returned to central London by car and were mobbed by crowds almost all the way.

In the few days that were left before the Coronation, they spent as much time as possible at Royal Lodge and Windsor Castle. After a relaxed lunch on May Day they drove, again through cheering crowds, to Wembley Stadium for the FA Cup Final – Sunderland beat Preston North End by three goals to one. They listened, clearly touched, as more than 90,000 people sang 'God Save the King'.[171]

The first Court of the new reign was held on 5 May. It was just as splendid and as formal as any that had been held by King George V and Queen Mary. In the Ball Room, the King and Queen sat on the dais before as many as 500 members of the Diplomatic Corps. Countess Spencer thought the Queen looked 'really beautiful' but she was not impressed by many of the ladies' curtsies, and remarked on the behaviour of the emissaries of the European dictators. 'The German ambassador, Herr von Ribbentrop, gave the King a Nazi salute & Signor Grandi [the Italian Ambassador] left the ball room as soon as possible, to avoid meeting any Abyssinians!'[172]*

All of Britain was preparing for a greater celebration than the 1935 Jubilee. There were official street decorations in every town, and shops and home owners made their own happy contributions to the gaiety. The London stores competed to produce the most splendid displays of imperial loyalty, with immense plaster casts and portraits of the King and Queen, masses of red, white and blue bunting. Selfridges was

---

* Ribbentrop, a supporter of Edward VIII and Mrs Simpson, had already given the Nazi salute in an even more enthusiastic manner, when he presented his credentials to the King. This had caused something of a scandal. The German diplomat Reinhard Spitzy recorded that, although the King had smiled weakly, his courtiers were furious and the press splashed the story, nicknaming the Ambassador 'Brickendrop'. The salutes nonetheless continued. Spitzy wrote that at this Court 'Ribbentrop delivered his three salutes in a rather more conciliatory fashion and not without a little humility.' (Reinhard Spitzy, *How We Squandered the Reich*, Michael Russell, 1997, pp. 70–1)

widely thought to have taken the prize and an Indian rajah was said to be so impressed by its decorations that he bought the whole lot, to be reinstalled in his palace.[173]

Huge crowds flocked towards London in special trains and chara-bancs. In almost every town and village Coronation committees were formed, May queens were chosen, fireworks were purchased, commemorative trees were planted. Maypoles were erected on village greens and children were taught how to dance around them, holding red, white and blue ribbons, bands practised, people of all ages trained for sports events, marquees were erected, bonfires built, veterans of the Great War polished their shoes and prepared to act as proud stewards throughout the country.[174]

On the evening of Sunday 9 May, congregations gathered in churches all over the country for special services at which prayers were offered for the King and Queen. As this worship was taking place, the Archbishop of Canterbury came to Buckingham Palace for a final talk and prayers with the King and Queen. Any unease about his reference to the King's stammer was clearly forgotten. 'They knelt with me,' he wrote later. 'I prayed for them and for their realm and Empire, and I gave them my personal blessing. I was much moved and so were they. Indeed there were tears in their eyes when we rose from our knees. From that moment I knew what would be in their minds and hearts when they came to their anointing and crowning.'[175]

There is no doubt that for both of them the Coronation was an act of great spiritual significance. Each of them was a devout Christian with a simple faith; each of them believed strongly in the sacred nature of monarchy and of the vows that they were about to take; they both believed that they were offering themselves before God and were being consecrated in the service of their people. The King himself, according to his biographer, was very grateful for the genuine affection that people had shown for him and the Queen since their unexpected accession.[176]

Crowds gathered all night, with many people sleeping on camp beds in the streets. The King and Queen were awoken at 3 a.m. by the testing of the loudspeakers on Constitution Hill – 'one of them might have been in our room,' wrote the King in his diary. From then on marching troops, bands and tension made sleep impossible. The King could eat no breakfast and had 'a sinking feeling inside'.[177]

The invited congregation had to be in the Abbey by around seven in the morning. Crowds cheered them along the roads. A special underground train took several hundred peers and peeresses in their full robes and wearing their coronets, together with Members of the House of Commons, from Kensington High Street to Westminster. The fare was threepence.[178]

The Queen had her own box in the Abbey which she filled with members of the Bowes Lyon family and a few particular friends. They included the faithful Beryl Poignand, Osbert Sitwell* and the Rev. Tubby Clayton. Owen Morshead, sitting with other members of the Household near by, left a touching account of the service in a long letter to his aunt. Peers, peeresses, bishops, judges, the Knights Grand Cross, in robes and regalia, the lustrous colours shining against the sober grey stone. Then the various processions began. The Princess Royal arrived 'between the two darling little Princesses in their full kit, their embryo trains looking as if they would grow with their wearers . . . little Princess Margaret very sweetly lifted up the front of her dress in ascending the steps, looking across surreptitiously to observe how her bigger sister was tackling it.'

After the Kents and the Gloucesters and other members of the family came one of the principal moments for which people had been waiting. 'As Queen Mary's noble figure appeared against the sombre woodwork of the choir-entry the impression was such as to give me a catch in the throat at the memory. She was ablaze with large diamonds the size of beans, and she wore around her silvered head the circlet of her former crown with the 4 arches removed. But it was not alone the glory of her personal appointments, but the majesty and grace of her bearing that made everyone hold their breath.'[179]

The King and Queen drove to the Abbey in the beautifully archaic Gold State Coach first used by George III in 1762. At the annexe built on the west door their two processions formed up. The Queen was to lead, but she was delayed when a chaplain passed out, just as her procession into the Abbey for her wedding fourteen years before had

---

* Sitwell had written an 'Ode for the Coronation of Their Majesties, May 12, 1937', which began:

> The King and Queen of England, what fair names
> That for a thousand years have lit the flames
> Within Their people's hearts; what trumpets sound
> Through timeless vistas as They both are crowned!

been held up by a fainting clergyman.* She entered the Abbey preceded by her cousin the Duke of Portland, who carried her new crown on a red velvet cushion. She seemed to Morshead:

> submissive and demure, and looking, despite her dazzling jewelry, curiously unfinished as to her costume: for not only had she no gloves (to facilitate the placing of the Ring upon her finger), but also her head was bare of any sort of covering. Her demeanour throughout was beautiful to observe, and it contributed greatly towards the impression which everyone seems to have carried away with them – namely that once the doors were closed and the various pieces duly disposed upon the board the pageantry and display fell away, revealing a deeply devotional service within the framework of the Holy Communion.[180]

Alan Don, the Archbishop of Canterbury's chaplain, was also watching her. 'As the Queen crossed the Theatre on her way to her chair of State under the Royal box, I looked at Lord and Lady Strathmore . . . and wondered what were their emotions as they watched their youngest daughter coming to be crowned as Queen. The Queen did not glance up at them (I expect that she scarcely dared), but took her place, looking neither to the right hand or to the left, to await the arrival of the King.'[181]

For most of the long service the focus was upon the King; the Queen stood or knelt at her chair immediately in front of the Royal Box. There, her daughter Princess Elizabeth, now just eleven, sitting next to Queen Mary, was following it all closely. 'I thought it all <u>very</u>, <u>very</u> wonderful and I expect the Abbey did, too. The arches and beams at the top were covered with a sort of haze of wonder as Papa was crowned, at least I thought so.'[182]

Once the King had been crowned and had taken the solemn oaths which were to dominate his life from now on, the Archbishop made his way towards the Queen. She knelt while he prayed, 'Almighty God, the fountain of all goodness: give ear we beseech thee to our

---

* The chaplain's faint in 1937 was recorded by King George VI himself. The 1923 incident appears only in Dorothy Laird's *Queen Elizabeth The Queen Mother*, Coronet, 1966; it may be that Laird confused the two occasions.

prayers, and multiply thy blessing upon thy servant ELIZABETH, whom in thy Name, with all humble devotion, we consecrate our Queen; defend her evermore from all dangers, ghostly and bodily; make her a great example of virtue and piety, and a blessing to the kingdom; through Jesus Christ our Lord, who liveth and reigneth with thee, O Father, in the unity of the Holy Spirit, world without end. Amen.'

Four duchesses held over her head the same canopy as was used for the anointing of the King. The Queen was anointed on her head only, whereas the King had been anointed on the palms of both hands, on the breast and on the crown of his head. The Archbishop placed the Queen's ring, rubies and brilliants, previously worn by Queen Adelaide, Queen Alexandra and Queen Mary, on the fourth finger of her right hand. And then Elizabeth Bowes Lyon was crowned queen. Lifting the crown above her head, the Archbishop said, 'Receive the Crown of glory, honour and joy; and God, the crown of the Faithful, who by our Episcopal hands (though unworthy) doth this day set a crown of pure gold upon your head, enrich your royal heart with his abundant grace, and crown you with all princely virtues in this life, and with everlasting gladness in the life that is to come, through Jesus Christ our Lord. Amen.'

As the Queen was crowned, a herald turned and made a sign to the rows of peeresses, at which hundreds of white-gloved arms rose up as each lady placed upon her head her own coronet. Princess Elizabeth was struck by this moment. 'When Mummy was crowned and all the peeresses put on their coronets, it looked wonderful to see arms and coronets hovering in the air and then the arms disappear as if by magic.'[183]

The Archbishop then gave the Queen her gold sceptre and ivory rod, both made for Queen Mary of Modena, wife of James II. Thus anointed, crowned and bearing her regalia, she proceeded to her throne. The Order of Service noted, 'And as she passeth by the King on his throne, she shall bow herself reverently to his Majesty, and then be conducted to her own throne, and without any further ceremony, take her place in it.' Together, the King and Queen then removed their crowns and received Holy Communion, probably the most moving and sacred moment of the tumultuous day for them both. They then walked together down the nave of the Abbey, outside to the Gold Coach which bore them back by a long route to the Palace. The rain poured down but this did not seem to dampen the excitement of the crowds who cheered them with wild enthusiasm.

That evening the King had to face the dreaded ordeal of his live broadcast from the Palace. In endless rehearsals with the Queen, with Logue and with Wood, he had stumbled, but on the actual day adrenalin overcame nerves and exhaustion and he was word perfect. 'It is with a very full heart that I speak to you tonight,' he said. 'Never before has a newly crowned King been able to talk to all his peoples in their own homes on the day of his Coronation . . . the Queen and I will always keep in our hearts the inspiration of this day. May we ever be worthy of the goodwill which I am proud to think surrounds us at the outset of my reign.' In evening dress, he and the Queen, who was wrapped in a white fur-trimmed stole, appeared five times on the Palace balcony to wave to the crowds still braving the rain.

Before midnight, Queen Mary wrote to them, 'I cannot let this day pass without once again telling you both how beautifully & reverently you carried out this most beautiful impressive service, I felt so proud of you both, & I felt beloved Papa's spirit was near us in blessing you on this wonderful day. I could not help feeling what that poor foolish David has relinquished for nothing!!! but it is better so & better for our beloved Country.'[184]

The Queen described her own experience in a letter thanking Archbishop Lang.

> I write to you with a very full heart . . . I was more moved, & more helped than I could have believed possible. It is curious, on thinking it over now, that I was not conscious of there being anybody else there at the Communion – you told us last Sunday evening that we would be helped and we were sustained & carried above the ordinary fear of a great ceremony. Our great hope now, is that as so many millions of people were impressed by the feeling of service and goodness that came from Westminster Abbey, that perhaps that day will result in strength and good feeling in individuals all over the world, and be a calming & strengthening influence on affairs in general.
>
> I thank you with all my heart for what you have been to us during these last difficult and tragic months – a good counsellor and true friend – we are indeed grateful. I am, Your affectionate friend Elizabeth R.[185]

CHAPTER ELEVEN

QUEEN CONSORT

1937–1939

'From thirty to forty, one battled and remade one's ideas'

THE HISTORIAN and royal biographer Noble Frankland observed that most biographies are about extraordinary people: they seek to explain how their subjects accomplished 'whatever it was that caught the eye of history', and they explore tensions related to ability, ambition and rivalry. The tension in a royal biography, however, 'is about how the ordinary man adjusts to the extraordinary position into which he is born'. The interesting question is not the position itself, nor how the subject reached it, but what sort of a fist he made of it.[1]

In the case of the non-royal bride of a royal prince, of course, it is marriage rather than birth that confers her position on her. As the subject of a biography, therefore, she crosses the boundary between Dr Frankland's definitions, for the story of how she achieved her marriage may well be part of the interesting question. This is certainly so in Queen Elizabeth's case. She was the first commoner to become queen consort since the seventeenth century – that in itself is of interest, at least to students of the British monarchy. Secondly, how she reached her position is of interest not just because it is an appealingly romantic tale, but also because it took place against a background of social and political ferment potentially damaging to the monarchy. Then there is the added curiosity that it was not a position she had sought. Indeed she rejected it at first. The story so far has tried to show why she inspired her royal suitor with so powerful a determination to win her hand. It has aimed also to show what she made of the position she took on.

The moment when the reluctant royal Duchess found herself becoming a queen *malgré elle* is an appropriate one at which to step back to consider her life as she had lived it since she had joined the Royal Family. In so doing we may ask how successful she had been in filling the lesser role into which she had married, and how well this had fitted her for the greater one into which she was now projected.

She had been understandably nervous of marrying into the first family of the land, a family far less easy-going and openly affectionate than her own. She was reluctant to have to live a life of much more formality, constraint and public scrutiny than she had ever known. But she had adapted superbly and had quickly learned how to win the approval and affection of both the King and Queen and the wider family.

She had disliked the autocratic streak in her father-in-law which alienated his sons from him, but she treated him with a combination of respect, humour and charm which won him over. Although she enjoyed dancing, cabarets and nightclubs as much as many contemporary young women, she retained a romantic, old-fashioned seemliness which the King contrasted favourably with the fast, modern girls whom he deplored. The warm relationship she established with him – knitting him socks and sharing jokes – enabled her to stand her ground without causing friction, to protect herself, her husband and his brothers from paternal wrath, and also to use her influence with the King to good effect in her public life.

With Queen Mary she was perhaps not quite as successful, although this is largely a matter of speculation, for the correspondence between them was invariably affectionate. In character, the two women were quite different, with Queen Mary as reserved and methodical as her daughter-in-law was outgoing and spontaneous. But each made an effort to treat the other considerately, and the Duchess showed tact in consulting her mother-in-law and sharing activities that both enjoyed: shopping, interior decorating, visits to art galleries. Importantly, too, the two confided in each other about the Prince of Wales and Mrs Simpson, a matter on which they saw eye to eye, and which undoubtedly drew them together.

There were disagreements, resentments, near-rebellion – over White Lodge, over the naming of Princess Margaret, over the numbers of Court functions which the King and Queen insisted the Duke and Duchess attend – in other words, whenever the young couple felt their own rights and independence threatened by unwarrantable interference. But from the start the young Duchess had the wisdom and self-control to keep such feelings in check, and to encourage her husband, who was easily angered and demoralized, to do the same. She could usually turn a situation to their advantage, or at least make the best of it. She was by nature cheerful, positive and optimistic – to a fault, some would say later. It was not a one-way process. At the start of her marriage, she knew little of what was expected of her as a royal duchess, but she had been very willing to learn and paid tribute to the King and Queen for all that they had taught her.[2]

As a daughter-in-law, then, she had filled her position with great success. As a wife, she achieved even more. That she and the Duke were happily married is evident from their letters and was obvious to those who saw them together both publicly and privately. The give and take in a marriage is so subtle and private a matter that no outsider can perceive the full truth of it. But she had clearly given her husband the self-assurance and joy that he had lacked. In particular, she helped him to overcome the stammer which had embittered his relations with his father. By the Duke's own account, the King had considered him unfit for a public role because of it. After the Duke's marriage, however, the King had gradually lost his prejudice against him, as the Duke appeared increasingly confident in public with his wife at his side. The Australasian tour, followed by the Duke's performance as lord high commissioner to the General Assembly of the Church of Scotland in 1929, set the seal on the King's regard for him – not entirely coincidentally, just as his respect for his eldest son waned. It was a change to which the Duchess had contributed a great deal. She had succeeded as a mother too; the births of her two daughters brought much happiness to her and her husband, while reassuring the Royal Family and the nation that the succession was safe even if the Prince of Wales did not marry.

With the marriages of the Dukes of Kent and Gloucester in 1934 and 1935 the Duchess had acquired two sisters-in-law within a year, after more than eleven years as sole daughter-in-law to the King and Queen. She was no longer the only buffer between the King and his younger sons; and the larger family circle eased some of the pressure on the Yorks to be constantly on call for Court functions, or to spend more time at Sandringham or Balmoral than they wished. As for the Prince of Wales, his charm, high spirits and love of amusement appealed to the same qualities in her, and she remained devoted and sympathetic to him. But in the 1930s their lives diverged, they met less often and he seemed resolutely fixed on a path which dismayed and alarmed her, and which she was convinced was wrong.

For all her commitment to her royal role, contact with her own family was vital to her wellbeing and she made sure that there was room for them in her life. If her parents were in London, she would lunch or dine with them when she could. She saw her brothers and their wives fairly often, especially David and his wife Rachel, whom he had married in 1929.* She saw her eldest brother Patrick and his wife Dorothy, to whom she had never been close, less frequently. Her sisters were habitual visitors, as were her nephews and nieces, especially the Elphinstone children, who came to stay at Birkhall in the summer holidays; and she and the Duke often stayed with the Elphinstones at Carberry when they had engagements in Edinburgh. Each year they and their daughters would spend several weeks at Glamis in the late summer and autumn, and at other times of the year they visited her parents in Hertfordshire.

In the first few years of their marriage, as we have seen, the Yorks had no really satisfactory home of their own, either in London or in the country. The gradual resolution of this problem was a minor triumph for both of them, which took patience on their part and forbearance on Queen Mary's. The exchange of White Lodge for 145 Piccadilly in 1927 was accomplished with the Queen's help, when she might have taken umbrage; when the King offered them Royal Lodge as a country home, they accepted it against Queen Mary's advice and won her round. In Scotland, meanwhile, they gradually established a claim on Birkhall as their base, although the King and Queen seemed not to understand why they preferred this extra expense to free accommodation at Balmoral.

By 1935 the pattern had been set: from January to early August the York family was based at 145 Piccadilly, with most weekends and much of April spent at Royal Lodge. They stayed at Windsor Castle with the King and Queen for a few days in April, sometimes over Easter. From early August to mid-October they were in Scotland, with visits to Glamis at the beginning and end, and six weeks or so at Birkhall in between. Then they returned to London, with occasional shooting weekends for the Duke – often accompanied by the Duchess – in the country, until Christmas, when they all went to Sandringham to stay with the King and Queen for about three weeks. Sometimes

---

* Rachel Bowes Lyon (1907–96), née Spender-Clay, was a niece of Viscount and Viscountess Astor. Like the Duchess of York, she was a keen fisherwoman.

the children would remain longer with their royal grandparents; at other times they would go to stay with the Strathmores.

Since the giddy days of the 1920s when, as Queen Elizabeth later expressed it, 'we did night club life madly for a few years, but also mixed with dinners & country house visits,'[3] the Duke and Duchess's social life had become quieter and more sedate, as the demands of both public and family life grew with their own maturity and sense of purpose. 'Out of the welter, one gradually found one's feet & head,'[4] she wrote. They still dined out frequently with friends and went to private dances – charity balls at the great London houses or hotels were an obligation. More often, the dinner parties they gave or attended were followed by film shows, trips to the theatre and occasionally to the ballet. Their circle of friends had changed little since their marriage. The Duchess had kept many of her girlhood friends, habitués of Glamis house parties and London dances – notably Doris and Clare Vyner, Lavinia Annaly, who had accompanied her to East Africa and was still an 'extra' lady in waiting, Katie Seymour and Helen Hardinge, James Stuart and his elder brother Francis, the Earl of Moray.* Prince Paul of Yugoslavia and his wife Princess Olga visited them on their trips to England. Patricia Herbert, now Lady Hambleden, remained a lifelong friend, as did Tortor Gilmour, who had shared the Yorks' Australasian tour with them; another friend was Audrey Field, formerly Coats, one of the flightier members of their set in the early 1920s.† Among the couples they saw most often were Teddy and Dorothé Plunket, whom they had known since their early married days; Maureen and Oliver Stanley were also good friends, she the daughter of Lord Londonderry, and once admired by the Duke, he a rising politician, the younger son of the Earl of Derby. It was not a fiercely intellectual set, but nor was it as frivolous as that of the Prince of Wales. The Duchess enjoyed people who had brains as well as charm and throughout her life she made sure that her close circle included people whom she found stimulating and amusing.

---

* Francis, Lord Doune (1892–1943), eldest son of seventeenth Earl of Moray, succeeded his father as eighteenth earl in 1930. He married Barbara Murray of New York in 1924.

† Following the death of her husband Dudley Coats in 1927, Audrey had married Marshall Field, of the wealthy Chicago department-store family, in 1930. They were later divorced and in 1938 she married the Hon. Peter Pleydell-Bouverie, son of sixth Earl of Radnor, whom she divorced in 1946.

As well as those of her own generation, there were older friends. She and the Duke were often entertained by her godmother Mrs Arthur James, whom she described as 'one of the survivors of the Edwardian era'.[5] Another Edwardian survivor and friend was Mrs Ronnie Greville, with whom they regularly spent a June or July weekend at Polesden Lacey. Each summer they also visited Trent Park in Middlesex, the home of the rich and hospitable Philip Sassoon, who entertained them lavishly at his London house as well. Here they met his cousin Hannah Gubbay, née Rothschild, who acted as his hostess and later inherited Trent Park: she was a friend of Queen Mary and became the Duchess's friend too. When public duties took them north, the Duke and Duchess might stay at Studley Royal with the Vyners, at Lumley Castle with Katharine (the Duchess's girlhood friend Katie McEwen) and Roger Lumley or at Darnaway in Morayshire with Francis and Barbara Moray; they were invited occasionally to Chatsworth, Longleat, Knowsley and other great houses. In the winter they spent shooting weekends at Elveden, Wilton and Lord Mildmay's house, Flete, in Devon.

This relaxed and agreeable social life amid a group of good friends was something of an innovation in the Royal Family. Had the Duchess been born a princess, she would not have been brought up among such people as her equals, and would have been far less able to form close and lasting friendships with them. Her friends had become the Duke's friends. Although the King and Queen appeared in society and the King had his shooting and sailing intimates, their sons yearned for a new, less formal life. For the Prince of Wales this quest ultimately led to complete rupture with the world of his parents, but for his younger brother and successor it helped shape his idea of kingship, in which the sovereign would be a far less remote figure than his father had been. It was a social life the Duchess thoroughly enjoyed: although a member of the Royal Family, her position was still sufficiently untrammelled for her to choose, and see, her own friends, yet exalted enough to include plenty of delightful evenings and weekends in beautiful surroundings at the grandest of houses in London or the country.

She had many friends, but she was well aware that the motives of those who sought her friendship might be suspect.[6] She said some years later that she had very few intimates, and in 1936 she was still asking herself who her real friends were.[7] Despite her caution, she retained several very close friendships, and in particular those which sprang from family contacts in her unmarried days, notably Arthur Penn, D'Arcy Osborne and Jasper Ridley. Less a confidant or mentor than a clever and well-placed friend was Duff Cooper, politician and diplomat; he and his wife Diana belonged to her social circle.

With these friends she discussed literature, art, education, social problems, domestic and international politics, people and places. She wrote them vivid and amusing letters, roving over serious subjects with a deceptively light touch. Given the reputation she acquired of reading nothing more challenging than the novels of P. G. Wodehouse, the books she discussed with D'Arcy Osborne, Duff Cooper and later Osbert Sitwell, all of whom kept her supplied with reading matter, come as a surprise. As we have seen, she read Graham Greene, Aldous Huxley, Radclyffe Hall.[8] She read Duff Cooper's biographies of Talleyrand and Earl Haig, and he recommended *The Tale of Genji*, the tenth-century Japanese romantic novel by Lady Murasaki, a work which delighted her.[9] Thornton Wilder sent her his *Woman of Andros*.[10] Osbert Sitwell too sent her his own prolific oeuvre, together with finds on subjects he thought would interest her, such as the letters of William Beckford.[11]

D'Arcy Osborne gave her the American Agriculture Secretary Henry Wallace's *Statesmanship and Religion*, which he said showed that politics could be combined with Christianity – a proposition after her own heart – and urged her to send it on to the Prince of Wales, as one of the future 'leaders of the world'.[12] It might not have had much effect on him. But the Christian faith she had learned as a child remained strong; like her mother, she took seriously the need to pass it on to her own children, and she was equally convinced of the importance of Christianity to the wellbeing of the nation as a whole, and of the power of prayer. Archbishop Lang remained a friend and counsellor; and her patronage of philanthropic causes showed that she was drawn to those with a Christian basis, like the Church Army and Toc H.

Owen Morshead later commented that the Queen was 'noticeably modern in her tastes, whether in books or pictures, or in her outlook on life; and this makes it easy for her to establish contacts in circles new to Court life.'[13] Where pictures were concerned, as duchess she had not yet the means, nor perhaps the motivation, to involve herself in the patronage of modern British artists that she would pursue so successfully as queen. But with the guidance of Dick Molyneux, a considerable connoisseur, and of Kenneth Clark, the Surveyor of the King's Pictures, she had begun to learn about the Royal Collection. She had some acquaintance with the younger artistic and literary scene; she liked the work of Rex Whistler, and she liked him; he wrote her a kind letter after the abdication and promised to design a bookplate for her;* modern ballet was another enthusiasm and Frederick Ashton became a lifelong friend.

Brought up in a traditionally Conservative family, she had decided political views which remained, on the whole, constant, although she was careful not to betray in public the strict neutrality required of members of the Royal Family. Her comments to D'Arcy Osborne on the first Labour government in 1924, flippant and whimsical in the manner of her youthful letters to him, conveyed a fundamental distrust. 'I am extremely Anti-Labour. They are so far apart from fairies & owls and bluebells & Americans & all the things I like. If they agree with me, I know they are pretending – in fact I believe everything is pretence to them.'[14] It was an intuitive antipathy, a sense, perhaps, that socialism sought to drag everything down into uniform and unimaginative drabness and political humbug. Her views matured, she could be critical of governments of right as well as left, and in fact she got on well with many Labour politicians, whether Ramsay MacDonald or the Labour Mayor of Sheffield; this sympathy continued all her life, Ernest Bevin and James Callaghan being later examples of socialists she liked.

In a different life she might have become politically active: indeed, despite her position, she did do so to the extent of sending 'a busload of servants', as she afterwards confided to Duff Cooper, to vote for him in the by-election in March 1931 in which he stood as official Conservative candidate against the Empire Free Trade candidate supported by Lords Rothermere and Beaverbrook.[15] It was not the battles of party politics that attracted her, however. It was that her public life had brought her increasingly into contact with poverty and unemployment and she felt that she knew what needed to be done. Despite the

---

* Reginald John 'Rex' Whistler (1905–44), artist, designer and illustrator, whose first great work was the mural in the café at the Tate Gallery in 1927. He illustrated his letters beautifully, including those to the Queen. He was commissioned in the Welsh Guards in 1939 and was killed in action in France.

occasional frustration her position caused her, her correspondence shows her both deeply concerned about social conditions and aware that sometimes she *could* do something about it.

Her views on the international political scene, like those of most of her correspondents, were inevitably dominated by the threatening developments in Europe and the worldwide economic crisis in the early 1930s. She shared the fears D'Arcy Osborne expressed to her about 'a regression from civilization under economic pressure', and about the growth of the malign forces of fascism and Nazism.[16] By nature more optimistic, however, she praised Britain's recovery from economic depression and considered that it was 'the only civilised country in Europe today'.[17] She had no illusions about the effectiveness of the League of Nations.[18]

By 1937 she had come a long way since the early days of her marriage when she had taken on a modest round of public duties. At first inclined to regard public engagements as mere 'stunts', often tedious, she had characteristically got what fun she could out of them – like the fundraising dinner in 1924 at which she looked forward to extracting as much money as possible from 'RICH SNOBS'.[19] Nevertheless she was lucky to find herself in a role for which she had a talent, and she had taken to it with an ease born of her natural self-confidence, and out of the early training she had received from helping her mother in charitable activities, and in the wartime convalescent hospital at Glamis. She had gradually built up her own long list of patronages, while at the same time accompanying her husband on many of his public engagements. As a pretty young woman with a charmingly friendly manner she often attracted more favourable press comment than her husband, and she could easily have outshone him and taken the starring role. She never did so.

Her handling of her public life became more professional and focused; she took care to select and combine engagements in different areas; she built up relationships with certain organizations and followed up promises to return, using her excellent memory for detail and instant rapport with people to skilful effect. She was well aware of how best to please – singling out individuals in crowds, concentrating her attention fully on each person she spoke to, and falling back on her acting skills where necessary. 'It amused me to hear that your sense of drama took you through any awkward moments of official entertaining!' she wrote to D'Arcy Osborne. 'It sometimes helps me when I am faced with difficulties in that line. What a lot of our life we spend in acting.'[20] It helped that she enjoyed it and genuinely liked people. But it would have been impossible to continue smiling and shaking hands so tirelessly if she had not known that what she did really helped, in terms of giving pleasure, raising funds for philanthropic works and extending the reach and popularity of the monarchy.

Meanwhile she had also learned a painful lesson: that her private life would have to take second place to her husband's and her own public role, never more so than during her six-month separation from the infant Princess Elizabeth in 1927. Sometimes she wondered whether it was worth it, especially when her efforts were wilfully shown in the wrong light by the press. But 'Keep the old flag flying' was her characteristic response.[21]

By any standards she had played her first part with great aplomb, and in so doing she had acquired the qualifications for the much more demanding and important role which she now had to fill. As duchess of York, however, she had enjoyed greater freedom, in both her private and her public life, than she would as queen. Now she would have to work harder than before, and here the observant Owen Morshead had reservations. 'She is full of ideas, public spirit, and good intentions,' he said; but he considered that she was much less energetic and punctilious than Queen Mary.[22] Or was private indolence perhaps the other side of the coin to her indefatigable sense of public duty?

What concerned the Queen in 1937, however, was not so much the many tasks that faced her and the King as the fear that they might not be accepted and liked, and that they could never adequately replace her glamorous brother-in-law. But as her mother put it, they were determined to do what was 'really good & best for the Empire'. Lady Strathmore's heart ached, she said, when she thought of the burden on her daughter – 'but she is so more than wise, & foreseeing & full of tact, & the King takes her advice so wonderfully & charitably, that I do feel very proud as well as anxious.'[23]

★

THE CORONATION was a process, not just an event. The consecration of the King and Queen in Westminster Abbey was undoubtedly the most significant moment of the year, but it was followed by many engagements, public and semi-public, in which the new King and Queen were introduced to their people.

Two days after the Coronation the King presented medals to detachments of overseas troops, and there was a dinner at the Foreign Office, followed by a state ball at Buckingham Palace. That night the King and Queen went out on the balcony again and were cheered with great enthusiasm by the crowds braving the rain in the Mall. After a welcome weekend resting at Royal Lodge the King and Queen, together with Queen Mary, attended the Duke and Duchess of Sutherland's ball at Hampden House in Mayfair. Queen Mary wrote in her diary that it was 'a lovely sight, all the Royalties and Representatives were there, the tennis court was turned into a ball room with the fine tapestries hanging on the walls'.[24]

Next day there was an official luncheon with the Lord Mayor of London at the Guildhall, and then the King, Queen and Princess Elizabeth took the train to Portsmouth and embarked on the royal yacht, *Victoria and Albert*, to prepare for the review of the fleet at Spithead. It was a magnificent occasion to which eighteen countries had sent warships. From the flagship the King sent out the traditional signal, 'Splice the mainbrace.'

The rest of May's engagements included a thanksgiving service at St Paul's on Empire Day and a dinner given by the Prime Minister at 10 Downing Street. This was by way of a farewell, for Stanley Baldwin had decided to resign, having skilfully guided the new King and Queen to the throne. Both regretted his departure and the King wrote to him of his 'real sadness' at accepting his resignation.[25] Baldwin was made an earl and a Knight of the Garter, and his wife a Dame Grand Cross of the Order of the British Empire. After a farewell lunch with the King and Queen at Buckingham Palace, Lucy Baldwin wrote to the Queen, 'Both our hearts are beating so warmly in gratitude to you both that I felt I must put pen to paper & try and express a little of what we feel.'[26] Baldwin was succeeded by Neville Chamberlain, the Chancellor of the Exchequer.

The King and Queen then made the customary post-Coronation visits to the four quarters of the United Kingdom – Scotland, Ireland, Wales and England. The country they visited was changing fast. Britain had been led out of the worst of the Depression by a housing boom, and by the accompanying growth in consumer industries. There had been one million telephones in the country in 1922 – by 1938 there were three million. Shops were full of electrical goods, often made of newly versatile plastic materials. In the 1920s, motor cars had belonged only to the rich. Now they were becoming cheaper and ever more popular.

Bypasses were being built to spare town centres from heavy traffic. These were soon lined with new suburban villas. 'Roadhouses' became popular if not fashionable. They sprang up all along the Great West Road and other highways; some even boasted swimming pools and invited people to 'Swim, Dine and Dance'. Road accidents were frequent and the Ministry of Transport introduced more regulations to try to improve safety. In 1934 driving tests had been introduced and that year the minister, Leslie Hore-Belisha, had given his name to the orange beacons which began to mark road crossings for pedestrians, and introduced speed limits of thirty miles an hour for towns. Motorists complained, and one magazine criticized the Belisha beacons as giving London the feel of 'being prepared for a fifth rate carnival'.[27] This feeling was increased by the new neon lighting with which shops could now decorate their fronts.

Social science and social research became new disciplines; advertising firms made more use of 'market research' which meant sending young women (because they were treated more politely than men) from door to door asking people questions about their likes and dislikes. From Dr Gallup in America came the innovation of asking people, over time, to tell pollsters their changing views on a wide range of subjects. A more ambitious project was Mass Observation, which proposed to involve ordinary people in surveys and observations about pretty well everything. It was to be the science of everyday life. It was ridiculed by newspapers – 'Mass Eavesdropping' was one description, and, although the zoologist Julian Huxley supported the scheme, the *Spectator* declared of its methods: 'Scientifically they're about as valuable as a chimpanzee tea party at the Zoo.'[28]

There was a lot to discover, particularly in regard to the lives of the poor. The Depression of the early 1930s had ended and economic recovery was well under way by the time of the Coronation. Industrial share prices doubled in value between 1932 and 1937. But it was a slow process and in 1937 there were still over 1,600,000 people unemployed. Conditions were especially harsh in the so-called Special Areas of the country – in some mining and industrial areas more than half of the workforce was still without jobs.

The King and Queen found their tours, especially of deprived areas, tiring but rewarding. They imposed an especial strain on the

King, who knew that he had to try to disprove rumours that he was sickly and could barely speak. Nonetheless they both began to realize that they could do the job, and with that realization came enjoyment. Lord Harewood, the King's brother-in-law, said to him, 'You're getting through a lot of work, and I've never seen you looking better, or seeming happier.' To which the King replied, 'I am working hard and I am liking my job ... It makes such a difference now that when I come home I'm not for certain going to be told that I've done whatever it may be all wrong.'[29]

The two Princesses accompanied their parents on part of the Scottish tour. In Edinburgh the Queen was installed as the only Lady of the Order of the Thistle. She went shopping in the rain in George Street and enthusiastic crowds broke through the police and surged around her car. They had 'two very strenuous, and inspiring days in Wales', the Queen wrote. 'The courage of the people in itself is inspiring when one thinks of the terrible times they have been through, & still are, in the mining valleys of S. Wales. But Hope is in the air, and I saw more [coal-]black faces, & saw more smoking chimneys than when I was there a few years ago, which pleased us very much.'[30]

In Northern Ireland also they received a warm welcome, despite threats of IRA violence. Newspapers on the continent carried an account of an assassination attempt against them. In fact a customs post was set on fire, some railway trucks were mined and a land mine exploded in Belfast. But the crowds were large and bubbling with enthusiasm.[31] The trip was considered a great success. According to Commander Oscar Henderson, the Governor's Private Secretary and the man who had organized their visit to Northern Ireland in 1924, the King had 'firmly cemented the feelings of the people of Ulster to himself and The Throne. For The Queen all our people now have a love which it is impossible to put into words.'[32]

In the course of this summer the Queen became colonel-in-chief of two regiments, the Black Watch and the Queen's Bays. The relationships she built up with many different units of the armed services meant a great deal to her – and to those units. She never liked to be seen to have favourites but perhaps the most important to her was the Black Watch, in which her brother Fergus had served and died in the 1914–18 war. The previous Colonel-in-Chief had been King George V; she was appointed at the time of the Coronation and remained close to the regiment all of her life.

In July 1937 she made her first visit to the Queen's Bays at Aldershot, soon after her appointment as their colonel-in-chief. This former cavalry regiment had recently become fully mechanized, a process which caused much anguish among many of the men. The Queen seems to have had an extraordinary impact. The regimental commander, Lieutenant Colonel E. D. Fanshawe, was grateful for her support, writing that until now there had been such shortages of men and equipment that it was difficult 'to keep the "spirit" really going. Ever since Her Majesty's appointment as Colonel an entire change has taken place. – Now, after the visit on Saturday, I have no fear for the future – She has done more good than it is possible to imagine.'[33]

Their main tours complete, the King and Queen were able to leave for a holiday at Balmoral, their first visit there since their Coronation. Instead of taking the train as usual direct from London to Ballater, the nearest railway station to the Castle, they alighted in Aberdeen and drove with their daughters the sixty miles to Balmoral. The road was lined with hundreds of people in all the villages through which they passed. They drove under scores of welcoming arches and swathes of bunting; even remote cottages and hamlets flew whatever flags they could muster. When they reached the Balmoral estate, they exchanged their car for a carriage which was pulled not by horses but by scores of estate workers, with pipers marching at the head of the column; 'altogether the cavalcade looked like a rather gay funeral!' the Queen wrote to Queen Mary. 'It was very delightful to be welcomed like that, but also very amusing.'[34]

At last they were able to relax with their daughters, even though the constant turnover of guests made the Castle often seem more like a hotel than a home. For the King and Queen outdoor life was the most important – just as it had been in their respective childhoods. The hills, rivers and gardens dominated everything – except on Sundays. There was stalking for the men, more gentle walks for women, picnics by waterfalls for adults and children, with a kettle boiled on a fire between four stones. There were friendly games of cricket on the lawn. Days were warm but there was already a frost at night. Those who had known the Castle before thought the best of times had come again; those for whom this was a first visit were enchanted.

Their guests that summer included some of the traditional figures spurned by King Edward VIII, among them the Archbishop of Canterbury and the Prime Minister. Neville Chamberlain liked both the King and the Queen. He had said of the then Duchess of York that she was 'the only royalty I enjoy talking to, for though she may not be an intellectual she is always natural and moreover appears always to be thoroughly enjoying herself'. Since becoming prime minister in May he had made it his business to see as much as he could of the King.[35] On his visit to Balmoral he went shooting, fishing, picnicking with the King and Queen, and even gooseberry picking with the Queen. The King told his mother, 'he is getting over his natural shyness which makes me the same'.[36]

As for Cosmo Lang, he was overjoyed to be back at Balmoral after the unhappy hiatus of Edward VIII's reign. Writing to the Queen afterwards he said, 'When I remember last year, with all its anxieties, how can we fail to see the hand of God in the changes which have been so marvellously wrought, in the wonder of the Coronation, in the rapid but secure establishment of Your Majesties in the confidence and affection of the people.'[37]

The Queen invited her own friends – she wanted Balmoral to be fun as well as formal. Osbert Sitwell loved the landscape, the gaiety, the comfort and the charming atmosphere that the Queen created. The King teased him for not being able to walk, like him, twenty-five miles over the hills. Sitwell greatly enjoyed the Ghillies' Ball. 'Such fun,' he told one friend. 'The most complicated reels, valetas and odd dances, like Elizabethan times, quite devoid, the whole thing, of class feeling.'[38]

James Stuart's American sister-in-law Barbara, Countess of Moray, stayed as well; she enjoyed herself 'wildly' – her only complaint was that no one asked her to dance the Spanish Gavotte at the ball. That aside, she told the Queen, she felt 'one hundred times the better for seeing you'.[39] So did the Queen's friend Dick Molyneux and the artist Rex Whistler, who decorated his thank-you letter with a Scottish trophy and a thistle and rose bouquet. Molyneux behaved with his usual exuberance, and afterwards sent an appropriately nonsensical bread-and-butter letter, written in pidgin French. He closed in English, 'Oh! Madam, besides all the fun, it was good to see you and the King so well – and everything I've prayed for.'[40]

*

NOT EVERYTHING was light hearted. The short time that they had to reign before war engulfed their kingdom and Empire seems at least in retrospect to have been filled with tensions, if not crises. The most painful for the family arose from continuing problems with the Duke of Windsor. This was not surprising. His predicament was unprecedented and complicated. Almost alone in Austria, while he waited for Mrs Simpson's decree nisi to become absolute, he grew distressed. In mid-January 1937 he had written the King a long letter in which he said he wanted to do all he could to help and support him. But he begged the King to help stop the attacks upon himself and Wallis emanating from government and Court officials: 'you and the family can help us so much by giving us your support just now and creating a dignified background for our marriage and our married life.'[41] The Duke followed this letter with many others and, more painfully for his brother, with the constant telephone calls in which he laid out his advice, his problems and his demands. The King came to find the calls so upsetting that after a time he actually refused to take them. The Duke of Windsor was horrified to have his access cut off.[42]

Money was a source of endless argument, especially when the Duke's lies about his financial situation emerged. In early 1937 opposition to a pension for him grew in the House of Commons and the King wrote to him to say he must now tell him the truth. 'I understood from you when I signed the paper at the Fort that you were going to be very badly off.'[43] Agreement was not reached until 1938. In the meantime much bitterness accrued.

Even more important than money to the Duke and his future wife were the manner of their marriage and the matter of her title. They were both determined that at least some members of his family should attend their wedding in order to give it the royal seal of approval. The Duke believed he had failed the woman he loved – instead of the throne she so obviously deserved, she was imprisoned by the hounds of the world's press in an ignominious villa in the south of France. Their marriage must make amends. It must be as grand and as official as possible. Mrs Simpson's decree absolute was expected to be granted on 27 April 1937, and she decided that they should wait till after the Coronation for their wedding. Then, she thought, the world's attention could turn from that 'event' to them.[44]

As so often, the burden of seeking a solution fell upon the able shoulders of Walter Monckton. The couple were set upon having a

Church of England service, and the Duke instructed Monckton to find a suitable member of the priesthood to officiate. Mrs Simpson thought that the King should be able to depute a bishop to conduct the ceremony, notwithstanding the fact that the Church did not countenance divorce. Monckton suggested that one of the King's chaplains could officiate. But that was out of the question. Lord Wigram, the King's Private Secretary, told Archbishop Lang that he would 'hound out' of the College of Chaplains any one of them who agreed to such a thing.[45] In the event a 'scallywag clergyman', as Owen Morshead described him, a parish priest from Yorkshire, volunteered his services.[46]

Wigram also took the view that for any member of the family to attend the wedding 'would be a firm nail in the coffin of monarchy'.[47] The King, the Queen and Queen Mary agreed absolutely: quite aside from their personal feelings, they were concerned about public opinion. 'I suppose you get endless letters as I do,' Queen Mary had written to the King, 'imploring us not to go out for the wedding as it wld do great harm, especially after the terrible shaking the Monarchy received last Decr.'[48] The King informed Monckton that no member of the family would attend the ceremony and none of his chaplains would undertake it. With great difficulty, the King composed a letter to the Duke setting out the bad news, and adding, 'I can't treat this as just a private family matter, however much I want to.'[49] The Duke became even more embittered.

More contentious still was the matter of the future Duchess's title. The Royal Family decided early on that she must not be granted the title of Her Royal Highness (HRH). This was a difficult and controversial decision if only because of the precedent of the Queen herself. Upon her marriage to the Duke of York in 1923, in accordance with the general rule that a wife takes the status of her husband, she had become 'Her Royal Highness the Duchess of York'. In early 1937 the King's Private Secretary was advised by Parliamentary Counsel that the same rule applied for Mrs Simpson, and that it would not be possible for her to hold a different rank from her husband. That was what the Duke assumed. He also believed that the title was essential. Mrs Simpson considered that the title HRH was 'the only thing to bring me back in the eyes of the world'.[50]

Queen Mary was horrified. She wrote to the King in early February, 'It is unfortunate that he does not understand our point of view with regard to the HRH and that this rankles still, but there is no doubt you must stick to this decision as it wld make great difficulties for us to acknowledge her as being in the same category with Alice & Marina.'[51]

Wigram wrote to the Home Secretary, Sir John Simon, 'His Majesty hopes that you will find some way to avoid this title being conferred.'[52] The family did not expect this marriage to last and if the Duke married again, then the next wife would have to be an HRH too – so would any of his children. 'This would mean that instead of confining the Royal Circle to those in the lineal succession all sorts of outsiders might be admitted and this would lower the dignity of the Crown.'[53] The King told Baldwin the question was simple: 'Is she a fit and proper person to become a Royal Highness after what she has done to the country; and would the country understand it if she became one automatically on marriage?' He thought not, and his family agreed with him – they thought that the monarchy had been degraded quite enough already.[54]

A solution was devised, with some reluctance, by the politicians and lawyers, who feared the King might be seen to be kicking his brother when he was down. It was for the King to issue new letters patent based on the argument that the abdication created a situation entirely without precedent, that the Duke had renounced the throne not only for himself but also for his descendants and that the style and title of HRH had hitherto been attached only to members of the Royal Family who were within the line of succession.

In fact, the decision did not cause much concern in Britain. Winston Churchill, the Duke's erstwhile supporter, was surprisingly emphatic in his support for the King's position, saying no government would wish to create Mrs Simpson a royal highness. Clive Wigram lunched with the editor of *The Times*, Geoffrey Dawson, and was delighted when Dawson agreed that this was the proper course – the paper endorsed the arrangement as 'a logical appendix to the events of last December'.[55] The Duke and his fiancée were predictably angered and the Duke wrote harsh letters to his mother and brother. They chose 3 June as the day for their wedding – this was King George V's birthday. Queen Mary told the Queen that the choice of date hurt her very deeply; 'of course she did it, but how can he be so weak, I suppose it is out of revenge that none of the family is going to the wedding.'[56]

Inevitably the British papers were now dwelling at some length on the forthcoming ceremony. Queen Mary told the Queen that she found it all 'sickening'.[57] The Queen agreed with her that the bad newspapers were 'too horrible' and 'so mischievous' about David. But she gave him the benefit of the doubt, saying that he could not realize the harm that the newspapers were doing. As for the wedding, 'It must be too ghastly for you, and I feel so enraged when I think of June 3rd that I can hardly speak.'[58] On the day of the wedding the Queen wrote a line to her mother-in-law: 'My darling Mama, We have been thinking so much about you today, with your memories of past days, and all the new anxieties added, and just send this little line of love to say how much we are with you in thought and sympathy & loving admiration.'[59]

Queen Mary could not bear to spend such an emotional day doing nothing and so she drove down to Sussex to see Lady Loder's garden at Leonard's Lee, where she found quiet and some peace. The Duke of Windsor sent her 'a nice telegram' but she was disgusted by the stories in the evening papers and by the fact that any clergyman, even a 'scallywag', had gone out to conduct the ceremony without permission. She took comfort in the fact that the family was of one mind over it all.[60]

Worries about the Duke and Duchess of Windsor continued to preoccupy both King and Queen. One concern was that the Windsors might soon try to return to Britain. Lord Beaverbrook was campaigning for this through his *Express* newspapers. The entire family was against it – at the very least it would cause controversy around the monarchy and, worse, it might well lead to demonstrations, perhaps some in favour of the Duke and some against the Duchess. Either way the prospect did not please. The King still felt vulnerable and informed Queen Mary that he had been worried about his brother's return 'for ages' and had told Chamberlain and other ministers 'that I did not wish to be let down, & that after all [is] said & done, I did step into the breach & that I was not the culprit for what had happened'. He thought they had understood the strength of his feelings and realized 'how important it is to prevent any untoward & premature return'.[61]

In this, as in all such matters, the Queen agreed with her husband. Much later, in talking about the drama of the abdication, she identified the core of King George VI's anxiety about his brother's return to England. 'He couldn't come back. You can't have two Kings.' She knew that the King had to 'take hold'.[62] Queen Mary was sympathetic. 'Poor Bertie,' she wrote to the Queen, ' I fear D. still gives him & us all great trouble, he is terribly selfish & only thinks of his & her point of view & of their position in life, not a bit of this Country & of all of us – of course we know she is at the back of it.'[63]

Quite apart from fears over the Duke's return, there were still complicated negotiations about the financial settlement to be made for him and a specific concern was a libel suit which the Duke had brought against the author of a book, *Coronation Commentary*. This alleged that Mrs Simpson had been his mistress and that he had been drinking too much before the abdication. The King, the Queen and their Household were appalled at the thought of the Duke being cross-examined in court. But the Duke was cockahoop, believing that he might make a considerable sum of money.[64]

Walter Monckton, who was still negotiating on behalf of the Windsors, wrote to the Queen in mid-September 1937 to say that he was 'distressed to hear how much the King is worried over His brother & I do want You to know that nothing will be too much trouble to me if I can help in any way & at any time'. He wanted to reassure her and the King that there was no immediate cause for anxiety and suggested that 'until these troubles are overpast', he might send regular reports to the King indicating whether or not there were any troubles ahead.[65]

The Queen appreciated Monckton's efforts. She said that she was 'most touched that you should think of writing so sympathetically and with such understanding and I appreciate your thought most deeply. I think that it would be an excellent thing if you were to write to the King at fairly regular intervals, for I feel that one of the main sources of anxiety of mind is the difficulty experienced of getting authentic news from abroad.' The possible libel case she thought degrading and damaging to the monarchy.[66] In the end, with Monckton's assistance, the libel case was settled without the Duke being cross-examined and he did indeed win substantial damages.[67] But anxieties about the Duke and Duchess were always present, as the Queen told Queen Mary at the end of their Balmoral stay.[68]

Understandably so – at the beginning of October the Duke sprang another unwelcome surprise, and also committed a fundamental mistake. He went to Germany and met Hitler. The German trip was to be followed by a similar tour in the United States, and both were, according to the press statement he issued on 3 October, 'for the purpose of studying housing and working conditions'. Innocent sounding, but tensions with Germany were already high over Hitler's expansionist ambitions. The news came to the King and Queen at Balmoral as 'a bombshell & a bad one too'.[69] 'He never sent a word to me about his plans,' the King complained to Queen Mary, '& I have told my Ambassadors that the Embassy Staff cannot help him in any official sense ... The world is in a very troubled state, & there is plenty to worry about, & D. seems to loom ever larger on the horizon.'[70]

The British Ambassador in Washington, Sir Ronald Lindsay, happened to be on home leave at this time, and was summoned to Balmoral to discuss the matter with the King. He argued that the Duke should be offered the full courtesies of the Embassy. But the King, together with Alexander Hardinge and Alan Lascelles, his Private and Assistant Private Secretaries, all disagreed, arguing that the Duke was behaving abominably, embarrassing the King and trying to stage a comeback. Moreover, 'his friends and advisers were semi-Nazis'.

'But the Queen was quite different,' Lindsay recorded.

> While the men spoke in terms of indignation, she spoke in terms of acute pain and distress, ingenuously expressed and deeply felt. She too is not a great intellect but she has any amount of 'intelligence du coeur'. Her reactions come straight from her heart and very strongly and a heart that is in the right place may be a very good guide. In all she said there was far more grief than indignation and it was all tempered by affection for 'David'. 'He's so changed now, and he used to be so kind to us.' She was backing up everything the men said, but protesting against anything that seemed vindictive. All her feelings were lacerated by what she and the King were being made to go through. And with all her charity she had not a word to say for 'that woman'. I found myself being deeply moved by her.*

---

* Lindsay thought that the King still did not feel safe on the throne, 'and up to a certain point he is like the medieval monarch who has a hated rival claimant living in exile. The analogy must not be pressed too far because I don't think George wanted the throne any more than Edward, and if he is there it is owing to a sense of duty which Edward lacked and not owing to a love of power which one sometimes thinks Edward may have after all. But in some ways the situation operates on the King just as it must have done on his medieval ancestors – uneasiness as to what is coming next – sensitiveness – suspicion. I greatly wonder

In the end, the agreed compromise was that in Washington the Windsors would not be invited to stay at the Embassy but would be given a dinner party there.[71]

When the Duke and Duchess arrived in Germany, they were escorted everywhere by Nazi officials, who made a point of calling the Duchess 'Her Royal Highness', and the Duke was granted an interview with Hitler at Berchtesgaden, the Führer's Alpine retreat. As his biographer has pointed out, the trip was not a crime, but it was ill advised, and the most serious and damaging result was that it convinced the Nazis that he was sympathetic to their cause.[72] Moreover, his apparent endorsement of National Socialism aroused widespread criticism in the United States, in the face of which he lost his nerve and cancelled his visit there.[73]

*

AFTER THEIR Scottish holiday ended, the King and Queen continued their Coronation tour with visits to Hull, York, Saltaire, Bradford, Halifax, Batley, Leeds, Wakefield and Sheffield. This part of the tour was made easier because they could stay with the Princess Royal and the Earl of Harewood at Harewood House.

At the end of October the King had to preside over his first opening of Parliament. He was anxious about having to read the speech from the throne, setting out his government's priorities, and so was the Queen, but she felt that it went off well. 'I must admit that I was very very nervous during the whole ceremonial!' she told Queen Mary, but she appreciated the way in which the speech demonstrated the link between the Crown and Parliament.[74]

November and December brought the Queen more official engagements, a state visit by the King of the Belgians, the Armistice Day commemoration at the Cenotaph, and a few lighter entertainments, including a matinée at the Royal Academy of Dramatic Art, the Marina Ice Ballet, *Macbeth* at the Old Vic, and a BBC Concert at the Queen's Hall, after which the composer William Walton wrote and thanked her for coming. If she could attend concerts from time to time, 'it would indeed make all the difference to music.'[75] With Princess

what Edward really wants. They all say he has no will but what is hers, and what does she really want? Is she really ambitious? Perhaps; and opinion at the palace has no doubt of it, but is certainly violently prejudiced.' (*The Crawford Papers: The Journals of David Lindsay, 27th Earl of Crawford*, ed. John Vincent, Manchester University Press, 1984, pp. 616–21)

Elizabeth she went to a performance of *Where the Rainbow Ends*. At Buckingham Palace, 'Grey Owl', a 'Red Indian' naturalist later revealed to be Archibald Belaney all the way from Hastings, gave a talk on Canadian animals to the Queens and the Princesses.

In early December the Queen had a rare treat: she went to a private lunch party with friends. 'I enjoyed it enormously. My first luncheon party out since Dec 1936.' Hannah Gubbay was the hostess and one of the other guests was Osbert Sitwell, who gave her a book on gardens. Thanking him, she told him how much she appreciated his 'unfailing and loyal friendship'. Reflecting the widespread nervousness about the state of the world, she told him how much she loved his writing and asked him to 'Write us something hopeful & courageous for next year. After all, this is a grand little country, & as we can never be warlike, let us at least have some pride in it – we must be serious about <u>something</u>.'[76]

Christmas 1937 at Sandringham was a relief – in 1935 the King had been dying, in 1936 the King had just gone over the water. Now, everyone – King, Queens, family, friends, Household, staff – could enjoy the end of the first year of a new and optimistic reign which they all hoped would prosper. In the party was Dick Molyneux, to whom the Queen had sent a characteristic invitation: 'My dear Dick, Will you come to Sandringham for Xmas and help us with [three drawings of bottles, each larger than the last, labelled Claret, Burgundy and Champagne respectively] pull a few [drawing of a cracker] & help us with that [drawing of a Christmas tree]? I hope that you are free – (not too free of course). Yours sincerely, Elizabeth R.'[77]

After the King's Christmas Day broadcast, which he did well in spite of his nervousness, both the King and the Queen could relax a little. There was only one slight family mishap. Before Christmas the Queen sent the Duke of Windsor a present, a set of antique dessert knives and forks with porcelain handles. In a letter to accompany them she wrote that she hoped that 'perhaps they <u>might</u> appeal to you, who like old things . . . Anyway, they take best wishes for Xmas & the New Year, of health & happiness to both of you. With love, Yours Elizabeth.'[78] Unfortunately this letter was not posted with the parcel, and the Duke, evidently puzzled by a set of cutlery with no note, wrote saying he assumed he must have been sent the present in error – he offered to return it.[79] The Queen was embarrassed and responded at once: 'Darling David, When I received your little note this morning,

I rushed to my writing table, and after hunting about amongst the letters on it, I <u>found</u> the lost letter. I am furious and disappointed, because I left it addressed & ready to post, and have no idea what can have happened . . . you must have thought it very odd.'[80]

The Duke replied that he was surprised to get any gift. 'Since your note of November 23rd nineteen hundred and thirty six, in which you stated that "we both uphold you always", so many things have happened to contradict this statement, things which I know from my own experience as King, lay in Bertie's power to prevent, that it is not easy to believe that we are the recipients of so beautiful a gift. At the same time, we both appreciate and thank you for your thought of us.'[81]

★

EARLY IN THE new year the Queen was yet again laid low by influenza. So was Princess Elizabeth, and they wrote to each other pencilled letters from their respective sickbeds.

> Her Royal Highness
> The Princess Elizabeth
> In Bed
> Sandringham.

> My darling Angel, Thank you so very much for your dear little letter . . . I believe that I have got the same disease as you have, only I <u>was</u> sick, & you <u>felt</u> sick! I hope that your throat is better, and drink plenty of orange juice with plain water mixed.[82]

The next day, the Queen's letter was addressed to her daughter at 'Gettingupforlunch, The Nursery'. She was glad that the Princess was feeling better. 'I am feeling much better too, but still a little achy and still living on tea! I hope by tomorrow that I shall be eating Irish stew, steak & kidney pudding, haricot mutton, roast beef, boiled beef, sausages & mutton pies, not to mention roast chicken, fried chicken, boiled chicken, scrambled chicken, scrunched up chicken, good chicken, nasty chicken, fat chicken, thin chicken, <u>any</u> sort of chicken.'[83]

While she was in bed she read Leo Rosten's Hyman Kaplan stories, which D'Arcy Osborne had sent her. Once more, Osborne had judged his friend well. She found the New York Jewish humour of the stories 'heavenly'. But her relationship with Osborne operated on many levels: as well as exchanging jokes they debated issues of state and morality. He was one of the few people to whom she talked and wrote in absolute confidence. Now, she told him she was worried about the sort of leadership she and, more especially, the King should provide. The Queen feared that since young people had given up on religion,

> they look more & more to individual leadership, or rather leadership by an individual, and that is going to be very difficult to find. It is almost impossible for the King to be that sort of leader. For many years there was a Prince of Wales, who did all the wise & silly & new things that kept people amused & interested, & yet, because he did not, or would not realize that they did not want that sort of thing from their King – well he had to go.
>
> It seems impossible to mix King and ordinary vulgar leadership – so what can we do? We don't want Mosleys, perhaps something will turn up. In the old days Religion must have given the people a great sense of security & <u>right</u>, and now there seems to be a vague sense of <u>fear</u>. Or am I sensing something that isn't there at all. Perhaps it is me . . . What a sadness that things aren't going any better in this troubled world.[84]

Osborne agreed with her.[85]

On 4 February 1938 Hitler made himself supreme commander of the Wehrmacht (the German armed forces) and later that month he demanded that the Austrian government 'invite' German troops into Austria. 'It was nothing less than the end of Austria's independence,' wrote Duff Cooper in his diary. 'A portentous development in European history about which nobody in England seems to give a damn.'[86]

After Austria, Czechoslovakia was the next country threatened by Hitler. Throughout the spring and early summer of 1938 the Sudeten Germans, who had been incorporated into the new Czechoslovak state after Austria-Hungary's defeat in 1918, were instructed by Berlin to make more and more impossible demands upon the government in Prague, in order that Hitler could claim that they were being persecuted. Chamberlain made it clear in Parliament that Britain would not risk war with Germany to defend Czechoslovakia's integrity and, in a vain effort to prise Mussolini away from Hitler, Britain signed the so-called Easter Accords with Italy. The main effect of these was to recognize Italian conquests in Africa. Anthony Eden resigned as foreign secretary in protest and was replaced by Lord Halifax. The dictators marched on.

In these ominous circumstances the King and Queen were making plans for their first state visit. President Lebrun of France, which was Britain's principal democratic ally in Europe, had invited them to Paris at the end of June. The purpose of the visit was both to demonstrate the strength of the renewed monarchy and to cement the Anglo-French Entente Cordiale in the face of German and Italian threats.* It would be the first British state visit to France since that of King George V and Queen Mary in April 1914, only a few weeks before both countries were at war with Germany. Many people believed that a similar disaster was inevitable once again. Others hoped that demonstrations of solidarity by the democracies could help to drive away the danger.

The Queen asked her new dressmaker Norman Hartnell to create a collection of dresses for Paris. In his memoirs, Hartnell recalled that the King showed him at Buckingham Palace portraits by Winterhalter of the Empresses Eugénie of France and Elisabeth of Austria, wearing crinolines. The King made it clear to him that this romantic, swaying style was favoured. And so that was what Hartnell fashioned.

While the preparations for Paris were gathering pace, the health of the Queen's mother declined seriously. She had been ill for many months and for part of the time had to stay in a London nursing home, where the Queen visited her frequently. She was able to move back to the family home in Bruton Street but grew weaker through the early summer of 1938. On 22 June her condition worsened. The Queen, her father, the King and other members of the family gathered at Lady Strathmore's bedside. At two o'clock in the morning of 23 June she died.

Her daughter Elizabeth had often said that she had been 'dreading this moment' since childhood; now that it had come, she found it hard to grasp.[87] 'We are all feeling very unhappy,' she wrote at once to the Archbishop of Canterbury; 'my mother was so much the pivot

---

* The Entente Cordiale was the name give to a series of agreements made between Britain and France in 1904 following the historic visit to Paris by King Edward VII. The Entente marked the end of centuries of conflict between the two countries and laid the basis for their co-operation in the First World War and thereafter.

of the family, so vital and so loving and so marvellously loyal to those she loved, or the things she thought right – an Angel of goodness & fun.'[88] Her mother had indeed been an extraordinary matriarch; she possessed a genius for family life, as *The Times* noted. The loss of four children, especially her firstborn, Violet, at the age of eleven, left wounds which never healed, but also gave her unusual understanding of others. She never felt self-pity; she was a person to whom everyone, within and without the family, turned for advice or consolation. The Queen received hundreds of letters of condolence from people all over the world who had been touched by her mother. The Duke of Windsor sent a telegram from Antibes: 'Sincerest sympathy in your great loss. David'.[89]

It was just five days before the state visit to Paris. Both governments were anxious not to cancel the visit. There was some discussion about whether the Queen should stay at home and the King make the trip alone. But she was determined to accompany him as promised. President Lebrun suggested the visit be postponed for three weeks, which was agreed. Writing to thank Neville Chamberlain for his condolences, the Queen said she was sorry about the postponement 'but as it was all Galas and Banquets and garden parties, it would have seemed rather a mockery to take part so soon, and the French have been very good about it, do you not think so?'[90]

Lady Strathmore's funeral was arranged at Glamis for 27 June and the family asked Arthur Penn, as one of their oldest friends, to arrange a simultaneous memorial service in London. Penn was deeply affected by Lady Strathmore's death. He recalled in a letter to the Queen the 'incomparable devotion between mother & daughter'. He had so many 'perfect pictures' of her mother – 'in days long ago at St James Square, when you were coming out & we were all friends together – at St Paul's Walden in summer days, – & most of all at Glamis'. He pictured Lady Strathmore sitting at the head of the dining-room table, at her piano playing Scarlatti and Bach by candlelight, '& most of all in her white sitting room, which seemed from every corner to radiate the kindness & character of its occupant'. The last time he was at Glamis he found her in the evening 'alone, sitting quietly by herself resting contentedly after the exodus of a tribe of her grandchildren ... I thought then how happy a picture she presented, surrounded by those who loved her, & of these I know you were always foremost.'[91] The Queen treasured this letter.

She concealed her misery from most and travelled with the King up to Glamis overnight on 25 June. In her childhood home she and other members of the family sat together for a time in her mother's sitting room and, she told Penn, 'found comfort even in that'.[92] The funeral began with a short private service in the chapel where the family had worshipped all their lives. She found it 'exquisite in its simplicity and beauty'.[93]

Then the coffin was borne by farm-cart to the burial ground half a mile away, followed by a long line of mourners, including the King. The Queen and her father, who was calm and buoyed by his religious faith, came in a car. When the cortège was at the graveside the heavens opened and torrents of rain soaked the mourners. The King persuaded his wife and father-in-law to remain in the car while he helped carry the wreaths to the graveside, including the cross of white carnations and blue irises from Princess Elizabeth and Princess Margaret, who remained in London. The Queen and her father then joined the King, and they stood in the lashing wind and rain for the service of committal taken by the Bishop of St Andrews.[94] The Queen liked the wildness – 'The elements taking a part made the whole mournful affair less agonizing.'[95]

Afterwards she and the King went north to rest – not to Balmoral but to Birkhall. Alone with her husband in the mountains and woods, she received and wrote many letters. She told Queen Mary that her mother had had a real sense of perspective – 'she gave things their due importance, and the things that did not matter were relegated to the background – that is so rare in women, & a great gift'. She assured her mother-in-law, 'You have it <u>very</u> strongly darling Mama.'[96]

The Queen received reports of the memorial service, held at St Martin in the Fields in London at the same time as the funeral in Glamis. Cosmo Lang sent her his own address, in which he had said of Lady Strathmore, 'She raised a Queen in her own home, simply, by trust and love, and as a return the Queen has won widespread love. Her charm and graciousness were not due to any conscious effort but the simple outflow of her spirit.'[97] The Queen wrote to thank him, saying his words were '<u>perfect</u> . . . Thank you, <u>thank you</u>, dear friend & good counsellor.'[98]

Arthur Penn wrote in more intimate fashion about the London service. He thought the music had lifted it out of the melancholy which Lady Strathmore would have hated. The congregation was both distinguished and diverse and included 'a considerable number of what Lord Curzon used to term "the rascality"' – which just went to show how widely she was loved. The church had been filled; Penn drew a moving portrait of Barson, the family butler, 'who advanced down the aisle with his battered old face full of grief, making apologetic & deprecatory noises at being given the place to which his long & faithful service so amply entitled him'.[99] The Queen thanked Penn '<u>from my heart</u>'. Birkhall had brought her solace, she said. 'I have climbed one or two mountains, & spent my days amongst them, and feel very soothed – they are so nice & big & everlasting & such a lovely colour.'[100] She picked a spray of bell heather to send to her daughters.[101]

After only a few days the peace had to end and it was back to London to rush through the preparations for Paris. The Queen had to make serious decisions about her wardrobe. She was in mourning and the coloured dresses that Hartnell had made were quite unsuitable. She was confronted with the possibility of having to wear only black and purple. According to Hartnell's own account, he then pointed out that there was an alternative: white was also a colour of royal mourning – after all Queen Victoria had insisted on a white funeral.[102] White was a bold proposal. But after some discussion the King and Queen agreed – instead of black, the Queen would be all in white. The couturier gathered all his seamstresses and in a fortnight all of the principal outfits had been remade. The Queen had to have endless new fittings and wrote to Queen Mary, 'I am nearly demented with rushing up & down & trying to order & try on all my white things for Paris!'[103]

It was worth all the trouble. The new dresses were exquisite and their effect was mesmerizing. As a result, Hartnell became official Court dressmaker to Queen Elizabeth, designing all her important outfits for the next four decades.

*

ON 19 JULY THE King and the Queen, who was still dressed in black, embarked at Dover on the Admiralty yacht, *Enchantress*. They crossed the Channel in thick mist, escorted by eight E-class destroyers – *Electra*, *Escort*, *Express*, *Esk*, *Escapade*, *Eclipse*, *Echo* and *Encounter* – and an air escort of eighteen Anson planes. In mid-Channel they were received by seven French destroyers, all flying the Union flag at their masthead, and the fleet made its way to Boulogne. From there the royal party took the train to Paris, a city the Queen had loved since her first adventurous visits as a young woman.

They stepped into the heart of the city at the restored ceremonial railway station in the Bois de Boulogne. On the train the Queen had changed and appeared in the first of Hartnell's dazzling white creations, a two-piece dress and coat edged with silver fox. From that moment, she captured Paris. Throughout, her dresses seemed to suit her personality exactly and were deemed to be lovely even by the fashion-conscious French. A 101-gun salute welcomed them and thousands of white doves were released. From the Eiffel Tower flew what was possibly the largest Union flag ever made, measuring 1,500 square yards.[104] Public buildings were lavishly decorated and tens of thousands of shops and homes displayed the flags of the two countries and photographs of the King and Queen. In deference to the Queen's ancestry, even the Loch Ness monster made an appearance on the Seine.[105]

Special apartments had been decorated for them at the Quai d'Orsay, the French Foreign Ministry, overlooking the river, at a cost of some eight million francs. Paintings, furniture and tapestries were brought from the Louvre and from the palaces of Versailles, Fontaine-bleau and Chantilly; the Queen's bed had belonged to Marie Antoin-ette, the King's to Napoleon. Silk had been specially woven – the Queen was even asked what colour she would like – for the walls of the Queen's room. The chef from the Hôtel Crillon came to cook for them in an electric kitchen built for their visit.[106] Luxurious modern bathrooms had been installed, one silver and the other gold. (Only a few years later, during the Nazi occupation, Field Marshal Göring was reported to have filled what had been the King's dressing room with cupboards for a hundred uniforms.)[107]

Although the French took security very seriously – King Alexander I of Yugoslavia had been assassinated during his state visit to France in 1934 – the atmosphere was joyous and seemed to some of the English officials not unlike the Jubilee or the Coronation. Cheering crowds greeted the King and Queen everywhere they went. Lady Diana Cooper wrote, 'Each night's flourish outdid the last. At the opera we leant over the balustrade to see the Royal couple, shining with stars and diadem and the Légion d'Honneur proudly worn, walk up the marble stairs preceded by *les chandeliers* – two valets bearing twenty-branched candelabra of tall white candles.' The Queen was wearing a spreading gown of oyster-coloured satin, the skirt draped in festoons held by clusters of cream velvet camellias. The Dowager Duchess of Rutland, standing with Diana Cooper and the Winston Churchills (who had been invited by the French government), said, 'I felt proud of my nation. The French went mad about the King and Queen. Winston was like a school boy he was so delighted.'[108]

President Lebrun and his wife were charming. At one occasion the Queen noticed the President looking askance at her: she was wearing the Légion d'Honneur, which he had just conferred on her, on the wrong shoulder. She hurriedly changed it.[109] She said later she was overwhelmed by the welcome they received everywhere, and she was struck that the French hardly talked to her about the English. 'It was all Scottish and Scotland that they seemed to be interested in.' She talked as much as she could in French, 'but when I was stuck for a word I just put my hand upon my heart and they supplied me with one.'[110]

The visit was a triumph for them both, but in particular for the Queen. One French newspaper exulted, 'We have taken the Queen to our hearts. She rules over two nations.'[111] Another paper, L'Oeuvre, published a humorous article, 'Hors d'oeuvre', with the subheading 'Honni soit qui mal y pense'. The writer expressed regret that protocol meant that the King & Queen had separate bedrooms, for otherwise perhaps the good food and wine and hospitality of France might have led to the birth of a 'dauphin' on 20 April 1939, and the Princesses would have been told, 'C'est un petit frère que papa et maman ont acheté à Paris et qui arrive aujourd'hui.'[112]

There was much to rejoice about in the present because there was so much to fear in the future. The overarching theme of all the events and of the constant applause was of two democracies embattled but united against brutal threats. Every opportunity was taken by both the hosts and the visitors to emphasize their alliance and their commitment to peace. At the Elysée banquet in their honour, the King said, 'It is the ardent desire of our Governments to find, by means of international agreements, a solution of those political problems which threaten the peace of the world and of those economic difficulties which restrict human well-being.'[113]

On the final day of the visit they were entertained at Versailles. The Queen was wearing another floor-length spreading dress of white organdie, embroidered all over with open-work broderie anglaise. Her white leghorn hat was trimmed with a ribbon of black velvet.[114] At Louis XIV's magnificent Palace, they reviewed 50,000 French soldiers as they marched past the King. Churchill was much moved and spoke of the French troops as the bulwark of European freedom.[115] Unfortunately, the fly-past by the French air force was delayed until the afternoon and took place during a concert in the chapel of the Palace. Suddenly the music was interrupted by the roars of wave after wave of military planes passing overhead. Rather than reassuring, the display was macabre and unsettling – certainly that was how the experience remained in the memories of the King and the Queen.[116]

That last night, the royal couple enjoyed many curtain calls on the balcony of the Quai d'Orsay as thousands of people in the streets below demanded, by enthusiastic cheering, to see them. Lady Diana Cooper joined the throng and wrote, 'I can never forget it. To the French the Royal Visit seemed a safeguard against the dreaded war. That at least is what they told me but I could see nothing to allay my fears.'[117]

She was right. The uninvited guests, Hitler and Mussolini, loomed over all those enchanted evenings. On the last day of the visit, in a reminder of why another war seemed too terrible to contemplate, the King and Queen visited Villers-Bretonneux to unveil a memorial to the 11,000 members of the Australian Imperial Forces who fell in France during the 1914–18 war and had no known grave. After the King had laid his official wreath, the Queen spontaneously approached the memorial and laid on it a bunch of red poppies from the surrounding fields which had been given to her that morning by a schoolboy.[118]

The French love affair with the Queen and her husband was intense. Neville Chamberlain wrote to the King, praising him and saying, 'the Queen's smile as usual took every place by storm'.[119] Duff Cooper congratulated the Queen, quoting a friend in Paris who had said that the visit had had an extraordinary effect in increasing French confidence. 'Never since Armistice night have I seen such vibration of happiness and relief from an unknown nightmare ... Everyone says that the Queen has something magnetic about her which touches the masses as well as the lucky few who know her.'[120] In his diary, Cooper wrote that the French enthusiasm for the King and more especially for the Queen surpassed description. 'This at least is good, but I view the

near future with great disquiet and if we are at peace when Parliament
meets on November 1st I think we shall be fortunate.'[121]

*

BACK HOME THERE was a heat wave. The King and Queen and their
daughters went first to the Solent where the King attended Cowes
Week briefly – unlike his father, he was not a yachtsman. The Queen
took her daughters picnicking in the New Forest and to visit Osborne,
Queen Victoria's home on the Isle of Wight. Then, more slowly than
usual, they made their way to Scotland, in the *Victoria and Albert*. The
sea was calm and they could all relax; the Queen thought the officers
were charming; they 'devised all kinds of amusing things to entertain
us!' They stopped off at Southwold in Suffolk for the King to make his
annual visit to his Duke of York's Camp. He was rowed to the shore
and carried aloft by the boys for a happy meal around the campfire,
before returning to the yacht. North they continued, arriving at
Aberdeen on a perfect hot day; the Queen remarked how pretty the
harbour looked with the gaily painted trawlers bobbing on the blue
sea.[122]

At Balmoral they did their best to have a holiday despite the
deepening political darkness on the continent. Georgina Guérin was
there again for the Princesses – they had lessons every morning and
then rode their ponies; afterwards the women and children usually
joined the men out on the hill for lunch. After tea back at the
house, the Princesses sometimes played the radio-gramophone in the
drawing room, or there was cricket on the lawn for anyone who
wanted to join in, and at about seven o'clock the house party
changed for dinner.[123] Life was a little less formal than under King
George V. Etiquette was nonetheless imposing and at dinner, white
tie was still *de rigueur*. A typical evening meal that August was clear
soup, fish, beef, grouse, chocolate pudding, iced pudding, cheese souf-
flé, peaches, plums and grapes, with several different wines. Seven
pipers played around the table at dessert. Afterwards cigarettes were
smoked, by women as well as men. Sometimes there was a film
show.[124]

The peaceful hills and heather could not conceal Europe's march
towards the war which everyone feared. Although many people
regarded Hitler with horror, it was from their memories of 1914–18
that their anxiety derived. People tried to reassure themselves that

Germany was too complex and had too rich a culture to be reduced to simple black and white, good and evil. They could agree that some of the decisions made about Germany at Versailles were unjust, or at least unworkable. The Sudeten Germans had indeed been incorporated without consultation into the new state of Czechoslovakia after the First World War. Their problems under the social democrat government in Prague were grossly exaggerated by the Nazi propaganda machine, but some problems did exist.

Those who argued for compromise, or appeasement, in both France and Britain had a fundamental belief which was both decent and compelling. It was that even the enemies of reason must in some fashion be susceptible to logic and persuasion. It was hard for men and women of goodwill to believe that the Nazis were 'a political movement whose animating principles were paranoid conspiracy theories, blood-curdling hatreds, medieval superstitions, and the lure of murder'.[125] But that is what they were.

By August 1938 Hitler was declaring that the condition of the Sudeten Germans under their Czech rulers was intolerable. German troops began conducting extensive manoeuvres around the Czech border. The danger that Germany would use force was growing every day. The French had made clear that they would abide by their treaty commitments to Czechoslovakia. If France went to war Britain would be dragged in. Neville Chamberlain took the train up to Balmoral to see the King at the end of August, still believing that peace could prevail. Back in London he wrote to the King that matters were developing only slowly and that he had a 'hunch' that the use of force might be avoided.[126] But on 12 September Hitler made a vicious speech at Nuremberg, laced with contempt for the Czechoslovak state and its ministers and demanding a revolt in the Sudetenland.

Thousands of people began to flee London and Chamberlain decided on a dramatic move – he, who had never been in an aeroplane, would fly at once to see Hitler. The King decided that he should return to the capital and on 14 September he took the night train from Ballater. Queen Mary approved, writing to him that the public took confidence in seeing the Royal Standard flying over the Palace and thus knowing that the King was in residence. She, like almost everyone, had been shocked by Hitler's speech. 'I was horrified at his voice & shouting & at what he said, so theatrical & awful.' But she thought it 'a brilliant idea' for the Prime Minister to fly to see the German dictator, 'for even if nothing comes of it, he will have made, in England's name, the beau geste for peace'. If war did come, she said, 'it will be to prevent Germany from dominating most of Europe, not to back up the Czechs for their foolishness in treating the Sudetens so badly.'[127]

Over the next ten days Chamberlain made not one but three visits to Germany – to Berchtesgaden, to Bad Godesberg and finally to Munich, in ever more desperate attempts to propitiate the dictator. In this he had the grateful support of the vast majority of the British people, and of their King and Queen. On 19 September, after Chamberlain's first meeting with Hitler, the King wrote to the Queen in Balmoral. 'My own darling Angel, I fear you must be feeling anxious as to how things are developing here.' He did not like to use the telephone, so he was sending her a lot of papers to read. Knowing that she felt she should be with him, he wrote, 'Please don't think of coming down here yet, as it might make people feel nervous. We will keep you well informed as to the daily progress of the situation, & just carry on as usual.'

Among the papers he sent were the minutes of Sunday's Cabinet meeting in which Chamberlain gave his impressions of Hitler. 'I wish he could have got more out of him,' the King told the Queen; but perhaps that would happen when Chamberlain returned the following Wednesday. He added, ' I don't much care for our new guarantees of the new Czechoslovakian frontier against unprovoked aggression, as again how can we help them in this event. What we want is a guarantee from Hitler that he won't walk into it in 3 or 4 months' time. However, the French & ourselves are in agreement on this point.' At the end of the letter, the King wrote, 'All my love Angel & I miss you too terribly.'[128]

The Queen missed him too; she felt miserable and thought she ought to be in London at such a time. On 21 September she did travel south, leaving the Princesses at Balmoral. She meant it to be only a short trip, but she found her husband under such strain that she stayed away longer than she had planned.[129]

London was grim. Air-raid precautions were put into effect on 25 September, cellars and basements were commandeered, hospitals were cleared for war-wounded, schoolchildren crowded the railway stations for evacuation to the countryside. Trenches were dug in Hyde Park, to give some notional shelter from air raids, Londoners were registered for gas-mask distribution, anti-aircraft guns were mounted on bridges and close to Buckingham Palace.

As the spectre of war approached, the greater grew the sense of urgency to avoid it. The King felt strongly the need to help in any way he could. His Private Secretary Alec Hardinge, although himself opposed to appeasement, suggested that the King send a personal appeal to Hitler, 'as one ex-Serviceman to another', urging him to spare the youth of Europe another terrible war. It might have no effect, but it would be 'the only real contribution that Your Majesty could make to a peaceful solution by approaching the question from an entirely non-political angle'.[130] The King put this idea first to the Foreign Secretary, Lord Halifax, on 15 September when Chamberlain was on his first trip to Germany. Halifax advised waiting for his return.[131] On 26 September the King told the Prime Minister of his proposal. He had prepared a draft, with Hardinge's assistance. But Chamberlain considered that such an advance would be unwise; he feared that Hitler might send an insulting reply.[132]

On 27 September the King and Queen had a long-standing engagement to launch the world's largest passenger liner, her namesake, the *Queen Elizabeth*, sister ship to the *Queen Mary*, on the Clyde. At the last minute the crisis prevented the King from leaving London. The Queen had to go on her own; worse still, she would have to make the speech at the launch ceremony. She left London by train on the evening of the 26th; all the stations were filled with children being sent out of the capital. Fears of an imminent German attack were very real. At Glasgow she was joined by her daughters, who had been brought down from Balmoral, and together they toured the Empire Exhibition. According to *The Times*, 'A great multitude of people gave them a welcome which the tension of the moment seemed to charge with a deeper and more personal feeling than would have coloured enthusiasm at a less critical time.'[133]

At John Brown's shipyard the great new liner lay, over a thousand feet long, ready to run out to sea at the Queen's command. Piled beside the vessel on each side were massive drag-chains, weighing more than 2,000 tons, to slow her impetus as she took to the water for the first time. The Queen's speech was broadcast live by the BBC and heard by millions of people across the country. She told them of the King's deep regret in having to cancel his journey to Clydeside and said that she had a message from him. 'He bids the people of this country to be of good cheer, in spite of the dark clouds hanging over them and, indeed, over the whole world.' She spoke confidently and clearly, describing the ships that plied across the Atlantic 'like shuttles in a mighty loom, weaving a fabric of friendship and understanding between the people of Britain and the people of the United States'.[134]

The last props holding the ship in place were removed. Very slowly she began to move to cries of 'She's off!' The Queen quickly stepped forward to say, 'I name this ship Queen Elizabeth and wish success to her and all who sail in her,' and released the bottle of champagne to break against the bow. As the great ship's stern hit the water, a riot of steam whistles mingled with the roar of the drag-chains as they rushed out into the sea after her.[135] 'I was so proud of Elizabeth taking on that ordeal of broadcasting the speech at a moment's notice, when I could not do it myself,' the King wrote to May Elphinstone afterwards.[136]

To Neville Chamberlain, the only way to peace seemed to be to allow Hitler to occupy the Sudetenland. On the night of 27 September, exhausted, he made the broadcast for which he would ever be remembered – 'How horrible, fantastic, incredible it is that we should be digging trenches and trying on gas masks here because of a quarrel in a faraway country between people of whom we know nothing.' Duff Cooper considered the speech 'the most depressing utterance', expressing more sympathy for Hitler than for Czechoslovakia.[137] Churchill also was indignant. But millions of people agreed with Chamberlain. The King himself was moved and sent him a message of sympathy and praise.

In both Paris and London there was a sense that the next day, 28 September, would be the final day of peace. The King held a Privy Council meeting to declare a state of emergency and to agree the mobilization of the fleet. That afternoon, as Chamberlain was recounting to the Commons the doleful events of recent days, he was handed a piece of paper containing an invitation from Hitler to an immediate four-power conference with Mussolini and the French Prime Minister Edouard Daladier in Munich. The House was ecstatic.

In Munich the dictators received the two dark-suited parliamentary leaders of France and Britain. They offered scant improvement on the terms for the dismemberment of Czechoslovakia, but Hitler gave Chamberlain a solemn undertaking that these were his last territorial demands. The Prime Minister chose to accept this assurance. He persuaded Hitler also to sign a piece of paper stating that their agreement was 'symbolic of the desire of our two peoples never to go to war again'. When Chamberlain landed at Heston aerodrome outside London he waved this paper to wild applause and read its words aloud; at Downing Street later he declared that it brought 'peace and honour' and 'peace for our time'.

The King had sent him an invitation to come straight to Buckingham Palace, where his wife Anne had also been invited. The King and Queen then took the Chamberlains out on to the balcony overlooking the Mall. They were given an emotional ovation. Crowds sang 'For He's a Jolly Good Fellow' deep into the night. Queen Mary wrote to congratulate the King. 'What an excellent photo of you two with Chamberlains in the papers . . . The paper the P.M. & Hitler signed is most interesting, let us hope that at last our 2 countries will come together.'[138]

For her part, the Queen wrote to Anne Chamberlain saying that she had been thinking of her 'during these last agonising weeks, knowing & understanding something of what you must be going through. It is so hard to wait, & when it is on the shoulders of your husband that such tremendous responsibilities rest, then it is doubly hard. But you must feel so proud & glad that through sheer courage & great wisdom he has been able to achieve so much for us & for the World.'[139] Anne Chamberlain replied, thanking her for her letter 'so full of understanding'.[140]

Chamberlain's Munich agreement was welcomed wholeheartedly not only in Britain but, as the historian Andrew Roberts has pointed out, by 'the vast majority of the English-speaking peoples'. Chamberlain received telegrams of congratulation and relief from the Prime Ministers of Canada, South Africa and Australia along with tens of thousands of letters and other messages from around the world. 'Appeasement was not simply a political phenomenon. The Church of England supported it on spiritual grounds, ex-servicemen's organizations supported it as a way to avoid war, and the management of corporate Britain embraced it as the best way to avoid damaging Britain's economic strength.'[141] The stock market leaped. The press was almost united in praise.

Given such euphoria, the Royal Family's enthusiasm for Munich was understandable. But the extent to which the King and the Queen so publicly embraced Chamberlain and his policies, on the balcony of the Palace, was imprudent, if not unconstitutional. The Queen herself later acknowledged the mistake.* The monarch must always be above party politics and the Munich agreement was, despite its popularity, controversial and was still subject to a debate and vote in the House of Commons. Indeed Labour and the Liberals voted against it. One minister, Duff Cooper, resigned in protest.

On the night of 2 October the King and Queen were able to return to Balmoral. The Queen wrote to Queen Mary praising the King's calm and courage. He was helped by his complete confidence in Chamberlain, 'but the consequences are so vast, of even Peace, that one's brain is in a whirl'.[142] To Osbert Sitwell she said that the recent terrible days were a nightmare of horror and worry that had made her feel years older. 'But one good thing is the fact that it was possible for sanity and Right to prevail at such a moment, and another, the marvellous way that the people of the country played up. They did not know very much of what was going on, and their courage & balance was (as usual) wonderful.'[143] In another letter to Sitwell later that year, under her signature she drew a little Union flag flying on a staff and wrote, 'Keep the old flag flying, Hooray! (I feel strongly about this.) ER'[144]

From D'Arcy Osborne in Rome came a letter praising her for having returned to London when so many people were fleeing the city. Osborne had arrived in Rome to take up his post as British ambassador to the Holy See in 1936; he was to remain *en poste* until 1947. Throughout the war, this cultured and sensitive man braved all dangers and difficulties, serving with great courage and distinction, and

---

* In an interview in March 1991 with the historian D. R. Thorpe for his official biography of Alec Douglas-Home, Queen Elizabeth made clear that she understood all the implications of what had happened. She said that when Chamberlain and his party, which included Douglas-Home (then Lord Dunglass), arrived at the Palace she had been struck by the fact that they were all exhausted rather than elated. (D. R. Thorpe, *Alec Douglas-Home*, Sinclair-Stevenson, 1996, p. 85) The balcony appearance was a constitutional error, she told Thorpe, though she believed it was a 'venial' one, because the British people were so relieved by Chamberlain's agreement. 'But one must remember it was relief for ourselves, not relief for Czechoslovakia,' she added. (Author's interview with D. R. Thorpe) For his part, Alec Hardinge subsequently commented: 'I have since been reproached for what the King did on this occasion. For me, who was among those with no faith in the prospect of conciliating Hitler, it all went much against the grain; but it seemed to me to be the correct policy for the Sovereign in the circumstances – namely, to give full and public support to the Government.' (Alec Hardinge's notes for autobiography, Hon. Lady Murray Papers)

helping both Jews and Allied soldiers to escape the fascists. For much of the time he was a virtual prisoner in Vatican City; he was able to maintain contact with the Foreign Office but his correspondence with the Queen inevitably became infrequent.

For now, however, Osborne applauded the Munich agreement and thought that the crisis had shown 'the undoubted horror of war among all the peoples'.[145] In similar vein the Archbishop of Canterbury wrote to the Queen, 'I am so thankful that the King was spared the ordeal which his good father had to face in 1914.'[146] Queen Mary agreed; she told the Queen she had no time for those who carped about Munich. She wished that, instead of finding fault, people would back Chamberlain '& help him in finding a real solution of the world's difficulties'.[147]

Eloquent among the critics was Winston Churchill. On 5 October in the Commons debate on Munich, he made one of his most powerful speeches. 'All is over. Silent, mournful, abandoned, broken, Czechoslovakia recedes into the darkness.' He understood the rapture that had greeted Chamberlain on his return from Munich. But he was sure that Britain would soon face demands that she surrender territory or liberty; freedom of speech would be curtailed. He argued that massive rearmament, particularly of the air force, was now vital, for Britain's defences had been grossly neglected. He warned, 'This is only the first sip, the first foretaste of a bitter cup which will be proffered to us year by year unless, by a supreme recovery of moral health and martial vigour, we arise again and take our stand for freedom as in the olden time.'[148]

Churchill was right. The euphoria was short lived. The Germans honoured almost none of the promises made at Munich. Within weeks, Hitler had reneged on his assurance that he had no more territorial ambitions and had begun to threaten the Lithuanian city of Memel and the Free City of Danzig. On the night of 9/10 November the Nazis' anti-Jewish pogroms reached a new level of barbarity with the destruction of Jewish property throughout Germany, Austria and the Sudetenland during what became known as Kristallnacht. Churchill described these attacks as 'the deep repeated strokes of the alarm bell' which should be a call to action.[149]

*

DESPITE THE darkening situation abroad, at home public life for the King and Queen continued. Among the Queen's engagements that autumn, she visited the Hospital for Sick Children in Great Ormond Street, the War-Disabled ex-Servicemen's Exhibition at the Imperial Institute and the Queen's Hospital for Children in Bethnal Green, and she received members of the International Labour Organization of the League of Nations. There were moments of relaxation, doubly welcome because of the stress of recent events. After a stay with her brother David and his wife at St Paul's Walden in late November, she wrote to Rachel, 'It was all so perfect – the house looking so lovely, the colours and flowers so exquisite, and that heavenly feeling of ease and friendliness which did us both so much good.'[150] At Christmas the Royal Family gathered as usual at Sandringham. But the Queen fell ill again – exhaustion had brought on influenza – and she took to her bed for a week after Christmas.

After she returned to London at the end of January 1939 the Queen conducted a normal mix of duties – among her engagements, she attended a congress for the leisure industry, an exhibition of Scottish art at the Royal Academy, the British Industries Fair at Earls Court, and a festival for the Women Helpers of one of her favourite charities, Toc H, at the Albert Hall. She continued to need the encouragement of her family and friends. Jasper Ridley wrote to praise her and the King: 'the way in which you have seized hold of the situation and are running it for the good – altho' it surprises me not at all – is so wholly admirable.'[151]

A less obvious force for good was still the Duke of Windsor. Since the summer of 1938 the patient Walter Monckton had been attempting to mediate between him and his family over his desire to return to England, with his wife, as early as that November. Monckton and the Prime Minister discussed the problem with the King and Queen at Balmoral. The Prime Minister was not averse to the Duke of Windsor's return, and felt that he could even be given a public role similar to that of the King's younger brothers. According to Monckton, the King was 'not fundamentally' against this. But, as he recorded later, 'I think the Queen felt quite plainly that it was undesirable to give the Duke any effective sphere of work. I felt then, as always, that she naturally thought that she must be on her guard because the Duke of Windsor to whom the other brothers had always looked up, was an attractive, vital creature who might be the rallying point for any who might be critical of the new king who was less superficially endowed with the arts and graces that please.'[152] As a result of these discussions the King wrote to his brother to say that he should postpone his return until 1939.

Queen Mary and the Queen remained opposed to the Windsors' return. The press had taken up the question, and letters from the public hostile to the very notion were being received at Buckingham Palace and Marlborough House. The Queen sent several of the letters she had received to Monckton, remarking, 'I do hope that it will be possible to put people's minds at rest <u>soon</u>, as such gossip reacts badly on the King & Queen.'[153]

Monckton continued to use his good offices to dissuade the Duke, but in February 1939 he asked to see Queen Mary in order to pass on a message enquiring whether she would receive both Duke and Duchess if they came to London. On the King's advice his mother decided not to see Monckton, but sent him a message saying that she could not receive them.[154] Monckton was in a difficult position and he asked the King to give the Duke some hope that he and the Duchess would eventually be received. 'To put the matter at its lowest, I find it increasingly difficult to keep him quiet ... I should hate to see any open controversy about it.'[155]

Shortly afterwards, the Duke vented his fury with his family over the dedication of his father King George V's tomb in St George's Chapel. He believed that his contribution to the cost of the tomb had not been adequately recognized, and that he had not been kept properly informed of the date of its dedication. In response to a kind letter from Queen Mary to him, the Duke wrote in evident anger that her letter was 'extremely illuminating, altho' I greatly regret that it shld have taken so sacred an occasion to disclose so much that is unpleasant, & to destroy the last vestige of feeling I had left for you all as a family'. He had by now turned totally against the sister-in-law he had loved, the new Queen, and he ended his letter, 'You, by your final refusal to receive Walter Monckton last month, & BERTIE, BY HIS IGNOMINIOUS CAPITULATION TO THE WILES OF HIS AMBITIOUS WIFE, have made further normal correspondence between us impossible.'[156] Queen Mary was distressed by this outburst and she at once sent a note to her daughter-in-law asking her to come and see her. The Queen did so and, though no record of the meeting exists, it can be assumed that she tried to comfort her mother-in-law.[157]

The Duke of Windsor was an unwelcome distraction. Over all hung the menace of fascism. Chamberlain had still not abandoned his hopes of preserving some sort of peace. But at the same time he did allow rearmament to continue. Production of Hurricane and Spitfire planes increased and the Air Ministry was swiftly building its Home Chain network of early-warning radar stations. Not all politicians approved. Clement Attlee, the Labour leader, wrote to his brother Tom, 'Neville annoys me by mouthing the arguments of complete pacifism while piling up armaments.'[158] In fact such rearmament was the only possible justification for a period of appeasement – and arguments over the extent to which the government used the year's grace after Munich to build up British military capabilities continue to rage today.*

In mid-February the King and Queen travelled to Tyneside where the King launched *King George V*, the first British battleship built in fourteen years. They inspected the Vickers Armstrong armament works at Elswick where tanks, tracked vehicles, bombs, guns and aircraft components were being manufactured, and also visited various hospitals, health clinics and training centres. A few days later at the British Industries Fair at Olympia, they were shown anti-aircraft guns. The Queen attended a House of Commons debate on a government bill to build fifty camps, to be used by schoolchildren if peace prevailed, or by refugees from the cities if war broke out.

It became more and more obvious that Munich had done nothing to diminish Hitler's appetite. On 15 March 1939 German troops marched into Prague. From the balcony of Hradčany Castle, the seat of the kings of Bohemia, Hitler declared that Czechoslovakia no longer existed.

Three days later the King and Queen listened together to a broadcast speech in which Chamberlain had finally to admit that Hitler had lied to him. He warned the German dictator that sacrifices for peace were over and that Britain would never surrender 'the liberty

---

* In spring 1939 one could indeed still argue that appeasement had bought Britain time to rearm and to improve her air defences – the number of RAF squadrons rose from five to forty-seven. And if and when war finally came, it would be true to say that Britain could not have done anything more to avoid it. In the 'Munich Winter' chapter of *The Gathering Storm*, Churchill acknowledges that in the 'vital sphere' of air power and air defences Britain improved her position after Munich, but he concluded, 'Finally there is this staggering fact: that in the single year 1938, Hitler had annexed to the Reich and brought under his absolute rule 6,750,000 Austrians and 3,500,000 Sudetens, a total of over ten million subjects, toilers and soldiers. Indeed the dread balance had turned in his favour.'

that we have enjoyed for hundreds of years'. The King immediately wrote to Chamberlain to support him and to say that his efforts for peace would not have been wasted 'for they can have left no doubt in the minds of ordinary people all over the world of our love of peace & of our readiness to discuss with any nation whatever grievances they think they have.'[159]

Across the Channel there were hopes that British inaction in the face of aggression was over. On 21 March the French President and Madame Lebrun arrived in London for a return state visit; the King and Queen entertained them to lunch at Windsor on 23 March. At the Guildhall banquet in the President's honour the eminent French journalist Ludovic Naudeau, reporting on the visit for *L'Illustration*, noticed with satisfaction that, as the guests arrived, Winston Churchill received almost as much applause as Neville Chamberlain. Naudeau saw this as a sign that Britain was at last awake and undeceived, ready to heed Churchill's perspicacious warnings and demands for rearmament.[160]

At the end of that month rumours of an impending German attack on Poland – even more of a 'faraway country' than Czechoslovakia – led Chamberlain to offer a guarantee of that country's integrity. France joined Britain. On Good Friday Italy invaded Albania and London gave similar guarantees to Romania and Greece. Britain had now declared herself to be standing solidly against the dictators and their serial aggression.[161] At the end of April 1939 Chamberlain announced that, for the first time ever in time of peace, the British government would introduce compulsory military service, despite opposition from the Labour and Liberal parties.

Such huge changes in British policy towards Europe and the dictators led, of course, to great debates, public and private. Within Buckingham Palace, as everywhere else, there were disagreements. Alec Hardinge, a consistent critic of Chamberlain and of Munich, was troubled to find himself disagreeing with the Queen, who still wished to give the Prime Minister's policies the benefit of the doubt.* After

---

* Hardinge had long opposed appeasement. In early September 1938 he wrote himself a memorandum to answer the question 'Can there be friendship between democracies and totalitarian states?' His answer was negative. No democratic government could be real friends with states which, 'with the acquiescence of their peoples, abolish individual freedom, preach intense nationalism, make war on religions, and subordinate them to the barbaric worship of race, show complete disregard for the sanctity of obligations and never cease to denounce and

a long conversation with her at the end of April 1939, Hardinge wrote that she found it hard to see what Britain had done wrong. She said that she did not like the idea of conscription, nor the creation of a large army to defend other people's frontiers. 'Her whole judgement is based on what is right or wrong to do, not on its consequences.' She resented Britain being blamed over Czechoslovakia. Furthermore, she feared that in the end Britain would be left 'holding the baby'. ('How right she was we did not clearly see then,' Hardinge added in 1941.)

Hardinge noted that the Queen was 'angelic' in her disagreement with him. But he was disturbed by the conversation 'because HM's judgement and common sense are so right always'. When the King joined them, he did not seem worried about the idea of conscription, even though the unions were much opposed to it. Hardinge said he thought that the unions could be talked round – 'upon which the King said, "Who by?" and the Queen at once answered, "you'll have to do it, of course – darling." '[162]

Hardinge clearly believed both that the Queen's influence counted for a great deal with the King and that this was usually for the good – though not on the matter of appeasement. Many years later Hardinge told the King's official biographer that early in his reign the King would refuse to discuss business with him but invariably went to talk to the Queen instead, returning with a decision which Hardinge attributed to her. And as Hardinge observed, her views were further to the right than those of her husband.[163]

Whether or not Hardinge's retrospective analysis was correct, there is no doubt that the Queen knew far more about affairs of state than did either Queen Alexandra or Queen Mary. But it is difficult to gauge the extent of her influence. She was utterly discreet and never talked,

pour scorn on the principles that we hold most dear'. In April 1939 he wrote in another memorandum that, as a result of appeasement, the dictators had been able to secure a much stronger strategic position on the continent. Each successive coup – Austria, Czechoslovakia and Albania – had added enormously to their actual armed power, as well as to their prestige. Each had effectively neutralized the advances made in British rearmament. Chamberlain's policies meant that the Eastern Front was destroyed; smaller countries now doubted the democrats' resolve and had been forced to come to terms with the dictators; fear of derailing appeasement had led to acquiescence in the victory of the fascists in Spain; optimistic forecasts of the intentions of the dictators had misled the British people and induced an unjustified complacency; finally, Hardinge argued, it had given the impression to foreign countries, large and small, that Britain could no longer be relied upon. (Hon. Lady Murray Papers) nor wrote even in letters to her family, about this aspect of her partnership with the King.

But it is clear that, although Hardinge had at first found the new King inarticulate and indecisive, his own guidance, together with the Queen's constant support of her husband, had gradually increased the King's self-confidence. George VI was quoted as saying that after he became King he discovered that he was for the first time in his life able to make up his own mind.[164] It was a happy experience and it meant that his relationship with the Queen began to change; the couple became more interdependent and she began to rely also on him. Her sister Rose said, 'In fundamental things she leant on him; I have always felt how much the Queen depended on the King.'[165]

*

THE LAST WEEKS of April and the first few days of May 1939 became hectic as the King and Queen made final preparations for a six-week visit to Canada and the United States. The government had debated whether the international crisis was so threatening that the trip should be cancelled. There were even rumours that the Germans might intercept their ship on the ocean and take them captive. That was not a pleasing thought – nor was it a deterrent. At dinner at Windsor the Queen talked to the US Ambassador, Joseph P. Kennedy, about the seriousness of the situation.* Kennedy had always been a supporter of appeasement and, even now, considered that a war between Britain and Germany should be avoided at all costs. Nonetheless he was impressed by the Queen. 'She wanted still very much to go to the USA no matter how dangerous it was because not to go would give satisfaction to the enemies. What a woman.'[166]

---

* Joseph P. Kennedy (1888–1969), American businessman and ally of President Roosevelt, Ambassador to Great Britain 1938–40. After the war began, his enthusiasm for appeasement became defeatism and he argued against US aid to Britain. In November 1940 he gave a newspaper interview in the United States in which he asserted, 'Democracy is finished in England. It may be here.' His son John F. Kennedy was President of the United States 1961–3.

CHAPTER TWELVE

ACROSS THE ATLANTIC

1939

'This has made us'

'I AM STARTING to read the unexpurgated edition of "Mein Kampf",' wrote Queen Elizabeth to Queen Mary, who may have been rather startled to be asked, 'Have you read it, Mama?'[1]*

The letter to Queen Mary was written on 8 May 1939 from the Canadian Pacific liner *Empress of Australia*. The King and Queen were at the start of the journey to Canada and the United States which was to take them away from the tense and anxious atmosphere in Europe for the next six weeks. The Queen's choice of reading matter showed where her concerns lay. The King had been reluctant to leave Britain as it became ever clearer that Hitler could not be appeased. But the government's advice was that war was not yet imminent, and that the international crisis rendered the tour more, rather than less, advisable. The visit would both demonstrate and strengthen the solidarity of the Empire against the threat to world peace, and boost Anglo-American friendship.

A tour of Canada had first been proposed by Lord Tweedsmuir,† the Governor General, in early 1937 and was promoted by the Canadian Prime Minister, Mackenzie King, when he came to London for the Coronation. President Roosevelt encouraged the idea of combining the tour of Canada with a trip to the United States. The

---

* Adolf Hitler published the two volumes of *Mein Kampf* (My Struggle) in 1925 and 1926. The book, part autobiography and part political treatise, outlined his hatred of Judaism and communism and expressed his belief that Germany must abandon democracy, rearm and acquire new European territories to fulfil her destiny. An expurgated English-language edition, omitting much of the anti-Semitism, was published in 1933. An unexpurgated English version, translated by James Murphy, was published in London in 1939.

† First Baron Tweedsmuir (1875–1940), Governor General of Canada 1935–40, and better known as the author John Buchan.

President invited the Princesses too, but the King felt that they were too young.[2] The announcement of the visit was well received, particularly in Canada. 'People talk about nothing else,' Lord Tweedsmuir reported. 'I suggest a very informal and unofficial visit to the United States, as being far more likely to please the American people. That I know is President Roosevelt's own idea, which he confided to my Prime Minister.'[3]

This cautious, indeed downbeat, approach to the American visit was Roosevelt's preference for both political and personal reasons. He could not afford to antagonize the isolationists in Congress and the press who believed that the United States should remain outside any European conflict. But, certain that war between Britain and Germany was inevitable, he hoped that the presence of the King and Queen on American soil would strengthen the friendship between the two English-speaking nations and sway Congress towards Britain. As his wife Eleanor later wrote, Roosevelt thought that 'we all might soon be engaged in a life and death struggle, in which Great Britain would be our first line of defence'.[4] The American part of the tour was thus of enormous significance, but it was also important to Canada that the King's journey should be seen to be primarily for the benefit of Canadians.

Much has been written about this tour.* Despite the hopes of Canadian officials, the American visit came to outweigh the Canadian journey because of the personal relationship the King was able to form with President Roosevelt and the effect this, as well as the public success of the tour, had upon American attitudes to the war when it came. But the visit to Canada was especially significant. Not only was it the first visit by a British sovereign to an overseas dominion, but King George VI was the first sovereign to be crowned king of Canada, since the 1931 Statute of Westminster had established the status of Canada and the other Dominions as autonomous dominions under the Crown. From Britain's point of view, furthermore, the visit was vitally important in guaranteeing the support of Mackenzie King and Canada in the event of war, for the Canadian Prime Minister had been a convinced appeaser, determined to keep Canada out of any European hostilities.

---

* The most comprehensive account is that given in *The Roosevelts and the Royals* by Will Swift, John Wiley & Sons, 2004.

The trip also gave both King and Queen their first opportunity to gauge, in person, the feelings of the people of the wider Empire towards them – and that in a country where King Edward VIII had acquired popularity through his visits as Prince of Wales and his purchase of a ranch in Alberta.* The challenge was political as well as personal: there were isolationists in Canada as well as in the USA – the support of French Canadians for the British cause could not be taken for granted. In the event, they succeeded beyond all expectation and for Queen Elizabeth this tour was the beginning of a long and affectionate relationship with Canada; she would visit it more than any other country, returning thirteen times.

They were to have travelled in the battlecruiser HMS *Repulse*, but the King considered it unwise to deprive the navy of a warship at this dangerous time. So it was in the liner *Empress of Australia* that they set sail on 6 May from Portsmouth, accompanied by a suite of ten. The two Princesses, aged thirteen and eight, came to see them off, together with Queen Mary and other members of the Royal Family. 'I hated saying good-bye to you & Margaret,' their mother wrote to Princess Elizabeth next day. 'I shall miss you horribly, but be good & kind,' she said, adding, 'P.S. My handwriting is very wobbly, because the ship is shivering like someone with influenza! P.P.S. Papa is writing to Margaret.'[5]

Their first few days afloat were not improved by rough seas and by what looked like a deliberate attempt by the Duke of Windsor to cause trouble. He accepted an invitation to broadcast an appeal for peace to the American people direct from the First World War battlefield of Verdun. The timing was not entirely of his choosing and his speech was an uncontroversial plea to statesmen to do all they could to avoid war. But it was tactless to make the broadcast while the King was on his way across the Atlantic. The Queen could only have seen it as an attempt to steal her husband's thunder. 'I see on the news bulletin today, that David is going to broadcast to America this evening,' she wrote to Queen Mary on 8 May. 'I do wonder whether this is true, and if it is, how troublesome of him to choose such a moment.'[6] The Duke spoke fluently and his speech was well received by many listeners;[7] but it did seem to be a gesture of appeasement

---

* This was the EP Ranch in Alberta, which the Prince bought after visiting Canada for the first time in 1919, and in which he took great interest. He kept it until the early 1960s.

designed to upstage the King. The Duke of Kent agreed with the Queen, and Alec Hardinge, writing to the King, commented that it was 'ludicrous' of the Duke to think that such a speech could do any good.[8]

Three days later the Duke seemed a minor irritant – the whole journey suddenly appeared to be in jeopardy. The ship was enveloped in thick fog and surrounded by icebergs. She stopped, not for a few hours, but for days. The Queen wrote home to her daughter:

> Here we are creeping along at about one mile per hour, & occasionally stopping altogether, for the 3rd day running! You can imagine how horrid it is – one cannot see more than a few yards, and the sea is full of icebergs as big as Glamis, & things called 'growlers' – which are icebergs mostly under water with only a very small amount of ice showing on the surface. We shall be late arriving in Canada, and it is going to be very difficult to fit everything in, and avoid disappointing people. It is very cold – rather like the coldest, dampest day at Sandringham – double it and add some icebergs, & then you can imagine a little of what it is like![9]

The blasts of the ship's foghorn echoed off the icebergs 'like the twang of a piece of wire. Incredibly eery,' she told Queen Mary. 'We very nearly hit a berg the day before yesterday, and the poor Captain was nearly demented because some kind cheerful people kept on reminding him that it was about here that the Titanic was struck, & just about the same date!' It was an alarming experience: 'one kept on imagining that a great iceberg was bearing down on the ship, & starting up at night with a beating heart,' the Queen wrote.[10] The fog finally cleared on 14 May, 'and we saw the sea covered with floating ice, a few big bergs, and a great mass of pack ice hemming us on three sides. We went round it for a bit, and then ploughed through one side of the pack into open water. It was an amazing sight,' she reported.[11]

Tommy Lascelles, the King's acting Private Secretary for the trip,* faced with reorganizing the beginning of the tour, commented that it was a near-run thing: any longer delay would have thrown the entire programme off track. Thanks to 'ingenious juggling', condensing the

---

* Alec Hardinge had been left behind to keep watch on the international situation, and it was Lascelles who had done the preparatory 'recce' for the tour earlier in the year.

Ottawa visit from four days into two and a half, 'we have re-mosaic'd the first four days so that nothing is left out.' And there was a silver lining – the delay had provided the King with a longer rest: 'it is the only really idle & irresponsible spell he has had since he acceded; there has been nothing for him to do, & Hitler has hardly been mentioned since we left England.'[12]

On the morning of 17 May, in fine weather, the *Empress of Australia* and her British and Canadian naval escorts finally steamed up the St Lawrence to L'Anse du Foulon – Wolfe's Cove – where the royal party was to disembark. The cliffs above the harbour were lined with thousands of spectators who had been gathering since early morning. At 10.30 Prime Minister Mackenzie King and the Justice Minister Ernest Lapointe went on board to welcome the King and Queen. Mackenzie King's diary, recording their conversation, showed that the Queen was well aware of the personal contribution she could make to the success of the tour as a Scottish queen: she spoke at once of Scotland's links with France, and the number of Scots who had come to Canada.[13] Nor were Canadian Scots about to forget this. The demands for her attention from émigré Scots became a leitmotif of the tour.

A few minutes later they came ashore. The King was wearing the full-dress uniform of an Admiral of the Fleet, the Queen was elegant in a pale-grey dress of light wool, with long slit sleeves edged with fur and a hat with a becomingly upswept brim. She stepped off the gangway first, remarking as she did so that this was the first time she had set foot on Canadian soil.[14] (It was the King's second visit: he had been to Canada as a naval cadet in 1913.) After being presented with a long line of dignitaries, they were driven to the Quebec Parliament to receive provincial and municipal addresses.

Both the luncheon which followed and dinner that night were held at Château Frontenac, the grandiose Canadian Pacific Railway hotel whose towering green roof still dominates the Quebec skyline. The lavish luncheon was followed by a speech by Mackenzie King expressing pride that Canada had been chosen for the King's first visit to his Dominions and stressing, for the benefit of French Canadians, that the King and Queen had come ashore at the same spot as the French founders of Canada. The King's reply, beginning in English and ending in French, betrayed his nerves but was well received. 'When the King began to speak, he was certainly moved and it was a little difficult to understand him,' wrote one of the French Canadian officials organizing the trip. 'He quickly recovered himself and continued his address in a firm voice. He was warmly applauded.'[15]

After lunch, the King and Queen drove round the city to a warm, if quiet, welcome. But crowds of excited children in the Parc des Champs de Bataille on the Plains of Abraham, site of the bloody battle between the armies of General Wolfe and the Marquis de Montcalm in 1759, cheered loudly and waved flags; others sang 'Dieu bénisse notre Roi et notre Reine'.

Yousuf Karsh, the Governor General's official photographer for the tour, photographed the party. For tea at the residence of the Lieutenant Governor of Quebec the nuns of the Hôtel-Dieu in the city had worked for a month creating two towering cakes surmounted by replicas of the King's and Queen's Coronation crowns. At Château Frontenac in the evening, the Queen wore a diamond tiara and a pink crinoline dress adorned with gold sequins and 'La France' roses. The Lieutenant Governor, Esioff-Léon Patenaude, seated next to her, was struck when she correctly identified three guests as having the air of 'educators' – they were all heads of universities – and two others as judges; she asked to meet them, and they were sought out after dinner. Only the intervention of Lascelles, announcing that it was time for the King and Queen to leave, prevented further presentations at the end of this exhausting first day.[16] They spent the night at the Citadel, the Governor General's Quebec residence.

The first twenty-four hours had certainly been a success. One observer commented, 'Sa Majesté la Reine avait conquis tous les Québécois.'[17] Asked what impression the King and Queen had made in Quebec, and whether French Canadians were loyal to England, Patenaude replied that less than 5 per cent of the French Canadian population shared the anti-British feelings expressed by certain soap-box orators, and that it had been a great thing for the people to see the King: they now felt that he belonged to them, as king of Canada. Indeed, French Canadians were eager to play a part in the visit. They clamoured for invitations to Château Frontenac; a country priest wrote to ask for commemorative medallions for the schoolchildren in his parish, although they would not see the King and Queen; a mayor begged for the couple to stop at his town.[18]

At Quebec the King and Queen embarked on a train which was to be their base for most of the rest of the tour, covering some 9,510 miles in twenty-nine days. It was the Governor General's official train, which had been redecorated and extended to twelve carriages to carry the large party. The two royal carriages were painted in silver and blue, with the royal arms on each; the bedrooms were furnished in grey-blue and pink for the Queen and blue and white for the King. There was a wood-panelled office for the King, sitting rooms and a handsome dining room; and pull-down maps on rollers to follow their route across Canada. There was a carriage for the Prime Minister, who accompanied them throughout the tour. The train was comfortably, indeed luxuriously, appointed, although there was scarcely room for the Queen's clothes: she needed a prodigious wardrobe for the multiple occasions and climate changes ahead, and Norman Hartnell had provided for all.[19] Towards the end of the tour, one of the accompanying journalists calculated that she had made forty-eight appearances in thirty-two different outfits.[20]

The royal staff of nineteen included three British police officers. But at the King's special request there were also four stalwart Royal Canadian Mounted Police orderlies in the party. Their task was to act as bodyguards in case of over-enthusiastic crowds.[21] Eight more Mounties travelled with the train.

After a brief stop at Trois Rivières, where the King and Queen alighted to meet the Mayor and City Council, they arrived at Montreal in the early afternoon of 18 May, to a welcome as warm as that in Quebec City but far noisier. 'So far, this tour is a roaring success,' Tommy Lascelles reported. 'I've never seen such splendid crowds . . . we must have seen well over a million people in Montreal alone.'[22] The guard of honour was provided by the Black Watch of Canada,* affiliated to the British regiment of which Queen Elizabeth had become colonel-in-chief in 1937. She became colonel-in-chief of the Canadian regiment ten years later, and maintained a close interest in it throughout her life.

Montreal had been preparing for the nine-hour royal visit for months, and the arrangements were lavish. The street decorations alone cost hundreds of thousands of dollars – the city was decked with floral arches,

---

* The Black Watch (the Royal Highland Regiment) of Canada also provided streetliners: so long was the processional route that there were not enough men, and the streetliners had to 'leapfrog' along the route. (Information from Tom Bourne, son of Colonel John Bourne of the Black Watch of Canada)

royal portraits and immense pylons covered with coloured bunting. Houses were painted and balconies rented out to spectators. As the King and Queen arrived, the schoolchildren massed in the East Baseball Park forgot to sing the National Anthem and burst out into spontaneous cheering instead.[23] Their host in Montreal was the Mayor, Camillien Houde, a colourful character. Earlier in the year he had made a speech asserting that if there were a war between England and Italy, the French Canadians, who were Roman Catholics, Latins and natural fascists, would side with Italy.[24] He posed the kind of challenge that the Queen enjoyed – she had charmed hostile 'Bolshevik' politicians in Australia; a maverick right-winger should prove no more difficult. Houde was indeed entranced by her and he is reputed to have said to the King, as huge crowds cheered them, 'You know, Your Majesty, some of this is for you.'[25]*

The thousand guests bidden to the dinner given by the City of Montreal had kept dressmakers and tailors employed for weeks, according to the local press. The Queen, this time, wore not a crinoline but a close-fitting silver-blue brocade gown embroidered with silver sequins and rhinestones, and a diamond tiara, three-strand necklace and earrings. When she and the King entered the hall, the guests abandoned protocol and broke into applause and cheers. Thereafter the dinner proceeded with much gaiety through its six courses and vintage champagne. The Quatuor Alouette sang traditional French Canadian folk songs as well as Scottish, Irish and English tunes, and the press reported that the King and Queen joined in with 'Drink to Me Only with Thine Eyes' and 'Alouette, Gentille Alouette', of which the Queen asked for a copy of the lyrics to take home.[26]

Next morning, 19 May, the royal train arrived in Ottawa, to be greeted by Lord and Lady Tweedsmuir. The Governor General's role in the tour was small: as the King's representative he stepped down, symbolically, while the King himself was in Canada. But during the two and a half days the King and Queen spent in Ottawa, days crammed with pomp and ceremony, Lord Tweedsmuir was able to observe them at first hand, and his comments were perceptive, particularly about the Queen. The city was thronged with spectators who had come in from the surrounding countryside;

---

* Her triumph was only temporary, however. Camillien Houde was interned in 1940 for urging men to refuse conscription.

thousands of Americans also came. The principal event of the first day in Ottawa was the session of Parliament over which the King presided. For the ceremony the Queen wore one of the more spectacular crinolines designed for her by Hartnell, with a long golden train.* 'The Q. is looking radiantly beautiful, & has them all gasping like goldfish – particularly the American press-men,' Tommy Lascelles reported.[27]

Saturday 20 May had been designated the King's official birthday, since he would be in the United States on 8 June, the date on which the birthday was normally celebrated. To mark the day, Trooping the Colour was held on Parliament Hill. While the King took the salute, the Queen watched from a window with Lord Tweedsmuir. 'When the crowd saw her,' Tweedsmuir observed, 'nothing would induce several thousand of them to look at the Trooping. They simply kept their eyes glued on Her Majesty and shouted like dervishes.'[28]

The Canadian government had been anxious for her to perform a ceremony to commemorate her visit, so after the Trooping she laid the foundation stone of the Supreme Court Building. Her deftly worded speech acknowledged the compliment to women which the ceremony represented, and also used her Scottish heritage to advantage. 'Perhaps it is not inappropriate that this task should be performed by a woman, for woman's position in civilized society has depended upon the growth of law,' she began. She continued in French, pointing out that Scottish and French Canadian law shared their source in Roman law.[29]

Afterwards, showing her instinct for the unexpected but welcome gesture, the Queen asked Lord Tweedsmuir to take her and the King to meet the masons working on the building. Some of them were Scots, and, as Tweedsmuir recorded, 'they spent at least ten minutes in Scottish reminiscences, in full view of 70,000 people, who went mad!'[30] This episode has been seen as the first instance of a royal 'walkabout', though it is worth remembering that the King and Queen had done much the same as Duke and Duchess of York in Australia in 1927. The following day, in beautiful weather, the King unveiled the National War Memorial – and then, Tweedsmuir reported,

---

* This dress she later presented to Canada and it was put on display in the Public Archives in Ottawa.

A most extraordinary scene followed. The King and Queen, and my wife and myself were absorbed in a crowd of six or seven thousand ex-soldiers, who kept the most perfect order among themselves, and opened up lanes for Their Majesties to pass through. There was no need of the police, and indeed the police would have had no chance. It was a wonderful example of what a people's king means, and it would have been impossible anywhere else in the world. One old fellow shouted to me, 'Ay, man, if Hitler could see this!' It was also extraordinarily moving, because most of these old fellows were weeping.[31]

Writing to a friend about these two occasions, Tweedsmuir declared that the Queen had 'a perfect genius for the right kind of publicity. The unrehearsed episodes here were marvellous.'[32] Both King and Queen, he remarked to Hardinge, had an infallible instinct for 'the small unscheduled things that count most'.[33] Throughout the tour, the press reports are peppered with accounts of impromptu breaks in the official programme when the pair stopped to talk to individuals, or appeared unannounced from the royal train. One Ottawa journal described the royal couple as 'democracy enthroned, not enthralled'.[34]

At the garden party at Government House on their second day in Ottawa, Lord Tweedsmuir was amazed to see, among the cheering guests, the Archbishop and other French Canadian ecclesiastics shouting, 'Vive le Roi!' and 'Vive la Reine!' This was followed by a Parliamentary dinner at Château Laurier. After it the King and Queen appeared on the balcony to acknowledge the cheers of a crowd of some 100,000 in the central square, and then surprised officials by returning to shake the hands of all 800 of the guests at the dinner.[35] Rufus Pope, one of the Senators, said to the Queen, 'Ma'am I would fight for you. Yes I would fight for you until hell is frozen.'[36]

All this was noticed in Europe. Georges Vanier,* the Canadian Minister in Paris, reported on the close attention the royal visit was receiving in France. 'The departure of the King and Queen from England at a time of acute national anxiety is seen as a proof of the cool, phlegmatic, and solid character of their Anglo-Saxon ally,' he wrote. Accounts of the King's speeches in French were well received,

---

* Georges Vanier (1888–1967). After a distinguished military and diplomatic career he became the first French Canadian governor general of Canada in 1959.

as was the attention paid to French Canadians.[37] In Italy, predictably, reactions were less favourable. The Italian press 'has paid studiously little attention' to the visit, the British Ambassador wrote, and such reports as it published were derogatory. Some newspapers mocked the idea that the visit augured well for Anglo-French collaboration, expressing surprise that the French had ever given up this former possession.[38] In Germany, meanwhile, having reported that the bad weather in the North Atlantic had spoiled the trip, the press did its best to play it down.[39]

'Their Majesties are very well, and in excellent spirits,' commented Lord Tweedsmuir the day after their departure from Ottawa. 'I am just a little doubtful as to how they will last the course. Canada has given them a pretty heavy programme, but they seem to want to add to it.'[40] On the way to Toronto, the King and Queen waved to the crowds from the rear platform of the train as it ran slowly through towns; this was often repeated as they travelled west.

In Toronto next day, in addition to the provincial and municipal welcoming ceremonies, the Queen had another engagement of her own. She had accepted the colonelcy-in-chief of the Toronto Scottish Regiment in 1937; now she inspected her regiment and presented them with new colours, making a short speech alluding to the ties uniting Canada and her native Scotland. 'Rousing Cheers Given for "Girl from Glamis"' announced the Toronto *Globe and Mail*.[41] There were more echoes of Scotland: while officially the King and Queen were enjoying periods of rest in the Lieutenant Governor's Chambers in the Legislative Buildings that day, they were in fact receiving individuals privately, including the son of a shepherd at Glamis whom the Queen had asked to meet,* and Sir William Mulock, a distinguished Canadian elder statesman, who presented her with funds collected by the Black Watch in Toronto to endow beds at a Black Watch Home in Scotland.

She had also asked to meet in Toronto the President of the Canadian Mothercraft Society. This was the only Canadian society to which she had as yet given her patronage, underlining the importance

---

* David Williamson, the shepherd's son, told the press afterwards that she had recalled playing with him when they were children. Also there to meet the Queen was a former member of the Girl Guides troop which she had organized at Glamis, Mrs Francis MacAndrew French, whose father was a tenant farmer there. (Toronto press report, 23 May 1939, RA F&V/VISOV/CAN/1939/Press cuttings/Vol. I, p. 114)

she attached to the teaching of maternal skills, for the Mothercraft Training Society was one of her earliest patronages in England. The Queen's public role in promoting charitable work was, in theory, suspended during the Canadian tour, but in this way she contrived to give a favourite cause a private boost;[42] she did the same for the Canadian Toc H League of Women Helpers in various cities across the country.[43]*

Their final engagement in Toronto was another landmark for Queen Elizabeth: the Woodbine Spring Meeting, to which they were invited at the suggestion of the President of the Ontario Jockey Club.[44] The King and Queen drove round the course in the state landau before watching the highlight of the meeting, the King's Plate, for which Queen Victoria had given fifty guineas in 1860. No one could have guessed then that racing would become the Queen's passion, or that she would return frequently to Woodbine, where she watched the running of what became the Queen's Plate six times, culminating, in 1989, on the fiftieth anniversary of this visit. After the race the King and Queen drove through the crowded streets of Toronto again, stopping at the Christie Street Military Hospital, where they overran their schedule, talking to war invalids.

That night, as the royal train journeyed west, a crowd estimated at 20,000 at Sudbury stood silently during a twenty-minute stop at 1 a.m. – the press had published a request that the King and Queen be allowed to sleep. On another occasion they were not so lucky: the steward of the royal carriages, Wilfred Notley, recorded that he was awakened at 6 a.m. by an out-of-tune rendering of the National Anthem attempted by patriotic citizens who had spent the night camped beside the train at Kenora, one of its overnight stopping places. Summoned by bells to the royal car, Notley found a half-awake King in the passageway, protesting at the noise. The Mounties diplomatically silenced the din with assurances that the King would come out later, which he duly did.[45]

The temperature dropped as the royal train headed north and

---

* Another unofficial but much publicized presentation took place in the Lieutenant Governor's offices that day: that of the Dionne quintuplets from Callander. The little girls, aged not quite five, curtsied and presented bouquets to the Queen, putting their arms round her neck and kissing her when it was time to leave. Mackenzie King found this episode particularly heart warming, and reported that the Queen 'was very nice about it, and seemed rather to enjoy it'.

westwards. On 23 May, as they travelled along the shores of Lake Superior, the Queen wrote again to Princess Elizabeth:

> I am afraid that I never had one single minute in Ottawa to write to you, and this is the first opportunity on the train. All day we have been passing through lovely wild country. Rather like Scotland on a large scale. Great rivers & lochs and pine woods, and for hours right along the great Lake. It was <u>bright</u> blue, with many little wooded Islands ... Papa & I have had a wonderful welcome everywhere we have been. The French people in Quebec & Ottawa were wonderfully loyal; & in Montreal there must have been 2,000,000 people, all very enthusiastic ... Yesterday in Toronto it was the same, and we feel so glad that we were able to come here ... Papa & I are bearing up very well. Tho' we are working very hard – from morning to night, we go in open cars & the good air keeps us well. The train stops at little stations to get water or coal or ice, & there is always a crowd, & we go out & talk to the people. Yesterday there were some Indians with a baby in its wooden cradle, & <u>always</u> someone from Scotland! Usually Forfar or Glamis![46]

It was raining when they arrived in Winnipeg on 24 May, but the King and Queen kept their car open for their drive around the city and were cheered by large crowds including many Americans: forty-two special trains had been run from the United States. In his Empire Day broadcast, the King described their journey as 'a deeply moving experience'. Across the Atlantic, he said, 'the Christian civilization of Europe is now profoundly troubled and challenged from within'. He pointed to the example of Canada in overcoming internal strife, and to the success of Canada and the United States in resolving differences between them without force or threats.[47]

Late that evening, when the train had made its customary stop at a small station for the night, the Queen took up her letter to Princess Elizabeth again: 'We spent the day in Winnipeg, a large town where all the business is done for the thousands of miles of farms round about. It rained in the morning, but cleared up in the afternoon, when we drove 28 miles, with cheering people & children all the way!'[48] The train had now taken to stopping at deserted spots on the line so that they could get out and walk about, a relief from the hours they spent in the public eye at one reception after another. At one such halt, the

Queen organized a race for members of their suite which had them all puffing along the track. 'She is full of life and charm,' commented Mackenzie King.[49]

In Saskatchewan on 25 May they were given another vociferous welcome at the provincial capital, Regina. Their host was the Lieutenant Governor, Archie McNab, who had to be reminded to remove his unaccustomed silk hat for the National Anthem. His homespun manner, the local press reported, 'called forth a happy response from the sovereigns'.[50] The royal train left Regina after a state dinner at Government House. Later, during a short stop in heavy rain at Moose Jaw, the King and Queen again faced a drenching in their open car as they drove through the town. In Calgary, home of the celebrated stampede, as the Queen wrote to Princess Elizabeth, 'we saw a lot of Indians, and quite a lot of cowboys on "bucking broncos" who came dashing along with us'.[51] They made an unscheduled stop at an Indian encampment on their drive through the city and shook hands with Duck Chief, head of the Blackfoot tribe. 'R. Dimbleby, BBC announcer, gave an atmosphere broadcast, assisted by Interpreter Little Dog,' the Calgary press reported.[52] It was the first royal tour on which Richard Dimbleby, later one of the BBC's most renowned correspondents, reported.

The seemingly endless journey across the prairies was enlivened by several incidents recorded by Wilfred Notley, the steward in the royal carriages. In his somewhat macabre words, 'a beautiful box not unlike a child's coffin' was delivered to the King: it proved to contain a dozen ducks, frozen solid, a present from one of the lieutenant governors. 'Remind me to have this man arrested for shooting game out of season,' said the King to Notley.* In Banff, where the royal party were to spend the night at the Banff Springs Hotel, the train crew took some rare time off in the village while their charges went hungry: someone had forgotten to order dinner either at the hotel or on the train.[53] A late dinner was eventually served at the hotel. The Queen wrote to Princess Elizabeth that the hotel was 'boiling' like all Canadian houses. 'We opened every window, and I expect all the poor habitants will get pneumonia! This morning we climbed a mountain

---

* It was probably Lieutenant Governor McNab of Saskatchewan. The Regina press reported that a gift box of prairie fowl had been sent to the royal train. (RA F&V/VISOV/CAN/1939/Press cuttings/Vol. I, p. 211)

nearby which took about 50 minutes. It was very like Balmoral only much bigger, & the pine trees smelt delicious in the hot sun. This afternoon Papa & I went for a Buggy ride!! . . . Two nice grey horses & we rolled along on high old wheels – very wobbly but great fun.'

They watched a moose feeding on waterlily bulbs, and beavers building a dam, and also saw black bears and other animals. It was a relief to get away from 'roaring crowds and incessant noise even tho' one is glad that the people are pleased to see us'. The Queen felt that they were bearing up well and added that the next two weeks would be tiring but worthwhile work, 'for one feels how important it is that the people here should see their King, & not have him only as a symbol'.[54]

Banff was supposed to be a day of rest from the press as well, but the King and Queen had long since learned the importance of good relations with journalists and allowed themselves to be photographed outside the hotel after lunch. They had held a reception in Ottawa for the eighty-strong press corps accompanying them on the tour in a pilot train, and the Queen later commented to Queen Mary that the journalists were 'really very nice, and were so shy and polite! The Americans are particularly easy and pleasant, and have been amazed I believe at the whole affair. Of course they have no idea of our Constitution or how the Monarchy works, and were surprised & delighted to find that we were ordinary & fairly polite people with a big job of work.'[55] Lascelles was delighted: 'I hope people at home realise what a wow this adventure is being,' he wrote. 'It is on a crescendo rather than a diminuendo – I hope T[heir] M[ajesties] will be able to stand the strain for another 17 days.'[56]

In his diary, Mackenzie King recorded a frank dinner conversation with the Queen about the dangers of fascism and war. The Queen told him how much all those men who had died in the Great War were now missed; she felt that a great struggle had begun between right and wrong, but that right would win in the end. According to Mackenzie King, she agreed with him that Hitler himself probably did not want war and she still thought that Chamberlain had acted correctly; war would otherwise have been certain. 'She said that England had done splendidly: had gone as far as she could in every way for peace. Was prepared to go to any length but to be strong to save the situation. She thought other nations were looking more and more to Britain for leadership. I was quite impressed with the earnestness with which she spoke.' At the end of the meal she said, 'I have been talking pretty freely. It is very nice to be able to say what you think.'[57]

Almost every day brought more bad news. 'Europe seems to be moving dangerously nearer to war,' Mackenzie King wrote on 25 May. He added, nonetheless, 'I am not without hope that this visit may help to let the peoples of Europe see how firmly the democracies are standing together.'[58]

The King too was pleased with the trip, but became uneasy as they travelled ever further from Europe. Commenting on the situation to Alec Hardinge, he wrote, 'I am glad Hitler & Mussolini are behaving fairly well but they may blow up again at any moment. I am longing for this visit to be over & to be back again.'[59] His anxiety sometimes revealed itself in the outbursts of temper which his Household and family called 'gnashes' or sometimes 'Nashvilles'. In the privacy of the royal train, to help him relax, the Queen would contrive opportunities for one particular Mountie, who amused the King, to take him cups of tea.[60]

Another twenty-four hours' travel brought the King and Queen to a spectacular welcome in Vancouver on the morning of 29 May. As elsewhere, they were both praised for their spontaneity, making extra stops and talking impromptu to people. This was a skill which had come easily to the Queen since the earliest days of her marriage, and which the King had acquired under her influence. It was often remarked upon in Canada. 'She dazzled me,' wrote one guest at the civic luncheon in Vancouver. 'As she greets you she seems as though she actually would like to know you.'[61] That evening they left for the British Columbian capital, Victoria, on board the SS *Princess Marguerite*, passing through a formation of Indian war canoes at the Lion's Gate. 'She's the most charming woman in the world' was the verdict of the ship's captain.[62]

The next day, 30 May, there were formal municipal and provincial welcome ceremonies; the press photographs show the Queen looking elegant in a slender, full-length pale-lilac dress, a spray of orchids pinned to the shoulder with a diamond bar, and, according to one reporter, the largest hat she had worn so far, of lilac straw. At the state luncheon which followed, the King made an eloquent speech referring to Victoria as 'Canada's Western gateway', and to Canada's role, looking as she did both east and west, in furthering friendly relations between the two hemispheres. A reporter watching the Queen noticed that she became tense and serious as he spoke; her eyes never left his face, while he exchanged glances with her at the beginning and end of the speech. Then she relaxed.[63]

After a 'brilliant spectacle, the most heart-lifting scene that the King and Queen have participated in during their stay in Canada', when the King presented colours to the Canadian navy in bright sunshine against a backdrop of snow-capped mountains and the deep blue of the Juan de Fuca Strait, their official engagements were over for the day. But another unofficial, Scottish gathering awaited the Queen. In the grounds of Government House, she met and was photographed with some fifty emigrant 'men of Angus', several of whom had worked on the Glamis estate.[64]

On 31 May they finally turned around and began the long train journey eastwards and homewards. Lady Tweedsmuir had stocked the train with books: the Queen enjoyed reading 'all M. R. James's Ghost Stories all over again!'[65] From Jasper, where they stopped to spend a day in the National Park and a night in a log cabin at the Jasper Park Lodge, the Queen wrote to Queen Mary: 'We arrived here this morning, and have just come in after a very beautiful drive & walk up to the Edith Cavell Glacier – where it was snowing!' She wished that they could have had two days of rest there, 'for we are working hard, and one day is really not much use for relaxation. However it's better than nothing, and a great relief to get out of the train.' For all the enthusiasm of the welcome given them everywhere, she was not unaware of one sub-text of their tour, commenting: 'We have had a most touching reception everywhere – it has really been wonderful and most moving. All Canada is very pleased at the way the French Canadians received us, and [they] are hopeful that the visit will bring lasting results in uniting the country. They are terribly divided in many ways – and the provincial Gov:ments especially are jealous and suspicious of the Federal Government. But they are so young that I expect they will achieve unity in the end.'[66]

Edmonton was the last provincial capital on the tour: once again the streets were thronged. 'The volume of cheering equalled anything Edmonton has seen on sound newsreels of European crowds listening to some jaw-thrusting dictator talk about forests of bayonets and rivers of blood,' reported one Canadian journalist. Twice the King and Queen made unscheduled stops, once to receive presents of beaded white buckskin from a group of Cree Indians, and then at the University Hospital, to talk to disabled ex-servicemen and child patients whose beds had been brought outside. 'She's a swell-looking girl,' one veteran told a reporter, delighted that both King and Queen had shaken hands with him as they walked among the beds. Another paid her a compliment and was rewarded with a smiling word of thanks. 'And did she smile! Oh boy – a million dollars' worth, that's all! I'll never forget it.'[67]

At Saskatoon, where they made a two-hour stop on 3 June for the usual mayoral reception and drive through the city, the Queen met yet another former Strathmore employee, John Batterson, who had worked at Glamis in 1908–9, and whom she remembered. They made another impromptu break in their programme, mingling with the crowds at the station when the Queen asked to meet a group of First World War nurses there. At Melville later that evening, when the Queen, ever on the lookout for fellow Scots, stopped to talk to a police officer who had served in the Black Watch, the King laughed that it was a wonder that there were any Scots left at home.[68]

The next day the inhabitants of Sudbury, who twelve days earlier had stood silently by the track at 1 a.m. so as not to wake the King and Queen during their journey westwards, were rewarded with an hour's visit. One banner proclaimed that its bearers had 'Come 400 miles'.[69] That evening there was an unscheduled addition to their programme: they were taken down a nickel mine clad in white oilskin coats and miners' helmets and carrying torches. Over the next two days, in a letter to Princess Elizabeth, the Queen summed up their increasingly hectic progress, from the empty expanses of the west into the populous reaches of Ontario close to the American border.

> Here we are flying along round terrific corners through quite wild and untouched country – along the side of beautiful lakes & thousands of miles of woods & bush. We left the cultivated land the day before yesterday, & have been travelling hard & without stopping except for little places where we water & coal. There are usually a large bunch of children who have probably come over a hundred miles by canoe down the lakes, as there are no roads up here . . .
>
> June 6th
> We have been almost continually 'on show' all today, passing through a very thickly populated part of Canada after Toronto,

and at every hour there are thousands & thousands of people waiting at the various stops. They are so happy to have 'the King' with them, & sometimes I have tears in my eyes when one sees the emotion in their faces.[70]

At Windsor, Ontario, they made only a brief stop at the station on the evening of 6 June. Nonetheless, a crowd of almost half a million, swelled by a large influx of Americans reported to have been crossing the border at the rate of 30,000 an hour, had come to greet them. The throngs around the train were so dense that its departure was delayed while the track was cleared.[71]

The next day the temperature soared and the King suffered in the heavy uniform of a field marshal while the Queen raised one of her parasols. They smiled their way through six more receptions at stations along the route and a gymnastic display by 1,200 children at Hamilton. Finally, they drove from St Catharine's to Niagara. 'The roar of the Cataracts was hushed to a whisper' by the cheering crowds, according to the local press. They had now been joined by Sir Ronald Lindsay, the British Ambassador to the United States, because the American part of their journey was about to begin.

At 9.30 p.m. the royal train left Niagara Falls; five minutes later, at the end of the suspension bridge, the Canadian officials (except the Prime Minister and his staff) stepped off and, as the official programme put it, 'At this point the responsibility for the Royal Train will be accepted by the United States.'[72] But the Queen, with the King's support, insisted on keeping the Mounties with them.[73]

In a 'dingy brick border station in a decrepit neighbourhood of Niagara Falls' the US Secretary of State, Cordell Hull, and a welcoming committee greeted the King and Queen.[74] It was a historic moment: the first visit by a reigning British monarch to the United States. But it was fraught with potential hazards.

As Eleanor Roosevelt noted, President Roosevelt had invited the King and Queen to Washington in the hope of creating a bond of friendship between America and Britain.[75] But throughout the United States memories of the First World War were still fresh. In 1935 Congress had passed the Neutrality Act, aimed at keeping the United States out of any European war. President Roosevelt had attempted to modify the act so as to allow the supply of munitions to Britain and France, but met fierce opposition in the Senate.

In these circumstances the royal visit might well have been regarded with suspicion. In order not to give the impression of embroiling the United States in an unwelcome alliance, Lord Halifax, the Foreign Secretary, did not accompany the King and Queen, as he would normally have done. Indeed, the King had thought it best to take no minister in attendance at all. But he had reckoned without Mackenzie King, who was determined not to be cast aside at the frontier 'like an old boot', and won his fight to remain with the King throughout the tour.[76] President Roosevelt saw no political disadvantage in the Canadian Prime Minister's presence: he could be passed off as a frequent visitor to Washington and a personal friend.

For their part, the King and Queen could not expect an exuberant welcome from an American public still dazzled by memories of a popular and glamorous ex-king who had given up his throne for a bride from Baltimore. The President had received a disobliging assessment of the royal couple from the American Ambassador in Paris, William Bullitt, who had met them during their state visit to France a year before. The 'little Queen', he wrote to Roosevelt, was 'a nice girl', whom he found 'pleasant' because she reminded him of the female caddies who carried his clubs at Pitlochry; he thought the President would like her, 'in spite of the fact that her sister-in-law, the Princess Royal, goes about England talking about her "cheap public smile"' – not a remark the Princess Royal is likely to have made. Of the King he said, 'The little King is beginning to feel his oats, but still remains a rather frightened boy.'[77]

American newspapers were not immediately enthusiastic; in *Scribner's Magazine*, an article by Josef Israels II insisted that a large part of the USA believed that Edward VIII should still be king and that George VI, 'a colorless, weak personality' who allegedly suffered from epilepsy, was very much on probation. As for the Queen, she was 'far too plump of figure, too dowdy in dress, to meet American specifications of a reigning Queen'.[78] The Washington *Evening Star* commented that, despite official denials of a political agenda, the visit was a sensational piece of diplomacy for European consumption, planned by the British government to dramatize the natural ties between the British and American peoples. The *New York Times* called the visit 'a pageant with a meaning': whatever policy differences might exist, the two peoples stood together on fundamentals, and the least Americans could do was to give spiritual aid and comfort to sister democracies. The fact that the representatives of one of these democracies were called King and Queen was 'a historical pleasantry. The British throne continues to exist because the British people regard it as a safeguard against tyranny . . . The liberties of England could not be destroyed without danger to our own.'[79]

In London, *The Times* carefully and a little disingenuously under-lined the non-political nature of the visit, describing it as 'a brief and delightful diversion from the strenuous programme of the Canadian tour . . . No political motive has prompted the visit. The two Govern-ments understand one another well enough, and have no need to ask King and President to interrupt the pleasures of social intercourse with business of State.'[80]

There were down-to-earth concerns. Lascelles wrote to his wife that the plans made by the American government were chaotic, 'and how we shall get through the elaborate programme of the next few days without a series of the most hopeless "box-ups", I don't know'. He blamed the President's 'happy-go-lucky temperament', adding that the British Embassy had been scarcely more efficient. The atmosphere on board the royal train was light-hearted, nonetheless. As the train rolled towards Washington it became the scene of a mobile investiture ceremony on foreign territory: the King, 'giggling in a most disarming fashion', knighted Lascelles, who had been appointed KCVO in the Birthday Honours, while Sir Ronald Lindsay and George Steward, the press liaison officer, were given the insignia of GCB and CVO respectively.[81] At midnight the King and Queen went out on to the rear platform when the train stopped for a while at Buffalo, and talked to groups of spectators.

The train halted at Baltimore before arriving at Washington, and the King and Queen got off briefly. According to Joseph Kennedy's diary of 21 July 1939, the Queen told him later that a woman looking exactly like the Duchess of Windsor came up to her with a bouquet. 'I didn't know what to think. I knew she came from Baltimore and after I realized it couldn't be she, I thought it must be her sister. Anyhow, I had a few uncomfortable minutes.'[82]

At 11 a.m. on Thursday 8 June, the King and Queen arrived at Washington's Union station, 'in the most stupendous heat!' as the Queen recorded. The temperature and humidity were made worse by their formal clothes, the King wearing the full-dress uniform of an Admiral of the Fleet. The Queen was 'looking cool' according to the press, but evidently not feeling it, in a full-length pearl-grey dress and jacket with deep cuffs of fur, gloves and a hat. 'I really don't know how we got through those 2 days of continuous functions mostly out of doors, as it really was ghastly. It is very damp heat, & one could hardly breathe,' she wrote to Queen Mary.[83]

President and Mrs Roosevelt greeted them at the station. The King and the President exchanged formal greetings and 'a historic hand-shake', setting off what one Washington newspaper described as 'a tumultuous reception in which the Capital outdid itself to make welcome the first reigning British King and Queen ever to set foot on American soil'.[84] Eleanor Roosevelt, who wrote a regular newspaper column called 'My Day', was quick to observe the Queen's character-istic way of reacting to crowds, as they drove together to the White House: 'She had the most gracious manner and bowed right and left with interest, actually looking at the people in the crowd so that I am sure many of them felt that her bow was for them personally.'[85]

At the White House, the King and Queen met the chiefs of mission of Washington's diplomatic corps before, at last, they could change into lighter clothes and sit down to an informal lunch with the Roosevelts, their three sons and their wives – and, of course, Macken-zie King. The lunch was followed by a sightseeing drive around Washington. During this drive the Queen seems to have given a revealing glimpse of her attitude to her own role. According to Eleanor Roosevelt's memoirs, the Queen expressed surprise that Mrs Roosevelt had been criticized in the press for attending a meeting of WPA workers,* for she thought that people with grievances should be allowed to air them, 'and it is particularly valuable if they can do so to someone in whom they feel a sense of sympathy and who may be able to reach the head of the government with their grievances.'[86] 'Both women were committed to serving as their husband's eyes and ears, and actively advised their mates,' the historian Will Swift concluded from these remarks, in his account of the Washington visit.[87] It is a tempting conclusion, and it is undoubtedly true that Queen Elizabeth kept her husband informed of what she saw and heard. But, as Swift pointed out, Eleanor Roosevelt sent barrages of memoranda to her husband, and that was definitely not the Queen's style.

---

* The Work Projects Administration was an agency set up under Roosevelt's New Deal in 1935, to provide jobs for the unemployed in public works projects.

The humidity continued to be debilitating. According to Joseph Kennedy, the Queen told him that afterwards she lay on the floor in her room at the White House, the hottest place she had ever been to (despite the newly installed air conditioners), to recover.[88] That evening they still had a state dinner and a reception to face. For this the Queen wore a crinoline of white tulle sprinkled with gold paillettes; she sat between the President and Vice-President Garner for the dinner. Harold Ickes, the American Secretary of the Interior, whose diaries provide a jaundiced view of the royal visit, remarked scathingly on the over-familiar behaviour of the Vice-President, who had no breeding and put his arm round the King as if he were a 'poker crony'. He also commented that the King and Queen 'looked like pigmies' beside the Roosevelts.[89] The heat was still relentless: according to Harold Ickes's wife, 'men's shirts buckled in the middle and collars wilted. Women, including the unfortunate Queen, turned beetlike.'[90]

At the end of the dinner the President made a short speech emphasizing the harmonious relations between the USA and Britain, and the King replied in kind; in the interlude after the ladies had left the table, the men conversed in what appeared to be prearranged groups. The King's group included a noted isolationist, Senator William E. Borah.[91] Even now, the day was not yet ended. Two hundred more guests arrived to hear a concert which included negro spirituals, cowboy ballads, folk songs sung by the Coon Creek Girls of Pinchem-Tight Hollow in Kentucky, folk dances by the Soco Gap Square-Dance Team and a finale of 'art music' – songs by American and European composers – sung by the radio star Kate Smith, the Metropolitan Opera's baritone Lawrence Tibbett and Marian Anderson, the black contralto, whose fine voice Mrs Roosevelt admired.[92]

To the astonishment of the King and Queen, the next day was even hotter – 97 degrees in the shade – and it proved even more strenuous. At the White House in the morning Eleanor Roosevelt gave one of her frequent press conferences to women journalists; she praised the Queen's interest in social problems, and then – after issuing stern warnings that they must not write that the Queen had attended the press conference – ushered in her guest. The King surprised the eighty-four women by coming too.[93] It was then back to the British Embassy, where they received members of the British community, including ex-servicemen, in the garden, before driving to the Capitol to be received by members of the Senate and the House of Representatives. The King was congratulated by one senator on being 'a very good Queen-picker'. A Democratic congressman who the previous day had sent the King a telegram demanding the repayment of Britain's war debt to the United States, stayed away; one of his Texan colleagues, seeing the Queen, remarked, 'If America can keep Queen Elizabeth, Congress will regard Britain's war debt as cancelled.'[94]

They lunched with the Roosevelts in the presidential yacht, USS *Potomac*, sailing to Mount Vernon, the home of George Washington.* The King placed a wreath on George Washington's tomb; the Queen was presented with a bouquet by the Mount Vernon gardener. Afterwards they drove with the Roosevelts to Fort Hunt, Virginia, to visit the Civilian Conservation Corps camp, a New Deal project for unemployed youths. They had particularly asked to see this; it was a project which related to their own concern about unemployment in Britain, and the King's boys' camps had given him some expertise in the field. They impressed Eleanor Roosevelt by talking to each boy. From there they drove to Arlington Cemetery, where the King laid wreaths; an 'informal' tea at the White House followed – informal, but hardly relaxing, for some sixteen heads of government agencies concerned with social and economic programmes were assembled to meet them. Eleanor Roosevelt commented that evening: 'The young royalties are most intelligent. At the tea they asked everyone questions & left them with the feeling that their subject was of interest & well understood. At dinner the King told me he felt that he had learned a great deal. She seems equally interested.'[95] The long hot day ended with a dinner, given by the King and Queen for the Roosevelts at the British Embassy, and then they left to rejoin their train at Union station. They waved goodbye on the rear platform of their train, the Queen resplendent in her rose-tulle Hartnell crinoline and diamond tiara.

In a letter to Princess Elizabeth, the Queen described their two 'burning, boiling, sweltering, humid furnace like days' in Washington. There was no doubt that they had been a personal success for her.

---

* Through Colonel Augustine Warner who settled in Virginia in the mid-seventeenth century, Queen Elizabeth shared a common ancestry with George Washington and General Robert E. Lee. Her paternal grandmother, Frances Dora Smith, was the great-great-great-great-great-great-granddaughter of Colonel Warner, while George Washington was his great-great-grandson. George Washington was therefore Queen Elizabeth's second cousin six times removed. General Lee was descended from Colonel Warner's daughter, Sarah.

D'Arcy Osborne wrote to her later: 'A friend of mine in Washington sent me a cable while you were there which simply said, "You have always known what you were talking about. She stole the show."'[96] This was certainly the tone of the Washington press. 'Three cheers for the King – and four for the Queen' was one verdict; 'Give the Queen a Crowd and She Mows 'em Down' was another.[97] Some, however, noted that she had 'a pleasant way of remaining in the background until such times that her presence is required', and that she smiled affectionately at her husband when he spoke, while 'he returns the attention with a swifter, shyer glance.'[98]

The train took them overnight to Sandy Hook, New Jersey where they embarked in the American destroyer USS *Warrington*, to sail to the Battery in New York City. It was a trying day: there were miscalculated timings and unscheduled presentations, and the programme slid inexorably out of control in the hands of two 'vociferous showmen', the Mayor of New York, Fiorello La Guardia, and the President of the World's Fair, Grover Whalen.[99] The King and Queen were greeted by the Governor of New York, Herbert Lehman, and by Mayor La Guardia, and driven through Manhattan to the World's Fair in Queens,* their open car showered with ticker tape, cheered by enormous crowds of between three and four million. One New York newspaper noted approvingly that the King had hit the right democratic note by appearing in the morning dress of 'an ordinary English gentleman' rather than in a showy uniform, but also commented that he looked very tired and waved mechanically. The Queen, who wore a plain blue crêpe dress and cape and a spectacular hat with an ostrich-feather plume, giving her extra height, was less visibly tired, and was able to 'do the honors for both in waving to the crowd'. The drive with the wisecracking Mayor took forty minutes longer than scheduled. Then Whalen insisted on presenting some 500 extra people to them. After shaking some 200 hands – and receiving a fascist salute from the Italian Commissioner to the Fair – the King had had enough.[100]†

---

* The Queen had lent her Wilson Steer painting, *Chepstow*, to the British Pavilion's exhibition of modern British painting. (Kenneth Clark to Queen Elizabeth, 17 December 1938; 2, 13 February 1939, n.d. [postmark 20 February 1939], RA QEQM/PRIV/HH; RA QEQM/PRIV/PIC)

† At the lunch given for them in the Federal Buildings at the World's Fair, according to the *New York Times*, among the waiters serving the King and Queen was a former steward to the Strathmore family, Joseph Lewis, who had worked at Glamis, St James's Square and St Paul's

They were well behind schedule for their next engagement, a brief visit to Columbia University (chosen because it had been founded by royal charter in the reign of King George II), and by the time they reached their final destination, President Roosevelt's country home at Hyde Park in Dutchess County, after an eighty-mile drive, they were an hour and a half late. They were greeted by the President, his wife and his mother, Sara Roosevelt, a formidable matriarch who had little in common with her daughter-in-law Eleanor beyond a disapproval of alcohol. Offering the King a martini, doubtless very welcome, the President said, 'My mother thinks you should have a cup of tea; she doesn't approve of cocktails.' 'Neither does my mother,' answered the King, as he took the drink.[101]

The King and Queen spent only a night and a day at home with the Roosevelts, but it was enjoyable for both of them. Springwood, the Roosevelt family home for over seventy years and Franklin Roosevelt's birthplace, was an unpretentious but comfortable house on the banks of the Hudson. The King and Queen loved it; 'at moments one really feels that one is at home in England!' she wrote to Queen Mary. 'Especially here, where we arrived about 8 last night – one might be in an average English country house, with a wide hall, & big sitting rooms & rather small hot bedrooms.' She added that at dinner that night the President had proposed Queen Mary's health 'in the most touching terms & quite impromptu, addressing himself to his own Mother who was sitting opposite him. It was so nice & friendly, & of <u>course</u> I found tears coming into my eyes!'[102] It was Eleanor Roosevelt herself who – to the fury of her mother-in-law – revealed in her 'My Day' column that a side-table had collapsed, sending part of the dinner service crashing to the floor, and that a butler had tripped on the library steps, dropping a tray loaded with drinks.[103]

After dinner the King, the President and Mackenzie King remained in the library, discussing the danger of war. The King and Roosevelt had already established a rapport. 'He is so easy to get to know & never makes one feel shy,' the King himself wrote; he wished his ministers talked to him as the President did.[104] He came to regard the visit to Hyde Park as the high point of the whole tour; out of it arose a strong

Walden and had served meals to Lady Elizabeth Bowes Lyon as a girl. He had subsequently worked for Henry Clay Frick (of the Frick Collection), and was now captain of waiters at the Waldorf Astoria.

friendship and a continuing correspondence with the President.[105] Their
talks that night and next day, of which the King made detailed notes,
showed that Roosevelt was anxious to co-operate with Britain and
Canada in naval defence in the Atlantic. He was also working to con-
vert American public opinion 'on to the right tack' in case of war in
Europe, and to get the Neutrality Act amended to make it less difficult
for the USA to help Britain. Mackenzie King's record of the conversation adds that Roosevelt proposed helping Canada set up aircraft-
manufacturing plants. Although the President was over-optimistic about
what he could achieve against the isolationists in Congress, these
conversations laid the foundations for the very real boost which the
USA was later able to give to Britain's naval resources through the
Bases-for-Destroyers deal and the Lend-Lease Agreement.

The next day was Sunday, and the King and Queen went with the
Roosevelts to the Episcopal Church of St James in Hyde Park village.
Again, the Queen felt very much at home. 'The service is exactly the
same as ours down to every word,' she reported to Queen Mary, '&
they even had the prayers for the King & the Royal family. I could not
help thinking how curious [it] sounded, & yet how natural.'[106] Up to a
point: President Roosevelt had specifically asked the rector to make
the service just like matins in an English country church.[107] Afterwards
the Queen had the fun of talking to her daughters on the transatlantic
telephone before she and the King were driven by President Roosevelt
up to the cottage he had recently built on the Hyde Park estate. She
later said that she had been more frightened by this than by any
wartime experience, because, to cope with the fact that the President's
legs were paralysed by polio, the car was specially adapted to be driven
with hands alone. Roosevelt drove at high speed, talking, pointing out
sights and waving his cigarette holder about, as well as operating the
controls. 'There were several times when I thought we could go right
off the road and tumble down the hills.'[108]

The picnic lunch which followed has become the best-known
feature of the entire visit – again thanks to Eleanor Roosevelt's column,
as she sighed over the letters of protest she had received from
compatriots objecting to the food she proposed to serve. 'There were
a lot of people there,' wrote the Queen to her daughters, 'and we all
sat at little tables under the trees round the house, and had all our
food on one plate – a little salmon, some turkey, some ham, lettuce,
beans & HOT DOGS too!'[109] The BBC's Richard Dimbleby spent so

long reading to his listeners from the National Sausage Casing Manu-facturers' pamphlet about the construction and history of the hot dog that he hardly seemed to mention the King and Queen at all.[110]

Then they moved on to Eleanor Roosevelt's own little cottage, where the King and the President and his sons bathed in the swimming pool, while the Queen sat in the shade and watched. 'It was deliciously peaceful, and the first really quiet moment we have had for WEEKS,' she told Princess Elizabeth. 'This evening, after dinner we are leaving, & tomorrow morning we start the last week of our trip. I must say that I don't think that I could bear very much more, as there comes a moment when one's resistance nearly goes.'[111] 'My complexion is ruined!' she wrote to Queen Mary.[112]

The royal train had been driven from New Jersey to Hyde Park station, and here the King and Queen said their last farewells to the Roosevelts. The train pulled out to the strains of 'Auld Lang Syne' sung by the assembled spectators. It was an emotional moment for all of them. Eleanor Roosevelt wrote that the threat of tragedy in Europe weighed on every single person there, and the song evoked friendship, sadness and uncertainty for the future. 'I think the King and Queen, standing on the rear platform on the train as it pulled slowly away, were deeply moved. I know I was.'[113]

Their departure from the United States prompted a flood of press comment on the political implications of the visit. A special dispatch in the *Washington Post* noted that the King and the President had had several 'man-to-man chats', and assumed that they had touched upon 'parallel actions' between Britain and the USA; the King and Queen had succeeded in focusing world attention on the ties of blood and sentiment between the two countries, just as Chamberlain had intended.[114] The *Washington Evening Star* concentrated on the reaction in Europe: the vituperation in the Nazi press showed the resentment caused by the 'tightening of the democratic bond' which was the unofficial but no less tangible result of the visit; but it also quoted the *Manchester Guardian*'s warning that the strikingly friendly reception given to the King and Queen by the American public did not mean that Congress would rescind the Neutrality Act.[115] In London, *The Times* again insisted that there was 'nothing political in the visit', and used the occasion to stress how well the King and Queen were playing their representational role, carrying on and broadening the precedents set by King George V and Queen Mary.[116]

The Queen's contribution was substantial. At least one observer gave her credit for a complete volte-face in American public opinion. 'In admiration of this one woman, America has somehow blinded herself to Chamberlain, has forgotten Munich, and now sees only the strong British nation again.'[117] One press report from New York remarked on her 'faculty for rapt attention to the persons presented to her, her quick, intelligent grasp of the background and the connections between people and things, such as the war veterans and their identifying war medals and berets'[118] – expertise which she had acquired through her marriage into a family very well versed in uniforms and decorations.

Eleanor Roosevelt was not entirely uncritical. She liked her and thought her 'perfect as a Queen, gracious, informed, saying the right thing & kind but a little self-consciously regal', although, as she more forgivingly remarked, who would not be self-conscious in the Queen's place? 'Turning on graciousness like water is bound to affect one in time!' Later she recalled that she was fascinated by the Queen, 'who never had a crease in her dress or a hair out of place. I do not see how it is possible to remain so perfectly in character all the time.'[119] Evidently the President's wife thought her guest played her role a little too professionally; but she was also acknowledging a personality, a style and a task very unlike her own. At the same time she warmly approved of the Queen's interest in social problems, and of her thoughtfulness in small things – like thanking their chauffeur for his careful driving.[120]

For her part, the Queen was touched by the kindness the Roosevelts had shown her and the King; she thought them a charming and united family and praised their easy, polished manners. The President she thought delightful, and '<u>very</u> good company'.[121] He was more than that for the King, who told Mackenzie King that he had never met anyone with whom he could talk so freely as Roosevelt; he felt 'as though a father were giving me his most careful and wise advice'.[122]

*

WHEN THE ROYAL train crossed the border again into Canada, the *Montreal Gazette* announced 'King George and Queen Elizabeth are back today in their own country.' It was 'Vive le Roi!' and 'Vive la Reine!' again as they drove through cheering French Canadian crowds in Sherbrooke. The weather was dramatically different – there had been a hurricane and a bitterly cold wind was still blowing. The gruelling pattern of their Canadian tour was resumed, with visits to the provincial capitals of New Brunswick, Nova Scotia and Prince Edward Island, processions through the streets and official welcomes and luncheons with the lieutenant governors and premiers of each province, interspersed with stops at smaller towns. If the King was busy with correspondence or 'state affairs', the Queen would descend to the platform alone, and 'the crowds thrill at her smile and the wave of her hand'. Most of the reporters who had been with them since 17 May were still 'hanging on grimly to the end of the Royal visit'.[123]

They sailed in driving rain to Charlottetown, Prince Edward Island, and the planned garden party at Government House was washed out, but the island's people turned out in their thousands nevertheless. When the King and Queen rejoined their train that evening after sailing back to the mainland for two more mayoral receptions, a display of temper by the King showed that the strain of the tour was telling on him. As he stood with the Queen on the rear platform waving goodbye to a large crowd at New Glasgow station, the train failed to move. The engine was missing. Going back inside the train, the King – who was in naval uniform – flung his sword down the passage in disgust, narrowly missing the steward, Wilfred Notley, who told the tale in his memoirs. 'The poor Queen', meanwhile, was 'left outside waving her handkerchief and the people standing in the rain and the pipes piping away'.[124]

At Halifax on Thursday 15 June, the last day of the Canadian tour, the King and Queen were greeted once again by the Governor General, Lord Tweedsmuir, and his wife, who had sailed down from Quebec in the *Empress of Britain* for the farewell ceremonies. The streets were thronged and the sun shone as they toured the city, watched a children's pageant and talked to disabled ex-servicemen. After lunch the King and Queen both made farewell speeches, which were broadcast throughout the Dominion. The Queen's speech, 'delivered with graceful ease and lucidity' according to the *Montreal Gazette*, described her delight in seeing Canada; 'but what has warmed my heart in a way I cannot express in words', she said, 'is the proof you have given us everywhere that you were glad to see us.' She ended, 'Au revoir et Dieu vous bénisse.'[125] At 8.20 that evening the *Empress of Britain* sailed away from Halifax to the blaring of whistles from accompanying craft and the shouts of thousands lining the harbour.

Amid all the favourable comment, Mackenzie King was not the only one to see the tour as a much needed boost to national unity: a Canadian lawyer remarked that the country had seemed to be in danger of falling apart, but the royal visit had awakened dormant patriotism. 'I think the Empire will find us in our proper place if and when trouble arises.' Another observer commented that, if war should come, the royal visit might mean far more volunteers from Canada and 'a sympathetic USA which won't stay out nearly so long as the last time'.[126]

It was not quite the end. Newfoundland, the oldest English colony and not yet a province of Canada, lay on their route home. On 17 June, in the capital city of St John's, the King and Queen stood on the spot where Sir Humphrey Gilbert had staked a claim to the island in the name of Queen Elizabeth I in 1583. It was a day of great excitement for the population of fishermen, farmers and miners who gathered along their route and in the capital. The King made a broadcast tribute to the courage and resilience of Newfoundlanders, both in the First World War and in the severe economic stress of recent years. At the end of the eight-hour visit the weather turned threatening, and the return journey to their ship via the three Royal Naval vessels escorting them, which the King and Queen had arranged to visit, was something of a challenge. In heavy seas they jumped from a trawler to a launch, and thence to another, becoming drenched from head to foot in the process.

As the *Empress of Britain* set sail, Lady Tweedsmuir watched on the shore while the crowds cheered and the figures of the King and Queen became smaller and smaller and were lost to sight. 'The line from Antony and Cleopatra came into my mind. I tried to push the thought away, but it kept coming back: "The bright day is gone and we are for the dark." '[127]

*

ON BOARD, AS the *Empress* sailed east and homewards, the King and Queen could finally rest. The voyage home was uneventful; there were cinema shows in the evening and a cricket match between the army and the navy, in which the Queen played for the navy. Five days later, in Yarmouth Bay on the Isle of Wight, there was a joyous reunion: the two Princesses came aboard to join their parents for the last two hours of their voyage. They had a family lunch party at which they all sang favourite songs, including 'Under the Spreading Chestnut Tree' and 'Doing the Lambeth Walk'.[128] And then the triumphal progress home began.

Flotillas of pleasure steamers, yachts and small boats crammed with cheering people accompanied the ship up the Solent and Southampton Water; more crowds gathered on the shore. Queen Mary came to meet them at Southampton, with the King's sister and two brothers and their spouses. The train track to London was lined with more well-wishers; at Waterloo they were greeted by the Prime Minister. The route to Buckingham Palace was thronged, and they were given a tumultuous reception; the Members of both Houses of Parliament were assembled in Parliament Square to welcome them home. Harold Nicolson recorded that when the Royal Family came into the Square, 'We lost all dignity and yelled and yelled. The King wore a happy schoolboy grin. The Queen was superb. She really does manage to convey to each individual in the crowd that he or she has had a personal greeting.' Then, echoing Lady Tweedsmuir, he added, 'she is in truth one of the most amazing Queens since Cleopatra.'[129]

Outside the Palace, where the King and Queen came out twice on to the balcony, tens of thousands of people cheered, waved flags and sang 'Land of Hope and Glory' and 'God Save the King' all evening. Then they chanted 'We want the King' and 'We want the Queen' and out the family came on to the balcony overlooking the Mall, and still the cheering went on and on – and they had to come out again.

The next day, 23 June, their return was celebrated with a luncheon at Guildhall. The tour had opened the King's eyes to a wider world and new ideas, and given him new confidence in himself and in his role as monarch. He spoke movingly and effectively, celebrating Canada and Britain, their shared institutions and their love of liberty. The enthusiastic welcome given to him and the Queen by Canadians was, he thought, 'an expression of their thankfulness for those rights of free citizenship which are the heritage of every member of our great Commonwealth of Nations'. He and the Queen had undertaken their journey to foster such ideals and to show that the Crown could be 'a potent force for promoting peace and goodwill among mankind'. If they had in some sort succeeded, that would be 'a source of thankfulness to us all our lives long'.

The speech brought tears to the eyes of the King's audience and was seen at home and abroad as a declaration that Britain would defend her democratic way of life.[130] Mackenzie King read it in Canada and cabled to Tommy Lascelles: 'I am sure that no Sovereign has ever uttered words fraught with greater good for mankind.' Lascelles replied that the King's performance had indeed been remarkable and that even 'hardened experts' like Churchill, Baldwin and the Archbishop of Canterbury had been much moved. The King himself recognized with obvious pleasure that public speaking was no longer 'hell' for him.[131]

If the tour had marked the King's coming of age as a monarch, for the Queen also the warmth and admiration with which she had been received came as a great psychological boost. 'This has made us,' both King and Queen said of the tour.[132] The Queen had grown confident in her role, not only in the more formal and ceremonial mode expected of her at home, but also in the hail-fellow-well-met ambiance of the North American continent. At the time of the abdication the Queen observed that King Edward VIII had lost 'the common touch' and was cut off from 'ordinary human feeling'.[133] In Canada and the United States in 1939 she and the King demonstrated that they were different. They showed themselves able to shed formality and take a close interest in all sorts and conditions of men, and the King began to speak explicitly of forming a more open and flexible idea of kingship than that of his father.[134] As he put it to Mackenzie King, it should be built on first-hand knowledge of his peoples and of their affairs.[135] It was a concept in which his wife was well qualified to support him.

The timing of the voyage, at this moment of great international tension, had also given the Queen a strong sense of the value of the Commonwealth. Writing to Lady Tweedsmuir after their return, she said: 'Our chief emotion is one of deep thankfulness that [the tour] was such a success, for more & more one feels that a united Empire is the only hope for this troubled world of today. Sometimes I wonder whether we are not already fighting a War. A war of love & right thinking against the forces of evil.' She acknowledged that they had dreaded returning to the 'horrible feeling' of acute anxiety that had sapped their strength before their departure for Canada; but, she continued, 'We find everybody very calm, very determined, and beginning to lose patience with the Nazi leaders, who seem determined to put a wrong construction on whatever any of our leading politicians say, and are still, I fear certain that England will not fight. We must continue to pray that some means of preserving Peace will be found, and that Germany will realize that aggression & cruelty lead to destruction.'[136]

★

THE SUMMER TO which they returned was balmy. Holiday trains had standing room only. Beaches were packed. But gas masks were carried now. There was a feeling in the air that war could not be far away and that the last minutes of peace must be enjoyed. On 19 July the King and Queen gave a ball at Buckingham Palace for Prince and Princess Paul of Yugoslavia, who had arrived at short notice for a private visit – Prince Paul was now regent of his country, during the minority of the fifteen-year-old King Peter (the godson whom the Duke of York had held nervously on a cushion at his christening in 1923). Some 800 people came to dance to Jack Jackson's orchestra, and the ball went on until dawn; even Queen Mary stayed until 2.30 a.m.[137] It was the last ball at the Palace before the war.

Two days later the King and Queen, with the Princesses, embarked in the royal yacht *Victoria and Albert* for a brief holiday which included a visit to the Royal Naval College at Dartmouth, where the King had studied. The Queen's old friend Freddy Dalrymple Hamilton was still Captain of the College and their host. They were given an enthusiastic reception; in the dining hall all 500 cadets 'leaped to their feet & cheered themselves to a standstill for about 3 minutes. A quite unrehearsed item & shook me to the core!' Dalrymple Hamilton recorded.[138] The King amused the cadets by reading out his own misdemeanours from the College Punishment Book.[139] This visit was often said to be the occasion of Princess Elizabeth's first meeting with Prince Philip of Greece, now a cadet at the College, but they had already met at the Duke of Kent's wedding in 1934 and at family gatherings since then.

The King had been longing to get back to Balmoral and at the beginning of August they were at last able to go north.[140] He had decided to hold this year's Duke of York's Camp in the grounds of Abergeldie Castle, near Balmoral; it was in full swing on the banks of the Dee and, the Queen thought, going very well. After a day or two it was impossible to distinguish the industrial boys from the public school boys, she told Queen Mary.[141] The King himself acted as camp chief and took the boys on expeditions each day; the Queen and the Princesses came to supper at the camp and the boys were invited to tea at Balmoral. On the final night the King lit the traditional bonfire and his pipers played 'Auld Lang Syne' and the National Anthem. It was to be the last such camp.

The march to war compelled the King to return south to inspect the Reserve Fleet at Weymouth. He was impressed and, back at Balmoral, wrote to his mother, 'It is wonderful the way in which all the men have come back for duty at this time, & I feel sure it will be a deterrent factor in Hitler's mind to start a war. If we can only get through these 2 months without a crisis all would be well.'[142] Hoping against hope, the King and Queen invited a series of shooting parties to Balmoral later in August and early September – 'with, let us pray, no warlike interruptions this year', wrote the Queen to Queen Mary.[143]

That was not to be. On 22 August the astonishing and awful news broke that the Soviet Union and Germany had signed a non-aggression pact. Almost everyone realized that the war which they had tried so long to avoid was now imminent. This embrace between the two most deadly dictatorships in the world would allow Hitler to launch an assault first on Poland and then on the West. At the same time, the Soviets could seize eastern Poland and hope that the Germans and the West would then fight each other to destruction. (The Soviet Union was later to be praised for the enormous sacrifice she made in the defeat of Hitler; such praise tended to ignore the crucial fact that had Stalin not allied his country with Hitler in August 1939, much of this sacrifice might never have been called for.)

In London the Cabinet met for three and a half hours; Chamberlain recalled Parliament, and the King at once took the night train back to London, leaving his wife and children in Scotland. On 25 August the government signed a formal treaty of alliance with Poland which committed Britain to her defence if attacked. From Sandringham Queen Mary wrote to the Queen: 'I feel deeply for you too I having gone through all this in Aug. 1914 when I was the wife of the Sovereign.'[144]

Desperate negotiations with Berlin continued to the end. The King sent the Queen copies of Chamberlain's final letter to Hitler and Hitler's reply. The German leader had, he told her, made yet another offer to Britain. 'We have no idea as to its nature but in the meantime we are working out counter proposals if the offer is not too outrageous . . . All hope has not gone anyhow for the moment.' He ran out of space at the bottom of the page and so wrote across the top, 'All my love Angel, & I wish I were with you. Ever your very loving Bertie.'[145]

Last-minute appeals for peace were sent to Berlin and Warsaw by Pope Pius XII, by President Roosevelt and by many others. Mackenzie King argued that the King and Queen could save the situation by making a direct appeal to Hitler. And he urged that the Queen's name should be associated 'in an appeal on behalf of women and children who would become innocent victims in any world conflict'.[146] Such suggestions fell on fertile soil: the King and Queen were still deeply anxious to try to prevent another war. On 27 August the King again suggested to the Prime Minister, as he had a year before, that he write a personal letter to Hitler. Once again Chamberlain demurred, arguing that the right psychological moment had not yet come.[147]

The problem of what to do with the Duke and Duchess of Windsor in the event of war now loomed. The King wrote to tell Queen Mary that he had provisionally arranged for them to return to England. The Duke would be given 'a civilian job under the Regional Commissioner for Wales. They would both stay in Wales.'[148] Neither his mother nor his wife wished to see the Duchess of Windsor; Queen Mary told the Queen that she thought she was dangerous.[149]

On the night of 28 August the Queen kissed her children goodbye and took the night train to London. She hated being parted from them, but wanted to wait on events before risking their coming back to the capital. If war did break out they would go to Birkhall, in case Balmoral was targeted by bombers. She also wrote to her eldest sister Rose asking her to look after the Princesses in the event that something befell her and the King. Rose replied promising that in such circumstances, 'I would give up everything to try & make the two darlings happy, & try my very best to smooth their lives . . . I have always loved them.'[150] In London the Queen found her husband 'very calm and cheerful' despite all the anxieties. She wrote to Queen Mary, 'It is indeed terrible that the world should be faced with a War, just because of the wickedness and sheer stupidity of the Nazis. One can only go on hoping & praying, that a solution will be found.'[151]

On the last day of August, the evacuation of three million mothers and children was announced. Railway stations were thronged with families, labels tied around the necks of the children; parents were weeping. Sandbags were piled around government buildings and Buckingham Palace. The most valuable paintings in the National Gallery were packed up for distribution to secret hiding places around the country. People finally began to realize that the unimaginable was happening – in this beautiful summer weather the world that they loved was about to come to an end.

Buckingham Palace and Windsor Castle began their own sombre preparations. The King and the Prime Minister had decided that both should be kept open, but the Palace with only a skeleton staff.[152] Many in the Royal Household departed for military service; most of the remaining staff started to move out of London to Windsor. Beds and bunk beds had to be brought into the Castle and rooms found for scores of people. The Castle windows were sandbagged, lights on the Long Walk were extinguished, visitors were barred, steel shelters were erected for the sentries, everyone was rehearsed in air-raid drill. The carriage horses in the Buckingham Palace Mews were sent to Windsor and put to work on the farms. The finest pictures and other works of art in both Palace and Castle were removed and stored underground at Windsor. Display cases were emptied of miniatures, gems, porcelain and glass; furniture was turned to face the wall. The great cut-glass chandeliers which illuminated the state rooms at Windsor were lowered to three feet from the floor so as to diminish the impact of any fall. Blackout restrictions were severe; all the skylights were covered in black paint, turning into gloom the splendour of the Waterloo Chamber, King Charles II's dining room and the Grand Staircase. The windows of the rooms still being used were covered with a lacework of glue and wire netting.

All hopes evaporated on 1 September 1939 when the Germans invaded Poland. The following day Britain issued an ultimatum: if Hitler withdrew his troops, the British government would endeavour to broker peace between Germany and Poland. On the morning of Sunday 3 September the British Ambassador to Berlin delivered a final note to the German government stating that unless Germany undertook to withdraw her troops from Poland by 11 a.m., Britain would declare war.

At 11.15 that morning Neville Chamberlain announced to the nation that no such undertaking had been given and Britain was at war with Germany. France declared war a few hours later. Next day, the Queen sat down at her writing table in Buckingham Palace; her four-page note deserves to be quoted in its entirety:

> I wish to try & set down on paper some of the impressions that remain from that ghastly day – Sunday September 3rd 1939. And yet when one tries to find words, how impossible, & how inadequate they are to convey even an idea of the torture of mind that we went through.
>
> Having tried by every means in our power to turn Hitler from his purpose of wantonly attacking the Poles, and having warned him of the consequences if he did so, and having been practically ignored by the Nazis, we knew on the night of Sept 2nd, that our request for a withdrawal of German troops from Poland would be refused, so that we went to bed with sad hearts.
>
> I woke early the next morning – at about 5.30. I said to myself – we have only a few hours of Peace left, and from then until 11 o'clock, every moment was an agony.
>
> My last cup of tea in peace! My last bath at leisure; and all the time one's mind working on many thoughts. Chiefly of the people of this Country – their courage, their sense of humour, their sense of right & wrong – how will they come through the wicked things that War lets loose. One thing is, that they are at their best when things are bad, and the spirit is wonderful.
>
> At 10.30 I went to the King's sitting room, and we sat quietly talking, until at 11.15 the Prime Minister broadcast his message from Downing Street, that as the Germans had ignored our communications, we were at War. He spoke so quietly, so sincerely, & was evidently deeply moved & unhappy.
>
> I could not help tears running down my face, but we both realized that it was inevitable, if there was to be any freedom left in our world, that we must face the cruel Nazi creed, & rid ourselves of this continual nightmare of force & material standards. Hitler knew quite surely that when he invaded Poland, he started a terrible war. What kind of a mentality could he have?
>
> As we were thinking these things, suddenly from outside the window came the ghastly, horrible wailing of the air raid siren. The King & I looked at each other, and said 'it can't be', but there it was, and with beating hearts we went down to our shelter in the basement. We felt stunned & horrified, and sat waiting for bombs to fall.

After half an hour the all clear went, & we returned to our rooms, & then had prayers in the 44 room.* We prayed with all our hearts that Peace would come soon – real peace, not a Nazi peace.[153]

---

* The 1844 Room – a drawing room on the ground floor of Buckingham Palace, so named because it was occupied by Tsar Nicholas I of Russia in 1844.

CHAPTER THIRTEEN

THE QUEEN AT WAR

1939–1941

'Dear old BP is <u>still standing</u>'

IN THE DAPPLED end of a lovely summer, it was hard to understand what lay ahead. The Queen was outwardly calm but she found it difficult to adjust to the fact that she and her husband were now reigning over a country at war. It was true, as her friend Arthur Penn put it to her, that, unspeakable though war was, at least the long suspense was over. 'Looking back on the past year or more,' he wrote, 'I realise that this shadow was behind one's shoulder at every turn: pleasures had a bitter taste, laughter a hollow ring & nothing seemed quite in tune. Now it is as if one had at last braced oneself for a long deferred but inevitable operation, & we can only pray for an early & complete recovery.'[1] But the Queen really had hoped that war could be avoided. She would have been appalled if she could have known that this looming struggle in Europe would spread throughout the world over the next six years and cause death and destruction on a terrible scale.

At first, she felt 'so miserable & disappointed & exhausted that life was almost horrible'.[2] But she knew that she had to pull herself together, summon her faith and stand up for what was right. She thought that 'After the first ghastly shock', the country 'has settled down grimly, quietly, and with the utmost determination, to try and rid the world of this evil thing that has been let loose by those idiotic Germans'.[3] In similar vein, she wrote to Queen Mary, 'Oh the Germans! If <u>only</u> they would choose decent leaders, then perhaps we would not need to go through the agony of War every 20 years.'[4] She had no more illusions about Hitler's intentions; she sent a copy of *Mein Kampf* to Lord Halifax, the Foreign Secretary, but advised him not to read it through 'or you might go mad, and that would be a pity. Even a skip through gives one a good idea of his mentality, ignorance and obvious sincerity.'[5]

She and the King took comfort in the fact that the Empire rallied to Britain at once. Australia was proud to declare war within seventy-five minutes of hearing the announcement that Britain was at war. New Zealand followed swiftly and in Canada the motion to declare war was approved without a division. Thanks to the passionate and cogent intervention of General Smuts, who subsequently became prime minister, the South African Parliament also voted for war. In the entire Commonwealth, only the Republic of Ireland insisted on being neutral.*

The Queen quickly realized that her role now was to sustain morale, with the King, all around the country. The Crown was the centre which must hold and be seen to hold. On 5 September they visited the London Civil Defence Region Headquarters and inspected ARP (Air Raid Precautions) posts and shelters; another of their early trips was by launch down the Thames to the London Docks where they saw a merchant ship being painted naval grey and watched the unloading of 4,000 tons of grain from a cargo ship which had arrived from South America.[6] On 6 September the Queen made the first of many wartime visits to her regiments with a surprise call at the headquarters of the London Scottish, the territorial regiment of which she was honorary colonel. As she left the canteen 'the cheers made the roof ring,' the regimental gazette reported.[7] She also met women of the Auxiliary Territorial Service, whose London headquarters were in the same building. In August she had been appointed commandant-in-chief of all three women's services: the Auxiliary Territorial Service (ATS), the Women's Royal Naval Service (the Wrens) and the Women's Auxiliary Air Force. She was already colonel-in-chief of three regiments in the regular army – the King's Own Yorkshire Light Infantry, the Black Watch and the Queen's Bays – and honorary colonel of another territorial regiment, the Hertfordshire Regiment.

To rousing cheers everywhere, the Queen also visited civilian organizations, including the Red Cross, the ambulance services, hospitals and the YWCA. She was heartened by a letter from the Archbishop of Canterbury, Cosmo Lang, telling her what an important part she

---

* In the next six years the Irish Prime Minister, Eamon de Valera, never once criticized Hitler or the Nazis. When Hitler committed suicide in April 1945, de Valera immediately visited the German envoy in Dublin to express his condolences – and later stated that he had been not only correct but wise to do so.

had to play in the war, both as the Queen and as a woman. He was sure that the women of Britain, who had offered themselves for the war effort, would look to her for leadership and he knew that she would do everything to encourage them, not least in 'spreading the spirit of your own sympathy and understanding and calm fortitude. Indeed I feel inclined to say to Your Majesty what was said in the Bible story to Queen Esther – "Who knoweth whether thou art come to the Kingdom for such a time as this." '⁸ Esther, portrayed in the Old Testament as a woman of faith and patriotism, whose piety and courage enabled her to save her people from destruction, was a challenging but apt role model for the Queen.

Like Esther, the Queen was compelled by the terrible drama of the next five years to accept a role of immense importance. She would never have sought it but it was a part for which she was by nature well suited. It fell to her to support the King as leader of his people in a time of total war. She saw her duty plainly. Replying to the Archbishop she wrote,

> I know, as do all our people, that we are fighting evil things, and we must face the future bravely. I shall try with all my heart to help the people. If only one could do more for them – they are so wonderful.
>
> One thing I realise clearly, that if one did not love this country & this people with a deep love, then our job would be almost impossible.
>
> The only hope for this world is love. I wish in a way that we had another word for it – in the ordinary human mind love has so many meanings, other than the sense in which I use it.⁹

For the next six years she would use her innate ability to convey hope and encouragement to all those engaged in the war, and her instinctive warmth and sympathy to comfort those in distress. All that had been instilled in her by her mother and other members of her family, all that she had learned in looking after soldiers at Glamis in the First World War, and all the public skills that she had acquired since entering the Royal Family, she put now to the service of the country.

The country and its government began to adapt. Chamberlain brought two of his severest Conservative critics, Winston Churchill and Anthony Eden, into the Cabinet, at the Admiralty and the

Dominions Office respectively. Air-raid sirens were sounded, London was blacked out at night and the sky above was filled with barrage balloons. Country houses were taken over for hospitals, schools or the military. Cinemas were closed (they soon reopened) and, as we have seen, hosts of children were rushed to safety in the country or overseas (many soon returned). Government expanded again, as it had after 1914 – there would be new Ministries of Information, Economic Warfare, Shipping, Food and Home Security, among others.[10]

Many changes were required of the Royal Family and the House-hold. Queen Mary was at Sandringham when war began. On Sunday 3 September the rector set up his wireless in the nave of the church and, with the other worshippers, she listened in her pew to Neville Chamberlain's announcement that the country was at war.[11] That evening, in tears, she listened to the King's broadcast; his voice reminded her of her husband's.[12]

The King feared that if she stayed in Norfolk, so close to the coast, Queen Mary could be bombed or even kidnapped by German raiders.[13] (This was a sensible concern, as the German attempt to capture Queen Wilhelmina of the Netherlands a few months later showed.) Queen Mary thought leaving town was 'not at all the thing'.[14] But the King persuaded her that her presence in Marlborough House would cause everyone unnecessary anxiety; reluctantly she agreed to go to Badmin-ton, the Gloucestershire home of her niece's husband, the Duke of Beaufort. She proceeded, with her luggage and her servants, across the country from Norfolk in a long and stately convoy of vehicles. The Duchess watched their arrival 'with a certain apprehension'.[15] Queen Mary, now aged seventy-two, was not accustomed to country life and she found Badminton rather old fashioned. But she determined to adapt as necessary. Before long, she had found an outlet for her remarkable energy and passion for orderliness in constant expeditions to rid the estate of ivy and to clear brushwood.

Among the members of the Royal Household who left for their regiments was the Queen's Private Secretary, Captain Richard Streat-feild. Her Treasurer and friend Arthur Penn, who was now regimental adjutant in the Brigade of Guards, agreed to come in two or three times a week to help with her correspondence. He was to act as her private secretary throughout the war.

The question of what war would mean for the Duke and Duchess of Windsor was still a concern. They were in Antibes when war was declared. His biographer states that, although the Duke felt the war could and should have been avoided, he knew he must now support the British cause. The King offered the Windsors a plane to fly them to Britain, but they asked for a destroyer instead – and made their way to Cherbourg to cross the Channel.[16] If they had hoped for reconciliation with the family, they were disappointed. According to a letter the Queen wrote to her friend Prince Paul of Yugoslavia, she had sent a private message to the Duchess saying she was sorry she could not receive her. 'I thought it more honest to make things quite clear.'[17] To Queen Mary she wrote, 'I haven't heard a word about Mrs Simpson – I trust that she will soon return to France and STAY THERE. I am sure that she hates this dear country, & therefore she should not be here in war time.'[18]

The King had agonized over what sort of war work to offer his brother. He had changed his mind about giving him an administrative post in Wales, and now thought it would be best for the Duke to remain abroad. So a job with the new British Military Mission to France was devised. On 14 September he and the Duke met at Buckingham Palace – the Queen was out. The King told him of the post on offer; accounts differ as to the level of the Duke's enthusiasm. The meeting passed without incident, though the King thought it 'very unbrotherly' and was struck that the Duke was 'in a very good mood, his usual swaggering one, laying down the law about everything'.[19] In his diary, and in a letter to the Prime Minister the same day, the King recorded that there were no recriminations on either side; nor, however, had his brother shown the slightest remorse. 'He seemed to be thinking only of himself, & had quite forgotten what he had done to his country in 1936.' On the contrary, 'He looked very well & had lost the deep lines under his eyes.'[20] The Queen had already expressed a view on that – who had those lines instead? she asked. Her husband.[21]

Now she was irritated; she reported that the Duke had come to see his brother 'just as if nothing had happened! Never asked after Mama or me (who he loathes) or the children or anything family, and never communicated with Bertie again!' Her view of her brother-in-law had hardened; she had written affectionately to him at Christmas in 1937, but the Duke's increasing hostility towards her and Queen Mary for refusing to receive his wife, his dishonesty over his wealth and his visit to Hitler could not but have roused her antipathy. Perhaps above all she resented his indifference to the harm he had done her husband and their country. 'Odd creature, he is exactly like Hitler in thinking that anybody who doesn't agree with him is automatically wrong.'[22] By the end of the first month of the war, the Duke and Duchess were back in France to begin his attachment to the Military Mission.

One of the King's other early wartime visitors was Joseph Kennedy, still American Ambassador to the Court of St James's. The King was upset by Kennedy's defeatism, his dismissal of Britain and her Empire and above all by the impact his views must have in Washington. He immediately wrote a frank letter to remind him that the US, Britain and France were the three great democracies in the world and two of them were now fighting that which they all detested, Hitler and his Nazi regime. 'We stand on the threshold of we know not what. Misery & suffering of War we know. But what of the future? The British Empire's mind is made up. I leave it at that.'[23] Kennedy replied that the people of America were sympathetic and wanted to help Britain and France economically, but did not want to go to war.[24]

On 18 September, the Queen went back to Scotland to see her daughters; she had been concerned about them. A few days earlier she had written to 'My darling Lilibet' at Birkhall to say that she and the King had seen the Australian rugby team who had arrived the day before war was declared and now had to turn around and go straight back. She enclosed little kangaroo pins the team had given her for the Princesses. 'I am longing to see you again my darling – please give Margaret a big hug from me, & get M to give you a big one from me, as you can't hug yourself very well! Your very loving Mummy.'[25] The Princesses, meanwhile, were enjoying an outdoor life in fine weather at Birkhall, under the eye of their French 'holiday governess', Georgina Guérin. Their cousins Margaret Elphinstone and Diana Bowes Lyon* came to stay. What made these holidays different from all others, however, were the evacuees. 'We have got hundreds all around about from Glasgow,' Princess Elizabeth reported in a letter to Marion Crawford.[26]

During the week the Queen spent with her daughters she went to

---

* Margaret Elphinstone (b. 1925), youngest daughter of the Queen's sister May Elphinstone; Diana Bowes Lyon (1923–86), fourth daughter of the Queen's brother John ('Jock') and his wife Fenella.

see some of these evacuees, women and children who had been moved out of slums to protect them in case of attack on the city, and who were being cared for on the Balmoral and Abergeldie estates. Many of them did not like country life, she recalled later. 'Do you know what frightened them most?' she said. 'They couldn't bear the noise of the trees.'²⁷ She discovered that many of the mothers had taken their children back to Glasgow when the threatened bombardment had not materialized, and she disapproved, writing to Queen Mary, 'I do think that it would be so much better if the wives stayed with their husbands, & let the children stay safely in the country.'²⁸

She herself returned to her husband after a week. Shortly after-wards Marion Crawford and the Princesses' French teacher Madame Montaudon Smith came up to Balmoral, and lessons were resumed, partly by correspondence with their other teachers.* They joined a weekly sewing party and knitted for the soldiers; Princess Margaret knitted and played the gramophone alternately, Crawfie reported.²⁹

While she was in Scotland the Queen had visited the Black Watch at their depot at Perth, where she had a poignant encounter which illustrated the turmoil of emotions that the war had unleashed in her. Among the officers, she suddenly saw her nephew John Elphinstone. She had never seen him in uniform before. 'It gave me such a shock to see John in his Black Watch uniform,' she wrote to Queen Mary, 'for he suddenly looked exactly like my brother Fergus who was killed at Loos, & in the same regiment. It was uncanny in a way, & desperately sad to feel that all that ghastly waste was starting again at the bidding of a lunatic.'³⁰ And yet, she asked in another letter, was it waste? 'Humanity must fight against bad things if we are to survive, and the spiritual things are stronger than anything else, and cannot be destroyed, thank God.' She felt as if the last twenty years had been swept away and the last war had joined up with this new one. 'Perhaps we never finished it after all.'³¹

One of the Queen's early wartime tasks was to make a broadcast to the women of the Empire. Appeals for her to do so had come from home and abroad, sometimes from unexpected quarters. Harold Laski, the socialist Professor of Political Science at the London School of

---

* Princess Elizabeth continued with the historical essays set her by Henry Marten, the Vice-Provost of Eton, and the Princesses' German teacher, Hanni Davey, sent them exercises.

Economics, wrote in early September urging the Queen to broadcast a reassuring message to the despondent British mothers whose children had been evacuated.[32] From Canada Lord Tweedsmuir went so far as to suggest a monthly broadcast to the Empire describing what the British people, especially the women, were doing. It would also be heard in the United States, he pointed out, where 'the Queen has become a legendary figure.' The idea of a regular broadcast had been pressed upon him by many in the USA, he said. After all, 'It was the American women who brought their country into the last war.'[33] Indeed, the Queen had already been asked to broadcast direct to America, but the British Ambassador in Washington advised against any such attempt to put pressure on a nation which at this stage was determined to keep out of the war.[34] Nevertheless, suggestions of a direct broadcast by the Queen to the United States continued to be made. For the moment, however, it was not the American effect that preoccupied her.

In the inter-war years of high unemployment she had disapproved strongly of women taking men's jobs, as she saw it.[35] But now women were needed to do essential work in support of the armed services and industry, and the Queen was keen to give them all the encouragement she could. This was the theme of her first wartime broadcast. It was not easy to choose the right words. She wanted her message to be simple, but was then concerned that the draft might be 'too homely' and that it did not mention God. She asked Cosmo Lang to suggest what she might say 'about our faith in divine guidance'.[36]

The day chosen for the broadcast was Armistice Day, 11 November 1939. She began by referring to the significance of the day, to the sacrifice it commemorated and to the peace which after only twenty years had been broken. 'I know that you would wish me to voice in the name of the Women of the British Empire, our deep and abiding sympathy with those on whom the first cruel and shattering blows have fallen – the women of Poland. Nor do we forget the gallant womanhood of France, who are called on to share with us again the hardships and sorrows of war.' War had always called for the fortitude of women in bearing anxiety and bereavement, but in this war 'we, no less than men, have real and vital work to do'. Not simply in new and interesting duties in various fields of National Service, but also in 'the thousand and one worries and irritations in carrying on War-time life in ordinary homes'. She sympathized with the women separated from husbands and children. 'The King and I know what it means to be parted from our children.'* She went on to praise those who had taken in evacuees, and assured them and all those working to keep their homes going that they were giving real service to the country.

> Women of all lands yearn for the day when it will be possible to set about building a new and better world, where peace and goodwill shall abide. That day must come. Meantime, to all of you, in every corner of the Empire, who are doing such fine work in all our Services, or who are carrying on at home amidst the trials of these days, I would give a message of hope and encouragement.

She ended, 'We put our trust in God, who is our Refuge and Strength in all times of trouble. I pray with all my heart that He may bless and guide and keep you always.'[37]

The speech was well received, not only by the Archbishop.[38] Many more letters came from members of the public and Lord Wigram told the Queen that the Chairman of the BBC, Sir John Reith, considered that it was 'one of the best broadcasts that have ever gone out to the world'.[39] One mother wrote with emotion of how the broadcast had helped her out of her despair when her young son joined the army, leaving her alone and ill. 'When your quiet words echoed in the room you seemed to be speaking direct to me, and gradually I saw how much a little home meant, and how important it was to keep on carrying on . . . I now feel I have had a new lead and know exactly what to do. Without that lead one little home might have faded out, and if that was the case with one, how many more must have cause to bless and thank you.'[40]

The Queen settled at once into the busiest period of her life, constantly visiting factories, hospitals, schools, first-aid posts, branches of the Women's Voluntary Service (WVS) and other workplaces and talking to as many people as she could. 'I feel that it is so important that the people can feel free and able to tell me anything they like,'

---

* An early draft of this part of the speech in her own hand reads: 'We too are parted from our children. When I told our little daughters that I was going to broadcast they said "oh Mummy please give our love to all the children", so I do that now – God bless you all.' (RA QEQMH/PS/SPE)

she said. In her view people were settling down to a war which they loathed: but they were determined to resist aggression.[41] She had noticed one way in which the people's cheerfulness showed itself: people were beginning to make jokes about Hitler. 'That is rather a good sign, for they usually joke about things when they are too serious to be taken seriously – if you know what I mean. He is usually known as Old Nasty. Very childish!' she wrote to Prince Paul of Yugoslavia.[42]

She had not lost her own sense of humour. Prince Paul had written asking her to send him one of the photographs Cecil Beaton had taken of her in the summer – the first time he had photographed her.* She promised to send the Prince one. 'Mr Beaton, who is mincing away at some light war work, will execute my order as soon as possible. I believe he is a telephone operator. Can you not imagine him saying, "Number darling? 2305? Oh divine, my dear, etc etc." '[43] She might make fun of Beaton to her friends, but she showed her appreciation of his superb series of photographs of her when, in November 1939, she authorized the publication of a selection of them. They were greeted with delight, and were judged a great propaganda success.

Cecil Beaton wrote a sharp but admiring account of the audience at which she made her selection. He thought her clothes ugly and dowdy and her jewellery messy, but concluded that it did not matter what she wore: nothing could detract from the impression of goodness, sympathy and overwhelming charm which she conveyed. She looked engagingly wistful but was businesslike; she made 'quietly witty remarks with every breath', and was humorous, full of fun and very shrewd. He described her as 'a genius', like a great artist, with an infallible instinct and an ability to make an asset of her own limitations. She could get on with all kinds of people by being genuinely interested in them, and she recognized the 'excitement' that painters or writers felt in their work. 'She is ideal as Queen of England for she is the personification of all that is best & a "real" Lady.'[44]

A very different project for a portrait of the Queen, which gave her much amusement, was about to begin at this time. She liked the

---

* Cecil Beaton (1904–80), photographer and designer, worked for *Vogue* and was renowned for his society portraits and fashion photography. On the recommendation of Prince Paul's wife Princess Olga, he had been summoned to Buckingham Palace in July 1939 to take a series of photographs of the Queen.

work of Augustus John and had already bought several of his pictures.*
In October 1939, John wrote to Mollie Cazalet,† a mutual friend, saying
he would like to paint an informal portrait of the Queen. 'I would stay
in some pub and no doubt there's a suitable room in the castle for
painting. If she had a pretty costume with a hat I'm sure it would be a
success . . . Please, please propose it to Her Majesty.'⁴⁵ The Queen
agreed, and began sitting to him in December – although in evening
dress with a tiara rather than day dress. He found her 'a perfect sitter,
she never asks questions & talks of all sorts of interesting things. If
only I can please Her Majesty as much as she pleases me then I shall
be a happy man.'⁴⁶ John had a habit of tinkering endlessly with his
pictures and the sittings continued, sometimes with musical entertainment.

'I loved sitting to A. John,' she wrote later.

> He was such fun & never drew breath except when the Griller
> Quartette came & played next door and put him off completely.
> He quite rightly said that he couldn't possibly listen and paint.
> Myra Hess‡ came and played one day, & that was so delicious
> that it put him off even more! The day that the Griller Quartet
> was coming to play, I was sitting to A. John & he was painting
> hard, when my page came into the room and said in rather a
> trembling voice 'The gorillas have arrived', which terrified us
> both, and I expect that poor A. John had a vision of several
> shambling baboons coming in to say how much too long my nose
> was, & wasn't one eye higher than the other.⁴⁷

The painting was never actually finished but the Queen was delighted
when, in 1961, she was presented with the work, and wrote to tell the
artist so. It hung in her drawing room for the rest of her life.⁴⁸

---

* Augustus John, OM, RA (1878–1961), post-impressionist painter and draughtsman, was
known for his Bohemian lifestyle and acclaimed for his portraits.

† Maud (Mollie) Cazalet, who had been a friend of Cecilia Strathmore, was the wife of
William Cazalet, and mother of Thelma Cazalet-Keir, a girlhood friend of Queen Elizabeth, of
Victor Cazalet MP and of Peter Cazalet, later to become Queen Elizabeth's racehorse trainer.

‡ Myra Hess (1890–1965) was a celebrated British pianist. During the Second World War,
when concert halls were closed, she organized popular lunchtime concerts at the National
Gallery, and played in many herself. For this contribution to maintaining the morale of the
populace of London, she was created a Dame Commander of the British Empire (DBE) in
1941.

At the same time the King and Queen were both having much more formal state portraits painted by Gerald Kelly, a distinguished portraitist and later president of the Royal Academy. Kelly had been lodging at Eton while he worked at Windsor Castle, but after the outbreak of war he gratefully accepted an invitation from the Queen to move into Windsor Castle until he finished his work.[49] The Royal Family were rather surprised that the artist ended up living for much of the war with them in the Castle. Fortunately he was witty and entertaining. The historian Kenneth Rose noted, 'It was said that to prolong his stay he would steal down to the studio at dead of night to erase the previous day's work.'[50] The paintings were finally ready to go on show after the war ended in 1945. That year he was also given a knighthood – the band at the investiture played 'Anybody Here Seen Kelly?'

*

THE KING AND Queen, like almost everyone else, were surprised that, once Hitler's Polish campaign was over, the first six months of the war should be so quiet. There were tragic exceptions: on 13 October 1939, just a week after the King had been to visit the fleet at Scapa Flow in Orkney, a skilful U-boat commander penetrated the boom defences and sank the battleship *Royal Oak*, with considerable loss of life. But the so-called Phoney War lasted through the winter until the spring of 1940. The Allies conducted very few offensive operations on the ground and somewhat more in the air. At sea, however, the Battle of the Atlantic was already under way: Allied convoys bringing vital supplies from North America were so often devastated by the German navy that Britain's survival was threatened.

At the opening of the first wartime Parliament at the end of November the usual ceremonial was abandoned and, instead of their Parliamentary robes, the King wore naval uniform and the Queen was dressed against the cold in velvet and furs embellished with pearls. Chips Channon thought she had never looked 'so regal and beautiful'. The King held the Queen's hand as he walked slowly out of the Chamber. Channon contrasted the quiet solemnity of this occasion with the vulgar fanfare in which the Nazis indulged.[51]

In the first week of December the King went to visit the British Expeditionary Force in France. The Queen felt that while he was gone there should be one member of the Royal Family at the Palace, though she knew it would not make 'the slightest difference to anybody'.[52] 'I am living here alone, & am the only member of the family in London!!' she wrote to Prince Paul in Belgrade. 'Keep the old flag flying. Hooray!'[53] The King's trip was timely – morale was not high among troops deployed in bitter cold for action which never seemed to come. Lieutenant Colonel Piers Legh, the King's equerry (and later Master of the Household), wrote to the Queen that his visit, although strenuous and uncomfortable, was 'an inspiration in itself' for the soldiers, and the King 'showed a vital interest & understanding of the difficulties and problems which confront the highest and lowest of all ranks of the BEF'.[54] One member of the Force put it strongly: 'We feel ready for any number of Hitlers now!'[55]

That year the King made his most famous Christmas broadcast. He felt it was his task to try and dissipate the apathy that the quiet stalemate of the Phoney War was creating.[56] He related what he had seen of the tasks of the Royal Navy and the RAF whose pilots, he said, 'were daily adding to the laurels that their fathers had won'. Of the soldiers he had just visited in France, he said, 'Their task is hard. They are waiting, and waiting is a trial of nerve and discipline.' He ended by warning his listeners of 'the dark times ahead of us' and said,

> A new year is at hand. We cannot tell what it will bring. If it brings peace, how thankful we shall all be. If it brings us continued struggle, we shall remain undaunted. In the meantime I feel that we may all find a message of encouragement in the lines which, in my closing words, I would like to say to you: 'I said to the man who stood at the Gate of the Year, "Give me a light that I may tread safely into the unknown." And he replied, "Go out into the darkness, and put your hand into the Hand of God. That shall be to you better than light, and safer than a known way." '* May that Almighty Hand guide and uphold us all.[57]

*

ONCE HIS SPEECH was over, he and his family could relax and enjoy a quiet holiday at Sandringham. The Princesses had come down from Birkhall on 20 December. There was a joyful reunion; the King had

---

* These lines, from the poem 'God Knows', had been sent to the King as he was composing his speech. The poem had been written by Minnie Louise Haskins (1875–1957), a lecturer at the London School of Economics, and had been published privately in 1908.

not seen his daughters for four months. The Queen loved having her children back. 'They do help one to forget the ever present worries & troubles of these horrible days.'[58] She wrote to Queen Mary that on Boxing Day, while they were out with the shooting party, '3 large bombers came over very low, & the children were thrilled because they thought that they saw black Swastikas on the wings. However, I think they proved to be our own aircraft.'[59] The King and Queen decided that the girls should not go back to Scotland after Christmas but stay at Royal Lodge. 'Birkhall is too far off, & at their age, their education is too important to be neglected,' the King recorded in his diary.[60]

For the first three months of 1940, as the Phoney War continued, the King and Queen carried out engagements specifically intended to boost morale wherever men and women, in and out of uniform, were contributing to the war effort. Every visit brought letters of thanks and evidence of the heartening effect of their presence. The King described in his diary his visit to the 1st Canadian Division at Aldershot. 'I met many officers I had already met in Canada . . . I was told that our visit to Canada had made it far easier for the 1st Canadian Division to come over so soon as a Division, & that the French Canadians from Quebec have come to fight for their Queen!!'[61]

At the end of February the Queen went to Edinburgh for two busy days of solo engagements, and stayed with the Elphinstones. As ever, her family provided an escape for her, and she left feeling refreshed and revitalized, as she told May. 'The last few months have been such a ghastly climax to two anxious years, and sometimes one feels very depressed, tho' not able to show it! . . . Life in London is so intensely worrying & anxious, that I was really <u>longing</u> for a change of thought & scene.' The King had come to join her for more Scottish engagements and they were now staying in the royal train. 'B and I got out of the train this evening, just before dark,' she wrote, '& walked up a stubble field, & along a little road between beech trees. So quiet & refreshing.'[62] The next day she and the King went aboard HMS *Rodney*, the flagship of the Commander-in-Chief of the Home Fleet, Admiral of the Fleet Sir Charles Forbes, on the Clyde.

Inevitably, in spending so much time at her husband's side, whether on his visits or during the long evenings when he painstakingly read through the mass of telegrams, reports and assessments he received daily, the Queen was acquiring much first-hand knowledge of the affairs of war. In addition, in January 1940 she and the King had begun giving a Monday-night dinner for members of the War Cabinet, other government ministers or officials, and occasionally foreign diplomats. At the dinner on 18 March the Queen gave Winston Churchill, First Lord of the Admiralty, some lines from William Wordsworth's poem *The Excursion* which had caught her imagination. She had copied them out in her own hand, and added across the top: 'I suppose written when Europe was terrified of Napoleon?'

> At this day
> When a Tartarean darkness overspreads
> The groaning nations; when the impious rule,
> By will or by established ordinance,
> Their own dire agents, and constrain the good
> To acts which they abhor; though I bewail
> This triumph, yet the pity of my heart
> Prevents me not from owning that the law,
> By which mankind now suffers, is most just.
> For by superior energies; more strict
> Affiance with each other; faith more firm
> In their unhallowed principles; the bad
> Have fairly earned a victory o'er the weak,
> The vacillating, inconsistent good.

It was the relevance of the last three lines which particularly struck her, she recalled many years later. Churchill treasured the gift, had it framed and kept it thereafter.[63]

Through these contacts with the country's leaders, and through her own increasingly full programme, she was developing stronger views and a clearer concept of her own role. It was one which was wholly in support of her husband, but also much more active and independent than that of Queen Mary in the First World War. In part, this reflected the expansion of the role of women in general. It was also due to her own personality: she was less retiring than her mother-in-law, and more confident that she could make her own contribution without overstepping the mark as the sovereign's consort. Lastly, it was undoubtedly due to others' appreciation of her effectiveness in boosting morale and winning public support for whatever cause she took up. At the same time she was determined to make her own views known, and not to be taken for granted.

Thus, following the success of her broadcast to the women of the Empire, she was in frequent demand to make speeches and send messages. In February 1940 the Minister of Health, Walter Elliot, drafted an announcement on evacuation policy and, in the hope of boosting public support, he added a statement that the Queen would be sending a message of appreciation to all householders who took in evacuee children. Unfortunately, however, he had failed to consult the Queen herself in time, and earned a rebuke from her: she thought it wrong that her name should be associated with a government measure in advance of its adoption. 'You are a good Scotsman, and will appreciate my caution I hope.' Nevertheless she approved the message, which was sent to more than 320,000 households.[64]

A moral dilemma arose for her over another request. The American Young Women's Christian Association asked her, as patron of the British YWCA, to broadcast to their National Convention in April 1940 on the eighty-fifth anniversary of the foundation of the YWCA. Alec Hardinge cautioned that a broadcast by her might be taken by Americans as propaganda for the Allied cause, but she discounted this, and was anxious to accept. Then, however, she learned from the King that Britain was about to mine neutral Norway's territorial waters in order to stop the export of oil and other vital supplies to Germany. The Queen realized the necessity of this. 'We've got to beat the Germans,' she wrote;[65] but she also understood that sinking ships in neutral territorial waters might anger other neutral countries – the United States included – and she feared that her broadcast at this time might add fuel to the fire, as well as making her look hypocritical. She consulted Lord Halifax who replied that he understood her qualms but assured her that the mine-laying off Norway was justified.[66]

She did make her speech – but in a less conspicuous form than originally proposed. It was addressed not direct to the American YWCA, but to an anniversary celebration at the British YWCA headquarters on 13 April, from which it was broadcast. 'Never, I suppose, has the Association had a more responsible part to play in the world than today,' she declared. 'Christian standards and values are being challenged at all points, and a purely material conception of life offered in their places.' It was for younger members to take up the challenge, as individual witnesses to the eternal truths and as one great fellowship, pledged to Christian ideals.[67] She made no direct reference to the war, but her words reflected her view of the threat to

Christianity which the war represented. There seem to have been no diplomatic repercussions.

The episode illustrates the inner conflict she shared with other Christian idealists before and since in times of war. Hardinge had been concerned, a year earlier, that she made judgements purely on the morality of an action without regard to its consequences.[68] Once war broke out she was as determined as any of her compatriots that it must be won; but she continued to believe that Christian values must be upheld and dishonourable conduct by the enemy should not be repaid in kind.[69]

*

IT WAS JUST under three years since the Coronation. Now the Phoney War or *Sitzkrieg* finally ended and within weeks real war brought Britain to the edge of disaster. On 9 April Hitler swooped on Denmark and attacked Norway. Norway resisted, and declared war on Germany; Britain promised all the help in her power, but the British naval and expeditionary forces were unable to protect their ally against the co-ordinated German assault. By 4 May almost all Norway was in German hands.

This shocking, sudden defeat released months of pent-up frustration with the government's lacklustre performance. It was now clear beyond argument that Neville Chamberlain could not be a war leader. He was a man of peace who could never seek victory; he hated making any decision that might cause casualties on either side. At the same time he was right to fear that Britain's conscript army, only two years old, was not well trained enough to take on the Wehrmacht. The disaster in Norway proved the point. On 7 May the Commons began a passionate two-day debate on Norway which ended with so many Conservative MPs deserting their Prime Minister that his position became untenable. In a stunning rebuke, the Conservative backbencher Leo Amery adopted Cromwell's words to the Long Parliament: 'You have sat too long here for any good you have been doing. Depart, I say, and let us have done with you. In the name of God, go!' The King and Queen, still loyal to Chamberlain, were dismayed.[70]

On 10 May Hitler's troops poured into Holland, Belgium, Luxembourg and France. Given the emergency, Chamberlain was determined to remain as prime minister at the head of a national government, but the Labour Party refused to serve under him. That afternoon, he went to Buckingham Palace to offer his resignation. Chamberlain recommended that the King send for Churchill. The King did so. Churchill still aroused considerable suspicion, not least because of his attempt to use the abdication crisis to secure his own advancement and to undercut Stanley Baldwin.

By Churchill's own account, 'His Majesty received me most graciously and bade me sit down. He looked at me searchingly and quizzically for some moments and then said: "I suppose you don't know why I have sent for you?" Adopting his mood, I replied "Sir, I simply couldn't imagine why." He laughed and said "I want you to form a Government." I said I would certainly do so.'[71] The King wrote in his diary: 'He was full of fire & determination to carry out the duties of Prime Minister.'[72]

The Queen wrote Chamberlain a warm letter: 'I can never tell you in words how much we owe you. During these last desperate & unhappy years, you have been a great support & comfort to us both, and we felt so safe with the knowledge that your wisdom and high purpose were there at our hand ... Although one knew that carnage had to come, it is hard to sit here and think of those splendid young men being sacrificed to Hitler. You did all you could to stave off such agony and you were right.'[73]

She never changed her opinion of Chamberlain. Asked many years later if history had been unkind to him, she said, 'Yes. I think he was a good man. I think he really tried. And whatever people say, it gave us that year. Because, as usual, they had practically got rid of the army. So that gave us one year to rearm, and build a few aeroplanes.'[74] Queen Mary wrote to the King to commiserate on the loss of a prime minister in whom he had confidence '& were able to talk to as a friend, whereas W. is so uncertain! Let us hope & pray all may be for the best in the end.'[75]

The next few weeks were probably the most dangerous Britain would face in the entire twentieth century. The King had still to appreciate Churchill. 'I cannot yet think of Winston as PM,' he wrote in his diary on 11 May.[76] But it was not long before he and the Queen came to realize that Churchill was far from 'uncertain'.

The new Prime Minister immediately began to rally a nation adrift. He invited the Labour leader Clement Attlee, Chamberlain and the Liberal leader Sir Archibald Sinclair to join his government. In the first of many epic speeches to the Commons and on the BBC he warned on 13 May, 'We are in the preliminary stage of one of the greatest battles in history . . . I would say to the House, as I said to those who have joined this Government, "I have nothing to offer but blood, toil, tears and sweat." ' Britain's policy, he declared, 'is to wage war by sea, land and air, with all our might and with all the strength that God can give us: to wage war against a monstrous tyranny, never surpassed in the dark, lamentable catalogue of human crime. That is our policy.'[77]

Such resolution was tested at once; May 1940 was merciless. The speed at which European powers and thrones collapsed before the onslaught of the Germans and their allies was terrifying. Denmark and Norway were followed by the fall of Holland, Luxembourg, Belgium and then Britain's most significant ally of all, France.

Hitler tried to capture the royal families of Europe. On 13 May the King was woken at 5 a.m. by an unprecedented telephone call – another monarch beseeching help. Queen Wilhelmina of the Netherlands 'begged' him to send the Royal Air Force to help defend her country, which was being overrun by the Germans. The King passed her request on to everyone concerned. 'It is not often one is rung up at that hour, and especially by a Queen. But in these days anything might happen, & far worse things too.'[78]

Queen Wilhelmina immediately fled her palace, only narrowly avoiding capture by German forces sent to seize her. Braving German bombs, she managed to get to the Hook of Holland and aboard the British destroyer *Hereward* which happened still to be there. She hoped to be taken to the south of Holland where her troops were still resisting. But the speed of German advances made that impossible and the *Hereward* carried her to Harwich instead. With great reluctance she went by train to London.

The King hurried to Liverpool Street station to greet the Dutch monarch and bring her to Buckingham Palace. The doughty Queen had little more than the clothes she was wearing, and a tin hat.[79] On 15 May came the news that the Dutch army had surrendered. The Queen did everything she could to make the royal refugee comfortable in the now rather spartan Palace, until Queen Wilhelmina moved to a house in Eaton Square at the end of the month. Princess Juliana, her daughter, had arrived in England with her husband and children on the same day as her mother. Princess Irene, the infant daughter of Princess Juliana, was to have been baptized in Amsterdam. Queen

Elizabeth suggested that the ceremony take place instead in the chapel
at Buckingham Palace where her own daughters had been christened.[80]
Soon afterwards Princess Juliana and her family left for Canada, where
they lived for the rest of the war. From there the Princess wrote to
thank the Queen for all the comforting hospitality she had given them,
'culminating in the very lovely atmosphere you made for little Irene's
christening'.[81]

After the Dutch, the Norwegians – King Haakon VII, the King's
uncle by marriage, and his son Crown Prince Olav – were the next to
arrive. For almost two months they had been hunted around their
country but had evaded capture. When King Haakon finally realized
that the Germans had seized every village and every fjord of his
kingdom, he too decided to leave and, with his son, was secreted
aboard a British ship. On 10 June the King met them at Euston station
and took them to Buckingham Palace.

The Queen was very fond of both father and son, and welcomed
them. But she was concerned about the extra strain that the royal
refugees placed upon the depleted staff. Later she remembered that in
one air raid she had to step over the recumbent King and his son,
'both snoring away' on the floor of the Palace shelter. 'It really was
too peculiar!'[82] She tried to find them another home as 'tho' we love
having them, it is rather a bore never to be alone'.[83] Eventually they
took Lord Harewood's house in Green Street, Mayfair.

As Europe collapsed, 'there was an appalling feeling of apprehension in the Palace. And the most wonderful comradeship,' one lady in
waiting recalled. The Queen remained calm.[84] Since the beginning of
the year she had carried out some fifty-five engagements in London
and the south-east, both on her own and with the King, as well as
visiting Bristol, Cardiff, Edinburgh, Glasgow, the Midlands, Lancashire
and Dorset for more engagements. She went to see her regiments
when she could, inspecting the Queen's Bays in Dorset on 14 May, but
the emphasis in her programme was on women, and civilian
organizations.

The news from the continent grew daily worse. The German army
attacked through the narrow lanes of the Ardennes and crossed the
River Meuse, which the French had thought impassable. By 15 May
the French army was retreating helter-skelter and the French Prime
Minister, Paul Reynaud, telephoned Churchill to tell him that the
battle was lost and the road to Paris was open to the Germans.

On 16 May German troops broke through the Maginot Line, the supposedly impregnable fortifications along France's eastern border. The British Expeditionary Force in Belgium and northern France was under real threat of being cut off from the sea by the German advance. Churchill broadcast a warning that 'the long night of barbarism will descend, unbroken even by a star of hope, unless we conquer, as conquer we must; as conquer we shall'.[85]

The position of the British troops in France became even more perilous when on 25 May King Leopold of the Belgians surrendered and made the fateful choice to stay with his people rather than follow his government into exile. This decision aroused horror in London, where a united European front against the Nazis was considered essential, and the King wrote to Leopold, whom he liked, expressing his great concern. King Leopold would not change his mind.

On 26 May the King and Queen, together with Queen Wilhelmina, attended a service at Westminster Abbey as part of a National Day of Prayer. Across the country millions gathered; the Archbishop of Canterbury called the war 'a mighty conflict against the powers of evil'.

The country was praying first of all for a miracle to rescue the British troops encircled near Dunkirk. That prayer was granted. Hitler delayed his Panzer attack on the BEF and the remnants of French and Belgian units. And the Channel was like a merciful mill pond. Between 26 May and 5 June an extraordinary flotilla of British vessels, including many yachts and other 'small ships', managed to rescue more than 300,000 British and French soldiers from the beaches of Dunkirk. Day by day the King wrote in his diary the numbers of men brought off the beaches so far – 80,000 by 30 May, 133,000 British soldiers and 11,000 Frenchmen by 31 May, 224,000 British and 111,000 French by Wednesday 5 June. The Queen went to visit some of the first wounded soldiers to return at a Ministry of Health emergency hospital.[86]

The Queen was relieved that Arthur Penn's nephew Eric got off the beaches. 'I can only say with all my heart – Thank God.'[87] But among the troops who did not reach Dunkirk was the 1st Battalion The Black Watch, in which her nephew John Elphinstone was serving. They were forced to surrender near Abbeville, after fierce fighting with the Germans. Only nine men and one officer got away. The Queen was deeply concerned; eventually the news came that John

Elphinstone had been captured. He spent almost five years in prisoner-of-war camps, including Colditz.[88]*

Deliverance aside, Dunkirk was a shocking defeat, and while the evacuation was taking place the War Cabinet even discussed whether Britain should take up a suggestion that Mussolini might negotiate an overall peace. On 28 May Halifax and Chamberlain argued that all options should be considered. This was a critical moment in British history. Churchill listened to the proposals for a negotiated settlement, but said he thought that the chances of Hitler offering 'decent terms' were a thousand to one against. He declared that 'nations which went down fighting rose again, but those who surrendered tamely were finished.' To a meeting of other ministers he expressed the same feelings – 'If this long island story of ours is to end at last, let it end only when each one of us lies choking in his own blood upon the ground.'[89] 'In response to this Macbethian challenge,' wrote the war historian John Keegan, 'Cabinet ministers, Conservative, Liberal and Labour alike, jumped from their seats to pummel him on the back.'[90] Churchill himself later wrote that if he had faltered at that moment 'I should have been hurled out of office.'[91]

Churchill's furious determination was crucial. On 4 June, warning the House of Commons that Britain faced imminent invasion, he declared, 'We shall go on to the end . . . we shall fight on the beaches, we shall fight on the landing grounds, we shall fight in the fields and in the streets, we shall fight in the hills, we shall never surrender.' From now on, the flame of British patriotism, lit by Churchill and tended assiduously by the King and Queen, burned through years of setbacks and tragedy with astonishing resilience.

Meanwhile, under German onslaught, the French had withdrawn most of their troops and were re-forming to await an attack on the Somme. Churchill made four flights to France to encourage resistance, and the King sent President Lebrun a telegram sympathizing with French losses and exhorting France to continue the struggle. Over the next week the French army launched an attack on a broad front in northern France, and appealed for more help; the British prepared to

---

* John Elphinstone (1914–75) was particularly close to his aunt, the Queen, and when he was released from Colditz in 1945 she was the first person he called. After the war he settled in Scotland and in 1951 bought Drumkilbo, an estate on the borders of Angus and Perthshire.

send out two more divisions, including the 1st Canadian Division. On 8 June the King and Queen went to see the Canadians at Aldershot; the King recorded that Canada was fielding the only division with all its equipment and artillery. Then, as the German armies poured across France and bombed Paris for the first time, French resistance faltered.

Everywhere the news was terrible. On 10 June Italy declared war on the Allies and immediately bombed the British island of Malta. On 12 June Churchill reported to the King that the French were outnumbered three to one and might have to surrender very soon. However, as the King noted, 'A young General de Gaulle is ready to carry on a "war of columns", mobile units against German tanks. Marshal Pétain is a defeatist, & says all is lost. Aged 84.'[92]

On Friday 14 June, the day on which the Germans entered an undefended and almost deserted Paris, the Queen broadcast – in French – a message of encouragement to the women of France. 'Je voudrais ce soir dire aux femmes de France, de cette France héroïque et glorieuse qui défend, en ce moment, non seulement son propre sol, mais les libertés du monde entier, les sentiments d'affection, et d'admiration, que leurs souffrances et leur courage éveillent en nos coeurs,' she began. She praised the ardour with which the French army was fighting, but her thoughts were primarily with the women who were watching in anguish the immense struggle in which their sons, husbands and brothers were engaged. 'Pour moi qui ai toujours tant aimé la France, je souffre aujourd'hui comme vous.' She recalled the enthusiasm and generosity with which she and the King had been received in Paris in 1938 and she saluted the sacrifices Frenchwomen were now prepared to make to save their country. 'Une nation qui a, pour la défendre, de tels hommes, et pour l'aimer, de telles femmes, doit, tôt ou tard, forcer la victoire' – a nation defended by such men and loved by such women must sooner or later attain victory.

Finally, she spoke of her recent conversations with wounded French soldiers who had come over from Dunkirk, and whom she had visited at the Wellhouse Emergency Hospital on 6 June. She had talked to each in French, and asked how they were feeling. All, even the most severely wounded, she said, had replied almost gaily with one short phrase: 'Ça va.' She was sure that the time would come when the two peoples, British and French, would be able to exchange the same words: 'Maintenant, ça va.'[93]

The Queen had been helped to draft the speech by the anglophile

French writer André Maurois, who had been Churchill's interpreter on the Western Front in 1916, and was in unhappy exile in London.[94] After the broadcast Maurois wrote to her praising the way she had delivered it.[95] He acknowledged that the broadcast probably came too late to help stiffen French resolve not to surrender. But he felt that it would give his countrymen hope for the future. The British government was sufficiently impressed for Anthony Eden, who was foreign secretary once again, to write to the Queen in January 1941 asking her to make another, similar broadcast (although in the event the idea was shelved), as her message had 'created a profound impression in France'.[96]

The day after the Queen's broadcast, General Charles de Gaulle arrived in Britain and set himself at the head of a campaign to rally French forces outside France, shortly to become the Free French movement. On 22 June the French government surrendered. Britain was now on her own and the prospects were terrible – Churchill warned Roosevelt that if Britain were defeated, 'you may have a United States of Europe under Nazi command far more numerous, far stronger, far better armed than the New World.'[97]

In response to a sympathetic letter from Eleanor Roosevelt,[98] the Queen wrote,

> Sometimes one's heart seems near breaking under the stress of so much sorrow and anxiety. When we think of our gallant young men being sacrificed to the terrible machine that Germany has created, I think that anger perhaps predominates, but when we think of their valour, their determination and their great grand spirit, pride and joy are uppermost.
>
> We are all prepared to sacrifice everything in the fight to save freedom, and the curious thing is, that already many false values are going, and life is becoming simpler and greater every day.[99]

Despair would have been understandable. But the country's solitary stand gave rise to a single-minded determination and, almost, elation. The King wrote to Queen Mary, 'Personally I feel happier now that we have no allies to be polite to & pamper.'[100] Many British people appeared to agree with this sentiment. Air Chief Marshal Sir Hugh Dowding, Air Officer Commanding Fighter Command, remarked 'Thank God we're alone now' – he would no longer have to deploy his limited number of fighters over the continent.

Churchill, knowing how vital the battle in the air would be, had appointed his friend Max Beaverbrook, the newspaper proprietor, to be minister for aircraft production. By the middle of June Beaverbrook had managed to raise the number of aircraft being manufactured every week from 245 to 363.[101] In the Commons on 19 June Churchill made two more of his historic declarations, announcing that the Battle of France was over and he now expected the Battle of Britain to begin. 'Upon this battle depends the survival of Christian civilisation,' he insisted. 'Let us therefore brace ourselves to our duty, and so bear ourselves that, if the British Empire and its Commonwealth last for a thousand years, men will still say, "This was their finest hour." '[102] Such rhetoric induced optimism which seemed astonishing if not downright foolish to onlookers abroad. As the *New Yorker*'s London correspondent Mollie Panter-Downes wrote, 'It would be difficult for an impartial observer to decide today whether the British are the bravest or merely the most stupid people in the world.'[103]

Brave or stupid, in these circumstances it was entirely proper that the bond between King and Prime Minister grew ever stronger. One impediment had long since gone. 'I am getting to know Winston better, & I feel that we are beginning to understand each other,' the King wrote to Queen Mary. 'His silly attitude over D. in 1936 is quite over ... Winston is definitely the right man at the helm at the moment.'[104] Churchill had indeed reconsidered his initial support of King Edward VIII. Malcolm MacDonald later recalled a conversation during the Battle of Britain when Churchill told him that 'King George and Queen Elizabeth are a far finer, more popular and more inspiringly helpful pair than the other would have been. We could not have a better King and Queen in Britain's most perilous hour.'[105] The King began to look forward keenly to their weekly meetings, and by the autumn of 1940 these had changed from formal audiences into private Tuesday lunches. The Queen was generally present.*

Churchill commented that the intimacy which developed between him and the King was unprecedented since the days of Queen Anne and his own ancestor, the Duke of Marlborough.[106] Just as unprecedented, however, was the presence of the Queen at these private

---

* On one occasion when she was unable to attend she wrote to Churchill, 'I am so sorry not to be at "the picnic" today, and hope that conversation will flow unchecked by that incessant prowl round the table by attentive varlets!' (13 April 1943, CAC CHAR 20/98A/56)

conversations between the King and his Prime Minister. The King's diary does not record any interventions by the Queen. Nevertheless she said, many years later, that she felt very much a part of a team with the King, and he 'got on terribly well, like a house on fire', with Churchill.[107] By now the King and Queen symbolized resistance to Hitler not only in Britain but also in all the occupied nations of Europe.

Britons were now organizing to resist invasion. In the south-east, there was widespread fear of Germans parachuting or gliding down from the skies, perhaps even disguised as nuns. Locals sabotaged possible landing sites: golf courses, sports fields, downland and fields were scattered with junk – old cars, old cookers, ploughs, tree trunks – anything to prevent an aircraft from touching down. Road signs were removed, so as not to assist any enemy who did arrive. The names of villages and even railway stations were taken down.[108]

The government had called for all able-bodied men between the ages of fifteen and sixty-five who were not already engaged in the war effort to step forward and become Local Defence Volunteers. (Thus was born the Home Guard, eventually to be portrayed as 'Dad's Army', in the affectionate television series which became one of Queen Elizabeth's favourite programmes in later years.) Immediately, over a quarter of a million people offered their services and began to gather in pubs and meeting rooms across the country to discuss how they could serve. By the end of June the 'force' had grown to a million and a half. Men and boys began to drill with broomsticks instead of rifles, pitchforks instead of anti-aircraft guns.

In Windsor Castle Owen Morshead became the head of the Castle's Home Guard. He wrote to Queen Mary to tell her how the King and Queen were coping and said that they had talked to the night patrols in the Castle, which was a great encouragement to them. He thought the King 'seemed rather oppressed and tired – sick of reading & reading the endless stream of Cabinet papers and war reports sent daily to him, and waiting & waiting. It is a misfortune for him in these days that he has to know so much of what is going on – where ignorance is bliss. Happily the Queen is a perpetual tonic, with her sunny and buoyant nature.'[109]

The King and Queen were determined to protect themselves. Both of them took shooting lessons (the King was already an accomplished shot) and the King carried a rifle as well as a revolver in his car. Joseph Kennedy noted in his diary a story told him by Brendan

Bracken, now a minister in the government. On one of Churchill's weekly visits to the King at Buckingham Palace he found him in the garden shooting at a target with a rifle. The King told his Prime Minister that 'if the Germans were coming, he was at least going to get his German and Churchill said if he felt that way about it, he would get him a Tommy Gun so he could kill a lot of Germans and he is getting him one'.[110]*

The Queen was equally resolute. She told Harold Nicolson that she was taking instruction every morning in firing a revolver. 'I shall not go down like the others,' she said. 'I should die if I had to leave.'[111] Nicolson was much cheered by her pluck and the resolution and good sense of both King and Queen. He wrote to his wife Vita, 'he was so gay and she so calm. They did me all the good in the world . . . *We shall win*. I know that. I have no doubts at all.'[112]

Through these months thousands of children were being evacuated from the major cities in anticipation of German bombing. Most were sent to the country but others, especially children of the well-to-do, were dispatched for safety to the United States or to the Dominions. The King and Queen had discussed with Churchill the threat to their own children; on 18 June the King had asked Churchill if he thought the Princesses would be a liability in the event of invasion. 'No,' the Prime Minister replied.[113] The Queen had no doubts. She made it clear that evacuation was not what she wanted for herself or for her children. She has been often quoted (though the precise moment is obscure) as saying, 'The children could not go without me, I could not possibly leave the King, and the King would never go.'

That being so, the security of the Royal Family was a major concern. On one occasion, King Haakon asked the King what would happen if German parachutists suddenly descended into the grounds of the Palace. The King's biographer explained what happened next:

> Obligingly King George pressed the alarm signal and, together
> with the Queen, they went into the garden to watch the result.

---

* Soon after Victory in Europe Day in May 1945, Churchill praised the King for his weapons training and recalled that 'if it had come to a last stand in London, a matter which had to be considered at one time, there is no doubt that His Majesty would have come very near departing from his usual constitutional rectitude by disregarding the advice of his Ministers'. In other words, the King would have wanted to fight the Germans himself rather than be taken to safety. (Hansard, 15 May 1945)

There followed an anti-climax; nothing happened at all. An anxious equerry, dispatched to make inquiries, returned with the report that the officer of the guard had been informed by the police sergeant on duty that no attack was pending 'as he had heard nothing of it'. Police co-operation having been obtained, a number of guardsmen entered the gardens at the double and, to the horror of King Haakon but the vast amusement of the King and Queen, proceeded to thrash the undergrowth in the manner of beaters at a shoot rather than of men engaged in the pursuit of a dangerous enemy. As a result of this incident precautions were revised and strengthened.[114]

The most important of these was the Coats Mission, a hand-picked body of officers and men from the Brigade of Guards and the Household Cavalry who, equipped with armoured cars, stood always ready to spirit the King and Queen into a secret place of safety in the country should the Germans really threaten them.[115]*

At Buckingham Palace the first royal air-raid shelter was somewhat amateurish and probably afforded little or no protection against a direct hit. It was a basement room which had been used by the housekeeper. The ceiling was reinforced by steel girders and there were steel shutters across the high window. The furniture was somewhat eclectic – it included gilt chairs, a regency settee and a large Victorian mahogany table. The shelter was decorated with many of the valuable small Dutch landscapes which had been brought downstairs. Hating the shelter as she did, the Queen said later that she had developed an unreasonable dislike for these little scenes of cows and bridges over canals.[116]

There were emergency steps to reach the window, axes on the wall, oil lamps, electric torches, a bottle of smelling salts and a pile of glossy magazines to help while away the hours. In the room next door, the Household took shelter – they were blessed with a piano, but the King was not amused when one of the refugee courtiers attempted a rousing singsong. The Queen's dressers and other staff had another nearby room, to which many of the Palace's priceless

* The Coats Mission was commanded by Major James Coats (1894–1966), later third baronet. He married in 1917 Lady Amy Gordon-Lennox, a great friend of Queen Elizabeth all her life, and sister of Lady Doris Vyner. Another old friend of the Queen, Audrey Pleydell-Bouverie, née James, had been married to James's brother Dudley.

clocks had been moved for safe keeping. Their loud ticking provided a useful distraction to those awaiting bombardment. Rats provided another, less welcome diversion.[117]

Throughout that summer, as daily dogfights took place across the skies, the Queen continued her visits to troops, hospitals, voluntary services, factories, aerodromes and training centres, carrying out more than twenty solo engagements in June and July and another ten jointly with the King. On 31 July she visited the Free French troops under the leadership of General de Gaulle at Olympia. De Gaulle did not prove an easy ally, but he soon became something of a favourite with her. On the same day she went to see another group of French soldiers, waiting to be repatriated, at White City. A Breton soldier to whom she spoke was impressed by her calm and smiling face, and wrote afterwards, 'cette Reine ne peut pas être vaincue car elle est la justice même et la vraie conception de la vie démocratique.'[118]

For the first time in their married life there was no holiday in Scotland that year, and the Queen celebrated her birthday on 4 August in a low-key manner.

*

INEVITABLY HITLER'S dash across Europe led to new, more serious concerns with regard to the Duke of Windsor. With the approval of the British Military Mission to which he was attached, he left Paris as the Germans advanced in May; he and the Duchess paused briefly in the south of France before having to flee the advancing Germans into Spain on the night of 20 June.

Berlin had ambitions for the Duke. Ribbentrop, the former Ambassador to London and now the German Foreign Minister, knew that the Duke had been sympathetic to Germany and that he considered the war unnecessary. The fascist government of General Franco was aligned with Berlin and the Germans now tried to have the Duke detained in Spain. Churchill, concerned, telegraphed the Duke asking him to move at once to neutral Lisbon, whence a flying boat would carry him and the Duchess back to England. The Duke's reply ignored the fact that Churchill was leading Britain in its most perilous hour – he insisted that before he returned he be given guarantees that he and the Duchess would be royally treated in England, and would be extended regular invitations to Buckingham Palace. To badger the Prime Minister on such matters at a time when Britain faced imminent invasion was, as his biographer put it, 'conduct that cannot be condoned'.[119]

The Windsors did then move on to Lisbon, but even there they were subject to German conspiracies. Ribbentrop first sent men to flatter the Duke with praise and promises and then an SS officer with the mission to cajole and if necessary force the Duke back to Spain. At Buckingham Palace Alec Hardinge made notes on an intelligence report: 'Germans expect assistance from Duke and Duchess of Windsor. Latter desiring at any price to become Queen. Germans have been negotiating with her since June 27th.'[120]

Churchill then devised the idea of getting the couple far from German reach by making the Duke governor of the Bahamas. The Royal Family were not keen – the King wrote to his mother, 'I at once said that "she" would be an obstacle as D's wife.' But none of the family wanted the Windsors in England at this time and, as the King put it to Queen Mary, 'it was imperative to get him away from Lisbon.'[121] Queen Mary was equally unenthusiastic but she replied, 'Under the circumstances I think this is the best arrangement for D.'[122]

The Queen, perhaps, had the greatest misgivings, and she expressed them very clearly in a handwritten memorandum. Although she knew that the appointment had already been decided, she asked Alec Hardinge to send her notes to the Colonial Secretary, Lord Lloyd. The language she used about the Duchess was strong, and undoubtedly reflected the feelings that she had harboured since 1936. But her views on the Windsors' suitability for public office were shared not only throughout the Royal Family* and Household, but also by members of the public, some of whose letters criticizing the Duke and Duchess she sent on to Lord Lloyd.[123]

She wrote that she was certain that, if the Duke was made governor of the Bahamas, 'a very difficult situation will arise over his wife.' Home and marriage ties were 'sacred' to the average Briton and the fact that the Duchess 'has three husbands alive, will not be pleasing

---

* Princess Alice, Countess of Athlone, newly arrived in Canada, where her husband had been appointed governor general, wrote to the Queen that it was 'a bitter blow to the Monarchy ... I am terribly grieved & it puts all of us Governors' wives in a horrid position; we are supposed to stand for all that's best in British home & social life, & now what's the use – & how can we make any difference between people who place themselves outside the pale when one of the King's representatives has a wife completely outside the pale.' (11 July 1940, RA QEQM/PRIV/RF)

to the good people of the Islands'. Britons were used to 'looking up' to the King's representatives, but 'The Duchess of Windsor is looked upon as the lowest of the low – it will be the first lowering of the standard hitherto set, and may lead to unimaginable troubles, if a Governor's wife such as she, is to lead and set an example to the Bahamas.' Her objections, she stressed, were 'on moral grounds, but in this world of broken promises and lowered standards, who is to keep a high standard of honour, but the British Empire . . . These few words are written from the point of view of general policy – they are not personal. I feel strongly that such an appointment may lead to great troubles.' She thought, moreover, that it would displease the Americans, which might be dangerous.[124]

Hardinge told her that he knew that Lord Lloyd, like most others, shared her views, but thought the appointment was a lesser evil than the only alternative – the Windsors' return to Britain. 'I think that she will do harm wherever she is – but there is less scope for it in a place like the Bahamas than elsewhere – and the native population probably will not understand what it is all about!'[125]

The Duke had new demands. He insisted that his former servants be released from active service to accompany him to the Bahamas and that he and the Duchess be allowed to visit New York en route. Churchill absolutely refused to allow the second request but eventually and reluctantly agreed that one valet be discharged in order to return to him. Even then the Windsors' departure was still not certain. The Germans made sure that the Duke was told that the British Secret Service were planning to assassinate him on the voyage and that he would be far safer under the German wing in Spain. It took another visit from the redoubtable Walter Monckton to convince him to leave; he and the Duchess finally set sail on 1 August.[126]

The extent to which the Duke would ever have co-operated with the Nazis cannot be known. On one occasion, the King wrote, 'Winston told me that D.'s ideas and his pro-Nazi leanings would have been impossible during the crisis of the last three years.'[127] That was undoubtedly true, but does not in itself imply treasonable intent. The considered view of the Duke's biographer, Philip Ziegler, is that 'there seems little doubt that he did think Britain was likely to lose the war and that, in such a case, he believed he might have a role to play.' Despite all this, Ziegler concluded that in the awful event of a German victory the Duke's belief in the British meant that 'he could not have allowed himself to rule by favour of the Germans over a sullen and resentful people.'[128]

★

As THE DUKE and Duchess sailed west, the next stage of Hitler's assault began with the unprecedented, indeed revolutionary use of air power to break Britain's will and ability to resist a seaborne invasion. The campaign had begun in early July with bombing raids on south-coast ports, and gathered in intensity, spreading through the south-east and on to London. Having given up hope of forcing Britain to the conference table, Hitler knew that no invasion could take place until the Germans controlled the air over Britain and the English Channel. He flung the mass of the Luftwaffe against London itself. For ten days the bright and sunny skies over south-eastern England were filled with the roar of warfare as wave after wave of German bombers growled across the coast towards London and young men in their Spitfires and Hurricanes rose up to shoot them down.

This new phase of the Battle of Britain was deadly. On 8 August the Luftwaffe began a systematic attack on airfields and aircraft factories, and managed to bomb many of them out of action. In the last week of August and the first week of September 1940 there were 600 enemy aircraft attacking Britain every day. In those two weeks, the RAF lost 290 aircraft. On the night of 7 September, 200 German bombers broke through the RAF defences and hit London, killing 300 people and injuring over 1,300 more in the next few hours. The docks in the East End were set alight and hundreds of fires attracted swarm after swarm of enemy aircraft. That night, to add to the horror, the Chiefs of Staff issued the code word 'CROMWELL'. An invasion was thought to be imminent.

And so it went on every night – by the middle of the month more than 2,000 civilians had been killed and 8,000 wounded, most in London itself. The courage of 'the few' in the RAF was extraordinary and gave Britain an essential victory – their resistance to the Luftwaffe until the equinox gales arrived in the fourth week of September meant that Hitler had had to postpone Operation Sea Lion, the invasion of Britain. Nonetheless, the bombing continued week after week and London was raided again and again and again.

On Sunday 8 September, Buckingham Palace itself received its first direct hit. A delayed-action bomb was dropped; it did not explode and next morning the King worked in his office above where it lay. In the middle of Monday night it went off, blowing out all the windows of his office and many others, and damaging the indoor swimming pool. Some of the Palace ceilings came down, but the main structure was not seriously affected.

During the week which followed, the King and Queen made their first visits to the devastated East End. They were given emotional welcomes by people picking through the rubble of their streets with extraordinary cheerfulness; they had lost everything but were still determined to try to rebuild their homes and their lives. The sight of their King and Queen walking among them and talking to many of them with obvious interest and concern was immensely reassuring. The King wrote to his mother, 'we have seen some of the awful havoc which has been done in East London, & have talked to the people who are quite marvellous in the face of adversity. So cheerful about it all, & some have had very narrow escapes.'[129]

On the morning of 13 September the King and Queen themselves were nearly killed. In a deliberate attack, a German bomber emerged from low cloud, flew straight up the Mall and dropped a stick of bombs on the Palace. The Queen described what happened in a long letter to Queen Mary:

> My darling Mama
> I hardly know how to begin to tell you of the horrible attack on Buckingham Palace this morning Bertie & I arrived there at about ¼ to 11, and he & I went up to our poor windowless rooms to collect a few odds and ends.

There was an air raid in progress and she went to find the King to see if he was coming down to the shelter.

> He asked me to take an eyelash out of his eye, and while I was battling with this task, Alec came into the room with a batch of papers in his hand. At this moment we heard the unmistakable whirr-whirr of a German plane. We said, 'ah a German', and before anything else could be said, there was the noise of aircraft diving at great speed, and then the scream of a bomb. It all happened so quickly, that we had only time to look foolishly at each other, when the scream hurtled past us, and exploded with a tremendous crash in the quadrangle.
> I saw a great column of smoke & earth thrown up into the

air, and then we all ducked like lightning into the corridor. There was another tremendous explosion, and we & our 2 pages who were outside the door, remained for a moment or two in the corridor away from the staircase, in case of flying glass. It is curious how one's instinct works at these moments of great danger, as quite without thinking, the urge was to get away from the windows. Everybody remained wonderfully calm, and we went down to the shelter. I went along to see if the housemaids were alright, and found them busy in their various shelters.

Then came a cry for 'bandages', and the first aid party, who had been training for over a year, rose magnificently to the occasion, and treated the 3 poor casualties calmly and correctly. They, poor men, were working below the Chapel, and how they survived I don't know.* Their whole workshop was a shambles, for the bomb had gone bang through the floor above them. My knees trembled a little bit for a minute or two after the explosions! But we both feel quite well today, tho' just a bit tired.

I was so pleased with the behaviour of our servants. They were really magnificent. I went along to the kitchen which, as you will remember, has a glass roof. I found the chef bustling about, and when I asked him if he was alright, he replied cheerfully that there had been un petit quelque chose dans le coin, un petit bruit, with a broad smile. The petit quelque chose was the bomb on the Chapel just next door! He was perfectly unmoved, and took the opportunity to tell me of his unshakeable conviction that France will rise again![130]

The King and Queen decided to conceal how nearly they had died, even from Churchill. In the second volume of his memoirs, *Their Finest Hour*, Churchill wrote, 'Had the windows been closed instead of open, the whole of the glass would have splintered into the faces of the King and Queen, causing terrible injuries. So little did they make of it that even I . . . never realised until long afterwards . . . what had actually happened.' Their near-escape was not made public until after the end of the war.†

---

* One, Alfred Davies, died of his injuries later.

† Queen Elizabeth's friend D'Arcy Osborne, then virtually imprisoned in Vatican City, was appalled when he heard on the BBC of the Palace bombing. Owen Chadwick, who recorded Osborne's extraordinary wartime service in *Britain and the Vatican during the Second World War*, recounted, 'When Buckingham Palace was bombed, Osborne went wild with rage (the only

On the day of the bombing, after lunch in their shelter, they drove
again to the East End of London. The Queen was horrified and moved.
'The damage there is ghastly,' she told Queen Mary.

> I really felt as if I was walking in a dead city, when we walked
> down a little empty street. All the houses evacuated and yet
> through the broken windows one saw all the poor little pos-
> sessions, photographs, beds, just as they were left. At the end of
> the street is a school which was hit, and collapsed on the top of
> 500 people waiting to be evacuated – about 200 are still under the
> ruins. It does affect me seeing this terrible and senseless destruc-
> tion – I think that really I mind it much more than being bombed
> myself. The people are marvellous, and full of fight. One could
> not imagine that life could become so terrible. We must win in
> the end.
>
> Darling Mama, I do hope that you will let me come & stay a
> day or two later. It is so sad being parted, as this War has parted
> families.
>
> With my love, and prayers for your safety, ever darling Mama,
> your loving daughter in law Elizabeth
>
> PS Dear old BP is still standing and that is the main thing.[131]

But in one way the bombing of the Palace was helpful to the King
and Queen – and to the country. Some Members of Parliament had
worried in the first days of the Blitz that, if the bombing was
concentrated on working-class areas, resentment would grow. The
Queen said, famously and more than once, that she was glad that the
Palace had been bombed because it meant that she could 'now look
the East End in the face'.[132] And it was true that it did help create a
closer bond. The King told Queen Mary that he thought their visits to
the bombed areas helped people 'who have lost their relations &
homes, & we have both found a new bond with them as Buckingham
Palace has been bombed as well as their homes, and nobody is
immune.'[133]

The Queen now found that people would ask her how she felt
about being attacked. A voluntary worker in one stricken area related
that 'the first thing all the women say to her, as they try to salvage

---

time in all these events, though not the only time he was angry) and persuaded the Pope to
send the King and Queen a telegram of congratulation on their escape.' (p. 137)

their own pathetic bundles of belongings from their ruined homes, is "Did the Queen lose all her pretty things too?" '[134] On one such visit to south-east London, Lord Woolton, the Minister of Food, was with them.

> The Queen asked me about the morale of the people who had been bombed: when we were coming through a very slummy district a crowd gathered around the carriage and called out, 'Good Luck' and 'God Bless You' and 'Thank YMs for coming to see us'. I knew the district and had been there only a week before. I said, 'You asked me about morale. All these people have lost their homes.' The Queen was so touched she couldn't speak for a moment, I saw the tears come into her eyes and then she said, 'I think they're wonderful.'[135]

At one communal feeding centre, there was a moment, noted Woolton, at which 'a very dirty child' in its mother's arms grabbed at the Queen's pearls. A photographer ran around trying to get a picture but she had just moved away. Woolton, standing behind the Queen, murmured to her, 'Your Majesty, you've broken a press man's heart.' 'Without showing the slightest sign that she had heard,' Woolton recorded, 'she moved back into position for the baby again to play with her pearls, and so that the pressman could take his photograph. The incident was, in fact, the only thing recorded in the press!'[136] Woolton appreciated the simplicity of both the King and Queen. 'They were so easy to talk to and to take round, and fell so readily into conversation with the people whom they were seeing, without any hesitation or affectation, or side. They were, in fact, very nice people, doing a very human job.'[137]*

That certainly was the impression they gave. After their trip to Bermondsey, the Chairman of the National Council of Girls' Clubs, Mrs Walter Elliot, wrote to the Queen's lady in waiting, 'Everyone in Bermondsey believed that Her Majesty came to see them because she had heard that there had been a direct hit on a shelter, and had wanted

---

* In February 1941 Lord Woolton suggested to the Queen that a mobile canteen service to be dispatched to bombed areas of London should be named 'The Queen's Messengers'. She agreed, and in March formally accepted the first convoy of eighteen canteens sent to Buckingham Palace for her inspection. She later visited the Queen's Messengers in operation at bomb sites. (Bodleian Library, MS Woolton 2)

to help them. It is impossible to over-estimate what this visit has meant ... The people felt as if an angel had passed through their midst. This must have been said often before, but it was the literal truth.'[138]

From Chicago the Queen received a poem which began:

> Be it said to your renown
> That you wore your gayest gown
> Your bravest smile, and stayed in Town
> When London Bridge was burning down,
>   My fair lady.[139]

In fact her gowns in wartime were a constant worry. The King looked elegant in uniform throughout the war; the Queen had more difficulty deciding what she should wear. She knew that press photographs tended to reveal her plumpness rather than her clear skin, let alone her charm. Her dressmaker, Norman Hartnell, advised that she must stand out in the crowd and that since most of the people she mingled with would be darkly if not drably dressed, she should wear light colours. In his autobiography he recalled the problem of how she should appear when visiting the victims of the bombing. 'In black? Black does not appear in the rainbow of hope. Conscious of tradition, the Queen made a wise decision in adhering to the gentle colours, and even though they became muted into what one might call dusty pink, dusty blue and dusty lilac, she never wore green and she never wore black. She wished to convey the most comforting, encouraging and sympathetic note possible.'[140] In such clothes, and often in high heels, she certainly stood out in the bombed streets. Her gentle ostentation was deliberate and it seems to have been effective. It was encouraging for people who had lost almost everything to see that the Queen still had her style.[141]

She was careful to abide by the rules for 'austerity' clothes – the amount of material, the number of seams, the amount of adornment and width of collar and belt. For receptions at the Palace or the Castle more elegant dresses were needed, but restrictions still applied. Embroidery was forbidden, so Hartnell 're-tinted and re-arranged' dresses from pre-war years. Many of them were the clothes he had created for the Canadian tour. In one case he painted by hand garlands of lilac and green leaves on a voluminous white satin gown. The

Queen also encouraged him to accept a Board of Trade request to design utility clothes for the public.[142]

★

THROUGHOUT THE Battle of Britain the King and Queen drove to London almost every day and slept at Windsor Castle with their daughters. A large dugout had been constructed for the Royal Family under the Brunswick Tower, at the northern corner of the East Terrace. The King and Queen did not like this hole in the ground (which was also quite far from their rooms) and from early September 1940 they usually slept on the ground floor of the Victoria Tower (now Queen's Tower) which had been protected outside by huge concrete frames filled with sand, while more extensive reinforcing works took place. The whole tower was clothed in scaffolding and a ten-inch raft of concrete, steel and asbestos was built across the roof, while the four rooms in the cellar were given added protection by constructing a four-feet-thick roof of concrete and girders across the ground floor. 'At least there we can sleep undisturbed, unless we are attacked by dive bombers,' the King wrote to Queen Mary. 'We still have the deep underground shelter to go to as a last resort, which is safe.'[143]

In the early days of the war, the inhabitants of the Castle were alerted to air raids not only by outside sirens but also by loud electric bells which clanged through the corridors. In one early air raid everyone made their way to their shelters – everyone, that is, except the nine-year-old Princess Margaret. Then, according to Owen Morshead, 'After a little time Miss Crawford was sent like the dove out of the ark to retrieve her, and after threading her way along endless deserted passages, she found the child still in her bedroom. She was on her knees before her chest of drawers, the room in disarray, hurriedly searching for a pair of knickers to go with her skirt.'[144]

Reminiscing later, Queen Elizabeth recalled that one of the Princesses' nannies always wore a nightcap to the shelter – 'I think she thought it was to be decent in the war.' She herself wore a gown which Hartnell had made especially for air-raid nights, and he also made her a black-velvet case for her gas mask.[145]

Windsor was attacked on two consecutive nights in October 1940, although the Castle was not hit. This, the Queen wrote to her sister May, was 'the first time that the children had actually heard the whistle & scream of bombs. They were wonderful, & when I went to say good-night to Margaret in her bed, I said that I hoped she wasn't frightened etc, & she said "Mummy, it was just like when you take a photograph that doesn't come out – all grey & blurred, & you see several hands & arms instead of one", & it is so true, really very much what one feels like.'¹⁴⁶ After the raid, the Queen visited bombed areas of Windsor and followed up by sending blankets to some whose houses had been destroyed.

The Castle was never warm in winter – the high rooms were hard to heat, the wind whistled through the tall windows. The King would sometimes sit in his room with a travelling rug wrapped around his feet, having failed in every other way to cope with the draught along the floor. In an attempt to ease the cold, electric radiators were installed in the window bays.¹⁴⁷

Now the western end of St George's Hall boasted a temporary stage on which the two Princesses and their friends from time to time gave entertainments. They played the piano and tap-danced, and put on a performance of the Mad Hatter's Tea Party from *Alice in Wonderland* – Princess Margaret distinguished herself as the Dormouse. Among their constant audience was a company of Grenadier Guards, stationed in the Castle mews to protect the Royal Family. They were welcomed – otherwise the Princesses were often alone with their governesses, a Castle official and perhaps Gerald Kelly the portraitist.

In October 1940 Neville Chamberlain, who had suddenly fallen gravely ill and had had to resign from the War Cabinet, was near death. The King and Queen drove to visit him. Chamberlain was very touched, and his wife Anne wrote to the Queen to thank them for their characteristic kindness.¹⁴⁸ Chamberlain died on 10 November; Churchill was a pallbearer at his funeral and was generous in his tribute in the House of Commons, saying that all Chamberlain's noble hopes for peace had been disappointed and cheated by a wicked man.¹⁴⁹

Although by the autumn the threat of imminent invasion had receded, London was still under constant attack. The King and Queen's first married home in London, 145 Piccadilly, was destroyed. Kensington Palace was bombed and then a land mine exploded just opposite Buckingham Palace in St James's Park, blowing out all the windows and frames in the front of the Palace. By now there was scarcely a pane of glass left intact – the windows had to be boarded up with cardboard.[150] The Queen was dismayed that the beauty of Georgian and Regency London was being smashed – and concerned that the eventual rebuilding would be without taste. (She was right.) 'It really makes one wild with rage to see all the insane destruction of beautiful & often dearly loved buildings.'[151] She wished the German Embassy had been bombed instead. 'I believe the interior had been made very vulgar by that horrible Ribbentrop, & it would have been no loss.'[152]

In Stoke Newington in mid-October 1940 the King and Queen watched as people were being dug out of flats which had collapsed upon them. The horror was compounded by the fact that a bomb had burst a water main and many who survived the bombs were then drowned. She and the King knew that such expeditions were essential, but 'I do hate these visits so desperately Mama,' she wrote to Queen Mary. 'I feel quite exhausted after seeing and hearing so much sadness, sorrow, heroism and magnificent spirit. The destruction is so awful, & the people too wonderful – they deserve a better world.'[153] She was determined, however moved or upset she was, not to show her emotions. 'Sometimes even Chief Constables wept, but she never broke down,' one lady in waiting said.[154] But the Queen felt it all intensely. 'It makes one furious seeing the wanton destruction of so much,' she wrote to her sister May. 'Sometimes it really makes me feel almost ill. I can't tell you how I loathe going round these bombed places, I am a beastly coward, & it breaks one's heart to see so much misery & sadness.'[155]

In their visits around the city, there were often air-raid warnings 'and I think we must have taken refuge in every single police station in London. We were always given a cup of very, very strong tea.' On the trips around the country, they lived a lot on the train and when it stopped at night she would walk up to the cab to chat with the engine drivers – 'they were nearly always the most delightful people, great characters, with proper engines. Such nice men.'[156]

She tended to wake early in those days and to lie in bed worrying. She thought of all the blows that had already befallen Britain and all those which could still come. But she had hope. 'We have had to take such great reverses, as only a truly great people can take disasters, and possibly so much disappointment & horror will steel our people, & take them to great heights of sacrifice and courage.'[157] She also felt, as many did, that the war was bringing out the best in people. Before the war materialism held sway, but now, as she wrote to Queen Mary in October 1940, 'the people are living a truly Christian life – being good neighbours & living for each other as never before; which, with the things of the spirit, seem to me to be real Christianity.'[158]

The national ordeal continued. In November 1940 British aircraft sank most of the Italian fleet at Taranto, and then the Eighth Army drove the Italians out of Egypt and most of Libya. But it was a false dawn. Hitler sent Lieutenant General Rommel and the Afrika Korps to North Africa and Rommel reversed the British victories, threatening the Allied oil supplies in the Middle East. The second six months of the real war were, if anything, worse than the first.

In December 1940 Lord Lothian, the British Ambassador to Washington, died *en poste* of food poisoning. A Christian Scientist, he had refused to call in a doctor. He had been a superb ambassador, a friend of Roosevelt for twenty-five years, and was admired throughout America. It was imperative to replace him quickly and within a week Churchill chose Lord Halifax, the Foreign Secretary. The King and Queen were both sorry to see Halifax and his wife go – the Queen found Dorothy Halifax, still one of her ladies in waiting, 'a real pillar of strength', but she felt sure the Americans would like and admire them as much as she and the King did.[159] She was right.

The second Christmas of the war came. The royal Christmas card that year was a photograph of the King and Queen standing in the bomb-damaged Palace. The two Princesses took part in a nativity play at Windsor Castle organized by Hubert Tannar, the headmaster of the primary school in Windsor Great Park. Princess Elizabeth was one of the three kings. According to Marion Crawford, she 'looked like Edward V in her Coronation Crown and tunic of pink and gold' as she walked the length of St George's Hall with her gift to the infant Jesus; Princess Margaret took the part of a child whose gift was herself, and sang 'Gentle Jesus' at the crib.[160] Her proud father recorded that she 'played her part remarkably well & was not shy'. He was overcome by the emotions the play evoked. 'I wept through most of it. It is such a wonderful story.'[161]

On 27 December they motored up to Norfolk to have a few days' rest on the Sandringham estate. The big house had been closed for the duration of the war; surrounded as it was by barbed wire, and with many shrubs and trees cut down on the orders of the King, the Queen thought it looked forlorn and uncherished.[162] They now lived in

Appleton, a small house near by which had been the home of Queen Maud of Norway, who had died in 1938. It was a less obvious target for German bombers than Sandringham itself. They were protected by an armoured-car unit and four Bofors guns, and there was a reinforced concrete air-raid shelter in the trees close by. The staff had filled Appleton with carpets and furniture from Sandringham House. It was warm and comfortable and the Queen and her daughters were happy to be there intimately *en famille*. 'The children are looking quite different already,' she wrote to Queen Mary in early January 1941. 'I am afraid that Windsor is not really a very good place for them, the noise of guns is heavy, and then of course there have been so many bombs dropped all round, & some so close.'¹⁶³

The snow was thick on the ground but the King went out shooting every day and, his wife said, looked much the better for it. The Queen tried to relax.¹⁶⁴ In the fresh chill of Norfolk, they could all reflect on the terrible year that Britain had endured. Thanks largely to the encouragement of Churchill and the mistakes of Hitler, Britain had survived – just. The King summed up 1940 in his diary as 'a series of disasters for us'. But 'Winston coming in as PM & Labour serving with him in his government stopped the political rot . . . Then the Blitzkrieg by the German Air Force by day & night against aerodromes & London which we countered magnificently. Civilian defence services & morale of people splendid . . . The 2nd six months have certainly shown the world what we can stand . . . Hitler has not had everything his own way.'¹⁶⁵

Through Christmas and New Year the air raids over London were particularly destructive. The Queen was 'enraged beyond <u>words</u>' by the bombing of the Guildhall and many of the other landmarks of the City of London on the night of 29 December 1940.¹⁶⁶ That one night of attack caused about 700 fires; fire crews rushed into the City from all over the Home Counties. As well as the Guildhall, eight Wren churches, five railway stations and sixteen Underground stations were damaged or destroyed.¹⁶⁷ 'I am beginning to really <u>hate</u> the German mentality – the cruelty and arrogance of it.'¹⁶⁸

Before returning to London the King and Queen visited many of the airfields in the Sandringham area. Blizzards and ice on the roads made their journeys slow and perilous, 'and everywhere we arrived there was a "Jerry" overhead! It became quite a joke in the end,' she wrote to her niece Elizabeth Elphinstone. But it was worth while; she was, as always, moved and encouraged by the modesty and the calmness of the men she met. She contrasted their calmness with her own fear. 'I am still just as frightened of bombs, & guns going off, as I was at the beginning. I turn bright red, and my heart hammers – in fact I'm a beastly coward, but I do believe that a lot of people are, so I don't mind! Well darling, I must stop . . . Tinkety tonk old fruit, & down with the Nazis.'[169]

She enjoyed the Sandringham Women's Institute party where the ladies put on patriotic tableaux. 'If only you could see them,' she wrote to the Duke of Kent. 'Dear Mrs Way, as Neptune, glaring furiously through a tangle of grey hair and seaweed, & Miss Burroughs (the Verger's daughter) as Britannia were HEAVEN. The words were spoken by Mrs Fuller's cook, who was draped in the Union Jack, and it was all perfect.'[170]

The prospects in early 1941 – the second year of Britain's standing alone – were terrible. While the bombing continued, the Battle of the Atlantic became ever fiercer as German U-boats stepped up their campaign to sink the convoys bringing supplies from North America. America was, as always, the key. The King and Churchill had a shared concern to draw the United States more firmly to Britain's side. Indeed that was one of Churchill's principal ambitions. It took a long time to achieve.

Churchill had warned Roosevelt as early as summer 1940 that 'the voice and force of the United States may count for nothing if they are withheld too long.'[171] But, despite Roosevelt's sympathy for the embattled democracy of Britain, it was not easy. Americans were indeed impressed by the courage of the British in resisting Hitler – the radio broadcasts of Edward R. Murrow during the Blitz gained Britain enormous admiration. But the great bulk of the American people, to say nothing of the political class, showed no enthusiasm for being dragged into another European war. When Roosevelt was re-elected in November 1940, the King wrote to say how thankful he and the Queen and all Britons were. The President replied, 'I am, as you know, doing everything possible in the way of acceleration and in the way of additional release of literally everything that we can spare.'[172] But this was provided only on the strictest commercial terms. By the end of 1940 Britain's orders were already in excess of her gold and dollar reserves, and the country had to promise to liquidate her remaining assets in the United States to guarantee future deliveries.

In January 1941 Harry Hopkins arrived in London as the personal representative of President Roosevelt. The King and Queen met him and the Queen commented that he was 'very helpful, and all out for our cause. A very nice American.'[173] Hopkins thought well of her too; they took cover together during an air raid and he wrote afterwards, 'The Queen told me that she found it extremely difficult to find words to express her feeling towards the people of Britain in these days. She thought their actions were magnificent and that victory in the long run was sure, but that the one thing that counted was the morale and determination of the great mass of the British people.'[174]

Hopkins arranged with Churchill a new basis for the purchase of American material, which was intended to make arms and supplies available to governments whose defence was considered vital to the defence of the United States. The Lend-Lease Act, passed by Congress on 11 March, gave Britain extended credit, allowing the country to buy equipment, oil and other supplies, which would not have to be paid for until the end of the war. This was as generous as the United States could be, but it meant that Britain was now, in effect, mortgaged to the United States. (The war debt was finally paid off in 2007.)

There was a renewed fear of invasion. The King talked to Churchill about the risks to his family, and to the government. The Prime Minister told him that he planned to stay in London as long as possible. The King knew that he would have to remain with the government – he could not delegate his powers. But the Queen and the Princesses would be rushed to the country.

The Queen had a frightening experience in February 1941. One evening she went into her room at the Castle and a man sprang out at her from behind the curtains and grabbed her ankles. According to her biographer, Dorothy Laird, she said afterwards, 'For a moment my heart stood absolutely still.' She understood that the man was mentally disturbed and worried that if she screamed he might attack her. So she said quietly, 'Tell me about it.' The man began to recite his troubles – he was a deserter and his family had been killed in the Blitz – and as he spoke, she moved calmly and quietly across the room to ring the bell. 'Poor man, I felt so sorry for him,' she said later. 'I realised quickly that he did not mean any harm.'[175] Harmless or not, it was an alarming breach of security. The intruder had been taken on as an electrician from the Ministry of Labour and his references had not been checked. The Office of Works gave him a pass and he was able to walk straight into the Castle, into the private rooms – and out again. Lord Wigram, who as Governor of the Castle was responsible for security, was horrified and ordered that regulations be tightened.[176]

That month the King and Queen visited Manchester after a particularly heavy air raid. She saw that the little homes which had clustered around factories had collapsed 'like packs of cards'. As always, she was impressed by the people's spirit, despite all that had happened to them.[177]

The British reaction to suffering moved Robert Menzies, the Australian Prime Minister, who paid a visit to London at this time. He stayed the night at Windsor and dined alone with the King and Queen. They impressed him. 'He shows no trace of stammer and speaks often loudly with a kind of excitement. She looks older but as fascinating as ever,' he wrote in his diary. 'She is as wise as possible and has the shrewdest estimate of all the Cabinet.'[178]

There were lighter moments. At the beginning of March 1941 the King and Queen journeyed north to visit the Scottish cities. At Glamis's tiny railway station they were pleasantly astonished to be met by a Polish guard of honour. As the King said, 'No one in their sanest moments would have thought such a thing possible a very few years ago.'[179] They lunched with General Sikorski at Forfar and inspected his troops. 'They were very nice,' the Queen told Princess Elizabeth, '& we walked along miles of coast which they are guarding. We were asked occasionally to go down what looked like a large rabbit hole, & how we did it, I don't know! But we <u>did</u>, & came out again very nearly doubled up!'[180] She was impressed by the Poles' exquisite manners: 'what with extremely good-looking young Counts and Princes loose in the countryside, I tremble for the love-stricken young ladies of North East Scotland!'[181]

While she was at Glamis, Princess Elizabeth and Princess Margaret wrote to give her the news from Windsor. There, their education continued under the care of their governess. Princess Elizabeth, now rising fifteen, was still being taught history by Henry Marten. In February 1941 Marion Crawford wrote a long letter to Queen Mary reporting on the Princesses' progress. Mr Marten, she said, tended to forget who his audience was, and would occasionally bark, 'Is that quite clear to you, gentlemen?' But he saw 'great stuff' in his pupil, and thought she could compare very well with Etonians a year older than her. She had given a very competent hour's lecture on explorers from Columbus to the present day, and had just finished a course on American history on which she had an essay to write.

Both Princesses loved playing the piano and often entertained the Household with duets, Miss Crawford wrote. She thought that Princess Margaret had developed 'wonderfully'; she was more of a companion for Princess Elizabeth, and she was 'a joy to teach – always asking questions'. The two Princesses were making excellent progress in French, and at family lunches they spoke only French to their governess. All in all, Marion Crawford assured their grandmother, 'The children are happy and well; and are having knowledge poured in as fast as I can pour it in.'[182]

At one stage the Queen became concerned lest the visits she and the King made to bombed towns were actually attracting more German attacks. On 20 March 1941 they took the train to Plymouth, which had been heavily bombed. That night as they were on the train back to London, 'the foul Germans made a very heavy attack on the town & dockyard. What brutes they are – I am certain that they first go for the working class houses, hoping to break the spirit of our people.'[183] Once back at Windsor she wrote to Lady Astor, MP for Plymouth, to say that since hearing of the bombing she had been 'thinking of you all without ceasing . . . That is one of the hard things about being King and Queen of a country that one loves so much. Every time this sort of murderous attack is made, we feel it, as if our own children were being hurt. All we can all do, is to do our very best, and leave the rest in God's hand.'[184]

The war continued badly. The German U-boats in the Atlantic sank half a million tons of British shipping in March 1941 alone. Louis Mountbatten lost his destroyer, HMS *Kelly*, in the Mediterranean during the evacuation of Crete. The cruisers *Gloucester* and *Fiji* were sunk. The Blitz continued – particularly against the ports where convoys berthed – and against London. Shortages grew worse and worse. One egg and a few ounces of meat a week were now the standard ration. Cigarettes could still be bought but alcohol was hard to find. Heating fuel and petrol for cars were short, clothing was rationed, people shivered. Even Churchill sometimes succumbed, privately, to the black dog of despair.[185]

The Balkans became a new area of great concern in the spring of 1941. Hitler demanded that Prince Paul, the Regent of Yugoslavia, allow German troops to march through Yugoslavia to subjugate Greece. Despite appeals from King George VI, the Prince felt he had

no alternative and at the end of March 1941 he signed a pact with the
Axis powers – Germany, Italy and Japan. The Germans advanced
inexorably through the Balkans and by the end of May the entire
peninsula was in fascist hands. Prince Paul and Princess Olga went into
exile first in Greece, then in Kenya, and spent the rest of the war in
South Africa; King George II of Greece escaped and, via Cairo, came
to London.

Prince Paul's conduct saddened the King and Queen, whose friend
he had been for so long. Queen Mary was shocked that he had
behaved as he did.[186] But the Queen responded that she felt sorry for
him – 'he has made such a mess of his job in the eyes of the world,
and that after struggling with immense difficulties for some very
unhappy years for himself. Of course, one knows that he is very
timorous & sensitive & subtle minded, but things have got too serious
in the world, for any country to be able to sign a pact with Germany,
& yet be pro-English or neutral. It just doesn't work & he must have
known it.'[187] To Lord Halifax in Washington she wrote, 'I am sure
that he was afraid & perhaps weak, but with all his faults I would trust
him before any of these politicians. He was always terrified of a coup
d'état, as of course it would mean the disintegration of such an
uncomfortably sham country.'[188] It was an acute observation.

Throughout this dark period, the Queen's life continued with
many visits intended to raise morale around the country. In early 1941
these included the 2nd Canadian Division, the WVS Salvage Centres
in Paddington, the American Eagle Club in Charing Cross Road,
London police stations, bombed areas of East and West Ham, New
Scotland Yard, the Red Cross, the British Legion Conference, the Staff
College at Camberley and the Royal Military Academy at Sandhurst,
the London Auxiliary Ambulance Service at County Hall, the RAF
aerodromes of Bomber Command, a battalion of the London Scottish
in Sussex, war factories in the north-east of England, the Glider
Training Squadron, the Maurice Hostel Community Club in Hoxton.

Lord Harlech, the North-Eastern Regional Commissioner for Civil
Defence, accompanied her on a visit to Sheffield, and afterwards
described it to Harold Nicolson, who reported to his wife: 'He says
that when the car stops, the Queen nips out into the snow and goes
straight into the middle of the crowd and starts talking to them. For a
moment or two they just gaze and gape in astonishment. But then
they all start talking at once. "Hi! Your Majesty! Look here!" She has

that quality of making everybody feel that they and they alone are being spoken to.'[189]

★

THROUGH ALL OF this, the relationship between Churchill and the King and Queen became ever closer. Churchill wrote to the King, 'I have greatly been cheered by our weekly luncheons in poor old bomb-battered Buckingham Palace, & to feel that in Yr. Majesty and the Queen there flames the spirit that will never be daunted by peril, nor wearied by unrelenting toil.'[190] At the lunches they digressed into subjects other than the war. The Queen had impressed Churchill by sending him the lines from Wordsworth in early 1940 and he realized the pleasure she took in the spoken and written word. He gave her a copy of H. W. Fowler's *Dictionary of Modern English Usage*, saying, 'He liberated me from many errors & doubts.'[191] She in turn found Fowler 'entrancing . . . very amusing and extremely instructive'.[192]

On 6 May 1941 Churchill came to the Palace to tell the King and Queen of an imminent operation to get more tanks and aircraft to General Wavell in Egypt. Because they were required at once, he was planning to send them by the risky route through the Mediterranean to Alexandria. On the evening of Friday 9 May, he wrote to the Queen – she had probably left for Windsor – to let her know how the operation was going. 'Madam, Tiger started with 306 [tanks]. One claw was torn away & another damaged last night. The anxiety will last for another day at least. More than half is over.'[193] She thanked him for sending news of Operation Tiger. 'Even though he lacks a claw or two, it is to be hoped that he will still be able to chew up a few enemies. Any risk was well worth taking.'[194] The King was able to record that the operation had been safely completed and that 250 tanks and fifty aircraft had arrived at Alexandria. One ship with fifty tanks on board had struck a mine and sunk in the Narrows – this was presumably the 'one claw' to which Churchill referred.[195]

On 10 May London suffered another gigantic raid by 400 bombers – on that one night almost 1,500 people were killed, 1,800 were injured, 2,000 fires were started and 11,000 houses were reduced to rubble. Both Houses of Parliament were hit, part of Waterloo station was destroyed, Bow Street Church was flattened, Westminster Abbey was damaged.[196] The Queen was outraged, and wrote to her mother-in-law, 'Alas, poor London, an even more violent & cruel raid on

Saturday night. Our beautiful national shrines and monuments – It seems such <u>sacrilege</u> that they should be destroyed by such wicked lying people as the Germans.'[197]

By June over two million British homes had been destroyed – more than half of them in London.[198] Air-raid shelters for the homeless were getting better. The Queen noticed that the bigger ones in the East End now had bunks and running water and that the social services had improved as well. But she and the King had begun to wonder 'what will happen after the war, when the people will want to go back' to areas such as Stepney which had been completely destroyed. 'Of course they were terribly overcrowded anyway, but it will be a great problem, for new houses will take time to build. There will be many very difficult moments, I feel.'[199]

What was truly astonishing was how well almost everyone coped with this continual grinding assault – in many ways everyday life continued, as normally as possible. Mail was delivered, trains ran (if not always on time), streets were swept (even more than usual), taxis plied for hire, telephones worked, restaurants stayed open and so did nightclubs, weddings were often celebrated in churches which had no roofs. Shattered shop windows were restored or boarded – as the historian Andrew Roberts has recorded, their owners even competed with cheeky slogans: 'If you think this is bad, you should see my branch in Berlin.'[200]

Hitler's attack on Russia in June 1941 was not immediately seen as the fatal error that it later proved. Indeed, as the Wehrmacht cut deep into the Soviet Union there were many who feared that another Blitzkrieg might well bring the Nazis another huge success. In summer 1941, with the vast losses in the Atlantic and the German capture of Crete, the war was going very badly for Britain.

The Queen was now able to exploit a personal link in the United States. Her youngest brother, David, was posted to the British Embassy in Washington. His mission was to create a Political Warfare Executive (PWE) in both Washington and New York. Bowes Lyon developed a good relationship with President Roosevelt as well as with the Ambassador, Lord Halifax, and was a useful, personal and independent channel of information to the King and Queen. Like every other Briton in the States he saw his task as trying to persuade the President and the American people that much more should be done to support the

British war effort. He understood the scale of the Queen's personal success during her 1939 visit to the USA with the King, and he felt that she could do more to capitalize on that. He wrote to pass on a request that she write an article for an American magazine.[201] Instead, she agreed to make a radio broadcast to the women of America; such a broadcast was diplomatically more acceptable now than it had been when first proposed in 1939 because she was able to thank the many Americans who were actively helping the war effort, not least in giving medical supplies.[202] A text was drafted, which she amended and then sent to Churchill for his advice, adding, 'I fear it is not very polished – a good deal of my own.'[203]

Churchill made suggestions, and the broadcast went out on 10 August 1941. It was effective. The Queen talked of the heavy burden being borne by the British people and of their unshakeable constancy under attack: 'hardship has only steeled our hearts and strengthened our resolution. Wherever I go, I see bright eyes and smiling faces, for though our road is stony and hard, it is straight, and we know that we fight in a great Cause.' She thanked Americans for all the help that they had already given – canteens, ambulances, medical supplies – and spoke in detail of all the tasks that women were now undertaking in the armed services, in factories, in the fields, in hospitals.

> It gives us great strength to know that you have not been content to pass us by on the other side; to us, in the time of our tribulation, you have surely shown that compassion which has been for two thousand years the mark of the Good Neighbour . . .
>
> The sympathy which inspires it springs not only from our common speech and the traditions which we share with you, but even more from our common ideals. To *you*, tyranny is as hateful as it is to us; to *you*, the things for which we will fight to the death are no less sacred; and – to my mind, at any rate – your generosity is born of your conviction that we fight to save a Cause that is yours no less than ours: of your high resolve that, however great the cost and however long the struggle, justice and freedom, human dignity and kindness, shall not perish from the earth.
>
> I look forward to the day when we shall go forward hand in hand to build a better, a kinder, and a happier world for our children. May God bless you all.[204]

President Roosevelt wrote at once to the King asking him to tell her that the broadcast was 'really perfect in every way and that it will do a great amount of good'.[205]

★

THE QUEEN'S forty-first birthday was spent at Windsor. Queen Mary sent her good wishes and her prayers for peace and victory '& that you may be given health & strength to carry on the help & comfort you have given to many since the war started. You have given so much help too, to my & your dear Bertie, help for which I shall ever be grateful as your joint loving Mama.'[206] Among her many other letters of congratulation was one from the Bishop of St Albans, who praised her and the King for the 'quiet steady lead' that they were giving the country 'in these grim but glorious days'.[207]

The Queen and her daughters were able to get to Scotland for a welcome holiday in the second half of August 1941. The King joined them a few days later; he had remained in London to see Churchill on his return from his first, secret wartime meeting with Roosevelt in Newfoundland. Churchill sailed in the new battleship *Prince of Wales*, and Roosevelt in the USS *Augusta*. They met at Placentia Bay, Newfoundland and, although they got on together splendidly, Churchill was disappointed that the President's ability to assist Britain was still restricted by the continued isolationism of Congress.

The Queen loved being in the sharp fresh air, seeing her husband and daughters relax, and walking in the hills. Within a few days she thought the Princesses were looking 'ten times better, with pink cheeks and good appetites!'[208] It felt healing to both mind and body – 'Also one stores up energy for whatever may lie ahead.'[209] Years later she recalled to her elder daughter, 'Balmoral is such a very happy house, and I remember thinking when we came up in those awful days of 1941 & 42 how clean it felt, in a way pure, & I still feel that now.'[210]

Mackenzie King, the Canadian Prime Minister, came to stay for two nights and described in his meticulous diary a lunch in a little cottage across the moors. There were no staff – the Princesses laid the table and decorated it with lettuce leaves. He found Princess Elizabeth 'very sweet' and natural in her conversation, and Margaret entertaining. 'She would cross her eyes to amuse the company. The Queen told her to stop doing that for fear they might become fixed in that position and the King had also to tell her the same.'[211]

From Balmoral they returned south to the stress and destruction. By the end of the year they were living more at Buckingham Palace – the Queen thought it was 'not too bad considering the lack of windows and general atmosphere of dust and distraction'.[212] The losses touched her, as everyone else. One of her footmen, Mervyn Weavers, who had joined the RAF, was missing. 'He went off in a Wellington, & never came back. I fear that there is little hope. Oh this cruel war, & the sorrows the German spirit has brought to so many young wives, for he was happily married.'[213] Tragedy struck the Queen's own family too. Her nephew John, Master of Glamis, son of her eldest brother Patrick, was killed in action on 19 September 1941 in Egypt, while serving with the Scots Guards.

*

The Queen was listening to the wireless in her room when she heard the news of Pearl Harbor on Sunday 7 December 1941. 'I remember going through to the King and saying "Do you know, I've just heard the most extraordinary thing on the wireless. The Japanese have bombed the Americans. It can't be true."' It was indeed true and she said later that she realized at once what it meant.[214] America would now at last enter the war.

Next day both Houses of Congress declared war on Japan, and Britain immediately did the same. Obligingly (and unnecessarily) Hitler then declared war on the United States – this was arguably his biggest single mistake of the war. The King sent a telegram of sympathy to President Roosevelt, now the leader of Britain's most important ally. 'We are proud indeed to be fighting at your side against the common enemy. We share your inflexible determination and your confidence that with God's help the powers of darkness will be overcome.'[215] American troops began to be shipped to Britain.

The King and Queen set off on the royal train for a prearranged visit to the mining villages of South Wales. En route the Queen wrote Queen Mary a long letter in which she lamented that Hitler had so far had so much more 'luck' than Britain. 'But we seem to be gradually pulling up, and if only the poor Americans keep calm & start working in earnest, we may get sufficient weapons to cope with the Germans.'

She thought it would take time for the US 'to learn total war methods, which those horrid Japanese have much used. I do feel rather sorry for them (the US), tho' they have persistently closed their eyes to such evident danger, for they are a very young and untried nation.'[216]

But there was shocking news to come. While they were in South Wales, the Queen noticed that Tommy Lascelles had been called to the telephone. She then saw him returning towards them 'with a face of doom. We thought, oh, what's happened now?'[217] Lascelles had just been told that two of Britain's principal ships, the battleship *Prince of Wales* and the battlecruiser *Repulse*, had been sunk by Japanese planes off the coast of Thailand. 'And that was a dreadful blow. I've never forgotten that,' the Queen said half a century later.[218]

The loss of these two great ships cast the country into despair. The King and Queen felt a similar sense of horror. As soon as they were back on the royal train, the King wrote to Churchill to say how shocked he and the Queen were to hear of this 'national disaster'. He went on: 'I thought I was getting immune to hearing bad news, but this has affected me deeply as I am sure it has you. There is something particularly "alive" about a big ship which gives one a sense of personal loss apart from consideration of loss of power.'[219] Many crewmen were saved but more than 800 were lost, including Admiral Sir Tom Phillips, Commander-in-Chief Eastern Fleet, Churchill's host on the voyage to Newfoundland only weeks before.

The horror of these losses killed any sense of jubilation over the entry of the United States into the war. As 1941 ended the Queen was weary. But she retained her faith in the spirit and the wisdom 'of this wonderful people of ours'. Writing a New Year's note to Queen Mary in Badminton, she said, 'I expect, that we shall have a very difficult time in this New Year, for the Americans have been caught out, and things must work up to a climax, but I do feel confident, don't you Mama? Confident in the values and good sense of the British people, & confident that good will prevail in the end. We send you every loving wish for a happier New Year, and may it help to bring victory to our cause.'[220]

CHAPTER FOURTEEN

YEARS LIKE GREAT BLACK OXEN

1942–1945

'My heart aches for our wonderful brave people'

THE SOMBRE, defensive and defiant mood of the war is caught in images of Windsor Castle. The Round Tower, Castle Hill and St George's Gate stand darkly, dramatically brooding against an ever blacker sky. These were the wartime visions of the Castle painted by the artist John Piper at the request of the Queen. His watercolours were controversial at the time but they were immediately recognized as, and remain today, an extraordinary invocation of Britain at war – the age-old fortress of the monarch standing strong against the forces of darkness.[1]

It was the bombardment of London in 1940 and 1941 that inspired the Queen's decision to have the Castle painted; she feared lest all or part of it be destroyed by the Germans. Her original idea, which she discussed with her friend Jasper Ridley, was to commission a series of watercolours 'in the manner of Sandby',[2] who had painted 200 or so watercolours of the Castle during the reign of George III. Ridley consulted Kenneth Clark and together they introduced her to the work of John Piper at an exhibition at the National Gallery.* She liked what she saw and gave him the commission. Piper was honoured and excited. In all he produced twenty-six watercolours. They were not quite what the Queen had expected – indeed they were far removed from the meticulous topographical records of Paul Sandby. But they were a remarkable body of topographical draughtsmanship, which

---

* John Piper (1903–92), British artist renowned for his landscape and architectural paintings, as well as for his abstract work. During the Second World War he was commissioned to record bomb damage in London and elsewhere, and he became an official war artist in 1944. He designed the stained-glass windows for Coventry Cathedral, built in the 1960s to replace the cathedral destroyed by bombing in the Second World War.

captured well the dark menace of the war. In the words of one art historian, 'the towers of the Castle assume an eerie quality of animation, like sentinels beneath impending apocalyptic clouds'.[3]

The Queen herself seems to have been surprised. Nonetheless, she was pleased enough to ask Piper to do a second set of drawings and Clark wrote to her to say, 'I have told Piper he must try a spring day & conquer his passion for putting grey architecture against black skies.'[4] Such advice had little effect. When the second series was finally completed, Clark had to tell the Queen that 'Black skies prevail, but the poor fellow has done his best to put in a little blue, & the general tone is less stormy.'[5] Later, the King made a joke to the artist that became famous. As they looked at the pictures together, he said, 'You seem to have had very bad luck with your weather, Mr Piper.'[6] This inspired the cartoonist Osbert Lancaster to paint a caricature of Piper sitting in the pouring rain as he drew, with the caption, 'Mr Piper enjoying his usual luck with the weather.'[7]

Whatever the Queen's original reservations may have been, she seems to have understood that she had commissioned a work of considerable importance – in the second half of her life she hung Piper's paintings prominently in her London home and showed them to visitors with evident pleasure. Moreover she remained in friendly touch with Piper and in 1968 suggested that he should be invited to design the coloured-glass windows for the King George VI Memorial Chantry at St George's Chapel.[8]

Piper's work was only one of her artistic interests. The arts flourished during the war and the Queen was as involved as she could be. Her interest was not new. It had begun with her maternal grandmother, Mrs Scott, in whose Florentine home she had stayed as a child, and who took her to the Uffizi and the Pitti Palace. By the time the war began, the Queen had been a keen collector and patron of the arts for several years. Her tastes were not avant garde but they were progressive. In 1938 she had purchased Augustus John's portrait of George Bernard Shaw; Kenneth Clark wrote to express his pleasure that she was buying the work of a living painter. 'Under Your Majesty's patronage British painters will have a new confidence, because you will make them feel that they are not working for a small clique but for the centre of the national life.'[9] In an editorial *The Times* echoed Clark's approval: 'The Queen has decided that contemporary British painting matters . . . and it will be against all experience if, according to their means, the decision is not followed by many of her subjects – to the raising of the general level of taste, and to the practical advantage of good artists.'[10]

She relied heavily, as other royal patrons have done, on the advice of a few friends and experts, in particular Jasper Ridley and Clark, who was himself considered very modern at the time. During the war he gave great help to young British painters as chairman of the War Artists Advisory Committee. He devised a project called 'Recording Britain', financed by the Pilgrim Trust, to help landscape artists who might not otherwise find work. The Queen commended his efforts and he thanked her, saying that he thought that appreciation of art had actually increased during the war, partly as a result of the Queen's own interest.[11]

In the middle of the war, she made one of her most important purchases – *Landscape of the Vernal Equinox* by Paul Nash. Ridley, who arranged the purchase, described Nash to her as the best 'intellectual' painter in England. It was a visionary painting of Wittenham Clumps, an ancient British camp in the Thames Valley, portrayed as in a dream, with the sun and moon together in the sky. Ridley commented that Nash put 'brains and ideas' into his paintings, and 'when there is a gradually discovered meaning in a picture, it has the effect of MAGIC, as you say; and magic is an agreeable and domestic relic of the old old world, which is not the same thing as the grand new world'.[12] Ridley's remarks give an insight into the Queen's own response to art – magic and a certain fey wistfulness had always been important to her. The picture kept its allure for her. 'It's a wonderful picture, imaginative and fascinating,' she said to Eric Anderson many years later. Not all of her family were so sure – Princess Margaret recalled that 'We said, poor Mummy's gone mad. Look what she's brought back. At the age of twelve we weren't, I suppose, into that sort of thing.'[13]

⋆

THE ROYAL FAMILY spent the first three weeks of 1942 at Appleton House near Sandringham. While they were there the Queen received her first ever food parcel. It was from J. P. Morgan, the American banker who had shot with them before the war. She wrote and thanked him, explaining that the cheese had caused the greatest stir and would always be most welcome as they never had any themselves, feeling it should be kept for the industrial workers. She feared that it would be a long time before they would meet again in the hills of Scotland. But 'somehow the world seems to have balanced itself better with the United States <u>in</u> the fight against evil thinking and evil doing.'[14]

Similar confidence was expressed by Churchill when he saw the King on his return from his first visit to Roosevelt since America had entered the war. The King noted in his diary that Churchill told him 'he was confident now of ultimate victory, as USA were longing to get to grips with the enemy & were starting on a full output of men & material. UK & USA were now "married" after many months of "walking out".'[15]

But it would be a long time before the marriage bore obvious fruit. The first half of 1942 was terrible for the Allies. German U-boats sank more and more American and British ships in the North Atlantic, and in February 1942 the German naval command was able to run three heavy warships, *Scharnhorst*, *Gneisenau* and *Prinz Eugen*, out of Brest and right up the Channel home into German waters, despite sustained British air assault upon them. As Churchill had predicted, worse was to come. With Malaya overrun by the Japanese, Singapore, the Far Eastern jewel in the imperial crown, surrendered to the enemy on 15 February. Eighty thousand British soldiers there were taken prisoner. The King and Queen were already feeling the effects of so much bad news. 'Bertie & I have been very tired & troubled of late,' the Queen acknowledged to her mother-in-law. But she still insisted on keeping faith: 'one must have confidence in the good sense & wonderful fighting spirit of this wonderful people of ours.'[16]

Even at the darkest moments of the war, humour remained important to her, as it did to most of the British people. Writing to Elizabeth Elphinstone, now working as a nurse in Edinburgh, about her making a trip south, she said,

> I rang up old Hitler, & quite politely asked him to make up his mind for once and all about his beastly old invasion. If he wasn't going to risk it, well & good, but if he <u>was</u> going to come, well, for goodness sake he must decide – <u>now</u>. I told him, that apart from the trouble of having to mine the beaches, and the perpetual sharpening of the Home Guards' pikes, that my niece Miss E was having her plans held up, and she really must be considered a little.

After a good deal of havering and evasions, I pinned him down to saying that the end of March was O.K., so that you will be able to come South with a clear conscience and no risk of being cut off from your hospital & kin and kith . . . I shall look forward to seeing you so <u>VERY</u> much. I am afraid that London is rather gloomy, with nobody to ring up or to go & see. Sometimes one feels quite lonely, it is so rare to see a friend, but how very exciting when one dear old face turns up![17]

There was one happy family moment that spring. Princess Elizabeth, who was nearly sixteen, was to be confirmed. Her parents asked Cosmo Lang, about to retire as Archbishop of Canterbury, to carry out the service. Lang had been publicly much criticized for his alleged 'cant' at the time of the abdication, but the Royal Family relied upon him. Queen Mary described him as 'our friend in weal & woe'.[18] The service, on 28 March in the Private Chapel at Windsor Castle, was simple and touching. The family were all moved by the young Princess taking her solemn vows before the old Archbishop. The Queen thought Lang was 'wonderful, so straightforward and so inspiring', and was sad that this would be his last appearance at a family festival.[19]

On Easter Sunday the Princess took her First Communion. She walked with her parents, on 'a deliciously clear early morning', from Royal Lodge to the Royal Chapel, the little church just beyond the garden. Then they came home to breakfast. 'It was so nice to be together & quiet after these years of war & turmoil & perpetual anxiety, for even a few moments of true peace,' the Queen wrote to Queen Mary. She said that she had learned that 'peace is only of the mind really. If only we can bring a true peace to this poor suffering world after this War is over, well, all the anguish & sorrow will have been worth while.'[20]

Much as the Queen regretted the departure of Cosmo Lang, so long both friend and spiritual adviser, it was at this time that she began to find a kindred spirit in Edward Woods, the Bishop of Lichfield. He was to become, in the words of a member of her family, 'her personal Bishop' for many years, and he helped both her and the King with speeches. In early May 1942 he came to preach at Windsor and stayed with the King and Queen for the weekend. 'We talked on many subjects & he has got the right ideas,' the King recorded in his diary;[21] afterwards Bishop Woods wrote to the Queen saying he had been impressed by her interest in prayer and healing, and would send her some of his writings on the subject. He agreed with her about 'the need of an occasional "retreat" or quiet day, in which to <u>recover</u> one's soul & spiritual balance'.[22]

The place of God in this war was, of course, a matter of anxious debate, at least among committed Christians like the Queen. Later in the year Woods recommended that she read Romans 8,* 'that never failing fount of comfort & strength'. He thought that all the suffering of the war would be utterly unbearable 'unless one cd be sure – and every Christian <u>can</u> be sure – that God is down in the midst of it all, & that out of all this raw material of evil He is creating something good'.[23] The Queen agreed with this. She believed, like many, that the war between Britain and Germany was between a nation that was still fundamentally Christian and one which had abandoned faith for godless 'materialism'. The horrors of fascism showed what could happen when a great nation forsook the teachings of Christ. She had always found both strength and comfort in prayer; the suffering and the fears of war made her, and the King, more devout. It was not unusual. Churches were much fuller during the war than they had been in the late 1930s.

The Queen worried about the divine purpose constantly and she prayed every day. She continued to correspond with the Bishop of Lichfield on private spiritual matters as well as on the broader subject that preoccupied them both – how to renew the influence of Christianity in the life of the nation, and particularly through education.[†] He sent her many books. In one of his letters to her Woods wrote, 'I think many people are needlessly fearful about the Church "interfering in politics", hardly perhaps realising that, if Christianity is <u>true</u>, then it must affect – and <u>redeem</u> – a man's environment, the whole framework of his life, as well as his "soul".'[24] It was a view which she shared.

Disasters continued. The Japanese swept the Allies out of the Philippines and the South Pacific, they captured Burma and they

---

* This is the chapter which includes the well-known verses: 'Who shall separate us from the love of Christ? Shall tribulation, or distress, or persecution, or famine, or nakedness, or peril, or sword? . . . For I am persuaded that neither death, nor life, nor angels, nor principalities, nor powers . . . shall be able to separate us from the love of God which is in Christ Jesus our Lord.' (Romans 8:35, 38–9)

† Most of her letters to Edward Woods were unfortunately lost in the 1980s in a fire.

positioned themselves at the gates of India. At the end of April 1942 the Luftwaffe began a series of attacks on England's heritage which became known as the Baedeker Raids. These bombing assaults were directed at such historic towns as Exeter, Bath, Norwich, York and Canterbury – ancient towns which had no war industries and which were targets only for cultural assault.

Over 1,500 people were killed in these raids; the King and Queen were outraged by the destruction.[25] Visiting Exeter after two nights of bombing, they walked through the ruins of one of the oldest cities in England; it had been hit on two separate nights, the main street was smashed to pieces, three historic buildings, five churches, St Luke's College and the old City Hospital (built in 1700) were demolished, and so were at least 2,000 houses.[26]

Their visit to Bath made a considerable impression upon a young schoolboy, Raymond Leppard, who later became an international conductor and a friend of Queen Elizabeth. They went all around Bath, he wrote, 'climbing over rubble, talking to everyone, unguarded and caringly sympathetic'. Leppard was serving meals at an improvised soup kitchen for the homeless and saw the 'magical and powerful' effect they had. 'At that moment they were the symbol of the spirit of England and people's contact with it uplifted hearts and the triumph of good was assured.'[27] With Queen Mary they watched a demonstration of a tank battle by the Guards Armoured Division; the Queen was impressed, but was reminded of the realities of warfare. 'I cannot bear to think what they must be going through in Libya, fighting this terrible battle in the burning heat,' she wrote.[28]

One of the Queen's regiments, the Queen's Bays, was deployed in North Africa. It had arrived in the desert in December 1941 and suffered considerable losses of men and tanks when trying to stem Rommel's advance north of Jedabya at the end of January 1942. From there, Lieutenant Colonel Tom Draffen wrote to Arthur Penn with news for the Queen of their actions and casualties. Penn wrote back saying that the Queen shared their sorrow over the dead, and anxiety for the missing. She regularly wore the regimental brooch which the officers had given her and 'She charges me to send you all every possible good wish and to assure you of her constant thoughts.'[29]

At the beginning of June 1942 they were in Scotland; the King inspected the fleet and the Queen went to the Palace of Holyroodhouse which had had its windows broken, but no worse, by nearby bombing. They then spent two days on the royal train in Cambridge-shire visiting RAF stations.

They were able to relax at the Oaks and the Derby, being run at Newmarket, and the King was delighted that his filly Sun Chariot won the Oaks. But the Derby was a disappointment. His runner, Big Game, was described by the Queen as 'such a beautiful & kindly disposed animal, as well as a good race horse!' but he faded.[30]

That month there was another disaster in North Africa – the strategic Libyan port of Tobruk, which had been captured by British forces in January 1941, fell after a week's siege. Rommel was then able to push eastwards to Egypt. The news reached Britain on a perfect summer's day; the King was depressed and worried about what it would mean for all the British troops deployed there.[31]

At the end of June the King and Queen made an official visit to Ulster where they stayed with their friends, the Duke and Duchess of Abercorn. At Harland and Wolff's shipyard they were mobbed by a boisterous, happy crowd.[32] The next day came a visit to a new and vital installation – the United States army camp near Ballykinler. There they saw some of the troops who had been shipped across the ocean since the attack on Pearl Harbor. They were impressed by the charm and intelligence of the officers and by their excellent equipment, especially 'a remarkable little portable wireless sending and receiving set, which they call a "walkie talkie"'.[33]

Back in England the Queen made more visits to war-related organizations, including the Red Cross, the ATS units in South-East Command (where she was pleased by the improvement in morale since the year before),[34] the Royal Military College at Sandhurst, the Clothing Branch of the Officers' Families Fund at the Royal School of Needlework (an organization in which she had a lifelong interest). In North Wales she and the King visited aircraft factories and steelworks and saw the oak tree in which King Charles had hidden at Boscobel. In Lichfield they visited the Cathedral and had tea with the Queen's new mentor, the Bishop Edward Woods. She was pleased to discover that he had three sons in the Church.[35]

That summer, her goddaughter Elizabeth, Doris and Clare Vyner's daughter, who had just joined the Wrens, died after a harrowing two-week struggle with meningitis. Both the King and Queen wrote the Vyners heartfelt letters of condolence.[36] Then on 25 August 1942 came a family tragedy.

The King and Queen were at Balmoral. That day the weather was appalling and in the evening while they were dining with their guests the King was called to the telephone. He came back to the table in clear distress and passed a card to the Queen on which he had written in pencil, 'Darling, what shall we do about ending dinner? I am afraid George has been killed flying to Iceland. He left Invergordon at 1.30 pm & hit a mountain near Wick.'[37] The Queen caught the eye of the Duchess of Gloucester, who was sitting next to the King, and signalled her to rise with the other ladies and leave the room. 'In the drawing room,' the Duchess said later, 'we all assumed the news must be of Queen Mary's death . . . Then the Queen left us and came back with the King who told us that it was the Duke of Kent who had been killed.'[38]

The war had brought out the best in the Duke. He had asked to be given military duties, and was created an air commodore in the Royal Air Force. His task was to oversee and inspect RAF facilities both at home and abroad. In 1941 he had visited the Canadian flying schools which were training pilots for the defence of Britain, and had journeyed also to the United States where President and Mrs Roosevelt were charmed by him. On the day he died he was aboard a Sunderland flying boat bound from Invergordon to an RAF base in Iceland. The plane should not have taken off in such poor conditions. Flying too low in thick fog it hit the top of a hill on the Duke of Portland's Langwell estate. All sorts of conspiracy theories have since been attached to the Duke's death but it seems to have been a simple case of pilot error.

The King and Queen were both distraught. The King confided to his diary that, at the funeral four days later in St George's Chapel, he had great difficulty in preventing himself from breaking down. No other family funeral had affected him so much.[39] The Queen knew that she too would miss the Duke greatly. She thought of him more as a brother than a brother-in-law – 'I could talk to him about many family affairs for he had a quick & sensitive mind & a very good & useful social sense, & we had a great many jokes too.'[40] To her brother David in Washington, she wrote that the Duke's death was 'such a dreadful waste, and he was doing such very good work, and becoming so helpful to Bertie. We shall miss him very much.'[41]

A real question now was how best to help the Duke's widow, Princess Marina. The King, trying to assuage her grief, arranged for her sister, Princess Olga of Yugoslavia, then in exile in South Africa with her husband Prince Paul, to come and stay with Princess Marina at her home, Coppins, in Buckinghamshire. This was far from simple because Prince Paul was now regarded as a man who had collaborated with the Germans. Both women were grateful.[42]

Queen Mary was especially affected – George was her favourite son. She was moved to receive a 'most dear telegram' from her eldest son, the Duke of Windsor, asking for details of what had happened.[43] She replied in an eight-page letter, the first lines of which illustrated her deep sorrow: 'Most darling David, In this terrible hour of grief at the passing of our darling precious Georgie, my thoughts go out to you, who are so far away from us all, knowing how devoted you were to him.' At the end of this letter she wrote, 'I send a kind message to your wife who will help you to bear your sorrow.'[44]

The Duke replied by hand, and when his mother saw his writing after so many years, she 'gave a gasp of pleasure', she told him.[45] He thanked her for her sweet letter and said that but for Wallis's love and comfort he would have felt very lost. Apparently still unable to comprehend the evil against which Britain was fighting, he said he thought George's death had brought home 'the utter useless cruelty of this ghastly war'. He still had the 'deep-rooted conviction' that it could have been avoided, but he realized that it could not now end until German plans for world domination had been frustrated. He was greatly pained by the six-year split with his mother and he still hoped that it could be mended and that he could bring Wallis to see her. 'I can never begin to tell you how intensified has become our great love for each other in the five years we have been married.'[46]

To his brother the King, the Duke wrote more harshly about the King's 'attitude' towards him. He added of their mother, 'She is certainly a most courageous and noble person and it is hard that in her later years, she should have yet another great and bitter blow to bear. Her fortitude is indeed an example to us all.'[47] The King sent this letter to their mother; Queen Mary copied out these words and added, 'I think this was very touching & nice of David.'[48]

Queen Mary, happy that 'the ice has at last been broken', was optimistic that the family crisis was finally past and that relations with the Duke could be more amiable in future.[49] However, within a few weeks, the Duke had written to the Prime Minister to ask once more that the title of HRH be 'restored' to his wife.[50] Churchill consulted

42. The Duke and Duchess visiting the shipyard building the RMS *Duchess of York*, 1928.

43. The Duchess receiving an honorary D.Litt. at the University of Oxford in 1931.

44. The Duke and Duchess with the Black Watch at Glamis in 1935.
She was appointed colonel-in-chief at the time of the Coronation in 1937.

45. Laying a wreath at the Cenotaph on Armistice Day, 1931.

46. With disabled veterans of the First World War in June 1932.

47. The Duchess with Girl Guides and Brownies in Stepney in 1933.

48. The Duchess in January 1935, lighting lamps for new branches of Toc H, the charity of which she was patron for over seventy years.

49. The Duchess playing with Princess Elizabeth in the sandpit at Glamis.

51. The Duchess in the uniform of the St John Ambulance Brigade, of which she was commandant-in-chief from 1937.

50. The Duchess, the Princesses and the Duchess of Kent, at St Paul's Cathedral for the service celebrating the Silver Jubilee of King George V on 9 May 1935.

52. The Duchess with the Princesses on the steps at Birkhall.

53. Sir Oswald Birley's portrait of the Windsor Wets. Seated, left to right: the
Earl of Airlie, Sir Reginald Seymour, the Duke of Devonshire, the Duke of Beaufort,
the Duke of Rutland, the Earl of Erne, the Hon. Sir Richard Molyneux; standing behind,
left to right: the Earl of Eldon, the Duke of Norfolk, the Earl of Halifax. Standing behind
the screen, the Countess of Eldon. The coat with the scarlet collar and cuffs worn by six
of the men is the Windsor uniform, introduced by George III in 1779. The portraits on the
wall behind are of the Duke of York, the Duchess of York and the Duchess of Beaufort.

54. The Duke, Duchess and the Princesses on a family holiday.

55. Wallis Simpson and the Duke of Windsor in April 1937 shortly before their wedding.

56. The new King and Queen on the balcony at Buckingham Palace after their coronation on 12 May 1937. Left to right: Queen Elizabeth, Princess Elizabeth, Queen Mary, Princess Margaret, King George VI.

57. The Queen with her train bearers, left to right: Lady Iris Mountbatten, Lady Margaret Bentinck, Lady Ursula Manners, Lady Diana Legge, Lady Elizabeth Percy and Lady Elizabeth Paget.

58. The Queen, photographed in July 1939 by Cecil Beaton.

the King, who wrote to his mother that he thought it was impossible 'to reverse a decision taken with much thought only 6 years ago. Elizabeth agrees with this too. Time is a great healer we know but this is not the moment I feel to rake up the past. This worry coming on top of all one's other work is too bad.'[51] Queen Mary agreed with the King and Queen that 'this tiresome question' of the Duchess's title should not be raised again.[52]

The strain of these weeks told upon the Queen. After the Duke of Kent's funeral she returned to Balmoral and took to her bed with a bad cold which developed into bronchitis; she had to cancel all her engagements for several weeks. The Queen was broad minded in her choice of medical treatment. Since her marriage she had, under the influence of Dr John Weir, come to share the Royal Family's faith in homeopathy. Throughout her life she would hand out arnica tablets to anyone with a bruise or worse. She described the homeopathic philosophy thus to Osbert Sitwell: 'the approach to illness is intelligent and each individual is treated as a person & not only as an interesting case of so and so. If it comes off, the treatment seems very successful, but of course it can be rather slow.'[53] Not everyone at Court was persuaded about the success of Dr Weir's methods. Tommy Lascelles wrote of him, 'I've known him now for over twenty years, and at one time allowed him to dose me with some of his curious little powders. I like him as a man; as a healer of the sick, how much of him is Aesculapius and how much Quack, I have never been able to determine.'[54]

The Queen was not dogmatic about homeopathy; she also accepted the advances of modern medicine. In one of her wartime bouts of tonsillitis, Dr Miles of Forfar, in whom she had confidence, gave her a new drug, M&B, which, she said, 'eats up the bad germs like lightning'.[55]*

In September 1942 Mrs Ronnie Greville died. She had good qualities and remarkable energy, but her snobbery, her anti-Semitism and her partiality for Hitler in the 1930s had made her many enemies.

---

* The Second World War saw an acceleration in medical science. M&B was first produced by the firm May & Baker in 1936 – it was the first effective antibiotic that could be used for a variety of infections, including sore throat and pneumonia. It was mass produced during the war. Churchill was prescribed it in 1943 and announced, 'This admirable M&B, from which I did not suffer any inconvenience, was used at the earliest moment and after a few weeks' fever the intruders were repulsed.'

She had been a generous friend to the King and Queen for almost twenty years and the Queen admired her tenacity. She told Osbert Sitwell: 'I shall miss her very much indeed, (as I know you will, for she was truly devoted to you), she was so shrewd, so kind, so amusingly unkind, so sharp, such fun, so naughty . . . and altogether a real person, a character, utterly Mrs Ronald Greville and no tinge of anything alien.'[56] Sitwell wrote to the Queen to describe Mrs Greville's funeral at Polesden Lacey – he found it a sad occasion, because she had no near relations. The Queen, touched by Sitwell's letter, remembered all the long-ago, carefree weekends at the house – 'they seem so far off and delectable.'[57]

A few days later the Queen learned to her surprise that, while leaving Polesden Lacey to the National Trust, Mrs Greville had left her jewellery to her – including a magnificent diamond necklace that was said to have belonged to Marie Antoinette. She had also left £20,000 to Princess Margaret.[58] The Queen was very touched by her bequest from 'the dear old thing', she told Queen Mary, admitting that she admired beautiful stones – 'I can't help thinking that most women do!'[59] Her mother-in-law was not above a tease, and responded that no one had ever left her such jewellery, 'but I am not really jealous, I just mention this as it came into my mind!'[60]*

Resting in bed at Balmoral was in a way welcome – 'the first time that I have been laid aside in peace & quiet since the war. I needed it very badly, & it was heaven seeing nobody at all except a nice tactful nurse & a Scottish doctor or two.'[61] At the end of September, Dr Weir recommended another fortnight convalescing. She clearly needed it – and wrote to Arthur Penn that she had 'narrowly escaped death from the antidote to pneumonia'.[62]

While she was unwell, she read widely. Alongside her abiding love of P. G. Wodehouse, who always cheered her up, she was now also much taken with Damon Runyon – indeed she and Arthur Penn appreciated Runyonesque repartee. In one letter to him she showed that she was on the road to recovery; thanking him for a book, she

---

* Mrs Greville also left Osbert Sitwell £10,000, which made him feel 'very rich'. A few months after her death he returned to Polesden Lacey to visit Aline, her old French maid who still lived there. He reported to the Queen that the rest of Mrs Greville's staff, known to him and her at least as 'the Crazy Gang', had been disbanded, but that they had 'brought off a big coup with the sale of Mrs Ronnie's cellar – an appropriate finale'. (Osbert Sitwell to Queen Elizabeth, [18] April 1943, RA QEQM/PRIV/PAL/Sitwell)

wrote, 'The author definitely knows his potatoes, and I think the whole story is absolutely the berries. The way that dame Pearl gets a ripple on, there was a baby for you – oh boy.'[63]

Books were always companions, and others that she enjoyed during the war included some by Robert Louis Stevenson, William Beckford's *Travels* and 'heavenly stories' by F. Marion Crawford, a nineteenth-century American author of adventure novels. She was not impressed by a few unidentified 'horrid modern books by horrid journalists'.[64] She exchanged books with Tommy Lascelles – he sent her one of Eric Ambler's thrillers, *Epitaph for a Spy*, and she lent him *Sir Richard Burton's Wife* by the explorer's great-niece, Jean Burton.[65] Osbert Sitwell sent her the typescript of the first volume of his autobiography. The Queen told him she loved it and it had done her the world of good – 'I immediately felt better after the first chapter, & called for a steak half way through the second, and have never looked back since.'[66]

Following the daily news of the war, she wrote to the King, 'It is really terrible what the Germans are doing now in Europe, they seem to have lost every vestige of decent behaviour . . . their true nature is coming out. Beasts.' She thought the German treatment of Allied prisoners at Dieppe was 'pure barbarism' but it was a great mistake for the British to indulge in any tit-for-tat behaviour.* 'Because they murder & rob, is no reason why we should follow their bad example. I was very distressed when I read it in the paper.'[67]

*

LIKE WINSTON CHURCHILL, the King and Queen both knew that nothing was more vital to Britain than the United States. General de Gaulle claimed that Churchill had once told him that he woke up every morning wondering how that day he could please President Roosevelt.[68] At the end of their American visit in summer 1939, the King and Queen had invited the Roosevelts to visit Britain. But the impetus for a trip came from the President himself. Sumner Welles, the Under Secretary of State, told Lord Halifax that the President

---

* An Allied raid on the German-occupied port of Dieppe in northern France in August 1942, carried out by a largely Canadian force, was a disastrous failure, with more than half of the 6,000 raiders either killed, wounded or captured. An Allied battle plan, discovered by the Germans, proposed that German prisoners should be shackled. Hitler gave orders that the same be done to Canadian prisoners. In retaliation, Churchill ordered that German POWs in Canada be shackled. Both orders were soon rescinded.

would like his wife to go to Britain to see as much as possible of the work of the Women's Voluntary Service. They asked for an invitation to be extended by the Queen. She quickly sent a formal message to Mrs Roosevelt saying, 'The King and I would be so pleased if you would care to pay a visit to England in the near future to see something of the varied war activities in which the women of Great Britain are now engaged.'[69]

The visit was fixed for the middle of October 1942, but to the Queen's embarrassment it had to be delayed because of her illness.[70] She finally returned from the peaceful beauty of the Highlands to the grime of wartime London on the night of 19 October. Writing to Queen Mary to tell her of Mrs Roosevelt's imminent arrival, she said, 'The whole affair is such a deadly secret owing to the flying risk'; she hoped the President's wife could spend a night with Queen Mary at Badminton. 'It is so dreary at Buckingham Palace, so dirty & dark and draughty,' and she felt very sorry for the housekeeper and the maids who had to keep a half-ruined house halfway presentable.[71] She decided to lend Mrs Roosevelt her own bedroom; she had had some small sheets of isinglass put into the window frames whose larger panes had been blown out. The preparations showed her that it was quite difficult putting up even a single guest in the Palace at this time. Fortunately Mrs Roosevelt travelled very simply, with just one secretary.[72]

The President's wife was delayed by bad weather, and finally arrived in London on 23 October; the King and Queen met her at Paddington station and took her to tea at the Palace with the Princesses. Eleanor Roosevelt found Princess Elizabeth 'very attractive, quite serious, with a good deal of character. She asked a great deal of questions about life' in the United States.[73] Mrs Roosevelt was far from demanding, but she was shocked by the conditions in which Britons had to live, even in the Palace. The Queen showed her to her rooms and Mrs Roosevelt observed the draughts, the lack of window panes and the black line painted around the bath showing just how little water was allowed to be drawn. In her diary she wrote that the Palace was 'an enormous place and without heat. I do not see how they keep the dampness out.'[74]

That night the King and the Queen gave a dinner for her – the Churchills, Lord Woolton, the Minister of Food, General Smuts and the Mountbattens were among the guests. Woolton told her that the indifferent food – fishcakes, cold chicken and ham with salad and two vegetables – was much the same as would be found in any house in England, and would have shocked the King's grandfather. Mrs Roosevelt did note, however, that it was served on gold and silver plate.[75]

The food may not have been memorable but there was a great air of excitement at the Palace that evening. General Montgomery had that day launched at El Alamein the offensive that would eventually destroy German power in North Africa. The Prime Minister was understandably distracted. Even the showing of the new Noël Coward film, *In Which We Serve*, a hymn to the courage of the navy based on Louis Mountbatten's command of HMS *Kelly*, did not divert him. He was, according to Tommy Lascelles, 'like a cat on hot bricks' waiting for news from the desert battlefield;[76] he finally telephoned 10 Downing Street himself and, on hearing that the initial reports were favourable, came back to the party singing 'Roll Out the Barrel' with great enthusiasm and rather less sense of tune.[77] Britain's first victory in three years of warfare was close at hand.

Next day the King and Queen took their American visitor to a lunch attended by heads of British women's services and organizations. Conscription of women under thirty had been introduced at the end of 1941 – they were allowed to choose between the auxiliary services and industrial jobs. The mobilization had been remarkable: according to figures sent to the Queen subsequently by Ernest Bevin, the Minister of Labour and National Service, fully 90 per cent of single women between the ages of eighteen and forty were now employed in industry, civil defence or the forces and the corresponding figure for married women with children under fourteen was no less than 76 per cent.[78]

That afternoon the King and Queen took their guest by car to see St Paul's Cathedral and many of the bomb-damaged areas in the City and East End of London. Eleanor Roosevelt was stunned. London, she said, 'is flat for blocks'. She realized that parts of the world's common heritage had been destroyed, but most shocking of all to her were the countless homes which had been razed.

The following day Mrs Roosevelt left the Palace to embark on an arduous tour of Britain, both to visit American camps and airfields and to see how the British were facing the hardship of war in factories and bombed towns all over the country, talking to hundreds of people. She had a sense of the cold, of the shortages, of the blackout and, particularly extraordinary to an American, of the terrifying nearness of the enemy. It was 'a curious feeling', she said, to stand at Dover and see the enemy lines just a few miles across the Channel. She was struck by English stoicism and enthusiasm and by how everyone contributed to one goal – victory. She found enormous gratitude for American help and *everyone*, she said, was welcoming to American soldiers.[79]

Mrs Roosevelt travelled extensively, and visited Queen Mary at Badminton. 'I liked her, she is so nice & very intelligent, has a wonderful grasp of things & is evidently impressed at what our women are doing – what a good thing she came over to see things for herself,' wrote Queen Mary.[80] Lascelles commented of the President's wife, 'she looks like a she-camel, and is tough; but I like her, and see dignity, even greatness in her.'[81] The Queen thought her guest charming, understanding of and sympathetic to 'our ideals & difficulties'.[82]

There was only one minor irritation provoked by Mrs Roosevelt's visit: she tried – and failed – to persuade the Queen to grant an interview to a friend of hers who was also in London, Mrs Bruce Gould, of the American magazine, *Ladies' Home Journal*. The Foreign Office supported the idea with vigour but the Queen had no such wish. Tommy Lascelles wrote succinctly in his diary that Americans failed to recognize the unique position of the King and Queen. It would be no more appropriate for them to give interviews than it would be for the Pope to go to a race meeting, or the President to a bawdy house. He thought the British public had no time for a 'chatty' monarch – indeed that was why Edward VIII could never have made a good king.[83]

Back in the White House Mrs Roosevelt gave a press conference in which she said she had been greatly impressed by the fact that in Britain 'there is only one thing in everyone's mind, and that is "we are fighting the war",' whereas in America there was much less pressure. She also noted how standards of living had fallen for everyone; 'for instance, in Buckingham Palace, they will not light a fire in the fireplace until December 1st. That's the uniform rule.'[84] The war, she thought, was changing Britain fundamentally and it would never be able to 'go back to the old system. The change is in the whole old social scale. Certain types of living will never be possible again. The people are now working side by side, getting to know each other well, as they never did before, from all classes.' She thought the length of the war still to come depended on how much Americans were prepared to sacrifice to help.[85]

Lascelles sent a transcript of this press conference to the Queen, who thought that her guest had drawn 'quite a good & sober picture of this incredibly gallant country'. Mrs Roosevelt, she thought, had wisely understated the hardships and sacrifices because she did not want to appear too pro-British.[86]

★

ON TUESDAY 3 NOVEMBER the Prime Minister was due at the Palace for his weekly lunchtime discussion with the King and Queen. Churchill endeavoured not to be late for his King, but this lunchtime he was delayed and, the Queen later told his daughter Mary, the King became irritated.[87] Eventually the Prime Minister arrived at the Palace, carrying before him a red dispatch box. He strode towards the King, bowed and made an extraordinary announcement. 'He said', the King recorded in his diary, ' "I bring you victory." '[88] The Queen was astonished. 'I remember we looked at each other,' said the Queen later, 'and we thought, "Is he going mad?" ' She added, 'We had not heard that word since the war began.'[89]

Churchill knew what he was saying. The King was overjoyed by the contents of the dispatch box. He wrote in his diary that night that it contained two top-secret intercepted 'Boniface' radio signals from Rommel to Hitler.★ In these messages, wrote the King, 'Rommel gave Hitler a very depressing account of the battle in Egypt from his point of view. He was greatly outnumbered by troops & tanks & armoured vehicles, & was short of petrol & ammunition in the forward areas & in the rear areas there was none . . . This is very good news . . . What rejoicing there will be.'[90]

★ 'Boniface' was the word used by Churchill and his circle for intelligence derived from the top-secret decryption of German communications. Much of the German cipher traffic was encrypted on Enigma machines, one of which had been handed to the British by Polish intelligence shortly after the outbreak of war; it was used by the decoders at Bletchley Park in Buckinghamshire. Enigma decrypts, one of the most important secret achievements of the war, were later called Ultra. General Dwight D. Eisenhower, the western Supreme Allied Commander, later described Ultra as being 'decisive' to Allied victory. The secret was kept until 1974 when F. W. Winterbotham published the first history of the codebreaking, *The Ultra Secret*.

Whether or not the Queen was privy to the closely guarded and vital secrets about British decryption of German messages cannot be known. It may be doubted that they were revealed to her. But they were revealed to the King, and he took her into his confidence on almost every matter during the war. Indeed, given the closeness of their relationship it would have been strange if he had not done so. Long afterwards, when asked if she had shared the King's wartime burdens and whether he had told her much, she replied, 'Oh yes, he told me everything. Well one had to, you see, because you couldn't not, in a way. There was only us there. So obviously he had to tell one things. But one was so dreadfully discreet, that even now I feel nervous sometimes, about talking about things. You know, you knew something and you couldn't say a word about it, when you heard people talking absolute nonsense.'[91]

Next day, 4 November 1942, the King received another welcome telegram. General Alexander, Commander-in-Chief, Middle East, cabled Churchill that after twelve days of heavy & violent fighting the Eighth Army had inflicted a heavy defeat on Rommel's forces at El Alamein. Churchill sent Alexander's telegram to the King, who pinned it into his diary, in which he wrote that day: 'A Victory at last. How good it is for the nerves.'[92] That night, when a BBC announcer interrupted programming to advise listeners that the best news for years would be broadcast at midnight, his voice was said to be trembling with excitement.[93]

Alamein was a catharsis. But of course the thousands of personal tragedies continued. That same day the Queen had to send condolences to her friends the Halifaxes in Washington – their son Peter had been killed in the fighting in Egypt.[94] Dorothy Halifax thanked her for her sympathy and, with the stoicism which so many people displayed during the war, replied, 'We now rejoice with Your Majesties at the good news of the battle in Egypt in which Peter was allowed to play a small part.'[95]

When the scale of the victory at El Alamein was confirmed and the success of American and British landings in Morocco and Algeria – Operation Torch – became clear, Churchill warned against euphoria. 'Now this is not the end. It is not even the beginning of the end. But it is, perhaps, the end of the beginning.'[96] Some rejoicing was called for and the government ordered that church bells, silenced since June 1940, be rung in celebration. Nothing symbolized better the renewal of hope than the bells pealing from towers and spires in every parish of the land.

In 1943 Stalin began to inflict serious defeats upon the Germans in Russia. Britain and America made more and more progress in North Africa. On 4 February, General Alexander sent his celebrated telegram to the Prime Minister: 'SIR, The orders you gave me on August 15, 1942 have been fulfilled. His Majesty's enemies, together with their impedimenta, have been completely eliminated from Egypt, Cyrenaica, Libya and Tripolitana. I now await your further instructions.'[97] The next instruction was to inflict total defeat on the Axis forces still in Africa. This was finally achieved with the surrender of the last-remaining enemy troops on 13 May 1943. 'It is an overwhelming victory,' wrote the King.[98]

The Queen was both infected and a little concerned by the new optimism. 'I am sure that this year is going to be a difficult one,' she wrote to Osbert Sitwell, 'because everyone is expecting so much. I am always a little alarmed when a sense of optimism sweeps the country, tho' I have infinite trust in the level heads of the Britons who live in these Islands.' She was more concerned about the perhaps inevitable disagreements between Britain and her allies. She had appreciated the 'arm-stretching sensation of freedom and independence' of the terrifying days when Britain was alone in 1940. Now she was 'conscious of a closing in of too many countries with all their jealousies, bitternesses, & unintelligent criticisms, and yet this must be a wrong feeling, for it is so very important to keep together & work together to win the peace.'[99]

Relationships among the Allies were certainly changing and not to Britain's advantage. At the Casablanca meeting with Roosevelt in January 1943, Churchill persuaded the American President that the cross-Channel invasion of Europe would have to be postponed till 1944, and in the meantime the Mediterranean campaign should be emphasized, with an invasion of Sicily. From now on the overwhelming might of America and the increasing power of Russia combined to diminish British influence among the 'Big Three'.[100]

The Queen continued her visits to places, people and institutions involved in the war effort, often with the King, sometimes alone. At the end of January they visited aerodromes around Norwich. They found it an interesting day, much less formal than usual, the King noted in his diary. They listened as four pilots were briefed for a mission over Holland in low-flying Typhoons and then watched them take off. Fog forced them back. At Ludham they met No. 167 Squadron, '& while we were there one of the pilots returned having just shot down his first Junkers 88. We were all thrilled but he was quite calm.'[101]

As the Allies made progress in different theatres on the ground, so the Luftwaffe attacks on Britain were stepped up again. The Queen was appalled – 'They are dropping bombs just <u>anywhere</u>.' On 4 February 1943 she visited Lewisham Hospital to see the children who had survived an attack on a school; she took them some bananas that Lord Louis Mountbatten had brought from Casablanca for her daughters.* The sight of these children touched and horrified her. 'It made me all the more determined to beat those unspeakable Huns, to see those little faces, so good and so hurt for the sake of Nazi propaganda. I grind my teeth with rage. But it happens every day – pure murder.'[102] On another occasion, she recalled later, she met a woman in the East End 'leaning on what was left of her little gate. The house in fact had gone behind her. And she said to me, "We're not going to be done in by that there 'itler." I remember it quite vividly.'[103]

In recent months the Queen, like many others, had become more and more aware of the scale of Nazi evil. The German regime had, since January 1942, institutionalized and quickened their attempt to liquidate all the Jews in Europe. The precise plans were secret, but Hitler publicly made his intentions clear.† He had told a huge crowd of cheering supporters in Berlin that the result of the war would be 'the complete annihilation of the Jews'.[104]

News of these diabolical efforts had begun to emerge in the course of 1942. In early December the Queen received a telegram from several women's organizations in Jerusalem, imploring her to use her influence to awaken the conscience of the world and help save the Jewish people from extinction by the 'Nazi Moloch'. At the same time

---

* The Matron at Lewisham Hospital wrote to thank the Queen for her visit and added that she 'would also like to thank the Princesses for their very generous gift of bananas, and to say how much the children enjoyed them, even little "Betty" who had never seen a banana before.' (RA QEQMH/PS/ENGT/1943: 4 February)

† In January 1942 the Nazi leadership had secretly devised plans for the more systematic destruction of the Jews. The minutes of this conference held at Lake Wannsee near Berlin survive – replete with such euphemisms as 'evacuating the Jews to the East' and 'dealt with appropriately'.

Harriet Cohen, CBE, a well-known concert pianist, wrote requesting the Queen's intercession on behalf of 'the (entire) European Jews – children old people & men & women; 5,000,000 of whom, by Xmas – i.e. in three weeks time will be exterminated in the Abattoirs, the slaughter-houses (literally) in Poland'. She pointed out that 'If a whole race can be exterminated it means there can be no truth in what we are fighting for. Will Your Majesty use Your Loving Interest, that Maternal Kindness for which your Subjects literally adore Your Majesty, to intercede with the King's Ministers – and the world's Rulers (Allied & Neutral) for the Jews.'[105] There is no record of what action the Queen took in response to this particular request. But she had become increasingly appalled by German conduct. In October 1942 she had written to Queen Mary, 'Is it not terrible the way the Germans are behaving all over Europe. The mask is off at last, & the true savagery is emerging.'[106]

In December 1942 the government published, with its American and Soviet counterparts, a Joint Declaration condemning 'in the strongest possible terms' what it described as 'this bestial policy of cold-blooded extermination'. In Parliament on 17 December the Foreign Secretary Anthony Eden read out the Declaration himself, stating that he regretted having to inform the House that Jews in occupied Europe were being subjected to 'barbarous and inhuman treatment'. The House then stood in a two-minute silent tribute.

*

RADIO WAS AN immensely important weapon of war. The BBC was used most effectively by Churchill, whose ringing invocations of the spirit of victory were vital to national morale. Broadcasts by the King and Queen were more rare but they too played a crucial role in sustaining the conviction that the nation was united around a just and essential cause. Neither of them did it lightly, the King because of his stammer, the Queen because she found the writing of any broadcast something of an ordeal. Tommy Lascelles commented that she had 'a great dislike of being what she calls "turned on like a tap"; moreover, she demands a considerable time for preparation & reflection before making any sort of public utterance'.[107] But in early 1943 she agreed to broadcast again to the women of the Empire and agonized over what to say.

The Queen was socially conservative and did not want the war to revolutionize women or indeed to revolutionize anything. Thus she wrote to Alec Hardinge, 'one would like to congratulate women on the way they are tackling men's jobs, & yet they must be ready to stand down (& by) after the war'.[108] To Cosmo Lang, the retired Archbishop of Canterbury, she said that she wanted both 'to praise & urge on to war work, & yet remind that the home & preferably a Christian one is more important than anything else'.[109]

She sought the help of her spiritual adviser the Bishop of Lichfield, but a week before the broadcast was due she was still not happy and showed it to Tommy Lascelles, asking that he do anything, 'however drastic, to give it a little punch'.[110]* He agreed that the draft was poor and sat up till 2 a.m. writing another three pages which he then returned to the Queen.[111] She adapted and adopted some of his ideas and then sent the new version to Churchill who made his own suggestions, which she liked.[112]

In the final version, which was broadcast on 11 April 1943, she started by saying that she wanted this talk to be a meeting between herself and 'my fellow-countrywomen all over the world'. She did not have a special message but there was something deep in her heart that she knew that they should be told – 'and probably I am the best person to do it.' Sometimes, after reading a book that inspired hope and courage, she continued, 'we have wished that, though we are strangers to him, we could meet the author and tell him how much we admire his work, and how grateful we are for it.' In the same way,

> I would like to meet *you*, this Sunday night. For you, though you may not realise it, have done work as great as any book that ever was written; you too, in these years of tragedy and glory, of crushing sorrow and splendid achievement, have earned the gratitude and admiration of all mankind; and I am sure that every man who is doing his man's share in the grim task of winning

---

* It was often difficult to write speeches for the Queen. In 1939 A. A. Milne, the author of *Winnie the Pooh*, had written a broadcast for the Queen at the request of the Ministry of Information. It was, in the words of the historian Frank Prochaska, 'patronising'. 'Men say we gossip,' the Queen was to tell her listeners, 'perhaps we do. It is nice sitting cosily with a friend and saying, "Did you hear this?" and "did you hear that?" But please, please don't let us gossip now.' The Director General of the BBC had thought the draft broadcast 'generally admirable' and it was sent to the Palace for approval. It was not delivered. (Frank Prochaska, *Royal Bounty*, p. 223, quoting PRO INF 1/670. 37)

this war, would agree that it is high time that someone told you so.

Women might feel that she was exaggerating, and ask what they had done compared with what their men had endured 'dodging submarines in the Atlantic or chasing Rommel across Africa'. But they had given all that was good in themselves to the same cause, 'our cause, the cause of Right against Wrong'. Women's work, she said, was:

> just as valuable, just as much 'war-work' as that which is done by the bravest soldier, sailor or airman who actually meets the enemy in battle.
>
> And have you not met that enemy too? You have endured his bombs; you have helped put out the fires he has kindled in our homes; you have tended those he has maimed; brought strength to those he has bereaved . . . in a hundred ways you have filled the places of the men who have gone away to fight; and, coping uncomplainingly with all the tedious difficulties of war-time – you . . . have kept their homes for them against the blessed day when they come back.

In a paragraph added by Churchill, she said, 'Many there are whose homes have been shattered by the fire of the enemy. The dwellings can be rebuilt, but nothing can restore the family circle if a dear one has gone for-ever from it. A firm faith in reunion beyond this world of space and time, and a fortitude born of the resolve to do one's duty and carry on to the end, are true consolations. I pray they may not be denied to all who have suffered & mourn.'

The Queen went on to say that all women loved their family life, homes and children and so did their men. 'These men – both at home and abroad – are counting on us at all times to be steadfast and faithful.' Women as home-makers had a great part to play in rebuilding family life as soon as the war ended, but it should be done on the strength of spiritual life. If 'the years to come are to see some real spiritual recovery, the women of our Nation must be deeply concerned with Religion, and our homes the very place where it should start; it is the creative and dynamic power of Christianity which can help us to carry the moral responsibilities which history is placing upon our shoulders. If our homes can be truly Christian, then the influence of that spirit will assuredly spread like leaven through all the aspects of our common life, industrial, social and political.' She thanked people for their prayers for her and the King and their family. 'We need them and try to live up to them. And we also pray that God will bless and guide our people in this Country and in our great family throughout the Empire, and will lead us forward, united and strong, into the paths of victory and peace.'[113]

It was all in all a formidable statement of her beliefs in the Christian Church and in the role of women in both wartime and the family. After the broadcast she wrote to thank Lascelles for his help and commented, 'What agony these things are! It's funny, but when I talk into those dumb-looking little microphones, I think of the grey & narrow streets of places like South Shields or Sunderland. If one can help those gallant people, everything is worthwhile.'[114]

Lascelles noted in his diary, 'The Q delivered her broadcast, & did so very well. In its final form, it was the joint work of Winston Churchill, the Bp. of Lichfield, & myself – a curious trio of collaborationists, who are unlikely ever to be in literary partnership again.'[115] Nevertheless its sentiments were the Queen's own. Thanking Churchill for his assistance, she said, 'I put it just as you wrote it, and I am certain that those words will comfort many an aching heart.'[116] Churchill replied with his usual graciousness, 'I am glad the few words I suggested were acceptable. The Broadcast was an outstanding success. Yr Majesty's voice was clear & captivating & I heard from every side nothing but praise & expressions of pleasure & high sentiment.'[117] That was true – the speech drew a flood of congratulatory letters from people who took comfort from her words.

She tried to wear the praise lightly. Later in the year, when her brother David asked her to speak to a women's Christian group, she replied, 'honestly darling I don't feel very holy at the moment, & couldn't think of a word to say to them. Just because I said last spring that I believed in Christianity and home life, I am considered practically a mother superior and clergymen raise their hats to me with a sort of special gusto!'[118]

*

A FEW DAYS after the broadcast the Queen and the Princesses attended a poetry reading at the Aeolian Hall in New Bond Street, which Osbert

Sitwell had organized to help 'keep the arts alive'.[119] He had persuaded her to attend and had been consulting her on the details for weeks.[120] The reading was given in aid of the Free French Fund and it was, as can be imagined, quite an occasion – a gathering of some of the greatest talents, and greatest egos, in the world of letters at the time. Among the ladies and gentlemen of letters were Edmund Blunden, Vita Sackville-West, Walter de la Mare, who was dwarfed by the lectern, Osbert's sister Edith, looking flamboyant as ever, and Lady Gerald 'Dottie' Wellesley, who was thought by many to be inebriated, although she denied it. The Queen and her daughters sat in the front row looking very serious. According to Sitwell's biographer, Philip Ziegler, 'the Princesses kept their eyes on the performers with decorous and disconcerting fervour, except when T. S. Eliot incanted from "The Waste Land", at which point they had to try hard not to giggle. They enjoyed it even more when W. J. Turner exceeded by far his allotted span of six minutes and was loudly heckled by his fellow poets.'[121] Decades later Queen Elizabeth recalled that 'they all got so angry with each other because they all went on too long.' She singled out Edith Sitwell for praise, remarking that she 'read beautifully'. All in all, she thought it very kind of Osbert Sitwell to try and educate her daughters but the great company of poets was more humorous than anything else.[122]

The Queen was certainly determined to do everything she could to shore up civilization and the arts. She took pleasure in attending the popular lunchtime concerts at the National Gallery, where Dame Myra Hess performed. There is a photograph of the Queen sitting next to Kenneth Clark at one of the concerts, wearing a trilby-shaped hat with a veil and looking eager and alert.

Clark's support continued to be essential to the Queen. Throughout the war they kept up a correspondence on the arts and, in particular, how best to safeguard the Royal Collection. The Queen was always concerned that it be protected from German attacks, and in 1940 she had even suggested that some of the most valuable paintings be sent to Canada, disguised as luggage for Lord Athlone, the Governor General. The idea was dropped on government advice, and the pictures remained stored in the basement of Windsor Castle. But when in 1942 Owen Morshead arranged for the priceless collections of drawings, miniatures and manuscripts from the Royal Library to be moved to the National Gallery's stores in a disused mine in North Wales, at the King and Queen's request the most precious paintings were dispatched there too.[123]

The Queen's anxiety for such works seems to have extended beyond the Royal Collection. The diarist James Lees-Milne recorded in 1942 that the Queen telephoned the Duchess of Wellington to see if it could really be true, as she had been told, that nothing had yet been removed from Apsley House (the Hyde Park Corner residence of the Dukes of Wellington). When the Duchess confirmed that this was so, the Queen announced, 'Well, then, I am coming round at 11 with a van to take them to Frogmore.' She and the King came over at once and started making lists of what was to stay and what was to go. She said, 'You mustn't be sentimental, Duchess. Only the valuable pictures can go.'[124]

*

THE DEFEAT OF the Germans and Italians in North Africa gave the King an opportunity he had long sought – to visit his armies in the field. Any such trip made the Queen nervous but she agreed with the King that it was important, and he had not been in the field since visiting the British Expeditionary Force in northern France at the beginning of the war. He discussed the idea with Churchill at their Tuesday 'picnic' on 23 March. The Prime Minister favoured the idea.

The King prepared for the worst, leaving instructions that, should he not return, the Queen must 'take the entire charge of & go through all my personal papers' which were locked in various boxes in Buckingham Palace, Windsor Castle and Royal Lodge. Only the Queen should read his diaries which should then be placed in the Royal Archives. 'I do not wish anyone else to read them. My wife will know if there is anything in them which should be used in reference to these days of war.'[125]

On 11 June the King set off from Northolt aerodrome, travelling incognito as 'General Lyon' on a converted Lancaster bomber which Churchill used. The Queen waited anxiously at the Palace. At 8.15 the following morning she learned that the plane had been heard near Gibraltar. An hour and a half later, she was told that thick fog had prevented the plane landing in Gibraltar and it was flying on to Africa. There was then complete silence for more than another hour. She was frightened. 'Of course I imagined every sort of horror, & walked up &

down my room, staring at the telephone!' she wrote to Queen Mary soon after she had heard that her husband had landed in Algiers.[126]

From there the King sent a wireless message to the Queen, 'Arrived safely after pleasant flight. All well. Lovely hot weather. Interesting programme arranged. Eisenhower and others dined Saturday, others come tonight. Three French generals lunched today. Best love.'[127] The Queen replied that she was 'so thankful' that he had had a comfortable journey. 'I was very relieved to hear that you had arrived safely . . . and I am counting the days until you return. I do hope that the warm sun will do you good, and that the change of everything will be a real tonic – I am sure you badly need it after these 4 years of grinding work and anxiety.' Lilibet, she told him, was down with a cold and Margaret had gone to Frogmore to help the Sea Rangers (the nautical section of the Girl Guides) cook their lunch. 'I think of you all the time, and do pray that you will have a really interesting & not too exhausting time. All my love darling from your very loving E.'[128]

The King's journey made the sort of headlines that the Queen loved to see for her husband.[129] On the day it was announced, she was almost mobbed by enthusiastic crowds in the East End who swarmed over her car.[130] She wrote to tell him that 'there is great excitement and admiration combined . . . I don't like to write too freely as I said before, not knowing what might happen to this letter, but I think of you all the time, & am so happy to know what pleasure you are giving to everybody in Africa, as well as everybody here.'[131]

The King's guide for much of the trip was Harold Macmillan, Britain's Minister Resident at Allied Forces Headquarters in North Africa. Macmillan thought Palace officials had failed to set priorities well, and in particular had done far too little to include the Americans in the King's trip. He thought this disastrous – General Eisenhower was after all Supreme Commander of the Allied (Expeditionary) Force in North Africa and thus the King's host.[132] Macmillan succeeded in getting the imbalance corrected; in the course of his gruelling two-week trip, the King met Eisenhower, gave a garden party for British and American officers and visited GIs in one of their camps. More time, of course, was spent with the British Eighth Army and the King knighted General Montgomery in recognition of his triumph at El Alamein. Like others with him, the King suffered throughout the trip from what he called 'Gyppy Tummy' and he lost nearly a stone, but he was very happy with what he was able to do.[133]

The most important and most dangerous part of the trip was his visit to Malta. This vital fortress in the Mediterranean had suffered ruthless bombing and blockade by Axis forces for over two years. With astonishing courage the islanders had held out and in April 1942 the King had awarded his personal decoration, the George Cross, to the people and the garrison of the island. This helped the morale of the islanders but their ordeal continued until after Rommel's defeat. The Battle of Malta was, according to the King's biographer, 'one of the most valiant and glorious episodes of the war'. Not surprisingly, the King was determined to go to the island. Equally unsurprisingly, his advisers – and his wife – were nervous about the idea: Sicily, only sixty miles to the north, was still in fascist hands.

The King prevailed. He travelled by sea and by night from Tripoli on the cruiser HMS *Aurora*. Early on the morning of 20 June the news of his imminent arrival was announced on the island. The church bells burst into prolonged clamour and thousands of people rushed to the harbour side to cheer with wild abandon as the King, elegant in a white uniform, stood and saluted in front of the bridge as *Aurora* slowly drew near. The cheering went on and on and, the King told his mother, 'brought a lump to my throat, knowing what they had suffered from 6 months of constant bombing'.[134]

The King sent the Queen a wireless message from Malta. 'All very delighted with my visit . . . Very interesting & strenuous tour in lovely weather. Hope all is going well at home. Best love to you & the children.'[135] Throughout, he was crowded by weeping, cheering people and bombarded with geraniums which stained his brilliant uniform. At the end of the emotional day, perhaps one of the most important in his reign, the Lieutenant Governor, David Campbell, said to the King, 'You have made the people of Malta very happy today, Sir.' To this the King replied, 'But I have been the happiest man in Malta today.'[136]

While he was away, the Queen acted as Counsellor of State and fulfilled some of the King's duties. Since the King would miss his usual Tuesday meeting with Churchill on 22 June, she invited the Prime Minister to lunch with her alone. Clementine Churchill wrote on his behalf to accept the invitation and to say that he had given instructions that the Queen be kept fully informed of all events while the King was away.[137]

The Queen wrote to tell the King that she had only had to sign '4 little ERs' on documents requiring the monarch's signature and hoped she had not yet let him down.[138] On 22 June she held an investiture at Buckingham Palace. There were several hundred people, mostly servicemen and women, to be awarded their honours. The ceremony took much longer than usual because she spent more time than the King in talking to each of those being honoured.[139] Among them were Wing Commander Guy Gibson, aged twenty-four, who had led the Dambusters raid in mid-May in which bouncing bombs were dropped on the reservoirs of the Ruhr to destroy the dams and the hydro-electric power of Germany's industrial heartland. After completing his own bombing run, Gibson had circled slowly to draw enemy fire from other aircraft doing the run. The losses had been serious – fifty-three of the 133 crew on this mission had been killed.

The Queen already had a personal interest in the Dambusters because at the end of May she and the King had visited their squadron, No. 617, at Scampton in Lincolnshire. There Gibson and Barnes Wallis, the scientist who had designed the bouncing bomb, explained to them how the raid had been conceived and carried out.[140] The Queen now took great pleasure in awarding Gibson the Victoria Cross, Britain's highest award for gallantry in face of the enemy. 'I always felt very proud of that,' she said years later.[141] Gibson, one of the most celebrated heroes of the war, was killed in action in September 1944.

The King had a calm and comfortable flight back from Fez to Northolt, where he landed at 6 a.m. on 25 June, an hour ahead of schedule. Churchill met him and they talked about the trip while they drove together to Buckingham Palace. The King recorded in his diary, 'I found Elizabeth in bed waiting anxiously for me. It was lovely seeing her again. She had had very little sleep, & it was then only 7.0 am.'[142]

*

THE TRIP WAS a great success, encouraging to the troops in North Africa, to the alliance with the United States, to the defenders of Malta, to the people of Britain and to the King himself.

There was just one unhappy consequence. Problems arising from the journey seem to have caused the final break between the King and his Private Secretary, Alec Hardinge, who had served him since he came to the throne. Hardinge was a fine man with many outstanding qualities. He had devotedly served King and country since being appointed assistant private secretary to King George V in 1920. He had acted honourably as Edward VIII's private secretary, but had quickly recognized the King's inadequacies. King George VI had profited greatly from his wisdom and experience as he grew into his role as monarch, and Hardinge had understood much earlier than many people (certainly the King and Queen) the dangers of appeasement. But he was not an easy man, and under the pressures of war his relationship with the King – not easy himself – became strained. The Queen and others in the Royal Family and Household felt that the King needed a private secretary with whom he was more compatible.[143]

While the King and Hardinge were in Africa, the Queen discussed this and other problems with Tommy Lascelles, the King's Assistant Private Secretary. Thanking him for his kindness and understanding, she wrote, 'If I was a trifle indiscreet – well who better qualified to listen than yourself! It is so important to be able to discuss rather delicate matters in a broadminded and I hope balanced way, and there are very few people in this world alas! to whom one can occasionally speak freely.'[144]

Lascelles wrote in his diary, 'For some years past I have been the unwilling target of a "Hardinge must go" barrage inside this house [that is, Buckingham Palace], from the King and Queen downwards.' He said that he had turned a deaf ear to such criticism because he believed that Hardinge's administrative talents outweighed other considerations. But by now Lascelles had come to realize that Hardinge and the King 'were so temperamentally incompatible that they were rapidly driving each other crazy'. Hardinge had become more isolated, and less able to delegate; his colleagues, according to Lascelles, found him 'impossible'.[145] This reached a climax at the time of the African journey, when Lascelles considered that Hardinge had failed to give him sufficient briefing or authority to conduct business properly during the King's absence.[146] On his superior's return Lascelles protested and the two men exchanged bitter letters; Lascelles threatened to resign, prompting Hardinge, who was exhausted and in poor health, to write to the King on 6 July tendering his own resignation.

The King was surprised but relieved. In his diary he noted, 'I replied accepting his resignation as I was not altogether happy with him.'[147] He told Tommy Lascelles he wanted him to become his private secretary. Hardinge was astonished and no doubt upset by the King's alacrity. Next morning he asked the King point blank if he really wanted him to resign. 'I told him I did, saying that I was very grateful for all he had done for me in the last 7 years. It was difficult for me to have to do this but I knew that I should not get this opportunity again. It came as a real shock to him I could see,' the King wrote in his diary.[148]

Many members of the Household believed that the Queen had played a large part in Hardinge's removal. Oliver Harvey, then the Private Secretary of Anthony Eden, wrote in his diary that the resignation of the 'strong, sensible, progressive minded Private Secretary' had been 'largely caused by the Queen who was determined to get him out'.[149] Perhaps. The Queen was more aware than anyone of the tension that existed between Hardinge and the King.[150] It would have been strange if she had advised the King not to accept the resignation. As ever, she sought anything that could improve the King's peace of mind.

Hardinge's wife Helen, who had been close to the Queen since girlhood, was hurt. She wrote to the Queen: 'I am not distressed about Alec's resignation which looks right to me but I am sad at what has led to it.' She said that she had been told by trustworthy people that the Queen had been trying to get rid of her husband for a long time. 'I do not know whether it is true or not – but if by any chance it should be – Your Majesty only had to send for me and tell me what you thought.'[151] The Queen immediately did send for Lady Hardinge, who recorded in her diary of 8 July: 'Went to see the Queen. She's very angry at me for believing they could have ill wished Alec.'[152]

On 17 July the Palace issued a statement saying that Hardinge had resigned on grounds of ill health, and that the King had appointed Sir Alan Lascelles in his place.[153] It was to be a close and fruitful relationship. Queen Mary was thankful.[154] When she next visited Windsor, Queen Mary thought that as a result of Hardinge's departure the atmosphere at Windsor had 'changed completely!'[155]

*

During July 1943 the Queen inspected ATS units of the London District and Anti-aircraft Command, an ARP first-aid post in Wimbledon, Joint War Organization convalescent homes and Red Cross depots in Surrey. She examined the new County of London Plan for post-war rebuilding (about which she had already expressed misgivings in letters quoted above) and with Princess Elizabeth she went to the Royal Academy. She attended the 1,000th Lunchtime Concert at the National

Gallery, she presented colours to the Royal Regiment of Canada and the South Saskatchewan Regiment, and she visited the Radiovision Factory, in the Euston Road, where she showed special interest in what was called 'invisible light-ray', or television development. Arthur Murray, the director who showed her around, was impressed that she understood all the technology he explained to her.[156]

After a few days at Appleton and a visit to her father at Glamis she and the King and the Princesses repaired to Balmoral. She was overjoyed that for the first time in the war she was able to invite friends to stay. 'I can hardly believe that I am really writing these words,' she said in her invitation to Bobbety Cranborne's wife Betty, 'as it seems such years and years since one ever thought of such things.'[157]

It was a happy holiday which the Queen tried to prolong for the Princesses so that they should have as much fresh Scottish air as possible to fortify them against another cold winter at war. Lady Cranborne brought with her a new popular gramophone record, 'Coming In on a Wing and a Prayer', which made the Queen and the Princesses weep a little every time they played it.* 'We were all so delighted to have such a gloriously glutinous song introduced to us.'[158]

> We're coming in on a wing and a prayer
> We're coming in on a wing and a prayer
> Tho' there's one motor gone we will still carry on
> We're coming in on a wing and a prayer
> What a show, what a fight
> Yes we really hit our target for tonight
> How we sing as we fly through the air
> Look below there's a field over there
> With a full crew on board and our trust in the Lord
> We're coming in on a wing and a prayer.

By the third quarter of 1943, Allied victories were more frequent. The Red Army was forcing the Germans back on the Eastern Front. Mussolini was overthrown and Italy changed sides. But there were growing tensions among the Allies. Churchill was increasingly concerned about Stalin's post-war ambitions in Europe, a concern which

---

* 'Coming In on a Wing and a Prayer' was sung by Anne Shelton with Ambrose and his Orchestra. The music was by Jimmie McHugh and the lyrics by Harold Adamson.

Roosevelt did not always share. Indeed, having been Churchill's great friend, Roosevelt now fondly imagined he could create an equally trusting relationship with Stalin. To Churchill's dismay he now often found himself the odd man out among the Big Three, Roosevelt, Stalin and himself. He shared such fears of Britain's diminishing status with the King and Queen.

The travels of the King and Queen around the country and their visits to factories, barracks and schools continued. Tommy Lascelles constantly advised where their presence would be most beneficial to the war effort. In October 1943 he wrote to the Queen, 'At the moment, the two obvious activities of vital importance are Bombing and Coal. Perhaps the troops that are being kept waiting, not too patiently, for some future continental adventure, come next.' He also suggested visits at Christmas to clubs and hospitals used by troops from overseas.[159]

After a visit to Queen Mary in November 1943, the King and Queen returned to London and gave lunch to two Saudi Arabian princes; the Queen reported to her mother-in-law that 'the two brothers were most beautiful; true Arabs with marvellous dignity & lovely manners. It was rather a strain having to talk through an interpreter, but it all seemed to go smoothly. They brought Bertie a diamond studded sword from King Ibn Saud, & they were very pleased when Bertie drew out its curved blade, & said that it would do to cut Hitler's head off!'[160]

*

IT WAS NOT easy for the Queen to combine her wartime duties with her responsibilities to, and love for, her daughters. She was unable to spend much time with them except at weekends. There was, perhaps, another factor. She had always dedicated herself to supporting her husband; since the abdication this had become an even stronger priority for her, and both as wife and as queen she felt that her place was at his side. She was nevertheless aware of how difficult it was to grow up in a nation at war and she did all she could to preserve the normal pleasures of childhood for them. She ended one letter to Arthur Penn, 'I must scram as the children have already eased off their ponies.'[161]

The Queen realized that there were similarities between her own life among the soldiers at Glamis in the First World War and that of her daughters, particularly Princess Elizabeth, at Windsor now: 'what a beastly time it is for people growing up. Lilibet meets young Grenadiers at Windsor and then they get killed, & it is horrid for someone so young.'[162] Among such young men was Francis Wigram, son of Lord Wigram, King George V's Private Secretary and now Governor of Windsor Castle. The Queen had liked him very much and was nervous about what to say when Lord Wigram came to meet them at the station soon after his son's death. She thought this was 'a very brave thing to do. Of course I could hardly say anything for the lump in my throat, but so like the wonderful old thing, he started off at once saying, "Isn't it sad about Francis", and helping us out as he always does.'[163]

The success of the nativity play in 1940 had led to a series of pantomimes written, as usual, by Hubert Tannar, in which the Princesses acted with children from his school. At Christmas 1943 the Princesses were heavily involved in *Aladdin*. Costumes were conjured up from old curtains and blackout material. 'The oldest jokes are being resurrected & used boldly once more,' said the Queen, but 'some dreadfully Japanese touches are creeping in, such atrocities as "Nip off to Nippon" & such things!'[164] The characters of the two Princesses were by now well developed. Princess Margaret, now thirteen, was still constantly mischievous and provocative. Tommy Lascelles told the Queen that one of her dancing partners had enjoyed her company greatly but had been embarrassed by her freewheeling gossip. The Queen thanked him, saying he should not hesitate to tell her such things, 'and even if it is something I don't like, if it is said kindly & tactfully I shall never mind'.[165]

Princess Elizabeth was growing into a poised, serious but open young woman. In early 1942 the King had appointed her colonel of the Grenadier Guards,* who were protecting the family at Windsor; she immediately took a great interest in the regiment, her father recorded, and on her sixteenth birthday she had inspected a regimental parade in the Quadrangle at the Castle.[166] General Smuts met her at the end of 1943 – 'He seems pleased with Lilibet, which is nice, as I think he is a good judge,' said the Queen.[167] The Princess made a great impression on a young Grenadier and friend of the family, Mark

---

* The previous Colonel, Prince Arthur, Duke of Connaught, third son of Queen Victoria, had died on 16 January 1942.

Bonham Carter, who went to see her as colonel of his regiment. According to Arthur Penn, he arrived nervous but 'when he came out he was in a state which I can best describe as exaltation . . . I have seen this effect, in another generation, so often that it is almost what the lawyers call "common form", but it gave me such pleasure to see it reproduced that I felt I must tell Your Majesty.'[168]

The Princess was also showing signs of an interest in Prince Philip of Greece; this was a friendship about which her parents had some concerns, if only on account of her age. Prince Philip was the nephew of King Constantine of Greece, but he was closely related to the British Royal Family – his maternal grandmother, Victoria Marchioness of Milford Haven, was Queen Victoria's granddaughter and lived in Kensington Palace. Both she and his mother, Princess Alice, were born in Windsor Castle. His father, Prince Andrew of Greece, was King George V's first cousin. Prince Philip himself was born in the family home on Corfu but when he was eighteen months old his parents had to flee with him and his four elder sisters on a British warship after a Greek revolutionary court sentenced his father to death.

The family then lived in somewhat reduced circumstances outside Paris. By the early 1930s the Prince's parents had drifted apart; his mother developed psychiatric problems and then sought solace in religion, while his father based himself in Monte Carlo. The young Prince Philip continued to see each of his parents and spent a good deal of time in Germany with his sisters, who had all married German princes. He went first to preparatory school at Cheam in Surrey, then to Salem in Germany, which was run by the progressive educationalist Kurt Hahn.

When Hahn was driven out of Germany by the Nazis in 1933, he founded a new school, Gordonstoun, in north-eastern Scotland, and Prince Philip became a pupil. An adventurous, good-looking and athletic boy with precocious curiosity, the Prince flourished there. 'Often naughty, never nasty,' Hahn wrote of him. Even as a boy the Prince set high standards – for himself and for others. In his final report, Hahn summarized his character: 'Prince Philip is a born leader, but will need the exacting demands of a great service to do justice to himself. His best is outstanding – his second best is not good enough.'

In January 1940, after passing out of the Royal Naval College at Dartmouth, having been awarded the King's Dirk as the best all-round cadet of his term, Prince Philip began a distinguished career in the

Royal Navy. He had a good war and was mentioned in dispatches after the Battle of Matapan in 1941; in charge of searchlights on HMS *Valiant*, he had enabled the sinking of two Italian cruisers.

In December 1943 the King and Queen held a small dance for their daughters at Windsor Castle. The Queen was much impressed by the good behaviour of the young men; they seemed to appreciate the beauties of Windsor – 'I fear that they are all starved of colour and beautiful things to look at, in these days.'[169] To Princess Elizabeth's disappointment Prince Philip was struck by flu and confined to bed in Claridge's ('of all gloomy places', said the Queen).[170] But in the end he was well enough to come to the pantomime; he stayed the weekend after it and they all laughed a great deal. He then spent Christmas with them and, according to Princess Elizabeth, 'we had a very gay time, with a film, dinner parties and dancing to the gramophone'.[171] According to Tommy Lascelles, they 'frisked and capered away till near 1 a.m.'.[172]

As well as being good looking, Prince Philip was a strong character, full of opinions. He seems to have been aware early on that the Queen, another such character, might not always appreciate his exuberance. In his thank-you letter to her after Christmas 1943, he wrote that he hoped that 'my behaviour did not get out of hand'. He said that he also hoped it would not be too presumptuous if he now added Windsor to Broadlands (the Mountbattens' home) and Coppins (the Kents' home) as his favourite places; 'that may give you some small idea of how much I appreciated the few days you were kind enough to let me spend with you.' The young Prince and the Queen had evidently been talking about what he should do next. 'In thinking it over I have come to the conclusion that you were right and that if I had the freedom to choose I would stay in this country and not go to America.'[173] After a subsequent visit to Windsor, Prince Philip told the Queen how much he loved being with them – 'It is the simple enjoyment of family pleasures and amusements and the feeling that I am welcome to share them. I am afraid I am not capable of putting all this into the right words and I am certainly incapable of showing you the gratitude I feel.'[174]

Early in 1944 Queen Mary heard a rumour that the King of Greece was planning to suggest his cousin Prince Philip as a possible suitor for Princess Elizabeth. Queen Mary thought Prince Philip was in some ways very suitable. The King liked him too but, according to Queen

Mary, wondered if an Englishman, through and through, might not be more popular with the people of Britain.[175] (Hugh Euston, son and heir to the Duke of Grafton, and now a young Grenadier who had been stationed at the Castle, was high on the King's list of suitable young men.) Queen Mary wrote to the King hoping that he would not think her interfering, 'But as you know well I adore Lilibet, & her future means much to me, tho' I am too old to be able to expect to see much of it!'[176]

The King confirmed the rumour about Prince Philip and said that he liked him – 'he is intelligent, has a good sense of humour and thinks about things in the right way.' But he and the Queen both thought that their daughter was 'too young for that now, as she has never met any young men of her own age'.[177] Queen Mary was relieved, 'as L is much too young, & after all the country will have to have a say in the matter. P. sounds extremely nice.'[178]

Despite their concerns about age, neither the King nor the Queen did anything to discourage the growing friendship between their daughter and the Prince. Meanwhile, Princess Elizabeth took on more public duties, particularly after her eighteenth birthday in April 1944. To her mother's and grandmother's delight, she now became a Counsellor of State.* She often accompanied her parents on official appointments and began to carry out engagements on her own.

*

BY THE SPRING of 1944 the Queen believed that, although the Allies were finally marching towards victory, an immense struggle still lay ahead. Longing for peace vied with anger. Writing to her mother-in-law she said, 'One feels quite exhausted by the immensity of the huge battlefields, stretching right across the world, and by the great amount of misery caused by the Germans. What people – words fail one . . . if only we could crush the Germans, and bring a true peace to this poor suffering world.'[179]

Weariness reigned. For the King's birthday, Queen Mary had sent him greetings and sympathy over 'this terrible war which never seems to come to an end & which gives you such endless work in so many

---

* In 1943 the King had asked Parliament to amend the Regency Act of 1937 to enable Princess Elizabeth to become a Counsellor of State at eighteen, instead of at twenty-one as under the existing law.

different ways'. She thought it was 'far, far worse' than the previous war.[180] The King replied that he hoped very much that the war would end in 1944 'as really everybody is getting worn out with work & anxiety'.[181]

The Queen's public life in 1944, the last full year of the war, did not much change. While she was still at Sandringham in January she chaired the AGM of the local Women's Institute, and gave out prizes at the Sunday School Treat. After returning to London, she visited the headquarters of Bomber Command (whose aircrews won her lifelong admiration for their exemplary courage), the Yorkshire coalfields and air force stations, the New Zealand Forces Club and the American Red Cross Club. On a very cold day she, the King and Princess Elizabeth attended the England vs Scotland football match at Wembley (England won 6–2), and she inspected the 5th, 1st and 7th Battalions of the Black Watch. She toured bombed-out areas in south and west London and watched the beating of the retreat by pipes and drums of the 51st Highland Division. On 7 March she attended the 'Back to Work' Exhibition for Disabled Men at Burlington House, and later in the month reviewed troops in Yorkshire and then, together with Princess Elizabeth, toured South Wales.

In April the family had a happy spring break at Sandringham. 'The beauty of the countryside was amazing,' the Queen wrote to Osbert Sitwell. 'It was so lovely that one could hardly bear it . . . One could watch the leaves unfolding and the lilac coming out, & the double cherry trees blazing. How lovely it was. I noticed that some of the young soldiers minded the beauty very much – it is true that the war does make anything as glorious as England in April very agonising.' And then, in elegiac vein, she quoted Turgenev:

> Years of gladness,
> Days of joy,
> Like the torrents of spring,
> They hurried away.

'It's all very sad,' she added.[182]

Spirits had to be sustained nonetheless. There were enjoyable interludes during family weekends at Windsor. In early May the King and Queen gave a small dance with Ambrose's band. It was a cheerful affair, Owen Morshead reported to Queen Mary, in large part because the King was in wonderful form, dancing every dance until four in the morning; 'and so did the Queen, who characteristically chose the shyest boys from the Sandhurst contingent and put them completely at their ease'. It was not just the Queen who enjoyed herself. 'Both Princesses too danced till the gunpowder ran out at the heels of their shoes.'[183]

The Allies were in the last weeks of preparing for the invasion of Europe. The Queen found the preparations for D-Day a time of enormous tension. The thought of all the deaths to come lay, she said, 'heavy on the heart & mind'.[184] Churchill felt the same. On the night of 5 June 1944, the day before D-Day, he said to his wife Clementine, 'Do you realise that by the time you wake up in the morning twenty thousand men may have been killed?'[185] The immediate casualties were in the event less terrible than expected, but still, as the Queen put it, 'so many precious people' lost their lives.[186] By the end of the month almost 8,000 Allied soldiers had been killed since D-Day, more than half of them American.[187]

Both the King and Churchill had wished to accompany the invading troops, and the Queen had encouraged the King to go. But Lascelles was appalled, and had dissuaded the King, who then had a fierce argument with Churchill, one of the worst he had ever had, when he insisted that the Prime Minister must not go either. Churchill gave way – but with bad grace.[188]

On the night of D-Day the King made a broadcast to the country. The Queen had insisted that it should be he, not the Prime Minister, who did this. She had discussed the matter with Queen Mary during a stay at Badminton with her daughters. 'One suggestion of yours which I think is admirable', Queen Mary wrote to her afterwards, 'is that Bertie shd talk to the Country when invasion starts, & not leave it to the P.M. or the Archbishop to do so, Bertie's message will be far more popular. Do persuade him to do so.'[189]

The King took a great deal of trouble – the Bishop of Lichfield helped craft the words and Lionel Logue once again helped him deliver them. He reminded the British people of what they had suffered and achieved so far: 'Four years ago, our Nation and Empire stood alone against an overwhelming enemy with our backs to the wall. Tested as never before in history, in God's providence we survived the test . . . Now once more a supreme test has to be faced.' He asked everyone throughout the land to take part in a worldwide vigil of prayer 'as the great crusade sets forth'.[190]

Ten days later, on 16 June, the invasion had proceeded well; the fighting was now far enough inland for the King to be able to cross the Channel to the Normandy beaches where he spent the day with General Montgomery. The Queen was overwhelmed by emotion. In church on Sunday 18 June, as the Allies were pushing further into France, she told Osbert Sitwell, 'I weakly let a tear leave my eye, thinking of the sorrows of so many good, brave people & feeling unhappy for them.' As she did so, 'I felt a small hand in mine, & the anxious blue eyes of Margaret Rose wondering what was the matter.' Holding her daughter's hand, the Queen remembered 'with a pang' that she had been in exactly the same situation with her own mother, Lady Strathmore, during the First World War. 'I remembered so vividly looking up at my mother in church, & seeing tears on her cheeks, & wondering how to comfort her. She then had 4 sons in the army, & was so brave. I could not bear to think that my daughter should have to go through all this in another 25 years. It must not be.'[191]

That same morning, as the Queen and Princess Margaret were praying together, death came to another church in which they worshipped, the Guards Chapel in Birdcage Walk. Hitler had just launched his latest weapon against Britain – the pilotless V1 bomber. These robotic machines were described as flying bombs and came to be known as doodlebugs. They were in some ways more horrifying than almost anything that had come before. They made a sinister growling noise, rather like an ill-tuned motorcycle, and they flew at 400 mph in a straight line from launch sites across the Channel until their engines cut out. Then they fell to earth causing massive explosions and, in built-up areas, terrible damage. When people heard the engine of a doodlebug stop, they knew that it was falling and was about to explode somewhere near by and so would throw themselves under tables, into doorways, down cellar steps.

These random killers came in swarms of thousands. 'It was as impersonal as the plague,' wrote Evelyn Waugh, 'as though the city were infested with enormous, venomous insects.'[192] On one occasion, while dictating a telegram to Roosevelt, Churchill broke off his argument to inform the President, 'At the moment a flying bomb is approaching this dwelling.' He continued his dictation regardless and then added, 'Bomb has fallen some way off but others are reported.'[193]

One of the lines along which the doodlebugs were directed seemed

to pass directly over the Houses of Parliament and then Buckingham
Palace. On the morning of 18 June, a V1 engine cut out just after it
had crossed the Thames and it fell, between Parliament and Palace,
straight on to the Guards Chapel while the Sunday-morning service
was being conducted. The nave of the chapel was smashed to pieces.
The chancel and the altar were unscathed and, astonishingly, the
candles remained alight. But the carnage was terrible. Sixty-three
servicemen and women and fifty-eight civilian worshippers were killed;
over a hundred more were wounded. Many of those who died that
morning were known to the King and Queen. Among them was Olive,
the sister of Arthur Penn. The Queen immediately wrote to her friend,
'I simply cannot <u>tell</u> you how much I feel for you over this ghastly
tragedy this morning . . . I feel quite stunned by it all and <u>what</u> you
must feel – I do pray that you may be helped and sustained. Oh
Arthur, it all seems so terrible – we must be brave – I know you are
and I shall try all I know in <u>case</u> I can help.'[194]

In the first sixteen days of the V1 bombardment 1,935 civilians
were killed, and by 6 July the toll had risen to 2,752.[195] In the first
month the doodlebugs destroyed 10,000 houses and damaged almost
200,000 more (compared with 63,000 homes destroyed during the
whole 1940–1 Blitz).[196] Hundreds of thousands of people fled the city.
Buckingham Palace was under real threat – after the Guards Chapel
was hit, another doodlebug fell on Constitution Hill, blowing out
seventy-five yards of the garden wall.[197] The King, the Prime Minister
and the Queen took to holding their Tuesday meetings in the Palace
air-raid shelter.

After four exhausting years of war the Queen, like many others,
thought the doodlebugs were an infernal new punishment – 'there is
something very inhuman & beastly about death dealing missiles being
launched in such an indiscriminate manner.'[198] Evidently fearing the
worst, she wrote a letter to Princess Elizabeth 'in case I get "done in"
by the Germans!', explaining that she had left her own things to be
divided between her and Princess Margaret and offering advice on
how her jewellery might be shared. 'Let's hope this won't be needed,
but I <u>know</u> that you will always do the right thing, & remember to
keep your temper & your word & be loving – sweet – Mummy.'[199]
The King, presumably with the same dangers in mind, wrote a longer
letter to Princess Elizabeth explaining the provisions of his will.[200]

As well as worrying about her human charges, the Queen worried for those works of art still in the various palaces. Kenneth Clark told her he thought the thick walls of Windsor would protect the pictures there – he was more worried about the paintings at Hampton Court where flying glass was a greater danger. The National Gallery store was full and he suggested that, if the doodlebug campaign were likely to continue, perhaps some pictures should be taken to Balmoral.[201]

Churchill was so appalled by the destruction and death wrought by the flying bombs that he considered using non-lethal poison gas on the launch sites and even on the cities of the Ruhr.[202] When that option was rejected, the only other defence was to shoot the flying bombs down over Kent and Sussex before they reached London. The RAF rushed all the available anti-aircraft guns close to the coast. In mid-July 1944 the King and Queen visited gun sites in Sussex and Surrey. The Queen described the way in which both the battery and fighter planes tried to shoot down the doodlebugs. 'An occasional fighter came hurtling past on the tail of one of the robots, and one flew straight into the bursting shells, & my heart nearly stopped, as he started to wobble about, and we thought he'd been hit. However, the bomb crashed a little further on, & the fighter seemed to recover. But really war is <u>very</u> exhausting!'[203]

As usual, the poor areas of south and east London suffered most from the new bombardment. The King and Queen visited victims in Lambeth on 29 June. Later, however, the Queen was infuriated when she was refused permission to visit other areas hit by flying bombs. She complained to Tommy Lascelles that 'the government does not want us to visit our own bombed out people.'[204] This, he replied, was 'not quite fair' – and he told her that the government was trying to conceal from the Germans where exactly their bombs were falling. If she or the King visited bomb sites, the Germans would hear of it and would be able to adjust the trajectories in order to hit more built-up areas. Reluctantly the Queen had to accept this argument.[205] She knew there were many other places where their presence was solicited. They visited airfields from which planes were scrambled at no notice to try and shoot down the flying bombs. Both of them were inspired by the bravery and the modesty of the young pilots.[206]

The King was the next source of anxiety for the Queen. On 23 July he departed on a ten-day visit to his troops in Italy under the command of General Alexander. From 23 July until 3 August, he visited battlefields old and current, watching fighting and artillery bombardments.

The night before his departure, the King wrote to his wife, 'My darling Angel, As I am going away tonight on a journey by air I feel it is always wise to put one's affairs in order. I am not thinking that something might happen to me while I am away from you, but there are some matters which might want clearing up.' He stressed that she would 'naturally go on living at Buck. Pal, in this Castle, Sandringham & Balmoral for the present until such time as Lilibet is on her own. I hope Royal Lodge, Appleton & Birkhall will always be your house on the private estates. The former is our home; the house we built & made for ourselves in Windsor Park.'[207]

On the evening he left, the Queen and Princess Elizabeth drove with the King to Northolt aerodrome to see him off. The Queen looked around the converted Lancaster bomber and thought it was quite comfortable. But when she went up to the cockpit, an extraordinary thing happened: 'the first thing I saw through the glass was a flying bomb caught in the searchlights, & coming straight for the plane! I really felt, well this is too much, & averted my eye in anger! Luckily it buzzed over & was going strong when I looked again! What emotions one goes through these days.'[208] She was always nervous when the King was off on such trips, but she tried to hide it – 'he feels so much not being more in the fighting line, and I know that it heartens the troops, & one swallows one's anxieties!'[209]

While the King was away, the Queen and, for the first time, Princess Elizabeth acted as Counsellors of State. The Queen kept herself busy, visiting the Girl Guide and Rangers camp at Frogmore, and ATS units at Bagshot, Aldershot and Windsor as well as the 2nd Battalion of the Home Guard under the command of her brother Mike. He had been left physically unfit by his experiences in the First World War and in 1939 he had been rejected by the army on medical grounds. The Queen had always been moved by these volunteers, and she said that as she looked at 'these very English & some not-so-young men – it was something very difficult to put into words, such an unyielding spirit & yet so modest – I felt a lump in my throat and a great thankfulness & also a great humbleness too.'[210] The effect was mutual, to judge by the letter of thanks her sister-in-law Betty Bowes Lyon wrote to her after the visit. The Queen, she said, had inspired a sense that 'you were theirs – part of them & that they loved you so much they would happily die for you'.[211]

From General Alexander's headquarters in Italy the King wrote to tell her he was having 'a very interesting time seeing a lot in lovely hot weather, a bit too hot for me but I'm dressed in shorts & a shirt . . . I have seen the Air Force, the US 5th Army & the Poles . . . Early starts in the morning, but I wake at 6.30 & bathe in the lake with Alex. He is a charming host & has told me a lot of his own thoughts . . . I have only been away a week & I feel it is 10 years. I hope you are not too lonely angel.'[212] She had written to him hoping that 'the tum tum tummy is behaving nicely, & not revolting at the climate, or the chianti, or the macaroni or spaghetti!'[213] She was cheered by his letter – 'I can tell everything is going alright,' she told Tommy Lascelles.[214]

In Naples the King saw the Queen's friend D'Arcy Osborne, who was still His Majesty's envoy to the Holy See. He had not enjoyed the nine months of German occupation, he told the Queen. It was 'terribly oppressive, never knowing if the Gestapo would not come at any moment'. He said that Yeats summed up his feelings about the war:

> The years like great black oxen tread the world
> And God the herdsman goads them on behind
> And I am broken by their passing feet.[215]

The King returned the day before the Queen's birthday on 4 August; Queen Mary and other members of the family contributed to a Fabergé cornflower for her – she loved it and thought it 'so beautifully unwarlike!'[216] Queen Mary decided not to come over from Badminton to celebrate – she was concerned that if she met a robot plane the shock would give her an allergic reaction.[217] The Queen thought she was probably wise – there were constant warnings and explosions on the afternoon of her birthday; she was longing to get the children away from Windsor 'because life is rather un-normal, & though they are so good & composed, there is always the listening, & occasionally a leap behind the door, and it does become a strain'.[218]

Once more Balmoral beckoned. There they could relax after two such violent months and she could watch her daughters with 'very bright eyes & pink cheeks again'. The liberation of Paris had begun but it was an end to the bombardment of London that she wanted. 'I don't think that anybody has any conception of the strain & horrible-ness of the whole thing, and people are so wonderful about it all. Up here, away from it, I find that I think all the time of those little rows of houses, & everyone carrying on so splendidly amongst all the ruin & death – one feels almost conscience stricken to be so peaceful & quiet. It is marvellous too!'[219]

After Paris was freed in August 1944 and Churchill had had a joyous reception there, the Queen asked the Prime Minister, 'Do you think that there is any chance of London being "Liberated" in the coming months? My heart aches for our wonderful brave people, they have been tried so high, & of course can go on, but it really is rather a bore to feel that one might be blown to pieces at any moment. There is no limit to their courage & cheerfulness and I long for them to have a lightening of their burden.'[220]

At the beginning of November 1944 the Queen learned that her father, who had been suffering from an attack of flu, was gravely ill. She immediately made plans to take the night train to Glamis, and telegraphed her younger brother David at the British Embassy in Washington: 'FEAR NOT MUCH HOPE BUT HE IS VERY PEACEFUL BEST LOVE DARLING ELIZABETH'.[221] David arranged to come at once, but Lord Strathmore died peacefully in his sleep on 7 November. His youngest son felt that in wartime circumstances he could not justify flying home 'when all is over'.[222] The Queen understood, but missed David greatly during the three sad days she spent at Glamis for the simple funeral.[223] Lord Strathmore's coffin, covered with a Union flag, was drawn to the burial ground on a farm cart by two horses while pipers from the Black Watch played 'Flowers of the Forest'.[224] The King walked behind the coffin with other men of the family; the Queen followed in a car with her sisters.

She had many letters, she told David, which stressed their father's 'kindness to one and all'.[225] She thanked Churchill for his sympathetic letter, saying, 'It is a very sad moment for us all, my father loved us, and we loved him, and it was so comforting for me to go home, and feel even now, with old age coming on, that I was a loved child – that has gone, but I am very grateful to have had it so long.'[226]

With the end of the war for the first time really in sight, the Queen was distressed by the decision to disband one of her favourite wartime institutions, the Home Guard. She saw it as emblematic of the 'good brave self sacrificing British people',[227] working together in their amateur but committed manner to defeat the evils of fascism. After a visit to one battalion in July 1944, she wrote to the commanding officer, 'As I went down the ranks I thought with pride & gratitude of the splendid spirit of loyalty and determination which brought the Home Guard into being during those critical days of 1940.'[228] The King broadcast thanks to the Home Guard for their 'steadfast devotion' which had 'helped much to ward off the danger of invasion'.[229]

★

AT THE END of 1944 the Queen began an association which gave her and others pleasure for the rest of her life – she became a bencher of the Middle Temple, one of the four Inns of Court, the professional associations to which every English barrister must belong. Since the foundation of the Inns in the Middle Ages, no monarch or consort had ever joined any of them, and no woman had ever before been a member of the parliament of an Inn.

Like many of the historic buildings in London, the Middle Temple had been badly damaged by bombing. The Queen's installation took place on 12 December 1944, in the New Parliament Chamber, whose windows had been blown out. One light was suspended from the ceiling by its flex. But good cheer was had nonetheless. The tables were set in the form of an E and were laid with the Middle Temple silver which, like the contents of the wine cellar, had survived.[230] The simple menu – Clear Soup, Roast Turkey, Apple Tart and Cheese and Biscuits – was made more memorable by Pol Roger 1928, Château Margaux 1924, Taylor's Port 1912 and 1878 brandy. In her speech the Queen displayed a sense of history:

> Though I am, I understand, the first of my sex to become a Bencher of this Inn, I like to feel that I am continuing a tradition rather than creating a precedent, for it is, after all, but a few paces from here that another Queen Elizabeth visited this Society in the Hall which was built with her permission, and indeed was so intimately associated with her that it was referred to by the Treasurer as 'The Queen's House' . . . I feel this sense of the past to be very heartening at present when we see all about us so much overlaid by those hazards through which, please God, we can today see a light beginning to shine.

Our walls may crumble, she continued, but more precious were the unshaken and unshakeable virtues and graces of the Inn. In particular 'the honourable administration of the Law and the unswerving impartiality between rich and poor'.[231] In response, the Master Treasurer rose and toasted 'Our new Bencher the Queen'. For the rest of her life she rarely missed the annual dinner of the Inn.

★

THE PANTOMIME season at Windsor was upon them again and, the Queen wrote, 'Windsor is ringing with words like lights, cut it, grease paint, Mother Hubbard, finale, opening chorus etc.'[232] They called this pantomime *Old Mother Red Riding Boots* and performed it in the Waterloo Chamber just before Christmas. The King thought the 1944 pantomime was 'better than ever & [the Princesses] both did their parts very well & enjoyed them'. This year, as he prepared his Christmas broadcast, he noted, 'I did not have Logue with me. I knew I did not need his help.'[233]

As the German armies retreated there were increasing anxieties about the wreckage that would be left behind, and about the march of Soviet communism westwards. Churchill was especially worried about Poland, on whose behalf Britain had originally gone to war, and Greece. In Athens, after the flight of the Nazi occupiers, growing violence between communists and royalists filled the streets. The Queen believed that such violence was perhaps inevitable given what had happened – 'one feels that occupation of a country by the Germans leaves a terrible legacy of anarchy & cruelty & a weakening of moral forces – Indeed the Nazis are the forces of Evil. May the coming year see the end of this ghastly struggle & a return to law & order in Europe is my fervent prayer.'[234]

She was dismayed by the way in which the press and the BBC appeared to support the communist side in Greece. 'One could hardly believe', she wrote to Queen Mary, 'that the Press and intellectuals of the socialist party could be so blind as to back up a gang of bandits who wanted to seize power by force. We have suffered so much in the fight for what is called Freedom, it was very sad that at this moment people could be so misled as to what freedom means. It certainly doesn't mean government by tommy gun.'[235]

The Queen was able, by early 1945, to spend more time writing to and seeing her friends, though she found letters difficult. 'There is so little to write about except war,' she said.[236] Among the friends of whom she had not seen enough was Dick Molyneux, co-founder of the Windsor Wets. He wrote to her in the middle of March and she replied immediately:

It is curious that your letter arrived today, because last night the King & I were saying that we had not seen you for AGES, and I said that I would write & ask you to come and spend a weekend at our little weekend cottage. And, lo and behold! on my table this morning what do I see? That well-known writing – is it? Can it be? Yes! No – Yes; it is! I suppose that my thoughts whizzed out of the window here, turned sharp right, cut across the Green Park, past the Ritz, down Berkeley Street, and entering your flat, elbowed their way through the guests thronging your hall, & crashed into your mind . . .

Down with Hitler! Your friend E.R.[237]

On 12 April 1945 the King and Queen were appalled to hear of the death of President Roosevelt from a cerebral haemorrhage. Queen Mary called it 'a positive catastrophe',[238] and the King replied that the news had been 'a great shock to me & we shall feel his loss very much.'[239] Roosevelt was succeeded by the then little-known Vice-President, Harry Truman.

By now, the war was nearly won. London was 'liberated' as the Queen had asked: all the doodlebug launch sites across the Channel had been captured or destroyed from the air; the mobile launchers of the V2 rocket bombs, whose trajectory could not be intercepted and whose death toll had been even higher, were also rendered ineffective. Mussolini was seized by Italian partisans on 27 April and executed the next day; two days later Hitler committed suicide in the squalor of his Berlin bunker. Victory was finally announced on 8 May 1945. In his diary the King wrote, 'The day we have been longing for has arrived at last, & we can look back with thankfulness to God that our tribulation is over.'[240]

The 8th was a Tuesday and after Churchill's weekly lunch with the King the Prime Minister returned to 10 Downing Street to put the finishing touches to his victory speech, to be broadcast by the BBC and relayed by loudspeakers around Whitehall that evening. It was short and resolute, and he ended with the words: 'the evil doers lie prostrate before us.' The crowds in the streets gasped at this phrase. 'Advance Britannia!' the Prime Minister shouted.

The streets of every town in the country were filled with singing, dancing, frolicking people. Tens of thousands of them gathered in the Mall in front of Buckingham Palace. The Palace balcony had been surveyed to ensure that it was still structurally sound after all the bombs that had exploded near by. That evening the King, the Queen and the Princesses appeared on the balcony – for the first time together. Huge happy crowds roared for the family to come back out again and again. Among the throng was Noël Coward: 'The King and Queen came out on the balcony, looking enchanting. We all roared ourselves hoarse . . . I suppose this is the greatest day in our history.'[241] The Princesses begged their parents to allow them into the throng to celebrate. The King agreed. 'Poor darlings, they have never had any fun yet,' he wrote in his diary.[242] With a party of young officers, the Princesses danced through the city unrecognized as hundreds of thousands of people cheered and cheered their parents.

The King was exhausted and in his victory broadcast he stumbled over his words more than usual. In common with millions of his subjects, he felt the strain of the war terribly. He looked shattered. He and the Queen found all the expressions of gratitude and praise for them overwhelming. They were especially moved by the tribute Churchill paid them.[243] In a speech to the Commons, the Prime Minister was lyrical in his description of all that the King had done to help sustain the war effort. He then told the House that it would be 'altogether unfitting' if he did not also speak of the King's 'gracious consort, the Queen'. She, he said, 'has been everywhere with him to scenes of suffering and disaster, to hospitals, to places shattered the day before by some devastating explosion, to see the bereaved, the sufferers and the wounded, and I am sure that many an aching heart has found some solace in her gracious smile.'[244]

The Queen summed up her own feelings in a letter to Osbert Sitwell:

I feel rather numbed by the emotions of the last weeks, and on top of all the great anxieties of the last years, this has made me feel stunned as well, so you will understand a rather stupid letter, I hope! . . . It is almost impossible to believe that the dreadful war is over, and Germany truly beaten – the sense of relief from bombs and rockets is very agreeable at the moment, and I hope that people won't forget too soon. They have shown such a noble and unselfish spirit all through the country during these long years of war, and I long for them to keep at the same high level in the days to come.

Our people respond so magnificently when they are asked to do hard things, to die, to smile amongst the wreckage of their homes, to work until they crack, to think of their neighbours before themselves; and the more difficult things you ask of them, the more response you get. It's been so wonderful; and all that spirit will be needed now, more than ever, for the whole world looks (even if some unwillingly) to these Islands for leadership in decent living and thinking. We <u>must</u> do it somehow.[245]

CHAPTER FIFTEEN

WAR TO PEACE

1945–1947

'Oh how I hate utility and austerity'

WITH THE END of the war in Europe, as the full horrors of Belsen, Buchenwald and Auschwitz were uncovered, it had become ever more clear that this war really had been, as Churchill had often declared, a war against evil and a new Dark Age. But, now that it was finally won, the vast costs of the effort, both personal and national, became starkly evident. In Europe alone more than fourteen million people had died; the economic structure of the continent had been ruined. Now millions of the survivors became refugees, wandering all over Europe, which was quickly divided, first by influence and then by physical barriers, between east and west. The Queen found it hard to believe that the Germans could have been responsible for so much misery.

She wrote to her mother-in-law to say that she and the King 'have aged a lot, and look rather haggard & ravaged! & one's clothes are so awful!'[1] The Queen was now in her mid-forties, a more mature, indeed more matronly figure than when the war began. Both she and the King had expended enormous physical, mental and emotional resources in the previous five years. The King, whose health had always been poor, was exhausted by the physical and moral strain. And he knew that it was not over yet. 'I have found it difficult to rejoice or to relax as there is still so much hard work ahead to deal with,' he wrote in his diary ten days after VE Day. 'Russia & America & U.K. have got to work together to put Europe straight again after this upheaval.'[2] And there was still the war in the east to be won. A tragic reminder of this was the news that Clare and Doris Vyner's son Charles had just been killed in his plane in action over Rangoon. The Queen was horrified. 'Oh Doris I cannot bear to think of your sorrow . . . All my most loving thoughts are with you all the time; if you ever want me I shall come at once, even just to be with you a moment.'[3]

The King needed to rest. But he could not. From the Queen's point of view, the story of the next six years was of tumultuous change in British society and of catastrophic decline in the King's health.

At the end of the war, London was a drab and filthy city, with thousands of homes, churches and other public buildings bombed beyond repair, the dust from myriad bomb sites blowing everywhere. Buckingham Palace was not destroyed, but it would take years to repair the damage and restore both the Palace and Windsor Castle to their pre-war state.

Through the summer of 1945, the King and Queen tried to construct a normal family life around their daughters. But they both knew that the war had made them into such public figures that they had no chance of returning to a relatively secluded private life. They undertook victory tours in many different parts of the United Kingdom; they attended countless march-pasts and rallies or services to celebrate the achievements of many different groups, regiments, associations. They visited the Channel Islands – the only part of British Crown territory occupied by the Germans. The Queen was impressed by the spirit of the islanders and, as a result of this visit, she decided to make a special gift to the Islands to commemorate their loyalty and Christian spirit – it took the form of specially made church plate, crucifix and candlesticks for the two main churches in Jersey and Guernsey.

Letters of praise and relief flooded into Buckingham Palace. The King replied to a letter from Cosmo Lang to say that he and the Queen had been overwhelmed by everyone's great kindness. 'We have tried to do our duty in these 5 long exacting years.' Now there could be only a moment for rejoicing, as there was so much more work to do to recover from 'all the suffering & destruction which Hitler has caused. But we also have much to be thankful for & the people of this Country won't let us down.'[4]

However, the people, wearied by the war, wanted political change. Politics had been, in effect, suspended since 1940, and the Labour leader Clement Attlee had served loyally as Churchill's deputy in the Coalition government. Churchill now wished to prolong the Coalition until the war with Japan was won. But the Labour Party decided at its annual conference in May 1945 to end the Coalition at once. Queen Mary thought this was 'disgusting & ungrateful' after all Churchill had done. She also thought that, since a peace conference involving all the big powers was about to convene in Potsdam, it should be Churchill who led Britain.[5] Churchill himself felt the same. Ever since VE Day, his main preoccupation had been with the Soviet Union – he feared that a new 'period of appeasement' would lead to a 'third World War'.[6]

The King and Queen agreed. They believed, in common with millions of others, that because of her heroic stand in 1940–1 and her dogged fighting ever since, Great Britain should still be considered a great power in 1945. Britain's armed services were more powerful than ever and Britain's global Empire was being restored. London now shared with the Allies in the governance of Germany, Austria and Italy. The Mediterranean was a British lake. The North African littoral, southern Persia and Greece were all under British control. British armies were keeping the peace and defending British interests around the world. The Royal Navy boasted 3,500 ships and the Royal Air Force enjoyed widespread international bases and prestige. It was not surprising that many Britons, proud of their individual and national achievements, believed that Britain would soon be able to re-establish her pre-war dominance of the international system.

But the war had vastly strengthened others, in particular the United States and the Soviet Union. People were slow to understand, but Britain now faced, in the words of John Maynard Keynes, a 'financial Dunkirk'.[7] To defeat the Nazis, Britain had nearly exhausted her gold and dollar reserves, worn out her industrial base and become increasingly dependent on American munitions, shipping and foodstuffs – each of these was essential to the war effort.[8] Moreover, for all Churchill's intimate relationship with Roosevelt, by the time of his death the American President had been negotiating over his head with Stalin.

Parliament was dissolved on 15 June. Polling began on 5 July but instead of the usual one day was extended for much longer to enable the troops stationed overseas to vote. The result – a stunning victory for the Labour Party with a majority of 146, and the rejection of Churchill and the Conservatives – was announced on 26 July.

The King and Queen were, to say the least, disappointed. That evening, Churchill drove to the Palace to tender his resignation. It was, wrote the King in his diary, 'a very sad meeting'; he told Churchill he thought the people were very ungrateful.[9] A few days later he wrote to Churchill to tell him:

how very sad I am that you are no longer my Prime Minister. During the last 5 years of war we have met on dozens, I may say on hundreds of occasions . . . Your breadth of vision & your grasp of the essential things were a great comfort to me in the darkest days of the War, & I like to think that we have never disagreed on any really important matter. For all those things I thank you most sincerely . . . I shall miss your counsel to me more than I can say. But please remember that as a friend I hope we shall be able to meet at intervals.[10]

Churchill replied with similar emotion.

The Queen set out her views to Queen Mary:

The election has been rather a shock, and I think that Bertie felt it very much, as Winston has been such a great support and comfort all through these terrible years of war. He is a great man, of great vision, and his leadership has meant so much to so many. People's memories are short, alas!, and one must try now to build up another good sound government. But the material is not too inspiring.

With a great war raging, & a Potsdam Conference sitting, really [it] is not the time to have a change of Government! We both feel tired, & today has been very depressing, but Bertie is wonderful, and tho' he looks rather pinched in the face, he is so calm & good, tho' I know he is worried to death. You have been through all these things Mama, & understand it all so well – it is hell, isn't it.[11]

Churchill himself was both devastated and philosophical. The waste of his talents upset him. 'The knowledge and experience I had gathered, the authority and goodwill I had gained in so many countries, would vanish,' he recalled later. But when his doctor, Charles Moran, spoke of the 'ingratitude' of the British people, Churchill replied, 'I wouldn't call it that. They have had a very hard time.' To another aide he said, 'They are perfectly entitled to vote as they please. This is democracy. This is what we've been fighting for.'[12]

Two men who later became friends and admirers of the Queen were pleased by the news. The Oxford philosopher and diplomat Isaiah Berlin danced a jig in celebration. Noël Coward, the actor–entertainer who had played an important wartime propaganda role and was certainly no left-winger, was sanguine. 'It may not be a bad idea for the Labour boys to hold the baby,' he recorded in his diary. 'I always felt that England would be bloody uncomfortable during the immediate postwar period.'[13]

In August 1945, President Truman unexpectedly and, he later acknowledged, unwisely, cut the economic lifeline of Lend-Lease, whose creation Churchill had called 'the most unsordid act in the history of any nation'. The sudden end of this vital support meant that Britain had to negotiate new loans from the United States; the terms seemed onerous. There was even less money to pay for both imperial and post-imperial commitments and for the socialist revolution which the Labour Party had been elected to carry out. The government immediately had to cut imports of food, tobacco, textiles, fuel. But that did not mean that Labour would, or could, change its policies. The historian Robert Rhodes James put it succinctly in his biography of the King: 'The series of economic miseries that were to demoralise and eventually to destroy the post-war Labour government had begun.'[14]

*

THE FAMILY WAS at Windsor for the first weekend in August 1945; Saturday the 4th was a special day, the Queen's forty-fifth birthday and a good outing for the King at the races – Rising Light won him the first victory by one of his own horses that he had ever seen. That evening they gave a small dance at the Castle to celebrate both the Queen's birthday and the end of the war in Europe.

On 6 August the first atom bomb was dropped on Japan with the second following three days later. Unconditional surrender followed swiftly and on 15 August the Pacific war was finally also over.

That same day the King and Queen proceeded, in an open landau drawn by four greys, to open the first peacetime Parliament since 1938. The crowds gave them a tumultuous welcome. Inside Parliament, Chips Channon noted that 'the many new socialists looked dazed and dazzled.' When the royal procession entered he thought the Queen, in aquamarine blue, was 'dignified and gracious'. The King announced the end of the war, and then mentioned the first radical measures of his new socialist government – the nationalization of the mines and of the Bank of England.[15]

The King made a radio broadcast that night in which he said, 'The war is over. You know, I think, that those four words have for the

Queen and myself the same significance, simple yet immense, that they have for you. Our hearts are full to overflowing, as are your own. Yet there is not one of us who has experienced this terrible war who does not realise that we shall feel its inevitable consequences long after we have all forgotten our rejoicings of today.'[16] But rejoice they did; that night the crowds gathered again outside Buckingham Palace and shouted for the King and Queen to come on to the balcony. James Lees-Milne, the diarist, was in the crowd and recorded, 'They were tiny. I could barely distinguish her little figure swathed in a fur, and something sparkling in her hair. The gold buttons of his Admiral's uniform glistened. Both waved in a slightly self-conscious fashion and stood for three minutes. Then they retreated. The crowd waved with great applause, and all walked quietly home.'[17]

At the end of August they went to Balmoral, exhausted. It was a happy family time. The Queen's friend and lady in waiting Cynthia Spencer described days in the hills and on the rivers, with them all singing 'descants and ditties' as they were driven from one place to another 'in a super-shining motor bus'.[18] A month at Balmoral was followed by a busy week in Edinburgh; with the Princesses they stayed at Holyroodhouse and attended Scotland's Victory Parade. After dinner on 27 September they listened to the massed bands and pipes and community singing. As the Queen put it, 'All the good staid citizens of Edinburgh let themselves go in an orgy of yelling & dancing, feeling decently disguised by the covering of the dark. It was the first time they had ever done such a thing, & it did them a lot of good.'[19]

The family remained in Scotland for the autumn, a vital break for the King, but he still felt drained. He even rather envied Churchill in defeat. The hero of victory had gone on holiday after the electorate rejected him in July 1945. Later he visited the King, who observed to Tommy Lascelles, 'When Winston was last here he was a tired man. Now he's back from two months' complete holiday in the Italian Lakes; brisk, chubby, pink as a baby, at the top of his form once more. That's where these people score. I can't ever get a holiday like that. I never get a chance to recuperate like they do.'[20]

Lascelles thought there was a good deal of truth in this. So did the Queen, who worried constantly about her husband's health. Duty pursued the King to Royal Lodge, Sandringham or Balmoral. Every day he had to read state papers, Cabinet minutes, and other documents that required his signature. He would stay up too late and smoke too much.[21] At Balmoral he had to spend as much time every day with his secretaries as in London – the only relief that Scotland afforded him was from the endless audiences that he had to hold every day in the capital. These were exhausting for him because he took considerable trouble with each person. By the end of the afternoon he would be 'dead beat'.[22] The King told the Duke of Gloucester, 'I feel burned out . . . I have been suffering from an awful reaction from the strain of the war I suppose.'[23]

He found that no medicine, not even Dr Weir's homeopathic powders, did him much good. The only cure was being out in the open air. The Queen told Queen Mary, 'to my joy Bertie has taken to stalking again, which means he has more energy, & it is doing him good. He was very tired when we got up here at the end of August, for the summer had been very exhausting.'[24]

★

THE DUKE OF Windsor was a continuing concern. He had announced his resignation as governor of the Bahamas at the end of 1944 and had left for the United States in May 1945. The question was where he and the Duchess would now live. His family hoped they would not wish to settle in England. Churchill informed him in no uncertain terms that, although the King would always see him, Queen Mary was 'inflexibly opposed' to meeting the Duchess. 'I imagine that this view is shared by the Queen,' he added.[25] That autumn the Duke wrote an affectionate letter to his mother and said that he would like to come and stay with her in October.[26] Queen Mary was delighted – she had not seen her eldest son since his abdication. The Queen was glad for Queen Mary's sake, knowing that 'it is very hard for a mother to be parted from her son.' But the Duke then immediately upset members of the family by giving press conferences en route to London. The Queen's view was that he should have said that his visit was private and have refused to see the press.[27]

When the new Prime Minister, Clement Attlee, came to Balmoral for the Prime Minister's traditional autumn weekend, the Duke was a central topic of discussion. The King was pleased with Attlee's attitude; he told Queen Mary that the Prime Minister 'agrees with me that he cannot live here permanently owing to his wife & he is not prepared to offer D. any job here or anywhere.' The King thought the family should remain firm, particularly about 'her' – 'She does not like either us or this country, & the life she has been accustomed to live no longer exists here.' He thought his brother still did not realize 'the irrevocable step he took nine years ago & the ghastly shock he gave this country'.[28]

The Duke came, alone, and Queen Mary was happy to have her 'dear eldest son' with her for a week. 'Very nice he was,' she told Owen Morshead later, 'quite like old times; very well informed, knew everything that was going on. But still persisting about my receiving his wife, when he <u>promised</u> he'd never mention the subject to me again. His last words when he was going away – "Well goodbye – and don't forget: I'm a married man now." Don't forget, indeed: as if one ever could!'[29]

When the King came down from Balmoral to see the Duke, the Queen stayed in Scotland. The brothers spent two hours together at Buckingham Palace on 6 October 1945. It was, said the King in a letter written immediately afterwards to his mother, an 'amicable & quiet' conversation. Indeed it went better than the King and Queen had feared. The Duke said he was anxious to help improve Anglo-American relations when he returned to the United States. The King explained that as an ex-king the Duke could neither live in Britain nor work abroad for the Crown. His post in the Bahamas had been a wartime expedient. On the subject of the Duchess, the Duke said that he should take all the blame for what had happened in 1936, and if only the Duchess were recognized by the family all would be well. The King seems to have been touched by his brother and did not repeat how badly the family felt he had behaved. 'I could tell that he is very happily married & that he wants to do his best for her in their future life together. But we cannot help him in this & I don't see how we ever can.'[30]

Queen Mary agreed entirely with the King.[31] Tommy Lascelles noted in his diary that when the Duke left on 11 October he felt 'rather as one did on hearing the all clear after a prolonged air-raid'.[32] The Duke considered living in the United States, but in the end he and the Duchess made their principal home in France for the rest of their lives.

*

THE KING AND the Queen both understood that fundamental shifts were occurring in Britain and that these might affect the Crown's relationship with the people. They were both determined to protect that relationship. Labour's July 1945 victory showed that the electorate did not want to relive the misery of the mass unemployment of the 1930s. They had chosen a government committed to radical change and a huge extension of public ownership and nationalization of the means of production.

It was not an implicit attack upon the monarchy. Indeed, the Labour Party had long ago made its peace with the Crown. In 1923 the Party Conference had defeated overwhelmingly a motion that republicanism should be the policy of the Labour Party. That decision was in good part a tribute to the success of Edward VII and George V in increasing royal involvement with social and charitable causes. As the historian Frank Prochaska put it, 'Just as the crown intended, the slum visits, the dispensaries and the cottage hospitals, the youth clubs and playing fields, the training schemes and workshops, the consoling words at the pit heads and in the canteens, had taken the republican edge off socialism.'[33]

After the abdication the new Queen had immediately seen that service to social causes would be her main responsibility. Charities and voluntary effort were at the forefront of her interest. And although she was happy to take on national institutions, she was determined also to keep up her local patronages and associations. Indeed throughout her life she retained this affection for the small, the local and the particular.

But at the same time the intellectual leaders of the Labour Party were convinced that centralized planning was more important to meeting modern needs than traditional associations based on family and civil society.[34] Individualism fell from fashion; state action, or collectivism, came to be seen as more 'noble' than charity work. The war had disrupted social norms; more and more women went to work, tens of thousands of children were separated from their parents, people had to move from areas in which their families had lived for centuries. Order gave way to change, voluntarism to compulsion, stability to destruction. Total war demanded total commitment and made charitable remedies seem inadequate. The state sector grew inexorably.

During the war, nothing had shown the popular march of the state more clearly than the Beveridge report published a few days after the victory at El Alamein at the end of 1942. It had called, in effect, for a comprehensive 'social service state' based on a free health service, child allowances and full employment. The report seemed to chime in with the mood of optimism and patriotism of the time; well written, almost populist, it became a bestseller at once, with a cheap edition for the armed forces. The Queen at first had had her doubts about promising social security before world security was achieved. 'It is much better not to promise things that may be impossible to bring to pass.'[35] But the ideas were quickly embraced by all parties. In March 1943 Churchill had made his first broadcast in a year; in it he drew on Beveridge's ideas and talked of the need for a national health service, universal national insurance and far wider educational opportunities.

The new Labour government's belief in 'common ownership of the means of production' would affect if not weaken traditional friends of the monarchy in the financial and commercial sectors and would tend also to 'subdue and dispirit those civil institutions from which the monarchy drew so much of its strength'.[36] In recent decades the Royal Family had developed their relations with the charitable and voluntary sections of society. After the 1945 election, a real question for them was this: as the government nationalized more and more of the economic structures and social services, what space would be left for civil society?

The King and the Queen understood that the Labour government had a clear mandate for its changes. They may not have agreed with all the government's policies but they grew to appreciate almost all members of the Cabinet, especially Ernest Bevin, who had distinguished himself as a member of the wartime coalition and was now a clear-sighted foreign secretary. He was the sort of traditional Labour patriot whom the Queen had always admired.

Labour's Prime Minister, Clement Attlee, was the opposite of Winston Churchill. He was a slim, short man of few emotions and fewer words, but he was precise and determined, and both the King and Queen liked him. With perception, the Queen said later of him, 'He wouldn't strike one as a star, but he was a practical little man. I think at first he was quite cagey, you know, difficult to get on with, but then he soon melted. But I think he was very practical. Seemed to get a grip of things.'[37]

But both the King and Queen came to fear that at home the government was being too radical too soon. In November 1945 the King noted in his diary that he had told Herbert Morrison, Attlee's deputy, that the legislative programme was too crowded. Morrison responded that the government had to carry out its proposals as soon as possible.[38] To the Duke of Gloucester, the King wrote, 'My new Government is not too easy & the people are rather difficult to talk to.'[39] But he always gave his government his support.

The Queen was well aware of the additional strain that her husband's anxieties about the governance of Britain placed upon him. She had a romantic view of the country, one in which perhaps Britain's glorious history was more important than her present straitened circumstances. It was a challenge for the Queen to come to terms with the austerity imposed by the Labour government. Her contradictory feelings were later carefully described by her biographer, Dorothy Laird. 'Her physical courage in the face of danger had been flawless; now another, and possibly more difficult kind of courage was required.'[40] The King had to give his constitutional support to a socialist government which was determined to create a social revolution in a badly battered country, and the Queen had to support him in this. Both had misgivings.

*

THEIR FIRST Christmas of peace was spent at Sandringham House, which had been closed since 1940. She wrote to her old friend Dick Molyneux, in jocular mood: 'Bowling through Berkeley Square today, it suddenly struck me to ask whether you were planning to spend Xmas anywhere particular, or whether you would care to come & spend it with us at hideous ugly germ ridden old Sandringham?' She hoped he could come for at least a few days. 'If you are already too engaged, a merry Xmas! if not you just wait. E R.'[41]

Molyneux accepted happily. There was a small party staying in Norfolk. It included Arthur Penn, Michael Adeane, the King's Deputy Private Secretary, Delia Peel, the Queen's friend and lady in waiting, Owen Morshead and Anthony Blunt, the new Surveyor of the King's Pictures.* No one was in better form than Queen Mary – she seemed to be the life of the party, 'youthful, skittish and generally rejuvenated . . . really full of fun and giggles. She dances given any chance at all,

---

* Anthony Blunt (1907–83) had been appointed surveyor in succession to Sir Kenneth Clark at the beginning of 1945. He remained in the post until the end of the reign, and was Surveyor of the Queen's Pictures from 1952 to 1972. He was knighted in 1956, but after he was exposed as a Soviet spy in 1979 he was stripped of his knighthood.

coming out shooting (with stick and umbrella) & generally contributes to any jolly fun.'[42] Queen Mary herself said she loved resuming 'the old life' and trying to forget the 'six horrible war years'.[43]

The new year was made sad for the Queen and the Princesses by the death at Sandringham of Alah Knight, who had looked after them all as children and was integral to the family. The Queen's sorrow was eased by the presence of her brother David. 'It really was a great shock, & a great sadness, & you were such a wonderful help. One still feels that she is quietly upstairs. It's curious,' she wrote to him shortly afterwards.[44]

Another recent death had been that of the Queen's longest-serving lady in waiting, Lady Helen Graham. She had been with the Queen since 1926 and served her with diligence, humour and affection. 'I loved & admired dear Nellie – she helped me through so much when I was young & silly,' said the Queen. 'She was such fun too.' The Queen took comfort in the continuing friendship and service of Delia Peel.[45]

In early 1946 Arthur Penn resigned his temporary wartime post as her Private Secretary, to be replaced by Major Thomas Harvey. But she did not want to lose Penn and, in writing to thank him for his long service, asked him to become her Treasurer – 'it would be nice to have a treasure as a Treasurer.'[46] He was touched by her words and replied, 'it is I who should be thanking you.' He was eager to take on the new job – 'If you had asked me to be your bootboy I should have leapt at it, & to be your Treasurer, that honourable post, would be a joy indeed. I shall certainly muddle, and probably embezzle, but it will be with the best possible intentions, I do promise, & perhaps I shan't embezzle much.'[47]

The King and Queen had to decide how best to rebuild the formal life of the Court now that peace had come – and now that British society was altering so profoundly. There was much advice. Jasper Ridley argued in a letter to the Queen that Britain had a unique history of orderly change, largely because of the influence of the Crown. 'We have, after all, had a 30-year beastly upheaval in the world, and I reckon that at the end of it the Crown is more universally acknowledged as right and necessary than ever before. Surely a grand feather in your caps.'[48]

In early 1946, they revived the pre-war practice of inviting people to 'dine and sleep' at Windsor Castle. Dick Molyneux reminded the

Queen that during George V's reign the Castle had become 'almost like a vast empty museum, with Their Majesties living in a corner; such a waste of that splendid place & establishment'. He thought this must never happen again. If they asked up to sixty people a week, and their friends at weekends, they could make their court 'the envy of the world, the centre of what is left of good society, a wonderful example to the young and an inspiration to everybody to be worthy of it'.[49]

At the end of April 1946 they had the Churchills to stay at Windsor. Churchill had recently been in Fulton, Missouri where he had made a deeply considered speech about the communist 'Iron Curtain' descending across Europe from Stettin in the Baltic to Trieste in the Adriatic. This speech became one of the defining texts of the post-war world; the King recognized its importance at once and told him 'how much good it had done in the world'.[50] After the weekend Clementine Churchill wrote to thank the Queen, saying how honoured and 'warmed' they had been by the King and Queen's 'grace and kindness'.[51]

On 8 June 1946, ten months after Victory in Japan Day, the official victory parade was at last held. Twenty-one thousand troops and civilians took part. But the growing split with the Soviet Union, and the bloc of countries it now controlled, meant that no Russian, Polish or Yugoslav troops were present. The King took the salute in the Mall, with the Queen standing beside him. On the dais with them were the Princesses and, among others, Crown Prince Olav of Norway, Princess Juliana and Prince Bernhard of the Netherlands, and Prince Felix of Luxembourg. The King had commanded that the tattered Royal Standard flown on the cruiser *Arethusa* in which he had crossed the Channel to visit his troops after D-Day should fly from the dais.[52] The next day there was a service at Westminster Abbey to give thanks for victory.

At the end of June the King and Queen, taking the Princesses with them, travelled to Scotland for a week of official engagements, based at Holyroodhouse in Edinburgh. They visited Falkirk, Stirling, Grangemouth and Linlithgow; the Queen took the salute at a march-past of Red Cross units at Holyroodhouse; they attended a service in St Giles' Cathedral and a drumhead service and parade for the twenty-fifth anniversary of the British Legion in Scotland; they gave a garden party, and returned to London overnight on 3 July. The rest of July and early August were filled with visits to Sandhurst, to Canterbury, to North

Wales, as well as constant engagements in and around London and two garden parties at Buckingham Palace. Thus it continued until the family departed for Balmoral on 8 August, where among the guests was Prince Philip of Greece. In September the King and Queen made a quick trip south to accompany Prime Minister Attlee, his wife Violet and Sir Stafford Cripps to the 'Britain Can Make It' exhibition. 'But no one can get it' was the Queen's pithy private comment.[53]

Back in Scotland, she and the Princesses drove from Balmoral to the Clyde to spend the day on the Cunard liner *Queen Elizabeth* which the Queen had launched in 1938. The liner had served as a troopship throughout the war and now she had been refitted for her original purpose. The Queen thought the ship beautiful and comfortable – she was glad to see good British taste and workmanship – 'oh how I hate utility and austerity, don't you?' she wrote in a note to the King. 'It's all wrong. Well, darling, I must fly, the children have just returned from the engine room, and tea is calling.'[54]

The state of the arts, in the broadest sense, remained a central interest for her. She had been concerned throughout the war about protecting artists and their work from the brutal assaults of the time. Osbert Sitwell had invited her, just before the war's end, to attend the Authors' Society Jubilee in June 1945. This included a John Gielgud recital of pieces by Tennyson, Thomas Hardy and John Masefield, the Poet Laureate. Sitwell told her how 'delighted and enchanted' 400 authors 'good and bad' were to see her.[55] She enjoyed the occasion and agreed to attend a more ambitious gathering in 1946 at which Flora Robson, Edith Evans, John Gielgud and others read from Shakespeare, Marlowe, Milton, Chaucer and many other classics, while T. S. Eliot, Dylan Thomas and Walter de la Mare read from their own works.

She had been anxious about the fate of the paintings and other works of art in the Royal Collection evacuated for safekeeping during the war. Now they were all being brought back, cleaned and restored where necessary. In autumn 1946 she involved herself in an exhibition, 'The King's Pictures', at the Royal Academy, a selection made by Anthony Blunt and Ben Nicolson, the Deputy Surveyor of the King's Pictures. It was the first large art show to be held in London since the end of the war and was a great success. More than 366,000 visitors came to the exhibition.

The Queen held a private view for family and friends on 20

November 1946. The evening ended with an unexpected supper in one of the rooms at the Academy. It was an enjoyable occasion – an example of what one courtier later described as the Queen's ability to make Court life 'fun'.[56] Queen Mary thought the mix of 'treasures & interesting people was a great success, very clever of Elizabeth to have thought of it, & the supper was a great surprise.'[57] The Queen was pleased; she enjoyed seeing the pictures well lit and well shown and the occasion encouraged her dream to build a gallery at Buckingham Palace to show the Royal Collection on a more regular basis.[58] (This was finally achieved in 1962.)

*

THE END OF the war did not diminish the Queen's interest in her regiments. In October 1945 she sent the Toronto Scottish a warm message as they embarked on their voyage home. 'I rejoice to think that you will soon see those who are most dear to you ... You are returning home covered with glory most well deserved and I trust that some day I shall see you again in your own dear land. Goodbye and God speed.'[59] Her connections with the Canadian armed forces were reinforced when she subsequently accepted the appointment of colonel-in-chief of the Black Watch (Royal Highland Regiment) of Canada.

In early 1946 she was upset by the disbandment of the 5th Battalion (Angus). She drafted a telegram to the regiment in which she said, 'I was grieved to hear this news as the 5th Battalion The Black Watch having such close ties with my family and my native County of Angus has a special place in my heart.' She thanked them for 'their devoted service' and asked to be kept informed where the men were posted.[60] There was happier news a few weeks later when one of the most accomplished staff officers of the war, Lord Wavell, became colonel of the regiment. She wrote to him saying that she wanted to associate herself with the pleasure that his appointment had given to all ranks, and telling him she hoped he would call upon her if he needed backing against the War Office. In a typical expression of purpose, she declared, 'There are certain things that one <u>must</u> fight for, and it is [no] use giving in.'[61]

The war had left the Queen with the conviction that Christianity was vital to the recovery of the country. She detested what she saw as the irreligious 'materialism' of the Nazi and communist creeds, and she was increasingly concerned by the decline in traditional religious belief in Britain. Education seemed to her to be the key to reversing this trend, and she was therefore enthusiastic about a scheme first put to her in 1944, to set up a centre 'for the study of the Christian philosophy of life'.[62] It was the brainchild of Amy Buller, whose book *Darkness over Germany* had been sent to the Queen in 1943 by her friend the Bishop of Lichfield, a supporter of the scheme. Miss Buller was a remarkable Christian pedagogue and a scholar of German culture who had travelled widely in Germany during the 1930s. She had been appalled by the ease with which the Nazis had seduced ordinary decent Germans, and she feared that, if such a civilized country as Germany could be so warped, Britain bore a similar risk. She believed that Western civilization was in decline because of the weakening of Christianity. The Queen was struck by the book and asked to meet the author. In March 1944 she did so; Amy Buller called this meeting 'my miracle'.[63]

Miss Buller's faith and enthusiasm impressed the Queen; when she spoke of her ambition to create a college to inculcate Christian principles, the Queen said she would like to help. She was as good as her word. The most serious immediate problem was to find it a site. The Queen asked Queen Mary whether part of the Royal College of St Katharine's in Regent's Park, of which Queen Mary was patron, could be used. Amy Buller, she said, hoped to attract teachers of psychology, science and medicine and other disciplines from universities all around the country for 'many of them seem to be almost pagans, and there seems to be absolutely <u>nowhere</u> where clever people can go to study & discuss the Christian way of life from an intellectual angle'.[64]

In the event no home could be found for the college until 1947, when Cumberland Lodge, a former royal residence in Windsor Great Park, fell vacant, whereupon the King and Queen decided to offer it to Miss Buller's foundation. They lent furniture, pictures and other household goods to the college, known first as St Catharine's, Cumberland Lodge, and renamed King George VI and Queen Elizabeth's Foundation of St Catharine's in 1966. Miss Buller became warden and Elizabeth Elphinstone assistant warden. A distinguished academic, Sir Walter Moberly, who had been chairman of the University Grants Committee and was the author of an important work, *The Crisis in the Universities*, was appointed principal. Like the Queen and Amy Buller he was a firm believer in the value of Christian insight in academic studies.

St Catharine's was – and remains – a Christian foundation but it brought together those with widely divergent political and religious views. Much of its early work was a strenuous attempt to bring out into the open the assumptions which underlie different points of view and to encourage students to persist in such investigations. It promoted the civilized values which had arisen from the millennia of Christianity. The Queen wrote to Elizabeth Elphinstone, 'I do take it very seriously, and am quite certain that it is doing, & will do, immense good.'[65] For decades to come St Catharine's offered university staff and students the opportunity to examine their own studies and explore the nature of man and society and the Christian interpretation of life as against the various secular alternatives. Its lasting success owes much to the Queen's patronage.

*

THROUGHOUT 1946 IT became ever more clear that the principal consequence of the war was the extreme poverty of the country. The Labour government's promise to extend state ownership and thus to build a New Jerusalem in Britain's 'green and pleasant land' had been enthusiastically accepted by the electorate in 1945, but inevitably disappointment and even disillusion followed. London remained a wrecked city; too often to the victors their country seemed neither green nor particularly pleasant. Bread had not been rationed during the war – but now it was. All other foods, clothing and fuel were in short supply or even rationed. The spiv had become an important character in the wasteland of post-war Britain: black-market goods were eagerly sought – by those who had the cash. Austerity was the watchword. On the other hand, for millions of people in Britain, perhaps the majority, the post-war years were not overwhelmingly bleak. On the contrary this was the first time in which they could feel security – with full employment, national insurance and national assistance, the advent of a national health service. There was rationing but, by contrast with the years after the end of the First World War, this meant that the poor could obtain food, and limited goods were shared out more equitably. The Labour government was much criticized but it did not lose a single by-election in the immediate post-war years and its vote in many working-class areas actually grew.

The war had demonstrated Britain's dependence on soldiers from the Empire. And now Britain depended on the Empire for much of her food and raw materials. Royal tours to Australia, New Zealand, Canada and elsewhere were envisaged as a means of giving thanks to the peoples of the Dominions. South Africa was chosen as the first such destination. During the war the King and Queen had discussed such a tour with their friend Field Marshal Smuts, the South African Prime Minister. For Smuts, the tour was politically important, as a means of uniting the country and bolstering his position against the Nationalist Party, which proposed to transform the existing segregation into apartheid and which was generally anti-British. The formal invitation, when it came in 1946, was addressed also to the two Princesses. For the King and Queen this interlude away from home, with their two growing daughters, had a certain poignancy, particularly since it seemed unlikely that 'we four' would remain a simple quartet for very long.

Their departure in early 1947 coincided with the most bitter winter in recent memory. The cold, combined with post-war rationing and the general austerity embraced and imposed by the government, made Britain a truly wretched place. The workings of Big Ben froze solid, as did the Thames. Much production just stopped – the ice and snow forced the coalmines and the ports to close. There was a fuel crisis and constant power cuts. Life was miserable. When the time came for their voyage to begin, both the King and the Queen were reluctant to leave.

The Queen had read widely about both the history and the natural life of South Africa. She understood that the journey would be complicated. Unlike Australia, New Zealand and (to a lesser extent) Canada, South Africa was neither homogeneous nor automatically inclined towards Britain. Instead, two races – the Dutch and the British – competed with each other over their visions and their shares of the country and their relationships with the huge indigenous black population, the Coloureds and the Indians. There were two capitals (Cape Town and Pretoria), two national anthems, two national flags. The King and Queen saw it as one of their primary purposes to try and bring as much unity as possible to the divided nation. The King was invited to open Parliament in Cape Town.

Both he and the Queen had lessons in Afrikaans; the Queen took with her for the voyage the lists of the phonetic equivalents of words and phrases given her by her tutor.[66] Norman Hartnell designed most of the clothes for her and her daughters; in the Queen's case they had a certain theatricality that served to project her presence to the forefront of every occasion. Her hats, designed by the Danish milliner Aage Thaarup, introduced the swept-up brim, which she liked because it did not hide her face or her smile.

The immediate Household staff for the tour numbered ten; they included Tommy Lascelles and Michael Adeane (Private Secretary and Assistant Private Secretary), Tom Harvey, the Queen's Private Secretary, Lieutenant Commander Peter Ashmore and Group Captain Peter Townsend (equerries), Edmund ('Ted') Grove (Chief Clerk). The Queen took Lady Harlech and Lady Delia Peel as ladies in waiting, and Lady Margaret Egerton was lady in waiting to the Princesses. The Queen also had two maids and her own hairdresser. An official tour diary was kept by the King's Press Secretary, Captain Lewis Ritchie, RN. Ted Grove wrote long letters home to his wife which formed a more intimate private diary of the trip.

On 1 February 1947 they sailed from Portsmouth in HMS *Vanguard*, a new battleship which Princess Elizabeth had launched on Clydeside in 1944; their quarters were made slightly more comfortable by the Queen's choice of soft furnishings and familiar satinwood furniture borrowed from the royal yacht. As on previous voyages, prints of familiar scenes adorned the walls: the Queen chose the 'Cries of London' series. Off the Isle of Wight, the double column of the Home Fleet made a fine sight. As Princess Elizabeth identified the warships for her sister, the Queen was busy with her cine camera filming it all. Their passage through the Bay of Biscay, however, was rough and disagreeable. The King and the two Princesses kept to their cabins. On the second and third days, only the Queen felt strong enough to dine with the Household. 'She was certainly looking better than I felt,' Ted Grove wrote home.[67]

News of their discomfort was published in London and the ever affectionate Arthur Penn wrote to the Queen to commiserate about 'the extreme disloyalty of the weather which has dogged you . . . Even the mainbrace has had to be spliced, I learn, which gives one some idea of the savagery of the tempest.' He said that he 'felt very low when I turned my back, on Friday, on the ship which was bearing away so many of the people who contribute most to the happiness of my life . . . It's disgusting being without you, but I knew it would be.'[68]

By the fifth day they had passed the Azores, and with the warm weather the King and Queen started to enjoy life on board ship. A friendly sense of fun and games developed. One night under a full moon the Queen, the two Princesses and Lady Margaret Egerton danced an eightsome reel with four ship's officers on the quarterdeck. Rather as Elizabeth Bowes Lyon used to correspond with her governess, Princess Elizabeth reported to Crawfie: 'The officers are charming, and we have had great fun with them . . . There are one or two real smashers, and I bet you'd have a WONDERFUL time if you were here.'[69]

Amusement on board was 'home-grown'; the ship's company gave a floorshow one night, on others Delia Peel played the piano for community singing; films were shown in the King's dining room. The press photographers begged for something to reveal and captured the family party playing deck games with the naval officers: in the background the royal parents, always impeccably dressed, watched their daughters. All took some part in the traditional high jinks of Crossing the Line. The King and Queen, veterans of King Neptune's demesne, were given Oceanic season tickets; the Princesses had their noses powdered with a gigantic puff and were given a candied cherry instead of a soap pill.[70]

On the calmer seas, the royal party were able to visit the escorting ships, including the aircraft carrier HMS *Implacable*, which the Queen had launched in Glasgow in 1942. Now she told the ship's company: 'To me that was one of the most memorable days in those long years of war.' She had followed the voyages of 'her ship' with warm interest. '*Implacable* made a notable contribution to our final victory, and I need not say that it was with deep pride that I heard of her achievements.'[71]

Inevitably, the holiday spirit was dampened by the King's growing anxiety about news of the ever worsening situation in Britain. He felt that, having shared so many trials with his people during the war, he should now be there to show sympathy and solidarity with them. Princess Elizabeth wrote regularly to Queen Mary, and admitted to their feelings of frustration: 'We hear such terrible stories of the weather and fuel situation at home, and I do hope you have not suffered too much. While we were dripping in the tropics, it was hard to imagine the conditions under which you were living, and I for one felt rather guilty that we had got away to the sun while everyone else was freezing!'[72] On the eve of their arrival in Cape Town, the King sent a telegram to Attlee, suggesting that he should come home by air. Attlee thought this would only increase the sense of national crisis and politely rejected the idea. But the King's feeling of guilt continued.[73]

For the Princesses, never before out of Britain, the landfall in South Africa was exciting. Princess Elizabeth wrote to her grandmother: 'When I caught my first glimpse of Table Mountain I could hardly believe that anything could be so beautiful.'[74] As the ship approached land, a great cheer went up from the dockside. The Queen came ashore wearing an ice-blue dress with floating panels bordered with South African ostrich feathers and a matching hat, also trimmed with feathers. The town was in fiesta mood. 'There is bunting everywhere and thousands more people have crowded into the town from the surrounding districts ... The Queen with her charm has captured them all,' Ted Grove told his wife.[75]

The first formal ceremony was a solemn procession of both Houses of Parliament to present loyal addresses to the King and Queen at Government House, and in the first of many additions to the programme the King invested Field Marshal Smuts with the Order of Merit. One evening the Queen added a personal touch to the work of reconciliation between Britain and the descendants of the Boers whom Britain had fought at the turn of the century. After dinner with Smuts at Groote Schuur, the prime-ministerial residence that had once been the home of Cecil Rhodes, she handed back to him the family bible of Paul Kruger, President of the Transvaal during the Boer War and a national hero who had died in 1904. The bible had been looted during the Boer War and taken to England; now the little ceremony, in which the Queen laid this immense and beautifully bound volume in Smuts's hands, struck Lascelles as 'a remarkable picture in the kaleidoscope of history'.[76]

For South African society, the garden party at the Governor General's country house, Westbrook, was a high spot. Princess Elizabeth and Princess Margaret, who wore short afternoon frocks, were surprised that all the ladies of Cape Town were in long dresses.[77] The Queen, however, met their highest standards: ostrich feathers decorated not only the sleeves of her long gown and her hat, but also her parasol. The radio carried enthusiastic reports of their progress throughout the country. Enid Bagnold, the author of *National Velvet*, who had come to South Africa in part to see the tour, wrote, 'The King and Queen's every breath and movement is blown through Africa at all hours on the wireless, so that I myself am worked up and await with excitement to know what they are wearing. There was a woman commentator in Cape Town who completely lost her head and kept shouting on the first day "But she's lovely. Oh, she's lovely, lovely." And the Princesses, "Oh, they're lovely, lovely." '78

All of them, but particularly the Princesses, were amazed by the warmth of the sunshine as well as of the welcome. They could hardly believe the vast blue skies, the vibrant colours, the cornucopias of food. The Princesses were no less astonished by the shops and gazed in the windows as they drove by. They had never seen anything like it in England, the Queen later recalled. 'Rolls of silk, garden chairs, all the things you hadn't seen at all. A young person growing up in the war was totally cut off from those sort of things.'79 A visit to the races at Kenilworth for the Cape of Good Hope Derby was made more enjoyable when the Queen and the Princesses backed the winner. That night at a ball for the non-European community, the Queen was visibly delighted by a cheerful interpretation of an old-fashioned quadrille. Entranced, the family stayed on long after they should have departed. Ted Grove wrote that the 5,000 dancers, in their evening dress, 'made a glorious pageant of colour'.80

But the reality of segregation could not be disguised. The King had asked that the third morning be given to the children of the Cape Peninsula. Schoolchildren lined the royal route to Simonstown: whites on one side of the road and Coloureds and blacks on the other, all from separate schools. The Queen and the Princesses each received baskets of flowers from three little girls: one of English extraction, one of Dutch and the third Bantu.

Nor could the political divisions be ignored. They spent a day in the rural Cape, visiting the wine-growing region, in valleys shadowed by the gaunt ridges of the Drakenstein mountains. Intensely National-ist, country people had lived simply there for three centuries, following old Dutch traditions. In Stellenbosch no Union flag flew and many of the Boers had refused to fight for the British Crown during the war. 'I think that the visit is going well,' the Queen reported to Queen Mary, adding, 'There are so many serious racial problems, but so far all sections of the community have been most welcoming. Yesterday we went out to Paarl & Stellenbosch, two very Nationalist & Afrikaans speaking towns, and had the most delightful reception – very nice country people, and they had prepared a picnic on the top of a mountain with a staggering amount of home made food! Lovely old Dutch recipes and French Hugenot dishes – Bertie & I were stunned by so much, & then we descended the mountain & had luncheon under the trees, again a mass of food & we nearly burst!'[81] In fact the workload and the stress were so great that the King lost weight in the course of the tour.

The climax of their days in the Cape was the state opening of Parliament by the King. The Queen had already put her tutoring in Afrikaans to use in informal conversations; the King's challenge was more daunting – to make a speech in Afrikaans to Parliament. For the ceremony the Queen was dressed formally in white silk crêpe, with the blue ribbon of the Garter. She wore Queen Mary's enormous, heavy tiara made for the Delhi Durbar in 1911 from diamonds originally given by De Beers to Queen Mary and George V when they visited South Africa as Duke and Duchess of York in 1901.[82]

With the success of Cape Town behind them, the royal party set off into the other provinces of South Africa. Their 'White Train' or 'Wittrein', with its smartly dressed engine drivers and stewards, was painted ivory and gold. The fourteen coaches were fully air-conditioned and insulated against heat and cold. Internally the suites were wood panelled and the corridors were lined with walnut veneer. Wireless and telephonic communication was built in. There was a carriage for the Household staff, where the clerks of the Private Secretary's office could continue working on matters relating to home as well as to the tour. Mail was delivered and collected daily. Day after day the train passed through beautiful countryside, farmland, vineyards and ravines and across rivers; years later the Queen remembered 'the dim blue hills everywhere' in the distance.[83]

The train was a place of escape, but it was also a trap in that it compelled endless impromptu encounters at station after tiny station and village after village. At every stage of its long progress through the Union, the family were pressed with opportunities to greet the enormous crowds of country people waiting by the line for them to pass by. Sometimes the train simply slowed through little halts to give time for waving; on occasion at night the Princesses were already in their dressing gowns when they were needed to appear at the doors to wave. The Queen advised them to put on their jewellery – this would make their dressing gowns look like long dresses. The Queen told Queen Mary that the constant stopping was rather exhausting but they liked to do it because the people 'are so nice, & some come a very long way, carrying babies, & standing patiently for hours, & one meets the ordinary citizens this way.'[84]

At an ostrich farm at Le Roux, outside Oudtshoorn, the Queen and the Princesses cut tail feathers from an ostrich. The owner of the farm, Basie Meyer, said he hoped that changing fashions in the USA and Britain would return their pre-war prosperity to the ostrich farmers of South Africa. To help do just that, the Princesses, as well as the Queen, had made a point of incorporating ostrich feathers in many of their tour clothes. That night in the dusk they heard for the first time a crowd of Bantu children singing, in slow haunting rhythm, as the train drew into a siding happily called Konigsrust – King's Rest.

Rest was always the problem. Prime Minister Smuts saw the tour as political rather than recreational and he worked his guests very hard. When they were by the Indian Ocean, they could sometimes bathe and have picnics or *braaivleis* on the shore and the Princesses tried to ride as often as they could, on mounts lent to them locally. But most days were gruelling. The rule for royal tours was to keep Sunday as a day of rest and simple worship. This tour offered some unusual services, the first of which was at George. By the estuary of the Touws river an arbour had been created, a table with a white cloth had been laid, and a lectern was cut from the branch of a tree. Here the Bishop of George held a service, which was a more sympathetic affair than those in the Dutch Reformed churches which the family had to attend, where they could understand little or nothing.

In place after place, crowds of Bantu men and women lined the track; as the train passed by they would break into the Bantu anthem, 'Nkosi Sikelel'i Afrika' (Lord, bless Africa). The Queen loved the singing. She had few solo engagements on the tour, but her spontaneity, her sense of fun and her instinct for what would do people good infected the whole tour. Enid Bagnold described her uncanny ability to relate to both scores of individuals and massive crowds. Writing to her friend Lady Diana Cooper, she observed,

> She is like Irving* after a First Night and oneself at the stage door. I watched her closely . . . when she was inspecting ex-servicemen right under my nose . . . She has an extraordinary control of every

---

* Sir Henry Irving (1838–1905), the most celebrated English actor of his day.

facial muscle, a very delicate control, so that she makes valuable every look and half smile in a very experienced way. We others, and the Princesses, just smile or don't smile, but the Queen has a bigger range and a delicacy of holding or tilting her head or casting a small look for an instant that gives a rain of pleasure here and there and on whoever gets one of the fragments. It's the sort of thing one sometimes sees Edith Evans do on the stage when she is half listening, half smiling at someone.[85]

The historical rift with Britain was strongest of all in the Orange Free State. In one town the nervous tension on the arrival of the royal party was eased by the Mayor, a Mr Hart. When he took off his hat it was evident that his hair was full of bees, and that he did not appear to be bothered. This gave rise to some hilarity.[86] During the visit to the Orange Free State they entered Basutoland, a British protectorate. At Umtata, on the border, the King and Queen stood up in their car as it drove slowly past the crowds. All were aware of the historic nature of the visit – Basutoland had never been conquered by either the British or the Dutch; now people came in their thousands to pay homage.

It was a magnificent spectacle. 'For days the Basuto had been riding in from the mountains and it was estimated that 60–70,000 had assembled for the great Pitso [the gathering of tribes under their chiefs] . . . The steep hillside was covered with Bantus including prisoners of both sexes and the inmates of the leper hospital.'[87] About 40,000 of the assembly were on horseback. As the King and Queen approached the dais the crowds shouted 'Pula!' – rain. In some districts the drought had been unbroken for three years. The day after the royal party arrived the rains came, and the King was seen as a rain-maker.

In Natal the Royal Family enjoyed a break in the Natal National Park Hostel. The flowers there, as elsewhere, were a dazzling sight; the Queen wrote to her sister May that 'the profusion & terrific colours just took my breath away! . . . hibiscus, & frangipani and morning glory (which at once made me think of Mother) not to mention roses & lilies and delphiniums and chrysanthemums & dahlias all mixed up together!'[88] When they flew into Eshowe they were greeted at the aerodrome by what appeared to be a chaotic crowd of Zulus. Then the mêlée resolved itself into a highly organized but wild war-dance. 'It was an impressive sight,' Princess Elizabeth wrote, 'with

5,000 warriors singing and stamping their feet, ending up with a terrific charge to the edge of the dais where we were. This they were allowed to do only because Mummy begged them to be allowed to come nearer.'[89]

In Benomi in the East Rand there was an unfortunate incident. The King and Queen were particularly tired that day and everyone was tense, according to Peter Townsend. Suddenly, to the Queen's great consternation, they saw a policeman rushing forward as another man sprinted up and grabbed hold of their car. The Queen misunderstood what was happening and was terrified that it was an assault; she beat the man off with her parasol, breaking it. In fact he was an ex-serviceman, named Kayser Sitholi, who was desperate to show the King his loyalty by giving him a sum of money, as was the custom of native tribesmen greeting their chief. Sitholi, who meant no harm to anyone, was dragged off. The King and Queen were both aghast; the King asked Townsend to find out if the man was all right. 'I hope he was not too badly hurt.'[90]

The Queen liked Durban. 'They are very English & Scottish there, & cling to the old links with Great Britain,' she wrote to Elizabeth Elphinstone. The churches were full of young people, a nice change from home. And even the old Boer farmers who were 'brought up Republicans & to look upon England as an enemy have come to greet us'.[91] Pretoria, the administrative capital of South Africa, was the official climax of the tour. The Queen established a rapport with the Mayor of Pretoria, despite his communist background. 'He confided to Mummy that he had been shut up without evidence, and that he had never even cut a telephone wire or blown up a railway line!' wrote Princess Elizabeth.[92]

The excitement of the crowds in both Pretoria and Johannesburg was palpable. But the demands were relentless and the Queen was concerned about the strain on the King. However warm the welcome, he was constantly worrying about conditions in Britain. She told Queen Mary: 'This tour is being very strenuous as I feared it would be, & doubly hard for Bertie who feels he should be at home . . . We think of home all the time.'[93] Sometimes his frustration got the better of the King and he lost his temper. He found the officiousness of the Afrikaner police irksome, as did the rest of his family. The *Cape Times* apparently reported that on one country walk he remarked that they had shaken off the Gestapo at last. On other occasions he could become exhausted and irritated by the constant pressure of the crowds. The Queen would stroke his arm or his hand to calm him. The royal biographer Elizabeth Longford was told that he was infuriated by the Nationalists' hostility to Smuts and burst out to the Queen, 'I'd like to shoot them all!' To which she replied soothingly, 'But Bertie, you can't shoot them *all*.'[94] Ted Grove commented that he did not think the King 'could have got through it all without the love and devotion of the Queen. We admired the way she cared and watched over him during the tour when sometimes the continual heat and travel in the confined space of the Royal Train did nothing to improve his occasional bouts of temper.'[95]

In his public speeches the King tried to remind his audiences of all that Britain had endured in the previous eight years; he told Queen Mary that he felt the South Africans, whose lives were much more comfortable, should be reminded of 'the trials going on at home'. He and the Queen and Princesses were often embarrassed by the amount of food that was always spread before them.[96]

One evening, the King ordered that the train be stopped beside a fairly distant beach. The British journalist James Cameron, who was covering the trip, recorded that the police roped off a pathway from the train and down it walked 'a solitary figure in a blue bathrobe, carrying a towel. The sea was a long way off, but he went. And all alone, on the great empty beach, between the surging banks of the people who might not approach, the King of England stepped into the Indian Ocean and jumped up and down – the loneliest man, at that moment, in the world.'[97]

It was tiring for the Queen as well. She may have been a brilliant actress who could be relied on to give a wonderful performance, but her feelings were genuine and the constant need to display them was exhausting. Enid Bagnold stood by the track to watch the White Train pass by. 'Suddenly there was the Queen in her garden dress, sitting in the window. I waved and she gave one more sickly wave like a dying duck, a sketch of her other waves. She looked as though she would die if she saw just one more woman to wave to.'[98] Bagnold was sympathetic and correct. The Queen confessed to Elizabeth Elphinstone that 'I am rather gaga & tired' and 'It is a curious thing how driving through crowded streets full of eager people seems to draw life out of one.'[99] Later she repeated: 'One feels quite sucked dry some-times – I am sure that crowds of people take something out of one – I can almost feel it going sometimes, and it takes a little time to put it back!'[100]

It was a daunting programme for everyone. They spent thirty-five nights on board the train. Many more miles were covered in a fleet of Daimlers and in aircraft. 'Mouse' Fielden, Captain of the King's Flight, who became a long-term friend of the Queen, remarked later that 'it was not until the South African Tour in 1947 that the King really began to enjoy flying'. Both King and Queen understood the freedom, speed and excitement offered by air travel. They particularly enjoyed communicating with one another on the intercom system when flying in separate planes.[101]

They flew up to the British colonies of Northern and Southern Rhodesia, where there was much less tension than in South Africa. The Queen relaxed in Government House in Salisbury, happy that, unlike many of the South African houses in which they stayed, it was a real home. She liked the Governor, Major General Sir John Kennedy, and his wife. Sir John later recalled that on the day they arrived at Salisbury he took the King out for a walk in the grounds of Government House, where there was a tree planted by King Edward VIII as Prince of Wales. 'The King stopped and looked at it reflectively, and then he said, "My brother never had the good fortune I had when I married my wife."'[102] They made a visit to the grave of Cecil Rhodes in Matabeleland; on the stony hillside, the heel of one of the Queen's high-heeled shoes broke. The press party made quite a show of the fact that Princess Elizabeth gave her shoes to her mother and completed the day in her stockinged feet. 'So like Mummy', said the Princess, 'to set out in those shoes.'[103]

In Salisbury, the Queen could indulge in a little shopping; she bought nylon stockings, crystallized fruit and chocolates for friends and family back home starved of such delicacies. She had a few solo engagements: visits to the Queen Elizabeth's Welfare Clinic in Salisbury, to a gathering of representatives of women's organizations at Government House, for the presentation of Red Cross certificates. Wearing her Black Watch regimental badge, she spoke to a contingent of Rhodesian members of the Black Watch in Bulawayo. Altogether she found Rhodesia 'most attractive, a very agreeable mixture of British & good colonial, and a nice feeling of freedom everywhere'.[104] She maintained a close affection for the country for many years to come.

Back in Johannesburg, Smuts arranged a private meeting with the exiled Prince and Princess Paul of Yugoslavia. The Queen was now pleased to have a reunion with them. She wrote at once to Princess Marina, Duchess of Kent, to tell her how her sister Olga was. The Duchess was deeply grateful. 'It is sweet of you to write the way you do, so full of heart,' she replied to the Queen.[105]

Towards the end of their trip an important moment arrived. Princess Elizabeth came of age on reaching her twenty-first birthday. On 21 April – a public holiday in South Africa – she took the salute at a march-past of the military garrison in Cape Town; she attended a large youth rally and then in the evening she made a remarkable broadcast pledging to devote her life to her people.

I should like to make that dedication now. It is very simple. I declare before you all that my whole life, whether it be long or short, shall be devoted to your service and the service of our great Imperial Commonwealth to which we all belong. But I shall not have strength to carry out this resolution unless you join in it with me, as I now invite you to do; I know that your support will be unfailingly given. God help me to make good my vow; and God bless all of you who are willing to share in it.[106]

Queen Mary listened in London, and wrote to the Queen afterwards that the broadcast was 'perfect . . . and of course I wept.'[107] The night was completed with fireworks by the ocean and a ball for the younger generation; it was attended by Field Marshal Smuts, who gave a speech in honour of the Princess and presented her with a diamond necklace. The next day, the Queen was pleased to receive an honorary degree of Doctor of Laws from the University of Cape Town. Smuts made a short speech, to which the Queen replied – the only formal speech she made throughout the journey.

The tour was finally over. When they embarked from Cape Town, Smuts and the King made warm formal speeches of farewell, and then the Queen paid her own tribute in a few impromptu words, thanking the women and children of South Africa for their welcome.[108] 'Tot siens' (so long, or *au revoir*) both King and Queen said in Afrikaans – a phrase the Queen liked and would use throughout her life.*

---

* The visit did not give Smuts the boost he might have expected. He lost the 1948 election;

From the ship, Queen Elizabeth wrote a long letter to May Elphinstone about the natural glories and the political difficulties of South Africa. She had enjoyed the tour, though she had been exhausted by it and was looking forward to being home – 'a little bit of England & Scotland will be heaven!'[109] Now, she and the King knew, they were sailing back to face many difficult, often emotional, issues – the continued deprivation of the British people, more radical social changes by the government, the independence of India, the jewel in the crown of Empire – and, perhaps most difficult of all, the independence of their beloved elder daughter. It had become clear to them both while they were in South Africa that her affection for Prince Philip would not pass – it was deep and real.

Tommy Lascelles thought that Princess Elizabeth was one of the great successes of the trip. 'She has come on in the most surprising way, and all in the right direction. She has got all P'cess Mary's solid and endearing qualities plus a perfectly natural power of enjoying herself without any trace of shyness.' She had a good healthy sense of fun, he said. 'Moreover, when necessary, she can take on the old bores with much of her mother's skill, and never spares herself in that exhausting part of royal duty.' She had 'an astonishing solicitude for other people's comfort' and:

> she has become extremely businesslike, and understands what a burden it is to the Staff if some regard is not paid to the clock. She has developed an admirable technique of going up behind her mother and prodding her in the Achilles tendon with the point of her umbrella when time is being wasted in unnecessary conversation. And when necessary – not infrequently – she tells her father off to rights. My impression, by the way, is that we shall be subscribing to a wedding present before the year is out.[110]

---

although he won more votes than the Nationalists, they were concentrated in large urban majorities in safe seats.

CHAPTER SIXTEEN

JOY AND SORROW

1947–1952

'He was such an angel to the children & me'

ON 10 JULY 1947 this statement was released from Buckingham Palace: 'It is with the greatest pleasure that the King and Queen announce the betrothal of their dearly beloved daughter the Princess Elizabeth to Lieutenant Philip Mountbatten, RN, son of the late Prince Andrew of Greece and Princess Andrew (Princess Alice of Battenberg) to which union the King has gladly given his consent.'

The personal dimension of monarchy can give a sense of continuity to national life which republics lack. The life of a royal family is punctuated by events which are familiar to everyone. Births, weddings, illnesses, deaths, follow each other with the sort of predictability every family knows and understands. The wedding of Princess Elizabeth was followed over the next three years by a series of events which were to be emotionally charged for the Queen – her own silver wedding anniversary, the births of her first grandchildren, Prince Charles and Princess Anne, and then the long-drawn-out illness of her husband.

Unlike her younger sister, Princess Elizabeth was reserved and thus often seemed shy. Her biographer Elizabeth Longford thought 'reticent' was a better word. 'Reticence has its own good reasons for silence; connected with the inner citadel.'[1] The Queen had never encouraged the strictly academic instruction of her daughters and each of them (particularly Princess Margaret) regretted this. Both Princesses felt under-educated, although Marion Crawford had been a conscientious governess, and the addition of other teachers such as Henry Marten and Toni de Bellaigue had broadened their horizons. In one important respect, however, the Princesses' training had been impeccable and this had come from their parents, as they accompanied them on more and more public engagements.

In March 1946 Princess Elizabeth had made a successful visit to

Northern Ireland. The Queen's sister Rose, Lady Granville, whose husband Wisp was Governor, wrote to the Queen saying that her daughter looked lovely and had inherited her mother's 'wonderful gift of looking as if she was loving it all'. She watched people listening to the Princess make a speech and 'I saw a sort of change come over them – & you could see them thinking that there was something else beside youth & charm, & what is so nice, looking as if they were patting their own backs about it, as if she belonged to them – which I suppose she does, in a sort of way!! . . . You must feel very proud of her darling – I would be!'[2]

Proud, yes, but the Queen was more and more worried about press intrusion into the lives of her daughters, particularly by the *Mail* and *Express* groups.[3] The area of greatest allure to newspapers was any suggestion of young romance. Princess Elizabeth's name was sometimes linked, privately at least, with well-born officers of the Grenadier Guards who had been stationed at Windsor Castle during the war and whose company she enjoyed. But the Princess's real interest always lay with Prince Philip of Greece, who was still on active service with his ship in the Far East. Their friendship was promoted, sometimes too forcefully, by Philip's uncle, Lord Mountbatten, whose social enthusiasms could interfere with his sense of decorum.

After Prince Philip returned to Britain in early 1946 he and the Princess saw more of each other. Lady Airlie recalled a conversation in which Queen Mary told her that the young couple had been in love for at least eighteen months: 'but the King and Queen feel that she is too young to be engaged yet. They want her to see more of the world before committing herself and to meet more men. After all she's only nineteen and one is very impressionable at that age.'[4]

Prince Philip, five years older than the Princess, was nothing if not determined. In June 1946, now serving as an instructor at HMS *Glendower*, a naval training establishment in North Wales, he wrote to the Queen to apologize for having committed the 'monumental cheek' of inviting himself to the Palace. But 'However contrite I feel there is always a small voice that keeps saying "nothing ventured, nothing gained" – well, I did venture and I gained a wonderful time.'[5] In early September 1946 the Queen invited him to Balmoral and it was during this holiday in the hills that he and the Princess decided to become engaged and to tell her parents.

After he left Balmoral, the Prince wrote an exuberant letter to the

Queen: 'I am sure I do not deserve all the good things which have happened to me. To have been spared in the war and seen victory, to have been given the chance to rest and re-adjust myself, to have fallen in love completely and unreservedly, makes all one's personal and even the world's troubles seem small and petty.' At last, he said, life had a purpose.[6]

> I only realize now what a difference those few weeks, which seemed to flash past, have made to me. I arrived still not accustomed to the idea of peace, rather fed up with everything with the feeling that there was not much to look forward to and rather grudgingly accepting the idea of going on in the peacetime navy.
>
> This holiday alone has helped to dispel those feelings. The generous hospitality and the warm friendliness did much to restore my faith in permanent values and brighten up a rather warped view of life. Naturally there is one circumstance which has done more for me than anything else in my life.[7]

But being in love did not make the Prince docile. Later that year he wrote to the Queen to apologize for getting carried away and starting 'a rather heated dicussion'. Politics seem to have been the problem. The Prince's views were a considerable way to the left of those of the Queen and he had by now come to the conclusion that trying to shift her from her instinctive conservatism was counter-productive. He hoped she did not think him 'violently argumentative and an exponent of socialism' and would forgive him 'if I did say anything I ought not to have said'.[8]

The Prince's strong views were not the issue. The King and Queen knew well by now that he and their daughter were in love and wished to marry. But they persuaded them to wait until their return from South Africa before the engagement was announced. Just before the family's departure, Prince Philip came to say goodbye and then wrote to the Queen to thank her for a remark she had made to him that day. 'I can only take it that you referred to Lilibet when you said that my fate "was in someone else's hands". It was the most heartening thing you could have said to keep my spirits up while you are away.'[9] Princess Elizabeth and Prince Philip wrote to each other constantly while she was in South Africa. The enforced separation did nothing to diminish their ardour – it may even have strengthened it. After the family's return, Prince Philip told the Queen he was sure that the delay had been right, but he and the Princess now wanted to start their new life together.[10]

Letters that the Queen wrote at the time show that she was supportive, if also anxious about her daughter's decision. 'You can imagine what emotion this engagement has given me,' she wrote to Tommy Lascelles. 'It is one of the things that has been in the forefront of all one's hopes & plans for a daughter who has such a burden to carry, and one can only pray that she has made the right decision, I think she has – but he is untried as yet.'[11]

On 7 July 1947 the Queen wrote to her sister May to tell her 'very secretly' (underlined in black and red) that Lilibet had 'made up her mind' to become engaged to Philip Mountbatten. While they were abroad Prince Philip had become a naturalized British citizen (as he was entitled to do, having served in the Royal Navy) and had taken his uncle's name, Mountbatten. 'As you know,' the Queen continued, 'she has known him ever since she was 12, & I think that she is really fond of him, & I do pray that she will be very happy.' They were keeping it all 'a deadly secret' because if the press found out 'they are likely to ruin everything.'[12] She wrote also to Arthur Penn, saying that she knew he would understand the emotion she was feeling. Her daughter, she wrote, 'has thought about it a great deal, and had made up her mind some time ago'. At the end of the letter she added, 'I say, Arthur, how annoyed the Grenadiers will be!'[13]

Penn was devoted to the Princess, whom he invariably called 'The Colonel' – 'In the last 18 months,' he wrote to the Queen, 'she has clothed herself with a new beauty of character – & of appearance, if I may say so.'[14] He thought that history was repeating itself, at least with regard to the press: he still had a letter from the Queen about her own engagement in 1923 in which she had written, 'Aren't the papers awful?' Nonetheless, he thought that 'their columns only reflect the intense interest & goodwill felt by thousands who don't know the Colonel ... What a daughter to have.' Penn realized how torn the Queen must be at the prospect of her daughter leaving home.[15]

The announcement of the engagement on 10 July was a rare shaft of happiness at a grim time both at home and abroad. The independence and partition of India was only weeks away and the sub-continent was already riven by bloody rioting. In Palestine Britain found herself caught between the Zionist Jews who, after the Nazi Holocaust, were even more determined to create a Jewish national home, and the settled Arab population who wanted no such thing. Some Zionists resorted to terrorism against British forces in Palestine in protest against Britain's failure to do more for their cause. Two British sergeants were captured and hanged by Jewish terrorists, and 4,500 European Jewish refugees on board the ship *Exodus* were prevented by the British from landing. The Russian Foreign Minister V. M. Molotov had denounced the offer by the US Secretary of State, George Marshall, to mount the financial rescue of Europe. This Soviet rejection was seen as a serious blow to the recovery of the continent.

Victorious Britain seemed to be on her knees. As well as bread rationing, controls on the imports of petrol, tobacco and paper were imposed. The Dominions began to send food parcels to the mother country. In New Zealand, branches of the Women's Institute decided to adopt and sustain their English counterparts. The Treasury was drawing up a secret 'famine food programme'. Clement Attlee announced a crisis austerity plan for the British economy, food rations were cut further, foreign travel allowances for British citizens were abolished, a coal strike in Yorkshire closed the Sheffield steelworks. The King was appalled by all that was happening to the country; in many ways he thought the situation even worse than in wartime. 'One feels so powerless to do anything to help,' he confessed to his mother.[16]

In such austere conditions, news of Princess Elizabeth's engagement brought widespread happiness and many letters of congratulation to the Queen. Queen Ingrid of Denmark wrote asking for advice on clothes for the wedding and opined that the Queen must be happy about the marriage – 'You couldn't have a more good-looking son-in-law'.[17] D'Arcy Osborne wrote that she would have to make difficult decisions for the wedding; faced with the choice between austerity and traditional pageantry, he thought most people would prefer the latter. Tongue firmly in cheek, he wondered if she would invite Stalin.[18]

The press became more and more demanding – at least by the standards of the day. Norman Hartnell begged the King and Queen for help, declaring that he was being persecuted by reporters for refusing to reveal details of the Princess's wedding dress. With this plea the Palace Press Secretary, Commander Richard Colville, sent a note to the Queen suggesting a formal statement to the press that it was the Princess's wish that the details of her dress be kept secret.[19] Colville also reported to the Queen that members of the Women's Press Club of London had asked him such questions as what cosmetics the Princess would wear on her wedding day; whether her mother and sister would help her to dress; whether the bridegroom would kiss the bridesmaids. He had asked whether journalists thought such details worthy of publication. They had said yes. He had then made it clear to them that he, the Press Secretary, 'was not prepared to publicise the private lives of the Royal Family'. He was, however, prepared to provide details of the family's charitable and welfare works.[20]

The King decided to invest the Princess with the Order of the Garter on 11 November; he did the same for Prince Philip on 19 November so that the Princess would be senior to her husband in the Order. His future son-in-law was to be created a royal highness and the titles of his peerage would be Duke of Edinburgh, Earl of Merioneth and Baron Greenwich. He told Queen Mary that he knew this was a lot to take on all at once, 'but I know Philip understands his new responsibilities on his marriage to Lilibet.'[21] More than 3,000 presents came from all over the world. They were unpacked, put on display by men from the Grenadier Guards, and catalogued by Beryl Poignand.

In straitened times, the question of what allowance the Princess and her new husband should receive from the Civil List to cover the official expenses of their Households was problematic. The King asked for £50,000 for the couple. He found the Chancellor of the Exchequer, Hugh Dalton, difficult on the matter. Dalton suggested £30,000, some of which would be taxable. But on 13 November Dalton had to resign after revealing details of his new budget to a journalist just before he informed the House of Commons itself. The new Chancellor, Stafford Cripps, accepted the royal request for £50,000 for the young couple.

Among the celebrations, the King and Queen gave a dance at the Palace on the evening of 18 November. Duff Cooper, now ambassador to France, and Lady Diana came on the Golden Arrow from Paris. They talked to the King and Queen, and Duff recorded in his diary, 'She has grown very large, but she looked queenly and was very well dressed. They were both very friendly. The King was most outspoken, first aside to me and then aside to Diana, in his criticism of his ministers . . . Princess Elizabeth was looking really charming – everything that a princess in a fairy tale ought to look like on the eve of her wedding.'[22]

Two days later, on 20 November, the wedding took place in

Westminster Abbey. It was an emotional occasion for the whole family. When the Princess and her husband left by carriage from the Palace for their honeymoon, she was concerned that she had not said proper goodbyes. She wrote to her mother, 'My mouth, my eyes, everything was jammed with rose petals and I felt as if I might cry if there was any more delay!'[23]

The young couple spent the first part of their honeymoon at Broadlands, the Mountbatten home in Hampshire. There the Princess received a loving letter from her father: 'I was so proud of you & thrilled at having you so close to me on our long walk in Westminster Abbey,' he wrote, 'but when I handed your hand to the Archbishop I felt that I had lost something very precious. You were so calm & composed during the Service & said your words with such conviction, that I knew everything was all right.' He was relieved that she had told her mother that the delay they had imposed on her engagement and marriage was for the best.

I was rather afraid that you had thought I was being hard hearted about it. I was so anxious for you to come to South Africa as you knew. Our family, us four, the 'Royal Family' must remain together with additions of course at suitable moments!! I have watched you grow up all these years with pride under the skilful direction of Mummy, who as you know is the most marvellous person in the World in my eyes, & I can, I know, always count on you, & now Philip, to help us in our work. Your leaving us has left a great blank in our lives but do remember that your old home is still yours & do come back to it as much & as often as possible. I can see that you are sublimely happy with Philip which is right but don't forget us is the wish of
    Your ever loving & devoted
    PAPA[24]

From Broadlands, the Princess wrote equally loving letters to her parents. To her mother she said, 'Darling Mummy, I don't know where to begin this letter, or what to say, but I know I must write it somehow, as I feel so much about it. First of all, to say thank you . . . I tried to say the other evening how much I appreciated all you have done for me, but somehow it wouldn't come. It's been such fun being together – all four of us – and I hope that we shall have just as much fun, now that you have got a son-in-law!' She hoped her mother had not been too miserable at the wedding. 'I was so happy and enjoying myself so much, that I became completely selfish and forgot about your feelings or anyone else's!'

She thought her mother had looked wonderful: 'Not just "the bride's mother" but you – and in the middle of all the fuss and bustle, you were as helpful and wonderful as ever. (I do hope this doesn't sound sentimental, because it isn't meant to be – just the truth). I think I've got the best mother and father in the world, and I only hope that I can bring up my children in the happy atmosphere of love and fairness which Margaret and I have grown up in. I feel it will be easier for me with such a vivid example and personal experience to guide me!' The Princess went on to say that she and Prince Philip felt completely at ease together – 'we behave as though we had belonged to each other for years! Philip is an angel – he is so kind and thoughtful, and living with him and having him around all the time is just perfect.'[25]

The Queen loved this letter; she re-read it many times, she told the Princess – 'and each time I feel more thankful for our darling little daughter!' She assured Princess Elizabeth that her parents were 'so happy in your happiness', having always hoped that she would be able to make a marriage of the heart as well as the head. 'We both love Philip already as a son.' She looked forward to having just as much fun as before now that 'we four' had become 'we five'. She wrote that she had thought about her daughter 'for nearly every minute' since she had driven away. 'Darling Lilibet, no parents ever had a better daughter, you are always such an unselfish & thoughtful angel to Papa & me, & we are so thankful for all your goodness and sweetness . . . That you & Philip should be blissfully happy & love each other through good days and bad or depressing days is my one wish – a thousand blessings to you both from your very very loving Mummy.'[26]

From Hampshire the newlyweds travelled, with corgis, to Birkhall; the Princess, used to the Highlands in the summer, found the November corridors cold and draughty but the rooms were wonderfully warmed by large log fires. She wrote again to her mother to tell her how 'blissfully happy' she was, but she was beginning to realize what terrific changes marriage brought to life. She did want to ask her mother's advice, in particular about how to square her husband's feelings with the formalities of the Court. 'Philip is terribly independent, and I quite understand the poor darling wanting to start off properly, without everything being <u>done</u> for us.' She hoped to enable her husband to be 'boss in his own home' and she knew how difficult this would be, living in her old rooms at Buckingham Palace and subject to endless protocol. She was right – it was indeed hard for the Prince to remain his own man. He considered some of the courtiers to be overly conservative and stuffy; they found him abrasive and were unsympathetic. But it was essential for him to strive to maintain his independence and authority over the years ahead.

The Princess ended her letter by writing, 'It is so lovely and peaceful just now – Philip is reading full length on the sofa, Susan is stretched out before the fire, Rummy is fast asleep in his box beside the fire, and I am busy writing this in one of the arm chairs near the fire (you see how important the fire is!). It's heaven up here!'[27]

The new Duke of Edinburgh also wrote deeply affectionate letters in which he poured out his love for his new wife to his new mother-in-law. In one he said:

> Lilibet is the only 'thing' in this world which is absolutely real to me and my ambition is to weld the two of us into a new combined existence that will not only be able to withstand the shocks directed at us but will also have a positive existence for the good . . . Cherish Lilibet? I wonder if that word is enough to express what is in me. Does one cherish one's sense of humour or one's musical ear or one's eyes? I am not sure, but I know that I thank God for them and so, very humbly, I thank God for Lilibet and for us.[28]

*

THE NEXT GREAT family celebration was of the King and Queen's Silver Wedding anniversary. It was an important and emotional moment for both of them – and for the country. The King's biographer rightly quoted Walter Bagehot, who had stated, 'A princely marriage is the brilliant edition of a universal fact, and as such it rivets mankind.' Eighty years before, with the happy marriage of Queen Victoria and Prince Albert very much in mind, he had written, 'We have come to believe that it is natural to have a virtuous sovereign, and that domestic virtues are as likely to be found on thrones as they are eminent when there.'[29]

The marriage, at the threshold of which Lady Elizabeth Bowes Lyon had hesitated so long, had been a triumph. Both had brought great love, support and happiness to the other. Their evidently happy life together with their daughters had given great joy and a sense of confidence in the monarchy, particularly during the war. The family's happiness was itself an object of national celebration.

On the morning of 26 April 1948, the King and Queen celebrated Holy Communion at the Palace and then drove with Princess Margaret in an open landau to St Paul's Cathedral, Princess Elizabeth and Prince Philip following in a second open carriage. It was an exquisite spring day and the streets were lined with troops and filled with huge crowds cheering in the sunshine. That afternoon, after a joyful service, they drove in an open car some twenty-two miles through London's streets, greeted by more enthusiastic crowds. Back at the Palace they appeared several times on the balcony to acknowledge the cheering people in the Mall and that evening they both broadcast to the nation. The King said it was 'unforgettable' to realize how many thousands of people 'wish to join in the thankfulness we feel for the twenty-five years of supremely happy married life which have been granted to us'.[30]

The Queen spoke, clearly from the heart: 'The world of our day is longing to find the secret of community, and all married lives are, in a sense, communities in miniature. There must be many who feel as we do that the sanctities of married life are in some ways the highest form of human fellowship, affording a rock-like foundation on which all the best in the life of the nations is built.' Remembering her parents and 'my own happy childhood', she said, 'I realise more and more the wonderful sense of security and happiness that comes from a loved home. Therefore at this time my heart goes out to all those who are living in uncongenial surroundings and who are longing for the time when they will have a home of their own.'[31]

Congratulations and tributes, public and private, were numerous. The National Association of Master Bakers, Confectioners and Caterers baked a vast three-tiered, red, white and blue cake weighing some 240 pounds while the Poet Laureate, John Masefield, offered his own praise:

> To These, today (to them a sacred day)
> Our hopes become a praying that the stress
> Of these, their cruel years, may pass away
> And happy years succeed, and Wisdom bless.

The King and Queen were both surprised and much moved by the tributes that came from Britain and from all over the world. 'We were both dumbfounded over our reception,' the King told his mother.[32] The day after their anniversary, they gave a formal dance at the Palace. Duff Cooper, back again from Paris for the occasion, had a long talk with the Queen 'which is always a great pleasure for me. She was as charming as ever and talked so sensibly about everything.' Nye Bevan, the Minister of Health, was there 'in an ordinary blue suit' – rather than in white tie and tails, like everyone else. Cooper thought the Queen would say something to him about it when he came towards them 'but he must have sensed danger for he swerved off.'[33]

Bevan may have been concerned that the Queen would have more serious questions to ask him than about his dress. The government's plans, which Bevan was leading, to create a national health service and the consequent nationalization of the hospitals were causing the Royal Family concern.

*

THE LABOUR PARTY had been elected precisely to extend public ownership, and a national health service was one of the basic building blocks of its proposed welfare state. The King and the Queen both understood this, but they were also devoted to the idea of individual service and a serious question for the monarchy now was where a nationalized health service would leave royal patronage.

At the end of the war there was a patchwork of about a thousand charity-funded hospitals in Britain and hundreds of them had links to the Crown. Members of the Royal Family had preserved these links for generations. These hospitals were unevenly spread across the country and of varying quality but Frank Prochaska later speculated that what he called 'the old Guard', including Queen Mary, the Queen and the Duke of Gloucester, must have seen the nationalization of the charitable hospitals as an act of vandalism comparable to the dissolution of the monasteries.[34]

Be that as it may, Nye Bevan's bill to nationalize the hospitals passed through Parliament in November 1946 and was due to take effect in July 1948. During the interregnum, members of the Royal Family 'made a concerted effort to bolster morale in the hospitals by visiting many of them and making symbolic donations'.[35] In his 1946 Christmas broadcast, the King had taken up the topical word 'reconstruction' to speak of the need for 'spiritual reconstruction', saying 'If our feet are on the road of common charity ... our differences will never destroy our underlying unity'.[36]

Similarly, the Queen never criticized government policy, but time and again she emphasized the need for individual service and for Christian commitment. Thus, praising Tubby Clayton, the creator of Toc H, the Christian charity which she had admired for years, she said, 'In a world where the individual may sometimes seem almost to lose his individuality, submerged beneath the mass movements of which we hear so much, we may well be heartened by remembering that we stand here today because of the inspiration of one man.'[37] (Clayton's church, All Hallows Berkyngechirche by the Tower, had been badly bombed during the war and he toured the United States afterwards seeking funds for its restoration. In 1948 the Queen laid the foundation stone of the east wall of the restored church.)

But the spirit of the time demanded centralization and collectivism. Labour ministers were convinced that the state was the embodiment of social good and that only state action could transform society. To the dismay of the Queen, whose faith was at her core, even the Church of England endorsed and embraced this concept. She was concerned that the Church seemed to be always in retreat in face of the march of what, like many others, she called 'material values'.

Despite imminent nationalization, the Royal Family maintained the links with those hospitals with which they were most closely associated. In March 1948, the Queen visited the Queen Elizabeth Hospital in Gateshead and made clear once more her enthusiasm for individual efforts, declaring that state control did 'not absolve us from the practice of charity or from the exercise of vigilance. The English way of progress has always been to preserve good qualities and apply them to new systems.'[38] In May that year she was guest of honour to mark Hospitals' Day at the Mansion House. The future of the NHS could not be predicted, she said, but it would still need charitable volunteers – she called on hospitals to enrol charitable workers so as to 'show that sympathy and compassion were still freely given'.[39] That same month Princess Elizabeth attended the annual Court of Governors of the Queen Elizabeth Hospital for Children in Hackney, of which she was president and her mother patron. Referring to the members of the Court whose years of work would soon be rewarded by compulsory retirement, she was frank: 'I feel a very special regret because of the long connection my family has had with this hospital.'[40]

Nationalization proceeded, but the charities were determined to try and keep royal patronage alive. Perhaps to its chagrin, certainly to its surprise, the Labour government found that such patronage was still needed. Indeed a Home Office memorandum warned that any withdrawal of royal patronage might be construed as royal disapproval of the new NHS – and that would not do for either side.[41] In fact there was a silver lining. Now that both the municipal hospitals and the former charitable hospitals were all under the same NHS umbrella, royal patronage could be extended to the municipal hospitals as well. As Prochaska put it, 'Not even Bevan, that scourge of social distinction, could bring himself to blackball the royal family from the NHS.' In 1948 Queen Mary had, with regret, resigned as president of the London Hospital – in July 1949 she and the Hospital were both pleased when she returned as joint patron with the King.[42] The Queen felt the same about St Mary's Paddington, of which she was president. Her title was changed to Honorary President and she remained involved with St Mary's for the rest of her life.

As with the hospitals, so with her regiments and the other organizations for which she felt an affection – the Queen tended to remain with them for ever. One of the least expected, perhaps, was the London Gardens Society, of which she became patron in 1947 and which was soon a favourite. One letter thanked her for a visit to the London Cottage Back Gardens in July 1947. 'Dear Mam, We was very pleased to see you to see our gardens and we always says you seem happier when you come amongst the likes of us than in the Palace lot and having to act queen when you aint been born to it and must be hard work for you. We liked your pretty clothes and you are always welcome to come to us when you wants a friend. Our kids and our chaps send there love to you, From all of us with Gardens.'[43]

With the exception of 1953, when she was unwell, the Queen visited gardens in one London borough or another every year from 1949 to 2001 (the penultimate year of her life). The tours originally included about six or seven different gardens – sometimes merely a good windowbox display at a council flat. By the end of her life the tour was reduced and it became a tradition for her to end it with a visit to a police station or fire station where there was some form of garden, and where she would join the officers for a drink. All of these visits gave pleasure to generations of London gardeners.

*

To the Queen's delight, Princess Elizabeth had become pregnant some three months after her marriage. She and Prince Philip were still living in Buckingham Palace, and the baby was due to be born there in November 1948. The home that the King had planned for them at Sunninghill had burned down. (In summer 1949 they were finally able to move to Clarence House, a house rebuilt by Nash in the 1820s for the Duke of Clarence next to St James's Palace.)

The Queen now had a rare tussle with Tommy Lascelles. A stickler for precedent, she was displeased to learn that Lascelles had persuaded the King to dispense with the tradition that the Home Secretary had to be in attendance at a royal birth. She asked that the decision be reversed. But Lascelles pointed out that the Dominions would also expect to be represented, so that in all there might be seven ministers sitting outside Princess Elizabeth's room while she gave birth. The King was horrified and told Lascelles that he would drop the tradition.

The Queen was of a different opinion. Fearing as she did that the avalanche of reform was sweeping away the old world which she loved and represented, she wrote to Lascelles, 'I feel that we should cling to our domestic traditions and ceremonies for dear life.'[44] He replied that he would never suggest discontinuing any ceremony which maintained the Crown's dignity, but he felt that this one probably had the opposite effect. 'Surely it is better to dispense with a thing that has no real significance, or dignity, rather than to allow it to become a source of friction & bitterness – of which there is quite enough in the Empire already?' He thought the Home Secretary's archaic presence was in fact 'an unwarrantable & out-of-date intrusion into Your Majesties' private lives'.[45] The Queen was at last persuaded.

By this time she had a much greater concern. The imminent birth of their first grandchild coincided with a serious deterioration in the King's health. The South Africa tour had exhausted him – he had lost seventeen pounds in weight in the course of those strenuous weeks. And, as his biographer discreetly put it, 'his temperament was not one which facilitated a rapid replenishing of nervous and physical reserves.'[46] Through 1948 he had been suffering from cramp in the feet and legs. He did not complain, but he kept a note of it. The problem eased when he was on holiday at Balmoral – he found he could spend a day on the hills without being tired, but by October 1948 the symptoms had got worse. His left foot was numb and the pain in it kept him awake at night. The affliction then spread to the right foot.

It was a busy time. The King and Queen were preparing for a visit to New Zealand and Australia, with Princess Margaret, in spring 1948, to complement that which they had just made to South Africa. The King and Queen of Denmark were about to arrive and on 26 October the King had to preside over a full state opening of Parliament for the first time since the war. The Queen was very concerned and that same day she told Tommy Lascelles she wanted to talk to him about 'making a real break for the King' for treatment for his legs. 'I am not at all happy about it.'[47] The King was examined by a team of doctors who agreed that his condition was so serious that he would have to cancel the proposed tour of Australia and New Zealand. The King and Queen were reluctant, but eventually, under pressure, they agreed. The King refused to cancel his current engagements, which included a review of the Territorial Army and the Remembrance Day service at the Cenotaph.

On 12 November Professor James Learmonth, one of Britain's leading cardiovascular specialists, examined the King and confirmed that he was suffering from the onset of arteriosclerosis; the doctors feared that his right leg might have to be amputated. The Queen explained to Queen Mary, 'I have been terribly worried over his legs, and am sure that the only thing is to put everything off, and try & get better. I am afraid that Australia & NZ will be desperately disappointed – but what else could one do – I do hope they will understand that it is serious.'[48]

The King insisted that Princess Elizabeth be told nothing of his condition until after the birth of her child, which was awaited with excitement around the nation. Then as now the first news of a royal birth was posted on the railings of the Palace. Queen Mary was rather surprised that scores of people were queuing all night for the news 'with sandwiches, like a film queue!' Prince Charles was born in the afternoon of Sunday 14 November. Princess Elizabeth and Prince Philip were delighted to be parents. She wrote to her aunt, May Elphinstone, that her son was 'too sweet for words' and already had a very loud voice. 'I can still hardly believe that I really have a son of my own – it seems quite incredible – and wonderful!'[49] The Queen, who was to play a large part in her first grandson's life, was very touched by the pleasure people felt at the arrival of 'such a darling baby'.[50] She wrote to Queen Mary, 'One has lived through such a series of crises & shocks & blows these last years, that something as happy & simple & hopeful for the future as a little son is indeed a joy.'[51]

Whether happy or anxious, the Queen continued her engagements. Queen Mary praised her for her calm and her courage in the face of the King's illness.[52] The King was now confined to bed, his legs clamped eight hours a day in a device called an occluder which was intended to improve his circulation. The treatment was successful and by early December the danger of amputation had passed. Nonetheless, the doctors felt that their patient should not be moved at least until the end of the month. This meant that the family would have to forgo their usual Christmas gathering at Sandringham.

Churchill gave the Queen a copy of the fruit of his new leisure, his book *Painting as a Pastime*. Thanking him, she referred to the deep emotions of recent months, and added, 'tho' sometimes one feels that they have been almost too vampire & have drained away something of the joy of living, yet one also feels closer than before to the good beating heart of the British people. God bless the people – they are good people, and when one feels depressed or frustrated (this often) a little talk with a painter, or a plumber or a steel worker or a nice angry English gentleman soon puts one right!'[53]

On 8 December she dined with Bobbety and Betty Salisbury* at their house in Swan Walk, Chelsea. Among the guests was Isaiah Berlin, whom Betty Salisbury described to her as 'brilliantly clever, a Fellow of All Souls, very amusing when one can understand a word he says – which is seldom'.[54] All his life Berlin spoke softly and with a lisp which meant one had to listen carefully to his words. The Queen was delighted – she found him 'just as nice & amusing as I had hoped',[55] and the dinner began a long friendship between her and the philosopher which lasted until Berlin's death in 1997.† One passion

---

* The former Lord Cranborne had become the fifth marquess of Salisbury on the death of his father in 1947.

† Berlin was not uncritical of Queen Elizabeth. In 1959 he described to a friend a dinner at which he, Queen Elizabeth and Maria Callas were among the guests. 'They were like two prima donnas, one emitting white and [the] other black magic. Each tried to engage the

they shared was for England. Berlin had arrived with his family as a Jewish refugee from Petrograd in 1921 and since then had fallen in love with his new country. According to his biographer, he believed England to be the very wellspring of the liberalism which inspired his life: 'that decent respect for others and the toleration of dissent are better than pride and a sense of national mission; that liberty may be incompatible with, and better than, too much efficiency; that pluralism and untidiness are, to those who value freedom, better than the rigorous imposition of all-embracing systems, no matter how rational and disinterested, better than the rule of majorities against which there is no appeal'. All of this Berlin believed to be 'deeply and uniquely English'.[56] These were sentiments with which the Queen agreed absolutely – and it was a joy for her to hear her own patriotism echoed so beautifully by so wise a man. In later years she came to enjoy annual lunches with Berlin and the other engaging Fellows of All Souls.

In his Christmas broadcast that year, the King spoke of his Silver Wedding, of the birth of his first grandchild and of his illness. He had been much distressed to have 'to postpone, on the advice of my doctors, the journey for which my peoples in Australia and New Zealand had been making such kindly preparations'. After Christmas his doctors decided that he was well enough to go to Sandringham, and there he was able to take short walks and even shoot a little. The Queen was relieved. She realized that she had been exhausted by the recent pleasures as well as the anxieties. 'Daughters getting engaged, and daughters marrying, and daughters having babies, & the King getting ill, & preparing for a tour of Australia & New Zealand, & then having to put it off – all these things are very filling to one's life.'[57]

---

attention of the table, Miss Callas crudely and violently, the Queen Mother with infinite gracefulness and charm of a slightly watery and impersonal kind . . . I sat between the Q.M. and Lady Rosebery and enjoyed myself . . . The Q.M., on the other hand, discussed the subject of courage and ventured the proposition that wholly fearless men are often boring. I pounced on that and produced a list of men distinguished in public life – such as General Freyberg and other V.C.s – whom we then duly found boring. It was such a conversation as might have occurred in about 1903 with the then still young Princess May [the future Queen Mary]. I enjoyed it in an artificial sort of way and thought the Q.M. not indeed particularly intelligent nor even terribly nice, but a very strong personality – much stronger than I thought her – and filled with the possibility of unexpected answers . . . In short I enjoyed my evening a good deal.' (Isaiah Berlin to Rowland Burdon-Muller, 7 July 1959, Isaiah Berlin, *Enlightening: Letters 1946–1960*, ed. Henry Hardy and Jennifer Holmes, Chatto & Windus, 2009, pp. 691–3)

Back in London, the King resumed a restricted programme of work. But he was not yet well. In early March 1949 his team of doctors concluded that the main artery in his right leg was still obstructed and, in order to improve circulation, they recommended that he should have a right lumbar sympathectomy. He was upset – his first thought was that all the restrictions already imposed on him had been a waste of time. But the doctors persuaded him that he had in fact done himself a lot of good and had avoided amputation of the leg. They considered carrying out the procedure in the Royal Masonic Hospital, but then decided to install a complete operating theatre in rooms at the front of the Palace. Before the operation took place on the morning of Saturday 12 March the Queen went with her daughters to communion at the Chapel Royal, St James's Palace. The King was calm. 'I am not in the least worried,' he said.[58] Crowds had gathered outside the railings and news placards soon carried the good news: 'He's all right.'

He was, but Professor Learmonth told him that he must not risk a recurrence of thrombosis, and he could not lead such an energetic or full life as before. It was not easy for him, psychologically or practically, to accept this.[59] As the Queen put it, it was hard for him to get any respite from 'the enormous problems which seem to rise up so often and which loom so darkly over the world'.[60] But, as a result of his incapacity, much of his work would have to be undertaken by his wife and daughters. The Queen was heard to speak of 'the person who once prayed to be granted not a lighter load but a stronger back'.[61]

She needed it not just to shoulder the burden of the King's incapacity but also to deal with what she saw as hurtful disloyalty close to home.

*

EARLY IN 1949 MARION Crawford, the Princesses' governess, retired at the age of forty. Then began the lamentable episode for which she was to be remembered far more than for her fifteen years of devoted service as teacher, companion and friend to the Princesses: the unauthorized publication of her memoirs entitled *The Little Princesses*. By the standards of the late twentieth and early twenty-first century, Miss Crawford's revelations might seem harmless, indeed charming. But at the time her conduct was seen as an unforgivable betrayal. Recent research by Hugo Vickers shows the chief villains of the piece to be a pair of unscrupulous American journalists and Marion Crawford's husband.* But Miss Crawford herself behaved in ways which bordered on blackmail and deliberately defied her trusting employer, the Queen.

On 1 January 1949 the Queen wrote affectionately to 'My dear Crawfie', urging her not to think that her retirement would mean severing all connection with the Royal Family. Crawfie had shared their joys and sorrows for years, and they looked upon her 'now & always as a true & trustworthy friend'. The letter continued: 'I can never tell you how grateful I am for all your devotion & love for Lilibet & Margaret. It was such a great relief to me during the war, to know that you were by their side, through sirens, guns, bombs & pantomimes – keeping everything cool and balanced, & good humoured. Thank you with all my heart.'[62] Now, the Queen wrote, Crawfie would be able to devote more time to 'the hub of your universe', Major George Buthlay, a retired army officer whom she had married in September 1947. He had been found a good job in a bank by members of the Household, the couple had been given a grace-and-favour house in Kensington Palace and Crawfie retired on a full-salary pension.

But that was not enough. Marion Crawford was anxious to develop, if not at first to exploit, her royal connections. She wrote to the Queen saying she had had many requests from the American and British press to speak or write about the Royal Family, but claimed that she had no desire to do so and would rather continue in royal employment; she also hoped that her husband could be helped by being given royal bank accounts to administer.[63]

The Queen, distracted by the King's illness, did not immediately respond. Then Bruce and Beatrice Gould, the editors of the American magazine *Ladies' Home Journal*, sent a writer, Dorothy Black, to see Marion Crawford in London to try and persuade her to write articles or a book about the Princesses. Crawfie put this suggestion to the Queen in February 1949.[64] This time the Queen saw the former governess, and in early April she wrote that she she felt 'most definitely' that Crawfie should not write and sign articles about the Princesses. She knew that Crawfie understood the need for people in positions of confidence with the Royal Family to be 'utterly oyster'

---

* See Vickers's illuminating account of this affair, based largely on the papers of Bruce and Beatrice Blackmar Gould at Princeton University, in *Elizabeth The Queen Mother*, pp. 279–91.

and urged her to say 'No No No to offers of dollars for articles about something as private & as precious as our family'. The Queen was ready to help her find a new teaching post.[65]

Although disappointed, Miss Crawford appeared to accept the Queen's request.[66] But in May 1949 the Goulds came to London and induced her to sign a contract under which she would write her story with the help of Dorothy Black. By August the manuscript was finished. Crawfie's agreement with the *Ladies' Home Journal* required the manuscript to be approved by the Queen before publication. In early October 1949 the Goulds sent it to her through Lady Astor, with whom they were on friendly terms. But the Queen was given only three weeks to respond – publication had been set for January 1950, and it was clear that the Goulds intended to go ahead with or without her approval.

The Queen was appalled both by the manuscript and by what she saw as Marion Crawford's breach of promise. She wrote a six-page letter telling Lady Astor of the shock and distress she and the King felt; they could only think that 'our late & completely trusted governess has gone off her head, because she promised in writing that she would not publish any story about our daughters'.[67] Her Private Secretary, Major Tom Harvey, reinforced the message, writing to Lady Astor that such a memoir was 'utterly alien to the spirit and custom of Their Majesties' households and staff'. He added: 'Nevertheless, The Queen realises that nothing much can be done about it.'[68] Perhaps unwisely, Harvey did not ask that publication be abandoned. Instead, he sent Lady Astor a list of 'passages to be considered for amendment'. These included several inaccuracies pointed out by Princess Elizabeth, who was as horrified as her mother by her governess's conduct.[69] But Major Harvey added a robust rider, to the effect that even in amended form 'the existence & publication of this article remain entirely repugnant to The King and Queen.'[70]

The Goulds remained ruthlessly committed to their commercial project.[71] On receiving Major Harvey's list of requested omissions Gould cabled Nancy Astor: 'WE WILL AGREE MOST MODIFICA-TIONS PARTLY NATURAL DESIRE UNOFFEND YOUR FRIENDS PARTLY WISH EASE GOVERNESS POSITION FOR HER SAKE ALSO BECAUSE ANY RETALIATION UPON HER WOULD INEVI-TABLY LEAK AMERICAN PRESS TRADITIONALLY LOVES DEFEND UNDERDOG'.[72] 'Slight blackmail,' commented the Queen, to whom Lady Astor brought the cable; 'but encouraging as to our suggested omissions.'[73]

Publication went ahead, without the objectionable passages but with further adaptations and inventions made by the Goulds to create the effect they desired. The series boosted the circulation of the *Ladies' Home Journal* by half a million.[74] Later in 1950 *The Little Princesses* was serialized in Britain in *Woman's Own*, and published in book form by Cassell & Co. The Palace insisted, however, that letters from the Princesses be removed from the British publications.[75]

Marion Crawford was allowed to keep both her house and her pension, but her relationship with the Royal Family never recovered. In November 1950 she and her husband moved to Aberdeen. She continued to write – or to permit others to use her name in writing – about the Royal Family, until the unfortunate occasion in 1955 when she allowed an article about Trooping the Colour and Royal Ascot to be published under her name, despite the fact that both events had been cancelled.

It was a painful and unpleasant episode in the Queen's life, and it showed how vulnerable the Royal Family was to betrayal by those around them whom they trusted.

*

IN AUGUST 1950 THE Queen celebrated her fiftieth birthday. *The Times* marked the occasion with an enthusiastic leader:

> It would be impossible to over-estimate the reinforcement that the King has derived from the serene and steady support of the Queen. She has sustained him in sickness and in health, at all times taking her full share of the burdens of royal service and in the time of great anxiety that befell her during the King's grave illness ... She speaks to all men and women on the level of common experience ... She is never afraid to challenge the oversophisticated of the age in which she lives; she ignores the cynics and the pessimists and holds up for admiration the things that are lovely and of good report.[76]

After her birthday, the King was well enough to travel up to Balmoral but the Queen waited in London until, on 15 August, her second grandchild, Princess Anne, was born.

That summer and early autumn the weather at Balmoral was cold with incessant gales. But the King was still able to get out walking most days and the Queen thought he was really better. He made a device whereby a pony could pull him up hills with the help of a long trace fastened around his waist. It had a quick-release mechanism, similar to that found on RAF parachutes, in case the pony bolted. All in all, the care he took of himself encouraged his doctors to agree that if he continued to make good progress he and the Queen might be able to make their delayed visit to Australia and New Zealand in 1952. It was a blessed relief, the Queen told Queen Mary.

Princess Elizabeth and her 'darling children' came to stay, and when they left the Queen found the house 'very empty & forlorn'. In another early indication of the growing affection between her and her grandson, she wrote to Queen Mary, 'Charles is really too angelic, and is such a clever child. His memory is prodigeous, and he takes a deep interest in everything. He is such a friendly little boy, and everyone here loves him.'[77]

At the end of 1950 Princess Elizabeth and Prince Philip were in Malta, where he was now stationed. They had a pleasant time, living as normal a life as was ever to be possible for them, along with other young naval couples. But their children remained in Britain and spent Christmas 1950 with their grandparents at Sandringham. The Queen wrote to her daughter about Prince Charles, 'I can't tell you how sweet he was driving to the station before Xmas. He sat on my knee, occasionally turning to Papa & giving himself an estatic hug, as if to say, isn't this fun. He sits bolt upright doesn't he, just like you used to.' He had also enjoyed Christmas itself. 'He was thrilled with the Tree, & after gazing at it, tried to pinch the silver balls, and then had great fun helping to unpack everybody else's parcels!'[78]

Prince Philip, in particular, was worried that the grandparents would spoil his children. The Queen assured her daughter that she was not doing so. But Charles often came to her bedroom in the morning '& likes to sit on the bed playing with my little box of rather old lip sticks! They are all colours, & they rattle & he loves taking the tops off'. Princess Margaret sometimes played 'Blaydon Races' to him on the piano after tea. 'He likes that because it has a line "all with smiling faces", so it's called 'Miling faces . . . And as for Anne! Well, she is too delectable for words . . . I know that you will be enchanted with her when you see how she has developed. She is so pretty & neat

& <u>very</u> feminine! Philip will see such a huge difference, I am sure she'll give him a tremendous glad eye!'[79]

The Queen's letters to her elder daughter in Malta contained more and more references to horses and racing. This was an interest which she was developing at the beginning of the 1950s and which became a passion for life. But the greater passion now was for her grandchildren. 'I can't tell you what a difference it makes having those heavenly little creatures in the house,' she told their mother, 'everybody loves them so, and they cheer us up more than I can say.'[80]

*

IN MAY 1951 THE King and Queen opened the Festival of Britain which the government had decided to stage on the one hundredth anniversary of Prince Albert's Great Exhibition of 1851. The Festival was both a prayer to the future and a tribute that the country paid herself for having defeated Nazism and for remaining a bastion of freedom. It extolled the virtues of Britishness and Britain's contributions to civilization. The unapologetic patriotism echoed the Queen's own fierce love of Britain.

Throughout the year the King's health remained a subject of anxiety and speculation. At the end of May 1951, he looked quite unwell at a service in the Abbey at which he installed his brother the Duke of Gloucester as Grand Master of the Order of the Bath. He was compelled to retire to bed, apparently suffering from influenza. 'The doctors can find nothing wrong with my chest so rest & quiet is the only thing for it,' he wrote to Queen Mary.[81] But he did not make the recovery expected and X-rays showed a shadow on his left lung. He was told he had a condition known as pneumonitis, which was not as serious as pneumonia, and should be resolved with daily injections of penicillin. 'Everyone is very relieved,' he told Queen Mary.[82]

But for most of the summer of 1951 he had to rest at Royal Lodge and Sandringham, depressed by the fact that he could not 'chuck out the bug', as he put it.[83] He was unable to undertake a planned visit to Northern Ireland and so Princess Margaret went with the Queen – it was a strenuous but successful visit, throughout which the Queen kept in touch with her husband by telephone.

When King Haakon of Norway (the King's Uncle Charles) arrived for an official visit in early June, it was the Queen who had to meet him and Princess Elizabeth who read the King's speech at the state banquet in his honour. Princess Elizabeth also had to take her father's place at the King's official birthday parade, Trooping the Colour. Queen Mary praised her granddaughter to the King: 'it must have been an ordeal for her, but she was so calm & collected all through the Ceremony, it was really a pleasure to watch her.'[84]

The King remained optimistic, writing to Queen Mary that since his official engagements were light, 'I feel now that I have got the chance of a rest I had much better take it & get really well. I am sure the doctors, especially Weir, will want me to rebuild my strength. It is no use getting ill again.'[85] He was not strong enough to attend a Buckingham Palace garden party in early July 1951 and the Queen pressed Queen Mary to come and join her. 'I am rather horrified at the idea of being alone,' she wrote.[86]

The day before the Queen's fifty-first birthday they moved up to Balmoral where she hoped that the Scottish air would work its usual beneficial effect upon the King. He was weaker than the year before but she was relieved that at first he did seem to improve and was able to enjoy shooting and Princess Margaret's twenty-first birthday celebrations. Singsongs were part of evenings at Balmoral and Princess Margaret could be counted upon to write the most witty lyrics. But on this occasion a song was written and sung to her – it was a reworking of 'Clementine':

> Oh my darling oh my darling oh my darling Margaret
> She's the pride of old Balmoral, far the nicest girl I've met . . .

> Round the table, round the table, where this happy scene is set
> Let us raise our brimming glasses to our darling MargarET[87]

Everyone enjoyed the party, but then the weather became cold and the King caught a chill and a sore throat.

The Queen insisted that his doctors come to Scotland to examine him, and they prevailed upon him to return for one day to London on 8 September for further examinations and X-rays. By this stage, they had begun to have their suspicions of what was really wrong with him. Clement Price Thomas, a specialist in malignant diseases of the chest, joined the list of consultants. After examining the new X-rays, the team decided the King must have a bronchoscopy of the left lung so that a biopsy could be carried out.[88]

The King reluctantly agreed to return once more to London but he insisted that the Queen remain at Balmoral to continue her holiday. 'I am telling no one about this new development,' he wrote to his mother.[89] The Queen was miserable to be left in Scotland. 'I do pray that the doctors will be able to find something to help the lung recover,' she told Queen Mary.[90]

The biopsy, performed on 15 September, revealed a malignant growth in the lung. The doctors decided that the only solution was to remove his entire lung. But the first medical bulletin, published on 18 September, mentioned that 'structural changes' had developed in the lung and that the King had been advised to stay in London for further treatment. This news alone was shocking enough. A further bulletin on 21 September stated that the doctors 'have advised His Majesty to undergo an operation in the near future. This advice the King has accepted.' When Churchill asked his doctor Charles Moran why the doctors had spoken of 'structural changes', Moran replied, 'Because they were anxious to avoid talking about cancer.'[91] The word was never used, either to the King or to anyone else, but he was suffering from lung cancer, almost certainly caused by his heavy smoking – though that link was not then widely understood.

The Queen flew down at once from Scotland. She sent a note to Queen Mary inviting her to tea the next day, 22 September. The King, she said, 'is so wonderfully brave about it all, and it does seem hard that he should have to go through so much.'[92] The King dreaded the thought of another operation. 'If it's going to help me to get well again I don't mind but the very idea of the surgeon's knife again is hell,' he admitted to a friend.[93]

On the morning of the King's operation, 23 September, the Queen left the Palace and went quietly with her daughters to take Holy Communion and pray for the King at Lambeth Palace with the Archbishop of Canterbury, Geoffrey Fisher.[94] By the time they returned to Buckingham Palace thousands of silent people were standing in drizzling weather around the Victoria Memorial, waiting for the bulletin to be posted on the railings; millions more listened to the radio. Messages of love and support came flooding in from all over the country and the world. Winston Churchill told Tommy Lascelles, 'I did a thing this morning that I haven't done for many years – I went down on my knees by my bedside & prayed.' Lascelles told the Queen that everyone in the Palace felt the same.[95] Lascelles was suffering his own anguish – his beloved son John had just died. The Queen understood his grief and told him how grateful she was that he was nonetheless able to give her such unfailing support.[96]

The Queen had an agonizing wait of more than three hours while the surgeons carried out their work. Like them, she feared the risk of a sudden thrombosis as well as what they might discover. The King survived the operation and the Queen was reassured by the doctors. 'What a long hell the morning has been! Endless waiting, & I thought of you so much darling Mama,' the Queen reported to Queen Mary that afternoon. Clement Price Thomas, she said, was 'very satisfied with the operation, which is a marvellous relief . . . He said that we must be anxious for 2 or 3 days, because of reaction & shock etc, but his blood pressure is steady, & his heart good. It does seem hard that he should have to go through so much, someone as good as darling Bertie who always thinks of others – but if this operation is successful, he may be much stronger in the future . . . Such moments are true torture. One must have real faith & trust in the goodness of God.'[97] In similar vein she said to Tommy Lascelles, 'I am sure that today the King was utterly surrounded by a great circle of prayer, and that he has been sustained by the faith of millions. There must be great strength in such an uprising of spiritual forces.'[98]

Outside the Palace, the crowds surged around the bulletin attached to the railings that afternoon. It stated that the King had undergone a lung resection and that, although anxiety must remain for some days, his post-operative condition was satisfactory. But the danger of thrombosis remained very real. Sometimes her worries became too much for the Queen; she would secretly slip out of the Palace and go to the flat of her oldest friend, Doris Vyner, for comfort.[99]

The leaders of all parties in the House of Commons signed a letter of good wishes and support. At the height of the crisis, the Duke of Windsor asked to see the Queen and she declined; she still thought of him as partly to blame for the King's troubles.[100] But when the Duke sent a kind note, she replied, thanking him: 'It does seem hard that poor Bertie should have to go through so much, and ill-health is such a big extra burden on the top of all the other burdens, but you can imagine he has been very brave & most patient, and one can only pray that this operation will give him some health back . . . I am very touched that you should suggest coming here one day, I think that I had better wait & see how Bertie gets on before making any arrangements, as all depends on that.'[101] A few weeks later, in November, the Duke was back and this time Queen Mary asked the King to persuade the Queen to see him – 'to bury that hatchet at last, he seemed so anxious to see her again when he was here that awful week of yr illness, but E. could not face it, however perhaps now she might feel able to manage it.'[102] With the King still frail, she did not feel she could.

The Queen agreed with Lascelles that to lift day-to-day business from the King a Council of State should be appointed, consisting of her and the Princesses. The King was able to sign the warrant authorizing the appointment of counsellors. Then, at the request of Clement Attlee, who could no longer sustain the narrow majority with which his government had been returned to office in the election of 1950, he signed the proclamation dissolving Parliament. An election was called for 25 October. It was a time of political turmoil – but all talk was of the King's illness. Harold Nicolson was asked by the *Spectator* to prepare an obituary and noted in his diary on 24 September, 'The King pretty bad. Nobody can talk about anything else – and the Election is forgotten. What a strange thing is Monarchy!'[103]

The King spent several weeks in bed, with the Queen much at his side, attempting to cheer him up, except when she had a cold and had to avoid the risk of infecting him. His condition improved. In early October the Queen was able to tell her sister May that his pain had lessened and he was now able to sit up in bed. 'The doctors are amazed at the way things have gone (so far), and I do believe that he has been tremendously helped, & held up, by the great circle of prayer & affection which surrounded him.'[104]

He and the Queen were much cheered by the success of Princess Elizabeth and Prince Philip on a tour of Canada. The Canadian government had suggested that this be postponed in view of the King's illness, but after a short delay they set off on 7 October. The Princess's Private Secretary, Martin Charteris, carried with him sealed envelopes containing the draft Accession Declaration and a Message to both Houses of Parliament to be opened in the event of the King's death.

Over nearly 10,000 miles, the Canadians gave the young couple a delirious reception which recalled the 1939 trip by the King and Queen. The Princess was struck that young women screamed when her husband waved and men shouted, 'Good old Phil.'[105] As the tour continued each of them became more confident – the Princess was pleased at her husband's 'succès fou' and the way his 'legend' got around.[106]

At home, the Queen was delighted to receive many warm letters of congratulation from Canadians. She wrote the Princess a long letter telling her that her father was getting stronger. 'His voice is still very hoarse, but he is beginning to take an interest in things again, and once he makes a start, he will, I am sure get on quicker. It must be slow I suppose, but the doctors are pleased, & he is a little more cheerful.' She said she longed to hear her daughter's impressions of everything, 'the French, the Mounties, the delicious people at the little unexpected stops'. She and the King were 'so proud of you & Philip, & so glad that it is all going so well. We think of you all the time, & with all the rush & tiredness, one stores up wonderful experiences, & perhaps a little more understanding & wisdom – doesn't one?'[107] The Queen managed to talk to the Princess a few times on the crackling transatlantic line; her daughter found that such calls made her feel 'much refreshed and strengthened'. She was happy to hear her son, Prince Charles, 'piping away' and to hear her father sounding stronger.[108]

The King continued to improve and by mid-October he was able to tell Queen Mary that his doctors and nurses had looked after him 'most beautifully' and that 'thank goodness there were no complications & everything has gone according to plan'.[109] He was well enough to resume worrying about the country and the forthcoming election. The Queen shared his concerns. 'Any government that comes in here next week is in for a mess,' she wrote to Princess Elizabeth in Canada. But her faith in the 'marvellous sense of balance' of the British people was undiminished.[110]

On 25 October 1951 the Conservatives, led by Winston Churchill, were returned to office with an overall majority of seventeen. The King and Queen both revered Churchill. His arrival at the Palace at 5.45 on the evening of 26 October to accept, for the second time, the King's invitation to form a government was a happy reunion. The King was not well enough to receive his new ministers individually and on 6 November his speech to the new Parliament had to be read by the Lord Chancellor. But he and the Queen were able to go to Royal Lodge for a weekend at the end of November for the first time since his operation. Sunday 2 December was declared a day of National Thanksgiving for the King's recovery.

The family spent Christmas together at Sandringham and this year the King's day was not dominated by anxiety over his live broadcast. The Queen had persuaded him that it must be recorded in advance. This was wise; the BBC engineer, Robert Wood, who had often helped him, brought his equipment to Buckingham Palace and he and the Queen helped the King through the recording. The King had to halt for a rest every few words and the whole session took more than two hours. It was harrowing for them all and Wood wrote later, 'It was very, very distressing for him, and the Queen and for me, because I admired him so much and wished I could do more to help.' In the event, the anguish of the recording was not evident to his world of listeners even if his voice did sound 'husky, hoarse, a wheezing as if he had a heavy cold audible between phrases'.[111]

He made his gratitude clear. 'For not only by the grace of God and through the faithful skills of my doctors, surgeons and nurses have I come through my illness, but I have learned once again that it is in bad times that we value most highly the support and sympathy of our friends. From my peoples in these islands and in the British Commonwealth and Empire – as well as from many other countries – this support and sympathy has reached me and I thank you now from my heart.'[112]

The King was able to go out into the Norfolk countryside over Christmas and to shoot with a light gun. Queen Mary was with them for the holiday and after she returned to Marlborough House in mid-January 1952 the King wrote to tell her how much they all missed her. He was seeing his doctors the following week '& I hope they will be pleased with my progress'. The letter ended: 'Best love to you, I remain, Ever, Your very devoted son, Bertie'. On the back of the envelope Queen Mary later wrote, in a tiny hand, 'Bertie's last letter to me'.[113]

On 30 January the family was back in London together; they went to see the popular musical *South Pacific* at Drury Lane. This occasion was both to celebrate the King's recovery and to mark the departure next day of Princess Elizabeth and Prince Philip to Kenya. After their success in Canada, they were embarking on the first leg of the long Australasian tour which the King and Queen had had to forgo. (Instead the King and Queen were planning to make a private trip, for convalescence and holiday, back to South Africa.)[114]

At London Airport next morning, the King stood, hatless and gaunt, in the cold wind, waving goodbye to his daughter and heir as the British Overseas Airways' Argonaut, *Atalanta*, sped down the runway and into the air. Those who had not seen him for some time were shocked by his appearance; those who had been closer to him over recent months were encouraged that he was well enough to be there. The Queen hated saying goodbye; two days later she wrote to the Princess: 'I could <u>not</u> help one huge tear forcing its way out of my eye, & as we waited to wave goodbye, as you taxied off, it trembled on my eyelashes.' She was sure that the young couple would give pleasure wherever they went. Expressing her own philosophy of life, she wrote, 'People react to goodness & kindness in a wonderful way.' She ended by referring to their proposed trip to South Africa: 'Papa seems pretty well, & I do hope that a good soaking from the sun will do him good. But he does hate being away from all his responsibilities and interests – & I don't expect we shall stay long!'[115]

On 1 February the Queen and the King took their grandchildren back to Sandringham. On the train, the three-year-old Prince Charles spent a good hour going up and down 'to see if Anne is alright', his grandmother wrote to his mother. And then he 'made a wonderfully unwholesome tea of half a crumpet, 2 chicken sandwiches, one ham sandwich and the ice cream!' That evening the Princess called her parents from Nairobi. Next day the Queen and Princess Margaret took the children to the beach at Brancaster; Prince Charles rushed to paddle in the cold sea.[116]

The King was in good spirits; he wrote cheerful letters to Sir John Weir to thank him for all the excellent medical care he had given him since 1934, and to Lord Halifax, Chancellor of the Order of the Garter, to whom he described a new form of Garter dress he had devised.[117] On 5 February he went out shooting rabbits. It was Keepers' Day, a relaxed informal shoot of the sort he enjoyed. James Macdonald, his servant for twenty years, said later that the King shot 'superbly' and was 'as gay and happy' as he had ever seen him. At the end of the afternoon the King thanked the keepers and that evening he said, 'Well Macdonald, we'll go after the hares again tomorrow.'[118]

While the King was at his sport, the Queen and Princess Margaret drove to the nearby village of Ludham to see one of her favourite painters, Edward Seago.* He showed them his latest works and he

---

* Edward Seago (1910–74), self-taught landscape painter and portraitist who spent most of his life in Norfolk.

took them for a cruise on his boat, which was moored at the end of his garden. Warmed by a coal fire in the cabin, they made a happy call on Delia Peel at her house at Barton Turf, and Seago gave the Queen new paintings to show the King.

Back at Sandringham that evening, the Queen went at once to see the King 'as I always do, & he was in tremendous form & looking so well and happy'.[119] Seago's paintings were laid out and they looked at them together; the King, she took the trouble to tell Seago a little later, 'was enchanted with them all'.[120] They had an enjoyable dinner with Princess Margaret; the King was cheerful and his wife was delighted. At around 10.30 p.m. they said good night and the King retired to the ground-floor room he was now using as a bedroom so as to avoid climbing the stairs. At around midnight a watchman in the garden saw him adjusting the new latch which had been fitted to his window to allow more air into the room.

At 7.30 the next morning Macdonald brought the King's early-morning tea, opened the curtains and drew the bath. When the King did not stir, Macdonald went to his bedside. The King was lying peacefully; he had not moved from his usual position and there were no signs of any discomfort. Macdonald shook his shoulder gently. Getting no response he touched the King's forehead, which was cold. He knew that the King was dead; he immediately sent word to the Queen's dresser and went himself to report to Sir Harold Campbell, the King's equerry.[121] 'I was sent a message that his servant couldn't wake him,' the Queen wrote to Queen Mary a few hours later. 'I flew to his room, & thought that he was in a deep sleep, he looked so peaceful – and then I realized what had happened.'[122]

The Household had devised a code word for this awful possibility. Lascelles called Edward Ford, the Assistant Private Secretary, in London, and said, 'Hyde Park Corner.' He told Ford to go and give the news at once to the Prime Minister and to Queen Mary. At 10 Downing Street, Ford found Churchill in bed, with papers scattered all over the blankets, a chewed cigar in his mouth. He said, 'I've got bad news, Prime Minister. The King died last night. I know nothing else.'

'Bad news? The worst,' said Churchill.

The old statesman was devastated. He threw aside all the papers on his bed, exclaiming, 'How unimportant these matters are.'[123] A little later, his secretary, Jock Colville, found the Prime Minister sitting with tears in his eyes, staring straight ahead. He tried to cheer him up by saying that he would get on well with the new Queen, 'but all he could say was that he did not know her and that she was only a child'.[124]

Edward Ford next had to make his melancholy way to Marlborough House to inform Queen Mary. Jock Colville's mother, Lady Cynthia, was in waiting and she went to Queen Mary's room to give her the news. Queen Mary seemed to have a premonition: 'Is it the King?' she asked Lady Cynthia.[125] Later that day she wrote in her diary, 'I got a dreadful shock when Cynthia asked to see me at 9.30, after breakfast, to tell me that darling Bertie had died in his sleep early today ... The news came out about 10.30. Later letters kept arriving & flowers from kind friends.'[126]

At Sandringham Lascelles asked Queen Elizabeth, as she was now properly called since her daughter had become 'The Queen',* to approve the announcement. He had made it as simple as possible: 'The King, who retired to rest last night in his usual health, passed peacefully away in his sleep early this morning'. The King's body was moved in its coffin on a cart to the little family church where his father had lain sixteen years before him. In the streets of London people stopped their cars and stood at attention in the streets to show their respect. Many wept openly. In America, the House of Representatives carried unanimously a resolution of sympathy and adjourned in respect for the King.

That same day, Queen Elizabeth wrote to Queen Mary:

My darling Mama,
    What can I say to you – I know that you loved Bertie dearly, and he was my whole life, and one can only be deeply thankful for the utterly happy years we had together. He was so wonderfully thoughtful and loving, & I don't believe he ever thought of himself at all. He was so <u>devoted</u> to you, & admired & loved you. It is impossible for me to grasp what has happened, last night he was in wonderful form & looking so well ... It is hard to grasp, he was such an angel to the children & me, and I cannot

---

* In accordance with practice at the British Court, as queen consort Queen Elizabeth was always referred to as 'The Queen', and not as 'Queen Elizabeth'. As the King's widow, however, she was referred to by her name, as Queen Elizabeth, like Queen Alexandra and Queen Mary before her. 'The Queen' now meant only her daughter, the reigning Queen. The same practice has been followed in this book. The widowed Queen Elizabeth was now queen dowager, and because her daughter was on the throne she was also queen mother, a title used for centuries among royal families throughout Europe and beyond.

bear to think of Lilibet, so young to bear such a burden – I do feel for you so darling Mama – to lose two dear sons, and Bertie so young still, & so precious – It is almost more than one can bear – Your very loving Elizabeth.'[127]

Queen Mary thanked 'Dear darling Elizabeth' for her 'wonderful letter to poor old me'. The old Queen was deeply touched by all that her daughter-in-law had said 'about the great affection between our darling Bertie and us all. I cannot get over the fearful shock you must have had when you realised that he had died in his sleep. You have been such a wonderful wife to him in "weal & woe" & such a prop when things were a little difficult and he was upset, this must be a comfort to you in your great grief and I feel this very much indeed.'[128]

*

IN KENYA THE new Queen and Prince Philip had spent the previous night in the countryside at Treetops, a simple treehouse overlooking a waterhole to which animals came at night. They were horrified, at every level. Grief mingled with the knowledge that this meant the end of their independent life together. Prince Philip, according to his Private Secretary, 'looked as if you'd dropped half the world on him'.[129] They began their journey home that night and on the plane Martin Charteris asked his employer what name she would take as monarch. 'My own name of course – what else?' she replied. She would be Queen Elizabeth II. Shortly before the plane arrived at London Airport she changed into the black mourning clothes which had travelled with her in case of just such an eventuality. 'What happens when I get there?' she asked. As the plane taxied to a halt, she saw the big black Palace cars – 'Oh, they've sent the hearses,' she said, using the name she and her sister had always used for the royal limousines.[130] All in black, the new Queen walked down the steps of the plane to be met by Churchill, Attlee, Eden and other political leaders. She and Prince Philip managed a few smiles and then climbed into one of the 'hearses'; a photographer caught a poignant image of the Queen in the corner of the back seat, her eyes cast down.

Churchill, in his own car, was in tears as he drove back to London, dictating a radio broadcast he was to make that night. He spoke of the King as 'a devoted and tireless servant of his country' and said that the announcement of his death 'struck a deep and solemn note in our lives which, as it resounded far and wide, stilled the clatter and traffic of twentieth century life in many lands and made countless millions of human beings pause and look around them'.

Churchill's sentiments, on this as on many occasions, epitomized the monarchist feelings that prevailed in a country where at least a third of the people thought the Queen had been chosen by God. 'The King', declared Churchill, had 'walked with death, as if death were a companion he did not fear . . . In the end death came as a friend; and after a happy day of sunshine and sport, and after "good night" to those who loved him best, he fell asleep as every man or woman who strives to fear God and nothing else in the world may hope to do.' Now the 'Second Queen Elizabeth' was ascending the throne at the same age as the first, nearly 400 years earlier. Despite his grief, the Prime Minister said, 'I, whose youth was passed in the august, unchallenged and tranquil glories of the Victorian era, may well feel a thrill in invoking, once more, the prayer and the anthem, "God Save the Queen".'

After the new Queen had arrived at Clarence House, one of her first visitors was Queen Mary. 'Her old Grannie and subject must be the first to kiss Her hand,' she said.[131] Thus the eighty-four-year-old woman, who had lived through five reigns, curtsied to her new queen. Queen Mary felt keenly the enormous responsibility that her grand-daughter now had to take on at the age of only twenty-five. 'But she has a fine steadfast character,' she wrote to Queen Elizabeth, '& will I know always do her best for our beloved country and her people all over the world – and dear Philip will be a great help.'[132]

Elizabeth II and Prince Philip drove to Sandringham. The new Queen understood that the loss of the King was especially terrible for her mother and sister to bear. She had a job as well as her young family – for Queen Elizabeth and Princess Margaret 'the bottom has really dropped out of their world'.[133]

Queen Elizabeth was utterly calm – too calm, felt some of those around her. She began to reply to many of the thousands of letters which were sent to her. She wrote almost at once to thank Edward Seago and Delia Peel for helping to make the day before the King died such a happy one. To Tommy Lascelles, she wrote:

> I do want to try & tell you something of the deep gratitude I feel
> for all your loving and wonderful service to the King through

perhaps the most difficult years any sovereign has passed through. Your advice & support were greatly cherished by the King – he respected your judgement completely, & how often I have heard him say, 'I must discuss this with Tommy' . . . I, who loved him most dearly, want to thank you with all my heart for all you have done to help him. I am glad beyond words that you will be at the side of our daughter.

I am, Yours sincerely, Elizabeth R.

PS The King was very <u>fond</u> of you.[134]

Lascelles was much moved, and thanked her, saying, 'It is an inexpressible comfort to me to know that The King felt I was not letting him down.' Her 'beautiful' letter had 'brought me a peace of mind that I haven't known for a long time; and I am deeply grateful.'[135]

Until 11 February the King's coffin lay in the church at Sandringham, draped in the Royal Standard and watched over all the time by estate workers. On the morning of the 11th it was conveyed, on the same gun carriage that had borne his father's coffin, to Wolferton station whence it was taken to London. At King's Cross station the young Queen, her grandmother, her mother and her sister were photographed standing in deepest black, heads bowed and darkly veiled as they watched the coffin of the man they had loved so long being taken from the train.

The King's body lay in state for the next four days in Westminster Hall while more than 300,000 people, dressed in their best, sombre and often well-worn clothes, waited quietly in the winter cold, in lines four miles long, to pass by and pay their respects to the unexpected King whom they had come to love and depend upon. For at least a month millions of people wore black mourning armbands.

On Friday 15 February the King's coffin was taken to Windsor and brought on a gun carriage drawn by officers and ratings of HMS *Excellent* to St George's Chapel in the Castle, where the funeral was held. Winston Churchill's wreath read simply 'For Valour'.

That evening Queen Elizabeth wrote to Lascelles: 'Today has been the most wonderful & the most agonising day of my life – Wonderful because one felt the sincerity of the people's feelings, & agonising because gradually one becomes less numb, & the awfulness of everything becomes real.'[136]

CHAPTER SEVENTEEN

QUEEN MOTHER

1952–1955

'Perhaps they would like me to retire decently to Kew'

QUEEN ELIZABETH'S sense of loss was beyond description. She and the King had lived so much as one, their love had been so deep, that the sudden separation was a physical as well as a spiritual shock. Grief engulfed her.

She had given the Duke of York what he had always longed for, a happy family life. As his wife, she had dedicated herself to him. She had enabled him to transform himself from an unconfident young man into an active and effective working member of the Royal Family. She had given him confidence and social grace. She had helped him control his temper and his debilitating stammer. After the horror of the abdication she above all had given him the courage to carry the unwanted burden of kingship. In the war she had been his equal partner in sustaining the people of Britain throughout the six long years of suffering. Afterwards she had supported and calmed him through the difficult, austere years of social change. And then she had devoted herself to his care in his extended series of illnesses. The King always talked of his family as 'We Four'. But, within 'We Four', 'We Two' were the closest of all.

Those nearest to Queen Elizabeth saw more clearly than the world at large that it was a relationship of mutual dependence. It has become a commonplace to say that, without her, the King could never have become 'the great and gallant King he proved to be', as a friend in later life observed. 'But perhaps what is not so widely known is the fact of her great reliance on him, on his wisdom, his integrity, his courage . . . How deeply she must have missed him and what courage it took for her to continue, alone, the work they had done so magnificently together.'[1] From a charming, vivacious, aristocratic but unsophisticated girl, she became a much loved queen. It was as 'the

King and the Queen' that they had become the symbols of British defiance and victory during the war. Now she was alone.

The shock was perhaps the greater because the past two generations of her own family had enjoyed and celebrated long marriages. When she was three years old her grandparents had celebrated their Golden Wedding, and in 1931 she had helped her own parents do the same. Instead of being able to repeat this pattern, after only twenty-eight years of marriage, the husband who adored her had died at the age of fifty-six.

Throughout the early weeks of her bereavement she was comforted by the letters of love and sympathy that poured in from friends, relations and strangers. Churchill was eloquent as always: 'All feel how Yr Majesty's devotion & love made it possible for him to reach the pinnacle on wh. he stood at his death. There must be some comfort in this. But then there is the future. Boundless hopes are centred in yr daughter's gleaming personality & reign; and these will find enduring expression in the place Yr Majesty will hold in all our thoughts as long as we live.'[2] His wife Clementine was scarcely less moved, saying that she wrote 'to express our love and gratitude to you Madam for all you both have given us all the years of your Marriage. You have shewn us what family life can be, not merely a domestic state, but a warm glowing existence full of interest and variety.'[3] She was right; their obvious celebration of family life was one of the qualities which had most endeared the King and Queen to the people of Britain.

Tributes came from America, too. General Eisenhower sent a three-page letter, expressing admiration for the King and devotion to Queen Elizabeth.[4] Eleanor Roosevelt wrote with understanding: 'There is nothing one can say to lighten the burden of your sorrow. Later you may be able to think with happiness of the life of service you & the King lived together & then you may be glad to feel how many, many of us appreciated the King's great qualities & were grateful for what you both meant to the world, as well as to your own people. May God give you faith & strength & consolation.'[5]

When the Duke of Windsor heard the news of his brother's death he immediately sailed from New York, where he was staying, to attend the funeral. His Duchess remained behind and advised him less than delicately, 'Now that the door has opened a crack try and get your foot in, in the hope of making it open even wider in the future because that is the best hope for WE [Wallis and Edward] . . . Do not mention or ask for anything regarding recognition of me.'[6] She urged him to see Queen Elizabeth and try to explain what he had felt at the time of the abdication. 'After all there are two sides to every story.'[7]

Queen Mary added her own grieving voice on the Duke's behalf. She wrote to Queen Elizabeth to 'beg & beseech of you & the girls to see him & to bury the hatchet after 15 whole years . . . I gather D. is awfully upset as in old days the 2 brothers were devoted to each other before that dreadful rift came. I feel grieved to have to add this extra burden on you 3 just at this moment but what can I do & I feel that you are so kind hearted that you will help me over what is to me a most worrying moment in the midst of the misery & suffering we are going through just now.'[8] Queen Elizabeth was not enthusiastic but, together with her daughters and Prince Philip, she did see the Duke, who came to tea at Buckingham Palace on 13 February, the day of his arrival. 'So that feud is over I hope, a great relief to me,' Queen Mary wrote to the Athlones.[9]

That was perhaps over-optimistic. But, before he left, the Duke wrote to Queen Elizabeth asking to see her again, this time alone. 'I can well understand your not wanting to be bothered by people at this terribly sad moment in your life. But I would very much like to have a talk with you alone before I return to America . . . I feel for you so very deeply and would like to say so in person.'[10] She reluctantly agreed, and he called on her at Buckingham Palace on 27 February.[11]

The Duke himself made notes of his meetings with his estranged family. 'Mama as hard as nails but failing,' he wrote. 'When Queens fail they make less sense than others in the same state. Cookie [the Windsors' unflattering nickname for Queen Elizabeth] listened without comment and closed on the note that it was nice to be able to talk about Bertie with somebody who had known him so well.' Writing to his wife, he said, 'Cookie was as sugar as I've told you,' and went on to write in bitter and insulting terms of his family's coldness to him, describing his mother and sister-in-law bitterly as 'ice-veined bitches'.[12] Notwithstanding such private thoughts, a few weeks later, in May, he sent Queen Elizabeth another apparently affectionate letter asking to see her on his next visit to London.[13] She agreed and invited him to tea on 27 May, as she did once again in November that year.

Despite the depth of her grief, in outward matters Queen Elizabeth showed fortitude. Less than a fortnight after the death of the King, she announced that in future she wished to be known as 'Queen Elizabeth

The Queen Mother', although privately she disliked the title – 'horrible name', as she described it.[14] With the help of Tommy Lascelles, she drafted an eloquent, personal message to the nation. The left-leaning *News Chronicle* called it 'a statement without parallel in the history of kingship'.

> I want to send this message of thanks to a great multitude of people – to you who, from all parts of the world, have been giving me your sympathy and affection throughout these dark days. I want you to know how your concern for me has upheld me in my sorrow, and how proud you have made me by your wonderful tributes to my dear husband, a great and noble King.
>
> No man had a deeper sense than he of duty and of service, and no man was more full of compassion for his fellow men. He loved you all, every one of you, most truly. That, you know, was what he always tried to tell you in his yearly message at Christmas; that was the pledge that he took at the sacred moment of his Coronation fifteen years ago.
>
> Now I am left alone, to do what I can to honour that pledge without him. Throughout our married life we have tried, the King and I, to fulfil with all our hearts and all our strength the great task of service that was laid upon us. My only wish now is that I may be allowed to continue the work we sought to do together.
>
> I commend to you our dear Daughter: give her your loyalty and devotion: though blessed in her husband and children she will need your protection and your love in the great and lonely station to which she has been called. God bless you all: and may He in His wisdom guide us safely to our true destiny of Peace and Good Will.[15]

*

HEREDITARY MONARCHY can be both efficient and unkind, as the old phrase 'The King is dead, long live the King', suggests. The real national sorrow at the death of King George VI was immediately followed by happiness at the prospect of the young Queen coming to the throne. The torch had been passed to a new generation.

But this meant that the Queen Mother was now, in effect, the *ancien régime*. She suddenly found that she was no longer the mistress of any home. Buckingham Palace was a tied cottage – as well as a tied

office – for the monarch, and the Queen and Prince Philip would need
to move from Clarence House into the Palace where the King and
Queen had lived since 1937. The Queen Mother would have to find
another house in London and she could no longer consider Windsor
Castle, Balmoral or Sandringham home.

The prospect of leaving the Palace distressed her. On at least one
occasion she collapsed in tears on discussing her inevitable move with
the Queen – and immediately wrote to apologize. She suggested to
the Queen that she and Prince Philip should move into the Belgian
Suite on the ground floor of the Palace – these were the rooms which
the King and Queen had occupied during the war. That would give
her time to move out of her own rooms on the first floor 'without
any ghastly hurry, and I could be quite self contained upstairs, meals
etc, and you would hardly know I was there . . . It is so angelic of you
both to tell me I can stay on for a bit at B.P., and I am most grateful
for your thoughtfulness. I know that it took Granny some months to
pack up everything, & I fear that I shall need some time too. But what
is a few months in a lifetime anyway! Thank you darling for being
such an angelic daughter.'[16]

Queen Elizabeth and Queen Mary continued to sustain each other
and, in Queen Mary's eloquent words, they talked together 'of much
that was in our poor tattered hearts'.[17] Queen Elizabeth's doctor, Sir
John Weir, sent her some homeopathic powders that he thought might
relieve her suffering.[18] Edward Woods, the Bishop of Lichfield, wrote
to say, 'I always knew that Your Majesty's faith & encouragement
would never fail in this supreme test; I have no doubt, Ma'am, that
you yourself are the main human source of strength & comfort to the
dear Princess Margaret & the others of the Family circle.' He sent her
a book, *Why Do Men Suffer?* by Leslie D. Weatherhead, and tried to
console her with the thought that 'suffering ("accepted" at God's
hands) is really a form of action.'[19]

She was concerned that she would now have nothing to do. At the
age of only fifty-one, much younger than Queen Alexandra and Queen
Mary when their husbands died, she did not feel ready for the relatively
retired life they had led in widowhood. Although both had continued
to carry out public engagements and to support their favourite
charities, neither had sought any constitutional role.

Queen Elizabeth, however, was anxious at least to be able to act
as a Counsellor of State when the Queen was away, as she had during

the King's reign. She told Lascelles, 'Naturally I would like this, as it would give me an interest, & having been one, it seems so dull to be relegated to the "no earthly use" class.'[20] But, under the existing legislation, after the death of her husband she was no longer eligible to serve in this capacity.* Lascelles thought that it would be both right and popular to change the law in the Queen Mother's favour and, with the agreement of the Queen, he immediately wrote to the Prime Minister and the Lord Chancellor to ask if it could be done.[21] It could, and in April the Queen approved a submission from the Prime Minister proposing to amend the Regency Act to include the Queen Mother's name following that of the Duke of Edinburgh and before the other Counsellors.[22] It was a slow process, and the new Regency Act did not pass into law until November 1953. It contained another new departure: the Duke of Edinburgh was designated regent in case Prince Charles should succeed before the age of eighteen, instead of Princess Margaret, who under the 1937 Act would have become regent.†

The position of the Duke of Edinburgh was a matter about which the Queen Mother showed concern – she asked that he be able to play a part in the Coronation. Lascelles suggested that the Prince should be made chairman of the Coronation Commission, and this was done.[23] But she found herself in conflict with her son-in-law over the name and style of the dynasty. The Prince's destiny and his day-to-day existence had been changed massively by the accession of his wife. Her premature transformation from heir to reigning monarch made his life in every way more difficult. He had been head of his young family. Now his wife was taken over by the venerable Court of her father. The Private Secretary, the Lord Chamberlain, the Keeper of the Privy Purse and Treasurer, the Master of the Horse, the Surveyor of the Queen's Pictures – all of these and many more wanted to serve their new monarch and wanted her to see them do so. They wanted access to the Queen, not to her husband.

Prince Philip saw himself as a man first and a prince second, and

---

* The Regency Act of 1937, amended in 1943, required the appointment, in the event of the Sovereign's illness or temporary absence from the country, of Counsellors of State, who were to be the Sovereign's spouse and the four persons of full age next in line to the Throne. Queen Elizabeth, of course, fulfilled neither requirement.

† In June 1953 a spurious link was fostered by the press between this change and Princess Margaret's private life – the story of her romance with Peter Townsend had just broken. In fact the changes to the Regency Act had been in preparation well before this.

as such he wanted recognition as head of his family. He thought that, in accordance with the normal practice, his children should take their father's name. He had taken the family name, Mountbatten, when he became a naturalized British subject but he now proposed Edinburgh as an alternative. However, behind suggestions of any name change, some members of the Cabinet suspected the hand of Earl Mountbatten, who was reported to have said that since 7 February a Mountbatten had sat upon the throne. Queen Mary was dismayed – she believed that her husband had founded the house of Windsor for all time, and she was not prepared to see the name changed to Battenberg or Mountbatten.[24] The Queen Mother seems to have agreed – Harold Macmillan, then the Conservative Minister for Housing, commented in his diary that she 'of course favours the name of Windsor and all the emphasis on the truly British and native character of the Royal Family. It is also clear that the Duke has the normal attitude of many men towards a mother-in-law of strong character, accentuated by the peculiar circumstances of his position.'[25] The Cabinet took the same view as the two dowager Queens and insisted to the new young Queen that her family must still be known as Windsor. It was not easy for Prince Philip. In the end, largely due to Dickie Mountbatten's insistence, a compromise was agreed – the name Mountbatten-Windsor was adopted, to be used in future for those of the Queen's descendants who were not entitled to be called Royal Highness. The name of the royal house remained Windsor.

The Queen Mother had to contemplate changing not only her residence but also her Household; as was customary, everyone formally resigned at the end of the reign. But she was anxious to keep many of the same people around her. She invited Lord Airlie to remain as her Lord Chamberlain – he accepted, ready to serve at her pleasure, but reminded her, 'Your Majesty will not forget the telegram – "Be Off" – when Your Majesty has had enough of me.'[26] Similarly, she wrote to her Treasurer Arthur Penn, 'Please do continue, & I expect that there will be less to do in the future, or do you think that there will be much more, with less money & more to spend it on! I fully expect to be bankrupt, & would very much like to have you at my side when that happens!'[27] There would indeed be much more for her to do, and money would always be a problem. On her widowhood, her Civil List allowance, for her official duties, was fixed at £70,000 a year; it remained at this level for the next twenty years.

Shock can dull grief and when the shock of the King's death began to wear off, the Queen Mother felt increasingly wretched. To her brother David she wrote that she could not envisage life without the King – 'he was so much, & such a big part of one's own life, & things can never be the same again without his energy, & fun & goodness & kindness. He really was the kindest and most <u>selfless</u> person I have ever known . . . At the moment one simply cannot take any interest in <u>anything</u>.'[28] Everything was painful; some of her letters echoed the sensibility which had led her to observe in 1944 that young soldiers contemplating the horrors of war found the beauty of the countryside hard to bear. To Lascelles she wrote that a beautiful day 'is almost unbearable, & seems to make everything a thousand times worse. I suppose it will get better some day.'[29]

She appreciated the rallying of friends. Thanking Bobbety Salisbury for his comforting letter, she wrote,

> tho' sorrow is such an immensely <u>personal</u> thing that it is with one all the time, yet the feeling that other people <u>understand</u> what one is going through does give one courage.
>
> The King was so wonderfully better, and for that I am very grateful, because he was so gay & so full of plans for the future, and I am quite sure did not contemplate death coming so soon.
>
> I had so hoped that he might have had a few years when he could have eased up a little, & done some of the things he loved doing, such as planning gardens & vistas, & changing all the pictures round, and had perhaps some less violent & uneasy years in contrast to the last rather terrible twelve. But it was not to be.
>
> At the moment everything seems very pointless, but I am sure that one must not be too sorry for oneself – it's like looking in the glass when one is weeping, it makes everything much worse![30]

Her friends did all they could. Doris Vyner was as important as any and the Queen continued to slip around to her flat secretly, as she had in the last months of the King's illness, just to be alone with kindness and companionship she had known almost all her life. Doris understood how desperately she had needed the King and she commented that without him her 'mainspring' had gone. Indeed Doris pointed out to mutual friends whom she trusted that although everyone thought that the Queen had energized the King and kept him up to his work, in fact the opposite was true. The initiatives almost all came from the King – he had had to make the decisions. Now she was quite lost without him.[31]

D'Arcy Osborne understood some of this. He wrote to her from Rome late one night and said he would not read his letter through in case he then threw it away as he had already done other such letters to her. He wished he could help her in all the painful adjustments she was facing.[32] Betty Bowes Lyon, the wife of her brother Mike, told her that she had a very rare gift with people, like the gift of healing, 'and You MUST GO ON using it.'[33] Understandably, she became more dependent upon her own family, in particular her brother David, who helped to put her life and finances into order and perspective. She told him, 'now that Bertie has gone, you are the only person to whom I can turn ... Thank you again darling for all your angelicness, Your very loving, Elizabeth.'[34]

She rarely let her grief show, and her ladies in waiting saw little of her anguish. Katie Seymour, who had known her since they were both in their teens, wrote: 'She varies from day to day, never shows anything but supreme self control.'[35] If she did break down, she was embarrassed. In April she wrote to Delia Peel to apologize for being 'so silly' and for being unable to tell her to her face how much she valued her help.[36] She did express herself quite openly to Osbert Sitwell, saying that she felt it so hard to realize that the King had gone. 'He was so young to die, and was becoming so wise in his Kingship. He was so kind too and had a sort of natural nobility of thought and life, which sometimes made me ashamed of my narrower & more feminine point of view.'[37]

One letter in particular nourished her. It was from Lord Davidson, who sent her his account of how he had encouraged the nervous Duke of York to pursue his quest for her in 1922. Davidson wrote, with great charm, that he had kept the story in the secret recesses of his memory and was only now releasing it 'because in Your Majesty's terrible loneliness I believe that it may bring one tiny grain of comfort'.[38] She thanked him warmly: 'As you told me your story so well, & so delicately, I must tell you that we were ideally happy, due to the King's wonderful kindness & goodness and thought for others. I never wanted to be with anyone but him.'[39]

Her mood changed all the time, as might well have been expected. To Arthur Penn she wrote, 'It is difficult to make any real plans as yet.'[40] She confided to Lady Salisbury that sorrow was devastating. 'I find everything a perpetual battle & struggle. But, as you know, the King never gave in, and I am determined to try & do what he would have wished.'[41] She wrote in similar vein to Cecil Boyd-Rochfort, the royal racehorse trainer.[42] At the end of April she went to a dinner with friends. According to Osbert Sitwell, 'a sudden roar' went up at the dining table which he took to be an indication of delight from everyone that the Queen Mother was among them once more.[43] She thought that 'the noise was so terrific and the plunge for me so sudden that I felt slightly bewildered'.[44]

Meanwhile she observed formalities. She received deputations from the Houses of Lords and Commons who presented addresses of condolence; she replied to each address. During the spring she fulfilled other commitments. Her first major official engagement after the death of the King took place on 13 May 1952. It was in fact an initiative of her own. She had always made a point of trying to see her regiments before they were sent off overseas, and when she heard that the 1st Battalion of her beloved Black Watch had been ordered to the war in Korea,* she asked if a visit to the battalion could be arranged for her.[45] Despite a bad cold she flew to Scotland to inspect them at Crail Camp in Fife. Dressed in black, she wore the diamond regimental brooch that General Sir Archibald Cameron had presented to her when she became colonel-in-chief in 1937. Five hundred men paraded before her, each wearing a black armband. She praised the regiment 'so dear to my heart and to many of my family'; then she met relatives and Old Comrades, visited the sergeants' mess and lunched with the officers before flying back to London.[46]

On 23 May she and Princess Margaret had an adventure. Together with Lord and Lady Salisbury, they visited the de Havilland factory near Hatfield and were taken for a four-hour flight in the Comet, the revolutionary jet airliner, over Geneva and Mont Blanc. On board was Sir Miles Thomas, the Chairman of the national airline, the British Overseas Airways Corporation (BOAC), who later wrote an account of

---

* The Korean War began in June 1950 with the invasion of South Korea by the communist North. The brutal conflict became a Cold War battleground with China and the Soviet Union supporting the North and the United States, Britain and other nations fighting for the South under the flag of the United Nations. An armistice was declared in July 1953 but the two Koreas remained in a state of permanent hostility thereafter, and in May 2009 the armistice was abrogated by the North.

the flight in his autobiography, *Out on a Wing*. The Comet flew over Italy and the north of Corsica as well; they reached 500 mph and Queen Elizabeth asked how fast they could go. The pilot suggested she push the control column forward – they reached 525 mph, touching the red danger section on the airspeed indicator. The aeroplane began to 'porpoise', showing that it was at the limit of its aerodynamic stability. Comets later proved to have a structural weakness which led to fatal crashes until the fault was put right, and Thomas wrote that he shuddered whenever he remembered this flight.[47] Queen Elizabeth, however, was quite unperturbed by the aircraft's erratic movement. 'The Viking will seem a little slow after this,' she said, and sent a radio message to No. 600 Squadron of the Royal Auxiliary Air Force at Biggin Hill, of which she was Honorary Air Commodore. 'I am delighted to tell you that today I took over as first pilot of the Comet aircraft. We exceeded a reading of Mach 0.8 at 40,000 feet. What the passengers thought I really would not like to say!'[48]

In early June 1952 she went north to Scotland, first – and rather sadly – to Balmoral. Every part of it evoked memories of the King, she told Queen Mary. 'He was always so full of plans & ideas for improving house & garden, & we spent so many happy hours here. Life seems incredibly meaningless without him – I miss him every moment of the day.'[49] After a week, she flew on up to Wick to stay with Clare and Doris Vyner in Caithness, on the very northern tip of mainland Britain, close to John o'Groats.

Caithness is a barren, surprisingly flat county, sometimes called 'the Lowlands beyond the Highlands'. Windswept and austere, it forms the north-eastern corner of Britain. For much of the Victorian era, fishing for herring – 'the silver darlings' – provided most of the work and the income of Caithness, and when that fishing declined, so did the population. By the early 1950s Caithness was really the end of Britain, one of the poorest regions of the country, with many unmade roads and very few people.

The Vyners had a home almost as far north as the land stretched, on Dunnet Head, a fist of rock which jabs out into the Pentland Firth just south of the Orkney Islands. Their large white house was romantically named The House of the Northern Gate. It was utterly alone and remote, and the wind used to lift the carpets. It was the first place Queen Elizabeth had been to since February that had no associations with the King and she gained relaxation and peace from it.[50] To her great surprise, this visit to Caithness offered her a new interest, one which was to provide her enormous pleasure for the rest of her life.

One day she drove with the Vyners east along the little coast road towards John o'Groats. Between the road and the waves, she said much later, they suddenly saw 'this romantic looking castle down by the sea'. They drove down the track towards it and found it was quite empty. 'And then the next day we discovered it was going to be pulled down and I thought this would be a terrible pity. One had seen so much destruction in one's life.'[51] The Castle, named Barrogill, had a superb position, right on the sea, overlooking Orkney, but it was in terrible condition. It had been commandeered during the war and used for troop accommodation. No maintenance had been carried out. The roof was in a disastrous state, and a violent storm in spring 1952 had caused serious damage. Now no one wanted it. The Queen Mother was immediately attracted to the Castle, and was determined to preserve it.

The owner, Captain Imbert-Terry, was delighted by her interest. He offered to give the Castle to her for nothing. This she declined, but she accepted his suggestion of a nominal price of £100. She decided to change the name from Barrogill to its more romantic original name, the Castle of Mey. It was the only house that ever belonged to her.

The Vyners were overjoyed that she was to become their neighbour in the wild. Doris Vyner wrote to her: 'You've no idea what a wonderful thing it is for us all this – to be able to be of use – and to have such an enthralling thing to think about instead of the usual gloomy thoughts.'[52] Clare Vyner arranged for the Queen Mother to buy some more land along the coast at a cost of some £300; the grazing would provide an income of about £30 a year and, when a small shoot was developed, it could bring in a rent of about £200 a year. 'It would thus all work in quite economically for you & although not a good shoot would amuse Your Majesty's guests & give food for the table.'[53] Doris Vyner went around local antique shops and found old and inexpensive furniture for her to buy – one extensive list cost £124. She also arranged for electricity to be brought to the Castle.[54] She wrote to Queen Elizabeth, 'I do long for Castle Mey, because I know you'll feel happy in a way there. I'm sure the King would love you to be by the sea looking at that such important part of his life – Scapa Flow etc etc, Oh dear – you are so brave.'[55]

For the time being the Queen Mother kept her plan secret. It was not until early August that she told Arthur Penn, her Treasurer, of what she had in mind. She planned to 'escape there occasionally when life became hideous', she told him. 'Do you think me <u>mad</u>?'[56] The news of her purchase came out in the newspapers towards the end of August 1952, and she wrote to her friends and family explaining what she had done. Perhaps nervous of the likely reaction of her cautious mother-in-law, in her letter to Queen Mary she played down the task she had taken on. She had been told that the Castle was going to 'crumble away', she wrote, 'and I felt that it was such a wrong thing to happen to an interesting old place'.[57]

Queen Mary owned that she had been surprised to learn from the press the 'exciting' news that Queen Elizabeth had bought herself an isolated castle. She feared she would not see it 'as my travelling days are over'.[58] May Elphinstone wished that Mey were not so far away.[59] To the Queen Mother that was part of the attraction – she loved being in Caithness because it was Scotland, to which she was devoted, and yet a part of Scotland which had no memories of happier days. She saw the Castle as emblematic of her own life. It gave her and many of her friends and courtiers great joy in the decades to come.

*

AS THE SUMMER of 1952 progressed, she started to undertake more official engagements. In the first ten days of July she received representatives of the Royal Society of Arts, attended a concert given by the Bar Musical Society at the Middle Temple, paid visits to the Home for Retired Congregational Ministers and their wives in Sussex and to the Royal College of Art, received several ambassadors and their wives, attended a garden party at Lambeth Palace, and made her annual visit to the London Garden Society.

She had been dreading going alone to Sandringham that summer – as Queen Mary wrote in a sympathetic letter, being there for the first time alone 'must have been a severe test to your shattered nerves'. She understood what her daughter-in-law was going through: 'all the intimate things one was accustomed to discuss with one's husband & how one misses the talks', and felt deeply sorry for her.[60]

Doris Vyner was more optimistic – she hoped that Queen Elizabeth would feel the King's presence close to her at Sandringham.[61] To her surprise and gratitude, that was indeed how Queen Elizabeth felt at

Sandringham that summer. She attended the King's Lynn Festival to
hear a recital by her friend and future lady in waiting Ruth Fermoy,
and visited the Sandringham Flower Show, another hardy perennial of
hers through the decades to come. She went to a concert by the
London Symphony Orchestra, conducted by Sir John Barbirolli, in St
Nicholas's Church at Dersingham; Vaughan Williams was in the
audience and his Fifth Symphony was performed.

These were friendly, unpretentious local events and she loved
them. Edward Seago, who came to stay, and Cynthia Spencer, who
was in waiting on her, commented on the peacefulness that surrounded her at Sandringham.[62] She was aware of it herself and wrote
to Queen Mary, 'I have felt more at peace than any time since
February. Being surrounded by people who loved Bertie, has made me
feel very close to him.'[63] To her daughter, the Queen, she wrote that
'I felt an amazing feeling of relief & peace, which I have not felt since
Papa died. It was just as if Sandringham opened its arms to me, & I
sank into them thankfully.' Although the house was utterly bound up
with the King, 'I love the people & all that happens here, & to be
amongst them is a relief & a healing.' She reminded her daughter that,
when Queen Mary was widowed, the King had told her that she must
still treat Sandringham as her home. 'I would so love it if you would
say that to me too.' She would not come often but she would love to
know she could come once in a while.[64] The Queen replied at once to
her mother that she was 'very, very thankful' that the visit had been
so happy. 'I had been in a fever in case it would prove too much
agony for you.' She said that 'of course' her mother must continue to
treat Sandringham as her home and go there whenever she wanted.[65]

After her birthday, the Queen Mother, as always in August,
removed to Scotland. First she stayed with the Vyners, making more
plans for Mey, and then she went back to the Highlands and Balmoral.
She had to prepare for another daunting change: she was to move out
of Balmoral and into Birkhall, where she would live without her
family. She was concerned; the house had many memories of happy
days at the beginning of her marriage but since then she had come to
see Balmoral as her Scottish home and after so many years in the
Castle, Birkhall seemed very cramped.[66] To her sister May she wrote
that it was 'rather awful' being there instead of at Balmoral and that
she felt completely lost without her husband.[67]

Even so, she had some friends to stay, among them D'Arcy

Osborne, whom she taught to play canasta.[68] She told him afterwards how glad she had been of his presence – 'You were one of the very few friends I wanted to see – you were so kind & understanding, and I was so very grateful to you. Next year I hope to be more brave.' For the moment she took comfort in her grandchildren, Charles and Anne. 'Charles is a great love of mine,' she said to Osborne. 'He is such a darling & so like his mother when she was a small child.'[69]

The peace and optimism she had felt at Sandringham did not last through that autumn. 'I suppose that one will never feel the same again. I talk & laugh & listen, but one lives in a dream, & I expect that one's real self dies when one's husband dies, and only a ghost remains.' What upset her, she said, were people who looked at her with a penetrating expression and asked, 'are you feeling BETTER', and those who said ' "but what a wonderful death for the King – how that must comfort you". If only they knew!'[70]

Gradually she came out of herself. Edith Sitwell sent her a copy of her new literary anthology, *A Book of Flowers*. This turned out to be an inspired gift. Queen Elizabeth wrote to her:

> I started to read it, sitting by the river, and it was a day when one felt engulfed by great black clouds of unhappiness and misery, and I found a sort of peace stealing round my heart as I read such lovely poems and heavenly words.
> I found a hope in George Herbert's poem, 'Who could have thought my shrivel'd heart, could have recovered greennesse. It was gone quite underground.' And I thought how small and selfish is sorrow. But it bangs one about until one is senseless, and I can never thank you enough for giving me such a delicious book wherein I found so much beauty and hope.[71]

She was still considering how exactly she should continue her official life. The uncertainty was difficult for her ladies in waiting too, as she postponed making any decision about which of them she wished to keep in her new Household. Arthur Penn wrote to Lady Spencer about their anxieties; as a lifelong friend, he understood Queen Elizabeth well. He was both sympathetic to the ladies and frank, if not tart, about a particular failing of their mistress: 'The Queen, bless her heart, has cultivated procrastination to a degree which is really an art – when one is vexed, as I fear I often am, one should recall that the Bowes Lyons are the laziest family in the world. Against this reflection it becomes remarkable that she accomplishes so much.'[72] Penn believed he understood why Queen Elizabeth had not yet informed her ladies of her intentions. 'I think it possible that this omission may be the reflection of what has been apparent from the first, a sturdy repudiation of any idea that HM has any intention, because she is widowed, of relinquishing all to which she has become accustomed.'[73] She did not give up any of her ladies.

During the autumn of 1952, Queen Elizabeth had a long conversation with Winston Churchill. According to his daughter Mary Soames, Churchill took it upon himself to tell Queen Elizabeth that, despite the death of the King and the accession of the Queen, she still had an enormously important part to play in British public life.

She had met Churchill at dinner with the Salisburys on 1 August, and she wrote afterwards to Betty Salisbury, 'Winston was so angelic about the King – he has such tender understanding, & I was so touched & helped.'[74] Then she saw him again in Scotland; he was staying at Balmoral for the Prime Minister's annual autumn visit and asked if he could come to see her at Birkhall. Her lady in waiting, Jean Rankin, told him to arrive unannounced, and on 2 October he drove over. 'He was absolutely charming & very interesting,' Queen Elizabeth wrote to Lord Salisbury, 'and I realised suddenly how very much I am now cut off from "inside" information. He is truly a remarkable man, & with great delicacy of feeling too.'[75] This may have been the crucial conversation during which he persuaded her that she still had a vital national role. Jean Rankin saw that his visit made a difference to Queen Elizabeth. 'I think he must have said things which made her realise how important it was for her to carry on, how much people wanted her to do things as she had before.'[76]

Throughout that autumn she began to pick up the pace of her private interests and her official work. The journal of her activities maintained by her ladies in waiting from the 1950s until the end of her life shows how her interests were concentrated: church, army and charities dominated her public life; in private, music, ballet, art and – a relatively new interest – horses drew her attention, and spilled over into her choice of patronages and engagements. Many of her public duties she now carried out with Princess Margaret at her side. Among the official engagements she undertook in Scotland were a visit to the oil refinery at Grangemouth, and the unveiling of the War Memorial to the Commandos at Spean Bridge. As always, she visited the Lord

Roberts' Workshops in Dundee and the Black Watch Memorial Home at Dunalistair. (This became an annual visit until the 1990s.) In mid-October she went back to London but there was little let-up. In the weeks leading up to Christmas her diary was full. There were visits to her regiments, to almshouses, to prize givings, concerts and recitals, the theatre and the ballet, the unveiling of monuments and many official dinners.

She had another important preoccupation: the search for a biographer for the King. It would not be an easy book to write, she thought. 'There can be very few Kings of England whose reigns were so harried and harassed by troubles & worries & anxieties on such an immense scale,' she wrote to Lascelles.

> First the abdication, & all the agony of mind. I doubt if people realise how horrible it all was to the King & me – to feel unwanted, & to undertake such a job for such a dreadful reason – & it was a terrible experience. Then the War with all its agony, & then 'after the War', which was a dreadful strain upon the King. I suppose that we have been through a revolution and, as usual, people hardly realised what was happening to them. All this crammed into 15 short years – it is a dizzy thought.[77]

Lascelles proposed John Wheeler-Bennett, a distinguished military historian, as official biographer. He wrote vividly and accurately, Lascelles considered, and had a reputation as a trustworthy historian; coincidentally he had also been a pupil of Lionel Logue.[78] (He had a stammer induced when a German bomb was dropped on his school during the First World War.) Moreover he had spent much time as a traveller and writer in Germany between the wars and was one of the first British commentators to recognize the evil of Nazism.[79] He was, in fact, well qualified to inspire Queen Elizabeth's confidence, and to give her reason to believe that he would be sympathetic to the challenges faced by the King.

She saw Wheeler-Bennett just before Christmas 1952, liked him, and agreed that he should be given the task. Early in 1953 she promised to send him, through Lascelles, the diaries the King had kept during the war – a decision which took much thought, for the King had intended them to be kept closed in the Royal Archives. 'And yet I feel that it is very important for someone like Wheeler B to read this day to day account of these terrible days.'[80]

Later in the year she invited the author to stay at Birkhall to gather atmosphere and information.[81] He gained insights, but at a certain cost. Sir Robert Bruce Lockhart later recorded that Wheeler-Bennett:

> gave us an amusing account of his visit to Balmoral to see the Queen and to Birkhall to see the Queen Mother. At Balmoral the Queen kept off the book till the last morning when she took Jack for a long eight (?) mile walk. Jack, who was not dressed nor shod for such a walk and was more or less 'beat' when he got back to Balmoral, collected his suitcase and drove over to Birkhall. The Queen Mother promptly took him for an afternoon walk as long as his morning walk with the Queen. When they returned to the house, Jack wilted visibly. The Queen Mother said to him: 'Did my daughter, by any chance, take you for one of her walks this morning?' Jack admitted that she had. 'Then', said the Queen Mother, 'champagne is the only remedy.'[82]

She continued to talk to him regularly as he worked on the book, and invited him to Sandringham as well as Birkhall. Obviously the abdication was one of the most important and most difficult episodes to cover, and perhaps the one about which the Queen Mother felt most strongly. Indeed, when Helen Hardinge, wife of Alec Hardinge, the King's former Private Secretary, had sent the Queen the manuscript of her book *The Path of Kings* in 1951, the only passage to which the Queen had objected dealt with the abdication, and was critical of the Duke and Duchess of Windsor. 'I don't like the idea of you writing about this agonising interlude in our history. I am quite certain that you would be wise to say very little on this subject – It only does harm, and the effect on people is sometimes so different to what you think it may be . . . Please take it out. Your loving friend, ER.'[83]

Wheeler-Bennett naturally conducted many interviews on the subject of the abdication – he spoke to the Duke of Windsor himself, but not to the Duchess – and wrote about the crisis at some length. His account was judicious; like almost everyone who studied the subject he came to feel a great deal more sympathy for King George VI than for Edward VIII. His painstaking, lucid biography, published in 1958, demonstrated well the author's regard for his subject; Queen Elizabeth was pleased.

For Christmas 1952 the whole family gathered as usual at Sandringham. Queen Mary was increasingly frail – the death of her son the

King was a blow from which she could not recover. She spent much of the holiday in her own rooms, only coming down to join the family for tea. The Queen Mother stayed at Sandringham until late January, and she visited areas of the east coast hit by the worst flooding in decades. She was filled with admiration for the courage of homeless people and wrote to the Queen, 'it was terribly like the war all over again, the same defiance, the same "I don't care" & I felt quite shattered & exhausted by memories, & the sad reality of the present tragedy'.[84] She returned to Royal Lodge and on the first anniversary of the King's death she took communion, with Princess Margaret, at the Royal Chapel. This service became an annual fixture for the rest of her life.

By this time, Queen Mary was nearing death. To one old friend, Lady Shaftesbury, she said, 'I suppose one must force oneself to go on until the end?' 'I am sure', replied Lady Shaftesbury, 'that Your Majesty will.'[85] She did; her duty all ended, Queen Mary died peacefully at Marlborough House on the evening of 24 March 1953. A week later tens of thousands of people stood silent and bareheaded as the coffin of a dignified and admired queen, who seemed to have been always with them, was carried 'slowly and majestically' away. Her biographer commented that 'by undeviating service to her own highest ideals, she had ended by becoming, for millions, an ideal in herself'.[86] Her death brought another huge change for her daughter-in-law. She and Queen Mary had enjoyed and suffered much together ever since Queen Mary had warmly welcomed Elizabeth Bowes Lyon into the family in 1923. Not only was an important bond with the past severed but Queen Elizabeth was now the senior member of the Royal Family.

In early April 1953 she travelled north to Fountains Abbey where she dedicated the monument Clare and Doris Vyner had erected to their children Elizabeth and Charles. Writing to Doris afterwards, she praised her friends' composure at what must have been a moment of anguish, and spoke of the solace she had found in being with them. 'Once again I subsided into the delicious feeling of "being with friends". There is nothing like it to heal wounds.'[87]

The question of a London residence for the Queen Mother had been resolved with the decision that she should move to Clarence House, which was now being prepared for her. Arthur Penn kept her informed of progress and offered advice on the colours of the walls to go with her old curtains, which were to be reused there.[88] It was not a house that she liked, however, and, after the death of Queen Mary, Queen Elizabeth expressed a wish to move to Marlborough House instead – it was much more suitable, and it had a garage and good staff accommodation. Moreover, it probably did not need much spending on it. She was annoyed that Members of Parliament had been commenting on the costs of altering Clarence House for her. She said to Arthur Penn, 'Perhaps they would like me to retire decently to Kew and run a needlework guild?' If there were any more such complaints, she said, 'you must tell them angrily how little has been done and how loathsome it [Clarence House] is.'[89] Nonetheless, Queen Elizabeth and Princess Margaret finally moved into Clarence House in May 1953, a few weeks before the Coronation. The Queen eventually gave Marlborough House to the Commonwealth Secretariat.

Queen Elizabeth had to face another loss at this time. Her brother Mike suddenly and unexpectedly died at the age of fifty-nine. Among her siblings, Mike had been one of the closest to the King. They had shot together and laughed together. He was seen in the family and by his friends as a genial and generous man, possessed of great charm and 'devoid of jealousy'.[90] His death on 1 May 1953 meant that Queen Elizabeth had now lost five of her brothers, all in youth or middle age.*

★

THE DATE OF the Coronation was fixed for Tuesday 2 June 1953. Churchill had been against having it in 1952 because he felt that the country's economic crisis was so serious that not a single working day should be lost. 'Can't have coronations with bailiffs in the house,' he said.[91] The Queen overcame her reluctance to have the whole event televised. Thus, for the first time a coronation would be taken to the entire nation, not just confined within the sight of its leaders. People scrambled to buy the new-fangled sets and gave the nascent television industry a huge boost. Excitement gathered as winter gave way to spring 1953. Houses were painted red, white and blue. Street parties

---

* Of Queen Elizabeth's six brothers, Alec (the third) had died in 1911 aged twenty-four, Fergus (the fourth) in 1915 aged twenty-six, Jock (the second) in 1930 aged forty-three and Patrick (the eldest) in 1949 aged fifty-four.

and many other forms of celebration were planned. Some called it hysteria but, rather, it was a sense of vindication; the people's reward to themselves for the immense sacrifice and effort of the war.

The Queen Mother was understandably concerned about what she would wear. Before her death, Queen Mary had offered to lend her her own Coronation robe, an offer which Queen Elizabeth had accepted with gratitude; it would save the difficult task of altering the robe made for her own Coronation in 1937.[92] Norman Hartnell made her dress and, in his memoirs, wrote about the difficulty of perfecting the hang of the heavily embroidered skirt 'bordered with golden tissue and with jewelled feather embroideries'. It had to be mounted 'on an underskirt of ivory taffeta laced with bands of horsehair and further strengthened with countless strands of whalebone'.[93] With it the Queen Mother wore a triple diamond necklace, large dropdiamond earrings and a diamond waterfall stomacher, together with the Riband of the Garter and the Family Orders of her husband and daughter.

On the morning of 2 June, she was wildly cheered by the crowds standing in the rain as she drove in a glass coach to Westminster Abbey. One journalist, Anne Edwards, described her progress through the Abbey as William Walton's *Orb and Sceptre* thundered from the organ: 'On she came up the aisle with a bow here to Prince Bernhard, a bow there to the row of ambassadors, and up those tricky steps with no looking down like the Duke of Gloucester, no half turn to check her train like the Duchess of Kent, no hesitation at the top like Princess Margaret, no nervous nods of her head like Princess Mary. She is the only woman I know who can slow up naturally when she sees a camera.'[94]

The Coronation brought her a mix of emotions. There was sadness but also pride that she and the King had managed to take an institution in crisis and restore it to its place at the centre of popular imagination and esteem. The emotional power of the monarchy that Queen Elizabeth II now inherited had been revived by the extraordinary diligence and dedication of her father and mother. For the service, Queen Elizabeth sat in the front row of the Royal Gallery with the four-and-a-half-year-old Prince Charles. A photograph shows her standing behind the Prince, looking thoughtful as her daughter made the same vows as she and the King had made only sixteen years before.

At Buckingham Palace after the Coronation there was merriment bordering on chaos. Cecil Beaton found it hard to corral all his subjects together for the group photographs. He described the Queen Mother as 'dimpled and chuckling, with eyes as bright as any of her jewels' and 'in rollicking spirits'. She asked him if he needed more time. 'Suddenly I felt as if all my anxieties and fears were dispelled . . . The great mother figure and nannie to us all, through the warmth of her sympathy bathes us and wraps us up in a counterpane by the fireside.' She gathered her over-excited grandchildren in her arms and Beaton saw 'a terrific picture' as she bent to kiss Prince Charles's hair. 'Suddenly I had this wonderful accomplice – someone who would help me through everything.'[95]

*

IMMEDIATELY AFTER the Coronation the first family crisis of the new reign broke into the open. It was a drama played out painfully in public, an augury of what was to come over the decades ahead as the Royal Family had to adjust to a more populist and intrusive age. Princess Margaret had fallen in love with Peter Townsend, a married member of the Royal Household sixteen years her senior.

Wing Commander Townsend had a heroic record as a Royal Air Force pilot; he was good looking and charming, if a trifle self-regarding. He had married during the war and had two young sons, but the marriage was not happy.[96] He had joined the Royal Household in 1944 and, as we have seen, quickly became a family favourite. Queen Elizabeth had described him to D'Arcy Osborne as 'a very nice, ultra sensitive ex-flying man, who was in the Battle of Britain, & nearly flew himself into a nervous decline'.[97] He had travelled with the family on the South African trip in 1947, when he had helped soothe the tired and troubled King,[98] and in 1948 when Princess Margaret was just eighteen he accompanied her to Amsterdam to attend the installation of Princess Juliana as queen of the Netherlands. At a dance afterwards the Princess danced with him and one report had it that she was utterly radiant.[99] Townsend himself commented, in an internal Palace report, that the dance was stuffy, overcrowded and far from enjoyable.[100]

Princess Margaret was bright, beautiful, mercurial and wilful. On her fifth birthday, Kenneth Rose has recorded, she captivated the playwright J. M. Barrie, the creator of Peter Pan, a guest at Glamis. 'Is that really your very own?' he asked of a present by her plate. She replied, 'It is yours and mine,' a delightful response which Barrie put into his next play, *The Boy David*.[101] As the younger child, she was spoiled by her parents – indeed it seems that within the family only Queen Mary was not captivated by her naughty winsomeness.[102] It would not be surprising if she had felt competitive with her elder sister, recognizing that so much more was both given to and required of her. Sharp witted, she always regretted that she had not had a fuller education – she blamed her mother for the fact that she had not even had the tutorials in history that Princess Elizabeth was given.

Nonetheless, after the war she became an attractive asset to the causes she chose to represent, and at home she savoured the role of joker and entertainer. She was, as her mother told D'Arcy Osborne, 'a great delight to us both. She is funny, & makes us laugh (en famille!), and also loves people & seeing & doing things – I do hope that she will be useful.'[103] After her elder sister's marriage to Prince Philip, she became an object of press obsession in respect of her alleged romantic life. The press in those days was mild by comparison with what it became, but its attentions seemed constant and were often unwelcome.

Princess Margaret visited Paris in November 1951 and afterwards Duff Cooper, the British Ambassador, wrote to the Queen to say how much he and his wife Diana had enjoyed entertaining her; 'by her charm, her wit and her beauty she made it a wonderful evening for everybody.' He also congratulated the Queen on the work of Princess Elizabeth. 'There are moments when I feel a little pessimistic about the future. It is a symptom, I suppose, of old age. But when I reflect upon the good fortune of our Empire in the possession of two such wonderful Princesses my heart is filled with pride, confidence and gratitude.'[104] The Queen was thrilled by such praise of her daughters. 'One's love for one's children is one of the real & enduring things of life, and your letter gave me a moment of great pleasure – & I thank you with all my heart.'[105]

Peter Townsend himself wrote later of the Princess:

She was a girl of unusual, intense beauty, confined as it was in her short, slender figure and centred about large purple-blue eyes, generous, sensitive lips and a complexion as smooth as a peach. She was capable, in her face and in her whole being, of an astonishing power of expression. It could change in an instant from saintly, almost melancholic, composure, to hilarious, uncontrollable joy. She was by nature generous, volatile. She was a *comédienne* at heart, playing the piano with ease and verve, singing in her rich, supple voice the latest hits, imitating the famous stars. She was coquettish, sophisticated. But what ultimately made Princess Margaret so attractive and lovable was that behind the dazzling façade, the apparent self-assurance, you could find, if you looked for it, a rare softness and sincerity.[106]

She had many admirers, but it was with Townsend that she fell in love. Her family may not have known, but she became closer and closer to him, all the more so after the death of the King. Indeed, the loss of her father created a chasm in Princess Margaret's life. They had been particularly close; he had always indulged her and she had teased, delighted and flirted with him. Unlike her elder sister, when the King died Princess Margaret had no new role with which to occupy herself. She was utterly bereft.

Her letters at the time show the depth of her grief. To her uncle David Bowes Lyon she wrote of her father: 'He was so tremendously the heart and centre of our family and together with Mummie made us a whole and complete family, united by the deepest love and respect. I think I told you how he always thought of us as one, as opposed to 4 different people.'[107] 'We were such a very happy and close family,' she told Diana Cooper, 'and we are so lucky to have countless lovely memories of my darling Papa.'[108] She resented the fact that he was worked so hard after the war. She felt he had never been allowed to rest between the horrors of war and the strains of the 'Socialist Experiment'.[109]

At the time of the King's death Townsend was already in the midst of his divorce, still an uncommon course of action which often aroused dismay if not contempt. But since his wife had admitted adultery, he was seen as the innocent party in the action and he was such a favourite of the Queen Mother that he was given the task of organizing her new Household, and preparing Clarence House for her and Princess Margaret to live in. This appointment alone suggests how little the Queen Mother may have known of the relationship which developed further during 1952 as each of these unhappy people sought solace in the company of the other.

Some were more clear sighted. Towards the end of the Queen Mother's stay at Balmoral in September 1952, Tommy Lascelles spoke about the matter to Townsend himself. By Lascelles's own account, 'He wished to consult me on some routine matter. When that business was finished I told him it was being commonly, and widely, said that he was seeing too much of Princess Margaret.' The Private Secretary reminded the younger courtier that in their profession there was one cardinal and inviolable rule: 'that in no circumstance ought any member of a royal household to give cause for such talk, particularly if the member of the Royal Family concerned was the Sovereign's sister, and the member of the Household a married man'. According to Lascelles, Townsend left the room without responding.[110]

In November 1952 Townsend obtained his divorce. Just before Christmas he went to see Lascelles again and told him that he and the Princess 'were deeply in love with each other and wished to get married'. This may have been the occasion, which later became public knowledge, on which Lascelles told Townsend, 'You must be either mad or bad.'[111] But Lascelles recorded that he replied only that Townsend must realize that there were 'formidable obstacles' to any such marriage. He asked who else in the family had been informed and Townsend said only the Queen and the Duke of Edinburgh. Lascelles suggested that the Queen Mother must be told and Townsend agreed. In fact, according to Lascelles, she was not informed until February 1953.[112] When the Princess and Townsend did finally tell her, she listened, according to Townsend, 'with characteristic understanding' and 'without a sign that she felt angered or outraged – or that she acquiesced – and the Queen Mother was never anything but considerate in her attitude to me. She never once hurt either of us throughout the whole difficult affair.'[113]

That may be so, but she was very upset. She discussed the matter with the Queen and then she wrote to Lascelles. 'I would like to talk to you, soon please. I have nobody I can talk to about such dreadful things.'[114] 'The Queen Mother wept when I talked to her,' Lascelles told Jock Colville, Churchill's Private Secretary. 'I have never seen her shed tears before.'[115] She said that she was 'quite shattered by the whole thing'. She felt that if the King had been still alive 'it would never have happened'.[116] In one sense that was incorrect, in that the Princess had fallen in love with Townsend well before her father died. But, had the relationship progressed so far while the King was living, he might have understood its dangers and intervened earlier than the Queen Mother had done.

One of the Queen Mother's characteristics within the family was that she never looked for trouble. In fact she had a tendency to ignore difficult situations. She had been brought up to believe that duty defined almost everything. Her shock was genuine – it had probably just not occurred to her that her daughter could be in love with a married (or divorced) courtier. She did not feel herself equipped to deal with such crises. But she felt comforted by the fact that Lascelles could 'understand the human side of such tragedies – for so they are to the young'.[117]

Lascelles may have understood the tragic side of the story, but he was not the most sympathetic interlocutor for the young couple. Understandably enough, he saw it as his duty above all to protect the Queen and her position as head of Church and state in what was still an overwhelmingly Christian country. He does not seem to have explained to Princess Margaret and Townsend themselves their full predicament. As Elizabeth Longford put it in her 1983 biography of the Queen, for which she received considerable assistance from Princess Margaret, 'Lascelles was never to give the anxious lovers that clear-cut if bleak picture of their position, legal and otherwise, which they needed.' The implications of the Royal Marriages Act were not explained to them. 'Today Princess Margaret feels that if they had understood from the start the hopelessness of the situation, Peter would have departed and no major tragedy would have ensued.'[118]

The affair became public as the Queen was crowned. On Coronation day, journalists outside the Abbey noticed the Princess pick a little piece of fluff off Townsend's jacket. For the American reporters this was more than enough evidence of what had been rumoured for months. Nine days later Lascelles wrote to the Queen Mother warning her that the story could break any day in the American press and that the British papers would quickly follow suit.[119]

Lascelles said that his only concern was 'whether The Queen, Head of Church & State, & the high priestess, so to speak, of the ideal of family life – whether she should or should not be advised to allow her sister to marry a divorced man in a registry office'. He argued that he and the Queen's ministers were bound to consider this, 'for it is, after all (and especially since 1936), fundamentally a State matter.'[120]

He sent Queen Elizabeth a summary of the key law in this matter, the Royal Marriages Act of 1772. This had been introduced by King George III, after one of his brothers contracted an unsuitable marriage, in order to prevent his children doing the same. The act made it illegal for any lineal descendant of George II to marry without the sovereign's consent (other than the issue of princesses who married into foreign families). If the sovereign refused consent, a member of the Royal Family might, after reaching the age of twenty-five, marry legally without it, unless both Houses of Parliament expressly disapproved within twelve months of notice being given of the intention to marry.

In such a matter the Queen had to act upon the advice of her ministers, whatever her personal sympathies for her sister. Lascelles was certain that, if the Queen asked her Privy Counsellors to approve the marriage, nine out of ten would refuse to do so, and that the attitude of the Commonwealth would be the same. He was convinced that the only way of avoiding trouble and protecting the Queen was for Townsend to go away for an indefinite period.[121]

On 13 June Lascelles called Churchill's Secretary, Jock Colville, on the scrambler phone and told him he wished to come and see the Prime Minister to talk about the crisis. Churchill was at Chartwell, his beloved country house in Kent. Lascelles drove there and warned the Prime Minister that the American press was about to carry detailed articles about the affair. Churchill's initial reaction was typically romantic. In Colville's account the Prime Minister exclaimed, 'What a delightful match! A lovely young royal lady married to a gallant young airman, safe from the perils and horrors of war!' Colville interrupted to point out that that was not how Lascelles saw the situation and Clementine Churchill broke in to say, 'Winston, if you are going to begin the Abdication all over again, I'm going to leave! I shall take a flat and go and live in Brighton.'[122]

The Prime Minister evidently reflected. Lascelles reported to the Queen Mother that Churchill felt he could not recommend consent being given to the marriage unless Princess Margaret first renounced all her royal rights, including her right of succession to the throne, her title of royal highness, and probably her share of the Civil List. If she did so, he saw no objection to the couple marrying in a registry office.[123] Churchill did, however, insist that the Queen Mother must not take Townsend with her on her forthcoming trip to Southern Rhodesia and that he must be found another job elsewhere for at least a year.[124] Two years later, commenting on a private account of the affair written by Lascelles, Jock Colville was anxious to set the record straight: Churchill, he said, 'was in reality opposed to any attempt to prevent their marrying'. So long as Princess Margaret renounced her rights to the throne, he would even have argued strongly for a Parliamentary income for her. But shortly afterwards Churchill suffered a stroke which put paid to further intervention on his part, although, according to Colville, his views remained the same.[125]

The day after this Chartwell meeting, 14 June, the *People* newspaper published an article demanding 'They Must Deny It Now' – the 'scandalous rumours' of the Princess being in love with a divorced man were, 'of course, utterly untrue'. This public exposure forced a choice. Princess Margaret could either renounce Townsend now and for ever – or she could wait two years until she was twenty-five. Then, under the Royal Marriages Act, she could expect to be free to make her own decision. She and Townsend talked with anguish together. They decided not to renounce their love – they would wait out the next two years, after which they would be able to marry, subject to Parliamentary consent.

Two days after the *People* article, Arthur Penn took Townsend out to dinner and advised him to make himself scarce for the time being. Reporting afterwards to the Queen Mother, Penn wrote that Townsend had a charming character but 'it may perhaps lack a strength . . . Poor boy: what a grey picture for him, & poor dear little Princess Margaret whom I have known ever since she was born. I am so sorry for her.'[126]

On 17 June Townsend himself wrote to the Queen Mother to say that he had had a long talk with Lascelles and that they were now on good terms again. He was bitterly disappointed not to be able to go with her and the Princess to Rhodesia but agreed to accept whatever was decided for the best – this turned out to be a post as air attaché at the British Embassy in Brussels. 'I do hope however that Princess Margaret & I may see a little of each other before she goes away, as I want so much to take care of her over this difficult bit.' He understood the problems that the romance had caused and concluded, 'Your Majesty is going through so much for us and I can never thank you enough for your kindness and your help, and for the way you have stood by Princess Margaret. We will never forget how much you are thinking of the Queen too, and will always do everything we can to consider her.'[127]

The ordeal, for suitor, daughter, mother and other members of the Royal Family, was far from over.

★

THE AGE OF empire was ending and, following India's independence in 1947, decolonization was gathering force throughout Africa. All through the 1950s Britain came under increasing pressure, from her own financial limitations, from the United Nations and then from the Organization of African Unity, to hand over her colonial powers to African nationalists. But in 1953 the tide of anti-colonialism still seemed resistible and the British government attempted to find alternatives to full independence. That summer London created a federation out of the former colony of Southern Rhodesia and the protectorates of Northern Rhodesia and Nyasaland. Its status was complicated – it was a federal realm of the British Crown, not a colony; it was eventually intended to become a dominion within the British-led Commonwealth of Nations.*

On 30 June 1953 the Queen Mother, accompanied by Princess Margaret, set off for the new Federation. She had been invited to Rhodesia, which she had much liked on the Royal Family's 1947 tour of southern Africa, some months after the death of the King. She acknowledged in a letter to Lord Salisbury, 'I must admit I had to screw myself up a good deal to finally say that I would go'; but because she admired the legacy of Cecil Rhodes, and because she hoped to contribute to the success of the Federation, she had now agreed to undertake the tour.[128] This was to be the first of many official overseas visits that Queen Elizabeth carried out as a widow.†

---

* The Federation collapsed on 31 December 1963 because black African nationalists continued to demand greater power than the dominant white populations were prepared to concede. Northern Rhodesia achieved independence as the new nation of Zambia, Nyasaland became Malawi, and Southern Rhodesia (by an illegal and unilateral declaration of independence in 1965) became Rhodesia, but still under white rule. When Rhodesia won full independence in 1981 the new government changed its name to Zimbabwe.

† Her trips abroad in the next twenty years included: 1954, the United States and Canada; 1956, France; 1957, the Federation of Rhodesia and Nyasaland; 1958, Canada, Honolulu, Fiji, Australia and New Zealand, Mauritius, Uganda, Malta; 1959, Kenya and Uganda, Italy and France; 1960, the Federation of Rhodesia and Nyasaland; 1961, Tunisia; 1962, Canada; 1963, France; 1964, the Caribbean; 1965, Jamaica, France, Canada and Germany; 1966, Canada, Honolulu, Fiji, Australia and New Zealand; 1967, Canada. She made some twenty-four more

The revolution of jet travel was about to shrink the world as never before and her first trip was made in the new British passenger jet, the Comet, in which she had enjoyed her trial flight in May 1952.

For the Queen Mother, Rhodesia was absorbing and enjoyable; for Princess Margaret, inevitably, it was less of a pleasure. They journeyed through much of the country on the same White Train that they had taken in 1947; the stewards were all South African and one of them had been with them then. At their first dinner on board, they were served no fewer than eight courses – 'I sent for the menus & pruned,' Queen Elizabeth wrote home. Princess Margaret was made ill by the chilly air-conditioning, which added to her misery.[129] It was not surprising that she was reported by the press to be unsmiling and sullen on the trip. It was indeed very hard for her to endure the public scrutiny on top of her personal sense of loss.

In Bulawayo on 3 July the Queen Mother opened the Central African Cecil Rhodes Centenary Exhibition in front of a crowd of about 20,000, and two days later she and the Princess went to pay their respects at Rhodes's grave in the Matopo Hills. It was intended to be a private visit, but a great crowd of people assembled around them at the service which was held there. According to the Governor, special care was taken to include in the programme 'a considerable number of events for the Africans, in every town and district which was visited'.[130] A crowd of 5,000 schoolchildren gathered in Gwelo on 7 July to see the Queen Mother open the Queen Elizabeth Memorial Gates at Chaplin School. After more engagements the train continued on its way, often stopping for her to greet local people. It brought back more memories of 1947: as she wrote to the Queen that evening, 'it seems a very short time since we were all alighting at the same places, & being urged back into the train by Papa!' She was impressed with the progress since then. 'I am sure that this country has a great future, tho' it will have to go through the teething troubles of Federation!'[131]

After more visits in the Umtali area, she and Princess Margaret had two welcome nights off the train, but since the Princess still felt wretched she flew back to Salisbury, while Queen Elizabeth continued the trip on her own. She met the boys of Eagle School and the residents of Melsetter district and Cashel; at Nyanyadzi she drove

official tours abroad, and several semi-private trips involving official engagements, over the years until 1989.

through African irrigation farms, then met the residents at Birchenough Bridge and took tea in the Bikita Native Reserve. She visited the ancient ruins at Great Zimbabwe – according to legend the Queen of Sheba's capital city – and the nearby Morgenster Mission Hospital. Back in Salisbury, she laid the foundation stone of the new University College on 13 July.

The journey was strenuous – her host, Major General Sir John Kennedy, the Governor of Southern Rhodesia, apologized that the programme was so heavy and wished that there could have been more lions and picnics in game reserves. But he thought her trip had done untold good, 'and it has, I believe, given everyone, of all races, a feeling of confidence about the future – which is just what was needed at this moment'.[132]

Queen Elizabeth loved Rhodesia for its sheer physical beauty – 'range after range of blue mysterious hills, fading into far far away. And a great plain stretching away for ever between the mountains. The light is exquisite, the sun bright & hot & the air cool. I love the immensity of Africa, one feels a great rhythm all the time.'[133] She had a maternalistic view of the British Commonwealth and believed that the white settlers were doing good not only for themselves but also for the black African populations. She thought the country had a great future. She also loved the fact that there were 'NO DEATH DUTIES!'[134]

Despite her concern for Princess Margaret, the Queen Mother had recovered much of her *joie de vivre*. Those with her remembered much laughter and high spirits on the trip. Everywhere she went she seemed to enjoy herself, and thousands of people, white and black alike, were happy to see her doing so. The Governor's wife, Lady Kennedy, wrote to thank her for all she had done for the country and 'for so much kindness, for all the heavenly fun & gaiety & for so much laughter'.[135] A guest at a reception in Salisbury at the end of her tour observed that she looked 'as fresh as a daisy' after gruelling days. 'I have never seen a more serene person. One cannot describe her as beautiful and yet she is a beautiful woman.'[136]

From Rhodesia, she and the Princess flew to Uganda and then back towards London. In Khartoum, where the plane refuelled, the two royal ladies were offered warm champagne, which they sipped sitting in garden chairs on the tarmac, after a 'gloriously incoherent deaf conversation' with some Sudanese religious leaders.[137] The Queen and Prince Philip came to London airport to meet them.

Three weeks later, after her fifty-third birthday, Queen Elizabeth travelled as usual to the Highlands. She stayed first at Balmoral with her children and grandchildren; it was 'heaven', she said, 'laughing & talking & being a family' which, she thought, 'is the only thing worth living for'.[138] Then she moved down the road to Birkhall, to which she had invited the Salisburys 'to stay in extreme discomfort' in her 'TINY' house for a week's shooting.[139] But her guests enjoyed it. Lady Salisbury wrote afterwards that Birkhall 'was the "warmest and cosiest" place in Scotland, both inside and out'.[140] Her husband thought the house delightful and to be back on the hill without the King was touching. 'The King had been so much the guiding spirit of the place, one felt he was still there all the time, watching us and blessing us with his presence.'[141]

Not long afterwards, the Queen Mother had new duties to fulfil when the Queen and Prince Philip departed for a five-month tour of the Commonwealth. For the first time in the new reign, she was required to exercise the powers conferred on her by the new Regency Act as Counsellor of State. The other Counsellors were Princess Margaret, the Duke of Gloucester, the Princess Royal and the Earl of Harewood. Over the ensuing months she and Princess Margaret held seven meetings of the Privy Council to carry out the Queen's constitutional duties on her behalf; they also received numerous British ambassadors who kissed hands on appointment to their postings, and newly appointed foreign ambassadors presenting their letters of credence. She held six investitures at Buckingham Palace and one of those whom she knighted was the 'dear', 'priceless', 'angelic' George Robey of her teenage letters to Beryl Poignand. She invested John Christie, the creator of the Glyndebourne opera house in Sussex, as a Companion of Honour. She also gave audiences to ministers and on at least two occasions she received Winston Churchill. 'I had a visit from Winston last week,' she wrote to the Queen in March 1954. 'What a privilege to have lived in his day – He is a truly great man.'[142] Churchill's health was failing but he resigned only in April 1955, making way for Anthony Eden.

Her duties were familial as well as formal – while the Queen and Prince Philip were abroad, the Queen Mother was *in loco parentis* to

Prince Charles and Princess Anne. She took great pleasure in this task. While the children were staying with her at Royal Lodge, she took them to Shaw Farm in Windsor Home Park. Afterwards she sent their mother a mock-dramatic account of their gleeful progress from one lethal farmyard hazard to the next, turning on taps, setting heavy metal objects swinging above their heads, climbing on tottering straw bales and rusty farm machinery bristling with sharp blades, and relishing a 'dear little cat hunt', during which the 'quite nice' corgis and Sealyhams turned into ravening wolves. The final delights were a cart full of manure – and a baby in a pram. 'They cooed and patted its hands and leant lovingly & heavily over it! "Mummy has promised us a baby" I heard Charles saying proudly . . . Having leant over the pigs, & fed the cows etc etc etc, we came home – the children fresh as paint, & me? – well, perhaps well exercised is the word! But they have been so good, and talk about you and Philip a lot.' She told the Queen how she missed her, and said she had not seen much of Princess Margaret. 'This I am very glad of for her sake, as she has been lunching & dining out a good deal.'[143]

That Christmas the Queen Mother presided at Sandringham and reported to the Queen that the children had enjoyed themselves 'galloping down the passage' to see the tree and gasping at it with ' "oh's" & "ah's" & isn't it BEAUTIFUL'. Earlier, at Windsor, she had enjoyed the Servants' Ball where she waltzed with Lord Freyberg, the distinguished former Governor General and Commander-in-Chief of New Zealand who was now Governor of Windsor Castle. It was 'very exciting as it was the dance when balloons descend from the roof, & Lord Freyberg went mad & banged housemaids out of his way, & pushed poor old ladies aside in a mad desire for balloons'.[144] Perhaps this spectacle would have prompted Isaiah Berlin to revise his later assessment of Lord Freyberg as 'boring'.*

Prince Charles, she added, had started lessons with Miss Peebles.† But, characteristically insouciant about formal lessons, his grandmother was determined that he should have fun. She reported that the children were enjoying playing Dumb Crambo in the evenings. 'It is a great success, & they adore acting, tho' the rhyming is slightly vague.

---

*   See note on pp. 638–9.

†   Catherine Peebles, the children's governess from 1953 to 1968, who had previously taught the Gloucester Princes and Prince Michael of Kent.

Something to rhyme with "stop" – "pheasant" said Charles triumphantly – that's the way it was played at first, but now they are getting
much better at rhyming.'[145]

Apart from the children, the letters between mother and daughter
dealt at length with their mutual interest in horses. With a light touch,
the Queen Mother's letters to her daughter at this time also sought to
advise and encourage her in the public role she herself understood so
well. 'We follow your journeys very well by the papers, and some
good newsreels,' she wrote. 'How well one knows the procedure, &
how monotonous it becomes. But one simply can't think of any other
way of letting people see the Sovereign, than getting up on a dais &
driving round town.' She hoped Prince Philip was not tired – 'It makes
just the whole difference in the world doing things together . . . I find
that doing things without Papa nearly kills one – he was so wonderful.'[146] She remembered how tired they had both become during their
own visit to New Zealand and Australia in 1927 – 'and yet, thank
goodness, one is uplifted & carried on by the wonderful loyalty &
affection. And one feels again, how moving & humble-making, that
one can be the vehicle through which this love for country can be
expressed. Don't you feel that?'[147]

The Queen wrote back long letters filled with vivid descriptions of
incidents and encounters on their trip as well as questions and advice
about the horses back home. 'Racing is incredible out here,' she wrote
from New Zealand; 'tremendous enthusiasm everywhere. They all bet
like mad and like their marathons of eight races at a dose!'[148] She was
also able to telephone, and her mother wrote to tell her how much
she liked talking to her, but with the children always 'poised to snatch
the receiver' she often failed to give her all the news.[149]

In early March 1954 the Queen wrote from Melbourne expressing
her excitement that she would see her children three weeks earlier than
originally planned. *Britannia*, the new royal yacht,* was sailing to the
Mediterranean to pick up the Queen and Prince Philip, and the children
would be on board. She was sure that they would have changed a lot
in the past six months; she was also concerned that they might not even
recognize their parents.[150] Her mother reassured her, with a gentle hint
that it was important to try to remember what it was like to be five or

---

* *Britannia* replaced the *Victoria and Albert*, which had been withdrawn from service in 1937
before acting as an accommodation ship in Portsmouth. She was broken up in 1954.

six years old: 'one really felt very deeply about things, and you may find Charles much older in a very endearing way. He is intensely affectionate & loves you & Philip most tenderly – I am sure that he will always be a very loving & enjoyable child to you both.' She had taken Princess Anne to the Royal Chapel near Royal Lodge where the little girl had amused everyone by singing very loudly and tunelessly. 'She is very intelligent, & very sensitive & very funny!'[151]

The reunion finally took place in Tobruk, on board the *Britannia*. 'The children are enchanting and it is so wonderful to be with them again!' the Queen wrote to her mother. When she and Prince Philip came aboard, both children 'gravely offered us their hands . . . partly I suppose because they were somewhat overcome by the fact that we were really there and partly because they have met so many new people recently! However the ice broke very quickly and we have been subjected to a very energetic routine and innumerable questions which have left us gasping!'[152]

*

ON 20 OCTOBER 1954 the Queen Mother began one of the most important journeys of her life. She embarked for New York in the *Queen Elizabeth*, which she had launched in 1938, to begin a three-week tour of the United States and Canada. She had been dreading the trip because she would not be accompanied by any member of the family. But she felt obliged to go because the centrepiece was to be the presentation of funds raised in memory of the King, to be spent on training in the USA of young people from the Commonwealth. In the event the trip was a personal triumph which convinced her that she did have an important part still to play in public life.

The outbound passage was rough, but she had always been a good sailor. In New York she stayed with the British Permanent Representative to the United Nations, Sir Pierson Dixon.* His official residence, outside Manhattan in Riverdale, was comfortable and she marvelled in particular at the abundance of American bathrooms and the endless supplies of 'millions of towels, large medium, small, tiny, face flannels, in great profusion' with which she was provided.[153] She had a busy time seeing much of New York both formally and informally. As she

---

* Sir Pierson Dixon (1904–65), British diplomat. Permanent Representative of the United Kingdom to the United Nations 1954–60, Ambassador to France 1960–4.

had expected, at first she found it hard 'not having any family to laugh with'.[154] Concealing this, she visited the Metropolitan Museum of Art, attended a luncheon given by the Pilgrims, the Anglo-American society, visited the American Bible Society where she was presented with a special edition of the King James Bible, and toured the United Nations headquarters in the company of the then Secretary General, Dag Hammarskjöld. When first shown the detailed programme for the day, which included meeting journalists at the UN, she had commented 'How ghastly.'[155] But she did not let her feelings about the press show at all. Indeed press men and women, a tough crowd, praised her for treating them well.[156]

She was guest of honour at the Charter Dinner of Columbia University, which she had visited with the King in 1939, and she received an honorary degree of Doctor of Laws. A ball was given in her honour by the Associated Commonwealth Societies of New York, and she had a private lunch with Eleanor Roosevelt, at Hyde Park – another echo of the memorable 1939 visit. It was a touching reunion of two women who had each contributed enormously to her country's wartime effort. There was fun to be had as well. She went to see the popular musical *The Pajama Game*, loved the tunes and wished Princess Margaret had been there.[157] She 'adored' the Empire State Building[158] and visited a children's day-care centre and a home for Aged British Men and Women. On 3 November the Mayor of New York gave her a luncheon and that night the English Speaking Union a dinner. It was at this formal occasion that the cheque honouring the King's memory was presented to her.

She found the formal dinners the worst part of the American trip. She hated dining on a dais in full evening dress and tiara, stared at by the world under 'a terrible glare of television & film lights'. Eating in public 'really is a nightmare, & they give one gigantic bits of meat, bigger than this sheet of paper, practically raw, & then instead of gravy, they pour a little blood over it. Oh boy.'[159] At the English Speaking Union dinner her lady in waiting observed that she only toyed with her food, and when she returned to the Dixons' house, she had a plate of scrambled eggs on a tray, enjoying the informal picnic infinitely more.[160]

A shopping expedition made to various New York department stores on the afternoon of Friday 29 October was intended to be private but everywhere she went she was pursued by packs of relentless British journalists and crowds of excited American women. In Saks Fifth Avenue, she, her lady in waiting Jean Rankin, the manager and three Secret Service men 'made a sharp & cunning dash into the lift, which we stopped between floors, & held a council of war'. They decided to sneak up to the top floor but, as they stepped out there, 'a gate opened opposite us, & a <u>horde</u> of ladies poured out, shouting in triumph. We flew for shelter to "Ladies shirts", & inside a sort of gazebo of police we tried to do a little shopping.' This proved impossible, so they 'decided to make a dash for the ground floor . . . It was all so like a Marx brothers film.'[161]

President Eisenhower, who had been elected to the White House in 1952, sent his private plane to bring her to Washington where she had another full week of formal appearances, visits and meals, including visits to the White House, the National Gallery of Art and tours in Virginia and Maryland, both of which she found 'delightful'.[162] She found life in the Eisenhower White House stiffer than it had been with the Roosevelts, and surrounded with more protocol. But, according to the British Ambassador, Sir Roger Makins, the Eisenhowers took evident pleasure in entertaining her as an old friend.[163] The Makinses were informal too and at least once they all had a midnight supper on the stairs of the Ambassador's residence.[164] Despite such informality, security was much tighter than in 1939. Her Secret Service people were just like nannies who, she told the Queen, 'look after one, & look also faintly disapproving or rather loving. I'd like to have one or two to bring home.'[165]

In Virginia she delighted in the kindness and the southern drawls – 'Miiiighty kind, mam, they say, taking longer than you can believe to say "mighty".'[166] Altogether, she was delighted with her trip. She found Americans charming, courteous and reassuringly old fashioned. She was also moved by the fact that many people recalled her 1939 visit with the King, and although they did not quite understand how the monarchy worked, 'they are prepared to look kindly on the <u>family</u>.'[167]

From Washington, she flew to Ottawa on Friday 12 November. The Canadian part of her trip was briefer and more demure than that to the States, but it was happy nonetheless – 'she was on home soil', reported the High Commissioner.[168] Her time was spent mostly in Ottawa and, among her engagements, she opened the Bytown bridges. She drove through the city, visited City Hall and went to a performance of *Whiteoaks* at the Canadian Repertory Theatre, held in aid of the Canadian Mothercraft Society of which she was patron. (She was aware that such voluntary organizations needed visible royal support if they were to survive at a time when most medical care was being publicly funded.) The visit rekindled affection for Canada, the Commonwealth country to which she returned most often in the remaining years of her life.

On the afternoon of 17 November the Queen Mother flew back to New York to embark in the *Queen Mary*. She gave a private dinner party on board that night and the next morning, after a leave-taking ceremony in the Verandah Grill, the ship set sail. The voyage home was much calmer than that on the way out.

Those who had witnessed the trip were in no doubt about its success. Senior British officials abroad would not be expected to criticize members of the Royal Family. But the enthusiasm of their reports on the way Queen Elizabeth carried out her duties was clearly not feigned. From Ottawa, the High Commissioner reported home that the Queen Mother had done an immense amount to strengthen ties between Britain and Canada.[169] Similarly from Washington Roger Makins enthused that she had been 'flawless'. The informal moments – the visit to the theatre, sightseeing, the shopping expedition, her readiness to stop and talk to people – had endeared her to the American public. Her warmth was 'so foreign to the copybook idea of Royalty in the American mind' that she had captivated everybody.[170] Makins offered a proper cost–benefit analysis: 'One of our most valuable assets in the world to-day is the fund of American goodwill toward Great Britain . . . I can think of no single action, calculated or uncalculated, which could have made a more substantial contribution to that fund of goodwill than the visit of Her Majesty Queen Elizabeth The Queen Mother.'[171]

Edward L. Bernays, one of the founders of public relations in America, came to a similar conclusion, writing to *The Times* and the *New York Times* that Americans had expected the Queen Mother, like other British people, to be 'stuffy, snobbish, snooty and unapproachable'. But in her they discovered to their delight 'warmth, sincerity, frankness, democratic bearing and interest in American institutions and a vigor that no one had imagined a Queen could have . . . The Queen Mother showed Americans that there is every reason to admit that they like the English.'[172]

Probably her most cherished response came in a private letter from

Winston Churchill in which he praised the success of her visit: 'The maintenance, and continuous improvement, of friendship between the English-speaking peoples, and more especially between these Islands and the great North American Democracies, is the safeguard of the future. Your Majesty has made a notable contribution to this end, and I think it is fitting that the Ministers of the Crown should be among the first to recognise it.'[173]

She had enjoyed the trip much more than she had expected. And she realized, perhaps for the first time, what a strong impact she could have as an ambassador for Britain. Her success stimulated her; now she could see that she could play a useful part in promoting both the monarchy and Britain herself in overseas visits. In the years to come foreign travel – to France, to Africa, to Australasia and to Canada again – would be a very important part of her work.

*

IN AUTUMN 1955 Princess Margaret had to face the second crisis in her relationship with Peter Townsend. On 21 August she turned twenty-five and so, under the Royal Marriages Act, she was free to marry without the permission of the sovereign.

The last two years had not been entirely bleak. The Princess was vivacious and, if moody, also witty and often charming. She did not want for admirers. One of them, Billy Wallace,* confessed to Queen Elizabeth that for seven years he had been 'a devoted, if unsatisfactory, admirer' of the Princess.[174] Others courted the young Princess too and she was seen around town, always chic and sometimes carrying an elegant cigarette holder, with such men as Colin Tennant, son of Lord Glenconner who had been one of Elizabeth Bowes Lyon's admirers, Dominic Elliot[†] and Mark Bonham Carter.

At the beginning of 1955 Princess Margaret had made a successful tour of the Caribbean. She liked the rhythms of life there and her

---

*   William Euan Wallace (1927–77), son of Captain Euan Wallace MP, Conservative politician, and his wife Barbara, daughter of the architect Sir Edwin Lutyens. A debonair man about town, he remained a good friend of Princess Margaret. He married Elizabeth Hoyer Millar in 1965.

†   Hon. Dominic Elliot (b. 1931), son of fifth Earl of Minto. He too was a good friend of the Princess for many years. He married Countess Marianne Esterházy in 1962.

enjoyment showed; a Nassau paper commented that she resembled her mother in her warmth, humanity, simplicity and interest in people.[175] But, as the end of her two-year waiting period neared, it became clear that she and Townsend would not be left in peace to make their decision. Press speculation increased, with some papers being supportive, others merely aggressively engaged. 'Come on Margaret! Please make up your mind,' shrilled the *Daily Mirror* just before her birthday, which she spent quietly at Balmoral.

It was painful for her, for her mother and for the rest of the Royal Family. The Queen Mother did not find it easy to discuss intimate matters of the heart. Sometimes, as in many such emotional crises, letters were easier. In early September, she wrote warmly to her daughter about her dilemma:

> My darling Margaret, I sometimes wonder whether you quite realise how much I hate having to point out the more difficult and occasionally horrid problems.
>
> It would be so much easier to gloss them over, but I feel such a deep sense of responsibility as your only living parent, and I seem to be the only person who <u>can</u> point them out, and you can imagine what anguish it causes me.
>
> I suppose that every mother wants her child to be happy, and I know what a miserable and worrying time you are having, torn by so many difficult constitutional and moral problems.
>
> I think about it and you all the time, and because I have to talk over the horrid things does not mean that I don't suffer <u>with</u> you, or that one's love is any less. I have wanted to write this for a long time, as it is something which might sound embarrassing if said.
>
> Your very loving Mummy[176]

Princess Margaret replied at once: 'Darling Mummie, Your letter did help so much. Thank you for writing it – as you said it's easier to write than say – but please don't think that because I have blown up at intervals when we've discussed the situation, that I <u>didn't</u> know how you felt. I knew only too well that you were feeling for one tremendously.' She went on to say that there were very few people to whom she could talk about her feelings, and that it was very difficult to make such decisions alone. 'Oh dear, I meant to tell you how much your letter meant, & I've only poured out a lot of complaints. But it did, and you will now know that I know what you are feeling when we next talk.'[177]

She told her mother that Peter Townsend was coming over from Brussels in mid-October for them to meet and talk. Before he arrived, Queen Elizabeth talked to her daughter on the telephone from the Castle of Mey – she felt she had to be guarded 'because one feels that so many people are listening most eagerly'. But, she then wrote, 'I did want to say, darling, that I know what a great decision you have to make fairly soon, & to beg you to look at it from every angle, and to be quite sure that you don't marry somebody because you are sorry for them. Marriage is such a momentous step and so intimate, and it is far, far better to be a little cruel & say "No" to marriage unless you are quite quite sure.' She thought that some people made wonderful friends and confidants but less successful husbands. 'Poor Peter has had a ghastly time, but I am sure that he would agree that a marriage could not be truly happy unless both were prepared to face the extraordinary difficulties with clear consciences. Oh I do feel for you darling – it is so hard that you should have to go through so much agony of mind.'[178]

For Princess Margaret, the way had seemed plain. She believed that now she had turned twenty-five, should she still wish to marry Peter Townsend, the government, and by extension Parliament, would allow her marriage to go ahead without further ado, as the Royal Marriages Act permitted. It was not so simple.

Anthony Eden, Winston Churchill's successor as prime minister, was himself divorced, but he could not or would not do battle on behalf of the Princess. After taking soundings among his Cabinet colleagues he indicated that, if asked for advice, the government could not recommend that the marriage should go ahead. And if the Princess decided to marry nonetheless, it was clear that Parliament, which under the Royal Marriages Act would have to give its permission, would not allow the third in line to the throne to enter into a marriage which the Church would not recognize. She would have to renounce her royal status.[179]

On 26 October, *The Times* published a fierce editorial in which it declared that, if she chose Townsend, she would have to abandon her royal status and she would be letting down the Queen, the symbol of people's 'better selves'.[180]

The external pressures upon Princess Margaret were immense. So were the internal conflicts. She was in love but her mother had always instructed her children, as Lady Strathmore had instructed hers, that duty came first. A convinced Christian, the Princess was of her time and she believed in the sanctity of marriage. She was also intensely loyal to her sister and to the institution in which she had grown up. She was well aware of the agony of her mother and father, and the consternation in the country, when King Edward VIII had insisted on marrying a divorced woman.

In this crisis, it is clear from the evidence, her mother and her sister both hoped above all for the Princess's happiness; they were both careful not to push her either way. But all three of them understood how hard it would be for her if she had to renounce the whole basis of her life and change her close relationships within the Royal Family. She made up her mind.

According to the Princess herself, when she and Townsend met shortly afterwards at Clarence House, they both decided at the same moment that 'It's not possible. It won't do.' The Princess went to inform the Archbishop of Canterbury, Dr Geoffrey Fisher, of her decision and he responded at once, 'What a wonderful person the Holy Spirit is.'[181]

The Princess and Townsend then worked together on a statement for her to release to the press. This went through several drafts and the final version began, 'I would like it to be known that I have decided not to marry Group Captain Peter Townsend.' She had been aware that, subject to her renouncing her rights of succession, she could have contracted a civil marriage, 'But, mindful of the Church's teaching that Christian marriage is indissoluble, and conscious of my duty to the Commonwealth, I have resolved to put these considerations before any others.' The statement, on which the Queen Mother also gave her advice, went on to say, 'I have reached this decision entirely alone, and in doing so I have been strengthened by the unfailing support and devotion of Group Captain Townsend.'[182] The statement was issued on 31 October 1955. The *Daily Mirror* headline was 'DUTY BEFORE LOVE'.

The Princess received thousands of sympathetic letters and Jean Rankin helped her to reply to them. One was from her former teacher, Toni de Bellaigue, to whom the Princess was devoted. Jean Rankin wrote to her, 'She is absolutely wonderful about it all. Fortunately

they both decided at the same time that they could not marry & so
there was not the agony of one changing. Since they reached this
decision some days before it was announced – they have both become
progressively more sure.' She said that the Princess, having been
through agonies, was 'amazingly calm now' but she expected there
would be a reaction at some time. 'It seemed too much for any person
to bear – this hideous publicity – and criticism. Our newspapers are
really abominable . . . Queen Elizabeth looks very tired. The strain of
these last weeks is telling.'[183]

Three weeks later Princess Margaret herself wrote to Toni de
Bellaigue. 'I must tell you quickly that Peter and I are calm & rather
peacefully happy' – because they had both decided 'at exactly the same
second that we couldn't get married. That was it – we did it together,
so you see instead of feeling it a tremendous wrench, we were in fact
joined even more strongly together by the fact that our love had been
strong enough to enable us to take the more difficult course, and there
we were, & our love had triumphed, in a way neither of us had ever
dreamt could give us any satisfaction or happiness. But it has.' Her
faith, she said, had helped both of them: 'we always dared to believe it
was God's love we were given a little of to love with, only we thought
he meant us to marry – until we found out it was not so. Then, all
our love, and what we had tried to do by it might have seemed in
vain. But by the strength we were given to make this decision and the
feeling of renewal we felt after it, we think humbly, that perhaps this
is what He ordained.'[184]

Queen Elizabeth had escaped for a night to the peace and calm of
St Paul's Walden with her brother David.[185] She also spent a weekend
with the Salisburys in Dorset in mid-November (if she knew of
Bobbety's hostility to Princess Margaret's abandoned plans, she no
doubt respected his views), and wrote to them afterwards saying, 'you
give me fresh courage when I see you. I felt so dreadfully shattered in
mind & body after that agonising experience over darling Margaret.'[186]
She wrote a kind letter to Peter Townsend, for which he thanked her,
and he assured her that he would give Princess Margaret every help in
remaking her life. 'I know that she now feels a great peace of mind in
having reached the right decision, and so do I . . . I hope Your Majesty
will be able to realise how conscious I have felt of your understanding
throughout a time which has given you so much anxiety.'[187]

The problem now for Princess Margaret, as her mother, her sister and other members of the family understood, was to find ways for her to occupy her time. She enjoyed an income of £5,000 a year from the Civil List, in return for which she carried out the public duties of a junior member of the Royal Family; she was colonel-in-chief of several regiments and patron of a number of charities, including the Royal Ballet, which became one of her most important and enduring interests.

After the Princess's final separation from Townsend, she was undoubtedly bereft and did not find it easy to confide her feelings to other members of her family. In the autumn of 1956 she undertook a trip to the Indian Ocean in *Britannia* to visit Mauritius, Zanzibar, Tanganyika and Kenya. She still had moments of misery, but was, she said, cheered by her mother's telephone calls and 'glorious' letters which made her laugh out loud. Yet she still hankered after Townsend and periodically felt depressed, as she told her mother in a letter written towards the end of her trip.[188]

After her return, she and her mother continued living together at Clarence House. This was not an ideal arrangement for either of them; Princess Margaret considered having a house of her own but rejected it, she said, on grounds of both loneliness and expense. 'It may come, but of course I might marry someone.'[189]

CHAPTER EIGHTEEN

FAVOURITES

1956–1960

'That's racing'

THE GRAND NATIONAL has long been one of Britain's greatest horse-races, and certainly its most dramatic. While the Derby, run every summer at Epsom, is the most important flat race of the year, the National, which takes place at the end of every winter, at Aintree, near Liverpool, is the most eagerly awaited over jumps. It is a punishing and unpredictable steeplechase, and many of its obstacles – Becher's Brook, the Chair, the Canal Turn – have become household names. The race is often run over ground made heavy by winter rains; horses frequently fall and there are sometimes fatalities. There is something gladiatorial about the challenge of the race – and the watching of it.

In 1956 the race had a relatively small field of twenty-nine runners.[1] Among them was a strongly built ten-year-old Irish-bred horse named Devon Loch who had a distinguishing white star on his forehead. He was trained by Peter Cazalet, one of the top trainers in the country. His jockey was Dick Francis, a superb rider.* His owner was the Queen Mother. And on 24 March she came with the Queen and Princess Margaret to watch him run. He started at odds of 100/7 and there were high hopes that he would win.

By the Canal Turn on the second circuit of the course, Francis was lying second and felt sure he could now carry the day. He eased off. 'Never before in the National had I held back a horse and said, "Steady boy". Never had I felt such power in reserve, such confidence in my

---

* Dick Francis CBE (b. 1920), one of the most successful National Hunt jockeys of his time. He won over 350 races, and raced in Queen Elizabeth's colours 1953–6. In 1957 he had to retire from the track after a serious fall and subsequently became an equally successful author of racing thrillers.

mount, such calm in my mind.'[2] After the last fence Francis just let the horse go and Devon Loch rushed towards the finishing post, leaving the next horse, ESB, ten lengths behind.[3] The roar of the crowds in the stands, happy that the Queen Mother was within yards of victory, was stupendous. On top of the stand the royal party was beside itself with excitement, joining in the cheers, gripped by the tension and the thrill of imminent victory. Then, disaster. Suddenly Devon Loch pricked back his ears; his back legs stiffened and splayed – and he 'pancaked' on to the ground. Horrified, Francis tried to gather him up and urge him along the last few yards to the post, but Devon Loch could hardly move and ESB passed him to win.

It was a terrible moment for jockey, trainer and owner. Like her daughters and almost everyone else at Aintree, the Queen Mother was appalled. But she knew how to deal with disappointment. 'I must go down and comfort those poor people,' she said.[4] 'Please don't be upset,' she said to Francis. 'That's racing.'[5]* She never liked to speak of the incident again.

*

THE PASSION for steeplechasing came relatively late to Queen Elizabeth. But it became a vital part of her life, particularly after the death of the King. The Royal Family has had an interest in horses and in racing since the days of Queen Elizabeth I. But they had almost always concentrated on flat racing. In 1949 the King had been well enough for the family to attend Royal Ascot and, to everyone's delight, his filly Avila won the Coronation Stakes. At a dinner at Windsor Castle that week the Queen sat next to Anthony Mildmay, a glamorous and celebrated figure in British steeplechasing since his reins broke when he was leading, only two fences from home, in the Grand National of 1936. After the war he went into partnership with his old schoolfriend Peter Cazalet to turn Cazalet's estate, Fairlawne in Kent, into one of the best racing stables in the country. They did well. Mildmay's special love was for steeplechasing, which had always been the poor relation

---

* Devon Loch recovered and later in 1956 he came second in the King George VI Chase at Kempton Park to Rose Park, another Cazalet-trained horse. He was then injured and retired. The Queen Mother gave him to Noël Murless, one of the Queen's trainers, and his daughter Julie rode him constantly until he had to be put down, aged seventeen, in 1963. (Sean Smith, *Royal Racing*, p. 60)

of flat racing; as a result it was less dominated by business interests than the flat and attracted a more louche and amusing crowd. Mildmay judged correctly that the Queen would enjoy its devil-may-care spirit. Before the evening was out he had persuaded her and Princess Elizabeth to buy a steeplechaser together.

Mildmay and Cazalet acquired a horse called Monaveen for the two royal ladies. Cazalet saw that the eight-year-old bay gelding was brave and strong and decided he would be ideal. Most important, he thought he would be a winner. Fairlawne's records describe Monaveen as a 'bold jumper and a courageous horse when in front or disputing the lead'. Such winning qualities are attractive to any owner; to the Queen and the Princess, desperately concerned as they were about the health of the King, and worried by the austerity and hardships of post-war Britain, it would be a hugely welcome diversion. Cazalet had chosen well. In his first outing under Princess Elizabeth's colours, at Fontwell Park, a charming small racecourse in Sussex, Monaveen romped home. Queen and Princess were both overjoyed, but there was a sad event that summer – Anthony Mildmay disappeared while swimming off the Devon coast. His death was a great loss, not just to the racing community.

Through the rest of 1950 Monaveen won several more races, including most importantly, the Queen Elizabeth Chase at Hurst Park. Within three months his prize money was almost three times what he had cost his owners and they both enjoyed following his outings. At the end of the year the Queen went to watch him run again at Hurst Park. She saw him off with high hopes, but in the middle of his race he fell and broke a leg. He was immediately put down. The Queen was devastated – she longed to weep but, being in public, she could not; she felt her voice cracking as she tried to control her emotion. A few days later she wrote about her sadness to Princess Elizabeth, who was with her husband in Malta. 'Somehow, Monaveen was all mixed up with a "first venture", & Anthony, & all the fun & excitement of last year, & sharing with you, and it seemed so sad that such a gallant & great hearted horse should have to be put to rest.'[6] The Princess was equally horrified.

By now mother and daughter had decided not to own another horse together. The Princess knew that at some stage she would have to assume responsibility for the Royal Stud, and she decided to concentrate on flat racing and to expand her interest in breeding. The

Queen wanted to stay with steeplechasing and, according to Princess Margaret, she was so enthusiastic about the sport that she 'wouldn't share with anybody now'.[7]

Before Monaveen's death she had bought Manicou, and this strong and handsome horse also did her proud, winning several races within months. He was a dark bay; on his forehead he boasted a bright white star and he had two splendid white socks. Not surprisingly, she loved him. On Boxing Day 1950 the Queen decided at the last minute that she could not bear to miss seeing him run that day at Kempton Park at Sunbury on Thames, and so she ordered up her car and rushed off from Sandringham over icy winter roads.

The field was strong and she did not expect Manicou to win. But to her delight he did.[8] At home, the rest of her family was enthralled – Princess Margaret recounted, 'We all nearly died with our ears glued to the wireless!'[9] On the way back in the dark the Queen's driver had to deal with thick fog as well as icy roads; they crept along with the back wheels swinging wildly. It was 8 p.m. before she got home to Sandringham. 'But it was the greatest fun – & I loved every moment of it.'[10]

The roller-coaster continued. Manicou ran poorly at Kempton Park in March 1951 and her hopes were dashed when he was beaten at Cheltenham by Silver Flame. He never won another race, and then became incurably lame, a misfortune that befell several of her horses. But she remained very fond of him and at stud he sired many horses, including The Rip, who later came to be one of her favourites.[11]

Formal mourning after the death of the King, quite apart from her own profound grief, kept Queen Elizabeth away from the racing scene in 1952; there are few letters between her and her daughter about their mutual interest until after the Coronation in June 1953. (The Queen's horse, Aureole, was running in the Derby at Epsom immediately after the Coronation; to the disappointment of the owner and many others he was beaten into second place.) In December that year Dick Francis rode the Queen Mother's horse M'as-tu-vu at Lingfield. He rode a good race and thought he was well ahead in the final straight. 'But suddenly I heard a terrific lot of noise and shouting from the sidelines, which is a thing jockeys don't hear normally, and I thought: "My God, I'm being tackled." I didn't dare look round, I just sat down and rode hard for the winning post. When I'd passed it I stood up in my irons and looked round and the opposition was lengths and lengths back. It was in the early days of royal winners and the noise was just the crowd giving us a great reception.'[12]

When the Queen and Prince Philip set off on their long Common-wealth tour at the end of 1953, she and her mother resumed writing their equine epistles. In January 1954 the Queen Mother recounted a visit she and Princess Margaret had made to the Newmarket stables of Cecil Boyd-Rochfort, who had been the King's trainer since 1942. She described the condition of each of their horses and ended by reverting to one of her favourites: 'Dear Manicou looks such a picture . . . He has got something special, hasn't he darling?'[13]

Over the next five decades, mother and daughter derived enor-mous pleasure from their shared passion for racing. Indeed the successes and failures of jockeys, trainers and mounts and the going at different racecourses featured large in many of their letters to each other. Wherever they were, they exchanged the news and the gossip of the turf. As always with racing there were more disappointments than triumphs, but it was all utterly absorbing. Racing was all the more enjoyable because, unlike the routines of royal life, it was so gamey, so full of bounders, such fun, so unpredictable, so exciting. Yet at the same time, the racetrack remained reassuringly constant.

*

HER ENTHUSIASMS defined the Queen Mother. When Major Tom Harvey retired as her Private Secretary in 1951, he gave her a crystal engagement-card holder designed by Laurence Whistler and engraved with verses which summed up well her different private and public enthusiasms:

> PLEASURES – A myriad to rehearse! . . .
> The likely horse . . . The lucky 'hand' . . .
> The leaping trout . . . The living verse . . .
> The favourite waltz . . . The floodlit dome . . .
> The crowds, the lights, the welcome . . .
> – and (sweet as them all) the going home!
>
> DUTIES! . . . The emblazoned document . . .
> The microphone, while nations listen . . .
> The moments when the ranks present . . .
> This tape to cut . . . That stone to lay . . .
> Another Veuve Clicquot to christen
> The great bows that slide away![14]

Harvey remained a friend of Queen Elizabeth until he died. In reorganizing her life after the death of the King, Queen Elizabeth depended on family, friends and courtiers like him. Her most constant support and protector throughout these difficult years remained Arthur Penn, her friend since childhood and her Treasurer since 1946.

Penn was humorous and cultivated; an ardent monarchist, he was devoted to Queen Elizabeth. She relied not only upon his benevolent supervision of her Household, but on his good taste, scouring sale rooms and antique shops on her behalf to find mirrors, tables or pictures at reasonable prices with which to complete the furnishing of her homes. He did his best to impose some order on her finances, both public and private, and to discourage her from unlimited expansion of her overdraft at Coutts, a private bank whose management was understanding of royal debt.

Such indulgence was helpful. Queen Elizabeth did not spend conspicuously on her homes, but bouts of cautious parsimony alternated with a certain insouciance. Arthur Penn began one of his letters to her: 'This is a boring letter, being about money, and if there is an odious subject that is it'[15] – which matched her attitude perfectly. She found it difficult to control her outgoings, and her horses and the Castle of Mey, for which she paid out of her private funds, were a heavy burden.[16] 'She certainly had a hazy idea of costs,' wrote one of her ladies in waiting later, 'but greedy she was not and her extravagances as measured by those of modern celebrities could be reckoned almost modest.'[17]

She was aware that royal expenses were under more and more Parliamentary scrutiny and at Sandringham over Christmas and New Year 1953–4, when the Queen and Prince Philip were on their Commonwealth tour, she made a point of telling the Queen that she had tried to keep costs down by having as few staff as possible.[18] Nonetheless she felt then (and always) that she had to maintain 'a certain standard, such as large motor cars & special trains, and all the things that are expected of the mother of the sovereign'.[19]

The letters between Queen Elizabeth and Arthur Penn are a poignant testimony to the affection between a queen and her friend and servant. By 1956, however, Penn was seventy and he told her he thought he should now bow out. Hating to lose someone so vital to her, she begged him to 'continue the drudgery of battling with my horrid finances' for some time yet. But, she added, when he really did find the job too burdensome he must tell her, so he could resign as her Treasurer '& become Keeper of my Conscience & prod it when I am preparing to buy two Chippendale mirrors, instead of paying off the overdraft at Coutts'.[20] On another occasion she sent him a teasing note saying, 'I have lost all your money at Ascot – I do hope you don't mind.'[21]

He stayed. But he felt weaker still and, two years later, he wrote another letter of charm and courtesy, reminding her that when he had last suggested retirement 'you most generously asked me to tarry'. He was almost seventy-three and 'my best service to you now is to slip unobtrusively away'.[22] Still she would not have it. She told him she was 'deeply distressed' by his letter. 'You do more for me than anyone else, so there.' She repeated that she could never have continued her public work after the death of the King without his help, pointing out that 'trying to start a completely new life by oneself is quite the most difficult and horrible thing that one could imagine, and I am deeply, deeply grateful for all you did then, & after'.[23]

Penn's burden was lightened after Martin Gilliat became her Private Secretary in 1955. Like Penn and many others whom the Queen Mother favoured, Gilliat was a military man who had been schooled at Eton. During the war he was mentioned in dispatches before being captured at Dunkirk; after escaping from two other German prisoner-of-war camps, he was imprisoned at Colditz, whence he attempted constantly to escape. After the war he had served with Lord Mountbatten in India and most recently he had been military secretary to Field Marshal Slim as governor general of Australia.[24]

A tall, convivial and clubbable man who dabbled in financing theatre productions, he was an excellent planner and quickly mastered the range of the Queen Mother's interests, concerns, duties and friendships. He shared her enthusiasm for the turf and played a large part in her racing life. She became both dependent on and fond of him. But it was characteristic of the informal way in which she oversaw Clarence House that he came to her on trial and thirty years later, according to Kenneth Rose, he joked that he was still waiting to hear if his appointment would be made permanent.[25]

*

ONE OF Martin Gilliat's first duties for the Queen Mother was to accompany her on a visit to Paris in March 1956. She had been invited to open the Franco-Scottish exhibition at the French National Archives in the Hôtel de Rohan. She flew to Le Bourget on 13 March. Sir Gladwyn Jebb, the British Ambassador, had not doubted that happy memories of her last visit, in 1938 with the King, would ensure the success of this one. But he was astonished at the warmth of her reception. 'Although the visit was completely unofficial and had not received any very great advanced publicity in the press,' he reported, 'the streets from Le Bourget to the Embassy were completely lined, in places 10 or 20 deep.'[26]

Queen Elizabeth opened the exhibition that afternoon with an expertly delivered speech in French and, after dinner at the British Embassy, returned to the Hôtel de Rohan for a French government reception. Next day she lunched with the President, René Coty, at the Elysée Palace, and then drove out to Versailles. There she was entertained to tea by all the Commonwealth ambassadors at the Grand Trianon, which had been placed at their disposal by the French government 'as an exceptional mark of friendship to Her Majesty'.[27] In the evening the Jebbs held a reception for her at the Embassy at which, according to a report reaching Lady Salisbury, she was 'dazzling'.[28]

There were more memories of the past. Queen Elizabeth's first French governess, Madame Guérin, came to see her with her daughter Georgina, who had taught the Princesses before the war. This episode gave rise to critical comment by Lady Jebb about her royal guest: she noted in her diary that Queen Elizabeth delighted in mimicry, and mimicked the governess. 'I find her a puzzling person,' she wrote. 'So sweet, so smiling, so soft, so charming, so winning, so easy and pleasant. And yet there is another side, which sometimes reveals itself, rather mocking, not very kind, not very loyal, almost unwise.'[29] Nonetheless, the Ambassadress wrote to Queen Elizabeth afterwards complimenting her on the pleasure her visit had given. 'The people of Paris, and indeed of France, have always held the late King and Your Majesty in a very special place in their hearts, and they were truly glad to welcome you again.' She thought that the visit had helped convince the French that they still had British support.[30]

Sir Gladwyn Jebb went even further, writing to the Foreign Secretary: 'There is no doubt at all to my mind that this kind of visit has a very profound and salutary political effect. Just when the French were feeling low about things in general, and more particularly about Algeria ... it was heartening for them to have physical proof of sympathy from their closest ally in the person of so charming and intelligent a member of the Royal Family.'[31]

Despite public successes, however, private loneliness was always with her. To recapture the sense of family life, her regular visits to Windsor for Easter and Sandringham for Christmas were vital. After her return to England and the disappointment of Devon Loch at the Grand National, Queen Elizabeth was grateful for her week at Windsor. Writing to the Queen afterwards she thanked her daughter for 'so much sweetness & thought and care for your venerable parent'. Above all, she treasured the companionship of family. 'You can't imagine how deadly everything is when one is alone – When one is young one feels that life goes on for ever, & I was utterly happy with Papa & you & Margaret.' She hoped that the Queen would have more children. 'I longed for more children, but somehow everything seemed against us.'[32]

The family spent Christmas together at Sandringham. Through February and March 1957 the Queen Mother undertook official engagements almost every weekday. In April she went to the Castle of Mey, where she 'got hold of' a television and watched 'some excellent tho' rather foggy pictures' of the Queen and Prince Philip on an official visit to Paris – she told the Queen that she thought her clothes looked 'perfect'.[33] On the anniversary of her Coronation, 12 May, the Worshipful Company of Gardeners presented her with a replica of her Coronation bouquet; this became a tradition which continued for the rest of her life. On 29 June she made a brief visit to France to unveil the Dunkirk Memorial commemorating the evacuation of the British Expeditionary Force in 1940.

Then came the major event of the Queen Mother's year. At the beginning of July 1957 she left for another official visit to the Federation of Rhodesia and Nyasaland. Her principal task was to open the new University College at Salisbury, the foundation stone of which she had laid in 1953, and to be installed as its president. Her role was especially significant because she was also Chancellor of the University of London, with which the new University College was linked. She was to tour all three countries of the Federation.

Prince Charles, together with Princess Margaret and Princess Anne, came to see her off at London Airport, and climbed aboard the Britannia aircraft to inspect the ingenious layout of the cabins for the Queen Mother and her ladies in waiting, with couches, tables and chairs which converted into beds. Also on board was Queen Elizabeth's wardrobe for the tour – some sixty items including twenty-nine outfits with matching hats, eleven extra day dresses and four extra evening dresses.

After a twenty-one-hour flight, they landed in Salisbury and over the next few days Queen Elizabeth went to a tobacco auction, visited a nursery school for African children and received several deputations. On 5 July, she was installed as president of the University College of Rhodesia and Nyasaland. Her speech emphasized the high academic standards and the multi-racial status of the new University.

They travelled on to Bulawayo for more engagements, and Queen Elizabeth attended an *indaba*, or tribal gathering, in the Matopos Hills. It was a 'moving and memorable occasion' as tribal sentinels stood with their spears and shields on the tops of surrounding hills. She was elaborately dressed for the occasion, in a white lace dress with her Garter ribbon and star and Family Orders, and wearing a white hat adorned with white feathers touched with Garter blue. There were ritual dances of welcome, gifts and acts of homage to Queen Elizabeth; her speech of thanks was translated into two languages and she invested four chiefs with the Queen's medal.[34]

Afterwards the party flew to Northern Rhodesia, first to Lusaka and then to Ndola in the copper belt, where in fierce heat at Luanshya Queen Elizabeth, now dressed in miner's kit of white protective coat, overshoes, helmet and lamp, was taken 1,500 feet down a copper mine. Conditions were said to be ideal – 'a high, light, airy mine, where it is apparently quite safe to smoke. The press in full force!' At another mine at Kitwe she was shown molten copper ore being poured from the furnace. 'Unfortunately the wind changed at the crucial moment, and the whole party were nearly asphyxiated by sulphur fumes.' She then drove through the African township and spent the night in the mining company's guest house. Her lady in waiting, Olivia Mulholland, commented that it was an exhausting 'but absorbingly interesting' day.[35]

On 10 July she took a 'bumpy flight in a small and not very comfortable plane', a Heron, to the town of Broken Hill where there was a reception and a lunch and she then decided to do a spontaneous 'walkabout' – such as she and her husband had first done in New Zealand in 1927. 'This produced immense enthusiasm and she was given an ecstatic welcome.' Back in Lusaka she received a deputation from Queen Elizabeth's Colonial Nursing Service,* and then unveiled a plaque at the High Courts of Justice. She laid the foundation stone for the new Anglican cathedral, attended a garden party at Government House and presented Silver Drums to the 1st Battalion The Northern Rhodesia Regiment and watched the Beating Retreat – 'a ceremony quite beautifully carried out, and the bugle calls most moving and romantic as the African light began to fail'.[36]

Next morning, 12 July, she was on another flight, this time to Chileke, where she was met by the Governor of Nyasaland and Lady Armitage; she visited and named the Queen Elizabeth Hospital, had lunch with the Chief Justice, attended a garden party at the Limbe Country Club and then had a pleasant evening drive to Government House in Zomba, pronounced by Olivia Mulholland the most beautiful place they had yet visited, with glorious views of the surrounding mountains.

At a state *baraza* (an open public meeting) for African chiefs from the whole territory, she delighted the crowd by appearing in a blue and white evening dress with a sparkling tiara, a mass of diamond jewellery and the Garter ribbon over her shoulder. More than a hundred chiefs took part in a colourful and impressive ceremony and the Queen Mother shook hands with each of them. In the evening she decided to drive up the hair-raising road to the top of the Zomba Mountain to see the view and the profusion of wild flowers; the whole party repeated the experience the next day in convoy, raising clouds of red dust, for a picnic tea. 'There were unanimous regrets at leaving such a lovely spot,' Olivia Mulholland recorded. They would have enjoyed a rest, but they had to return to Salisbury next morning.[37]

The last day, 16 July, was particularly exhausting with several public engagements, a hot and dusty race meeting and a state banquet. After that the party was driven straight to the airport with the Queen Mother still in evening dress and tiara. 'A most romantic departure as HM boarded the plane with the floodlights on, the whole thing looking like a scene from a musical comedy.'[38] They landed at London Airport in the pouring rain and were met by Princess Margaret. The Queen

---

* Queen Elizabeth had become patron of the service in 1953; its name was later changed to Queen Elizabeth's Overseas Nursing Service Association.

and Prince Philip came to Clarence House and they all dined together before dispersing, exhausted and somewhat dazed but confident that the trip had been a great success.

The acting British High Commissioner reported home that Queen Elizabeth's tour had had a positive effect on race relations in the Federation. Her engagements had been very much multi-racial, sometimes in spite of opposition. 'For her part, Her Majesty emphasised again and again the pleasure with which she saw the representatives of all races, and this gracious influence in favour of racial tolerance cannot fail to be of effect throughout the country . . . now that these barriers of race prejudice have once been lowered other people will be less fearful of trying to behave in a liberal way in future.'[39]

*

QUEEN ELIZABETH undertook her longest tour at the beginning of 1958. It gave her considerable pleasure that as a result she would fly right around the world before her very modern son-in-law Prince Philip had done so. She left feeling unwell, after she and other members of the family had contracted a rather vicious form of flu at Sandringham.

She had been invited by the government of Australia to open the British Empire Service League biennial conference in Canberra on 17 February, and preceded this with a ten-day visit to New Zealand. She flew out of London on a BOAC DC-7 on the morning of 28 January. Her first brief stop was Montreal where the plane landed to refuel in a blinding snowstorm. Her flight continued across the Prairies and the Rockies to Vancouver, where she arrived at 11.30 p.m. local time. The snow had been replaced by drenching rain. Almost twenty-four hours after leaving London, she was tired, but when she landed she said she was 'so glad to be here'.

Travelling via Honolulu and crossing the international dateline, she touched down in Fiji on the afternoon of Friday 31 January. There was no question of rest – instead she was accorded a formal reception first by the Governor and then by the Mayor of Lautoka, and was asked to watch a display of Fijian song and dance. After a short night's sleep, she took off for the last leg of the journey out to New Zealand, arriving in the afternoon of 1 February. There, after a journey of 12,700 miles, she was greeted by the Governor General and Lady Cobham.

Throughout February and the first week of March she conducted an extensive and relentlessly busy tour of New Zealand and Australia. It included all the usual paraphernalia of royal tours – civic receptions, garden parties, inspections of schools and universities, farms and showgrounds; the presentation of colours to military units, luncheons and dinners with local and national politicians, church services, drives from airport to hotel, hotel to airport in long convoys of cars. Sir James Scholtens, the assistant director of the Australian tour, later recalled that her programme was indeed very heavy and was 'saturated with' events.[40]

Still exhausted by the journey out, she had a nasty recurrence of her flu symptoms in the Cathedral Church of St Paul at Wellington. As she described it to the Queen, 'My head started to go round just like it did in London before I left, & my knees trembled so much that the service paper rattled & rustled! It was really an agony, & the first time in my life that such a thing has happened to me.' She found that the worst thing was being alone without anyone in the family. 'When one has someone either to help, or be helped by, nothing seems quite so devastating – Luckily, I shall be far too old soon for any more Australasian tours!'[41]

When she finally shook off her illness, the Queen Mother enjoyed herself much more and wrote home saying how touching her welcome had been. The Australian papers were gossipy, but 'so far they are quite polite, & go on the old stories of how tired I am, & how much my feet hurt, & how tired the staff is, & how I must dye my hair otherwise how could it still be dark etc etc!! Quite harmless, & quite funny sometimes.'[42]

Later she described herself as 'just hanging on'; the tour was so packed that there was hardly time for breathing. But luckily the weather was lovely 'and one feels revived'.[43] She found the loyalty to the Crown and to Britain 'burning'.[44] She was annoyed to think that the English newspapers were not covering her efforts, but in fact the British press followed her tour quite extensively and both her daughters told her so. Princess Margaret wrote, 'We see nothing but delicious hot sunny photographs of you with millions & millions of people waving. I can almost hear that exhausting noise!'[45] There were compensations. Queen Elizabeth wrote to her unmarried daughter that on a sheep station she had met the owners' 'very beautiful nephews, all called Bill. The real country Australian is really a knock out. Very tall, with long legs encased in tight trousers, blue eyes, a drawl and a Stetson – they are too charming for words and the American cowboy is a mere nothing compared.'[46]

Sydney was another matter. The city, she said, 'nearly killed me!' The organizers kept slotting in new events – on one morning she had three children's rallies 'in boiling sun', then visits to a factory and a housing estate, followed by a garden party, after which she had to give out presents to people who had helped with the tour. She did not like this ritual – it was 'always at the end of a busy day, & one gradually thanks them less & less, until the poor deputy transport officer gets a mere whisper'.[47] On one memorable day, because of the intense rivalry between the two towns, she had to fit in both Hobart, the capital of Tasmania, and Launceston, a hundred miles away, on a day trip by air from Melbourne. Her entourage was daunted; but the Queen Mother, rarely unable to enjoy herself, found it hilarious.

> I went to Tasmania for lunch yesterday. That's the form! It was a gloriously crazy day, & I haven't laughed so much for years! First of all, we arrived in a howling gale, which is always faintly funny.
>
> Sir Ronald Cross had an A.D.C. from the Grenadiers who was having ghastly trouble with a huge bearskin, & I thought he had gone mad when he conducted me firmly to the <u>back</u> of the Guard of Honour – I had visions of inspecting their backs, when on a word of command, they revolved, & we faced each other bravely. Then on arrival at their house, there was drawn up a lot of Army nurses to inspect. As I started down the line, a particularly vicious blast took <u>all</u> their hats off, & being round & flat, they rolled away like little bicycles!
>
> Then the public address system broke down when I was making my very boring speech, & then we had a mad chauffeur who obediently slowed down on approaching a group of people, and then accelerated violently when passing them, so all the poor things saw was a pair of white shoes, as I was thrown back against the seat & my feet shot into the air. Let us hope that they thought they saw little white hands waving.[48]

There were some days off and the relaxation that she enjoyed the most was visiting studs or going to the races. Early in the trip around New Zealand, at Trentham racecourse, near Wellington, she presented the St James's Cup to Sir Ernest Davies, a colourful businessman and former mayor of Auckland, whose horse Bali Ha'i had just won. To her astonishment, 'he roared up to the microphone' and announced that he wanted to give her the horse 'as a present from all the sports people of New Zealand!! You can imagine my feelings!' she wrote to the Queen. 'And at once I thought of you and Margaret saying, "what has Mummy done now".'[49] She wrote also to her trainer Cecil Boyd-Rochfort asking him to take the gift horse into his stable.[50] In the event, Bali Ha'i was an excellent horse and raced well for her after he had arrived in England.

Right through to the end came more civic ceremonies, more mayoral receptions, more awards to be given, parades of ambulance workers, tours of housing projects, inspections of factories, more garden parties, further civic receptions, meetings of youth organizations and attendance at a schoolchildren's rally in Perth, until on the evening of Friday 7 March Queen Elizabeth left on one of Qantas's best planes, a Super Constellation named *Southern Star*, bound for London. As she flew north and west, she was pleased with her tour and was looking forward to dinner with her family on Monday night (she never liked being alone on the evening she returned from a trip). And then the unforeseen happened.

The refuelling in the Cocos Islands was without incident. But about two hours before arriving in Mauritius for another fuelling, a cylinder seized in one of the plane's four engines. Serious damage was caused. Cyclones in the Mauritius area added to anxiety about a safe landing. To everyone's relief they made it into Plaisance airport, but it then became clear that the engine's cowling needed to be replaced. The intended one-hour stopover had to be extended – and extended. In the end the necessary repairs delayed them for three nights. The weather was dreadful: airless and steamy, crackling with violent electrical storms or pouring with rain. But Queen Elizabeth made the best of her enforced holiday. The Governor concocted an impromptu programme and she was cheered by crowds of delighted Mauritians wherever she went. She toured Port Louis, and at Pamplemousses she inspected the araucaria tree she had planted in 1927 on the way back from Australia; she drove up into the mountains for a picnic. Everywhere she went, she met with enthusiastic crowds.

She was offered another aircraft to continue, but knowing how upset her Qantas crew (and their superiors back home) already were, she said that she preferred to stay with her Qantas flight. Back in Australia Sir Allen Brown, the director general of her visit and a keen writer of rhymes, concocted a telegram about her plight:

> A cowling's just a piece of tin
> To keep the aircraft engine in
> But without it one gets vicious
> Especially if in Mauritius

Anticipating that Martin Gilliat would be more upset than his mistress, he added,

> I fear the rage of Comrade Martin,
> Because the aircraft won't get startin'
> Yet tell him that the loudest howling
> Will not replace the missing cowling[51]

On 11 March, after a new cowling had eventually arrived from Australia, she flew away, church bells pealing, people shouting fare-wells as she waved goodbye from the steps of the plane.[52]

Her greatest concern was for Kenya where she had been scheduled to open Nairobi's new airport during another stopover. The delays had made this impossible and she sent a message to the Governor of Kenya saying how sad she was about this, but expressing confidence that 'on another voyage, which I hope will not be too far in the future, my aircraft will land at your new airport'.[53] It happened just one year later.

Instead of Nairobi, her plane was routed by Entebbe where she landed in the middle of the night. Once again, engine trouble pro-longed what was to have been a refuelling stop. Once again, she was offered another aircraft but declined. A further eighteen hours late, she took off for Malta. She was almost home but even here there was trouble and another delay of at least twelve hours was promised. So finally she agreed to transfer to a BOAC plane and completed the journey to London, landing on the morning of 13 March, sixty-eight hours late. When the desolate Qantas manager in London apologized, she reassured him, 'It could have happened to anyone. I feel very sorry for the crew; they all worked so hard.'[54]

Typically, she saw the incessant delays in her flight home more as an adventure than as a setback. She had reason to be pleased with her trip; in one letter home she wrote, 'I have been deeply touched by their very true feelings of love, & <u>amazed</u> at their enthusiastic reception.'[55]

*

ALL IN ALL the Queen Mother was becoming an avid traveller. She had enjoyed flying since her first flight in 1935, and she loved to be the Royal Family's pioneer in the air. She was one of the first in the family to fly by helicopter, which she loved – indeed it became a method of transport she enjoyed till the very end of her life.

She was also gaining confidence in her own ability to represent her country abroad. She was widely, visibly present in Africa as what Harold Macmillan later called 'the winds of change' swept through the continent, fanning nationalist sentiments and removing British colonial rule. Ghana was the first African colony to become independent, in 1957, and it was followed by Nigeria, Sierra Leone, Tanganyika (Tanzania), Uganda, Kenya, Nyasaland (Malawi) and Northern Rhodesia (Zambia) through the 1960s. All became members of the British Commonwealth. Its growth, as the Queen herself later said, marked 'the transformation of the Crown from an emblem of dominion into a symbol of free and voluntary association. In all history this has no precedent.'[56]

In early 1959 Queen Elizabeth made an official tour to Kenya and Uganda. It was nostalgic for her, the first time she had been to Kenya since she and the Duke of York had been there in 1924–5. The visit to Kenya was arranged partly in order to make up for the previous year's cancelled visit to open Nairobi Airport. This time the British government considered cancelling the visit again, because of political unrest in the colony. The African elected members of the Kenya Legislative Council had decided to boycott any official functions during the visit, but their leader Dr Kiano sent Queen Elizabeth a personal message assuring her of their esteem for her and the Royal Family.[57] The authorities in Nairobi were unworried, and persuaded the Colonial Office that cancellation was unnecessary.[58] She was met at Nairobi airport on the afternoon of 5 February by the Governor of Kenya, Sir Evelyn Baring, and his wife Molly. The Governor had devised a sophisticated programme for her and his efficient staff guided her with care around the country.

East Africa had been suffering serious drought, but, soon after she arrived in the almost waterless Masai district of Narok, not for the first

time in royal history fate obligingly took a hand. At a picturesque
baraza with Masai tribesmen, some in lion-skin headdresses, Queen
Elizabeth made a speech expressing a hope for rain. 'An hour later the
skies opened & an inch fell in 20 minutes,' recorded her lady in
waiting. 'The Masai were convinced that HM had magic powers.'[59]
Princess Margaret congratulated her on being a rain-maker: 'The BBC
man read it out quite seriously and dead-pan which made it sound
even more unbelievable. It reminded me so much of when Papa said
"Pula" in Bechuanaland. That worked too!'[60]

Queen Elizabeth travelled widely through Kenya by train, sitting
for hours on the observation platform and being welcomed with huge
enthusiasm at every halt and road crossing, where hundreds of people
had gathered and waited to glimpse her, even at night.[61] Evelyn Baring
commented that from the train she had a real glimpse of true rural
Kenya. 'There were European farmers, Asian traders, Africans working
on farms or in forest villages, and the forest officers in charge of them.'
At one station there was a farmer with five couple of fox hounds
which he hunted himself, 'since in Kenya the eccentric English individ-
ualist is not yet a thing of the past'.[62]

On Valentine's Day the train crew sent her cards. The best was
hand drawn, with a background of a smiling sun above mountains and
a little train weaving past hearts and cherubs:

> To show you our affection this is a simple sign
> And tell you most sincerely, you are our Valentine
> The only thing that worries us when we are on the line,
> Is that there is no corridor between our coach and thine.

At the bottom of the card was a line of black Africans waving Union
flags and a fat bald white man, also waving his flag.[63]

She drove through the Nyeri Reserve, past crowds of cheering
Kikuyu tribesmen, to spend a night in the new Treetops Hotel (the
original cabin in which Princess Elizabeth had stayed in 1952 had been
burned down in the Mau Mau revolt in 1954) and enjoyed the wild
animals. Rhino, buffalo, baboon, the rare giant forest hog and many
shapes and sizes of antelope appeared that night for her and her party
– but, alas, no elephants.

Next day she spoke for some time with a group of Kikuyu chiefs
before flying back to Nairobi. Baring was struck that the Kikuyu were
more enthusiastic than almost any of the other African tribes and that

the cheering in Nyeri 'was the loudest heard during the visit'. It was particularly remarkable because this was an area 'where the struggle against the Mau Mau had been at its hottest'. The Governor believed that Queen Elizabeth's presence in their lands 'gave to many Kikuyu there a feeling that the bitter story of the past was closed, and she appeared as a symbol of a new and a better era'.[64] Similarly the two *barazas* held with the Masai and with the Elgeyo and Marakwet tribes seemed great successes. 'Here there was no sign of political trouble and there were no dark memories of the Emergency to forget. The people received Her Majesty with great enthusiasm.'[65]

African nationalist politicians had tried to persuade the citizens of Nairobi not to turn out in the streets to cheer her. To the great relief of the Governor their attempts failed; she was welcomed heartily everywhere, and by everyone – Africans, Asians and Europeans. In Mombasa the Arab population greeted her with courtesy. There were dances in her honour at a reception for women of all races.[66]

She was struck by the achievements of the colony. In Nairobi she visited the King George VI Hospital for Africans and, according to the Governor, was impressed by the standard of medical care dispensed. Everywhere she went she seemed to be delighted – and this in turn pleased everyone she met. The Governor concluded that her visit was 'a most outstanding success. It made a profound impression on all the people of Kenya. In my view it has, in an indirect but a powerful way, assisted the recent more hopeful political developments in this complex and often troubled country.'[67] Lady Baring wrote to the Queen Mother, 'There has been a most genuine drawing together of all sorts of people & races & groups as a direct result of your coming.'[68]

'Kenya was very crowded as to programme,' Queen Elizabeth wrote to Princess Margaret, 'but goodness, what a beautiful country it is!' The only drawback, she said, was that people constantly told her how much they had enjoyed Princess Margaret's own visit two years before. The sheikhs in Mombasa had 'looked gravely at my flushed & streaming face, & red eyes (v. small too) and said "We DID so love having Princess Margaret here – I do hope she comes again soon, soon."'[69]

On 18 February she flew from Nairobi to Kisumu on Lake Victoria for a brief visit, and then on to Entebbe, the capital of neighbouring Uganda, still a British protectorate. In Kampala, as chancellor of the University of London she visited the University College of Makerere, which had a close relationship with her university. There, suffering from the heat in her Chancellor's robes, she presented doctorates and opened the new University Library. On the green college lawns she was surrounded by students and academics in coloured robes, all anxious to talk to or at least glimpse her. It was a relaxed occasion.

That afternoon she opened the new headquarters of the Uganda Sports Union, and watched boxing, athletics, hockey, tennis and cricket. Everyone was impressed when the Kabaka's brother, Prince George Mawanda, hit two magnificent sixes clean out of the ground. This was followed in the evening by the Uganda Royal Tattoo in a crowded stadium. Among the displays the Queen Mother watched was, rather astonishingly, a reconstruction of the Battle of Leik Hill in Burma, during the last war, by the 4th King's African Rifles. This was followed by African, Indian and Scottish dancing, and music by military and police bands. The whole Tattoo, she told Princess Margaret, was 'so gloriously English that it was almost funny'. All was most enjoyable except, she wrote, 'I had a lizard in my room all night, & it hung over my bed looking at me with bulging eyes. I felt quite embarrassed.'[70]

She visited the Western, Northern and Eastern provinces of Uganda, travelled to two national parks and sailed on Lake Victoria, Lake Albert and the Nile, spotting birds, hippos and crocodiles. She was pleased that she was often taken on the same route and to the same places that she and the Duke had visited in 1925 – the trip that she later described as the best time of their lives. In each province she listened to kind addresses of welcome.

At Paraa in the Murchison Falls National Park a special cottage overlooking the Nile had been built for her visit; there she watched a spectacular display by Acholi dancers, each of whom wore a large headdress of ostrich feathers. To general delight she repaid the compliment by wearing her tiara.[71] In Jinja, in the Eastern Province, the welcome was even more enthusiastic with thousands of people lining the streets. She was presented with many gifts, including a bag of coffee from Bugisu, accompanied by a plea that Her Majesty 'influence the British people to take to drinking more coffee and less tea'. She loved it all, and in her farewell speech said that the 'spirit of courage, confidence and enterprise' she had seen 'bodes well for the future of Uganda'.[72]

As she left, the *East African Standard* asserted that her tour was one of the most successful ever undertaken by a member of the Royal

Family. In his report to Alan Lennox-Boyd, the Colonial Secretary, the Governor praised Queen Elizabeth's demeanour throughout, stressing that 'the unqualified success of the visit was attributable above all to the Queen Mother herself, to Her Majesty's visible affection for and interest in all those she met and to her gracious and friendly manner to all on all occasions'. Over 950 people were presented formally to her and the Governor noted that she had 'a friendly and informal word for scores of others and a gracious smile and wave for thousands'. He thought that it all amounted to 'a personal triumph'.[73]

It was not just loyal colonial administrators who thought this. George Thomas, the Labour Member of Parliament for Cardiff West and future Speaker of the House of Commons, returning from a trip to Kenya, wrote to Martin Gilliat that everywhere he had heard 'profound appreciation' of the good the Queen Mother had done. The Arab community in Mombasa 'were quite ecstatic' at the interest she had shown in them, and all other races felt the same. 'It is not my habit to write to pay this sort of tribute but in view of the tremendous surge of appreciation of this Royal visit I am breaking a rule! It will do no harm for you to know that people like myself feel the impact of what this visit meant. Above all I felt that it had been a real tonic for those folk who have the sticky job of everyday administration in that difficult country'.[74]

*

SOON AFTER Queen Elizabeth's return from Africa she prepared for a trip to Rome with Princess Margaret. It was an unofficial visit but she was to have an audience with Pope John XXIII and unveil a monument to Byron in the Borghese Gardens. She wrote a happy letter to D'Arcy Osborne, saying, 'I can't believe that at last I am coming to Rome! It really is too exciting, and I am looking forward to it all so much – It is the first time in my life that I am to visit a place just for pleasure.'[75] She told him that she had already been inundated with anxious letters from Protestants about her visit to the Pope. 'I wish that one could convey to these people (who are simple & good) that if one goes to Rome, the Pope, being a Sovereign, must be visited out of politeness if nothing else. There is great ignorance & fear still about the R. Catholic religion – possibly because they are so well organised.'[76] The visit went well and included lunch with D'Arcy Osborne and a lunch at a trattoria on the Via Appia Antica. The British Ambassador to Italy, Ashley

Clarke, reported that the Romans were usually cynical about distinguished foreign visitors to the city. But the warmth of the welcome given to the Queen Mother and Princess Margaret was striking.[77]

On the way home they stopped in Paris at the suggestion of Lady Jebb, whose husband was still British ambassador. She had proposed that the Queen Mother visit the International Floral Exhibition and the exhibition of British furniture, 'The Century of Elegance in England', at the Musée des Arts Décoratifs.[78] Queen Elizabeth rarely needed encouragement to visit Paris, one of her favourite cities, and, while there, she was pleased to have lunch with General de Gaulle, now President of France.

In her published diaries, Lady Jebb painted an unflattering portrait of Princess Margaret, whose 'disagreeable' behaviour she contrasted with her mother's 'sparkling and delightful' manners. The Princess, she said, 'wishes to convey that she is very much the Princess, but at the same time she is not prepared to stick to the rules if they bore or annoy her, such as being polite to people.' She claimed that the Princess faked a cold to get out of engagements and that her only interests were to have her hair coiffed by the famous hairdresser Alexandre and to have a fitting for a Dior dress. Lady Jebb complained about the Princess to the Queen Mother's lady in waiting, Patricia Hambleden, who, she claimed, was not surprised and observed that the Queen Mother would not be concerned in any way by her daughter's behaviour: 'Nothing will disturb her happiness.' Lady Jebb asked if Queen Elizabeth had always been so philosophical and Lady Hambleden replied, 'Yes, I think she always had this quality. And a sort of serenity, and of being unhurried.'[79]

A year later, in May 1960, Queen Elizabeth made her second visit to the Federation of Rhodesia and Nyasaland and spent nineteen days there. This was perhaps her favourite part of the British Empire in Africa. She listened to the growing concerns of the white minority in Southern Rhodesia but was told by people she trusted that relations between black and white were likely to get much worse. Major General Sir John Kennedy, the former Governor, thought the white settlers were 'diehard' and 'unrealistic'.[80]

Once again there were fears that, given what the Governor of Nyasaland called 'the uneasy political atmosphere', there might be boycotts or 'unhappy incidents'.[81] In the event there were none at all. The principal purpose of Queen Elizabeth's visit was to open the

Kariba Dam, intended to provide hydro-electric power for the copper belt. She made numerous other visits to schools, factories and farms; one child whose school she had visited wrote an essay about her saying 'she had gloves studded with rubies ... Her shoes were pink, studded with diamonds ... The jewels on her dress and her tiara twinkled like stars ... On her gloves were small emeralds.'[82]

She travelled widely throughout the Federation, visiting small towns far from the usual beaten track. She went to Barotseland, which delighted her. 'No roads, and a vast plain, which every year is inundated by the mighty Zambesi, too beautiful for words, because the water is just going down now, & the tall grass is growing through the water, & this endless vista of shimmer & light is really fascinating.'[83] More schools, tea plantations, farms, tobacco estates and hospitals welcomed her. Near Blantyre, the capital of Nyasaland, she unveiled a war memorial to African and European servicemen who had fallen in the two world wars. She spoke movingly of the sacrifices that colonial soldiers had made for Britain and laid a wreath of poppies on the memorial, which bore the inscription 'Lest we forget'.

The Governor of Nyasaland noted that it was above all the Queen Mother's 'charm and dignity' which ensured the great success of the visit at such a politically difficult time. 'Tales of her friendliness and personal charm' spread quickly and as a result what began as small crowds grew to throngs of thousands.[84] She was pleased too. Martin Gilliat wrote to the Governor to say that her hopes had been 'fulfilled beyond her keenest expectations'.[85]

From this period on Queen Elizabeth followed the affairs of all of eastern and southern Africa with great attention. She admired what the white settlers had achieved while understanding that 'the winds of change' must indeed produce just that – and would lead to black majority rule. In the case of Southern Rhodesia she grew more and more concerned by the gulf between the whites and the blacks, by the white minority government's later unilateral declaration of independence, and by the way in which subsequent British governments handled the crisis.

*

IT WAS NOT just the Empire that was having to change at the end of the 1950s. The imperial monarchy at home also began to come under scrutiny, along with many other British institutions. The years following the failure of British intervention in the Suez crisis of 1956 were a time of national reassessment. The Conservative Prime Minister, Anthony Eden, resigned and was replaced by Harold Macmillan. The country was still poor and battered, struggling to recover from the immense exertion of winning the war. There were still bomb sites all over London and other great cities. Added to the expense of rebuilding were the costs of nationalization and the welfare state embarked upon by the radical Labour governments of 1945–51 and accepted by the Conservative government that succeeded them.

Britain was still an overwhelmingly white nation. The first immigrants from the British colonies, particularly the West Indies, had begun to arrive in 1947, but there were only 36,000 a decade later. Class divisions had been diminished but not ended by the war. Social rank was easily identified by accents and clothing, even by men's hats. The monarchy was not just accepted but was enjoyed by the overwhelming majority of the population. But, even for the monarchy, change had begun.

In 1953 the Royal Family had profited from a romantic sense of renewal and hope after the coronation of Queen Elizabeth II. But public attitudes by the end of the decade were much more questioning. There was love still, but it was no longer unconditional. The period of scepticism was triggered (or was subsequently seen to be triggered) when a young peer, Lord Altrincham (John Grigg), criticized the Queen in *National Review*, a small magazine he owned. He called her speeches 'prim little sermons' and said that her background and training were too limited and her advisers too narrowly chosen. He thought she needed 'a truly classless and Commonwealth Court'. His remarks were thoughtful and intended to be supportive of what he called 'the genius of constitutional monarchy'. Privately, some of the Queen's own advisers considered that such comments were helpful and that it was time for the Palace to shed its 'tweedy' image. But such criticism was unprecedented and raised a public storm.

In these circumstances, the arrival of Antony Armstrong-Jones in the royal firmament was propitious – he was far from the tweedy set that Lord Altrincham had criticized. A young and attractive society photographer, his uncle was Oliver Messel, a well-known artist and theatrical designer. Armstrong-Jones had been at Eton and had then coxed the winning Cambridge boat in the 1950 boat race against Oxford.

His friendship with Princess Margaret began to develop in 1958 after they were introduced by Elizabeth Cavendish, a sister of the Duke of Devonshire. His bohemian lifestyle was instantly attractive to the cloistered but somewhat rebellious Princess. He had a studio and flat in the Pimlico Road and also a hideaway south of the Thames in Rotherhithe, in those days a very unfashionable part of London that would have seemed exotic to someone nurtured in the greatest palaces and castles of the land.

Armstrong-Jones sent Princess Margaret long-playing gramophone records of a popular musical, *Irma la Douce*, and then invited her to see it.[86] She took her mother into her confidence and Queen Elizabeth asked Armstrong-Jones to lunch at Clarence House. The Princess warned him that if he came she would 'bore you by forcing you to look at my photograph of Mama in the heather which has blown up very nicely. It's interesting (to me) for its textures . . . Altogether it would be too sad if you cannot come!'[87] The lunch went well; the Queen Mother liked this engaging young artist and encouraged her daughter to pursue the friendship. Armstrong-Jones liked the Queen Mother too – he enjoyed her coquettish familiarity touched with formality. Their friendship became close and was to survive to the end of her life.

Armstrong-Jones took scores of photographs of the Princess, as he did of all his friends. In April 1959 she asked him to photograph her 'properly' and suggested he come to Royal Lodge for the weekend of 1 May.[88] That summer they fell in love and by August she was writing to him joyful letters from Balmoral. 'You've made me happy. Are you pleased? I am . . . I left London tremendously NOT in turmoil. Are you aware how much that means to me – having travelled unhappily, bumping about.' Now, by contrast, she had 'golden dreams' and found herself 'smiling unconsciously. What a short time it is since April really. Three months, not counting the last blissful weeks . . . every time you came to stay it was nicer than the last . . . my sister is glorious, my b[rother] in l[aw] better now and the children are cockahoop, camping the night in a stalking house. Darling do write back and tell me everything that happens to you, every detail please.'[89]

All that summer they wrote to each other, letters filled with endearment. On her birthday, 21 August, she waited in her room for his call and next day she wrote to tell him again how happy she now was. 'Dare one say that word . . . I'm afraid of stating it.' She had been unhappy for a long time but now she thought she really was happy – 'because I feel peaceful and unworried and you are nice and gentle, very rare'. Later that evening the family, she told him, 'sat for hours after dinner singing songs round the table, and then on and on in the drawing room'.[90]

At the end of August President Eisenhower, near the end of his second term in office, took up a long-standing invitation to visit the family in Scotland. The Princess wrote a long and hilarious description of the occasion. 'Excitement, arrangements, arrangements, nonsense talked, wrong information, confirmation of wrong information, diet sheets, screening by G men, last minute refutation of wrong information, that went on before his arrival put us all in a frenzy of nerves.'

Prince Philip met Eisenhower's flight and drove with him to Balmoral. The Queen and the Princess walked down the drive and waited just around a corner and out of sight of the horde of photographers outside the gate. Prince Philip had forgotten that they were planning to do this and his first reaction, he said afterwards, was 'who are those two idiotic women?'[91] They took Eisenhower into the hills and the Queen cooked him drop scones on a barbecue. Then it was 'on for a drink with my glorious Mum at a party at Birkhall where everybody produced cameras so that instead of faces there were just a lot of old lenses on the lawn'.[92]

In October Armstrong-Jones came to stay at Balmoral and he and the Princess enjoyed exploring together all the places the Princess loved the most. They visited the Queen Mother at Birkhall too. He showed the Princess how to take better photographs and took many himself. Afterwards, he sent her a parcel of hundreds of photographs – she handed them around with pride and was particularly pleased if someone said, 'What a marvellous Armstrong-Jones portrait,' and she could say 'I took that one myself.'

While the family was at Balmoral the general election called by Harold Macmillan took place on 8 October, and on election night, the Princess stayed up in 'the nerve centre' (the equerries' room) watching the results; she was much cheered when Macmillan and his Conservative Party won another victory.[93]

Later, after a visit to Glamis, the Princess wrote to tell Armstrong-Jones that it gave her such pleasure to be there 'and it brings back hundreds of blissful memories of a sunny childhood and loving, fond grandparents'. She was about to take the train 'back to London and you. I love you passionately and peacefully and I've thought of you every second which has resulted in long periods of day dreaming out of which I have to be literally shaken. I have missed you all the time darling and can't wait to see you.'[94]

On 27 February 1960, shortly after the birth of Queen Elizabeth's third grandchild, Prince Andrew, the Court Circular announced: 'It is with the greatest pleasure that Queen Elizabeth the Queen Mother announces the betrothal of her beloved daughter The Princess Margaret to Mr Antony Charles Robert Armstrong-Jones, son of Mr R. O. L. Armstrong-Jones, QC, and the Countess of Rosse to which engagement the Queen has gladly given her consent.'

The news was greeted with astonishment – Armstrong-Jones had never been mentioned as a possible suitor – and great pleasure. Many people felt that Princess Margaret had been dealt a poor hand over Peter Townsend; the fact that she could now be happy was doubly pleasing. And the fact that the Queen's sister was marrying neither prince nor duke nor even aristocrat found favour with many. He was widely described in the press as a 'commoner', though the *Daily Mail* reassured its readers that both his parents were from the landed gentry. By comparison with his new family, he was seen as somewhat raffish. His boyish good looks, his wide smile, the fact that he worked for a living and his obvious talent endeared him to many people, and to the spirit of the more populist age.

Some of Armstrong-Jones's friends were concerned that the love match might also in the end prove a mismatch. And some members of the family were not sure what to make of it all. The Duchess of Gloucester wrote to Queen Elizabeth to say that she and her husband had been 'wondering how you feel about Margaret's great venture'. She thought 'her "Tony"' looked very nice in the photographs '& sounds an interesting & rather unusual sort of character'. The fact that they had never come across him 'all makes it so much more difficult to know what to say or think about it. Anyway it is very exciting news.'[95]

The Queen Mother was pleased. In a letter she wrote to the Archbishop of Canterbury* she said, 'I feel very happy about it, and feel sure too, that Margaret has found someone with whom she can

---

* The letter was never sent, as she noted on it herself, and remained among her papers – probably, therefore, an oversight on her part.

be happy . . . they went to Holy Communion together on the first Sunday after they became engaged, which seems encouraging for the future.'[96] She presented the beaming couple to the world at a gala evening at the Royal Opera House. They all waved from the royal box while the audience in the stalls and the circles cheered with evident pleasure.

Preparations for the wedding went on alongside the Queen Mother's normal official life. In early April there was a charming interlude. The President of France and Madame de Gaulle made a state visit to London. De Gaulle had always been one of the Queen Mother's heroes. She stood on the balcony of Clarence House to watch his carriage drive up the Mall to Buckingham Palace. When the carriage was opposite Clarence House it stopped; the General stood up and saluted her.[97] Later he and his wife came to tea at Clarence House, and the Queen Mother and Princess Margaret attended the state banquet in his honour at Buckingham Palace.

The wedding took place at Westminster Abbey on 6 May 1960. It was the first great royal event since the Coronation. Now, seven years later, the country was bursting into the 1960s and what the Queen's biographer Elizabeth Longford called 'a period of brittle animation'.[98] The Mall was decorated with arches of roses, the sun shone; the crowds, according to Noël Coward, 'looked like endless, vivid, herbaceous borders'. 'We want Margaret,' they shouted. Three million more people watched the ceremony on television.

Queen Elizabeth wrote to her daughter on her honeymoon in terms which many mothers would understand. 'After the tremendous bustle and noise and beauty of your wedding day, you suddenly disappeared, and I feel that I haven't seen you since you were about 9 years old!' She thought the wedding was perfect – 'I felt that it was a real wedding service, holy & beautiful, and you looked heavenly darling.'[99] From *Britannia* Tony Armstrong-Jones, thanked his mother-in-law for 'the wonderful feeling of warmth and welcome' she had given him; he had never in his life been as contented as during the weekends at Royal Lodge.[100]

Princess Margaret told her mother that every minute of her wedding 'was a dream of happiness' – and she thanked her 'for being so absolutely heavenly all the time we were engaged, you were so encouraging and angelic and it is something that is difficult to express on paper because it is really thanking you for being you'.[101]

CHAPTER NINETEEN

THE HEART OF THE MATTER

'I would LOVE to be Patron'

IN THE 1960s Britain embarked on an extensive social revolution, one which led to more questioning of ancient institutions than ever before. It was uncomfortable for members of the Royal Family. The social historian Asa Briggs suggested later that culturally and politically the year 1956 had seemed to mark the symbolic break with the past. That was the year of John Osborne's play *Look Back in Anger*, of James Dean's *Rebel without a Cause*, of Elvis Presley's 'Heartbreak Hotel', of Bill Haley and the Comets' 'Rock around the Clock'. It was also the year, as we have noted, of the failed British intervention at Suez, which showed the British more clearly than anything else that their country was no longer the Great Power that it had been.[1]

The country was becoming richer – and the number of families owning refrigerators, washing machines and cars was increasing all the time. The sociologist Ferdinand Zweig saw such a domestic revolution as leading to 'a deep transformation of values', the development of other ways of thinking and feeling, a new ethos, new aspirations and cravings. It was the beginning of the era of what *The Economist* called 'the deproletarianised consumer'. What this would mean was not clear – and *The Economist* agreed that 'deproletarianised societies' would not necessarily become 'more discriminate, more moral and more self-reliant'.[2]

In schools and universities students became more assertive. Everywhere authority was questioned. Even hospital matrons and station masters were no longer allowed to run their own empires. A new orthodoxy began to emerge in Britain, at least among the urban intellectual elite, which later came to be known as the chattering classes. Deference began to die and was replaced by indifference, scepticism and satire. Established institutions – the state, the Church, the education system and the monarchy – were suddenly questioned and satirized, if not challenged.

The most powerful harbinger of change was probably television. In 1955 the BBC had lost its monopoly of television broadcasting, after anguished Parliamentary debate, and new commercial companies flourished and competed thereafter. In 1960 there were ten million combined radio and TV licences in the country; within four years the number had doubled and the coming of colour in 1968 led to another surge in the sale of television sets and the numbers of viewers. In the 1960s, the BBC's mission changed: it had begun as a temple to arts, science, the glory of God and the propagation of knowledge.* Now its Director General, Hugh Greene, began to push the BBC away from its traditional culture of decorous reserve 'right into the centre of the swirling forces that were changing life in Britain'.[3]

Such television shows as *That Was The Week That Was* poked fun at the establishment. This popular programme's first satirical sketch about the Royal Family was broadcast in March 1963. The producer, Ned Sherrin, claimed that it had in fact been suggested by Princess Margaret. 'I think she'd been watching the programme,' said Sherrin. 'Anyway she said, "Why don't you do something about the ridiculous way that they report us?"'[4] The sketch, called 'The Queen's Departure', described the Queen setting out from the Pool of London in a barge which started to sink. As it went down, the commentary became more and more reverential until it finally ended, 'The Queen is swimming for her life' and the band struck up the National Anthem.

The explosion of pop music was also a powerful harbinger of change. So was the public's attitude to sex, and it was sex that claimed the political career of John Profumo, Minister for War in the Conservative government; he admitted lying to the House of Commons about his relationship with a call girl, Christine Keeler. His resignation weakened Harold Macmillan's government, and shortly afterwards Macmillan himself, believing (wrongly) that he was gravely ill, resigned and recommended that the Queen send for Lord Home, the Foreign

---

* The inscription above the door of the original BBC headquarters in Portland Place read, 'This Temple of the Arts and Muses is dedicated to Almighty God by the first Governors of Broadcasting in the year 1931, Sir John Reith being Director-General. It is their prayer that good seed sown may bring forth a good harvest, that all things hostile to peace or purity may be banished from this house, and that the people, inclining their ear to whatsoever things are beautiful and honest and of good report, may tread the path of wisdom and uprightness.'

Secretary, in his stead. She did so. Home, a Scottish friend of Queen Elizabeth, led the Conservatives into an election in 1964. After thirteen years in power, they narrowly lost to the Labour Party, under the leadership of Harold Wilson, who promised, rather oddly, that 'the white heat of the technological revolution' would transform Britain.

In social terms, the Wilson government, re-elected with a larger majority in 1966, did embark on more radical legislation than any before it. The age of voting was lowered to eighteen, the Sexual Offences Act permitted homosexual acts between consenting adults over the age of twenty-one, and abortion was legalized. Capital punishment was abolished. The Lord Chamberlain's powers of theatrical censorship were removed in 1968. The Divorce Reform Act of 1969 made it easier to end a marriage. Sexuality was discussed and explored more openly than ever before. Along with access to the birth-control pill, these liberalizing measures would have a huge impact on society in the decades ahead.

In these 'Swinging Sixties' the Royal Family was judged remote by the vanguard of the London-led cultural revolution. But others, less enamoured of the new standards with which society was experimenting, saw the monarchy and particularly Queen Elizabeth as symbols of the tried and traditional values of Britain.

*

'THE VERY important thing is to be <u>busy</u>,' Queen Elizabeth believed.[5] It was advice she herself had followed after the death of the King and ever since. Although nothing could replace her loss, in the end she had found a new role and renewed zest for life in her public responsibilities.

As she grew older, she continued to bear a workload under which many much younger people would have faltered. Above all she displayed unceasing enthusiasm and diligence on behalf of the charities, regiments and other bodies of which she was patron, president, colonel-in-chief, honorary colonel or a dozen other titles. Her list of patronages grew to over 300, and she continued to accept new ones until the last year of her life. Her interest in people and curiosity about them kept her enjoyment of this work alive; and she would not have been human if she had not been gratified by the public acclaim it brought her. But in any event 'retirement' was not a concept she entertained for herself; the sense of duty with which she had been brought up remained with her. Having become aware of the contribution she could still make, she played her part conscientiously.

Royal patronage of charitable organizations has a long history: successive monarchs not only considered it their duty to their people to support good works, but also recognized that it helped maintain the position of the monarchy. Indeed Frank Prochaska argued in *Royal Bounty* that it was of paramount importance to the monarchy: it brought the Royal Family into contact with a wide spectrum of the population, and it underpinned the monarch's role at the head of civic society.

Prochaska used the term 'welfare monarchy' to describe this role. But, as he pointed out, the growth of the welfare state in the twentieth century represented a potential conflict. The first twenty years of Queen Elizabeth II's reign were the heyday of state-directed health and social services in Britain. It was then almost universally accepted that the government should provide health, welfare and much else on a centralized basis. Voluntarism of the sort epitomized by charities supported by the Royal Family seemed almost to be quaint and outdated. Do-gooders or volunteers were not always made to feel welcome, let alone important. And yet, remarkably, they did not go away. To take just one example: in 1962 – fourteen years after the National Health Service was founded – there were 800,000 volunteers in one organization of which Queen Elizabeth was patron, the National League of Hospital Friends. The Labour government of the mid-1960s was in many circumstances ideologically opposed to the voluntary sector, and so, in general, was the civil service. But when Richard Crossman became Secretary of State for Health and Social Security in 1968 he was 'staggered' by the extent of voluntary help in the now twenty-year-old Health Service and he saw its value.[6] Indeed, he realized that the Labour Party's obsession with centralized planning and welfare provision had done 'grievous harm' to philanthropy.

The monarchy's links with the voluntary sector increased. In the mid-1960s, a Mass Observation survey showed that the public identified the Royal Family with their welfare role much more than any other. The survey also showed some correspondents feeling that the Crown was 'a bulwark' against the danger of government taking away too many democratic freedoms.

Merely to note a few of the organizations to which Queen

Elizabeth gave her patronage and the work she did for them over many years – some since she had become duchess of York – is to realize the extent to which the monarchy had been woven into the fabric of British life. There was hardly any aspect of it she did not touch. In her choice of societies and institutions, and in her speeches and messages to them, one can glimpse the nature of her priorities and her vision of the world. Clearly only a few of her patronages can be mentioned here, but a chronological sample can at least show the growth of her interests.* At the same time, it must be admitted that any selection goes against her own firm rule that all should be treated equally. 'Favourite' was a word she always avoided as invidious, whether it was a colour, a flower, food or drink, but most especially if it was a patronage or a regiment.

There is no question, however, that the University of London, of which she became chancellor in 1955, was in a league of its own for her and became one of her principal interests in the second half of her life. King George VI's uncle, the Earl of Athlone, had been chancellor of the University since 1932. Queen Elizabeth had no wish to anticipate the retirement of 'Uncle Alge', but after he had indicated in early 1954 that he did want to step down at the age of seventy-nine, she happily allowed herself to be elected as his successor.[7] In her acceptance speech she said, 'It is my hope that I may be able to forge a personal link between myself and this great University.'[8] And indeed she did. 'It was the spark', Sir Martin Gilliat said later of her appointment, 'which set off this tumultuously varied way of life.'[9]

It helped her to remain in touch with young people, which was something she always sought to do. She was chancellor for twenty-five years, handing over to the Princess Royal in 1980. During this time she carried out 208 engagements for the University and made 132 speeches. Diligently every spring she went to the Albert Hall for the annual graduation ceremonies (Presentation Day), and every winter to Senate House for Foundation Day, when honorary degrees were conferred. Each year she and Gilliat would pore over the long list of the University's colleges and schools, acdemic institutes, halls of residence, libraries and clubs, planning her visits so as to ensure that every aspect of the life of the University was included at some point, from the Institute of Archaeology and Classical Studies to the Sailing

---

* See Appendix B for a complete list of Queen Elizabeth's patronages.

Club, from the CDC 6600 Computer Centre to the Percival David Foundation of Chinese Art at the School of Oriental and African Studies. The University's activities, and thus her visits, were not restricted to London: she went, for instance, to the Marine Biology Station on the Isle of Cumbrae, the British School in Tehran and the British Cultural Centre in Paris, all of which came under 'the marvellous umbrella of the University', as she put it.[10]

Her efforts helped the University's fundraising. In the 1970s, for instance, she strongly supported an appeal which garnered £1,800,000 for a new library for the London School of Economics. She opened the library in July 1979 and after congratulating all who had been assiduous in raising the money she invoked the name of John Ruskin, the distinguished Victorian educationalist: 'Ruskin, in a lecture, once made the somewhat stern observation: "What do we, as a nation, care about books? How much do you think we spend altogether on our libraries, public or private, as compared with what we spend on our *horses*?"' This brought the house down.[11] Lord Annan, the Vice-Chancellor of London University for many years, recalled that whenever she visited any part of the University 'the whole morale of the place shot up. She had that gift of encouraging people simply by being there and taking an interest in what they did.'[12]

One of the features of the University which she particularly liked was its association with the Commonwealth through the universities with which it was linked. One of these was the University of Rhodesia: in 1957 she had opened the University College of Rhodesia at Salisbury and she was its president until it became a university in its own right in 1971. In 1963 she agreed to be president of the Golden Jubilee Congress of the Association of Universities of the Commonwealth, a great gathering of distinguished academics. She attended the Congress's ceremonies for three days in July.

As chancellor she was able to put forward names for honorary degrees each year until 1975; her nominees included her childhood friend Professor Lord David Cecil, as well as Field Marshal the Earl Alexander of Tunis, Sir John Barbirolli, Benjamin Britten, Yehudi Menuhin, Sir Frederick Ashton, Sir Isaiah Berlin and Lord Goodman, the prominent solicitor. She was pleased when Princess Margaret was awarded an honorary doctorate of music in 1957; this she conferred on her daughter at a special ceremony at the Senate House.

Lord Annan recorded that, although she would never interfere in matters of policy, Queen Elizabeth might well express regret at changes. She did not like it when colleges had to be amalgamated and she was unhappy when the University sold the Athlone Press, named after her predecessor. Annan knew when she wanted something done. 'She would just lift her eyebrows slightly and give you a quizzical look as if to say: "I wonder if you could do that." And you knew you ought to do it!' It was equally clear when she did not like something. 'She simply had a way of slightly indicating if things could be done this way rather than that way.' He recalled one occasion in which a member of the House of Commons became rather 'tired and over-emotional' and 'to see the Queen Mother disentangle herself from his advances was really a lesson in courtly and firm behaviour'.[13]

She maintained her interest in the University to the end of her life. She was admitted to honorary fellowships of several colleges, and in September 1999 she approved the proposal that a chair of British History at the Institute of Historical Research should bear her name. David Cannadine was the first to be appointed Queen Elizabeth The Queen Mother Professor of British History, and the subject he chose for his inaugural lecture in 2003 was, appropriately, the historiography of the modern British monarchy. In it he touched upon the themes of this chapter: welfare and warfare, as he put it – royal links with charitable organizations and with the armed services.[14]

In fact, thanks to her popularity and longevity, Queen Elizabeth provided the historian with a striking and unprecedented case study in successful royal patronage, in the form of her ninetieth- and hundredth-birthday parades, which brought together on public display the evidence of her involvement with an extraordinary variety of charitable organizations, educational, medical and learned institutions and elements of the armed services.

In her long life the first patronage Queen Elizabeth had accepted, and retained for almost eighty years, was, appropriately, of Scottish origin. She agreed to become patron of the Girls' Guildry, a Church of Scotland Sunday School organization, just before her marriage in April 1923. She went to her first engagement with the Guildry in Glasgow in September 1924, noting in her diary, 'B. went off to do industrial things & I went to a rally of the Girls' Guildry – about 4000 girls. Very good thing.'[15] In the 1930s she gave them the 'Duchess of York trophy' for an annual needlework competition. Two weeks after the war began in 1939 one of her ladies in waiting wrote to the General Secretary to say that the Queen now felt it was more important 'that quantities of knitted and other garments' should be made by the girls, rather than that they should compete with each other.[16] When the Guildry amalgamated with its English and Irish counterparts in 1965 to become the Girls' Brigade, she became joint patron with the Duchess of Gloucester, who had been patron of the English organization (the Girls' Life Brigade).

Another natural leitmotif of her early patronages was the First World War. She became president of the Royal British Legion Women's Section in 1924. The Legion, formed in 1921 by bringing together the four previous ex-servicemen's organizations, was intended both to perpetuate the memory of those who died in the service of their country and to educate public opinion to the view that support for disabled ex-servicemen and their dependants was a public duty. The emblem of the Legion became the poppy, which had grown so abundantly in the fields of Flanders. Within just a few years of the First World War, the Legion had become one of the most important organizations in British society. Poppy Day was fixed for the Saturday before Remembrance Sunday, which is always the second Sunday in November, close to Armistice Day, 11 November. Every year the Royal British Legion organizes a Festival of Remembrance at the Royal Albert Hall, in the presence of senior members of the Royal Family; the ex-servicemen march to the Cenotaph in Whitehall the following day. Each year the Legion also lays out a Field of Remembrance of poppies on wooden crosses in the churchyard of St Margaret's, Westminster. From its beginning the Duchess and then Queen felt a special affinity with the organization.

In April 1934 she attended the annual conference of the Women's Section. Her handwritten speech commended the work of the section in providing country and seaside holidays for children in 'distressed areas', and praised a new scheme to provide special training for widows and dependants of ex-servicemen who were in a poor state of health but were obliged, 'through their dire need', to seek employment. 'Schemes such as these, which show permanent results in securing the health & happiness of our children, & a means of livelihood & a future free from care, for the women, are worthy of our very best efforts.'[17]

She continued to support them for the next six decades. In May 1991 she attended the national conference in Bournemouth, and in 1999, to mark the seventy-fifth anniversary of her presidency, there was a parade of standards through the garden at Clarence House. Three hundred and forty standards from branches all over the country and 120 marchers led by the Band of the Irish Guards marched past Queen Elizabeth, who took the salute from the steps of the Garden Room. It was an astonishing spectacle which lasted some fifteen minutes, with a sea of blue and gold standards carried by women of all ages and sizes. Queen Elizabeth loved it, as she did the Legion.[18]

It seems to have been her mother's involvement with the Church of England Children's Society which led the Duchess of York to accept its patronage in 1924. In 1947, she sent a message on the Society's Diamond Jubilee in which she said, 'The care of children is near to my heart, and is all the more dear to me because my Mother for so many years took such a deep interest in the Society.'[19] Over the years she attended Founders' Day Festivals at the Royal Albert Hall and in 1986 she opened the Society's new headquarters in Margery Street, in the Finsbury district of London. She supported many appeals to raise funds to help the children, dispatching another member of the Royal Family if she was unable to go.

Other children's charities looked to her for support: one was the Children's Country Holiday Fund, which Queen Elizabeth first took on as Duchess of York after the death of Queen Alexandra in 1925. The Fund organized holidays for underprivileged city children, and the Duchess's visit to a holiday camp in Epping Forest for a thousand slum children in 1923, one of her first public engagements after her marriage, may have sparked her lifelong interest in this organization. Even in the late 1990s there were plenty of children who needed the Fund's help.

Another long-lasting patronage had its origins in the First World War. This was Toc H, a worldwide movement which began as a club for soldiers opened in 1915 in Belgium by the Rev. Philip 'Tubby' Clayton. The club was intended to allow all ranks to mix freely, an unusual concept at the time. It was at first called Talbot House after a friend of Clayton, the Rev. Gilbert Talbot, who was killed in battle. But the name Talbot House soon became known to the soldiers of the Ypres Salient as Toc H, Toc being the army signaller's code for 'T'.

The club became an invaluable home from home for thousands of young soldiers whose morale had been damaged, if not destroyed, on the battlefield. After the Great War, Clayton transformed Toc H into an international Christian organization, designed to express ideals of co-operation and friendship across the barriers that often divide communities. Much of its work came to involve the improvement of children's lives. Each branch of Toc H had a little lamp similar to that used by Tubby Clayton which members lit for their 'ceremony of light' at meetings. Toc H was incorporated by Royal Charter in 1922.

Queen Elizabeth's involvement with Toc H seems to have begun during her Australian tour as Duchess of York in 1927, when she was given a banner by the Australian League of Toc H. On her return this was presented to Tubby Clayton at a short ceremony at his church in London, All Hallows Berkyngechirche by the Tower. Soon after that she became patron of the Toc H League of Women Helpers.

In July 1939, when she and the King visited the Royal Naval College at Dartmouth, she surprised and gratified a college servant by immediately noticing his Toc H badge and speaking to him about the movement.[20] (This was one of many examples of her sharp eye for badges and other insignia, military or civilian.) In 1948, as we have seen, at the request of Tubby Clayton she laid the foundation stone for the rebuilding of his church, which had been bombed during the war, and she regularly accepted Clayton's requests for messages thereafter. When Tubby Clayton died in 1972 Martin Gilliat wrote warmly to the Director of Toc H of Queen Elizabeth's long and close association with his work.[21]

St Mary's Hospital, Paddington, one of the great London teaching hospitals, asked the Duchess of York to be its president in 1930. She accepted the invitation. Her first official visit to the hospital was in 1934 and in 1936 she opened the first phase of the new Nurses' Home, and then a new wing for paying patients. In 1945 she granted her patronage to the 5,000th performance of *Me and My Gal*, the proceeds of which went to the hospital.[22] When the National Health Service was introduced, the Queen made it clear that she had no wish to give up her role. Sir Arthur Penn wrote to the House Governor of St Mary's saying, 'I do not suppose that there would be a desire on the part of any authority to suggest the termination of Her Majesty's Presidency of St Mary's Hospital, which I am sure she will never contemplate readily.'[23] The Minister of Health, however, decreed that the position of president of an NHS hospital could no longer exist, and so the Queen became honorary president.[24] Throughout the decades to come she continued to pay visits to the hospital; she presented prizes to nurses, attended the centenary celebrations at the medical school, and opened the east wing of the medical school and the new nurses' training school. She laid the foundation stone of the new paediatric Accident and Emergency wing of the hospital and opened the completed building, which was called the Queen Elizabeth The Queen Mother Wing.[25]

The Queen Mother's links with another institution to which she gave her name, Queen Elizabeth's Foundation for Disabled People, went back to 1934 when she launched the fundraising drive for what was then called the Cripples' Training College, at a public meeting at Mansion House. The project was the brainchild of the formidable Georgiana Buller, who had been made a Dame of the Order of the British Empire (DBE) for her hospital work in the First World War and afterwards devoted herself to the rehabilitation of the disabled. In 1935 the Duchess opened the College at Leatherhead Court in Surrey. Her handwritten speech extolling its work survives in her papers.[26] In 1942 she agreed to the College's name being changed to Queen Elizabeth's Training College for the Disabled, and still later to its renaming as a foundation. She became its patron in 1953. In 1960 she visited it for its silver jubilee, and over the years opened various new buildings and supported fundraising efforts.[27]

Not surprisingly, national women's organizations often sought her patronage, but some she enjoyed supporting on a small and local scale. One of the domestic organizations near to both her home and her heart was the Sandringham Women's Institute, whose meetings she appears to have first attended in 1924. After she became queen she was appointed joint president with Queen Mary and every year she wrote out her own speech for the annual general meeting. In 1943 she praised the women for all the 'splendid' war work they had been doing: 'The collections of rose-hips, of horse-chestnuts, of rags & bones, the jam making, the savings group, the knitting, & the 90 per cent wartime supper dishes are some of the ways in which you here are helping to win the war.'[28] In January 1945, with victory in sight, she reported the King's praise of all their work. In the final effort to beat the Germans, she knew, Sandringham Women's Institute 'will do their bit'.[29]

In 1951 she quoted poignant words from the King's 1950 Christmas broadcast: 'Our motto must be, whatever comes, or does not come, I will not be afraid, for it is on each individual effort that the safety and happiness of the whole depends. And what counts is the spirit in which each one of us fulfils his or her appointed task.'[30] These were sentiments which informed her own approach to life. In 1954, after the devastating east-coast floods of the previous year, she praised the Sandringham WI for all the help they had given their neighbours in distress. 'It is encouraging to think that when disaster strikes, self is forgotten, & the uplifting thought, "Love thy neighbour" is uppermost in people's minds.'[31]

Twenty-two years later, at a time of advances in feminist legisla-tion, she insisted that 'the WI were pioneers in many of the moves towards a fairer society, and for the equal treatment of women in that society. And talking of that, what about the new Sex Discrimination Act? What are we going to do if the husbands & fathers demand to join, & win the competition for a covered coat hanger or knitted bootees?'[32] In her 1987 speech she praised the caring nature of the WI. 'The Annual Report tells of countless acts of kindness to the elderly, the lonely and the sick – and to be cherished & knowing that someone cares, must be of infinite comfort to the recipients. This is an important side of community life.'[33] Her message was always one of positive action and determined optimism.

Queen Elizabeth became president of the British Red Cross Society in January 1937 when King George VI became patron. (She had been elected to the governing council in 1923.) The Society, incorporated by Royal Charter in 1908, was part of the International Red Cross organization. By the middle of the twentieth century the British Red Cross was one of the largest and most effective charities in the country.

During the Second World War, the British Red Cross worked closely with the St John Ambulance Brigade and played a vital role in helping civilian victims of German bombing. Queen Elizabeth's child-hood home, St Paul's Walden Bury, was used as a Red Cross convalescent home, as it had been in the First World War. Throughout the war the Queen identified herself with Red Cross work, attended its services in Westminster Abbey, visited Red Cross depots and exhibi-tions and sales to raise money for its work. After the death of the King she became vice-president of the Society and her daughter the Queen became patron and president. For the rest of her life Queen Elizabeth remained involved with it and after her death the Society launched the

Queen Mother Appeal which by June 2002 had raised some £250,000 to be used specifically for the expansion and modernization of their vital tracing and messaging services.[34]

One of the charities to which she gave most financial assistance was the Soldiers', Sailors' and Airmen's Families' Association. She became patron in 1937 but was much more closely involved after 1946, when Mrs Constance Cooke, widow of the Captain of HMS *Barham*, a ship which was sunk during the war with heavy loss of life, sought help to set up a rest home for bereaved widows and children. The Queen thought there was a genuine need for such a home but, after much discussion, felt that a fund would be more useful, so that money from it could be used by *Barham* widows as they pleased. In 1948 the Queen's Fund was set up and the initial sum raised was £10,000. The Queen contributed generously to it, using at first some money from the Queen's Canadian Fund.* She continued to take an active interest in how the Fund's money was spent (she often called it 'her' fund), and raised her own contributions from £2,500 a year in 1960 to £15,000 a year from 1993 onwards.[35]

A patronage which reflected a personal passion was the Aberdeen Angus Cattle Society, of which King George VI became patron and she patroness in 1937. There had been royal patrons since the time of Queen Victoria, and Glamis lay in one of the principal districts from which the breed took its name. The Strathmores kept a herd of the cattle and the King and Queen began their own small herd on the farm at Abergeldie, near Balmoral. After the King's death Queen Elizabeth became patron, and started her own herd at the Castle of Mey in 1964. She was increasingly involved with the society, and in later years regularly invited the Society's President and its long-serving secretary, Captain Ben Coutts, to Mey. In October 1970 she opened the new headquarters of the Society in Perth and watched the final judging of the supreme championship at the bull sale, presenting the

---

* This fund, set up in 1941 on the initiative of a Canadian Battle of Britain pilot, Flight Lieutenant Hartland de M. Molson, raised huge sums in Canada, initially for British victims of air raids, under the chairmanship of John G. McConnell. The organizers wanted it to be associated with Queen Elizabeth, and she allowed it to use her name, and also agreed to a later proposal that its work should extend throughout the Empire, and to victims of all kinds of enemy attack. By December 1941 it had raised £145,000; by VE Day $1,655,252 had been collected. It ceased to make appeals after May 1945, and its funds were used to support the WVS and SSAFA. (RA QEQMH/PS/CSP/Queen's Canadian Fund)

Balfour Trophy to the winning owner. The Society gave her a heifer calf for her herd, called Queen Mother of Clackmae.

Her interest in the breed was noted in farming communities far and wide, and over the years she attended meetings of national Aberdeen Angus Associations and sent messages of support to those in the United States, Canada, Australia and New Zealand. It was an entirely happy connection; she delighted in both the cattle and the people who bred them, and the breeders rejoiced in her support. An Aberdeen Angus bull took part in both her ninetieth- and her hundredth-birthday parades.

In 1938 she joined the King as a patron of the Royal College of Music and from 1946 an award given to young British-born performers was named the Queen's Prize in her honour. After the death of the King she became president of the College, with the responsibility of approving the nominations of honorary fellows and Council members. The date of the annual concert and prize giving was always fixed to suit her diary. In 1981 she was pleased to be asked to confer an honorary doctorate of music on Prince Charles, to whom she handed on the presidency in 1993, when she became president emerita and gave £60,000 to fund a scholarship.[36]

Her pleasure on becoming a master of the Bench of the Middle Temple in 1944 has already been noted. In 1957 she opened the Queen Elizabeth Building and the following year she attended a service for the rededication of the Temple Church and also opened the new library. In the early 1960s the Middle Temple arranged for some of its overseas students to spend a weekend at Cumberland Lodge; this proved so successful that arrangements were made for two weekends a year to be reserved for them. Whenever possible she invited a number of the students to drinks at Royal Lodge after morning service at the Royal Chapel. She often attended Grand Night in the summer and she made a point of dining every year (except for a few occasions when she was unwell) with the Benchers on Family Night. Her last such dinner took place on 5 December 2001.[37]

A musical fixture close to her heart was the King's Lynn Festival, of which she had been patron since her friend and lady in waiting Ruth Fermoy launched it in 1950. The tradition developed that she would hold a house party at Sandringham during the Festival at the end of July. Every year at this time the Queen gave over the house to her mother, and thus sometimes became a guest in her own home.

Lady Fermoy died in 1993 but Queen Elizabeth continued her patron-age every year until the end of her life.[38]

The Friends of St Paul's Cathedral sprang from members of the St Paul's Watch who had helped to save the Cathedral from fire and destruction in the war, and Queen Elizabeth was happy to give them her patronage in 1952. She loved the Cathedral and its Friends and she attended their Festival Service every year from 1953 to 2001, missing only five years in the 1960s and 1970s.[39]

Just as she had done after Queen Alexandra's death in 1926, she took on extra patronages after the death of Queen Mary in 1953. One such was Queen Mary's Clothing Guild, which had been created by Queen Mary to provide clothing for needy people. Members had their own groups of workers who either made or bought articles of clothing for the Guild. Each member was expected to provide two articles a year; these were all collected in the autumn and unpacked and displayed in November at the Imperial Institute, and later at St James's Palace. Queen Elizabeth always attended the Guild's AGM and would invite a guest speaker, who lunched with her at Clarence House beforehand. Her choices were typically unpredictable, ranging from the female comedians Elsie and Doris Waters (who starred as Gert and Daisy), and their brother the actor Jack Warner (who played the reassuring policeman Dixon of Dock Green in one of the earliest TV soap operas), to Clement Freud, the broadcaster, politician and humor-ist, and Churchill's daughter Mary Soames. She was fond of Jack Profumo who, since his political downfall in 1963, had redeemed himself by good works in London's East End, and she invited him three times. She also took the Guild's Scottish branch, run by Clare Russell at Ballindalloch Castle, under her wing and attended its viewing day. When a proposal was made to expand the Guild and put it on a more commercial footing, she resisted, arguing that its personal scale was what made it so appreciated.[40] By the end of her life the Guild's finances had improved markedly – subscriptions and donations reached £10,000 and it had received two large legacies.[41]

Another of Queen Mary's patronages had been the National Trust, of which she was president, and this too Queen Elizabeth took over in 1953. Given her love of history, tradition and culture it was an appropriate appointment – she was already patron of the National Trust for Scotland. Over the years she visited a large number of the Trust's properties throughout the country. After the hurricane which

59. The Queen in Paris, July 1938. Her wardrobe of 'mourning white' was designed for her by Norman Hartnell following the death of her mother in June that year.

60. The Queen launching the Cunard liner *Queen Elizabeth*, 27 September 1938.

61. The King and Queen on the royal train as they leave Toronto, June 1939.

62. The Queen driving through Washington D.C. with Eleanor Roosevelt, 8 June 1939.

63. The King and Queen talking to a shipyard worker on a wartime tour of the North-west, 2 September 1940.

64. The Queen on a wartime tour of south London, talking to bombed-out residents, 11 September 1940.

65. 'Dear old B.P. is <u>still standing</u>!' The King and Queen surveying the damage after the bombing of Buckingham Palace on 9 September 1940.

66. The Queen visiting an air-raid shelter in an Underground station, at the height of the Blitz, in November 1940.

67. The King and Queen talking to young air-raid victims having their supper at a rest centre in November 1940.

68. The King and Queen visiting a bomb site in London, April 1941.

69. With the Princesses at a wartime poetry reading on 14 April 1943. Left to right: Arthur Waley, Princess Elizabeth, Osbert Sitwell, the Queen, Princess Margaret and Walter De La Mare.

70. The Princesses on stage in the 1944 Windsor Castle pantomime, *Old Mother Red Riding Boots*.

71. VE Day, 8 May 1945.

72. 'We four' on tour in South Africa, 1947, with the police crew of the White Train.

73. The King and Queen en route to St Paul's Cathedral for a service to celebrate their Silver Wedding, 26 April 1948.

74. The Queen presenting the King with a cup for the best Aberdeen Angus at the Royal Norfolk Show, May 1950.

75. Four generations of the Royal Family at the christening of Princess Anne, 21 November 1950. Left to right: Queen Mary, the King, Princess Elizabeth holding Princess Anne, the Duke of Edinburgh, Prince Charles, the Queen.

76. The three Queens awaiting the coffin of King George VI, February 1952.

uprooted thousands of trees across south-east England in October 1987 Angus Stirling, the Director General of the Trust, wrote Queen Elizabeth a long report setting out the damage to its properties. She annotated his letter: 'Please thank him for his excellent letter. Perhaps you could tell him what the Queen said yesterday. "We must stop sobbing and start planting."'[42]

In 1966 she took on another university chancellorship – at Dundee, a town she had known since childhood. She was installed in October 1967, reminding students that their 'rights' brought with them obligations.[43] The following year she attended the installation as rector of the University of the actor Peter Ustinov, who later recalled that it was at the height of the student revolts across Europe and the United States. As the solemn procession arrived, the students pelted it with rolls of lavatory paper like streamers. Ustinov recalled, 'The Queen Mother stopped and picked these up as though somebody had misplaced them. "Was this yours? Oh, could you take it?" And it was her sang froid and her absolute refusal to be shocked by this, which immediately silenced all the students.' Ustinov, a good judge of character as well as of comic timing, admired her greatly. 'She is capable of riding any sort of wave that comes along and coming out the other side looking exactly as she did when she went in ... an extraordinary pool of calmness seems to spread around her.'[44]

Smaller charities held her attention too, and one of these was, for obvious reasons, the Injured Jockeys Fund, though she did not grant it her patronage until 1973. If she were asked for a charity which could benefit from fundraising events, she often suggested this one. From time to time she lunched with the trustees; her lunch with them at the Goring Hotel on 6 December 2001 was her last public engagement.[45]

Her enjoyment of music, as we have seen, was often reflected in her patronage. She was fond of Benjamin Britten and his companion the singer Peter Pears; they were her guests at Sandringham in 1968 and 1970, and to their delight she agreed in 1974 to become president of their Aldeburgh Festival.[46] The following year she visited Britten and Pears at home in Aldeburgh and attended a 'Patron's Choice' concert of music she had suggested, beginning with Britten's Prelude and Fugue for strings and ending with Berlioz's *Nuits d'Eté* sung by Janet Baker.[47]* In later years she went to concerts and receptions in aid

---

* Benjamin Britten's health was failing following a stroke, but that year the Queen

of the Festival held in London, and at the 2002 Festival a special performance was given in her memory.[48]

Some tiny organizations gave her particular amusement. Close to Sandringham, in a small house called Stores Bungalow, lived an enthusiast called Arthur Hammond Browne who had founded what he called the Sandringham Fur and Feather Show. This was for farmyard birds and small animals, and was to be held each year in conjunction with the Sandringham Flower Show. At the age of eighty in January 1977 Arthur Browne wrote to ask the Queen Mother if she would be patron for this year of the Silver Jubilee. She had no doubts – 'I would LOVE to be Patron of the S F & F Society for 1977!' she noted for her Treasurer. 'I do love enthusiasts, don't you?'[49]

Browne offered her a pair of Buff Orpington chickens, which she accepted, agreeing that he should look after and exhibit the birds on her behalf. The pair won many prizes and became quite famous; she loved getting Browne's letters describing the shows to which he took them. Of one letter she commented, 'He's quite right. The Olympics are <u>nothing</u> compared with F & F!'[50] In 1988 Browne wrote to say he was too old to look after her birds any longer; they were taken on by Will Burdett, the President of the Poultry Club, of which the Queen Mother was also patron from 1977 onwards. Her interest continued. When she heard of a young boy who lost his Buff Orpingtons to a fox, she asked Burdett to send him some eggs, which he did. The twelve-year-old Tom Clarke hatched the eggs successfully, became a junior member of the Buff Orpington Club and some years later went on to win Supreme Championship at the Poultry Show at Alexandra Palace.[51]

Queen Elizabeth found any requests involving the military hard to resist and in 1983 she agreed to a personal appeal that she become president of the Victoria Cross and George Cross Association. This held special significance for her because the George Cross had been instituted by King George VI in September 1940, at the height of the Battle of Britain, to honour acts of heroism, primarily by civilians. She had always looked on holders of these two medals with admiration. Most years thereafter she attended their service at St Martin in the Fields in Trafalgar Square and she gave the President's Tea Party

---

commissioned him to compose a short piece as a surprise present for Queen Elizabeth's seventy-fifth birthday. The result was *A Birthday Hansel*, a setting for voice and harp of poems by Robert Burns.

at St James's Palace. In the last year of her life she attended both events.[52]

Age did not deter her from accepting new patronages and taking a lively interest in them – in February 2000 she agreed to become patron of the Clan Sinclair Trust, set up by her neighbour at Mey, the Earl of Caithness. With her characteristic flair for the picturesque phrase, she altered the last words of the message drafted for her for the Trust's brochure from 'the edge of the North Sea' to 'the wild shores of the North Sea'.[53] In September 2001 she agreed to become patron of the Longhope Lifeboat Museum Trust.[54] And in January 2002 Sir Peter O'Sullevan, the horseracing commentator, asked her to be patron of his charitable trust which raised money for racing and animal charities. She agreed.[55]

Other charities with which she was long involved have already been mentioned – such as the Royal Foundation of St Katharine in Ratcliffe, another of the patronages in which she succeeded Queen Mary. Then there was Cumberland Lodge, in which she had invested so much hope for the spiritual improvement of graduates when the foundation was set up after the end of the war. Through the decades the College, while retaining its belief in Christian ethics, came to provide a relaxed but also challenging environment in which different groups of people could meet to look beyond their own disciplines to the wider issues affecting society.

Queen Elizabeth kept in close touch with the Lodge, its recurrent financial problems and its development. Since it was so close to Royal Lodge in Windsor Great Park, she often visited. At the time of her eightieth birthday the then Principal, Walter James, wrote that the work she had done for Cumberland Lodge 'is, it is fair to say, the most striking contribution to university life made by a member of the Royal Family this century'.[56]

Her interest in Cumberland Lodge never flagged, and in 2001 she agreed to the naming of two new fellowships – the King George VI Fellowship and the Queen Elizabeth Fellowship – at the Lodge. Her involvement remained personal as well as institutional, and many who attended sessions at Cumberland Lodge found themselves invited to meet her at Royal Lodge. The preacher to Harvard University, Peter Gomes, attended one such occasion. 'Tell me, Professor Gomes,' she said, as he sat down beside her, 'do you give them good news from the pulpit? I do so like good news on a Sunday.'[57] (After her death

Professor Gomes preached at a memorial service held for her in Boston.)

*

AS DAVID CANNADINE has pointed out, the monarchy's links with the armed services go back to the days when the sovereign himself led his troops into battle. Those days are gone, but the sovereign is still the head of the armed forces, and successive monarchs have been careful to maintain the connection, visiting their forces, taking a close interest in military appointments and reforms, and sending their sons to serve in the army or navy.

An important element of this relationship is that of the honorary appointments, particularly in the army, which the monarch has either held in person or has delegated to other members of the Royal Family. These provide powerful personal links. An admired figurehead as colonel-in-chief or honorary colonel gives great encouragement to a regiment, boosting cohesion and morale; if the figurehead is royal, the effect is enhanced. Visits, parades, the presentation of colours, messages of congratulation or encouragement and an active interest in the affairs of the regiment, all help foster the vital sense of the regiment as a family, and its inherent pride in itself.

Female members of the Royal Family are almost always sought for such tasks, and Queen Elizabeth was particularly well qualified. The daughter and sister of army officers, she had seen her brothers go off to war and experienced the anxiety and loss this can bring to families; she had also got to know and like ordinary soldiers in the convalescent hospital at Glamis, and had seen the effects of war on them. She was imbued with the spirit of service in which she had been brought up and saw the military ethos as an absolutely essential part of what it meant to be British.

It is hardly surprising, therefore, that she took a close and persistent interest in all the regiments of which she became colonel-in-chief or honorary colonel. She did whatever was expected of her – visits, messages, presentation of colours or guidons,* receiving commanding officers on change-over. But her individual style showed itself in such thoughtful gestures as sending Canadian violets to a Canadian regiment which found itself in Britain and facing war for the first time, in 1941,[58]

---

* The term used for regimental colours in the cavalry.

or encouraging commanding officers to write to her with news of the regiments. She assiduously read and commented on their letters and even regimental annual reports. There was a pattern: she was invariably in favour of whatever gave regiments and other units their individuality and sense of identity, whether uniforms, badges, rank titles or – most especially – territorial connections. She deplored the loss of these through the reductions and mergers which happened increasingly in her later years as one government after another cut down on British military spending. She maintained that the old county names were very valuable in recruiting and that uncertainty created by successive strategic reviews was terrible for morale. As for the sacrifice of regimental bands, that was 'a real disaster . . . such a stupid way to economise'.[59]

The first regiment of which she was appointed colonel-in-chief was the King's Own Yorkshire Light Infantry (KOYLI); this was in 1927, and she visited them at their depot at Pontefract in 1928. That year she approved the affiliation of KOYLI with the Saskatoon Light Infantry (to which she presented colours during the Canadian tour of 1939) and a further link with the 51st Battalion of Australian Infantry. She kept in touch with the regiment by holding periodic at-homes for officers.

With the reorganization of the infantry in 1967, it was decided that KOYLI should be amalgamated with the Somerset and Cornwall Light Infantry, the King's Shropshire Light Infantry and the Durham Light Infantry to form the Light Infantry. The Queen Mother accepted the appointment of colonel-in-chief of the new regiment in 1968, with Princess Alexandra, who had been colonel-in-chief of the Durham Light Infantry, as her deputy. She was as conscientious as always in following the regiment's affairs, visiting them, presenting colours, reading and annotating their annual reports.

She nevertheless kept up a special link with 'her' former regiment, KOYLI. In June 1997 she attended a luncheon at Claridge's given by the Officers' Club to mark the seventieth anniversary of her becoming their colonel-in-chief. This was followed by another such lunch in June 2000, her last KOYLI engagement.

Of all the regiments with which she was involved, one of the most important to her was, as we have already seen, the Black Watch (Royal Highland Regiment), in whose ranks three of her brothers had served and one, Fergus, had been killed in 1915; her nephews Timothy Bowes Lyon (Patrick's second son) and John Elphinstone served in the regiment in the Second World War. The Queen was appointed colonel-in-chief just four days after the Coronation in May 1937, and later that year she became patron of the Black Watch Association as well. In December 1937 the senior officers of the regiment presented her with a regimental brooch which she wore on all Black Watch occasions.

She followed the regiment's fortunes closely during the war, and successive colonels of the regiment wrote to keep her informed. She was, as we have seen, distressed by news of the capture of almost the entire 1st Battalion during the Dunkirk evacuation in June 1940, but she recognized the need to remain positive and sent an encouraging message to the Colonel of the regiment, welcoming the proposal to re-form the 1st Battalion.[60]

In November 1941 the Queen addressed the 6th Battalion, which was about to leave for North Africa, at Danesbury Stables in Stockbridge. She congratulated the men on their 'splendid bearing'. She trusted that 'it may not be long before you return safely to your dear ones at home, with your task accomplished, and duty nobly done.'[61]

In his letter of thanks General Wauchope, who had succeeded General Cameron as colonel, wrote: 'It may interest Her Majesty that the two phrases they most appreciated were: that she hoped that they might soon return to their families & homes after they had accomplished their task: that when they were abroad, she would often wear the Black Watch brooch, and whenever she did she would think of the 6th Battalion.'[62] In February 1944 she visited three battalions in one day at camps in Buckinghamshire – the 1st, 5th and 7th, all of which had been in action in North Africa and had contributed to victory at El Alamein. The three battalions were soon to be among the forces taking part in the Normandy landings.

Her concern for the Black Watch continued throughout the postwar years – particularly when cutbacks were imposed. Again and again, she visited units in Berlin, in Northern Ireland, in Scotland – taking salutes, lunching with the officers and taking part in cherished ceremonies. On the sixtieth anniversary of her appointment as colonel-in-chief, in September 1997, she made a forty-minute helicopter journey from Birkhall to visit the 1st Battalion at Fort George in Invernessshire. Her last engagement with the regiment was her attendance at the 3rd (Volunteer) Battalion Drumhead Service and luncheon afterwards at Glamis Castle on 20 September 1998. Now ninety-eight herself, she made the one-and-a-half-hour drive from Birkhall to Glamis; in the afternoon the old colours which she had presented in 1975 were ceremonially escorted off the parade ground, to be laid up in Glamis Castle.[63]

Her attention often had a remarkable effect on regiments. In July 1937, as recently appointed colonel-in-chief of the Queen's Bays, the Queen visited them at Aldershot, just two months after the Coronation. The commanding officer, Lieutenant Colonel E. D. Fanshawe, wrote, 'Ever since Her Majesty's appointment as Colonel an entire change has taken place. Now, after her visit on Saturday, I have no fear for the future. She has done more good than it is possible to imagine.'[64] During the war the Queen's Bays served with distinction with the Eighth Army in Egypt against Rommel.

Throughout the war the Queen was sent reports and letters by the Colonel and by commanding officers, who told her of actions in which the regiment had been engaged and its successes and losses. In his reply to one such letter, Arthur Penn wrote in April 1942 that the Queen shared their sorrow at their losses and their anxiety over men missing in action and that 'direct news is always extremely welcome.'[65] The news was not always serious. 'The Queen has learnt with interest', Arthur Penn wrote to the commanding officer in 1943, 'of the arrangements you are contemplating for Christmas and hopes that the pigs, which have made a fresh addition to the booty already credited to your Regiment, may provide a satisfactory substitute for the turkeys who have failed to put in the appearance which is generally considered the principal justification for their existence.'[66]

Thirteen years later, in 1957, Queen Elizabeth was informed of the decision to amalgamate the Queen's Bays with the King's Dragoon Guards. She was again dismayed and Martin Gilliat wrote to the Colonel saying, 'I have had an opportunity of showing your letter to the Colonel-in-Chief, and I feel that no words of mine are needed to emphasise how sad Queen Elizabeth is that amalgamation should have been ordained for the Regiment.'[67] It went ahead, however, and she paid a valedictory visit at Tidworth on 1 November 1958. The new regiment was named 1st The Queen's Dragoon Guards and she inspected and addressed it on a number of occasions, both at home and overseas, throughout the decades to come. Her involvement was unfailing through the Gulf War in the early 1990s and up until the year before her death. When the commanding officer sent her his annual report in January 2001 – a four-page document covering all aspects of regimental activities – she could barely see to read. But she clearly still cared and wrote on it, 'How can a Regiment function with only 300 men?'[68] That November she received the new commanding officer of the regiment for the last time.

The Royal Army Medical Corps came under her care after the death in 1942 of Prince Arthur, Duke of Connaught, Queen Victoria's third and longest-lived son. Succeeding him as colonel-in-chief, the Queen first visited the corps depot at Boyce Barracks, Crookham, in December 1943. To commemorate the Golden Jubilee of the corps in 1948, these barracks were renamed after her. Thereafter she kept in touch with the affairs of the RAMC through periodic reports, and regularly exchanged messages with them.

In 1947 she became colonel-in-chief of the 7th Queen's Own Hussars. In 1958 they were compelled to merge with the 3rd King's Own Hussars and she became colonel-in-chief of the newly formed regiment, called the Queen's Own Hussars. She kept in constant touch with them too and sympathized with them over the continual cuts imposed upon them. On one of the regiment's annual reports she wrote, 'How well all these Regiments cope with such difficult modern circumstances.'[69]

With the Hussars she showed her concern particularly with regard to their horses. In 1974 when told that Crusader, their drum horse, was to be retired, she sought another for them. The Crown Equerry, Sir John Miller, who was in charge of the Royal Mews, found a suitable horse belonging to the St Cuthbert's Co-operative Society in Edinburgh; the price was £300. The regiment accepted him with pleasure and named him Dettingen. When, in 1988, Dettingen had to be destroyed, she found a replacement with the Crown Equerry's help. It was a great occasion when she presented the new drum horse, Peninsula, to the Colonel and commanding officer of the regiment in her own garden at Clarence House on 4 May 1988.

The regiment amalgamated with the Queen's Royal Irish Hussars in 1993 to become the Queen's Royal Hussars (the Queen's Own and Royal Irish), and, despite her sadness, Queen Elizabeth agreed once again to become colonel-in-chief. In June 1997, just a few weeks before her ninety-seventh birthday, she travelled in the royal train with the

Duke of Edinburgh, who was deputy colonel-in-chief, to present a new guidon to the regiment at Cambrai Barracks at Catterick in Yorkshire. She slept aboard the train and next day she and the Duke inspected the regiment in a Range Rover. The old guidons were marched off, the new one consecrated, and Queen Elizabeth made a short speech congratulating the regiment.[70]

After meeting past colonels and others, and lunching in the officers' mess, she and the Duke flew back to London. Many of the officers and men marvelled at the stamina and will of their colonel-in-chief. It was not yet exhausted: in November 1999 she attended the regimental reception in St James's Palace, and her last engagement with the regiment was to receive the commanding officers at Clarence House on 22 February 2001.

Another 1947 appointment was that of colonel-in-chief of the Manchester Regiment, which in 1958 was merged with the King's Regiment (Liverpool). Like all other mergers this one caused unhappiness, but Brigadier R. N. M. Jones, the Colonel of the King's Regiment, wrote to Queen Elizabeth to say how delighted they were that she was to be colonel-in-chief of the new combined King's Regiment (Manchester and Liverpool). 'There is nothing else that could go such a long way towards softening the blow of the loss of our separate identity.'[71] Over the next four decades, she was always in touch, sending messages of congratulation or of sympathy, as when Kingsmen lost their lives in terrorist attacks in Londonderry in October 1990.[72]

In July 1993 she presented new colours to the 1st Battalion, congratulating them on their bearing and on the way in which they had upheld the high traditions of the regiment on operations in Northern Ireland.[73] In 1998, after receiving the Colonel's report, she commented on the envelope, 'This is a wonderful record. I do hope that the 2 Territorial Companies survive. It is so important.'[74]

In 1953, in honour of her Coronation, the Queen appointed her mother colonel-in-chief of the 9th Queen's Royal Lancers. During the next few years the regiment was serving in Germany and she was unable to visit them there; but in 1960 she presented a guidon to the regiment at Tidworth and attended a regimental dinner and ball in London. Later that year the regiment was amalgamated with the 12th Royal Lancers to form the 9th/12th Royal Lancers (Prince of Wales's), and Queen Elizabeth was appointed colonel-in-chief of the new regiment. She visited them in Northern Ireland and in Germany, and, in keeping with her practice of finding homes for all her retired racehorses, in 1969 she gave them Bel Ambre and later Barometer.

Queen Elizabeth was always nostalgic about her home county of Hertfordshire, and in 1949 she had become colonel-in-chief of the Bedfordshire and Hertfordshire Regiment, retaining the appointment when the regiment amalgamated with the Essex Regiment to form the 3rd East Anglian Regiment in 1958. In 1964 there was a further series of mergers and the Royal Anglian Regiment was formed; the Queen Mother was appointed colonel-in-chief, with Princess Margaret and Princess Alice, Duchess of Gloucester becoming deputy colonels-in-chief; all three royal ladies attended a reception at St James's Palace to celebrate the formation of the new regiment in November that year. Over the ensuing years Queen Elizabeth followed the fortunes of the regiment, always regretting mergers which reduced its strength and its territorial links, and doing all she could to ensure that at least cap badges and regimental buttons were maintained where possible.

In February 1988 the Queen Mother received a representative group from the Royal Anglian Regiment at Clarence House to mark the fiftieth anniversary of her becoming honorary colonel of the Hertfordshire Regiment, part of the Territorial Army. In the Territorials the appointment of honorary colonel is the equivalent of that of colonel-in-chief in the regular army. This was one of several honorary colonelcies which she accepted over the years. The Hertfordshire Regiment (TA) had a distinguished war and took part in the Normandy landings in June 1944. Queen Elizabeth had been once more upset when in 1960 she learned that the new order of battle for the Territorial Army did not contain the name of the regiment after its proposed amalgamation with the 5th Battalion The Bedfordshire Regiment. 'The lack of imagination shown by the War Office is too depressing,' she remarked privately.[75] There was much correspondence between Clarence House, the War Office, David Bowes Lyon (who was now lord lieutenant of Hertfordshire) and various generals over the thorny question; at one point the Queen Mother commented, 'What a very irritating letter!'[76] But she and her brother eventually won this particular battle: in July 1961, the War Office finally agreed that the regiment's new name should be the 1st Battalion the Bedfordshire and Hertfordshire Regiment (TA). Eventually, when the regiment was incorporated into the 3rd East Anglian Regiment, of which she was colonel-in-chief, she relinquished the honorary colonelcy.

Even earlier than the Hertfordshire Regiment, the 14th London Regiment (London Scottish) had claimed her as honorary colonel in 1935. As has already been mentioned,* she had used all her powers of persuasion with King George V to allow her to take it on:

> You know that they consist of Scottish business people, clerks, and city workers who give up hard earned leisure to doing a little soldiering, and for years now, they have been pining and panting for you to make me their Colonel . . . I would like it very much, as I have taken an interest in the London Scots for some time now, and as it is really rather like being President of something, I could perhaps help them in some ways. Lord Haig was their Colonel for years, and you know how sentimental my countrymen are, so they won't have anybody else, unless it is your loving and dutiful daughter in law, who hates troubling you about the matter, but who thinks it better really to put the facts as clearly as possible.[77]

No doubt she also remembered the 'London Scotties' who had been among her favourite convalescent soldiers at Glamis in the First World War. In later years the regiment repaid her interest by providing her with a piper in London, who piped at Clarence House on her birthdays.

As a master bencher of the Middle Temple, Queen Elizabeth took a special interest in the Inns of Court Regiment, and in November 1949 – the year in which she served as treasurer of the Middle Temple – she visited the regiment at Lincoln's Inn. In 1954 she presented colours to it and in 1957 she agreed to become joint honorary colonel with the Marquess of Reading. She became honorary colonel of the City of London Yeomanry (Rough Riders) soon after the death of the King in 1952. The Rough Riders were linked to another of her regiments, the Queen's Bays, and she was saddened when, because of government-imposed changes in 1956, this association had to end.[78] Only four years later the Rough Riders were subject to another amalgamation – with the Inns of Court and City Regiment. She exclaimed, 'my goodness what traditions & feeling of service they are

* See p. 342.

destroying in the Territorials', but she took some comfort in the fact that since she was honorary colonel of both regiments, the officers and men of each would 'remain under her care'.[79] The new regiment was known as the Inns of Court and City Yeomanry.

Queen Elizabeth's association with the women's services began in August 1939 with her appointment as commandant-in-chief of all three branches – the Women's Royal Naval Service (later Women in the Royal Navy), the Auxiliary Territorial Service (later the Women's Royal Army Corps), and the Women's Auxiliary Air Force (later the Women's Royal Air Force, then Women in the Royal Air Force). During the war she visited units of all the services (and gave the ATS permission to play tennis in the garden at Buckingham Palace, although she decided against hockey on the lawn).[80] In later years she attended many receptions and reunions, received the heads of the three services on their appointment and departure, and took an active interest in changes of design of badges and uniform. 'Very difficult to look nice in this' was one comment, on a new uniform for WRNS personnel in 1991 when they were to serve at sea in Royal Navy ships.[81] She was always keen that they retain their individuality as women's services, and thus was unenthusiastic about the idea, adopted in 1968, that the titles of officers in the WRAF should become identical to those of the RAF.[82] Later she stated her disagreement with plans to incorporate the women's services fully into the navy, army and air force respectively, but felt she had to bow to the 'inevitable'.[83]

In a special category of its own was Queen Elizabeth's informal, but important, link with the Irish Guards. In 1965 the Colonel of the regiment, Lord Alexander of Tunis,* asked whether she would consider taking on the annual task of presenting shamrock[†] to the regiment at its St Patrick's Day parade. It was a tradition instituted by Queen

---

* Field Marshal Harold Alexander, first Earl Alexander of Tunis KG OM (1891–1969). During the Second World War he served as a commander in Burma, North Africa and Italy, eventually rising to become Supreme Commander of the Allied Forces Headquarters. In 1946 he succeeded Lord Athlone as Governor General of Canada and in 1952 he returned to Britain to become minister of defence in Winston Churchill's Cabinet before retiring from public life in 1954.

[†] The shamrock was grown specially for the regiment in County Cork, and every serving member received a sprig; hitherto it had been provided by the regiment, but Queen Elizabeth decided to pay for it herself. The initial annual cost of about £25 rose to more than £1,700 over the next thirty years.

Alexandra in 1905, after whose death in 1926 Princess Mary (later Countess of Harewood and Princess Royal) had continued the tradition until she herself died in 1965. Queen Elizabeth agreed to keep up this royal link, of which the Irish Guards were very proud, although because St Patrick's Day, 17 March, fell at a busy time in her annual racing programme she feared she might not always be able to attend the presentation.[84] In the event she became so fond of the Irish Guards that she rarely missed it from 1968 until the late 1990s, often flying out to Germany for the ceremony when the regiment was stationed there. Because every serving member of the regiment received a sprig, this sometimes meant deliveries of shamrock, on the Queen Mother's behalf, to out-of-the-way places – once to a jungle airfield and a beach in Belize, another time to a camp near Mount Kenya, where the ceremony was watched by 'two giraffe, several baboons and a group of local Samburu warriors'.[85]

From 1972 a further link with the Irish Guards was formed when Captain Charles Baker was appointed equerry to Queen Elizabeth for two years. This was a break from the tradition by which the regiments of which she was colonel-in-chief supplied her equerries. Captain Baker was followed by a captain from the Black Watch, but from 1976 all her equerries – thirteen more, each serving for two years – came from the Irish Guards. This was because the appointment, which was not full time, could easily be combined with a post at the regimental headquarters at Wellington Barracks in Birdcage Walk, not far from Clarence House. The officer would spend the morning at Clarence House and the afternoon at Wellington Barracks, unless he was needed for specific engagements with the Queen Mother.

Outside Great Britain, Queen Elizabeth had other military relationships which she treasured, with Canada, South Africa, Australia and New Zealand. She became colonel-in-chief of the Toronto Scottish Regiment in 1937, and presented the regiment with new colours during her tour of Canada with the King in 1939. During the war the regiment served with the Canadian forces in Europe, and in April 1940 the Queen visited them at Aldershot; they mounted the guard at Buckingham Palace later that month. When the regiment returned to Canada at the end of the war, she sent a farewell message congratulating them on their 'splendid achievements on the field of battle' and hoping to see them again 'in your own dear land'.[86]

She did indeed see them again, on almost all of her many visits to

Canada over the next forty-five years. She always included a walkabout among the ordinary soldiers, often attending garden parties and receptions for her three Canadian regiments. She also received visiting officers or members of the regimental association at Clarence House on many occasions, and Lieutenant Colonel Robert Hilborn, a former commanding officer of the regiment, became her honorary Canadian equerry. In November 2000 'Queen Elizabeth The Queen Mother's Own' was added to the title of the regiment.

The Black Watch (Royal Highland Regiment) of Canada was affiliated with its namesake in Scotland, and it was natural that Queen Elizabeth should be asked to be colonel-in-chief, an appointment she took on in 1947. She often received visiting officers of the Black Watch at Clarence House; one of her most frequent visitors was Colonel John Bourne, who had witnessed the 1939 royal tour as a junior officer and rose to become honorary colonel in 1970. Queen Elizabeth's last contact with the regiment was in January 2002, when she sent a message of congratulation on its 140th anniversary.[87]

Her third Canadian regiment was the Royal Canadian Army Medical Corps, which later became the Canadian Forces Medical Services. All three regiments took part in her birthday tributes on Horse Guards Parade in 1990 and 2000.

Military medicine interested Queen Elizabeth. In Australia she was colonel-in-chief of the Royal Australian Army Medical Corps, a post to which the Queen appointed her in honour of her own Coronation in 1953. In 1977, in honour of the Queen's Silver Jubilee, she was appointed colonel-in-chief of the Royal New Zealand Army Medical Corps. 'Good old loyal N.Z.', she remarked when she heard that the corps was to serve in the Gulf War in 1991.[88]

Following her visit to Australia in 1958 Queen Elizabeth had become honorary air chief commandant of the Women's Royal Australian Air Force, and she sent a message to the Director of the WRAAF on its twenty-first anniversary in 1972. The appointment came to an end when the women's services were integrated into the Royal Australian Air Force in 1977.

Her relationships with regiments in South Africa became more problematic as the South African government's commitment to apartheid grew. In 1947, after the Royal Family's visit, the government submitted a list, for the King's approval, of regiments which desired to have a member of the Royal Family as colonel-in-chief. The government recommended that the Queen should become colonel-in-chief of the Cape Town Highlanders and of the Witwatersrand Rifles.

In 1948 the Commandant of the Cape Town Highlanders asked if they could be named the Queen's Own Cape Town Highlanders. Permission was granted. The Witwatersrand Rifles were affiliated to the Cameronians. In November 1956 Queen Elizabeth was also appointed colonel-in-chief of the Transvaal Scottish Regiment, which was affiliated to the Black Watch. She liked all these connections but they had to end when South Africa left the Commonwealth to pursue its apartheid policies in May 1961. She accepted the inevitable: that all her South African colonelcies-in-chief had to lapse. But she did not consider herself bound to break off all contact with her regiments. Martin Gilliat wrote to Commandant Loveland of the Cape Town Highlanders (which dropped the prefix 'Queen's Own'), 'Queen Elizabeth will always continue to take the closest interest in the achievements and welfare of her Regiment.'[89] And so she did. In October 1961 a letter was sent from Clarence House to Commandant Hone who was to succeed Commandant Loveland, assuring him of Queen Elizabeth's continuing interest.[90] When Commandant Loveland visited London in March 1970, he was received (unofficially) by the Queen Mother, as were officers of her other South African regiments in later years. All three regiments sent contingents to her ninetieth- and hundredth-birthday parades.

Rhodesia, another country of which she was fond, posed problems too. In 1954 she was appointed honorary commissioner of the British South Africa Police.* She took up the appointment willingly, saying, 'I have vivid memories of the smartness and efficiency of the British South Africa Police on my visit to Southern Rhodesia and it has given me particular pleasure therefore to be able to accept the appointment of your Honorary Commissioner. I would be grateful if you would convey to All Ranks my best wishes and my hope that I may have the opportunity of visiting them again in the not too far distant future.'[91]

---

* The British South Africa Police (a Rhodesian force) had its origin in the British South Africa Company's Police which was formed under the powers conferred by the Charter granted to the company in 1889 by Queen Victoria. The services of the BSAP to the Empire were recognized as early as 1904 when a banner in recognition of these services was presented to the force at Mafeking by Lord Milner on behalf of the King.

After the white minority government of Rhodesia made its unilateral declaration of independence in 1965, she tried to maintain
unofficial contacts with the country, receiving lengthy reports on the
welfare of the British South Africa Police until 1970. But in March that
year, after Rhodesia had declared herself a republic, the Foreign and
Commonwealth Office advised that Queen Elizabeth's appointment as
honorary commissioner of the Police Force should be suspended. She
wrote a note saying, 'Suspend but not Sever! It could be cunningly
written in.'[92] There were then ten more years of increasing bloodshed
between the Rhodesian security forces and black nationalist guerrillas
before a transfer of authority was brokered in 1980 by the new British
government led by Margaret Thatcher. In the country's first-ever
elections held on the basis of universal suffrage, the white minority
regime finally lost power to a black government led by one of the
principal guerrilla leaders, Robert Mugabe, and the independent
country was renamed Zimbabwe. Hopes for a great future for Zimbabwe were to be dashed. The Queen Mother and other friends of the
country watched in dismay as, over the next twenty years, Mugabe's
regime became increasingly corrupt and brutal, eventually destroying
one of the most fertile and one of the richest countries in Africa.

In South Africa, apartheid was eventually defeated by the moral
force of Nelson Mandela and the political skills of President de Klerk,
and to the great pleasure of the Queen and the Queen Mother South
Africa returned to the Commonwealth. A special service, which the
Queen Mother attended, was held in Westminster Abbey on 20 July
1994 to mark the occasion. In March 1995 the Queen made her first
visit to the country since her family trip in 1947; she was moved by
the reception she was given, particularly in the black townships where
the inhabitants lined the streets in far greater numbers than for any
other visitor, cheering and waving placards saying 'THANK YOU FOR
COMING BACK'.[93]

*

MONARCHY OFFERS constancy. No member of the Royal Family had
the opportunity to demonstrate that quality better than the Queen
Mother. Remarkably, during what turned out to be not the end but
the central period of her life, the political pendulum swung decisively
in Britain. With the coming of the Labour government in 1964 after
thirteen years of Conservative rule, it had seemed that the move of

society towards government provision of all services was inevitable. It appeared that the role of the charitable sector, supported as it was by the monarchy, would inevitably decline. This was certainly what many Labour politicians wished should happen. They wanted no return to the 1930s and what one young socialist, Robin Cook, characterized as 'a flag-day NHS'.[94]

But after Margaret Thatcher won power for the Conservative Party in 1979, collectivist nostrums and activities came under criticism. It was argued that since 1945 collectivism had not proved itself vastly superior to voluntarism; a more balanced view of the potential of philanthropy began to emerge. From within the Royal Family the most trenchant analysis of overwhelming centralized state power came from Prince Philip. In one speech he observed that government was no longer satisfied with such traditional, neutral concerns as peace and security – 'but now it is interested in morality and behaviour and legislating for the common good. The fact is that the liberty of the individual is a vital part of the common good also.' He criticized not only the collectivist mentality in Britain but, even more fiercely, the myths of Marxism – above all for its dismissal of the voluntary and altruistic elements in human nature.[95] A few years later he was bolder still and was quoted as saying that the monarchy had helped Britain 'to get over . . . the development of an urban industrial intelligentsia reasonably easily'.[96]

As the twentieth century drew to a close, it became clear that members of the Royal Family were still in constant demand to represent different sections of civil society. This was a surprise to some commentators but not so much to members of the family who saw the impact that their charitable and philanthropic work continued to have, year after largely unchanging year. In 1966, Princess Alice, Countess of Athlone, the last-surviving grandchild of Queen Victoria, reflected that royalty was 'an arduous profession' which allowed its members few opt-outs. 'Their daily tasks, for months ahead, are prescribed and set out in a diary of engagements from which only illness can excuse them. None but those trained from youth to such an ordeal can sustain it with amiability and composure. The royal motto "ich dien" is no empty phrase. It means what it says – I serve.'[97] That was certainly true of Princess Alice herself, who had been tireless in her charitable works. It was equally true of Queen Elizabeth, who continued to add new charities and organizations to her patronages right up until the end of her life. This aspect of her work brought both institutional and individual dividends.

The constitutional historian Vernon Bogdanor has argued in his book *The Monarchy and the Constitution* that the future of the monarchy lies 'in the practical employment of its symbolic influence'.[98] Queen Elizabeth's public life and work showed exactly what he meant. The wide and complex web of her organizations kept her in touch with hundreds of different aspects of the changing world around her, and guaranteed that she received a massive postbag. Some of these letters were 'fan mail', some were chatty letters from lonely people who wrote regularly and who were referred to as 'old friends' by the ladies in waiting whose duty it was to reply. Other letters were requests for advice or help from people who clearly believed that Queen Elizabeth could be of more assistance to them than the impersonal organs of the state.

One of her ladies in waiting, Lady Angela Oswald, said later, 'People treated her as a mixture of Agony Aunt, Information Office, Advice Bureau, Solve-the-Problem organisation. They wrote when they had nowhere else to turn.' The ladies in waiting would discuss with Queen Elizabeth how best to help each individual – often one of her many patronages could assist – and, in later years, Fiona Fletcher, the Lady Clerk, ran an extensive filing system of Queen Elizabeth's contacts which enabled specific assistance to be given. The benefit, to thousands of different people over the decades, was real. Her unique, personal value as a charitable fundraiser was noted by her friend Deborah, Duchess of Devonshire at a performance of *Die Fledermaus* at the Royal Opera House in aid of the Putney Hospital for Incurables, with which Queen Elizabeth had a long association. 'Good Cake* came and turned it into a gala. One forgets between seeing her what a star she is & what incredible and wicked charm she has got.'[99]

The Queen Mother's philanthropic reach by the last decade of her life was remarkable, but most other senior members of the Royal Family played similar roles with their patronages and regiments. Indeed, this fruitful interchange showed the robustness of British philanthropic traditions despite the rise of the state. It has been argued that consistent royal involvement in the realm of voluntary action,

---

* 'Cake' was the nickname that the Duchess gave to the Queen Mother after being deeply impressed long before by her enthusiasm at a wedding when the cake was cut.

with its diversity, its principled rivalry and its love of the *ad hoc* remedy, had given the nation 'immeasurable moral and democratic benefit'.[100]

At the same time, the monarchy offered a constitutional landmark and institutional continuity which made the costs of social change appear easier to bear.[101] Queen Elizabeth spoke to this issue in January 1993, when she gave her annual talk to the Sandringham Women's Institute. Looking back fifty years, she recalled the time 'when the skies above us were filled with aircraft of the American 8th Air Force, stationed all around us in East Anglia'. She went on to affirm her faith in the unaltered core of her country: 'Many changes have come about since those days of War, some good, and some not so good, but through all those changing scenes of life we can feel the strong beat of the English heart.'[102] It was in this heart that she trusted above all.

CHAPTER TWENTY

AT HOME

'One feels so beautifully far away'

FOR QUEEN ELIZABETH one decade glided into another, with the basic pattern of her days, weeks, months and years being fairly constant. Thus in outward form the action on stage in 1963, for example, would in many ways have been repeated in 1983 or 1993, with the cast of characters much the same, merely older. Her constant pleasures – from P. G. Wodehouse to Sandown Park, from the Black Watch to Middle Temple, from her corgis to the royal yacht *Britannia* – did not change.

Each year she spent Christmas with the Royal Family, until 1964 at Sandringham and after that at Windsor until 1988, when the family reverted to spending Christmas at Sandringham. They were always at Sandringham for the New Year and, unless she was unwell, in which case the Queen took her place, Queen Elizabeth never missed her first fixture there in January: the annual general meeting of the Sandringham Women's Institute. She visited the studs at Sandringham and Wolferton at least twice a week during her stay. Every year on 6 February, the anniversary of the King's death, she took communion, usually with other members of the family. In later years she would spend this day at Royal Lodge.

For most of the second half of the winter and early spring she would be based at Clarence House with weekends at Royal Lodge. Easter was always with the family at Windsor and in May she would make her first visit of the year to Scotland, in the early years to the Castle of Mey, where she was constantly improving the house and the garden and where, in 1960, she bought the neighbouring Longoe Farm to pursue her growing interest in breeding Aberdeen Angus cattle and North Country Cheviot sheep. Latterly she went to Birkhall in May and invited friends to stay for the fishing. Then she would return south.

Summer's annual events included the Derby, Trooping the Colour on Horse Guards Parade, the Garter Service at Windsor, and Royal Ascot. In July she went back to Norfolk for the King's Lynn Festival and the Sandringham Flower Show. After her birthday on 4 August, she would go to Mey for a longer holiday, then a weekend with the Queen and other members of the family at Balmoral, after which she would move down the road to her home, Birkhall, until the end of October – with one final week at Mey. Then it was back to London and Royal Lodge until Christmas. Within this fairly well-fixed timetable there were many events that were ringfenced, on both the private and the public sides of her life.

Regular engagements included, in March, the annual general meeting of Queen Mary's London Needlework Guild at St James's Palace – she attended this every year until 2001. A favourite fixture was dinner with the members of the Garden Society, for an evening of horticultural talk. And every year until she ceased to be chancellor in 1980 there were the University of London graduation ceremonies at the Royal Albert Hall. She attended gala performances of ballet or opera in aid of the Royal Ballet and Royal Opera Benevolent Funds; the Royal Variety Performance was also a regular engagement until 1988. Then there was the Royal College of Music's annual prize giving and concert which she attended from 1952 till 1992, when she retired as president and was elected president emerita, and the Middle Temple Family Night dinner every December.

The First World War remained always in her consciousness. She made sure that in November she planted her personal Cross of Remembrance in the Field of Remembrance at St Margaret's Church, Westminster, attended the Royal British Legion Festival of Remembrance at the Royal Albert Hall and watched the Remembrance Day Ceremony at the Cenotaph from the Home Office balcony. Often, though not annually, she would attend the Royal Tournament at Earl's Court, until this ended in 1996. Similarly, in early December she liked to visit the Royal Smithfield Show, of which she was annual president in 1983, 1987 and 1989.

Most years she carried out around a hundred official engagements – occasionally more.* Many more requests – usually about 200 – had

---

* These figures can be compared with those of other – younger – members of the Royal Family. In a sample year, 1984, Queen Elizabeth carried out 115 engagements at home and 16

to be refused every year. Most years included at least one official overseas visit.

*

HER GREATEST pleasure throughout was family. She and the Queen talked to each other almost every day on the telephone if not in person. The Buckingham Palace switchboard operator, putting through the call, would say 'Your Majesty, I have Her Majesty on the line.' When they were not talking of their shared obsession with horses and racing, family matters dominated their conversations. Queen Elizabeth took a keen interest in her grandchildren, particularly Prince Charles. The bond between them, forged while his parents were on their long Commonwealth tour in 1953–4, grew stronger as the years passed. In 1961, while his parents were in India, Queen Elizabeth visited the twelve-year-old Prince at his preparatory school, Cheam, in Surrey; he was suffering from a bad attack of measles and came home to Royal Lodge to convalesce. He soon recovered, 'much to his disappointment!' said his grandmother, and she took him with her to Buckingham Palace for Prince Andrew's first birthday party. Afterwards, writing to the Queen, she reported that Andrew was 'looking absolutely angelic . . . the noise was terrific, & everyone enjoyed themselves very much. The cake was cut, with great difficulty, by Andrew, & the proceedings ended by me escaping at about 5.30.'[1]

Later that year, when the Queen was on a visit to Ghana, the Queen Mother took Princess Anne to Cheam to see Prince Charles's school play, and wrote to tell the Queen about it afterwards. She was not allowed to mingle with the other parents, she said, but was firmly segregated in another room, where she was given 'boiling sherry'. She described the play as an adaptation of *Richard III*:* 'after a few minutes on to the stage shambled a most horrible looking creature, a leering vulgarian, with a dreadful expression on his twisted mouth; & to my

---

abroad; Princess Margaret 161 at home and 25 abroad; the Queen 391 at home and 121 abroad; the Prince of Wales 204 at home and 112 abroad. (Information kindly supplied by Tim O'Donovan)

* This was *The Last Baron*, by David Munir. According to Jonathan Dimbleby's biography of the Prince of Wales, Prince Charles had been understudy for the Duke of Gloucester (that is, the future Richard III), but had to take over when the boy playing the Duke suddenly left the school. Dimbleby records that 'there were sniggers when he intoned a prayer which included the line "And soon may I ascend the throne", but he got a good write-up in the *Cheam School Chronicle*.' (Jonathan Dimbleby, *The Prince of Wales*, p. 43)

horror I began to realise that this was my dear grandson! He was the Duke of Gloucester, & acted his part very well, in fact he made the part quite revolting!' The headmaster told Queen Elizabeth that he was pleased with the young Prince's progress. Passing on his comments to the Queen, she added a remark reflecting both her general attitude to the upbringing of children and, perhaps, her anxiety for this particular child. 'So often, in children, they suddenly develop, and gain confidence, & if they are naturally gentle & considerate, they probably become all the stronger in character.'[2]

The family was at this moment discussing where Prince Charles should be educated next. Prince Philip argued for his own school, Gordonstoun, in north-eastern Scotland. He thought it would suit the Prince best and that its remoteness would protect him somewhat from the intrusions of the media. Moreover, though far from London, Gordonstoun was within relatively easy reach of Balmoral and Birkhall. The Queen Mother, however, made a strong case for Eton, where her brothers and many of her friends had been educated. Recognizing that her grandson was sensitive, even vulnerable, she thought Eton would be by far the best place for him.[3] Moreover, the school was just across the River Thames from Windsor Castle and many of the sons of his parents' friends would be there. At Gordonstoun, by contrast, 'he might as well be at school abroad.'[4] It would be 'an alien world' in which he would be 'terribly alone & cut off'.[5] Prince Philip's view prevailed. On family matters the Queen almost always deferred to her husband's judgement, conscious that although she was queen he was head of the family.

Queen Elizabeth was tactful, but she was dismayed by Prince Philip's choice. She was right – Prince Charles was unhappy and felt isolated at Gordonstoun. She did all she could to aid and comfort him at what she called in one letter 'that glorious salubrious bed of roses known as Gordon's Town',[6] and he visited her often at Birkhall; after one weekend there, he wrote, 'All the way back in the car I kept wanting to go back and stay longer at Birkhall.' He listed all the times in the week at which he was allowed to receive telephone calls.[7] She urged members of the family to telephone him to cheer him up – he was 'a brave little boy', she said.[8] The Prince's dislike of Gordonstoun did not ease as he grew older.

She thoroughly approved of his ultimate educational destination, Trinity College, Cambridge, where the former Conservative politician

Rab Butler was master.* 'I am <u>delighted</u> that you are going to Trinity – I am sure that you will enjoy it to the full, & be able to make the most of the opportunity of getting to know that splendid character Lord Butler – I feel sure too, that he is one of the few <u>wise</u> men just now, & full of humour as well as being a statesman.'[9] She gave him a painting by Edward Seago for his room in the College.

Her complement of grandchildren was completed by the birth of the Queen and Prince Philip's fourth and last child, Prince Edward (1964), and by the two children of Princess Margaret and Lord Snowdon, Lord (David) Linley (1961) and Lady Sarah Armstrong-Jones (1964). The Queen Mother played an important role in the lives of these last two grandchildren – they spent a great deal of time at her homes, particularly in the 1970s – and they too came to love her deeply as they did their aunt, the Queen.

*

THERE WERE SADNESSES too. Her 1960s, like each of her decades, were regularly punctuated by the deaths of many people close to her. The first was Arthur Penn, her oldest, most devoted friend and courtier.

His last months of service to her (she still had not released him completely) were marred when in May 1960 the British press picked up a report in an American newspaper that Queen Elizabeth was about to marry him. She was in Northern Rhodesia when the story broke and her office dismissed it as 'complete and absolute nonsense'.[10] Her Private Secretary, Martin Gilliat, said she took it 'in very good part',[11] but Penn was mortified by what he called 'this most embarrassing absurdity'. He felt that having successfully avoided any publicity through twenty-five years of royal service, 'this reversal has been most odious.'[12]

He became ever more frail and at the end of November 1960 he wrote to Queen Elizabeth in a shaky hand that 'the medicine men' could not succeed in stabilizing him. He felt he had to be patient and count his 'very numerous' blessings. 'But I wish I could be with Your Majesty & be of some service to you.'[13] He died on 31 December that year. Queen Elizabeth was greatly saddened and wrote to his sister,

---

* R. A. Butler (1902–82), leading Conservative Party politician, known as Rab. Architect of the 1944 Education Act, Butler had a high reputation and became one of the few politicians to serve as chancellor, home secretary and foreign secretary. He was twice passed over for the premiership.

saying that 'to be able to turn to Arthur for wise counsel in so many different situations, to be able to share the pleasure of beautiful things and to laugh, was something that has meant more to me that I can ever say, both in happy days and sad days. How wonderful to have lived a life such as Arthur lived. Spreading gaiety and kindness around him, and goodness and courage as well.'[14]

Penn's death was followed in February 1961 by that of Queen Elizabeth's elder sister May Elphinstone, at the age of seventy-seven. Remembered affectionately by her daughter Margaret as 'permanently in an old tweed coat tied round the waist with a piece of string and gumboots, bent double over something in the garden',[15] she had a strong social conscience and had worked in the slums of Edinburgh, and in the Women's Voluntary Service during the war.

Later in 1961 Queen Elizabeth suffered the sudden death of her younger brother David, who still lived at St Paul's Walden with his wife Rachel and son Simon. Not everyone found David Bowes Lyon easy, but brother and sister were devoted to each other. Suddenly, at Birkhall on 12 September, he had a heart attack and he died the next day. His funeral took place at the Episcopal church at Ballater on 15 September and that evening the Queen Mother, the Queen, Prince Philip and members of the Bowes Lyon family accompanied the coffin on the night train south. David was buried at the familiar little church at St Paul's Walden.

The Queen knew what a gap this would leave in her mother's life and did her best to cherish her in these days – for which Queen Elizabeth wrote to thank her, and to say how devoted David had been to his niece too – 'he really loved you, & would have done anything for you.' He was one of the few people upon whom she could rely to tell her the truth and his death was 'like a light going out in one's life, we have always been so close, I knew what he was thinking even.'[16]

Soon after the funeral, Queen Elizabeth went up to the Castle of Mey. Relaxing there, she said, made her feel calmer. But she continued to find life bleak without the other 'Benjamin'. Almost a year after his death she went to stay with his widow Rachel at St Paul's Walden, and afterwards wrote to say how grateful she was for Rachel's understanding of her own love of David. She added, 'He has left something so strong, hasn't he – perhaps that is really the point of human life and living, to give, & to create new goodness all the time.'[17]

This probably represents as good a statement of her view of the purpose of life as any other – *to give and to create new goodness all the time*. But she knew also how hard that was – on a later occasion she told Rachel how much she admired 'the way you face life & its obligations – & oh what a battle it is sometimes.'[18]

Her last surviving sibling, Rose, Lady Granville, died in November 1967; Queen Elizabeth had visited her twice earlier that year at her home in Scotland. Rose was not only thought to be the great beauty in the family – 'a lovely person with a slow, gravelly voice', one of her nieces remembered[19] – she was much loved for her kindness.

Queen Elizabeth's old friend D'Arcy Osborne was also beginning to falter; he had continued to live in Rome and worked on behalf of street children in the city. In early 1962 Osborne told her that he had had a hard winter. She sent him her sympathy and expounded her rather sanguine view of international affairs: 'The world staggers on, from one crisis to another, but I have a feeling that human beings are beginning to become accustomed to these rather bogus upheavals, & take them more philosophically than the slightly hysterical reporters & newscasters!'[20]

Osborne was well enough to come and stay with her at Birkhall that autumn.[21] She was worried about his finances, which had always been precarious, and she did something about it – a few months later she told him, 'D'Arcy, one or two of your old & loving friends have sent a small sum to your banking account in Rome, in case it might come in handy some time. They hope you won't mind, it is just to show their true affection.'[22] He replied at once, 'Madam, Dear Ma'am, How KIND!' Her generosity would, he wrote, enable him to take taxis when tired and would give him 'the invaluable benefit of peace of mind and freedom from fussing over small and ignoble matters'.[23]

In 1963 D'Arcy Osborne became the duke of Leeds,* on the death of his distant cousin the eleventh Duke, brother of Queen Elizabeth's sister-in-law Dorothy. It was too late for him to enjoy this transition; he died in Rome in April 1964. One of his friends wrote to the Queen

---

* The first Duke of Leeds had been Sir Thomas Osborne. Better known as the Earl of Danby, he was a minister of Charles II and was impeached by the Whigs and imprisoned in the Tower. Danby was one of those who invited William of Orange to England in 1688 and his adherence to the plot was important to the Whigs because he was a leading Tory; the dukedom was his reward from the new king, William III. D'Arcy Osborne was the twelfth and last duke.

Mother that they had held a 'goodbye' ceremony around his bed, and his ashes were buried, with emotion, 'on a golden Roman spring day' in the English cemetery.[24]

Next it was her girlhood governess and friend Beryl Poignand who died. In early 1963, Queen Elizabeth, knowing that she was unwell, had helped arrange for her admission first into the London Homeopathic Hospital and then into the Parkfield Nursing Home in Kingston, run by the Friends of the Poor and Gentlefolk's Help, of which she was patron.[25] In December 1964 Queen Elizabeth visited her – it was the last time she saw the woman to whom she had been so close when they were both young. A month later Beryl fell and broke her hip; she died after a few days, aged seventy-seven. The Queen Mother wrote to Mrs Leone Poignand Hall, Beryl's cousin, 'She shared our joys & sorrows to the full, & I have nothing but happy and loving thoughts in my mind when I think of her.'[26]

In 1964 Edith Sitwell died, and Queen Elizabeth wrote sympathetically to Osbert, to whom his sister's loss was a real blow; he himself was ill, and spending much time at his house at Montegufoni, in Italy. Their mutual friend Hannah Gubbay, hostess at many luncheons which both had enjoyed, died in 1968; 'there will never be anyone like her again,' Queen Elizabeth wrote to Sitwell. 'The last time I lunched with her, she seemed desperately frail & crippled, but just as funny & crisp as ever. We all spoke of you, & wished that you could have been there.'[27] Sitwell invited her to visit him in Italy; but he died in May 1969. She grieved, and sent a telegram expressing her 'truly heartfelt sympathy in this moment of great sorrow' to his brother Sacheverell.[28]

All such deaths reminded her how 'curiously alone' she had become – even in the 1960s. 'Nearly all my family have gone, & so many old friends, and sometimes one feels very solitary. But I suppose that happens to everyone who lives past 60, and one must not allow the fact to depress one.'[29] In a later, more upbeat moment, she acknowledged that with ageing 'there are compensations, such as loathing the idea of going to a Night Club and things like that!'[30]

A poignant commemoration of her greatest loss came on 31 March 1969, when Queen Elizabeth, with most of the Royal Family, attended the dedication of the King George VI Memorial Chapel in St George's Chapel, Windsor, as the last resting place of her husband. His coffin had remained in the Royal Vault beneath St George's since his death. It had originally been intended that a tomb should be made for him in

St George's Chapel itself, like those of his parents and grandparents. Various sculptors were suggested to make an effigy of the King to be placed on the tomb.* Jacob Epstein† was approached, although Queen Elizabeth was concerned that his bold style might be inappropriate for the setting. She herself saw 'the possibility of something exceptional', in the words of Sir Arthur Penn, from the hand of Henry Moore. She wanted to discuss it with Moore personally if he were willing to undertake it. But she was reluctant to press him, and the idea was evidently dropped.[31] In the end it was decided that rather than a tomb with effigies, a chantry chapel should be built for the King, opening off the north aisle of St George's. There were delays because the Fine Arts Commission had understandable reservations about the effect of a modern addition to an architectural masterpiece of the Perpendicular Gothic style. But the architects succeeded in creating a simple and harmonious building lit by narrow lancet windows with stained glass designed by John Piper. Queen Elizabeth was pleased with the result, which she described as 'a truly peaceful & holy place.'[32]

*

QUEEN ELIZABETH'S principal home for the second half of her life was Clarence House. Despite her initial dismay at having to move there after the death of the King, she gradually grew to accept it as an effective London base. With the help of friends and advisers she decorated it well and imbued it with a sense of continuity.

Standing off Stable Yard next to St James's Palace, Clarence House was built by John Nash in 1825–8 for the Duke of Clarence, later King William IV. Through the nineteenth century the house was lived in by a succession of junior members of the Royal Family. After the last of these, the Duke of Connaught, died in 1942, the house served for the rest of the war as the headquarters of the British Red Cross Society

---

* Another effigy was to be made of Queen Elizabeth at the same time, so that she would be represented at the age she was when the King died, when the time came for her own burial. This was in accordance with royal tradition; effigies of the widowed Queen Victoria, Queen Alexandra and Queen Mary were made not long after their husbands' deaths for the same reason.

† At the time when the project was put to Epstein, he was engaged in making a bas-relief of Queen Elizabeth's friend Bishop Woods, who had died in 1953, for Lichfield Cathedral. Epstein expressed interest, and was sure he could make effigies that would not be out of place in St George's Chapel. But Queen Elizabeth's advisers decided otherwise. (RA QEQM/PRIV/MEM)

and the St John Ambulance Brigade. It was damaged by bombing and had to be extensively restored before becoming the married home of Princess Elizabeth and the Duke of Edinburgh in 1949.

The front door of the house is approached through black-painted wooden gates on Stable Yard Road, a private street off the Mall. Inside the gates, a gravel drive of barely more than a car's length leads to the pillared portico. From there it is just one step into the small outer hall where stood a musical clock given to her and the Duke of York by the citizens of Glasgow for their wedding – it was surmounted with a Scottish lion on a crown and was made by 'John Smith of Pittenweem, North Britain'. The broad inner hall is the backbone of the house and the Queen Mother used it as a gallery for paintings, tapestries and mirrors.

Past an early seventeenth-century tapestry, acquired in 1950, was Simon Elwes's sketch of Queen Elizabeth in Garter robes, made for his large painting, which hung on the wall opposite, of the King investing Princess Elizabeth with the insignia of the Order of the Garter in the Throne Room at Windsor Castle in April 1948. It is a delicate portrait of a poignant moment as the King made his beloved daughter a member of the oldest and most distinguished Order of British chivalry, 600 years after the founding of the Order.

Elwes's painting, which was completed only in 1953 after the death of the King, is an important part of the collection built up over decades by Queen Elizabeth. The art historian John Cornforth, in his admirable study of Clarence House, points out that the Garter picture 'is part of a chronological story that reflects the intensity of the period in which Queen Elizabeth was most active in acquiring pictures by living artists'.[33] After the grim menace of the 1930s and the war, and the grey immediate post-war years, there was something 'doubly celebratory' about the Garter picture. Victories had been won, evil had been defeated, and the King was handing the promise of the future to his daughter.[34]

That sense of what had been avoided is also illuminated by a painting further down the hall by James Gunn – it is a conversation piece of several soldiers entitled simply *Field Marshal Montgomery in his Mess Tent in Belgium in 1944*. This shows the Field Marshal himself in a flying jacket and corduroy trousers, sitting around a table with his aides. Gunn had been with them in Belgium in August and September 1944 as the Allies advanced towards Berlin. Eindhoven was relieved while the artist was there. There is on many of the faces, and certainly on that of Montgomery, a quiet smile of satisfaction. The Queen saw the painting at the Royal Academy in 1945 and bought it; Montgomery was chagrined and tried to acquire it for himself. She declined to release it and Gunn eventually painted another version for the Field Marshal.[35]

Off the main corridor is the Lancaster Room, which Queen Elizabeth used as a waiting room for those whom she was to receive in audience. It was dominated by the watercolours of Windsor Castle under lowering skies by John Piper, which the Queen had commissioned in 1941.

Leading off the hall is a corridor filled with paintings and mementoes of horses and racing and therefore known as the Horse Corridor. In 1963 Queen Elizabeth added to this collection with a painting by J. F. Herring which represented Cotherstone, a Derby and 2000 Guineas winner owned by John Bowes. Even more striking is another Herring – a sketch of the twelfth Earl of Strathmore on horseback. And at the east end of the corridor hung pictures of some of the Queen Mother's own horses – The Rip, Double Star and Makaldar.

In the Garden Room the Queen Mother hung over the fireplace the celebrated unfinished portrait of her which Augustus John began at the end of 1939. It was a difficult commission to complete in the brutal circumstances of war, but the result is rather magical – almost a portrait of a fairy queen. In the upright figure dressed in a Hartnell gold and white crinoline, bedecked in glittering jewels and holding red roses in her lap, John captured much of this Queen's sparkling gaiety.

It was presented to her as a gift in 1961 and she wrote to John, 'What a tremendous pleasure it gives me to see it once again. It looks so lovely in my drawing room and has cheered it up no end! The sequins glitter and the rose and the red chair give a fine glow and I am so happy to have it.'[36] John was overjoyed by her letter and replied that now that the picture was on her wall, 'I am convinced that with all its faults, there is something there which is both true and lovable. I have really thought so all along but have not dared to say so.'[37]

Close by was another, very different portrait – she is not in light crinolines but in black, she is uncrowned and looks, as she was, half a decade older and seasoned by the worries of war. There is realism rather than magic in this sketch which James Gunn painted, a few months after the war ended, for a large portrait of her as Royal Bencher of the Middle Temple.[38]

Other portraits of her in the house included the profile done for her mother by John Singer Sargent at the time of her marriage, and a sketch for a portrait by Graham Sutherland which was to have hung at Senate House in the University of London.* The idea of a Sutherland portrait had been long in gestation. In 1951 she had had some doubts about the artist when he was suggested for a regimental portrait. She had seen his painting of Somerset Maugham, which, in the words of Arthur Penn, showed 'a cynical and desiccated old turtle'.[39] By 1959, when the University gave Sutherland the commission, she evidently had fewer qualms. She agreed to his suggestion that she should wear a feathered hat and gave him seven sittings in March 1961. According to his biographer Roger Berthoud, Sutherland 'found that her flow of conversation made concentration difficult, and he was not used to coping with a face so relatively cherubic and unlined.'[40] He produced a sketch which was a good start, but he came to the conclusion that he would not be able to paint a portrait that the University would like and so the project was abandoned. There were many who thought this was a pity – the art historian, friend of Queen Elizabeth and later Director of the National Portrait Gallery Roy Strong remarked that 'Sutherland focuses on what his predecessors omitted, the acute intelligence of the sitter beneath the beguiling humour.'[41]

Instead of Sutherland, at Queen Elizabeth's request London University commissioned a portrait of her from Pietro Annigoni in 1962.† She gave him about twenty one-hour sittings in spring 1963. The artist wrote later that he warmed more to her than to any other members of the Royal Family he had painted. Both artist and sitter liked the

---

* Graham Sutherland OM (1903–80), multi-talented English artist who was an official war artist in the Second World War. His most famous portrait was probably that of Somerset Maugham (1949). But the most notorious was that which he painted of Winston Churchill in 1954. Lady Churchill disliked it so much that she had it destroyed. In 1962 Sutherland created a huge tapestry, *Christ in Glory*, for the new Coventry Cathedral which replaced the original building bombed in the war.

† Pietro Annigoni (1910–88), acclaimed Italian fresco painter and portraitist whose work was influenced by Renaissance rather than modernist traditions. Among his most celebrated subjects were Queen Elizabeth II (1954), Princess Margaret (1957) and Pope John XXIII (1962).

finished portrait, which showed her with a wry smile and her tasselled mortarboard set at a jaunty angle. But the Court and Senate of the University were disappointed. According to Annigoni, they complained that they had asked her to be painted holding her mortarboard in her hand. Instead she had worn it, saying to Annigoni, 'Why shouldn't I put it on my head? After all when I go the University I have to wear it.'[42]

Upstairs in the corridor leading to the Queen Mother's own rooms was the arresting large watercolour portrait of her with a bonnet hanging from her arm, painted by Savely Sorine at the time of her marriage in 1923.

Just as Augustus John and Cecil Beaton were bold choices for portraitists in the 1930s, so was Sutherland in the 1960s and, even more so, John Bratby of the so-called Kitchen Sink School in the late 1970s. He was in the process of creating his 'Hall of Fame' of people who had marked and influenced the century and was rather surprised when Queen Elizabeth accepted his request to paint her. Sir Oliver Millar, then Surveyor of the Queen's Pictures, was in favour of the proposal. He considered Bratby 'a very entertaining and exciting painter' and thought that in joining his Hall of Fame Queen Elizabeth would be in 'delightful and – largely – congenial company'. Bratby painted two pictures of her in day clothes; after the first sitting he commented, 'I found Her Majesty to be splendid and enchanting.' He offered her a small painting of a sunflower as a present, which she accepted. But his request to paint her again, in formal attire with a tiara, was turned down. Later, after her first visit to Venice, in 1984, Bratby gave her a drawing of Punta della Dogana, which she hung in the Morning Room at Clarence House, alongside paintings by Sickert and Augustus John.[43]

Apart from the portraits of herself, the house was filled with her collection of art, including other pictures and busts of members of the Royal Family and of her own family. They included King William IV, Queen Victoria (more than once), King George V and of course King George VI, her mother, her father, her daughters – and many more.

John Cornforth observed that in the Clarence House collection there was much romanticism and much patriotism – and it is indeed that combination which informed so much of the Queen Mother's life, both publicly and privately.[44] But there was also another quality to be found in her collection – the excitement she had shown since girlhood in mystery and magic.

The collection suggests that she preferred sketches or unfinished works rather than more polished (sometimes ponderous) formal portraits. Aside from those already mentioned, the house contained works by Philip de László, Edward Seago (who gave her many small paintings for her birthday and at Christmas) and others. Throughout the house were objects and paintings and drawings which had been brought to her attention over the years by her artistic guides, Jasper Ridley, Kenneth Clark and Arthur Penn. In 1938 she had bought two paintings by living artists – Wilson Steer's *Chepstow Castle* and Augustus John's portrait of George Bernard Shaw with his eyes closed, *When Homer Nods*. In the Morning Room at Clarence House was one of the most 'modern' and visionary paintings in her collection, Paul Nash's *Landscape of the Vernal Equinox*, which had puzzled her daughter when she bought it in 1943.

In her own sitting room at Clarence House, Queen Elizabeth had a big desk latticed with photographs and busts of her family, horses and dogs, and another writing table equally laden with memorabilia, in front of the fire. There was an agreeable clutter in the room, with shopping bags on the floor serving as filing cabinets for letters and bills, mixed from all decades. The room included one of Gerald Kelly's wartime sketches for the state portraits he painted of the King and Queen. On her large mahogany desk was the Whistler glass engagement-card holder.

*

THROUGHOUT MOST of these decades, Queen Elizabeth's Household and her staff remained as constant as her kindness, her dislike of change and her powers of persuasion could ensure. As with Arthur Penn, she would never willingly let go of anyone she valued. This was demanding – but few of her Household or staff appear to have been in any great rush to leave.

Her establishment was always grand, but it was also quirky and friendly, perhaps more tolerant of eccentricity than some royal households. Just as Queen Elizabeth enjoyed having unconventional people among her friends, so she accepted foibles in the men and women who served her that other royal establishments might have considered a little risqué. The tone for this was set, not only by herself, but also

by her good-natured and open minded Private Secretary, Sir Martin
Gilliat.

Gilliat would see her every morning at about 10.30 with the mail
and any official papers she had been sent. A constant source of pleasure
both to Queen Elizabeth and to other members of the Household, as
well as to his many friends outside the Palace and around the world,
Gilliat was a great joy at any party and was always able to break the
ice, which was sometimes very thick between nervous guests around
the Queen Mother. He had exhibited this skill many years before when
he had met the shy young King Bhumibol of Thailand. Everyone was
standing around nervously when Gilliat said to the King, 'Your
Majesty, I understand that you are an expert at standing on your head.
Do please show us.' The King obliged and the party then 'went like
wedding bells'.[45]

Alongside Gilliat was the man with the most difficult task in the
Queen Mother's Household – her Treasurer. After the death of Sir
Arthur Penn this job was held for many years by Sir Ralph Anstruther.
He was a precise and meticulously dressed martinet whose job was to
try and impose order if not limits on Queen Elizabeth's spending. He
was daunting in his appraisals of others and a stickler for proper dress,
particularly among the equerries when they arrived to work at
Clarence House. He insisted on highly polished black lace-up shoes (he
regarded shoes without laces as 'bedroom slippers') and detachable
starched white collars at all times in London, and he himself never
travelled anywhere without at least one black tie and a bowler hat in
case he had to attend a funeral. He did not speak of 'the tube' but of
'the Underground Tubular Railway', and preferred 'wireless sets' to
'radios'.

Together with Gilliat and Anstruther worked her assistant Private
Secretary Alastair Aird, another ex-army officer. He had joined her
Household as equerry in 1960, took on the role of comptroller in 1974,
and became the lynchpin of her Household, in charge of her homes
and their contents, her staff and her entertaining. In close support from
1959 was her press secretary John Griffin, a former officer of the 24th
Lancers and then of the Queen's Bays, who fitted well into the easy-
going Household. With the press he was laconic, taking the view that
the fewer words he uttered, the better he was doing his job. Like
others, he stayed and stayed in Queen Elizabeth's service – until he

suffered a debilitating stroke in 1990, after which she used to invite him and his wife Henrietta to come as guests to Scotland.

Her senior Household were all devoted to Queen Elizabeth but they were aware that her style of living, as 'the last great Edwardian', could excite criticism in the more egalitarian times at the end of the twentieth century. Ralph Anstruther, in particular, had to be concerned about the size of her entourage, as well as the cost of her clothes, her horses and her entertaining at home – no easy matter when she liked everything to be of the best.

Her parties tended to go with a swing. She described to Princess Margaret one ecclesiastical reception she gave. 'I gave a cocktail party for 200 Bishops from overseas – by the time that 8 o'clock came, they were in cracking form!' They tucked into all the canapés '& tossed down martini after martini, especially the Americans who I am sure had been entertained on warm sherry for weeks before!'[46]

She frequently gave lunch and dinner parties, usually for about twelve people. Guests always loved these invitations: the food was good, the cocktails were mixed and the wine was poured with generous aplomb by her uniformed stewards, and the atmosphere was merry. On fine summer days lunch was often served at a table under the trees in the garden. Harold Macmillan, the former Conservative Prime Minister, thanked her for one such 'picnic', saying that it had 'all the pleasures of informality and none of its disadvantages. A rustic bank is all very well in its way, but it is apt to be uncomfortable and there is always the danger of earwigs.'[47] Roy Strong noted, 'The Clarence House ritual is that of an Edwardian great house and the sight of eighteen people sitting at a dining-room table laid overall alfresco with three menservants ministering to their needs was pure 1890s.'[48]

Among the jovial and frequent guests were Woodrow Wyatt, a slightly rakish former Labour politician and prolific journalist who became a devotee of Margaret Thatcher and was also chairman of the Horserace Totalisator Board. She enjoyed his gossipy wit as well as his love of racing and often dined with him. Equally, if differently, entertaining was Bruno Heim, who became in 1982 the Vatican's first apostolic nuncio to Great Britain and Northern Ireland, marking the establishment for the first time of full diplomatic relations between the United Kingdom and the Holy See. (This was of significance to Queen

Elizabeth because of her long friendship with D'Arcy Osborne.) Heim was a cultivated man, an authority on ecclesiastical heraldry, and a generous host at his own home where he entertained Queen Elizabeth and many others with his own excellent cooking, generous martinis and champagne enhanced with a twist of sorrel.

Lady Gladwyn, wife of the former Ambassador in Paris,* recounted a night at the Opera. She and other guests gathered to wait rather formally at Clarence House for their hostess. 'Suddenly there seemed a movement in the air, a widening of our circle, a rustle of skirts, and in came, with the greatest of informality and the highest of spirits, the Queen Mother. Sparkling with diamonds, in a pink tulle crinoline, and breaking any ice there might have been, she exuded an excited joy that was almost unqueenly.' Lady Gladwyn was fascinated: 'such is her power to charm and dazzle, that it does not seem to matter one whit that her inherent stoutness is now completely out of control.' Other people worried about weight for reasons of health or vanity. 'Not her. Obviously she relishes her food, her sweets and her champagne, and is not going to spoil her enjoyment of life by bothering about diet and exercise.' Cynthia Gladwyn was not sure how much the Queen Mother enjoyed *Figaro*. 'She sat straight as a ramrod and completely still . . . I thought from where I sat that I could detect a little weariness, a little sadness in her profile.' (In fact ramrod straight was how Queen Elizabeth always sat: she had been brought up to believe that a lady's back should never touch the back of her chair.) Lady Gladwyn said that as soon as there was a chance to applaud and comment, Queen Elizabeth's gaiety returned and she encouraged everyone to clap as loudly as they could and to shout encore.[49]

Not for nothing did Frances Campbell-Preston later recall that when she started to work as one of the women of the bedchamber – ladies in waiting in daily attendance – for Queen Elizabeth in the 1960s, 'I stepped back into a world which had died for me in 1939 – a world of butlers, chefs, housekeepers, housemaids, pages and footmen in smart uniforms, kitchen maids, chauffeurs and gardeners.'[50] She carried out her duties with wit and brio and became one of Queen Elizabeth's longest-serving ladies in waiting. Another was Lady

---

* Sir Gladwyn Jebb had been created Baron Gladwyn in 1960.

Grimthorpe, who was appointed in 1973 and later became the senior lady in the Household. In 1990 she took over the duties of the Mistress of the Robes – attending Queen Elizabeth at important engagements and arranging the rota of ladies in waiting – after the death of the Duchess of Abercorn, who had held the post since 1964. Elizabeth ('Skip') Grimthorpe was the daughter of Queen Elizabeth's girlhood friend Katharine McEwen, who had become countess of Scarbrough.

The ladies lived with Queen Elizabeth for two weeks at a time. One of their principal tasks, as we have seen, was to deal with the thousands of letters, often requests for help, which she received every year. There were social as well as secretarial duties. Dame Frances Campbell-Preston (as she later became) commented, 'The job was very nebulous. There were no rules. You did have to answer letters, help plan her engagements, chat up her guests, but no one told you what to do. You did as you liked. She didn't want stereotypes. She wanted to gossip with you. She was huge fun, but you never got very intimate with her. There was always a line.' This was perhaps because of her nervousness about the danger of being quoted, or misquoted in the press. 'She hated being asked questions,' said Dame Frances. 'If you asked her how she had liked Churchill, it would be a blank wall. She was very guarded and didn't want to be caught out.'[51] Many other members of the Royal Family share that concern.

The engine room at Clarence House was the equerry's room. The equerry, typically seconded from one of the Queen Mother's regiments for a two-year tour of duty at Clarence House, sat behind a large partner's desk with a telephone and an internal communications box to various parts of the house and to the Mews at Marlborough House. His principal tasks were to help organize the Queen Mother's private and official travel arrangements while in London and to act as host in her other homes. It was not an especially challenging role and the Queen Mother was a forgiving employer. On one occasion in the early 1970s an equerry overslept and missed an important engagement at which he was supposed to be in attendance. He was forgiven – and received an alarm clock the next day for his pains.

The equerry's office boasted a large drinks cupboard behind a door disguised by a selection of regimental histories and the like. The office acted as a general meeting place for the Household, and outside guests could be invited there. The equerry's working day would usually be interrupted at about noon when his male colleagues gathered in the room. Many of Sir Martin Gilliat's friends, who included a number of former Colditz comrades, would come to see him before lunch.

The staff whom the Queen Mother saw most often were her maid, her dresser and her two pages. One of the longest serving of her pages, Bill Baker, had worked for her since 1927 and retired in 1975. Walter Taylor, steward at Clarence House, served for almost as long, from 1936 until his death in 1978. These two were succeeded, respectively, by Reginald Wilcock and his friend William Tallon. Queen Elizabeth relied greatly upon them both in later life. Tallon was a cultivated but flamboyant man who became the great character on her staff. His off-duty behaviour as a boulevardier raised eyebrows; with his bouffant hair, his gift for bold repartee and his fondness for a drink, he had various escapades in his private life which might have embarrassed other employers – but if senior members of her Household ever complained about his conduct, she would suggest to them that, although their jobs were always under review, Tallon's was not.[52] After Queen Elizabeth's death Tallon was offered large sums of money by newspapers to tell her secrets. He refused.

From 1970 onwards there was also her chef Michael Sealey, who described himself as 'a loquacious West Country yeoman'. Sealey had been third assistant chef at Buckingham Palace since Coronation year and the offer to work for Queen Elizabeth came, he said, out of the blue. Her taste in food was simple and, he thought, derived from early life at Glamis. He said later that choosing the menus was a two-way street. She loved goujons of sole (which she had been served on her triumphant 1938 visit to Paris), and haddock – 'She would have had that every night. I once tried monkfish and she sent a message "Tell Chef we won't have that again." '[53] She insisted on fresh food in season; the only frozen food that Sealey ever served her were peas in Russian salads. She thought Spanish strawberries tasted like turnips. Among other dislikes were smoked salmon (which other people gave her too often), oysters, coconut and capers. She loved omelettes. One of her favourite dishes, which Sealey made time and time again, was *Oeufs Drumkilbo*. Named after the Elphinstone family home in Perthshire, the dish had been created by their Baltic cook; it consisted of diced hard-boiled eggs, lobster, shrimps, tomato, cream and mayonnaise, served cold in aspic.[54]

Most of the staff at Clarence House saw Queen Elizabeth only rarely. Indeed for some it was only when she gave out Christmas presents. 'We used to call it school prize giving,' recalled Lucy Murphy, who started working at Clarence House as lady clerk to the Private Secretary in 1967, and was still there in 2002. Everyone was allowed to choose his or her own gift, which was then presented, unwrapped, by the Queen Mother at individual audiences where only William Tallon and the housekeeper were present.

*

WHEN SHE WAS based in London, Queen Elizabeth spent as many weekends as possible at Royal Lodge, the pale-pink-washed house in Windsor Great Park on which she and the Duke of York had lavished so much time and affection. She continued to love the house along with new generations of the family. In the 1950s Prince Charles and Princess Anne spent long weekends and parts of the school holidays playing in the Welsh Cottage which had been given to Princess Elizabeth in 1932. In the upstairs nursery at Royal Lodge there were still the rocking horses and many of the toys – a Noah's Ark and a host of animals – with which both Princesses had played, and from the mid-1960s onwards it was the turn of Princess Margaret's children, David and Sarah, to enjoy them.

Royal Lodge was a comfortable, easy house, whose focal point was still the magnificent saloon which the Duke and Duchess of York had restored in the 1930s, and which was depicted in the National Portrait Gallery's well-known conversation piece by James Gunn, showing the King and Queen and the two Princesses in 1950. The room was dominated by the five tall and elegant French windows which gave on to the terrace. Over the fireplace hung, appropriately, a portrait of the Lodge's original denizen King George IV by Sir Thomas Lawrence. Facing each other on either side of the fireplace were two sofas, one covered in pink damask and the other in green. Other groups of chairs were gathered close to the windows. Tables were piled with books and big pots of flowers. On one end wall hung a fine verdure tapestry from Brussels. A large red and blue Persian carpet covered most of the floor.

Next door was the Octagon Room where visitors might wait before seeing Queen Elizabeth in the saloon. There was a green-marble fireplace with an old-fashioned three-bar electric fire in the hearth, a hexagonal table piled with books, panelled walls, bookcases filled with worn-looking leatherbound sets, family photographs on the piano. On the wall were the John Singer Sargent pendant portraits of the Duke and Duchess of York at the time of their marriage. The curtains were pink and the armchairs and sofas covered in flowered chintz. The carpet, with a twelve-sided central panel, became very worn over the years, by people and also by dogs. The desk, by the French window, was filled to overflowing with family photographs and large cache-pots of flowers.

Upstairs the bedrooms and bathrooms remained as the Duke and Duchess of York had designed them, simple and somewhat tired. Queen Elizabeth was always reluctant to change familiar, much-loved furnishings and, as the years went by, Royal Lodge showed its age. Doors could get stuck, light switches tended to flash, the central heating and the plumbing were unpredictable. All this, together with the clutter of Wellington boots and gardening clothes just inside the front door, enhanced the feeling of old-fashioned country-house living at Royal Lodge, and the sense of continuity was reflected in the garden tombstones of the corgis who had barked before.

Here, as at her other homes, Queen Elizabeth developed annual rituals. She would have two pheasant-shooting weekends. Every spring she welcomed a lawn meet for the Eton College Hunt (Beagles). In March she had what was called the Musical Weekend (sometimes also called the Geriatric Weekend within her Household) at which she entertained those of her friends who were less interested in shooting or fishing. In the last two decades of her life, the guests often included Archbishop Runcie and his wife Lindy, Peter Carrington and his wife Iona, Fitzroy and Veronica Maclean, Sir John (later Lord) Sainsbury, merchant and philanthropist, and his wife Anya, a former principal ballerina with the Royal Ballet. She admired the Sainsbury family for both its business success and its record of philanthropy. In 1985, John Sainsbury, the chairman of the company, invited her to make her one and only visit to the modern phenomenon of a supermarket, the big Sainsbury store in Cromwell Road. There she spoke to surprised and delighted customers and staff and told the French manager of the wine department (in French) of her fondness for claret. She appreciated the Sainsburys' generous interest in ballet and much approved of their donation of the new wing of the National Gallery at the end of the

1980s. The original, modernist design was fiercely criticized, including by the Prince of Wales who described it as 'a monstrous carbuncle on the face of a much loved and elegant friend'. Many architects never forgave the Prince but, after a long controversy, the modernist plans were scrapped, a more harmonious design by the firm of Venturi, Rauch and Scott Brown was approved instead, and the new Sainsbury wing opened to acclaim in 1991.[55]

Other frequent guests at Royal Lodge included Lord David Cecil, the Duke and Duchess of Grafton, and Lord Gowrie, Conservative politician and poet, and his wife Nitie, whose father, Count Fritz-Dietlof von der Schulenburg, had been executed for his part in the July 1944 plot to kill Hitler. There was always fine poetry and music at these weekends, provided by such poets as Stephen Spender and John Betjeman, actors like Sir John Gielgud, and young musicians, some-times from the Royal College of Music. Like other guests, Spender found these weekends 'magical' and told her, 'I think you float on the pleasure that you give to all those around you.'[56]

One Royal Lodge house party was amusingly evoked by another guest, the diplomat Sir Charles Johnston, who described the fun and games after dinner, with Lord Ballantrae playing the piano while the guests danced in and out of the room led by the 'dynamic little figure' of the Queen Mother, 'arms up in Highland attitudes', until 'we all got noisy and over-excited and the ex-bish of New York began to lose his collar.'[57]

She had met the 'ex-bish', Horace Donegan,* on her trip to the United States in 1954, when she had heard him preach on the importance of family life. Thereafter, as Hugo Vickers expressed it in his biography of her: 'The Queen Mother warmed to him, and, once he had found her, he never let her go.'[58] Bishop Donegan appreciated the martinis that flowed at Royal Lodge. One year he had so many, Lord Carrington recalled, that he was unable to remember Grace when Queen Elizabeth asked him to say it. 'After dinner she said to

---

* The Rt Rev. Horace Donegan (1900–91), Bishop of New York 1950–72. Born in England, he moved with his family to the United States when he was ten. He was a strong advocate of the rights of women, black people and the poor, and according to his obituary in the *New York Times* he transformed the social consciousness of his New York diocese. He was made an honorary Companion of the Order of the Bath in 1957. (*New York Times*, 30 November 1991)

Martin [Gilliat] "You really must not give him so many martinis next year." The next year I *heard* Martin saying to him, "Have another martini Bish – it will steady your nerves for Grace." [59]

Royal Lodge was also the base for many of her expeditions to see her racehorses and attend race meetings. Horses enlivened the whole of the second half of her life. She read *Sporting Life* every day and she had installed in Clarence House a rather primitive loudspeaker system, such as usually exists only in betting shops, to relay minute-by-minute news from racetracks around the country.

Her racing colours, derived from those of the 'racing' twelfth Earl of Strathmore, were blue with buff stripes, blue sleeves and a black cap with a gold tassel. She brought a new excitement and glamour to steeplechasing and she was welcomed warmly at every racecourse. An early annual meeting that she always wished to attend was the Royal Artillery Meeting at Sandown Park in February. To coincide with the Grand Military meeting in early March, she held a house party and gave a reception for owners, trainers, jockeys and race officials every year. Then came the National Hunt Festival at Cheltenham. For some years she stayed with Lady Avice Spicer at Spye Park for Cheltenham, but later she drove down daily from Royal Lodge, where she always had a house party for the meeting.

At the end of April there was the Whitbread Gold Cup at Sandown Park. Billy Whitbread, who had started this sponsorship, was one of those flamboyant characters she enjoyed. After attending the Derby, with the Queen, the Queen Mother always went to Royal Ascot, and the King George VI and Queen Elizabeth Stakes at the end of July. She had house parties at Royal Lodge for the latter.

Her first important race meeting of the winter was the Hennessy Gold Cup at Newbury for which she would have a different group of friends to stay at Royal Lodge. At the Ascot Christmas meeting on the Saturday before Christmas, she would have a children's lunch party in the royal box for the grandchildren and great-grandchildren of friends. It was often a riotous affair, for Martin Gilliat was adept at making children roar with laughter. Father Christmas drove down the race-course, and crowds of children would gather round the entrance to the Royal Box, where the Queen and Queen Elizabeth gave out the presents – sweets and chocolates – from his sack. When Christmases were at Windsor, Queen Elizabeth always went to the King George VI steeplechase at Kempton Park on Boxing Day.

In addition to all these regular meetings, she tried to go wherever she had a horse running. She and Michael Oswald, her Racing Manager, once went to Warwick by train; the steward brought her tea in his own earthenware teapot instead of the standard British Rail metal one, which he didn't think good enough. 'How nice,' she said, whereupon he gave it to her. She used it often thereafter at Royal Lodge, Birkhall and Sandringham.[60]

Of her trainers, Peter Cazalet probably gave her the most fun, both with the horses he trained and at his beautiful house, Fairlawne in Kent. Cazalet's grandfather, Edward, who had made a fortune through trade with Russia, had become the squire of the neighbouring village of Shipbourne and had acquired Fairlawne in the 1870s. He had added to the house and built the Queen Anne-style stables which his grandson used to create his racing establishment in the late 1940s. Cazalet's first wife, Leonora, was the stepdaughter of P. G. Wodehouse. She had died during the war and in 1949 Cazalet married Zara Strutt, a bubbly and attractive woman who immediately began to enhance Fairlawne and became a lifelong friend of Queen Elizabeth. The Cazalets appreciated fine living and throughout the 1950s and 1960s, as Cazalet built up the racing successes of Fairlawne, his wife entertained generously. Every December, they would throw a big house party to coincide with the races at nearby Lingfield, a small Surrey racecourse. Weekends at Fairlawne were glamorous and fun and the Queen Mother enjoyed them. All in all she stayed with the Cazalets about twenty times.

On one occasion Peter Cazalet's son Anthony, aged about nine, invited Queen Elizabeth for a drive in the ancient car he drove about the grounds. To Zara Cazalet's consternation Queen Elizabeth replied, 'Oh yes, I would love to,' and sat on the floor of the banger, which disappeared into Fairlawne's Home Woods, while Mrs Cazalet uttered anxious cries of 'Where *are* they?' Eventually they returned, both smiling happily, and Queen Elizabeth remarked on what a wonderful time she had had.

Among her fellow guests at Fairlawne were the film star Elizabeth Taylor, Noël Coward and the historian Elizabeth Longford and her husband Frank, the Labour peer, who lived near by. Once when Coward was at Fairlawne the Cazalets invited to lunch a couple they had met in Tahiti; the wife's father had written about the mutiny on the *Bounty*. They presented the Queen Mother with a Cartier box. Its contents were unexpected: a nail from the *Bounty*. Never at a loss at such moments, she received it with her usual charm. Afterwards, Noël Coward teased her for the way she had exclaimed in tones of wonderment, 'Oh, a *nail*!', 'as if it was a Crown Jewel!'[61]

At Noël Coward's weekends there would always be at least one singsong around the piano. Queen Elizabeth, like everyone else, loved Coward's affectionate parodies of British manners. Particular favourites were 'Mad Dogs and Englishmen Go Out in the Midday Sun', 'The Stately Homes of England' and 'Don't Let's Be Beastly to the Germans'.[62]

Peter Cazalet always ensured that the Queen Mother had horses running at Lingfield during these weekends. These included Double Star, The Rip, Laffy, Makaldar and Escalus. Double Star had been found in Ireland by Cazalet; he had cost £4,000, a considerable sum in 1956, but he justified this, winning the Ashdown Handicap Chase at Lingfield three times; overall he won seventeen out of the fifty races in which he was entered between 1956 and 1963.

Perhaps her best racing weekend there was in December 1961 when she had three winners – Laffy, Double Star and The Rip. The Rip was by Queen Elizabeth's own early favourite, Manicou, out of a mare called Easy Virtue, which was owned by Jack Irwin, the son of the landlord of the Red Cat pub at Wootton Marshes near Sandringham. The Queen Mother acquired him for 400 guineas, which turned out to be a bargain.

He was sent to be broken in by Major Eldred Wilson DSO, the senior tenant farmer on the Sandringham estate, who had been a prisoner of war and on his return became a successful farmer and horseman. He brought on Queen Elizabeth's young horses and became a friend to her; she liked to compliment him by saying that he had 'a touch of Irish in him'. Wilson had been a brave point-to-point rider and, after he retired, he continued to live on the estate. She visited him at home every July and each year the same conversation was repeated, the same jokes rehearsed, the same laughter enjoyed. She made similar visits to other retired members of her staff and Household every year until the end of her life.

Wilson did a fine job with The Rip, who won four races in a row in 1962; in the 1964 Hennessy Gold Cup he was placed third behind the illustrious Arkle and Ferry Boat. Altogether The Rip won thirteen races under the Queen Mother's colours. Among her other more successful horses, Double Star and Chaou II each won seventeen races.

In 1964 she had her one-hundredth win with a rather temperamental horse, Gay Record, in the Sevenoaks Chase at Folkestone. To celebrate, she held a dance to which she invited all her friends from the racing world and many from the acting world as well and, according to Dick Francis, danced with all the jockeys.[63]

During the Cazalet years Queen Elizabeth had up to sixteen jumpers in training with him and with other trainers. After his death in 1973 she cut back somewhat – the expenses were not sustainable – and usually had fewer than ten, many of them with Fulke Walwyn at his stables at Lambourn in Berkshire. Walwyn had his own distinguished racing history and, when he was a jockey, had actually won the Grand National on Reynoldstown in 1936. He had fewer winners for the Queen Mother than Cazalet, but his winners won bigger races. The first race he won for her was, appropriately, the Fairlawne Chase at Windsor, with Game Spirit, and the next the Reynoldstown Pattern Hurdle at Wolverhampton, with Sunnyboy. In 1975 he won her the popular Schweppes Hurdle at Newbury with Tammuz, ridden by Bill Smith. It carried a purse of over £9,000 – her most valuable win up to that time. For her 200th and 300th winners, her rumbustious friend Dick Wilkins, a stockjobber in the City of London and a man of generous instincts and proportions, gave her parties at the Savoy.

Racing and horses afforded her not just seasonal but daily pleasure. Like her daughter, she was a good judge of horseflesh and had an encyclopaedic knowledge of racing form. She and the Queen were both patrons of the Jockey Club, and when the National Hunt Committee, of which she was patron, merged with the Jockey Club, she became joint patron.

Sir Michael Oswald recalled that, unlike many owners, she took an interest in everyone from stable boys and girls upwards. 'Very few people looking at a horse pay any attention to the person holding the horse. She always spoke to them and shook hands before looking at the horse.' Oswald thought that the Queen Mother understood well what people wanted from her. If she found herself surrounded by people with cameras at an event, she would smile and wave to each side of the road. She invariably stopped to talk to people in wheelchairs. 'She always wanted to make sure that people who wanted to see her went away happy.' She would often repeat the maxim she had learned from her mother – 'There is no one who is really boring – if you find someone so, it must be because of you.' She had wonderful manners and to the end of her life she would try to get out of her chair to shake people's hands. She managed to remember people year after year.[64]

She was loyal to horses as well as trainers. She would never sell a horse; instead homes would be found for them with her regiments, or with local farmers who could use them for hacking, and she would send them off on permanent loan. None of this came cheap and, throughout, her racing had to be subsidized by the Queen. After one particularly disappointing year, the Queen offered to pay her mother's bill from Peter Cazalet. The Queen Mother accepted gratefully, signed the bill and wrote underneath the total, 'Oh dear'.[65]

After Devon Loch's disastrous collapse in the 1956 Grand National, probably the most thrilling race in which she was involved was the 1984 Whitbread Gold Cup in which she ran Special Cargo. That year's race was in a class of its own, as the *Sunday Times* correspondent, Brough Scott, related. In the final uphill stretch, after twenty-four fences had been jumped, four horses – Special Cargo, Lettoch, Diamond Edge and Plundering – strained towards the post. In the Royal Box, the Queen Mother was visibly excited. Plundering then fell away and, with only a hundred yards to go, Diamond Edge was gaining on the leader, Lettoch. But Special Cargo was now within two lengths and flying fast. 'All three were together as the post flashed by. First thoughts were that none could be a loser.' There were long minutes of suspense as the judges considered the photographs. Queen Elizabeth was unable to move until she knew the result.[66] Special Cargo had won by a fraction; overjoyed she rushed down to the winner's enclosure, where her pale-blue coat matched her jockey's silks.[67]

*

THE MOST REMOTE of her houses, the Castle of Mey, was the most personal – in good part, no doubt, because it was the only one that actually belonged to her. She was able to invest Mey, and her stays there, with her own individual spirit and tastes. Her principal visit every year from 1956 onwards was made in August, immediately after her birthday, and she used to say that it was 'the beginning of the holidays' and the end of the 'term' in London. She loved the fresh air and the open space that the Castle offered, with the ever changing view of clouds and sea and the shadows on Orkney beyond. Another great advantage was that 'at the furthest tip of these islands, one feels so beautifully far away and the newspapers come too late to be readable'.[68]

Her visits to Mey started privately and modestly, but developed into what her neighbour Lord Thurso called 'a mini season' in Caithness. Local landowners made sure they were in residence when she came, and many threw parties in the hope of attracting her; she gave a cocktail party every summer which was a major event. There was no question but that her ownership of Mey put Caithness on the map.

The Castle itself required constant maintenance even after she had completed the basic structural repairs in the 1950s. Because it was built of porous sandstone, it was very hard to keep the damp out. In addition, as the years went by, water seeped through the roof, and lead work was found to be missing; the initial repairs had been inadequate.

The furnishings developed and moved over time. Many of the original pieces she and the Vyners had bought locally, in Miss Miller Calder's shop in Thurso. A huge clam-shell jardinière stood in the front hall, packed with flowers while the Queen Mother was in residence. In the hall there was a chronometer from King George V's racing yacht *Britannia*, which struck the bells of the watch instead of the hours. The London firm of Lenygon and Morant, which worked for the Queen Mother in her other homes, was responsible for much of the internal design and decoration, and supplied curtains and other furnishings. She and those around her were pleased with the results. In 1959 Arthur Penn wrote to her to say, 'What a very rewarding & memorable visit your Castle gave us all this spring. It was bristling with triumphs.'[69]

Today the house is preserved as it was in her lifetime. The main room on the raised ground floor is the drawing room, whose windows face both inland and north towards the sea and the Orkney Islands. A large sixteenth-century Flemish wool tapestry hangs on the north wall. When she was in residence a peat fire burned continuously in the grate. Next door to the drawing room is the equerry's room. On the desk the red leatherbound hymnal and prayer book which the equerry carried for her to church every Sunday can still be seen. In this and other rooms are paintings and miniature model casts of some of her most successful cattle.

Beyond the equerry's room is the Library where, in later life,

Queen Elizabeth dealt with her correspondence every day – 'my Hunka-Munka room', she called it. On her desk are three of her favourite photographs, slightly faded by time – the King in uniform in 1943, the King in South Africa, the King with her and Princess Elizabeth – and various objects, including a little corgi from the Buckingham Palace gift shop. On a small Formica table by the wall sits an elderly television, on top of which are photographs of Princess Elizabeth and Princess Margaret, dressed for a wartime pantomime. Against one wall stands a handsome upright piano in a walnut case, which the Queen Mother bought in Inverness and which she encouraged Ruth Fermoy and others to play after dinner.

The most striking room in the house is the dining room, at the western end. This was added in 1819 by the twelfth Earl of Caithness as an extension to the original Castle. On the east wall Queen Elizabeth hung a spectacularly vivid tapestry of her coat of arms, which she had commissioned from the Dovecote Studio in Edinburgh in 1950.[70] It was designed by Stephen Gooden RA, a distinguished book illustrator and line engraver, and was woven on an ancient loom using Cheviot wool specially spun and dyed in Scotland. In the fireplace at the opposite end of the room is a beautiful cast-iron fire-back created by Martin Charteris, the Queen's long-serving Private Secretary and a friend of the Queen Mother. The piece depicts the Queen Mother's ER cipher and the royal yacht *Britannia* among local flora and fauna. Above the fireplace is a naive painting of the Castle from the sea painted by R. I. Gray in 1884. It is an oddly prophetic picture. In the field in front of the Castle there is a herd of black cattle; offshore a yacht lies at anchor. Just over a century later *Britannia* could have been seen sailing past Queen Elizabeth's herd of Aberdeen Angus cattle. On either side of the fireplace is an oil painting by Prince Philip, an accomplished amateur painter.

Next door to the dining room is the butler's pantry, which by the end of the century had become almost a museum piece of 1950s domestic design, with white metal doors and drawers, a wheezing, ancient gas-fired refrigerator and an old electric oven in which plates were warmed. Connecting the pantry with the much more modern kitchen below is a steep and narrow staircase and a small dumb-waiter food lift. But the dumb-waiter was hand operated and made a great deal of noise – the footmen and pages preferred to run up and down stairs balancing heavy trays rather than disturb the guests with its wailing mechanism.

At the opposite end of the house, Queen Elizabeth's bedroom is reached up the stone stairs in the turret, which she managed to navigate until the end of her life. (In the 1950s she restored the lift that the Imbert-Terrys had installed, but she rarely used it except for regular Sunday-morning descents to talk to the chef and his staff in the kitchen, after which she would insist on walking up the narrow stairs before leaving for church.) Her bedroom has north-, east- and south-facing windows which enabled her to keep an eye not only on her cattle and sheep but also on the comings and goings of guests in the driveway. Ceilings and walls are all painted light blue; her bed covers and the headboard are also blue and have faded gently with the years. The room is modestly furnished with a simple blue-painted wardrobe and mahogany chest of drawers.

Near her room is a bedroom with a small four-poster bed with pale-blue hangings. This is called Princess Margaret's Bedroom, although the Princess never spent a night there. She did not much like 'Mummy's draughty castle'. At the western end of the corridor is Lady Doris Vyner's Bedroom; this looks out on the Castle's walled garden, which Queen Elizabeth cherished. The garden is surrounded by the fifteen-foot high Great Wall of Mey, as it became known, to shield the flowers, shrubs and vegetables from the worst of the elements. Everything grown there had to be chosen for its resistance to wind and sea spray. Queen Elizabeth was pleased to be able to grow even her favourite old rose, Albertine, on the south-facing wall between the garden and the Castle; within the garden a complicated network of seven-foot-high hedges of privet, currant and elder protected flower-beds of marigolds, pansies, dahlias, primulas, nasturtiums and sweet peas. A wide variety of fruits and vegetables was grown for the dining table.[71]

Near the Castle is Longoe Farm, where she insisted, despite the expense, on raising her livestock. Whenever she was at Mey she would walk down through the gardens and policies (fields) between the Castle and the sea to visit her animals and talk to those who cared for them, especially the McCarthy family who farmed the land. She took great pleasure in showing off the cattle and sheep to knowledgeable farmers and stockmen who occasionally came on organized visits, and in

getting their views – 'the more forthright and frank the better!' said
Martin Leslie, her factor. At such visits tea, chocolate cake and drams
of whisky were served in the dining room. 'Afterwards a Page reported
on the whisky consumption and the hostess got much satisfaction, and
amusement, judging how well her hospitality had been received while
marvelling at her guests' capacity.' She would show her cattle and
sheep at both local and national shows. Whenever Leslie went up to
Mey in her absence, she would ask him to telephone her to tell her
'how the people are, how the stock are looking, what Caithness is
looking like and if the weather is fine and the skies are beautiful'.[72]

The Mey Visitors' Book is a large brown-leather volume. Its first
page is inscribed 'Arrival at Wick Airport 1952' and a photograph
shows Queen Elizabeth at the bottom of the steps of a plane, being
greeted by the Vyners. She is all in black, wearing a string of pearls
and a long fur stole. This is followed by photographs of her and the
Vyners on a trawler and taking a picnic on the cliffs. The first
signatures of guests appear in October 1959 – they include Queen
Elizabeth's niece Elizabeth Elphinstone, Martin Gilliat and E. H.
'Mouse' Fielden, an RAF veteran who had been appointed the first
captain of the King's Flight by King Edward VIII in 1936 and was
reappointed in the next two reigns.

Fielden was a courageous man; during the war he had won the
Distinguished Flying Cross for flying British agents in and out of
occupied France in tiny Lysander planes. In 1941 he brought back a
bottle of that year's wine and presented it to the King. According to
the historian Kenneth Rose, the King served the bottle to Winston
Churchill, at one of their weekly lunches, 'teasing his guest by refusing
to say how he had come by it'.[73] Fielden worked hard within the post-
war Whitehall bureaucracy to ensure the best and safest planes for his
royal charges; he was an exuberant and delightful man and became a
long-standing friend of Queen Elizabeth.

These and many other guests – both friends and members of her
Household – Elizabeth Basset, David McMicking, Olivia Mulholland,
Adam Gordon, Ruth Fermoy and her niece Margaret Elphinstone, with
her husband Denys Rhodes, came frequently over the decades. In 1970
and in later years Archie Winskill,* the Captain of the Queen's Flight

---

* Air Commodore Sir Archibald Winskill (1917–2005), a fighter pilot in the Battle of Britain,
was appointed captain of the Queen's Flight in 1968.

and a popular guest, was often invited – it was of him that Queen Elizabeth was reported to have said, 'It's people like Archie who make it worth putting lipstick on.'

During the 1970s the guests at Mey were younger and occasionally more high-spirited. The Visitors' Book is filled with more colour snapshots of picnics and individuals. One shows a picnic basket close to piles of rusting steel tubing and is entitled 'Lunch in a rubbish dump'. In 1973 a young officer in the Blues and Royals of whom she was fond, Andrew Parker Bowles, was invited with his wife Camilla. Parker Bowles's father Derek was an old and close friend of Queen Elizabeth.

There was grouse shooting at Mey for the guests, but the birds became more and more scarce, as elsewhere in Scotland; the keeper, who was only six months younger than his employer, organized days of walked-up grouse shooting until he was well into his nineties. Lunches were almost always out, at various favourite picnic places which included Captain's House, a cottage with spectacular views of the Castle and the Pentland Firth, and Ralph Anstruther's nearby home at Watten.

In 1975 a young man named Ashe Windham arrived at Mey. Windham, who served in the Irish Guards from 1976 to 1987, was a friend of Lord ('Mikie') Glamis, the son of Queen Elizabeth's nephew Fergus, seventeenth Earl of Strathmore. He invited Windham to come with him to visit his great-aunt at Mey; she liked the young man and from that first encounter grew many years of service and friendship from Windham.

Every Sunday at Mey she worshipped in her own pew at Canisbay Church. From 1959 the minister was the Rev. George Bell. He and his wife were nervous when they first met the Queen Mother but she put them at their ease, inviting them to the Castle every year.[74] On Bell's retirement the Queen Mother provided him with a cottage, and when he fell ill, she visited him. After his death, Mrs Bell said, 'she was a tremendous support to me ... I am sure she realised exactly how I felt, because she had experienced the same thing, at a much younger age too.'[75] Mrs Bell, still regularly invited to the Castle, would entertain the Queen Mother and her guests with comic recitations of popular Scottish poetry, for which she had a talent. One in particular, 'Bella Macrae', was a great favourite and Queen Elizabeth named a horse after the heroine. Another was 'McAllister Dances before the King', the tale of a Scotsman who went to London and stunned the King and particularly the Queen with his prowess as a dancer. The last two verses raised especial smiles when Mrs Bell recited them at Mey:

> And then the gracious queen herself
>   Came shyly o'er to me
> And pinned a medal on my breast
>   For everyone to see.
>
> Her whisper I shall ne'er forget,
>   Nor how her eyes grew dim.
> 'Ach, where were you, McAllister,
>   The day I married him!'

When Mrs Bell succumbed to Alzheimer's, Queen Elizabeth continued to ask her to tea, with her daughter Christine Shearer.[76]

George Bell's successor at Canisbay Church, the Rev. Alex Muir, found the Queen Mother interested in church affairs and always keen to discuss the hymns and the sermons. He thought that she had 'a very strong and genuine faith, which I'm sure has been a great support to her. She loves to worship God.'[77] Muir had a guitar which he not only played in the pulpit but brought to dinner at the Castle. The Queen Mother encouraged her guests to sing along with his hymns and songs, which included a Glasgow street favourite (here Martin Leslie's wife Catriona, who knew the song, was the only one to join in), 'Ye Cannae Shove Yer Grannie aff a Bus'.[78]

Britannia's visit was a high point every summer. The Queen would start her annual holiday aboard, sailing around the Western Isles and then around the north coast of Scotland before disembarking finally at Aberdeen. This was one of the most cherished breaks of the year for both the monarch and her family.

The yacht anchored off Scrabster, the nearest port to Mey, and the family came ashore and motored over to the castle. There Queen Elizabeth laid on a splendid lunch, with *Oeufs Drumkilbo* usually on the menu. Then the Queen would often lead a party down to the beach to clean up rubbish and make a bonfire. Sometimes there was croquet on the lawn. After tea the yacht party returned to Scrabster. Then in the early evening the local coastguards would bring to the Castle all the time-expired maroons and flares from the north of Scotland which they would let off as the yacht steamed past on its way to Aberdeen. *Britannia* and her escorting frigate would reply with fireworks while the Mey party lined the Great Wall of Mey and waved dog towels, tea towels and handkerchiefs.

It became a habit for the Queen and her mother to exchange doggerel over ship-to-shore radio, via the Coast Guard. One year came these words from the yacht, to be sung to the tune of 'O Worship the King':

> We send our best thanks
> For lunch and good cheer
> Though skies may be grey
> Warm welcome was there
> Pavilioned in Splendour
> The Castle of Mey
> Gave all of the family
> A wonderful day.[79]

*

AT THE END of her summer holiday at Mey, Queen Elizabeth would travel 180 miles south to her other Scottish home, Birkhall, hidden in the trees of the Balmoral estate and lulled by the waters of the River Muick rushing beside it. Here she spent several weeks every year in spring and in early autumn. It is an attractive house, a typical Scottish lodge built of stone, harled and painted white. The front door faces east, is approached by stone steps and has a canopy above it supported by tree trunks painted 'Balmoral grey'.

In the mid-1950s the Queen paid to have the house extended for her mother; a corrugated-iron-roofed extension was torn down and in its place was built a drawing room and a wing of bedrooms – single rooms for bachelors on the ground floor and doubles above. A round tower containing a staircase connected the old and new wings. Arthur Penn played a large part in redesigning and redecorating the house at that time. After it had been completed, it was realized that no provision had been made for a downstairs gentlemen's lavatory. Penn helped devise such a closet space under the tower staircase and Queen Elizabeth performed an opening ceremony in which the lavatory was filled with flowers from the garden and she declared it open by pulling the chain and saying 'I name this "Arthur's Seat".'[80] The house is on raised ground, surrounded to the north by trees. The grass terrace on the south side sweeps down to a typical Scottish garden, with rows of vegetables between gravel paths and flower borders.

Birkhall had its own particular smell which, to those who visited often, had its own poignancy. It was the aroma of juniper twigs burned on the fire, mingled with the scents of roses and sweet peas which filled the house in the early autumn. There was the smell of smoking lavender too, from the incense burner which William Tallon would swing as he walked down the corridors to summon the guests for dinner. The house breathed warmth, life and laughter, according to one frequent guest.[81]

Features of Birkhall's earlier days remained: the tartan carpets, and the extraordinary collection of Spy and Ape cartoons of famous Victorians and Edwardians, left to the house by a former occupant and courtier, Sir Dighton Probyn VC.* They lined the main corridor and the stairs, providing guests with endless subjects of conversation. Queen Elizabeth added her own works of art – many of her Seago paintings were hung in the drawing room and dining room, and Kathleen Scott's sensitive sculpture of King George VI stood near the entrance to the drawing room. In the dining room, bronze figures of Highlanders running, tossing the caber, putting the shot and throwing the hammer stood on the sideboard and sometimes on the dining table. The walls were lined with Queen Elizabeth's collection of eight grandfather clocks – an echo of her youth, for the dining room at Glamis was also full of clocks. She enjoyed pointing out to guests their different characters. The cacophony when they chimed – which was seldom precisely together – interrupted conversation to comical effect.

Queen Elizabeth liked to go to Birkhall in May for the fishing and because it afforded her a complete re-run of spring. Long after the daffodils at Royal Lodge had withered, their northern cousins on the banks of the Dee were beginning to emerge from winter sleep. There was still snow on the slopes of Lochnagar, and the river teemed with life as the salmon forged upstream in search of spawning places. In a crevice on the rock face opposite the Polveir pool there was a dipper's nest, and every year Queen Elizabeth took great pleasure in observing the movements of the parents and wondering how they were raising their young.[82]

At her Scottish homes, Queen Elizabeth often wore aged blue

---

*   See note on p. 310.

tweed jackets and tartan skirts and a blue felt hat with a sprig of heather and a feather held in place by a badge containing a cairngorm stone. She called such clothes 'old friends – you never get rid of old friends'. Everywhere she went she was accompanied by the latest in many generations of corgis.

She did not believe there was much purpose in having guests in the Highlands unless they took advantage of the great outdoors. After lavish traditional breakfasts, guests were supposed to be usefully employed either shooting on the hill, fishing or walking. She leased Corndavon moor from the Invercauld Estate next to Balmoral for many years, as the King had done.

A particular feature of her shoots was the tradition, followed from 1965 to 1974, of having student beaters from St Andrews and Aberdeen Universities. There was no shortage of applicants for a month on the moors. Michael Briggs, one of the students from St Andrews, recalled the sheer sense of fun she displayed. 'One of her favourite little things was to glance across at Lochnagar and say, "Isn't Lochnagar looking beautiful today?" And then she would bend down and say, "Isn't Lochnagar beautiful, even upside down!" She would have us in stitches because you knew she was going to do it.' At the end of the month, Queen Elizabeth always gave a cocktail party for the student beaters. 'The last time, we all presented her with a crystal rose bowl. I had to give a little speech and one of her wonderful friends, Mr Dick Wilkins, came up to me afterwards and said, "I saw a tear in Her Majesty's eye when you were speaking."' [83]

The Corndavon lease ran out in 1974 and she decided not to renew it. Instead she took individual days on the hill when she had a house party that was particularly dedicated to shooting. From now on the focus of many of her guests shifted to the river. Queen Elizabeth had fished most of her life, at first mainly for trout. Salmon fishing became a passion in the second half of her life. Her ghillie at Balmoral, Charlie Wright, said of her, 'she was a good fisher, she had good casting and was excellent at playing a fish. She liked catching fish herself, but she was even happier if her guests did so.' [84] Evening fishing was much favoured at Birkhall. Once Queen Elizabeth was out very late and came back in the dark carrying, in triumph, a twenty-pound salmon. 'This is what kept me,' she declared. [85] She continued fishing in her favourite pools on the Dee until her early eighties.

Her other passion, which she indulged particularly at Birkhall, was for eating outside. Picnics there, as at Mey, could take place in high winds and even snow. She had favourite picnic places, which included the old Schoolhouse by the Gairn and the lodge at Loch Callater which, though dank, had magnificent views. The fare was generous; good drinks, little sausages from Ballater, prawn croquettes, *Oeufs Drumkilbo*, asparagus – for starters. Then game or chicken pie, cold lamb cutlets, ham or cold beef, with baked potatoes wrapped in foil. In especially bad weather, 'picnics' could be held in the porch or even in the drawing room. Queen Elizabeth liked the informality and the sense of adventure involved. Picnics, she also claimed, were easier on the staff. Perhaps some were.

Back at the house there was tea to be taken in the drawing room, which featured an old gramophone with long-playing records of such old favourites as the Crazy Gang, and an equally aged television set for watching videos (rarely if ever the news). Ruth Fermoy would play the piano and Queen Elizabeth sang the old favourites – 'Smoke Gets in Your Eyes' or 'The Lambeth Walk'.

Often she played Racing Demon, with no holds barred. Frances Campbell-Preston wrote, 'She enjoyed winning.' She considered herself devilishly good at the game and she did usually win – not only because of her skill but also because other guests worried that they might be asked to catch the midnight train south if they won too often. Almost everyone understood that. The Duke of Atholl, another competitive card player, did not. When, at the end of one evening, it appeared he had not won, he asked that the scores be counted once more. The discomfited equerry did so; it then seemed that the Duke had indeed scored the most points. It was a pyrrhic victory. He was not asked again.[86]

As time went by, the evenings became quieter – fewer singsongs and games of cards, more videos, usually *Dad's Army* or *Keeping Up Appearances*; *Fawlty Towers* was another favourite. But the hostess insisted on dancing Scottish reels with her guests until the very end of her life.

Guests at Birkhall felt they had been happily transported into a world without time or travail. One of them, Sir Pierson Dixon, wrote of 'the charm and rhythm of life' there, and thanked Queen Elizabeth for 'thrilling hours on the moors', for lunches by the river, and for 'Lucullan dinners', quizzes and games. He had been refreshed and enlightened by his experience, and although he was now far away, 'in the mind's eye Birkhall is close and brilliant.'[87]

CHAPTER TWENTY-ONE

QUEEN VOYAGER

1961–1967

'It would be so delicious to go to France'

QUEEN ELIZABETH became, in her sixties and beyond, an even more avid traveller, for both duty and pleasure. Her North American, African and Australasian tours in the 1950s had shown that she could still contribute to the role of the monarchy in maintaining and strengthening Britain's links with the Commonwealth, and in fostering good relations with foreign countries. As she grew older she lost none of her enthusiasm for such visits. Their number did not diminish until she reached her seventies, although like royal tours in general they tended to become shorter, partly because of easier and faster air travel. The pattern changed – there were no more trips to sub-tropical Africa. She made one more tour to New Zealand and Australia, but otherwise within the Commonwealth she travelled mostly to Canada. Her contribution to diplomatic relations at home and abroad was still valued: visiting heads of state called at Clarence House, she attended state banquets in their honour, and she made two unusual and diplomatically significant foreign visits, to Tunisia and Iran, as well as briefer trips within Europe.

Spring 1961 saw her embarking in *Britannia* to Tunisia on a visit instigated by the Foreign Office as a demonstration of British goodwill. No member of the Royal Family had previously visited the country, which had gained its independence from France in 1956. The President, Habib Bourguiba, was seen as an important voice of moderation in Africa; moreover he had frequently made gratifying public comments on Britain's handling of decolonization. To return the compliment, the Foreign Office suggested that a visit by the Queen Mother would 'do much to confirm our regard for Bourguiba and our interest in Tunisia'. She would be a particularly appropriate envoy because it appeared that Tunisians, especially women, already regarded her with interest and affection.[1]

The royal yacht set off in fine weather down the English Channel. Among those on board was Brigadier Bernard Fergusson,* whom Queen Elizabeth had invited to join the royal party because he knew Tunisia well and was a fluent French-speaker. His hostess, Fergusson wrote to his wife, was in excellent form, cracking endless jokes, including her own line in funny voices, from Cockney to French. In the Bay of Biscay they were able to spend a lot of time on deck. They were all eating too much, Queen Elizabeth said, 'and I forgot to bring my skipping-rope. I shall have to do this instead.' Whereupon 'she went gliding off across the sun deck doing mock eurythmics throwing her hands up in the air at every hop ... She is so obviously enjoying herself madly.'² They stopped in the British dependent territory of Gibraltar where the crowds were 'almost delirious'. Even Spaniards joined in with enthusiasm, which they had not been allowed to do during an earlier visit by the Queen and Prince Philip.³

When *Britannia* set sail again, the weather in the Mediterranean deteriorated. And, as they approached Tunis, so did the situation in Algeria, where rebellion broke out among the French troops stationed there. There were fears that Tunisia might be drawn into the conflict and Queen Elizabeth sent word to President Bourguiba offering to postpone her visit. The answer was *non*.⁴

Before landing, she prepared meticulously for her speech in French in honour of Monsieur le Président – although she said that it didn't matter a hoot what she said as no one ever listened. They arrived at Tunis on 24 April, with a gale blowing, but in bright sunshine. The banquet at which she spoke that night was not easy. The President was tired and worried about Algeria, Tunisian officials altered the seating plan at the last moment and even Queen Elizabeth could not make the conversation flow.⁵ Nonetheless, according to Fergusson, she gave her speech 'quite charmingly, smiling at the President with every sentence.' Dinner, served with fruit juices,

---

* Brigadier Sir Bernard Fergusson (1911–80), created Lord Ballantrae in 1972. His father, Sir Charles Fergusson, was Governor General of New Zealand during the visit of the Duke and Duchess of York in 1927; Sir Bernard held the same appointment from 1962 to 1967 and was thus Queen Elizabeth's host during her visit to New Zealand in 1966. His wife Laura was the sister of Queen Elizabeth's long-serving lady in waiting, Dame Frances Campbell-Preston. Another link was the Black Watch, in which Fergusson served, becoming colonel of the regiment from 1969 to 1976.

included 'brik à l'oeuf', a deep-fried pancake containing an egg. Back on board, Queen Elizabeth called for champagne and they all dissected the evening. She described how her brik had exploded and covered her chin with egg.[6]

The next day after various formal engagements Queen Elizabeth gave the President a return banquet aboard *Britannia*. This was a much more enjoyable occasion than the night before; the British Ambassador, Anthony Lambert, called it 'a masterpiece' – because of Queen Elizabeth's 'warm and gracious personality'. The Belgian Ambassador, the doyen of the diplomatic corps, whispered to Lambert, 'I feel I am in a dream; so does everyone else.' The effect on the President was the most marked – he seemed to relax and tell Queen Elizabeth his entire life story.

Over the next two days arrangements were constantly altered by the Tunisian hosts, a practice which Lambert hoped their guest found diverting rather than fatiguing. She visited a women's organization, a foundling hospital and the Islamic Museum in Tunis; at Medjez el Bab she saw the Commonwealth War Cemetery (where there were the graves of many officers and men of her own regiments). To the Ambassador's alarm she was driven through the narrow streets of Kairouan, where religious feeling ran very high, and was shown the Great Mosque. She visited Sousse and Monastir, the President's birthplace. At a reception for 250 people which she gave on board *Britannia*, British Embassy staff 'worked like a team of well-trained collies', cutting out and bringing forward individuals for presentation, so that she spoke to at least a hundred of them. All in all, the Ambassador declared the visit 'a brilliant success' for Anglo-Tunisian relations and 'one more personal triumph for Her Majesty'. The universal verdict was 'La Reine Mère a conquis tous les coeurs.'[7]

In June that year Queen Elizabeth was obliged to cancel several engagements after breaking a bone in her foot. 'It is a great bore', she wrote to D'Arcy Osborne, 'because one cannot get a shoe on, & therefore I cannot hop round Hospital wards, shipyards, Universities, garden parties, picture galleries, boys' schools, girls' schools, race meetings, Agricultural Shows, Civic Centres, slum clearances, Horse Shows, regimental reviews, and all my usual treats!'[8] Nevertheless she managed to get to Newcastle on Tyne on 27 June to launch the *Northern Star*, a Shaw Savill liner. It was on this occasion that she was presented with the unfinished portrait by Augustus John for which she had sat in the early months of the war, and which the directors of Shaw Savill and of the Vickers Armstrong shipyard had acquired. She was delighted.

Business could always be combined with pleasure, if only because of Queen Elizabeth's natural inclination to enjoy herself; but on her visit to Northern Ireland in April 1962, when among other engagements she attended the 350th anniversary celebrations of the town of Enniskillen, visited her regiment the 9th/12th Royal Lancers at Lisanelly camp and opened the new Department of Physics at Queen's University, there was the special bonus of a racing victory. At Downpatrick racecourse she watched her horse Laffy win the major race 'in front of an enthusiastic and record crowd'.[9] This trip was followed at the end of the month by a pleasurable cruise in *Britannia* to Cornwall, where she visited a spring flower show and had tea with a young farmers' club in Truro. In Devon she opened the Tamar Bridge and then spent a day island-hopping by helicopter in the Scillies before sailing back to Portsmouth.

*

IN JUNE 1962 Queen Elizabeth made her first visit to Canada since 1954. The main purpose was to celebrate the centenary of the Black Watch (Royal Highland Regiment) of Canada, of which she was colonel-in-chief. The regiment was based at Montreal, but at the request of the Canadian government she agreed to 'balance' her stay there with a visit to Toronto, the home of her other regiment, the Toronto Scottish, and of the famous Woodbine racecourse.[10] That set the pattern for several more Canadian visits – care was taken to include both regiments, and both English- and French-speaking areas.

There was a second purpose to the visit: the Canadian government was, perhaps optimistically, keen to establish that members of the Royal Family could come to Canada for limited trips in the same way as they visited different parts of Britain. This visit was therefore kept as low key and easy for her as possible.[11] She had a full programme nonetheless; in Montreal this included six Black Watch engagements, a garden party and several civic events. One day's engagements filled fifteen hours.

The next four days were spent in Ottawa, where Queen Elizabeth was the guest of the Governor General, Major General Georges Vanier, and carried out another dozen engagements, including the presentation, as colonel-in-chief of the Royal Army Medical Corps, of an RAMC sword to her other Canadian regiment, the Royal Canadian Army Medical Corps. She attended a civic luncheon at which, as her lady in waiting Jean Rankin commented, 'iced water was drunk', and dined with the Prime Minister, John Diefenbaker.[12]

For her Toronto visit Queen Elizabeth stayed at Batterwood House in Port Hope with Vincent Massey, who had been governor general at the time of her 1954 visit, Her last day, Saturday 16 June, began with a long hot drive into Toronto for a civic reception where the guard of honour provided by the Toronto Scottish Regiment fired a royal salute which was so loud that it smashed windows. After an official lunch she was able to escape to one of her favourite places – a racecourse. At the Woodbine track she watched one of Canada's premier races, the Queen's Plate Stakes. That night she flew home with the eloquent thanks of the Governor General, who wrote that Canadians 'will never forget the grim war years when a gracious Queen stood strong and steadfast beside a noble and gallant King'.[13] She had endeared herself to them again and 'Your Majesty has a great part to play for the Crown throughout the Commonwealth.' That was certainly her hope.[14]

*

As EVENTS turned out, her next official Commonwealth tour was not for another three years. Meanwhile there were more short trips in *Britannia* in the British Isles. She sailed to the Channel Islands for four days in May 1963, her first visit since she had been there with the King in 1945. The trip was nearly disrupted by gale-force winds. A local press photograph shows Queen Elizabeth, her petal hat firmly anchored with a large scarf tied under her chin, seated next to the indomitable Dame of Sark, Sybil Hathaway, who had stoutly resisted the German occupation. Despite the wind, the two women drove around the island in the Dame's open carriage – no cars were allowed on Sark. She flew on to Jersey in weather so bad, her lady in waiting Jean Rankin recorded, that the spectators were appalled. *Britannia* was forced to take refuge in a sheltered bay; even so, the heavy swell made it difficult for Queen Elizabeth to get aboard from the royal barge, and dinner at Government House had to be cancelled. On the last day she toured Alderney, strong winds and choppy seas notwithstanding.[15]

In July she paid a visit to the Isle of Man, presiding at the island's parliament, the Tynwald, and attending its Banquet. She drove to Douglas in a horse-drawn tram and met crowds of children and, along with other engagements in the island, again gave a dinner party on board *Britannia* before setting sail for Portsmouth. On her way home she stopped at St Mawes in Cornwall for a convivial lunch with Dick Wilkins.

In October she flew to Northern Ireland, where she opened the War Memorial Building in Belfast and was given a standing ovation at a civic luncheon. In cold and windy weather at the Abercorn Barracks at Ballykinlar next day the 1st Battalion 3rd Royal Anglian Regiment, of which she was colonel-in-chief, paraded for her and she presented medals. A trip to the Maze racecourse had been included in her programme that afternoon, but visibility was so poor that it was almost impossible to see the horses, and the day ended unhappily, with a charity film premiere of what turned out to be 'a very bad film', according to the lady in waiting, *Rampage* starring Robert Mitchum and Jack Hawkins.[16]

A few weeks earlier Queen Elizabeth had agreed to make a tour of several weeks to Australia and New Zealand in 1964. She had been invited to open the third Adelaide Festival of Arts, of which she was patron; visits to other states and to New Zealand were built around that. All was arranged. Then on Sunday 2 February, she felt unwell and was admitted to the King Edward VII Hospital. It was entirely unexpected – the frequent attacks of flu or tonsillitis she had suffered when she was younger were now behind her and she rarely admitted to being ill. She hated even taking her temperature; she thought that a tiny homeopathic tablet or powder would cure her of any complaint – and she tended to think that most complaints were imagined, anyway. Her Scottish childhood had taught her that nothing was better than open windows in the bedroom or a stiff walk in the wind to 'blow the germs away'.[17]

Not this time. Clarence House announced that she was to have an emergency appendectomy, and she underwent surgery on 4 February.* Martin Gilliat immediately sent telegrams around the world to cancel the tour. Sackfuls of letters and vast quantities of flowers

---

* Sir Ralph Marnham (Sergeant-Surgeon to the Queen 1967–8) carried out the operation; Dr D. E. F. Johnson was the anaesthetist.

arrived for her at the hospital. Within a few days she was receiving members of her family and then her friends. Prince Philip wrote to say 'how happy and relieved I am that everything has gone off (come out!) so well'.[18] Prince Charles, writing from Gordonstoun, told her that after he had had his appendix removed in 1962 he made the mistake of watching Eric Sykes and Hattie Jacques on television. 'I literally nearly split my sides laughing. My goodness it was agony! . . . I wish I could come and visit you like you visited me, but as I'm at this horrible place, it's impossible.'[19]

She returned home to Clarence House on 16 February. Her surgeons advised that she undertake no public engagements for two months. But a two-week convalescent cruise in the Caribbean on board *Britannia* proved therapeutic. She visited more than a dozen islands and the Queen commented that her programme looked 'madly busy and not at all what I had envisaged as a rest cruise for you'.[20] But she thoroughly enjoyed it all. Sometimes they anchored off secluded beaches, and while the rest of her party swam, Queen Elizabeth collected shells. They had an evening picnic on a beach in Montserrat. 'One of the sailors played an accordion and we danced a reel by the light of the moon. As the beach sloped, we found ourselves dancing gradually down to the water, & the last grand chain was well into the sea.'[21]

In the Antipodes, however, disappointment over the cancelled tour was real and widespread. Allen Brown, the bard of her last tour and now Australian High Commissioner in London, sent a poem to Martin Gilliat:

> Trusting Fate would be propitious
> This time we left out Mauritius.
> But indeed as if to spite us
> Fate called in appendicitis.
> Why should Fate thus aim at you
> Something we would never do?
> Let us take firm hold of Fate
> 'Get well at a rapid rate.'
> And though there's no one wants to wait
> Pencil in another date.[22]

She was willing to do that right away. Gilliat reported to Bernard Fergusson, now Governor General of New Zealand, that she was 'quite open-minded' about a visit in one or two years' time.[23] (The next Adelaide Festival would be in March 1966.) She herself wrote to Fergusson about how badly she felt about having let everyone down. After so many inoculations and so many dress fittings, 'I should not be prone to typhoid or small pox or yellow fever for some years, & tho'' perhaps the chiffons will be a little old fashioned by the time I get out to you, I hope to be fairly healthy.'[24]

★

ON 24 JANUARY 1965 the news reached Sandringham at breakfast time that Winston Churchill had died. It was a solemn moment for Britain. While Churchill lay in state in Westminster Hall, 300,000 people filed past his coffin. At St Paul's Cathedral on 29 January he was given the first state funeral for a person not of royal rank since that of the Duke of Wellington in 1852. The ceremony was attended by 6,000 people and all senior members of the Royal Family, including the Queen and the Queen Mother. Fifteen heads of state were there and 112 countries were represented. The ceremony was sombre but stirring and, as Churchill promised, there were 'lively hymns'. The historian Andrew Roberts later wrote that Churchill's funeral 'marked the end of a distinctive epoch in British history, one that had been as glorious as it was long'.[25] Indeed, the era of British imperialism into which both Churchill and Queen Elizabeth had been born was gone. But over the years to come Queen Elizabeth remained true to the concept of British greatness which Churchill had defended, preserved and personified. In particular she did everything she could to sustain the Commonweath, Britain's inspired attempt to come to terms with the end of, and the legacy of, Empire. Her daughter the Queen was, if anything, even more passionately committed to the ideals of the Commonwealth.

Three weeks after Churchill's death, Queen Elizabeth set off for a visit to Jamaica, where she had been invited to receive the first honorary degree awarded by the University of the West Indies, of which Princess Alice, Countess of Athlone, was chancellor. The journey out on 18 February involved an exhausting wait in a 'super heated VIP lounge' at Kennedy Airport, and two more flights before Queen Elizabeth and her party arrived at King's House, Jamaica, at 5 a.m. London time.[26]

On the evening of 20 February her degree of Doctor of Letters was conferred upon her by Princess Alice. She made a short speech of thanks, which was followed by an unexpectedly long peroration by Adlai Stevenson, the distinguished American statesman. As a result it was 10.30 p.m. before the reception for her could be held. By now she was tired, but when a steel band played, she asked to be shown the local Ska dance.

The next morning, Holy Communion at St Andrew's Parish Church took some time – over 800 people had come to share the sacrament with her. Then she had a spectacular, twisting drive up into the hills above Kingston to lunch at the military camp of New-castle. That evening at a special service at the University Chapel, the lights all failed and a torch had to be found so that Princess Alice could read the lesson. When power was restored a dog appeared and wandered up and down the aisle. 'It was an unusual service!' noted Queen Elizabeth's lady in waiting.[27]

She was enjoying her trip, Queen Elizabeth wrote to Princess Margaret, but 'I always have very bad luck with the drinks! Perhaps because I am considered a frail invalid, I am always given delicious fruit drinks with so little alcohol that one feels quite sick! Then I ask timidly if I might have just a <u>very</u> little gin in it, & then too much is put in, & I have to ask for a little more ice to stop my throat being burnt, & so it goes on! This is usually at Government Houses, I may say.'[28]

No such problem was likely to arise when she went to lunch with Noël Coward at his house, Firefly Hill. It was a small party and lunch was a delicious curry cooked in a coconut shell. She always enjoyed Coward's wit and she invited him to stay at Sandringham for the King's Lynn Festival that July to hear the Russian cellist, Mstislav Rostropovich.* 'Should I brush up my Russian?' Coward asked her. 'It is limited at the moment to "How do you do?" "Shut up you pig" and "She has a white blouse". But I am eager to improve.'[29]

On the afternoon of 26 February, after a drive through cheering crowds, Queen Elizabeth flew home via New York. On the last leg of the journey, overnight to London, her party let themselves go. 'Dinner on board the aeroplane was very gay and lasted so long that

---

* Mstislav Rostropovich (1927–2007) was publicly disgraced in the USSR for his support of his friend Alexander Solzhenitsyn in 1974 and left Russia in 1978 to live permanently in the USA, where he became director and conductor of the US National Symphony Orchestra.

no one had more than an hour's sleep.'[30] The British High Commissioner in Jamaica reported to the Commonwealth Secretary that Queen Elizabeth impressed everyone with her charm and 'zestful interest' and that the visit 'will have served to strengthen the attachment to the Throne of an already "loyalist" country'.[31]

*

ANOTHER LOYALIST country, another visit: in June 1965 Queen Elizabeth returned to Canada, this time in honour of the Toronto Scottish, whose fiftieth anniversary was to be celebrated. By now, however, the Canadian government's expansive attitude towards royal visits – the more the merrier – had given way to an understandable reluctance to foot the bill for visits which were purely for the benefit of local organizations. This led to a testy correspondence between Canadian officials and Martin Gilliat. The Toronto Scottish, together with the Ontario Jockey Club, which had invited her to attend the running of the Queen's Plate, agreed to pay the costs of the trip. But Queen Elizabeth was worried about her regiment taking on such an expense, and asked Gilliat to approach the British government to pay for her flights to and from Canada. This was agreed; but the Canadian government, which had not been consulted, was affronted, and finally a compromise was reached by which the regiment paid for her journey out on a commercial flight and the Canadian government provided a Royal Canadian Air Force Yukon to fly her home.[32]

She flew to Toronto on the afternoon of 23 June and stayed with her party at Windfields, the home of Mr and Mrs E. P. Taylor, who shared her enthusiasm for racehorses. The following day after several engagements in the city she was taken to see Taylor's stud farm and some fifty-five thoroughbred yearlings. In the evening her regimental duties began with the presentation of former officers of the Toronto Scottish and of its precursor, the 75th Battalion. Then there was a dinner given by the Empire Club in honour of the regiment.

Over the next three days Queen Elizabeth presented colours to the regiment at a ceremony attended by some 22,000 people, and went to a service for the laying up of the old colours at the Knox Presbyterian Church. Among other engagements she lunched with Vincent Massey at Batterwood, and watched the Queen's Plate Stakes at the Woodbine racetrack. When she left, she drove the ten miles to the airport in an open car along a road lined by thousands of cheering people. She arrived back in London on 28 June.

Two weeks later she flew to Germany to visit British regiments and units in the British Army of the Rhine, accompanied by Princess Marina, Duchess of Kent. At Celle they watched an impressive parade by the 11th Hussars, in which the Duchess's son Prince Michael was serving, on their 250th anniversary. Then Queen Elizabeth went to Minden to visit the 1st Battalion The Black Watch; she took the salute and inspected a guard of honour, but the Highland Gathering which had been planned was washed out by a thunderstorm. The last day was devoted to another of her regiments, the 9th/12th Royal Lancers at Osnabrück, where she watched a mounted parade and attended a regimental fête before flying back to London.

★

IN MARCH 1966 she set off for the postponed tour of Australia and New Zealand, flying with Qantas via Ottawa, Vancouver and Fiji. In Adelaide the official and formal engagements included many drives through crowded streets, a civic welcome at the Town Hall, a reception for the media, luncheons and a tour of floral and handicraft exhibits put on by 600 members of the Country Women's Association. There were more floral creations in the Victoria Parks: the *tour de force* was a carpet of flowers made in an aboriginal design. She attended a performance of the Australian Ballet, went to a reception for the Royal Australian Army Medical Corps, of which she was colonel-in-chief, mingled at a garden party with 6,000 guests, and opened the new Flinders University. She and her lady in waiting, Frances Campbell-Preston, drove there in an open car 'in a gale, mostly crouched on the floor of the car & clutching their hats & arrived a little battered and blinded to be received by the Chancellor'.[33]

In her speech, the Queen Mother noted the remarkable development of Adelaide and praised universities as the centre of hope. 'We live in an age in which higher education has become a matter of national concern,' she said.[34] Dinner at Government House was followed by a concert by the Australian Youth Orchestra. The music was rousing but even that 'did not quite succeed in keeping all members of the party awake all the time'.[35] Next day the Queen

Mother made an unscheduled visit to the National Gallery where Sir Hans Heysen, an endearing figure dressed in knickerbockers, showed her around an exhibition of his own paintings.* She made a final speech praising the Festival and its 'far-sighted' organizers and then spent a pleasant afternoon at the races.[36]

On this as on other such trips, Queen Elizabeth was irritated only if there was too much formality or protocol. She was always looking for ways to make officials relax and, if engagements were going well, she stayed on, thus pleasing her interlocutors but upsetting the schedule. She enjoyed slip-ups. Frances Campbell-Preston recorded that 'Martin assured me that nothing pleased "People" [as he called her to mislead any eavesdroppers] more' than if the lady in waiting 'did something wrong or arrived in the wrong place at the wrong time'.[37]

Across the country in Perth, 'People' had another five busy days. These included a visit to an Aquatic Carnival at the Beatty Park Aquatic Centre which was packed with 5,000 children for her visit. As she arrived, the announcer on the public address system declared 'The Queen Mother is now in the Pool' – this raised a storm of laughter and cheering which continued unceasing until she left, rather deafened, an hour and a half later. On returning to Government House she found the drive lined with members of the Boys' and the Girls' Brigades, and got out of her car to walk down the ranks and talk to as many of the young people as possible. From Perth she went to Fremantle where, among other engagements, she gave a speech to a room full of teenagers. Frances Campbell-Preston recorded that she had 'rather dreaded' this occasion, but that it went off very well in the event.[38]

It was then on to Canberra where she was overjoyed to have a rendezvous with Prince Charles. He had been released from Gordonstoun to be an exchange student for two terms at Timbertop, the rural outpost of Geelong Grammar school in Victoria. Princess Margaret wrote to her mother to say that she was so happy that she and

---

* Sir Hans Heysen, born in Germany in 1877, had emigrated with his family to Australia as a child. He was particularly recognized for his watercolours of the Australian bush, and won the Wynne Prize for landscape painting nine times. He lived in the Adelaide Hills until his death in 1968. The people of Adelaide presented Queen Elizabeth with two Heysen watercolours, *Brachina Gorge* and *Timber Haulers*. The former was included in the exhibition of her watercolours and drawings in Edinburgh and London in 2005–6. (Susan Owens, *Watercolours and Drawings from the Collection of Queen Elizabeth The Queen Mother*, pp. 150–1)

Prince Charles were together 'for I have never known a grandson more devoted than Charles is to you.' She said that she and her sister, the Queen, had had glowing accounts of their mother's 'usual smash-hit success. "Her Majesty, in powder blue, stepped from the plane, radiant"!'[39]

The most enjoyable part of the trip for Queen Elizabeth and Prince Charles was a visit to the Snowy Mountains hydro-electric project in New South Wales. Between visits to dams and power stations, they stayed in the delightful Queen Elizabeth Cottage at Island Bend where the Prince and other members of the party fished. He and his grandmother spent so much time joking together that they reduced the whole party to giggles, which proved hard to control when the Commissioner of the Snowy Mountains Authority and his wife came to dine, give a lecture and show a film. According to Frances Campbell-Preston, 'suppressed – & not so suppressed – laughing went on to our guests' bewilderment as they weren't consciously adding to the fun'.[40]

The Australia tour ended on 7 April after a return visit to Canberra and a dinner party attended by the Prime Minister and Mrs Harold Holt. (Holt later disappeared off a beach in Victoria – his body was never found.) Prince Charles returned happily for his last few weeks at Timbertop and the Queen Mother and party flew to Fiji, where *Britannia* was waiting to take her on the next part of her tour.

Embarking on the yacht was 'rather a splendid moment, a little like arriving home', wrote Frances Campbell-Preston, doubtless echoing the Queen Mother's own views.[41] On Easter Saturday the ship docked in Suva for the formal welcome from a Fijian chief. The short formal visit to Suva was somewhat spoiled by rain, but Queen Elizabeth held a reception and a dinner aboard the yacht before sailing for New Zealand. She landed at Bluff on 16 April in pouring rain, and was greeted by the Governor General, Sir Bernard Fergusson, his wife Laura – Frances Campbell-Preston's sister – and the Prime Minister and his wife.

Her punishing schedule over the coming weeks was made possible by *Britannia*, both an agreeable means of transport and a refuge after long days of exposure to the crowds and the elements. When there were evenings in the yacht with no engagements, Queen Elizabeth encouraged everyone to let their hair down. Laura Fergusson had heard that after-dinner games were obligatory and was daunted, but they turned out to be both silly and easy, 'and she is such enormous fun playing them. It's gloriously childish and very restful as a result.'[42]

In town after town across New Zealand, the Queen Mother was greeted by huge crowds, of all ages, cheering her along streets from one civic reception to another. In Wellington on 25 April she marked Anzac Day at the National War Memorial in Wellington – she always found such moments of remembrance for the war dead intensely moving. The engagements continued. On 1 May, after Sunday service in St John's Anglican Church at Te Awamutu, she flew to Auckland where, despite torrential rain, the crowds packing the streets and the wharf by *Britannia* were so dense that it took an hour for her car to reach the yacht. Next day there was a civic reception and a performance by children dancing and doing gymnastics in Eden Park.

On one quiet day off, there was enough sunshine to go fishing on Lake Wanaka. Queen Elizabeth was not greatly amused by having to pose, in waders, tweed jacket, a green felt hat and pearls, casting with an unfamiliar rod, for a horde of photographers. They 'looked as though they were going to swallow her', according to Laura Fergusson, but the deal was that they would then leave her alone, and they did.[43]

Near the end of her trip, she received a contingent of London Scottish Old Comrades, was greeted by '26,000 children yelling their heads off quite uninhibitedly',[44] made a quick private visit to a stud and attended a reception at Government House. On her last day, she opened a new Science Building at the University of Auckland and received an honorary degree. She went to the races at Ellerslie, and gave a dinner in *Britannia* followed by a reception on board for 300 people, as rain leaked through the awning.

Next morning there was long 'farewelling' (a term they had picked up in Australia), to the officers and crew of the yacht before Queen Elizabeth left for the airport. Admiral Morgan had organized the Royal Marine Band to play 'Will Ye No Come Back Again?' while the entire ship's company stood and saluted on the top deck. 'There was hardly a dry eye,' wrote Frances Campbell-Preston.[45] Once again the roads to the airport were lined with thousands of people.

Queen Elizabeth's enjoyment is evident from the letter recalling the best moments that she wrote to thank the Fergussons. There were some things that really mattered to her in the fast-changing world of the 1960s. 'The love & loyalty of the NZ people is something I shall always treasure – long may it be part of their philosophy of life.'[46]

The flight home was long; the aircraft landed to refuel in both Honolulu (where she joined in a dance by hula girls in her honour) and Vancouver (where, during her one-day stopover, she visited City Hall and attended a formal lunch). She arrived back in England to find, to her joy, that spring was there – 'the cherries are bowed down with blossom, & the birches & chestnuts a most tender green.'[47]

Politics was another matter. Towards the end of her trip she had written to her son-in-law Lord Snowdon, saying that she loved New Zealand's 'great mountains and lakes and rivers' but was rather longing to get home 'and hear those yelling dogs, and play with the grandchildren and burn with rage at politics!'[48] She disliked the Labour government's mishandling – as she saw it – of taxation. Harold Wilson's administration was into its second year of reforms and was now planning a selective employment tax which she feared would 'hit many excellent institutions very hard'.[49] And she hated what she saw as the government's 'mismanagement of the Rhodesia question'.[50] In November 1965 the white Rhodesian government had made its unilateral declaration of independence (UDI) rather than move swiftly towards black majority rule, as demanded by the British government.

*

ON HER RETURN she resumed her round of public engagements. She presided at the presentation of degrees of the University of London at the Albert Hall; she went to Cardiff for the service of dedication of the Welsh National Book of Remembrance in Llandaff Cathedral and the opening of an extension to the Royal Gwent Hospital in Newport. In Sheffield she received an honorary doctorate of music and visited her regiment, the Queen's Own Hussars, at Catterick Camp. In Northern Ireland in early July she visited another of her regiments, 1st The Queen's Dragoon Guards, at Omagh. Such visits had their own protocol and form – there was a regimental dismounted parade, during which the Queen Mother addressed the regiment; an inspection of the Old Comrades; photographs with the warrant officers and sergeants and with the officers; luncheon in the officers' mess; and finally informal meetings and chats with the NCOs and troopers and their wives.

At the end of July, as usual, she attended the King's Lynn Festival, which included a thrilling performance of Benjamin Britten's *The Burning Fiery Furnace* given by the English National Opera at St Margaret's Church, with Peter Pears singing Nebuchadnezzar. Afterwards Pears and Britten stayed with her at Sandringham. She celebrated her sixty-sixth birthday in London and went with her daughters to the theatre to see *The Prime of Miss Jean Brodie*. Next day she flew up to Wick for her summer visit to the Castle of Mey and Birkhall.

In September 1966 she launched HMS *Resolution*, the first of Britain's Polaris-class nuclear submarines, now to be the front line of the country's independent nuclear deterrent, and a few days later flew by helicopter to land on the deck of one of her favourite ships, HMS *Ark Royal*, which she had launched in 1950. She enjoyed her day watching various types of aircraft landing and being catapulted off the deck, the firing of live ordnance, air-sea rescue and mid-air refuelling. On her departure her helicopter circled the carrier and, the lady in waiting recorded, 'Queen Elizabeth waved her scarf through the open door. A Russian trawler snooped about all day & had to be warned off because of the firing. It was a very special day.'[51]

After a busy autumn, filled with engagements, on 6 December she gave a lunch party at Clarence House and attended a reception given by the Women's Royal Voluntary Service* at St James's Palace. After dinner that evening she checked quietly into the King Edward VII Hospital.

Queen Elizabeth had been diagnosed with cancer of the colon. The tumour was successfully excised in an operation on 10 December.[52]† Members of her family visited her and from Gordonstoun Prince Charles wrote, 'I hope they're looking after you well. Mummy said that you had difficulty getting around two gi-normous policemen wedged into the corridor outside your room.'[53] She was still in hospital over Christmas and so, on Christmas Day, the Queen, with Princess Margaret, Prince Charles and Princess Anne drove down from Sandringham to see her. She left hospital on 28 December and convalesced at Clarence House until she felt well enough to travel to

---

* The WVS was awarded the honour of adding 'Royal' to its title in 1966.

† The operation was carried out by the same team, Sir Ralph Marnham and Dr D. E. F. Johnson, as for the appendectomy in 1964.

Sandringham in the middle of January. She had no recurrence of the disease.

Rumours subsequently spread that she had had a colostomy. This was not true. Her office was careful to say very little on the subject, but some years later Sir Richard Bayliss, physician to the Queen, wrote to Queen Elizabeth's lady in waiting, Olivia Mulholland: 'I understand that there have been a number of letters about the colostomy operation which Queen Elizabeth is alleged to have had. We of course know that this is incorrect and I think it is time that as unobtrusively as possible this lie is countered.'[54] But the rumours that the operation had included a colostomy persisted. Many people who had to endure that operation themselves derived comfort from the belief that even someone with as active a life as Queen Elizabeth could manage so well after such a difficult procedure.

It is perhaps worth pointing out that, even though the operation did not include a colostomy, the cancer from which she had suffered was serious. The illness crystallized concerns within her family and Household about the pace at which she was still performing her duties as she approached her seventieth birthday.

In most respects her health remained remarkably good. She no longer suffered from the frequent bouts of tonsillitis that she had endured as a young woman. She still believed in the power of homeopathy. Sir John Weir had been succeeded by Dr Marjorie Blackie as her homeopathic doctor, and, after Dr Blackie died, Dr Anita Davies, who was a conventional as well as a homeopathic doctor, took over. Dr Davies would create an individual mix of 'constitutional powders' for each patient. She also treated Queen Elizabeth for the painful ulcers which developed on her legs with propolis, a resinous mixture produced by bees which is thought to reduce inflammation naturally. She prescribed hawthorn for blood pressure and belladonna for sore throats. Queen Elizabeth also continued to swear by the healing power of arnica – in both tablet and ointment form. She handed it to any of her guests who bruised themselves.

Following her operation, she cancelled nine engagements during the first three months of 1967. Altogether that year her public engagements were down to fifty-two, which included eight for the University of London. She spent January as usual at Sandringham where, she said, the Norfolk air made her feel much better, then February and March at Clarence House and Royal Lodge, with frequent expeditions to race meetings. Her first public engagement was the annual meeting of Queen Mary's London Needlework Guild at St James's Palace on 21 March, and on 27 April she dined with the London Scottish Regiment.

That May she made a significant broadcast to mark the fiftieth anniversary of the enrolment of women on active service. In her address, heard throughout much of the world on the British Forces Broadcasting Service, she referred to the 'pioneers' of the First World War and told of her own memories of women serving in the Second – 'of WREN Boat-Crews, who never failed in their task, regardless of the weather; of cheerful girls of the ATS, on bleak Anti-Aircraft Gun sites; of WAAF Radio Operators, who were on watch – night and day – detecting the approach of enemy aircraft'.[55]

After her spring holiday at Birkhall she left for another tour of Canada, this time of the Maritime Provinces. (Martin Gilliat had at first turned down the invitation but the Governor General and the Prime Minister of Canada had begged the Queen Mother to reconsider.[56] She did, and kept to her promise despite her cancer operation.) She flew first to New Brunswick to join *Britannia*, which was in Canada for the Queen's visit to Expo 67, the world's fair at Montreal. Once again, her trip was crowded in every sense. On the first day, at St John, after a mayoral lunch she visited the Veterans' Hospital, where she talked to patients lying on their beds in the sunshine and then – although it was not on the programme – agreed to the Mayor's request to unveil a plaque to open Rockwood Park, where she was 'like the Pied Piper' surrounded by thousands of children, according to the lady in waiting's diary.[57] Next day, among other engagements in Fredericton, she was given an official welcome at the Legislative Building and watched a parade of the Canadian Black Watch. That evening *Britannia* sailed from St John and the Queen Mother came on deck in a pale-yellow evening gown and, while the band played 'Auld Lang Syne', waved to the large crowds on the dockside.

The next few days brought thick fog which made navigation difficult, and rain which forced changes of plan at Dalhousie University in Halifax, Nova Scotia – an open-air ceremony had to be moved into an overheated ice rink. Voyages from port to port in *Britannia* and car journeys as often as possible in open cars made this a pleasurable visit. On Sunday 16 July she and her party attended St

Andrew's Anglican Church at Sydney and then the yacht anchored off a deserted island on which the company picnicked and spent an afternoon enjoying wild flowers, walking, fishing and even water-skiing. The Queen Mother presided benignly and signed the book of the island's only inhabitants, the lighthouse keeper, his wife and baby.

After the yacht had berthed at Charlottetown on Prince Edward Island, the Queen Mother opened the new Provincial Government Building. The royal party was then offered a mammoth lunch of soup, lobster and an entire stuffed chicken each. A garden party at Government House took place in a rainstorm which apparently daunted neither guests nor the Queen Mother, who walked around the garden talking to people under an umbrella. That evening she saw a musical version of L. M. Montgomery's *Anne of Green Gables*, which is set in the island.

In St John's, Newfoundland, the Queen Mother was greeted by at least a thousand children yelling and cheering in the Memorial Stadium; she pleased them by giving an unscheduled address. After a good lunch, a hot afternoon watching Trooping the Colour by the Royal Newfoundland Regiment was followed by an even muggier ordeal in a sweltering marquee while more than a hundred officers, wives and officials were presented to her. The day ended with a reception on board the yacht.

Next day, the last of the visit, there were more formalities and a farewell dinner on board – after which Admiral Morgan invited the Queen Mother and her party to the wardroom where they had fun, games and a singsong conducted by the Bandmaster till 1.15 a.m. On Saturday 22 July she flew back to London, sending a telegram to the Admiral to thank him and all the officers and yachtsmen 'from my heart' for 'such a very happy' voyage. 'I hope you will have an excellent passage home and No Fog.'[58] It had been a hugely successful tour. Once again Canadians had shown that they loved her and she had shown that she loved Canada.

*

IT WAS SEVEN years before she went back again. In June 1974 she was invited by the Canadian government to present colours once again to her two regiments, the Black Watch of Canada and the Toronto Scottish. She flew to Toronto in a Canadian Armed Forces Boeing 707 that was carrying home about a hundred families from the Canadian Army stationed in Germany and Cyprus. Queen Elizabeth walked through the aeroplane talking to them.

The hospitable Taylors again put their comfortable house, Windfields, at her disposal. Her first full day in Toronto, 26 June, was exhaustingly long and ended with an interminable dinner and speeches at which 1,500 guests were served eight courses. 'HM should have returned to Windfields at 10.30 pm & in fact did so at 1 am,' noted the lady in waiting, Frances Campbell-Preston.[59] The next day she flew to Montreal for the Black Watch ceremonies. French Canadian separatist aspirations had given rise to a tense political situation, and so her visit was restricted to regimental business, and to a single day.

On Friday 28 June, back in Toronto, she met Canada's young and debonair Prime Minister, Pierre Trudeau. A civic reception, a walkabout and two speeches later she was allowed a brief rest in the Royal Suite of the Four Seasons Sheraton Hotel. 'This was the only moment on the whole tour when HM admitted to feeling utterly exhausted,' wrote Frances Campbell-Preston, 'but after a few minutes of rest she was quite alright.'[60] A civic luncheon for over a thousand people followed; and that evening she presented the new Queen's colour to the Toronto Scottish in a stadium filled with some 25,000 enthusiastic people who cheered her as she drove around in an open car.

Saturday was race day but first she met officers from the Royal Canadian Army Medical Corps. Then it was off to the races at Woodbine where, after a night of heavy rain, the conditions were appalling. The horses ran, with difficulty, in a sea of mud, and the colours of the jockeys were completely obliterated by the time they reached the finishing post. Nonetheless, the Queen's Plate was run and Queen Elizabeth presented the trophy to the winning owner and congratulated the bedraggled but jubilant jockey.

The Toronto Scottish Regiment had another turn on Sunday 30 June when, after lunch with the officers, she attended a service at Knox Presbyterian Church for the laying up of the old colours and then took the salute at a march-past. That evening she dined with officers of all her Canadian regiments and they had a nostalgic evening watching a film of her 1939 visit with the King.

Next day was Dominion Day, a public holiday, and she drove to the Legislative Building, Queen's Park, for a brief ceremony where she

presented Gold Awards on behalf of the Duke of Edinburgh's Award.*
She then flew home on another troop flight and once again talked to
soldiers and their families heading for Europe. The trip had encouraged
her to believe that her role in Canada was unusual and valuable. It
was a widely shared view. Pauline McGibbon, the future lieutenant
governor of Ontario, subsequently wrote of the Dominion Day ceremonies, 'The affection that literally flowed to the Queen Mother
from young and old can only be understood if one was present. It was
a revelation to both my husband and myself.'[61]

*

ONE OF QUEEN Elizabeth's most important official visits was to Iran in
April 1975, only four years before the fall of the Shah in the face of an
Islamic revolution which was to change the world.

The Shah, a bulwark of Western policy in the Middle East and also
an aggressive champion of high oil prices, had sent an invitation to her
in 1974 to visit Iran whenever it suited her, and the Foreign Secretary,
James Callaghan, urged her to accept on the grounds that close
relations with Iran were very important to Britain. Moreover, the
Shah, very conscious of his own royal status, would much appreciate
a visit by Queen Elizabeth.[62] It was rather a gruelling undertaking, but
she seems to have had no doubts about accepting it.

She left on Monday 14 April, in what was by now rather an elderly
RAF Comet, and flew to Tehran, where she was met by the British
Ambassador, Anthony Parsons, his wife Sheila and various Iranian
courtiers and officials. She was taken to the relatively new Saad-Abad
Palace, used by the Shah in summer, which had large and lavish
reception rooms but surprisingly few bedrooms; only Queen Elizabeth,
her dresser and Ruth Fermoy stayed there.

She had a full programme; on the first day she met the Shah's
wife, Empress Farah, and other members of his family. She went to
the Empress's Nursery Society Orphanage, one of almost 8,000 such
orphanages established throughout Iran. That first day she also had
lunch with the Shah's twin sister, Princess Ashraf, and attended a
garden party in the wisteria-clad grounds of the British Embassy. There

---

* The Duke of Edinburgh's Award, launched by the Duke in 1956, helped young people
from all backgrounds to participate in challenging activities, have adventures and make new
friends.

she met all 400 guests; the 'rather strenuous' day ended close to midnight.[63]

The next morning she flew to Shiraz and was taken to visit the sumptuous tent city which the Shah had erected at Persepolis in 1971 to celebrate the 2,500th anniversary of the Persian monarchy. These celebrations, which were directed more towards foreign guests than the Persian people, were later seen as symbolic of the excesses of the Shah's rule and an important element in the rise of the Islamic movement against him. Queen Elizabeth was reported to be 'greatly impressed by all she saw'.[64]

Every day was overfilled and tiring but she stood up to it well. She impressed with her consideration all those with whom she came into contact. Indeed, Lady Parsons commented that Persians were struck and 'slightly puzzled' by the Queen Mother's 'kindness and good manners to everyone regardless of their status or importance'.[65] They were not used to such courtesy from members of their own royal family.

From Shiraz she flew on to Isfahan, landing in heavy rain, and spent much of the day sightseeing. A reception for the British community was followed by a banquet given by the Governor General of Isfahan, and next morning she returned to Tehran. That afternoon, after a visit to the Commonwealth War Graves Commission Cemetery, she laid the first brick at the site of the British Institute of Persian Studies, had 'endless presentations', and finally at 8.30 p.m. arrived at the Niyavaran Palace for dinner with the Shah and his wife. This was followed by an entertainment consisting of folk dancing and singing, in which the last item was, curiously, 'Annie Laurie'.[66]

Parsons cabled the Foreign Office that her visit had been 'a triumph'. She had 'cast her spell' across a wide spectrum of Persian life. He thought that the most touching of the many tributes paid to her came from his driver, who spent much of his time with the servants and police who had looked after the Queen Mother. 'He told my wife that they said that they had never looked after anyone who had shown them so much kindness and attention, who had taken such trouble to speak to each of them personally and to take an interest in them as individuals.' This was rare praise in a country where hierarchical lines were rigid and people at all levels only looked upwards and ignored those less fortunate than themselves. 'I hope that the Persian courtiers and other members of the Persian hierarchy who took note of Her Majesty's conduct will have learnt some lessons.'[67]

Whatever the lessons learned, less than four years later the Shah was driven into exile, his Imperial Court broken and dispersed, by a brutal Islamic revolution, the effects of which were felt long afterwards.

*

QUEEN ELIZABETH's official visits around the world (and particularly to Canada) continued. She also developed a happy new habit in the 1960s of making private visits to France, and by the 1970s and 1980s these had became an annual event. She had loved the country and its people ever since her visits as a young woman in the early years of the century and she longed to be able to explore it more. In 1955 she told Sir Alan Lascelles that she had always wanted to visit the châteaux of the Loire – '& it would be so delicious to go to France without any real timetable or set programme.'[68] It was not until 1962 that a private trip to the Loire seemed possible, but then there were more delays because of difficulties with the French over Britain's application to join the Common Market.

The visit was postponed until April 1963. In January 1963, President de Gaulle uttered his magisterial 'Non' to Britain's admission to the European Economic Community. The Queen Mother was not outraged. Her natural loyalty was to the Commonwealth, many of whose members were alarmed by the probable loss of trading privileges if Britain joined the EEC. Moreover, she retained her wartime affection for de Gaulle and seems to have been almost amused by his démarche. 'Everyone is slightly indignant about de Gaulle's rather high handed pronouncement on the Common Market, & indeed he might have saved everyone a great deal of work & worry if he had said it before! So like him!'[69]

Queen Elizabeth's visit to the Loire went ahead, with the Foreign Office anxious to emphasize the private and informal nature of the trip. Lord Home, the Foreign Secretary, did his best to persuade Queen Elizabeth that the British Ambassador, Sir Pierson Dixon, should not accompany her for more than a day. Martin Gilliat was instructed to respond that, since Pierson Dixon had arranged the whole trip and was an old friend, it would be sad if he could not be with her throughout.

'Queen Elizabeth very much hopes that Lord Home will see his way to agree with her in this matter.' He did.[70]

Acting as her French tour director was the Vicomte de Noailles, who became a firm friend over the next few years. She flew out on 17 April with her friends Hugh and Fortune Euston (later the Duke and Duchess of Grafton) and Ruth Fermoy; Ralph Anstruther, a fluent French-speaker, went ahead with the motor cars. They stayed at the nineteenth-century Château d'Artigny, a hotel at Montbazon, in lovely countryside overlooking the River Indre. On the first night, before dinner, the President of the Council of Indre et Loire made a long speech of welcome which was eventually cut short because he was overcome with emotion.[71]

Over the next week she visited several of the most celebrated châteaux – Chambord, Cheverny, Chenonceaux, Azay-le-Rideau and Villandry – as well as some lesser-known ones including La Guéritaulde, Couzières and Rochecotte. The owner of Cheverny, the Marquis de Vibraye, was a widower and something of a character in the French hunting world. To welcome the Queen Mother, he had his hunt servants lined up on the steps, dressed in scarlet, playing their hunting horns. After an excellent lunch the mounted huntsmen and hounds paraded in front of the château. The Queen Mother, who loved seeing people and animals in their habitat, enjoyed herself talking to many of the hunt servants and visiting the kennels.

She went also to Chinon and the Abbey of Fontevraud. Lunch at the Château de Rochecotte was followed by tea with the Duc and Duchesse de Blacas at the Château d'Ussé, which was said to be the original fairy-tale castle of the Sleeping Beauty. The château too needed resuscitation. In the drawing room the legs of a sofa were resting on the joists, the floorboards having disintegrated.

Everything was kept as informal as possible, though even on such a private visit the Queen Mother aroused intense enthusiasm and curiosity and local officials and dignitaries all begged for access to her. She made speeches in French and talked to as many ordinary people as she could. One night she and her party dined in a little restaurant – a pleasure which she could rarely enjoy.

Madame Guérin, her old French governess, came to have tea with her at the hotel on 19 April, a lovely sunny afternoon. It was their last meeting: Madame Guérin died not long afterwards, and Queen Elizabeth wrote to her daughter Georgina sending her condolences and speaking affectionately of the governess 'qui a été si près de nous dans notre enfance'.[72]

On the final day, 21 April, she flew to Fontainebleau to tour the palace and have a grand lunch with Charles de Noailles in the Pavillon de Pompadour, and then back to London. She and her friends all agreed that they had had a marvellous time. 'We certainly had more than our usual laughs,' wrote Lord Euston to her afterwards.[73]

Over subsequent years she covered almost every region of France, visiting Provence, Burgundy, Normandy, Bordeaux, the Dordogne, the Languedoc and Lorraine. Each trip took roughly the same form. In April or May she would fly out, usually to a small local airport; with her would be the Eustons, Ruth Fermoy and Ralph Anstruther, who later compiled an account of her journeys and had it bound into a book for her.[74] She would be accompanied by a staff of about half a dozen, including a police officer, her page, her dresser and sometimes her hairdresser; her equerry would drive out with the chauffeurs bringing her two cars. It was quite a group.

In Provence in 1965 she was lent the fifteenth-century Château Légier at Fontvieille, close to the windmill which inspired Alphonse Daudet's *Lettres de mon moulin*. She loved the architecture and the ambience of Provence; she toured the fountains of Aix-en-Provence with the mayor, and visited the Roman temple (the Maison Carrée) and the Jardin de la Fontaine at Nîmes. She lunched with the Marquis and Marquise de Saporta at Fonscolombe, and at the beautiful Château de Vézénobres, untouched since the eighteenth century.

She and her party spent the best part of two days in and around Avignon, the former Papal State: they visited the Château de Castille, briefly home of the exiled Stuart royal family after the failed 1715 rising, and now owned by an Englishman, Douglas Cooper, who had filled it with a remarkable collection of paintings by Picasso, Braque and others. They sauntered on the bridge where 'on y danse tout en rond' and visited the Palais des Papes; they went to the ancient town of Arles, where the Arena was being prepared for a bull fight, and the wilderness area of the Camargue. *Paris Match* commented on her tireless progress: 'La reine mère sillonne [criss-crosses] infatigablement la Provence.'[75] At the fortress-like Château d'Ansouis, perched on top of a rocky spur in beautiful country, and home to generations of the Sabran family, she was entertained by Lord Euston's cousin the Duchesse de Sabran-Pontevès, to a feast including whole black truffles.

She and her party enjoyed the relaxed atmosphere of Provence – Hugh Euston commented that the people were 'ideal, much better (& funnier) than the ones in Touraine [on her visit to the Loire two years before]'.[76]

At the end of her trip, on 10 April, Queen Elizabeth paid a visit to the Hôtel de Ville at Fontvieille and was received by the Mayor – he was thought to be a communist but had bought a new suit for the occasion and made a charming speech. On arrival at the Château de Castries, the Duc met Queen Elizabeth at the door holding a lighted candelabrum, as was the custom when the King of France visited a subject. When she left the next day for London, the maid at the Château Légier, who had cooked excellent meals for the party, remarked, 'La Reine Mère est bien plus commode que Madame.'[77]

On a shorter visit to Normandy and Brittany in May 1967, Queen Elizabeth used the royal yacht *Britannia* (in which she had just completed a tour to the West Country) as her base, and had on board Dick Wilkins and her niece Margaret Elphinstone with her husband Denys Rhodes, together with Ruth Fermoy and Ralph Anstruther. Martin Gilliat and Alastair Aird were also in the party and Charles de Noailles joined them. Bad weather rather spoiled the visit, but she enjoyed seeing both the Bayeux Tapestry and Mont-Saint-Michel. Aboard *Britannia*, Ruth Fermoy took her familiar place at the piano and there was singing and dancing.[78]

By the late 1960s Charles de Noailles, unlike the Queen Mother, was flagging; he stood aside and the role of her escort was taken on by Prince Jean-Louis de Faucigny-Lucinge, an elegant Frenchman of her own generation. He had known Queen Elizabeth since the 1930s, and during the war he had been at the French mission in Britain when, he recalled later, 'she was very kind to the French.'[79] He came from an ancient family, and he had connections with great houses all over the country. He was a most sophisticated tour guide and also arranged Italian trips for her.

He found her an easy client. 'When we first arrive people are delighted, but probably sometimes a little nervous. Not for long though; she's such a charmer. It's that extraordinary natural niceness she has, and then that kindness.'[80] He thought her love of France was in her Scots blood and she in turn was 'adored' by the French, he said. 'There's not a village we pass where people are not at their windows or in the street waving at her. I think she's about the most popular person I know, and in France certainly.' Her vitality, he thought, came from her curiosity, her sense of fun and her natural good health. He thought her perceptive and able to see people as they really were. She rightly had a sense of her mission and role, and while people were excited to see her he never saw anyone become familiar – 'they wouldn't do it because she inspires natural respect in people.'[81]

Her sense of fun was very much to the fore on these trips and many of them featured moments that could have come from the pages of her beloved P. G. Wodehouse. On a trip to Burgundy, in 1976, the Prince arranged for them to stay at the Château de Sully, as guests of the Duc and Duchesse de Magenta. It was a chilly April; after dinner, attended by a canon of Autun Cathedral who (according to Anstruther) 'wore a trendy white polo-neck sweater and was obliged reluctantly to say Grace', they all went on to the balcony and, in a light frost, fed the carp in the moat. The next day the canon showed Queen Elizabeth his Cathedral; a choir of children held pink roses and sang Purcell in her honour.[82]

An unhappy incident occurred when the Captain of the Gendarmerie who was escorting the cars was thrown from his motorcycle into a ditch. Fortunately he just missed hitting a telegraph pole, but even so he broke his arm in two places and looked alarmingly white as he lay on the ground. The Queen Mother and the Duchesse de Magenta covered him with a rug and a coat and they waited for forty-five minutes, picking violets and cowslips by the roadside, 'keeping a watchful eye on the Captain' until an ambulance finally arrived.[83]

At Cluny, the Queen Mother admired the stallions of the State Stud; at Tournus she stopped to see the Cathedral, its pink brick pillars aglow in the afternoon light. Lunching at La-Roche-en-Brénil with the Montalembert family she met again a dancing partner from debutante days, Comte Willy de Grünne. At one dinner, the Préfet's wife produced from her bag a mouth organ which she gave to Queen Elizabeth. When the Queen Mother retired to her room, she was serenaded by the son-in-law of the house, who for some reason was known in the family as 'Naughty Boy', playing a hunting horn outside. The Queen Mother responded by playing the 'Marseillaise' on her mouth organ from the window.[84]

In 1977 came the turn of the great vignerons in Bordeaux. She stayed at Château Mouton with Baron Philippe de Rothschild, who showed her his cellars and then drove her to lunch with the Baron and Baronne Elie de Rothschild at Château Lafite. In Pauillac the entire town seemed to be on the streets to welcome her; in one village the local pony club formed a guard of honour, all waving Union flags. It was a shorter visit than usual and so at a lunch at the Château de Beychevelle she met all the owners whose great estates she did not have time to visit – Latour, Margaux, Pontet Canet, Yquem.[85]

When she went to the Dordogne in 1978 she was received by the Mayor of Limoges and the British Consul General, Robert Ford. Her hostess on this occasion was the Baronne Henry de Bastard. Her house, the Château de Hautefort, had just been restored for the second time – after the first restoration one of the neighbours' children had apparently dropped a cigarette and burned it down.

On the first evening of her visit Queen Elizabeth attended a pre-dinner reception at the château for the Mayor and local notables. 'This was a great success,' noted Anstruther wryly, 'too great, in fact, as they were still there after dinner.' She was fascinated by the prehistoric cave paintings at Lascaux which were opened especially for her. That was followed by lunch in a charming country hotel and then a visit to the beautiful town of Sarlat.[86]

Her host and hostess in Lorraine in 1979 were the Prince and Princesse de Beauvau-Craon, at their magnificent early-eighteenth-century château, Haroué. The Queen Mother's hostess was struck by the fact that, along with her police officer, her dresser, two chauffeurs, a footman and a page (whose main task appeared to be mixing extremely dry martinis), she brought a hairdresser with a broken arm. This, the Princesse gathered, was because Queen Elizabeth wanted him to see France.[87]

As with all of her visits, this one began with a reception for the local authorities. The Mayor and the municipal council came to Haroué for drinks and presented her with a medal, which she examined closely and gave to Ralph Anstruther, saying, 'Gardez-moi ce trésor.' They were enchanted. According to her hostess, 'Elle rayonnait' – she radiated warmth; although the visit was officially incognito, going about with her was 'rather like following a pop star'; people waved out of their windows and exclaimed, 'Qu'elle est mignonne!'[88]

There was a long drive in pouring rain to Sélestat in Alsace, for lunch at a restaurant with Commandant Paul-Louis Weiller, an air ace in the Great War. The restaurant served soup with frogs' legs in it, even though Clarence House had insisted that she did not like them. Laure de Beauvau-Craon recalled that Weiller had been called 'froggie' in England in his youth, and was determined to make his English guests pay the penalty. Outside the window, a band played gamely in the rain.

It had become part of the pattern of the visits that Johnny Lucinge would organize a private dinner at a restaurant, and this time it took place at Le Capucin Gourmand in Nancy. A crowd of striking workers gathered outside the restaurant: according to Princesse de Beauvau-Craon, they had been locked out of their factory and wanted to force the Préfet, who was among the diners, to intervene, although *Le Figaro* reported later that they had intended to kidnap the Queen Mother to draw attention to their dispute. An unlikely story, perhaps; but it seems an angry crowd surrounded her Daimler as she left the restaurant. According to the Princesse, the Queen Mother behaved like 'un toréro face au taureau'. She walked slowly towards the strikers, beamed at them and started to talk to them. She got an ovation and shouts of 'Vive la Reine!'[89]

She loved the beautiful library at Haroué and one evening, as she sat there with a glass of champagne, hearing that Ralph Anstruther and others in her party were missing, she said, 'They must have found a low joint in Nancy.' Her host and hostess told her that the family had buried its silver in the grounds of the château during the war but never found it again. To their surprise the plane which arrived to take Queen Elizabeth home brought out a large package from Harrods which she had ordered – it was a metal detector. Sadly, after digging several holes in the garden the Princesse discovered only water pipes, and her husband put an end to her searches.[90]

In 1980 Queen Elizabeth stayed with Monsieur and Madame Kilian Hennessy in Cognac, where she was offered brandy from the year 1800 to taste, before visiting historic châteaux and Romanesque churches.[91] In May 1981, she returned to the Loire, eighteen years after her first visit, and stayed at the moated Château de Serrant, near Angers; this was once the property of an Irish Jacobite family which had assisted Bonnie Prince Charlie in the '45, and now belonged to the Prince and Princesse de Ligne-La Tremoille. She watched a display by the Cadre Noir at the cavalry barracks at Saumur, and went to Gennes to lay a wreath of poppies at the memorial to the cavalry cadets who had defended the bridge over the Loire in 1940 and held up the

German advance; they were nearly all killed.[92] She was delighted with this trip, writing to Ralph Anstruther, 'I thought that this year it was better than ever.'[93]

In 1982 she made what was inevitably a rather formal trip to Paris to open the new wing of the Hertford Hospital, of which she was patron. She stayed at the British Embassy and called on President Mitterrand. Johnny Lucinge gave a cocktail party at his flat and among the many guests was Princess Olga, the widow of her old friend Prince Paul of Yugoslavia, who had died in 1976.

In 1983 it was the turn of Champagne, where she stayed again with the Kilian Hennessys in a house which had belonged to the Chandon family. Champagne flowed throughout an excellent dinner. She was driven around the miles of Moët and Chandon cellars in an electric car.[94] In Epernay she talked to a survivor of the Ravensbrück concentration camp, Madame Servagnat, who with her husband had been in the wartime Resistance and had helped British airmen shot down over France. Queen Elizabeth praised her courage. 'Vous avez donné l'exemple,' Madame Servagnat replied.[95]

In 1984 the Queen Mother visited the Sarthe region, south-west of Paris, and stayed with the Comte and Comtesse René de Nicolay at the Château du Lude on the River Loir. The streets of the little town of Le Lude were decked with Union flags and Tricolours, the Mayor received her with a 'vin d'honneur' and the town band played 'God Save The Queen' and the 'Marseillaise' before enthusiastic crowds.[96] 'She is very *bon vivant*,' the Comtesse later recalled.[97]

At the Château de Bournel, a large nineteenth-century house in Franche Comté, the following year the Marquis de Moustier was on the doorstep to greet her, but the rest of the family were all off hunting a dormouse in the dining room. Eventually they were presented to her. This house, which had wonderful views of the 'ligne bleu des Vosges', was unusual in France in that it had passed intact from father to son for many generations. After visiting Besançon and other sights of the area, the Queen Mother was presented with a substantial and very heavy local cheese which was much appreciated after her return to Clarence House.[98]

One should not underestimate the difficulty to which Queen Elizabeth's guide, Johnny Lucinge, was put in organizing these tours. The diarist James Lees-Milne, who could be unkind, recalled talking about it to Lucinge:

He has taken the place of Charles de Noailles in that he stays annually at Sandringham with the Queen Mother and pilots her around France each summer. Told me the difficulty was finding suitable hosts who were rich enough and possessed large houses with rooms enough and servants enough to accommodate her retinue, consisting of himself, Lady Fermoy, the Graftons, two maids, two valets, two detectives. He had just come from Sandringham and said the Q.M. is the only member of the Royal Family one could call cultivated. She has humour, and is never overtly critical. Interested, reads her prep. before making visits.[99]

Johnny Lucinge's daughter, the Marquise de Ravenel, later recalled that when her father ran out of castles in France, he looked to Italy, where fortunately he had good friends.[100] Queen Elizabeth was happy to go there.

In October 1984 she visited Venice on behalf of the Venice in Peril Fund. This was the first time she had been to the city since she and the Duke of York had travelled on the Orient Express to the wedding of Prince Paul of Yugoslavia and Princess Olga in 1923. All they saw of Venice then was the railway station.

She joined the royal yacht *Britannia* at Ancona and sailed into Venice on 25 October. As well as her usual guests, she had invited the archiect Sir Hugh Casson and his wife on this trip.* He had accepted with great pleasure in a note adorned with a watercolour sketch of a corgi reclining in a gondola, adding that he had ordered himself a sailor suit.[101] She entertained on board numerous Italian officials and nobles and, although her health was now failing, the ninety-year-old explorer and writer Freya Stark came from her villa at Asolo in the Veneto.† Queen Elizabeth had long admired Dame Freya's work, and in 1976 she had invited her to stay at the Castle of Mey; they had kept in touch since then with letters and Christmas cards.

---

* Sir Hugh Casson KCVO (1910–99), President of the Royal Academy 1976–84. Friends with several members of the Royal Family, he designed the interior of the royal yacht *Britannia* and helped teach Charles, Princes of Wales to paint in watercolours. Casson's wife Margaret was also a distinguished architect.

† Freya Stark DBE (1893–1993), British travel writer who became one of the first Western women to travel through the Arabian deserts and Persian wilderness.

The weather was poor and the tides were extreme during this visit. Rear Admiral Paul Greening, the Flag Officer in command of the royal yacht, was nervous that Queen Elizabeth's frequent tardiness might cause problems. It did. On one occasion her launch ran aground in the mud,[102] and the church of San Nicolò dei Mendicoli, where parishioners were eagerly awaiting her, could be reached only by taking all the other passengers out of her motor boat.[103] In St Mark's Square, sudden rain forced her into the Caffè Florian, where she and her party were given a welcome tea. She was accompanied everywhere by swarms of photographers who, naturally, demanded that she be seen in a gondola. Her staff finally gave in and she made a short gondola ride with Admiral Greening. 'A really memorable spectacle,' commented the lady in waiting.[104]

Afterwards Hugh Casson sent her a booklet of sketches of the trip, which delighted her. 'Every page brings back memories,' she wrote to him, 'mostly blissful, and one or two funny, like the speeches in Church! The Service was marvellously chaotic, & most enjoyable – wasn't it? It is quite difficult to take in so much beauty in a few days, and your heavenly and lovely drawings will always be a great joy to me.'[105]

Johnny Lucinge arranged a trip to Tuscany in 1986. She stayed with Duke Salviati and his wife in their country house at Migliarino. Sir Harold Acton was among those who came to dine with her there.* The next morning the Duke showed her around his greenhouses; he had started a business propagating seedlings for export and now employed 300 local people. For lunch they drove to the Villa Reale at Marlia, which had belonged to Napoleon's elder sister, Elise, when she was Duchess of Lucca and Grand Duchess of Tuscany.

One of the high points of the trip for the Queen Mother was a visit to the Villa Capponi, where she had stayed with her grandmother before the First World War. She looked again at the view over Florence she had first seen some eighty years earlier, then drove to Sir Harold Acton's home at La Pietra. In yet another villa with an exquisite garden, she met Pietro Annigoni, who gave her a book of

---

* Sir Harold Acton KBE (1904–94), British writer, scholar and aesthete who lived much of his life on his family estate Villa La Pietra near Florence. A generous and entertaining host, he had a remarkable circle of friends who loved to make pilgrimages to La Pietra. He left the villa to New York University.

the frescos he had just painted for Padua Cathedral. On the last evening, Johnny Lucinge took her party to dinner at the restaurant Solferino in the village of Marcario-in-Piano; after an excellent alfresco meal, in the company of a group of friendly doctors from Lucca, the party drove to Pisa to see the Tower, the Cathedral and the Baptistery. The Queen Mother talked with a group of students who had a guitar and were singing Neapolitan songs.[106]

In her six-page letter of thanks, she told Johnny Lucinge that he must be a magician to be able to conjure up such beautiful houses. The Duke, she said, 'with his splendid Graeco-Roman head made us feel so happy' and the villas, 'the gardens, the picnics, the fun of it all, will always remain a happy wonderful memory'. She loved the evening at Pisa and the charming restaurant dinner, with all the doctors. 'I couldn't help wondering about their patients.'[107]

In 1987 she visited the Palladian villas of the Veneto. She stayed at the Hotel Cipriani in Asolo and saw Freya Stark again. In the Villa Maser she admired the frescos by Veronese, and visited the only country church that Palladio built; the same afternoon, in Castelfranco, she visited the eighteenth-century theatre – a young boy played the British National Anthem on the piano as she arrived. She then went to the Duomo San Liberale to see Giorgione's *Madonna and Child*. She went shopping for local china and tried the fiery local grappa; wherever she went she was greeted by enthusiastic crowds.[108]

In June 1988 she took her party to Sicily and Naples in *Britannia*. She was not feeling well when she flew out from London and was rather dreading her crowded schedule. But the Mediterranean sunshine revived her and she carried out an exhausting round of official and private visits with her habitual zest and energy. In Salerno she laid a wreath at the Commonwealth War Graves Cemetery at Battipaglia, and met the gardener and his son who together had looked after the graves since 1945.[109]

She entertained on board *Britannia* – one night her grandson Prince Andrew, who had joined the Royal Navy in 1979 and whose ship HMS *Edinburgh* was in the Bay of Naples, came to dinner – and she was fêted and feasted in beautiful palazzi in both Sicily and Naples. The Archbishop showed her over the exquisite Cathedral at Monreale above Palermo, and then gave the party tea in his palace.[110] Hugh Casson, whom she had again invited aboard, was impressed by her stamina; after each full day's sightseeing 'at six-thirty every evening she'd give a party on the ship for all the local dignitaries, and at eight-thirty it would be a dinner party, and at midnight she'd have the officers from the wardroom for a last drink before going to bed.'[111] The British Ambassador in Rome, Sir Derek Thomas, agreed – he reported to the Foreign Office that 'Her sparkling personality, her unflagging energy, and her keen enjoyment of life – so manifestly undulled by the passage of years – were universally admired by all whom she met.'[112]

She enjoyed the Italian trips but her greater love remained France. When Prince Jean-Louis asked her at the end of the Sicilian trip, 'What about next year, Your Majesty?' she replied, ' "Oh you know, I miss France a lot." So that made me understand that she'd like to come back.'[113] But the Prince, her second cicerone and only three years her junior, was beginning to tire. In 1989 he took Queen Elizabeth to the Languedoc, where her party stayed in a quiet, comfortable hotel, the Hôtel de la Réserve, in Albi on the banks of the River Tarn. There they visited the Toulouse-Lautrec family house, which now belonged to a young friend of Johnny Lucinge, Bertrand du Vignaud de Villefort, and his sister, whose mother was a Toulouse-Lautrec. The Prince had in fact asked the young man to take over his role.

The tour-director designate quickly discovered what he was up against. On the afternoon of the Queen Mother's arrival, after the customary reception for local dignitaries, he had left a short interval for the eighty-eight-year-old traveller to rest. Instead, he found himself hurriedly improvising a visit to two local villages in response to a telephoned request for 'something to do before dinner'.[114]

Two days later the party visited Toulouse on the same day that the right-wing politician Jean-Marie Le Pen was holding a rally there. The authorities were anxious to get Queen Elizabeth away before this began; she wanted to stay and said – mischievously – that she would love to meet Le Pen. In the event she left before the rally, having proved, according to Sir Ralph Anstruther's account, a greater attraction than the politician. She questioned du Vignaud about Le Pen; although conservative in her own ideas, she was worried by the tendency he represented.[115]

Nineteen-ninety saw her in Brittany; she took a French naval barge up the River Odet to Quimper and had an excellent picnic lunch on board. In Quimper itself, the enthusiastic crowds were too big for her to be able to carry out a planned tour of the Old Town. At lunch the next day the Naval Pipe Band from Lorient played for her. They had gone to great trouble to learn a Scots tune – they had chosen the dirge 'Flowers of the Forest'.[116] In 1991 she made what proved to be her last French trip. Appropriately, it was to Savoie, where Johnny Lucinge's family had once ruled over Faucigny as an independent state. She stayed at the Hôtel Royale in Evian and toured châteaux, gardens and churches on the edge of Lake Geneva and in the mountains near by, and laid a wreath on the memorial to Resistance fighters at the cemetery at Les Glières.[117]

In early May 1992 she added Spain to her European list, when she was invited by the Duke and Duchess of Wellington to spend a private weekend at their house near Granada. The trip included a picnic lunch and a drive round one of the estates granted to the first Duke of Wellington by a grateful Spain after the Peninsular Wars. The next day the Wellingtons gave a lunch party to which the King and Queen of Spain came, and on the last evening Queen Elizabeth visited the Alhambra in Granada.

The last of these happy private excursions was to Umbria that same month. The only sadness to the trip was that Johnny Lucinge was not well enough to accompany her. (He died later that year.) On her first evening in Perugia, Queen Elizabeth gave a reception at her hotel, the Brufani, at which the Abbot of St Peter's Church invited her to come and see his church there and then – which she did.

In Cortona she visited the Museo Diocesano, with its small but exquisite collection of paintings by Fra Angelico, Duccio and Signorelli. In the hot afternoon she walked up the steep cobbled street to the Church of San Nicolò and then drove to Santa Maria del Calcinaio, a beautiful, simple fifteenth-century church with a fine sixteenth-century stained-glass window. The next day the Marchese and Marchesa Antinori gave her an excellent lunch at their fortress-like home, Castello della Sala, with wine from the family vineyard, and she then drove to see the Cathedral in Orvieto – a large crowd in the piazza cheered her. On her final day she visited both basilicas in Assisi, saw the tomb of St Francis, and talked through a grille to members of a silent order of nuns.[118]

In all the thirty years during which she made her twenty-two private tours in Europe, little changed from year to year. She moved in an exquisitely geared time machine, cocooned against the harsher realities of the modern world. Her travelling companions remained constant and vigilant; on each occasion she was generously and charmingly entertained by members of the local nobility or even royalty; and each year she saw beautiful churches, castles, palaces, houses, museums, monuments, gardens and landscapes, in two countries which she had loved since she was young. Her hosts went to immense trouble to ensure that she was received everywhere as a dowager queen should be – regally.

CHAPTER TWENTY-TWO

UNDER SCRUTINY

1968–1981

'Let's go down to the old Bull and Bush'

As ONE DECADE succeeded another, Britain continued to alter with almost bewildering speed. In retrospect and perhaps in cliché, the 1960s were deemed the decade of change, but the social revolution that began there had no neat ten-year ending. Rather, its reverberations continued to work through society in all the years that followed. The 1970s, Queen Elizabeth's eighth decade, were notable for economic failure, for weak government and for the abandonment of old social nostrums. Many time-honoured British institutions – the Church of England, the armed services, the law and the monarchy itself – faced unprecedented challenges and demands for reform. Patterns of authority were discarded. Relativism, the belief that no point of view is superior to another, became the new creed. People of conservative bent became concerned that society was disintegrating, even that Britain was facing its twilight.

The traditional family was in decline as the nucleus of society. More marriages ended in divorce, and the numbers of children born out of wedlock rose inexorably. More women went to work, more people lived alone. Minorities demanded more rights more vocally. University students became more rebellious. Football hooliganism and mugging on the streets became more common. Decimal coinage replaced pounds, shillings and pence in 1971, unsolicited credit cards were sent by banks to their customers, spending became more fashionable than saving, inflation soared, the first of many housing booms gathered pace, the price of oil shot up after the Arab–Israeli Yom Kippur War of 1973, supermarkets grew and so did the numbers of immigrants from disparate parts of the former empire.[1]

The nature of secondary education changed as a result of decisions by the Labour government after 1964. For decades selective grammar schools had been a great help to clever working-class children, but Tony Crosland, Harold Wilson's Education Secretary, declared that he was going to 'destroy' every grammar school in the country.[2] Comprehensive schools, less exclusive and less academic, were promoted instead. The result was startling – in 1970 some 34 per cent of British secondary-school children were in comprehensive schools; by 1980 the numbers had swollen to 80 per cent. It would be fair to say that this change did not always seem to lead to a widespread improvement in standards.

Numbers in higher education doubled in the 1960s with the opening of new universities – first, Sussex (at Brighton) in 1961, followed by York, Kent (at Canterbury) and Essex (at Colchester). Numbers of students continued to increase in the 1970s but cuts in government expenditure took some of the gloss off the new institutions. The hope that large numbers of children would take to science and engineering was not realized – sociology was preferred.

In addition to social change, the United Kingdom was under brutal assault from the Irish Republican Army with its frequent murderous attacks in Ulster and in British cities, in pursuit of its demand for a united Ireland. Terrorist atrocities and the consequent deaths of both civilians and members of the armed forces (including some from regiments of which Queen Elizabeth was colonel-in-chief) became a dismal refrain throughout the next thirty years. Queen Elizabeth followed closely the fortunes of her own regiments which were involved in the defence of the United Kingdom. She said that she prayed for Northern Ireland every night.[3]

Queen Elizabeth was aware of the magnitude of the changes that were taking place. 'It is almost incredible to think of what has happened in the last 30 years, compared with, say 30 years in one's grandfather's time,' she wrote to a friend at the time of her seventieth birthday.[4] Much of it she may have disliked. But she was always careful not to give public voice to her anxieties. Moreover, she was usually both optimistic and philosophical – she did not see it as part of her duties to tilt at windmills.

Such a battery of changes was bound to affect the monarchy and the Royal Family. As the Duke of Edinburgh had said, 'The monarchy is part of the fabric of the country. And, as the fabric alters, so the monarchy and its people's relations to it alters.'[5] With society becoming so much more open, some Palace officials felt by the end of the

1960s that the Royal Family itself needed to be more accessible. Until now relations with the press had been deliberately kept formal and as distant as possible.

When Lord Brabourne, Lord Mountbatten's son-in-law, suggested making a film of the family at work and play, the Duke of Edinburgh took up the idea and the Queen agreed to it. *Royal Family* was broadcast by the BBC and then by ITV in June 1969, and the BBC estimated that 68 per cent of the British public had watched it. The film was sold to 140 countries. It was a remarkable documentary which gave people all over the world the opportunity to see for the first time the annual pattern of the monarch's life, to hear her voice at home and to see her and her children interact (if somewhat stiltedly). Viewers saw the Queen on formal occasions and at ease; she was seen discussing her clothes with her dresser and Foreign Office telegrams with her Private Secretary, at Balmoral and on board *Britannia*. Prince Philip was shown boating with his young son, Prince Edward; at a picnic Prince Charles made salad dressing while Princess Anne tried to get the barbecue going. On the Berkshire downs the Queen and Princess Anne watched racehorses exercise in the morning mist. This first authorized glimpse into the Royal Family's daily life was far more revealing than anything Crawfie or other royal servants had ever disclosed.

The film was made in good faith as an attempt to portray the family in a more modern, open manner, and it was received in this spirit by many members of the public. It was a huge success at the time and showed the most attractive side of the family itself and of its individual members. Such openness was almost revolutionary. But it carried risks; those who hoped that this one act of collaboration would sate the appetites of the media had made a sad misjudgement. Perhaps inevitably many journalists saw it as a challenge: the Royal Family had breached the walls of privacy from the inside, so their private lives were now fair game.

The theatre critic Milton Shulman maintained that with the film the Royal Family was replacing an old image with a new one. The old image, that of George V and George VI and, till now, of Queen Elizabeth II, had been of authority and remoteness – this had now given way to one of 'homeliness, industry and relaxation'. He noted that 'Every institution that has so far attempted to use TV to popularise or aggrandise itself has been trivialised by it.'[6]

The Queen's biographer Ben Pimlott later asked, 'Was it right for a fourth estate worth its salt, to accept such a calculated piece of media manipulation as a given? If royal "privacy" was no longer sacrosanct, why should its exposure be strictly on royalty's own terms?'[7] In fact, real though the dangers were, the Royal Family had no alternative to becoming more open to the world. Had they refused to do so at the end of the 1960s, they would have been dismissed and denounced as utterly irrelevant to the modern age. They were damned if they did and damned if they did not.

The film was immediately followed by another big media event which put the Royal Family at the centre of the national stage. This was the Investiture of Prince Charles as Prince of Wales by the Queen at Caernarvon Castle, on 1 July 1969, in his twenty-first year. It was an effort to show the monarchy as both self-renewing and involved in all parts of the United Kingdom. It was a deliberately theatrical event; the Queen appointed the Duke of Norfolk, the Earl Marshal, to co-ordinate the ceremony together with Lord Snowdon, who designed the setting and the costumes with the demands of powerful television cameras very much in mind.

In retrospect it was easy to mock both Snowdon's efforts and, indeed, the entire ceremony, as 'mock-Arthurian'.[8] The Queen and the Prince themselves saw the funny side of it all and the dress rehearsal threatened to reduce them both to giggles; but the actual ceremony was conducted faultlessly.[9] The Queen, the Duke of Edinburgh and the Prince were enthroned in the courtyard of Caernarvon Castle under a perspex canopy. Four thousand guests seated on scarlet chairs watched as the Prince, clad in the Snowdon vision of medieval garb, kneeled before his mother who was dressed for 1969, and swore an oath of loyalty to the Queen. She in turn placed a gold coronet on his head. The Prince wrote in his diary that he was very moved by it all.[10]

So was Queen Elizabeth; she congratulated Snowdon on his efforts, saying that the Investiture was all 'so perfect and arranged with such marvellous taste that I feel I must send you one line of heartfelt congratulation on a really super result . . . It is so lovely to know that this day, so important to you, is also a sort of turning point for the people of our country. You've done so much to achieve this, well done. Your loving MOTHER IN LAW, ER'.[11]

★

ROYAL FAMILY and the Investiture came at a time of increased pressure upon the royal finances. Indeed the costs of the monarchy now became an issue for the first time since the Queen came to the throne. Six years of Labour government made this almost inevitable. The needs of the state seemed to grow inexorably. Government expenditure on health and social services, which consumed 16 per cent of Gross National Product in 1951, had risen to 29 per cent in 1975, or almost half of all public expenditure that year.[12]

As a result, Labour politicians and others on the left began again to examine royal expenditure. Money for the monarch and the Royal Family has always been a contentious matter in the House of Commons. Parliament first took responsibility for the expenses of the Royal Household after the Revolution of 1688. Since 1760 every monarch has agreed to surrender the income from the Crown Estates to Parliament, and in return Parliament gives the monarch an annual provision known as the Civil List. The amount used to be fixed at the start of every reign and was supposed to remain fixed at that level thereafter.

By 1969 inflation had eaten away at the Civil List, which had been fixed at £475,000 in 1952. Salaries at Buckingham Palace were famously low. That year Prince Philip surprised everyone when he gave a television interview in North America and warned that the Royal Family was about to go into the red and 'we may have to move into smaller premises, who knows?'[13]

Harold Wilson, a Labour Prime Minister who was devoted to both the Queen and the monarchy, did not want the issue of royal finances to become party political. He sought and obtained the agreement of Edward Heath, the leader of the Conservative Party, that there should be a new select committee on the Civil List, to be set up after the forthcoming election.

In May 1970, when the polls looked favourable to Labour, Wilson called an election. To widespread surprise, the Conservatives won and the Queen called upon Edward Heath to form her new government. He went ahead and set up the Select Committee. It was chaired by the new Conservative Chancellor of the Exchequer, Anthony Barber, but included also such dedicated republican critics of the monarchy as William Hamilton, Labour MP for Fife. In May 1971 the Committee began its examination of royal finances. The hearings were tough. Indeed, Pimlott suggested that the Select Committee put the monarchy more seriously on the defensive than at any time since 1936.[14]

The Queen's Private Secretary, Sir Michael Adeane, came before the Committee and explained in detail the work that the Queen undertook and why there was a need for an increase in the Queen's public income, the Civil List, to £980,000. The Queen's work, he said, was endless and unending – no retirement for her.[15] The costs of the royal yacht *Britannia*, the royal train and other perquisites were examined closely. There was much speculation on the size of the Queen's personal fortune. Huge and inflated sums were put around and newspaper editorials criticized the fact that she paid no tax. As for the Queen Mother, the Committee complained that no explanation had been given for the increase in her Civil List allowance – £95,000 was now requested, instead of the £77,000 set in 1952. The Lord Chamberlain, Lord Cobbold, said that it was his 'personal view' that it should be considered 'as something of the nature of payment for services rendered over years of peace and war'. The Committee, arguing that her duties were likely to contract as the years went by, recommended that her annuity be reduced and that she be paid no more than a retired Prime Minister.

When the Committee's recommendations came up for debate in the House of Commons in December 1971 there was fierce criticism, particularly of the Queen Mother and Princess Margaret, from the Labour benches. William Hamilton denounced the monarchy's supporters on the Committee as 'diligent sycophants'. Why did the Queen Mother need £95,000 a year? He listed by name all her Household with their titles. 'That is a total household of 33,' he said. 'I ask the House: what the blazes do they do? What do the Ladies of the Bedchamber do that the Women of the Bedchamber do not do? Why all the extras? . . . What size of bed chamber is this?' He did not mention that the ladies in waiting received only a dress allowance but no pay, or that the extras were all retired and unpaid. Instead he declared that it was 'obscene' that the Queen Mother was getting such monies while old folk in his constituency were dying from cold and starvation. He was even more insulting about Princess Margaret, 'an expensive kept woman' who did 'even less than her old Mum'.[16] In fact Queen Elizabeth had in that year undertaken eighty-six official engagements and seven for the University of London; 187 further invitations had had to be turned down.

The criticisms were disagreeable and Lord Snowdon telephoned and wrote to his mother-in-law to sympathize. She thanked him, saying she was 'deeply, deeply touched' by his words, 'for of course one can't help minding such venomous observations, especially coming from our revered House of Commons!'[17]

In the end, the Conservative-dominated House ignored the recommendations of the Committee, passed a generous settlement and fixed the Civil List for the next ten years so as to avoid such a debilitating debate every year. Anthony Barber managed to secure victory on one of Buckingham Palace's greatest concerns – that the Queen should not be forced to divulge the details of her personal wealth and that she be allowed to retain the monarch's traditional immunity from paying tax. Nonetheless, a precedent had been created – from now on the Civil List would be scrutinized by newly appointed Royal Trustees who included the Prime Minister and the Chancellor, and who would recommend whether or not any increases should be entertained in future. In other words, the monarchy would have to justify the expenses it incurred.

They changed the guard at Buckingham Palace in spring 1972. Having achieved the new settlement, Michael Adeane retired after nineteen years as the Queen's Private Secretary. He was replaced by Martin Charteris, formerly Private Secretary to Princess Elizabeth and then Assistant Private Secretary to the Queen. Charteris's succession heralded a change of mood, even of atmosphere. He was probably the liveliest and most amusing Private Secretary the Queen had had. A clubbable and kind man, he was less cautious than his predecessors. He was an incurable romantic and used to say that he had fallen in love with Princess Elizabeth when he came for his first interview in 1950 and had loved her ever since. He had a feel for the monarchy and its place in British society. Its purpose, he said, was to spread a carpet of happiness. It should never be ahead of the times but would be in trouble if it fell far behind.[18] Queen Elizabeth might not always agree on the need for change. But when such arguments were expressed with Charteris's charm and bonhomie, they were hard to resist. He added joy to both Buckingham Palace and Clarence House.

*

IN FEBRUARY 1972, the Queen made an official tour of countries in South-east Asia and in her absence Queen Elizabeth and Princess Margaret acted as Counsellors of State. Political events were taxing.

The National Union of Mineworkers had called the first national coal strike since 1926 and employed flying pickets to close a major coal depot. It was a cold winter and the strike caused significant disruption and power cuts across the country. On 9 February Queen Elizabeth and Princess Margaret were required to approve the declaration of a state of emergency. Queen Elizabeth's private sympathy for the miners – who counted among the 'real people' she enjoyed and admired[19] – was widely shared and the government was unable to muster support for a hard line. It capitulated. Miners' wages rose in 1972 by 16 per cent, twice the rate of inflation. There was growing strife in Ireland too. On 24 March Queen Elizabeth had to sign papers in connection with the announcement of direct rule in Ulster.

On a more cheerful note, she undertook four investitures, a duty she always found a pleasure. After she had knighted the playwright Terence Rattigan in November 1971, he wrote to congratulate her on the way she conducted such ceremonies, remarking that, for almost everyone receiving honours, 'those few proud but nerve-wracking seconds of confrontation represent the high pinnacle of their lives.' It was apparent to him how conscious she was of this.[20] She was indeed. At a later investiture she met a young sailor who had displayed great bravery after an accident in his nuclear submarine. He had – she wrote to the Queen – 'crept through scalding steam in darkness to see what was wrong'. She said to him, 'That must have been a terrible experience,' to which he replied, 'Not half as terrible as this.' She liked that answer and noted that he was indeed 'white with apprehension & fear!'[21]

At Royal Lodge in the spring of 1972 she entertained members of the Eton Beagles to a lawn meet for the first time. This became a cherished annual event and took place every year except two until her death. She loved the gathering of the hounds and the boys, whose school she continued to think was the best in the world. The meet, a win at Sandown Park by one of her favourite horses, Game Spirit, and her constitutional duties helped take her mind off a death she minded very much – that of the Marquess of Salisbury. Since the 1930s she and the King had counted Bobbety and Betty Salisbury among their closest friends.

Another death in 1972 broke a less happy link with the past. The health of the Duke of Windsor, still living in Paris, had been deteriorating for some time. Prince Charles, under the influence of his 'honorary grandfather', Lord Mountbatten, had taken a sympathetic interest in the plight of his great-uncle. He believed that reconciliation was to be desired. There had been a few contacts since the mid-1960s. In 1965 the Duke had been admitted to the London Clinic for an eye operation and the Queen visited him there. She then invited the Duke and Duchess to the unveiling of a plaque in memory of Queen Mary at Marlborough House in 1967. Queen Elizabeth was there too; this was her first meeting with the Duchess since before the abdication. There is no record of any conversation they may have had. Queen Elizabeth and the Duke met again – for the last time – at the funeral of Princess Marina, Duchess of Kent, in 1968.

Prince Charles thought that such brief encounters were not enough and in 1970, according to his biographer Jonathan Dimbleby, he suggested that the Duke and Duchess of Windsor should be invited for a weekend. He was curious about the Duchess, and thought 'it would be fun to see what she was like . . . It is worthwhile getting to know the better side of her.'[22]

The Prince raised the idea with his grandmother but, in Dimbleby's words, 'it was immediately apparent to him how difficult she would find it to be reconciled with the man whom she held responsible for consigning her husband to an early grave.'[23] On the other hand, Robert Fellowes, later the Queen's Private Secretary, subsequently commented, 'Queen Elizabeth would not have minded the Prince of Wales being kind to the Duke of Windsor. She was herself very kind to the Duchess. On the rare occasions when I talked to her about the Duchess she showed no animosity at all, but rather sympathy for the Duchess's plight.'[24]

But there would be no visit. In May 1972, the Queen called on her uncle while she was on a state visit to France. Ten days later, he died. The Queen sent a sympathetic telegram to the Duchess and expressed pleasure that she had been able to see him before his death.[25]

The Duke had stated his wish to be buried at Frogmore and the Duchess came to stay at Buckingham Palace for the funeral. The Queen and Prince Charles dined with her; the Queen Mother, who was suffering a mild attack of shingles, did not. Queen Elizabeth's feelings at this time can only be guessed at; she herself left little trace of them in writing. Her well-informed and sympathetic biographer Elizabeth Longford wrote that the funeral was a 'considerable ordeal' for her. 'The Queen Mother was gentle with [the Duchess], as became a Queen, taking the sadly bemused woman by the arm.'[26] Longford also speculated that Queen Elizabeth would have been less than human if she had not reflected that her own married life had been somewhat shorter than the thirty-five years that the Duchess had shared with the Duke. But as one of her ladies in waiting remarked, 'she was perfectly all right about meeting the Duchess.'[27] Once, she had found this impossible. Without the Duchess, however, she would never have been queen, a role of which she had made a great success and which she had enjoyed. Moreover, although the burdens of kingship took a heavy toll upon George VI, it was lung cancer that killed him, and a frequent cause of lung cancer is smoking.

Queen Elizabeth felt subdued at this time; in one of the few letters which give a hint of her feelings, she told Betty Salisbury that she had been cheered by her example of 'great spirit and courage' for she had been feeling 'rather depressed, what with one thing and another'. The death of the Duke, and all the memories it aroused, may have been more difficult for her than she had anticipated.[28] In 1976, when Queen Elizabeth was on an official visit to Paris, the possibility of her calling on the Duchess of Windsor was discussed, but the Duchess was too ill to receive her. Instead Queen Elizabeth sent a large bouquet of roses with a signed card of good wishes.[29]

The Duchess lingered, her health deteriorating; she died on 24 April 1986, aged eighty-nine. Her body was flown to England and after a service in St George's Chapel attended by members of the Royal Family including Queen Elizabeth, she was buried next to her husband at Frogmore.

Public opinion was divided about Queen Elizabeth's responsibility for the estrangement with the Windsors. After the Duchess's death, letters between the Duke and Duchess were published in the *Daily Mail*.* Some of them contained vituperative comments about Queen Elizabeth and other members of the family. She received letters of support and sympathy which she appreciated, while others were less kind and continued to blame her.[30] Her own words, reflecting on the abdication in her nineties, bear repetition here. Of the Duke she said, 'He must have been bemused with love, I suppose . . . You couldn't

---

* This was the serialization of *Wallis and Edward: Letters 1931–1937*, edited by Michael Bloch, published in 1986.

reason with him. Nobody could.' She added, 'The only good thing is I think he was quite happy with her.'[31]

*

IN 1973 PRINCESS ANNE had become the first of Queen Elizabeth's grandchildren to marry. She chose Captain Mark Phillips, a good-looking army officer who shared her love of horses and showjumping. They had a son, Peter, born in 1977, and a daughter, Zara, in 1981, both of whom inherited their parents' sporting prowess.

But the wedding was followed by less joyful news. Princess Margaret – the target of intolerant attitudes towards divorce in the 1950s, and probably the member of the Royal Family subjected to the most criticism by the Select Committee on the Civil List – became the first in the Queen Mother's immediate family to divorce. Her marriage to Lord Snowdon had begun with great happiness, enhanced by their two children, David and Sarah. The Princess, who had artistic instincts that went beyond her passionate support of ballet, had enjoyed the art-loving, sophisticated world and the easy-going life to which Snowdon had introduced her. He had resumed his career as a photographer, principally with the *Sunday Times*, with great success, but he had been attacked in the press for attempting to combine his professional activities with his position in the Royal Family. He did find these increasingly hard to reconcile. Nor was he by nature monogamous. By the 1970s the strains between the couple had become considerable. Their unhappiness was well known within the family and among their friends.

As the rift between them grew, Princess Margaret seems to have rejected the manners of the society in which her husband was at home and retreated into the certainty and order of the world in which she had grown up. The biographer Kenneth Rose recorded that Chips Channon had observed when she was only eighteen that she had 'a Marie Antoinette aroma about her'.[32] Even her closest friends could not predict when her mood might change from gaiety to hauteur. Although she loved her mother, she was not always kind to her – indeed she could be rude. On one occasion Lady Penn (who was married to Arthur Penn's nephew Eric) said to Queen Elizabeth, 'I can't bear to see the way Princess Margaret treats you.' To which Queen Elizabeth replied, 'Oh you mustn't worry about that. I'm quite used to it.'[33]

On the other hand, Princess Margaret's son David Linley later recalled that 'she was a fantastic mother to me and Sarah. She was unusual, with strong senses of religion, fun and family.'[34] She still wrote the same sort of poems and doggerel that had so entertained guests at Balmoral in the early post-war years. She wrote prayers too. Queen Elizabeth and Snowdon had always had an excellent relationship – she loved his sense of humour as well as admiring his talent as a photographer. Linley recalled that she was adept in trying to defuse arguments between his parents.[35]

The Snowdons came to live increasingly separate lives in their apartment at Kensington Palace. In 1973 friends introduced the Princess to a young man named Roddy Llewellyn with whom she embarked on a relationship. Snowdon moved out and in March 1976 an official announcement of their separation was issued. Divorce followed.

Queen Elizabeth and the Queen were particularly upset by what had happened. Each of them remained close to Lord Snowdon as well as to Princess Margaret in the years that followed. The couple's children spent a great deal of time with Queen Elizabeth, at Royal Lodge and Birkhall in the school holidays and on many other family occasions, such as Christmas in Norfolk. She loved them both and she worried that they felt the break-up of their parents' marriage very deeply.[36] Over the years ahead she enthusiastically supported David in his later career as a furniture maker, and Sarah as an artist.

Linley recalled, 'She was always there for us. She was always such fun. Lunches at Royal Lodge were hilarious. The laughter of my grandmother, my mother and my sister was utterly contagious. She came to every school I went to. She and my mother bought me my first plane and a saw when I was at school. She commissioned me to make a cigar box and then an easel. She had great ideas – including "wasp scissors" – these had paddles instead of blades to catch wasps. Later she became the first shareholder in my furniture company.'[37]

Family and family occasions became ever more important to Queen Elizabeth with the years. After her stays at Sandringham, Windsor or Balmoral, she always sent grateful letters to the Queen. 'I have always been a "family" person,' she wrote on one occasion, 'and the chance of being together & occasionally discussing family matters in an unhurried atmosphere, is very helpful.'[38] At Sandringham, there were all the familiar outings that she loved: lunch parties with neighbours like Anthony Gurney, going out with the guns, watching their horses jump at Eldred Wilson's farm, 'delightful horse chat over the cup of coffee afterwards, visiting the stud grooms, sympathising over Bradley's knees, Sunday lunch with George Dawnay, oh! it's endless pleasure! . . . it is the highlight of one's year.'[39]★

★

BRITAIN'S PROBLEMS worsened in the late 1970s. Inflation and unemployment rose; the unions seemed to be beyond political control. In February 1974 Edward Heath narrowly lost power after an election fought largely on the question of 'Who runs Britain?' Harold Wilson returned to office and, after another election in October that year, strengthened Labour's position in the Commons. But his government was unable to deal with the country's structural problems and in March 1976 he suddenly resigned and was succeeded by James Callaghan. Later that year the government had to apply to the International Monetary Fund for a loan – it was granted only on the condition that large cuts in government expenditure be imposed. There was an abiding sense of failure in both Parliament and the country.

Queen Elizabeth did what she could to 'keep the old flag flying'. In October 1976 she went to Paris to open the new British Cultural Centre. After a crowded three days which both she and the French enjoyed, the British Ambassador, Sir Nicholas Henderson, wrote, 'She came to Paris at a time when Britain's fortunes seemed in French eyes to be at a particularly low ebb: the pound was falling heavily and there was widespread pessimism about the country's capacity to pull through. Her Majesty, by the way she went about her work, managed to embody those qualities of resilience and good humour in adversity that the French associate with us.'[40]

In 1977, a quarter-century since the death of the King, the Queen celebrated her Silver Jubilee. Given Britain's economic malaise, there was concern both within government and at the Palace at how extensively this anniversary should be marked. Martin Charteris argued that twenty-five years on the throne was a significant achievement which people would wish to celebrate. Events proved him right. The

---

★   Anthony Gurney and George Dawnay were, along with Harry Birkbeck, farmers and neighbours to Sandringham in Norfolk whom Queen Elizabeth enjoyed visiting. Eldred Wilson was the senior tenant farmer on the Sandringham Estate, a skilled horseman who broke in Queen Elizabeth's horses. Len Bradley was the retired stud groom at Wolferton.

Queen had a happy tour of Commonwealth countries and then millions of people across Britain came out to celebrate. In London alone 4,000 street parties were held. Altogether the popular enthusiasm provided an endorsement of all that the Queen, with support from other members of her family, particularly her husband and her mother, had achieved in the previous twenty-five years. 'She had a love affair with the country,' said Martin Charteris.[41] She was genuinely touched by it all. 'I am simply amazed, I had no idea,' one courtier recalls her as saying over and over again.[42]

Queen Elizabeth attended many of the celebrations with the Queen, including a dinner given by the Secretary of State for Scotland at Edinburgh Castle in May, the lighting of the bonfire on Snow Hill in Windsor Great Park, which was the signal for beacons to be lit around the country, on 6 June, and the thanksgiving service at St Paul's Cathedral the next day. Her lady in waiting noted that 'there were tremendous crowds out for the full length of the route & deafening cheers.'[43]

During her visit to the Castle of Mey that summer she attended a Jubilee Ball in the somewhat utilitarian Assembly Rooms in Wick. The evening, arranged by Lord and Lady Thurso, was a great success. The Queen Mother was expected to stay for an hour or so but, resplendent in tiara and long evening dress, she arrived at 9 p.m. and danced till 1.30 a.m. Most of the dances were Scottish reels, which she had loved since childhood. She treasured the evening, reeling into the small hours, and thereafter she always referred to it as 'the Great Ball'.[44]

In a way, perhaps, the celebration and the enthusiasm for the Queen represented a nostalgic longing for what Britain had once been. At the beginning of the Queen's reign Britain was still the strongest economic and military power in Europe, even though exhausted and depleted by the effort of war. By the end of the 1970s Britain seemed to be a country in free fall.

This impression was supported by the realities. Inflation was still soaring, causing fear and distress, and the winter of 1978–9 brought a series of strikes by road transport workers, ambulance drivers, grave-diggers, dustmen and others. Not for nothing did the period become known as 'the winter of discontent'. At the height of it, while the Queen undertook an official tour of the Middle East in February 1979, Queen Elizabeth acted as Counsellor of State, a task which as always she much enjoyed. She kept the Queen up to date. 'Here, everything rumbles along in the same old way, strikes everywhere, and yesterday the Civil Service joined in, and . . . people arriving by air had a marvellous time smuggling at the airports, because the customs men were on strike!'[45]

That spring the Labour government lost a vote of confidence and called a general election for 3 May. The Conservative Party, led now by Margaret Thatcher, campaigned against the 'extremism' of Labour and against the power of the unions. On election day there was a swing away from Labour of 5.2 per cent, the largest since 1945, and the Conservatives won power. This turned out to be one of the most significant elections since the end of the war. Mrs Thatcher was convinced that by the end of the 1970s Britain was not working. She was determined to confront the unions and change for ever the bipartisan tradition of government by consensus, which she thought weak, irresponsible and a major reason for British economic and industrial decline. Her prescriptions for change were to be painful and controversial, and they aroused fury at the time, but eventually they came to be more widely accepted.

Queen Elizabeth was too discreet to make known her view on the election and the different parties. She hated the spectre of British decline. But James Callaghan, who had succeeded Harold Wilson as Labour prime minister in 1976, was one of the Labour politicians whom she had always liked. The respect was mutual; among other things, Callaghan appreciated that in conversation with him she often asked after the wellbeing of the miners in his Cardiff constituency.[46]

Her attitude towards the unions was mixed. She did not like the harsh militancy of left-wing leaders who used industrial disputes for political purposes. But she liked traditional unionists (as had King George VI) and she often sympathized with their grievances. Some years later, after a visit to Smithfield Market, she was pleased when she was invited by Ron Todd, the General Secretary of the Transport and General Workers Union, to become an honorary member of the union, 'in line with the precedent set by your late husband, HM King George VI, who became an honorary member of the Union in the time of the late Ernest Bevin'.[47]

'Would you tell Ron Todd (splendid name!)', she instructed Martin Gilliat, 'that as an Hon. Bummaree* I would be delighted to become

---

* Bummarees were porters at Smithfield Meat Market; Queen Elizabeth was an honorary

an honorary member of the Union, and especially to follow the King as an Hon. Member (I remember the occasion) & I greatly admired & respected Ernie Bevin – a proper Englishman.'[48]

★

AT THE END of June 1979 Queen Elizabeth made another official visit to Canada, the country which had come to symbolize best for her the old Commonwealth. The original invitation had been from the Province of Ontario to attend the 120th running of the Queen's Plate at the Woodbine races and undertake engagements with her Canadian regiments.

At first, Toronto was to be the only destination and Queen Elizabeth looked forward to a simple trip built around the regiments and the race. But then the province of Nova Scotia asked that she come there too. As often happened, her office's requests that she be given no more than two engagements a day were ignored. Instead, Canadian officials inserted more and more engagements, grander parties and more speeches into the programme. On the afternoon she arrived in Halifax, Nova Scotia (when it was already evening London time), she found she had to wave to assembled crowds from an uncomfortable closed car (the brakes on the open car had failed at the last moment), attend two receptions and then wait two hours for an official dinner. The party was able to retire to bed only at 4 a.m. London time.

The main event of the Nova Scotian visit, the opening ceremony of the International Gathering of the Clans, took place the following day at the Halifax Metro Centre, a stadium filled with 9,000 people clad in kilts and tartan sashes. Queen Elizabeth, wearing her sash, made a speech, which was followed by a three-hour tattoo, sometimes very noisy indeed, with some 500 military and civilian performers. It was a long evening.

After flying to Toronto the next morning she talked with a hundred

---

freeman of the Butchers' Company. Queen Elizabeth always enjoyed her Smithfield lunches. Deborah, Duchess of Devonshire described one of them with her customary eloquence: 'Smithfield looms, Cake to lunch there, much raising of glasses & toasts to Tom, Dick and Harry, any excuse really. I love going in her wake through the crowds, she has an extraordinary effect on the populace, the faces when she's passed unexpectedly are v revealing, giggles, amazement, cameras too late, only getting backs of people like me. Worth seeing.' (*In Tearing Haste: Letters between Deborah Devonshire and Patrick Leigh Fermor*, ed. Charlotte Mosley, John Murray, 2008, p. 211) recipients of Gold Medals of the Duke of Edinburgh's Award Scheme, and then attended a reception for officers of her three regiments, the Canadian Forces Medical Services, the Black Watch of Canada and the Toronto Scottish Regiment. That evening the Lieutenant Governor, the Hon. Pauline McGibbon, gave a dinner for 1,500 people. Queen Elizabeth endeared herself to the Black Watch pipers by talking to them at length before the dinner.[49]

Saturday 30 June was the day of the big race. In the morning she drove to the Sunnybrook Medical Centre to meet veterans and spoke to more than a hundred of them, as her lady in waiting recorded. Lunch at Windfields, the private house in which she was again staying, was 'nearly a rather fraught meal' because her host, E. P. Taylor, had 'locked up all the drink & gone to the races with the key'. Happily he returned 'in the nick of time' just before lunch.[50] There had been much rain and the Woodbine racetrack was a sea of mud; horses and riders emerged looking filthy. Against his trainer's advice one owner, Major Donald Willmot, insisted on running his horse, Steady Growth, a 'flat-footer' unsuited to muddy conditions, because the Queen Mother was there.[51] To everyone's surprise he won. Queen Elizabeth presented the trophy, and that evening enjoyed a dinner given by the Ontario Jockey Club, where she remained until after midnight.

After one more day of engagements including a regimental garden party Queen Elizabeth flew home, arriving at Clarence House after 1 a.m. on Tuesday 3 July. Over a scrambled-egg supper, she and her companions held a 'post mortem' with 'a great deal of laughter ... It was generally accepted that it had all been a great success,' noted her lady in waiting; 'she is undoubtedly greatly loved in Canada.'[52]

*

THAT SUMMER Queen Elizabeth took on another pleasant responsibility. She was installed as the 160th lord warden of the Cinque Ports at Dover, the first woman ever to hold the post. Her appointment had been proposed in 1978 by the Prime Minister, James Callaghan.

The group of strategic ports, facing continental Europe at the Channel's narrowest point, has existed since before the Norman Conquest; they were the Anglo-Saxon successors to the Roman system of coastal defence. The original five ports were Hastings, Romney, Hythe, Dover and Sandwich – Rye and Winchelsea were added later. After the Norman invasion King William I gave them special jurisdiction.

They provided the core of the King's fleet until the fourteenth century but then they lost their monopoly and declined. Nonetheless, they retained a symbolic importance. In recent years the most distinguished holder of the title had been Winston Churchill, who took it on at the height of the war in 1941 and kept it until his death in 1965. He had been followed by Queen Elizabeth's friend and admirer Robert Menzies, the former Prime Minister of Australia, monarchist and anglophile.

On the evening of Monday 30 July, together with Princess Margaret and Prince Edward, Queen Elizabeth embarked in the royal yacht at Greenwich to sail to Dover for her installation. Princess Margaret's children, David and Sarah, joined her next day. Over the years to come she much enjoyed her summer visits to the Kent coast. She based herself at the lord warden's apartments in Walmer Castle near Deal and every year her staff, led by the indomitable William Tallon and the housekeeper, would load a van with furniture, silver, cutlery, glass, kitchen equipment, wine and food so that Walmer Castle, which lay empty for most of the year, was transformed into a miniature royal palace for the two days that she was there. The kitchen was tiny but her chef Michael Sealey did the best he could and she enjoyed entertaining local dignitaries and friends from London in style. On several occasions she invited the biographer Kenneth Rose. In one letter of thanks he wrote that his heart glowed with pride to see the lord warden's flag flying from the battlements of Walmer. 'I shall never forget standing on the terrace with Your Majesty, gazing across to France: a magic moment, as if time had run back to fetch the age of King Henry V.'[53]

*

ON MONDAY 27 August 1979 Queen Elizabeth was lunching with friends and members of her Household at her favourite salmon pool, Polveir, on the River Dee, when a policeman came to speak to Alastair Aird, her Deputy Private Secretary. He brought terrible news. Lord Mountbatten had been killed in an explosion in his small boat just outside the harbour of Sligo in Ireland.

Mountbatten and his family had been staying, as they did every August, at Classiebawn Castle, a large Gothic house which his wife Edwina had inherited and which Mountbatten adored. He had come here without problems for many years despite the increasing menace of the IRA throughout the 1970s. Security was lax. He and members of his family went out most days on a twenty-nine-foot fishing boat, *Shadow V*, which was left unprotected in the harbour for long periods. The IRA hid a bomb on board and it was detonated as Mountbatten steered the boat out to sea. He was killed instantly. So were his fourteen-year-old grandson, Nicholas Knatchbull, and the young Irish boatman, Paul Maxwell. Mountbatten's daughter Patricia, her husband John Brabourne (who had made the film *Royal Family*), his mother and Nicholas's twin brother Timothy were seriously injured. John Brabourne's mother died next day.

Queen Elizabeth was appalled by the news. Shortly afterwards the Queen, with Princess Margaret and her children, came to join her at Polveir. 'Everyone horrified – deeply distressed,' her lady in waiting recorded in the diary.[54] Prince Charles was told the news in Iceland; he was overcome by the loss of the man he described that night in his journal as 'a combination of grandfather, great-uncle, father, brother and friend'.[55] He flew back to Scotland to grieve with his family.

On 4 September the Queen Mother, together with the Queen, Princess Margaret and the Prince of Wales, took the train to London together for Lord Mountbatten's funeral in Westminster Abbey next day. It was a grand and stirring event; Mountbatten had meticulously planned every moment himself.

A few days later she gave tea at Birkhall to the new Conservative Prime Minister, Margaret Thatcher. Mrs Thatcher had recently returned from the Commonwealth Heads of Government conference in Lusaka, which had threatened to end with a disastrous breakdown between Britain and black African states over the Rhodesian issue. In fact it ended in success – the Lusaka Accord set up a new constitutional conference in London to resolve the future of Rhodesia.

The views of the two women on this occasion are not recorded, but both were believed to have sympathy for the white minority settlers. In a prompt thank-you letter, Mrs Thatcher wrote that it had been a great pleasure to talk to the Queen Mother about Rhodesia; she reported that the first day of the constitutional conference 'went all right – thanks to our British calm and refusal to be put out by the posturing of the "Patriotic" Front'.[56] But the views of the Front were largely accepted; in fairly short order, the conference agreed the end of white-settler rule, a new constitution, free elections and the creation of a new independent state, to be named Zimbabwe, under an elected black majority government.

At their Birkhall tea Queen Elizabeth had given the Prime Minister a silver brooch, which Mrs Thatcher told her she would always treasure.[57] The two women also shared a belief in the greatness of Britain and the important role that the monarchy played in the cohesion of British society. Margaret Thatcher was resolved to reduce the role of government in both the public and private sectors, and her government was the first since 1945 seriously to question state provision of services. This meant that the importance of voluntarism, which the monarchy had always championed, was now being recognized once more in government.[58]

Queen Elizabeth had a habit, much enjoyed by her friends, of raising or lowering her glass in dinner-table toasts. For those of whom she disapproved, such as some socialist politicians, 'The Dear Old Liberal Democrat Mixup Party' (as she referred to the merged Liberal and Social Democrat Parties) and the Forestry Commission (which she blamed for planting too many ugly conifers on pristine Scottish moors), she would propose a toast of 'Down with . . .', while lowering her glass out of sight below the table. For those she favoured the toast was more traditional, with the glass held up. 'Up with de Gaulle' was one. For Mrs Thatcher, the glass was always high.

*

IN THE YEAR of Queen Elizabeth's eightieth birthday an important new building and an important new relation came into her life.

The year began badly, at least as far as her horses were concerned; in fact they had been a 'disaster' recently. The problem with jumpers, she used to say, was that one always had to wait a long time to discover how good they would really be '& one's hopes are always high'.[59] So disappointment would be all the greater. As she told the Queen in a thank-you letter after her usual New Year's stay at Sandringham, Upton Grey had swollen hind legs, Rhyme Royal had a cough and was very stiff, Special Cargo (one of her best horses) was better but not ready to run, Cranbourne had run well, but got stuck in the mud, Queen's College kept falling about – all in all she was despondent.[60] Later she wrote to the retired trainer, Cecil Boyd-Rochfort, that she had had a bad season – 'Nothing but legs and backs etc, so must hope that next season they will be more healthy! It is very difficult to find a decent horse at a decent price nowadays.'[61]

Throughout this period her own legs were continuing to give her pain. Ischaemic damage, sometimes caused by the paws of affectionate corgis, was one of the principal and most painful ailments from which she suffered. In London she saw the royal physician, Sir Richard Bayliss, before going to Royal Lodge with Princess Margaret and Elizabeth Elphinstone. She remained there until after the annual service in memory of the King, in the Royal Chapel on 6 February.

One great sadness in the early part of 1980 was the death of Lady Doris Vyner. They had been intimate friends for more than sixty years and Lady Doris was the last real link to Queen Elizabeth's youth. Queen Elizabeth arranged a memorial service for her in the Chapel Royal at St James's Palace, after which she gave a lunch at Clarence House for the family.[62]

In May she travelled north as usual for her fishing fortnight, although this year she stayed at Craigowan, in the grounds of Balmoral Castle, as the Queen was having a new kitchen built at Birkhall as her birthday present to her mother. The Queen and Princess Margaret were well aware that their mother's homes all became a little tired as the decades passed, because she hated to spend money on furnishings, redecoration or even maintenance. From her sixties onwards she would say, 'I won't be around much longer. It's not worth it.' Guests enjoyed shabby lino in the bathrooms, frayed curtains and damaged lampshades in the bedrooms. Sometimes when she was away her daughters would have chairs re-covered in identical material so that she would not notice anything had changed. When the Queen gave her mother a new carpet for the drawing room at the Castle of Mey it had to be indistinguishable from the one it replaced.

Queen Elizabeth's house parties in Scotland were more prolonged and more spontaneous than the musical weekends at Royal Lodge. As time went by, Birkhall seemed increasingly like another world, totally separated from modern Britain. Some visitors found it quite magical, almost like walking through the wardrobe door into Narnia. The same guests returned year after year; as a rule only death ended their annual invitations. Among the early regulars were John and Magdalen Eldon, good friends over many decades, he a remarkable naturalist, she a great beauty and one of the few female members of Queen Elizabeth's Windsor Wets club; the Sutherlands, the Linlithgows and

Billy Fellowes, the retired agent from Sandringham, and his wife Jane; they were the parents of the Queen's Private Secretary in the 1990s, Robert Fellowes. Dick Wilkins, her ebullient and witty stockjobber friend, was often invited though he was not a great sportsman. He would go fishing with a ghillie and tended to sit on the bank until the ghillie caught something, whereupon he would seize the rod and, if lucky, reel the creature in. His account of his triumph at dinner would be splendid.

For her eightieth birthday her friends and members of her House-hold had decided to combine the pleasures of moor and stream and eating alfresco; they clubbed together to build her a log cabin at Polveir. On the morning of Saturday 17 May the presentation ceremony took place.

The beauty and excitement of the spring day was sadly dashed by a telephone call. Queen Elizabeth's beloved niece, Elizabeth Elphin-stone, had died of a heart attack during the night. The news was broken to Queen Elizabeth by her nephew, Fergie Strathmore, who with his wife Mary was to have driven Elizabeth to Birkhall. According to Mary Strathmore, 'There was a long pause on the line after Fergie told her. Then Queen Elizabeth said, 'We have to go ahead. We can't let everyone else down.'[63]

It was a terrible shock – Elizabeth Elphinstone had been a brides-maid at her aunt's wedding to the Duke of York and the two women had always been close; the difference in their ages was only eleven years and they were more like sisters than aunt and niece. Her sudden death cast a dark shadow over an otherwise lovely day, particularly for the Queen Mother. But Queen Elizabeth refused to allow her own sadness to diminish the pleasure of others. She was driven the short distance from Birkhall through the dappled Caledonian pines along the river to Polveir and was happily surprised to find there such a large gathering of friends from far and wide.* She was pre-sented with the key to the cabin in a box wrapped in birthday paper and tied with a large bow. Entering for the first time, she found it fully furnished with a long table and chairs all ready for lunch. She admired the chimneypiece, which had been built with local stone by

---

* The guests included Lord and Lady Abergavenny, Lord and Lady Dalhousie, Lord and Lady Strathmore and their son Michael, Lord Glamis, Martin and Catriona Leslie, Brian and Carey Basset, Sir Martin Gilliat and many more.

two craftsmen as their last job before retirement. A long and lively lunch ensued, though Elizabeth Elphinstone was missed throughout that day, and beyond.

The new cabin quickly became a much loved spot. Queen Elizabeth sent dozens of thank-you letters to all those friends who had contributed to its cost. It had 'settled in most happily between the river and the pine trees, and I have spent many blissful hours there, in fact I cannot think what we did before it arrived,' she wrote.[64] From now on she used it on holiday after holiday, year after year for the rest of her life. If only because it was warmer than the huts and old Victorian cottages often used for picnics, her guests appreciated it too, particularly if, with the passing of the years, they felt the cold on the moors or in the river more acutely. (Picnics at Mey, by contrast, remained draughty.)

Her equerry Ashe Windham recalled that after breakfast at Birkhall he would telephone Queen Elizabeth in her room and she would ask, 'What is the fishing like today?' Often he would reply, 'Not so good, Ma'am, but it's a lovely day for a picnic.' 'What a good idea,' she would reply. 'Let's go down to the old Bull and Bush'[65] – her name for the cabin. The staff from Birkhall would light the wood-burning stove and bring down lunch. For the Queen Mother this would often start with a gin and Dubonnet; she and the guests would sometimes cook little sausages from Ballater on the stove. A fish mousse and cold meats would follow and the picnic would often end with the jam-puff exercise. Guests were expected to slice off the top and fill the brittle pastry with cream before manoeuvring it into their mouths. Old hands would put a drop of cream in the bottom; newcomers tended to be more enthusiastic with their helpings and covered themselves with cream.

Until she was no longer able to do so, Queen Elizabeth, invariably dressed in her beloved blue kilt skirt, blue coat and blue hat, would walk part of the way back to Birkhall, supported latterly by two sticks. She insisted she needed them only for balance, which was sensible enough since she was so small and frail that it seemed the slightest gust could blow her over. Once home she would sit on one of the two seats built into the wall on either side of the porch talking to her guests as they arrived after ambling back from Polveir.

*

The formal celebrations for her eightieth birthday in August gathered pace throughout the year. She was touched by the suggestion of the Dean of St Albans that a carving of her head be placed in the porch of the Abbey to commemorate her birthday.[66] She was happy for the British Gladiolus Society to name a new seedling after her but asked that it be called Queen Mother rather than Queen Mum.[67] The Zoological Society gave her 4,000 tickets for London Zoo and Whipsnade, which were distributed among thirty of her charities connected with children. The Queen gave a party at Windsor Castle, a joint celebration for Princess Alice, Duchess of Gloucester, the Duke of Beaufort and her mother. Among the guests were some of Queen Elizabeth's hosts and hostesses from France – she was pleased because the news 'will whizz round France (or rather Paris!)'.[68]

Lady Fermoy and Sir Martin Gilliat took her to see Noël Coward's *Private Lives* at the Duchess Theatre on 11 June. Two weeks later Dick Wilkins gave her a birthday dinner at the Savoy to which the Queen, Prince Philip and Princess Margaret also came. In July she attended two days of celebrations in Edinburgh, after which she returned to the south for a tour of the Cinque Ports based in *Britannia*.

The Poet Laureate, John Betjeman, now elderly and unwell, wrote a poem which he described as 'late and tired Tennyson'; but as he told Martin Gilliat, 'I wanted to make a personal tribute to a wonderful friend and a thanksgiving for the spreading oaks and hospitality of Royal Lodge and that ground floor bedroom and those church services with the family and the young thereof.' In the fourteen-line poem, the Laureate began:

> We are your people
> Millions of us greet you
> On this your birthday
> Mother of our Queen.
> Waves of goodwill go
> Racing out to meet you
> You who in peace and war
> Our faithful friend have been.

He was not sure whether the lines should be published, and indeed they did not do him justice, but he was pleased when Gilliat told him that Queen Elizabeth would like them released for her birthday.[69]

On 15 July her birthday was marked by a thanksgiving service at St Paul's Cathedral. She drove with Prince Charles in an open carriage to the service and massive crowds cheered her along the route. It was a moment to reflect on the remarkable role she had played since the death of the King in personifying the continuity of monarchy. For almost thirty years she had devoted her personality and her energy to the support of her daughter, her country and the institutions she loved. In his tribute, the Archbishop of Canterbury, Robert Runcie, spoke appositely: 'The Queen Mother has shown a human face. Royalty puts a human face on the operations of government.' The Prince of Wales put it another way, writing to her afterwards, 'You give so many people such extraordinary happiness, pleasure & sheer joy.'[70]

Two days later she met many friends and admirers at a celebratory afternoon garden party at the Palace – she seemed untiring and did not leave until 6 p.m. There was a birthday carnival at her childhood home, St Paul's Walden Bury, dinner with the Lord Mayor of London at the Mansion House, and then on 24 July she attended the Royal Tournament. This was a special birthday edition of the then annual military tattoo and embraced all of the many units of the armed forces with which she was associated. That evening she gave a party at Clarence House for the colonels of all those regiments and other organizations which had taken part.

She loved and was touched by it all. Almost all. The only birthday celebration she did not much enjoy was one which was repeated rather too often across the country – planting the first of a group of eighty rose trees in her honour. It seemed to her that she had to do it 'all over the place, & if I ever get to 81, there won't be room anywhere in England & Scotland for any more Roses, thank goodness.'[71]

At the end of July she went, as usual, to Sandringham for the Flower Show and the King's Lynn Festival. It was the centenary year of the show and she was presented with a cheque for plants from the Committee; she then returned to London where she received a deluge of letters, cards, telegrams, birthday cakes and bouquets of flowers. At Clarence House her staff had reckoned on some 20,000 messages, on the basis that Winston Churchill had received 23,000 for his eightieth birthday. In the event there were more than 30,000 for Queen Elizabeth, and extra staff had to be brought in, some of whom worked twelve-hour shifts, seven days a week for a month, to reply to all well-wishers.[72]

On the morning of her birthday she went out of the gate of Clarence House to wave to the large crowd; there was a fly-past of ten Jet Provosts in E formation at noon, her daughters and four of her grandchildren came to lunch and that evening she went with Prince Charles to a gala at the Royal Opera House. Her grandson was again much moved by the enthusiasm expressed for her.[73]

Parliament was well represented in tributes. On 5 August the Lord Chancellor, Lord Hailsham, and the Speaker of the House of Commons, George Thomas (two of the parliamentarians closest to her), came to present messages of congratulation along with eight members of each House. She entertained them to drinks in the garden.

Finally, on 6 August she was able to get away from it all and fly to Mey where, she told Prince Charles, she would 'sink back into obscurity'. 'Some obscurity . . . !' he commented.[74] Before leaving, she wrote to thank her daughter the Queen for all the celebrations – 'such happy affairs, & enjoyed by everyone who was there'.[75] The Queen replied with an emotional thank-you letter to her mother: she said that the family had loved it all and 'rejoiced in the huge and loving feeling of thanksgiving for all that your life represents which has come from all walks of the people who make up this country and Commonwealth, and especially your own family. I only hope you have been buoyed up by knowing what people feel. From your very loving Lilibet'.[76]

A few days later the Queen, Prince Charles and other members of the family sailed in *Britannia* through bad weather up the west coast of Scotland for their annual Western Isles cruise culminating in lunch at Mey. In preparation, the day before, Queen Elizabeth and Ruth Fermoy spent an hour shelling peas. On 14 August a happy day was had with the usual picnic lunch and much cheer.

At the end of her Mey holiday that year Queen Elizabeth flew south for the traditional family weekend at Balmoral, before moving on to Birkhall. She was always slightly saddened to forsake the family at Balmoral to drive down the road to Birkhall alone. Now she found that the cabin eased that annual move. Leaving Balmoral at lunch time and breaking the journey at the Bull and Bush, in a spot that she loved, made the transition much less painful.[77]

*

THAT SUMMER Queen Elizabeth enjoyed the arrival not only of her new picnic place, but also of her future granddaughter-in-law. This was something to which she had long been looking forward. She had sat near her three grandsons in church at Crathie on a previous summer Sunday, admiring them in their kilts, and thinking how proud their mother the Queen must be of them – 'so good looking & gay and clever. And such good company! How I hope that they will all find dear, charming, pretty, intelligent, kind, & GOOD girls to marry!'[78]

In the media, if not within the family, most speculation at this stage inevitably centred on the Prince of Wales and his possible choice of bride and thus of the future Queen. The Prince often took his girl friends to meet his grandmother. After she had invited him and one young woman to the opera in early 1980, he wrote to Queen Elizabeth, 'She so enjoyed it and I do hope you approved of her in that short time.'[79] The Prince knew that, to win Queen Elizabeth's approval, a young woman would have to have a clear sense of duty alongside her other qualities.

In the second half of 1980 he became close to Lady Diana Spencer, the pretty nineteen-year-old daughter of Viscount Althorp, later Lord Spencer, by his wife Frances, the daughter of Lord Fermoy. The Spencers had a long history of service at Court and both Lady Diana's grandmothers, Cynthia Spencer and Ruth Fermoy, had served Queen Elizabeth as ladies in waiting; indeed, Ruth Fermoy was one of her oldest friends. It has been alleged that Queen Elizabeth and Lady Fermoy had somehow contrived to bring about the marriage of their grandchildren. There is no evidence of this but, like others in the Royal Family, Queen Elizabeth seems to have been pleased with the Prince's choice.

From the start, the relationship between the two young people was crowded by the media. As soon as her name was linked to that of the Prince, Lady Diana became a star of the world's press, the face that would sell millions of magazines and newspapers for years to come. Journalists now observed fewer and fewer boundaries; members of the Royal Family – now known as 'the royals' – became more and more the subjects of front-page speculation, innuendo, pursuit and attack. The obsession of the press with Lady Diana was sometimes welcome to her, but it was often invasive if not brutal. It made any pretence at normal life impossible.

The couple's engagement was announced on Tuesday 24 February 1981. 'Great excitement at the happy news,' the Queen Mother's lady in waiting wrote in the diary. That day Lady Diana arrived to stay for a few days at Clarence House and the Queen Mother gave a dinner party for her and Prince Charles. As an engagement present for Lady Diana she had chosen a sapphire and diamond brooch. Lady Diana thought it was a 'staggering' gift, and told her, 'I have never owned a piece of jewellery like that & will be proud to wear it when I'm with Charles – I only hope that I'll be able to do it justice!' She added, 'I could not have been happier at Clarence House, & to me it was the ideal place to escape to after all the excitement. Thank you for allowing me the opportunity of living there. One of the nicest things of being married to Charles is that I will be able to see more of you!'[80]

Prince Charles was evidently delighted with his fiancée. In one letter to friends quoted by his biographer Jonathan Dimbleby, he wrote, 'I do believe I am very lucky that someone so special as Diana seems to love me so much ... Other people's happiness and enthusiasm at the whole thing is also a most "encouraging" element and it makes me so proud that so many people have such admiration and affection for Diana.'[81]

In early March 1981 Prince Charles brought his fiancée to spend the weekend at Royal Lodge with his grandmother; they all attended one of the Queen Mother's favourite race meetings, the Grand Military Meeting at Sandown Park. Prince Charles rode Good Prospect in the Gold Cup race; the horse fell but no harm came to either horse or rider. The Prince thanked his grandmother for a lovely weekend: 'it was particularly special that Diana was there too.'[82] After another such visit to Royal Lodge a few weeks later, the Prince told his grandmother, 'Diana, I know, adored every minute of our stay.'[83]

The prospect of the royal wedding – the marriage of the future king of England and the first time a prince of Wales had married since the reign of Queen Victoria – fast became a subject of national and indeed international fascination. It was a welcome diversion from the economic and political difficulties of the time. Nineteen-eighty-one was a hard year. The Thatcher government's radical, monetarist attempt to address Britain's structural and financial problems was leading to a large rise in unemployment. Discontent grew and there were riots in London, Liverpool and other towns in protest against what seemed to many to be harsh economic measures.

Fairy tale usurped reality, at least for a time. Hundreds of pages of newspaper supplements and magazine articles covered every aspect of the event. Thousands of items of memorabilia were launched with enthusiasm upon the market. 'Charles & Di' was emblazoned on everything. It was not just marketing, though that certainly was no barrier. Prince Charles was one of the most popular figures in the Royal Family at the time; he was regarded as a serious and decent young man, who worked hard and enjoyed pleasing the myriad people whom he had to meet. And Lady Diana seemed to be the perfect young bride, an exquisite future queen of the United Kingdom.

In April 1981 the Prince made an official visit to Australia and New Zealand, Venezuela and the United States. In a long letter to his grandmother he wrote that people had been very kind and welcoming. He continued, 'I must say, I am missing Diana a great deal & she seems to be missing me! She has written lots of letters that get better & better & funnier & funnier & seems to be doing wonderfully at home.'[84] But in fact Lady Diana was finding it difficult to adjust to the pressures of her new life and Queen Elizabeth – who had once been in a similar position herself – was concerned. She told Sir John Johnston, who as comptroller of the Lord Chamberlain's Office was in charge of the protocol for the wedding, 'I think she's having difficulty finding her way.'[85]

That summer, as the family and the country prepared for the royal wedding, Queen Elizabeth continued with her usual blend of duties and pleasures. In May she made one of her private trips to France and on 2 June she much enjoyed launching the new aircraft carrier *Ark Royal* at the Swan Hunter yard at Wallsend. Next day she attended the Derby which was won by Shergar, the superb horse owned by the Aga Khan which was later stolen and killed by the IRA. A few days later she opened the physiotherapy department and swimming pool at King Edward VII's Hospital for Officers, familiarly known as Sister Agnes. The money for the pool had been raised in part by the Royal Warrant Holders Association as their eightieth-birthday present to the Queen Mother, who had then selected the hospital to receive their gift.

The Queen's Birthday Parade on 13 June 1981 was marred by two incidents. The public and dangerous one occurred when someone in the crowd fired shots near the Queen as she rode down the Mall, and frightened her much loved horse, Burmese. Fortunately both horse and rider were experienced (this was their eighteenth Trooping together) and neither was hurt. The Queen continued almost as if nothing had happened. It emerged that the gunman was firing only blanks, but that was not evident at the time – the Queen's skill, her sangfroid and her courage were impressive and led to a new surge of monarchist fervour and patriotism just before the wedding.

Unseen that same day was an accident which befell the Queen Mother – as she was leaving Horse Guards Parade, she slipped and hurt her leg. It took a very long time to heal. Despite her injury, she insisted on going ahead with a planned visit to Canada in early July – Canada was a leitmotif of her eighties. She made four trips there during the decade. But she was hobbling badly throughout the trip and when she returned she was in such pain that she had to cancel a number of engagements. She was nevertheless determined to recover in time for the wedding of her grandson on 29 July.

On 28 July, the eve of the wedding, there was much coming and going at Clarence House. Bridesmaids' dresses and pages' uniforms arrived. That night a huge firework display was to be staged in Hyde Park, attended by the Royal Family and their principal guests. Half a million people were expected to line the streets and fill the park to see the Prince of Wales light the first in a chain of beacons to blaze across the country, and to hear Handel's *Music for the Royal Fireworks* played in front of a specially constructed pyrotechnic Palace in the Park.

Queen Elizabeth had invited the bride, together with her sister Lady Jane, the wife of Robert Fellowes, Assistant Private Secretary to the Queen, to stay at Clarence House that night. It was a low-key evening with no dinner party. In fact the generations separated early. The two young women had supper alone together in their upstairs sitting room, while the two grandmothers, Queen Elizabeth and Lady Fermoy, had theirs in front of the television in the main drawing room on the first floor. Frances Campbell-Preston, who was in waiting, joined them and, in her private record of the evening, noted that the Queen Mother was in excellent spirits. They watched *Dad's Army* and then the news which was followed by an interview with Prince Charles and Lady Diana. 'Diana is awfully good,'[86] said Queen Elizabeth. Then came the fireworks and Queen Elizabeth provided good-natured commentary on all the important guests appearing on the screen. All in all, Frances Campbell-Preston concluded, it was a joyful evening – 'the Queen Mother in the most marvellous form'.[87]

Next day, vast crowds – perhaps over half a million people – gathered along the route between Buckingham Palace and St Paul's Cathedral. Queen Elizabeth drove to the Palace with the Dowager Duchess of Abercorn, her Mistress of the Robes, in attendance on her, to join the Queen's procession. She took her place with other members of the Royal Family under the dome of Wren's magnificent Cathedral and greatly enjoyed the service. Back at the Palace, the family appeared on the balcony and the Prince kissed his bride to roars of approval from the crowds in the Mall. Then they set off, as his father and mother had done almost thirty-three years before, to start their honeymoon at the Mountbatten home, Broadlands, in Hampshire, and completed it in the royal yacht *Britannia*.

Both bride and groom wrote Queen Elizabeth thank-you letters. The new Princess of Wales expressed herself with charm – 'Dearest Ma'am, I cannot explain just how much it meant to me to spend my last night in your home. Everyone was <u>so</u> kind & I ended up a thoroughly spoilt bride to be.' She thanked Queen Elizabeth 'from the bottom of my heart'. And as a postscript she added, 'I will try my <u>hardest</u> to make your grandson happy & give him all the love & support he needs & deserves. I still can't get over how lucky I am & it will take me the rest of my life to recover!'[88]

CHAPTER TWENTY-THREE

POETRY AND PAIN

1981–1999

'It's no good sitting back. Your *devoir*, your duty'

IF THE LOG CABIN at Polveir, happily placed between river and trees, had been a perfect eightieth-birthday present, a gift which Queen Elizabeth valued highly ten years later was a poem by Ted Hughes, the Poet Laureate. He wrote her an epic of the century, hers, his and everyman's. He called it 'A Masque for Three Voices' and considered it 'a drama of the modern age'.[1] He used a variety of tones to bring different moments from the Queen Mother's life into focus 'against a procession of simple historical tableaux'.

Hughes was a passionate man and a patriot. He thought that any country needing to defend itself must call upon its 'dormant genetic resource', its 'sacred myth', and in Britain's case that was the Crown. In 1939 'the mantle of this palladium settled on the Queen Mother, who was then Queen.' He believed that 'She rose to the occasion in such a way that she became the incarnation of it.'

His poem began with a statement of the importance of monarchy:

> A royalty mints the sovereign soul
> Of wise man and of clown
> What substitute's debased those souls
> Whose country lacks a crown
> Because it lies in some Swiss bank
> Or has been melted down . . .

The century, he wrote, 'dawned at your first smile / Lit with another wonder'. Hughes took the reader through both the innovations and the horrors of the twentieth century, the Great War, Einstein, the Ford motor car, Mickey Mouse, Stalin, Hitler, Mussolini. But in the 1930s, he wrote, tyranny 'alchemised its antidote, the true' – and by 'the true' he meant the Coronation of King George VI and Queen Elizabeth.

He ended in the present day with new generations who had never known what the First and Second World Wars meant, nor 'how the Queen Mother comes to be at the centre of Britain's experience of the drama by which the 20th century will be remembered'.[2]

> Much like the heart that carries us about,
> The fearless hope beneath the fearful doubt,
> You have worn the Nazi and Soviet Empires out . . .
> Your birthday shares this present with the world.
> Simply yourself, like the first smile you smiled,
> A small blue figure, bending to a child.

Queen Elizabeth took the poem with her to the Castle of Mey in August 1990. It was a good place, she told him, to concentrate: 'There is only the sea and an immense sky, and the images that you create in your great poem seem to float in one's mind, in fact every time I read it a new one appears.' Thanking him, she said that she was full of admiration for its beauty and was amazed that he had been able to put into glorious words the whole history of the previous ninety years. 'And slipping from horror words like Stalin and Hitler suddenly into lovely things like a salmon lying under a white stone. There is a white stone in my favourite pool on the Dee, Polveir, and there is nearly always a fish under it, just moving in a languid way against the stream. And you even remembered when Mickey Mouse came upon the scene!' She felt she did not have words enough to tell him 'what immense joy your poem has given me, it is so beautiful and so moving, there are several passages that make me cry, and this happens every time I read it.'[3]

*

TED HUGHES's tribute came at the end of a happy decade for Queen Elizabeth. She loved her eighties and thrived throughout them. When Dame Frances Campbell-Preston later reached what she considered the ripe old age of eighty and thought she ought to retire, Queen Elizabeth would have none of it. 'Congratulations. You will feel marvellous,' she said.[4] Dame Frances stayed *en poste*.

It is often said that people rarely make new friends late in life. With Queen Elizabeth this was not so. She remained particularly good at forging new friendships among younger people, often much younger than her. During her eighties and nineties many new friendships were begun, many older ones ripened and matured. Lady Diana Cooper, socialite, writer and wit, widow of Duff, gave bohemian lunch parties for Queen Elizabeth which she loved. After one typically convivial occasion at the Cooper home in Little Venice, west London, she remarked that it was 'great fun to watch the famous HOUSE POISON doing its work, voices rising, conversation becoming more & more sparkling, & even the dear faces of the clergy becoming a tiny bit roseate'.[5]

Another private fixture she much enjoyed was lunch with her friends Charles and Lady Katharine Farrell (niece of Lady Diana Cooper) at their house in Oxfordshire. As with letters to other friends, her thank-you letters to the Farrells, stretching over more than twenty years, have their own refrain. She often referred to the brilliance of the 'Palais de Glace' – the conservatory which they built on to their house and in which they often ate – and the 'ANNUAL INSPECTION' of the hedge they had planted in the garden. The lunches were merry, bucolic occasions. She enjoyed the neighbours and friends whom they invited and was especially intrigued by Paul Getty, the philanthropist whose love of English traditions in general and cricket in particular had a Wodehousian quality.

Her own invitations were cherished. Her guests – whether they were shooting friends or bibliophiles or music lovers or fishermen and women or walkers or racegoers – loved her stylish, generous entertainment at Clarence House and Royal Lodge, Birkhall, the Castle of Mey and, in July, at Sandringham.

Outside her intimate circle, she had her critics. James Lees-Milne, the diarist, commented ungallantly on her appearance. 'Her teeth, which are her own, are bad. She has little finger nails upturned at the ends – not pretty. Her hair straight, wispy, stringy. Nevertheless, she has dignity and charm – how often has that been said? – however evanescent; and stamina. For 1½ hours she stood – never once sat – talking to total strangers and making herself agreeable.'[6]

Lees-Milne criticized her for 'sugary insincerity', which he found quite unlike the bright, direct dignity and humour of the Queen. He recorded a story told him by Johnny Lucinge, the impresario of her French visits, who had stayed with her at Sandringham for the Flower Show in 1983. There, local women were displaying their pet rabbits.

One old lady, very eccentric and untidy, had an awful exhibit, an ancient, bald rabbit like a melon which she adorned with ribbons and furbelows. The other old ladies did their best to shield the spectacle from the Queen. But the Q. made straight for her, talked to her only and stroked the animal. When urged by Fortune Grafton to walk on to some other stall she lingered, turning her head towards the proud owner as though most loath to leave. All the other respectable old lady competitors furious, of course. This is an example of her compelling charm, he says.

Lees-Milne himself sounds unconvinced.[7]

But even he was wary when the novelist Penelope Mortimer came to interview him for 'yet another biography of the Queen Mother'. She had brought a tape recorder which alarmed him and 'so long as the machine was whizzing I remained discreet.'[8] Mortimer's biography was probably the most unsympathetic ever written about the Queen Mother.*

Writing of Queen Elizabeth's many charitable appearances, Mortimer said:

The Queen Mother Image is dressed, coiffeured, transported, deposited. When the performance is over it is fetched, deposited, fed, cleaned and put carefully away for the night. If the Queen Mother beckons, someone notices; if she calls, someone comes. All she has to do when she drops fresh as a daisy from the sky is to generate love, delight and enthusiasm . . . It may be increasingly difficult for an octogenarian to climb into the helicopter, but once air-borne the flight is effortless, skimming over the dull, pedestrian world, skimming over empty spaces and uneasy silences, over neglect and indifference, landing only where the lights shine and the climate is entirely dependable. One day she will simply spin out of sight, emerging God knows where to carry on with the angels.[9]

But there were other authors whom she helped with their books – she assisted Kenneth Rose with his well-received biography of George V. Rose, diarist extraordinaire of the *Daily Telegraph*, was one of the few journalists whom she trusted. He sent her flowers with

---

* Penelope Mortimer, *Queen Elizabeth: A Life of the Queen Mother*, 1986.

kind notes on her wedding anniversary every year. She also talked to her friend the Cambridge historian Professor Owen Chadwick, in preparation for his book *Britain and the Vatican during the Second World War*. This paid what she thought was overdue tribute to D'Arcy Osborne's wartime achievements as British ambassador to the Vatican. Chadwick, like Queen Elizabeth herself, admired Osborne for both his courage and his delightful personality and she enjoyed talking with him. On another occasion, ever true to her love for P. G. Wodehouse, she advised him to read Gussie Fink-Nottle's prize-giving speech in *Right Ho, Jeeves*. Chadwick did so, with great pleasure, and wrote to tell her that his laughter had caused consternation in the silent college library.[10]

One of the great new friends of her eighties was Ted Hughes. They met when he spoke at the King's Lynn Festival and Queen Elizabeth invited him and his wife Carol to dinner at Sandringham. The following year she invited them to Royal Lodge for her Musical Weekend. She asked him to read some of his poems, which he did 'with some trepidation'. He need not have worried; he was captivated by her and she by him.[11]

Hughes was a dedicated countryman and fisherman. Queen Elizabeth liked that sort of person and she also found his looks – tall, craggy and well built – 'very striking'.[12] Writing to his brother after one visit to Birkhall, Hughes said, 'the morale and general spirits in her group is always incredibly high. And she never alters in the slightest way. Interested in everything, amused by everything. Her secret is – one of her secrets – to be positive about everything. Another must be – to be pretty strong. She climbs about the steep gardens. Stands & walks for hours at a time. There's something about her that's kept very young – like a young woman. But everybody is so fond of her that she escapes the psychological isolation – for most old people inescapable.'[13]

*

ISOLATED SHE never was. Through this decade she watched with pleasure (and sometimes concern) her grandchildren growing older and her great-grandchildren's infancy. She continued with her private trips to France and with her official visits abroad, particularly to Canada. The pattern of her years remained much the same as it had always been, with the regular commitments to her charities, her regiments, her ships – and of course her horses. Not all of these engagements need to be rehearsed; at the risk of showing favouritism (which she always tried to eschew) a few landmarks should be recorded.

Spring 1982 saw her carrying out her military obligations, presenting shamrock to the Irish Guards at Pirbright on 17 March and visiting her regiment, 1st The Queen's Dragoon Guards, in Northern Ireland at the end of April. Earlier that month an unexpected war had broken out when Argentina seized the Falkland Islands, a British colony in the South Atlantic. The British government immediately declared its intention of regaining the islands; a task force was prepared and dispatched. Prince Andrew went out with the force as a naval helicopter pilot in HMS *Invincible*. With her habitual horror of war, Queen Elizabeth wrote to the Queen, 'One feels such a dark cloud in one's mind over the Falklands'; she longed for a solution to be found.[14]

In early June she lunched privately with Mrs Thatcher at Chequers, the Prime Minister's official country residence, and shortly afterwards President and Mrs Reagan arrived in England on an official visit, during which the American leader made clear his support for British determination to recapture the Falklands. Queen Elizabeth attended the banquet for the Reagans at Windsor Castle. The war ended with British victory on 14 June.

Queen Elizabeth was to have flown by helicopter from Royal Lodge to Margate for the start of her Cinque Ports visit on 8 June. But one engine failed just after takeoff and the helicopter had to make an emergency landing. She seemed not in the least alarmed; after lunch at home she took a plane of the Queen's Flight from Heathrow to Marston in Kent instead.

She had a busy summer which included a visit to Barnard Castle in County Durham to open three galleries at the Bowes Museum, in which her family connection gave her a personal interest.* She travelled to Glasgow for the Centenary Service of the St Andrew's Ambulance Association and a visit to the Royal Scottish Academy of Music and Drama; and she paid a two-day visit to Germany to see her regiments – the 9th/12th Royal Lancers and the 1st Battalion The Black Watch. On 16 July she returned to Scotland to celebrate the centenary of the University of Dundee, and on 26 July she attended

---

* See p. 11. She had given a number of her dresses and hats to the costume department of the museum.

the Falklands thanksgiving service at St Paul's Cathedral before driving
to Sandringham for the King's Lynn Festival and her usual July house
party. Her birthday that year had a special resonance; Prince William,
the first son of the Prince and Princess of Wales, was christened by the
Archbishop of Canterbury at Buckingham Palace. After the ceremony
the family celebrated both events at a lunch at the Palace.

Towards the end of her customary Scottish holidays she paid her
annual visit to the Lord Roberts Workshops for disabled soldiers in
Dundee, named a British Railways locomotive *The Queen Mother* at
Aberdeen and attended the Perth Bull Sales where she was delighted
that her Aberdeen Angus bull won Reserve Junior Champion. Back in
London she and Princess Margaret acted as Counsellors of State while
the Queen was in Australia. She wrote to her daughter: 'Thinking of
you in great heat & chiffon, I write, as usual, in a downpour of rain
and thick wool!' and sent her horse news – mostly bad at this point.
She had been following the tour on television and thought of how
hard the Queen worked, compared with how little she was doing.[15]

In fact she had been far from idle, but an enforced rest followed.
During a shooting weekend at Royal Lodge a fishbone lodged in her
throat at dinner one evening, and she had to have an operation to
remove it. Letters and flowers arrived from many people, including
Margaret Thatcher, who sent 'affectionate good wishes' from everyone
at 10 Downing Street, and Lord Snowdon. 'Do look in if you are down
our way. It would be lovely to see you,' she wrote back to him from
Royal Lodge. 'A thousand thanks, ever your affec Ex M in L.'[16]

After two weeks she was able to resume her public life and in early
December went to Southampton to visit the liner *Queen Elizabeth 2*,
the Cunard Line's successor to *Queen Elizabeth*, which she had launched
in 1938, and she unveiled a plaque to mark the ship's role as a troop
carrier in the Falklands War.

On St Patrick's Day 1983 she flew to Münster in West Germany to
present shamrock to the Irish Guards stationed there. The cheers they
gave her 'were deafening and straight from the heart'.[17] A very
different ceremony took place later in April when Queen Elizabeth
opened a Luncheon Club and Day Centre for the West Indian Elderly
in Railton Road, Brixton, a part of south London with a large West
Indian population. There had been violent riots there in 1981, and the
Mayor of Brixton had asked her to make this visit as a way of restoring
confidence in the area. She toured the building while children danced

and sang to a steel band. The visit was a great success and the director of the Brixton Neighbourhood Community Association thought that she had 'kindled a ray of hope for the future of our neighbourhood'.[18]

Perhaps the next most significant public event of her eighty-third year was her visit to Northern Ireland, still in the throes of the Troubles. In 1958, a more peaceful time, she had visited the Territorial Auxiliary and Volunteer Reserve Association for Northern Ireland for their fiftieth anniversary. Now they asked her to come again to celebrate their seventy-fifth. She decided to do so, but after the news leaked to the press the visit had to be cancelled. It was then quietly rearranged and she flew to Northern Ireland to preside over the association's parade at St Patrick's Barracks, Ballymena, on Monday 20 June. Afterwards Lieutenant General Sir Robert Richardson, General Officer Commanding Northern Ireland, wrote that her determination to come, despite the press leaks and threats from the IRA, 'impressed everyone, yet again, with her personal courage'. The visit was 'a triumph'.[19]

In another symbol of the lasting strength of her commitments, on 4 March 1984 she helped celebrate the fortieth anniversary of Cumberland Lodge. She could take satisfaction in the fact that this institution, which she had hoped would contribute to a more Christian future for Britain, had at least survived in a much more secular age.

Later that month she unveiled a memorial in Westminster Abbey to Noël Coward, whose wit had given her so much pleasure and whose death in 1973 she had much regretted. On 5 June that year she honoured her hero General de Gaulle, unveiling a blue plaque on his wartime residence in Carlton Gardens. On the evening of 30 July she was quietly admitted to the King Edward VII Hospital in Marylebone. There she underwent a simple excision for carcinoma of the breast and the doctors were confident that the entire tumour had been removed.* Her spirits were high and her lady in waiting's diary recorded that she 'came home on the morning of 2 August "in very good form"'[20] – then she dived gaily into the celebrations of her eighty-fourth birthday.

*

---

* Mr William Slack, Sergeant-Surgeon to the Queen, carried out the operation and Dr Derek Cope was the anaesthetist.

ON 16 JULY 1985 Queen Elizabeth, on her eleventh visit to Canada, was flying from Regina, Saskatchewan, to Edmonton, Alberta. A sudden violent storm hit Edmonton and her Canadian military plane was at the last minute diverted to the military base of Cold Lake, Alberta. There was something akin to panic on the ground. The officers on the base had only a few minutes' warning of the royal arrival and they rushed around finding cars and a bit of carpet to be placed at the steps of the plane. As many of the top brass as could be gathered hurried over. When she came down the steps Queen Elizabeth greeted the welcoming party on the ground with words that some of them never forgot: 'Ah, Cold Lake! I've always wanted to come here.'[21]

Like other members of the Royal Family, Queen Elizabeth usually enjoyed herself when things went wrong. Surprises were often a welcome relief from the official round set months before. She seemed genuinely amused by this unexpected little adventure. In the officers' mess they rustled up refreshments and she talked happily to the officers and their wives until, after an hour and a half, the weather cleared enough for the pilot to resume the flight to Edmonton. The plane was some four hours late when it finally touched down at its destination.

This trip to Canada had been built around Queen Elizabeth's enthusiasm for Aberdeen Angus cattle. The Fifth World Aberdeen Angus Forum was being held in Edmonton. On the way across Canada she had spent three days in Toronto and attended the 126th running of the Queen's Plate Stakes at the Woodbine racetrack. She dined, as she liked to do, with the Ontario Jockey Club, and went to a garden party for her Canadian regiments next day. She made an unscheduled visit to the CN Tower, at that time the highest in the world, insisting that the morning's rain and mist had cleared sufficiently for the view to be worth while. Rather to the consternation of her tour staff, who were worried about the effect on her of the high-speed lifts, she made for the fastest lift and was ensconced at the top with a drink before the rest of the party arrived.* Next day, flying to Edmonton, she paused

---

* Her tour staff were not the only ones worried about her. The Queen was concerned about the heavy programme for this tour, and gave strict orders that no 'extras' should be added. When Queen Elizabeth expressed a wish to go up the CN Tower, Sir Martin Gilliat told Harris Boyd, the Canadian Federal Coordinator of the tour, that there was nothing for it – they

for a Provincial reception and luncheon at Regina before the unexpected detour to Cold Lake.

Restored by a good night's sleep at Soaring, the elegant modern
home of Mr and Mrs Sandy McTaggart, the Queen Mother resumed
her delayed programme in Edmonton. On Thursday 18 July she opened
the Forum, where, amongst others, she met delegates from Argentina
and farmers from Zimbabwe – the former Southern Rhodesia – whom
she remembered from a visit there. After lunch and a warmly welcomed
speech, she returned to the show and spent two hours viewing the
cattle and talking to almost all of the exhibiting farmers.

★

BACK HOME Queen Elizabeth spent her eighty-fifth birthday at Sandringham. The crowd at the church for Matins was so large that the
service was relayed to those who could not get inside. That evening
she enjoyed a concert by the Russian cellist Mstislav Rostropovich,
and a high-spirited dinner party which included the Queen, Princess
Margaret and the Prince of Wales. After dinner she danced with Sir
Frederick Ashton to music played by the Russian maestro. The Prince
of Wales wrote to her afterwards of his delight 'in you and Freddie
dancing that demented scarf dance to the accompaniment of Rostropovich's equally demented mazurka'.[22] Next day in London she was
greeted by large crowds outside Clarence House and on 6 August
she was treated to a birthday present by British Airways – a two-
hour flight in Concorde up to Scotland and back. Now she could say
that, having started her life in the horse age, she was a supersonic
traveller.

She returned to the Castle of Mey by a more mundane flight the
following day and summer in Scotland followed its usual pattern –
guests, fishing, stalking, shooting, picnics, Racing Demon and favourite
videos in the evenings.

Through the 1980s her health remained remarkably good. She still
swore by her herbal and homeopathic medicines and powders. Her
biggest problem remained the lesions on her legs; and she suffered

---

would have to arrange the visit. There was initial relief when the weather seemed to rule it
out; but Queen Elizabeth got her way in the end. She had not yet made her regular telephone
call to the Queen; Boyd suspected that she put it off until after the CN Tower visit, for fear of
being forbidden to go up. As he remarked later, the Queen Mother always went outside her
programme.

further occasional obstructions in her throat. In August 1986, she choked at dinner one night at Mey and refused all help until *Britannia* arrived the next day, when she reluctantly accepted a visit from the ship's doctor. She was in considerable discomfort but said there was no need to make a fuss. Finally, she agreed to be flown by helicopter to hospital in Aberdeen where she was X-rayed and kept in overnight. The lady in waiting's diary recorded that 'the doctors were amazed by her resilience, and attitude to what had been a very unpleasant, painful episode.'[23] Prince Charles wrote to tell her how relieved he was that she was all right and asked her to be more careful with fish dishes in future.[24] The rest of the holiday at Mey passed without incident and then, as usual, she went south to Balmoral and Birkhall.

Three weeks later, on 9 September 1986, she gave a remarkable demonstration of her continuing stamina. She flew from Birkhall by helicopter to Glasgow, where she opened the Pollok Leisure Centre, a £3½ million development in a deprived area of the city. This included a lunch (to which she had to climb two flights of stairs) and a visit to the new gallery housing the magnificent Burrell Collection of works of art. Then it was immediately off to Govan Shipbuilders, where she launched the MV *Norsea*, a £40 million P&O cruise ferry and the largest passenger-carrying ship built in Britain since 1969. When the ceremony was over she met members of the workforce and patients from the Princess Louise Scottish Hospital. She then drove to the Crest Hotel for a reception, meeting more people, before flying back to Birkhall for dinner and an evening of Racing Demon.

In October she stepped on 'a dead but vicious piece of wood'[25] while walking in Scotland. It seemed at first to be a mere graze but on her return to London her doctor advised that she avoid standing – advice which she cheerfully ignored. By 7 November the leg had become inflamed. She insisted on carrying out her usual Remembrance Day engagements. But she had to go into hospital again for five days and, to her regret, cancelled one of her favourite excursions – lunch with Charles and Kitty Farrell.

*

THE LOVE AFFAIR between Queen Elizabeth and Canada persisted throughout the 1980s. In 1986 Martin Gilliat's desk overflowed with requests for a major trip in 1987, including visits to four provinces with dozens of projected events. Gently he batted many of these back, suggesting that she might limit her visit to Montreal, in order to take part in the 125th anniversary celebrations of her regiment, the Black Watch of Canada. Reluctantly, the Canadian hosts agreed to a short-ened version of the trip and she left London on 4 June 1987, landing in Montreal that afternoon.

This was a visit with political importance. Queen Elizabeth was the first member of the Royal Family to return to French-speaking Quebec since the deterioration in relations between anglophone and francophone Canada in the 1960s – there had been riots when the Queen went to Quebec in 1964, and in 1967 President de Gaulle had made his inflammatory 'Vive le Québec libre' speech in Montreal. The Queen had been to Montreal for Expo in 1967 and for the 1974 Olympics, but only to these events – she had not ventured outside the grounds on to Quebec territory on either occasion. In a real sense, therefore, Queen Elizabeth was 'testing the waters' for the Queen; she even went to the spot where de Gaulle had spoken, and drew small but friendly crowds.

In Montreal, Queen Elizabeth stayed in a charming private house, but she found the food surprisingly unpleasant. Her staff discovered why – the chef had a health inspector standing beside him, ' "monitor-ing" every gesture, causing him to wash his hands in iodine about forty times a day & insisting on all meat being done to a frazzle'. Not only that – after the Queen Mother had eaten, any food left on her plate was taken for analysis. She complained in fairly strong terms and the culinary censorship was relaxed.[26]

On her first full day she made two long speeches, each of them partly in French, and her lady in waiting thought she must be tired. Not so – she considered her twenty-minute afternoon rest period far too long. Next morning she was dismayed to find she had a completely free morning so a visit to the Musée des Beaux Arts was hurriedly arranged, to see a Leonardo da Vinci exhibition. She apparently impressed her guides by her questions – and by speaking French throughout the visit.

That afternoon she went to Molson Stadium to see Trooping the Colour by the Black Watch. Colonel Victor Chartier, at that time the commanding officer, later recalled her impressive knowledge of the regiment's history. Talking to one veteran, she said, 'You weren't always with the Black Watch, were you?' She had seen the Italy Medal on his chest and she knew the Black Watch had not served there. She was right: the soldier had transferred temporarily to the Signallers, with whom he had been in Italy.[27]

After a regimental dinner at the Reine Elizabeth Hotel she passed a room where French Canadian high-school students were having a graduation party to noisy discotheque music. To the alarm of her flagging Household she asked to go in. The students recognized her at once and gathered around cheering, 'Vive la Reine.' She emerged a few minutes later, dancing.[28]

Before she left the city on 8 June the Queen Mother thanked all ten of her motorcycle escorts in French, and posed for photographs with them.[29] Her reception in Montreal had broken the ice in Quebec. When the Queen visited the city in October, she was given a friendly welcome.[30] No one doubted that Queen Elizabeth's earlier venture had helped to ease the Queen's way.

★

QUEEN ELIZABETH's last trip to Canada took place shortly before her eighty-ninth birthday. It was part of a crowded summer: she had inaugurated two new oilfields – Tern and Eider – at Aberdeen, made a private visit to the Languedoc in France and celebrated the tenth anniversary of becoming lord warden of the Cinque Ports with a visit to Dover in *Britannia*. At the end of the ceremonies she sailed in the royal yacht for France, disembarked at Caen and drove to Bayeux, where she unveiled a memorial window in the Cathedral and laid a wreath at the 50th (Northumbria) Division Memorial, commemorating the D-Day landings. In June she visited Oxford to mark the University's development programme, went to Tyne Tees Television in Newcastle and visited Hadrian's Wall to open a National Trust hostel. On 16 June she gave a reception at Clarence House for members of the French Resistance and the RAF Escaping Society and made a visit to RAF Scampton to see the RAF Central Flying School.

Then on 5 July she boarded a Canadian Armed Forces Boeing 707 to Ottawa. This trip had originally been envisaged to mark the fiftieth anniversary of the historic tour she had made with the King just before the outbreak of war. On arrival in Ottawa, in fierce heat, she was driven through the city in the open Buick that she and the King had used in 1939, for an official welcome on Parliament Hill. At tea with the Governor General afterwards she cut a birthday cake with the same knife she had used to cut a cake fifty years before. The ride back to the airport, in a modern car with a low seat and a small window, was less pleasant. Frances Campbell-Preston, who had been her lady in waiting on all her Canadian visits since 1967, recorded 'Poor Queen Elizabeth has to sit very bolt upright & wave frantically. Window sealed as car bullet proof and air conditioned. It's <u>extremely</u> tiring for her.'[31] They flew that evening to Toronto where, fortunately, she had been lent the comfortable home of Galen and Hilary Weston, friends of the Royal Family who were frequent guests at Royal Lodge.*

Next day, after a gargantuan civic luncheon, she had a long, humid afternoon inspecting a combined guard of honour of her two regiments, the Toronto Scottish and the Black Watch of Canada. She talked at length to the soldiers and as a result she was quite a long time in the heat without shade or water.[32] In London, Ontario, the following day, after another long hot lunch and an enjoyable meeting with veterans, it was on to Sir Frederick S. Banting Square to unveil a statue of the man who had discovered insulin in 1922 and thus saved the lives of millions of diabetics thereafter. She lit an 'eternal flame' to his memory.†

On Saturday 8 July there was yet another long luncheon in Toronto, this time with the officers of her regiments, then a tiring walkabout among the soldiers and some impromptu sightseeing. That evening, after a reception for her regiments and an enjoyable dinner with the Ontario Jockey Club, she met all the Club Trustees, two by two, over liqueurs and coffee. With the final pair, David Willmot and Bob Anderson, a young Aberdeen Angus cattle breeder, she talked and talked about her favourite cattle as she plied them with Drambuie. She told them of an alarming experience she had once had in a landau on an English racecourse; the coachman lost control of the team of horses and they ran on and on for three circuits. What did she do? Willmot

---

* Galen Weston, successful Canadian businessman whose fortune came from one of the oldest family businesses in Canada, the George Weston Food company. His wife, Hilary, served as lieutenant governor of Ontario 1997–2002. In the 1980s they took a long lease on Fort Belvedere, King Edward VIII's favourite home, in Windsor Great Park.

† Unfortunately this memorial was later vandalized and extinguished. Complicated plans were devised to enable her to light another flame in London and for it to be flown back to Canada, but this proved too difficult and eventually she authorized its relighting by someone else.

asked. She just gave the spectators a royal wave each time she went past the stands, she replied.[33]

Queen Elizabeth's last Canadian engagement, appropriately, was at the races – attending the 130th running of the Queen's Plate Stakes at the Woodbine racetrack that afternoon. The next day the royal party flew back to London. 'The tour had been punishing for HM at moments,' Dame Frances recorded; 'but she is so loved and venerated in Canada that it was impossible not to be buoyed up by the enthusiasm of so many nice people.'[34] Canadian officials and politicians asked for yet another visit in the early 1990s. The Queen was consulted and came to the reluctant decision that eighty-nine was old enough for such adventures. Thus the long and happy saga of Queen Elizabeth's trips to Canada came to an end in her ninth decade.[35]

*

IN 1990, LUNCHEONS, dinners, garden parties and other events were held all over the kingdom in honour of Queen Elizabeth's ninetieth birthday. Among them were celebrations organized by the Lord Mayor of London, by the Black Watch in Northern Ireland, by the Queen and Prince Philip at Holyrood. The tributes were substantial – it is probable that most of those who took part did not expect her to complete another decade.

The highlight came on 27 June 1990 when, accompanied by the Prince of Wales and Princess Margaret, she rode in a carriage to Horse Guards Parade, for a procession of tableaux in her honour. This was organized by Major Michael Parker, of the Queen's Own Hussars (one of her regiments), who had been planning military and royal events for many years. This time the display included many of the hundreds of organizations – military, medical, social, cultural, animal – that she patronized.[36]

Queen Elizabeth inspected the parade while Princess Margaret and the Prince of Wales watched together from a window overlooking Horse Guards Parade. The Queen was away on an official trip to Iceland and Princess Margaret wrote to tell her sister of the event, saying that their mother was 'looking very her in blue, while the choir, orchestra & massed bands played & sang "I was Glad" so of course Charles and I were sobbing'.[37]

The Princess gave the Queen a spirited description of the soldiers and the civilians marching gamely on behind.

Outstanding amongst the nurses, Guides, Distressed Gentlefolk, Vacani school of dancing, NSPCC etc were all the mayors & maces of the Cinque Ports, Middle Temple judges in their wigs, the Nat Trust (houses, gardens, the Coast) all dressed up & dancing past, followed by two huge bulls in trailers, one Highland, the other Aberdeen Angus looking incredibly stately, the Argonaut & Special Cargo, ridden, and Desert Orchid [racehorses] being led, dear old Sefton, the survivor of the horrible bomb in the Park,* Shetlands, many dogs trotting along very well and – wait for it, could it be – yes it _is_ – it's the Poultry Club! And 4 little hens were trundled past in cages!

Then there was 'a glorious noise' from the massed bands, a march-past by the King's Troop, and a fly-past by a Lancaster, a Hurricane, a Spitfire and the Red Arrows; all in all 'it was stupendous and I wish you had been there.'[38]

After the parade, when she arrived home at Clarence House Queen Elizabeth was pleased to see her racing manager Michael Oswald holding up a sign to tell her that the Queen's horse Starlet had won a race by eight lengths. So the day ended especially well. Later she said that one of its joys had been to see the Sandringham Women's Institute marching by. 'The sight of Mrs Beamis, Mrs Emmerson, Mrs Candy, Mrs Hall, Mrs Rispin and Mrs Whittaker stepping out bravely to the rousing tune of Blaydon Races was a great sight.'[39]

The celebrations continued. Queen Elizabeth gave audiences and received gifts and loyal birthday addresses from both Houses of Parliament at Clarence House. She embarked in the royal yacht at Portsmouth on 30 July and reviewed at least a thousand small yachts and boats which came out to greet her in the Solent. On 1 August _Britannia_ sailed up the Thames, through Tower Bridge and into the

---

* On 20 July 1982 the IRA exploded a nail bomb placed in a car in Hyde Park as a detachment of sixteen horses from the Queen's Life Guard (found from the Blues and Royals) was passing, en route to a changing of the guard. Three soldiers were killed, as were seven horses. Sefton suffered serious injuries including a severed jugular. Under the orders of Lieutenant Colonel Andrew Parker Bowles, a groom used his shirt to staunch the wound in Sefton's neck and after extensive surgery the horse survived. He became something of a national hero and in his name hundreds of thousands of pounds were raised to construct a new surgical wing at the Royal Veterinary College.

In an even worse atrocity, on the same day another IRA bomb exploded under the bandstand in Regent's Park when a band from the Royal Green Jackets was giving a concert. Seven members of the band were killed and many in the audience were wounded.

Pool of London. That afternoon, Queen Elizabeth drove around parts of the East End. She was touched that she was still greeted with intense affection half a century after she and the King had comforted people under German attack there. After a reception, a family dinner on board and fireworks, she slept in *Britannia*, returning to Clarence House the next day. That night Prince Charles gave a concert in her honour at Buckingham Palace.

The day before her ninetieth birthday, 3 August, was the hottest day recorded since 1911; Queen Elizabeth said she remembered clearly the heat of that distant summer.[40] On her birthday itself, she spent an hour in the sun collecting flowers from well-wishers. Lunch with her family was followed by a ballet gala at Covent Garden and then dinner with Ruth Fermoy at her flat – a long day. Then she flew to Mey where she settled down to the pleasure of reading Ted Hughes's poetic tribute.

The 1990s were to be much harder.

*

AT THE END of 1991, as the Queen approached the fortieth anniversary of her accession to the throne, she used her Christmas broadcast to reflect upon the momentous changes that had taken place during her reign, and particularly upon the recent fall of communism in eastern Europe where the people had 'broken the mould of autocracy'.

The fall of communism had an impact within Britain too. For decade after decade established politicians and pedagogues had expressed far greater enthusiasm for the work of centralized state powers than for that of voluntary associations. By the early 1990s the patronages of the Royal Family – including Queen Elizabeth and those younger members whose marital difficulties the press remorselessly chronicled – amounted to almost 3,500 organizations.

In her Christmas broadcast, the Queen said that she was 'constantly amazed by the generosity of donors and subscribers, great and small, who give so willingly and often towards the enjoyment of others. Without them . . . voluntary organizations would not exist.' She believed that voluntary service was the bedrock of Britain's democratic way of life and she pledged to continue the royal tradition of public service she had inherited and her own personal commitment to the nation.

The Queen's steady determination was reinforced by that of her mother. Indeed, throughout her nineties, despite increasing frailty, Queen Elizabeth continued to work for the organizations to which she had pledged herself. At a time of life when most people do almost nothing she willed herself to carry on. Physically this became more and more of a struggle, but she knew and would consider no other way.

That March she undertook her usual, pleasant responsibility to the Irish Guards and flew to Berlin to present them with shamrock on St Patrick's Day. In May she undertook another task that was close to her heart, flying for the day to Valençay in central France to unveil a memorial to the F (France) Section of the Special Operations Executive (SOE).* She had always admired the courage of the secret agents of SOE charged by Churchill in 1940 to 'set Europe ablaze' behind enemy lines. The men and women of SOE were sometimes known as Churchill's Secret Army and she had become patron of their discreet association, the Special Forces Club, in London. On this occasion, the fiftieth anniversary of the first SOE agent being dropped into France in May 1941, Queen Elizabeth took her piper, Pipe Major King, with her and he played 'The Flowers of the Forest' at the memorial ceremony. During the rest of 1991 she carried out seventy-five other public engagements at home during the year, while attending as many race meetings as ever, entertaining and being entertained by her friends, and taking her usual holidays in Scotland.

On 30 October she lunched, with her daughters, at Ascot race-course, to celebrate her 400th winner under National Hunt Rules, Nearco Bay. Several hundred people attended this happy occasion, including all the jockeys who had ridden for her. Several of her favourite horses were paraded. On 25 November she flew by helicopter to Portsmouth to visit the aircraft carrier HMS *Ark Royal*. As with the previous *Ark Royal*, which she had launched in 1950, she felt a great attachment to this ship. Indeed she looked upon both *Ark Royal* and HMS *Resolution*, the first Polaris submarine, which she had launched in 1966, very much as she did on her regiments – as an extension of

---

* SOE's mission was to conduct unconventional warfare against the Germans throughout Europe in preparation for the eventual Allied invasion. Many of the secret agents were betrayed, arrested by the Gestapo and executed or sent to concentration camps. The memorial that Queen Elizabeth unveiled in Valençay commemorated the ninety-one men and thirteen women members of SOE who had given their lives for the freedom of France. After Queen Elizabeth's death in 2002, the Princess Royal became patron of the Special Forces Club.

family for which she was responsible. She often visited both ships over the years, particularly when they were in dock for recommissioning; she had also visited *Ark Royal* three times at sea, landing on deck by helicopter. Their captains kept in touch with her.

After the customary family holiday at Sandringham over Christmas and the New Year of 1992, which she described to the Queen as 'better than ten bottles of tonic or twenty bottles of Arnica',[41] she acted as Counsellor of State during the Queen's absence in Australia. In March 1992, she attended the service and final parade of the Women's Royal Army Corps in Guildford: the WRAC was to be incorporated into the army. As so often when her regiments were disbanded, she was not only sad but felt strongly that it was a wrong decision that would be regretted in the future.[42]

At the end of April she spent two days in Scotland for public engagements; she then flew for a weekend to Spain to stay privately with the Duke and Duchess of Wellington, and then before the last of her private European visits, to Umbria, she went back to Birkhall for her annual two weeks' fishing with friends.

Ted Hughes was again among the guests and at a picnic below Lochnagar, as they listened to the wind in the trees, they had a conversation typical of their friendship. She asked him if he thought that trees could communicate with each other. The exchange kept coming back to him and he wrote a poem about the picnic. Sending it to her, he told her that he thought the verses were 'rough and playful', but there was also a mystical quality to them.[43] He wrote of her question:

> And what were the great pines whispering?
>   We would have liked to know.
> With rooty thoughts and needle tongues
>   They murmured: 'There they go
> Looking for mountain sunshine just
>   In time to meet the snow!
>   Toasting Queen Victoria
> For blazing the trail to Lochnagar.'[44]

She was at Royal Lodge when she received the poem, and wrote to tell Hughes that it transported her 'at once to my beloved hills, and to the "steep frowning glories of dark Lochnagar" (Lord Byron!!), and to the birds and the deer and the elusive salmon and the dear creaking pines. It is such a wonderful and <u>loving</u> poem, and I send you my most hearty thanks for giving us something so special.'[45]

She had a summer full of engagements. At the end of May 1992 she unveiled a statue of one of her heroes, Sir Arthur 'Bomber' Harris, the wartime leader of Bomber Command, outside the RAF Church, St Clement Dane's, in the Strand. (In 1988 she had unveiled a statue of Lord Dowding of Fighter Command near by.) Charged with destroying German industry, Bomber Command had a higher casualty rate than any other unit in the British armed forces. Queen Elizabeth knew well that, despite the appalling odds, its young airmen had flown into danger night after night, month after month. The missions included the saturation bombing of Dresden, where 35,000 people died in British attacks in February 1945. Dresden was an important military communications centre through which German troops passed to the Eastern Front, but after the war was won Harris had been the subject of fierce criticism because of such attacks. Some post-war historians even called British bombing policies 'war crimes'.

Queen Elizabeth had no time for such views. She knew that Britain now had a completely new relationship with the democratic state of Germany, but her heart was still with the heroes of the war against Nazi Germany.* She believed that Bomber Command, and Harris in particular, had been treated badly since the war. Far from seeing them as criminals, she thought that the young bomber pilots, whose airfields she and the King had often visited, were the bravest of the brave.† In April 1983 she had opened the Bomber Command Museum at Hendon,

---

* In November 1990, on the fiftieth anniversary of the bombing of Coventry, Queen Elizabeth had visited the city for a service of reconciliation attended also by Dr Richard von Weizsäcker, President of the Federal Republic of Germany. The ceremony called for Queen Elizabeth to exchange 'Symbols of Peace' with the President. These were her words: 'Mr President, I present to you this Cross of Nails from Coventry – a symbol of reconciliation, friendship and peace. May God bless the people of your country.' The President presented a 'Bell of Peace' to Queen Elizabeth. (RA QEQMH/PS/ENGT/1990: 14 November)

† In May 1982, the *Sunday People* had published a story that she had refused to attend Harris's ninetieth birthday as a 'deliberate slur'. Sir Arthur wrote to Martin Gilliat to say that he was used to this sort of 'sensational sneer and smear' and always just ignored it. Sir Martin clearly felt that he should reassure Harris and wrote to him: 'As you know from those far off days of World War II, both The King and Queen Elizabeth have always had a very special regard for you and it is a source of real sadness to Her Majesty that owing to long arranged commitments she cannot be at the 90th birthday dinner which is being given in your honour.' (RA QEQMH/PS/GEN/1982/Harris)

where Harris had come to welcome her. It was, according to the lady in waiting's diary, 'A very moving occasion, so full of memories for all concerned'.[46]

Now, eight years after Sir Arthur's death, as she unveiled his memorial, demonstrators tried to interrupt Queen Elizabeth's speech. She seemed surprised, but after a moment's pause she continued. (Subsequently the statue had to be protected by police because it was frequently defaced with red paint.) That day she entertained some of the RAF officers present to lunch at Clarence House and one of them, Air Marshal Sir John Grandy, wrote to her to say, 'We were all worried but your great calm and disarming smile, courage and brave example against that ridiculous attempt to upset you was superb.'[47]

*

FAR MORE upsetting than transient demonstrations was the turmoil afflicting her own family. It was the misfortune of the Royal Family that the globalization of the media was now making the so-called cult of celebrity into an ever more valuable commodity. Newspapers, fearful of losing market share to television and other media, became more invasive. Tabloid editors juggled the lives of real people with those of fictional characters from television soap operas for space on front pages. Actors and actresses were deliberately confused with their screen personalities. The borderlines between fact and fantasy became ever more blurred.

Exaggerations, inventions, lies about different members of the Royal Family became commonplace. The editor of the *Sun*, Kelvin Mackenzie, was reported to have instructed his staff, 'Give me a Monday splash on the royals. Don't worry if it's not true – so long as there's not too much fuss about it afterwards.'[48] Donald Trelford, editor of the *Observer*, a more sober paper, wrote, 'The royal soap opera has now reached such a pitch of public interest that the boundary between fact and fiction has been lost sight of . . . it is not just that some papers don't check their facts or accept denials: they don't care if the stories are true or not.'[49] No other European royal family was being subjected to such ruthless and sententious assault.

The revelation of problems and peccadilloes in the family was highly profitable. But there was a more important cause of tension. Though many journalists sought to deny or belittle the idea, a large majority of the population still believed that one of the Royal Family's functions was, in the words of the writer Rebecca West, to hold up to the public 'a presentation of ourselves doing well'.[50] When some of them did badly, we did not like what we saw of ourselves. And all too often we found it difficult to remember that the mirror of the media distorted as much as it revealed.

The marriages and divorces of younger members of the Royal Family have since been written about endlessly and often cruelly. These crises obviously touched Queen Elizabeth profoundly; she worried constantly about her grandchildren. But she rarely committed her views to paper. Such caution was characteristic: since joining the Royal Family in 1923 she had always made it a rule not to talk about members of the family with anyone outside it, not even with her own Bowes Lyon relations. Still less did she write to anyone about family matters. Given the ever increasing danger of leaks, her discretion was well placed.

What one can venture to say is that Queen Elizabeth, like other members of the Royal Family, had welcomed Lady Diana Spencer's entry into the family. In her public life, the Princess of Wales gradually showed that she could use her natural warmth and spontaneity to good effect. After a tour of Australia in early 1983 in which she had been the centre of obsessive media attention, Queen Elizabeth wrote to congratulate her. The Princess replied that she was 'enormously touched by your letter – the thought gave me a lot of happiness. Charles is the one who deserves all the credit by showing me what to do & how to do it, always patient & ready to explain. The whole Tour seems to have helped me a great deal on how to cope with my public duties, so all in all, a good experience!'[51]

Her success as a new member of the Royal Family was similar to that of the young Duchess of York in 1923. But, unlike the Duchess of York, personal contentment eluded her, as it did her husband. The births of their two much loved sons, Prince William in 1982 and Prince Harry in 1984, gave joy to them as well as to everyone else in the family. But hopes that motherhood would bring the Princess fulfilment proved illusory. Within the family, enthusiasm and hopes for the marriage gave way to anxiety and concern. The Prince's response was to retreat into his grandmother's concept of duty. He had always been diligent; now his work became ever more important to him. The Princess was younger and her unhappiness was more volatile. She began to move along a separate trajectory in both her personal life and her official duties, which she continued to carry out with aplomb. By 1986 the marriage had all but broken down.

The Waleses were not alone in their problems. Princess Anne, the Princess Royal, had become the first of Queen Elizabeth's grand-children to separate from her husband. She and Captain Mark Phillips were divorced in April 1992. By this time the marriage of Prince Andrew, Queen Elizabeth's second grandson, was also in trouble. He had met Sarah Ferguson in 1985 and they had subsequently fallen in love. She was a friendly, outspoken young woman and the match was welcomed not only by journalists who considered that Miss Ferguson was that famous cliché 'a breath of fresh air', but also by most of the Prince's family. Queen Elizabeth thought she was 'such a cheerful person, and seems to be so thankful & pleased to be part of a united family'.[52] (Sarah Ferguson's parents had divorced when she was a child.) The wedding, in July 1986, engendered widespread pleasure and on the same day the Queen created the Prince duke of York, the title held by both his grandfather, King George VI, and his great-grand-father, King George V. The new Duke and Duchess had two daughters, Princess Beatrice, born in 1988, and Princess Eugenie, born in 1990. But their marriage also deteriorated.

In these hard times Queen Elizabeth gave her grandchildren, particularly the Prince of Wales, as much support as she could. The Prince visited her often and loved to bring his sons to stay with her at either Birkhall or Royal Lodge. There were some in the Royal Household who wished Queen Elizabeth would give him robust advice. But that was not her style. She never liked to acknowledge, let alone confront, disagreeableness within the family. It was a character-istic which had earned her the nickname 'imperial ostrich' among some members of the Household. She thought her role was not to try and change people's courses but to be an anchor.

Nineteen-ninety-two began well with the sort of holiday which Queen Elizabeth most enjoyed, a family Christmas and New Year at Sandringham. In thanking her sister, Princess Margaret urged her, 'Do keep Mummy there as long as poss. And please say it to her otherwise she gets in a tizz about being there for so long.'[53]

While she was in Norfolk Queen Elizabeth received from Ted Hughes a special edition of his poems, *Rain-Charm for the Duchy*. She thanked him for the 'enchanting' book with its 'rich and rustling' paper, and for his accompanying letter 'with its thrilling description of landing a fish in such wild & stormy conditions. It must have been too exciting for words, & I felt an envious thrill myself when reading of the battle with the fish and the wind and the rocks.'[54]

The happy start to the year was brought to an abrupt end by the announcement that the Duke and Duchess of York were to separate. Worse was to come. In June 1992 the *Sunday Times* began to serialize a book called *Diana: Her True Story*. Highly sympathetic to Diana, this work created a sensation, particularly when it was revealed that the Princess had collaborated covertly with the author, Andrew Morton. This was deeply shocking to Queen Elizabeth. She had been sympathetic to both the Princess of Wales and the Duchess of York over the enormous pressures they faced from the media. But the washing of dirty linen in public was utterly abhorrent to Queen Elizabeth. Her entire life was based upon obligation, discretion and restraint. The Princess's public rejection of her husband and his life was contrary to everything that Queen Elizabeth believed and practised. She also regretted it when, subsequently, Prince Charles discussed his private life in a wide-ranging series of interviews with Jonathan Dimbleby for a film and a book. 'It's always a mistake to talk about your marriage,' she said to Eric Anderson. But she was proud of the Prince's achievements, such as the Prince's Trust,* and she hoped that the book, a serious study of his career,† would help history to judge him better.[55]

She did not cast the Princess aside at this time but she gave her grandson as much emotional support as she could. She also talked almost daily to her daughter the Queen, who was distraught about what was happening to her children and the fact that it was taking place so publicly. Queen Elizabeth often asked members of the Household, 'Is the Queen all right?' They in turn recognized that the frequent conversations between mother and daughter helped the Queen to maintain her sangfroid and sense of perspective.

Everyone in the family felt the impact of the unhappiness among the younger generation. Prince Philip exchanged a series of affectionate letters with the Princess in which he offered 'to do my utmost to help you and Charles to the best of my ability. But I am quite ready to concede that I have no talent as a marriage counsellor!' The Princess

---

* The Prince's Trust, the successful charitable organization founded in 1976 by the Prince of Wales, helps create opportunities for young people from underprivileged backgrounds.

† Jonathan Dimbleby, *The Prince of Wales*, 1994.

was grateful, and said she hoped to be able to draw on his advice in the months ahead, 'whatever they may bring'.[56]

Princess Margaret wrote to the Queen after staying with her at Balmoral in September 1992 thanking her and sympathizing with her worries about her children. She hoped that her sister was able to have a little peace in the familiar hills, adding, 'I personally found great comfort in being with you and in that particular place.' After leaving Scotland, Princess Margaret had been to Italy. 'I think you would be very touched at how many people expressed great sympathy for you,' she wrote. 'Everyone loves you all over the place, I was so pleased for you and you must be encouraged by this I hope.'[57]

Sorrows marched in battalions that year, and not only through the hearts of Queen Elizabeth's grandchildren. On 20 November 1992, while she was giving a lunch party at Clarence House, there came a distant echo of the fire at Glamis in 1916 – she was told that Windsor Castle was on fire. She drove down to Windsor to be with the Queen, who had already arrived from London and was watching in agony as her favourite home burned. Prince Philip was away and Queen Elizabeth invited her daughter to stay with her at Royal Lodge that weekend. Alone together they were able to talk over all the unhappinesses of the time. It helped. The Queen later thanked her mother, saying, 'It made all the difference to my sanity after that terrible day.'[58]

The injury of the fire was at once followed by insult. The Castle is Crown property and the fire damaged parts of the State Apartments and other reception rooms, not the Queen's private rooms. The fabric of the Castle is maintained at government expense, and the building was being rewired under this arrangement at the time when the fire broke out. Like other Crown or national properties, it is covered by government indemnity rather than commercial insurance. It was therefore not obviously unreasonable when the Minister responsible immediately announced that the government would pay for the restoration.

To the astonishment and embarrassment of the Prime Minister, John Major, who had succeeded Mrs Thatcher in 1990, there was a storm of protest led by the *Daily Mail*, ostensibly a Conservative and monarchist paper. The *Mail* published a front-page editorial under the headline 'Why the Queen Must Listen', asking 'Why should the populace, many of whom have had to make huge sacrifices during the bitter recession, have to pay the total bill for Windsor Castle, when the Queen, who pays no taxes, contributes next to nothing?' The *Mail*'s line was followed by other parts of the media. The matter was resolved by the Queen's decision to open the State Rooms of Buckingham Palace to the public during late summer from then on. The £37 million of repairs were carried out without any additional contribution from the public purse.

Four days after the fire, the Queen made a remarkable speech at Guildhall. She had flu and a temperature of 101, but she refused to cancel the engagement. Her voice hoarse, she used a phrase that became instantly famous – 1992, she said, 'is not a year on which I will look back with undiluted pleasure. In the words of one of my more sympathetic correspondents, it has turned out to be an *annus horribilis.*' (Her correspondent was Sir Edward Ford, the former Assistant Private Secretary to King George VI and then to the Queen.) She declared also that she understood that no institution – 'City, Monarchy, whatever – should expect to be free from the scrutiny of those who give it their loyalty and support, not to mention those who don't'. The Queen's lunchtime audience at Guildhall was touched and responded with a standing ovation.

On 26 November it became clear that the speech had been a prologue. John Major announced that the Queen and Prince Charles had agreed to pay tax on their private incomes and that £900,000 worth of Civil List payments that went to five members of the Royal Family would end. From now on only the Queen, the Duke of Edinburgh and the Queen Mother would continue to receive direct Parliamentary annuities; the Queen would reimburse the government for the allowances given to her children under the Civil List.

Before the decision on tax had been announced, the Queen asked her Private Secretary, Sir Robert Fellowes, to break the news to Queen Elizabeth. He knew that she would not be pleased. The Queen Mother understood that the country was changing so much that monarchy had, as always, to change to retain consent.* But, according to members of the family, she was concerned lest acceptance of such

---

* One change about which Queen Elizabeth had not been enthusiastic was the admission of women (apart from members of the Royal Family) to the Order of the Garter, the most senior British Order of Chivalry, which was in the gift of the sovereign. Her resistance was overcome when the Queen decided that one of the first non-royal women to be made a member of this great Order in modern times should be one of Queen Elizabeth's favourite politicians – Margaret Thatcher.

reform should imply criticism of the Queen and her predecessors, particularly the King, for not having paid tax earlier.

Fellowes made an appointment to see her at Clarence House one evening at 6 o'clock. 'The drawing room was in shadow with very few lights on. She gazed into the distance as I talked. When I finished there was a long pause and then she said, "I think we'll have a drink." ' He was relieved. 'In other words, she thought it was completely wrong, but she did not want to take it out on me. She didn't want to hear about it or dwell upon it.' He asked for a whisky and water; Queen Elizabeth had a martini.[59] The tax-reform plan had been almost completely ready when the fire forced a premature announcement. Many newspapers were ungracious.[60]

On 7 December the Prince of Wales dined with his grandmother and gave her the draft statement to be made by the Prime Minister on the separation between him and the Princess.[61] The announcement came on 9 December – 'a sad day at Clarence House', wrote the lady in waiting.[62]

Four days later there was a moment of pleasure to offset the gloom of the year. On Saturday 12 December the Princess Royal was married in Crathie Church to her second husband, Commander Tim Laurence, a naval officer and a former equerry to the Queen. The wedding clashed with one of Queen Elizabeth's house parties at Royal Lodge. But she left her guests to fly to Scotland for the ceremony, and after the reception at Balmoral she flew back in the evening for dinner at Royal Lodge.

Even an *annus horribilis* comes to an end. The family spent Christmas and New Year together at Sandringham. In her thank-you letter to her elder daughter, the Queen Mother said, 'I do hope that you feel rested and relaxed after all the ghastly happenings of last (& this) year. I do think that you have been marvellous, & so does everybody.'[63]

*

EARLY IN THE New Year Queen Elizabeth and the Prince of Wales together went to the Royal College of Music where she officially handed over to him the presidency of the institution which she had assisted diligently and with great pleasure for so many years. Then they went together to see the new apartment into which he was moving at St James's Palace; the Princess of Wales continued to live in their home at Kensington Palace. A few weeks later, after taking his boys back to their preparatory school, Ludgrove, the Prince went to supper with Queen Elizabeth at Clarence House – it was just the tonic he needed, he told her. 'It very nearly finished me off completely, seeing those two, pathetic little figures standing in the drive waving forlornly as I drove away.'[64]

Queen Elizabeth had another great anxiety. Martin Gilliat, still her Private Secretary, had been diagnosed with cancer; he was now very ill. Queen Elizabeth gave a dinner party to celebrate his eightieth birthday; there were about thirty guests, and Martin Charteris, the Queen's former Private Secretary and one of the few courtiers whose joie de vivre matched that of Gilliat, made a short speech praising his beloved colleague. After dinner they all had a singsong around the piano. They were as merry as they could be given the appearance of their friend.

Even now Gilliat did not feel he could leave Queen Elizabeth. He soldiered on for more than three months and, in the words of Martin Charteris, he was 'run to a shadow, visibly dying, jaundiced as a yellow guinea, scarcely able to walk', but still 'courageous, humorous and of wonderful morale until the end'.[65] Over the last weekend of his life, he worked from his flat in St James's Palace. On Monday 24 May he was at his desk when he said he felt more than usually unwell; he went into hospital that afternoon. Three days later he died.

Queen Elizabeth was suddenly without the much loved man ('dear, indomitable Martin', Ted Hughes called him)[66] who, with wit and good cheer, had organized both her public life and her private engagements, shared her racing interests, and protected her from the outside world for nearly forty years. The Queen wrote to her with sympathy: 'Darling Mummy, I have just heard about Martin's death – I am so very sorry. I know how much you will miss him after such a long time of relying on him – I felt much the same when my Martin left, only he was still around if I needed to ask anything difficult.'[67]

Queen Elizabeth felt Gilliat's death as keenly as that of Arthur Penn three decades earlier. Like Penn, Gilliat had been an essential stimulant in the cocktail of good humour in her Household. 'He was such a wonderful mixer,' she said later. 'One of the kindest of people. He was always helping somebody.'[68] Their relationship became second nature to them both. The artist Andrew Festing, who painted her twice in the early 1990s, thought they behaved more like brother and sister than Queen and courtier. 'They bickered,' he said. 'She would say to me, "When are you coming next?" and I would reply that I would ask Martin. "There's no point in talking to him. Fix it with me" she would say. Then Martin would tell me, "That's absurd. She's bonkers. Talk to me." '[69] Others observed that Gilliat was able to be tough with her when he felt that she was being wilful or extravagant, and saw to it that she did not always get her way. In his address at Gilliat's memorial service, Martin Charteris chose P. G. Wodehouse's words, 'like a prawn in aspic', to describe how well his friend had fitted into life at Clarence House.

Gilliat was succeeded as private secretary by Alastair Aird, who had worked for Queen Elizabeth since 1960. The Queen assured her mother that he would be 'very good',[70] and he was, though Aird later recalled that she found it difficult at first to adjust to his different style.[71] But his courtesy and attention to detail were invaluable to her.

More sadness was to come. A few weeks after Martin Gilliat's death, Ruth Fermoy was admitted into Edward VII Hospital for tests. Queen Elizabeth visited her there. Lady Fermoy had inoperable cancer and she died in early July. Queen Elizabeth took the Princess of Wales to the funeral of her grandmother in King's Lynn. Prince Charles came too. After the funeral the Prince and Princess joined the Queen Mother for a picnic at Wood Farm, Sandringham, and the Princess then flew back to London with her. The Princess's aunt Mary Roche wrote to Queen Elizabeth, grateful that she had been 'so caring and inclusive' towards Diana; she was touched to see Prince Charles and her niece 'so apparently close' and was filled with a wild hope that they could get back together again.[72]

Thus in a very short time two of the people to whom Queen Elizabeth had been closest for decades had gone. Their deaths, coming as they did on top of all her family's problems, left her feeling bereft. She wrote to Ted Hughes to say, 'We have lately been battered by tragic happenings and I found it hard to put pen to paper.'[73]

Hughes's friendship was a continued pleasure. He had come fishing at Birkhall again and, as usual, he kept the party entertained. The weather was wild – there was snow one morning, but the trees were venturing into bud. He wrote the Queen Mother another whimsical poem which invented a life for a young woman they had seen near their picnic place on the hill. Hughes called her Miss Dimsdale and

Queen Elizabeth loved the fantasy.[74] She even suggested a marriage between Miss Dimsdale and another of Hughes's imagined characters, the Rev. Cedric Potter. 'As they are both dream people could a dream wedding be a possibility?' she wrote to him. 'I can see the announcement in the Daily Telegraph – *A wedding has been arranged and will shortly take place between Julia eldest daughter of Doctor Dimsdale and Rev. Cedric Potter, Rector of Knoware.* I wonder where the happy union will take place. Possibly on the steep frowning glories of dark Lochnagar. Forgive all this nonsense, and with a thousand thanks, I am ever yours, Elizabeth R.'[75]

Later in summer 1993, during the traditional visit of *Britannia* to the Castle of Mey, the family set itself a special task: they gathered to build a cairn in memory of Martin Gilliat and Ruth Fermoy. Mikie Strathmore, Queen Elizabeth's great-nephew, whose idea the project had been, had brought with him from Glamis a stone block carved with the two friends' initials and dates, to be fitted into the cairn. It was an emotional day. Under a brilliantly clear Scottish sky, Queen Elizabeth supervised the construction while the Queen led the party in gathering nearby stones and piecing them together. The Queen's Press Secretary, Robin Janvrin, a former naval officer and diplomat, recalled that it was 'a real labour of love, a hugely symbolic moment in which all of the family there paid homage to two great old friends'.[76]

Nineteen-ninety-three was, in every way, hard for Queen Elizabeth. She was lame, her skin was in places as thin as tissue, and her legs bruised easily. But little or none of this was apparent to anyone but her personal maids and her doctor and nurses; she never complained and she rarely sought medical treatment. Her homeopathic doctor, Dr Anita Davies, prescribed propolis for her lesions. The Prince of Wales arranged for his Australian physiotherapist, Sarah Key, to treat her legs.

Notwithstanding such assistance, the Queen became increasingly worried about her mother's health as the decade went on, and thought that, with the infirmities of age, life was less fun and less easy for her. One constant risk was that she might fall, and the Queen sent her mother a special stick: 'Darling Mummy, Your daughters and your nieces would very much like you to TRY this walking stick! It has a magic handle which fits one's hand like a glove and therefore gives one confidence in movement, especially when feeling dizzy! Just at this moment, it would make the two Margarets, Jean* and me very happy and relieved if you would rely on its support!'[77]

Queen Elizabeth never warmed to such aids, and what she did not like she stubbornly resisted. One year at Mey, while she was at church, her staff installed handrails either side of the stairs down to the front door. She stared at them angrily for days before she agreed to use them. She still used the lift only to ride downstairs, and walked back upstairs. She did eventually make much use of another aid which the Queen provided – the golf buggy which her chauffeur John Collings had suggested would be useful. She did not like it at first, but when it was painted in her racing colours she used it at race courses and elsewhere. But not everywhere. On one occasion the Queen had the buggy sent up to Mey. It was returned next day.

Losing her eyesight was in some ways even harder. From the mid-1990s she was less and less able to recognize people who came into the room, though she disguised the fact well. She still liked to have her menu handwritten in French for every meal, but she could not read it. Nor could she read her speeches. She could still write cheerful letters, but it was more difficult. Thus 'please forgive my horrid hand writing but something has gone wrong with the focus of my eye so I hope that it is legible.'[78]

One of the pleasant events of 1993 was the wedding in October of Princess Margaret's son David Linley to Serena Stanhope at St Margaret's, Westminster. The reception was at St James's Palace and the newly married couple changed into their going-away clothes next door at Clarence House. To mark the occasion, Queen Elizabeth gave Princess Margaret a ruby ring, but rather than handing it to her she left it for her daughter to find when she was alone after the wedding. The Princess was touched, and wrote to thank her: 'It is typical of you to be so kind, just when one was feeling rather flat, after David's wedding, to think of giving it to me . . . a million thanks for such a lovely surprise.'[79]

Princess Margaret was now engaged on one of her periodic 'sortings' of her mother's papers, which were still filed haphazardly in various drawers and bags and pieces of furniture in her rooms at Clarence House and Royal Lodge. She wrote to her mother at Birkhall,

---

* Princess Margaret, Margaret Rhodes (née Elphinstone) and her sister Jean Wills.

'I am going back today to clear up some more of your room. Keeping the letters for you to sort later.'[80] Next day she wrote, 'Darling Mummy, I am sitting in your sitting room "doing a bit of sorting" . . . I've nearly cleared the chaise longue and made an attack on the fire stool.'[81] On the Princess's orders, large black bags of papers were taken away for destruction rather than for ultimate consignment to the Royal Archives. There is no record of just what was thus lost but Princess Margaret later told Lady Penn that among the papers she had destroyed were letters from the Princess of Wales to Queen Elizabeth – because they were so private, she said.[82] No doubt Princess Margaret felt that she was protecting her mother and other members of the family. It was understandable, although regrettable from a historical viewpoint.

Queen Elizabeth was not feeling well when she returned from Scotland in autumn 1993 and she undertook few engagements for the rest of that year. She spent Christmas and New Year at Sandringham and was unwell much of the time. It was, in her view, an awful waste of time, but at least she was ill in the family home in Norfolk – 'in London I would have died of depression.'[83] In 1994 her official engagements were down to thirty-eight and five had to be cancelled late in the day because of either bad weather or bad health. In February, the Queen embarked on a long tour of the Caribbean. Mother and daughter corresponded at length, with Queen Elizabeth, as usual, sending the Queen the latest horseracing news. It was snowing widely in England, she said, so most racing was cancelled – 'and the great Whitechapel is still waiting!' He was to have his first run over hurdles at Plumpton, in Sussex, the only course where the going was possible, but she was nervous lest he fall.[84]

On 22 February 1994 Queen Elizabeth entertained the Eton Beagles to the annual lawn meet at Royal Lodge. Now that her great-grandsons Prince William and Prince Harry were set to go to Eton, and Martin Charteris was the Provost, her affection for the school was reinforced. She became close to the Head Master, Eric Anderson, and his wife Poppy – who had made friends with Prince Charles when Anderson taught him at Gordonstoun in the 1960s. She enjoyed visiting the school; she made a point of talking to as many boys as she could on every occasion.

That year Queen Elizabeth began a series of long conversations with Anderson, at the suggestion of Prince Charles; many of her comments have been quoted already in this book. She greeted him over tea at Royal Lodge with the disarming words, 'I'm afraid Charles has been bullying you. I'm a very ordinary person. There is nothing very interesting about me.' She talked at length about the jolly conviviality of her childhood. Living at Glamis as a child, she said, was like being in a happy village – 'A big family was fun. You were brought up by your brothers and sisters as well as by your parents and the servants.' Talking of the authors and wits she had always enjoyed, she praised Joyce Grenfell, a favourite comedienne, Peter Sellers (a 1960s friend of the Snowdons) and, more recently, Alan Bennett, whose gentle ragging of British habits she loved. But 'Kitchen sink is not my cup of tea.'

Asked about the abdication she said, 'The terrible thing was that the two brothers were such *friends*. So it was such a terrible shock.' During the war, she *never* thought Britain would not win. 'The worse things are, the more the British become determined.' When Anderson told her that the country owed a lot to her and the King, she replied, 'Oh, I don't think so, I think it was the people who won the war. We happened to be there.'

She spoke well of many politicians, including Clement Attlee and other Labour leaders. All in all she had few complaints; optimism and faith in Britain always defined her. But 'one of the banes of my life' was that she tended to remind middle-aged men of their mothers. 'I recognize the glazed look that comes over their faces,' she said, 'a sort of glazed look of memory' just before they would tell her so. This happened famously with US President Jimmy Carter who, extolling the cherished likeness, kissed her full on the lips. 'I took a sharp step backwards,' she recalled. 'Not quite far enough.' She was quoted in the press as saying that no one had kissed her on the lips since her husband the King had died.

As for her present interests, she cited above all the need for preservation – 'I'm a great preserver.' She mentioned also the Shaftesbury Society, a Christian charity which helped disabled people and poor children. 'It's extraordinary,' she said, that in every town and village in Britain there were always people helping each other. 'You never hear about those, but it's going on all the time.' She recalled visiting an old ladies' home in Glasgow where they all looked very jolly – 'and I discovered that the boys from the local High School came along two or three times a week, took the old ladies out, took them for walks, jollied them up, got their newspapers. And you see, if you can get that mixture, it's wonderful.'

She loved that mixture for herself. 'I don't know what I'd do without my grandchildren, you know. We have great rags. They keep one up to date . . . We don't always agree on things, which is a very good thing, I think.' She was endlessly curious about the younger generations and their changing interests. But she also believed that values such as duty should remain eternal. She told Anderson that she had not understood the Princess of Wales's announcement, made after her separation, that she was giving up her charitable works. 'I can't believe she won't come out and do some things. I may perhaps bully her into doing things. It's no good sitting back. Your *devoir*, your duty. There we are back again. It's the same old thing. Your *devoir*.'[85]

In fact the Princess did resume her public life and became active in several causes, especially the campaigns to help AIDS sufferers and to ban land mines. But her marriage could not be saved. In 1996, the Prince and Princess of Wales were divorced, as were the Duke and Duchess of York. Throughout, Queen Elizabeth talked constantly to the Queen, and wrote to her, commiserating with her about all the strain that these events inevitably placed upon her.[86]

*

TED HUGHES's friendship was a great support throughout this difficult time. He could understand the horror of what was happening to the Royal Family; his own unhappy marriage had ended with the suicide of his wife Sylvia Plath and he had been publicly excoriated by her champions ever since. Like Queen Elizabeth herself, he knew how to be sympathetic and to give pleasure. After one visit to Birkhall he wrote to remind her of 'the skylines rolling away, the nearest browny-red heather, the next the dense green of pine-forest, & beyond that, highest and furthest, the snow-patched hills. You remember we tried to photograph it in our memories? The trees by the stream just coming into their new green. And the ranger's falcons that preferred a bath in the burn to hunting rabbits! And all our conversations about every-thing.'[87] She loved such letters and she told him so.

The deterioration in the health of her friends and then their deaths was an inevitable but sad theme of this decade. This year, two of her long-serving ladies in waiting, Patricia, Viscountess Hambleden, who had been a friend since their debutante days, and Lady Victoria Wemyss, both died; the latter, born a Cavendish-Bentinck and a cousin of Queen Elizabeth, was 104.

In June 1994 Queen Elizabeth took part in celebrations to mark the fiftieth anniversary of D-Day. On 4 June she flew by helicopter to HMS *Vernon*, Portsmouth, and embarked in the royal yacht; later, accompanied by the Princess Royal, she landed at Whale Island for the ceremony of Beating Retreat. The next morning, Sunday 5 June, a Drumhead Service was held on Southsea Common, which she attended with the Queen and the Duke and other members of the Royal Family, together with the assembled heads of state and statesmen representing the Allied nations during the war. She enjoyed such commemorations above all because they evoked the spirit of unity that had prevailed during the war. Of the Portsmouth celebration, she said, 'It's very strange. I think it brought people together in the most amazing way. They suddenly remembered that we were all together then . . . And it was a wicked thing we were fighting.'[88]

Queen Elizabeth's summer continued with all her usual fixtures – her progress to Walmer Castle, the King's Lynn Festival, her birthday at Clarence House (followed by *Romeo and Juliet* with Princess Margaret at Covent Garden), the Castle of Mey and then Birkhall. Whenever she was at Birkhall she would ask the Balmoral factor and his wife to dinner. Latterly that was Peter Ord, who had been the factor at Glamis before. He thought her interest was not just to get the latest news and gossip of the area but also to remind him of her views and values on the running of the estate. Her view, simply put, was that Balmoral belonged to the Queen and she could do with it as she wished. She was correct, but in practice the demands for public accountability grew all the time, even though Balmoral was one of the best-run private estates in Scotland.

She liked continuity in employment and felt a responsibility for all those who worked in the estates. 'If I wanted to get a good gardener, she might ask me to employ Jimmy's son, rather than an experienced man from outside,' said Peter Ord. She encouraged the employment of young people in order to try and keep the school rolls up. She always wanted to know who was with child, who was ill. She would say to new arrivals, as she did to the Ords, 'You are family now.'[89] It was an unashamedly paternalistic way of doing things – and it worked well in tempering more modern methods. The disadvantage, however, was that it sometimes led her to insist on retaining, out of loyalty, staff who were ineffective, which could cause exasperation in her family and Household.

After her return to London she suffered from considerable pain in her right leg, but she insisted on attending the 1994 Royal Smithfield Show at Earls Court, the Middle Temple Family Night dinner, and even a reception at St James's Palace given by the Cookery and Food Association. Despite rest and recuperation – over Christmas and New Year at Sandringham – her leg and her foot were now giving her so much trouble that she could not manage her favourite walks, but she managed to see 'dear old Bustino' and other horses.[90]

She nevertheless carried out thirty official engagements in 1995 and only three had to be cancelled because of her health. Wherever she went, she still managed to appear deeply interested in the people she met. One Member of Parliament later identified this quality. On a visit to his constituency, he said, she had lingered, saying, 'I am not in a hurry. I have time. Time is not my dictator; I dictate to time. I want to meet people.'[91] That remained true until the end. In May 1995 she enjoyed lunch as much as ever with her friends the Farrells in their 'salle de glace' – 'Chicken with Tarragon! What a treat!' She was happy to see Paul Getty transformed in health,[92] and ascribed this miracle, correctly, to his new wife Victoria, whom he had married in 1994 and who did indeed transform his life.

That summer Britain celebrated the fiftieth anniversary of the end of the war in Europe, VE Day. The festivities were remarkable; once again both monarchists and republicans were struck by the affection in which the monarchy was still held by large sections of the population, of all ages. On Saturday 6 May Queen Elizabeth inaugurated the celebrations in Hyde Park – after a Drumhead Service she spoke briefly, without notes, of all those 'whose courage and fortitude brought us the victory'.[93] The next day she accompanied other members of the Royal Family to the service of thanksgiving at St Paul's Cathedral and then to lunch at Buckingham Palace for all the heads of state visiting London.

On Monday 8 May Queen Elizabeth joined her daughters on the balcony of Buckingham Palace, to wave to the crowds just as they had done in May 1945. Only the King, husband and father, was gone. As a demonstration of the continuity of monarchy it could not be bettered. The cheering seemed endless. Queen Elizabeth loved seeing

the 'old patriotism' shine through again, 'but it was so funny being
there, just us three on the balcony.' She told the Queen, 'We are just
war relics.'[94]

Another 'war relic', Vera Lynn, sang 'We'll Meet Again'. Harry
Secombe and Cliff Richard also performed. There was vigorous singing
of 'Rule Britannia', 'Land of Hope and Glory' and the National
Anthem. A clutch of surviving wartime aircraft flew overhead, followed by the Red Arrows, and finally there were fireworks from the
roof of Buckingham Palace – making a noise very reminiscent of the
Blitz, the lady in waiting noted, and at one stage almost engulfing the
royal ladies in smoke. Some of the fireworks were supposed to drop
Union flags on little parachutes, but not all the parachutes opened and
one bundle fell on Queen Elizabeth's shoulder. Princess Margaret
recalled that the Queen then said, 'Come on, Mummy, I think you
had better get back.' 'Into shelter,' added Queen Elizabeth.[95]

The summer was punctuated by her usual engagements, including
her annual visit to the Cinque Ports, but in mid-July she quietly went
into King Edward VII's Hospital for the removal of a cataract in her
left eye.* No engagements were cancelled, and the operation did help
a little to improve her vision. For her ninety-fifth birthday, Queen
Elizabeth used the golf buggy to move among the usual crowd of
well-wishers at Clarence House. She then had lunch and dinner with
family and friends and next day flew to Scotland. Ted Hughes sent her
another birthday poem. 'How fortunate I am to have a friend who is
a great poet!' she thanked him. 'Lucky lucky me!'[96]

By November that year both hips were giving her considerable
pain. On 15 November she calmly went to lunch with friends at the
Ritz, and then was driven to King Edward VII's Hospital. She had
decided to have a right hip replacement. The operation was performed
successfully, though not without difficulty, by Roger Vickers the next
morning, assisted by the anaesthetist Dr Di Davis. Vickers, who had
taken over as the orthopaedic surgeon to the Queen in 1993, had been
reluctant to carry out the operation until it became essential. In the
event he found her to be a good patient. She stayed longer than most
patients in hospital, because she wanted to be able to walk unaided

---

* Mr Jonathan Jagger, Surgeon-Oculist to the Royal Household, performed the operation; Dr
Leonard Hargrove was the anaesthetist.

down the steps when she left. Afterwards she invited all the doctors and nurses and their spouses, and the cleaners of her room, to a party at Clarence House. They were moved and delighted.[97]

While she was at Sandringham after Christmas another member of her family, Rachel, widow of her much loved brother David, died. The roads around Sandringham were impassable with snow and ice and Queen Elizabeth was distressed that she could not get to St Paul's Walden for the funeral. She sent a tender letter to her nephew Simon, talking of his mother's brave spirit, her courage, her humour and 'her great loving kindness. I know that when my heart fails me I shall hear Rachel saying come on now, don't give up.'[98]

On 6 February, the anniversary of the King's death, Queen Elizabeth celebrated Holy Communion as usual at the Royal Chapel in Windsor Great Park. She received a heartening letter from the former chaplain of the Royal Chapel, the Rev. Anthony Harbottle, a devout and kindly man who had served with the Royal Marines during the war and was also a distinguished lepidopterist, the first person in Britain to breed the New Pale Clouded Yellow butterfly. He had become close to many members of the Royal Family, but particularly the Queen Mother, throughout his time as chaplain from 1968 to 1981. In 1972, on the twentieth anniversary of the King's death, she wrote to tell him that the family had all thought his sermon was 'perfect'. In February 1982, the first year after he had ceased to be chaplain, she wrote to tell him how much they missed his 'sympathy and under-standing' at the service.[99]

Every year thereafter Harbottle would write to her on the anni-versary of the King's death, and every year she would reply. Queen Elizabeth took comfort in his vivid statements of belief in an all-encompassing, loving God, the resurrection of the dead and the reunion of souls. Her faith was traditional and uncomplicated and she derived a great deal of support from it. She was more interested in liturgical tradition than in theological subtleties. She preferred, to put it mildly, the 1662 version of the Prayer Book and the Authorized or King James Version of the Bible. Her friend Lord St John of Fawsley, a regular guest at her home, said, 'It was the Prayer Book that she loved.'* She did not like such new-fangled ideas as 'the kiss of peace'

---

* Lord St John of Fawsley (b. 1929), formerly Norman St John Stevas, Conservative politician,

or even the handshake. 'When she saw it winging its way towards her, she stiffened and took evasive action. Her religion was loving kindness.'[100] Her devotion to the truths of the Christian gospel sustained her through sadness and nourished her sense of commitment to others.

Another friend and lady in waiting, Lady Elizabeth Basset, put it thus: 'In LIVING, her faith shines out almost unconsciously and speaks through her dedication to her country, in her tremendous sense of duty, and her endurance, her courage, and last but not least her sense of humour and enjoyment of life.'[101]

*

IN 1996 QUEEN ELIZABETH was cheered by the state visit of President Nelson Mandela to London, following South Africa's readmission to the Commonwealth. He came to tea with her at Clarence House on 9 July and she then attended the state banquet in his honour. She marvelled in the change that Mandela had peacefully brought about, and dared for the first time in decades to be hopeful about the beloved country.[102]

It was the summer of heroes. On 18 July she received the Dalai Lama, the exiled spiritual leader of Tibet. The meeting took place at a complex time, just one year before Hong Kong was due to revert from British rule to China. The Chinese government was always sensitive to criticism of its human rights record in Tibet. The day before Chinese officials had attacked a cross-party group of British politicians for inviting the Dalai Lama to address members of the Lords and Commons. Their actions, said a Chinese foreign ministry spokesman, 'will have an adverse affect on the Sino-British relationship'.

This was the first time that the exiled Tibetan leader had been received by a member of the Royal Family. It was a moving encounter and the Tibetan spiritual leader explained to the Queen Mother that as a boy in Tibet he had seen newsreel and pictures of her and the King in bombed-out London and had wanted to meet her ever since. The Dalai Lama seemed, in the words of Robert Ford, the Foreign Office official with him, to be 'captivated by the charm of Her Majesty'. This was very clear when he left her – he took her hand and placed it to

barrister, author and constitutional expert. Twice Minister of Arts, chairman of the Royal Fine Arts Commission 1985–99.

his bowed forehead, a mark of sincere respect and affection.[103] For years afterwards the Dalai Lama referred to this meeting in speeches and interviews, saying how impressed he had been by Queen Elizabeth's optimistic view of the world and of improvements that she had witnessed during the twentieth century. 'I was deeply impressed and inspired' by her, he said. Her optimism reinforced his own and he was further encouraged when Prince Charles inherited and expanded his grandmother's interest in the plight of Tibet.[104]

At the Sandringham Flower Show, in late July that year, Queen Elizabeth arrived in a carriage with Prince Charles; they then toured the stalls together in her golf buggy. Ted Hughes, who was again among her guests, captured it all in another poem, called 'The Prince and His Granny'. The second of the five verses ran:

> The Police Brass Band, they puffed and frowned
> To turn their duty into sound.
> They woke the flowers and the flowers swooned
> To meet the gaze of the Prince and his Granny.
> Then hearing the bees boom 'Taste our honey!'
> The Lemon Curd and the Marmalade
> Rose from the stalls, no matter who paid,
> And joined in the joys of the Royal Parade.[105]

She was 'thrilled and delighted' by it, she told him. First, she said, the Prince himself read it to his granny '(Very nicely)' and then she had read it herself 'again and again'. He had evoked lovely memories, she said, and she ended by sending 'an immense amount of gratitude from the Prince's Granny, Elizabeth R'.[106]

A disagreeable occurrence for her in 1996 was publicity over the size of her overdraft which suddenly hit the headlines – £4 million, the papers said. That she was extravagant and lived beyond her means had always been assumed – how could any retired person, even a queen, pay for so many homes, horses, staff and dresses? Her finances were managed by Ralph Anstruther until he fell ill and was replaced as Treasurer by Nicholas Assheton, the former deputy chairman of Coutts. She had a passbook from Coutts that would be brought by hand every quarter, written up by hand and detailing all her personal cheques. Most of them were to dressmakers and those close friends whom she helped. Her racing account was still looked after by Michael Oswald. There were inevitable financial shortfalls, even after her Civil

List annuity rose, eventually, to £643,000 to cover her official expenses. As we have seen, the Queen had elected always to cover her mother's racing losses and other expenses, and thus enable her to continue the style of life to which she was both accustomed and suited.

Her expenditure would doubtless have been much reduced had she not been so determined, despite her age, to continue leading a remarkably active public and private life. In 1997 she carried out fifty-four public engagements and many private ones. In early February there was an enjoyable family weekend at Royal Lodge for the christening of her great-grandson, Samuel Chatto, the son of Princess Margaret's daughter Sarah and her husband Daniel. Lord Snowdon was there for the christening and lunch and she made sure that he sat next to her.

Later that month she gave tea to the President of Israel, Ezer Weizman, and his wife during their state visit, and attended the banquet for them at Buckingham Palace on 25 February. Over the next two days she inspected the Royal Yeomanry, of which she was honorary colonel, in Chelsea, and paid a visit to the National Head-quarters of the British Red Cross Society. March followed the usual pattern, with race meetings at Sandown and Cheltenham and the presentation of shamrock to the Irish Guards at Pirbright on 17 March. So it continued throughout the year, with almost all her true and tried engagements, public and personal.

She had her usual fishing fortnight at Birkhall, and Ted Hughes came. He was recovering from an operation and Queen Elizabeth invited Carol Hughes to come too, although wives did not usually accompany their husbands on these occasions. As always he entered into the spirit of the place and loved his 'deeply restful and richly happy' days there.[107]

As lord warden of the Cinque Ports, she visited Walmer Castle from 18 to 21 July and went to Sandringham for the King's Lynn Festival a week later. Prince Charles was there as usual and wrote to her afterwards, 'I still can't believe that another year has passed and that, once again, we have walked round the flower & vegetable tent at Sandringham, talked to all those hardy annual people in the crowd and sung Cole Porter songs after dinner with Raymond Leppard.* As

---

* Raymond Leppard CBE (b. 1927), acclaimed musician and conductor who performed at venues all over the world, including the Royal Opera House, Glyndebourne, the Metropolitan

always, everything was a very special treat because it was with you.'[108] She was at Clarence House for her birthday lunch, before which the King's Troop of the Royal Horse Artillery paraded by in her honour. This year she invited Prince William and Prince Harry and their father wrote to her afterwards that his boys 'adored it'.[109]

She then left as usual for the Castle of Mey on 7 August. There was a sad moment at Mey that summer: *Britannia* made her last visit. The Conservative government of John Major had decided to decommission the royal yacht and this decision was confirmed by the new Labour government, led by Tony Blair. The yacht had been an effective seaborne embassy and trade platform for Britain for over forty years, as well as being the family's floating haven both when they were promoting Britain and when they were taking holidays.*

Britannia anchored off Caithness for the last time on 16 August 1997. The Queen came ashore to Mey leading a large family party which included Prince Andrew and his daughters Princesses Beatrice and Eugenie, Princess Anne and her husband, her children Peter and Zara, Prince Edward and his friend Sophie Rhys-Jones (whom he married in June 1999), and Princess Margaret's son and daughter, David Linley and Sarah Chatto, with their spouses.

Lunch that day was fun but somewhat melancholy. Conscious that without their resident muse, Martin Gilliat, their collective writing skills were much diminished, Queen Elizabeth's Household had gone for the best – they secretly asked Ted Hughes to come up with some lines to be sent to the Queen as she sailed away for the last time. His verse ended:

> Whichever course your Captain takes, you steer
> Into this haven of all our hearts, and here
> You shall be anchored for ever.

The reply from the yacht was similar in spirit:

Opera House in New York and Santa Fe, New Mexico. He was musical director of the Indianapolis Symphony Orchestra 1987–2001.

* The Queen had given her mother a last voyage in *Britannia* in July 1996. The yacht sailed to Cornwall, carrying a party of Queen Elizabeth's friends and Household including Lord and Lady Nicholas Gordon Lennox, Mr and Mrs Gerald Ward, Lady Grimthorpe and Sir Michael and Lady Angela Oswald. They visited the gardens at Trelissick, before sailing back up the Channel.

> My what a marvellous time we have had,
> Visiting you at your castellated pad.
> We couldn't have had a better time,
> Seeing the garden in its prime.
> Glasses filled with Dubonnet, gin and Pimm's,
> Loosened our tongues and our limbs!
>   Oh what a heavenly day,
>   Happy, glorious and gay.[110]

That autumn, the Queen and many members of the family attended the decommissioning of *Britannia* at Portsmouth. Queen Elizabeth did not go. As with other aspects of life she considered disagreeable, she turned away from the subject. Her friends and Household knew not to mention the yacht to her again.

On her departure from Mey, she spent the last weekend of August as usual at Balmoral before moving on to Birkhall. That weekend, on the night of 30–31 August 1997, came disaster. The Princess of Wales was killed in a car crash in Paris. Her drunken driver had been speeding to escape an insistent swarm of press photographers.

*

IN THE EARLY hours of Sunday morning, 31 August, the Queen wrote her mother a note to be given her when she awoke, telling her of the tragedy.

At Balmoral everyone's first concern was for the Princess's sons, William and Harry. Fortunately they were there with their father and the rest of the family, all of whom rallied to help them in different ways. But time to cope with shock and loss were not permitted to any of them. This at once became a national tragedy and the tone was set by the Prime Minister, Tony Blair, who a few hours after her death eulogized the Princess of Wales as 'the People's Princess'.

There was an extraordinary outpouring of grief across the country which grew more intense throughout the week. This was a remarkable testimony to the Princess's popularity, but some of it was self-indulgent and passions were inflamed by non-stop broadcasting of events and shrill demands from tabloid newspapers. 'SHOW US YOU CARE' one front page screamed at the Queen. Whether intentionally or not, such attacks upon the monarch helped deflect public attention from the fact that the Princess had died in a flight from press harassment.

In this turbulent week, the Queen was very much at the centre of the family, as well as the centre of the press storm. It is safe to say that, in the unchanging peace and seclusion of Balmoral, the family was stunned by this extraordinary, sometimes angry outpouring of emotion. So were millions of other people in the country. At the Castle Robin Janvrin, now the Queen's Deputy Private Secretary, calmly helped navigate a course through all the swirling cross-currents. At the end of an agonizing, perplexing week, the Queen, Prince Philip, Prince Charles and his sons flew down to London. They talked to people in the crowds outside the palaces. The Queen then made a live television broadcast in which she spoke, as both queen and grandmother, of her admiration for the Princess of Wales and her gratitude that people had shown how much they cared.

Queen Elizabeth also flew down to London on 5 September for the funeral on Saturday 6 September. She returned to Birkhall immediately afterwards to rejoin the friends who had already been invited to stay. Characteristically she said very little about it to her guests. A few days later, Princess Margaret wrote to her sister to express 'my loving admiration of you, how you kindly arranged everybody's lives after the accident and made life tolerable for the two poor boys . . . there, always in command, was you, listening to everyone and deciding on all the issues . . . I just felt you were wonderful.'[111]

But the public reaction to the death of the Princess brought home to many observers how much had changed in Britain since the death of King George VI and how hard it was for the monarchy to keep pace with these changes. It was, and remained later, difficult to define just what the widespread display of emotion meant. One argument, put forward by the constitutional historian Vernon Bogdanor, was that it showed that, although the British were still a monarchical people, they wanted a demystified monarchy, in touch with their needs, 'a practical monarchy'.[112] That is, in effect, another way of describing the welfare monarchy, represented by the work that Queen Elizabeth did throughout her life for her charities and other patronages.

There was another, not necessarily conflicting suggestion, that the week's events showed a yearning for the *ideal* of monarchy. Monarchs used to have a vital, sacred role in society, but few traces of this remained at the end of the twentieth century. Rowan Williams, the Anglican Archbishop of Wales (and later Archbishop of Canterbury), pointed out that in our secular society there was no easy way for the monarch to represent the sacred, the unquestioned given in human affairs. Perhaps, as Williams argued, what we saw was 'a potent lament for a lost sacredness, magical and highly personal, but equally a ritualised focus for public loyalty. The lost icon was not simply the dead princess; it was a whole mythology of social co-hesions around anointed authority and mystery – ambiguous, not very articulate and not easy for either right or left in simple political terms.'[113]

Life at Birkhall had to continue. On 8 September Queen Elizabeth flew to Fort George in Inverness-shire to visit the 1st Battalion The Black Watch; the visit marked the sixtieth anniversary of her appoint-ment as colonel-in-chief of the regiment. In the next few weeks the Prince of Wales brought his sons to stay with her twice at Birkhall.

After Queen Elizabeth returned to London her winter programme was less onerous than in the past but, as usual, she visited the Field of Remembrance at St Margaret's, Westminster on 7 November. She went to the Royal Smithfield Show at Earls Court on 27 November and, in fine form, attended the Middle Temple Family Night dinner on 4 December.

*

NINETEEN-NINETY-EIGHT began badly. While visiting the horses in the stable at Sandringham on 25 January, Queen Elizabeth slipped, fell and broke her left hip. She was taken by ambulance first to the hospital in King's Lynn for examination and then to King Edward VII's Hospital in London. She was in great pain and the ride was far from comfortable for her. In such circumstances, Ian Campbell, the doctor from Sandringham who accompanied her, was astonished when she said to him in the ambulance, 'You'll miss supper, won't you?' At the hospital she immediately ordered sandwiches for him and the nurse who had travelled with them.[114] That evening Roger Vickers, with Dr Robert Linton as anaesthetist, operated on her and replaced her broken hip. She returned to Clarence House on 17 February to convalesce.

She cancelled a mere seven official engagements as a result of the accident and operation. Altogether she had forty-six official engage-ments in 1998. She was able to make a brief appearance at the lawn meet of the Eton Beagles at Royal Lodge on 3 March, but she cancelled her Musical Weekend that year and she was disappointed to forgo her annual visit to the Irish Guards in Münster, Germany, to present them with shamrock. Her first public engagement was to attend the annual general meeting of Queen Mary's Clothing Guild in St James's Palace on 25 March.

After Easter at Windsor she flew to Scotland to spend two weeks at Birkhall. Ted Hughes, who was by now seriously ill with cancer, came again with his wife to experience what he had called, after his last visit, 'the healing warmth of your kindness to me'.[115] It was to be their final encounter. The fishing was not at its best that spring but Hughes was pleased because that gave them 'more time to lounge and loll and gaze and meditate'.[116] He particularly enjoyed an afternoon when, after lunch at Polveir, they just sat and listened to the river.

He had brought the Queen Mother his new book *Birthday Letters*,[117] a series of poems about his life with Sylvia Plath. When the Queen Mother asked him why he had published them, he replied that he thought it was important for him as 'a kind of purging', and he had done it both for his children and for himself.[118] Since he had published the book (and ignored everything the critics had said about it), 'I have felt vastly unburdened. It has quite changed my life and whole outlook for the better.' He thought that Queen Elizabeth had helped change his life too. 'When I remember your gesture and your words, "We must be strong!" I feel it like a huge smile of joy, like a surge from a tremendous battery, going through me as well. And I remember it constantly.'[119]

He needed all such strength to resist his illness. On 16 October he and Carol went to Buckingham Palace where the Queen bestowed upon him the Order of Merit.[120] A few days later, on 28 October 1998, Ted Hughes died.

Queen Elizabeth sent a wreath of yellow, white and cream flowers; they accompanied his coffin, and Carol Hughes then cast them upon the waters of his favourite river, the Torridge in Devon.[121] The following May Queen Elizabeth attended Hughes's memorial service in Westminster Abbey. She walked up the long aisle on the arm of Prince Charles. At the end, the congregation heard Hughes's rich Yorkshire voice reading the Song from Shakespeare's *Cymbeline*. As it echoed round the ancient church many were moved to tears.

Fear no more the heat o' the sun
    Nor the furious winter's rages;
Thou thy worldly work hast done,
    Home art gone, and ta'en thy wages.
Golden lads and girls all must,
As chimney sweepers, come to dust.

Until the end of Queen Elizabeth's life, Ted Hughes remained always in the pantheon of people to whom she raised high her glass at dinner.

CHAPTER TWENTY-FOUR

CENTENARIAN

1999–2002

'She laughs at the time to come'

THE YEAR 2000 was marked throughout the world by celebrations of the millennium and, in Britain, of the hundredth birthday of Queen Elizabeth. The year began with an event fashioned by the New Labour government: the opening of the Dome, a purpose-built stage on the Thames at Greenwich. It was intended to be a symbol of a new Britain and so it turned out to be, if not quite in the way which its creators had intended.

The occasion echoed an earlier celebration on the south bank of the Thames by an earlier Labour government. In 1951, a time of post-war austerity and rationing, the administration of Clement Attlee had staged the Festival of Britain. King George VI and Queen Elizabeth had opened the Festival together. Although neither of them felt entirely at ease with the political ambitions of the post-war Labour government, they admired many of its leaders and the sentiments of the Festival, conceived during Labour years, were ones which they could accept with pleasure.

The Festival's proclaimed intention was to display British achievements in 'one united act of national reassessment and one corporate reaffirmation of faith in the nation's future'. Fifty years on, the official statement of intent read like a guide to another planet – its proud purpose was to extol Britain's 'contributions to civilization' and it celebrated, among many historic events, St Augustine bringing 'a new infusion of Christianity to Britain'. The Festival acclaimed the British people whose 'native genius' was displayed in a pavilion called 'The Lion and the Unicorn'. These great creatures were thought to symbolize 'two of the main qualities of the national character: on the one hand, realism and strength, on the other fantasy, independence and imagination'. The spread of the English language around the world was celebrated and the King James Bible was described as 'still the great beacon for the language'; it had 'a resonance and radiance which have suffused all our later literature and speech'. Queen Elizabeth would certainly have agreed with that.

In the pavilion there were tributes to Shakespeare – 'who took the language in his hand and made words do things that had never been dreamed of' – and, among others, to Chaucer, Defoe, Swift, Sterne, Carlyle, Dickens, Lewis Carroll, T. S. Eliot, Gainsborough and Constable. The British were praised not just for their artistic achievements but also for their 'continuing impulse' to develop and enlarge basic freedoms. The examples given were Magna Carta, the struggle of the House of Commons with King Charles I, Milton's pamphlet *Areopagitica* ('a spearhead for the breakthrough into freedom of the press'), freedom for Catholic worship, freedom for labour, and the suffragettes.

The Festival's unashamed celebration of the British character and achievement was one with which Queen Elizabeth could have great sympathy. She believed absolutely in the spirit and resilience of the British people, in the strength of their constitutional system and in the benefits that British rule had brought to millions of people throughout the world. The fifty years of her widowhood had brought many benefits to the country at large. By the year 2000 Britain was more prosperous than at any time in her history. People had wider opportunities for individual happiness than ever before. Many of the taboos and the social stigmas that existed in the 1950s had gone. Women had greater power and freedom. Society was more fluid and in many ways more tolerant. There was more diversity – London was a cosmopolitan city. Wealth was spread more equally between classes. There was better housing, and much better food. Educational opportunities had widened – tertiary education was no longer the privilege of the few, as in the 1950s, but was now within the grasp of almost everyone.

But if education was broader, it was also sometimes shallower. More and more children were emerging from school without basic skills. In the early 1950s people's sexual behaviour was often unhappily restricted; by 2000 there appeared to be almost no restraints. Popular culture had become ever more explicit; discretion was unusual. Drugs posed a serious threat to the lives of young people. There was less respect for public service, tradition and authority than fifty years before. The concept of duty, central to Queen Elizabeth, seemed quite outdated to many of the young. Habits and beliefs that had held British society together had disappeared. Immigration had changed the face of many cities. Islam was now the fastest-growing religion in Britain. By contrast, Christian congregations were constantly diminishing; the Prime Minister, Tony Blair, himself a Christian, said, 'We enjoy a thousand material advantages over any previous generation and yet we suffer a depth of insecurity and spiritual doubt they never knew.'

British towns and much of the countryside had been completely changed. Motorways had been cut harshly through beautiful areas; the hearts of many towns had been ruined by insensitive developers, architects and planners. Suburbanization had destroyed local communities. Towns became cloned suburbs and the quirky or the original features of different places were often razed in the name of profits and efficiency. The English landscape was also losing character; orchards were cut down, small family farms were sold to make holiday homes; the landscapes (and the townscapes) celebrated by Queen Elizabeth's friend John Betjeman and, before him, by Thomas Gray, Constable and Turner, were vanishing. Independent shops were closing while green fields became shopping malls where security guards, closed-circuit cameras, piped music and the latest consumer temptations defined modern life.

Philip Larkin had expressed his dismay in his poem 'Going, Going':

> And that will be England gone,
> The shadows, the meadows, the lanes,
> The guildhalls, the carved choirs.
> There'll be books; it will linger on
> In galleries; but all that remains
> For us will be concrete and tyres.

In a way, the Millennium Dome reflected the intellectual and moral tenor of its time. It was built on the occasion of the 2,000th anniversary of the birth of Christ, the defining event of Western civilization, but Christ was a sideshow in the Dome, relegated to a few bland sentences in one small exhibit. The £800 million construction was the product of committees and its content was at best jolly, at worst vacuous. The names of commercial sponsors were more important than any enduring message – let alone any pride in the history and achievements of

Britain. In fact, the contrast between the Festival and the Dome illustrated one way in which Britain had changed in the previous half-century. The Festival displayed a poor but self-confident Britain, rejoicing in her singular accomplishments. The Dome represented a richer but far less self-assured nation.

On the Dome's opening night, 31 December 1999, the organizers paid lip-service to the Christian origins of the Millennium. The Archbishop of Canterbury, Dr George Carey, was allowed to read prayers just before midnight. The prelate tried to remind people that Christ had been born 2,000 years before, but he was surrounded by drunks and chivvied by impatient officials who wished to begin the real, secular celebrations. These included an appearance by the Queen and the Duke of Edinburgh who were required to join hands with the Prime Minister and his wife to sing 'Auld Lang Syne'.

Queen Elizabeth had a quieter evening – she dined at Sandringham with Princess Margaret and her racing manager, Sir Michael Oswald, and his wife Lady Angela. The celebrations of her birthday later in the year provided a remarkable contrast with those at the Dome.

*

QUEEN ELIZABETH was, by any measure, well into what one member of her Household called her 'running down' years. But running down did not mean giving up. In 1999 she had undertaken thirty-eight public engagements – only one was cancelled, because she had a chill. At Sandringham in January 2000 she had to miss one of her hardy annuals – attending the annual general meeting of the Sandringham Women's Institute – but managed the other – presenting a prize to a pupil of Springwood High School.* She also planted an oak tree at Sandringham to mark the 350th anniversary of the formation of the Coldstream Guards. Back in London she received various colonels of her regiments on changeover of command and gave sittings for portraits. She entertained the Eton Beagles at Royal Lodge. In March she went to Cheltenham and Sandown Park to attend the National Hunt, the Grand Military and the Royal Artillery race meetings – treasured fixtures every year.

---

* Each year Queen Elizabeth presented a book to the prizewinner, who would come to Sandringham with the Head Teacher to receive it. Springwood is a long-established comprehensive school in King's Lynn.

She still entertained generously, with her lunches, her weekend parties and more intimate invitations to tea. In early 1999 she and Princess Margaret invited the Director of the Royal Collection,* Hugh Roberts, and his wife Jane, then Curator of the Print Room, to look through a trunk of Strathmore papers that had 'turned up'. Greeted by Royal Lodge's longtime, sophisticated steward, Ron Wellbelove, Hugh Roberts thought he had stepped into a reincarnation of the famous James Gunn portrait of the Royal Family at tea in the same room in 1950: 'a tea-table was laid in the centre of the room, in front of the fireplace. Queen Elizabeth in cornflower blue dress with blue hat and veil, beautiful sapphire and diamond flower brooch; Princess Margaret in pale blue silk suit and diamond brooch, both just returned from Ascot where QE had had a winner.'

There were delicious, tiny sandwiches, toasted hot cross buns and little cakes to eat – and two teapots. Queen Elizabeth asked her guests, 'Would you like Margaret's special tea, or my ordinary?' The Princess's tea was served in a pretty yellow teapot, Queen Elizabeth's was still in the basic brown pot she had been given by the train steward on the way to Warwick races.[1]

When the Princess and the Robertses delved into the trunk, Queen Elizabeth studied the photographs with a magnifying glass. She was able to identify and provide a running commentary on almost everything and everyone. She thought some of the portrait studies of her as a young woman were too serious or 'yearning'. After an hour of sorting, she offered them all a drink; Princess Margaret mixed a stiff martini for her mother and the rest of them had whisky. Queen Elizabeth and Hugh Roberts had a Trollopean discussion about St George's Chapel – she was glad to hear that the new dean was much liked and that the canons were not at each other's throats. She spoke wistfully of Ted Hughes. 'He knew about *everything*, it didn't matter what – and wrote some charming things for me – birthdays and whatnot.'

One of her staff then came in to announce, in something of a

---

* The Royal Collection includes paintings, drawings, manuscripts, books, furniture, ceramics, gold, silver, glass, clocks and many other works of art collected by British monarchs and other members of the Royal Family over centuries. It is unique in the sense that, unlike the collections of other European royal houses, the British Royal Collection is the property of the Crown, not the state.

solecism, that 'Queen Elizabeth' was on the telephone. 'Who?' asked
Queen Elizabeth. 'Oh, you mean the Queen.' The Curator and the
Director took their leave, their car laden with plastic bags filled with
photographs which were then incorporated in the Royal Photographic
Collection at Windsor, while others were sent to Glamis by Queen
Elizabeth.[2]

That year Queen Elizabeth looked forward to the annual lunch
with Charles and Kitty Farrell in May even more than usual because it
marked her friends' fiftieth wedding anniversary. 'How blissful and
how wonderful,' she wrote. 'I expect that the HEDGE will be many
feet higher.'[3] After the lunch party she told Lady Kitty what joy she
had had seeing 'all those delightful people chatting and boozing outside
the salle de glace'.[4]

The turf retained its unchanging allure as a world of its own in
which she could be totally absorbed and in some ways the equal of
others. Almost every day in their telephone conversations she and the
Queen still discussed the breeding, the naming, the successes (and
failures) of their horses and their jockeys. Her racing reputation still
stretched across the world. Sir Michael Oswald received a cable from a
North Queensland Drinking Club called Liars' Lounge. Eighty-five of
them had won a filly in a lottery and they offered Queen Elizabeth a
1/86th share as a hundredth birthday present. She accepted with
alacrity and the message came back, 'Tell the Queen that the next
time she is here to drop in for a Cold One, and the shout's on me.'[5]

There were happy family events that year, including the wedding
of her grandson Prince Edward to Sophie Rhys-Jones, and the christening in the Royal Chapel at Royal Lodge of her great-grandson Arthur,
second son of Lady Sarah Chatto. The playwright Tom Stoppard was
a guest and he wrote Queen Elizabeth a letter of thanks for a day
which he would treasure. 'When I think of the long arc of life-and-
times that connects you and Arthur, all that history, it brings a lump
to the throat.'[6]

But there were family sorrows, too. In November Queen Elizabeth
gave a lunch party at Clarence House after the memorial service for
Lord Dalhousie, her Lord Chamberlain. Towards the end of the meal,
her niece Jean Wills (her sister May Elphinstone's second daughter)
had a heart attack. The Queen Mother quietly led her guests from the
room; Mrs Wills was given immediate medical attention but she died

several days later in hospital. It was a great shock, made easier for the Queen Mother only by her belief in the afterlife.*

In his annual letter to her on the anniversary of the King's death Anthony Harbottle expressed her own view well. 'There is no separation but an abiding oneness with our loved ones who have gone on ahead & are ever with us, giving us already a foot in heaven. It is a great & glorious thought, as Your Majesty knows so well.' She replied, 'I was so touched to receive your most thoughtful & beautiful letter, which arrived at exactly the right time. We were a little depleted at the service as John & Jean Wills have died, but it was all lovely & peaceful.'[7]

*

CELEBRATIONS HONOURING Queen Elizabeth's centenary tumbled one after another, through the spring and summer. She enjoyed them all. On 27 June she was given a luncheon at the Guildhall; her neighbour, the Archbishop of Canterbury, absent-mindedly picked up her wine glass rather than his own. 'Hey, that's mine!' she said quickly.[8] On 21 June the Queen gave a reception and dance at Windsor Castle to mark the major birthdays of Queen Elizabeth, Princess Margaret (seventy), the Princess Royal (fifty) and the Duke of York (forty).

On 11 July her life was celebrated in a service of thanksgiving at St Paul's Cathedral, attended by her entire family and many European crowned heads, the Grand Duke and Grand Duchess of Luxembourg, the King and Queen of Norway, the King and Queen of the Belgians, King Constantine and Queen Anne-Marie of the Hellenes and King Michael and Queen Anne of Romania. The Archbishop of Canterbury praised her public service – she had entered the hearts of the British people, he told her, 'and your own heart has been open to them ever since.' As she left, she paused to greet other centenarians who had been invited. 'Do you know, they were all in wheelchairs,' she said, with a touch of mischief. 'I spoke to them when I walked down the aisle.'[9]

On 18 July, the Lord Chancellor, Lord Irvine, together with other

---

* Hon. Jean Elphinstone (1915–99), second daughter of sixteenth Lord Elphinstone and Lady Mary Bowes Lyon, married 1936 Major John Wills. Major Wills, born in 1910, died a few weeks before his wife, in September 1999.

leaders of the House of Lords, brought to the Queen Mother a message from the House. Lord Strathclyde, the Conservative leader in the Lords, said later that when they made to leave, 'not wishing to impinge too much on her time or to weary her, she insisted that more drinks be brought and that we should tell her more about politics and in particular your Lordships' House.'[10] Her more formal response to their Lordships stated that 'I feel fortunate that during the last Century I have been given the opportunity to serve our Country in times of war and peace and I have always been helped and uplifted by the love of my family, by the fortitude and courage of our people, and by my faith in Almighty God.'

In the Commons, the Prime Minister Tony Blair moved a motion commending the Queen Mother on reaching her centenary year – the first time that the Commons had ever considered such a motion. He pointed out that throughout her life 'she has enthused countless people, for countless good causes, with her familiar smile, her sparkle and, of course, her wonderful hats.' Speaker after speaker paid tribute to the work she had done for the country since the abdication, her steadfastness during the war, her service to the monarchy and nation ever since.[11]

The high point of her birthday celebrations was the pageant in her honour in Horse Guards Parade, described in the Prologue to this book. The organizer, as for her eightieth and nineteenth birthday celebrations, was Major Michael Parker. In the mid-1990s Parker had had tea with the Princess of Wales and the Queen Mother. When the Princess said to her, 'We're all so looking forward to your hundredth birthday,' Queen Elizabeth replied, 'Oh, you mustn't say that, it's unlucky. I mean I might be run over by a big red bus.' Parker said he thought this was very unlikely, to which Queen Elizabeth replied, 'No, no, it's the principle of the thing. Wouldn't it be terrible if you'd spent all your life doing everything you were supposed to do, didn't drink, didn't smoke, didn't eat things, took lots of exercise, all the things you didn't want to do, and suddenly one day you were run over by a big red bus, and as the wheels were crunching into you you'd say "Oh my God, I could have got so drunk last night!" That's the way you should live your life, as if tomorrow you'll be run over by a big red bus.' And that, Parker thought, was exactly the way she did live. Moreover, 'she treated each day as a lovely surprise that was going to be wonderful.'[12]

All of her regiments and organizations wished to be included in the pageant, and Parker arranged that they should march past in motley groups of people, animals and vehicles, each supervised by two Guardsmen. 'You can have anything in your group, from an Aberdeen Angus bull to a Field Marshal,' Parker told the Guardsmen; 'but you are in charge. You must get them to keep up and move at the right speed.'

The plan was that the National Anthem would be played after Queen Elizabeth arrived in Horse Guards Parade, before she got out of her carriage to inspect the troops. Then came a message from Clarence House that Queen Elizabeth insisted on standing up in the carriage for the Anthem. Parker was alarmed, for it would be dangerous if the horses moved. He consulted precedents and found that Queen Victoria had remained seated in a coach while the Anthem was played. But the message came back: 'Queen Elizabeth is not Queen Victoria. She will stand.' Eventually he persuaded her that the National Anthem should be played as she drove on to the parade ground, rather than after she had arrived.

As we have seen, the day itself began badly with IRA bomb scares in London, cancelled trains and even the controlled explosion of a suspected bomb in Whitehall. The police were nervous. The officer in charge told Mike Parker that the whole event might have to be cancelled. Parker replied that such a surrender was out of the question, but if that was his considered view the officer would have to go and give the news to Queen Elizabeth himself. The man was horrified. The parade went ahead.[13]

It was a balmy evening, and on her dais Queen Elizabeth stood a great deal, chatted with Prince Charles, and clearly enjoyed the music and the singing. Beside her stood Major General Evelyn Webb-Carter, the General Officer Commanding London District, who told her what was passing in front of her so that she could react appropriately – and she did. The veteran actor Sir John Mills, aged ninety-two and totally blind, stood up before her in an open vintage Rolls-Royce and made a moving speech in her honour. Few of the thousands of people who took part realized how little of the festivities she herself could see.

Afterwards, Queen Elizabeth wrote to Parker to say that she had loved the contrast between the smart soldiers and the 'orderly rabble' which followed them. She said the parade had cheered people up all over the country – 'I thought it was marvellous.'[14]

★

THE CELEBRATIONS continued, and on 29 July Queen Elizabeth went to Ascot for the King George VI and Queen Elizabeth Diamond Stakes. As she drove down the course, children paraded wearing the colours of previous winners of the race and the band played 'Happy Birthday'.

Congratulations poured in – among them one heartfelt letter from Queen Fabiola of Belgium, widow of King Baudouin, who praised 'your generous gestures, your unique hats and striking dresses, together with your ever-present and welcoming smile';[15] Vladimir Putin, the Russian President, recalled her wartime concern for the people of Stalingrad; Tony Blair said she was being honoured for being 'a great example to us all of service'. Andrew Motion, who had succeeded Ted Hughes as poet laureate, wrote a long affectionate tribute to her birthday.[16] It ended:

> My dream of your birthday
> is more like a wedding,
> the August sky
> confused with confetti,
> and lit with the flash
> of our camera-gaze –
> the century's eyes
> of homage and duty
> which understand best
> the persistence of love.

On the morning of her actual birthday, 4 August, her long-serving page Reginald Wilcock brought her her morning teatray to her study as usual. On it was a silver cream jug, a birthday present from her staff. Wilcock was ill with leukaemia but had been determined to see this day. That evening he was taken to hospital and within days he was dead. Queen Elizabeth wrote a tender letter to his partner and friend, William Tallon, who, like Wilcock, had served her lovingly since the 1950s.

After her traditional appearance at the gates of Clarence House and the opening of the telegram from the Queen, came the carriage ride to Buckingham Palace with Prince Charles. She had been nervous about this, fearing that she might have to drive up an empty Mall. Sitting in the hall at Clarence House, she still seemed strangely reluctant. In the end Prince Charles gave her his arm and said, 'Come on, Granny – remember Hitler said you were the most dangerous woman in Europe.' Laughing together they set off in her landau – and to her relief the large crowds in the Mall cheered enthusiastically, particularly when she came out on to the balcony to wave.[17] After lunch with her family she went to see the team of people recruited to answer all the letters of good wishes that she had received, and in the evening she and the Queen and Princess Margaret went to see the Kirov Ballet perform at Covent Garden.

It was in every way a happy day and Prince Charles wrote to her, 'I will never forget the magical atmosphere that surrounded you with love, devotion and gratitude for all that you mean to people.'[18] As for Queen Elizabeth herself, she said to one friend that she could not understand what all the fuss was about. 'I was just doing my job.'[19]

*

HER 101ST SUMMER was spent, as usual, at Mey and then Birkhall. Back in London at the end of October, she received one more birthday tribute: the Governor General of Canada came to Clarence House to present her with the insignia of the Order of Canada. The autumn seemed set fair, until on the morning of 3 November she tripped and fell in her bedroom at Clarence House. She had broken her collar bone and had to remain in bed for six weeks. She was looked after principally by her dresser Jacqui Meakin and her page Leslie Chappell; these two cared for her with the utmost devotion in the months ahead.[20]

Outwardly, her final year, 2001, followed the pattern of the others which it seamlessly followed. She grew frailer and she suffered more pain, but she was determined to conceal it. Her real sadness was the constant deterioration in the health of her younger daughter. Princess Margaret had frequently been unwell since the 1970s, suffering migraines, laryngitis, bronchitis. She had endured depression, she had had part of her lung removed and in 1998 she had her first stroke. In March 1999 she severely scalded her feet in a bath in her house in Mustique and never really recovered from these burns, nor from a second stroke she suffered there.

In February 2001 Queen Elizabeth made her first public appearance after her collar-bone fracture, at the memorial service for Lady Elizabeth Basset, who had died on 30 November 2000 and with whom she had shared her devout faith. The service took place in the Savoy Chapel and according to the chaplain, the Rev. John Robson, Queen

Elizabeth seemed serious, sad and wistful in remembrance of her old friend. But still lively too – when he showed her to her car, 'she FLUNG her sticks into it in a most eloquent gesture as if to say, "Let us be rid of these pesky things!"'[21] That same month she presided as usual over the lawn meet of the Eton Beagles. Then she had her annual house party for the Grand Military Race Meeting at Sandown Park in March, but to her disappointment foot-and-mouth disease forced the cancellation of Cheltenham races.

In early June 2001 she lunched privately at All Souls in Oxford, an annual custom she much enjoyed. At the Sandringham Flower Show in July she toured every stall in her buggy and entertained her usual house party, including the Queen and the Prince of Wales. Her grandson, as always, marvelled at her stamina and wrote to her that 'no-one would ever have known that you were actually feeling pretty tired.'[22]

She was even more tired a few days later, during her racing house party at Royal Lodge for the King George VI and Queen Elizabeth Stakes at Ascot. She insisted on going to the races but when she returned home she almost collapsed. She was taken to King Edward VII hospital where she was discovered to be suffering seriously from anaemia. Blood transfusions were prescribed to make good the iron deficiency. Determined as ever, she demanded that the treatment be carried out overnight so that she could be back at Clarence House in time for her 101st birthday.[23]

In these circumstances, members of her Household expected her merely to wave from the window to the crowd which always gathered on 4 August.[24] But no, she insisted on going to the gate and greeting people in the street as she had always done. She then gave lunch to the Queen, the Prince of Wales and others in the family and that evening she went to the ballet at the Royal Opera House. Then, once again, she flew to her Castle in the north. Prince Charles wrote to thank her for the joy of being with her on her 101st birthday. 'It was so wonderful to see Your Majesty so transfused and with your iron constitution so comprehensively "re-ironed".' He thought that 'Evidence of the ironing operation was there for all to see when Your Majesty stepped boldly off the aeroplane . . . The fact that your dogs were carried down the steps reinforced the message about your "rude" health!'[25]

He was right, but it was to be her last summer in her Castle.

Among the guests were many of those friends who loved her most.* There was the familiar merriment, the jokes, the toasts to favourites high in the air and to unfavourites below the table, the video evenings, the pervading sense of happiness. But behind everything there was a sense of frailty if not finality. In the Guest Book are photographs of her sitting in the sun and walking in the mist, always clad in her familiar blue hat and coat and tartan skirt. Although the weather was unspeakable on the day of the Mey Highland Games she insisted on attending, buttoned up against driving rain and fierce wind.

In September, after saying goodbye with unusual emphasis to her staff, neighbours and friends at Mey, she drove south to Balmoral and Birkhall. And, again as usual, she stopped for lunch at Foulis Castle in Ross-shire, the home of Mrs Timmy Munro, a tradition that had been maintained since 1959. At lunch she engaged in a long conversation with the younger members of the family about the teenage fad for body piercing, a phenomenon of which she may have been aware because her great-granddaughter, Zara Phillips, had a pierced tongue. A few days later a three-page, handwritten thank-you letter arrived for Mrs Munro.[26]

At Birkhall she found that the Queen had had a stairlift installed for her. Prince Charles wrote to cheer the fact that 'you now have a form of mechanized assistance to ascend "les escaliers" without Your Majesty's feet touching the floor. Thank God for the wonders of science . . . !'[27] Her guests – many of them Prince Charles's stalking friends – enjoyed the usual fishing expeditions, picnics and evening videos. One night there was dancing and, twirling her sticks, she took part in an eightsome reel. She went with Prince Charles to Aberdeen for the unveiling of a statue of a bull for the North East Aberdeen Angus Breeders, to the pleasure of them all.[28]

But there was an elegiac note to her days. She said that she wanted to see her old ghillie, Charlie Wright, who had fished with her for decades. Wright, now eighty-two, had been captured with the 51st Highland Division at Saint-Valéry, covering the retreat at Dunkirk in

---

* Guests this summer included Queen Elizabeth's factor Martin Leslie and his wife Catriona, her former equerry Jamie Lowther-Pinkerton and his wife Susannah, Ashe Windham and his wife Arabella, her racing manager Michael Oswald and his wife Lady Angela, and John Perkins, a friend from Norfolk.

June 1940; as a result, he had spent five years as a prisoner of war. His father had been a stalker for the King, and Charlie Wright had himself worked at Balmoral first as a stalker and then as a river ghillie. After he retired from the river he still turned out for Queen Elizabeth's spring fishing parties.

She insisted on going to his home rather than asking him to hers. She was driven on a track along the bank of the Dee to the little humpbacked stone bridge, the Brig O'Dee,* which led across the river to his cottage. There is a photograph of Queen Elizabeth pulling herself on her sticks across the bridge by sheer will power. She took tea with Wright and his daughter Jane. Then she forced herself back across the bridge to the car. Charlie and Jane Wright were touched by her determination and her courtesy.[29]

One of the happiest occasions at Birkhall that year was a convivial picnic lunch at Loch Callater. Her guests and Household were all worried that she was too frail and should not go. As usual, she insisted. It was a blithe gathering and she enjoyed herself immensely. Many times in the months to come, as she grew weaker, she would say, 'I wish I was at Loch Callater.'

In November 2001, just before the annual Remembrance Day ceremony at the Cenotaph, she was strong enough to make her customary visit to the Garden of Remembrance at St Margaret's, Westminster. The Duke of Kent accompanied her and he was struck by the fact that, despite the cold, she spent an hour in the open air, greeting and talking to old soldiers.[30] A few days later she watched the Remembrance Day Parade from a window of the Home Office looking over Whitehall.

On 22 November she made an extraordinary trip – another visit to the aircraft carrier HMS *Ark Royal*, which she had launched in 1981 and which was now being recommissioned and rededicated after an extensive refit. She flew by helicopter to Portsmouth, landed on the carrier and was lowered into the ship's great hangar. It was a touching spectacle: 1,200 people were there to greet her and to take part in the rededication service. She summoned the strength to make a short speech and then, to the pleasure of the audience, she said to Captain David Snelson, 'Captain, splice the mainbrace.'[31]

---

* The Brig O'Dee was built in 1748 as part of the military pacification programme after the '45 Rebellion.

Before Christmas she felt strong enough to give interviews to two authors – one writing a PhD thesis on Dr Cosmo Lang, Archbishop of Canterbury at the time of the abdication, and the other the biographer of the Grand Duchess Xenia of Russia, who had spent forty years in exile in Britain and whom Queen Elizabeth had liked.[32]

And still she went on and on: she attended the Middle Temple Family Night dinner on 5 December and the next day she went to lunch with the Trustees of the Injured Jockeys Fund at the Goring Hotel. She went racing, for the last time, at Sandown Park on 9 December and to her great pleasure she saw her own horse First Love win – she delighted the crowd by going to the winner's enclosure to congratulate the jockey. She had had seventy-five winners at Sandown Park over her racing career – more than at any other racecourse.[33]

She had another fall before Christmas but, as usual, she refused to admit she was in pain. She carried out the engagements to which she had agreed; the last was the staff Christmas party in St James's Palace. There were about 200 people there; she consented to be wheeled around but whenever she stopped to talk to a group of people she insisted on standing up out of the chair. She did this some twenty times.[34]

Christmas, of course, was with her family at Sandringham. She and Princess Margaret flew there together by helicopter and landed in a blizzard. After her two strokes, Princess Margaret was now in a wheelchair. Queen Elizabeth was not well either; she developed a cough over Christmas and had to spend much of the holiday in her room. By early January 2002 she was better and able to come down and mingle with her family, but then she caught another virus which she could not shake off and she stayed in Norfolk when the Queen returned to Buckingham Palace. Princess Margaret was, if anything, in worse pain than her mother; she barely spoke. When the Princess left for London Queen Elizabeth carried out the family tradition of waving a white handkerchief in farewell as her daughter was wheeled out of the saloon to the car. It was their final parting.

The 6th of February marked the fiftieth anniversary of the death of the King, but Queen Elizabeth was not well enough to go to Royal Lodge for her customary service in the Royal Chapel. Instead, Canon John Ovenden, the chaplain there, drove up to Norfolk. He and Canon George Hall conducted the service in a small sitting room at Sandringham.

Queen Elizabeth would probably have stayed on in Norfolk, but three days later, on 9 February, the Queen telephoned her mother to say that Princess Margaret had died. The Princess had suffered another stroke the previous afternoon and then developed cardiac problems. She was taken to King Edward VII Hospital during the night and she had died there on Saturday morning. She was seventy-one. The death of a child is an intolerable burden to a parent, whatever their respective ages. But Queen Elizabeth knew her daughter had been suffering with no hope of respite.[35]

Prince Charles immediately went to Sandringham to comfort his grandmother. She told him that 'Margot's' death had probably been a merciful release. He agreed and shortly afterwards he sent her a letter in which he related that Anne Glenconner, one of the Princess's ladies in waiting and a good friend, 'told me that she had seen Margot on Wednesday last week and that she had said to Anne that she felt so ill that she longed "to join Papa" '. He added, 'I thought that this was so incredibly touching.'[36]

A few days after the Princess's death Queen Elizabeth fell again; she damaged her arm, which had to be carefully dressed by Dr Campbell. But she insisted on attending her daughter's funeral in St George's Chapel at Windsor. She was flown there by helicopter and manoeuvred with difficulty into a car to be taken to the Chapel. The service was tranquil; the melancholy but reassuring words of the 23rd Psalm – 'I will dwell in the house of the Lord' – seemed to many in the congregation to be apposite to the life and death of the devout, talented but troubled Princess, whose greatest joy was to be a loving mother to her two children. As the coffin was borne out of the Chapel, Queen Elizabeth struggled to her feet. Princess Margaret was cremated; she had asked that her ashes be interred in the King George VI Memorial Chapel in St George's. After the funeral, Queen Elizabeth went home to Royal Lodge for the last time.

This year was the fiftieth anniversary of the Queen's accession to the throne. The Golden Jubilee celebrations were due to begin with official visits by the Queen to Jamaica, New Zealand and Australia. Members of Queen Elizabeth's Household felt that she was determined not to cause any disruption to these tours and was intent on husbanding her remaining strength a little longer. The Queen telephoned her mother every day she was away and when she returned to Britain on

3 March she went straight from Heathrow Airport to Royal Lodge to see her.

Still Queen Elizabeth carried on and still she saw people; on 5 March she held a lawn meet and lunch for the Eton Beagles and discussed future dates with them. Then, as usual, she held her house party for the Grand Military Race Meeting at Sandown Park. On this occasion the Queen had arranged to receive her mother's guests. But at the last minute Queen Elizabeth appeared and greeted them herself. Her horse First Love distinguished himself by winning again at the race meeting – her last ever runner. She could not attend the Cheltenham races but she watched them on television. As luck would have it, the Gold Cup on 14 March was won by Best Mate, trained by Henrietta Knight, daughter of her great friend of many years, Guy Knight. She was ecstatic, her lady in waiting Angela Oswald recorded.[37]

Easter fell early that year, on 31 March, and by the week before Easter Queen Elizabeth was weakening further. She was visited regularly by her local doctor, Jonathan Holliday, the Apothecary to the Household at Windsor; and Gill Frampton, the nursing sister at the Castle, came every afternoon to change the bandages on her legs and to give her a light massage if she wished. She was not eating much now but she might take a small glass of champagne with scrambled eggs in the evening – this reminded her of late-night suppers with the Duke in the early days of her marriage, she said.[38] She had decided not to have a lady in waiting with her now, but her niece Margaret Rhodes came regularly to Royal Lodge from her own house a few hundred yards away in the Great Park. On Palm Sunday, Canon Ovenden held a service for her in the Saloon, the room in which she had entertained so many friends over so many years.

That week she made many telephone calls from her bedroom. Michael Oswald was pleased to hear her, but it was clear to him that she was saying goodbye; she gave him a list of things to do and people to thank for all that they had done for her. She rang Johnny Perkins, her faithful neighbour in Norfolk and frequent visitor to Mey, to thank him for freesias that he had sent her. She telephoned the Princess Royal and asked her to take some of her horses.

It was obvious that she would not be able to join the rest of the family for Easter at Windsor Castle. On Wednesday 27 March her Private Secretary, Sir Alastair Aird, went down to Royal Lodge to talk to her staff and to wish them a happy Easter. When Queen Elizabeth heard he was there she asked to see him. 'I found her in the Saloon sitting in a winged chair with her feet up and covered by a rug. I took a chair and sat immediately opposite her for her eyesight was very bad and she had very limited lateral vision. We discussed a few things and I told Queen Elizabeth whom I had seen recently – she always liked to be kept up to date with news of her Household and friends. She had a smile on her face and I suddenly had the feeling that this was the last time we would meet and that she was in her own way saying goodbye to me.'[39]

Over the next two days Queen Elizabeth weakened further; by Good Friday she was unable to lift her head from the pillow, but she remained in complete control. She asked Leslie Chappell to take a box from the drawer of her desk. In it he found a pair of cufflinks for himself and a brooch with her 'ER' cypher for Jacqui Meakin, a token of affection for their care.

On Saturday morning Dr Richard Thompson, Physician to the Queen, and Dr Jonathan Holliday came to see her. They realized she would not last the day. Dr Thompson called first the Queen and then the Prince of Wales, who was dismayed because he was in Switzerland and would not be able to return in time to be with his grandmother. The Queen, who was riding in the Park, went at once to Royal Lodge and Queen Elizabeth was able to say goodbye to her daughter.

Canon Ovenden arrived as Queen Elizabeth lapsed into unconsciousness. He held her hand, prayed aloud and read her a Highland lament:

> I am going now into the sleep,
> Be it that I in health shall wake;
> If death be to me in deathly sleep,
> Be it that in thine own arm's keep.
> O God of grace, to new life I wake;
> O be it in thy dear arm's keep,
> O God of grace that I shall awake![40]

Queen Elizabeth died at 3.15 in the afternoon of 30 March 2002, Holy Saturday, a contemplative day for Christians anticipating the resurrection. At her bedside were her daughter the Queen and her grandchildren, Sarah Chatto and David Linley.

The following afternoon her oak coffin was borne to the Royal Chapel and in the evening Canon Ovenden celebrated Evensong for all the members of her family who could be there.

*

QUEEN ELIZABETH'S funeral was to be the most solemn state occasion since the funeral of her husband the King, half a century before. She had been diligent in planning it herself and Operation Tay Bridge, as it was codenamed, was regularly updated. On Tuesday 2 April her coffin was driven from Windsor to the Queen's Chapel at St James's Palace, where her family, friends and Household were able to pay their respects in private.

The public part of the ceremonies began on the morning of Friday 5 April. The coffin was placed on the same gun carriage that had borne the remains of her husband the King fifty years before, to be carried from St James's Palace to lie in state in Westminster Hall. The coffin was draped in her personal Standard and on it lay the crown made for her Coronation in 1937. The Koh-i-nûr diamond, given to Queen Victoria, the first Empress of India, and now set in the crown of Queen Elizabeth, the last Empress, flashed in the sunlight. Next to the crown lay one wreath – the card read simply, 'In Loving Memory, Lilibet'. The procession began to the sounds of Mendelssohn's Funeral March played by the bands of the Scots Guards and the Irish Guards. As it moved off, the King's Troop of the Royal Horse Artillery started a twenty-eight-gun salute in Green Park. The boom of the guns echoed once every minute until the procession reached Westminster Hall.

In bright spring sunshine a quarter of a million people lined the streets. More than 1,600 servicemen took part, marching slowly to the beat of a muffled drum as the coffin was taken down the Mall and across Horse Guards Parade and thence past the Cenotaph on White-hall to Westminster. There were contingents from all the regiments associated with her, from both Britain and the Commonwealth. They included the Witwatersrand Rifles, the Transvaal Scottish, the Cape Town Highlanders, the Royal New Zealand Army Medical Corps, the Royal Australian Army Medical Corps, the Toronto Scottish and the Black Watch (Royal Highland Regiment) of Canada. Walking beside the coffin were ten pallbearers, eight of them colonels of her British regiments – the Royal Army Medical Corps, the Black Watch, the Light Infantry, the Royal Anglian Regiment, the King's Regiment, 9th/

12th Royal Lancers, the Queen's Royal Hussars, 1st The Queen's Dragoon Guards, the Royal Army Medical Corps – together with the Captain of HMS *Ark Royal* and the Commandant of the Central Flying School of the Royal Air Force.

The Queen Mother's grandsons, the Prince of Wales, Prince Andrew, the Earl of Wessex and Viscount Linley, together with Prince Philip, Princes William and Harry and Peter Phillips, all marched behind the coffin. Breaking with tradition, the Princess Royal marched with them. The Prince of Wales was visibly distressed; as Deborah, Duchess of Devonshire wrote of him, 'My poor friend's steely face made us all realise how much he loved her and relied on her.'[41] In the procession, Queen Elizabeth's grandchildren were followed by other members of the Royal Family and of the Bowes Lyon family, her Household and staff, including her Lord Chamberlain, the Earl of Crawford and Balcarres, and her Private Secretary Captain Sir Alastair Aird. Among the staff who marched were her page, William Tallon, her Head Chauffeur, John Collings and her Head Chef, Michael Sealey. Then came senior military personnel, including the Chief of Defence Staff, the Chief of Air Staff and the Chief of Naval Staff.

The Queen, with her niece Lady Sarah Chatto, drove by car to meet the coffin as it arrived at the door of Westminster Hall exactly thirty minutes after it left St James's, and as the last of the echoes of the twenty-eight guns fired in salute died away. Members of the House of Lords stood along the west side of the Hall and members of the Commons along the east as, led by Black Rod, the coffin was carried by the bearer party from 1st Battalion Irish Guards into the vast and magnificent medieval space.

Queen Elizabeth's coffin was placed on a catafalque in exactly the same spot where her husband had lain in 1952. The Queen and other members of the Royal Family gathered around and the Archbishop of Canterbury said prayers. Four officers of the Household Cavalry then took their places around the catafalque for the first Vigil of the Watch. Officers from many different regiments would stand guard day and night until the funeral. As had happened with the coffin of King George V, one watch was held by her four grandsons, Prince Charles, Prince Andrew, Prince Edward and Lord Linley.

After the short service, the Queen drove back along Whitehall to Buckingham Palace. Suddenly a ripple of applause ran through the crowd and the Queen was clapped all the way up the Mall. It was an extraordinary moment, a spontaneous burst of popular sympathy, a recognition of all that the Queen had had to endure in recent years, culminating in the death of her sister and her mother in such a short space of time. She was visibly moved and she said to one of those with her that this moment was one of the most touching things that had ever happened to her.[42]

That was just the beginning. For the rest of the week, the people of Britain confounded opinion-makers. The government had hugely underestimated the impact of her death – people came in their hundreds of thousands to pay their final respects to Queen Elizabeth and what she had represented. The scheduled opening hours had to be lengthened to twenty-two hours a day. Despite biting weather, people queued patiently, waiting their turn in lines that stretched along the Embankment and across the river, to pass by the coffin. The Women's Royal Voluntary Service (of which Queen Elizabeth had been patron and then president) passed along the lines, carrying flasks of hot tea.

Prince Charles broadcast an emotional tribute to his grandmother, 'the original life enhancer – at once indomitable, somehow timeless, able to span the generations. Wise, loving, with an utterly irresistible mischievousness of spirit.' Above all she understood the British character, 'and her heart belonged to this ancient old land and its equally indomitable and humorous inhabitants.' He had dreaded her death, which he somehow thought would never happen. He praised her for the fun, laughter and affection she had created around her, for her 'sparklingly wonderful letters' and for seeing the funny side of life – 'we laughed till we cried, and oh how I shall miss those laughs.' She had wisdom and sensitivity too, and she was 'quite simply, the most magical grandmother you could possibly have, and I was utterly devoted to her. Her departure has left an irreplaceable chasm in countless lives but, thank God, we're all richer for the sheer joy of her presence and everything she stood for.'[43]

The night before the funeral the Queen made a short television address in which she too spoke with emotion. She said, 'the extent of the tribute that huge numbers of you have paid my mother in the last few days has been overwhelming. I have drawn great comfort from so many individual acts of kindness and respect.' She hoped that at her mother's funeral 'sadness will blend with a wider sense of thanksgiving, not just for her life but for the times in which she lived – a century for this country and the Commonwealth not without its trials and sorrows, but also one of extraordinary progress, full of examples of courage and service as well as fun and laughter. This is what my mother would have understood, because it was the warmth and affection of people everywhere which inspired her resolve, dedication and enthusiasm for life.'[44]

The next morning, Tuesday 9 April, the bearer party from the 1st Battalion Irish Guards carried her coffin from Westminster Hall into the sharp sunlight and laid it again on the gun carriage. It was drawn by the King's Troop, the Royal Horse Artillery, to the Abbey for her funeral. Some 200 pipers and drummers, playing 'My Home' and 'The Mist Covered Mountains', accompanied the coffin. Nine senior members of the Royal Family followed behind; all were sombre. But the service was joyful, with lessons from Ecclesiastes and Revelation, and a reading from *Pilgrim's Progress*. The hymns included 'Immortal, invisible, God only wise' and 'Guide me, Oh thou great Redeemer'. The anthem was Brahms's setting of Psalm 84 – 'How lovely are thy dwellings fair'.

In his eulogy, the Archbishop of Canterbury, Dr George Carey, said that the vast crowds who had passed before her had understood that, in George Eliot's lovely phrase, there was about her 'the sweet presence of a good diffused'. He felt that the one verse in scripture which captured her best was from the Book of Proverbs: 'Strength and dignity are her clothing and she laughs at the time to come.' Her strength and her dignity were clear; her laughter 'reflects an attitude of confident hope in the face of adversity and the unpredictable challenges of life'. Moreover, she had a deep, simple and abiding faith 'that this life is to be lived to the full as a preparation for the next'. He ended by quoting again from the Book of Proverbs. 'It says simply of a woman of grace, "Many have done excellently, but you exceed them all."'

After the blessing and Last Post, Garter King of Arms proclaimed the Styles and Titles of Queen Elizabeth, which served to remind the congregation of the great history of her country in which she had so memorably played her part:

> Thus it hath pleased Almighty God to take out of this transitory life into His Divine Majesty the late Most High, Most Mighty, and Most Excellent Princess Elizabeth, Queen Dowager and Queen Mother, Lady of the Most Noble Order of the Garter, Lady of the

77. The Royal Family on the balcony at Buckingham Palace following the Coronation of Queen Elizabeth II, 2 June 1953.

78. Manning a stall at the Abergeldie Bazaar, August 1955.

79. Queen Elizabeth with her corgi Honey at the Castle of Mey, October 1955.

80. On tour in Rhodesia with Princess Margaret, June 1953.

81. Arriving at the Vatican with
Princess Margaret for a papal audience,
22 April 1959.

82. With Princess Margaret and Antony
Armstrong-Jones, after the announcement
of their engagement in February 1960.

83. Queen Elizabeth patting her horse, Devon Loch, for good luck before the Mildmay Memorial Cup at Sandown Races in January 1956.

84. With the jockey Dick Francis at Windsor Races in January 1969.

85. Backstage at the Royal Ballet with Margot Fonteyn, Princess Margaret and Lord Snowdon.

86. Progressing through the Melbourne suburbs, Australia 1958.

87. The Queen Mother in Rotorua, New Zealand, talking to Maori women after a performance of their Poi dance, May 1966.

88. On tour in Canada in 1967.

89. With the Duchess of Kent at the needlecraft stall at Sandringham Women's Institute Flower Show, 1978.

90. Celebrating St Patrick's Day with the Irish Guards at Windsor Barracks, 17 March 1980.

91. A birthday lunch in the gardens of Clarence House, 1984. Left to right: Lt. Col. Sir John Miller (Crown Equerry), Ruth, Lady Fermoy (lady in waiting), the Prince of Wales, Queen Elizabeth, Lord Maclean (Lord Chamberlain).

92. With the chefs of the Hôtel de la Réserve in Albi, May 1989.

93. A farewell lunch at the Château de Saran with the Comte de Chandon, after touring the cellars at Möet & Chandon while on holiday in France in 1983.

94. Queen Elizabeth at the pageant to celebrate her hundredth birthday.

Most Ancient and Most Noble Order of the Thistle, Lady of the Imperial Order of the Crown of India, Grand Master and Dame Grand Cross of the Royal Victorian Order upon whom had been conferred the Royal Victorian Chain, Dame Grand Cross of the Most Excellent Order of the British Empire, Dame Grand Cross of the Most Venerable Order of the Hospital of St John, Relict of His Majesty King George the Sixth and Mother of Her Most Excellent Majesty Elizabeth The Second by the Grace of God of the United Kingdom of Great Britain and Northern Ireland and of her other Realms and Territories Queen, Head of the Commonwealth, Defender of the Faith, Sovereign of the Most Noble Order of the Garter, whom may God preserve and bless with long life, health and honour and all worldly happiness.

As Queen Elizabeth's coffin was borne from the Abbey by the Irish Guardsmen, the organ played Bach's Prelude and Fugue in E flat, while high above the bells of the Abbey were rung half muffled to a peal of Stedman Caters, comprising 5,101 changes. Outside the Abbey, pipers from all her regiments played the forlorn lament, 'Oft in the Stilly Night'.

Followed by the royal cortège, her coffin was driven up the crowded Mall towards Buckingham Palace as two Spitfires and a Lancaster bomber flew overhead in a final wartime tribute. Along the route to St George's Chapel in Windsor Castle thousands of people had gathered to watch her pass by for the last time. Some people crossed themselves, some bowed, others waved or threw flowers or raised glasses in a last toast.

That evening, in the King George VI Memorial Chapel, in the presence of her daughter, her grandchildren and her great-nephew Lord Strathmore, Queen Elizabeth was laid to rest beside the King, together with the casket containing the ashes of their daughter Princess Margaret, her epic journey finally completed.

EPILOGUE

ELIZABETH BOWES LYON might reasonably have expected to live a pleasant and relatively privileged but inconspicuous life, marrying into a family like her own, raising children, supporting her husband, her community and her charitable causes, and ending her days quietly, rich in good works and grandchildren. Instead, fate dealt her an extraordinary hand. This book has attempted to show what she made of it, to discern the qualities which enabled this young Scottish aristocrat, who surprised herself by marrying into the Royal Family, play such a central role, as wife and mother, as grandmother and great-grandmother, in the life of the nation.

Queen Elizabeth's century, the twentieth, started (as the historian John Roberts pointed out)* with both optimism about the march of progress and pessimism about the tide of materialism. No one could then have predicted either the horrors or the scientific and social advances to come. One hundred years later, Roberts wrote, facts are more accessible than ever but the events of the twentieth century will go on acquiring new meanings 'as they drop below the horizon of memory'. All we can do now is look back upon these years 'and search them for guidance'.[1] In that respect, the long life of Queen Elizabeth offers a fruitful study.

'England Expects' was the watchword of the Age of Empire into which she was born. She was of the last generation of aristocrats who felt able to accept their superior social position with no feeling of guilt but rather a sense of duty and of obligation. Her own Christian principles, instilled by her parents, gave her grace and an inner strength throughout her life. Allied to that was her sense of joy. The happy,

---

* See above, p. 16.

mischievous spirit in her letters to Beryl Poignand was still there more than eight decades later.

It would not be quite correct to say that she had a common touch – rather that she had an innate ability, inherited and learned, to mix with everyone. This was first apparent in her friendships with the wounded soldiers at Glamis during the First World War. Throughout her life she dealt without condescension to those less fortunate or less prominent than herself, and treated those in higher positions, like King George V and Queen Mary, with respect.

After she married the Duke of York she immediately transformed his life, bringing him the love, understanding, sympathy and support for which he had always craved. She inspired him, she calmed him and she enabled him for the first time in his life to believe in himself. Her sense of humour awoke his own, her natural gaiety lightened him. Their marriage was a rare union in which each complemented and enhanced the other. Their joy in each other and in their children fulfilled public expectations in an age when the Royal Family was seen as a model and an ideal.

In 1936, without the added confidence which his wife had imparted to him, and the loyal and loving support which she and their children continued to give him, the Duke of York might never have been able to make a success of his unwanted kingship after his brother's abrupt departure. Even before her coronation the unexpected Queen adapted to the new demands and responsibilities that were upon her. 'We are not afraid. I feel that God has enabled us to face the situation calmly,' she wrote at the time.[2] Thereafter she discovered how well her vivid and open personality was suited to the role.

In the thirty-two months they had before the war broke out, the King and Queen came to embody the cause of the democracies both at home and abroad, in their visits to France, Canada and the United States. The Queen was a triumph wherever she went, though the affection she and the King won in America did not quickly translate into wartime support. On their return from Canada in summer 1939, the nation cheered them home. Harold Nicolson expressed a widely shared belief when he wrote, 'She is in truth one of the most amazing Queens since Cleopatra.'[3]

Her horror at the prospect of another war so soon after 1918 led her, like the King, to support Chamberlain's efforts to avoid it, but once war was declared she committed herself totally to victory.

'Humanity must fight against bad things if we are to survive, and the spiritual things are stronger than anything else, and cannot be destroyed, thank God.'⁴ No one can measure the importance of the Queen's presence alongside the King in London throughout the war. During the brutal days of the Blitz their unannounced appearances among the rubble of bombed homes brought immense comfort. There could perhaps never be a better symbol of the difference between constitutional monarchy and dictatorship than the way in which the King and Queen endured the war alongside their people until victory was achieved. 'For him we had admiration, for her adoration' summed up the views of many.⁵ And for her part she never faltered in her belief in the British people.

Peace in 1945 brought new anxieties, particularly for the King, as Britain's Labour government embarked upon not only reconstruction but also radical reform. The Queen was not naturally predisposed to such changes, but she never lost her optimism; she and the King looked forward eagerly to the future and when he fell ill she always believed that he would recover.

When the King died in February 1952, grief overwhelmed her. Perhaps only her family and a few close friends knew how much she had depended on her husband and how much his loss undermined her. Her anguish was profound. Her spontaneous purchase of the Castle of Mey was a symptom of her grief, but it was a happy decision. Though impractical and expensive to run, the only home she ever owned gave her and her friends much pleasure for the rest of her life.

Once she had recovered her equilibrium, she brought to her new role a distinctive combination of wisdom, sympathy and vivacity, underpinned by a sturdy determination. She sometimes said to friends, 'I am not as nice as I seem,' and as a young woman she had written, 'What a lot of our life we spend in acting.'⁶ But that's true enough of most of humanity, after all; what matters is the use to which the 'seeming niceness' and the acting are put. Queen Elizabeth's natural charm and inbred good manners undoubtedly helped her achieve what she wanted, both personally and in her public role. But it would be wrong to dismiss those qualities as a façade. In personal terms, the devotion of her family, friends and, perhaps above all, employees speaks for itself. In public the enduring, unflagging interest and sympathy she showed for others over so many decades – no doubt with occasional bouts of acting – surely reveals a genuine engagement,

answered by the genuine popularity she earned. Her unaffected enjoyment of the good things of life, especially dry martinis and champagne,
and her indulgence in horseracing, both the most aristocratic of sports
and the most popular form of gambling, won her great affection. Her
joie de vivre was such that all of her life she lit up not only rooms that
she entered but every occasion in which she took part. The name
which she took, Queen Mother, she did not at first like but the title
came quickly to symbolize the role she played in both her family and
the nation.

She loved to preserve. The England in which she grew up was a
home, filled with familiar and well-loved rituals. Many of these became
unfashionable in the second half of her life. But she still treasured them
– in her regiments, her ships, her universities and her 300 or so
charities and other organizations. By celebrating traditions, she both
enriched and prolonged them in a more impatient age. The remarkable
breadth of her patronages gave her a public presence and, indeed,
influence in many areas of national life. This could have been difficult
for the Queen but her mother never usurped her daughter's position.
Deeply conscious of the monarch's role, Queen Elizabeth always
remained in the picture but never placed herself in the centre of the
frame. She was always aware that it is a principal task of a hereditary
monarch to pass the crown to someone well prepared for this unique
responsibility, and she rejoiced in the success of her daughter. Indeed,
during the Queen's Golden Jubilee, which was celebrated only weeks
after her mother's death, millions of people across the country displayed their enthusiasm for Elizabeth II, providing remarkable proof of
the affection which the monarch and the institution still enjoyed. They
sensed that both Queens embodied the Shakespearean royal ideal of
'Christian service and true chivalry'.

Queen Elizabeth's dislike of change may have slowed down the
pace of royal reform which is always necessary to retain consent.
There were changes which the Queen and her advisers might have
chosen to make earlier, had there been no concern about upsetting
Queen Elizabeth. Against this must be weighed the fact that her
remarkable popularity helped soften criticism of the monarchy, particularly in the miseries of the 1990s. The press had become unforgiving
of almost everyone else in the family, but she remained largely above
criticism. Even her extravagance was accepted, and usually with a
smile – because of who she was. In those family crises, she was

sometimes criticized for not intervening directly in the lives of her grandchildren. But that is never easy in any family; she saw her task rather to support and sustain the Queen in any way she could throughout not only the *annus horribilis* but the rest of that painful decade.

The core of her popularity and the major feature of the second half of her life was surely her permanence, both in her principles and in the pattern of her life. As she grew older, she showed great courage in not allowing the infirmities of the years to compel her into retirement. There was something immensely reassuring in her insistence on carrying out her commitments year after year, and the stamina which enabled her to do so. Britain changed enormously but she remained constant. This had particular resonance for all those who were feeling rudderless in the wake of the immense social upheavals of the late twentieth century. Her high spirits and her love of the traditions and the quirkiness of Britain were an inspiration to millions.

In closing, one could recall that at the beginning of the Second World War, the Archbishop of Canterbury wrote to her, 'I feel inclined to say to Your Majesty what was said in the Bible story to Queen Esther – "Who knoweth whether thou art come to the Kingdom for such a time as this." '[7] That was true in 1939 and it remained so to the end of her life.

The Bowes Lyon

Family Tree

Robert I the Bruce,   m.   Isabella of Mar
King of Scotland   (d. before 1302)
(1274–1329)

Marjorie Bruce,   m.   Walter Stewart,
Princess of Scotland   6th High Steward of Scotland
(c.1296–1316)   (1296–1327)

Robert II,   m.1   Elizabeth Mure   m.2   Euphemeia Ross,
King of Scotland   of Rowallan   Countess of Moray
(1316–90)   (d. before 1355)   (d. 1388/9)

Sir John Lyon   m.   Jean Stewart   David, 1st Earl of Caithness,   m.   Unknown daughter
of Glamis   (b. before 1355,   Earl Palatine of Strathearn   of
(d. 1382)   d. after 1404)   (b. before 1360   Alexander de Lindsay
                                          d. before 1389)

Sir John Lyon   m.   Elizabeth   Eupheme Stewart,   m.   Patrick Graham,
of Glamis   Countess of Caithness   Earl of Strathearn
(d. c.1435)   (born c.1375, d. 1434)   (d. 1413)

Isabella Ogilvy   m.   Patrick, 1st Lord Glamis
(c.1410–85)   (c.1400–60)

Alexander, 2nd Lord Glamis   John, 3rd Lord Glamis m. Elizabeth Scrymgeour
(d. 1486)   (d. 1497)

John, 4th Lord Glamis   m.   Elizabeth Gray
(d. c.1500)   (d. c.1526)

George, 5th Lord Glamis   John, 6th Lord Glamis m.   Janet Douglas
(d. 1505) no issue   (d. 1526)   (d. 1537)

Janet Keith   m.   John, 7th Lord Glamis
                  (d. before 1559)

Elizabeth Abernethy   m.   John, 8th Lord Glamis
(d. before 1581)   (c.1544–78)

Lady Anne Murray   m.   Patrick, 9th Lord Glamis
(1579–1618)   and 1st Earl of Kinghorne
                     (1575–1615)

John, 2nd Earl of Kinghorne   m.1   Lady Margaret Erskine   m.2   Lady Elizabeth Maule
(1596–1646)   no issue   (d. 1659)

Lady Helen Middleton   m.   Patrick, 3rd Earl of
(d. 1708)   Strathmore and Kinghorne
                     (1643–95)

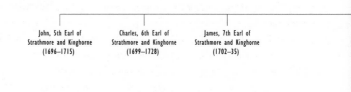

| John, 5th Earl of Strathmore and Kinghorne (1696–1715) | Charles, 6th Earl of Strathmore and Kinghorne (1699–1728) | James, 7th Earl of Strathmore and Kinghorne (1702–35) |

| Charlotte Barrington m. (1826–54) | Thomas, 12th Earl of Strathmore and Kinghorne (1822–65) |

without issue

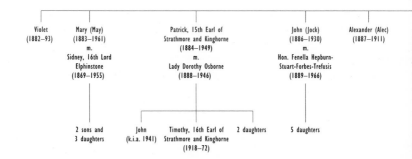

| Violet (1882–93) | Mary (May) (1883–1961) m. Sidney, 16th Lord Elphinstone (1869–1955) | Patrick, 15th Earl of Strathmore and Kinghorne (1884–1949) m. Lady Dorothy Osborne (1888–1946) | John (Jock) (1886–1930) m. Hon. Fenella Hepburn-Stuart-Forbes-Trefusis (1889–1966) | Alexander (Alec) (1887–1911) |

| 2 sons and 3 daughters | John (k.i.a. 1941) | Timothy, 16th Earl of Strathmore and Kinghorne (1918–72) | 2 daughters | 5 daughters |

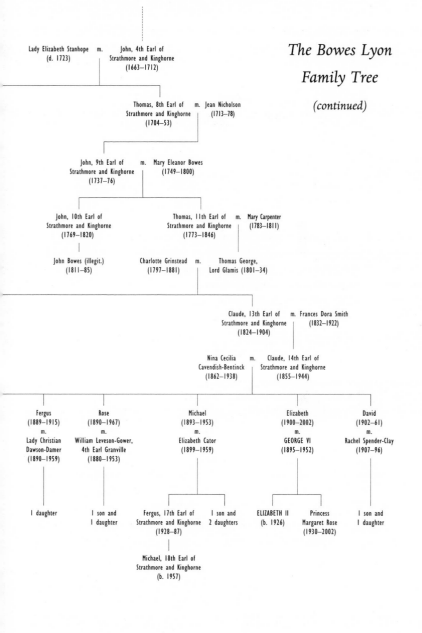

The Bowes Lyon

Family Tree

(continued)

Lady Elizabeth Stanhope m. John, 4th Earl of
(d. 1723) Strathmore and Kinghorne
(1663–1712)

Thomas, 8th Earl of m. Jean Nicholson
Strathmore and Kinghorne (1713–78)
(1704–53)

John, 9th Earl of m. Mary Eleanor Bowes
Strathmore and Kinghorne (1749–1800)
(1737–76)

John, 10th Earl of
Strathmore and Kinghorne
(1769–1820)

Thomas, 11th Earl of m. Mary Carpenter
Strathmore and Kinghorne (1783–1811)
(1773–1846)

John Bowes (illegit.)
(1811–85)

Charlotte Grinstead m. Thomas George,
(1797–1881) Lord Glamis (1801–34)

Claude, 13th Earl of m. Frances Dora Smith
Strathmore and Kinghorne (1832–1922)
(1824–1904)

Nina Cecilia m. Claude, 14th Earl of
Cavendish-Bentinck Strathmore and Kinghorne
(1862–1938) (1855–1944)

Fergus
(1889–1915)
m.
Lady Christian
Dawson-Damer
(1890–1959)

Rose
(1890–1967)
m.
William Leveson-Gower,
4th Earl Granville
(1880–1953)

Michael
(1893–1953)
m.
Elizabeth Cator
(1899–1959)

Elizabeth
(1900–2002)
m.
GEORGE VI
(1895–1952)

David
(1902–61)
m.
Rachel Spender-Clay
(1907–96)

1 daughter

1 son and
1 daughter

Fergus, 17th Earl of
Strathmore and Kinghorne
(1928–87)

1 son and
2 daughters

ELIZABETH II
(b. 1926)

Princess
Margaret Rose
(1930–2002)

1 son and
1 daughter

Michael, 18th Earl of
Strathmore and Kinghorne
(b. 1957)

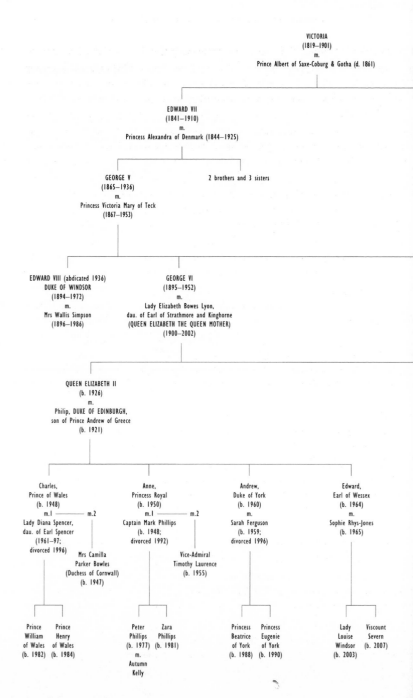

VICTORIA
(1819–1901)
m.
Prince Albert of Saxe-Coburg & Gotha (d. 1861)

EDWARD VII
(1841–1910)
m.
Princess Alexandra of Denmark (1844–1925)

GEORGE V
(1865–1936)
m.
Princess Victoria Mary of Teck
(1867–1953)

2 brothers and 3 sisters

EDWARD VIII (abdicated 1936)
DUKE OF WINDSOR
(1894–1972)
m.
Mrs Wallis Simpson
(1896–1986)

GEORGE VI
(1895–1952)
m.
Lady Elizabeth Bowes Lyon,
dau. of Earl of Strathmore and Kinghorne
(QUEEN ELIZABETH THE QUEEN MOTHER)
(1900–2002)

QUEEN ELIZABETH II
(b. 1926)
m.
Philip, DUKE OF EDINBURGH,
son of Prince Andrew of Greece
(b. 1921)

Charles,
Prince of Wales
(b. 1948)
m.1 ———— m.2
Lady Diana Spencer,
dau. of Earl Spencer
(1961–97;
divorced 1996)

Mrs Camilla
Parker Bowles
(Duchess of Cornwall)
(b. 1947)

Anne,
Princess Royal
(b. 1950)
m.1 ———— m.2
Captain Mark Phillips
(b. 1948;
divorced 1992)

Vice-Admiral
Timothy Laurence
(b. 1955)

Andrew,
Duke of York
(b. 1960)
m.
Sarah Ferguson
(b. 1959;
divorced 1996)

Edward,
Earl of Wessex
(b. 1964)
m.
Sophie Rhys-Jones
(b. 1965)

Prince   Prince
William   Henry
of Wales   of Wales
(b. 1982)   (b. 1984)

Peter   Zara
Phillips   Phillips
(b. 1977)   (b. 1981)
m.
Autumn
Kelly

Princess   Princess
Beatrice   Eugenie
of York   of York
(b. 1988)   (b. 1990)

Lady   Viscount
Louise   Severn
Windsor   (b. 2007)
(b. 2003)

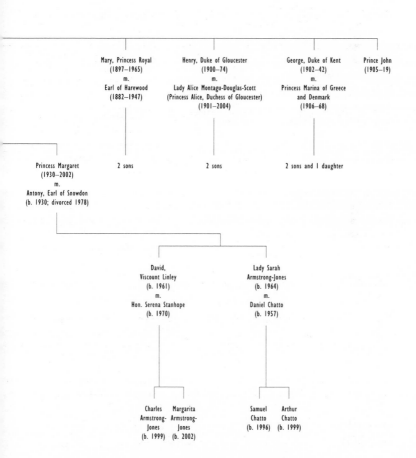

The Saxe-Coburg & Gotha
(1837–1917)
and Windsor
Family Tree

3 brothers and 5 sisters

Mary, Princess Royal
(1897–1965)
m.
Earl of Harewood
(1882–1947)

Henry, Duke of Gloucester
(1900–74)
m.
Lady Alice Montagu-Douglas-Scott
(Princess Alice, Duchess of Gloucester)
(1901–2004)

George, Duke of Kent
(1902–42)
m.
Princess Marina of Greece
and Denmark
(1906–68)

Prince John
(1905–19)

Princess Margaret
(1930–2002)
m.
Antony, Earl of Snowdon
(b. 1930; divorced 1978)

2 sons

2 sons

2 sons and 1 daughter

David,
Viscount Linley
(b. 1961)
m.
Hon. Serena Stanhope
(b. 1970)

Lady Sarah
Armstrong-Jones
(b. 1964)
m.
Daniel Chatto
(b. 1957)

Charles
Armstrong-
Jones
(b. 1999)

Margarita
Armstrong-
Jones
(b. 2002)

Samuel
Chatto
(b. 1996)

Arthur
Chatto
(b. 1999)

Queen Elizabeth's Patronages

Aberdeen-Angus Cattle Society	1937–2002	Patroness 1937–1958; Patron 1958–2002
R. Academy of Arts American Associates (Sir Hugh and Lady Casson Fund)	1996	
R. Academy of Dramatic Art	1931–2002	
R. Academy of Music	1937–2002	
Adelaide Festival of Arts	1960–1999	
Aged Christian Friend Society	1937–2002	As Duchess of York, Countess of Inverness – Patron of Inverness Branch 1936–1937
Albany, The	1937–2002	Formerly the Deptford Fund and the Princess Alice New Albany Foundation
Aldeburgh Festival	1974–2002	
Ancoats Hospital	1926–2002	
Archer House Convalescent Fund	1931–1965 1965–1968	Formerly Archer House Home for Nurses. Subsequently administered by National Fund for Nurses
R. Agricultural Society of England	1959 1960 1998	Trustee President Hon. Trustee
Associated Board of the Royal Schools of Music	1953–2002	President
R. Association for Disability & Rehabilitation	1976–2002	Formerly Central Council for the Care of Cripples, then Central Council for the Disabled (1929–1976), amalgamated with the British Council for the Rehabilitation of the Disabled
Australian Red Cross Society	1941–2002	
Bar Musical Society	1957–2002	

Barnardo's	1936–2002	Formerly Dr Barnardo's
Barrowmore Village Settlement	1953–2002	
Bath Club, Ladies' Section	1937–1958?	Hon. Member 1936 Patroness 1937 until the Club closed
Battle of Britain Fighter Association	1977–2002	
Bedfordshire and Hertfordshire Historic Churches Trust	1992–2002	
Benenden Healthcare Society	1952–2002	Formerly (Post Office and) Civil Service Sanatorium Society
Benevolent Society of St Patrick	1955–2002	
Bible Reading Fellowship	1952–2002	
Bible Society	1943–2002	Formerly British and Foreign Bible Society
Birkbeck College	1937–2002	
Birmingham Royal Institution for the Blind	1937–2002	
R. Blind Asylum and School, Edinburgh	1937–2002	
Bomber Command Association	1987–2002	
Botanical Society of the British Isles	1965–2002	
Botanical Society of Scotland	1950–2002	
Brendoncare Foundation	1983–2002	
Bridewell Royal Hospital (King Edward's School, Witley)	1953–2002	President
Britain in Bloom Competitions	1976–1989	
British–American Benevolent Association	1937–1977	Formerly Queen Victoria Hospital, Nice
British & International Sailors' Society	1937–2002	Formerly British Sailors' Society
British Commonwealth Ex-Services League (Women's Auxiliaries)	1949–2002	
British Commonwealth Nurses War Memorial Fund	1946–1995	Formerly British Empire Nurses War Memorial Fund
British Dental Hospital	1926–1948	
British Equine Veterinary Association	1968–2002	
British Home and Hospital for Incurables, Streatham	1925–2002	
British Homeopathic Association	1982–2002	
British Hospital for Mothers and Babies, Woolwich	1953–1984	Hospital closed

R. British Legion Women's Section	1924–2002	President
R. British Legion Scotland (Women's Section)	1936–2002	Grand President
British Orthopaedic Association	1959–2002	
British Records Association	1952–2002	
British Red Cross Society	1937–2002	President 1937–1952 Vice/Deputy President 1952–1998 President 1998–2002
British Sporting Art Trust	1977–2002	
British Theatre Association	1952–1990	Formerly British Drama League
R. Brompton National Heart & Lung Hospital	1937–2002	Formerly Brompton Hospital for Diseases of the Chest
Bud Flanagan Leukaemia Fund	1982–2002	
Caithness Agricultural Society	1970–2002	
Caithness Heritage Trust	1991–2002	
R. Caledonian Horticultural Society	1937–2002	
R. Caledonian Schools Trust	1937–2002	Patroness. Formerly The Royal Caledonian Schools
R. Cambrian Academy of Art	1937–2002	
Cambridge Arts Theatre Trust	1981–2002	
Canada Memorial Foundation	1989–1994	Patron-in-Chief
Canadian Merchant Navy Prisoner of War Association	1994–2002	
Canadian Mothercraft Society	1931–2002	
Canadian Red Cross Society	1939–2002	
Careers for Women	1939–1993	Formerly Women's Employment Federation (–1972) then National Advisory Centre on Careers for Women (–1990)
Cassel Hospital	1954–2002	Formerly Cassel Hospital for Functional Nervous Disorders
Cavalry & Guards Club (Ladies' Side)	1976–2002	Formerly Guards' Club (Ladies' Annexe) 1937–1972
Centre for Policy on Ageing	1950–2002	Formerly National Corporation for the Care of Old People
Charing Cross Hospital	1937–2002	
Chelsea Physic Garden	1984–2002	First Patron
Children's Country Holidays Fund	1925–2002	
Children's Hospital at Westmead, The	1927–2002	Formerly Royal Alexandra Hospital for Children, Sydney
Children's Society, The	1924–2002	Formerly the Church of England Children's Society

Church Army	1943–2002	
Church of England Soldiers', Sailors' and Airmen's Clubs	1937–2002	
Church of England Temperance Society	1937–1967	
Cinque Ports Mayors' Association	1980–2002	First Patron
R. Cinque Ports Yacht Club	1978–2002	President
City & Metropolitan Welfare Charity	1937–1972	Formerly Metropolitan Convalescent Institution
Civil Defence Welfare Fund	1940–1950s?	Formerly Civil Defence (Services) Comforts Fund
Civil Service Retirement Fellowship	1977–2002	
Clan Sinclair Trust	2000–2002	
Colditz Association	1992–2002	
R. College of Midwives	1938–2002	Formerly Midwives Institute
R. College of Music	1938–1952 1952–1992 1993–2002	Patron President President Emerita
R. College of Nursing	1963–2002	
R. College of Obstetricians and Gynaecologists	1946–2002	And Hon. Fellow
R. College of Speech & Language Therapists	1959–2002	Formerly College of Speech Therapists
R. Commonwealth Society	1937–2002	
Commonwealth Trust	1989–2002	
Contemporary Art Society	1948–2002	
Cookery & Food Association	1953–2002	
Coronation Planting Committee	1936–1938	
Countess of Dufferin's Fund, New Delhi	1937–1948	
Courtauld Institute of Art Trust	1983–2002	
Crathie District Nursing Association	1938–1945	Honorary President
Crathie Women's Rural Institute	Pre-1953–2000?	
Cumberland Lodge (King George VI and Queen Elizabeth Foundation of St Catharine's, Cumberland Lodge)	1968–2002	Formerly St Catharine's Cumberland Lodge
Darwin Caledonian Pipe Band	1984–2002	
Dispensaire Français	1983–2002	

Dockland Settlements	1924–2002	
Douglas Bader Foundation	1983–1991	
Dover College	1979–2002	
Dover Museum	1991–2002	
Downpatrick Race Club	1989–2002	
Duchy Health Charity Limited	1983–2002	Formerly Duchy Hospital Truro and Cornwall Independent Hospital Trust
Dundee Dental Hospital	1934–2002	
Dundee University Operatic Society	1970–1981	
East Grinstead Medical Research Trust	1977–2002	Formerly East Grinstead Research Trust
East Ham Memorial Hospital	1931–2002	
Eastern Arts Board	1973–2002	Formerly Eastern Arts Association
Edinburgh Angus Club	1953–2002	
R. Edinburgh Hospital for Sick Children	1937–2002	
Edinburgh International Festival of Music and Drama	1948–2002	
R. Edinburgh Repository & Self-Aid Society	1937–2002	Royal Repository for the Sale of Gentlewomen's Work, Edinburgh, and Royal Scottish Society for the Self-Aid of Gentlewomen amalgamated in 1977
Elizabeth Finn Trust	1953–2002	Formerly Distressed Gentlefolk's Aid Association
Emily McPherson College, Melbourne	1970–1980	
Entertainment Artistes' Benevolent Fund	1946–2002	Formerly Variety Artistes' Benevolent Fund
Ex-Services Mental Welfare Society	1942–2002	Also known as Combat Stress
Ex-Flying Squad Officers' Association	2000	Patron for one year only
Family Service Units	1955–2002	
Federated Caledonian Society of Southern Africa	1958–2002	Patron-in-Chief
R. Female Orphanage, Beddington	1937–1968	The Beddington Fund was incorporated in the Shaftesbury Society
Fleming Memorial Fund for Medical Research	1959–1969	

Florence Nightingale Aid-in-Sickness Trust	1966–2002	Formerly Florence Nightingale Hospital
R. Foundation of St Katharine, in Ratcliffe	1953–2002	
Franco-British Society	1944–2002	
Friendly Almshouses	1938–2002	
Friends of Aberbrothock	1933–1948	
Friends of the Ashmolean Museum	1969–2002	
Friends of the Bowes Museum	1962–2002	
Friends of Canterbury Cathedral	1978–2002	
Friends of the Elderly	1937–2002	Formerly Friends of the Poor and Gentlefolk's Help
Friends of the Imperial War Museum	1986–2002	Patron-in-Chief
Friends of Lusaka Cathedral, Zambia	1962–2002	
Friends of Manchester Cathedral	1952–2002	
Friends of Norwich Cathedral	1951–2002	
Friends of the Norwich Museums	1959–2002	
Friends of Old St Peter's Church, Thurso	1966–2002	
Friends of St Magnus Cathedral, Orkney	1972–2002	
Friends of St Martin-in-the-Fields	1952–2002	
Friends of St Mary's, Haddington	1971–2002	
Friends of St Paul's Cathedral	1952–2002	
Friends of the Tate Gallery	1958–2002	
Friends of York Minster	1928–2002	
Future Fisherman Foundation, Auckland NZ	1989–1993	
Garden Society	1952–2002	
Garden Society of Scotland	1957–2002	
R. Gardeners' Orphan Fund	1953–2002	
Gardeners' Royal Benevolent Society	1969–1992	
General Lying-in Hospital	1937–1972	
Georgian Group	1947–2002	
Girls' Brigade, England & Wales	1967–2002	Formed on amalgamation of Girls' Life Brigade, Girls' Brigade Ireland and Girls' Guildry

Girls' Brigade Scotland	1923–2002	Formerly the Girls' Guildry HM was Patron before she was married
Girls' Friendly Society	1937–2002	
Girls' Friendly Society of Scotland	1937–1990	
Glasgow Angus Association	1952–1959	
Glasgow Angus & Mearns Benevolent Society	1927–1978	
Glasgow Caithness Benevolent Association	1956–1997	
Grand Antiquity Society of Glasgow	1927–2002	
Grand Military Race Committee	1969–2002	
Greater London Fund for the Blind	1931–2002	
Grenfell Association of Great Britain & Ireland	1934–1981	The Duke and Duchess of York granted their Patronage pre-1934
Grosvenor House Antiques Fair	1953–2002	Formerly Antique Dealers' Fair
Guide Association	1937–2002	Formerly The Girl Guides Association
Guild of Glass Engravers	1980–2002	
Guy's Hospital Ladies' Association	1923–?	President
R. Gwent Hospital	1937–2002	
Haddo House Choral Society	1958–2002	
Hepburn Starey Blind Aid Society	1935–2001	
Heritage Craft Schools, Chailey	1940–2002	
Hertford British Hospital, Paris	1937–2002	
Hertfordshire Society, CPRE	1970–2002	
Highland Home Industries	1923–1974	
Hillington & District Nursing Association	1937–1948	
R. Holloway and Bedford New College	1985–2002	Formerly Patron of Bedford College 1953–1985
R. Horticultural Society	1937–2002	
R. Hospital for Neuro-Disability	1923–2002	Formerly Royal Hospital and Home for Incurables, Putney
R. Hospital for Sick Children, Glasgow	1923–2002	
R. Household Cricket Club	1937–2002	
Hunters Improvement Society	1960–1961	
Injured Jockeys Fund	1973–2002	Formerly Injured National Hunt Jockeys Fund

Institute of Journalists – Orphan Fund	1953–2002	
Institute of Leisure & Amenity Management	1961–2002	Formerly Institute of Park and Recreation Administration
International Students Trust	1965–2002	
Jockey Club	1968–2002	Patron National Hunt Committee 1954–1968
Keats–Shelley Memorial Association	1950–2002	
King's Lynn Festival	1953–2002	
King's Lynn Preservation Trust	1972–2002	
Kingston-on-Thames Victoria Hospital	1923–	Patroness
League for the Exchange of Commonwealth Teachers	1977–2002	
League of Remembrance	1953–2002	
R. Liverpool Seamen's Orphan Institution	1937–2002	
London Angus Association	1933–1968	
London Caithness Association	1956–2002	
London Children's Flower Society	1974–2002	Formerly London Flower Lovers League
London Gardens Society	1947–2002	
London Hospitals Street Collections: Hospitals Week	1937–1948	
London Library	1952–2002	
London Schools' Guild of Arts & Crafts	1937–1955	
Longhope Lifeboat Museum Trust	2001–2002	
Lord Mayor's Air Raid Distress Fund	1941–1954	Including Empire Air Raid Distress Fund – Patron 1942
Magdalen Hospital, Streatham	1953–1972	
Manor Gardens Centre	1923–2002	Formerly North Islington Infant Welfare Centre
Marie Curie Cancer Care	1956–2002	Formerly Marie Curie Memorial Foundation
Mathilda Verne College of Music	1924–	Patroness
R. Medical Benevolent Fund Guild	1927–1972	
R. Mencap Society	1962–2002	Formerly R. (National) Society for Mentally Handicapped Children and Adults
R. Military Benevolent Fund	1953–1960	

Moor House School	1957–2002	
Mothercraft Training Society	1923–1952	President
Mothers' Union	1937–2002	
Mothers' Union, Scotland	1926–1983	
Museums Association	1955–2002	
National Association of Hospital & Community Friends	1952–2002	Formerly National Association of Leagues of Hospital Friends
National Children Adoption Association	1923–1978	
National Council of Nurses of Great Britain and Northern Ireland	1952–1963	
National Deaf Children's Society	1961–2002	
National Gardens Scheme	1979–2002	
R. National Hospital for Diseases of the Chest	1937–1964	Formerly R. National Hospital for Consumption, Ventnor
R. National Institute for the Blind	1937–2002	
R. National Lifeboat Institution	1937–2002	
National Operatic and Dramatic Association	1960–2002	
R. National Orthopaedic Hospital	1937–2002	
R. National Pension Fund for Nurses	1953–2001	
R. National Rose Society	1965–2002	
National Savings Committee	1943–1978	
National Society for the Prevention of Cruelty to Children	1924–2002	
National Training College of Domestic Subjects	1937–1962	
National Trust	1953–2002	President
National Trust for Scotland	1952–2002	
National Youth Orchestra of Great Britain	1953–2002	
R. Naval and R. Marine Children's Home, Portsmouth	1953–1997	
Naval Home Industry	1937–1965	Patroness
Norfolk Nursing Association	1946–1950	
Norfolk Record Society	1953–2002	
Norwich Philharmonic Society	1948–2002	
Nuffield Foundation	1945–2002	

Nuffield Trust	1945–2002	Formerly Nuffield Provincial Hospitals Trust
Octavia Housing and Care	1961–2002	Formerly St Marylebone Housing Association
Officers' Families Fund	1953–1989	
Old Contemptibles, London and South East Area	1987–1999	Patron-in-Chief
Ontario Jockey Club	1987–2002	
Oriana Madrigal Society	1926–1961	Patroness
Our Dumb Friends League	1926–1930	Patroness
Peter Pears Award	1989–1991	
R. Philharmonic Orchestra	1962–2002	
Post Office Arts Club	1932	
Poultry Club	1978–2002	
Princess Royal Maternity Hospital	1927–2002	Formerly Glasgow Royal Maternity Hospital Hon President 1927–1937 Patron 1937–2002
Professional Classes Aid Council	1955–2002	Patroness
Queen Alexandra Hospital Home, Worthing	1953–2002	President
Queen Charlotte's and Chelsea Hospitals	1937–2002	Formerly Queen Charlotte's Maternity Hospital
Queen Elizabeth Club for Officers	1941–1947	
Queen Elizabeth Hospital for Children, Hackney	1942–1998	
Queen Elizabeth's Foundation	1953–2002	Formerly Queen Elizabeth's Training College for the Disabled, and then for Disabled People
Queen Elizabeth's Overseas Nursing Service Association	1953–2002	
Queen Mary's Clothing Guild	1953–2002	Formerly Queen Mary's London Needlework Guild
Queen Victoria Hospital NHS Trust, East Grinstead	1949–2002	
Queens' College, Cambridge	1948–2002	Patroness
Queen's College, London	1937–2002	
Queen's College, Oxford	1937–2002	Patroness
Queen's Nursing Institute	1953–2002	Formerly the Queen's Institute of District Nursing

Queen's Nursing Institute, Scotland	1928–2002	Formerly the Queen's Institute of District Nursing Scotland President 1928–1953 Patron 1953–2002
Racing Welfare	1991–2002	Formerly Racing Welfare Charities
Railway Benevolent Institution	1937–2002	
Regular Forces Employment Agency	1937–2002	Formerly National Association for Employment of Regular Sailors, Soldiers and Airmen
Research into Ageing	1976–2002	Formerly British Foundation for Age Research, then Age Action Trust
Roads Beautifying Association	1930–1965	Patroness
Robert Mayer Concerts for Children	1937–1979	
Sadler's Wells Foundation	1937–2002	And Sadler's Wells Trust from 1980
Sailors' Families Society	1937–2002	Formerly Sailors' Orphans Home, Hull, then Sailors' Children's Society
R. Sailors' Rests (Portsmouth & Devonport)	1937–2002	
St Albans Cathedral Music Trust	1996–2002	Patron-in-Chief
St Andrew's Ambulance Association	1937–2002	
St John Ambulance Association & Brigade (Nursing Corps and Divisions)	1937–2002	Commandant-in-Chief
St Mary's Hospital, Paddington	1930–2002	President
St. Mary's Hospital Medical School	1954–2002	
Salmon & Trout Association	1953–2002	
Sandringham District Nursing Association	1937–1948	
Sandringham Women's Institute	1937–2002	President
R. School (for Daughters of Officers of the Royal Navy and Royal Marines)	1932–1937 1937–2002	President Patron
R. School for Deaf Children, Margate	1937–2002	
R. School of Church Music	1950–2002	
R. School of Needlework	1923–1937 1937–2002	President Patron
Schoolmistresses' & Governesses' Benevolent Institution	1937–2002	Formerly Governesses' Benevolent Institution
Schools Music Association	1961–2002	

Scotland's Churches Scheme	1995–2002	
R. Scottish Academy of Music and Drama	1944–2002	
Scottish Children's League of Pity	1924–	Patroness
Scottish Council for Voluntary Organisations	1950–2002	Formerly Scottish Council of Social Service
Scottish Disability Foundation	1983–2002	
Scottish National Institution for the War Blinded	1937–2002	
Scottish National Memorial to David Livingstone Trust	1961–2002	
Scottish Orthopaedic Council	1942–1955	
R. Scottish Society for Prevention of Cruelty to Children	1937–2002	
R. Scottish Society of Arts	1938–2002	
R. Scottish Society of Painters in Watercolours	1937–2002	
Scottish Women's Hospitals (Memorial) Association	1923–1958	President
Shaftesbury Homes and 'Arethusa'	1937–2002	
Shaftesbury Society	1937–2002	
Shetland Pony Stud Book Society	1980–2002	
Silk & Man-made Fibre Users Association	1953–1970	Formerly Silk and Rayon Users Association
Sir George Thalben-Ball Memorial Trust	1989–2002	President
Sir Peter O'Sullevan Charitable Trust	2002	
Sir Robert Menzies Memorial Trust	1979–2002	
R. Smithfield Club	1983	President of the Show
	1987	President of the Show
	1988	President of the Show
	1989	President of the Show
	1994	Vice-President
R. Society for India, Pakistan and Ceylon	1953–1975	
R. Society for the Prevention of Cruelty to Animals	1952–2002	
Society for the Protection of Ancient Buildings	1977–2002	
Society of Chiropodists and Podiatrists	1981–2002	Formerly the Society of Chiropodists

R. Society of Edinburgh	1948–2002	
R. Society of Musicians of Great Britain	1937–2002	
R. Society of Painters in Water-colours	1947–2002	
South London Hospital for Women	1925–1948 1948–1984	President Hon. President
Special Forces Club	1987–2002	
SSAFA Forces Help	1923–2002	Formerly Soldiers', Sailors' and Airmen's Families Association and Forces Help Society and Lord Roberts Workshops, amalgamated in 1997
Sunningdale Ladies Golf Club	1938–2002	Captain 1932
Teachers Housing Association	1937–2002	Formerly National Union of Teachers Benevolent & Orphan Fund
Teesdale Buildings Preservation Trust	1977–1999	
Textile Benevolent Association (1970)	1967–2002	
Thistle Foundation	1945–2002	
Three Choirs Festival	1938–2002	
Tidy Britain Group	1960–2001	Formerly Keep Britain Tidy Group
Toc H	1931–2002	
Tower Hill Improvement Trust	1935–2002	President, Ladies' Council 1934
Trefoil Guild	1960–2002	
Trinity Hospice	1926–2002	Formerly The Hostel of God
UK Youth	1927–2002	President, Girls Clubs 1927 Patron, Girls Clubs 1937 Patron, Girls & Mixed Clubs 1945 Patron. Nat. Assoc. Youth Clubs 1961 Patron, Youth Clubs UK 1988 Patron, UK Youth 2001
Unicorn Preservation Society	1974–2002	
United Associations of Great Britain and France	1937–1952	Patron with The King
R. United Kingdom Beneficent Association (Rukba)	1937–2002	
United Nursing Services (South Street) Club	1925–1992	
United Society for Christian Literature	1950–2002	
University College Hospital	1925–2002	

University of Aberdeen Development Trust	1982–2002	
University of Oxford Development Programme	1988–2002	
Vacani School of Dancing	1927–2002	
R. Veterinary College Animal Care Trust	1982–2002	
Victoria Cross and George Cross Association	1983–2002	President
R. Victoria Hall Foundation	1937–2002	
Victoria League for Commonwealth Friendship	1923–2002	
Victoria League in Scotland	1951–2002	
Victorian Order of Nurses for Canada	1955–2002	Grand President
Virginia Water & Long Cross District Nursing Association	1937–1948	
R. Wanstead Foundation	1939–2002	Formerly R. Wanstead School
West Cumbria Health Care NHS Trust	1970–2002	Formerly West Cumberland Hospital
West Ham Central Mission	1929–2002	Formerly Child Haven, then Greenwood Children's Home
Westminster Abbey Special Choir	1925–1985	
Westminster Children's Society	1933–2002	Formerly City of Westminster Health Society
Widows' Friend Society	1936–2002	
Windsor District Nursing Association	1945–1948	
R. Wolverhampton School	1937–2002	
Women's College Hospital, Toronto	1962–2002	
Women's Land Army Benevolent Fund	1941–1957	HM sent messages for reunions until the final one in 2001
Women's Royal Voluntary Service	1939–2002	President
World Angus Secretariat	1999–2002	
Young Women's Christian Association of Great Britain	1923–1937 1937–2002	Patroness, Girls' Section Patron, National Association
Young Women's Christian Association Central Club	1937–2002	

MISCELLANEOUS APPOINTMENTS

R. Agricultural Society	1959	Trustee
	1960	President
	1998	Hon. Trustee
Charterhouse, The	1953–2002	Royal Governor
Cinque Ports	1978–2002	Lord Warden and Constable of Dover Castle
Girton College, Cambridge	1948–2002	Visitor
Middle Temple, the Honourable Society of the	1944–2002	Master of the Bench
	1949	Treasurer
Hospital of Sir John Hawkins, Kt, in Chatham (Almshouses)	1978–2002	Governor as Lord Warden of the Cinque Ports
St John of Jerusalem, Order of the Hospital of	1927	Dame Grand Cross
University College of Rhodesia and Nyasaland	1954–1971	President
University of Dundee	1967–1977	Chancellor
University of London	1955–1980	Chancellor

NOTES

Abbreviations

BUA	Birmingham University Archives
CAC	Churchill Archives Centre, Cambridge
CHAR	Chartwell Papers
FCO	Foreign and Commonwealth Office
FO	Foreign Office
GLLD	Papers of first Baron Lloyd of Dolobran
LAC/BAC	Library and Archives Canada/Bibliothèque et Archives Canada
LASL	Papers of Sir Alan Lascelles
NLS	National Library of Scotland
RA	Royal Archives
RCIN	Royal Collection Inventory Number
SPW	St Paul's Walden Bury

PROLOGUE

1 Birthday card, RA QEQM/PRIV/RF
2 Prince of Wales to Queen Elizabeth, 6 August 2000, RA QEQM/PRIV/RF

ONE: AN EDWARDIAN CHILDHOOD 1900–1914

1 *The Book of Record: A Diary written by Patrick Third Earl of Kinghorne and First of Strathmore and other documents relating to Glamis Castle 1684–1689.* Rendered into modern spelling and punctuation from the edition published by the Scottish History Society in 1890 by David M. Gauld, privately printed, 2004
2 Charles E. Hardy, *John Bowes and the Bowes Museum*, Friends of the Bowes Museum, 1989, p. 10
3 James Wentworth Day, *The Queen Mother's Family Story*, Robert Hale, 1967, pp. 22–3
4 Ibid., p. 24
5 J. Foot, *Lives of Andrew Robinson Bowes Esq. and the Countess of Strathmore . . .* (1810), quoted in Hardy, p. 10
6 Wentworth Day, p. 27

7 *Streatlam and Gibside, the Bowes and Strathmore Families in County Durham*, Durham County Council, 1980

8 Wendy Moore, *Wedlock: How Georgian Britain's Worst Husband Met His Match*, Weidenfeld & Nicolson, 2009, p. 93

9 Wentworth Day, p. 36

10 Moore, p. 239

11 Ibid., p. 253

12 Rosalind K. Marshall, *Oxford Dictionary of National Biography*, Oxford University Press, 2004, article on Mary Eleanor Bowes

13 Wentworth Day, p. 85; Stafford M. Linsley, *Oxford Dictionary of National Biography*, article on John Bowes

14 Harry Gordon Slade, *Glamis Castle*, Society of Antiquaries of London, 2000, p. 11

15 Lord Frederick Hamilton, *The Days before Yesterday*, Hodder & Stoughton, 1920, p. 247

16 Ibid., pp. 242–3, 245

17 Letters between Lord Glamis and Cecilia Cavendish-Bentinck, undated, Glamis Archives

18 Thirteenth Earl of Strathmore, diary, 16 July 1881, Glamis Archives

19 1901 Census return for The Bury, St Paul's Walden

20 Lady Elizabeth Bowes Lyon, passport issued on 23 May 1921, Glamis Archives

21 Diana Lyttelton to Editor, *Woman's Weekly*, 6 & 11 July 1950; to Jennifer Ellis, 8 August 1952, RA QEQMH/PRS/4

22 Russell T. Grant to Queen Elizabeth, 14 October 1978, RA QEQMH/GEN/1978/British Astrological Society

23 Thirteenth Earl of Strathmore, diary, 21 August 1900, Glamis Archives

24 Grania Forbes, *My Darling Buffy*, Headline, 1999, pp. 3–7

25 Dorothy Laird, *Queen Elizabeth The Queen Mother*, Coronet, 1985, p. 39

26 Hugo Vickers, *Elizabeth The Queen Mother*, Hutchinson, 2005, pp. 1–2

27 Rev. Canon Dendle French to Elizabeth Leeming, 5 February 2005. See also Canon Dendle French to Lucy Murphy, 12 January 1983, RA QEQMH/GEN/1983/St Paul's Walden

28 J. M. Roberts, *History of the World*, Hutchinson, 1976, p. 885

29 Ibid.

30 Mark Girouard, *Life in the English Country House*, Yale University Press, 1978, p. 298

31 Richard Beaumont, *Purdey's: The Guns and the Family*, David & Charles, 1994, p. 104

32 Jill Franklin, *The Gentleman's Country House and Its Plan 1835–1914*, Routledge & Kegan Paul, 1981, p. 81

33 Notes on the Strathmore family and its homes compiled for the author by Elizabeth Leeming, elder daughter of the seventeenth Earl of Strathmore

34 Lady Cynthia Asquith, *The Duchess of York*, Hutchinson, [1927], p. 45

35 Ibid., p. 33

36 Asquith, *The Queen*, Hutchinson, 1937, pp. 22–3

37 Queen Elizabeth, conversations with Eric Anderson, 1994–5, RA QEQM/ADD/MISC

38 Asquith, *The Queen*, p. 24

39 Ibid., p. 25

40 Ibid., p. 49

41 Queen Elizabeth to Rachel Bowes Lyon, 19 July 1988, Bowes Lyon Papers, SPW

42 Laird, p. 40

43 Asquith, *The Queen*, p. 45

44 Ibid., pp. 45–6

45 Gordon Slade, pp. 31–2; notes on Glamis Castle by Elizabeth Leeming

46 Leeming notes

47 Gordon Slade, pp. 105–6

48 Ibid., p. 76

49 Queen Elizabeth, conversations with Eric Anderson, 1994–5, RA QEQM/ADD/MISC

50 Thirteenth Earl of Strathmore, diary 2 October 1903, Glamis Archives

51 Lady May Bowes Lyon, diary, February 1904, private collection

52 Queen Elizabeth, conversations with Eric Anderson, 1994–5, RA QEQM/ADD/MISC

53 Beryl Poignand to her mother, n.d. [20 November 1914], Poignand Papers

54 Leeming notes

55 Queen Elizabeth, conversations with Eric Anderson, 1994–5, RA QEQM/ADD/MISC

56 Leeming notes

57 Laird, p. 37

58 Leeming notes

59 Laird, p. 36

60 Leeming notes

61 Laird, p. 36

62 Raymond Asquith to Katharine Horner, 25 September 1905 (copy), RA QEQM/PRIV/HIST, quoted in *Raymond Asquith: Life and Letters*, ed. John Joliffe, Collins, 1980, p. 134

63 Forbes, pp. 8–9

64 Christopher Dingwall, *Glamis Castle: A History of the Designed Landscape*, Strathmore Estates, 2000, pp. 40–1; the Countess of Strathmore, 'Glamis, the Autumn Garden', *The Gardener's Year Book*, Philip Allen, 1928, p. 52

65 Mrs Scott to Lady Glamis, 10, 16 September 1903, Glamis Archives (CH)

66 Asquith, *The Queen*, p. 32

67 Ibid., p. 29

68 Ibid., pp. 36–7

69 Ibid., p. 41

70 Ibid., pp. 46–7

71 Ibid., pp. 47–8

72 Lord Strathmore to the Dowager Lady Strathmore, 14 February 1907, Glamis Archives

73 Lady Elizabeth Bowes Lyon to Lord Strathmore, 22 February 1907, Glamis Archives

74 Asquith, *The Queen*, p. 38

75 Lady Elizabeth Bowes Lyon to Lord Strathmore, 10 February 1909, Glamis Archives

76 Asquith, *The Queen*, p. 39

77 Elizabeth's friend Lavinia Spencer wrote several letters to her sympathizing over her troubles with Dorothy: 14 August, 17 September, 27 December 1915, 7 January 1916, 16 October 1919, Glamis Archives

78 Lady Elizabeth Bowes Lyon, diary, 1910, RA QEQM/PRIV/DIARY/1

79 Ibid.

80 Lady Elizabeth Bowes Lyon to Mlle Lang, 20 [21] January 1910, Glamis Archives

81 Elizabeth Longford, *The Royal House of Windsor*, Weidenfeld & Nicolson, 1974, pp. 51–2

82 King George V, diary, 6 May 1910, quoted in Kenneth Rose, *King George V*, Weidenfeld & Nicolson, 1983, p. 76

83 Lady Strathmore, diary, 7, 20 May 1910, Glamis Archives

84 Asquith, *The Queen*, p. 39

85 Lady Elizabeth Bowes Lyon to May Elphinstone, 16 July 1910, RA QEQM/OUT/ELPHINSTONE

86 Lady Elizabeth Bowes Lyon to May Elphinstone, 19 July 1910, RA QEQM/OUT/ELPHINSTONE

87 Lady Elizabeth Bowes Lyon to May Elphinstone, 5 August 1910, RA QEQM/OUT/ELPHINSTONE

88 Lady Elizabeth Bowes Lyon to Lady Strathmore, 13 December 1910, Glamis Archives (CH)

89 Lady Elizabeth Bowes Lyon to Lady Strathmore, 29 December 1910, Glamis Archives (CH)

90 Roberts, *History of the World*, p. 901

91 Exercise book, 1911, Bowes Lyon Papers, SPW

92 Ibid.

93 Queen Elizabeth, conversations with Eric Anderson, 1994–5, RA QEQM/ADD/MISC

94 Ibid.

95 Asquith, *The Queen*, p. 42

96 Elizabeth Leeming: Notes on shooting with the Strathmores; Elizabeth Leeming interview with Ronnie Carr, 8 February 2006

97 Laird, p. 45

98 Asquith, *The Queen*, p. 44

99 Frederick Dalrymple Hamilton, diary, 15, 18, 19 August 1911, private collection

100 Ibid., 20, 21 August 1911

101 Hon. John Bowes Lyon to Lady Strathmore, 24 July [1911], Glamis Archives

102 Hon. John Bowes Lyon to Lady Delia Spencer, 14 October 1911, Glamis Archives

103 Mrs Scott to Lady Strathmore, 29 October 1911, Glamis Archives

104 Lady Elizabeth Bowes Lyon, diary, 17–18 February 1912, RA QEQM/PRIV/DIARY/1

105 Frederick Dalrymple Hamilton, diary, 3, 4 March 1912, private collection

106 Ibid., 13–15 April 1912

107 Lady Elizabeth Bowes Lyon, diary, 1912, RA QEQM/PRIV/DIARY/1

108 Lady Elizabeth Bowes Lyon to Lady Strathmore, 10 May 1912, Glamis Archives

109 Lady Elizabeth Bowes Lyon to Lady Strathmore, 12 May 1912, Glamis Archives

110 Laurel Gray to Queen Elizabeth, 1 December 1948, RA QEQMH/GEN/1948/Gray

111 Terry Wolsey, *Elizabeth of Glamis*, Canongate, 1990, p. 11

112 Joan Woollcombe, 'A Royal Birthday', *The Lady*, 31 July 1969; Vickers, p. 10

113 Lady May Bowes Lyon, diary, 22 December 1904, private collection

114 Asquith, *The Queen*, p. 56

115 Ibid., p. 54

116 Queen Elizabeth, conversations with Eric Anderson, 1994–5, RA QEQM/ADD/MISC; Lady Elizabeth Bowes Lyon, diary, 2, 3 June 1913, Glamis Archives

117 Author's interview with Lady Penn

118 Queen Elizabeth, conversations with Eric Anderson, 1994–5, RA QEQM/ADD/MISC

119 School reports, 30 Sloane Street, January–February 1912, March 1913, Glamis Archives, Box 270

120 Lady Elizabeth Bowes Lyon, diary, April 1913, RA QEQM/PRIV/DIARY/2

121 Käthe Kübler, *Meine Schülerin – die Königin von England*, Hermann Eichblatt, Leipzig, 1937, pp. 7–8, 10 (translation)

122 Ibid., p. 10

123 Ibid., p. 12

124 Ibid., p. 13

125 Ibid., pp. 18–19

126 Lady Elizabeth Bowes Lyon to the Hon. David Bowes Lyon, 18 July [1913], Glamis Archives

127 Frederick Dalrymple Hamilton, diary, 19–20 July 1913, private collection

128 Lady Elizabeth Bowes Lyon, diary, 1913, RA QEQM/PRIV/DIARY/2

129 Kübler, pp. 25–7

130 Lady Elizabeth Bowes Lyon to the Hon. David Bowes Lyon, 30 November 1913, Bowes Lyon Papers (SPW)

131 Kübler, pp. 11–12

132 Lady Elizabeth Bowes Lyon to Lady Strathmore, 25 June 1914, Glamis Archives (CH)

133 Lady Elizabeth Bowes Lyon to Lady Strathmore, 26 June 1914, Glamis Archives (CH)

134 Beryl Poignand to her mother, n.d. [8 December 1914], Poignand Papers. The same story appeared in Lady Cynthia Asquith's biography of the Duchess of York

135 Lady Elizabeth Bowes Lyon to Lady Strathmore, 25 June 1914, Glamis Archives (CH)

136 Lady Elizabeth Bowes Lyon to Lady Strathmore, 12 June 1914, Glamis Archives (CH)

137 Lady Elizabeth Bowes Lyon to the Hon. Michael Bowes Lyon, Glamis Archives (CH)

138 Kübler, p. 31

139 King George V, diary, RA GV/PRIV/GVD/1914: 3, 4 August

140 Queen Elizabeth, conversations with Eric Anderson, 1994–5, RA QEQM/ADD/MISC

TWO: TENDING THE WOUNDED 1914–1918

1 Quoted in Samuel Hynes, *The Auden Generation*, The Bodley Head, 1976, p. 18

2 John Terraine, *The First World War*, Leo Cooper, 1983, p. 8

3 Winston Churchill, *The World Crisis 1911–1918*, ed. Martin Gilbert, Free Press, London, 2005, p. 109

4 King George V, diary, 3 August 1914, RA GV/PRIV/GVD

5 Gilbert, *The First World War*, HarperCollins, 1995, p. 37

6 Ibid., pp. 37, 38

7 David Cannadine, *The Decline and Fall of the British Aristocracy*, Yale University Press, 1990, p. 72

8 Hon. Michael Bowes Lyon to Lady Strathmore, 8 August 1914, Glamis Archives

9 Hon. Fergus Bowes Lyon to Lady Strathmore, 9 September 1914, Glamis Archives

10 Asquith, *The Queen*, p. 59

11 Beryl Poignand to her mother, 11 December [1914], Poignand Papers

12 Beryl Poignand to her mother, n.d. [5/6 December 1914], Poignand Papers

13 Beryl Poignand to her mother, 21 November 1914, Poignand Papers

14 Asquith, *The Queen*, p. 59

15 Beryl Poignand to her mother, n.d. [20 November 1914], Poignand Papers

16 French dictations, August–September 1914, Glamis Archives, Box 270

17 Lady Strathmore to Beryl Poignand, 16 September 1914, Glamis Archives (CH)

18 Lady Strathmore to Beryl Poignand, 9 October 1914, Glamis Archives (CH)

19 Beryl Poignand to her mother, n.d. [20 November 1914], Poignand Papers

20 Beryl Poignand to her mother, 21 November [1914], Poignand Papers

21 Beryl Poignand to her mother, 22 November [1914], Poignand Papers

22 Ibid.

23 Lady Elizabeth Bowes Lyon to Beryl Poignand, 21 October 1917, Glamis Archives (CH)

24 Beryl Poignand to her mother, 22, [25] November, [5/6], 11 December [1914], 13 July [1915], Poignand Papers

25 Beryl Poignand to her mother, 22 November [1914], Poignand Papers

26 Beryl Poignand to her mother, n.d. [November1914], [8], 9, 14/15 December 1914, Poignand Papers

27 Beryl Poignand to her mother, n.d. [8 December 1914], Poignand Papers

28 Beryl Poignand to her mother, 22 November [1914], Poignand Papers

29 Beryl Poignand to her mother, 14–15 December [1914], Poignand Papers

30 Asquith, *The Queen*, p. 61

31 Beryl Poignand to her mother, n.d. [5/6 December 1914], Poignand Papers

32 Asquith, *The Queen*, p. 61

33 Beryl Poignand to her mother, 11 December [1914], Poignand Papers

34 Asquith, *The Queen*, p. 62

35 Beryl Poignand to her mother, n.d. [5/6, 8 December 1914], Poignand Papers

36 Asquith, *The Queen*, p. 60

37 Beryl Poignand to her mother, n.d. [8 December 1914], Poignand Papers

38 Beryl Poignand to her mother, 14/15 December [1914], Poignand Papers

39 Lines by J. Chadwick Brooks, 1st Battalion The London Scottish, January 1915, autograph book, RA QEQM/PRIV/PERS

40 Beryl Poignand to her mother, 14/15 December [1914], Poignand Papers

41 Lady Rose Bowes Lyon to Lady Delia Peel, undated [December 1915], Glamis Archives

42 Lady Elizabeth Bowes Lyon to Beryl Poignand, 26 December 1914, Glamis Archives (CH)

43 Frederick Dalrymple Hamilton, diary, 31 December 1914, private collection

44 Lady Strathmore to May Elphinstone, 3 January 1915, RA QEQM/OUT/ELPHINSTONE

45 Lady Strathmore to May Elphinstone, 1 March 1915, RA QEQM/OUT/ELPHINSTONE

46 Frederick Dalrymple Hamilton, diary, 17 January 1915, private collection; Beryl Poignand to her mother, 23 [February 1915], Poignand Papers

47 Lady Lavinia Spencer to the Hon. Cecil Spencer, 8 February 1915, Althorp Archives

48 Beryl Poignand to her mother, 31 March [1915], Poignand Papers

49 Beryl Poignand to her mother, n.d. [20 February 1915], Poignand Papers

50 Lady Strathmore to May Elphinstone, 24 February 1915, RA QEQM/OUT/ELPHINSTONE

51 Lady Strathmore to May Elphinstone, 6 March 1915, RA QEQM/OUT/ELPHINSTONE

52 Elizabeth Leeming interview with Lady Mary Clayton

53 Beryl Poignand to her mother, 9 March [1915], Poignand Papers

54 Queen Elizabeth, conversations with Eric Anderson, 1994–5, RA QEQM/ADD/MISC

55 Beryl Poignand to her mother, 30 May, 2 June [1915], Poignand Papers

56 Beryl Poignand to her mother, 15 May [1915], Poignand Papers

57 Beryl Poignand to her mother, 12 [May 1915]; 31 March [1915], Poignand Papers

58 Beryl Poignand to her mother, 13 July [1915], Poignand Papers

59 Lady Elizabeth Bowes Lyon to Beryl Poignand, 9 August 1915, Glamis Archives (CH)

60 Lady Elizabeth Bowes Lyon to Beryl Poignand, 26 August 1915, Glamis Archives (CH)

61 Lady Elizabeth Bowes Lyon to Beryl Poignand, 16 April 1916, Glamis Archives (CH)

62 Lady Lavinia Spencer to Lady Elizabeth Bowes Lyon, n.d. [12 August 1915], Glamis Archives, Box 270

63 Lady Lavinia Spencer to Lady Elizabeth Bowes Lyon, 17 September 1915, Glamis Archives, Box 270

64 Lady Katharine Hamilton to Lady Elizabeth Bowes Lyon, 6 September 1916, Glamis Archives

65 Lady Elizabeth Bowes Lyon to Beryl Poignand, 31 July 1915, Glamis Archives (CH)

66 Lady Elizabeth Bowes Lyon to Beryl Poignand, 6 August 1915, Glamis Archives (CH)

67 Ibid.

68 Lady Elizabeth Bowes Lyon to Beryl Poignand, 9 August 1915, Glamis Archives (CH)

69 Lady Elizabeth Bowes Lyon to Beryl Poignand, 9 August 1915, Glamis Archives (CH)

70 Asquith, *The Queen*, p. 67

71 Information from Clare Elmquist, daughter of Lydie Lachaise

72 Lady Elizabeth Bowes Lyon to Lady Strathmore, 14 September 1915, Glamis Archives, Box 270/II

73 Lady Elizabeth Bowes Lyon to Beryl Poignand, 16 September 1915, Glamis Archives (CH)

74 Lady Elizabeth Bowes Lyon to Lady Strathmore 19 September 1915, Glamis Archives, Box 270/II

75 Elizabeth Leeming interview with Lady Mary Clayton

76 Hon. Fergus Bowes Lyon to Lady Elizabeth Bowes Lyon, 26 April 1911, Glamis Archives (CH)

77 Hon. Fergus Bowes Lyon to [Lady Strathmore], 16 February 1914, Glamis Archives (CH)

78 Hon. Fergus Bowes Lyon to [Lady Strathmore], n.d., Glamis Archives

79 Reported in letter from Beryl Poignand to her mother, 23 June [1915], Poignand Papers

80 Terraine, p. 91

81 Ibid., p. 92

82 A. J. P. Taylor, *English History 1914–45*, Oxford University Press, 1961, p. 46

83 *Daily Mail* (overseas edition), 23 October 1915, quoted in Lyn Macdonald, *1914–1918: Voices and Images of the Great War*, Penguin, 1988

84 Lieutenant G. B. Gilroy to Lady Strathmore, 30 September 1915, Glamis Archives

85 Notes by Lady Strathmore of accounts of the death of Capt. The Hon. Fergus B. Lyon by Lance Corporal Andrew Ross, 10 November 1915, and Sergeant Lindsay, [10 December 1915]; Lieutenant G. B. Gilroy to Lady Strathmore, 30 September 1915; Cameron of Lochiel to Lady Strathmore, 10 October 1915, Glamis Archives

86 Lady Strathmore to Private William Vanbrick, 25 October 1916, Glamis Archives

87 Asquith, *The Queen*, p. 72

88 Leeming notes

89 Lady Lavinia Spencer to Lady Elizabeth Bowes Lyon, 5, 17 October 1915, Glamis Archives; Beryl Poignand to her mother, [October 1915], Poignand Papers

90 Gilbert, *First World War*, pp. 224–5

91 Ibid., p. 200

92 Lady Elizabeth Bowes Lyon to Mrs Poignand, 23 October 1915, Glamis Archives (CH)

93 Lady Elizabeth Bowes Lyon to Beryl Poignand, 30 October 1915, Glamis Archives (CH)

94 Gilbert, *First World War*, p. 203

95 Lady Elizabeth Bowes Lyon to Beryl Poignand, 1 November 1915, Glamis Archives (CH)

96 Lady Elizabeth Bowes Lyon to Beryl Poignand, 23 December 1915, Glamis Archives (CH)

97 Lady Elizabeth Bowes Lyon to Beryl Poignand, 26 December 1915, Glamis Archives (CH)

98 Gilbert, *First World War*, p. 201

99 Lady Elizabeth Bowes Lyon to Beryl Poignand, 31 December 1915, Glamis Archives (CH)

100 Lady Elizabeth Bowes Lyon to Mrs Poignand, 6 February 1916, Glamis Archives (CH)

101 Lady Elizabeth Bowes Lyon to Lady Strathmore, 17 March 1916, Glamis Archives (CH)

102 Lady Elizabeth Bowes Lyon to Lady Strathmore, 24, 25 March 1916, Glamis Archives (CH)

103 Lady Elizabeth Bowes Lyon to Lady Strathmore, 25 March 1916, Glamis Archives (CH)

104 Henry Ainley to Lady Elizabeth Bowes Lyon, 19 March 1916, Glamis Archives, Box 270

105 Printed form signed by Margaret E. Goodman, Local Secretary, Oxford Local Examinations Board, 1916, RA QEQM/PRIV/PERS/Education

106 Lady Elizabeth Bowes Lyon to Beryl Poignand, 26 April 1916, Glamis Archives (CH)

107 Lady Elizabeth Bowes Lyon to Lady Strathmore, 28 March 1916, Glamis Archives (CH)

108 Lady Elizabeth Bowes Lyon to Lady Strathmore, 4 April 1916, Glamis Archives (CH)

109 Beryl Poignand to her mother, n.d. [4–5 April 1916], Poignand Papers

110 Lady Elizabeth Bowes Lyon to Lady Strathmore, 4 April 1916, Glamis Archives (CH)

111 Lady Elizabeth Bowes Lyon to Beryl Poignand, 1 May 1916, Glamis Archives (CH)

112 Elizabeth Leeming interview with Lady Mary Clayton

113 Frederick Dalrymple Hamilton, diary, 3 April 1916, private collection

114 Lady Elizabeth Bowes Lyon to Beryl Poignand, 27 April 1916, Glamis Archives (CH)

115 Lady Elizabeth Bowes Lyon to Beryl Poignand, 26 April 1916, Glamis Archives (CH)

116 Lady Elizabeth Bowes Lyon to Beryl Poignand, 11 May 1916, Glamis Archives (CH)

117 Lady Elizabeth Bowes Lyon to Beryl Poignand, 21 May 1916, Glamis Archives (CH)

118 Lady Elizabeth Bowes Lyon to Beryl Poignand, 4 June 1916, Glamis Archives (CH)

119 Terraine, p. 106

120 Gilbert, *First World War*, p. 258

121 Ibid., p. 275

122 Terraine, pp. 116–17

123 Lady Elizabeth Bowes Lyon to Beryl Poignand, 21 July, 11 August 1916, Glamis Archives (CH)

124 Lady Elizabeth Bowes Lyon to Beryl Poignand, 22 September 1916, Glamis Archives (CH)

125 Lady Elizabeth Bowes Lyon to Beryl Poignand, 17 September 1916, Glamis Archives (CH)

126 Ibid.

127 Ibid.

128 Asquith, *The Queen*, p. 78

129 Forbes, p. 84

130 Hon. Michael Bowes Lyon to Lady Elizabeth Bowes Lyon, 24 September 1916, Glamis Archives

131 Lady Strathmore to Beryl Poignand, 22 September 1916, Glamis Archives (CH)

132 Lady Elizabeth Bowes Lyon to Beryl Poignand, 1 October 1916, Glamis Archives (CH)

133 Lady Elizabeth Bowes Lyon to Beryl Poignand, 22 September 1916, Glamis Archives (CH)

134 Lady Elizabeth Bowes Lyon to Beryl Poignand, 10, 20 October 1916, Glamis Archives (CH)

135 Lady Elizabeth Bowes Lyon to Beryl Poignand, 10, 25 October 1916, Glamis Archives (CH)

136 Lady Elizabeth Bowes Lyon to Beryl Poignand, 20 October 1916, Glamis Archives (CH)

137 Lady Elizabeth Bowes Lyon to Beryl Poignand, 25 October 1916, Glamis Archives (CH)

138 Ibid.

139 Lady Elizabeth Bowes Lyon to Beryl Poignand, 26 October 1916, Glamis Archives (CH)

140 Lady Elizabeth Bowes Lyon to Beryl Poignand, 3 November, 1 December 1916, Glamis Archives (CH)

141 Lady Elizabeth Bowes Lyon to Beryl Poignand, 3 November 1916, Glamis Archives (CH)

142 Lady Elizabeth Bowes Lyon to Beryl Poignand, 5 September 1916, Glamis Archives (CH)

143 Wolsey, p. 20

144 Lady Elizabeth Bowes Lyon to Beryl Poignand, 11 February 1917, Glamis Archives (CH)

145 Lady Elizabeth Bowes Lyon to Beryl Poignand, 7 April, 19 March 1917, Glamis Archives (CH)

146 Lady Elizabeth Bowes Lyon to Beryl Poignand, n.d. [24 March 1917], Glamis Archives (CH)

147 Lady Elizabeth Bowes Lyon to Beryl Poignand, 28 March 1917, Glamis Archives (CH)

148 Autograph by W. H. Harrap, 12 March 1917, Glamis Archives

149 Roberts, *History of the World*, p. 916

150 Gilbert, *First World War*, p. 318

151 Lady Elizabeth Bowes Lyon to Beryl Poignand, 24 April [1917], Glamis Archives (CH)

152 Lord Strathmore to Lady Rose Leveson-Gower, telegram, 3 May 1917, Glamis Archives

153 Lady Elizabeth Bowes Lyon to Beryl Poignand, 10 May 1917, Glamis Archives (CH)

154 Lady Elizabeth Bowes Lyon to Beryl Poignand, 3 May 1917, Glamis Archives (CH)

155 Lady Strathmore to Lady Elizabeth Bowes Lyon, 3 May 1917, Glamis Archives

156 Colonel A. Stephenson to Lord Strathmore, 2 May 1917, Glamis Archives

157 Colonel A. Stephenson to Lady Strathmore, 8 May 1917, Glamis Archives

158 Lady Elizabeth Bowes Lyon to Beryl Poignand, 6 May 1917, Glamis Archives (CH)

159 Lady Elizabeth Bowes Lyon to Beryl Poignand, 12 May 1917, Glamis Archives (CH)

160 Asquith, *The Queen*, p. 52

161 Lady Elizabeth Bowes Lyon to Beryl Poignand, 22 May 1917, Glamis Archives (CH)

162 Lady Elizabeth Bowes Lyon to Beryl Poignand, 25 May 1917, Glamis Archives (CH)

163 Hon. Michael Bowes Lyon to Lady Strathmore, 4 May 1917, Glamis Archives, Box 69, bundle 9

164 Hon. Michael Bowes Lyon to Lady Elizabeth Bowes Lyon, 10 June 1917, RA QEQM/ PRIV/BL

165 Hon. Michael Bowes Lyon, diary, 23 June 1917, Glamis Archives

166 Lady Elizabeth Bowes Lyon to Beryl Poignand, [22 or 29] August 1917, Glamis Archives (CH)

167 Lady Elizabeth Bowes Lyon to Beryl Poignand, 15 September 1917, Glamis Archives (CH)

168 Hon. Michael Bowes Lyon to Lady Strathmore, 17 February, 24 April 1918, Glamis Archives

169 Lady Elizabeth Bowes Lyon to Beryl Poignand, 17 June 1917, Glamis Archives (CH); Clerk of Forfar School Board to Lady Elizabeth Bowes Lyon, 9 June 1917, Glamis Archives, Box 270

170 Lady Elizabeth Bowes Lyon to Beryl Poignand, 20 June 1917, Glamis Archives (CH)

171 Lady Elizabeth Bowes Lyon to Beryl Poignand, 28 June 1917, Glamis Archives (CH)

172 Ibid.

173 Lady Elizabeth Bowes Lyon to Beryl Poignand, 7 September 1917, Glamis Archives (CH)

174 Lady Elizabeth Bowes Lyon to Beryl Poignand, 16 July 1917, Glamis Archives (CH)

175 Lady Elizabeth Bowes Lyon to Beryl Poignand, [22 or 29] August 1917, Glamis Archives (CH)

176 Lady Elizabeth Bowes Lyon to Beryl Poignand, 7 September 1917, Glamis Archives (CH)

177 Lady Elizabeth Bowes Lyon to Beryl Poignand, 29 September 1917, Glamis Archives (CH)

178 Lady Elizabeth Bowes Lyon to Beryl Poignand, 9 October 1917, Glamis Archives (CH)

179 Ibid.

180 Lady Elizabeth Bowes Lyon to Beryl Poignand, 18, 21 October 1917, Glamis Archives (CH)

181 Lady Elizabeth Bowes Lyon to Beryl Poignand, 29 September 1917, Glamis Archives (CH)

182 Private C. Morris to Lady Elizabeth Bowes Lyon, n.d. [October 1917], RA QEQM/ PRIV/PAL

183 Lady Elizabeth Bowes Lyon to Beryl Poignand, 26 November 1917, Glamis Archives (CH)

184 Ibid.

185 Lady Elizabeth Bowes Lyon to Beryl Poignand, 8 November 1917, Glamis Archives (CH)
186 Lady Elizabeth Bowes Lyon to Beryl Poignand, 5 January 1918, Glamis Archives (CH)
187 Lady Elizabeth Bowes Lyon to Beryl Poignand, 22 November 1917, Glamis Archives (CH)
188 Lady Elizabeth Bowes Lyon to Beryl Poignand, 31 October 1917, Glamis Archives (CH)
189 Lady Elizabeth Bowes Lyon to Beryl Poignand, 22, 26 November 1917, Glamis Archives (CH)
190 Lady Elizabeth Bowes Lyon to Beryl Poignand, 13 December 1917, Glamis Archives (CH)
191 Lady Elizabeth Bowes Lyon to Beryl Poignand, 7 December 1917, Glamis Archives (CH)
192 Lady Elizabeth Bowes Lyon to Beryl Poignand, 5 January 1918, Glamis Archives (CH)
193 Lady Elizabeth Bowes Lyon to Beryl Poignand, 9 January 1918, Glamis Archives (CH)
194 Hon. Michael Bowes Lyon to Lady Strathmore, 17 February 1918, Glamis Archives
195 Lady Elizabeth Bowes Lyon to Beryl Poignand, 7 February 1918, Glamis Archives (CH)
196 Lady Elizabeth Bowes Lyon to Beryl Poignand, 26 February 1918, Glamis Archives (CH)
197 Lady Elizabeth Bowes Lyon to Beryl Poignand, 13 March 1918, Glamis Archives (CH)
198 Lady Elizabeth Bowes Lyon to Beryl Poignand, 22 March 1918, Glamis Archives (CH)
199 Hon. Victor Cochrane Baillie to Lady Elizabeth Bowes Lyon, 29 March 1918, RA QEQM/PRIV/PAL
200 Lady Elizabeth Bowes Lyon to Beryl Poignand, 22 March 1918, Glamis Archives (CH)
201 Lady Elizabeth Bowes Lyon to Beryl Poignand, 20 April 1918, Glamis Archives (CH)
202 Lady Elizabeth Bowes Lyon to Beryl Poignand, 29 April 1918, Glamis Archives (CH)
203 George Lancelot Thirkell to Lady Elizabeth Bowes Lyon, 3 May 1918, RA QEQM/PRIV/PAL
204 Lady Elizabeth Bowes Lyon to Beryl Poignand, 26, 29 May 1918, Glamis Archives (CH)
205 Lady Elizabeth Bowes Lyon to Beryl Poignand, 13 June 1918, Glamis Archives (CH)
206 Lady Elizabeth Bowes Lyon to Beryl Poignand, [20 and 25] June, 5 July 1918, Glamis Archives (CH)
207 Lady Elizabeth Bowes Lyon to Beryl Poignand, 25 June 1918, Glamis Archives (CH)
208 Lady Elizabeth Bowes Lyon to Beryl Poignand, 12, 31 August, 15, 21 September 1918, Glamis Archives (CH)
209 Lieutenant J. S. Reynolds to Lady Elizabeth Bowes Lyon, 30 September 1918, RA QEQM/PRIV/PAL
210 Lady Elizabeth Bowes Lyon to Beryl Poignand, 5 October 1918, Glamis Archives (CH)
211 Lady Elizabeth Bowes Lyon to Beryl Poignand, 22 October 1918, Glamis Archives (CH)
212 Queen Elizabeth, conversations with Eric Anderson, 1994–5, RA QEQM/ADD/MISC
213 Terraine, p. 185
214 Roberts, *History of the World*, p. 920
215 Lady Elizabeth Bowes Lyon to Beryl Poignand, 27 November 1918, Glamis Archives (CH)
216 Lady Elizabeth Bowes Lyon to Beryl Poignand, 5 January 1919, Glamis Archives (CH)
217 Lady Elizabeth Bowes Lyon to Beryl Poignand, n.d. [6 April 1919], Glamis Archives (CH)
218 Queen Elizabeth, conversations with Eric Anderson, 1994–5, RA QEQM/ADD/MISC
219 Lady Elizabeth Bowes Lyon to Beryl Poignand, n.d. [6 April 1919], Glamis Archives (CH)
220 Lady Elizabeth Bowes Lyon to Beryl Poignand, n.d. [6 April 1919], 17 April 1919, Glamis Archives (CH)
221 Lady Elizabeth Bowes Lyon to Beryl Poignand, 25 May 1919, Glamis Archives (CH)
222 Longford, *The Royal House of Windsor*, p. 76
223 Lady Elizabeth Bowes Lyon to Beryl Poignand, 11 August 1919, n.d. [August 1919], 22 August 1919, Glamis Archives (CH)

224 Lady Elizabeth Bowes Lyon to Beryl Poignand, 22 August 1919, Glamis Archives (CH)
225 Lady Elizabeth Bowes Lyon to Beryl Poignand, n.d. [late August–early September 1919], Glamis Archives (CH)

THREE: PRINCE ALBERT 1918–1923

1 Lady Elizabeth Bowes Lyon to Beryl Poignand, 22 November 1916, Glamis Archives (CH)
2 Lord Chamberlain's Annual Report, 1919, RA LC/AR/1919/48
3 RA QM/PRIV/QMD/1919: 17 June; RA GV/PRIV/GVD/1919: 17 June
4 Lady Elizabeth Bowes Lyon to Beryl Poignand, n.d. [1 July 1919], Glamis Archives (CH)
5 Lady Katharine Hamilton to Lady Elizabeth Bowes Lyon, 2 October 1919; Lady Lavinia White to Lady Elizabeth Bowes Lyon, 16 October 1919, Glamis Archives
6 Lady Elizabeth Bowes Lyon to Beryl Poignand, 28 December 1919, Glamis Archives (CH)
7 Lady Elizabeth Bowes Lyon to Beryl Poignand, Friday n.d. [9 January 1920], Glamis Archives (CH)
8 Lady Elizabeth Bowes Lyon to Beryl Poignand, n.d. [8 March 1920], Glamis Archives (CH)
9 RA QM/PRIV/QMD/1920: 9 March
10 Holyrood Palace menu, 5 July 1920, RA MRH/MISC/055/04; Lady Elizabeth Bowes Lyon to Beryl Poignand, 13 July 1920, Glamis Archives (CH)
11 Viscount Stuart of Findhorn, *Within the Fringe*, The Bodley Head, 1967, p. 57
12 Lady Elizabeth Bowes Lyon to Beryl Poignand, 13 July 1920, Glamis Archives (CH)
13 Mabell Airlie, *Thatched with Gold*, ed. Jennifer Ellis, Hutchinson, 1962, p. 166
14 John Wheeler-Bennett, *King George VI*, Macmillan, 1958. p. 4
15 RA VIC/MAIN/QVJ/1895: 14 December
16 Wheeler-Bennett, p. 8
17 Harold Nicolson, *King George V*, Pan Books, 1967, pp. 473–4
18 Wheeler-Bennett, p. 17
19 Sarah Bradford, *George VI*, Penguin, 2002, p. 47
20 Nicolson, *George V*, p. 154
21 Bradford, *George VI*, p. 62
22 Wheeler-Bennett, p. 60
23 Ibid., p. 57
24 Ibid., p. 76
25 Ibid., p. 77
26 Bradford, *George VI*, p. 87
27 Wheeler-Bennett, pp. 95–6
28 Ibid., p. 117
29 Robert Graves and Alan Hodge, *The Long Weekend*, Faber & Faber, 1940, pp. 23–4
30 Frank Prochaska, *The Republic of Britain 1760–2000*, Allen Lane, 2000, p. 178
31 Ibid., p. 174
32 Wheeler-Bennett, p. 157
33 Ibid., p. 164
34 Ibid., pp. 165–72
35 Ibid., pp. 126–32
36 Bradford, *George VI*, p. 92
37 Airlie, pp. 162–3

38 Princess Dimitri, 'Waltzing Matilda' (unpublished memoirs of Lady Loughborough), 1948, p. 38, private collection

39 Ibid., p. 39

40 Prince Albert to Prince of Wales, 7 April 1920, RA EDW/PRIV/MAINB/50

41 Prince Albert to Prince of Wales, 13 April, 16 May 1920, RA EDW/PRIV/MAINB/51, 53

42 King George V to Prince Albert, 7 June 1920, quoted in Wheeler-Bennett, p. 140

43 Prince Albert to King George V, 6 June 1920, RA GV/PRIV/AA61/27

44 Prince Albert to Prince of Wales, 25 May 1920, RA EDW/PRIV/MAINB/54A

45 Lady Elizabeth Bowes Lyon to Beryl Poignand n.d. [in envelope with postmark 9 March 1920], Glamis Archives (CH)

46 Lady Elizabeth Bowes Lyon to Beryl Poignand, n.d. [29 March 1920], Glamis Archives (CH)

47 Lady Elizabeth Bowes Lyon to Beryl Poignand, n.d. [7 April 1920], Glamis Archives (CH)

48 Queen Elizabeth, conversations with Eric Anderson, 1994–5, RA QEQM/ADD/MISC

49 Forbes, p. 117

50 Ibid., p. 125

51 Lady Elizabeth Bowes Lyon to Beryl Poignand, n.d. [22 March 1919, November 1919], Glamis Archives (CH)

52 Lady Elizabeth Bowes Lyon to Beryl Poignand, 11 June and 13 July 1920, Glamis Archives (CH)

53 Helen Cecil to Captain Hardinge, n.d. [18 September 1920], Hardinge Papers, Centre for Kentish Studies, Maidstone, U 2117-C2/33

54 Prince Albert to Prince of Wales, 21 July 1920, RA EDW/PRIV/MAINB/57

55 Longford, Queen Mother, p. 18

56 Lady Elizabeth Bowes Lyon to Beryl Poignand, n.d. [14 September 1920], Glamis Archives (CH)

57 Helen Cecil to Lady Milner, 15 September 1920, Bodleian Library, VM28/C 103/74

58 Captain Hardinge to Helen Cecil, 11, 13 September 1920, Hardinge Papers, Centre for Kentish Studies, U 2117-C1/19, 21

59 Helen Cecil to Captain Hardinge, n.d. [14 September 1920], Hardinge Papers, Centre for Kentish Studies, U 2117-C2/28

60 Helen Cecil to Captain Hardinge, n.d. [18 September 1920], Hardinge Papers, Centre for Kentish Studies, U 2117-C2/33

61 Helen Cecil to Captain Hardinge, n.d. [18 September 1920] and 20 September 1920, Hardinge Papers, Centre for Kentish Studies, U 2117-C2/35, 36

62 Helen Cecil to Captain Hardinge, n.d. [19 September 1920], Hardinge Papers, Centre for Kentish Studies, U 2117-C2/34

63 Lady Elizabeth Bowes Lyon to Beryl Poignand, n.d. [23 September 1920], Glamis Archives (CH)

64 Helen Cecil to Captain Hardinge, n.d. [19 September 1920], Hardinge Papers, Centre for Kentish Studies, U 2117-C2/34

65 Lady Elizabeth Bowes Lyon to Beryl Poignand, n.d. [23 September 1920], Glamis Archives (CH)

66 Helen Cecil to Captain Hardinge, n.d. [19 September 1920] and 20 September 1920, Hardinge Papers, Centre for Kentish Studies, U 2117-C2/34, 36

67 Helen Cecil to Captain Hardinge, 20 September 1920, Hardinge Papers, Centre for Kentish Studies, U 2117-C2/36

68 Helen Cecil to Lady Elizabeth Bowes Lyon, 21 September 1920, Glamis Archives, Letters from friends

69 Lady Elizabeth Bowes Lyon to Beryl Poignand, n.d. [23 September 1920], Glamis Archives (CH)

70 Duke of York to Lady Strathmore, 21 September 1920, Glamis Archives

71 Hon. James Stuart to Lady Strathmore, 21 September 1920, Glamis Archives

72 Lady Doris Gordon-Lennox to Lady Elizabeth Bowes Lyon, 21 September 1920, Glamis Archives, Letters from girlfriends; Helen Cecil to Lady Elizabeth Bowes Lyon, 21 September 1920, Glamis Archives, Letters from friends

73 Lady Doris Gordon-Lennox to Lady Elizabeth Bowes Lyon, n.d. [14 October 1920], Glamis Archives, Letters from girlfriends

74 Lady Elizabeth Bowes Lyon to Beryl Poignand, n.d. [November 1920], Glamis Archives (CH)

75 Lady Elizabeth Bowes Lyon to Beryl Poignand, n.d. [November or December 1920], Glamis Archives (CH)

76 Lady Elizabeth Bowes Lyon to Duke of York, Monday, n.d. [13 December 1920], RA GVI/PRIV/RF/26/01

77 Lady Elizabeth Bowes Lyon to Duke of York, n.d. [23 December 1920], RA GVI/PRIV/RF/26/02

78 Lady Elizabeth Bowes Lyon to Beryl Poignand, Friday, n.d. [31 December 1920], Glamis Archives (CH)

79 Lady Elizabeth Bowes Lyon to Duke of York, n.d. [6 January 1921], RA GVI/PRIV/RF/26/03

80 Lady Elizabeth Bowes Lyon to Beryl Poignand, Sunday, n.d. [9 January 1921], Glamis Archives (CH)

81 Lady Elizabeth Bowes Lyon to Duke of York, 10 January 1921, RA GVI/PRIV/RF/26/04

82 Lady Elizabeth Bowes Lyon to Beryl Poignand, n.d. [1 February 1921], Glamis Archives (CH)

83 Airlie, p. 167

84 Lady Elizabeth Bowes Lyon to Duke of York, n.d. [17 February 1921], RA GVI/PRIV/RF/26/05

85 Lady Elizabeth Bowes Lyon to Duke of York, 28 February 1921, RA GVI/PRIV/RF/26/07

86 Lady Elizabeth Bowes Lyon to Duke of York, n.d. [7 March 1921], RA GVI/PRIV/RF/26/08

87 Lady Strathmore to Lady Airlie, 5 March 1921, British Library, Add MSS 82762

88 Queen Mary to Lady Airlie, 9 March 1921, British Library, Add MSS 82748

89 Lady Elizabeth Bowes Lyon to Duke of York, n.d. [25 March 1921], RA GVI/PRIV/RF/26/08

90 King George V to Queen Alexandra, 10 April 1921, RA GV/PRIV/AA38/20

91 Duke of York, engagement diary, 9 April 1921, RA PS/PSO/GVI/C 352/1921

92 Lady Elizabeth Bowes Lyon to Beryl Poignand, 12 April 1921, Glamis Archives (CH)

93 Nicolson, *George V*, p. 444

94 Philip Ziegler, *King Edward VIII*, Collins, 1990, pp. 111–12

95 Lady Elizabeth Bowes Lyon to Beryl Poignand, Wednesday n.d. [18 May 1921], Glamis Archives (CH)

96 Helen Hardinge, *Loyal to Three Kings*, William Kimber, 1967, p. 23

97 Prince Paul of Serbia to Lady Elizabeth Bowes Lyon, 8 May 1921, Glamis Archives, Box 270

98 Lady Elizabeth Bowes Lyon to Duke of York, 28 May 1921, RA GVI/PRIV/RF/26/10

99 Lady Elizabeth Bowes Lyon to Beryl Poignand, 28 May 1921, Glamis Archives (CH)

100 Lady Elizabeth Bowes Lyon to Duke of York, 28 May 1921, RA GVI/PRIV/RF/26/10

101 Lady Elizabeth Bowes Lyon to Duke of York, 9 June 1921, RA GVI/PRIV/RF/26/11

102 Lady Elizabeth Bowes Lyon to Duke of York, n.d. [18 July 1921], RA GVI/PRIV/RF/26/12

103 Lady Elizabeth Bowes Lyon to Duke of York, 6 August 1921, RA GVI/PRIV/RF/26/13
104 Ibid.
105 RA QM/PRIV/QMD/1921: 9 September
106 Airlie, p. 167
107 Queen Mary to Duke of York, 28 September 1921, RA GVI/PRIV/RF/11
108 Duke of York to Queen Mary, 29 September 1921, RA QM/PRIV/CC11/19
109 Duke of York to King George V, 2 October 1921, RA GV/PRIV/AA61/88
110 Duke of York to Lady Elizabeth Bowes Lyon, 2 October 1921, Glamis Archives, Box 270
111 Lady Airlie to Queen Mary, 2 October 1921, RA QM/PRIV/CC47/684
112 Lady Elizabeth Bowes Lyon to Beryl Poignand, Friday, n.d. [7 October 1921], Glamis Archives (CH)
113 Lady Elizabeth Bowes Lyon to Duke of York, 4 October 1921, RA GVI/PRIV/RF/26/15
114 Lady Elizabeth Bowes Lyon to Duke of York, 11 October 1921, RA GVI/PRIV/RF/26/16
115 Duke of York to Lady Elizabeth Bowes Lyon, 12 October 1921, Glamis Archives, Box 270
116 Undated note from Lady Strathmore to Mollie Cazalet, enclosed with letter from Mollie Cazalet to Queen Elizabeth, 8 August 1938, RA QEQM/PRIV/PAL
117 Lady Elizabeth Bowes Lyon to Duke of York, 8 November 1921, RA GVI/PRIV/RF/26/18
118 Duke of York to Queen Mary, 18 November 1921, RA QM/PRIV/CC11/20
119 Lady Elizabeth Bowes Lyon to Duke of York, n.d. [23 November 1921], RA GVI/PRIV/RF/26/20
120 Lady Elizabeth Bowes Lyon to Beryl Poignand, n.d. [28 November 1921], Glamis Archives (CH)
121 Stuart, *Within the Fringe*, pp. 44–57
122 Queen Mary to Lady Elizabeth Bowes Lyon, 19 October 1921, RA QEQM/PRIV/RF
123 Queen Mary to Lady Strathmore, 26 November 1921, Glamis Archives
124 Lady Elizabeth Bowes Lyon to Duke of York, n.d. [23 November 1921], RA GVI/PRIV/RF/26/20
125 Lady Elizabeth Bowes Lyon to Duke of York, 16 December 1921, RA GVI/PRIV/RF/26/21
126 Lady Elizabeth Bowes Lyon to Duke of York, n.d. [December 1921], RA GVI/PRIV/RF/26/22
127 Glamis Visitors' Book, Glamis Archives
128 Vickers, pp. 47–8
129 Princess Margaret to Queen Elizabeth II, 8 March 1954, RA QEII/PRIV/RF
130 Queen Elizabeth, conversations with Eric Anderson, 1994–5, RA QEQM/ADD/MISC
131 Lady Elizabeth Bowes Lyon to Beryl Poignand, n.d. [28 November 1921], Glamis Archives (CH)
132 Princess Mary to Lady Elizabeth Bowes Lyon, 5 January 1922, RA QEQM/PRIV/RF
133 Duke of York to Queen Mary, 19 January 1922, RA QM/PRIV/CC11/23
134 Queen Mary to Duke of York, 22 January 1922, RA GVI/PRIV/RF/11
135 Duke of York to Queen Mary, 25 January 1922, RA QM/PRIV/CC11/24
136 Duke of York to Prince of Wales, 2 February 1922, RA EDW/PRIV/MAIN/B/67
137 Duke of York to Lady Elizabeth Bowes Lyon, 6 February 1922, Glamis Archives, Box 270; Lady Elizabeth Bowes Lyon to Duke of York, n.d. [7 February 1922], RA GVI/PRIV/RF/26/24
138 Lady Elizabeth Bowes Lyon to Beryl Poignand, n.d. [6 February 1922], Glamis Archives (CH)

139 Lady Elizabeth Bowes Lyon to Duke of York, 23 February 1922, RA GVI/PRIV/RF/26/25

140 Longford, *Queen Mother*, p. 23

141 Lady Elizabeth Bowes Lyon to Duke of York, n.d. [8 March 1922], RA GVI/PRIV/RF/26/26

142 Duke of York to Lady Elizabeth Bowes Lyon, 8 March 1922, RA QEQM/PRIV/RF

143 Lady Elizabeth Bowes Lyon to Duke of York, n.d. [12 March 1922], RA GVI/PRIV/RF/26/27

144 Duke of York to Lady Elizabeth Bowes Lyon, 16 March 1922, RA QEQM/PRIV/RF

145 Lady Elizabeth Bowes Lyon to Duke of York, 18 March 1922, RA GVI/PRIV/RF/26/28

146 Duke of York to Lady Elizabeth Bowes Lyon, 26 March 1922, RA QEQM/PRIV/RF

147 Hon. James Stuart to Lady Elizabeth Bowes Lyon, 24 March 1922, RA QEQM/PRIV/PAL

148 Vickers, p. 50

149 Lady Elizabeth Bowes Lyon to Beryl Poignand, n.d. [May 1922], Glamis Archives (CH)

150 Queen Mary to Lady Strathmore, 6 May 1922, Glamis Archives

151 Lady Strathmore to May Elphinstone, 16 May 1922, RA QEQM/OUT/ELPHINSTONE

152 Lady Elizabeth Bowes Lyon to Duke of York, n.d. [16 May 1922], RA GVI/PRIV/RF/26/29

153 Lady Elizabeth Bowes Lyon to May Elphinstone, n.d. [12 May 1922], RA QEQM/OUT/ELPHINSTONE

154 Lady Elizabeth Bowes Lyon to Beryl Poignand, n.d. [14 May 1922], Glamis Archives (CH)

155 Lord Gage to Lady Elizabeth Bowes Lyon, 26 May 1922, RA QEQM/PRIV/PAL

156 Lord Glenconner to Duchess of York, 7 May [1931], RA QEQM/PRIV/PAL

157 Lord Davidson to Queen Elizabeth, 26 February 1952, enclosing account of conversation with Duke of York, RA QEQM/PRIV/PAL

158 Duke of York to Queen Mary, 12 January 1923, RA QM/PRIV/CC11/21

159 Lady Elizabeth Bowes Lyon to Duke of York, n.d. [26 July 1922], RA GVI/PRIV/RF/26/30

160 Information from Donald Gillies, biographer of Lord Inverchapel. Donald Gillies suggests that Clark Kerr may have met Lady Elizabeth first the previous autumn in Scotland, but if so there is no evidence of this in her papers

161 Archibald Clark Kerr to Lady Elizabeth Bowes Lyon, 3 December 1922, RA QEQM/PRIV/PAL

162 Lady Elizabeth Bowes Lyon to D'Arcy Osborne, [26] October 1922, RA QEQM/OUT/OSBORNE

163 Lady Elizabeth Bowes Lyon to Duke of York, 12 September 1922, RA GVI/PRIV/RF/26/31B

164 Duke of York to King George V, 30 September 1922, RA GV/PRIV/AA61/128; Duke of York to Queen Mary, 30 September 1922, RA QM/PRIV/CC11/28

165 *'Chips': The Diaries of Sir Henry Channon*, ed. Robert Rhodes James, Penguin, 1967, p. 483

166 Rev. Dr John Stirton, diary, RA AEC/GG/026

167 Lady Elizabeth Bowes Lyon to Duke of York, 3 October 1922, RA GVI/PRIV/RF/26/34

168 Duke of York to Queen Mary, 4 October 1922, RA QM/PRIV/CC11/29

169 Lady Elizabeth Bowes Lyon to Duke of York, 7 November 1922, RA GVI/PRIV/RF/26/36

170 Duke of York to Lady Elizabeth Bowes Lyon, 8 November 1922, RA QEQM/PRIV/RF

171 Duke of York to Lady Elizabeth Bowes Lyon, 27 November 1922, RA QEQM/PRIV/RF

172 Duke of York to Lady Elizabeth Bowes Lyon, 30 November 1922, RA QEQM/PRIV/RF

173 Lady Elizabeth Bowes Lyon to Duke of York, n.d. [6 and 7 December 1922], RA GVI/PRIV/RF/26/42–43

174 Duke of York to Lady Elizabeth Bowes Lyon, 16 December 1922, RA QEQM/PRIV/RF

175 Lady Airlie to Lady Strathmore, draft, 23 December 1922, British Library, Add MSS 82763

176 Lady Elizabeth Bowes Lyon to Duke of York, 25 December 1922, RA GVI/PRIV/RF/26/47

177 Duke of York to Lady Airlie, 30 January 1923, British Library, Add MSS 82751

178 Duke of York to Lady Elizabeth Bowes Lyon, 29 December 1922, RA QEQM/PRIV/RF

179 Lady Elizabeth Bowes Lyon to Duke of York, 30 December 1922, RA GVI/PRIV/RF/26/48

180 Lady Elizabeth Bowes Lyon to Beryl Poignand, 2 January [1923], Glamis Archives (CH)

181 Lady Elizabeth Bowes Lyon to Duke of York, 4 January 1923, RA GVI/PRIV/RF/26/49

182 Lady Elizabeth Bowes Lyon, diary, 4 January 1923, RA QEQM/PRIV/DIARY/3

183 Lady Elizabeth Bowes Lyon, diary, 5 January 1923, RA QEQM/PRIV/DIARY/3

184 Bradford, *George VI*, p. 137; Vickers, p. 58

185 Bradford, *George VI*, p. 137

186 Lady Elizabeth Bowes Lyon, diary, 5 January 1923, RA QEQM/PRIV/DIARY/3

187 Lady Elizabeth Bowes Lyon, diary, 8 January 1923, RA QEQM/PRIV/DIARY/3

188 Lady Elizabeth Bowes Lyon to Duke of York, n.d. [8 January 1923], RA GVI/PRIV/RF/26/50

189 Lady Elizabeth Bowes Lyon, diary, 11 January 1923, RA QEQM/PRIV/DIARY/3

190 Queen Mary to Lady Airlie, 9 January 1923, British Library, Add MSS 82748

191 Queen Elizabeth, conversations with Eric Anderson, 1994–5, RA QEQM/ADD/MISC

192 Duke of York to Queen Mary, 12 January 1923, RA QM/PRIV/CC11/21

193 Lady Elizabeth Bowes Lyon, diary, 12 January 1923, RA QEQM/PRIV/DIARY/3

194 Lady Elizabeth Bowes Lyon, diary, 13 January 1923, RA QEQM/PRIV/DIARY/3

195 Lady Strathmore to May Elphinstone, 16 January 1923, RA QEQM/OUT/ELPHINSTONE

196 RA GV/PRIV/GVD/1923: 15 January; QM/PRIV/QMD/1923: 15 January

197 Lady Elizabeth Bowes Lyon to Arthur Penn, n.d. [15 January 1923], Penn Papers

198 Lady Elizabeth Bowes Lyon, diary, 15 January 1923, RA QEQM/PRIV/DIARY/3

Four: A Royal Wedding 1923

1 Lady Elizabeth Bowes Lyon, diary, 16 January 1923. RA QEQM/PRIV/DIARY/3

2 King George V to Lady Elizabeth Bowes Lyon, 15 January 1923, RA QEQM/PRIV/RF

3 Queen Mary to Lady Elizabeth Bowes Lyon, 15 January 1923, RA QEQM/PRIV/RF

4 Queen Mary to Lady Strathmore, 15 January 1923, Glamis Archives (CH)

5 Lady Strathmore to Queen Mary, 16 January 1923, RA QM/PRIV/CC47/737

6 Duke of York to Queen Mary, 16 January 1923, RA QM/PRIV/CC11/22

7 Lady Elizabeth Bowes Lyon to King George V, 17 January 1923, RA GV/PRIV/AA61/342

8 Lady Elizabeth Bowes Lyon to Queen Mary, 17 January 1923, RA QM/PRIV/CC 11/34

9 Lady Strathmore to May Elphinstone, 16 January 1923, RA QEQM/OUT/ELPHINSTONE

10 *Evening News*, 17 January 1923

11 Charles Graves, *The Bad Old Days*, Faber & Faber, 1951, pp. 70–1

12 Queen Mary to Duke of York, 18 January 1923, RA GVI/PRIV/RF/11

13 Lady Elizabeth Bowes Lyon, diary, 16–18 January 1923, RA QEQM/PRIV/DIARY/3

14 Prince of Wales to Duchess of York, 15 January 1923, RA QEQM/PRIV/RF

15 Lady Elizabeth Bowes Lyon to Arthur Penn, n.d. [18 January 1923], Penn Papers

16 Lady Strathmore to Arthur Penn, 18 January 1923, Penn Papers

17 Lady Elizabeth Bowes Lyon to D'Arcy Osborne, 17 January, 1923, RA QEQM/OUT/OSBORNE

18 Lady Elizabeth Bowes Lyon, diary, 19 January 1923, RA QEQM/PRIV/DIARY/3

19 Lady Elizabeth Bowes Lyon, diary, 20 January 1923. RA QEQM/PRIV/DIARY/3

20 Wheeler-Bennett, p. 151

21 RA GV/PRIV/GVD/1923: 20 January; RA QM/PRIV/QMD/1923: 20–21 January

22 Queen Elizabeth to Charles, Prince of Wales, n.d. [1960s], Clarence House Archives, 10086–600

23 RA QM/PRIV/QMD/1923: 20 January

24 Duke of York to Lady Leicester, 21 January 1923, Glamis Archives

25 Lady Elizabeth Bowes Lyon to May Elphinstone, n.d. [20 January 1923], RA QEQM/OUT/ELPHINSTONE

26 Lady Elizabeth Bowes Lyon to Beryl Poignand, 21 January 1923, Glamis Archives (CH)

27 Michael Bowes Lyon to Lady Elizabeth Bowes Lyon, 20 January 1923, RA QEQM/PRIV/BL

28 Lady Elizabeth Bowes Lyon, diary, 1 February 1923, RA QEQM/PRIV/DIARY/3

29 Lord Gage to Lady Elizabeth Bowes Lyon, 19 January 1923, RA QEQM/PRIV/PAL

30 Archibald Clark Kerr to Lady Elizabeth Bowes Lyon, 24 January 1923, RA QEQM/PRIV/PAL

31 Lady Elizabeth Bowes Lyon, diary, 21 January 1923, RA QEQM/PRIV/DIARY/3

32 Duke of York to Queen Mary, 23 January 1923, RA QM/PRIV/CC11/35

33 Queen Mary to Duke of York, 24 January 1923, RA GVI/PRIV/RF/11

34 King George V to first Lord Hardinge of Penshurst, 27 January 1923, RA QEQM/PRIV/PAL (enclosed with letter from Lord Hardinge to Queen Elizabeth, 22 July 1937)

35 Queen Mary to Lady Strathmore, 25 January 1923, Glamis Archives

36 Lady Elizabeth Bowes Lyon, diary, 22 January 1923, RA QEQM/PRIV/DIARY/3

37 Queen Mary to Duke of York, 24 January 1923, RA GVI/PRIV/RF/11

38 Wheeler-Bennett, pp. 187–8

39 Lady Elizabeth Bowes Lyon, diary, 23 January 1923, RA QEQM/PRIV/DIARY/3

40 Lady Elizabeth Bowes Lyon to Queen Mary, 25 January 1923, RA QM/PRIV/CC11/36

41 Lady Elizabeth Bowes Lyon, diary, 26 January 1923, RA QEQM/PRIV/DIARY/3

42 Lady Elizabeth Bowes Lyon to Duke of York, n.d. [25 January 1923], RA GVI/PRIV/RF/26/51

43 Duke of York to Lady Elizabeth Bowes Lyon, n.d. [25] and 26 January 1923, RA QEQM/PRIV/RF

44 Lady Elizabeth Bowes Lyon, diary, 27 January 1923, RA QEQM/PRIV/DIARY/3

45 King George V to Prince George, 31 January 1923, RA GV/PRIV/AA61/152

46 Lady Elizabeth Bowes Lyon, diary, 4 February 1923, RA QEQM/PRIV/DIARY/3

47 Duke of York to Lady Strathmore, 30 January 1923, Glamis Archives

48 Lady Strathmore to Duke of York, 1 February 1923, RA GVI/PRIV/PAL/S/32

49 Duke of York to Lady Airlie, 30 January 1923, pencil copy by Lady Airlie, British Library, Add MSS 82751

50 Lady Elizabeth Bowes Lyon to Beryl Poignand, 4 February 1923, Glamis Archives (CH)

51 Lady Elizabeth Bowes Lyon, diary, 6 February 1923, RA QEQM/PRIV/DIARY/3

52 RA QM/PRIV/QMD/1923: 8 February

53 Laird, p. 72

54 Lady Elizabeth Bowes Lyon, diary, 8 February 1923, RA QEQM/PRIV/DIARY/3

55 Lady Elizabeth Bowes Lyon, diary, 9 February 1923, RA QEQM/PRIV/DIARY/3

56 Duke of York to Lady Elizabeth Bowes Lyon, 11 February 1923, RA QEQM/PRIV/RF

57 Lady Elizabeth Bowes Lyon, diary, 12 February–2 March, RA QEQM/PRIV/DIARY/3

58 Lady Elizabeth Bowes Lyon, diary, 5 March 1923, RA QEQM/PRIV/DIARY/3

59 Lady Elizabeth Bowes Lyon to Duke of York, n.d. [13 March 1923], RA/GVI/PRIV/RF/26

60 Duke of York to Lady Elizabeth Bowes Lyon, 14 March 1923, RA QEQM/PRIV/RF

61 Duke of York to Lady Elizabeth Bowes Lyon, 13 March 1923, RA QEQM/PRIV/RF

62 Lady Elizabeth Bowes Lyon to Duke of York, n.d. [13 March 1923], RA GVI/PRIV/RF/26/54

63 Jock Smith to Louis Greig, 19 March 1923, RA ADYH/MAIN/8

64 Lady Elizabeth Bowes Lyon, diary, 21 March 1923, RA QEQM/PRIV/DIARY/3

65 Lady Elizabeth Bowes Lyon, diary, 23 March 1923, RA QEQM/PRIV/DIARY/3

66 Lady Elizabeth Bowes Lyon, diary, 24 March 1923, RA QEQM/PRIV/DIARY/3

67 Lady Elizabeth Bowes Lyon, diary, 28 March 1923, RA QEQM/PRIV/DIARY/3

68 Lady Elizabeth Bowes Lyon to Duke of York, [2 April 1923], RA GVI/PRIV/RF/26/59

69 Archibald Clark Kerr to Lady Elizabeth Bowes Lyon, 31 March 1923, RA QEQM/PRIV/PAL

70 Gordon George to Lady Elizabeth Bowes Lyon, 17 April 1923, RA QEQM/PRIV/PAL

71 Duke of York to Lady Elizabeth Bowes Lyon, 29 March 1923, RA QEQM/PRIV/RF

72 Lady Elizabeth Bowes Lyon to Duke of York, n.d. [29 March 1923], RA GVI/PRIV/RF/26/57

73 Lady Elizabeth Bowes Lyon to Duke of York, n.d. [31 March 1923], RA GVI/PRIV/RF/26/58

74 Duke of York to Lady Elizabeth Bowes Lyon, 1 April 1923, RA QEQM/PRIV/RF

75 Lady Elizabeth Bowes Lyon, diary, 4 April 1923, RA QEQM/PRIV/DIARY/3

76 Laird, p. 53

77 Lady Elizabeth Bowes Lyon, diary, 5–7 April 1923, RA QEQM/PRIV/DIARY/3

78 Lady Elizabeth Bowes Lyon, diary, 10, 11 April 1923, RA QEQM/PRIV/DIARY/3

79 *Graphic*, 21 April 1923, and Wedding Number

80 Lady Elizabeth Bowes Lyon to D'Arcy Osborne, 12 April 1923, RA QEQM/OUT/OSBORNE

81 Lady Elizabeth Bowes Lyon to D'Arcy Osborne, n.d. [28 June 1923], RA QEQM/OUT/OSBORNE

82 Laird, p. 57

83 Correspondence between Lord Stamfordham and H. R. Boyd, April–May 1923, RA PS/PSO/GV/C/O/1852/1–2

84 Gunter & Co. Ltd to Sir Derek Keppel, 13 February 1923, RA MRH/GV/FUNC/039/2A/01

85 Lord Cromer to Sir Frederick Ponsonby, 9 April 1923, RA LC/LCO/SPECIAL/1923/GVI WEDDING/20

86 Lady Strathmore to Sir Douglas Dawson, n.d. [21 April 1923], RA LC/LCO/SPECIAL/1923/GVI WEDDING/20

87 Lady Strathmore to Sir Douglas Dawson, 17 April 1923, RA LC/LCO/SPECIAL/1923/GVI WEDDING/20

88 Lady Elizabeth Bowes Lyon, diary, 13–20 April 1923, RA QEQM/PRIV/DIARY/3

89 Laird, p. 51; *Morning Post*, 19 April 1923; RA ADYH/MAIN/8/1923

90 *Daily Telegraph*, 26 April 1923

91 Laird, p. 49; *Morning Post*, 24 April 1923

92 Laird, p. 50; *The Times*, 24 April 1923

93 Lady Elizabeth Bowes Lyon, diary, 22 April 1923, RA QEQM/PRIV/DIARY/3

94 H. H. Asquith, *Letters to a Friend*, Geoffrey Bles, 1934, vol. 2, pp. 50–1

95 Frederick Dalrymple Hamilton, diary, 23 April 1923, private collection

96 RA QM/PRIV/DIARY/1923: 23 April

97 Lady Elizabeth Bowes Lyon, diary, 23 April 1923, RA QEQM/PRIV/DIARY/3

98 Lady Elizabeth Bowes Lyon, diary, 24 April 1923, RA QEQM/PRIV/DIARY/3

99 Lady Elizabeth Bowes Lyon, diary, 25 April 1923, RA QEQM/PRIV/DIARY/3

100 *Dundee Advertiser*, 22 February 1923, quoted in Laird, p. 49

101 Lady Elizabeth Bowes Lyon, diary, 25 April 1923, RA QEQM/PRIV/DIARY/3

102 RA QM/PRIV/DIARY/1923: 26 April

103 Lord Stamfordham to Sir John Baird, 18 April 1923; Lord Stamfordham to Rear Admiral Hugh Watson, 23 April 1923, RA PS/PSO/GV/PS/MAIN/38428/3–4

104 Laird, p. 55

105 *The Times*, 27 April 1923; *Yorkshire Post*, 27 April 1923; Laird, p. 58

106 Will Thorne to Lord Stamfordham, 23 April 1923, RA PS/PSO/GV/PS/MAIN/38428/8

107 Asquith, *Letters to a Friend*, vol. 2, pp. 52–3

108 Duff Cooper, *Diaries 1915–1952*, ed. John Julius Norwich, Weidenfeld & Nicolson, 2005, pp. 174–5

109 Memorandum and list, n.d., in RA LC/BP/Marriage of the Duke of York/1, 2

110 RA LC/ LCO/SPECIAL/1923/GVI WEDDING/2

111 *Morning Post*, 27 April 1923

112 Descriptions from *Illustrated London News*, quoted by Laird, pp. 59–60

113 Frederick Dalrymple Hamilton, diary, 26 April 1923, private collection

114 Ibid.

115 Laird, pp. 63–4

116 Lady Strathmore to Beryl Poignand, 10 May 1923, Glamis Archives (CH)

117 Laird, p. 65

118 RA F&V/WED/1923/GVI/MENU

119 RA ADYH/MAIN/1/G; *Daily Telegraph*, 26 April 1923

120 Duff Cooper, p. 175

121 Laird, p. 67

122 Ibid.

123 Duchess of York to Lady Strathmore, 26 April 1923, Glamis Archives (CH)

124 Duchess of York, diary, 26 April 1923, RA QEQM/PRIV/DIARY/3

FIVE: DUCHESS OF YORK 1923–1924

1 Duchess of York to Lady Strathmore, n.d. [27 April 1923], Glamis Archives

2 Ibid.

3 Lady Strathmore to Duchess of York, 27 April 1923, RA QEQM/PRIV/BL

4 Duke of York to Lady Strathmore, 28 April 1923, Glamis Archives

5 Lady Strathmore to Duke of York, 1 May 1923, RA GVI/PRIV/PAL/S/33

6 Duke of York to King George V, 27 April 1923, RA GV/PRIV/AA61/155

7 Duke of York to Queen Mary, 27 April 1923, RA QM/PRIV/CC11/40

8 Queen Mary to Duke of York, 28 April 1923, RA GVI/PRIV/RF/11

9 King George V to Duke of York, 29 April 1923, quoted in Wheeler-Bennett, pp. 154–5

10 Wheeler-Bennett, p. 155

11 Duchess of York, diary, 27–29 April 1923, RA QEQM/PRIV/DIARY/3

12 Duchess of York, diary, 3 May 1923, RA QEQM/PRIV/DIARY/3

13 Duchess of York, diary, 7 May 1923, RA QEQM/PRIV/DIARY/3

14 Duchess of York, diary, 8 May 1923, RA QEQM/PRIV/DIARY/3

15 Duchess of York to Beryl Poignand, 22 May 1923, Glamis Archives (CH)

16 Duchess of York, diary, 16, 17 May 1923, RA QEQM/PRIV/DIARY/3

17 Duchess of York, diary, 18–22 May 1923, RA QEQM/PRIV/DIARY/3

18 Duchess of York, diary, 23–25 May 1923, RA QEQM/PRIV/DIARY/3

19 Dowager Lady Bradford to Queen Mary, 4 June 1923, RA QM/PRIV/CC47/750

20 Duke of York to Queen Mary, 25 May 1923, RA QM/PRIV/CC11/42

21 Duchess of York, diary, 5 July 1923, RA QEQM/PRIV/DIARY/3

22 Duchess of York to Lady Strathmore, n.d. [18 October 1923], Glamis Archives, Box 270

23 Queen Mary to Duke of York, 16 June 1923, RA GVI/PRIV/RF/11

24 Duchess of York to D'Arcy Osborne, n.d. [28 June 1923], RA QEQM/OUT/OSBORNE

25 Owen Chadwick, *Britain and the Vatican during the Second World War*, Cambridge University Press, 1986, p. 14

26 Duchess of York, diary, 4 July 1923, RA QEQM/PRIV/DIARY/3

27 Hardinge, p. 39

28 Helen Hardinge, diary, quoted in Vickers, p. 72

29 Laird, pp. 79–80

30 Ibid.

31 Sir Frederick Ponsonby, *Recollections of Three Reigns*, 1952, quoted in Laird, p. 78

32 Wheeler-Bennett, p. 151; Laird, p. 78

33 Laird, p. 97

34 Wheeler-Bennett, p. 189; RA QM/PRIV/DIARY/1923: 28 June

35 Quoted in Charles Loch Mowat, *Britain between the Wars*, Methuen, 1966, p. 164

36 Laird, p. 76

37 Duchess of York to D'Arcy Osborne, 10 July 1923, RA QEQM/OUT/OSBORNE

38 *Scotsman*, 14 July 1923

39 Duchess of York, diary, 19 July 1923, RA QEQM/PRIV/DIARY/3

40 RA ADYH/MAIN/8

41 Frank C. Wilson, Lord Mayor of Liverpool, to Louis Greig, 28 July 1923, RA ADYH/MAIN/8/1923/25 July

42 Ernest Pearce to Duchess of York, 1 July 1923, RA QEQM/PRIV/PAL

43 Duchess of York, diary, 30 July–3 August 1923, RA QEQM/PRIV/DIARY/3

44 *Daily Telegraph*, 2 August 1923

45 Duchess of York, diary, 4 August 1923, RA QEQM/PRIV/DIARY/3

46 Prince of Wales to King George V, 21 August 1923, RA EDW/MAINA/2481

47 Duchess of York to Lady Strathmore, 10 September 1923, Glamis Archives (CH)

48 Duke of Kent to Duchess of York, n.d. [19 September 1923], RA QEQM/PRIV/RF

49 King George V to Duke of York, 20 September 1923, RA GV/PRIV/AA61/179; Queen Mary to Duke of York, 18 September 1923, RA GVI/PRIV/RF/11

50 Duke of York to Louis Greig, 24 September 1923, RA ADYH/MAIN/101/1923; Wheeler-Bennett, p. 192

51 Duchess of York to Duke of York, n.d. [27 September 1923], RA GVI/PRIV/RF/26/60

52 Duchess of York to Duke of York, n.d. [27 September 1923], RA GVI/PRIV/RF/26/61

53 Duchess of York, diary, 11 October 1923, RA QEQM/PRIV/DIARY/3

54 RA ADYH/MAIN/101/1923

55 Duke of York to Duchess of York, 27 September 1923, RA QEQM/PRIV/RF

56 Duchess of York to D'Arcy Osborne, 17 October 1923, RA QEQM/OUT/OSBORNE

57 Duchess of York to Lady Strathmore, n.d. [18 October 1923], Glamis Archives, Box 270

58 Wheeler-Bennett, p. 196

59 Duchess of York to D'Arcy Osborne, 17 October 1923, RA QEQM/OUT/OSBORNE

60 Duchess of York to D'Arcy Osborne, 17 October 1923, RA QEQM/OUT/OSBORNE

61 Duchess of York, diary, 20 October 1923, RA QEQM/PRIV/DIARY/3

62 Duchess of York to Lady Strathmore, 21, 26 October [1923], Glamis Archives; Duchess of York, diary, 20 October 1923, RA QEQM/PRIV/DIARY/3

63 Duke of York to King George V, 26 October 1923, RA GV/PRIV/AA61/189; Duchess of York to Lady Strathmore, 21 October [1923], Glamis Archives, Box 270

64 Duchess of York, diary, 21 October 1923, RA QEQM/PRIV/DIARY/3

65 Wheeler-Bennett, p. 193

66 Duchess of York to Lady Strathmore, 26 October [1923], Glamis Archives

67 Ibid.

68 Duchess of York, diary, 22 October 1923, RA QEQM/PRIV/DIARY/3; Duchess of York to Lady Strathmore, n.d. [26 October 1923], Glamis Archives

69 Duchess of York to Lady Strathmore, 26 October [1923], Glamis Archives

70 Duke of York to King George V, 26 October 1923, RA GV/PRIV/AA61/189

71 Graves and Hodge, p. 75

72 Ibid.

73 Nicolson, *George V*, p. 382

74 Ibid., p. 497

75 Ibid., p. 496

76 Duchess of York to Violet Cavendish-Bentinck, 21 December 1923, Glamis Archives (CH)

77 Duchess of York, diary, 22 December 1923, RA QEQM/PRIV/DIARY/3

78 Duchess of York, diary, 25 December 1923, RA QEQM/PRIV/DIARY/3

79 Duchess of York, diary, 13 January 1924, RA QEQM/PRIV/DIARY/4

80 Duchess of York, diary, 8 January 1924, RA QEQM/PRIV/DIARY/4

81 Graves and Hodge, pp. 118–19

82 Duchess of York to King George V, 14 January [1924], RA GV/PRIV/AA61/343

83 King George V to Duke of York, 8 January 1924, RA GV/PRIV/AA61/196, quoted in Wheeler-Bennett, p. 196

84 RA GV/PRIV/GVD/1924: 22 January

85 King George V to Queen Alexandra, 17 February 1924, RA GV/PRIV/AA38/65

86 Quoted by Nicolson, *George V*, pp. 499–500

87 Duchess of York, diary, 21 January 1924, RA QEQM/PRIV/DIARY/4

88 Duchess of York, diary, 26–27 February 1924, RA QEQM/PRIV/DIARY/4

89 Duke of York to Queen Mary, 9 October 1923, RA QM/PRIV/CC11/49

90 Duke of York to King George V, 16 October 1923, RA GV/PRIV/AA61/188

91 Louis Greig to Duchess of York, 15 November [1923], RA QEQM/PRIV/HH

92 Geordie Greig, *Louis and the Prince*, Hodder & Stoughton, 1999, p. 214

93 Ibid., pp. 209–15

94 Duchess of York, diary, 7 March 1924, RA QEQM/PRIV/DIARY/4

95 Duchess of York to D'Arcy Osborne, n.d. [17 March 1924], RA QEQM/OUT/OSBORNE

96 Niall Ferguson, *Empire*, Allen Lane, 2003, p. 318

97 Duchess of York, diary, 23 April 1924, RA QEQM/PRIV/DIARY/4

98 Wheeler-Bennett, pp. 206–7

99 King George V, speech, 23 April 1924, 'Speeches and Replies to Addresses by His Majesty King George V', printed for the Private Secretary's Office, RA

100 Laird, p. 85

101 Duchess of York, diary, 23 April 1924, RA QEQM/PRIV/DIARY/4

102 Duchess of York, diary, 7, 11 May, 4 June 1924, RA QEQM/PRIV/DIARY/4

103 Laird, p. 90

104 Dorothy Willis to Louis Greig, 13 July 1923: RA ADYH/MAIN/9/1923: 30 November

105 J. Machell to Basil Brooke, RA/ADYH/MAIN/12/1924: 16 July

106 Duchess of York, diary, 26 April 1924, RA QEQM/PRIV/DIARY/4

107 Queen Elizabeth to Queen Elizabeth II, 2 May 1988, RA QEII/PRIV/RF

108 Duchess of York, diary, 27 May 1924, RA QEQM/PRIV/DIARY/4

109 Wheeler-Bennett, p. 197

110 Duke of Abercorn to Duke of York, 22 March 1924, RA ADYH/MAIN/102; Duke of
     York to King George V, 24 March 1924, RA GV/PRIV/AA61/201

111 Duchess of York, diary, 19 July 1924, RA QEQM/PRIV/DIARY/4

112 Helen Hardinge, diary, 19 July 1924, quoted in Vickers, p. 84

113 Duchess of York, diary, 21 July 1924, RA QEQM/PRIV/DIARY/4

114 Helen Hardinge, diary, 21 July 1924, quoted in Vickers, p. 86

115 Duchess of York, diary, 22 July 1924, RA QEQM/PRIV/DIARY/4

116 Duchess of York, diary, 22–23 July 1924, RA QEQM/PRIV/DIARY/4

117 Duchess of York, diary, 24–25 July 1924, RA QEQM/PRIV/DIARY/4

118 Duchess of York, diary, 26 July 1924, RA QEQM/PRIV/DIARY/4

119 Duke of York to King George V, 22 July 1924, RA GV/PRIV/AA61/213

120 Rose, *George V*, p. 286

121 Nicolson, *George V*, p. 658n.

122 Ibid., p. 658; Rose, *George V*, pp. 91–2; Bradford, *George VI*, pp. 121–2

123 Bradford, *George VI*, p. 122

124 Duchess of York to Lady Strathmore, Sunday n.d., [14 September 1924], Glamis Archives

125 Duke of York to Duchess of York, 29 September 1924, RA QEQM/PRIV/RF

126 Duchess of York to Duke of York, Wednesday [1 October 1924], RA GVI/PRIV/RF/26/
     63

127 Duke of York to Duchess of York, 2 October 1924, RA QEQM/PRIV/RF

128 Duke of York to Queen Mary, 9 October 1924, RA QM/PRIV/CC11/64

129 Duchess of York, diary, 30 October 1924, RA QEQM/PRIV/DIARY/4

130 Duchess of York to Lady Strathmore, Saturday [1 November 1924], Glamis Archives
     (CH)

Six: On Safari 1924–1925

1   Duchess of York, diary, RA QEQM/PRIV/DIARY/4

2   Queen Elizabeth, conversations with Eric Anderson, 1994–5, RA QEQM/ADD/MISC

3   Winston Churchill to Duchess of York, undated, postmark 10 July 1924, RA QEQM/
    PRIV/PAL

4   Duchess of York, diary, 14 July 1924, RA QEQM/PRIV/DIARY/4

5   Duke of York to Queen Mary, 30 November 1924, RA QM/PRIV/CC11/67

6   Duchess of York to D'Arcy Osborne, 4 December 1924, RA QEQM/OUT/OSBORNE

7   Author's interview with Margaret Rhodes, 2004

8   Simon Schama, *A History of Britain*, vol. 3, pp. 448–9

9   Ibid., p. 463

10 Ferguson, *Empire*, p. 317

11 H. A. Macmichael to Basil Brooke, 30 July 1924, RA ADYH/MAIN/103/14

12 King George V to Duke of York, 28 November 1924, RA GV/PRIV/AA61/228

13 Queen Mary to Duke of York, 2 December 1924, GVI/PRIV/RF/11

14 Duchess of York to Lady Strathmore, n.d. [30 November 1924], Glamis Archives

15 Duchess of York to Lady Strathmore, n.d. [1 November 1924], Glamis Archives

16 Duchess of York to D'Arcy Osborne, 4 December 1924, RA QEQM/OUT/OSBORNE

17 Duchess of York, diary, 4 December 1924, RA QEQM/PRIV/DIARY/4

18 Duchess of York, diary, 5 December 1924, RA QEQM/PRIV/DIARY/4

19 Duchess of York, diary, 11 December 1924, RA QEQM/PRIV/DIARY/4

20 Duchess of York to Lady Strathmore, 20 December 1924, Glamis Archives

21 Duchess of York, diary, 18, 20 December 1924, RA QEQM/PRIV/DIARY/4; Duchess of
    York to Lady Strathmore, 20 December 1924, Glamis Archives; RA QEQM/PRIV/
    PERSONAL

22 Duke of York, diary, 22 December 1924, RA GVI/PRIV/DIARY/4

23 Duchess of York to King George V, 9 February 1925, RA GV/PRIV/AA61/345

24 Duke of York to King George V, 24 December 1924, RA GV/PRIV/AA61/232, quoted
    in Wheeler-Bennett, p. 200

25 Duchess of York to Lady Strathmore, 29 December 1924, Glamis Archives. She was so
    delighted with the flowers that she asked Mrs Lamb, the wife of the District
    Commissioner, to send a consignment of orchids and canna lilies to White Lodge on
    their return (RA ADYH/MAIN/104/23)

26 Duchess of York to Prince of Wales, 13 January 1925, RA EDW/PRIV/MAINB/76

27 Duchess of York to Lady Strathmore, 29 December 1924, Glamis Archives

28 Duchess of York to the Hon. David Bowes Lyon, 6 January 1925, Glamis Archives

29 Duchess of York, diary, 21 January 1925, RA QEQM/PRIV/DIARY/5

30 Duchess of York to D'Arcy Osborne, 31 January 1925, RA QEQM/OUT/OSBORNE

31 Duchess of York, diary, 23 January 1925, RA QEQM/PRIV/DIARY/5

32 Duchess of York, diary, 24 January 1925, RA QEQM/PRIV/DIARY/5

33 Duchess of York to King George V, 9 February 1925, RA GV/PRIV/AA61/345

34 Duke of York, diary, 29 January 1925, RA GVI/PRIV/DIARY/4

35 Duchess of York, diary, 4, 5 February 1925, RA QEQM/PRIV/DIARY/5

36 Duchess of York to Lady Strathmore, 16 January 1925, Glamis Archives

37 Duchess of York to Prince of Wales, 13 January 1925, RA EDW/MAINB/76

38 Ibid.

39 Prince of Wales to Duchess of York, 27 February 1925, RA QEQM/PRIV/RF

40 Duke of York to King George V, 31 January 1925, RA GV/PRIV/AA61/239

41 Duke of York to Queen Mary, 31 January 1925, RA QM/PRIV/CC11/71

42 Duchess of York to King George V, 9 February 1925, RA GV/PRIV/AA61/345

43 Duke of York, diary, 14 February 1925, RA GVI/PRIV/DIARY/4

44 Duke of York, diary, 15, 16 February 1925, RA GVI/PRIV/DIARY/4; Duchess of York,
    diary 15, 16 February 1925, RA QEQM/PRIV/DIARY/5

45 Duchess of York to Lady Strathmore, 14 February 1925, Glamis Archives

46 Sir Geoffrey Archer to Captain Basil Brooke, 13 October 1924, RA ADYH/MAIN/103/10

47 Captain Roy Salmon to his mother, 19 February 1925, private collection

48 Ibid.

49 Duke of York, diary, 20 February 1925, RA GVI/PRIV/DIARY/4

50 Duchess of York to Lady Strathmore, 27 February 1925, Glamis Archives

51 Duchess of York, diary, 22 February 1925, RA QEQM/PRIV/DIARY/5

52 Duchess of York, diary, 24 February 1925, RA QEQM/PRIV/DIARY/5

53 Duchess of York to Lady Strathmore, 27 February 1925, Glamis Archives

54 Captain Roy Salmon to his mother, 25 March 1925, private collection

55 Duchess of York, diary, 25 February 1925, RA QEQM/PRIV/DIARY/5

56 Duke of York, diary, 25 February 1925, RA GVI/PRIV/DIARY/4. According to the Duchess's diary, there were 'about 60 huge crocodiles!'

57 Address from Mukama of Bunyoro, 26 February 1925, RA ADYH/MAIN/103/3

58 Captain Roy Salmon to his mother, 25 March 1925, private collection

59 Duchess of York, diary, 27, 28 February 1925, RA QEQM/PRIV/DIARY/5

60 Captain Roy Salmon to his mother, 25 March 1925, private collection

61 Duchess of York to Lady Rose Leveson-Gower, n.d. [March 1925], Glamis Archives

62 Captain Roy Salmon to his mother, 25 March 1925, private collection

63 Duke of York, diary, 2 March 1925, RA GVI/PRIV/DIARY/4

64 Captain Roy Salmon to his mother, 25 March 1925, private collection

65 Duke of York, diary, 3 March 1925, RA GVI/PRIV/DIARY/4

66 Captain Roy Salmon to his mother, 25 March 1925, private collection

67 Duchess of York, diary, 4 March 1925, RA QEQM/PRIV/DIARY/5

68 Captain Roy Salmon to his mother, 25 March 1925, private collection. Although the Yorks did not return, Salmon did indeed meet the Prince of Wales, accompanying him on safari in Uganda in 1928 and 1930 and writing equally lively accounts to his mother

69 Ibid.

70 Geoffrey Archer, *Personal and Historical Memoirs of an East African Administrator*, Oliver & Boyd, Edinburgh and London, 1963, p. 192; Vickers, p. 95

71 Telegrams from Colonial Office to Basil Brooke, 16 December 1924, 29 January 1925, RA ADYH/MAIN/103/4

72 Duchess of York to Lady Rose Leveson-Gower, n.d. [March 1925], Glamis Archives

73 Duke of York, diary, 21 March 1925, RA GVI/PRIV/DIARY/4

74 Duke of York to Duchess of York 7 March 1925, QEQM/PRIV/RF

75 Duke of York to Prince of Wales, 6 March 1925, RA EDW/MAINA/2506

76 Duchess of York to May Elphinstone, 6 March 1925, RA QEQM/OUT/ELPHINSTONE

77 Ibid.; Duchess of York to Lady Strathmore, 30 March 1925, Glamis Archives, Box 270/II

78 Duke of York, diary, 14 March 1925, RA GVI/PRIV/DIARY/4

79 Duke of York, diary, 15 March 1925, RA GVI/PRIV/DIARY/4

80 Duchess of York to Lady Strathmore, 30 March 1925, Glamis Archives, Box 270/II

81 Duke of York, diary, 17 March 1925, RA GVI/PRIV/DIARY/4

82 Duchess of York, diary, 20 March 1925, RA QEQM/PRIV/DIARY/5

83 Duchess of York to Major R. H. Walsh, 24 October 1925, RA QEQM/OUT/WALSH

84 Account of Nuba gathering by D. A. D. L., 25 March 1925, RA ADYH/MAIN/103/4

85 Duke of York to Lady Strathmore, 21 March 1925, Glamis Archives

86 Duchess of York, diary, 31 March 1925, RA QEQM/PRIV/DIARY/5; Duchess of York to Lady Strathmore, 30 March–1 April 1925, Glamis Archives, Box 270/II

87 Duchess of York, diary, 2, 4 April 1925, RA QEQM/PRIV/DIARY/5; Duke of York, diary, 2 April 1925, RA GVI/PRIV/DIARY/4

88 Duchess of York, diary, 6 April 1925, RA QEQM/PRIV/DIARY/5

89 Ibid.

90 Archibald Clark Kerr to Duchess of York, 10 March 1925, RA QEQM/PRIV/PAL

91 Duchess of York to Queen Mary, 8 April 1925, RA QM/PRIV/CC11/74

92 Duke of York, diary, 7 April 1925, RA GVI/PRIV/DIARY/4; Duchess of York, diary, 7 April 1925, RA QEQM/PRIV/DIARY/5

93 Duchess of York, diary, 10, 11 April 1925, RA QEQM/PRIV/DIARY/5

94 Duchess of York to Major R. H. Walsh, 14 April 1925, RA QEQM/OUT/WALSH

95 Duchess of York to May Elphinstone, 15 April 1925, RA QEQM/OUT/ELPHINSTONE

96 Duchess of York to D'Arcy Osborne, 4 May 1925, RA QEQM/OUT/OSBORNE

97 Queen Elizabeth, conversations with Eric Anderson, 1994–5, RA QEQM/ADD/MISC

SEVEN: BIRTH OF A PRINCESS 1925–1927

1 Duchess of York, diary, 28 April 1925, RA QEQM/PRIV/DIARY/5

2 Extract from the Introduction to Lord Radcliffe, *Not in Feather Beds: Some Collected Papers*, Hamish Hamilton, 1968, pp. xvi–xvii

3 Graves and Hodge, p. 172

4 See Osbert Lancaster, *Progress at Pelvis Bay*, 1936, and *Pillar to Post: The Pocket Lamp of Architecture*, 1938, quoted in Graves and Hodge, pp. 173–4

5 Graves and Hodge, p. 185

6 Duchess of York, diary, 28 April 1925, RA QEQM/PRIV/DIARY/5

7 Duke of York to Prince of Wales, 27 May 1925, RA EDW/MAINA/2516

8 Wheeler-Bennett, p. 206

9 Ibid., p. 208

10 Duke of York to Prince of Wales, 27 May 1925, RA EDW/PRIV/MAINA/2516

11 Duchess of York, diary, 9 May 1925, RA QEQM/PRIV/DIARY/5

12 Duke of York to Prince of Wales, 27 May 1925, RA EDW/PRIV/MAINA/2516

13 Wheeler-Bennett, p. 208

14 See for instance Queen Mary to Duke of York, 30 May 1925, RA GVI/PRIV/RF/11

15 Harry Lench to Basil Brooke, 8 June 1925, RA ADYH/MAIN/14/1925: 4 June

16 James Gough to Basil Brooke, 8 June 1925, RA ADYH/MAIN/14/1925: 4 June

17 F. S. Dutton to Basil Brooke, 16 July 1925, RA QEQMH/PS/ENGT/1925/1A

18 Duchess of York, diary, 15 July 1925, RA QEQM/PRIV/DIARY/5; speeches by Duchess of York and Lady Astor in the *Woman Engineer*, Vol. II, No. 4, September 1925, RA QEQMH/PS/GEN/1934/E; Caroline Haslett to Basil Brooke, 20 July 1925, RA QEQMH/PS/ENGT/1925/1A

19 *Daily Telegraph*, 27 April 1926

20 Duke of York to Prince of Wales, 9 August 1925, RA EDW/MAINA/2528

21 Duchess of York's, diary, 17 July 1925, RA QEQM/PRIV/DIARY/5

22 Duchess of York's diary, 16 July 1925, RA QEQM/PRIV/DIARY/5; Duchess of York to Major R. H. Walsh, n.d. [summer 1925] and 21 June 1926, RA QEQM/OUT/WALSH

23 Duchess of York to Duke of York, 10 September 1925, RA GVI/PRIV/RF/26/65

24 Duke of York to Duchess of York, 11 September 1925, RA QEQM/PRIV/RF

25 Duke of York to Prince of Wales, 9 August 1925, RA EDW/MAINA/2528

26 RA QM/PRIV/QMD/1925: 16 October

27 Wheeler-Bennett, p. 208

28 Nicolson, *George V*, pp. 529–30

29 Duchess of York to King George V, 24 November 1925, RA GV/PRIV/AA56/105

30 Duke of York to Prince of Wales, 9 August 1925, RA EDW/MAINA/2528

31 Duchess of York to Duke of York, 10 September 1925, RA GVI/PRIV/RF/26/65

32 Duke of York to Lady Strathmore, 18 October 1925, Glamis Archives

33 Queen Mary to Duke of York, 20 October 1925, RA GVI/PRIV/RF/11

34 Duke of York to Queen Mary, 27 October 1925, RA QM/PRIV/CC11/81

35 Duchess of York to Queen Mary, 28 October 1925, RA QM/PRIV/CC11/82

36 Queen Mary to Duke of York, 29 October 1925, RA GVI/PRIV/RF/11

37 RA ADYH/MAIN/16/1925: 22 and 23 October

38 RA ADYH/MAIN/16/1925: 17 November

39 Colin Buist, reply to invitation from the Royal Overseas League, 7 July 1925, RA ADYH/MAIN/16/1925: 18 November

40 Duke of York to Duchess of York, 8 December 1925, RA QEQM/PRIV/RF

41 Duke of York to Duchess of York, 24 December 1925, RA QEQM/PRIV/RF

42 Duchess of York to May Elphinstone, 29 December 1925, RA QEQM/OUT/ELPHINSTONE

43 Duchess of York to D'Arcy Osborne, n.d. [postmark 11 January 1926], RA QEQM/OUT/OSBORNE

44 Duke of York to Queen Mary, 16 January 1926, RA QM/PRIV/CC11/85

45 Duke of York to Duchess of York, 11 January 1926, RA QEQM/PRIV/RF

46 Jane Walker-Okeover to Mrs S. Hudson, 23 February 2001, RA QEQMH/PS/GEN/2001/Hudson; Duchess of York to Mrs Annie Beevers, 8 January [1926], private collection

47 King George V to Duke of York, 26 January 1926, RA GV/PRIV/AA61/297; Duke of York to King George V, 31 January 1926, RA GV/PRIV/AA61/298; Queen Mary to Duke of York, 20 March 1926, RA GVI/PRIV/RF/11; Duchess of York to Nannie Beevers, 28 March [1926], private collection

48 King George V to Duke of York, 17 April 1926, RA GV/PRIV/AA61/307; Queen Mary to Duke of York, 17 April 1926, RA GVI/PRIV/RF/11

49 Queen Mary to Duke of York, 17 April 1926, RA GVI/PRIV/RF/11

50 Duke of York to King George V, 27 April 1926, RA GV/PRIV/AA61/310

51 RA QM/PRIV/QMD/1926: 21 April

52 Ibid.

53 Queen Mary to Duke of York, 23 April 1926, RA GVI/PRIV/RF/11

54 Duke of York to Queen Mary, 22 April 1926, RA QM/PRIV/CC11/87

55 Duke of York to Beryl Poignand, 23 April 1926, Glamis Archives (CH)

56 Lady Strathmore to Beryl Poignand, 24 April 1926, Glamis Archives (CH)

57 Duke of York to King George V, 27 April 1926, RA GV/PRIV/AA61/310

58 King George V to Duke of York, 28 April 1926, RA GV/PRIV/AA61/311

59 Taylor, *English History*, p. 239

60 Ibid., p. 240

61 RA GV/PRIV/GVD/1925: 29 July

62 Duff Cooper, p. 214

63 Ibid.

64 Rose, *George V*, p. 341

65 Taylor, *English History*, p. 245

66 Rose, *George V*, p. 340

67 Nicolson, *George V*, p. 540

68 Rose, *George V*, p. 342

69 Ibid., p. 343

70 Ibid., p. 341

71 Graves and Hodge, p. 165

72 Rose, *George V*, p. 343

73 Graves and Hodge, p. 167

74 Nicolson, *George V*, p. 543

75 Taylor, *English History*, p. 250

76 *Daily Mirror*, 26 May 1925

77 Duchess of York to Queen Mary, 15 September 1926, RA QM/PRIV/CC11/90

78 Duchess of York to Lady Strathmore, 9 August 1926, Glamis Archives (CH)

79 Prince of Wales to Lady Strathmore, n.d. [October 1926], Glamis Archives (CH)

80 Prince of Wales to Duchess of York, n.d. [October 1926], RA QEQM/PRIV/RF

81 RA ADYH/MAIN/19/1926: 26 August and 18 September

82 Mina Davidson to Lady Strathmore, 4 July 1926, RA ADYH/MAIN/20/1926

83 Wheeler-Bennett, p. 211
84 Graves and Hodge, p. 129
85 L. S. Amery to Lord Stamfordham, 10 March 1926, RA PS/PSO/GV/PS/MAIN/44029
86 Lord Stamfordham to L. S. Amery, 13 March 1926, RA PS/PSO/GV/PS/MAIN/44029
87 Lord Stonehaven to Lord Stamfordham, 6 April 1926, RA PS/PSO/GV/C/P/284/190
88 Wheeler-Bennett, pp. 212–14
89 Ibid., p. 212
90 Ibid., p. 213
91 Ibid.
92 Bradford, *George VI*, p. 161, quoting *News Chronicle*, 13 April 1953
93 Wheeler-Bennett, p. 214
94 Queen Mary to Duke of York, 2 and 15 July 1926, RA GVI/PRIV/RF/11
95 Duchess of York to Queen Mary, 15 September 1926, RA QM/PRIV/CC11/90; Queen Mary to Duke of York, 6 October 1926, RA GVI/PRIV/RF/11
96 Duchess of York to Lady Strathmore, 19 November 1926, Glamis Archives
97 Duchess of York to Nannie Beevers, 5 October 1926, private collection
98 Duchess of York to Major R. H. Walsh, 20 October 1926, RA QEQM/OUT/WALSH
99 Duchess of York to Nannie Beevers, 24 December 1926, private collection
100 Duchess of York to Queen Mary, 30 December 1926, RA QM/PRIV/CC11/93
101 Duchess of York, diary, 1–3 January 1927, RA QEQM/PRIV/DIARY/6
102 Duchess of York to Queen Mary, 30 December 1926, RA QM/PRIV/CC11/93
103 Duchess of York, diary, 3 January 1927, RA QEQM/PRIV/DIARY/6
104 Anne Ring (nom de plume of Beryl Poignand), *The Story of Princess Elizabeth*, John Murray, 1930, p. 24
105 Duchess of York, diary, 4 January 1927, RA QEQM/PRIV/DIARY/6
106 Duchess of York, diary, 5 January 1927, RA QEQM/PRIV/DIARY/6
107 Duchess of York, diary, 6 January 1927, RA QEQM/PRIV/DIARY/6
108 Duchess of York to Queen Mary, 9 January 1927, RA QM/PRIV/CC11/95
109 Duke of York to Queen Mary, 10 January 1927, RA QM/PRIV/CC11/96
110 Duchess of York, diary, 6 January 1927, RA QEQM/PRIV/DIARY/6
111 Queen Mary to Duchess of York, 18 February 1927, RA QEQM/PRIV/RF
112 Henry Batterbee, political secretary to the Duke of York, to Lord Stonehaven, Governor General of Australia, 7 January 1927, RA ADYH/MAIN/100/Personal correspondence

EIGHT: AN AUSTRALASIAN ASSIGNMENT 1927

1 Duke of York to King George V, 10 January 1927; RA GV/PRIV/AA62/2
2 Basil Brooke to R. S. Meiklejohn, 22 November 1927, RA ADYH/MAIN/85/Government Grant
3 Charles Stanley, Secretary of British Industries Fair Birmingham to Duke and Duchess of York, 23 February 1927, RA ADYH/MAIN/86/Farewell & congratulatory messages
4 Rear-Admiral H. W. Parker to Basil Brooke, 26 August 1926, RA ADYH/MAIN/91
5 Basil Brooke to Admiral Parker, 15 November 1926, RA ADYH/MAIN/91
6 Alfred Stevens to Basil Brooke, 23 October 1926, RA ADYH/MAIN/85/Supplies; list of books loaned, RA ADYH/MAIN/91/HMS Renown
7 Duchess of York to D'Arcy Osborne, 24 November 1928, RA QEQM/OUT/OSBORNE
8 T. H. Parker to Basil Brooke, 23 December 1926, RA ADYH/MAIN/85/Supplies
9 H. E. Reynolds, Pathé Frères Cinema Ltd, to Basil Brooke, 4 January [1927], RA ADYH/MAIN/91/Papers re correspondence on board HMS Renown

10 Correspondence re supplies for HMS *Renown*, August–December 1926, RA ADYH/MAIN/85/Supplies

11 Ibid.

12 Ibid.

13 Patrick Hodgson to Queen Mary, 20 January 1927, RA QM/PRIV/CC11/98

14 Duchess of York, diary, 7 January 1927, RA QEQM/PRIV/DIARY/6

15 Duchess of York to D'Arcy Osborne, 9 January 1927, RA QEQM/PRIV/OUT/OSBORNE

16 Duchess of York, diary, 5 February 1927, RA QEQM/PRIV/DIARY/6

17 Lord Cavan to King George V, 10 January 1927, RA PS/PSO/GV/PS/MAIN/44029

18 Lord Cavan to Clive Wigram, 13 January 1927, RA AEC/GG/6/2/2

19 Ibid.

20 Ibid.

21 Clive Wigram to Lord Cavan, 23 February 1927, Lord Cavan to Clive Wigram, 21 February 1927, RA AEC/GG/6/2/2

22 Lord Cavan to King George V, 21 January 1927, RA PS/PSO/GV/PS/MAIN/44029

23 Harry Batterbee to Lord Stamfordham, 24 January 1927, RA PS/PSO/GV/PS/MAIN/44029/Diary file

24 *Daily Gleaner*, 22 January 1927, enclosed with letter from Lord Cavan to Lord Stamfordham, 22 January 1927, RA PS/PSO/GV/PS/MAIN/44029

25 Duke of York to King George V, 26 January 1927, RA GV/PRIV/AA62/7

26 Duchess of York to Prince of Wales, 25 January 1927, RA EDW/PRIV/MAINB/81

27 Ibid.

28 Duke of York to King George V, 26 January 1927, RA GV/PRIV/AA62/7

29 King George V to Duke of York, 25 January 1927, RA GV/PRIV/AA62/6

30 Panama *Star & Herald*, 26 January 1927, RA ADYH/MAIN/86/Press cuttings/Panama

31 Ibid.

32 Duchess of York to Alah Knight, 27 January 1927, RA ADYH/MAIN/86/Private messages

33 Duke of York to Prince of Wales, 5 February 1927, RA EDW/PRIV/MAINB/82

34 Duchess of York to Queen Mary, 9 February 1927, RA QM/PRIV/CC11/101

35 Queen Mary to Duke of York, 31 and 25 January 1927, RA GVI/PRIV/RF/11

36 Queen Mary to Duke of York, 6 February 1927, RA GVI/PRIV/RF/11

37 Wheeler-Bennett, p. 220

38 Duchess of York to Queen Mary, 9 February 1927, RA QM/PRIV/CC11/101

39 Patrick Hodgson to Queen Mary, 14 February 1927, RA QM/PRIV/CC11/102

40 Lord Cavan to Lord Stamfordham, 15 February 1927, RA PS/PSO/GV/PS/MAIN/44029

41 *Fiji Times*, 18 February 1927, RA ADYH/MAIN/86/Press cuttings/Fiji

42 Richard Gardner Casey to Stanley Bruce, 28 July 1926, National Archives of Australia, Canberra, A1420

43 Wheeler-Bennett, p. 218

44 Duchess of York to Queen Mary, 8 March 1927, RA QM/PRIV/CC11/104

45 Lord Cavan to King George V, 24 February 1927, RA PS/PSO/GV/PS/MAIN/44029

46 Wheeler-Bennett, p. 218

47 Duke of York to Queen Mary, 22 February 1927, RA QM/PRIV/CC11/103

48 Sir Charles Fergusson to King George V, 25 February 1927, RA PS/PSO/GV/C/P/476/77; Wheeler-Bennett, pp. 218–19

49 Duchess of York to Queen Mary, 8 March 1927, RA QM/PRIV/CC11/104

50 Wheeler-Bennett, p. 219

51 Duchess of York to Queen Mary, 8 March 1927, RA QM/PRIV/CC11/104

52 Ibid.

53 Duchess of York to May Elphinstone, 17 March 1927, RA QEQM/OUT/ELPHINSTONE

54 Ibid.

55 RA Press cuttings from Yorks' tour to New Zealand and Australia

56 Duchess of York to Duke of York, 15 March 1927, RA GVI/PRIV/RF/26/67

57 Duchess of York to Queen Mary, 8 March 1927, RA QM/PRIV/CC11/104

58 Official Tour Diary, RA F&V/VISOV/AUSNZ 1927

59 Duke of York, diary, RA GVI/PRIV/DIARY/5: 28 February, 2 March 1927

60 Lord Cavan to King George V, 8 March 1927, RA PS/PSO/GV/PS/MAIN/44029

61 Taylor Darbyshire, *The Royal Tour of the Duke and Duchess of York*, Edward Arnold, 1927, p. 113

62 Patrick Hodgson to Queen Mary, 11 April 1927, RA QM/PRIV/CC11/108

63 Wheeler-Bennett, p. 220

64 Lord Cavan to Patrick Hodgson, 11 March 1927, RA/ADYH/MAIN/96

65 Darbyshire, p. 115

66 Wheeler-Bennett, p. 220

67 Harry Batterbee to Lord Stamfordham, 28 March 1927, RA PS/PSO/GV/PS/MAIN/44029/Diary file

68 Duchess of York to Duke of York, 15 March 1927, RA GVI/PRIV/RF/26/67

69 Duke of York to Duchess of York, 18 March 1927, Ian Shapiro Collection

70 Duchess of York to May Elphinstone, 17 March 1927, RA QEQM/OUT/ELPHINSTONE

71 King George V to Duke of York, 12 March 1927, RA GV/PRIV/AA62/14

72 Wheeler-Bennett, p. 221

73 Ibid.

74 Ibid., p. 223

75 Lord Cavan to Lord Stamfordham, 30 March 1927, RA PS/PSO/GV/PS/MAIN/44029

76 Harry Batterbee to E. J. Harding, Dominions Office, 28 March 1927, RA ADYH/MAIN/100

77 Lord Cavan to Lord Stamfordham, 30 March 1927, RA PS/PSO/GV/PS/MAIN/44029

78 Ibid.

79 King George V to Duke of York, 31 March 1927, RA GV/PRIV/AA62/18

80 Queen Mary to Duke of York, 30 March and 6 April 1927, GVI/PRIV/RF/11

81 Dr George F. Still to Duchess of York, 7 February, 2 March 1927, RA QEQM/PRIV/PAL; 30 March 1927, RA QEQM/PRIV/CHILD

82 See Lady Strathmore's letter to Queen Mary of 12 May 1927, RA QM/PRIV/CC11/113, referring to this and the pleasure it gave in Australia

83 Vivian Eastland to Duchess of York, 25 April 1927, RA ADYH/MAIN/96/Victoria 1

84 Harry Batterbee to J. A. P. Edgcumbe, 21 April 1927, RA ADYH/MAIN/100

85 Duchess of York to Queen Mary, 20 April 1927, RA QM/PRIV/CC11/109

86 Duchess of York to Lady Strathmore, 10 April 1927, Glamis Archives

87 Duke of York to King George V, 6 April 1927, RA GV/PRIV/AA62/20

88 Patrick Hodgson to Queen Mary, 11 April 1927, RA QM/PRIV/CC11/108

89 Ettie Harvey to Duchess of York, 9 April 1927; Nell Griffin-Oxley to Duchess of York, 21 April 1927, RA ADYH/MAIN/95/Brisbane 2

90 Sarah E. Muir to Duchess of York, 3 May 1927; schoolgirl to Duchess of York, [May] 1927, RA ADYH/MAIN/96

91 Duke of York to King George V, 21 April 1927, RA GV/PRIV/AA62/24

92 Duchess of York to Queen Mary, 20 April 1927, RA QM/PRIV/CC11/109

93 RA QM/PRIV/QMD/1927: 21 April; RA GV/PRIV/GVD/1927: 21 April
94 RA ADYH/MAIN/86/Private messages
95 Dr George F. Still to Duchess of York, 20 April, 9 May 1927, RA QEQM/PRIV/PAL
96 Duke of York to Minister of Defence, 21 April 1927, RA ADYH/MAIN/96/Melbourne 1
97 Lord Cavan to Lord Stamfordham, 26 April 1927, RA PS/PSO/GV/PS/MAIN/44029
98 Ibid.
99 Wheeler-Bennett, p. 206
100 Ibid., p. 227
101 Ibid., p. 228
102 Ibid., pp. 228–9
103 Duchess of York to King George V, 12 June 1927, RA GV/PRIV/AA62/32
104 W. Carrington to Duchess of York, 19 May 1927, RA ADYH/MAIN/97/Perth
105 Wheeler-Bennett, p. 230
106 Lady Strathmore to Queen Mary, 12 May 1927, RA QM/PRIV/CC11/113
107 Harry Batterbee to Lord Stamfordham, 26 May 1927, RA PS/PSO/GV/PS/MAIN/44029
108 Duke of York to King George V, 12 May and 12 June 1927, RA GV/PRIV/AA62/30
109 Queen Mary to Duke of York, 20 May 1927, RA GVI/PRIV/RF/11
110 Wheeler-Bennett, p. 231
111 Harry Batterbee to Major Casey, 14 June 1927, RA ADYH/MAIN/100
112 Queen Elizabeth, conversations with Eric Anderson, 1994–5, RA QEQM/ADD/MISC
113 Lord Cavan to Lord Stamfordham, 12 June 1927, RA PS/PSO/GV/PS MAIN/44029
114 Duchess of York to King George V, 12 June 1927, RA GV/PRIV/AA62/32
115 King George V to Duke of York, 12 June 1927, RA GV/PRIV/AA62/31
116 Queen Mary to Lady Strathmore, 14 May 1927, Glamis Papers

NINE: THE LONG WEEKEND 1927–1936

1 Roberts, *History of the World*, pp. 926–7
2 King George V to Duke of York, 30 June 1927, RA GV/PRIV/AA62/34
3 Duchess of York to Nannie Beevers, 18 July 1927, private collection
4 Bradford, *George VI*, p. 164
5 King George V to Queen Mary, 29 August 1927, RA QM/PRIV/CC4/277
6 Wheeler-Bennett, pp. 232–3
7 J. A. Edgcumbe to Basil Brooke, 24 June 1927, RA ADYH/MAIN/21/1927: 28 June;
    Duke of York, Engagement Diary, 11 July 1927, RA PS/PSO/GVI/C/352/1927
8 Prince of Wales to Duchess of York, [August 1927], RA QEQM/PRIV/RF
9 Prince George to Duchess of York, 17 August 1928, RA QEQM/PRIV/RF
10 Lady Cynthia Asquith to Ernest Pearce, 26 July 1927, RA QEQM/PRIV/TEXTS
11 Ernest Pearce to Duchess of York, 2 August 1927, QEQM/PRIV/PAL
12 Duchess of York to Beryl Poignand, 14 September 1927, Glamis Papers (CH)
13 RA ADYH/MAIN/21/1927: 20–21 September
14 Duchess of York to Queen Mary, 22 September 1927, RA QM/PRIV/CC11/119
15 King George V to Duke of York, 23 September 1927, RA GV/PRIV/AA62/43
16 King George V to Duke of York, 30 June 1927, RA GV/PRIV/AA62/34
17 Sir Hamar Greenwood to Patrick Hodgson, 30 November 1927, RA ADYH/MAIN/22/
    1927: 30 November
18 Lady (Lena Ashwell) Simson to Patrick Hodgson, 15 December 1927, RA ADYH/MAIN/
    22/1927: 13 December
19 RA PS/PSO/GV/PS/ARMY/38215

20 RA QM/PRIV/QMD/1927: 28 December

21 Duchess of York to Queen Mary, 26 January 1928, RA QM/PRIV/CC11/121

22 King George V to Duke of York, 28 January 1928, RA GV/PRIV/AA62/55

23 Queen Mary to Duke of York, 26 September 1928, RA GVI/PRIV/RF/11

24 Duchess of York to D'Arcy Osborne, 24 November 1928, RA QEQM/OUT/OSBORNE

25 RA GV/PRIV/GVD/1928: 21 November

26 Rose, *George V*, p. 355; Nicolson, *George V*, p. 554n.

27 Princess Mary to Prince of Wales, 6 December 1928, RA EDW/PRIV/MAINA/2602

28 Baldwin Papers, 177/36, quoted in Ziegler, *Edward VIII*, p. 194

29 Ziegler, *Edward VIII*, p. 192

30 Ibid., pp. 192–3

31 Duke of York to Prince of Wales, 6 December 1928, RA EDW/PRIV/MAINB/91

32 Wheeler-Bennett, p. 235

33 Ibid.

34 Rose, *George V*, p. 357

35 Nicolson, *George V*, p. 556

36 Rose, *George V*, p. 357

37 Wheeler-Bennett, p. 235

38 Duke of York to Queen Mary, 10 February 1929, RA QM/PRIV/CC11/130

39 Duchess of York to Queen Mary, 12 March 1929, RA QM/PRIV/CC11/133

40 Duke of York to Queen Mary, 10 February 1929, RA QM/PRIV/CC11/130; Queen Mary
    to Duke of York, 12 February 1929, RA GVI/PRIV/RF/11

41 Duchess of York to Queen Mary, 15 March 1929, RA QM/PRIV/CC11/135

42 Duchess of York to D'Arcy Osborne, 16 March 1929, RA QEQM/OUT/OSBORNE

43 Ibid.

44 Duchess of York to Queen Mary, 12 March 1929, RA QM/PRIV/CC11/133

45 Queen Maud of Norway to Queen Mary, 31 March 1929, RA QM/PRIV/CC45/759

46 Duchess of York to D'Arcy Osborne, 25 April 1929, RA QEQM/OUT/OSBORNE

47 Queen Mary to Duchess of York, 29 April 1929, RA QEQM/PRIV/RF

48 Wheeler-Bennett, p. 243

49 *Aberdeen Press*, 22 May 1929

50 Duchess of York to Queen Mary, 25 May 1929, RA QM/PRIV/CC11/137

51 Basil Brooke to Colonel Arthur Erskine, 31 May 1929, RA ADYH/MAIN/63/Transport

52 Quoted by Wheeler-Bennett, p. 246

53 Duchess of York to Queen Mary, 25 May 1929, RA QM/PRIV/CC11/137

54 Princess Elizabeth to Duchess of York, 22 May 1929, RA QEQM/PRIV/RF

55 Rose, *George V*, p. 361

56 Margaret Bondfield, *A Life's Work*, Hutchinson, 1949, p. 278

57 Rose, *George V*, p. 362

58 Queen Elizabeth, conversations with Eric Anderson, 1994–5, RA QEQM/ADD/MISC

59 Duchess of York to D'Arcy Osborne, 17 November 1929, RA QEQM/OUT/OSBORNE

60 Duchess of York to King George V, 21 August 1929, RA GV/PRIV/AA62/86

61 Duchess of York to D'Arcy Osborne, 10 October 1932, RA QEQM/OUT/OSBORNE

62 Duchess of York to King George V, 21 August 1929, RA GV/PRIV/AA62/86

63 Ibid.

64 Duchess of York to D'Arcy Osborne, 17 November 1929, RA QEQM/OUT/OSBORNE

65 Ibid.; Duchess of York to Osbert Sitwell, 11 November 1929, Sitwell Papers

66 Duchess of York to Queen Mary, 9 September 1929, RA QM/PRIV/CC11/143

67 Duke of York to King George V, 6 October 1929, RA GV/PRIV/AA62/100; Wheeler-
    Bennett, p. 250

68 Lady Helen Graham to Rev. J. I. McNair, 6 July 1929, RA QEQMH/PS/ENGT/1929: 5 October

69 ADYH/MAIN/33/1929: 29 October

70 Princess Elizabeth to Duchess of York, n.d. [January 1930], RA QEQM/PRIV/RF

71 Duchess of York to Nannie Beevers, 31 December 1929, private collection

72 Duke of York to Duchess of York, 6, 7, 8 January 1930, RA QEQM/PRIV/RF

73 Lady Strathmore to Beryl Poignand, 23 February 1930, Glamis Archives (CH)

74 Duchess of York to Nannie Beevers, 4 April 1930, private collection

75 Duchess of York to D'Arcy Osborne, 11 March 1930, RA QEQM/OUT/OSBORNE

76 Queen Mary to Duchess of York, 9 February 1930, RA QEQM/PRIV/RF

77 Duchess of York to Queen Mary, 14 April 1930, RA QM/PRIV/CC11/154

78 Queen Mary to Duchess of York, 15 [April] 1930, RA QEQM/PRIV/RF

79 Duchess of York to Nannie Beevers, 4 April 1930, private collection

80 Duchess of York to Queen Mary, 21 July 1930, RA QM/PRIV/CC11/158

81 Duchess of York to Queen Mary, 31 July 1930, RA QM/PRIV/CC11/159

82 Dr Frank Neon Reynolds, letters to his wife, Reynolds Papers

83 Duchess of York to Queen Mary, 5 August 1930, RA QM/PRIV/CC11/161

84 Duke of York to Queen Mary, 5 August 1930, RA QM/PRIV/CC11/160

85 Dr Reynolds to Mrs Reynolds, August 1930, Reynolds Papers

86 Dr Reynolds to Mrs Reynolds, [21] August 1930, Reynolds Papers

87 Lady Strathmore to the Hon. David Bowes Lyon, 26 August 1930, Bowes Lyon Papers, SPW

88 Reported by Sir Clive Wigram in letter to Lady Wigram, 22 August 1930, RA AEC/GG/6

89 Queen Mary to Duke of York, 22 August 1930, RA GVI/PRIV/RF/11

90 Queen Mary to May Elphinstone, 25 August 1930, RA QEQM/OUT/ELPHINSTONE

91 Colonel Herbert Spender-Clay to Rachel Bowes Lyon, 24 August 1930, Bowes Lyon Papers, SPW

92 Asquith, *The Queen*, p. 168

93 Ibid.

94 Lady Strathmore to the Hon. David Bowes Lyon, 26 August 1930, Bowes Lyon Papers, SPW

95 Basil Brooke to *Sunday Express*, 24 August 1930; statement by Sir Henry Simson, 24 August 1930, RA ADYH/MAIN/070/Birth of Princess Margaret

96 Queen Mary to Duchess of York, 25 August 1930, RA QEQM/PRIV/RF

97 Duke of York to Duchess of York, 25 August 1930, RA QEQM/PRIV/RF

98 Queen Mary to Duke of York, 22 August 1930, RA GVI/PRIV/RF/11

99 Duchess of York to Queen Mary, 27 August 1930, RA QM/PRIV/CC11/163

100 Duchess of York to Queen Mary, 6 September 1930, RA QM/PRIV/CC11/165

101 Duke of York and Princess Elizabeth to Duchess of York, 8 September 1930, RA QEQM/PRIV/RF

102 Duchess of York to Duke of York, 9 September 1930, RA GVI/PRIV/RF/26/70

103 Princess Elizabeth to Duchess of York, 10 September 1930, RA QEQM/PRIV/RF

104 Duchess of York to Duke of York, [12 September 1930], RA GVI/PRIV/RF/26/72

105 Duchess of York to Queen Mary, 28 August 1930, RA QM/PRIV/CC11/164

106 Duchess of York to Most Rev. Cosmo Lang, 10 September 1930, Lambeth Palace Library, Lang Papers 318 f. 186

107 Most Rev. Cosmo Lang to Duchess of York, 11 September 1930, RA QEQM/PRIV/PAL/Lang

108 Duke of York to Queen Mary, 15 September 1930, RA QM/PRIV/CC11/166; Duke of York to King George V, 29 September 1930, RA GV/PRIV/AA62/120

109 Duchess of York to Queen Mary, 22 October 1930, RA QM/PRIV/CC11/169

110 Duchess of York to Most Rev. Cosmo Lang, 10 September 1930, Lambeth Palace Library, Lang Papers 318 f. 186

111 Duchess of York to Dr Varley, 17 December 1930, RA GVI/OUT

112 RA QM/PRIV/QMD/1930: 25 December

113 Duchess of York to Queen Mary, 26 January 1931, RA QM/PRIV/CC11/175

114 Nicolson, *George V*, pp. 580-1

115 Graves and Hodge, pp. 254-5

116 King George V to Duke of York, 30 September 1931, RA GV/PRIV/AA62/147

117 Wheeler Bennett, pp. 257-9; Rose, *George V*, pp. 376-7

118 RA GV/PRIV/GVD/1931: 28 October

119 Ibid.

120 Ibid.

121 Graves and Hodge, p. 297

122 Duchess of York to D'Arcy Osborne, n.d. [January 1932], RA QEQM/OUT/OSBORNE

123 Duchess of York to Queen Mary, 16 September 1931, RA QM/PRIV/CC11/184

124 Duchess of York to Queen Mary, 22 October 1931, RA QM/PRIV/CC11/189

125 Patrick Hodgson to George Aylwen, 1 October 1931, RA ADYH/MAIN/41

126 Lord Mayor of Cardiff to Lady Helen Graham, 30 October 1931, RA QEQMH/PS/ENGT/1932/12

127 W. C. R. Martin to Lady Helen Graham, 18 February 1932, RA QEQMH/PS/ENGT/1932: 16 February

128 Duchess of York to D'Arcy Osborne, n.d. [January 1932], RA QEQM/OUT/OSBORNE

129 Queen Mary to Duke of York, 19 August 1931, RA GVI/PRIV/RF/11

130 Duchess of York to Queen Mary, 16 September 1931, RA QM/PRIV/CC11/184

131 Duchess of York to Queen Mary, 21 September 1931, RA QM/PRIV/CC11/186

132 Queen Mary to Duke of York, 22 September 1931, RA GVI/PRIV/RF/11; Duchess of York to Queen Mary, 8 December 1931, RA QM/PRIV/CC11/190

133 Duchess of York to Queen Mary, 21 October 1932, RA QM/PRIV/CC11/204

134 Jane Roberts, *Royal Landscape*, Yale University Press, 1997, p. 321

135 Duke of York to King George V, 29 April 1932, RA GV/PRIV/AA62/154

136 Wheeler-Bennett, p. 259

137 Roberts, *Royal Landscape*, p. 329

138 Wheeler-Bennett, pp. 259-60

139 Christopher Hussey, 'Royal Lodge', *Country Life*, 1 July 1939

140 Miss B. Hankey to Duchess of York, n.d. [May 1932], RA QEQM/PS/GEN/1932/Blaina

141 Queen Mary to Duchess of York, 31 July 1932, RA QEQM/PRIV/RF

142 Duchess of York to King George V, 5 August 1932, RA GV/PRIV/AA62/158

143 Ibid.

144 Queen Mary to Duke of York, 19 May 1932, RA GVI/PRIV/RF/11

145 Queen Mary to Duke of York, 24 May 1932, RA GVI/PRIV/RF/11

146 Duchess of York to D'Arcy Osborne, 10 October 1932, RA QEQM/OUT/OSBORNE

147 Duchess of York to Queen Mary, 21 October 1932, RA QM/PRIV/CC11/204

148 Duchess of York to D'Arcy Osborne, 30 November and 20 December 1932, RA QEQM/OUT/OSBORNE

149 D'Arcy Osborne to the Duchess of York, 26 January 1933, RA QEQM/PRIV/PAL/Osborne

150 Note by the Duchess of York on letter from Lady Londonderry to Lettice Bowlby, 27 July 1934, RA QEQMH/PS/GEN/1934/Women's Employment Federation

151 Lady Helen Graham to Lady Ruth Balfour, 30 November 1934, RA QEQMH/PS/GEN/1934/National Council of Women

152 Most Rev. Cosmo Lang to Duchess of York, 27 December 1932, RA QEQM/PRIV/PAL/Lang

153 Duchess of York to Most Rev. Cosmo Lang, 7 January 1933, Lambeth Palace Library, Lang Papers 318 f. 169

154 Queen Mary to Duchess of York, 5 February 1933, RA QEQM/PRIV/RF

155 Duchess of York to Queen Mary, 19, 30 January 1933, RA QM/PRIV/CC11/209, 210

156 Correspondence with Miss Thelma Evans of Rozevale Kennels, Reigate, RA ADYH/MAIN/070

157 Marion Crawford to Duchess of York, 21 November 1932, RA QEQM/PRIV/CHILD

158 Dermot Morrah, *Princess Elizabeth*, Odhams Press, 1950, p. 50

159 K. M. Murphy to Duchess of York, 5 April 1934, RA QEQMH/PS/GEN/Linguaphone Institute

160 Marion Crawford to Lady Cynthia Colville, n.d. [8 November 1937], RA QM/PRIV/CC14/62a

161 Ibid.

162 Ibid.

163 See Marion Crawford, *The Little Princesses*, Harcourt, Brace, New York, 1950, pp. 53, 97 for Lady Cynthia Colville's letters to Marion Crawford relaying Queen Mary's questions and comments

164 Queen Mary to Owen Morshead, 26 March 1941, RA QM/PRIV/CC48/957

165 Owen Morshead to Queen Mary, 25 July 1941, RA QM/PRIV/CC48/975

166 Information from the family of the Vicomtesse de Bellaigue

167 Queen Elizabeth to Princess Elizabeth, 29 December 1935, 6, 13, 27 May 1939, 27 June 1944, RA QEII/PRIV/RF, RA QEQM/PRIV/CHILD

168 Notes by Duchess of York, n.d. [1931–6], RA QEQM/PRIV/PERS

169 Duchess of York to Most Rev. Cosmo Lang, 12 January 1934, Lambeth Palace Library, Lang Papers 318 f. 174

170 ADYH/MAIN/51/1934: 16 February

171 QEQMH/PS/ENGT/1934: 21 February

172 Captain Lionel Scott to Harold Campbell, 7 July 1934, RA ADYH/MAIN/53/1934: 5–6 July

173 Duchess of York to Osbert Sitwell, 15 July 1934, Sitwell Papers

174 Queen Elizabeth to Sir Robin Mackworth-Young, 3 May 1976, RA QEQM/OUT/MOLYNEUX/140

175 Duchess of York to Hon. Richard Molyneux, 19 June 1931, 29 December 1935, RA QEQM/OUT/MOLYNEUX/46, 74

176 Duchess of York to Hon. Richard Molyneux, 18 August 1934, RA QEQM/OUT/MOLYNEUX/71

177 RCIN 403396

178 Queen Elizabeth to Sir Robin Mackworth-Young, 3 May 1976, RA QEQM/OUT/MOLYNEUX/140

179 Duchess of York to D'Arcy Osborne, 28 July 1934, RA QEQM/OUT/OSBORNE

180 Duchess of York to Osbert Sitwell, 2 August 1934, Sitwell Papers

181 King George V to Duchess of York, 7 August 1934, RA QEQM/PRIV/RF

182 Duchess of York to King George V, 6 August [misdated July] 1934, RA GV/PRIV/AA62/188

183 Duchess of York to King George V, 28 October 1934, RA GV/PRIV/AA62/200

184 Duchess of York to Queen Mary, 6 August 1934, RA QM/PRIV/CC11/225

185 Duchess of York to Duke of Kent, 27 August 1934, RA QEQM/OUT/GDK

186 RA GV/PRIV/GVD/1934: 19 September

187 Duchess of York to Beryl Poignand, 21 September 1934, Glamis Archives (CH)

188 Queen Mary to Duchess of York, 9 November 1934, RA QEQM/PRIV/RF

189 *The Times*, 30 November 1934

190 Lord Strathmore to Miss Cavie, 7 December 1934, Glamis Archives

191 *Daily Telegraph*, 30 November 1934

192 Duchess of York to King George V, 18 March 1935, RA GV/PRIV/AA62/215

193 RA GV/PRIV/GVD/1935: 6 May

194 Nicolson, *George V*, pp. 669–72

195 Prochaska, *Republic of Britain*, pp. 207–8

196 Ibid., p. 208

197 Nicolson, *George V*, p. 669

198 Prochaska, *Republic of Britain*, pp. 208–9

199 Nicolson, *George V*, pp. 662–8

200 Käthe Kübler to Duchess of York, 1 April 1933, RA QEQM/PRIV/PAL

201 Queen Elizabeth, conversations with Eric Anderson, 1994–5, RA QEQM/ADD/MISC.
     See also Vaughan Jones, *Daily Express*, 18 August 1946

202 D'Arcy Osborne to Duchess of York, 7 February 1934, RA QEQM/PRIV/PAL/Osborne

203 D'Arcy Osborne to Duchess of York, 14 March 1935, RA QEQM/PRIV/PAL/Osborne

204 Nicolson, *George V*, p. 665; Rose, *George V*, p. 388

205 Sir Eric Phipps to King George V, 12 September 1934, RA PS/PSO/GV/C/P/586/200

206 Sir Clive Wigram to Sir Eric Phipps, 16 January 1935, RA PS/PSO/GV/C/P/586/216,
     quoted in Nicolson, *George V*, p. 666

207 Rose, *George V*, p. 387

208 Ibid., p. 389

209 Norman Hartnell, *Silver and Gold*, Evans Bros, 1955, pp. 90–1

210 RA GV/PRIV/GVD/1935: 6 November

211 Sir Ian Malcolm to Duchess of York, 9 April 1935, RA ADYH/MAIN/58/1935: 30
     November

212 Sir Basil Brooke to Sir Ian Malcolm, 24 July 1935, RA ADYH/MAIN/58/1935: 30
     November

213 Sir George Clerk to Sir Basil Brooke, 5 November 1935, RA ADYH/MAIN/58/1935: 30
     November

214 Sir George Clerk to Sir Clive Wigram, 2 December 1935, RA PS/PSO/GV/C/P/1273/67

215 Duchess of York to D'Arcy Osborne, 10 January 1936, RA QEQM/OUT/OSBORNE

216 Wheeler-Bennett, p. 264

217 Princess Margaret to Duchess of York, 17 December 1935, RA QEQM/PRIV/RF

218 Jean Bruce to Duchess of York, 22 December 1935, RA QEQM/PRIV/CHILD

219 Alah Knight to Duchess of York, 24 December [1935], RA QEQM/PRIV/CHILD

220 Duchess of York to Princess Elizabeth, 29 December 1935, RA QEII/PRIV/RF

221 Princess Margaret to Duchess of York, 1 January [1936], RA QEQM/PRIV/RF

222 Duchess of York to Princess Elizabeth, 6 January 1936, QEII/PRIV/RF

223 Duchess of York to Queen Mary, 27 December 1935, RA QM/PRIV/CC12/18

224 Duchess of York to King George V, 30 December 1935, RA GV/PRIV/AA62/241

225 Duchess of York to Dick Molyneux, 29 December 1935, RA QEQM/OUT/
     MOLYNEUX/74

226 Owen Morshead to Paquita Morshead, 14 January 1936, RA AEC/GG/12/OS/1 (Morshead Papers)
227 Rose, *George V*, p. 400
228 Hon. Jean Bruce to Duchess of York, 10 January 1936, RA QEQM/PRIV/CHILD
229 RA GV/PRIV/GVD/1936: 16 January
230 Alan Lascelles to Joan Lascelles, 16 January 1936, CAC LASL 4/2/1
231 Alan Lascelles to Joan Lascelles, 18 January 1936, CAC LASL 4/2/4
232 Duchess of York to Queen Mary, RA QM/PRIV/CC12/22
233 Queen Mary, diary, RA QM/PRIV/QMD/1936: 19 January
234 Ziegler, *Edward VIII*, p. 241
235 Hardinge, p. 59
236 RA QM/PRIV/QMD/1936: 20 January
237 Rose, *George V*, p. 403
238 RA QM/PRIV/QMD/1936: 27 January
239 RA QM/PRIV/QMD/1936: 28 January
240 Arthur Penn to Duchess of York, 22 January 1936, RA QEQM/PRIV/PAL/Penn
241 Rose, *George V*, p. 406

TEN: ABDICATION 1936–1937

1 Laird, p. 160
2 Channon, *Diaries*, p. 53
3 Kenneth Rose, *Kings, Queens and Courtiers*, Weidenfeld & Nicolson, 1985, p. 73
4 Ziegler, *Edward VIII*, p. 202
5 Ibid., p. 203
6 Bradford, *George VI*, pp. 178–9
7 Ibid., pp. 179–80
8 Ziegler, *Edward VIII*, pp. 227–8
9 Bradford, *George VI*, p. 183
10 Ibid., p. 190
11 Ziegler, *Edward VIII*, p. 233
12 Rose, *George V*, p. 392
13 Airlie, p. 197, quoted in Ziegler, *Edward VIII*, p. 199
14 Ziegler, *Edward VIII*, pp. 236–7
15 Ibid., p. 243
16 Ibid.; Sir Alan Lascelles to A. G. Allen, 19 April 1956, CAC LASL 3/9/7
17 Owen Morshead, note, 20 December 1936, RA AEC/GG/12/OS/1
18 Ziegler, *Edward VIII*, p. 247
19 Ibid., p. 245
20 Helen Hardinge, diary, Hon. Lady Murray Papers
21 Francis Watson, *Dawson of Penn*, Chatto & Windus, 1950, p. 285
22 Kenneth Clark to Duchess of York, 28 March 1936, RA QEQM/PRIV/PAL
23 Duchess of York to Queen Mary, 11 March 1936, RA QM/PRIV/CC12/24
24 RA QM/PRIV/QMD/1936: 10–12 April
25 Duchess of York to Queen Mary, 21 May 1936, RA QM/PRIV/CC12/26
26 RA QM/PRIV/QMD/1936: 25 May; *Morning Post*, 26 May 1936
27 Duchess of York to Dick Molyneux, 12 June 1936, RA QEQM/OUT/MOLYNEUX/79
28 D'Arcy Osborne to Duchess of York, 5 June 1936, RA QEQM/PRIV/PAL/Osborne
29 RA QEQMH/PS/ENGT/1936/7

30 RA ADYH/MAIN/060/9 June 1936

31 Roger Lumley to Sir Basil Brooke, 21 July 1936, RA ADYH/MAIN/060/1936: 28 July

32 Duchess of York to Duff Cooper, 3 August 1936, CAC, Duff Cooper papers; Duff Cooper to Duchess, 14 August 1936, RA QEQM/PRIV/PAL

33 Duke of York to Clare Vyner, 3 August 1936, Vyner Papers

34 Queen Mary to Duchess of York, 9 August 1936, RA QEQM/PRIV/RF

35 Helen Hardinge, diary, 28 March 1936, Hon. Lady Murray Papers

36 Lord Wigram, memorandum, 13 March 1936, RA PS/PSO/GVI/C/019/315

37 Duchess of Devonshire to Lady Airlie, 25 February 1936, British Library, Add MSS 82766

38 Ziegler, *Edward VIII*, p. 281

39 Ibid., p. 291

40 Hardinge, pp. 101–3

41 Ziegler, *Edward VIII*, pp. 266–72, 273–5

42 Ibid., p. 273

43 Helen Hardinge, diary, 25 November 1936, Hon. Lady Murray Papers

44 Ziegler, *Edward VIII*, p. 274

45 Ibid., pp. 282–6

46 Ibid., p. 287

47 Duchess of York to Queen Mary, 14 September 1936, RA QM/PRIV/CC12/31

48 Queen Mary to Duke of York, 13 August 1936, RA GVI/PRIV/RF/11

49 Edward W. Watt, Lord Provost, to Sir Basil Brooke, 11 August 1936, with marginal notes by the Duke of York, RA ADYH/MAIN/060/23 September 1936

50 Duchess of York to Queen Mary, 19 September 1936, RA QM/PRIV/CC12/32

51 Ziegler, *Edward VIII*, p. 288 (see also Bradford, *George VI*, p. 225)

52 Ziegler, *Edward VIII*, p. 287, quoting Sir Walter Monckton

53 Ibid., pp. 287–8, quoting Sir Alan Lascelles

54 Queen Mary to Duke of York, 13 August 1936, RA GVI/PRIV/RF/11

55 Duke of York to Queen Mary, 13 October 1936, RA QM/PRIV/CC12/35

56 Duchess of York to Queen Mary, 11 October 1936, RA QM/PRIV/CC12/34

57 Ibid.

58 Queen Mary to Duchess of York, 14 October 1936, RA QEQM/PRIV/RF

59 Ziegler, *Edward VIII*, p. 291

60 Wheeler-Bennett, p. 277

61 Ibid.

62 Duchess of York to Queen Mary, 21 October 1936, RA QM/PRIV/CC12/36

63 Queen Mary to Duke of York, 22 October 1936, RA GVI/PRIV/RF/11

64 Rev. Alan Don, diary, 24 November 1936, Lambeth Palace Library, MSS 2864

65 Duchess of York to King Edward VIII, 29 October 1936, RA EDW/MAINA/3024

66 Duke of York to Queen Mary, 6 November 1936, RA QM/PRIV/CC12/38

67 Queen Mary to Duke of York, 8 November 1936, RA GVI/PRIV/RF/11

68 Wheeler-Bennett, p. 280

69 Ibid., p. 281

70 Duff Cooper, p. 229

71 Queen Mary to Lord Wigram, 15 July 1938, commenting on King Edward VIII's letter to her of 20 November 1936, quoted in Ziegler, *Edward VIII*, p. 324

72 Ziegler, *Edward VIII*, pp. 323–4

73 King Edward VIII to Queen Mary, 20 November 1936, RA EDW/ADD/ABD/1, quoted in ibid., p. 324

74 Queen Mary to Duchess of York, 17 November 1936, RA QEQM/PRIV/RF

75 Duchess of York to Queen Mary, n.d. [17 November 1936], RA EDW/ADD/ABD/1

76 Evelyn, Duchess of Devonshire, to Lady Airlie, 17 November 1936, British Library, Add MSS 82766

77 Duchess of York to Queen Mary, 20 November 1936, RA EDW/ADD/ABD/1

78 Ziegler, *Edward VIII*, p. 324

79 Duchess of York to King Edward VIII, 23 November 1936, RA EDW/PRIV/MAINB/111

80 Duchess of York to Helen Hardinge, 23 November 1936, Hon. Lady Murray Papers

81 Wheeler-Bennett, p. 283

82 Ziegler, *Edward VIII*, p. 302

83 Ibid., pp. 303–4

84 Ibid., pp. 305–7

85 Wheeler-Bennett, p. 284

86 Ibid., p. 284n.

87 King George VI's account of the abdication, quoted in ibid., p. 284

88 Duchess of York to Dick Molyneux, n.d. [3 December 1936], RA QEQM/OUT/MOLYNEUX/83

89 King George VI's account of the abdication, quoted in Wheeler-Bennett, p. 285

90 Ziegler, *Edward VIII*, p. 310

91 King George VI's account of the abdication, quoted in Wheeler-Bennett, p. 285

92 Frederick Dalrymple Hamilton, diary, 3 December 1936, private collection

93 Susan Williams, *The People's King*, Allen Lane, 2003, pp. 184

94 Alan Lascelles to George Allen, 19 April 1956, CAC, LASL 3/9/7

95 Lord Birkenhead, *Walter Monckton*, Weidenfeld & Nicolson, 1969, p. 138

96 Duke of York to Queen Mary, 5 December 1936, RA EDW/ADD/ABD/1

97 Duchess of York to Osbert Sitwell, 7 December 1936, Sitwell Papers

98 Owen Morshead, notes, 14 January 1937, RA AEC/GG/12/OS/1. A slightly different version of Queen Mary's words appears in her biography by James Pope-Hennessy: *Queen Mary*, Allen & Unwin, 1959, p. 576

99 Ziegler, *Edward VIII*, p. 311

100 Ibid., pp. 311–12; Bradford, *George VI*, p. 255

101 King George VI's account of the abdication, quoted in Wheeler-Bennett, p. 285

102 Duchess of York to May Elphinstone, 6 December 1936, RA QEQM/OUT/ELPHINSTONE

103 Lady Londonderry to Duchess of York, 5 December [1936], RA QEQM/PRIV/PAL; Duchess of York to Lady Londonderry, 7 December 1936, RA QEQM/OUT/MISC

104 Helen Hardinge, diary, 9 December 1936, Hon. Lady Murray Papers

105 King George VI's account of the abdication, quoted in Wheeler-Bennett, p. 286

106 Ibid.

107 Queen Mary's words to Harold Nicolson, quoted in Bradford, *George VI*, p. 198

108 RA QM/PRIV/QMD/1936: 9 December

109 Duchess of York to Queen Mary, 10 December 1936, RA EDW/ADD/ABD/1

110 RA QM/PRIV/QMD/1936: 10 December

111 Ziegler, *Edward VIII*, pp. 326–7

112 Frederick Dalrymple Hamilton, diary, 10 December 1936, private collection

113 Princess Royal to Duchess of York, 10 December 1936, RA QEQMH/PRIV/RF

114 King George VI's account of the abdication, quoted in Wheeler-Bennett, p. 287

115 Ziegler, *Edward VIII*, p. 331

116 Queen Elizabeth to Duke of Windsor, 11 December 1936, RA EDW/MAINA/3068

117 RA QM/PRIV/QMD/1936: 11 December

118 King George VI's account of the abdication, quoted in Wheeler-Bennett, p. 287

119 Queen Elizabeth to Most Rev. Cosmo Lang, 14 January 1937, Lambeth Palace Library, Lang Papers 318 ff. 181–3

120 Queen Mary to Queen Elizabeth, 11 December 1936, RA QEQM/PRIV/RF

121 Wheeler-Bennett, p. 288

122 Queen Elizabeth, conversations with Eric Anderson, 1994–5, RA QEQM/ADD/MISC

123 Lady Cynthia Asquith, *The King's Daughter*, Hutchinson, [1937], pp. 96–7; Ben Pimlott, *The Queen*, HarperCollins, 1997, p. 41

124 Queen Elizabeth to Most Rev. Cosmo Lang, 12 December 1936, Lambeth Palace Library, Lang Papers 318 ff. 177–80

125 Rev. Alan Don, diary, 14 December 1936, Lambeth Palace Library, MSS 2864

126 Most Rev. Cosmo Lang to Queen Elizabeth, 14 December 1936, RA QEQM/PRIV/PAL/Lang

127 Quoted in Bradford, *George VI*, p. 299

128 Owen Morshead, notes, 12 January 1937, RA AEC/GG12/OS/1

129 Letter to Victor Cazalet quoted in Bradford, *George VI*, p. 300

130 Queen Elizabeth to Queen Mary, 14 December 1936, quoted in Wheeler-Bennett, p. 296

131 Wheeler-Bennett, pp. 296–7

132 Queen Mary to King George VI, 11 December 1936, RA GVI/PRIV/RF/11

133 King George VI to Queen Mary, n.d. [11 December 1936], RA QM/PRIV/CC12/39

134 Queen Mary, Message to the Nation, 12 December 1936, RA QM/PRIV/CC49/99

135 Quoted by Bradford, *George VI*, p. 298

136 Owen Morshead, notes, 20 December 1936, RA AEC/GG12/OS/1

137 King George VI, broadcast, 1 January 1937, quoted in Wheeler-Bennett, p. 297

138 Queen Elizabeth to Queen Mary, 2 February 1937, RA QM/PRIV/CC12/42

139 Princess Beatrice to Queen Elizabeth, 12 December 1936, RA QEQM/PRIV/RF

140 Duchess of Beaufort to Queen Elizabeth, 12 December 1936, RA QEQM/PRIV/RF

141 Princess Alice to Queen Elizabeth, 12 December 1936, RA QEQM/PRIV/RF

142 Queen Mary to Lady Strathmore, 16 December 1936, Glamis Archives

143 Lady Strathmore to Sir John Weir, 19 December 1936, Glamis Archives

144 Owen Morshead, notes, 16 January 1937, RA AEC/GG12/OS/1

145 The Duke of Windsor, *A King's Story: The Memoirs of H.R.H. The Duke of Windsor*, Cassell, 1951, p. 278

146 Jasper Ridley to Queen Elizabeth, 10 December 1936, RA QEQM/PRIV/PAL/Ridley

147 Archibald Clark Kerr to Queen Elizabeth, 10 December 1936, RA QEQM/PRIV/PAL

148 Osbert Sitwell to Queen Elizabeth, 11 December 1936, RA QEQM/PRIV/PAL/Sitwell

149 Queen Elizabeth to Osbert Sitwell, 17 December 1936, Sitwell Papers

150 Queen Elizabeth to Osbert Sitwell, 19 February 1937, RA QEQM/OUT/SITWELL

151 Queen Elizabeth to D'Arcy Osborne, 16 December 1936, RA QEQM/OUT/OSBORNE

152 Bradford, *George VI*, p. 299

153 Walter Monckton, notes, September 1941, Bodleian Library, Monckton Papers, MT 22/220–2

154 Owen Morshead, notes, 17 January 1937, RA AEC/GG12/OS/1

155 Osbert Sitwell to Queen Elizabeth, 8 February 1937, RA QEQM/PRIV/PAL/Sitwell

156 Queen Elizabeth to Osbert Sitwell, 19 February 1937, RA QEQM/OUT/SITWELL

157 Queen Elizabeth, conversations with Eric Anderson, 1994–5, RA QEQM/ADD/MISC

158 Queen Elizabeth to Queen Mary, 23 March, 7 April 1937, RA QM/PRIV/CC12/45, 47

159 W. C. Johnson, Chairman, People's Palace, to Sir Alexander Hardinge, 21 December 1936, RA PS/PSO/GVI/PS/MAIN/00616/B/03

160 Earl of Cromer to Alan Lascelles, 22 December 1936, RA PS/PSO/GVI/PS/MAIN/00616/B/19

161 Countess Spencer, diary, 16 March 1937, Althorp Archives
162 Harold Nicolson, *Diaries and Letters 1930–1939*, ed. Nigel Nicolson, Collins, 1966, pp. 297–8
163 Clement Attlee to Tom Attlee, 17 April 1937, Bodleian Library, MS Eng.c.4792
164 Ziegler, *Osbert Sitwell*, Pimlico, 1999, p. 238
165 Lady Diana Cooper, quoted in Bradford, *George VI*, pp. 301–2
166 Queen Mary to King George VI and Queen Elizabeth, 26 April 1937, RA GVI/PRIV/RF/11
167 Pope-Hennessy, p. 584
168 Queen Mary to Queen Elizabeth, 23 February 1937, RA QEQM/PRIV/RF; Queen Elizabeth to Queen Mary, 11 March 1937, RA QM/PRIV/CC12/44
169 Longford, *Queen Mother*, pp. 63–4, and Laird, pp. 205–7
170 Robert Wood, *A World in Your Ear*, 1979, pp. 102–3, quoted in Bradford, *George VI*, pp. 278–9
171 Countess Spencer, diary, 1 May 1937, Althorp Archives
172 Countess Spencer, diary, 5 May 1937, Althorp Archives
173 Graves and Hodge, p. 367
174 Ibid.
175 Wheeler-Bennett, p. 311
176 Ibid. pp. 311–12
177 Ibid., p. 312
178 Graves and Hodge, pp. 367–8
179 Owen Morshead to Aunt Dora (copy), 14 May 1937, RA AEC/GG12/DIARY/1937
180 Ibid.
181 Rev. Alan Don, diary, 12 May 1937, Lambeth Palace Library, MSS 2864
182 Princess Elizabeth, 'The Coronation, 12th May 1937', account written for her parents, RA QEII/PRIV/PERS
183 Ibid.
184 Queen Mary to King George VI, 12 May 1937, RA GVI/PRIV/RF/11
185 Queen Elizabeth to Most Rev. Cosmo Lang, 15 May 1937, Lambeth Palace Library, Lang Papers 318 ff. 184–6

ELEVEN: QUEEN CONSORT 1937–1939

1 Noble Frankland, *History at War*, Giles de la Mare, 1998, p. 214. Dr Frankland is the author of biographies of Prince Henry, Duke of Gloucester, and of Prince Arthur, Duke of Connaught
2 Duchess of York to King George V, 5 August 1932, RA GV/PRIV/AA62/158
3 Queen Elizabeth to Princess Elizabeth, 21 December 1949, RA QEII/PRIV/RF
4 Ibid.
5 Mackenzie King, diary, 20 May 1939, LAC/BAC MG26-J13
6 Helen Hardinge, diary, quoted in Vickers, p. 76
7 Duchess of York to D'Arcy Osborne, 5 August 1931, 10 January 1936, RA QEQM/OUT/OSBORNE
8 Duchess of York to D'Arcy Osborne, 24 November 1928, 17 November 1929, RA QEQM/OUT/OSBORNE
9 Duchess of York to Duff Cooper, 1 October 1935, CAC, Duff Cooper Papers
10 Duchess of York to D'Arcy Osborne, 11 March 1930, RA QEQM/OUT/OSBORNE
11 Osbert Sitwell to Duchess of York, 12 August 1936, RA QEQM/PRIV/PAL/SITWELL

12 D'Arcy Osborne to Duchess of York, 15 August 1934, RA QEQM/PRIV/PAL/OSBORNE

13 Owen Morshead, notes, 7 July 1940, RA AEC/GG/12/OS/2

14 Duchess of York to D'Arcy Osborne, n.d. [postmark 17 March 1924], RA QEQM/OUT/OSBORNE

15 Duchess of York to Duff Cooper, 20 March 1931, CAC, Duff Cooper Papers

16 D'Arcy Osborne to Duchess of York, 27 August 1935, RA QEQM/PRIV/PAL/OSBORNE

17 Duchess of York to D'Arcy Osborne, 28 July 1934, RA QEQM/OUT/OSBORNE

18 D'Arcy Osborne to Duchess of York, 23 July 1937, RA QEQM/PRIV/PAL/OSBORNE

19 Duchess of York to D'Arcy Osborne, n.d. [postmark 22 March 1924], RA QEQM/OUT/OSBORNE

20 Duchess of York to D'Arcy Osborne, 13 July 1928, RA QEQM/OUT/OSBORNE

21 Duchess of York to D'Arcy Osborne, 17 November 1929, RA QEQM/OUT/OSBORNE

22 Owen Morshead, notes, 7 July 1940, RA AEC/GG/12/OS/2

23 Lady Strathmore to Major and Mrs Colvin, 14 January 1937, Glamis Archives

24 RA QM/PRIV/QMD/1937: 18 May

25 Wheeler-Bennett, p. 318

26 Lucy Baldwin to Queen Elizabeth, 1 June 1937, RA QEQM/PRIV/PAL

27 Graves and Hodge, p. 380

28 Ibid., pp. 402–3

29 Conversation reported by Owen Morshead in a letter to Paquita Morshead, 20 September 1937, RA AEC/GG/12/OS/1

30 Queen Elizabeth to Lord Nuffield, 15 July 1937, RA QEQM/OUT/MISC

31 Laird, pp. 214–15

32 Commander Oscar Henderson to Sir Alexander Hardinge, 3 August 1937, RA PS/PSO/GVI/PS/MAIN/01000/075/A/94

33 Lieutenant Colonel Evelyn Fanshawe to Captain R. J. Streatfeild, n.d. [26 July 1937], RA QEQMH/PS/ENGT/1937: 24 July

34 Queen Elizabeth to Queen Mary, 18 August 1937, RA QM/PRIV/CC12/54

35 Letters from Chamberlain to his sister Hilda, Chamberlain Papers, quoted by Bradford, *George VI*, pp. 347–9

36 King George VI to Queen Mary, 30 August 1937, RA QM/PRIV/CC12/55

37 Most Rev. Cosmo Lang to Queen Elizabeth, 4 September 1937, RA QEQM/PRIV/PAL/LANG

38 Ziegler, *Osbert Sitwell*, pp. 238–9

39 Countess of Moray to Queen Elizabeth, n.d. [autumn 1937] RA QEQM/PRIV/PAL

40 Hon. Sir Richard Molyneux to Queen Elizabeth, 12 September 1937, RA QEQM/PRIV/PAL/Molyneux

41 Ziegler, *Edward VIII*, p. 348

42 Ibid., p. 349

43 Ibid., p. 351

44 Bradford, *George VI*, p. 318

45 Lord Wigram to Most Rev. Cosmo Lang, 5 April 1937, Lambeth Palace Library, Lang Papers 318 ff. 136–7

46 Owen Morshead, diary, 3 June 1937, RA AEC/GG/12/DIARY/1937

47 Lord Wigram to Most Rev. Cosmo Lang, 5 April 1937, Lambeth Palace Library, Lang Papers 318 ff. 136–7

48 Queen Mary to King George VI, 10 April 1937, RA GVI/PRIV/RF/11

49 King George VI to Duke of Windsor, 11 April 1937, RA EDW/MAINB/116, quoted in Ziegler, *Edward VIII*, p. 355

50 Ibid., p. 357

51 Queen Mary to King George VI, 4 February 1937, RA GVI/PRIV/RF/11

52 Lord Wigram to Sir John Simon, 11 March 1937, RA PS/PSO/GVI/C/019/207

53 Lord Wigram, memorandum, n.d. [May 1937], RA PS/PSO/GVI/C/019/216

54 Ziegler, *Edward VIII*, p. 359

55 Lord Wigram, memorandum, n.d. [May 1937], RA PS/PSO/GVI/C/019/216; *The Times*, 29 May 1937

56 Queen Mary to Queen Elizabeth, 21 May 1937, RA QEQM/PRIV/RF

57 Ibid.

58 Queen Elizabeth to Queen Mary, 21 May 1937, RA QM/PRIV/CC12/49

59 Queen Elizabeth to Queen Mary, 3 June 1937, RA QM/PRIV/CC14/74

60 Queen Mary to Queen Elizabeth, 3 June 1937, RA QEQM/PRIV/RF

61 King George VI to Queen Mary, 14 September 1937, RA QM/PRIV/CC12/57

62 Queen Elizabeth, conversations with Eric Anderson, 1994–5, RA QEQM/ADD/MISC

63 Queen Mary to Queen Elizabeth, 30 September 1937, RA QEQM/PRIV/RF

64 Ziegler, *Edward VIII*, p. 376

65 Walter Monckton to Queen Elizabeth, 18 September 1937, RA QEQM/PRIV/PAL

66 Queen Elizabeth to Walter Monckton, 21 September 1937, RA GVI/OUT/MONCKTON

67 Ziegler, *Edward VIII*, p. 376

68 Queen Elizabeth to Queen Mary, 28 September 1937, RA QM/PRIV/CC12/59

69 King George VI to Walter Monckton, 5 October 1937, RA GVI/OUT/MONCKTON

70 King George VI to Queen Mary, 4 October 1937, RA QM/PRIV/CC12/60

71 Sir Ronald Lindsay to Lady Lindsay, 11 October 1937, quoted in *The Crawford Papers: The Journals of David Lindsay, 27th Earl of Crawford*, ed. John Vincent, Manchester University Press, 1984, pp. 616–21

72 Ziegler, *Edward VIII*, p. 392

73 *Crawford Papers*, pp. 616–21

74 Queen Elizabeth to Queen Mary, 26 October 1937, RA QM/PRIV/CC12/61

75 William Walton to Queen Elizabeth, 22 December 1937, RA QEQM/PRIV/PAL

76 Queen Elizabeth to Osbert Sitwell, 18 December 1937, Sitwell Papers

77 Queen Elizabeth to Hon. Sir Richard Molyneux, 7 December 1937, RA QEQM/OUT/MOLYNEUX/91

78 Queen Elizabeth to Duke of Windsor, 23 December 1937, RA EDW/MAINB/130

79 Duke of Windsor to Queen Elizabeth (copy), 12 January 1938, RA EDW/MAINB/127

80 Queen Elizabeth to Duke of Windsor, 15 January 1938, RA EDW/MAINB/129

81 Duke of Windsor to Queen Elizabeth (copy), 22 January 1938, RA EDW/MAINB/131

82 Queen Elizabeth to Princess Elizabeth, 4 January 1938, RA QEII/PRIV/RF

83 Queen Elizabeth to Princess Elizabeth, 5 January 1938, RA QEII/PRIV/RF

84 Queen Elizabeth to D'Arcy Osborne, 5 January 1938, RA QEQM/OUT/OSBORNE

85 D'Arcy Osborne to Queen Elizabeth, 27 January 1938, RA QEQM/PRIV/PAL/Osborne

86 Duff Cooper, p. 241

87 Queen Elizabeth to Arthur Penn, 30 June 1938, Penn Papers, and Queen Elizabeth to Neville Chamberlain, 2 July 1938, BUA NC 7/4/8

88 Queen Elizabeth to Most Rev. Cosmo Lang, 23 June 1938, Lambeth Palace Library, Lang Papers 318 ff. 188–9

89 Duke of Windsor to Queen Elizabeth, telegram, 23 June 1938, RA QEQM/PRIV/DEATH/STRATH

90 Queen Elizabeth to Neville Chamberlain, 2 July 1938, BUA NC 7/4/8

91 Arthur Penn to Queen Elizabeth, 23 June 1938, RA QEQM/PRIV/DEATH/STRATH

92 Queen Elizabeth to Arthur Penn, 30 June 1938, Penn Papers

93 Queen Elizabeth to Queen Mary, 28 June 1938, RA QM/PRIV/CC12/73

94 Laird, p. 220

95 Queen Elizabeth to Queen Mary, 28 June 1938, RA QM/PRIV/CC12/73

96 Ibid.

97 Address by the Archbishop of Canterbury, *The Times*, 28 June 1938; Glamis Archives

98 Queen Elizabeth to Archbishop Lang, 1 July 1938, Lambeth Palace Library, Lang Papers 318 ff. 191–2

99 Arthur Penn to Queen Elizabeth, 28 June 1938, RA QEQM/PRIV/DEATH/STRATH

100 Queen Elizabeth to Arthur Penn, 30 June 1938, Penn Papers

101 Queen Elizabeth to Princess Elizabeth, 28 June 1938, RA QEII/PRIV/RF

102 Longford, *Queen Mother*, pp. 70–1

103 Queen Elizabeth to Queen Mary, 13 July 1938, RA GV/CC12/75

104 Laird, p. 221

105 Bradford, *George VI*, p. 359

106 'Les Souverains Britanniques en France', special issue of *L'Illustration*, July 1938; Sir Eric Phipps to Sir Alexander Hardinge, 15 March 1938, RA PS/PSO/GVI/PS/SV/02718/1/038

107 Longford, *Queen Mother*, p. 71

108 Bradford, *George VI*, p. 360

109 Interview with Bertrand du Vignaud de Villefort on behalf of the author

110 Rev. Dr John Stirton, diary, 27–29 August 1938, RA AEC/GG/026

111 Longford, *Queen Mother*, p. 72

112 *L'Oeuvre*, June 1939

113 Quoted in Wheeler-Bennett, p. 343

114 Hartnell, p. 94

115 Bradford, *George VI*, p. 361

116 Wheeler-Bennett, p. 343

117 Lady Diana Cooper, *The Light of Common Day*, 1959, p. 223, quoted in Bradford, *George VI*, p. 361

118 Laird, p. 222

119 Neville Chamberlain to King George VI, 13 August 1938, BUA NC 7/3/25

120 Duff Cooper to Queen Elizabeth, 2 August 1938, RA QEQM/PRIV/PAL

121 Duff Cooper, diary, 23 July 1938, John Julius Norwich Papers

122 Queen Elizabeth to Queen Mary, 5 August 1938, RA QM/PRIV/CC12/77

123 Georgina Guérin to her parents, 31 August 1938, RA QEII/OUT/GUÉRIN/31

124 Rev. Dr John Stirton, diary, 27–29 August 1938, RA AEC/GG/026

125 Paul Berman, *Terror and Liberalism*, W. W. Norton, 2003, pp. 124–8

126 Wheeler-Bennett, p. 345

127 Queen Mary to King George VI, 15 September 1938, RA GVI/PRIV/RF/11

128 King George VI to Queen Elizabeth, 19 September 1938, RA QEQM/PRIV/RF

129 Queen Elizabeth to May Elphinstone, 24 September 1938, RA QEQM/OUT/ELPHINSTONE

130 Sir Alexander Hardinge to King George VI, 15 September [1938], RA PS/PSO/GVI/C/235/04

131 Sir Alexander Hardinge, memorandum, 29 September [1938], RA PS/PSO/GVI/C/235/06

132 Sir Alexander Hardinge, memorandum, 26 and 29 September 1938, RA PS/PSO/GVI/C/235/10

133 Laird, pp. 224–5

134 Queen Elizabeth, speech, 27 September 1938, RA QEQMH/PS/SPE

135 Laird, pp. 225–6

136 King George VI to May Elphinstone, 29 September 1938, RA QEQM/OUT/ELPHINSTONE

137 Duff Cooper, p. 268

138 Queen Mary to King George VI, 1 October 1938, RA PRIV/RF/11

139 Queen Elizabeth to Anne Chamberlain, 30 September 1938, BUA NC 13/11/656

140 Anne Chamberlain to Queen Elizabeth, 30 September 1938, RA QEQM/PRIV/PAL

141 Andrew Roberts, *The History of the English Speaking Peoples since 1900*, Weidenfeld & Nicolson, 2006, p. 249

142 Queen Elizabeth to Queen Mary, 2 October 1938, RA QM/PRIV/CC12/84

143 Queen Elizabeth to Osbert Sitwell, 11 October 1938, Sitwell Papers

144 Queen Elizabeth to Osbert Sitwell, 13 December 1938, Sitwell Papers

145 D'Arcy Osborne to Queen Elizabeth, 17 October 1938, RA QEQM/PRIV/PAL/Osborne

146 Most Rev. Cosmo Lang to Queen Elizabeth, 19 December 1938, RA QEQM/PRIV/PAL/Lang

147 Queen Mary to Queen Elizabeth, 5 October 1938, RA QEQM/PRIV/RF

148 Martin Gilbert, *Churchill: A Life*, Minerva, 1992, p. 598

149 Ibid., p. 604

150 Queen Elizabeth to Rachel Bowes Lyon, 22 November 1938, Bowes Lyon Papers, SPW

151 Jasper Ridley to Queen Elizabeth, 29 January 1939, RA QEQM/PRIV/PAL/Ridley

152 Lord Birkenhead, *Walter Monckton: The Life of Viscount Monckton of Brenchley*, Weidenfeld & Nicolson, 1969, p. 169

153 Queen Elizabeth to Sir Walter Monckton, 6 December 1938, RA GVI/OUT/MONCKTON

154 Queen Mary to King George VI, 3 February 1939, RA GVI/PRIV/RF/11; King George VI to Queen Mary, RA QM/PRIV/CC12/87

155 Walter Monckton to King George VI (copy), 10 February 1939, RA GVI/OUT/MONCKTON

156 Duke of Windsor to Queen Mary, 29 March 1939, RA QM/PRIV/CC9

157 Queen Mary to Queen Elizabeth, 31 March 1939, RA QEQM/PRIV/RF

158 Clement Attlee to Tom Attlee, 23 February 1939, Bodleian Library, Attlee Papers, MS Eng.c.4792

159 Wheeler-Bennett, p. 364

160 *L'Illustration*, special supplement on state visit of President Lebrun, 21–24 March 1939, Archives Nationales, Paris: Papiers des Chefs de l'État AG/1/69

161 Wheeler-Bennett, pp. 367–8

162 Sir Alexander Hardinge, memorandum, 26 April 1939, Hon. Lady Murray Papers

163 John Wheeler-Bennett interview with second Baron Hardinge of Penshurst, January 1954, RA AEC/GG/20

164 Laird, p. 185

165 Ibid.

166 *Hostage to Fortune: The Letters of Joseph P. Kennedy*, ed. Amanda Smith, Viking, 2001, pp. 326–9

TWELVE: ACROSS THE ATLANTIC 1939

1 Queen Elizabeth to Queen Mary, 8 May 1939, RA QM/PRIV/CC12/93
2 Wheeler-Bennett, pp. 371, 373
3 Lord Tweedsmuir to Sir Alexander Hardinge, 17 October 1938, RA PS/PSO/GVI/PS/VISCOM/03400/001A/01
4 Wheeler-Bennett, p. 382
5 Queen Elizabeth to Princess Elizabeth, 6 May 1939, RA QEII/PRIV/RF
6 Queen Elizabeth to Queen Mary, 8 May 1939, RA QM/PRIV/CC12/93
7 Ziegler, *Edward VIII*, pp. 398–400
8 Duke of Kent to Queen Elizabeth, 16 May 1939, RA QEQM/PRIV/RF; Sir Alexander Hardinge to King George VI, 9 May 1939, RA PS/PSO/AH, quoted in Ziegler, *Edward VIII*, pp. 399–400
9 Queen Elizabeth to Princess Elizabeth, 13 May 1939, RA QEII/PRIV/RF
10 Queen Elizabeth to Queen Mary, 15 May 1939, RA QM/PRIV/CC12/94
11 Ibid.
12 Sir Alan Lascelles to Joan Lascelles, 14–16 May 1939, CAC LASL 4/3/8
13 Mackenzie King, diary, 17 May 1939, LAC/BAC MG26-J13
14 Ibid.
15 Diary (translation) of Lieutenant Colonel D. B. Papineau, 17 May 1939, Archives Nationales du Québec, P569, S1, D1, P19
16 Ibid.
17 Ibid., 18 May 1939
18 L'Abbé J.-C. Desrosiers to A. Paquette, 5 May 1937, Archives Nationales du Québec, E4 1960–01–483/567; Dr J. Marcoux to Jean Bruchési, 16 February, 6 May 1939, Archives Nationales du Québec, E4 1960–01–483/268/154, 567
19 Hartnell, pp. 99–100
20 Canadian press report, 13 June 1939, RA F&V/VISOV/CAN/1939/Press cuttings/Vol. III, p. 125
21 Sir Alan Lascelles to Eric Mackenzie, Comptroller to the Governor General, 21 January 1939, RA PS/PSO/GVI/PS/VISCOM/03400/002/094
22 Sir Alan Lascelles to Joan Lascelles, 21 May 1939, CAC LASL 4/3/9
23 Molly Pulver Ungar, 'Emile Vaillancourt and the Royal Visit of 1939', paper given to the Canadian Historical Association, London (Ontario), 2005; Diary (translation) of Lieutenant Colonel D. B. Papineau, 21 May 1939, Archives Nationales du Québec, P569, S1, D1, P19
24 'Canada: Houde for Dictators', *Time*, 20 February 1939
25 Quoted in *Colombo's Canadian Quotations*, Hurtig Publishers, 1974, p. 267
26 Montreal press reports cited by Ungar, 'Emile Vaillancourt'; Diary (translation) of Lieutenant Colonel D. B. Papineau, 21 May 1939, Archives Nationales du Québec, P569, S1, D1, P19
27 Sir Alan Lascelles to Joan Lascelles, 21 May 1939, CAC LASL 4/3/9
28 Lord Tweedsmuir to Sir Alexander Hardinge, 22 May 1939, RA PS/PSO/GVI/PS/VISCOM/03400/001A/116
29 *Speeches by the King and Queen during Their Majesties' visit to Canada, 1939*, booklet published by the Government of Canada, 1939
30 Letter from Lord Tweedsmuir to a friend, quoted in Wheeler-Bennett, p. 380
31 Lord Tweedsmuir to Sir Alexander Hardinge, 22 May 1939, RA PS/PSO/GVI/PS/VISCOM/03400/001A/116

32 Letter from Lord Tweedsmuir to a friend, quoted in Wheeler-Bennett, p. 380

33 Lord Tweedsmuir to Sir Alexander Hardinge, 22 May 1939, RA PS/PSO/GVI/PS/VISCOM/03400/001A/116

34 Article by F. C. Mears, *Montreal Gazette*, [21 May 1939], RA F&V/VISOV/CAN/1939/Press cuttings/Vol. I, p. 98

35 Lord Tweedsmuir to Sir Alexander Hardinge, 22 May 1939, RA PS/PSO/GVI/PS/VISCOM/03400/001A/116

36 Journal of Their Majesties' Tour of Canada, USA, and Newfoundland, May and June 1939, RA PS/PSO/GVI/C/257/01

37 Georges Vanier to the Canadian Secretary of State for External Affairs, 20 May 1939, LAC/BAC RG7, G26, Vol. 93, File 2213-D General

38 Sir Percy Loraine to Viscount Halifax, 15 June 1939, RA PS/PSO/GVI/PS/VISCOM/03400/145/1

39 Canadian press report, 19 May 1939, RA F&V/VISOV/CAN/1939/Press cuttings/Vol. I, p. 97

40 Lord Tweedsmuir to Sir Alexander Hardinge, 22 May 1939, RA PS/PSO/GVI/PS/VISCOM/03400/001A/116

41 Toronto *Globe and Mail*, 23 May 1939, RA F&V/VISOV/CAN/1939/Press cuttings/Vol. I, p. 116

42 Sir Alan Lascelles to Shuldham Redfern, 22 March 1939, LAC/BAC RG7, G26, Vol. 93, File 2213-D(1); press release on guiding principles of Canadian tour, 5 January 1939, Archives Nationales du Québec, R4/00022, 1994–11–013

43 Correspondence re the Queen and Toc H, March–April 1939, RA PS/PSO/GVI/PS/VISCOM/03400/093/01–12

44 A. E. Dyment to W. L. Mackenzie King, 11 November 1938, LAC/BAC RG7, G26, Vol. 93, File 2213-D General

45 Journal of Their Majesties' Tour, RA PS/PSO/GVI/C/ 257/01; Wilfred Notley, diary, private collection

46 Queen Elizabeth to Princess Elizabeth, 23–24 May 1939, RA QEII/PRIV/RF

47 The King's Empire Day Broadcast, 24 May 1939, RA PS/PSO/GVI/PS/VISCOM/03400/033/44

48 Queen Elizabeth to Princess Elizabeth, 23–24 May 1939, RA QEII/PRIV/RF

49 Mackenzie King, diary, 25 May 1939, LAC/BAC MG26-J13

50 Ibid.; Regina press report, 26 May 1939, RA F&V/VISOV/CAN/1939/Press cuttings/Vol. I, p. 210

51 Queen Elizabeth to Princess Elizabeth, 27 May 1939, RA QEII/PRIV/RF

52 Calgary press report, 26 May 1939, RA F&V/VISOV/CAN/1939/Press cuttings/Vol. I, p. 233

53 Wilfred Notley, diary, private collection

54 Queen Elizabeth to Princess Elizabeth, 27 May 1939, RA QEII/PRIV/RF; Journal of Their Majesties' Tour, 27 May 1939, RA PS/PSO/GVI/C/257/01

55 Queen Elizabeth to Queen Mary, 1 June 1939, RA QM/PRIV/CC12/99

56 Sir Alan Lascelles to Joan Lascelles, 28 May 1939, CAC, LASL 4/3/11

57 Mackenzie King, diary, 19 May 1939, LAC/BAC MG26-J13

58 Mackenzie King, diary, 22, 25 May 1939, LAC/BAC MG26-J13

59 King George VI to Sir Alexander Hardinge, 28 May 1939, Hon. Lady Murray Papers

60 Information from Mrs Ted James kindly sent to the author by the Rev. Thomas M. Steel

61 Vancouver press reports, 29 May 1939, RA F&V/VISOV/CAN/1939/Press cuttings/Vol. I, pp. 252, 257

62 Ibid., p. 261

63 Victoria press report, [31 May 1939], RA F&V/VISOV/CAN/1939/Press cuttings/Vol. II, p. 12

64 R. V. D. Guthrie to Lord Airlie (extract), 13 March 1939; R. J. Streatfeild to R. V. D. Guthrie, 31 March 1939, RA PS/PSO/GVI/PS/VISCOM/03400/099/1, 2; Victoria newspaper articles, [31 May 1939], RA F&V/VISOV/CAN/1939/Press cuttings/Vol. II, pp. 14–15; Journal of Their Majesties' Tour, 30 May 1939, RA PS/PSO/GVI/C/251/1

65 Queen Elizabeth to Lady Tweedsmuir (copy), 28 June 1939, RA QEQM/ADD/OUT/MISC

66 Queen Elizabeth to Queen Mary, 1 June 1939, RA QM/PRIV/CC12/99

67 Edmonton press reports, 2 June 1939, RA F&V/VISOV/CAN/1939/Press cuttings/Vol. II, pp. 66–7, 71

68 Canadian press reports, June 1939, RA F&V/VISOV/CAN/1939/Press cuttings/Vol. II, pp. 90, 91, 94, 98

69 Journal of Their Majesties' Tour, 5 June 1939, RA PS/PSO/GVI/C/251/01

70 Queen Elizabeth to Princess Elizabeth, 5–6 June 1939, RA QEII/PRIV/RF

71 Canadian press reports, 6 June 1939, RA F&V/VISOV/CAN/1939/Press cuttings/Vol. II, pp. 147, 154; Journal of Their Majesties' Tour, 6 June 1939, RA PS/PSO/GVI/C/251/01

72 Canadian press reports, 6–7 June 939, RA F&V/VISOV/CAN/1939/Press cuttings/Vol. II, pp. 213, 214; RA PS/PSO/GVI/VISCOM/03400/003/01/114

73 Mackenzie King, diary, 6 June 1939, LAC/BAC MG26-J13

74 *Washington Star*, 8 June 1939, RA F&V/VISOV/CAN/1939/Press cuttings/Vol. III, p. 16

75 Eleanor Roosevelt, *This I Remember*, 1950, pp. 183–4, quoted in Wheeler-Bennett, p. 382

76 Wheeler-Bennett, p. 375

77 William Bullitt to President Roosevelt, 9 May 1939, quoted in Will Swift, *The Roosevelts and the Royals*, John Wiley, Hoboken, 2004, p. 107

78 Bradford, *George VI*, p. 377

79 *Washington Evening Star*, 7 June 1939; *New York Times*, 8 June 1939, RA F&V/VISOV/CAN/1939/Press cuttings/Vol. III, p. 8

80 *The Times* leader, 8 June 1939

81 Sir Alan Lascelles to Lady Lascelles, 7 June 1939, CAC LASL 4/3/16; Journal of Their Majesties' Tour, 7 June 1939, RA PS/PSO/GVI/C/251/01

82 *Hostage to Fortune: The Letters of Joseph P. Kennedy*, p. 351

83 Queen Elizabeth to Queen Mary, 11 June 1939, RA QM/PRIV/CC12/101

84 Washington press report, 8 June 1939, RA F&V/VISOV/CAN/1939/Press cuttings/Vol. III, p. 27

85 Swift, p. 114

86 Ibid., p. 115

87 Ibid.

88 Ibid., p. 118

89 *The Secret Diaries of Harold L. Ickes*, vol. 2, 1954, pp. 646, 650, quoted in ibid., p. 119

90 Kenneth S. Davis, *FDR: Into the Storm*, 1993, p. 448, quoted in Swift, p. 119

91 Journal of Their Majesties' Tour, 8 June 1939, RA PS/PSO/GVI/C/251/01

92 Swift, p. 121

93 Eleanor Roosevelt, 'My Day', 9 June 1939; press report by Emma Bugbee, 9 June 1939, RA F&V/VISOV/CAN/1939/Press cuttings/Vol. III, pp. 47–8

94 Swift, pp. 122–3

95 Joseph P. Lash, *Love, Eleanor*, 1982, quoted in Swift, p. 127

96 D'Arcy Osborne to Queen Elizabeth, 23 June 1939, RA QEQM/PRIV/PAL/Osborne

97 Swift, p. 126; 'He Came, We Saw, He Conquered', *Anglo-American Review*, July 1939, Vol. 2, No. 2

98 Washington press reports, 9 June 1939, RA F&V/VISOV/CAN/1939/Press cuttings/Vol. III, p. 57

99 Wheeler-Bennett, pp. 386–7

100 Washington press reports, 10 June 1939, RA F&V/VISOV/CAN/1939/Press cuttings/Vol. III, pp. 83–5; Journal of Their Majesties' Tour, 10 June 1939, RA PS/PSO/GVI/C/251/01

101 Wheeler-Bennett, p. 387

102 Queen Elizabeth to Queen Mary, 11 June 1939, RA QM/PRIV/CC12/101

103 Eleanor Roosevelt, 'My Day', [12 June 1939], quoted in press report, RA F&V/VISOV/CAN/1939/Press cuttings/Vol. III, p. 114; Swift, pp. 135–6

104 Wheeler-Bennett, pp. 388–9

105 Ibid., pp. 390–2; Mackenzie King, diary, 10 June 1939, LAC/BAC MG26-J13

106 Queen Elizabeth to Queen Mary, 11 June 1939, RA QM/PRIV/CC12/101

107 Swift, p. 139

108 Conrad Black, *Franklin Delano Roosevelt: Champion of Freedom*, 2003, p. 524, quoted in Swift, pp. 140–1

109 Queen Elizabeth to Princess Elizabeth, 11 June 1939, RA QEII/PRIV/RF

110 United Press report, [11 June 1940], RA F&V/VISOV/CAN/1939/Press cuttings/Vol. III, p. 114

111 Queen Elizabeth to Princess Elizabeth, 11 June 1939, RA QEII/PRIV/RF

112 Queen Elizabeth to Queen Mary, 11 June 1939, RA QM/PRIV/CC12/101

113 Laird, p. 239

114 *Washington Post* special dispatch, 11 June 1939, RA F&V/VISOV/CAN/1939/Press cuttings/Vol. III, p. 115

115 *Washington Evening Star* leader, 12 June 1939, RA F&V/VISOV/CAN/1939/Press cuttings/Vol. III, p. 130

116 *The Times* leader, 12 June 1939

117 Fred Leventhal, *Anglo-American Attitudes*, 2000, quoted in Swift, p. 150

118 Press article by Kathleen McLaughlin, 10 June 1939, RA RA F&V/VISOV/CAN/1939/Press cuttings/Vol. III, p. 89

119 Quoted in Robert Rhodes James, *A Spirit Undaunted*, Little, Brown, 1998, p. 163, and in Swift, pp. 148, 122

120 Swift, p. 147

121 Queen Elizabeth to Queen Mary, 11 June 1939, RA QM/PRIV/CC12/101

122 Wheeler-Bennett, pp. 389, 390

123 Muriel Adams and A. E. Fulford, Canadian press report, 13 June 1939, RA F&V/VISOV/CAN/1939/Press cuttings/Vol. III, p. 146

124 Wilfred Notley, diary, pp. 26–7, private collection

125 *Montreal Gazette* report, RA F&V/VISOV/CAN/1939/Press cuttings/Vol. III, p. 224; Speech by Queen Elizabeth, 15 June 1939, RA QEQMH/PS/SPE

126 Extracts of letters from a Canadian King's Counsel to A. G. Allen, n.d. [June 1939], RA QEQM/PRIV/MISC/OFF

127 Laird, p. 241

128 Bradford, *George VI*, p. 396

129 Nicolson, *Diaries and Letters 1930–39*, p. 405

130 Wheeler-Bennett, pp. 393–4

131 Ibid., pp. 392–4

132 Ibid., p. 392

133 Queen Elizabeth to Most Rev. Cosmo Lang, 12 December 1936, Lambeth Palace Library, Lang Papers 318 ff. 177–80

134 Wheeler-Bennett, p. 393

135 Mackenzie King, diary, 12 June 1939, LAC/BAC MG26-J13

136 Queen Elizabeth to Lady Tweedsmuir, 28 June 1939, RA QEQM/OUT/MISC

137 RA QM/PRIV/QMD/1939: 19 July

138 Frederick Dalrymple Hamilton, diary, 23 July 1939, private collection

139 Wheeler-Bennett, p. 397

140 King George VI to Arthur Penn, 8 July 1939, Penn Papers

141 Queen Elizabeth to Queen Mary, 8 August 1939, RA QM/PRIV/CC12/106

142 Wheeler-Bennett, p. 400

143 Queen Elizabeth to Queen Mary, 8 August 1939, RA QM/PRIV/CC12/106

144 Queen Mary to Queen Elizabeth, 23 August 1939, RA QEQM/PRIV/RF

145 King George VI to Queen Elizabeth, 25 August 1939, RA QEQM/PRIV/RF

146 Mackenzie King, diary, 26 August 1939, LAC/BAC MG26-J13

147 Sir Alexander Hardinge, memorandum, 27 August 1939, RA PS/PSO/GVI/C/111/3;
Wheeler-Bennett, pp. 402–3

148 King George VI to Queen Mary, 28 August 1939, RA QM/PRIV/CC12/108

149 Queen Mary to Queen Elizabeth, 1 September 1939, RA QEQM/PRIV/RF

150 Lady Granville to Queen Elizabeth, 6 September 1939, RA QEQM/PRIV/BL

151 Queen Elizabeth to Queen Mary, 31 August 1939, RA QM/PRIV/CC12/110

152 Sir Alexander Hardinge, memorandum, 27 August 1939, RA PS/PSO/GVI/C/111/3

153 Queen Elizabeth, notes, 4 September 1939, RA QEQM/PRIV/PERS

THIRTEEN: THE QUEEN AT WAR 1939–1941

1 Arthur Penn to Queen Elizabeth, 27 September 1939, RA QEQM/PRIV/PAL/Penn

2 Queen Elizabeth to Queen Mary, 26 September 1939, RA QM/PRIV/CC12/113

3 Queen Elizabeth to Prince Paul of Yugoslavia, 2 October 1939, photocopy enclosed with
letter from Prince Charles to Queen Elizabeth, 1 September 2000, RA QEQM/PRIV/RF

4 Queen Elizabeth to Queen Mary, 17 October 1939, RA QM/PRIV/CC12/114

5 Queen Elizabeth to Lord Halifax, 15 November 1939, Hickleton Papers, A2/278/26A 1

6 Laird, pp. 243–4

7 Ibid., p. 243

8 Most Rev. Cosmo Lang to Queen Elizabeth, 5 September 1939, RA QEQM/PRIV/PAL/
Lang

9 Queen Elizabeth to Most Rev. Cosmo Lang, Lambeth Palace Library, Lang Papers 318
ff. 196–8

10 Peter Clarke, *Hope and Glory: Britain 1900–1990*, Penguin, 1990, p. 191

11 RA QM/PRIV/QMD/1939: 3 September

12 Queen Mary to King George VI, 3 September 1939, RA GVI/PRIV/RF/11

13 King George VI to Queen Mary, 6 September 1939, RA QM/PRIV/CC12/111

14 Pope-Hennessy, p. 596

15 Ibid.

16 Ziegler, *Edward VIII*, pp. 402–3

17 Queen Elizabeth to Prince Paul of Yugoslavia, 2 October 1939, photocopy enclosed with
letter from Prince Charles to Queen Elizabeth, 1 September 2000, RA QEQM/PRIV/RF

18 Queen Elizabeth to Queen Mary, 26 September 1939, RA QM/PRIV/CC12/113

19 King George VI to Duke of Kent, 26 September 1939, quoted in Ziegler, *Edward VIII*,
p. 404

20 King George VI to Neville Chamberlain, 14 September 1939, quoted in Wheeler-Bennett, p. 417; King George VI, diary, 14 September 1939, RA GVI/PRIV/DIARY

21 Sir Robert Bruce Lockhart, *Diaries 1915–1938*, ed. Kenneth Young, Macmillan, 1980, p. 413

22 Queen Elizabeth to Duke of Kent, 5 October 1939, RA QEQM/OUT/MISC

23 Wheeler-Bennett, p. 420

24 *Hostage to Fortune: The Letters of Joseph P. Kennedy*, pp. 376–7

25 Queen Elizabeth to Princess Elizabeth, 15 September 1939, RA QEII/PRIV/RF

26 Princess Elizabeth to Marion Crawford, 11 September 1939, RA QEII/OUT/BUTHLAY

27 Queen Elizabeth, conversations with Eric Anderson, 1994–5, RA QEQM/ADD/MISC

28 Queen Elizabeth to Queen Mary, 26 September 1939, RA QM/PRIV/CC12/113

29 Marion Crawford to Queen Elizabeth, 23 October 1939, RA QEQM/PRIV/CHILD; Princess Elizabeth to Georgina Guérin, 30 December 1939, RA QEII/OUT/GUÉRIN/13

30 Queen Elizabeth to Queen Mary, 26 September 1939, RA QM/PRIV/CC12/113

31 Queen Elizabeth to Prince Paul of Yugoslavia, 2 October 1939, photocopy enclosed with letter from Prince Charles to Queen Elizabeth, 1 September 2000, RA QEQM/PRIV/RF

32 Professor Harold Laski to Lord Wigram, 12 September 1939, and to Sir Alexander Hardinge, 19 September 1939, RA PS/PSO/GVI/PS/MAIN/03959/2

33 Lord Tweedsmuir to Sir Alexander Hardinge, 2 October 1939 (extract), Lord Tweedsmuir to King George VI, 10 October 1939 (extract), RA PS/PSO/GVI/PS/MAIN/03959/1A

34 Lord Lothian to Sir Alan Lascelles, 25 September 1939, RA PS/PSO/GVI/PS/MAIN/03959/1B

35 Duchess of York to D'Arcy Osborne, 30 November 1932, RA QEQM/OUT/OSBORNE

36 Queen Elizabeth to Most Rev. Cosmo Lang, 6 November 1939, Lambeth Palace Library, Lang Papers 318 ff. 199–200

37 Queen Elizabeth's broadcast, 11 November 1939, RA QEQMH/PS/SPE

38 Most Rev. Cosmo Lang to Queen Elizabeth, 11 November 1939, RA QEQM/PRIV/PAL/Lang

39 Letters to Queen Elizabeth, November 1939, RA QEQM/PRIV/GEN, RA QEQM/PRIV/PAL; Lord Wigram to Queen Elizabeth, 12 November 1939, RA QEQM/PRIV/PAL

40 Anonymous letter to Queen Elizabeth, n.d. [12 November 1939], RA PS/PSO/GVI/PS/MAIN/04298

41 Queen Elizabeth to Prince Paul of Yugoslavia, 6 December 1939, RA QEQM/OUT/PAUY

42 Queen Elizabeth to Prince Paul of Yugoslavia, 2 October 1939, photocopy enclosed with letter from Prince Charles to Queen Elizabeth, 1 September 2000, RA QEQM/PRIV/RF

43 Ibid.

44 Vickers, p. 206

45 Augustus John to Maud (Mollie) Cazalet, 23 September 1939, RA QEQM/PRIV/PIC

46 Mollie Cazalet to Queen Elizabeth, 16 December 1939, RA QEQM/PRIV/PAL

47 Queen Elizabeth to Osbert Sitwell, 10 July 1947, Sitwell Papers

48 Susan Owens, *Watercolours and Drawings from the Collection of Queen Elizabeth The Queen Mother*, Royal Collection Publications, 2005, pp. 47–8

49 Gerald Kelly to Queen Elizabeth, 18 December 1939, RA QEQM/PRIV/PAL

50 Rose, *Kings, Queens and Courtiers*, p. 151

51 Channon, *Diaries*, p. 276

52 Queen Elizabeth to Lord Halifax, 9 December 1939, Hickleton Papers, A2/278/26A 2

53 Queen Elizabeth to Prince Paul of Yugoslavia, 6 December 1939, RA QEQM/OUT/PAUY

54 Wheeler-Bennett, p. 428; Colonel Hon. Piers Legh to Queen Elizabeth, 11 December 1939, RA QEQM/PRIV/OFF

55 Extract from a letter to Mollie Cazalet from a cousin in the British Expeditionary Force, enclosed with letter from Mollie Cazalet to Queen Elizabeth, 16 December 1939, RA QEQM/PRIV/PAL

56 Wheeler-Bennett, pp. 428–9

57 Ibid., pp. 429–30

58 Queen Elizabeth to May Elphinstone, 6 January 1940, RA QEQM/OUT/ELPHINSTONE

59 Queen Elizabeth to Queen Mary, 27 December 1939, RA QM/PRIV/CC12/116

60 King George VI, diary, 20 January 1940, RA GVI/PRIV/DIARY

61 King George VI, diary, 24 January 1940, RA GVI/PRIV/DIARY

62 Queen Elizabeth to May Elphinstone, 26 February 1940, RA QEQM/OUT/ELPHINSTONE

63 William Wordsworth, *The Excursion*, 1814, Book IV, lines in Queen Elizabeth's hand (original in possession of Winston Churchill, grandson of Sir Winston Churchill); Sir Martin Gilliat to Kenneth Rose, 22 May 1974, RA QEQMH/PS/GEN/1974/Rose

64 Sir Alexander Hardinge to Queen Elizabeth, 15 February 1940; Sir Walter Elliot to Queen Elizabeth, 15 February 1940, RA QEQM/PRIV/OFF; Queen Elizabeth to Sir Walter Elliot, 17 February 1940, RA QEQM/OUT/MISC

65 Queen Elizabeth to Sir Alexander Hardinge, 1 April 1940, Hon. Lady Murray Papers

66 Queen Elizabeth to Lord Halifax, 1 April 1940, Hickleton Papers, A2/278/26A 4; Lord Halifax to Queen Elizabeth, 1 April 1940, RA QEQM/PRIV/PAL

67 Queen Elizabeth's speech to YWCA, 13 April 1940, RA QEQMH/PS/ENGT/1940

68 Sir Alexander Hardinge, memorandum, 26 April 1939, Hon. Lady Murray Papers

69 Queen Elizabeth to King George VI, 10 October 1942, RA GVI/PRIV/RF/26/76

70 Wheeler-Bennett, pp. 439–43

71 Gilbert, *Churchill: A Life*, p. 642

72 King George VI, diary, 10 May 1940, RA GVI/PRIV/DIARY

73 Queen Elizabeth to Neville Chamberlain, 17 May 1940, BUA NCI/23/81A

74 Queen Elizabeth, conversations with Eric Anderson, 1994–5, RA QEQM/ADD/MISC

75 Queen Mary to King George VI, 12 May 1940, RA GVI/PRIV/RF/11

76 King George VI, diary, 11 May 1940, RA GVI/PRIV/DIARY

77 John Keegan, *Churchill*, Weidenfeld & Nicolson, 2002, pp. 123–4

78 King George VI, diary, 13 May 1940, RA GVI/PRIV/DIARY

79 Wheeler-Bennett, p. 450

80 Ibid., pp. 451–2

81 Princess Juliana of the Netherlands to Queen Elizabeth, 20 June 1940, RA QEQM/PRIV/FORRF

82 Queen Elizabeth, conversations with Eric Anderson, 1994–5, RA QEQM/ADD/MISC

83 Queen Elizabeth to Queen Mary, 24 July 1940, RA QM/PRIV/CC12/131

84 Laird, p. 246

85 Gilbert, *Churchill: A Life*, p. 647

86 Queen Mary to Queen Elizabeth, 29 May 1940, RA QEQM/PRIV/RF

87 Queen Elizabeth to Arthur Penn, 1 June 1940, Penn Papers

88 Leeming notes

89 Martin Gilbert, *Winston S. Churchill*, vol. VI, William Heinemann, 1983, pp. 418–21

90 Keegan, p. 125

91 Gilbert, *Churchill: A Life*, p. 651

92 King George VI, diary, 12 June 1940, RA GVI/PRIV/DIARY

93 Queen Elizabeth's speech to the Women of France, 14 June 1940, RA QEQMH/PS/SPE

94 André Maurois, *Mémoires*, Flammarion, Paris, 1970, pp. 301–2

95 André Maurois to Queen Elizabeth, 26 June 1940, RA QEQM/PRIV/PAL

96 Anthony Eden to Queen Elizabeth, 24 January 1941, RA QEQM/PRIV/OFF

97 Gilbert, *Churchill: A Life*, p. 661

98 Eleanor Roosevelt to Queen Elizabeth, n.d. [early June 1940], RA QEQM/PRIV/PAL

99 Swift, pp. 156–7

100 Wheeler-Bennett, p. 460

101 Gilbert, *Churchill: A Life*, p. 663

102 Ibid., pp. 363–4

103 Mollie Panter-Downes, *London War Notes 1939–1945*, ed. William Shawn, Longman, 1972, p. 70

104 King George VI to Queen Mary, 14 October 1940, RA QM/PRIV/CC12/138

105 Malcolm Macdonald to Queen Elizabeth, 27 December 1977, RA QEQM/PRIV/PAL

106 Wheeler-Bennett, p. 447

107 Queen Elizabeth, conversations with Eric Anderson, 1994–5, RA QEQM/ADD/MISC

108 Angus Calder, *The People's War: Britain 1939–1945*, Pimlico, 1992, pp. 120–2

109 Owen Morshead to Queen Mary, 10 June 1940, RA QM/PRIV/CC48/914

110 *Hostage to Fortune: The Letters of Joseph P. Kennedy*, p. 457

111 Harold Nicolson, *Diaries and Letters: 1939–1945*, ed. Nigel Nicolson, Collins, 1967, p. 100

112 Ibid.

113 King George VI, diary, 18 June 1940, RA GVI/PRIV/DIARY

114 Wheeler-Bennett, p. 464

115 Ibid.

116 Queen Elizabeth, conversations with Eric Anderson, 1994–5, RA QEQM/ADD/MISC

117 Laird, pp. 249–50

118 Eugène Keryell to Lady Grigg, 2 August 1940, RA QEQMH/PS/ENGT/1940/41

119 Ziegler, *Edward VIII*, p. 423

120 Ibid., p. 434

121 King George VI to Queen Mary, 7 July 1940, RA QM/PRIV/CC12/130

122 Queen Mary to King George VI, 8 July 1940, RA GVI/PRIV/RF/11

123 Letters from members of the public to Queen Elizabeth, September 1939 and undated, CAC GLLD/21/7A/3–6, 8

124 Notes by Queen Elizabeth, 6 July 1940 (copy), enclosed with letter from Sir Alexander Hardinge to Lord Lloyd, CAC GLLD/21/7A/1. Lord Lloyd burned the original handwritten memorandum from the Queen, but kept a typed copy which remains in the Lloyd Papers at the Churchill Archive Centre, Cambridge

125 Sir Alexander Hardinge to Queen Elizabeth, 7 July 1940, RA QEQM/PRIV/OFF

126 Ziegler, *Edward VIII*, pp. 428–33

127 Rhodes James, p. 219

128 Ziegler, *Edward VIII*, p. 435

129 King George VI to Queen Mary, 11 September 1940, RA QM/PRIV/CC12/134

130 Queen Elizabeth to Queen Mary, 13 September 1940, RA QM/PRIV/CC12/135

131 Queen Elizabeth to Queen Mary, 13 September 1940, RA QM/PRIV/CC12/135

132 Betty Spencer Shew, *Queen Elizabeth The Queen Mother*, 1955, p. 76, quoted in Wheeler-Bennett, p. 469

133 King George VI to Queen Mary, 14 October 1940, RA QM/PRIV/CC12/138

134 Myrtle Farquharson to Queen Elizabeth, 26 September 1940, RA QEQM/PRIV/PAL

135 Bradford, *George VI*, p. 430

136 Lord Woolton, diary, 11 October 1940, Bodleian Library, MS Woolton 2

137 Ibid.

138 Mrs Walter Elliot to Lettice Bowlby, 30 October 1940, RA QEQMH/PS/ENGT/1940/53

139 Edna Healey, *The Queen's House*, Michael Joseph, 1997, p. 306

140 Hartnell, pp. 101–2

141 Wheeler-Bennett, p. 467

142 Hartnell, pp. 101–2

143 King George VI to Queen Mary, 11 September 1940 RA QM/PRIV/CC12/134

144 Owen Morshead, notes, 12 November 1940, RA AEC/GG/12/OS/2

145 Queen Elizabeth, conversations with Eric Anderson, 1994–5, RA QEQM/ADD/MISC

146 Queen Elizabeth to May Elphinstone, 25 October 1940, RA QEQM/OUT/ELPHINSTONE

147 Owen Morshead, notes, 12 November 1940, RA AEC/GG/12/OS/2

148 Anne Chamberlain to Queen Elizabeth, 16 October [1940], RA QEQM/PRIV/PAL

149 Gilbert, *Churchill: A Life*, p. 683

150 Queen Elizabeth to May Elphinstone, 25 October 1940, RA QEQM/OUT/ELPHINSTONE

151 Queen Elizabeth to Queen Mary, 19 October 1940, RA QM/PRIV/CC12/139

152 Queen Elizabeth to Queen Mary, 31 October 1940, RA QM/PRIV/CC12/141

153 Queen Elizabeth to Queen Mary, 19 October 1940, RA QM/PRIV/CC12/139

154 Laird, p. 253

155 Queen Elizabeth to May Elphinstone, 25 October 1940, RA QEQM/OUT/ELPHINSTONE

156 Queen Elizabeth, conversations with Eric Anderson, 1994–5, RA QEQM/ADD/MISC

157 Queen Elizabeth to Queen Mary, 31 October 1940, RA QM/PRIV/CC12/141

158 Ibid.

159 Queen Elizabeth to Queen Mary, 7 January 1941, RA QM/PRIV/CC12/147

160 Marion Crawford to Queen Mary, 23 February 1941, Lambeth Palace Library, Lang Papers 318 ff. 67–9

161 King George VI, diary, 21–22 December 1940, RA GVI/PRIV/DIARY

162 Queen Elizabeth to George Duke of Kent, 14 January 1941, RA QEQM/OUT/MISC

163 Queen Elizabeth to Queen Mary, 7 January 1941, RA QM/PRIV/CC12/147

164 Queen Elizabeth to Winston Churchill, 21 January 1941, CAC CHAR/20/29A/38

165 King George VI, diary, 'Retrospect of 1940', RA GVI/PRIV/DIARY

166 Queen Elizabeth to Queen Mary, 7 January 1941, RA QM/PRIV/CC12/147

167 Roberts, *History of the English-Speaking Peoples since 1900*, p. 286

168 Queen Elizabeth to Queen Mary, 7 January 1941, RA QM/PRIV/CC12/147

169 Queen Elizabeth to the Hon. Elizabeth Elphinstone, 7 February 1941, RA QEQM/OUT/ELPHINSTONE

170 Queen Elizabeth to George, Duke of Kent, 14 January 1941, RA QEQM/OUT/GDK

171 Keegan, p. 131

172 President Roosevelt to King George VI (copy), 22 November 1940, RA PS/PSO/GVI/C/243/34

173 Queen Elizabeth to Queen Mary, 4 February 1941, RA QM/PRIV/CC12/151

174 Longford, *Queen Mother*, p. 80

175 Laird, pp. 251–2

176 Lord Wigram to Lady Airlie, 24 February 1941, British Library, Add MSS 82768

177 Queen Elizabeth to Queen Mary, 17 February 1941, RA QM/PRIV/CC12/153

178 Robert Menzies, *Dark and Hurrying Days*, National Library of Australia, 1993, pp. 66–7

179 King George VI to Queen Mary, 17 March 1941, RA QM/PRIV/CC12/157

180 Queen Elizabeth to Princess Elizabeth, 8 March 1941, RA QEII/PRIV/RF

181 Queen Elizabeth to Queen Mary, 21 March 1941, RA QM/PRIV/CC12/158

182 Marion Crawford to Queen Mary, 23 February 1941, Lambeth Palace Library, Lang Papers Papers 318 ff. 67–9

183 Queen Elizabeth to Queen Mary, 21 March 1941, RA QM/PRIV/CC12/158

184 Queen Elizabeth to Lady Astor (copy), 23 March 1941, RA QEQMH/GEN/1990/Wasley

185 Keegan, p. 133

186 Queen Mary to Queen Elizabeth, 10 April 1941, RA QEQM/PRIV/RF

187 Queen Elizabeth to Queen Mary, 13 April 1941, RA QM/PRIV/CC12/161

188 Queen Elizabeth to Lord Halifax, 23 April 1941, Hickleton Papers A2/278/26A/5

189 Nicolson, *Diaries and Letters 1939–1945*, p. 137

190 Churchill to King George VI, 5 January 1941, RA PS/PSO/GVI/C/069/07

191 Churchill to Queen Elizabeth, 3 February 1941, RA QEQM/PRIV/PAL

192 Queen Elizabeth to Churchill, 21 January 1941, CAC CHAR 20/29A/38

193 Churchill to Queen Elizabeth, 9 May 1941, RA QEQM/PRIV/PAL

194 Queen Elizabeth to Churchill, 12 May 1941, RA QEQMH/PS/GEN/1997/Gilbert

195 King George VI, diary, 13 May 1941, RA GVI/PRIV/DIARY

196 Roberts, *History of the English-Speaking Peoples since 1900*, p. 287

197 Queen Elizabeth to Queen Mary, 12 May 1941, RA QM/PRIV/CC12/164

198 Calder, *People's War*, p. 223

199 Queen Elizabeth to Queen Mary, 1 August 1941, RA QM/PRIV/CC12/170

200 Roberts, *History of the English-Speaking People since 1900*, pp. 286–7

201 Hon. David Bowes Lyon to Queen Elizabeth, n.d. [June 1941], RA QEQM/PRIV/OFF

202 File on Queen Elizabeth's broadcast to America, RA QEQMH/PS/GEN/1941/America

203 Queen Elizabeth to Churchill, 2 August 1941, CAC CHAR 20/20/32

204 Queen Elizabeth's broadcast, 10 August 1941, RA QEQMH/PS/GEN/1941/America

205 Wheeler-Bennett, p. 530

206 Queen Mary to Queen Elizabeth, 3 August 1941, RA QEQM/PRIV/RF

207 Rt Rev. Michael Furse to Queen Elizabeth, 3 August 1941, RA QEQM/PRIV/PAL

208 Queen Elizabeth to Queen Mary, 28 August 1941, RA QM/PRIV/CC12/173

209 Queen Elizabeth to Queen Mary, 5 September 1941, RA QM/PRIV/CC12/174

210 Queen Elizabeth to Queen Elizabeth II, 3 September 1982, RA QEII/PRIV/RF

211 J. W. Pickersgill (ed.), *The Mackenzie King Record*, vol. I: *1939–44*, University of Chicago Press and University of Toronto Press, 1960, pp. 254–7

212 Queen Elizabeth to Queen Mary, 9 December 1941, RA QM/PRIV/CC12/179

213 Ibid.

214 Queen Elizabeth, conversations with Eric Anderson, 1994–5, RA QEQM/ADD/MISC

215 Wheeler-Bennett, p. 533

216 Queen Elizabeth to Queen Mary, 9 December 1941, RA QM/PRIV/CC12/179

217 Queen Elizabeth, conversations with Eric Anderson, 1994–5, RA QEQM/ADD/MISC

218 Ibid.

219 Wheeler-Bennett, p. 533

220 Queen Elizabeth to Queen Mary, 28 December 1941, RA QM/PRIV/CC12/182

FOURTEEN: YEARS LIKE GREAT BLACK OXEN 1942–1945

1 The story of John Piper and Windsor Castle is recounted in Owens, pp. 34–41. See also Susan Owens, ' "Evocation or Topography": John Piper's Watercolours of Windsor Castle, 1941–44', *Burlington Magazine*, September 2005, pp. 598–605

2 Owens, p. 34

3 Ibid., p. 107
4 Ibid., p. 37
5 Ibid., p. 38
6 Ibid.
7 Ibid., p. 41
8 Ibid.
9 Ibid., p. 13
10 *The Times*, 5 April 1938
11 Owens, p. 19
12 Ibid., p. 30
13 Queen Elizabeth, conversations with Eric Anderson, 1994–5, RA QEQM/ADD/MISC
14 Queen Elizabeth to J. P. Morgan (incomplete draft), 19 January 1942, RA QEQM/OUT/MISC
15 King George VI, diary, 19 January 1942, RA GVI/PRIV/DIARY, quoted in Wheeler-Bennett, p. 535
16 Queen Elizabeth to Queen Mary, 14 February 1942, RA QM/PRIV/CC13/5
17 Queen Elizabeth to the Hon. Elizabeth Elphinstone, 27 February 1942, private collection
18 Queen Mary to Queen Elizabeth, 13 January 1942, RA QEQM/PRIV/RF
19 Queen Elizabeth to Queen Mary, 10 April 1942, RA QM/PRIV/CC13/10
20 Ibid.
21 King George VI, diary, 3–4 May 1942, RA GVI/PRIV/DIARY
22 Rt Rev. Edward Woods to Queen Elizabeth, 4 May 1942, RA QEQM/PRIV/PAL/Woods
23 Rt Rev. Edward Woods to Queen Elizabeth, 28 August 1942, RA QEQM/PRIV/PAL/Woods
24 Rt Rev. Edward Woods to Queen Elizabeth, 6 November 1942, RA QEQM/PRIV/PAL/Woods
25 Wheeler-Bennett, p. 540
26 Gladys Saunders, Mayoress of Exeter, to Queen Elizabeth, 10 May 1942, RA QEQMH/PS/ENGT/1942/41
27 Raymond Leppard, *On Music*, Pro/Am Music Resources, New York, 1993, pp. 442–3
28 Queen Elizabeth to Queen Mary, 10 June 1942, RA QM/PRIV/CC13/16
29 Lieutenant Colonel Tom Draffen to Arthur Penn, 21 February 1942; Arthur Penn to Tom Draffen, 30 April 1942, RA QEQMH/PS/ARMFOR/Former Regiments/Queen's Bays
30 Queen Elizabeth to Queen Mary, 10 June 1942, RA QM/PRIV/CC13/16
31 King George VI to Queen Mary, 22 June 1942, RA QM/PRIV/CC13/18
32 Sir Alan Lascelles, *King's Counsellor: The Wartime Diaries*, ed. Duff Hart-Davis, Weidenfeld & Nicolson, 2006, p. 33
33 Ibid., p. 34
34 Queen Elizabeth to Queen Mary, 20 July 1942, RA QM/PRIV/CC13/20
35 Ibid.
36 Queen Elizabeth to Lady Doris Vyner, 5 June 1942; King George VI to Lady Doris Vyner, 7 June 1942, Vyner Papers
37 King George VI to Queen Elizabeth, n.d. [25 August 1942], RA QEQM/PRIV/RF
38 Bradford, *George VI*, p. 456
39 King George VI, diary, quoted in Wheeler-Bennett, p. 548
40 Queen Elizabeth to Osbert Sitwell, 13 September 1942, Sitwell Papers
41 Queen Elizabeth to the Hon. David Bowes Lyon, 31 August 1942, Bowes Lyon Papers, SPW

42 Duchess of Kent to Queen Elizabeth, 8 September 1942, RA QEQM/PRIV/RF

43 Queen Mary to King George VI, 1 September 1942, RA GVI/PRIV/RF/11

44 Queen Mary to Duke of Windsor, 31 August 1942, RA EDW/PRIV/MAINB/156

45 Queen Mary to Duke of Windsor, 18 October 1942, RA EDW/PRIV/MAINB/161

46 Duke of Windsor to Queen Mary, 12 September 1942, RA QM/PRIV/CC9

47 Duke of Windsor to King George VI, 15 September 1942, RA GVI/PRIV/RF/02/16

48 Queen Mary, undated note with letters from Duke of Windsor, September 1942, RA QM/PRIV/CC9

49 Queen Mary to King George VI, 15 October 1942, RA GVI/PRIV/RF/11

50 King George VI to Queen Mary, 4 December 1942, RA QM/PRIV/CC13/30

51 Ibid.

52 Queen Mary to King George VI, 4 December 1942, RA GVI/PRIV/RF/11

53 Queen Elizabeth to Osbert Sitwell, 5 March 1943, Sitwell Papers

54 Lascelles, p. 100

55 Queen Elizabeth to Queen Mary, 23 August 1943, RA QM/PRIV/CC13/62

56 Queen Elizabeth to Osbert Sitwell, 27 September 1942, Sitwell Papers

57 Osbert Sitwell to Queen Elizabeth, 20 Sepember 1942, RA QEQM/PRIV/PAL/Sitwell; Queen Elizabeth to Osbert Sitwell, 27 September 1942, Sitwell Papers

58 Queen Elizabeth to King George VI, 30 September 1942, RA GVI/PRIV/RF/26/74

59 Queen Elizabeth to Queen Mary, 13 October 1942, RA QM/PRIV/CC13/24

60 Queen Mary to Queen Elizabeth, 16 October 1942 (misdated November), RA QEQM/PRIV/RF

61 Queen Elizabeth to Osbert Sitwell, 16 October 1942, Sitwell Papers

62 Queen Elizabeth to Arthur Penn, 30 September 1942, Penn Papers

63 Queen Elizabeth to Arthur Penn, 12 October 1942, Penn Papers

64 Queen Elizabeth to Osbert Sitwell, 16 October 1942, Sitwell Papers

65 Lascelles, pp. 58, 46

66 Queen Elizabeth to Osbert Sitwell, 16 October 1942, Sitwell Papers

67 Queen Elizabeth to King George VI, 10 0ctober 1942, RA GVI/PRIV/RF/26/76

68 Martin Gilbert, *Winston S. Churchill*, vol. VII, William Heinemann, 1986, p. 646

69 Queen Elizabeth to Eleanor Roosevelt, message in telegram from Sir Alexander Hardinge to British Ambassador in Washington, 12 September 1942, RA PS/PSO/GVI/PS/MAIN/06093

70 Queen Elizabeth to Sir Alexander Hardinge, 7 October 1942, RA PS/PSO/GVI/PS/MAIN/06093

71 Queen Elizabeth to Queen Mary, 13 and 19 October 1942, RA QM/PRIV/CC13/24, 26

72 Queen Elizabeth to Queen Mary, 19 October 1942, RA QM/PRIV/CC13/26

73 Transcript of Mrs Roosevelt's press conference after her visit to Britain, 18 November 1942, RA PS/PSO/GVI/PS/MAIN/06093

74 Wheeler-Bennett, p. 550

75 Ibid., p. 551

76 Lascelles, pp. 66–7

77 Wheeler-Bennett, p. 551

78 Tables on the mobilization of women, sent to the Queen on Bevin's instructions, 5 November 1942, RA QEQM/PRIV/MISCOFF

79 Transcript of Mrs Roosevelt's press conference, 18 November 1942, RA PS/PSO/GVI/PS/MAIN/06093

80 Queen Mary to Queen Elizabeth, 2 November 1942, RA QEQM/PRIV/RF

81 Lascelles, p. 69

82 Queen Elizabeth to Queen Mary, 2 November 1942, RA QM/PRIV/CC13/28

83 File on proposed interview, RA PS/PSO/GVI/PS/MAIN/06489; Lascelles, pp. 74, 82–4

84 Transcript of Mrs Roosevelt's press conference, 18 November 1942, RA PS/PSO/GVI/PS/MAIN/06093

85 Ibid.

86 Queen Elizabeth to Sir Alan Lascelles, 13 December 1942, RA PS/PSO/GVI/PS/MAIN/06093

87 Author's interview with Lady Soames

88 King George VI, diary, 3 November 1942, RA GVI/PRIV/DIARY

89 Queen Elizabeth, conversations with Eric Anderson, 1994–5, RA QEQM/ADD/MISC; Rhodes James, p. 223

90 King George VI, diary, 3 November 1942, RA GVI/PRIV/DIARY

91 Queen Elizabeth, conversations with Eric Anderson, 1994–5, RA QEQM/ADD/MISC

92 King George VI, diary, 4 November 1942, RA GVI/PRIV/DIARY

93 Calder, *People's War*, p. 304

94 Queen Elizabeth to Lady Halifax, telegram, 4 November 1942, Hickleton Papers, A2/279/13

95 Lady Halifax to Queen Elizabeth, 5 November 1942, Hickleton Papers A2/279/13

96 Winston Churchill's speech at the Mansion House, November 10 1942, Gilbert, *Churchill: A Life*, p. 734

97 General Alexander to Winston Churchill, telegram, 4 February 1943, quoted in Wheeler-Bennett, p. 563

98 Wheeler-Bennett, p. 564

99 Queen Elizabeth to Osbert Sitwell, 3 January 1943, Sitwell Papers

100 Keegan, *Churchill*, pp. 145–7

101 King George VI, diary, 28 January 1943, RA GVI/PRIV/DIARY

102 Queen Elizabeth to the Hon. David Bowes Lyon, 14 February 1943, Bowes Lyon Papers, SPW

103 Queen Elizabeth, conversations with Eric Anderson, 1994–5, RA QEQM/PRIV/ADD/MISC

104 Franklin Watts (ed.), *Voices of History 1942–43*, 1943, p. 121, quoted by Martin Gilbert, *Auschwitz and the Allies*, Michael Joseph, 1981, p. 20

105 Council of Jewish Women's Organizations to Queen Elizabeth, 3 December 1942, RA QEQM/PRIV/MISCOFF; Harriet Cohen to Queen Elizabeth, n.d. [December 1942], RA QEQM/PRIV/MISCOFF

106 Queen Elizabeth to Queen Mary, 13 October 1942, RA QM/PRIV/CC13/24

107 Sir Alan Lascelles to Lady Airlie, 29 December 1943, British Library, Add MSS 82768

108 Queen Elizabeth to Sir Alexander Hardinge, 19 March 1943, Hon. Lady Murray Papers

109 Queen Elizabeth to Most Rev. Cosmo Lang, 4 May 1943, Lambeth Palace Library, Lang Papers 318 ff. 202–3

110 Queen Elizabeth to Sir Alan Lascelles, 5 April 1943, CAC LASL 2/3/2

111 Sir Alan Lascelles to Queen Elizabeth, 5–6 April 1943, CAC LASL 2/3/3

112 Winston Churchill to Queen Elizabeth, 8 April 1943, RA QEQM/PRIV/MISCOFF; Queen Elizabeth to Winston Churchill, 13 April 1943, CAC CHAR 20/98A/56

113 Queen Elizabeth's broadcast, 11 April 1943, RA QEQMH/PS/SPE; RA QEQM/PRIV/MISCOFF; RA PS/PSO/GVI/PS/MAIN/03959/C

114 Queen Elizabeth to Sir Alan Lascelles, 11 April 1943, RA PS/PSO/AL/Box B

115 Lascelles, p. 122

116 Queen Elizabeth to Winston Churchill, 13 April 1943, CAC CHAR 20/98A/56

117 Winston Churchill to Queen Elizabeth, 16 April 1943, RA QEQM/PRIV/MISCOFF

118 Queen Elizabeth to the Hon. David Bowes Lyon, 17 October 1943, Bowes Lyon Papers, SPW

119 Ziegler, *Osbert Sitwell*, pp. 275–6

120 Osbert Sitwell to Queen Elizabeth, 7 March 1943, RA QEQM/PRIV/PAL/Sitwell

121 Ziegler, *Osbert Sitwell*, pp. 275–6

122 Queen Elizabeth, conversations with Eric Anderson, 1994–5, RA QEQM/ADD/MISC

123 Owen Morshead's correspondence re safekeeping of Royal Library material, RA AEC/GG12

124 Owens, p. 22

125 King George VI, instructions to Queen Elizabeth, 9 June 1943, RA QEQM/PRIV/RF

126 Queen Elizabeth to Queen Mary, 12 June 1943, RA QM/PRIV/CC13/54

127 King George VI to Queen Elizabeth, 14 June 1943, RA QEQM/PRIV/RF

128 Queen Elizabeth to King George VI, 14 June 1943, RA GVI/PRIV/RF/26/78

129 Queen Elizabeth to King George VI, 17 June 1943, RA GVI/PRIV/RF/26/79

130 Laird, p. 262

131 Queen Elizabeth to King George VI, 17 June 1943, RA GVI/PRIV/RF/26/79

132 Bradford, *George VI*, pp. 467–70

133 King George VI, diary, 24–25 June 1943, RA GVI/PRIV/DIARY

134 King George VI to Queen Mary, 28 June 1943, RA QM/PRIV/CC13/56

135 King George VI to Queen Elizabeth, message sent in note from Sir Alan Lascelles to Queen Elizabeth, 20 June 1943, RA QEQM/PRIV/MISCOFF

136 Wheeler-Bennett, p. 578

137 Clementine Churchill to Queen Elizabeth, 19 June 1943, RA QEQM/PRIV/PAL

138 Queen Elizabeth to King George VI, 14 June 1943, RA GVI/PRIV/RF/26/78

139 Alastair Philips in *Glasgow Herald*, quoted in Laird, p. 262

140 King George VI, diary, 27 May 1943, RA GVI/PRIV/DIARY

141 Queen Elizabeth, conversations with Eric Anderson, 1994–5, RA QEQM/ADD/MISC

142 King George VI, diary, 25 June 1943, RA GVI/PRIV/DIARY

143 Arthur Penn to Sir Alan Lascelles, 9 July 1943, CAC LASL/2/3/1

144 Queen Elizabeth to Sir Alan Lascelles, 26 June 1943, RA PS/PSO/AL/Box B

145 Lascelles, pp. 138–9

146 Vickers, p. 241

147 King George VI, diary, 6 July 1943, RA GVI/PRIV/DIARY

148 King George VI, diary, 7 July 1943, RA GVI/PRIV/DIARY

149 Rose, *Kings, Queens and Courtiers*, pp. 141–2

150 Rhodes James, p. 249

151 Helen Hardinge to Queen Elizabeth, 7 [July] 1943, RA QEQM/PRIV/PAL

152 Helen Hardinge, diary 8 July 1943, Hon. Lady Murray Papers

153 RA PS/PSO/GVI/PS/MAIN/06518

154 Queen Mary to Queen Elizabeth, 15 July 1943, RA QEQM/PRIV/RF

155 Queen Mary to Lady Airlie, 8 August 1943, British Library, Add MSS 82748

156 Arthur Murray to Lady Doris Vyner, 30 July 1943, RA QEQM/PRIV/PAL

157 Queen Elizabeth to Lady Cranborne, 31 July 1943, Hatfield House, Papers of Elizabeth, Marchioness of Salisbury

158 Queen Elizabeth to Lady Cranborne, 30 September 1943, Hatfield House, Papers of Elizabeth, Marchioness of Salisbury

159 Sir Alan Lascelles to Queen Elizabeth, 10 October 1943, RA QEQM/PRIV/PAL

160 Queen Elizabeth to Queen Mary, 20 November 1943, RA QM/PRIV/CC13/74

161 Queen Elizabeth to Arthur Penn, 7 October 1943, Penn Papers

162 Queen Elizabeth to the Hon. David Bowes Lyon, 17 October 1943, Bowes Lyon Papers, SPW

163 Queen Elizabeth to Queen Mary, 25 September 1943, RA QM/PRIV/CC13/64

164 Queen Elizabeth to Osbert Sitwell, 30 November 1943, Sitwell Papers
165 Queen Elizabeth to Sir Alan Lascelles, 1 February 1944, RA PS/PSO/AL/Box B
166 King George VI, diary, 26 February and 21 April 1942, RA GVI/PRIV/DIARY
167 Queen Elizabeth to Queen Mary, 20 November 1943, RA QM/PRIV/CC13/74
168 Arthur Penn to Queen Elizabeth, 20 November 1943, RA QEQM/PRIV/PAL/Penn
169 Queen Elizabeth to Queen Mary, 12 December 1943, RA QM/PRIV/CC13/76
170 Ibid.
171 Princess Elizabeth to Marion Crawford, 1 January 1944, RA QEII/OUT/BUTHLAY
172 Lascelles, p. 189
173 Prince Philip of Greece to Queen Elizabeth, 31 December 1943, RA QEQM/PRIV/RF
174 Prince Philip to Queen Elizabeth, 23 July [1944], RA QEQM/PRIV/RF
175 Queen Mary to King George VI, 6 March 1944, RA GVI/PRIV/RF/11
176 Ibid.
177 King George VI to Queen Mary, 17 March 1944, RA QM/PRIV/CC13/84
178 Queen Mary to King George VI, 20 March 1944, RA GVI/PRIV/RF/11
179 Queen Elizabeth to Queen Mary, 23 October 1943, RA QM/PRIV/CC13/69
180 Queen Mary to King George VI, 10 December 1943, RA GVI/PRIV/RF/11
181 King George VI to Queen Mary, 14 December 1943, RA QM/PRIV/CC13/77
182 Queen Elizabeth to Osbert Sitwell, 4 May 1944, Sitwell Papers
183 Owen Morshead to Queen Mary, 8 May 1944, RA QM/PRIV/CC48/1184
184 Queen Elizabeth to Osbert Sitwell, 21 June 1944, Sitwell Papers
185 Keegan, p. 153
186 Queen Elizabeth to Osbert Sitwell, 21 June 1944, Sitwell Papers
187 Gilbert, *Churchill: A Life*, p. 781
188 King George VI, diary, 30 May 1944, RA GVI/ PRIV/ DIARY; Wheeler-Bennett, pp. 601–6
189 Queen Mary to Queen Elizabeth, 18 May 1944, RA QEQM/PRIV/RF
190 King George VI to Queen Mary, 10 June 1944, RA QM/PRIV/CC13/90; Wheeler-Bennett, p. 607
191 Queen Elizabeth to Osbert Sitwell, 21 June 1944, Sitwell Papers
192 Evelyn Waugh, *Unconditional Surrender*, 1961, p. 245, quoted in Calder, *The People's War*, p. 560
193 Martin Gilbert, *Winston S. Churchill*, vol. VII, William Heinemann, 1985, pp. 812–13
194 Queen Elizabeth to Arthur Penn, 18 June 1944, Penn Papers
195 Gilbert, *Churchill: A Life*, p. 782
196 Wheeler-Bennett, p. 610
197 King George VI to Queen Mary, 25 June 1944, RA QM/PRIV/CC13/91
198 Queen Elizabeth to Queen Mary, 8 July 1944, RA QM/PRIV/CC13/93
199 Queen Elizabeth to Princess Elizabeth, 27 June 1944, RA QEQM/OUT/CHILD
200 King George VI to Princess Elizabeth, June 1944, RA QEQM/PRIV/RF (with letters from King George VI to Queen Elizabeth)
201 Kenneth Clark to Queen Elizabeth, 22 June 1944, QEQM/PRIV/PIC
202 Gilbert, *Churchill: A Life*, pp. 782–3
203 Queen Elizabeth to Queen Mary, 17 July 1944, RA/QM/PRIV/CC13/95
204 Queen Elizabeth to Sir Alan Lascelles (quoted in Sir Alan Lascelles to Queen Elizabeth, 29 March 1945), RA QEQM/PRIV/MISCOFF
205 Sir Alan Lascelles to Queen Elizabeth, 29 March 1945, RA QEQM/PRIV/MISCOFF
206 Queen Elizabeth to Queen Mary, 17 July 1944, RA QM/PRIV/CC13/95
207 King George VI to Queen Elizabeth, 22 July 1944, RA QEQM/PRIV/RF
208 Queen Elizabeth to Queen Mary, 26 July 1944, RA QM/PRIV/CC13/96

209 Ibid.
210 Queen Elizabeth to Sir Alan Lascelles, 29 July 1944, RA PS/PSO/AL/Box B
211 Betty Bowes Lyon to Queen Elizabeth, 25 July [1944], RA QEQM/PRIV/BL
212 King George VI to Queen Elizabeth, 29 July 1944, RA QEQM/PRIV/RF
213 Queen Elizabeth to King George VI, 26 July 1944, RA GVI/PRIV/RF/26/80
214 Queen Elizabeth to Sir Alan Lascelles, 31 July 1944, RA PS/PSO/AL/Box B
215 D'Arcy Osborne to Queen Elizabeth, 3 August 1944, RA QEQM/PRIV/PAL/Osborne
216 Queen Elizabeth to Queen Mary, 4 August 1944, RA QM/PRIV/CC13/97
217 Queen Mary to Queen Elizabeth, 30 July 1944, RA QEQM/PRIV/RF
218 Queen Elizabeth to Queen Mary, 4 August 1944, RA QM/PRIV/CC13/97
219 Queen Elizabeth to Queen Mary, 19 August 1944, RA QM/PRIV/CC13/98
220 Queen Elizabeth to Winston Churchill, CAC CHAR 1/380/52
221 Queen Elizabeth to the Hon. David Bowes Lyon, telegram, 6 November 1944, Bowes Lyon Papers, SPW
222 Hon. David Bowes Lyon to Queen Elizabeth, telegram, 6 November 1944, Bowes Lyon papers, SPW
223 Queen Elizabeth to the Hon. David Bowes Lyon, 14 November 1944, Bowes Lyon Papers, SPW
224 Laird, p. 267
225 Queen Elizabeth to the Hon. David Bowes Lyon, 14 November 1944, Bowes Lyon Papers, SPW
226 Queen Elizabeth to Winston Churchill, 14 November 1944, CAC, CHAR 1/380/52
227 Queen Elizabeth to Sir Alan Lascelles, 4 October 1944, RA PS/PSO/AL/Box B
228 Queen Elizabeth, message to Commanding Officer (Lieutenant Colonel Hon. Michael Bowes Lyon), 31 July 1944, RA QEQM/PS/ENGT/1944/43
229 Wheeler-Bennett, pp. 614–15
230 Laird, pp. 267–8
231 Queen Elizabeth's speech at Middle Temple, 12 December 1944, RA QEQMH/PS/ENGT/1944/39
232 Queen Elizabeth to Osbert Sitwell, 18 December 1944, Sitwell Papers
233 King George VI, diary, 21–26 December 1944, RA KGVI/PRIV/DIARY
234 Queen Elizabeth to Queen Mary, 28 December 1944, RA QM/PRIV/CC13/114
235 Queen Elizabeth to Queen Mary, 26 January 1945, RA QM/PRIV/CC13/117
236 Queen Elizabeth to D'Arcy Osborne, 14 February 1945, RA QEQM/OUT/OSBORNE
237 Queen Elizabeth to Hon. Sir Richard Molyneux, 20 March 1945, RA QEQM/OUT/MOLYNEUX/113
238 Queen Mary to King George VI, 13 April 1945, RA GVI/PRIV/RF/11
239 King George VI to Queen Mary, 23 April 1945, RA QM/PRIV/CC13/122
240 King George VI, diary, 8 May 1945, RA GVI/PRIV/DIARY
241 David Kynaston, *Austerity Britain 1945–51*, Bloomsbury, 2007, p. 212
242 King George VI, diary, 8 May 1945, RA GVI/PRIV/DIARY
243 King George VI to Queen Mary, 22 May 1945, RA QM/PRIV/CC13/124
244 Hansard, 15 May 1945
245 Queen Elizabeth to Osbert Sitwell, 14 May 1945, Sitwell Papers

FIFTEEN: WAR TO PEACE 1945–1947

1 Queen Elizabeth to Queen Mary, 18 September 1945, RA QM/PRIV/CC13/133
2 King George VI, diary, 18–20 May 1945, RA GVI/PRIV/DIARY

3 Queen Elizabeth to Lady Doris Vyner, 12 May 1945, Vyner Papers

4 King George VI to Most Rev. Cosmo Lang, 19 May 1945, Lambeth Palace Library, Lang Papers 318 f. 162

5 Queen Mary to King George VI, 27 May 1945, RA GVI/PRIV/RF/11

6 Gilbert, *Churchill: A Life*, pp. 843–5

7 Peter Hennessy, *Never Again*, Jonathan Cape, 1992, p. 94

8 Ibid.

9 King George VI, diary, 26 July 1945, RA GVI/PRIV/DIARY

10 Wheeler-Bennett, p. 637

11 Queen Elizabeth to Queen Mary, 26 July 1945, RA QM/PRIV/CC13/128

12 Gilbert, *Churchill: A Life*, pp. 854–6

13 *The Noël Coward Diaries*, 1982, p. 36, quoted in Kynaston, p. 78

14 Rhodes James, p. 283

15 Channon, *Diaries*, 15 August 1945, p. 501

16 'Speeches and Replies to Addresses by His Majesty King George VI', printed for the Private Secretary's Office, RA

17 James Lees-Milne, *Prophesying Peace: Diaries 1944–1945*, Chatto & Windus, 1977, 15 August 1945

18 Countess Spencer to Earl Spencer, 13 September 1945, Althorp Archives

19 Queen Elizabeth to Lady Cranborne, 7 October 1945, Hatfield House, Papers of Elizabeth, Marchioness of Salisbury

20 Owen Morshead, notes on conversation with Sir Alan Lascelles, 10 November 1945, RA AEC/GG/12/OS/2

21 Bradford, *George VI*, p. 594, quoting Alec Hardinge's subsequent remark that the King 'literally died for England'

22 Owen Morshead, notes on conversation with Sir Alan Lascelles, 10 November 1945, RA AEC/GG/12/OS/2.

23 Wheeler-Bennett, p. 654

24 Queen Elizabeth to Queen Mary, 18 September 1945, RA QM/PRIV/CC13/133

25 Winston Churchill to Duke of Windsor (copy), 31 December 1944, CAC CHAR/20/148/28

26 Queen Mary to King George VI, 27 August 1945, RA GVI/PRIV/RF/11

27 Queen Elizabeth to Queen Mary, 18 September 1945, RA QM/PRIV/CC13/133

28 King George VI to Queen Mary, 23 September 1945, RA QM/PRIV/CC13/135

29 Owen Morshead, notes on conversation with Queen Mary, 18 February 1946, RA AEC/GG/12/OS/2

30 King George VI to Queen Mary, 6 October 1945, RA QM/PRIV/CC13/137

31 Queen Mary to King George VI, 25 September 1945, RA GVI/PRIV/RF/11

32 Lascelles, p. 361

33 Frank Prochaska, *Royal Bounty*, Yale University Press, 1995, p. 206

34 Ibid., p. 218

35 Queen Elizabeth to Queen Mary, 19 February 1943, RA QM/PRIV/CC13/39

36 Prochaska, *Royal Bounty*, p. 229

37 Queen Elizabeth, conversations with Eric Anderson, 1994–5, RA QEQM/ADD/MISC

38 Wheeler-Bennett, p. 653

39 Ibid., p. 654

40 Laird, p. 272

41 Queen Elizabeth to Hon. Sir Richard Molyneux, 19 December 1945, RA QEQM/OUT/MOLYNEUX/115

42 Hon. David Bowes Lyon to Rachel Bowes Lyon, 1 January 1946, Bowes Lyon Papers, SPW

43 Queen Mary to King George VI, 31 January 1946, RA GVI/PRIV/RF/11; Owen Morshead, notes on conversation with Queen Mary, 18 February 1946, RA AEC/GG/12/OS/2

44 Queen Elizabeth to the Hon. David Bowes Lyon, 26 January 1946, Bowes Lyon Papers, SPW

45 Queen Elizabeth to Lady Delia Peel, 27 August 1945, Althorp Archives

46 Queen Elizabeth to Arthur Penn, 29 March 1946, Penn Papers

47 Arthur Penn to Queen Elizabeth, 1 April 1946, RA QEQM/PRIV/HH

48 Jasper Ridley to Queen Elizabeth, 27 January 1946, RA QEQM/PRIV/PAL/Ridley

49 Hon. Sir Richard Molyneux to Queen Elizabeth, 8 January 1946, RA QEQM/PRIV/PAL/Molyneux

50 King George VI, diary, 22–28 April 1946, RA GVI/PRIV/DIARY

51 Clementine Churchill to Queen Elizabeth, 26 April 1946, RA QEQM/PRIV/PAL

52 Laird, p. 274

53 Queen Elizabeth to Lady Cranborne, 25 September 1946, Hatfield House, Papers of Elizabeth, Marchioness of Salisbury

54 Queen Elizabeth to King George VI, 8 October 1946, RA GVI/PRIV/RF/26/82

55 Osbert Sitwell to Queen Elizabeth, 23 June 1945, RA QEQM/PRIV/PAL/Sitwell

56 Author's interview with Sir Oliver Millar

57 Queen Mary to King George VI, 22 November 1946, RA GVI/PRIV/RF/11

58 Queen Elizabeth to Osbert Sitwell, 12 November 1946, Sitwell Papers

59 Queen Elizabeth to Toronto Scottish, 20 October 1945, RA QEQMH/PS/ARMFOR/Toronto Scottish

60 Queen Elizabeth to 5th Battalion, The Black Watch (draft telegram), n.d. [February 1946], RA QEQMH/PS/ARMFOR/Black Watch

61 Queen Elizabeth to Lord Wavell, 9 April 1946 (incomplete draft), RA QEQM/OUT/MISC

62 Queen Elizabeth to Queen Mary, 13 November 1944, RA QM/PRIV/CC13/111

63 Helen Hudson, *Cumberland Lodge: A House through History*, Phillimore, 1989, p. 147

64 Queen Elizabeth to Queen Mary, 13 November 1944, RA QM/PRIV/CC13/111

65 Queen Elizabeth to the Hon. Elizabeth Elphinstone, 5 February 1950, RA QEQM/OUT/ELPHINSTONE

66 Afrikaans vocabulary lists, RA QEQM/PRIV/VIS

67 Sir Edmund Grove Papers

68 Arthur Penn to Queen Elizabeth, 5 February 1947, RA QEQM/PRIV/HH

69 Princess Elizabeth to Marion Crawford, 15 February 1947, RA QEII/OUT/BUTHLAY

70 RA F&V/VISOV/SA/1947/Diary of the Royal Visit to South Africa

71 Ibid.

72 Princess Elizabeth to Queen Mary, 16 February 1947, RA QM/PRIV/CC14/148

73 Wheeler-Bennett, p. 687

74 Princess Elizabeth to Queen Mary, 23 February 1947, RA QM/PRIV/CC14/149

75 Sir Edmund Grove Papers

76 Sir Alan Lascelles to Lady Lascelles, 22 February 1947, CAC LASL 4/4/4

77 Princess Elizabeth to Queen Mary, 23 February 1947, RA QM/PRIV/CC14/149

78 Enid Bagnold Letters, Diana Cooper Papers, Box VII, Eton College Library

79 Queen Elizabeth, conversations with Eric Anderson, 1994–5, RA QEQM/ADD/MISC

80 Sir Edmund Grove Papers

81 Queen Elizabeth to Queen Mary, 21 February 1947, RA QM/PRIV/CC13/169

82 Queen Elizabeth to Queen Mary, 9 March 1947, RA QM/PRIV/CC13/172

83 Queen Elizabeth, conversations with Eric Anderson, 1994–5, RA QEQM/ADD/MISC

84 Queen Elizabeth to Queen Mary, 9 March 1947, RA QM/PRIV/CC13/172

85 Enid Bagnold Letters, Diana Cooper Papers, Box VII, Eton College Library

86 Sir Alan Lascelles to his son, 10 March 1947, CAC LASL 4/4/9

87 RA F&V/VISOV/SA/1947/Diary of the Royal Visit to South Africa, 12 March 1947

88 Queen Elizabeth to May Elphinstone, 26 April 1947, RA QEQM/OUT/ELPHINSTONE

89 Princess Elizabeth to Queen Mary, 28 March 1947, RA QM/PRIV/CC14/152

90 Bradford, *George VI*, p. 519

91 Queen Elizabeth to the Hon. Elizabeth Elphinstone, 23 March 1947, RA QEQM/OUT/
    ELPHINSTONE

92 Princess Elizabeth to Queen Mary, 9 April 1947, RA QM/PRIV/CC14/153

93 Queen Elizabeth to Queen Mary, 9 March 1947, RA QM/PRIV/CC13/172

94 Longford, *Queen Mother*, p. 111

95 Note by Edmund Grove on King George VI and the South Africa Tour, 1947, Sir
    Edmund Grove Papers

96 King George VI to Queen Mary, 6 April 1947, RA QM/PRIV/CC13/174

97 Bradford, *George VI*, pp. 519–20

98 Enid Bagnold Letters, Diana Cooper Papers, Box VII, Eton College Library

99 Queen Elizabeth to the Hon. Elizabeth Elphinstone, 23 March 1947, RA QEQM/OUT/
    ELPHINSTONE

100 Queen Elizabeth to May Elphinstone, 26 April 1947, RA QEQM/OUT/ELPHINSTONE

101 Wheeler-Bennett, notes of interview with Sir Edward Fielden, RA AEC/GG/20

102 Sir John Kennedy to Queen Elizabeth, 14 January 1959, RA QEQM/PRIV/PAL

103 Longford, *Queen Mother*, p. 110

104 Queen Elizabeth to Queen Mary, 16 April 1947, RA QM/PRIV/CC13/176

105 Duchess of Kent to Queen Elizabeth, 20 April 1947, RA QEQM/PRIV/RF

106 Dermot Morrah, *The Royal Family in Africa*, Hutchinson, 1947, p. 124

107 Queen Mary to Queen Elizabeth, 22 April 1947, RA QEQM/PRIV/RF

108 Morrah, *Royal Family in Africa*, p. 128

109 Queen Elizabeth to May Elphinstone, 26 April 1947, RA QEQM/OUT/ELPHINSTONE

110 Sir Alan Lascelles to Lady Lascelles, 30 April 1947, CAC LASL 4/4/2/17

SIXTEEN: JOY AND SORROW 1947–1952

1   Longford, *Queen Mother*, p. 102

2   Rose Granville to Queen Elizabeth, 22 March 1946, RA QEQM/PRIV/BL

3   Sir Alan Lascelles to Queen Elizabeth, 12 December 1945, RA QEQM/PRIV/CHILD

4   Longford, *Queen Mother*, p. 106

5   Prince Philip to Queen Elizabeth, 12 June 46, RA QEQM/PRIV/RF

6   Prince Philip to Queen Elizabeth, 14 September 1946, RA QEQM/PRIV/RF

7   Ibid.

8   Prince Philip to Queen Elizabeth, 3 December [1946], RA QEQM/PRIV/RF

9   Prince Philip to Queen Elizabeth, 28 January [1947], RA QEQM/PRIV/RF

10 Prince Philip to Queen Elizabeth, 11 June [1947], RA QEQM/PRIV/RF

11 Queen Elizabeth to Sir Alan Lascelles, 7 July 1947, (draft letter, unfinished and possibly
    not sent; no final version in Lascelles's papers) RA QEQM/PRIV/HH

12 Queen Elizabeth to May Elphinstone, 7 July 1947, RA QEQM/OUT/ELPHINSTONE

13 Queen Elizabeth to Arthur Penn, 9 July 1947, Penn Papers

14 Arthur Penn to Queen Elizabeth, 13 June 1947, RA QEQM/PRIV/PAL/Penn

15 Arthur Penn to Queen Elizabeth, 9 July 1947, RA QEQM/PRIV/PAL/Penn

16 King George VI to Queen Mary, 14 September 1947, RA QM/PRIV/CC13/183

17 Queen Ingrid of Denmark to Queen Elizabeth, 13 October 1947, RA QEQM/PRIV/FORRF

18 D'Arcy Osborne to the Queen, 20 July 1947, RA QEQM/PRIV/PAL/Osborne

19 Normal Hartnell to King George VI and Queen Elizabeth, 15 October 1947; Commander Richard Colville to Queen Elizabeth, 17 October 1947, RA QEQM/PRIV/CHILD

20 Richard Colville to Queen Elizabeth, 10 November 1947, QEQM/PRIV/MISCOFF

21 King George VI to Queen Mary, 6 November 1947, RA QM/PRIV/CC13/188

22 Duff Cooper, p. 453

23 Princess Elizabeth to Queen Elizabeth, 22 November 1947, RA QEQM/PRIV/RF

24 Wheeler-Bennett, pp. 754–5

25 Princess Elizabeth to Queen Elizabeth, 22 November 1947, RA QEQM/PRIV/RF

26 Queen Elizabeth to Princess Elizabeth, 24 November 1947, RA QEII/PRIV/RF

27 Princess Elizabeth to Queen Elizabeth, 30 November 1947, RA QEQM/PRIV/RF

28 Prince Philip to Queen Elizabeth, 3 December [1947], RA QEQM/PRIV/RF

29 Wheeler-Bennett, pp. 760–2

30 'Speeches and Replies to Addresses by His Majesty King George VI', printed for the Private Secretary's Office, RA

31 Laird, p. 296

32 King George VI to Queen Mary, 3 May 1948, RA QM/PRIV/CC13/198

33 Duff Cooper, p. 463

34 Prochaska, *Royal Bounty*, p. 234

35 Ibid.

36 Ibid., p. 244

37 Laird, p. 279

38 Prochaska, *Royal Bounty*, p. 235

39 Ibid.

40 Ibid., p. 236

41 Ibid.

42 Ibid., p. 238

43 Letter to Queen Elizabeth from 'All in the Gardens', RA QEQMH/PS/ENGT/1947/31

44 Queen Elizabeth to Sir Alan Lascelles, 5 November 1948, RA PS/PSO/AL/Box B

45 Sir Alan Lascelles to Queen Elizabeth, 6 November 1948, RA QEQM/PRIV/CHILD

46 Wheeler-Bennett, p. 762

47 Queen Elizabeth to Sir Alan Lascelles, 26 October 1948, RA PS/PSO/AL/Box B

48 Queen Elizabeth to Queen Mary, 14 November 1948, RA QM/PRIV/CC13/211

49 Princess Elizabeth to May Elphinstone, 18 November 1948, RA QEQM/OUT/ELPHINSTONE

50 Queen Elizabeth to Lady Salisbury, 27 November 1948, Hatfield House, Papers of Elizabeth, Marchioness of Salisbury

51 Queen Elizabeth to Queen Mary, 20 November 1948, RA QM/PRIV/CC13/212

52 Queen Mary to Queen Elizabeth, 12 December 1948, RA QEQM/PRIV/RF

53 Queen Elizabeth to Winston Churchill, 27 December 1948, RA QEQM/OUT/MISC

54 Lady Salisbury to Queen Elizabeth, 7 December [1948], RA QEQM/PRIV/PAL/Salisbury

55 Queen Elizabeth to Lady Salisbury, 9 December 1948, Hatfield House, Papers of Elizabeth, Marchioness of Salisbury

56 Isaiah Berlin, *Personal Impressions*, ed. Henry Hardy, 2nd edn, Pimlico, 1998, p. 257

57 Queen Elizabeth to D'Arcy Osborne, 5 March 1949, RA QEQM/OUT/OSBORNE

58 Wheeler-Bennett, p. 769

59 Ibid., p. 768

60 Queen Elizabeth to Lady Violet Bonham Carter, 27 March 1949, Bodleian Library, MS BC 169/125–6

61 Laird, p. 301

62 Queen Elizabeth to Marion Crawford, 1 January 1949, RA QEII/OUT/BUTHLAY

63 Marion Crawford to Queen Elizabeth, 28 January 1949, RA QEQM/PRIV/HH

64 Marion Crawford to Queen Elizabeth, 8 March 1949, RA QEQM/PRIV/HH

65 Queen Elizabeth to Marion Crawford, 4 April 1949, from a copy in Princeton University Library, quoted in Vickers, p. 283. This appears to be the only extant copy

66 Marion Crawford to Queen Elizabeth, 15 April 1949, RA QEQM/PRIV/HH

67 Queen Elizabeth to Lady Astor, 19 October 1949, quoted in Vickers, pp. 285–6

68 Major Thomas Harvey to Lady Astor, undated draft, RA PS/PSO/QEII/PS/19/9/00/4

69 Notes by Princess Elizabeth, RA PS/PSO/QEII/PS/19/9/00/4; Lady Astor to Mr and Mrs Gould, quoted in Vickers, p. 286

70 Major Thomas Harvey to Lady Astor, undated draft, RA PS/PSO/QEII/PS/19/9/00/4

71 Bruce Gould to Lady Astor, 24 October 1949, RA PS/PSO/QEII/PS/19/9/00/4

72 Bruce and Beatrice Gould to Lady Astor, 27 October 1949, RA PS/PSO/QEII/PS/19/9/00/4

73 Queen Elizabeth to Major Thomas Harvey, undated memorandum [27 October 1949], RA PS/PSO/QEII/PS/19/9/00/4

74 Vickers, p. 289

75 Correspondence with *Woman's Own* and Cassell & Co., January–March 1950, RA PPTO/PP/GVI/MAIN/7606

76 Laird, p. 301

77 Queen Elizabeth to Queen Mary, 15 October 1950, RA QM/PRIV/CC14/15

78 Queen Elizabeth to Princess Elizabeth 29 December 1950, RA QEII/PRIV/RF

79 Ibid.

80 Queen Elizabeth to Princess Elizabeth, 7 April 1951, RA QEII/PRIV/RF

81 King George VI to Queen Mary, 26 May 1951, RA QM/PRIV/CC14/26

82 King George VI to Queen Mary, 31 May 1951, RA QM/PRIV/CC14/28

83 Wheeler-Bennett, p. 787

84 Queen Mary to King George VI, 6 June 1951, RA GVI/PRIV/RF/11

85 King George VI to Queen Mary, 12 June 1951, RA QM/PRIV/CC14/30

86 Queen Elizabeth to Queen Mary, 10 July 1951, RA QM/PRIV/CC14/32

87 RA QEQM/PRIV/POEM

88 Wheeler-Bennett, p. 788

89 King George VI to Queen Mary, 11 September 1951, RA QM/PRIV/CC14/35

90 Queen Elizabeth to Queen Mary, 17 September 1951, RA QM/PRIV/CC14/36

91 Bradford, *George VI*, pp. 600–1

92 Queen Elizabeth to Queen Mary, 21 September 1951, RA QM/PRIV/CC14/37

93 Wheeler-Bennett, p. 788

94 Queen Elizabeth to Princess Elizabeth, 22 September 1951, RA QEII/PRIV/RF

95 Sir Alan Lascelles to Queen Elizabeth, 23 September 1951, RA QEQM/PRIV/MISCOFF

96 Queen Elizabeth to Sir Alan Lascelles, 23 September 1951, RA PS/PSO/AL/Box B

97 Queen Elizabeth to Queen Mary, 23 September 1951, RA QM/PRIV/CC14/38

98 Queen Elizabeth to Sir Alan Lascelles, 23 September 1951, RA PS/PSO/AL/Box B

99 Owen Morshead, notes of conversation with Sir Richard Molyneux, 30 March 1953, RA AEC/GG/12/OS/2

100 Sir Alan Lascelles to Queen Elizabeth, 23 September 1951, RA QEQM/PRIV/MISCOFF, and Queen Elizabeth to Sir Alan Lascelles, 23 September 1951, RA PS/PSO/AL/Box B

101 Queen Elizabeth to Duke of Windsor, 25 September 1951, RA EDW/PRIV/MAINB/182

102 Queen Mary to King George VI, 17 November 1951, RA GVI/PRIV/RF/11

103 Bradford, *George VI*, p. 601

104 Queen Elizabeth to May Elphinstone, 5 October 1951, RA QEQM/OUT/ELPHINSTONE

105 Princess Elizabeth to Queen Elizabeth, 16 October 1951, RA QEQM/PRIV/RF

106 Princess Elizabeth to Queen Elizabeth, 4 November 1951, RA QEQM/PRIV/RF

107 Queen Elizabeth to Princess Elizabeth, 15 October 1951, RA QEII/PRIV/RF

108 Princess Elizabeth to Queen Elizabeth, 4 November 1951, RA QEQM/PRIV/RF

109 King George VI to Queen Mary, 14 October 1951, RA QM/PRIV/CC14/40

110 Queen Elizabeth to Princess Elizabeth 15 October 1951, RA QEII/PRIV/RF

111 Bradford, *George VI*, p. 605

112 Ibid.

113 King George VI to Queen Mary, 23 January 1952, RA QM/PRIV/CC14/42

114 Wheeler-Bennett, p. 605

115 Queen Elizabeth to Princess Elizabeth, 2 February 1952, RA QEII/PRIV/RF

116 Ibid.

117 King George VI to Sir John Weir (copy, enclosed with letter from Sir John Weir to Queen Elizabeth, 21 February 1952), 3 February 1952, RA QEQM/PRIV/PAL; King George VI to Lord Halifax, 4 February 1952, Hickleton Papers, A2/278/26/7

118 John Wheeler-Bennett, interview with James Macdonald, 20 October 1954, RA AEC/GG/20

119 Queen Elizabeth to Lady Delia Peel, 11 February 1952, Althorp Archives

120 Queen Elizabeth to Edward Seago (extract), n.d. [February 1952], RA QEQMH/PS/GEN/1989/Seago

121 John Wheeler-Bennett, interview with James Macdonald, 20 October 1954, RA AEC/GG/20

122 Queen Elizabeth to Queen Mary, 6 February 1952, RA QM/PRIV/CC14/44

123 Bradford, *George VI*, pp. 607–8: author's interview with Edward Ford

124 Ibid., p. 608

125 Ibid., pp. 607–8: author's interview with Edward Ford

126 RA QM/PRIV/DIARY/1952: 6 February

127 Queen Elizabeth to Queen Mary, 6 February 1952, RA QM/PRIV/CC14/44

128 Queen Mary to Queen Elizabeth, 7 February 1952, RA QEQM/PRIV/RF

129 Commander Michael Parker quoted in Bradford, *Elizabeth*, p. 66

130 Author's interview with Countess Mountbatten of Burma

131 Pope-Hennessy, p. 619

132 Queen Mary to Queen Elizabeth, 7 February 1952, RA QEQM/PRIV/RF

133 Queen Elizabeth II to John Elphinstone, 13 February 1952, RA QEQM/OUT/ELPHINSTONE

134 Queen Elizabeth to Sir Alan Lascelles, 12 February 1953, RA PS/PSO/AL/Box B

135 Sir Alan Lascelles to Queen Elizabeth, 13 February 1952, RA QEQM/PRIV/PAL

136 Queen Elizabeth to Sir Alan Lascelles, 15 February 1952, RA PS/PSO/AL/Box B

SEVENTEEN: QUEEN MOTHER 1952–1955

1 Notes by Lady Elizabeth Basset, 'Living Her Faith', June 1990, RA QEQMH/PS/PRIV

2 Winston Churchill to Queen Elizabeth, 14 February 1952, RA QEQM/PRIV/DEATH/ GVI

3 Clementine Churchill to Queen Elizabeth, 12 February 1952, RA QEQM/PRIV/ DEATH/GVI

4 General Eisenhower to Queen Elizabeth, 7 February 1952, RA QEQM/PRIV/DEATH/ GVI

5 Eleanor Roosevelt to Queen Elizabeth, 7 February 1952, RA QEQM/PRIV/DEATH/ GVI

6 Ziegler, *Edward VIII*, p. 537

7 Ibid.

8 Queen Mary to Queen Elizabeth, 10 February 1952, RA QEQM/PRIV/RF

9 Queen Mary to the Earl of Athlone and Princess Alice, 23 February 1952, RA QM/ PRIV/CC53/1566

10 Duke of Windsor to Queen Elizabeth, 18 February 1952, RA QEQM/PRIV/RF

11 Queen Elizabeth to Sir Alan Lascelles, 19 February 1952, CAC LASL 2/2/8

12 Michael Bloch, *The Secret File of The Duke of Windsor*, Bantam Press, 1988, pp. 264–5

13 Duke of Windsor to Queen Elizabeth, 18 May 1952, RA QEQM/PRIV/RF

14 Queen Elizabeth to Queen Elizabeth II, 28 June 1953, RA QEII/PRIV/RF

15 Queen Elizabeth's message, 18 February 1952, RA QEQMH/PS/RF/DEATH/GVI

16 Queen Elizabeth to Queen Elizabeth II, undated [1952], RA QEII/PRIV/RF

17 Queen Mary to Queen Elizabeth, 21 February 1952, RA QEQM/PRIV/RF

18 Sir John Weir to Queen Elizabeth, 21 February 1952, RA QEQM/PRIV/PAL

19 Rt Rev. Edward Woods to Queen Elizabeth, 28 February 1952, RA QEQM/PRIV/PAL/ Woods

20 Queen Elizabeth to Sir Alan Lascelles, 25 February 1952, RA PS/PSO/AL/Box B

21 Sir Alan Lascelles to Queen Elizabeth, 26 February 1952, RA QEQM/PRIV/MISCOFF

22 Sir Alan Lascelles to Queen Elizabeth, 1 April 1952, RA QEQM/PRIV/MISCOFF

23 Queen Elizabeth to Sir Alan Lascelles, 25 February 1952, RA PS/PSO/AL/Box B; Lascelles to Queen Elizabeth, 26 February 1952, RA QEQM/PRIV/MISCOFF

24 Elizabeth Longford, *Elizabeth R*, Weidenfeld & Nicolson, 1983, p. 155; John Colville, *The Fringes of Power*, Hodder & Stoughton, 1985, p. 641

25 *The Macmillan Diaries: The Cabinet Years 1950–1957*, ed. Peter Catterall, Macmillan, 2003, p. 150

26 Lord Airlie to Queen Elizabeth, 8 May [1952], RA QEQM/PRIV/HH

27 Queen Elizabeth to Arthur Penn, 1 April 1952, Penn Papers

28 Queen Elizabeth to the Hon. David Bowes Lyon, 20 March 1952, Bowes Lyon Papers, SPW

29 Queen Elizabeth to Sir Alan Lascelles, 25 February 1952, RA PS/PSO/AL/Box B

30 Queen Elizabeth to Lord Salisbury, 14 March 1952, Hatfield House, Papers of fifth Marquess of Salisbury

31 Owen Morshead, notes of conversation with Sir Richard Molyneux, 30 March 1953, RA AEC/GG/12/OS/2

32 D'Arcy Osborne to Queen Elizabeth, 11 March 1952, RA QEQM/PRIV/PAL/Osborne

33 Betty Bowes Lyon to Queen Elizabeth, 7 March 1952, RA QEQM/PRIV/BL

34 Queen Elizabeth to the Hon. David Bowes Lyon, 20 March 1952, Bowes Lyon Papers, SPW

35 Lady Katherine Seymour to Countess Spencer, 26 March 1952, Althorp Archives

36 Queen Elizabeth to Lady Delia Peel, 22 April 1952, Althorp Archives

37 Queen Elizabeth to Osbert Sitwell, 3 May 1952, Sitwell Papers

38 Lord Davidson to Queen Elizabeth, 26 February 1952, RA QEQM/PRIV/PAL

39 Queen Elizabeth to Lord Davidson, 31 March 1952, RA GVI/ADD/MISC/COPY

40 Queen Elizabeth to Arthur Penn, 1 April 1952, Penn Papers

41 Queen Elizabeth to Lady Salisbury, 28 April 1952, Hatfield House, Papers of Elizabeth, Marchioness of Salisbury

42 Queen Elizabeth to Cecil Boyd-Rochfort, 14 May 1952, RA QEQM/OUT/BOYD-ROCHFORT

43 Osbert Sitwell to Queen Elizabeth, 7 May 1952, RA QEQM/PRIV/PAL/Sitwell

44 Queen Elizabeth to Osbert Sitwell, 3 May 1952, Sitwell Papers

45 Oliver Dawnay to Major General R. K. Arbuthnott, 28 April 1952, RA QEQMH/PS/ARMFOR/Black Watch

46 Laird, pp. 315–16

47 Sir Miles Thomas, *Out on a Wing*, Michael Joseph, 1964, p. 313

48 Hugh Massingberd, 'She derived much pleasure from all that she did', *Daily Telegraph*, 1 April 2002; Squadron Leader J. P. Meadows to Oliver Dawnay, 24 May 1952, RA QEQMH/PS/ARMFOR/600 City of London Squadron RAAF

49 Queen Elizabeth to Queen Mary, 22 June 1952, RA QM/PRIV/CC14/55

50 *The Queen Mother Remembered*, ed. James Hogg and Michael Mortimer, BBC Worldwide, 2002, p. 161

51 Queen Elizabeth, conversations with Eric Anderson, 1994–5, RA QEQM/ADD/MISC

52 Lady Doris Vyner to Queen Elizabeth, n.d. [20 August 1952], RA QEQM/PRIV/PAL

53 Commander Clare Vyner to Queen Elizabeth, 23 August 1952, RA QEQM/PRIV/RES

54 Lady Doris Vyner to Queen Elizabeth, n.d. [3 December 1952], n.d. [December 1952], RA QEQM/PRIV/RES

55 Lady Doris Vyner to Queen Elizabeth, n.d. [21 July 1952], RA QEQM/PRIV/RES

56 Queen Elizabeth to Sir Arthur Penn, n.d. [6 August 1952], Penn Papers

57 Queen Elizabeth to Queen Mary, 31 August 1952, RA QM/PRIV/CC14/59

58 Queen Mary to Queen Elizabeth, 9 September 1952, RA QEQM/PRIV/RF

59 May Elphinstone to Queen Elizabeth, 5 September 1952, RA QEQM/PRIV/BL

60 Queen Mary to Queen Elizabeth, 25 June 1952, RA QEQM/PRIV/RF

61 Lady Doris Vyner to Queen Elizabeth, n.d. [21 July 1952], RA QEQM/PRIV/RES

62 Edward Seago to Queen Elizabeth, 27 July 1952, RA QEQM/PRIV/PAL/Seago; Countess Spencer to Earl Spencer, 26 July 1952, Althorp Archives

63 Queen Elizabeth to Queen Mary, 28 July 1952, RA QM/PRIV/CC14/57

64 Queen Elizabeth to Queen Elizabeth II, 21 July 1952, RA QEII/PRIV/RF

65 Queen Elizabeth II to Queen Elizabeth, 23 July 1952, RA QEQM/PRIV/RF

66 Queen Elizabeth to Queen Mary, 22 August 1952, RA QM/PRIV/CC14/58

67 Queen Elizabeth to May Elphinstone, 2 September 1952, RA QEQM/OUT/ELPHINSTONE

68 D'Arcy Osborne to Queen Elizabeth, 9 September 1952, RA QEQM/PRIV/PAL/Osborne

69 Queen Elizabeth to D'Arcy Osborne, 29 November 1952, RA QEQM/OUT/OSBORNE

70 Queen Elizabeth to Sir Alan Lascelles, 29 November 1952, CAC LASL 2/3/5

71 Victoria Glendinning, *Edith Sitwell: A Unicorn among Lions*, 1981, p. 299, quoted in Longford, *Elizabeth R*, pp. 147–8

72 Sir Arthur Penn to Countess Spencer, 29 August 1952, Althorp Archives

73 Ibid.

74 Queen Elizabeth to Lady Salisbury, 6 August 1952, Hatfield House, Papers of Elizabeth, Marchioness of Salisbury
75 Queen Elizabeth to Lord Salisbury, 3 October 1952, Hatfield House, Papers of fifth Marquess of Salisbury
76 *The Queen Mother Remembered*, p. 161
77 Queen Elizabeth to Sir Alan Lascelles, 29 November 1952, CAC LASL 2/3/5
78 Sir Alan Lascelles to Queen Elizabeth, 29 November 1952, RA QEQM/PRIV/TEXTS
79 Rose, *Kings, Queens and Courtiers*, pp. 279–80
80 Queen Elizabeth to Sir Alan Lascelles, 15 February 1953, CAC LASL 2/3/6
81 John Wheeler-Bennett to Queen Elizabeth, 27 September 1953, RA QEQM/PRIV/PAL
82 Sir Robert Bruce Lockhart, *Diaries 1939–1965*, ed. Kenneth Young, Macmillan, 1980, p. 755
83 Queen Elizabeth to Helen Hardinge, 2 May 1951, RA QEQM/PRIV/TEXTS
84 Queen Elizabeth to Queen Elizabeth II, RA QEII/PRIV/RF
85 Pope-Hennessy, p. 619
86 Ibid., p. 622
87 Queen Elizabeth to Lady Doris Vyner, 13 April 1953, Vyner Papers
88 Sir Arthur Penn to Queen Elizabeth, 7 January 1953 [misdated 1952], RA QEQM/PRIV/RES
89 Queen Elizabeth to Sir Arthur Penn, 12 April 1953, Penn Papers
90 *The Times* obituary notice by James Stuart, 7 May 1953
91 William Shawcross, *Queen and Country*, BBC Worldwide, 2002, p. 49
92 Queen Elizabeth to Queen Mary, 2 March 1953, RA QM/PRIV/CC14/62
93 Hartnell, p. 128
94 Longford, *Queen Mother*, p. 125
95 Cecil Beaton, *The Strenuous Years*, Weidenfeld & Nicolson, 1973, p. 147
96 Longford, *Elizabeth R*, p. 148
97 Queen Elizabeth to D'Arcy Osborne, 5 March 1949, RA QEQM/OUT/OSBORNE
98 Rose, *Kings, Queens and Courtiers*, p. 271
99 Longford, *Elizabeth R*, p. 148
100 Wing Commander Peter Townsend, report on Princess Margaret's visit to Amsterdam, 26 October 1948, RA PS/PSO/GVI/PS/MAIN/09087
101 Rose, *Kings, Queens and Courtiers*, p. 185
102 Ibid., p. 186
103 Queen Elizabeth to D'Arcy Osborne, 5 March 1949, RA QEQM/OUT/OSBORNE
104 Duff Cooper to Queen Elizabeth, 26 November 1951, RA QEQM/PRIV/PAL
105 Queen Elizabeth to Duff Cooper, 9 December 1951, RA QEQM/OUT/MISC
106 Quoted by Rose, *Kings, Queens, and Courtiers*, p. 273
107 Princess Margaret to the Hon. David Bowes Lyon, 21 February 1952, Bowes Lyon Papers, SPW
108 Princess Margaret to Lady Diana Cooper, Diana Cooper Papers, Eton College Library
109 John Wheeler-Bennett, interview with Princess Margaret, 15 April 1954, RA AEC/GG/20
110 Sir Alan Lascelles, undated note, CAC LASL 2/3/14
111 Peter Townsend, *Time and Chance*, Collins, 1978, p. 198
112 Sir Alan Lascelles, undated note, CAC LASL 2/3/14
113 Longford, *Queen Mother*, p. 123
114 Queen Elizabeth to Sir Alan Lascelles, 12 June 1953, CAC LASL 2/3/7
115 Longford, *Elizabeth R*, p. 152
116 Queen Elizabeth to Sir Alan Lascelles, 12 June 1953, CAC LASL 2/3/7
117 Ibid.

118 Longford, *Elizabeth R*, p. 151
119 Sir Alan Lascelles to Queen Elizabeth, 11 June 1953, RA QEQM/PRIV/CHILD
120 Ibid.
121 Ibid.
122 Sir John Colville to Sir Alan Lascelles, n.d. [1955], CAC LASL 8/7/6, and Longford, *Elizabeth R*, p. 152
123 Sir Alan Lascelles to Queen Elizabeth, 13 June 1953, RA QEQM/PRIV/CHILD
124 Ibid.
125 Sir John Colville to Sir Alan Lascelles, n.d. [1955], CAC LASL 8/7/6
126 Sir Arthur Penn to Queen Elizabeth, 17 June 1953, RA QEQM/PRIV/PAL/Penn
127 Peter Townsend to Queen Elizabeth, 17 June 1953, RA QEQM/PRIV/PAL
128 Queen Elizabeth to Lord Salisbury, 3 October 1952, Hatfield House, Papers of fifth Marquess of Salisbury
129 Queen Elizabeth to Queen Elizabeth II, 7 July 1953, RA QEII/PRIV/RF
130 Sir John Kennedy to Secretary of State for Commonwealth Relations (copy), 28 July 1953, RA QEQMH/PS/VIS/1953/SR
131 Queen Elizabeth to Queen Elizabeth II, 7 July 1953, RA QEII/PRIV/RF
132 Sir John Kennedy to Queen Elizabeth, 30 July 1953, RA QEQM/PRIV/PAL
133 Queen Elizabeth to Osbert Sitwell, 9 July 1953, RA QEQM/OUT/SITWELL
134 Ibid.
135 Lady Kennedy to Queen Elizabeth, 16 August 1953, RA QEQM/PRIV/PAL
136 Letter from Mrs Palmer of Swindon, 8 December 1953, quoting her brother-in-law's letter from Salisbury, RA QEQMH/GEN/1953/Palmer
137 Lady Kennedy to Queen Elizabeth, 16 August 1953, RA QEQM/PRIV/PAL
138 Queen Elizabeth to Queen Elizabeth II and Prince Philip, 23 August 1953, RA QEII/PRIV/RF
139 Queen Elizabeth to Lord Salisbury, 26 May 1953, Hatfield House, Papers of fifth Marquess of Salisbury
140 Lady Salisbury to Queen Elizabeth, 13 September 1953, RA QEQM/PRIV/PAL/Salisbury
141 Lord Salisbury to Queen Elizabeth, 17 September 1953, RA QEQM/PRIV/PAL
142 Queen Elizabeth to Queen Elizabeth II, 28 March 1954, RA QEII/PRIV/RF
143 Queen Elizabeth to Queen Elizabeth II, 14 December 1953, RA QEII/PRIV/RF
144 Queen Elizabeth to Queen Elizabeth II, 28 December 1953, RA QEII/PRIV/RF
145 Queen Elizabeth to Queen Elizabeth II, 10 January 1954, RA QEII/PRIV/RF
146 Ibid.
147 Queen Elizabeth to Queen Elizabeth II, 10 March 1954, RA QEII/PRIV/RF
148 Queen Elizabeth II to Queen Elizabeth, n.d. [early 1954], RA QEQM/PRIV/RF
149 Queen Elizabeth to Queen Elizabeth II, 28 March 1954, RA QEII/PRIV/RF
150 Queen Elizabeth II to Queen Elizabeth, 2 March 1954, RA QEQM/PRIV/RF
151 Queen Elizabeth to Queen Elizabeth II, 28 March 1954, RA QEII/PRIV/RF
152 Queen Elizabeth II to Queen Elizabeth, 5 May 1954, RA QEII/PRIV/RF
153 Queen Elizabeth to Queen Elizabeth II, 5 November 1954, RA QEII/PRIV/RF
154 Ibid.
155 Queen Elizabeth, note with memo from Oliver Dawnay, 1 October 1954, RA QEQMH/PS/VIS/1954/USA
156 John Russell to Oliver Dawnay, 22 November 1953, RA QEQMH/PS/VIS/1954/USA
157 Queen Elizabeth to Queen Elizabeth II, 5 November 1954, RA QEII/PRIV/RF
158 Queen Elizabeth to Osbert Sitwell, 8 February 1955, Sitwell Papers
159 Queen Elizabeth to Queen Elizabeth II, 5 November 1954, RA QEII/PRIV/RF

160 Laird, p. 326
161 Queen Elizabeth to Osbert Sitwell, 8 February 1955, Sitwell Papers
162 Queen Elizabeth to May Elphinstone, 13 December 1954, RA QEQM/OUT/ ELPHINSTONE
163 Sir Roger Makins to Sir Anthony Eden, 30 November 1954 (copy), RA QEQMH/PS/ VIS/1954/USA
164 Alice Makins to Queen Elizabeth, 22 November 1954, RA QEQM/PRIV/PAL
165 Queen Elizabeth to Queen Elizabeth II, 5 November 1954, RA QEII/PRIV/RF
166 Queen Elizabeth to Princess Margaret, 13 November 1954, Linley Papers
167 Queen Elizabeth to May Elphinstone, 13 December 1954, RA QEQM/OUT/ ELPHINSTONE
168 Archibald Nye, British High Commissioner, to Viscount Swinton, 29 December 1954, RA QEQMH/PS/VIS/1954/CAN
169 Ibid.
170 Sir Roger Makins to Sir Anthony Eden, 30 November 1954 (copy), RA QEQMH/PS/ VIS/1954/USA
171 Ibid.
172 Enclosure with letter from Bill Ormerod, British Information Services, New York, to Oliver Dawnay, 24 November 1954, RA QEQMH/PS/VIS/1954/USA
173 Winston Churchill to Queen Elizabeth, 25 November 1954, RA QEQMH/PS/VIS/1954/ USA
174 William Wallace to Queen Elizabeth, 24 May [1955], RA QEQM/PRIV/PAL
175 *Nassau Daily Tribune*, 4 March 1955, RA QEQM/PRIV/CHILD
176 Queen Elizabeth to Princess Margaret, 9 September 1955, Linley Papers
177 Princess Margaret to Queen Elizabeth, 10 September [1955], RA QEQM/PRIV/RF
178 Queen Elizabeth to Princess Margaret, 11 October 1955, Linley Papers
179 Longford, *Elizabeth R*, p. 176; *The Royal Encyclopedia*, Macmillan, 1991, p. 332
180 *The Times*, 24 October 1955
181 Longford, *Elizabeth R*, p. 177. Longford states that her source for this was Princess Margaret
182 Queen Elizabeth II to Queen Elizabeth, 31 October 1955, RA QEQM/PRIV/RF, and Princess Margaret, draft announcement, 31 October 1955, QEQM/PRIV/CHILD
183 Lady Jean Rankin to Toni Untermyer (Toni de Bellaigue), 2 November 1955, Bellaigue Papers
184 Princess Margaret to Toni Untermyer, 23 November 1955, Bellaigue Papers
185 Queen Elizabeth to Rachel Bowes Lyon, 31 October 1955, Bowes Lyon Papers, SPW
186 Queen Elizabeth to Lady Salisbury, 22 November 1955, Hatfield House, Papers of Elizabeth, Marchioness of Salisbury
187 Peter Townsend to Queen Elizabeth, 19 November 1955, RA QEQM/PRIV/PAL
188 Princess Margaret to Queen Elizabeth, 3, 5, 18 October 1956, RA QEQM/PRIV/RF
189 Princess Margaret to Toni Untermyer, 26 August 1957, Bellaigue Papers

EIGHTEEN: FAVOURITES 1956–1960

1 Sean Smith, *Royal Racing*, BBC Books, 2001, pp. 57–61
2 Ibid., p. 59
3 Ibid.
4 Nicolson, *Diaries and Letters 1945–1962*, p. 299
5 Dick Francis in *The Queen Mother Remembered*, p. 194; Longford, *Queen Mother*, p. 149

6 Queen Elizabeth to Princess Elizabeth, 12 December 1950, RA QEII/PRIV/RF

7 Author's interview with Lady Penn

8 Queen Elizabeth to Princess Elizabeth, 29 December 1950, RA QEII/PRIV/RF

9 Princess Margaret to the Hon. David Bowes Lyon, 27 December 1950, Bowes Lyon Papers, SPW

10 Queen Elizabeth to Princess Elizabeth, 29 December 1950, RA QEII/PRIV/RF

11 Smith, pp. 53–4

12 Dick Francis in *The Queen Mother Remembered*, p. 193

13 Queen Elizabeth to Queen Elizabeth II, 10 January 1954, RA QEII/PRIV/RF

14 Laird, p. 348

15 Sir Arthur Penn to Queen Elizabeth, 29 September 1952, RA QEQM/PRIV/HH

16 Queen Elizabeth to Sir Arthur Penn, 13 September 1954, Penn Papers

17 Unpublished memoirs of Dame Frances Campbell-Preston, quoted in Vickers, p. 401

18 Queen Elizabeth to Queen Elizabeth II, 10 January 1954, RA QEII/PRIV/RF

19 Queen Elizabeth to Sir Arthur Penn, 13 September 1954, Penn Papers

20 Queen Elizabeth to Sir Arthur Penn, 14 January 1956, Penn Papers

21 Queen Elizabeth to Sir Arthur Penn, n.d., Penn Papers

22 Sir Arthur Penn to Queen Elizabeth (draft), 23 September 1958, Penn Papers

23 Queen Elizabeth to Sir Arthur Penn, 25 September 1958, Penn Papers

24 Rose, *Kings, Queens and Courtiers*, pp. 129–30

25 Ibid.

26 Sir Gladwyn Jebb to Selwyn Lloyd, 20 March 1956 (copy dispatch), RA QEQMH/PS/VIS/1956/FRA

27 Report by Private Secretary to British Ambassador, attached to telegram of 20 March 1956, RA QEQMH/PS/VIS/1956/FRA

28 Lady Salisbury to Queen Elizabeth, n.d. [March 1956], RA QEQM/PRIV/PAL/Salisbury

29 *The Diaries of Cynthia Gladwyn 1946–71*, ed. Miles Jebb, Constable, 1995, p. 168

30 Lady Jebb to Queen Elizabeth, 24 March 1956, RA QEQM/PRIV/PAL

31 Sir Gladwyn Jebb to Selwyn Lloyd (copy dispatch), 20 March 1956, RA QEQMH/PS/VIS/1956/FRA

32 Queen Elizabeth to Queen Elizabeth II, 12 April 1956, RA QEII/PRIV/RF

33 Queen Elizabeth to Queen Elizabeth II, 10 April 1957, RA QEII/PRIV/RF

34 Lady in waiting's diary, 8 July 1957, RA QEQMH/QEQM/DIARY/LIW

35 Ibid., 9 July 1957

36 Ibid., 10–11 July 1957

37 Ibid., 13–15 July 1957

38 Ibid., 16 July 1957

39 E. L. Sykes, Acting UK High Commissioner, to Secretary of State for Commonwealth Relations, 23 July 1957, National Archives, Treaty Royal Matters, FO 372 7449 1957

40 Author's interview with Sir James Scholtens

41 Queen Elizabeth to Queen Elizabeth II, 9 February 1958, RA QEII/PRIV/RF

42 Queen Elizabeth to Queen Elizabeth II, 18 February 1958, RA QEII/PRIV/RF

43 Queen Elizabeth to Queen Elizabeth II, 1 March 1958, RA QEII/PRIV/RF

44 Queen Elizabeth to Queen Elizabeth II, 13 February 1958, RA QEII/PRIV/RF

45 Queen Elizabeth II to Queen Elizabeth, 20 February 1958; Princess Margaret to Queen Elizabeth, 25 February [1958], RA QEQM/PRIV/RF

46 Queen Elizabeth to Princess Margaret, 22 February 1958, Linley Papers

47 Queen Elizabeth to Queen Elizabeth II, 1 March 1958, RA QEII/PRIV/RF

48 Ibid.

49 Queen Elizabeth to Queen Elizabeth II, 9 February 1958, RA QEII/PRIV/RF

50 Queen Elizabeth to Cecil Boyd-Rochfort, 18 February 1958, RA QEQM/OUT/BOYD-ROCHFORT

51 Allen Brown to Queen Elizabeth, n.d. [March 1958], RA QEQM/PRIV/PAL

52 Sir Robert Scott, Governor of Mauritius, to the Secretary of State for the Colonies (copy dispatch), 14 March 1958, RA QEQMH/PS/VIS/1958/AUSNZ

53 Laird, p. 336

54 Ibid., p. 337

55 Queen Elizabeth to Queen Elizabeth II, 1 March 1958, RA QEII/PRIV/RF

56 Queen Elizabeth II, speech to City of London, 7 June 1977

57 Dr Kiano to Queen Elizabeth, telegram, 30 January 1959, RA QEQMH/PS/VIS/1959/KENUG/I/I

58 Acting Governor of Kenya to the Secretary of State for the Colonies (copy dispatch), 21 January 1959, RA QEQMH/PS/VIS/1959/KENUG

59 Lady in waiting's diary, 9 February 1959, RA QEQMH/QEQM/DIARY/LIW

60 Princess Margaret to Queen Elizabeth, 11 February 1959, RA QEQM/PRIV/RF

61 Laird, p. 339

62 Sir Evelyn Baring to Alan Lennox-Boyd (copy dispatch), 30 May 1959, RA QEQMH/PS/VIS/1959/KENUG/II/7

63 Valentine card sent to Queen Elizabeth, RA QEQM/PRIV/GEN

64 Sir Evelyn Baring to Alan Lennox-Boyd (copy dispatch), 30 May 1959, RA QEQMH/PS/VIS/1959/KENUG/II/7

65 Ibid.

66 Ibid.

67 Ibid.

68 Lady Mary Baring to Queen Elizabeth, 5 March 1959, RA QEQM/PRIV/PAL

69 Queen Elizabeth to Princess Margaret, 21 February 1959, Linley Papers

70 Ibid.

71 Sir Frederick Crawford to Alan Lennox-Boyd (copy dispatch), 6 March 1959, RA QEQMH/PS/VIS/1959/KENUG/II/7

72 Ibid.

73 Ibid.

74 George Thomas MP to Leiutenant Colonel Martin Gilliat, 7 April 1959, RA QEQM/PS/VIS/1959/KENUG/II/8

75 Queen Elizabeth to D'Arcy Osborne, 30 January 1959, RA QEQM/OUT/OSBORNE

76 Ibid.

77 Ashley Clarke to Selwyn Lloyd, 30 April 1959, RA QEQMH/PS/VIS/1959/ITAL/3

78 Lady Jebb to Queen Elizabeth, 25 January 1959, RA QEQM/PRIV/PAL

79 *Diaries of Cynthia Gladwyn*, pp. 235–8

80 Major General Sir John Kennedy to Queen Elizabeth, 2 January 1961, RA QEQM/PRIV/PAL

81 Sir R. P. Armitage to Iain Macleod (copy report), 25 June 1960, RA QEQMH/PS/VIS/1960/RHONY/III/4

82 Major General Sir John Kennedy to Queen Elizabeth, 2 January 1961, RA QEQM/PRIV/PAL

83 Queen Elizabeth to Princess Margaret, 22 May 1960, Linley Papers

84 Sir R. P. Armitage, to Iain Macleod (copy report), 25 June 1960, RA QEQMH/PS/VIS/1960/RHONY/III/4

85 Lieutenant Colonel Martin Gilliat to Sir R. P. Armitage, 1 June 1960, RA QEQMH/PS/VIS/1960/RHONY/III/3a

86 Princess Margaret to Antony Armstrong Jones, 27 October 1958, Snowdon Papers

87 Princess Margaret to Antony Armstrong Jones, 31 October 1958, Snowdon Papers

88 Princess Margaret to Antony Armstrong Jones, 19 April 1959, Snowdon Papers

89 Princess Margaret to Antony Armstrong Jones, 14 August 1959, Snowdon Papers

90 Princess Margaret to Antony Armstrong Jones, 22 August 1959, Snowdon Papers

91 Princess Margaret to Antony Armstrong Jones, 29 August 1959, Snowdon Papers

92 Ibid.

93 Princess Margaret to Antony Armstrong Jones, 9 October 1959, Snowdon Papers

94 Princess Margaret to Antony Armstrong Jones, 6 December [1959], Snowdon Papers

95 Duchess of Gloucester to Queen Elizabeth, n.d. [28 February 1960], RA QEQM/PRIV/RF

96 Queen Elizabeth to Most Rev. Geoffrey Fisher, Archbishop of Canterbury, 2 March 1960, RA QEQM/OUT/MISC

97 Lady in waiting's diary, 5 April 1960, RA QEQMH/QEQM/DIARY/LIW

98 Longford, *Elizabeth R*, p. 202

99 Queen Elizabeth to Princess Margaret, 22 May 1960, Linley Papers

100 Lord Snowdon to Queen Elizabeth, 19 May 1960, RA QEQM/PRIV/RF

101 Princess Margaret to Queen Elizabeth, 16 May 1960, RA QEQM/PRIV/RF

NINETEEN: THE HEART OF THE MATTER

1 Asa Briggs, *A Social History of England*, Weidenfeld & Nicolson, 1994, p. 319

2 Ibid., pp. 317–19

3 Ibid., p. 324

4 William Shawcross, *Queen and Country*, BBC Worldwide, 2002, p. 77

5 Queen Elizabeth to Rachel Bowes Lyon, 1 October 1961, Bowes Lyon Papers, SPW

6 Richard Crossman, 'The Role of the Volunteer in the Modern Social Service', in *Traditions of Social Policy*, ed. A. H. Halsey, 1976, p. 283, quoted in Prochaska, *Royal Bounty*, pp. 249–50

7 Sir Arthur Penn to Dr Percy Dunsheath, 18 February 1954, RA QEQMH/PS/PAT/University of London/Box I/MAIN/I

8 Queen Elizabeth's speech, 24 November 1955, RA QEQMH/PS/PAT/University of London/Box I/University of London Gazette

9 Longford, *Queen Mother*, p. 143

10 Note by Queen Elizabeth on first report of University Consultative Committee on Murray Report, February 1974, RA QEQMH/PS/PAT/University of London/Box II

11 Longford, *Queen Mother*, p. 147

12 Noel Annan in *The Queen Mother Remembered*, p. 125

13 Ibid., pp. 126, 128

14 *Times Literary Supplement*, 23 January 2004, pp. 11–13

15 Duchess of York, diary, 2 September 1924, RA QEQM/PRIV/DIARY/4

16 Lady Katharine Seymour to Miss May McKinlay, 16 September 1939, RA QEQMH/PS/PAT/Girls' Brigade

17 Duchess of York's speech, 24 April 1934, RA QEQMH/PS/PAT/British Legion (Women's Section)

18 Information from Lucy Murphy

19 Queen Elizabeth's message, 18 October 1947, RA QEQMH/PS/PAT/Church of England Children's Society

20 L. R. Shapley to A. S. Greenacre, 29 July 1939, letter forwarded to Queen Elizabeth by Rev. P. B. Clayton, RA QEQMH/PS/PAT/Toc H

21 Sir Martin Gilliat to Sir Alexander Giles, 20 December 1972, RA QEQMH/PS/PAT/Toc H
22 Sir Arthur Penn to Colonel Parkes, 18 March 1948, RA QEQMH/PS/PAT/St Mary's Hospital Paddington
23 RA QEQMH/PS/PAT/St Mary's Hospital Paddington
24 Keeper of the Privy Purse to Comptrollers and Ladies-in-Waiting to members of the Royal Family, 29 October 1948, RA QEQMH/PS/CSP/Hospitals
25 RA QEQMH/PS/PAT/PS/St Mary's Hospital Paddington
26 Duchess of York's speech, 27 June 1935, RA QEQMH/PS/ENGT/1935/23
27 RA QEQMH/PS/PAT/Queen Elizabeth's Foundation for the Disabled
28 Queen Elizabeth's speech, 1943, RA QEQMH/PS/PAT/Sandringham WI
29 Queen Elizabeth's speech, 1945, RA QEQMH/PS/PAT/Sandringham WI
30 Queen Elizabeth's speech, 1951, RA QEQMH/PS/PAT/Sandringham WI
31 Queen Elizabeth's speech, 1954, RA QEQMH/PS/PAT/Sandringham WI
32 Queen Elizabeth's speech, 1976, RA QEQMH/PS/PAT/Sandringham WI
33 Queen Elizabeth's speech, 1987, RA QEQMH/PS/PAT/Sandringham WI
34 Dr William Beaver to Nicholas Assheton, 27 June 2002, RA QEQMH/PS/PAT/British Red Cross
35 RA QEQMH/PS/PAT/SSAFA
36 W. M. Morgan to Sir Ralph Anstruther, 19 May 1993, RA QEQMH/PS/PAT/Royal College of Music
37 RA QEQMH/PS/PAT/Middle Temple
38 RA QEQMH/PS/PAT/King's Lynn Festival
39 RA QEQMH/PS/PAT/Friends of St Paul's Cathedral
40 Sir Ralph Anstruther to Angus Critchley-Waring, 1 August 1972, RA QEQMH/PS/PAT/Queen Mary's Clothing Guild
41 Statement of accounts, 11 January, 2002, RA QEQMH/PS/PAT/Queen Mary's Clothing Guild
42 Note by Queen Elizabeth on letter from Angus Stirling to Sir Martin Gilliat, 29 October 1987, RA QEQMH/PS/PAT/National Trust
43 Queen Elizabeth's speech, 19 October 1967, RA QEQMH/PS/PAT/University of Dundee
44 Peter Ustinov in *The Queen Mother Remembered*, pp. 212–15
45 RA QEQMH/PS/PAT/Injured Jockeys' Fund; RA QEQMH/PS/ENGT/2001: 6 December
46 Peter Pears to Queen Elizabeth, 7 April 1974, RA QEQMH/PS/PAT/Aldeburgh Festival
47 Peter Pears to Lady Fermoy, 27 September 1974, RA QEQMH/PS/ENGT/13 June 1975
48 Régis Cochefert to Sir Alastair Aird, 6 June 2002, RA QEQMH/PS/PAT/Aldeburgh Festival
49 Queen Elizabeth, note to Sir Ralph Anstruther, n.d. [January 1977], RA QEQMH/PS/PAT/Sandringham Fur & Feather
50 Queen Elizabeth to Sir Ralph Anstruther, n.d. [21 May 1980], RA QEQMH/PS/PAT/Sandringham Fur & Feather
51 *Poultry World*, January 1999, RA QEQMH/PS/PAT/Poultry Club
52 RA QEQMH/PS/PAT/Victoria Cross and George Cross Association
53 Queen Elizabeth, message sent with letter from Hon. Nicholas Assheton to Earl of Caithness, 21 March 2000, RA QEQMH/PS/PAT/Clan Sinclair Trust
54 Hon. Nicholas Assheton to Bernard Evans, 18 September 2001, RA QEQMH/PS/PAT/Longhope Lifeboat Museum Trust
55 RA QEQMH/PS/PAT/Sir Peter O'Sullevan Charitable Trust

56 Dr Walter James, article in *Times Higher Education Supplement*, 12 September 1980, RA QEQMH/PS/PAT/St Catharine's

57 Author's interview with Eric Anderson

58 Message from Queen Elizabeth to Lieutenant Colonel John H. Christie, accompanying a bowl of violets sent to the Officers' Mess, 27 April 1941, illustrated in *'Proud to be Your Colonel-in-Chief', 1937–2002*, Toronto Scottish Regiment, Toronto, 2003

59 Queen Elizabeth, annotations on Light Infantry annual reports, 1997, 1998; annotation on letter from Major General Peter Bush to Sir Martin Gilliat, 30 December 1981, RA QEQMH/PS/ARMFOR/Light Infantry

60 Arthur Penn to General Sir Archibald Cameron, 5 July 1940, RA QEQMH/PS/ARMFOR/Black Watch

61 Queen Elizabeth's speech, 20 November 1941, RA QEQMH/PS/ARMFOR/Black Watch

62 General Sir Arthur Wauchope to Arthur Penn, 22 November 1941, RA QEQMH/PS/ARMFOR/Black Watch

63 RA QEQMH/PS/ENGT/1998: 20 September

64 Lieutenant Colonel Evelyn Fanshawe to Captain R. J. Streatfeild, n.d. [26 July 1937], RA QEQMH/PS/ENGT/1937: 24 July

65 Arthur Penn to Lieutenant Colonel Tom Draffen, 30 April 1942, RA QEQMH/PS/ARMFOR/Queen's Bays

66 Arthur Penn to Lieutenant Colonel Alexander Barclay, 31 December 1943, RA QEQMH/PS/ARMFOR/Queen's Bays

67 Lieutenant Colonel Martin Gilliat to Colonel G. W. Draffen, 23 July 1957, RA QEQMH/PS/ARMFOR/Queen's Bays

68 Note by Queen Elizabeth on regimental annual report, January 2001, RA QEQMH/PS/ARMFOR/Queen's Dragoon Guards

69 Note by Queen Elizabeth on a letter from Lieutenant Colonel R. M. Carnegie to Sir Martin Gilliat, 11 October 1968, RA QEQMH/PS/ARMFOR/Queen's Own Hussars

70 Queen Elizabeth's speech, 13 June 1997, RA QEQMH/PS/ENGT/1997: 13 June

71 Brigadier R. N. M. Jones to Lieutenant Colonel Martin Gilliat, 4 March 1958, RA QEQMH/PS/ARMFOR/The King's (Manchester and Liverpool) Regiment

72 Queen Elizabeth to Lieutenant Colonel Malcolm Grant-Howarth, 24 October 1990, RA QEQMH/PS/ARMFOR/The King's (Manchester and Liverpool) Regiment

73 Queen Elizabeth's speech, 2 July 1993, RA QEQMH/PS/ENGT/1993: 2 July

74 Note by Queen Elizabeth on report by Brigadier J. J. Gaskell, 21 August 1998, RA QEQMH/ARMFOR/The King's (Manchester and Liverpool) Regiment

75 Note by Queen Elizabeth on letter from Brigadier J. A. Longmore to Lieutenant Colonel Martin Gilliat, 26 July 1960, RA QEQMH/PS/ARMFOR/Hertfordshire Regiment

76 Note by Queen Elizabeth attached to letter from Lieutenant General Sir Reginald Denning to Lieutenant Colonel Martin Gilliat, 2 January [1961], RA QEQMH/PS/ARMFOR/Hertfordshire Regiment

77 Duchess of York to King George V, 18 March 1935, RA GV/PRIV/AA62/215

78 Lieutenant Colonel Martin Gilliat to Lieutenant Colonel R. C. P. Wheeler, 28 November 1956, RA QEQMH/PS/ARMFOR/City of London Yeomanry (Rough Riders)

79 Note by Queen Elizabeth to Lieutenant Colonel Martin Gilliat, 29 August 1960, re letter from Lieutenant Colonel G. D. Thompson, RA QEQMH/PS/ARMFOR/Inns of Court Regiment; Lieutenant Colonel Martin Gilliat to Colonel Sir James Waterlow, 21 October 1960, RA QEQMH/PS/ARMFOR/City of London Yeomanry (Rough Riders)

80 Hon. Mrs Geoffrey Bowlby to Lady Maud Bailey, 29 October 1941, RA QEQMH/PS/ARMFOR/WRAC

81 Note by Queen Elizabeth on memorandum from Defence Services Secretary to Sir Martin Gilliat, 15 August 1991, RA QEQMH/PS/ARMFOR/WRNS

82 Sir Martin Gilliat to Air Commandant Dame Felicity Hill, 7 March 1968, RA QEQMH/PS/ARMFOR/WRAF

83 Note by Queen Elizabeth on letter from Brigadier G. K. Ramsay to Sir Alastair Aird, 8 March 1990, RA QEQMH/PS/ARMFOR/WRAC; note by Queen Elizabeth on memorandum from Sir Alastair Aird, 13 January 1994, RA QEQMH/PS/ARMFOR/WRAF

84 Lord Alexander of Tunis to Sir Martin Gilliat, 16 July 1965, and reply, 21 July 1965, RA QEQMH/PS/MISCOFF/Irish Guards

85 Lieutenant Colonel James Baker to Queen Elizabeth, 19 March [1979]; Lieutenant Colonel John Clavering to Queen Elizabeth, 18 March 1981, RA QEQMH/PS/MISCOFF/Irish Guards

86 Queen Elizabeth to Commanding Officer, Toronto Scottish, 20 October 1945, RA QEQMH/PS/ARMFOR/Toronto Scottish

87 RA QEQMH/PS/ARMFOR/Black Watch of Canada

88 Note by Queen Elizabeth on note from Sir Martin Gilliat, 21 January 1991, RA QEQMH/PS/ARMFOR/RNZAMC

89 Lieutenant Colonel Martin Gilliat to Commandant Denzil M. Loveland, 14 April 1961, RA QEQMH/PS/ARMFOR/South Africa

90 Lieutenant Colonel Martin Gilliat to Commandant C. St L. Hone, 27 October 1961, RA QEQMH/PS/ARMFOR/South Africa

91 Telegram from Queen Elizabeth to Acting Commissioner, BSAP, [12 February 1954], QEQMH/PS/ARMFOR/South Africa

92 Note by Queen Elizabeth on letter from John Graham, FCO, to Sir Martin Gilliat, 6 March 1970, RA QEQMH/PS/ARMFOR/South Africa

93 Pimlott, p. 565

94 Geoffrey Finlayson, *Citizen State and Social Welfare in Britain, 1830–1990*, 1994, p. 352, quoted in Prochaska, *Royal Bounty*, p. 256

95 Ibid., pp. 259–60

96 Ibid., p. 272

97 *For my Grandchildren: Some Reminiscences of Her Royal Highness Princess Alice, Countess of Athlone*, 1996, p. 7, quoted in Prochaska, *Royal Bounty*, pp. 261–2

98 Vernon Bogdanor, *The Monarchy and the Constitution*, Oxford University Press, 1995, p. 308

99 *In Tearing Haste: Letters between Deborah Devonshire and Patrick Leigh Fermor*, ed. Charlotte Mosley, John Murray, 2008, letter from Deborah Devonshire, 18 January 1980, p. 177

100 Prochaska, *Royal Bounty*, p. 279

101 Bogdanor, pp. 305–9

102 Queen Elizabeth's speech, January 1993, RA QEQMH/PS/PAT/Sandringham WI

TWENTY: AT HOME

1 Queen Elizabeth to Queen Elizabeth II, 17 February 1961, RA QEII/PRIV/RF

2 Queen Elizabeth to Queen Elizabeth II, 26 November 1961, RA QEII/PRIV/RF

3 Longford, *Queen Mother*, p. 135

4 Queen Elizabeth to Queen Elizabeth II, 23 May 1961, RA QEII/PRIV/RF

5 Queen Elizabeth to John Elphinstone, 6 June 1962, RA QEQM/OUT/ELPHINSTONE

6 Queen Elizabeth to Prince Charles, 5 January 1967, Clarence House Archives

7 Prince Charles to Queen Elizabeth, 21 May 1962, RA QEQM/PRIV/RF

8 Queen Elizabeth to John Elphinstone, 6 June 1962, RA QEQM/OUT/ELPHINSTONE

9 Queen Elizabeth to Prince Charles, 15 December 1966, Clarence House Archives

10 *The Times*, 21 May 1960

11 Martin Gilliat to Richard Colville, 22 May 1960, RA QEQMH/PRS/CSP/1/2

12 Sir Arthur Penn to Richard Colville, 21 May 1960, RA QEQMH/PRS/CSP/1/2

13 Sir Arthur Penn to Queen Elizabeth, 20 November [1960], RA QEQM/PRIV/PAL/Penn

14 Queen Elizabeth to Marjorie Penn, 7 April 1961, Penn Papers

15 Elizabeth Leeming interview with Margaret Rhodes

16 Queen Elizabeth to Queen Elizabeth II, 19 September 1961, RA QEII/PRIV/RF

17 Queen Elizabeth to Rachel Bowes Lyon, 1 August 1962, Bowes Lyon Papers, SPW

18 Queen Elizabeth to Rachel Bowes Lyon, 29 July 1965, Bowes Lyon Papers, SPW

19 Elizabeth Leeming interview with Lady Stair

20 Queen Elizabeth to D'Arcy Osborne, 13 February 1962, RA QEQM/OUT/OSBORNE

21 D'Arcy Osborne to Queen Elizabeth, 17 October 1962, RA QEQM/PRIV/PAL/Osborne

22 Queen Elizabeth to D'Arcy Osborne, 7 February 1963, RA QEQM/OUT/OSBORNE

23 D'Arcy Osborne to Queen Elizabeth, 19 February 1963, RA QEQM/PRIV/PAL/Osborne

24 Mrs Milton (Judy) Gendel to Queen Elizabeth, n.d. [April 1964], RA QEQM/PRIV/PAL

25 Note by Lady Jean Rankin, 28 October 1963, RA QEQMH/PS/GEN/1971/Poignand; Queen Elizabeth to Beryl Poignand, 12 October 1963, Glamis Archives (CH)

26 Queen Elizabeth to Mrs Leone Poignand Hall, 11 January 1965, private collection

27 Queen Elizabeth to Osbert Sitwell, 26 December 1968, RA QEQM/OUT/SITWELL

28 Queen Elizabeth to Sacheverell Sitwell, 5 May 1969, RA QEQMH/PS/GEN/1969/Sitwell

29 Queen Elizabeth to the Hon. Elizabeth Elphinstone, 14 September 1964, RA QEQM/OUT/ELPHINSTONE

30 Queen Elizabeth to Osbert Sitwell, 26 January 1967, RA QEQM/OUT/SITWELL

31 Correspondence between Sir Arthur Penn, the Dean of Windsor and others, 11 June 1954–29 June 1960; memorandum by Sir Arthur Penn, 29 March 1960, RA QEQM/PRIV/MEM

32 Queen Elizabeth to Lord Salisbury, 16 October 1969, Hatfield House, Papers of fifth Marquess of Salisbury

33 John Cornforth, *Queen Elizabeth The Queen Mother at Clarence House*, Michael Joseph, 1996, pp. 64–5

34 Ibid., pp. 61–5

35 Ibid., pp. 71–3

36 Michael Holroyd, *Augustus John*, vol. 2, p. 473, quoted in Owens, p. 48

37 Augustus John to Queen Elizabeth, July 1961, RA QEQM/PRIV/PIC

38 Cornforth, pp. 88–9

39 Sir Arthur Penn to Brigadier Kingstone, 21 May 1952, RA QEQMH/PS/POR/5

40 Roger Berthoud, *Graham Sutherland*, Faber & Faber, 1982, pp. 152, 243–4

41 Cornforth, pp. 109–10

42 Pietro Annigoni, *An Artist's Life*, W. H. Allen, 1977, pp. 140–3

43 John Bratby to Captain Alastair Aird, 10 February 1978, John Bratby to Queen Elizabeth, 22 February 1978, RA QEQMH/POR/18; Owens, p. 184; Cornforth, pp. 5, 29–30

44 Cornforth, p. 38

45 Frances Campbell-Preston, *The Rich Spoils of Time*, Dovecote Press, 2006, pp. 273–4

46 Queen Elizabeth to Princess Margaret, 24 July 1958, Linley Papers

47 Harold Macmillan to Queen Elizabeth, 18 June 1970, RA QEQM/PRIV/PAL

48 Roy Strong, *The Roy Strong Diaries 1967–1987*, Weidenfeld & Nicolson, 1997, p. 175

49 *Diaries of Cynthia Gladwyn*, pp. 285–7
50 Campbell-Preston, pp. 268–311
51 Author's interview with Frances Campbell-Preston, 5 February 2004
52 Ibid.
53 Author's interview with Michael Sealey
54 Ibid.
55 Queen Elizabeth, conversations with Eric Anderson, 1994–5, QEQM/ADD/MISC; *JS Journal*, April 1985; author's interview with Lord Sainsbury
56 Stephen Spender to Queen Elizabeth, 5 March 1986, RA QEQM/PRIV/PAL
57 Sir Charles Johnston's diary, quoted in Vickers, p. 431
58 Vickers, pp. 344–5
59 Author's interview with Lord Carrington
60 Author's interview with Sir Michael Oswald
61 Author's interview with Zara Cazalet
62 Ibid.
63 Dick Francis in *The Queen Mother Remembered*, pp. 193–5
64 Author's interview with Sir Michael Oswald
65 Smith, p. 235
66 Mrs Fulke Walwyn in *The Queen Mother Remembered*, pp. 196–8
67 *Sunday Times*, 29 April 1984, quoted in Laird, p. 372
68 Queen Elizabeth to Lady Katharine Farrell, 15 August 1979, Farrell Papers
69 Sir Arthur Penn to Queen Elizabeth, 8 April 1959, RA QEQM/PRIV/RES
70 *Friends of the Castle of Mey Newsletter*, April 2005
71 *The Castle & Gardens of Mey*, The Queen Elizabeth Castle of Mey Trust, 2008, pp. 65–71
72 Author's interview with Martin Leslie; *The Queen Mother Remembered*, p. 221
73 Rose, *Kings, Queens and Courtiers*, p. 105
74 *The Queen Mother Remembered*, p. 231
75 Ibid., p. 232
76 Author's interview with Christine Shearer
77 Rev. Alex Muir in *The Queen Mother Remembered*, pp. 234–5
78 Information from Martin Leslie
79 Castle of Mey Visitors' Book
80 Author's interview with Lady Penn
81 Interview with Lady Bacon on behalf of the author
82 Author's interview with Ashe Windham
83 Elizabeth Leeming interview with Dr Michael Briggs
84 Author's interview with Charlie Wright
85 Laird, pp. 373–4
86 Campbell-Preston, p. 306
87 Sir Pierson Dixon to Queen Elizabeth, 2 September 1963, RA QEQM/PRIV/PAL

Twenty-One: Queen Voyager 1961–1967

1 Foreign Office note, 'Proposal that HM The Queen Mother should visit Tunisia', 16 January 1961 (copy), RA QEQMH/PS/VIS/1961/TUN
2 Brigadier Bernard Fergusson to Laura Fergusson, 19 April 1961, Ballantrae Papers, NLS Acc 9259/87
3 Brigadier Bernard Fergusson to Laura Fergusson, 22 April 1961, Ballantrae Papers, NLS Acc 9259/87

4 Brigadier Bernard Fergusson to Laura Fergusson, 24 April 1961, Ballantrae Papers, NLS Acc 9259/87

5 Anthony Lambert to Lord Home, 4 May 1961 (copy), RA QEQMH/PS/VIS/1961/TUN

6 Brigadier Bernard Fergusson to Laura Fergusson, 24 April 1961, Ballantrae Papers, NLS Acc 9259/87

7 Anthony Lambert to Lord Home, 4 May 1961 (copy), RA QEQMH/PS/VIS/1961/TUN

8 Queen Elizabeth to D'Arcy Osborne, 20 June 1961, RA QEQM/OUT/OSBORNE

9 Lady in waiting's diary, 6 April 1962, RA QEQMH/QEQM/DIARY/LIW

10 John Diefenbaker to Major General Georges Vanier, 16 January 1962, LAC/BAC Acc 1988–89/081, Vol. 144, File 3185-K 1962

11 Acting British High Commissioner in Canada to Duncan Sandys, 25 June 1962 (copy), RA QEQMH/PS/VIS/1962/CAN

12 Lady in waiting's diary, 14 June 1962, RA QEQMH/QEQM/DIARY/LIW

13 Major General Georges Vanier to Queen Elizabeth, 16 June 1962, RA QEQMH/PS/VIS/1962/CAN

14 Major General Georges Vanier to Queen Elizabeth, 16 June 1962, RA QEQM/PRIV/PAL

15 Lady in waiting's diary, 8–13 May 1963, RA QEQMH/QEQM/DIARY/LIW

16 Lady in waiting's diary, 30 October 1963, RA QEQMH/QEQM/DIARY/LIW

17 Longford, *Queen Mother*, p. 141

18 Prince Philip to Queen Elizabeth, 16 February [1964], RA QEQM/PRIV/RF

19 Prince Charles to Queen Elizabeth, 7 February 1964 [misdated 1963], RA QEQM/PRIV/RF

20 Queen Elizabeth II to Queen Elizabeth, 25 March 1964, RA QEQM/PRIV/RF

21 Queen Elizabeth to Princess Margaret, 24 March 1964, Linley Papers

22 Allen Brown to Sir Martin Gilliat, 5 February 1964, RA QEQMH/PS/VIS/1964/AUSNZ (cancelled)

23 Sir Martin Gilliat to Sir Bernard Fergusson, Governor General of New Zealand, 20 February 1964, RA QEQMH/PS/VIS/1964/AUSNZ (cancelled)

24 Queen Elizabeth to Sir Bernard Fergusson, 9 April 1964, Ballantrae Papers, NLS Acc 9259/109

25 Andrew Roberts, *History of the English-Speaking Peoples since 1900*, pp. 467–9

26 Lady in waiting's diary, 18 February 1965, RA QEQMH/QEQM/DIARY/LIW

27 Ibid., 21 February 1965

28 Queen Elizabeth to Princess Margaret, 28 March 1965, Linley Papers

29 Noël Coward to Queen Elizabeth, 9 July [1965], RA QEQM/PRIV/PAL

30 Lady in waiting's diary, 26 February 1965, RA QEQMH/QEQM/DIARY/LIW

31 Sir Alexander Morley, British High Commissioner, Kingston, to Rt Hon. Arthur Bottomley, Commonwealth Secretary (copy), 1 March 1965, RA QEQMH/PS/VIS/1965/JAM

32 Correspondence between Sir Martin Gilliat, the Private Secretary to the Governor General and the Chief of Protocol, External Affairs, 31 December 1964–3 May 1965, LAC/BAC Acc 1988–89/081, Vol. 144, File 3185-K 1965

33 Lady in waiting's diary, 25 March 1966, RA QEQMH/QEQM/DIARY/LIW

34 Queen Elizabeth's speech, 25 March 1966, RA QEQMH/PS/VIS/1966/AUSNZ/I/3

35 Lady in waiting's diary, 25 March 1966, RA QEQMH/QEQM/DIARY/LIW

36 Queen Elizabeth's speech, 26 March 1966, RA QEQMH/PS/VIS/1966/AUSNZ/I/2

37 Campbell-Preston, p. 280

38 Lady in waiting's diary, 31 March, 1 April 1966, RA QEQMH/QEQM/DIARY/LIW

39 Princess Margaret to Queen Elizabeth, 8 April 1966, RA QEQM/PRIV/RF

40 Lady in waiting's diary, 4 April 1966, RA QEQMH/QEQM/DIARY/LIW

41 Ibid., 7 April 1966

42 Campbell-Preston, p. 280

43 Ibid., p. 283

44 Ibid.

45 Lady in waiting's diary, 4 May 1966, RA QEQMH/QEQM/DIARY/LIW

46 Queen Elizabeth to Sir Bernard Fergusson, 9 May 1966, Ballantrae Papers, NLS Acc 9259/109

47 Ibid.

48 Queen Elizabeth to Lord Snowdon, 21 April 1966, Snowdon Papers

49 Queen Elizabeth to Sir Bernard Fergusson, 24 May 1966, Ballantrae Papers, NLS Acc 9259/109

50 Queen Elizabeth to Lord Salisbury, 24 December 1966, Hatfield House, Papers of fifth Marquess of Salisbury

51 Lady in waiting's diary, 20 September 1966, RA QEQMH/QEQM/DIARY/LIW

52 Author's interview with Sir Richard Thompson

53 Prince of Wales to Queen Elizabeth, 10 December 1966, Clarence House Archives

54 Sir Richard Bayliss to the Hon. Mrs John Mulholland, 18 September 1979, RA QEQMH/ PS/GEN/1979/Searle Medical

55 RA QEQMH/PS/GEN/1967/Women's Services

56 Correspondence with Government House, Ottawa, May–July 1966, RA QEQMH/PS/ VIS/1967/CAN

57 Lady in waiting's diary, 11 July 1967, RA QEQMH/QEQM/DIARY/LIW

58 Queen Elizabeth to Rear Admiral P. J. Morgan, 22 July 1967, RA QEQMH/PS/VIS/ 1967/CAN

59 Lady in waiting's diary, 26 June 1974, RA QEQMH/QEQM/DIARY/LIW

60 Ibid., 28 June 1974

61 Pauline McGibbon to Governor General of Canada, 8 August 1978, LAC/BAC Acc 90–91/016, Vol. 156, File 896–7901

62 Thomas Brimelow to Sir Martin Gilliat, 17 May 1974, RA QEQMH/PS/VIS/1975/IRAN

63 Lady in waiting's diary, 15 April 1975, RA QEQMH/QEQM/DIARY/LIW

64 Ibid., 16 April 1975

65 Lady Parsons to Queen Elizabeth, n.d. [December 1975], RA QEQM/PRIV/PAL

66 Lady in waiting's diary, 18 April 1975, RA QEQMH/QEQM/DIARY/LIW

67 Sir Anthony Parsons to Rt Hon. James Callaghan, 30 April 1975 (copy), RA QEQMH/ PS/VIS/1975/IRAN

68 Queen Elizabeth to Sir Alan Lascelles, 17 January 1955, CAC LASL 2/2/20

69 Queen Elizabeth to D'Arcy Osborne, 7 February 1963, RA QEQM/OUT/OSBORNE

70 Oliver Wright to Sir Martin Gilliat, 7, 18 March 1963, Sir Martin Gilliat to Oliver Wright, 12 March 1963, RA QEQMH/PS/VIS/1963/FRA

71 Details of this and subsequent trips are taken from the account of her travels written by Sir Ralph Anstruther, RA QEQMH/PS/VIS

72 Queen Elizabeth to Madame Georgina Reinhold, 16 February 1965, RA QEII/OUT/ GUÉRIN/09

73 Lord Euston to Queen Elizabeth, 26 April 1963, RA QEQM/PRIV/PAL

74 RCIN 1164183; copy in Royal Archives, RA QEQMH/PS/VIS

75 Paris Match, 17 April 1965

76 Lord Euston to Queen Elizabeth, 13 April 1965, RA QEQM/PRIV/PAL

77 Anstruther account, 5 April 1965, RA QEQMH/PS/VIS

78 Ibid., 1–7 May 1967, RA QEQMH/PS/VIS

79 Prince Jean-Louis de Faucigny-Lucinge in The Queen Mother Remembered, pp. 110–13

80 Ibid.

81 Ibid.

82 Anstruther account, 27–28 April 1976, RA QEQMH/PS/VIS

83 Ibid., 28 April 1976, RA QEQMH/PS/VIS

84 Longford, *Queen Mother*, pp. 154–5; author's interview with Duke and Duchess of Grafton

85 Anstruther account, 25–28 April 1977, RA QEQMH/PS/VIS

86 Ibid., 1–2 May 1978

87 Interview with Laure, Princesse de Beauvau-Craon on behalf of the author

88 Ibid.

89 Ibid.; *Le Figaro*, 28 June 1979

90 Interview with Laure, Princesse de Beauvau-Craon on behalf of the author

91 Anstruther account, 6–9 May 1980, RA QEQMH/PS/VIS

92 Ibid., 14 May 1981

93 Queen Elizabeth to Sir Ralph Anstruther, 17 May 1981, RA QEQM/OUT/ ANSTRUTHER

94 Anstruther account, 6 May 1983, RA QEQMH/PS/VIS

95 Interview with Madame Servagnat on behalf of the author

96 Anstruther account, 12–25 June 1984, RA QEQMH/PS/VIS

97 Comte et Comtesse René de Nicolay in *The Queen Mother Remembered*, pp. 114–15

98 Anstruther account, 25–27 June 1985, RA QEQMH/PS/VIS

99 James Lees-Milne, *Holy Dread: Diaries 1982–1984*, ed. Michael Bloch, John Murray, 2001, 3 August 1983

100 Interview with Marquise de Ravenel on behalf of the author

101 Sir Hugh Casson to Sir Alastair Aird, 9 July 1984, RA QEQMH/PS/VIS/1984/ITA

102 Author's interview with the Duke and Duchess of Grafton

103 Laird, p. 376

104 Lady in waiting's diary, 27 October 1984, RA QEQMH/QEQM/DIARY/LIW

105 Queen Elizabeth to Sir Hugh Casson, 27 December 1984, RA AEC/GG/21

106 Anstruther account, 23–27 June 1986, RA QEQMH/PS/VIS

107 Queen Elizabeth to Prince Jean-Louis de Faucigny-Lucinge, July 1986, private collection

108 Anstruther account, 25–29 May 1987, RA QEQMH/PS/VIS

109 Ibid., 23 June 1988

110 Ibid., 20–25 June 1988

111 Sir Hugh Casson in *The Queen Mother Remembered*, pp. 116–22

112 Sir Derek Thomas to Sir Patrick Wright, 1 July 1988 (copy), RA QEQMH/PS/VIS/1988/ ITA

113 Prince Jean-Louis de Faucigny-Lucinge in *The Queen Mother Remembered*, pp. 110–13

114 Interview with Bertrand du Vignaud on behalf of the author

115 Ibid.

116 Anstruther account, 30 May–2 June 1990, RA QEQMH/PS/VIS

117 Ibid., 27–30 May 1991

118 Ibid., 26–29 May 1992

TWENTY-TWO: UNDER SCRUTINY 1968–1981

1 Briggs, *Social History of England*, pp. 324–6

2 Clarke, p. 286

3 David Burnside, MP for South Antrim, House of Commons Tribute to Queen Elizabeth, Hansard, 3 April 2002, column 821
4 Queen Elizabeth to Sir Bernard Fergusson, 19 September 1970, Ballantrae Papers, NLS Acc 9259/109
5 Shawcross, p. 104
6 Sarah Bradford, *Elizabeth*, Heinemann, 1996, pp. 359–60
7 Pimlott, pp. 378–88
8 Ibid., p. 390
9 *Noël Coward Diaries*, 27 July 1969, quoted in ibid., p. 391
10 Jonathan Dimbleby, *The Prince of Wales*, Little, Brown, 1994, p. 163
11 Queen Elizabeth to Lord Snowdon, 8 July 1969, Snowdon Papers
12 Prochaska, *Royal Bounty*, pp. 255–6
13 Prince Philip interview with NBC Television, 10 November 1969, quoted in Pimlott, p. 394
14 Pimlott, p. 402
15 Ibid., pp. 402–6
16 Hansard, Civil List debate, 14 December 1971, columns 278–400
17 Queen Elizabeth to Lord Snowdon, 16 December 1971, Snowdon Papers
18 Pimlott, pp. 409–10
19 Campbell-Preston, pp. 307–8
20 Terence Rattigan to Queen Elizabeth, 5 December 1971, RA QEQM/PRIV/PAL
21 Queen Elizabeth to Queen Elizabeth II, 24 February 1979, RA QEII/PRIV/RF
22 Private letter from the Prince of Wales, 11/12 March 1970, quoted in Dimbleby, p. 215
23 Dimbleby, p. 215
24 Author's interview with Lord Fellowes
25 *The Times*, 29 May 1972, quoted in Pimlott, p. 408
26 Longford, *Queen Mother*, pp. 162–4
27 Author's interview with Dame Frances Campbell-Preston
28 Queen Elizabeth to Lady Salisbury, 27 June 1972, Hatfield House, Papers of Elizabeth, Marchioness of Salisbury
29 Information from Lucy Murphy
30 Mrs Barnard to Queen Elizabeth, 16 May 1986, RA QEQMH/PS/GEN/1986/Barnard; Longford, *Queen Mother*, pp. 162–4
31 Queen Elizabeth, conversations with Eric Anderson, 1994–5, RA QEQM/ADD/MISC
32 Rose, *Kings, Queens and Courtiers*, p. 191
33 Author's interview with Lady Penn
34 Author's interview with Viscount Linley
35 Ibid.
36 Queen Elizabeth to Queen Elizabeth II, 29 August 1978, RA QEII/PRIV/RF
37 Author's interview with Viscount Linley
38 Queen Elizabeth to Queen Elizabeth II, 6 February 1981, RA QEII/PRIV/RF
39 Ibid.
40 Sir Nicholas Henderson to Anthony Crosland (copy), 3 November 1976, RA QEQMH/PS/VIS/1976/FRA
41 Author's interview with Lord Charteris, quoted in Shawcross, p. 117
42 Author's interview with Lady Susan Hussey, quoted in ibid.
43 Lady in waiting's diary, 7 June 1977, RA QEQMH/QEQM/DIARY/LIW
44 Author's interview with Lady Thurso
45 Queen Elizabeth to Queen Elizabeth II, 24 February 1979, RA QEII/PRIV/RF
46 Lady Jay, speech, Hansard, 13 July 2000

47 Ron Todd to Queen Elizabeth, 3 April 1986, RA QEQMH/PS/GEN/1986/Todd

48 Queen Elizabeth to Sir Martin Gilliat, n.d. [April 1986], RA QEQMH/PS/GEN/1986/Todd

49 Interview with Colonel Bruce Bolton, former Commanding Officer, Black Watch of Canada, on behalf of the author

50 Lady in waiting's diary, 30 June 1979, RA QEQMH/QEQM/DIARY/LIW

51 Interview with David Willmot on behalf of the author

52 Lady in waiting's diary, 2 July 1979, RA QEQMH/QEQM/DIARY/LIW

53 Kenneth Rose to Queen Elizabeth, 17 July 1995, RA QEQM/PRIV/PAL

54 Lady in waiting's diary, 27 August 1979, RA QEQMH/QEQM/DIARY/LIW

55 Dimbleby, p. 324

56 Margaret Thatcher to Queen Elizabeth, 10 September 1979, RA QEQM/PRIV/PAL

57 Ibid.

58 Prochaska, *Royal Bounty*, p. 256

59 Queen Elizabeth to Queen Elizabeth II, 25 June 1979, RA QEII/PRIV/RF

60 Queen Elizabeth to Queen Elizabeth II, 3 February 1980, RA QEII/PRIV/RF

61 Queen Elizabeth to Cecil Boyd-Rochfort, 11 July 1980, RA QEQM/OUT/BOYD-ROCHFORT

62 Author's interview with Margaret Vyner

63 Author's interview with Lady Strathmore

64 Queen Elizabeth to Sir Alan Lascelles, 18 October 1980, CAC LASL 2/2/24

65 Author's interview with Ashe Windham

66 Sir Martin Gilliat to the Dean of St Albans, 14 May 1980, RA QEQMH/PS/GEN/1980/St Albans

67 Frances Campbell-Preston to J. D. Marston, 28 July 1980, RA QEQMH/PS/GEN/1980/Gladiolus

68 Queen Elizabeth to Queen Elizabeth II, 23 June 1980, RA QEII/PRIV/RF

69 Sir John Betjeman to Sir Martin Gilliat, 14, 15 and 22 July 1980, and Sir Martin Gilliat to Sir John Betjeman, 21 July 1980, RA QEQMH/PS/GEN/1980/Betjeman

70 Prince of Wales to Queen Elizabeth, 16 July 1980, Clarence House Archives

71 Queen Elizabeth to Queen Elizabeth II, 22 October 1980, RA QEII/PRIV/RF

72 Information from Lucy Murphy

73 Prince of Wales to Queen Elizabeth, 6 August 1980, RA QEQM/PRIV/RF

74 Ibid.

75 Queen Elizabeth to Queen Elizabeth II, 5 August 1980, RA QEII/PRIV/RF

76 Queen Elizabeth II to Queen Elizabeth, 7 August 1980, RA QEQM/PRIV/RF

77 Queen Elizabeth to Queen Elizabeth II, 3 September 1982, RA QEII/PRIV/RF

78 Queen Elizabeth to Queen Elizabeth II, 29 August 1977, RA QEII/PRIV/RF

79 Prince of Wales to Queen Elizabeth, 30 March 1980, Clarence House Archives

80 Lady Diana Spencer to Queen Elizabeth, 3 March 1981, RA QEQM/PRIV/RF

81 Dimbleby, p. 343

82 Prince of Wales to Queen Elizabeth, 18 March 1981, Clarence House Archives

83 Prince of Wales to Queen Elizabeth, 18 May 1981, Clarence House Archives

84 Prince of Wales to Queen Elizabeth, 18 April 1981, Clarence House Archives

85 Author's interview with Lieutenant Colonel Sir John Johnston

86 Dame Frances Campbell-Preston, private diary

87 Ibid.

88 Princess of Wales to Queen Elizabeth, 30 July 1981, RA QEQM/PRIV/RF

Twenty-Three: Poetry and Pain 1981–1999

1 'A Masque for Three Voices' was first published in the *Weekend Telegraph*, 4 August 1990. The holograph presentation copy is in the Royal Library (RCIN 1165090)

2 Ted Hughes, *Collected Poems*, Faber & Faber, 2003, Appendix One, pp. 1219–22

3 Queen Elizabeth to Ted Hughes, 18 August 1990, RA QEII/OUT/HUGHES

4 Dame Frances Campbell-Preston, *The Times*, 27 February 2008

5 Queen Elizabeth to Lady Diana Cooper, 28 March 1981, Diana Cooper Papers, Eton College Library

6 James Lees-Milne, *Deep Romantic Chasm: Diaries 1979–1981*, ed. Michael Bloch, John Murray, 2000, p. 132

7 Lees-Milne, *Holy Dread 1982–1984*, 3 August 1983

8 Ibid., 15 July 1984

9 Penelope Mortimer, *Queen Elizabeth: A Life of the Queen Mother*, Viking, 1986, pp. 259, 267

10 Rev. Professor Owen Chadwick to Queen Elizabeth, 23 October 1986, RA QEQM/PRIV/PAL

11 Ted Hughes to Queen Elizabeth, 6 March 1988, RA QEQM/PRIV/PAL/Hughes

12 Queen Elizabeth, conversations with Eric Anderson, 1994–5, RA QEQM/ADD/MISC

13 Ted Hughes to Gerald Hughes, 18 May 1991, Ted Hughes Papers, Manuscript, Archives and Rare Book Library, Emory University

14 Queen Elizabeth to Queen Elizabeth II, 4 May 1982, RA QEII/PRIV/RF

15 Queen Elizabeth to Queen Elizabeth II, 18 October 1982, RA QEII/PRIV/RF

16 Margaret Thatcher to Queen Elizabeth, 23 November 1982, RA QEQM/PRIV/PAL; Queen Elizabeth to Lord Snowdon, 10 December 1982, Snowdon Papers

17 Lady in waiting's diary, 17 March 1983, RA QEQMH/QEQM/DIARY/LIW

18 Courtney A. Laws to Sir Martin Gilliat, 6 May 1983, RA QEQMH/PS/ENGT/1983: 20 April

19 Lieutenant General Sir Robert Richardson to Sir Martin Gilliat, 24 June 1983, RA QEQMH/PS/ENGT/1983: 20 June

20 Lady in waiting's diary, 2 August 1984, RA QEQMH/QEQM/DIARY/LIW

21 Author's interview with Dame Frances Campbell-Preston, 5 February 2004; Lady in waiting's diary, 16 July 1985, RA QEQMH/QEQM/DIARY/LIW

22 Prince of Wales to Queen Elizabeth, 8 August 1985, Clarence House Archives

23 Lady in waiting's diary, 16 August 1986, RA QEQMH/QEQM/DIARY/LIW

24 Prince of Wales to Queen Elizabeth, 19 August 1986, RA QEQM/PRIV/RF

25 Queen Elizabeth to Lady Katharine Farrell, 15 November 1986, Farrell Papers

26 Lady in waiting's diary, 5 June 1987, RA QEQMH/QEQM/DIARY/LIW

27 Interview with Colonel Victor Chartier on behalf of the author

28 Interviews with Colonel Victor Chartier and Harris Boyd on behalf of the author

29 Interview with Mrs Tom Price on behalf of the author

30 Interview with Jean Paul Roy on behalf of the author

31 Lady in waiting's diary, 5 July 1989, RA QEQMH/QEQM/DIARY/LIW

32 Ibid., 6 July 1989

33 Interview with David Willmot on behalf of the author

34 Lady in waiting's diary, 10 July 1989, RA QEQMH/QEQM/DIARY/LIW

35 Interview with Harris Boyd on behalf of the author

36 Interview with Michael Parker on behalf of the author

37 Princess Margaret to Queen Elizabeth II, 28 June 1990, RA QEII/PRIV/RF

38 Ibid.

39 Queen Elizabeth, speech to Sandringham Women's Institute, 15 January 1991, RA QEQMH/PS/PAT/Sandringham WI

40 Lady in waiting's diary, 3 August 1990, RA QEQMH/QEQM/DIARY/LIW

41 Queen Elizabeth to Queen Elizabeth II, 5 February 1992, RA QEII/PRIV/RF

42 Lady in waiting's diary, 25 March 1992, RA QEQMH/QEQM/DIARY/LIW

43 Ted Hughes to Queen Elizabeth, 20 May 1992, RA QEQMH/PS/GEN/1992/Hughes

44 Ted Hughes, 'The Picnic', RA QEQMH/PS/GEN/1992/Hughes

45 Queen Elizabeth to Ted Hughes, 5 June 1992, RA QEII/OUT/HUGHES

46 Lady in waiting's diary, 12 April 1983, RA QEQMH/QEQM/DIARY/LIW

47 Sir John Grandy to Queen Elizabeth, 1 June 1992, RA QEQM/PRIV/PAL

48 Pimlott, p. 521

49 Donald Trelford, 'Why Princess Anne horsewhipped the Press', *Observer*, 21 September 1986

50 Quoted in Shawcross, p. 169

51 Princess of Wales to Queen Elizabeth, 19 May 1983, RA QEQM/PRIV/RF

52 Queen Elizabeth to Queen Elizabeth II, 10 April 1986, RA QEII/PRIV/RF

53 Princess Margaret to Queen Elizabeth II, 21 January 1992, RA QEII/PRIV/RF

54 Queen Elizabeth to Ted Hughes, 25 January 1992, RA QEQM/OUT/HUGHES

55 Queen Elizabeth, conversations with Eric Anderson, 1994–5, RA QEQM/ADD/MISC

56 Duke of Edinburgh to Princess of Wales, 7 July 1992, Princess of Wales to Duke of Edinburgh, 12 July 1992, published in *Daily Telegraph*, 17 December 2007

57 Princess Margaret to Queen Elizabeth II, 18 September 1992, RA QEII/PRIV/RF

58 Queen Elizabeth II to Queen Elizabeth, 1 December 1992, RA QEQM/PRIV/RF

59 Author's interview with Lord Fellowes

60 Pimlott, pp. 558–61

61 Prince of Wales to Queen Elizabeth, 7 December 1992, Clarence House Archives

62 Lady in waiting's diary, 9 December 1992, RA QEQMH/QEQM/DIARY/LIW

63 Queen Elizabeth to Queen Elizabeth II, 3 February 1993, RA QEII/PRIV/RF

64 Prince of Wales to Queen Elizabeth, 18 March 1993, RA QEQM/PRIV/RF

65 Memorial Address, St Martin in the Fields, 8 July 1993

66 Ted Hughes to Queen Elizabeth, 11 July 1993, RA QEQM/PRIV/PAL/Hughes

67 Queen Elizabeth II to Queen Elizabeth, 27 May 1993, RA QEQM/PRIV/RF

68 Queen Elizabeth, conversations with Eric Anderson, 1994–5, RA QEQM/ADD/MISC

69 Author's interview with Andrew Festing

70 Queen Elizabeth II to Queen Elizabeth, 27 May 1993, RA QEQM/PRIV/RF

71 Author's interview with Sir Alastair Aird

72 Mary Roche to Queen Elizabeth, 16 July 1993, RA QEQM/PRIV/PAL

73 Queen Elizabeth to Ted Hughes, 18 July 1993, RA QEII/OUT/HUGHES

74 Ibid.

75 Queen Elizabeth to Ted Hughes, 10 June 1995, RA CPW/OUT/HUGHES

76 Author's interview with Lord Janvrin

77 Queen Elizabeth II to Queen Elizabeth, 24 June 1993, RA QEQM/PRIV/RF

78 Queen Elizabeth to Lady Katharine Farrell, n.d. [May] 1993, Farrell Papers

79 Princess Margaret to Queen Elizabeth, 12 October 1993, RA QEQM/PRIV/RF

80 Ibid.

81 Princess Margaret to Queen Elizabeth, 13 October 1993, RA QEQM/PRIV/RF

82 Author's interview with Lady Penn

83 Queen Elizabeth to Queen Elizabeth II, 7 February 1994, RA QEII/PRIV/RF

84 Queen Elizabeth to Queen Elizabeth II, 28 February 1994, RA QEII/PRIV/RF

85 Queen Elizabeth, conversations with Eric Anderson, 1994–5, RA QEQM/ADD/MISC

86 Queen Elizabeth to Queen Elizabeth II, 6 February 1996, RA QEII/PRIV/RF
87 Ted Hughes to Queen Elizabeth, 19 May 1994, RA QEQMH/PS/GEN/1994/Hughes
88 Queen Elizabeth, conversations with Eric Anderson, 1994–5, RA QEQM/ADD/MISC
89 Author's interview with Peter Ord
90 Queen Elizabeth to Queen Elizabeth II, 4 February 1995, RA QEII/PRIV/RF
91 Hansard, 11 July 2000
92 Queen Elizabeth to Lady Katharine Farrell, 29 May 1995, Farrell Papers
93 Queen Elizabeth's speech, 6 May 1995, RA QEQMH/PS/ENGT/1995
94 Queen Elizabeth, conversations with Eric Anderson, 1994–5, RA QEQM/ADD/MISC
95 Ibid.
96 Queen Elizabeth to Ted Hughes, 18 August 1995, RA CPW/OUT/HUGHES
97 Author's interview with Roger Vickers
98 Queen Elizabeth to Simon Bowes Lyon, 29 January 1996, Bowes Lyon Papers, SPW
99 Queen Elizabeth to Rev. Anthony Harbottle, 6 February 1982, Harbottle Papers
100 Archbishop of Canterbury and Lord St John of Fawsley, Hansard, 13 July 2000
101 Lady Elizabeth Basset, 'Living Her Faith', June 1990, RA QEQMH/PS/PRIV
102 Queen Elizabeth, conversations with Eric Anderson, 1994–5, RA QEQM/ADD/MISC
103 Robert Ford to Sir Alastair Aird, 5 August 1996, RA QEQMH/PS/GEN/1996/Dalai Lama
104 Pico Iyer to author, 2 October 2008
105 Ted Hughes, 'Christmas Card Rhymes, The Day of the Sandringham Flower Show', 22 December 1996, RA QEQM/PRIV/PAL/Hughes; typescripts in Royal Library, RCIN 1165092–3
106 Queen Elizabeth to Ted Hughes, 15 February 1997, RA CPW/OUT/HUGHES
107 Ted Hughes to Queen Elizabeth, 1 June 1997, RA QEQM/PRIV/PAL/Hughes
108 Prince of Wales to Queen Elizabeth, 5 August 1997, RA QEQM/PRIV/RF
109 Ibid.
110 Castle of Mey Visitors' Book
111 Princess Margaret to Queen Elizabeth II, 14 September 1997, RA QEII/PRIV/RF
112 Bogdanor, passim; Shawcross, p. 214
113 Rowan Williams, *Lost Icons: Reflections on Cultural Bereavement*, T. & T. Clark, 2000, pp. 65–6
114 Author's interview with Dr Ian Campbell
115 Ted Hughes to Queen Elizabeth, 1 June 1997, RA QEQM/PRIV/PAL/Hughes
116 Ted Hughes to Queen Elizabeth, 26 May 1998, RA QEQM/PRIV/PAL/Hughes
117 Queen Elizabeth's copy of *Birthday Letters*, dedicated by Ted Hughes, 15 May 1998, RCIN 1167528
118 Lady Penn, diary, Penn Papers
119 Ted Hughes to Queen Elizabeth, 26 May 1998, RA QEQM/PRIV/PAL/Hughes
120 Ted Hughes to Hilda Farrer, 19 October 1998, *Letters of Ted Hughes*, ed. Christopher Reid, Faber & Faber, 2007, pp. 736–7
121 Carol Hughes to Queen Elizabeth, 18 November 1998, RA QEQM/PRIV/PAL/Hughes

Twenty-Four: Centenarian 1999–2002

1 Note by Sir Hugh Roberts, 'Tea at Royal Lodge', 20 February 1999
2 Ibid.
3 Queen Elizabeth to Lady Katharine Farrell, 26 January 1999, Farrell Papers
4 Queen Elizabeth to Lady Katharine Farrell, 12 May 1999, Farrell Papers

5   Author's interview with Sir Michael Oswald
6   Tom Stoppard to Queen Elizabeth, 18 June 1999, RA QEQM/PRIV/PAL
7   Rev. Anthony Harbottle to Queen Elizabeth, 3 February 2000; Queen Elizabeth to Rev. Anthony Harbottle, 7 February 2000, Harbottle Papers
8   Lady Angela Oswald, diary compiled for the author
9   Ibid.
10 Hansard, 3 April 2002
11 Hansard, 11 July 2000
12 Interview with Sir Michael Parker on behalf of the author
13 Ibid.
14 Queen Elizabeth to Major Michael Parker, 2 August 2000, Michael Parker Papers
15 Queen Fabiola to Queen Elizabeth, 29 July 2000, RA QEQM/PRIV/FORRF
16 Andrew Motion to Sir Alastair Aird, 13 August 2000, RA QEQMH/PS/GEN/2000/Motion
17 Campbell-Preston, p. 309
18 Prince of Wales to Queen Elizabeth, 6 August 2000, RA QEQM/PRIV/RF
19 Elizabeth Basset, *Moments of Vision*, Ledburn Press, 2004, p. 140
20 Author's interview with Lady Angela Oswald
21 Sermon preached by the Rev. John Robson LVO, Chaplain of the Savoy Chapel, Sunday 7 April 2002
22 Prince of Wales to Queen Elizabeth, 29 July 2001, Clarence House Archives
23 Lady Angela Oswald, diary compiled for the author
24 Author's interview with Lucy Murphy
25 Prince of Wales to Queen Elizabeth, 8 August 2001, RA QEQM/PRIV/RF
26 Author's interview with Mrs Timmy Munro
27 Prince of Wales to Queen Elizabeth, 8 September 2001, RA QEQM/PRIV/RF
28 RA QEQMH/PS/ENGTPRIV/2001: 11 October
29 Author's interview with Charlie Wright
30 Author's interview with the Duke of Kent
31 *Navy News*, 27 November 2001
32 Rev. Robert Beaken to Queen Elizabeth, 4 December 2001, RA QEQMH/PS/GEN/2001/Beaken; Sir Alastair Aird to Mrs Coryne Hall, 4 December 2001, RA QEQMH/PS/GEN/2001/Hall
33 Author's interview with Sir Michael Oswald
34 Campbell-Preston, pp. 309–10
35 Author's interview with Leslie Chappell and Jacqui Meakin
36 Prince of Wales to Queen Elizabeth, 12 February 2002, Clarence House Archives
37 Lady Angela Oswald to author, 14 May 2009
38 Author's interview with Gillian Frampton
39 Sir Alastair Aird, account of the last days of Queen Elizabeth, RA QEQM/ADD/MISC
40 Author's interview with Canon Ovenden; *The Oxford Book of Prayer*, ed. George Appleton, Oxford University Press, 1985, p. 101
41 *In Tearing Haste: Letters between Deborah Devonshire and Patrick Leigh Fermor*, ed. Charlotte Mosley, John Murray, 2008, p. 332
42 Author's interview with lady in waiting
43 *Guardian*, 2 April 2002
44 *Daily Telegraph*, 9 April 2002

EPILOGUE

1 J. M. Roberts, *Twentieth Century*, Allen Lane, 1999, pp. 848–56
2 The Queen to Most Rev. Cosmo Lang, 12 December 1936, Lambeth Palace Library, Lang Papers 318, ff. 177–80
3 Nicolson, *Diaries and Letters 1930–1939*, p. 405
4 The Queen to Prince Paul of Yugoslavia, 2 October 1939, copy enclosed with letter from Prince of Wales to Queen Elizabeth, 1 September 2000, RA QEQM/PRIV/RF
5 John Wheeler-Bennett, draft obituary of Queen Elizabeth for *The Times*, October 1967, RA AEC/GG/20
6 Duchess of York to D'Arcy Osborne, 13 July 1928, RA QEQM/OUT/OSBORNE
7 Most Rev. Cosmo Lang to Queen Elizabeth, 5 September 1939, RA QEQM/PRIV/PAL/Lang

SELECT BIBLIOGRAPHY

ARCHIVES AND COLLECTIONS

Airlie Papers, British Library
Althorp Archives
Archives Nationales, Paris
Archives Nationales du Québec
Attlee Papers, Bodleian Library
Bowes Lyon Papers, St Paul's Walden Bury
Library and Archives Canada
Chamberlain Papers, Birmingham University Library
Churchill Papers, Churchill Archives Centre, Cambridge
Clarence House Archives
Diana Cooper Papers, Eton College Library
Duff Cooper Papers, Churchill Archives Centre, Cambridge
Glamis Archives
Hickleton Papers (papers of Earls of Halifax), Borthwick Institute, University of York
Ted Hughes Papers, Emory University, Atlanta, Georgia
Lang Papers, Lambeth Palace Library
Lloyd Papers, Churchill Archives Centre, Cambridge
Violet Milner Papers, Bodleian Library
Monckton Papers, Bodleian Library
Hon. Lady Murray Papers
Royal Archives, Windsor Castle
Papers of Elizabeth, Marchioness of Salisbury, Hatfield House
Papers of fifth Marquess of Salisbury, Hatfield House
Sitwell Papers

BOOKS

Airlie, Mabell (ed. Jennifer Ellis) – *Thatched with Gold*. Hutchinson, 1962.
Annan, Noel – *Our Age: Portrait of a Generation*. Weidenfeld & Nicolson, 1990.
Asquith, Cynthia – *The Duchess of York*. Hutchinson, [1927].
Asquith, Cynthia – *The Queen*. Hutchinson, 1937.
Asquith, Cynthia – *Queen Elizabeth*. Hutchinson, 1937.
Basset, Elizabeth – *Moments of Vision: A Memoir*. Ledburn, 2004.

Bloch, Michael – *The Secret File of the Duke of Windsor*. Bantam Press, 1988.

Bogdanor, Vernon – *The Monarchy and the Constitution*. Oxford University Press, 1995.

Bradford, Sarah – *Elizabeth: A Biography of Her Majesty the Queen*. Heinemann, 1996.

Bradford, Sarah – *George VI*. Penguin, 2002.

Briggs, Asa – *A Social History of England*. Weidenfeld & Nicolson, 1994.

Brown, Callum – *The Death of Christian Britain: Understanding Secularisation 1800–2000*. Routledge, 2001.

Campbell-Preston, Frances – *The Rich Spoils of Time*. Dovecote Press, 2006.

Chadwick, Owen – *Britain and the Vatican during the Second World War*. Cambridge University Press, 1986.

Channon, Henry (ed. Robert Rhodes James) – *'Chips': The Diaries of Sir Henry Channon*. Penguin, 1967.

Clarke, Peter – *Hope and Glory: Britain 1900–1990*. Allen Lane, 1996.

Cornforth, John – *Queen Elizabeth The Queen Mother at Clarence House*. Michael Joseph, 1996.

Dimbleby, Jonathan – *The Prince of Wales: A Biography*. Little, Brown, 1994.

Douglas-Home, Charles – *Dignified and Efficient*. Claridge Press, 2000.

Duff Cooper (ed. John Julius Norwich) – *Diaries 1915–1951*. Weidenfeld & Nicolson, 2005.

Forbes, Grania – *My Darling Buffy: The Early Life of the Queen Mother*. Headline, 1999.

Gilbert, Martin – *Churchill: A Life*. Minerva, 1992.

Gilbert, Martin – *First World War*. HarperCollins 1995.

Gordon Slade, Harry – *Glamis Castle*. Society of Antiquaries of London, 2000.

Graves, Robert and Alan Hodge – *The Long Weekend: A Social History of Great Britain 1918–1939*. Faber & Faber, 1940.

Greig, Geordie – *Louis and the Prince: A Story of Politics, Intrigue and Royal Friendship*. Hodder & Stoughton, 1999.

Hardinge, Helen – *Loyal to Three Kings: A Memoir of Alec Hardinge*. William Kimber, 1967.

Hardman, Robert – *Monarchy: The Royal Family at Work*. Ebury Press, 2007.

Hartnell, Norman – *Silver and Gold*. Evans Bros, 1955.

Hennessy, Peter – *Never Again: Britain 1945–51*. Jonathan Cape, 1992.

Hughes, Ted – *Collected Poems*. Faber & Faber, 2003.

Hughes, Ted (ed. Christopher Reid) – *Letters*. Faber & Faber, 2007.

Keegan, John – *Churchill: A Life*. Weidenfeld & Nicolson, 2002.

Lacey, Robert – *Majesty: Elizabeth II and the House of Windsor*. Weidenfeld & Nicolson, 1977.

Laird, Dorothy – *Queen Elizabeth The Queen Mother*. Coronet, 1985.

Lascelles, Alan (ed. Duff Hart-Davis) – *King's Counsellor: The Wartime Diaries of Sir Alan Lascelles*. Weidenfeld & Nicolson, 2006.

Longford, Elizabeth – *Elizabeth R*. Weidenfeld & Nicolson, 1983.

Longford, Elizabeth – *The Queen Mother: A Biography*. Weidenfeld & Nicolson, 1981.

Nicolson, Harold (ed. Nigel Nicolson) – *Diaries and Letters, 1930–1939*. Collins, 1966.

Nicolson, Harold (ed. Nigel Nicolson) – *Diaries and Letters, 1939–1945*. Collins, 1967.

Nicolson, Harold (ed. Nigel Nicolson) – *Diaries and Letters 1945–1962*. Collins, 1968.

Nicolson, Harold – *King George V: His Life and Reign*. Pan Books, 1967.

Owens, Susan – *Watercolours and Drawings from the Collection of Queen Elizabeth The Queen Mother*. Royal Collection Publications, 2005.

Pimlott, Ben – *The Queen: A Biography of Elizabeth II*. HarperCollins, 1997.

Pope-Hennessy, James – *Queen Mary: 1867–1953*. Allen & Unwin, 1959.

Prochaska, Frank – *The Republic of Britain, 1760–2000*. Allen Lane, 2000.

Prochaska, Frank – *Royal Bounty: The Making of a Welfare Monarchy*. Yale University Press, 1995.

The Queen Mother Remembered (ed. James Hogg and Michael Mortimer) BBC Worldwide, 2002.

Rhodes James, Robert – *A Spirit Undaunted: The Political Role of George VI*. Little, Brown, 1998.

Roberts, Andrew – *A History of the English-Speaking Peoples since 1900*. Weidenfeld & Nicolson, 2006.

Roberts, J. M. – *The History of the World*. Hutchinson, 1976.

Roberts, J. M. – *Twentieth Century*. Allen Lane, 1999.

Rose, Kenneth – *King George V*. Weidenfeld & Nicolson, 1983.

Rose, Kenneth – *Kings, Queens and Courtiers*. Weidenfeld & Nicolson, 1985.

The Royal Encyclopedia (ed. Ronald Allison and Sarah Riddell). Macmillan, 1991.

Scruton, Roger – *England: An Elegy*. Chatto & Windus, 2000.

Seward, Ingrid – *The Last Great Edwardian Lady: The Life and Style of Queen Elizabeth the Queen Mother*. Century, 1999.

Shawcross, William – *Queen and Country*. BBC Worldwide, 2002.

Sitwell, Osbert – *Rat Week*. Michael Joseph, 1986.

Smith, Sean – *Royal Racing*. BBC Books, 2001.

Strong, Roy – *The Story of Britain*. Hutchinson, 1996.

Swift, Will – *The Roosevelts and the Royals*. John Wiley & Sons, Hoboken, New Jersey, 2004.

Terraine, John – *The First World War*. Leo Cooper, 1983.

Vickers, Hugo – *Elizabeth The Queen Mother*. Hutchinson, 2005.

Wentworth Day, James – *The Queen Mother's Family Story*. Robert Hale, 1967.

Wheeler-Bennett, John – *King George VI*. Macmillan, 1958.

Williams, Susan – *The People's King: The True Story of the Abdication*. Allen Lane, 2003.

Ziegler, Philip – *King Edward VIII: The Official Biography*. Collins, 1990.

Ziegler, Philip – *Mountbatten: The Official Biography*. Collins, 1985.

COPYRIGHT ACKNOWLEDGEMENTS

The author and publisher would also like to thank the following for their kind permission to reproduce copyright material:

The Estate of Mabell Airlie, The Right Honourable the Earl of Arlie., GVCO and Hutchinson for *Thatched with Gold*; The Estate of Pietro Annigoni and The National Portrait Gallery for *An Artist's Life*; The Estate of Cynthia Asquith and Michael Asquith for *The Duchess of York* and *The Queen*; The Estate of Lord Bonham-Carter for H.H. Asquith's *Letters to a Friend: Vol 2*; Elizabeth Basset and Ledburn Press for *Moments of Vision*; BBC Books for *The Queen Mother Remembered*; The Estate of Cecil Beaton, Hugo Vickers and Rupert Crew Ltd for *The Strenuous Years*; Richard Beaumont and David & Charles for *Purdey's, The Guns and The Family*; Paul Berman and W.W. Norton & Co. Inc. for *Terror and Liberalism*; Roger Berthoud and PFD for (www.pfd.co.uk) for *Graham Sutherland* (© Roger Berthoud, 1982); The Estate of John Betjeman and John Murray for *Continual Dew*; Lord Birkenhead and Weidenfeld & Nicolson for *Walter Monckton*; Michael Bloch for *The Secret File of the Duke of Windsor*; Vernon Bogdanor and Oxford University Press for *The Monarchy and the Constitution*; The Estate of Margaret Bondfield and Hutchinson for *A Life's Work*, reproduced by permission of The Random House Group Ltd.; Sarah Bradford and Penguin Books for *George VI* and *Elizabeth* (both © Sarah Bradford); Asa Briggs and Barbara Levy Literary Agency for *A Social History of England*; The Estate of Robert Bruce-Lockhart and Macmillan for *Diaries 1939–1965*; Frances Campbell-Preston and Dovecote Press for *The Rich Spoils of Time*; Owen Chadwick and Cambridge University Press for *Britain and the Vatican during WWII* (1987); The Estate of Sir Henry Channon, the Estate of Robert Rhodes James, The Orion Publishing Group and Curtis Brown Group Ltd. for *Chips: The Diaries of Sir Henry Channon* (© Robert Rhodes James, 1967); John Robert Colombo and McClelland & Stewart for *Colombo's Canadian Quotations* (© John Robert Colombo, 1974); The Estate of Duff Cooper and Weidenfeld & Nicolson for *Diaries*; John Cornforth and Michael Joseph for *Queen Elizabeth the Queen Mother at Clarence House*; The Estate of Noel Coward and Weidenfeld & Nicolson for *Diaries*; The Estate of Taylor Darbyshire and Edward Arnold for *The Royal Tour of the Duke & Duchess of York*; Jonathan Dimbleby and David Higham Associates for *The Prince of Wales*; Durham County Council for *Streatlam and Gibside*; Grania Forbes and Hodder Headline for *My Darling Buffy*; Noble Frankland and Giles de la Mare Publishers for *History at War*; Jill Franklin and Routledge & Kegan Paul for *The Gentleman's Country House*; Martin Gilbert and The Orion Publishing Group Ltd for *First World War*; Martin Gilbert and Pimlico for *Churchill, A Life*; Martin Gilbert and Michael Joseph for *Auschwitz and the Allies*, reproduced by permission of The Random House Group Ltd.; The Estate of Lady Gladwyn, Lord Gladwyn and Constable & Robinson for *The Diaries of Cynthia Gladwyn*; Victoria Glendinning and The Orion Publishing Group Ltd for *Edith Sitwell, A Unicorn Among Lions*; Harry Gordon Slade and The Society of Antiquaries of Scotland for *Glamis Castle*;

The Estate of Robert Graves and The Estate of Alan Hodge, A.P. Watt and Carcanet for *The Long Weekend*; The Estate of Charles Graves and Faber & Faber Ltd. for *The Bad Old Days*; Geordie Greig and HodderHeadline for *Louis and the Prince*; The Estate of Helen Hardinge and HarperCollins for *Loyal to Three Kings*; The Estate of Norman Hartnell and Evans Brothers Ltd for *Silver and Gold*; Edna Healey and Michael Joseph for *The Queen's House*; Michael Holroyd and Chatto & Windus for *Augustus John*; The Estate of Ted Hughes and Faber & Faber for extracts from *Collected Poems* and unpublished works and letters; Michael Ignatieff and Chatto & Windus for *The Life of Isaiah Berlin*; John Keegan and Weidenfeld & Nicolson for *Churchill*; The Estate of Joseph P. Kennedy and Viking Books for *Hostage to Fortune*; The Estate of Dorothy Laird and HodderHeadline for *Queen Elizabeth the Queen Mother*; The Estate of James Lees-Milne, David Higham Associates, and John Murray Publishers for *Diaries 1944–5*, *Diaries 1979–81*, *Diaries: Holy Dread 1982–4*; Raymond Leppard and Pro/Am Music Resources for *On Music*; The Estate of Elizabeth Longford and Weidenfeld & Nicolson for *Elizabeth R*, *The Queen Mother* and *The Royal House of Windsor*; The Estate of Robert Menzies and National Library of Australia for *Dark and Hurrying Days*; The Estate of Deborah Morrah and Hutchinson Books for *Princess Elizabeth* and *The Royal Family in Africa*; Charles Loch Mowat and Methuen Publishing Ltd for *Britain Between the Wars*; The Estate of Harold Nicolson for *Harold Nicolson, Diaries and Letters*; The Estate of George Orwell and A.M. Heath & Co Ltd for *The Unknown Orwell*; The Estate of George Orwell, Bill Hamilton, the Literary Executor of the Estate of the Late Sonia Brownwell Orwell, and Secker & Warburg Ltd. for 'Awake Young Men of England' (© George Orwell); Susan Owens and Royal Collection Publications for *Watercolours & Drawings*; J.W. Pickersgill (Ed.) and University of Chicago Press for *The Mackenzie King Record* (1960); The Estate of Ben Pimlott and HarperCollins for *The Queen* (© Ben Pimlott, 1996); The Estate of Sir Frederick Ponsonby and The Lord Ponsonby for *Recollections of Three Reigns*; The Estate of James Pope-Hennessy and Allen & Unwin for *Queen Mary*; Frank Prochaska and Yale University Press for *Royal Bounty* (© Frank Prochaska, 1995); The Estate of Lord Radcliffe and Hamish Hamilton for *Not in Feather Beds*; The Estate of Robert Rhodes James and Little Brown Book Group UK for *A Spirit Undaunted* (© Robert Rhodes James, 1998); Andrew Roberts and Weidenfeld & Nicolson *for A History of the English Speaking Peoples*; J. M. Roberts and Penguin Books for *The History of the World*; Jane Roberts and Yale University Press for *Royal Landscape*; Kenneth Rose and Weidenfeld & Nicolson for *King George V* and *Kings, Queens and Courtiers*; Sean Smith and BBC Books for *Royal Racing*, reproduced by permission of The Random House Group Ltd.; Roy Strong and Weidenfeld & Nicolson for *Diaries 1967–87*; Will Swift and John Wiley & Sons for *The Roosevelts and the Royals*; The Estate of A.J.P. Taylor, The Oxford University Press and David Higham Associates for *Limited English History 1914–1945*; The Estate of John Terraine and PFD (www.pfd.co.uk) for *The Short History of World War I* (© John Terraine, 1983); The Estate of Peter Townsend and Editions Robert Laffont for *Time and Chance*; Hugo Vickers and Hutchinson & Co. for *Elizabeth The Queen Mother*; Francis Watson and Chatto & Windus for *Dawson of Penn*; The Estate of Evelyn Waugh and The Wylie Agency for *Unconditional Surrender*; James Wentworth Day and Robert Hale & Co. for *The Queen Mother's Family Story*; The Estate of John Wheeler-Bennett and Macmillan for *King George VI*; Terry Wolsey and Canongate Books for *Elizabeth of Glamis* (1990); Philip Ziegler, Chatto & Windus and Curtis Brown Group Ltd for *Osbert Sitwell*, reproduced by permission of The Random House Group Ltd.; Philip Ziegler, Pimlico and Curtis Brown Ltd. for *King Edward VIII*.

Every effort has been made to contact all copyright holders of material in this book. If any have been inadvertently overlooked, the publishers will be pleased to make the necessary arrangement at the earliest opportunity.

INDEX

NOTE: Titles and ranks are generally the latest mentioned in the text. In subheads Queen Elizabeth the Queen Mother is abbreviated to QE; King George VI (formerly Prince Albert, then Duke of York) is referred to as George.